ABNORMAL
PSYCHOLOGY

DSM-IV Multiaxial Classification System

Axis I	Axis II	Axis III
Clinical syndromes:	Mental Retardation	General Medical
Disorders Usually First Diagnosed in Infancy, Childhood, or Adolescence	Personality Disorders	Conditions
Delirium, Dementia, Amnestic and other Cognitive Disorders		
Substance-related Disorders		
Schizophrenia and Other Psychotic Disorders		
Mood Disorders		
Anxiety Disorders		
Somatoform Disorders		
Factitious Disorder		
Dissociative Disorders		
Sexual and Gender Identity Disorders		
Eating Disorders		
Sleep Disorders		
Impulse Control Disorders Not Elsewhere Classified		
Adjustment Disorders		

Axis IV
Psychosocial and Environmental Problems

Check:

_____ Problems with primary support group. Specify:

_____ Problems related to the social environment. Specify:

_____ Educational problem. Specify:

_____ Occupational problem. Specify:

_____ Housing problem. Specify:

_____ Economic problem. Specify:

_____ Problems with access to health care services. Specify:

_____ Problems related to interaction with the legal system/crime. Specify:

_____ Other psychosocial and environmental problems. Specify:

OMATOFORM DISORDERS

omatization Disorder
onversion Disorder
ypochondriasis
ody Dysmorphic Disorder
ain Disorder

ACTITIOUS DISORDERS

actitious Disorder

ISSOCIATIVE DISORDERS

issociative Amnesia
issociative Fugue
issociative Identity Disorder (Multiple Personality Disorder)
epersonalization Disorder

EXUAL AND GENDER IDENTITY DISORDERS

exual Dysfunctions
Sexual Desire Disorders: Hypoactive Sexual Desire Disorder;
Sexual Aversion Disorder / Sexual Arousal Disorders: Female
Sexual Arousal Disorder; Male Erectile Disorder / Orgasmic
Disorders: Female Orgasmic Disorder (Inhibited Female
Orgasm); Male Orgasmic Disorder (Inhibited Male Orgasm);
Premature Ejaculation / Sexual Pain Disorders: Dyspareunia;
Vaginismus / Sexual Dysfunction Due to a General Medical
Condition / Substance-induced Sexual Dysfunction
araphilias
Exhibitionism / Fetishism / Frotteurism / Pedophilia / Sexual
Masochism / Sexual Sadism / Voyeurism / Transvestic
Fetishism
ender Identity Disorders
Gender Identity Disorder: in Children; in Adolescents or Adults
(Transsexualism)

ATING DISORDERS

norexia Nervosa
ulimia Nervosa

LEEP DISORDERS

rimary Sleep Disorders
Dyssomnias: Primary Insomnia; Primary Hypersomnia;
Narcolepsy; Breathing-related Sleep Disorder; Circadian
Rhythm Sleep Disorder (Sleep-Wake Schedule Disorder) /
Parasomnias; Nightmare Disorder (Dream Anxiety Disorder);
Sleep Terror Disorder; Sleepwalking Disorder / Sleep Disorders
Related to Another Mental Disorder
leep Disorder Due to a General Medical Condition
Substance-induced Sleep Disorder

IMPULSE CONTROL DISORDERS NOT ELSEWHERE
CLASSIFIED

Intermittent Explosive Disorder
Kleptomania
Pyromania
Pathological Gambling
Trichotillomania

ADJUSTMENT DISORDERS

Adjustment Disorder
with Anxiety / with Depressed Mood / with Disturbance of
Conduct / with Mixed Disturbance of Emotions and Conduct /
with Mixed Anxiety and Depressed Mood

Axis II

Mental Retardation
Mild Mental Retardation / Moderate Mental Retardation /
Severe Mental Retardation / Profound Mental Retardation

PERSONALITY DISORDERS

Paranoid Personality Disorder
Schizoid Personality Disorder
Schizotypal Personality Disorder
Antisocial Personality Disorder
Borderline Personality Disorder
Histrionic Personality Disorder
Narcissistic Personality Disorder
Avoidant Personality Disorder
Dependent Personality Disorder
Obsessive-Compulsive Personality Disorder

OTHER CONDITIONS THAT MAY BE A FOCUS OF CLINICAL
ATTENTION

Psychological Factors Affecting Medical Condition
Medication-induced Movement Disorders
Relational Problems
Relational Problem Related to a Mental Disorder or General
Medical Condition / Parent-Child Relational Problem / Partner
Relational Problem / Sibling Relational Problem
Problems Related to Abuse or Neglect
Physical Abuse of Child / Sexual Abuse of Child / Neglect of
Child / Physical Abuse of Adult / Sexual Abuse of Adult
Additional Conditions That May Be a Focus of Clinical
Attention
Bereavement / Borderline Intellectual Functioning / Academic
Problem / Occupational Problem / Child or Adolescent
Antisocial Behavior / Adult Antisocial Behavior / Malingering /
Phase of Life Problem / Noncompliance with Treatment /
Identity Problem / Religious or Spiritual Problem / Acculturation
Problem / Age-related Cognitive Decline

SEVENTH EDITION

ABNORMAL PSYCHOLOGY

GERALD C. DAVISON
University of Southern California

JOHN M. NEALE
State University of New York at Stony Brook

JOHN WILEY & SONS, INC.

New York / Chichester / Weinheim / Brisbane / Singapore / Toronto

Cover   Ginko leaves/Andreas Bleckmann/nonstock

Executive Editor   Christopher J. Rogers
Developmental Editors   Madalyn Stone, Pui F. Szeto
Marketing Manager   Kimberly Manzi
Production Director   Pamela Kennedy
Senior Production Editor   Jeanie Berke
Text Designer   Madelyn Lesure
Cover Designer   Karin Gerdes Kincheloe
Senior Photo Editor   Mary Ann Price
Photo Researcher   Jennifer Atkins
Senior Illustration Coordinator   Anna Melhorn
Illustrator   Seventh Edition updated by Radiant Illustration & Design

Special thanks to Photo Researchers, a New York City photo agency, for their
various contributions to this book, including consulting on the stock and location photography.

This book was set in 10/12 Palatino by LCI Design and printed and bound by
R. R. Donnelley & Sons, Inc. The cover was printed by The Lehigh Press, Inc.

Library of Congress Cataloging-in-Publication Data:
Davison, Gerald C.
    Abnormal psychology / Gerald C. Davison, John M. Neale — 7th ed.
        p.   cm.
    Includes bibliographical references and index.
    ISBN 0-471-11122-8 (cloth: alk. paper)
    1. Psychology, Pathological.   I. Neale, John M., 1943–
    II. Title.
    [DNLM: 1. Psychopathology.   2. Mental Disorders.   WM 100 D265a
1997]
    RC454.D3   1997
    616.89—dc21
DNLM/DLC
for Library of Congress   97-21696
                                                                CIP

Printed in the United States of America

10 9 8 7 6 5 4 3 2

To
Kathleen C. Chambers, Eve H. Davison, and Asher Davison
and
Gail and Sean Neale

ABOUT THE AUTHORS

GERALD C. DAVISON is Professor of Psychology at the University of Southern California, where he was also Director of Clinical Training from 1979 to 1984 and Chair of the Department from 1984 to 1990. Previously he was on the psychology faculty at the State University of New York at Stony Brook (1966—1979). He received his B.A. from Harvard and his Ph.D. from Stanford. He is a Fellow of the American Psychological Association and has served on the Executive Committee of the Division of Clinical Psychology, on the Board of Scientific Affairs, on the Committee on Scientific Awards, and on the Council of Representatives. He is also a Charter Fellow of the American Psychological Society and a past president of the Association for the Advancement of Behavior Therapy. He served two terms on the National Academy of Sciences Committee on Techniques for the Enhancement of Human Performance. In 1988 Davison received an outstanding achievement award from APA's Board of Social and Ethical Responsibility, in 1989 was recipient of the Albert S. Raubenheimer Distinguished Faculty Award from USC's College of Letters, Arts and Sciences, and in 1993 won the university-wide USC Associates Award for Excellence in Teaching. His book *Clinical Behavior Therapy*, co-authored in 1976 with Marvin Goldfried and reissued in an expanded edition in 1994, is one of two publications that have been recognized as Citation Classics by the Social Sciences Citation Index. He is on the editorial board of *Behavior Therapy, Cognitive Therapy and Research, Journal of Cognitive Psychotherapy,* and *Journal of Psychotherapy Integration.* His current research program focuses on the relationships between cognition and a variety of behavioral and emotional problems. In addition to his teaching and research, he is a practicing clinical psychologist.

JOHN M. NEALE is Professor of Psychology at the State University of New York at Stony Brook, where he regularly teaches the undergraduate course in abnormal psychology. He received his B.A. from the University of Toronto and his M.A. and Ph.D. from Vanderbilt University. His internship in clinical psychology was as a Fellow in Medical Psychology at the Langley Porter Neuropsychiatric Institute. In 1975 he was a Visiting Fellow at the Institute of Psychiatry, London, England. In 1974 he won the American Psychological Association's Early Career Award for his research on cognitive processes in schizophrenia. In 1991 he won a Distinguished Scientist Award from the American Psychological Association's Society for a Science of Clinical Psychology. He has been on the editorial boards of several journals and has been associate editor of the *Journal of Abnormal Psychology.* Besides his numerous articles in professional journals, he has published books on the effects of televised violence on children, research methodology, schizophrenia, case studies in abnormal psychology, and psychological influences on health. Schizophrenia is a major focus of his research and for the past several years he has been studying the symptom of flat affect. He also conducts research on the influence of stress on health and is currently investigating how coping moderates this relationship.

PREFACE

It has been more than twenty-five years since we sat down to share our experiences teaching the undergraduate abnormal psychology course at Stony Brook. Arising from that conversation was the outline of a textbook on which we decided to collaborate, one that was different from the texts available at the time in its balance and blending of the clinical and the empirical/experimental; in its use of paradigms as an organizing principle; and in its effort to involve the reader in the problem-solving engaged in by clinicians and scientists. As young academics, we had no idea how our proposed effort would be received by our colleagues and their undergraduate students. We were therefore surprised and delighted at the favorable reception our first edition received when it was published in 1974, and our pleasure has only been enhanced by the continuing acceptance of the succeeding editions.

With each new edition, we update, make changes, and streamline features to enhance both the scholarly and didactic characteristics of the book. We also devote considerable effort to couching complex concepts in prose that is lucid and vivid. The domains of psychopathology and intervention have become increasingly technical. Therefore a good abnormal psychology textbook must engage the careful and focused attention of students so that they can acquire a deep understanding of the issues and the material. They deserve nothing less. We believe that this Seventh Edition maintains a proper balance between undiluted discussion of a complex subject matter and a student-friendly presentation that is engaging and informative. Feedback that we have received over the years from both instructors and their students indicates that we have been succeeding in this effort.

GOALS OF THE BOOK

In contemporary abnormal psychology there are few hard and fast answers. Indeed, the very way the field should be conceptualized and the kinds of questions that should be asked are hotly debated issues. In this book we have tried to present glimpses of possible answers to two primary questions: *What causes psychopathology?* and *Which treatments are most effective in preventing or reducing psychological suffering?*

Our goals in writing this textbook are not only to present theories and research in psychopathology and intervention but also to convey some of the intellectual excitement that is associated with the search for answers to some of the most puzzling questions facing humankind. A reviewer of an earlier edition once said that our book reads like a detective story, for we do more than just state the problem and then its solution. Rather, we try to involve the student in the search for clues, the follow-up of hunches, and the evaluation of evidence that are part and parcel of the science and art of the field. We try to encourage students to participate with us in a process of discovery as we sift through the evidence on the origins of psychopathology and the effectiveness of specific interventions.

SCIENTIFIC CLINICAL APPROACH

As in the preceding six editions of this book, we share a strong commitment to a scientific approach but at the same time appreciate the often uncontrollable nature of the subject matter and the importance of clinical findings. It has become commonplace in psychology to recognize the selective nature of perception, and we sound this theme throughout the book. We encourage readers to think critically and consider the merits of our and others' points of view. We believe we have succeeded in presenting fairly and comprehensively the major alternative conceptualizations in contemporary psychopathology.

PARADIGMS AS AN ORGANIZING PRINCIPLE

A recurrent theme in the book is the importance of major points of view or, to use Kuhn's (1962) phrase, paradigms. Our experience in teaching undergraduates has made us very much aware of the importance of making explicit the unspoken assumptions underlying any quest for knowledge. In our handling of the paradigms, we have tried to make their premises clear. Long after specific facts are forgotten, the student should retain a grasp of the basic problems in the field of psychopathology and should understand that the answers one arrives at are, in an important but often subtle way, constrained by the questions one poses and the methods employed to ask those questions. Throughout the book we discuss four major paradigms: *psychoanalytic*, *learning (behavioral)*, *cognitive*, and *biological*. When therapy is discussed, we also describe the *humanistic* and *existential* paradigm.

A related issue is the use of more than one paradigm in studying abnormal psychology. Rather than force an entire field into, for example, a biological paradigm, we argue from the available information that different problems in psychopathology are amenable to analyses within different frameworks. For instance, biological processes must be considered when examining mental retardation and schizophrenia; but for other disorders, such as depression, a cognitive behavioral theory seems essential as well; and for still others, for example, dissociative disorders, psychoanalytic theories can enhance our understanding. Over the course of our several revisions the importance of a *diathesis-stress* approach has become more and more evident. Emerging data indicate that many, perhaps most, disorders arise from subtle interactions between somatic or psychological predispositions and stressful life events. Our coverage continues to reflect these hypotheses and findings, strengthening our basic position that a diathesis-stress paradigm is necessary for understanding most psychopathologies.

ORGANIZATION OF THE SEVENTH EDITION

In Part 1 (Chapters 1–5) we place the field in historical context, present the concept of paradigms in science, describe the major paradigms in psychopathology and intervention, review the Fourth Edition of the Diagnostic and Statistical Manual of Mental Disorders (DSM-IV), discuss critically its validity and reliability, and then provide an overview of major approaches and techniques in clinical assessment. As in previous editions, specific disorders and their treatment are discussed in Parts 2 and 3 (Chapters 6–16). Our chapter on aging in our Third Edition in 1982 was the first such chapter in a book of this kind, and our current Chapter 16 remains, we believe, the most comprehensive discussion of this important and still inadequately studied set of topics in an abnormal psychology textbook. The final section, Part 4 (Chapters 17–20), on intervention is also retained, for we continue to believe that only a separate and extended consideration allows us to explore with the reader the many perplexing and intriguing problems encountered by health professionals who try to prevent or treat

mental disorders. Also, we have continued to update and strengthen our chapter on legal and ethical issues (20), which we are pleased to know has been assigned to law school classes as an accurate and analytical introduction to mental health law. This closing chapter is devoted to an in-depth study of the complex interplay between scientific findings and theories, on the one hand, and the role of ethics and the law, on the other, a core issue being the dialectical tensions between what science can tell us and what use is properly made of science in controlling the everyday lives of people.

CHANGES TO THE ORGANIZATION

In this Seventh Edition, we have a chapter each on sexual disorders (14) and on disorders of childhood (15) instead of the two chapters previously devoted to each of these topics. This has enabled us to focus and integrate better our examination of these two domains. We have moved our study of eating disorders from one of the earlier child chapters and expanded coverage of this increasingly important topical area in a new separate chapter (Chapter 9). We have not, however, reduced our coverage of child disorders; anxiety and mood disorders of children are now discussed in Chapters 6 and 10, respectively. These organizational changes result in a reduction of chapters to make the book more manageable for a one-semester course.

NEW TO THIS EDITION

Several themes and topics are new or expanded in this Seventh Edition.

CULTURAL AND CROSS-CULTURAL CONSIDERATIONS

We have included throughout the book considerable material on cultural factors in the study of psychopathology and intervention as well as discussion of the different ways abnormal behavior is conceptualized in cultures other than our own. For example, we examine in depth the ways that DSM-IV sensitizes clinicians and researchers to the role of culture in shaping abnormal behavior as well as the ways psychological abnormality is manifested in different parts of the world. In the anxiety disorders chapter (6), for example, we discuss kayak-angst, a form of panic disorder found among seal hunters who spend a great deal of time alone at sea. In the clinical assessment chapter (4), we have extended our earlier discussions of cultural bias in assessment and ways to guard against this selectivity in perception. Cultural influences are explored in the new eating disorders chapter (9), where societal conceptions of what is beautiful and desirable in body shape are presented as contributing factors in the extremes to which people will go to control their weight.

BIOLOGICAL FACTORS AND THE DIATHESIS-STRESS PARADIGM

Our book continues to pay major attention to biological factors in both etiology and treatment. Ongoing advances in neuroscience are bringing new and important knowledge about the origins of psychopathology and how better to prevent and treat it. Of particular note are biological findings bearing on the origins of obsessive-compulsive disorder, schizophrenia, mood disorders, conduct disorder, attention-deficit/hyperactivity disorder, autistic disorder, and Alzheimer's disease. However, as the saying goes, anatomy is not destiny, and we endeavor to avoid the unwarranted extremes of biological determinism as we maintain our focus on a diathesis-stress point of view. Thus, while improved twin and adoption studies as well as new neurochemical findings enhance our appreciation for the somatic substrates of abnormal behavior, considerable variance remains unexplained by these factors. Therefore, we must continue to explore the myriad and complex ways that biological predispositions interact with environmental factors, especially stressors that await us all as we negotiate our way.

EXPANDED COVERAGE

In addition to the foregoing and the kind of general updating that keeps our coverage current, we list below a small sampling of some of the major new material in this Seventh Edition:

- New discussion of the limits of reductionism in explaining complex human behavior (Chapter 2, pp. 29–30)
- New material throughout on contemporary psychodynamic theories and research (most chapters but especially Chapters 2, p. 39; 17, pp. 500–502; and 18, pp. 548–551)
- Advances in biochemical assessment (Chapter 4, p. 89)
- New Focus box on chaos theory and its implications for the limits of our understanding of complex human behavior in a complex world (Chapter 5, p. 104)
- Discussion of research on worry as a central

aspect of generalized anxiety disorder (Chapter 6, pp. 140–141)
- Anxiety sensitivity as a mediator of experimentally induced panic attacks (Chapter 6, pp. 136–138)
- Critical discussion of the role of childhood sexual abuse in various disorders, including dissociative disorder (Chapter 7, pp. 173–175), borderline personality disorder (Chapter 13, p. 339), and sexual dysfunctions (Chapter 14, p. 385–394), as well as the controversies surrounding recovery of repressed memories during psychotherapy (Chapter 7, p. 174) and some of the legal consequences arising from accusations made by some adult patients against their parents (Chapter 20, pp. 625–626)
- Similarities between dissociative and conversion disorders (Chapter 7, p. 172)
- Recent research on blood pressure among paramedics responding to emergencies (Chapter 8, p. 192)
- Latest laboratory research on social support (Chapter 8, pp. 186–187)
- Relationships between coping and breast cancer (Chapter 8, pp. 185–186; 202–203)
- New treatments for bulimia (Chapter 9, pp. 221–223)
- New research on bipolar disorder and creativity (Chapter 10, p. 228)
- Current studies on mixed anxiety and depression (Chapter 10, p. 230)
- Recent research on predicting depression from cognitive factors (Chapter 10, pp. 232–233)
- Latest work on G-proteins and bipolar disorder (Chapter 10, p. 242)
- Latest research on schizophrenia, showing how the field is moving away from dopamine toward a consideration of a broader range of neurotransmitters (Chapter 11, pp. 277–279)
- New material on predicting alcoholism from alcohol sensitivity (Chapter 12, p. 318)
- New efforts to prevent substance use and abuse in children and adolescents (Chapter 12, pp. 329–331)
- A dimensional approach to classifying personality disorders using the five-factor model of personality (Chapter 13, p. 348)
- Recent experimental evidence supporting the psychoanalytic hypothesis that homophobia arises from repressed homosexual inclinations (Chapter 14, p. 382)
- New information on the role of negative mood in child molestation (Chapter 14, p. 367)

- Expanded discussion of conduct disorder, including new data and theorizing on time-limited versus life-persistent patterns (Chapter 15, p. 416)
- The new classification system of the American Association of Mental Retardation, with its emphasis on support systems needed to maximize the person's potential (Chapter 15, pp. 426–427)
- Positive long-term outcomes of some of those afflicted with autistic disorder (Chapter 15, pp. 441–443)
- The possible role of estrogen in the course and treatment of Alzheimer's disease (Chapter 16, pp. 458–459)
- Latest research on tau proteins and neurofibrillary tangles in Alzheimer's disease (Chapter 16, pp. 456–457)
- New and expanded discussion of sleep disorders, including sleep apnea (Chapter 16, pp. 472–473)
- Consideration of gender role flexibility and advantages that women may have in accommodating changes brought by aging (Chapter 16, p. 452)
- New discussion of major issues in research on the outcomes of psychotherapy, such as the strengths and limitations of treatment manuals and the differences between efficacy and effectiveness studies (Chapter 17, pp. 491–494)
- Matching patients with treatments and the outcomes of Project Match, a major multisite study on the treatment of alcohol abuse (Chapter 18, pp. 550–551)
- Continuing developments in psychotherapy integration and eclecticism (Chapters 2, pp. 51–52 and 18, pp. 548–555)
- The nature and consequences of violence in intimate relationships (Chapter 19, p. 573)
- Expanded discussion of cultural and racial considerations in psychotherapy (Chapter 19, pp. 587–590)
- Latest research on predicting violence and its relationship to civil commitment (Chapter 20, pp. 604–606)
- Recently enacted sexual predator laws designed to implement preventive detention when the danger to the public is judged to be particularly high (Chapter 20, p. 606)
- Increased use of clinical case material throughout the text, much of it based on our own clinical work, to show how general scientific principles come to life in the complexities of individual cases

FEATURES OF THE BOOK OF PARTICULAR INTEREST TO THE STUDENT READER

There are several features of this book that are designed to make it easier for students to master and enjoy the material, elements designed to make it user-friendly.

- **Focus Boxes.**   There are many in-depth discussions of selected topics encased in focus boxes throughout the book. This feature allows us to involve the reader in a sometimes very specialized topic in a way that does not detract from the flow of the regular text. Sometimes a focus box expands on a point in the text; sometimes it deals with an entirely separate but relevant issue, often a controversial one. Reading these boxes with care will deepen the reader's understanding of the subject matter. (For a complete list of focus boxes, see page xx.)
- **Chapter-Opening Cases.**   The syndrome chapters, 6 through 16, open with extended case illustrations. These accounts provide a clinical context for the theories and research that occupy most of our attention in the chapter and help make vivid the real-life implications of the empirical work of psychopathologists and clinicians.
- **Chapter Summaries.**   A summary appears at the end of each chapter, and readers may find it useful to peruse it before beginning the chapter itself. These summaries give readers a good sense of what lies ahead. When the summary is reread after completing the chapter itself, it will enhance the student's understanding and provide an immediate sense of what has been learned in just one reading of the chapter.
- **Glossary and Key Terms.**   When an important term is introduced, it is boldfaced and listed after the chapter summary as a key term. A definition and/or discussion of that term immediately follows its appearance in the text. Of course, the term will probably appear again later in the book, in which case it will not be highlighted in this way. We have provided at the end of the book a glossary that includes all these terms.
- **DSM-IV Table.**   On the endpapers of the book is a summary of the current psychiatric nomenclature, DSM-IV. This provides a handy guide to where particular disorders appear in the "official" taxonomy, or classification. Readers will notice that we make considerable use of DSM-IV, yet in a selective and sometimes critical vein.

Sometimes we find it better to discuss theory and research on a particular problem in a way that is different from DSM's conceptualization.

- **References.** Our commitment to remain current and forward-looking is reflected in the inclusion of more than 1300 new references, over half of which were published from 1994–1997.

ANCILLARIES

A New Psychopathology Videotape featuring 10–15 minute video clips of patients, their problems, and the professional care they receive. This tape covers the major disorders. Available free to adopters. Contact your sales representative for details.

A New Classroom Presentation CD ROM containing the transparency set of art work for classroom presentation as well as the instructor's manual with lecture outlines, key terms, and chapter summaries. This can be customized into an organization that fits an instructor's individual presentation.

A Student Study Guide written by Douglas Hindman of the Eastern Kentucky University is available to help students read and study the textbook. For each chapter there is a summary of the chapter, a list of key concepts, important study questions, and practice tests written in collaboration with the test bank author to ensure consistency and to encourage active reading and learning. We believe that it is a very helpful study guide.

A New Davison and Neale Web Site with an on-line Faculty Resource page and an on-line Student Resource page, as well as active learning links to several interesting sites related to the field of abnormal psychology. http://www.wiley.com/college

Instructor Resource Manual with chapter summaries, lecture launchers, perspectives on each disorder's causes and treatment, key points students should know, key terms, discussion stimulators, and guides to instructional films; authored by Marian Williams of the University of California at Los Angeles.

Complete Test Bank is available in printed form as well as computerized programs on disks for Mac and IBM computers; authored by Marian Williams.

ACKNOWLEDGMENTS

It is a pleasure to acknowledge the contributions of a number of colleagues to this Seventh Edition. Their thoughtful comments have helped us to refine and improve the book.

Gordon D. Atlas
Alfred University

Manuel Barrera
Arizona State University

Ronald W. Belter
University of West Florida

Larry E. Beutler
University of California—Santa Barbara

Jack Blanchard
University of New Mexico

Ronald L. Blount
The University of Georgia

Wolfgang G. Bringmann
University of South Alabama

Carol Carlson
University of Wisconsin—Osh Kosh

Sarah Cirese
College of Marin

John D. Cone
United States International University—San Diego

James O. Davis
Southwest Missouri State University

Margaret T. Davis
University of Baltimore

S. Wayne Duncan
University of Washington

Mitchell Earleywine
University of Southern California

Anthony Fazio
University of Wisconsin—Milwaukee

Thomas C. Greenland
Kentucky State University

David A. F. Haaga
American University

Todd F. Heatherton
Dartmouth College

William Iacono
University of Minnesota

Harvey Irwin
The University of New England

Carlton James
Rutgers University

Russell T. Jones
Virginia Tech University

Carolin Keutzer
University of Oregon

Peter M. Lewinsohn
Oregon Research Institute—Eugene

Christopher Martin
Western Psychiatric Institute—Pittsburgh

David McCord
W. Carolina University

Richard J. McNally
Harvard University

David E. Powley
University of Mobile

James A. Schmidt
Western Illinois University

Sandra T. Sigmon
University of Maine

Hugh Stephenson
Ithaca College

Zvi Strassberg
State University of New York—Stony Brook

Bob Summer
University of California—Davis

Lisa Terre
University of Missouri—Kansas City

Fred W. Whitford
Montana State University

Thomas A. Widiger
University of Kentucky—Lexington

W. Joseph Wyatt
Marshall University

Helpful library research was provided at the University of Southern California by Eve H. Davison, Linda Ferry, and Todd O'Hearn. Special thanks go to Marian Williams for drafting and reorganizing major portions of Chapters 4 and 15, and to Todd O'Hearn for similar work on Chapter 19. Valuable clerical assistance was given by Jean Campbell, Rebecca Krakov, and Amanda Schelling.

Several chapters benefited greatly from discussions and advice from colleagues at Stony Brook — Joseph Schwartz, Arthur Stone, and Gerdi Weidner. Further assistance at Stony Brook was provided by Antonis Kotsaftis and Susanne Triesch.

We signed on with Wiley in 1971 and continued in this revision to enjoy the skills and dedication of our "Wiley family": Chris Rogers, Pui Szeto, Johnna Barto, Jeanie Berke, Mary Ann Price, Carrie Ann Sabato, Jenifer Cooke, Madalyn Stone, Maddy Lesure, Kimberly Manzi, Pam Kennedy, Caroline Ryan, and Laura Ierardi. Special thanks go to Leslie Carr, who provided many helpful editing and development suggestions as we continued our efforts to produce a readable and engaging text without sacrificing scientific accuracy or professional responsibility.

One of the things previous users have liked about our textbook is its readability and the way it engages the reader in a collaborative quest with the authors for answers to some of the most perplexing problems facing psychology. From time to time students and faculty colleagues have written us their comments on the book. These communications are always welcome. Readers may find it convenient to contact us via E-mail at abnormal @ wiley.com or write us by regular mail at Department of Psychology, University of Southern California, Los Angeles, CA 90089-1061 (Davison); or Department of Psychology, State University of New York, Stony Brook, NY 11794-1200 (Neale).

For putting up with occasional limited accessibility and mood swings, and for always being there for moral support, our thanks go to the most important people in our lives — Kathleen Chambers, Eve and Asher Davison (GCD), and Gail and Sean Neale (JMN), to whom this book is dedicated with love and gratitude. Finally, we have maintained the order of authorship as it was for the First Edition, decided by the toss of a coin.

June 1997

GERALD C. DAVISON
Los Angeles

JOHN M. NEALE
Stony Brook

CONTENTS IN BRIEF

CONTENTS

FOCUS BOXES

PART 1

INTRODUCTION AND BASIC ISSUES

Jedd Garet,
"What The Earth Is Really Like," *1984*

INTRODUCTION: HISTORICAL AND SCIENTIFIC CONSIDERATIONS

Slumping in a comfortable leather chair, Ernest H., a thirty-five-year-old city police officer, looked skeptically at his therapist as he struggled to relate a series of problems. His recent inability to maintain an erection when making love to his wife was the immediate reason for his seeking therapy, but after gentle prodding from the therapist, Ernest recounted a host of other difficulties, some of them dating from his childhood but most of them originating during the previous several years.

Ernest's childhood had not been a happy one. His mother, whom he loved dearly, died suddenly when he was only six, and for the next ten years he lived either with his father or with a maternal aunt. His father drank heavily, seldom managing to get through any day without some alcohol. Moreover, the man's moods were extremely variable; he had even spent several months in a state hospital with a diagnosis of manic-depressive psychosis. His father's income was so irregular that he could seldom pay bills on time or afford to live in any but the most run-down neighborhoods. At times Ernest's father was totally incapable of caring for himself, let alone his son. Ernest would then spend weeks, sometimes months, with his aunt in a nearby suburb.

Despite these apparent handicaps, Ernest completed high school and entered the tuition-free city university. He earned his miscellaneous living expenses by waiting tables at a small restaurant. During these college years his psychological problems began to concern him. He often became profoundly depressed for no apparent reason, and these bouts of sadness were sometimes followed by periods of manic elation. His lack of control over these mood swings troubled him greatly, for he had observed this same pattern in his alcoholic father. He also felt an acute self-consciousness with people who he felt had authority over him—his boss, his professors, and even some of his classmates, with whom he compared himself unfavorably. Ernest was especially sensitive about his clothes, which were old and worn compared with those of his peers; their families had more money than his.

It was on the opening day of classes in his junior year that he first saw his future wife. When the tall, slender young woman moved to her seat with grace and self-assurance, his were not the only eyes that followed her. Ernest spent the rest of that semester watching her from afar, taking care to sit where he could glance over at her without being conspicuous. Then one day as they and the other students were leaving class, they bumped into each other quite by accident, and her warmth and charm emboldened him to ask her to join him for some coffee. When she said yes, he almost wished she had not.

Amazingly enough, as he saw it, they soon fell in love, and before the end of his senior year they were married. Ernest could never quite believe that his wife, as intelligent as she was beautiful, really cared for him. As the years wore on his doubts about himself and about her feelings toward him would continue to grow.

He hoped to enter law school, and both his grades and his scores on the law-school boards made these plans a possibility, but he decided instead to enter the police academy. The reasons that he related to his therapist had to do with doubts about his intellectual abilities as well as his increasing uneasiness in situations in which he felt himself being evaluated. Seminars had become unbearable for Ernest in his last year in college, and he had hopes that the badge and uniform of a police officer would give him the instant recognition and respect that he seemed incapable of earning on his own.

To help him get through the academy his wife quit college at the end of her junior year, despite Ernest's pleas, and sought a secretarial job. He felt she was far brighter than he and saw no reason why she should sacrifice her potential to help him make his way in life. But at the same time he recognized the fiscal realities and grudgingly accepted her financial support.

The police academy proved to be even more stressful than college. Ernest's mood swings, although less frequent, still troubled him. And like his father, who was now confined to a state mental hospital, he drank to ease his psychological pain. He felt that his instructors considered him a fool when he had difficulty standing up in front of the class to give an answer that he himself knew was correct. But he made it through the physical, intellectual, and social rigors of the academy and was assigned to foot patrol in one of the wealthier sections of the city.

Several years later, when it seemed that life should be getting easier, he found himself in even greater turmoil. Now thirty-two years old, with a fairly secure job that paid reasonably well, he began to think of starting a family. His wife wanted this as well, and it was at this time that his problems with impotence began. He thought at first it was the alcohol—he was drinking at least six ounces of bourbon every night except when on the swing shift. Soon, though, he began to wonder whether he was actually avoiding the responsibility of having a child, and later he began to doubt that his wife really found him attractive and desirable. The more understanding and patient she was about his sometimes frantic efforts to consummate sex with her, the less manly he felt he was. He was unable to accept help from his wife, for he did not believe that this was the right way to maintain a sexual relationship. The problems in bed spread to other areas of their lives. The less often they made love, the more suspicious he was of his wife, for she had become even more beautiful and vibrant as she entered her thirties. In addition, she had been promoted to the position of administrative assistant at the law firm where she worked. She would mention—perhaps to taunt him—long, martini-filled lunches with her boss at a posh uptown restaurant.

The impetus for contacting the therapist was an ugly argument with his wife one evening when she came home from work after ten. Ernest had been agitated for several days. To combat his fear that he was losing control, he had consumed almost a full bottle of bourbon each night. By the time his wife walked in the door on that final evening, Ernest was already very drunk, and he attacked her both verbally and physically about her alleged infidelity. In her own anger and fear she questioned his masculinity in striking a woman and taunted him with the disappointments of their lovemaking. Ernest stormed out of the house, spent the night at a local bar, and the next day somehow pulled himself together enough to seek professional help.

Every day of our lives we try to understand other people. Even when their behavior is not as extreme as Ernest's, determining why another person does or feels something is a difficult task. Indeed, we do not always understand why we ourselves feel and behave as we do. Acquiring insight into what we consider normal, expected behavior is difficult enough; understanding human behavior beyond the normal range, such as that of the police officer just described, is even more difficult.

This book is concerned with the whole range of abnormality, its description, its causes, and its treatment. We face numerous challenges in this field. Foremost, we must have a tolerance for ambiguity, an ability to be comfortable with tentative, often conflicting information. Then, of course, we must have the endurance to work with that information, to study and research it. As you will see, the human mind remains elusive; we know with certainty much less about our field than we would hope. As we approach the study of **psychopathology**, the field concerned with the nature and development of abnormal behavior, thoughts, and feelings, we do well to keep in mind that the subject offers few hard and fast answers. Yet, as will become evident when we discuss our orientation toward scientific inquiry, the study of psychopathology is no less worthwhile because of its ambiguities. The kinds of questions asked, rather than the specific answers to those questions, constitute the essence of the field.

Another challenge we face in studying abnormal psychology is to remain objective. Our subject matter, human behavior, is personal and powerfully affecting, making objectivity difficult but no less necessary. The pervasiveness and disturbing effects of abnormal behavior intrude on our own lives. Who has not experienced irrational thoughts, fantasies, and feelings? Who has not felt profound sadness, even depression, that is more extreme than circumstances can explain? Many have known someone, a friend or perhaps a relative, whose behavior was upsetting and impossible to fathom, and you realize how frustrating and frightening it is to try to understand and help a person suffering psychological difficulties. Even if you have had no personal experience with the extremes of abnormal behavior, you have probably been affected by reports in the

news of terrifying actions of a person described as mentally disturbed who is found to have had a history of mental instability or even to have been confined at some time in a mental hospital.

Our closeness to the subject matter adds to its intrinsic fascination; undergraduate courses in abnormal psychology are among the most popular in psychology departments and indeed in the entire college curriculum. Our feeling of familiarity with the subject matter encourages us to study abnormal psychology, but it has one distinct disadvantage. All of us bring to our study preconceived notions of what the subject matter is. We have developed certain ways of thinking and talking about behavior, certain words and concepts that somehow seem to *fit*. For example, we may believe that a useful way to study fear is to focus on the immediate experience of fear, known as a phenomenological approach. This is one way of viewing fear, but it is not the only way. As behavioral scientists we have to grapple with the difference between what we may *feel* is the appropriate way to talk about human behavior and experience and what may be a more productive way of defining it in order to study and learn about it. When most people would speak of a "feeling of terror," for example, scientists studying fear might be more inclined to use a phrase such as "fear response of great magnitude." In doing so we would not be merely playing verbal games. The concepts and verbal labels we use to study abnormal behavior scientifically must be free of the subjective feelings of appropriateness ordinarily attached to certain human phenomena. As you read this book and try to understand the mental disorders it discusses, we may be asking you to adopt frames of reference different from those to which you are accustomed, and indeed different from those we ourselves use when we are not wearing our professional hats.

The case study with which this chapter began is open to a wide range of interpretations. No doubt you have some ideas about how Ernest's problems developed, what his primary difficulties are, and perhaps even how you might try to help him. We know of no greater intellectual or emotional challenge than deciding both how to conceptualize the life of a person with psychological problems and how best to treat him or her. In Chapter 2 we will refer again to the case of Ernest H. to illustrate how workers from different theoretical orientations might describe him and try to help him.

Now we turn to a discussion of what we mean by the term *abnormal behavior*. Then we will look briefly at how our view of abnormality has evolved through history to the more scientific perspectives of today.

WHAT IS ABNORMAL BEHAVIOR?

One of the more difficult challenges facing those in the field of abnormal psychology is to define **abnormal behavior**. Here we will consider several characteristics that have been proposed as components of abnormal behavior. We will see that no single one is adequate, although each has merit and captures some part of what might be the full definition. Consequently, abnormality is usually determined based on the presence of several characteristics at one time. Our best definition of abnormal behavior takes into account the characteristics of statistical infrequency, violation of norms, personal distress, disability or dysfunction, and unexpectedness.

STATISTICAL INFREQUENCY

One aspect of abnormal behavior is that it is *infrequent*. The **normal curve**, or bell-shaped curve, places the majority of people in the middle as far as any particular characteristic is concerned; very few people fall at either extreme. An assertion that a person is normal implies that he or she does not deviate much from the average in a particular trait or behavior pattern.

Statistical infrequency is used explicitly in diagnosing mental retardation. Figure 1.1 shows the normal distribution of intelligence quotient measures in the population. Though a number of measures are used to diagnose mental retardation, low intelligence is a principal criterion (see p. 424).

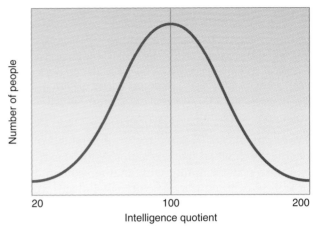

Figure 1.1 The intelligence distribution among adults, illustrating a normal, or bell-shaped curve.

When an individual's intelligence quotient is below 70, his or her intellectual functioning is considered sufficiently subnormal to be designated as mental retardation.

Although some infrequent behaviors or characteristics of people do strike us as abnormal, in some instances the relationship breaks down. Having great athletic ability is infrequent but few would regard it as abnormal. Only certain infrequent behavior, such as experiencing hallucinations or deep depression, falls into the domain considered in this book. Unfortunately, the statistical component gives us no guidance in determining what infrequent behavior psychopathologists should study.

Although abnormal behavior is infrequent, so too is great athletic talent like that of Gail Devers. Therefore, infrequency is not a sufficient definition of abnormal behavior.

VIOLATION OF NORMS

Another characteristic to consider when determining abnormality is whether the behavior *violates social norms* or threatens or makes anxious those observing it. This characteristic also rings true, at least partially. The anorexic's self-starvation fits the definition, as do the obsessive-compulsive person's complex rituals and the psychotic patient's conversation with imaginary voices. Violation of norms explicitly makes abnormality a relative concept; various forms of unusual behavior can be tolerated, depending on the prevailing cultural norms. Yet this component is also at once too broad and too narrow. Criminals and prostitutes violate social norms but are not usually studied within the domain of abnormal psychology; and the highly anxious person, who is generally regarded as a central character in the field of abnormal psychology, typically does not violate social norms and would not be bothersome to many lay observers.

In addition, cultural diversity can affect how people view social norms—what is the norm in one culture may be abnormal in another. This subtle issue is addressed throughout the book (see especially Chapter 4, pp. 96–98).

PERSONAL DISTRESS

Another characteristic of some forms of abnormality is *personal suffering*; that is, behavior is abnormal if it creates great distress and torment in the person experiencing it. Personal distress clearly fits many of the forms of abnormality considered in this

Prostitution is clearly a violation of norms, but does not necessarily indicate psychopathology.

book—people experiencing anxiety disorders and depression truly suffer greatly. But some disorders do not necessarily involve distress. The psychopath, for example, treats others coldheartedly and may continually violate the law without experiencing any guilt, remorse, or anxiety whatsoever. And some forms of distress—for example, hunger or the pain of childbirth—do not seem to belong to the field. Another difficulty in using personal discomfort as a defining characteristic is that it is inherently subjective. People decide and report on how much they are suffering. Levels of distress are diffi-

Personal distress is also part of the definition of abnormal behavior but unlike grief, which is an expected response to losing a loved one, the distress most relevant to psychopathology is not expected, given the situation in which it occurs.

cult to compare, since people's standards for defining their own psychological states can vary greatly.

DISABILITY OR DYSFUNCTION

Disability, that is, whether the individual is impaired in some important area of life (e.g., work or personal relationships) because of the abnormality, can also be a component of abnormal behavior. Substance-use disorders, for example, are defined in part by the social or occupational disability (e.g., poor work performance, serious arguments with spouse) created by substance abuse. Similarly, a phobia could indicate both distress and disability, for example, if a severe fear of flying prevented someone from taking a job promotion. As with suffering, disability applies to some, but not all, disorders. For example, transvestism (cross-dressing for sexual pleasure), which is currently diagnosed as a mental disorder if it distresses the person, is not necessarily a disability. Most transvestites are married, lead conventional lives, and usually cross-dress in private. Other characteristics that might in some circumstances be considered disabilities—such as being short if you want to be a professional basketball player—do not fall within the domain of abnormal psychology. As with distress, the absence of a more precise definition of disability does not

Abnormal behavior frequently produces disability or dysfunction. But some diagnoses, like transvestitism, are not clearly disabilities.

allow us to determine which disabilities belong and which do not.

UNEXPECTEDNESS

We have previously described how not all distress or disability falls into the domain of abnormal psychology. Distress and disability are considered abnormal when they are *unexpected* responses to environmental stressors (Wakefield, 1992). For example, anxiety disorders are diagnosed when the anxiety is unexpected and out of proportion to the situation, as when people who are well off worry constantly about their financial situation. On the other hand, hunger is an *expected* response to not eating and thus would be excluded as a state of distress that is relevant to abnormal behavior.

We have considered here several of the key characteristics of a definition of abnormal behavior. Again, none by itself yields a fully satisfactory definition but together they offer a useful framework for beginning to define abnormality.

What we present in a text such as this is a list of conditions that are currently considered abnormal. The disorders in the list will undoubtedly change with time. Because the field is continually evolving, it is not possible to offer a simple definition of abnormality that captures it in its entirety. The characteristics presented constitute a partial definition, but they are not equally applicable to every diagnosis.

HISTORY OF PSYCHOPATHOLOGY

As psychopathologists our interest is in the causes of deviant behavior. The search for causes has gone on for a considerable period of time. Before the age of scientific inquiry, all good and bad manifestations of power beyond the control of humankind—eclipses, earthquakes, storms, fire, serious and disabling disease, the passing of the seasons—were regarded as supernatural. Behavior seemingly outside individual control was subject to similar interpretation. The writings of early philosophers, theologians, and physicians who studied the troubled mind reported that deviancy reflected the displeasure of the gods or possession by demons.

EARLY DEMONOLOGY

The doctrine that an evil being, such as the devil, may dwell within a person and control his or her mind and body is called **demonology**. Examples of demonological thinking can be found in the records

Focus 1.1   The Mental Health Professions

The training of **clinicians**, the various professionals authorized to provide psychological services, takes different forms. To be a **clinical psychologist** (the profession of the authors of this textbook) requires a Ph.D. or Psy.D. degree, which entails four to seven years of graduate study. Training for the Ph.D. in clinical psychology is similar to that for the other psychological specialties; it requires a heavy emphasis on laboratory work, research design, statistics, and the empirically based study of human and animal behavior. As with other fields of psychology, the degree is basically a research degree, and candidates are required to research and write a dissertation on a specialized topic. Candidates in clinical psychology learn skills in two additional areas, which distinguishes them from other Ph.D. candidates in psychology. First, they learn techniques of assessment and **diagnosis** of mental disorders; that is, they learn the skills necessary to determine that a patient's symptoms or problems indicate a particular disorder. Second, they learn how to practice **psychotherapy**, a primarily verbal means of helping troubled individuals change their thoughts, feelings, and behavior to reduce distress and to achieve greater life satisfaction. Students take courses in which they master specific techniques under close professional supervision; then, during an intensive internship or postdoctoral training, they gradually assume increasing responsibility for the care of patients.

Other clinical graduate programs are more focused on *practice*. These programs offer the relatively new degree of Psy.D. (doctor of psychology). The curriculum is generally the same as that available to Ph.D. students, but with less emphasis on research and more on clinical training. The thinking behind this approach is that clinical psychology has advanced to a level of knowledge and certainty that justifies—even requires—intensive training in specific techniques of assessment and therapeutic intervention rather than combining practice with research.

A **psychiatrist** holds an M.D. degree and has had postgraduate training, called a residency, in which he or she has received supervision in diagnosis and psychotherapy. By virtue of the medical degree, and in contrast with psychologists, psychiatrists can also continue functioning as physicians—giving physical examinations, diagnosing medical problems, and the like. Most often, however, the only aspect of medical practice in which psychiatrists engage is prescribing **psychoactive drugs**, chemical compounds that can influence how people feel and think.

There has recently been a lively and sometimes acrimonious debate concerning the merits of allowing clinical psychologists with suitable training to prescribe psychoactive drugs. Predictably, such a move is opposed by psychiatrists, for it would represent a clear invasion of their professional turf. It is also opposed by many psychologists. Profits are an issue, but so is the question of whether a non-M.D. can learn enough

Clinicians with various degrees often work together in a team, as in this diagnostic conference.

about biochemistry and physiology to monitor the effects of drugs and protect patients from adverse side effects and drug interactions. This debate will undoubtedly continue for some time before any resolution is reached.

A **psychoanalyst** has received specialized training at a psychoanalytic institute. The program usually involves several years of clinical training as well as the in-depth psychoanalysis of the trainee. Although Sigmund Freud held that psychoanalysts do not need medical training, until recently most U.S. psychoanalytic institutes required of their graduates an M.D. and a psychiatric residency. It can take up to ten years of graduate work to become a psychoanalyst.

A **social worker** obtains an M.S.W. (master of social work) degree. Master's and doctoral programs for **counseling psychologists** are somewhat similar to graduate training in clinical psychology but usually have less emphasis on research.

The term *clinician* is often applied to people who, regardless of professional degree, offer diagnostic and therapeutic services to the public. Clinicians can be Ph.D.'s in clinical or counseling psychology, Psy.D.'s, holders of an M.S.W. degree, or psychiatrists. The term also applies to people, such as the authors of this textbook, who do both research and clinical work. A highly diverse group of people can be called **psychopathologists**. These people conduct research into the nature and development of the various disorders that their therapist colleagues try to treat. Psychopathologists may come from any number of disciplines; some are clinical psychologists, but the educational backgrounds of others may range from biochemistry to developmental psychology. What unites them is their commitment to the study of how abnormal behavior develops. Since we still have much to learn about psychopathology, the diversity of backgrounds and interests is an advantage, for it is too soon to be certain in which area major advances will be made.

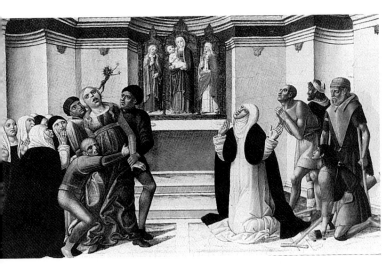

In the Dark Ages, the Christian church reclaimed an important role in treating the mentally ill. In this painting St. Catherine is exorcising a possessed woman.

of the early Chinese, Egyptians, Babylonians, and Greeks. Among the Hebrews deviancy was attributed to possession of the person by bad spirits, after God in his wrath had withdrawn protection. Christ is reported to have cured a man with an unclean spirit by casting out the devils from within him and hurling them onto a herd of swine (Mark 5:8–13).

Exorcism, the casting out of evil spirits by ritualistic chanting or torture, typically took the form of elaborate rites of prayer, noisemaking, forcing the afflicted to drink terrible-tasting brews, and on occasion more extreme measures, such as flogging and starvation, to render the body uninhabitable to the devils.

SOMATOGENESIS

In the fifth century B.C., Hippocrates (460?–377? B.C.), often regarded as the father of modern medicine, separated medicine from religion, magic, and superstition. He rejected the prevailing Greek belief that the gods sent serious physical diseases and mental disturbances as punishment and insisted instead that such illnesses had natural causes and hence should be treated like other, more common maladies, such as colds and constipation. Hippocrates regarded the brain as the organ of consciousness, of intellectual life and emotion; thus he thought that deviant thinking and behavior were indications of some kind of brain pathology. Hippocrates is often considered one of the very earliest proponents of **somatogenesis**—the notion that something wrong with the *soma*, or physical body, disturbs thought and action. **Psychogenesis**, in contrast, is the belief that a disturbance has psychological origins.

Hippocrates classified mental disorders into three categories: mania; melancholia; and phrenitis, or brain fever. Through his teachings the phenomena of abnormal behavior became more clearly the province of physicians than of priests. The treatments Hippocrates suggested were quite different from the earlier exorcistic tortures. For melancholia he prescribed tranquility, sobriety, care in choosing food and drink, and abstinence from sexual activity. Such a regimen was assumed to have a healthful effect on the brain and the body. Because Hippocrates believed in natural rather than supernatural causes, he depended on his own keen observations and made a valuable contribution as a clinician. He also left behind remarkably detailed records describing many of the symptoms now recognized in epilepsy, alcoholic delusion, stroke, and paranoia.

Hippocrates's physiology was rather crude, however, for he conceived of normal brain functioning, and therefore of mental health, as dependent on a delicate balance among four humors, or fluids of the body, namely, blood, black bile, yellow bile, and phlegm. An imbalance produced disorders. If a person was sluggish and dull, for example, the body supposedly contained a preponderance of phlegm. A preponderance of black bile was the

The Greek physician Hippocrates held a somatogenic view of abnormal behavior, considering psychopathology a disease of the brain.

The four temperaments, as depicted in this medieval painting, were thought by the followers of Hippocrates to result from excesses of the four humors. Top left: the irritable man. Top right: the melancholic man. Lower left: the sluggish man. Lower right: the changeable man.

explanation for melancholia; too much yellow bile explained irritability and anxiousness; and too much blood, changeable temperament. Hippocrates's humoral physiology did not withstand later scientific scrutiny. His basic premise, however, that human behavior is markedly affected by bodily structures or substances and that abnormal behavior is produced by some kind of imbalance or even damage, did foreshadow aspects of contemporary thought. In the next seven centuries, Hippocrates's naturalistic approach to disorder was generally accepted by other Greeks as well as the Romans, who adopted the medicine of the Greeks after their city became the seat of power in the ancient European world.

THE DARK AGES
AND DEMONOLOGY

In a massive generalization historians have often suggested that the death of Galen (A.D. 130–200), the second-century Greek who is regarded as the last major physician of the classical era, marked the beginning of the Dark Ages for all medicine and for the treatment and investigation of abnormal behavior in particular. Over several centuries of decay Greek and Roman civilization ceased to be. The churches gained in influence, and the papacy was declared independent of the state. Christian monasteries, through their missionary and educational work, replaced physicians as healers and as authorities on mental disorder.

The monasteries cared for and nursed the sick; a few were repositories for the classic Greek medical manuscripts, even though they may not have made use of the knowledge within these works. When monks cared for the mentally disordered, they prayed over them and touched them with relics or they concocted fantastic potions for them to drink in the waning phase of the moon. The families of the deranged might take them to shrines. Many of the mentally ill roamed the countryside, becoming more and more bedraggled and losing more and more of their faculties.

THE MENTALLY ILL AS WITCHES

During the thirteenth and the following few centuries, a populace that was already suffering from social unrest and recurrent famines and plagues again turned to demonology to explain these disasters. People become obsessed with the devil. Witchcraft, now viewed as instigated by the powerful Satan of the heretics, was seen as a heresy and denial of God. Then, as today, faced with inexplicable and frightening occurrences, people tended to seize on whatever explanation was available. The times conspired to heap enormous blame on those regarded as witches, and these unfortunates were persecuted with great zeal.

In 1484 Pope Innocent VIII, in a papal bull, exhorted the clergy of Europe to leave no stone unturned in the search for witches. He sent two Dominican monks to northern Germany as inquisitors. Two years later they issued a comprehensive and explicit manual, *Malleus Maleficarum* ("the witches' hammer"), to guide the witch hunts. This legal and theological document came to be regarded by Catholics and Protestants alike as a textbook on witchcraft. Those accused of witchcraft should be tortured if they did not confess; those convicted and penitent were to be imprisoned for life; and those convicted and unrepentant were to be handed over to the law for execution. The manual specified that a person's sudden loss of reason was a symptom of demonic possession and that burning was

the usual method of driving out the supposed demon. Although records of the period are not reliable, over the next several centuries it is thought that hundreds of thousands of women, men, and children were accused, tortured, and put to death.

For some time the prevailing interpretation has been that the mentally ill of the later Middle Ages were considered witches (Zilboorg & Henry, 1941). In their confessions the accused sometimes reported having had intercourse with the devil and having flown to sabbats, the secret meetings of their cults. These reports have been interpreted by contemporary writers as delusions or hallucinations and thus are taken to indicate that some of the so-called witches were psychotic.

More detailed examination of this historical period, however, indicates that most of the accused were not mentally ill. Careful analyses of the witch hunts reveal that although some accused witches were mentally disturbed, many more sane than insane people were tried. The delusion-like confessions were typically obtained during brutal torture; words were put on the tongues of the tortured by their accusers and by the beliefs of the times. Indeed, in England, where torture was not allowed, the confessions did not usually contain descriptions indicative of delusions or hallucinations (Schoeneman, 1977; Spanos, 1978).

Evaluations of other sources of information also indicate that witchcraft was not the primary interpretation of mental illness. From the thirteenth century on, as the cities of Europe grew larger, hospitals began to come under secular jurisdiction. Municipal authorities, gaining in power, tended to

In the dunking test, if the woman did not drown, she was thought to be in league with the devil, the ultimate no-win situation.

supplement or take over some of the activities of the church, one of these being the care of the ill. The foundation deed for the Holy Trinity Hospital in Salisbury, England, dating from the midfourteenth century, specified the purposes of the hospital, among them that the "mad are kept safe until they are restored of reason." English laws during this period allowed both the dangerously insane and the incompetent to be confined in a hospital. Notably, the people to be confined were not described as being possessed (Allderidge, 1979).

Beginning in the thirteenth century lunacy trials to determine a person's sanity were held in England. The trials were conducted under the Crown's right to protect the mentally impaired, and a judgment of insanity allowed the Crown to become guardian of the lunatic's estate (Neugebauer, 1979). The defendant's orientation, memory, intellect, daily life, and habits were at issue in the trial. Explanations for strange behavior typically linked it to physical illness or injury or to some emotional shock. In all the cases that Neugebauer examined, only *one* referred to demonological possession. The preponderance of evidence thus indicates that this explanation of mental disturbance was not as dominant during the Middle Ages as was once thought.

DEVELOPMENT OF ASYLUMS

Until the end of the Crusades in the fifteenth century there were very few mental hospitals in Europe, although there were thousands of hospitals for lepers. In the twelfth century England and Scotland had 220 leprosy hospitals for a population of a million and a half. After the principal Crusades had been waged, leprosy gradually disappeared from Europe, probably because with the end of the wars came a break with the eastern sources of the infection. With leprosy no longer of such great social concern, attention seems to have turned to the mad.

Confinement of the mentally ill began in earnest in the fifteenth and sixteenth centuries. Leprosariums were converted to **asylums**, refuges established for the confinement and care of the mentally ill. Many of these asylums took in a mixed lot of disturbed people and beggars. Beggars were regarded as a great social problem at the time; in sixteenth-century Paris the population of fewer than 100,000 included 30,000 beggars (Foucault, 1965). These asylums had no specific regimen for their inmates other than to get them to work; but during the same period hospitals geared more specifically for the confinement of the mentally ill also emerged. The Priory of St. Mary of Bethlehem was founded in 1243. By 1403 it housed six insane men, and in 1547 Henry VIII handed it over to the city of London, thereafter to be a hospital devoted solely to the confinement of the mentally ill. The conditions in Bethlehem were deplorable. Over the years the word *bedlam*, a contraction and popular name for this hospital, became a descriptive term for a place or scene of wild uproar and confusion. Bethlehem eventually became one of London's great tourist attractions, by the eighteenth century rivaling both Westminster Abbey and the Tower of London. Even as late as the nineteenth century, viewing the violent patients and their antics was considered entertainment, and tickets of admission

A tour of St. Mary's of Bethlehem (Bedlam) provides amusement for these two upper class women in Hogarth's eighteenth-century painting.

Shown here is the first American mental hospital, founded in 1773 in Williamsburg, Virginia.

to Bedlam were sold. Similarly, in the Lunatic's Tower constructed in Vienna in 1784, patients were confined in the spaces between inner square rooms and the outer walls, where they could be viewed by passersby. The first mental hospital in the United States was founded in Williamsburg, Virginia, in 1773.

It should not be assumed that the inclusion of abnormal behavior within the domain of hospitals and medicine necessarily led to more humane and effective treatment. Medical treatments were often crude and painful. Benjamin Rush (1745–1813), who began practicing medicine in Philadelphia in 1769 and was deeply involved in his country's struggle for independence, is considered the father of American psychiatry. He believed that mental disorder was caused by an excess of blood in the brain. Consequently, his favored treatment was to draw from "the insane" great quantities of blood (Farina, 1976)! Rush entertained another hypothesis, that many "lunatics" could be cured by frightening them. In one recommended procedure the physician was to convince the patient of his or her impending death. A New England doctor of the nineteenth century implemented this prescription in an ingenious manner. "On his premises stood a tank of water, into which a patient, packed into a

coffin-like box pierced with holes, was lowered. … He was kept under water until the bubbles of air ceased to rise, after which he was taken out, rubbed, and revived—if he had not already passed beyond reviving!" (Deutsch, 1949, p. 82).

MORAL TREATMENT

Philippe Pinel (1745–1826) is considered a primary figure in the movement for humanitarian treatment of the mentally ill in asylums. In 1793, while the French Revolution raged, he was put in charge of a large asylum in Paris known as La Bicêtre. A historian described the conditions at this particular hospital:

[The patients were] shackled to the walls of their cells, by iron collars which held them flat against the wall and permitted little movement. … They could not lie down at night, as a rule. … Oftentimes there was a hoop of iron around the waist of the patient and in addition … chains on both the hands and the feet. … These chains [were] sufficiently long so that the patient could feed himself out of a bowl, the food usually being a mushy gruel—bread soaked in a weak soup. Since little was known about dietetics, [no attention] was paid to the type of diet given the patients. They were presumed to be animals … and not to care whether the food was good or bad. (Selling, 1940, p. 54)

Pinel removed the chains of the people imprisoned in La Bicêtre and began to treat them as sick human beings rather than as beasts. Many who had been completely unmanageable became calm and much easier to handle. Formerly considered dangerous, they strolled through the hospital and grounds with no inclination to create disturbances or to harm anyone. Light and airy rooms replaced dungeons. Some who had been incarcerated for years were restored to health and eventually discharged from the hospital.

Freeing the patients of their restraints was not the only humanitarian reform advocated by Pinel.

Pinel's freeing the patients at La Bicêtre is the event often considered as the beginning of more humanitarian treatment of the mentally ill.

Consistent with the egalitarianism of the new French Republic, he believed that the mental patients in his care were essentially normal people who should be approached with compassion and understanding and treated with dignity as individual human beings. He surmised that if their reason had left them because of severe personal and social problems, it might be restored to them through comforting counsel and purposeful activity.

For all the good Pinel did for the mentally ill, he was not a complete paragon of enlightenment and egalitarianism in his treatment of them. The more humanitarian treatment he reserved for the upper classes; patients of the lower classes were still subjected to terror and coercion as a means of control—a telling commentary on the duplicity of prejudice in the birth of a new government (Szasz, 1974).

In the wake of Pinel's revolutionary work in La Bicêtre, the hospitals established in Europe and the United States were for a time relatively small and privately supported. A prominent merchant and Quaker, William Tuke (1732–1822), shocked by the conditions at York Asylum in England, proposed to the Society of Friends that it found its own institution. In 1796 York Retreat was established on a country estate. It provided the mentally ill with a quiet and religious atmosphere in which to live, work, and rest. Patients discussed their difficulties with attendants, worked in the garden, and took walks through the countryside. In the United States the Friends' Asylum, founded in 1817 in Pennsylvania, and the Hartford Retreat, established in 1824 in Connecticut, were patterned after the York Retreat. Other U.S. hospitals were influenced by the sympathetic and attentive treatment provided by Pinel and Tuke. In accordance with this approach, which became known as **moral treatment**, patients had close contact with attendants, who talked and read to them and encouraged them to engage in purposeful activity; residents led lives as normally as possible and in general took responsibility for themselves within the constraints of their disorders.

Two findings have emerged from a recent review of detailed case records of the York Retreat from 1880 to 1884 (Renvoise & Beveridge, 1989). First, drugs were the most common treatment and included alcohol, cannabis, opium, and chloral hydrate (knockout drops). Second, the outcomes do not appear very favorable; fewer than one-third of the patients were discharged as improved or recovered. Moral treatment may not have been all that it was cracked up to be.

Moral treatment was abandoned in the latter part of the nineteenth century. Ironically, the efforts of Dorothea Dix (1802–1877), a crusader for improved

By the nineteenth century a number of mental hospitals had been established along the principles of moral treatment. This woodcut shows patients at a New York hospital dance.

conditions for the mentally ill who fought to have hospitals created for their care, helped effect this change. Dix, a Boston schoolteacher, taught a Sunday school class at the local prison and was shocked at the deplorable conditions in which the

In the nineteenth century, Dorthea Dix played a major role in establishing more mental hospitals in the United States.

FOCUS 1.2   THE MENTAL HOSPITAL TODAY

Each year over two million Americans are hospitalized for mental disorders. In the 1970s concerns about the restrictive nature of confinement in a mental hospital led to the deinstitutionalization of a large number of mental-hospital patients. Budget cuts in the 1980s and 1990s have caused this trend to continue. But the problems of the chronic patient, who cannot be deinstitutionalized, have yet to be handled adequately (as we will discuss in more detail in Chapter 20). Treatment in public mental institutions is primarily custodial in nature. Patients are kept alive, but they receive little treatment; their existence is monotonous and sedentary for the most part.

Mental hospitals in the United States today are usually funded either by the federal government or by the state. (In fact, the term *state hospital* is taken to mean a *mental* hospital run by the state.) Despite their staggering costs they are often old, grim, and somewhat removed from major metropolitan centers. Many Veterans Administration hospitals and general medical hospitals also contain psychiatric wards.

In addition, there are private mental hospitals. Sheppard and Enoch Pratt near Baltimore, Maryland, and McLean Hospital, in Belmont, Massachusetts, are two of the most famous. The physical facilities and professional care in private hospitals tend to be superior to those of state hospitals for one reason: the private hospitals have more money. The costs to patients in these private institutions can exceed $1,000 per day and yet may not include individual therapy sessions with a member of the professional staff! Although many patients have medical insurance, usually with a ninety-day limit, such hospitals are clearly beyond the means of most citizens.

A somewhat specialized mental hospital, sometimes called a prison hospital, is reserved for people who have been arrested and judged unable to stand trial and for those who have been acquitted of a crime by reason of insanity (see p. 594). Although these patients have not been sent to prison, armed guards and tight security regiment their lives. Treatment of some kind is supposed to take place during their incarceration.

Even in the best hospitals patients usually have precious little contact with psychiatrists or clinical psychologists, a situa-

tion confirmed by careful observations of Gordon Paul and his co-workers. They found that most patients had no contact with staff for 80 to 90 percent of their waking hours and that the clinical staff spent less than one-fourth of their working time in contact with patients (Paul, 1987, 1988). Most of a patient's days and evenings are spent either alone or in the company of other patients and of aides, individuals who often have little more than a high school education. As with imprisonment, the overwhelming feeling is of helplessness and depersonalization. Patients sit for endless hours in hallways waiting for dining halls to open, for medication to be dispensed, and for consultations with psychologists, social workers, and vocational counselors to begin. Except for the most severely disturbed, patients do have access to the various facilities of a hospital, ranging from woodworking shops to swimming pools, from gymnasiums to basket-weaving shops.

Most hospitals require patients to attend group therapy—here, a general term indicating only that at least two patients are supposed to relate to each other and to a group leader in a room for a specific period of time. Some patients have a few sessions alone with a professional therapist. For the most part, however, traditional hospital treatment over the past forty years has been oriented toward dispensing drugs rather than offering psychotherapy. The institutional setting itself is used as a way to provide supportive care and to protect and look after patients whose conditions make it virtually impossible for them to care for themselves or that render them an unreasonable burden or threat to others (Paul & Menditto, 1992).

One nagging problem is that institutionalization is difficult to reverse once people have resided in mental hospitals for more than a year. We recall asking a patient who had improved markedly over the previous several months why he was reluctant to be discharged. "Doc," he said earnestly, "it's a jungle out there." Although we cannot entirely disagree with his view, there are at least a few advantages to living on the outside; yet this man—a veteran and chronic patient with a clinical folder more than two feet thick—had become so accustomed to the protected environment of various Veterans Administration hos-

inmates lived. Her interest spread to the conditions of mental hospitals and to the mentally ill of the time who had nowhere to go for treatment. Dix campaigned vigorously to improve the lot of the mentally ill; she personally helped see that thirty-two state hospitals were built. Unfortunately, the staffs of the large, public hospitals that were built to take in the many patients whom the private ones could not accommodate were unable to provide

individual attention (Bockhoven, 1963). Moreover, these hospitals came to be administered by physicians, who were interested in the biological aspects of illness and in the physical, rather than the psychological, well-being of mental patients. The money that once paid the salaries of personal attendants now paid for equipment and laboratories. See Focus 1.2 for an examination of the conditions in today's mental institutions.

pitals that the prospect of leaving was as frightening to him as the prospect of entering a mental hospital is to those who have never lived in one.

One treatment sometimes applied is **milieu therapy**, in which the entire hospital becomes a "therapeutic community" (e.g., Jones, 1953). All its ongoing activities and all its personnel become part of the treatment program. Milieu therapy appears to be a return to the moral practices of the nineteenth century. Social interaction and group activities are encouraged so that through group pressure the patients are directed toward normal functioning. Patients are treated as responsible human beings rather than as custodial cases (Paul, 1969). They are expected to participate in their own readjustment as well as that of their fellow patients. Open wards allow them considerable freedom. There is some evidence for the efficacy of milieu therapy (e.g., Fairweather, 1964; Greenblatt et al., 1965), the most convincing from a milestone project by Paul and Lentz (1977).

In this ambitious study Paul and Lentz demonstrated encouraging improvement in chronic, hard-core patients through both milieu therapy and a learning-based therapy. In the latter, patients were able to earn rewards for making their beds, observing social conventions, such as saying good morning, combing their hair, and attending classes in which they learned skills needed for living outside the hospital, as well as socializing with other patients. Described in more detail on pages 521–524, this learning-based therapy rewards patients for behaving in a particular way by giving them tokens that can be exchanged for privileges or other items patients desire. On a number of measures of the effectiveness of the therapies, the learning program was more successful than milieu therapy; both treatments were much superior to the routine hospital management of another group in an older Illinois state hospital. Since mental hospitals will be needed for the foreseeable future, especially by people who demonstrate time and again that they have difficulty functioning on the outside, this work is of particular importance. It suggests specific ways in which chronic patients can be helped to cope better not only within the hospital but after discharge as well.

Most dormitory rooms at state mental hospitals are bleak and unstimulating.

THE BEGINNING OF CONTEMPORARY THOUGHT

A RETURN TO SOMATOGENESIS

After the fall of Greco-Roman civilization the writings of Galen were the standard source of information about both physical and mental illness. It was not until the Middle Ages that any new facts began to emerge. One development that fostered progress was the discovery by the Flemish anatomist and physician Vesalius (1514–1564) that Galen's presentation of human anatomy was incorrect. Galen had presumed that human physiology mirrored the apes he had studied. It took more than a thousand years for autopsy studies of humans—not allowed during his time—to begin to prove that Galen had been wrong. Empirical medical science, in which knowledge is based on direct observation, received another boost from the efforts of the famous English physician Thomas Sydenham (1624–1689). Sydenham was particularly influential in advocating an empirical approach to classification and diagnosis that subsequently influenced those interested in mental disorders.

One of those impressed by Sydenham's approach was a German physician, Wilhelm Griesinger, who insisted that any diagnosis of mental disorder specify a biological cause, a clear return to the somatogenic views first espoused by Hippocrates. A textbook of psychiatry, written by Griesinger's well-known follower Emil Kraepelin (1856–1926) and first published in 1883, furnished a classification system in an attempt to establish the organic nature of mental illnesses. Kraepelin discerned among mental disorders a tendency for a certain group of symptoms, called a **syndrome**, to appear together regularly enough to be regarded as having an underlying physical cause, much as a particular medical disease and its syndrome may be attributed to a biological dysfunction. He regarded each mental illness as distinct from all others, having its own genesis, symptoms, course, and outcome. Even though cures had not been worked out, at least the course of the disease could be predicted. Kraepelin proposed two major groups of severe mental diseases: dementia praecox, an early term for schizophrenia, and manic-depressive psychosis. He postulated a chemical imbalance as the cause of schizophrenia and an irregularity in metabolism as the explanation of manic-depressive psychosis. Kraepelin's scheme for classifying these and other mental illnesses became the basis for the present diagnostic categories, which are described more fully in Chapter 3.

Though the workings of the nervous system were understood somewhat by the mid-1800s, not enough was known to reveal all the expected abnormalities in structure that might underlie various mental disorders. Degenerative changes in the brain cells associated with senile and presenile psychoses and some structural pathologies that accompany mental retardation were identified, however. Perhaps the most striking medical success was the discovery of the full nature and origin of syphilis, a venereal disease that had been recognized for several centuries.

The story of this discovery provides a wonderful picture of how an empirical approach, the basis for contemporary science, works. Since 1798 it had been known that a number of mental patients manifested a syndrome characterized by a steady deterioration of both physical and mental abilities and that these patients suffered multiple impairments,

including delusions of grandeur and progressive paralysis. Soon after these symptoms were recognized, it was realized that these patients never recovered. In 1825 this deterioration in mental and physical health was designated a disease, **general paresis**. Although it was established in 1857 that some patients with paresis had earlier had syphilis, there were many competing theories of the origin of paresis. For example, in attempting to account for the high rate of the disorder among sailors, some supposed that seawater might be the cause. And Griesinger, in trying to explain the higher incidence among men, speculated that liquor, tobacco, and coffee might be implicated. In the 1860s and 1870s Louis Pasteur established the **germ theory** of disease, which set forth the view that disease is caused by infection of the body by minute organisms. This theory laid the groundwork for demonstrating the relation between syphilis and general paresis. In 1897 Richard von Krafft-Ebing inoculated paretic patients with matter from syphilitic sores; the patients did not develop syphilis, indicating that they had been infected earlier. Finally, in 1905, the specific microorganism that causes syphilis was discovered. A causal link had been established between infection, destruction of certain areas of the brain, and a form of psychopathology. If one type of psychopathology had a biological cause, so could others. Somatogenesis gained credibility, and the search for more biological causes was off and running.

PSYCHOGENESIS

The search for somatogenic causes dominated psychiatry until well into the twentieth century, no doubt partly because of the stunning discoveries made about general paresis. But in other parts of western Europe, in the late eighteenth and throughout the nineteenth century, mental illnesses were considered to have an entirely different origin. Various psychogenic points of view, attributing mental disorders to psychological malfunctions, were fashionable in France and Austria. Many people in western Europe were at that time subject to hysterical states; they suffered from physical incapacities, such as blindness or paralysis, for which no physical cause could be found (see p. 156).

Franz Anton Mesmer (1734–1815), an Austrian physician practicing in Vienna and Paris in the late eighteenth century, believed that hysterical disorders were caused by a particular distribution of a universal magnetic fluid in the body. Moreover, he felt that one person could influence the fluid of another to bring about a change in the other's behavior. He conducted meetings cloaked in mystery and mysticism, at which afflicted patients sat around a covered *baquet*, or tub, with iron rods protruding through the cover from bottles underneath that contained various chemicals. Mesmer would enter a room, take various rods from the tub, and touch afflicted parts of his patients' bodies. The rods were believed to transmit animal magnetism and adjust the distribution of the universal magnetic fluid, thereby removing the hysterical anesthesias and paralyses. Whatever we may think of what seems today to be a questionable theoretical explanation and procedure, Mesmer apparently helped many people overcome their hysterical problems. The reader may wonder about our discussing Mesmer's work under the rubric of psychogenic causes, since Mesmer regarded the hysterical disorders as strictly physical. Because of the setting in which Mesmer worked with his patients, however, he is generally considered one of the earlier practitioners of modern-day hypnosis, which is discussed in more detail in Chapter 7 (p. 162). The word *mesmerize* is an older term for *hypnotize*. (The phenomenon itself, however, was known to the ancients of probably every culture, part of the sorcery and magic of conjurers, fakirs, and faith healers.)

Although Mesmer was regarded as a quack by his contemporaries, the study of hypnosis gradually became respectable. A great Parisian neurologist, Jean Martin Charcot (1825–1893), also studied hysterical states, not only anesthesia and paralysis, but blindness, deafness, convulsive attacks, and gaps in memory brought about by hysteria. Charcot initially espoused a somatogenic point of view. One day, however, some of his enterprising students hypnotized a normal woman and suggested to her certain hysterical symptoms. Charcot was deceived into believing that she was an actual hysterical patient. When the students showed him how readily they could remove the symptoms by waking the woman, Charcot changed his mind about hysteria and became interested in nonphysiological interpretations of these very puzzling phenomena.

At about this time, in Vienna, a physician named Josef Breuer (1842–1925) treated a young woman who had become bedridden with a number of hysterical symptoms. Her legs and right arm and side were paralyzed, her sight and hearing were impaired, and she often had difficulty speaking. She also sometimes went into a dreamlike state, or "absence," during which she mumbled to herself, seemingly preoccupied with troubling thoughts. During one treatment session Breuer hypnotized Anna O. and repeated some of her mumbled words. He succeeded in getting her to talk more freely and

Mesmer's procedure for transmitting animal magnetism was generally considered a form of hypnosis.

ultimately with considerable emotion about some very upsetting past events. On awakening from these hypnotic sessions she would frequently feel much better. With Anna O. and other hysterical patients Breuer found that the relief and cure of symptoms seemed to last longer if, under hypnosis, they were able to recall the precipitating event for the symptom and if their original emotion was expressed. Reliving an earlier emotional catastrophe and the release of the emotional tension produced by previously forgotten thoughts about the event was called *catharsis*. Breuer's method became known as the **cathartic method**. In 1895 one of his colleagues joined him in the publication of *Studies in Hysteria*, a book considered a milestone in abnor-

The French psychiatrist, Jean Charcot, lectures on hysteria in this famous painting. Charcot was an important figure in reviving interest in psychogenesis.

Josef Breuer, the Austrian physician and physiologist, collaborated with Freud in the early development of psychoanalysis. He treated only Anna O. by the cathartic method he originated. Becoming alarmed by what would later be called her transference and his own countertransference, he described his procedures to a colleague and turned her over to him.

Anna O., actually Bertha Pappenheim, was the patient in the celebrated case that Breuer treated with the cathartic method.

mal psychology. In the next chapter we examine the thinking of Breuer's collaborator, Sigmund Freud.[1]

SCIENCE: A HUMAN ENTERPRISE

In space exploration highly sophisticated satellites have been sent aloft to make observations. It is possible, however, that certain phenomena are missed because our instruments do not have the sensing devices capable of detecting them. Consider some recent discussion of the announcement on August 7, 1996, by the National Aeronautics and Space Administration (NASA) that signs that life once existed on Mars may have been found in a piece of

Martian rock that, it is believed, was catapulted into space by an asteroid about 16 million years ago and was drawn into Earth's gravity about 13,000 years ago. Found in Antarctica in 1984, this rock is the subject of study and speculation by chemists and space scientists as possibly containing signs of Martian microbes from 3.6 million years ago. Though controversy reigns about the validity of the findings, of relevance to us here are some comments regarding how one can decide that there are, indeed, signs that life once existed on the now-barren planet. How can we be certain that our own understanding of what is alive matches what may have once lived on Mars? Said a NASA astrophysicist, "Everything we know about life we learned from Earth" (cited in Cole, 1996, p. A1). Another scientist put it this way: "We're working with a sample of one: life on Earth. That's like trying to learn about fruit by studying only apples. We have to look at a lot of apples and oranges" (cited in Cole, 1996, p. A29).

Life on another planet can be looked for only with the instruments we have available, and the design of these instruments is determined not just by technology but by our preconceptions of what life is. Tests that are conducted on material from another part of the solar system rest on assumptions about the nature of living matter that may not match what might have evolved elsewhere.

---

[1]Anna O., the young woman treated by Breuer with the cathartic method, or "talking cure," has become one of the best-known clinical cases in all psychotherapy literature, and as indicated above, the report of this case and four others in 1895 formed the basis of Freud's important later contributions. But historical investigations by Ellenberger (1972) cast serious doubt on the accuracy of Breuer's reporting. Indeed, Anna O.—in reality Bertha Pappenheim, member of a well-to-do Viennese family—was apparently helped only temporarily by Breuer's talking cure! Carl Jung, Freud's renowned colleague, is quoted as saying that, during a conference in 1925, Freud told him that Anna O. had never been cured. Hospital records discovered by Ellenberger confirmed that Anna O. continued to rely on morphine to ease the "hysterical" problems that Breuer is reputed to have removed by catharsis. In fact, evidence suggests that some of her problems were biological, not psychological.

This discussion of space exploration is one way of pointing out that scientific observation is a human endeavor that reflects not only the strengths of human ingenuity and scholarship but also our intrinsic incapacity to be fully knowledgeable about the nature of our universe. Scientists are able to design instruments to make only the kinds of observations about which they have some initial idea. They realize that certain observations are not being made because our knowledge about the general nature of the universe is limited.

SUBJECTIVITY IN SCIENCE: THE ROLE OF PARADIGMS

Science is bound not only by the limitations imposed on scientific inquiry by the current state of knowledge, but also by the scientist's own limitations. We now return to the point with which we began this chapter—the challenge of remaining objective when trying to understand and study abnormal behavior. Every effort should be made to study abnormal behavior according to scientific principles. But science is *not* a completely objective and certain enterprise. Rather, as suggested by philosopher of science Thomas Kuhn, subjective factors as well as limitations in our perspective on the universe enter into the conduct of scientific inquiry.

Central to any application of scientific principles, in Kuhn's view, is the notion of **paradigm**, a conceptual framework or approach within which a scientist works. A paradigm, according to Kuhn, is a set of basic assumptions that outline the particular universe of scientific inquiry, specifying the kinds of concepts that will be regarded as legitimate as well as the methods that may be used to collect and interpret data. A paradigm has profound implications for how scientists operate at any given time, for "[people] whose research is based on shared paradigms are committed to the same rules and standards for scientific practice" (Kuhn, 1962, p. 11). Paradigms specify what problems scientists will investigate and how they will go about the investigation. Paradigms are an intrinsic part of a science, serving the vital function of indicating the rules to be followed. In perceptual terms a paradigm may be likened to a general perspective or approach, a tendency to see certain factors and not to see others.

In addition to injecting inevitable biases into the definition and collection of data a paradigm may also affect the interpretation of facts. In other words, the meaning or import given to data may depend to a considerable extent on a paradigm. We will describe the major paradigms of abnormal psychol-ogy in the next chapter, but for now we would like to give you an idea of how they operate.

AN EXAMPLE OF PARADIGMS IN ABNORMAL PSYCHOLOGY

Langer and Abelson (1974) were interested in how theoretical orientations or paradigms might affect how trained clinicians view the adjustment of a person, so they designed an experiment to examine this issue.

As we will discuss more fully in the next chapter, behavior therapy stems from the behaviorism-learning branch of psychology, which is concerned with the observation of overt behavior and views behavior as the product of certain kinds of learning. Behavior therapists believe that abnormal behavior is acquired according to the same learning principles by which normal behavior is acquired, and they tend to focus on overt behavior. More traditionally trained clinicians are apt to look for an inner, perhaps hidden, conflict that is causing disturbed behavior. They tend to view behavior as a means of inferring what is going on in the patient's mind. Often these inferences involve processes of which the patient is unaware. Langer and Abelson reasoned that because they were trained to focus on observable behavior, behavior therapists might be less swayed by being told that a person was ill than would traditionally trained clinicians, who would be more likely to see overtly normal behavior as masking hidden or unconscious problems. To test this supposition they conceived the following experiment. A group of behavior therapists and another of traditional clinicians with some training in psychoanalysis (see p. 38) were shown a videotape of an interview in progress between two men. Before viewing this videotape, half the participants in each group were told that the interviewee was a job applicant, the other half that he was a patient. The traditional clinicians who were told that the interviewee was a patient were expected to rate him as more disturbed than those who considered him a job applicant. The ratings of the two groups of behavior therapists were expected to be less affected by the labels and thus to be rather similar.

The videotape shown to all subjects depicted a bearded professor interviewing a young man in his midtwenties. The interviewee had been recruited through a newspaper advertisement that offered ten dollars to someone who had recently applied for a new job and was willing to be interviewed and videotaped. The fifteen-minute segment chosen from the original interview contained a rambling, autobiographical monologue by the young man in which he described a number of past jobs and dwelt on his conflicts with bureaucrats. His manner was considered by Langer and Abelson to be intense but uncertain; they felt that he could be regarded either as sincere and struggling or as confused and troubled.

A questionnaire measured the clinicians' impressions about the mental health of the interviewee. When the interviewee was identified as a job applicant there were no differences in the adjustment ratings given by the traditional clinicians and the behavior therapists. But the patient label, as expected, produced sharp differences (Figure 1.2). When the interviewee was identified as a patient the traditional clinicians rated him relatively disturbed—significantly more so than did the traditional clinicians who viewed the man as a job applicant. In contrast, the behavior therapists rated the "ill" interviewee as relatively well-adjusted, in fact, as no less well-adjusted than he was rated by the behavior therapists who thought he was a job applicant. Qualitative evaluations obtained from the clinicians supported their ratings. Whereas the behavior therapists described the man as "realistic," "sincere," and "responsible," regardless of label, the traditional clinicians who viewed him as a patient used phrases such as "tight, defensive person," "conflict over homosexuality," and "impulsivity shows through his rigidity."

Why, in this particular experiment, did the behavior therapists appear to be unbiased? Langer and Abelson explain it this way. The behavioral approach encourages clinicians to concentrate on overt or manifest behavior and to be skeptical about illness that is not readily apparent. Those with such an orientation had the advantage in this particular study because, however the interviewee rambled, his behavior on balance was not overtly disturbed.

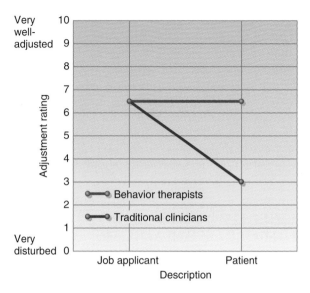

Figure 1.2   The mean adjustment ratings given the interviewee, depending on the investigators' description of him and the diagnosticians' training. Adapted from Langer and Abelson (1974). Copyright 1974 by the APA. Reprinted by permission.

The traditional therapists had been trained to look beyond what was most obvious in a client; therefore, they probably paid too much attention to the negative ramblings about bureaucrats and inferred that something was basically wrong with the man.

Langer and Abelson properly alert readers to the limitations of their experiment, reminding them that a different study—perhaps using an interviewee who was obviously disturbed—might put behavior therapists at a disadvantage. The purpose of the experiment and of this discussion of it is not to pit one orientation against another, but rather *to illustrate how a paradigm can affect perception*, causing us to attend to certain details and to overlook others.

SUMMARY

The study of psychopathology is a search for why people behave, think, and feel in unexpected, sometimes bizarre, and typically self-defeating ways. Much less is known than we would like; this book will focus on the ways in which psychopathologists have been trying to learn the causes of abnormal behavior and what they know about preventing and alleviating it.

Several characteristics are considered in evaluating whether a behavior is abnormal: statistical infrequency, violation of societal norms, personal distress, disability or dysfunction, and unexpectedness. Each characteristic tells something about what can be considered abnormal, but conceptions change with time, making it impossible to offer a simple definition that captures abnormality in its entirety.

The field of abnormal psychology has its origins in ancient demonology and crude medical theorizing. Since the beginning of scientific inquiry into abnormal behavior, two major points of view have vied for attention: the somatogenic, which assumes that every mental aberration is caused by a physical malfunction; and the psychogenic, which assumes that the sufferer's body is intact and that difficulties are to be explained in psychological terms. Today both are viewed as contributing to abnormal behavior.

Scientific inquiry is presented as a special way in which human beings acquire knowledge about their world. In a very important sense people may see only what they are prepared to see, and certain phenomena may go undetected because scientists can discover only the things about which they already have some general idea. There is subjectivity in science as there is in everyday perception and problem solving. By defining one's paradigm or scientific perspective, one is better able to keep track of subjective influences.

KEY TERMS

psychopathology
abnormal behavior
normal curve
clinicians
clinical psychologist
diagnosis
psychotherapy
psychiatrist
psychoactive drugs

psychoanalyst
social worker
counseling psychologists
psychopathologists
demonology
exorcism
somatogenesis
psychogenesis

asylums
moral treatment
syndrome
milieu therapy
general paresis
germ theory (of disease)
cathartic method
paradigm

Joan Genovese, "La Ruta," 1980

CURRENT PARADIGMS IN PSYCHOPATHOLOGY AND THERAPY

The subject of the last chapter was the nature of abnormality—its history and how it has been defined by characteristics such as personal distress and the violation of norms. In this chapter we consider current paradigms of abnormal behavior and treatment. A paradigm, again, is a set of basic assumptions that together define how to conceptualize, study, gather and interpret data, even how to think about a particular subject. There are several paradigms for conceptualizing abnormal behavior. Those we cover here focus both on understanding the etiology, or causes, of abnormal behavior and on therapeutic interventions. In Chapters 17 through 19, we will examine these perspectives on treating abnormal behavior in greater detail.

This chapter presents four paradigms of abnormal psychology: biological, psychoanalytic, learning, and cognitive. Current thinking about abnormal behavior tends to be multifaceted. The work of clinicians and researchers is informed by an awareness of the strengths and limitations of the various paradigms as well as of the role that environmental factors play in producing psychopathology. For this reason current views of abnormal behavior tend to be integrations of several paradigms. At the end of this chapter we will describe another paradigm— diathesis–stress—which provides the basis for an integrative approach.

In previous editions of this book, we also discussed the humanistic and existential paradigms at this point. In this edition, however, we are reserving our in-depth discussion of these paradigms for Chapter 17, where we examine and compare current approaches to therapy. Our reasoning is that proponents of the humanistic and existential paradigms usually object to thinking in terms of categories of disorders, such as schizophrenia and anxiety disorders, and these paradigms are seldom used to analyze how psychological problems develop—they focus more on personal growth than on disorder. Although different in some ways, humanistic and existential approaches share several important features: they emphasize free will; they regard as the most important determinant of behavior a person's phenomenological world, that is, how he or she construes and experiences events; they focus on people's abilities rather than on their disabilities; they are concerned with issues of the meaning of life and how one forges a place in it; and they encourage personal growth and fulfillment rather than emphasize the relief of psychological distress. Leading figures in these paradigms are Carl Rogers, Abraham Maslow, Viktor Frankl, and Frederic (Fritz) Perls.

Many people go about the study of abnormal psychology without explicitly considering the nature of the paradigm they have adopted. As this chapter will indicate and as we saw in Langer and Abelson's study in Chapter 1, however, the choice of a paradigm has some very important consequences for the way in which abnormal behavior is defined, investigated, and treated. Our discussion of paradigms will lay the groundwork for the examination of the major categories of disorders and of intervention that makes up the rest of the book.

THE BIOLOGICAL PARADIGM

The **biological paradigm** of abnormal behavior is a continuation of the somatogenic hypothesis described in Chapter 1. This broad, theoretical point of view holds that mental disorders are caused by aberrant somatic, biological, or bodily processes. This paradigm has often been referred to as the **medical model** or **disease model**.

The study of abnormal behavior is historically linked to medicine. Many early workers as well as contemporaries have used the model of physical illness as the basis for understanding deviant behavior. Within the field of abnormal behavior the terminology of medicine is pervasive. As Brendan Maher, a noted schizophrenia researcher, pointed out, "[Deviant] behavior is termed *pathological* and is classified on the basis of *symptoms*, classification being called *diagnosis*. Processes designed to change behavior are called *therapies* and are [sometimes] applied to patients in mental *hospitals*. If the deviant behavior ceases, the patient is described as *cured*" (1966, p. 22).

As we described earlier, when Louis Pasteur discovered the relation between bacteria and disease and soon thereafter postulated viruses, the germ theory of disease provided a new explanation of pathology. External symptoms were assumed to be produced through infection of the body by minute organisms and viruses. For a time the germ theory was the paradigm of medicine, but it soon became apparent that not all diseases could be explained by this theory. Diabetes, for example, a malfunction of the insulin-secreting cells of the pancreas, cannot be attributed to infection. Nor does it have a single cause. Heart disease provides another example. A multitude of factors—genetic makeup, stress produced by smoking and obesity, life stress, and perhaps Type A behavior (see p. 194)—are all related to the frequency of heart disease. Medical illnesses can be very different from one another in their causes. However, they all share one characteristic in common: some biological process is disrupted or not functioning normally. That is why we have chosen to call this the biological paradigm.

CONTEMPORARY APPROACHES TO THE BIOLOGICAL PARADIGM

There is a considerable literature, both research and theory based, dealing with biological factors relevant to psychopathology. Heredity probably predisposes a person, through physiological malfunction, to develop schizophrenia (see Chapter 11); depression may result from chemical imbalances within the brain (Chapter 10); anxiety disorders may stem from a defect within the autonomic nervous system that causes a person to be too easily aroused (Chapter 6); delirium and dementia can be traced to impairments in structures of the brain (Chapter 16). In each case a type of psychopathology is viewed as caused by the disturbance of some biological process. Those working with the biological paradigm assume that answers to puzzles of psychopathology will be found within the body. In this section, we will look at two areas of research within this paradigm in which the data are particularly interesting—behavior genetics and biochemistry.

BEHAVIOR GENETICS

When the ovum, the female reproductive cell, is joined by the male's spermatozoon, a zygote, or fertilized egg, is produced. It has forty-six chromosomes, the number characteristic of a human being. Each chromosome is made up of thousands of **genes**, the carriers of the genetic information (DNA) passed from parents to child. Each cell of the human

Behavior genetics studies the degree to which characteristics, like physical resemblance or psychopathology, are shared by family members because of shared genes.

body contains a full complement of chromosomes and genes in its nucleus.

Behavior genetics is the study of individual differences in behavior that are attributable in part to differences in genetic makeup. The total genetic makeup of an individual, consisting of inherited genes, is referred to as the **genotype**. An individual's genotype is his or her unobservable, physiological genetic constitution, in contrast with the totality of observable characteristics, such as level of anxiety, which is referred to as the **phenotype**. The genotype is fixed at birth, but it should not be viewed as a static entity. Genes controlling various features of development switch off and on at specific times, for example, to control various aspects of physical development.

The phenotype changes over time and is generally viewed as the product of an interaction between the genotype and experience. For example, an individual may be born with the capacity for high intellectual achievement, but whether he or she develops this genetically given potential depends on such environmental factors as upbringing and education. Hence any measure of intelligence is best viewed as an index of the phenotype.

On the basis of the distinction between phenotype and genotype we recognize that various clinical syndromes are disorders of the phenotype. Thus it is not proper to speak of the direct inheritance of schizophrenia or anxiety disorders; at most, only the genotypes for these disorders can be inherited. Whether these genotypes will eventually engender the phenotypic behavior disorder will depend on environment and experience; a predisposition, also known as a *diathesis*, may be inherited, but not the disorder itself.

The study of behavior genetics has relied on three basic methods to uncover whether a genetic predisposition for psychopathology is inherited—comparison of members of a family, comparison of pairs of twins, and the investigation of adoptees. The **family method** can be used to compare members of a family because the average number of genes shared by two blood relatives is known. Children receive half their genes from one parent and half from the other, so on average siblings and parents and children are identical in 50 percent of their genetic background. People who share 50 percent of their genes with a given individual are called first-degree relatives of that person. Relatives not as closely related share fewer genes. For example, nephews and nieces share 25 percent of the genetic makeup of an uncle. If a predisposition for a mental disorder can be inherited, a study of the family should reveal a correlation between the

The study of twins is an important aspect of research in behavior genetics. The key to the method is comparing concordance rates in MZ and DZ pairs.

number of shared genes and the prevalence of the disorder in relatives. The starting point in such investigations is the collection of a sample of individuals who bear the diagnosis in question. These people are referred to as **index cases**, or **probands**. Then relatives are studied to determine the frequency with which the same diagnosis might be applied to them. If a genetic predisposition to the disorder being studied is present, close relatives of the index cases should have the disorder at a rate higher than that in the general population.

In the **twin method** both **monozygotic (MZ) twins** and **dizygotic (DZ) twins** are compared. MZ, or identical, twins develop from a single fertilized egg and are genetically the same. DZ, or fraternal, pairs develop from separate eggs and are on average only 50 percent alike genetically, no more alike than any two siblings. MZ twins are always the same sex, but DZ twins can be either the same sex or opposite in sex. Twin studies begin with diagnosed cases and then search for the presence of the disorder in the other twin. When the twins are similar diagnostically they are said to be concordant. To the extent that a predisposition for a mental disorder can be inherited, **concordance** for the disorder should be greater in MZ pairs than in DZ pairs. When the MZ concordance rate is higher than the DZ rate, the characteristic being studied is said to be heritable.

Although the methodology of the family and twin studies is clear, the data they yield are not always easy to interpret. Let us assume that chil-

dren of agoraphobic parents—people suffering from a cluster of fears centering on being in open spaces and leaving home—are themselves more likely than average to be agoraphobic. Does this mean that a predisposition for this anxiety disorder is genetically transmitted? Not necessarily. The greater number of agoraphobics could as well reflect the child-rearing practices of the phobic parents as well as the effects of the children's imitating adult behavior.

The ability to offer a genetic interpretation of data from twin studies hinges on what is called the equal environment assumption. As noted, concordance among twins for psychopathology is a result of the operation of both genetic and environmental factors. The equal environment assumption states that for whatever diagnosis is being studied, the environmental factors that are partial causes of concordance are equally influential for both MZ and DZ pairs. In a review of the evidence for the equal environment assumption Kendler (1993) concluded that for the most part, it is reasonable, although further study is needed. Twin research thus offers a better opportunity to draw inferences about genetic diatheses for psychopathology than does the family method.

The study of children adopted and reared completely apart from their abnormal parents is not subject to the aforementioned problems. Though infrequent, this situation has the benefit of eliminating the influence of being raised by disordered parents. (The study of MZ twins reared completely apart would also be valuable, but this situation occurs so rarely that there is virtually no research using this method to study psychopathology. We will see in Chapter 13, however, that research involving separated twins does exist in the study of the inheritance of personality traits.) A high frequency of agoraphobia in children reared apart from their agoraphobic parents would offer convincing support for the theory that genetic factors figure in the disorder.

BIOCHEMISTRY IN THE NERVOUS SYSTEM

The nervous system is composed of billions of neurons. Although differing in some respects, each **neuron** has four major parts: (1) the cell body; (2) several dendrites, the short and thick extensions; (3) one or more axons, but usually only one, long and thin, extending a considerable distance from the cell body; and (4) terminal buttons on the many end branches of the axon (Figure 2.1). When a neuron is appropriately stimulated at its cell body or through its dendrites, a **nerve impulse**, which is a change in

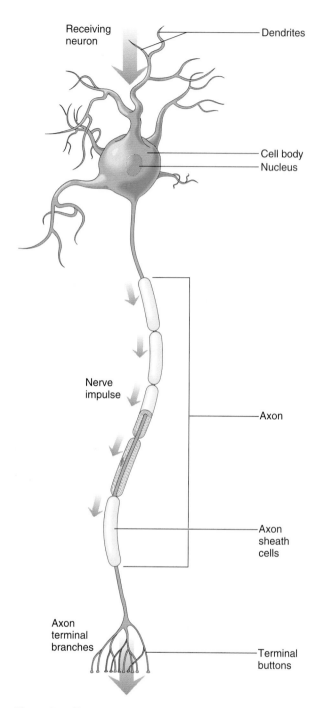

Figure 2.1   The neuron, the basic unit of the nervous system.

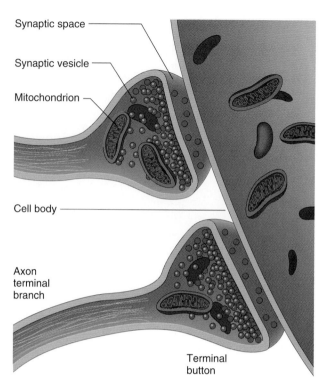

Figure 2.2   A synapse, showing the terminal buttons of two axon branches in close contact with a very small portion of the cell body of another neuron.

the electric potential of the cell, travels down the axon to the terminal endings. Between the terminal endings of the sending axon and the receiving neurons there is a small gap, the **synapse** (Figure 2.2).

For a nerve impulse to pass from one neuron to another it must have a way of bridging the synaptic space. The terminal buttons of each axon contain synaptic vesicles, small structures that are filled with **neurotransmitters**, chemical substances that

are important in transferring a nerve impulse from one neuron to another. Nerve impulses cause the synaptic vesicles to release molecules of their transmitter substances, which flood the synapse and can then interact with receptor sites in the postsynaptic neuron.

Once a neuron has fired and released its transmitter, the last step is for it to be returned to its normal state. Not all of the released neurotransmitter has found its way to postsynaptic receptors. Some of what remains in the synapse is broken down by enzymes, and some is pumped back into the presynaptic cell through a process called **reuptake**.

Several key neurotransmitters have been identified and implicated in psychopathology, including norepinephrine, dopamine, and serotonin. Norepinephrine is a neurotransmitter of the peripheral sympathetic nervous system, where it is involved in producing states of high arousal. Both serotonin and dopamine are neurotransmitters of the brain and are important in mediating the effects of rewards and punishments. Another important brain transmitter is gamma-aminobutyric acid (GABA), which inhibits some nerve impulses; a deficiency in this transmitter may allow states of high arousal to occur and thus may be involved in the anxiety disorders.

Theories linking neurotransmitters to psychopathology usually propose that a given disorder is caused by either too much or too little of a particular transmitter (e.g., mania results from too much norepinephrine, anxiety disorders result from too little GABA). Neurotransmitters are synthesized in the neuron through a series of metabolic steps, usually beginning with an amino acid. Each reaction along the way to producing an actual transmitter is catalyzed by an enzyme. Too much or too little of a particular transmitter could result from an error in these metabolic pathways. Similar disturbances in the amounts of specific transmitters could result from alterations in the usual processes by which transmitters are deactivated after being released into the synapse.

Finally, contemporary research has focused to a large extent on the possibility that the receptors are at fault. If the receptors on the postsynaptic neuron were too numerous or too easily excited, the result would be akin to having too much transmitter released. For example, the delusions and hallucinations of schizophrenia are thought to result from an overabundance of dopamine receptors.

BIOLOGICAL APPROACHES TO TREATMENT

An important implication of the biological paradigm is that prevention or treatment of mental disorders should be possible by altering bodily functioning. Certainly if a deficiency in a particular biochemical substance is found to underlie or contribute to some problem, it makes sense to attempt to correct the imbalance by providing appropriate doses of the deficient chemical. In such cases a clear connection exists between viewing a disorder as a biological defect and attempting to correct the fault through a biological intervention.

For example, phenylketonuria (PKU) is a form of mental retardation caused by a genetically determined enzyme deficiency that results in the body's inability to metabolize phenylalanine into tyrosine. State laws require routine testing of an infant's blood for excess phenylalanine; if the test is positive a specific diet low in the amino acid is prescribed. Children otherwise doomed to profound mental deficiency can thereby be brought closer to the normal range of intelligence (Chapter 15). The prevention of such disorders is an example of a successful intervention to correct a biological anomaly.

Other biological interventions in common use do not necessarily derive from knowledge of what causes a given disorder. Tranquilizers, such as Valium, can be effective in reducing the tension

associated with anxiety disorders, perhaps by stimulating GABA receptors. Antidepressants, such as Prozac, in widespread use for depression, increase neural transmission in serotonin neurons by inhibiting the reuptake of serotonin. Antipsychotic drugs, such as Thorazine, used in the treatment of schizophrenia, reduce the activity of dopamine neurons by blocking their receptors. Stimulants are often employed in treating children with attention-deficit disorder; they increase the levels of several transmitters, thereby helping the children pay attention. These somatic therapies are not yet known to be related definitively to possible causes of these disorders. Further, a person can hold a biological theory about the nature of a mental problem, yet recommend psychological intervention. Recall from Chapter 1 that Hippocrates proposed *non*somatic therapies—rest for melancholia, for example—to deal with mental disorders that he considered somatic in origin. Contemporary workers also appreciate that nonbiological interventions can have beneficial effects on the soma.

EVALUATING THE BIOLOGICAL PARADIGM

Over the past two decades biological research has made great progress in elucidating brain-behavior relationships. Biologically based research on both causes and treatment of psychopathology is proceeding at a rapid rate, as we will see when we discuss specific psychopathologies in later chapters. Although we view these developments in a positive light, we also want to caution against reductionism, a faulty position taken by some biologically oriented researchers.

Reductionism refers to a view that advocates reducing whatever is being studied to its most basic elements or constituents. In the case of mental disorders the position proposes reducing complex mental and emotional responses to simple biology. Using this logic, the argument could be taken even further to propose that biology be reduced to atomic physics. In its extreme form reductionism asserts that psychology will ultimately be nothing more than biology. In philosophical circles reductionism is rarely taken seriously. Once basic elements, such as individual nerve cells, are organized into more complex structures or systems, such as neural pathways or circuits, the properties of these systems cannot be deduced from the properties of the constituents. The whole is greater than the sum of its parts. A good example is provided by the theory of movement of the earth's mantle or crust known as plate tectonics. The earth's outer shell is made up of about a dozen large plates and several smaller ones. Movement of the plates at their boundaries is what causes most earthquakes. Although the earth's plates are made up of rock and the rock of atoms, tectonic movement cannot be accounted for at all by our knowledge of atoms. Similarly, in the field of abnormal psychology, problems such as delusional beliefs, dysfunctional attitudes, and catastrophizing cognitions may well be impossible to explain biologically, even with a detailed understanding of the behavior of individual neurons (Turkheimer, in press).

THE PSYCHOANALYTIC PARADIGM

The central assumption of the **psychoanalytic** or **psychodynamic paradigm**, originally developed by Sigmund Freud (1856–1939), is that psychopathology results from unconscious conflicts. We will spend considerable time looking at the significant impact of Freud in the development of this paradigm; however, the focus of this paradigm has shifted through the years, and we will examine those changes as well.

CLASSICAL PSYCHOANALYTIC THEORY

Classical psychoanalytic theory refers to the original views of Freud. His theories encompassed both the structure of the mind itself and the development and dynamics of personality.

STRUCTURE OF THE MIND

Freud divided the mind, or the psyche, into three principal parts, id, ego, and superego. These are metaphors for specific functions or energies. According to Freud, the **id** is present at birth and is the part of the mind that accounts for all the energy needed to run the psyche. It comprises the basic urges for food, water, elimination, warmth, affection, and sex. Trained as a neurologist, Freud saw the source of all the id's energy as biological. Only later, as the infant develops, is this energy, which he called **libido**, converted into psychic energy, all of it unconscious, below the level of awareness.

The id seeks immediate gratification, operating on what Freud called the **pleasure principle**. When the id is not satisfied tension is produced, and the id strives to eliminate this tension as quickly as possible. For example, the infant feels hunger, an aversive drive, and is impelled to move about, sucking, in order to reduce the tension arising from the unsatisfied drive. Another means of obtaining gratification is **primary process** thinking, generating

Sigmund Freud was the founder of the psychoanalytic paradigm, proposing both a theory of the causes of mental disorder and devising a new method of therapy.

images—in essence, fantasies—of what is desired. The infant who wants mother's milk imagines the mother's breast and thereby obtains some short-term satisfaction of the hunger drive through a wish-fulfilling fantasy.

The next aspect of the psyche that develops is the **ego**. Unlike the id, the ego is primarily conscious and begins to develop from the id during the second six months of life. Whereas the id resorts to fantasy if necessary, the task of the ego is to deal with reality. The ego does not employ primary process thinking, for fantasy will not keep the organism alive. Through its planning and decision-making functions, called **secondary process** thinking, the ego realizes that operating on the pleasure principle at all times, as the id would like to do, is not the most effective way of maintaining life. The ego thus operates on the **reality principle** as it mediates between the demands of reality and the immediate gratification desired by the id.

The ego, however, derives all its energy from the id and may be likened to a horseback rider who receives energy from the horse he or she is riding. Whereas a horseback rider directs the horse with his or her own energy, not depending on that of the horse for thinking, planning, and moving, the ego derives *all* its energies from the id and yet must direct what it is entirely dependent on for energy.

The final part of the psyche that emerges is the **superego**, which operates roughly as our conscience and develops throughout childhood. Freud believed that the superego developed from the ego much as the ego developed from the id. As children discover that many of their impulses, such as biting or bed-wetting, are not acceptable to their parents, they begin to take on or introject parental values as their own in order to enjoy parental approval and to avoid disapproval.

The behavior of the human being, as conceptualized by Freud, is thus a complex interplay of three parts of the psyche, all vying for the achievement of goals that cannot always be reconciled. The interplay of these forces is referred to as the **psychodynamics** of the personality. Theorists who follow some of Freud's ideas are also referred to as psychodynamic theorists.

Freud was drawn into studying the mind by his work with Breuer on hypnosis and hysteria (see p. 19). The apparently powerful role played by factors of which patients seemed unaware led Freud to postulate that much of our behavior is determined by forces that are inaccessible to awareness. Both the id's instincts and many of the superego's activities are not known to the conscious mind. The ego is primarily conscious, for it is the metaphor for the psychic systems that have to do with thinking and planning. But the ego, too, has important unconscious aspects, the defense mechanisms, that protect it from anxiety (these will be discussed shortly). Freud considered most of the important determinants of behavior to be **unconscious**.

STAGES OF PSYCHOSEXUAL DEVELOPMENT

Freud conceived of the personality as developing through a series of four distinct **psychosexual stages**. At each stage a different part of the body is the most sensitive to sexual excitation and therefore the most capable of providing libidinal satisfaction to the id. The **oral stage** is the first stage of psychosexual development. From birth to about eighteen months the demands of the infant's id are satisfied primarily by feeding and the sucking and biting associated with it. As a result, the body parts involved with this stage are the lips, mouth, and tongue. From about eighteen months to three years of age, the child's enjoyment shifts to the anus. During this **anal stage** the child's main source of libidinous pleasure comes from passing and retaining feces. The **phallic stage** extends from age three to age five or six, and maximum gratification of the

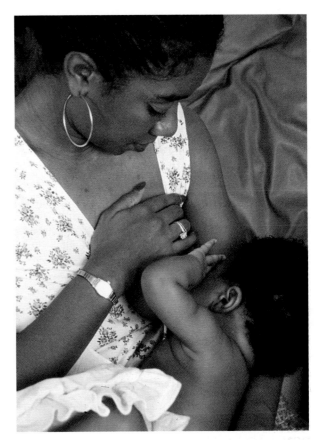

The first psychosexual stage is the oral stage. During this stage maximum gratification of id impulses comes from sucking.

The second psychosexual stage is the anal stage. The site of pleasure shifts to the anus and toilet training typically begins.

id now occurs through genital stimulation. Between the ages of six and twelve the child is in a **latency period**. During these years the id impulses do not play a major role in motivating behavior. The final and adult stage is the **genital stage**, during which heterosexual interests predominate.

During each stage the growing person must resolve the conflicts between what the id wants and what the environment will provide. How this is accomplished determines basic personality traits that last throughout the person's life. For example, a person who in the anal stage experiences either excessive or deficient amounts of gratification, depending on the toilet-training regimen, develops a **fixation** and is likely to regress to this stage when stressed. Such a person might develop obsessive-compulsive disorder and become stingy and obsessively clean.

Perhaps the most important crisis of development occurs during the phallic stage, around age four. Then, Freud asserted, the child is overcome with sexual desire for the parent of the opposite sex; at the same time he or she views the parent of the same sex as a rival and fears retaliation. The threat of dire punishment from the parent of the same sex may cause the child to *repress* the entire conflict, pushing these sexual and aggressive urges into the unconscious. This desire and repression (discussed in the next section) are referred to as the **Oedipus complex** for the male and the **Electra complex** for the female. The dilemma is usually resolved through increased identification with the parent of the same sex and through the adoption of society's mores, which forbid the child to desire his or her

Freud believed that all children develop desires for the parent of the opposite sex. Fearing punishment for expressing these desires, the conflict is repressed, creating the Oedipus complex for boys and the Electra complex for girls.

parent. Through the learning of these moral values the superego develops. According to Freud, resolving the Oedipus complex or the Electra complex is extremely important to the child's ongoing sexual development; failure to do so may lead the child to feel guilty about sexual desires, to fear intimacy, or to develop other difficulties in romantic relationships.

NEUROTIC ANXIETY

When one's life is in jeopardy one feels **objective anxiety**, or **realistic anxiety**, the ego's reaction, according to Freud, to danger in the external world. The person whose personality has not developed fully, perhaps because he or she is fixated at one or another stage, may experience **neurotic anxiety**, a feeling of fear that is unrealistic and not connected to any real threat. Freud initially viewed neurotic anxiety as stemming from the blockage or repression of unconscious impulses; a person afraid of small spaces, for example, experiences this neurotic anxiety because he or she has repressed the need for closeness.

Later, Freud came to view neurotic anxiety quite differently, not as stemming from a *lack of expression* of unconscious impulses, but arising from *fear of the disastrous consequences* likely to ensue if a previously punished id impulse were allowed expression. The boy afraid of closed spaces is really afraid of expressing his desire for sex and intimacy, a desire

Too much or too little gratification during one of the psychosexual stages may lead to regression to this stage during stress.

that was perhaps mocked or thwarted in his child-hood. The girl afraid of dirt who cleans obsessively is actually afraid of her childhood fascination with her messy feces, perhaps as a result of parents who were overly strict and disapproving or disgusted when she was toilet training.

Perhaps because Freud's earlier views held that repression of id impulses would create neurotic anxiety, we often hear that Freudians preach as much gratification of impulses as possible, lest a person become neurotic. But this is not the case. For Freudians the essence of neurotic anxiety is repression. Being unaware of conflicts lies at the core of neurotic anxiety, rather than simply being reluctant, unwilling, or unable to reduce the demands of the id. A celibate Catholic priest and nun, for example, are not considered candidates for neurosis provided that they consciously acknowledge their sexual or aggressive tendencies. Such individuals do not have to act on these felt needs to avoid neurotic anxiety. They must only remain aware of these needs whenever the needs vie for expression.

DEFENSE MECHANISMS: COPING WITH ANXIETY

According to Freud and elaborated by his daughter Anna (A. Freud, 1966), herself a famous psychoanalyst, the discomfort experienced by the anxious ego can be reduced in several ways. Objective anxiety, rooted in reality, can often be handled by removing or avoiding the danger in the external world or by dealing with it in a rational way. Neurotic anxiety may be handled through an unconscious distortion of reality by means of a defense mechanism. A **defense mechanism** is a strategy, unconsciously utilized, to protect the ego from anxiety. Perhaps the most important is **repression**, which pushes impulses and thoughts unacceptable to the ego into the unconscious. Repression not only prevents awareness but also keeps buried desires from growing up (Wachtel, 1977). By remaining repressed these infantile memories cannot be corrected by adult experience and therefore retain their original intensity. Another defense mechanism, important in paranoid disorders (see Chapter 11), is **projection**, attributing to external agents characteristics or desires that are possessed by an individual and yet are unacceptable to conscious awareness. For example, a hostile woman may unconsciously find it aversive to regard herself as angry at others and may project her angry feelings onto them; thus she sees others as angry with her. Other defense mechanisms are **displacement**, redirecting emotional responses from a perhaps dangerous object to a substitute, for instance, yelling at one's spouse instead of at one's boss; **reaction formation**, converting one feeling, such as hate, into its opposite, in this case love; **regression**, retreating to the behavioral patterns of an earlier age; **rationalization**, inventing a reason for an unreasonable action or attitude; and **sublimation**, converting sexual or aggressive impulses into socially valued behaviors, especially creative activity.

All these defense mechanisms allow the ego to discharge some id energy while not facing frankly the true nature of the motivation. Because defense mechanisms are more readily observed than are other symptoms of a disordered personality, they very often make people aware of their troubled natures and thus provide the impetus for consulting a therapist. It should be noted that contemporary psychoanalytic theorists allow for the use of some defense mechanisms to be adaptive and healthy. A period of denial after the death of a loved one can help in adjusting to the loss. Sublimation of one's sexual impulses into hard work or creativity can be useful in coping with one's sexual impulses when intercourse is not a feasible alternative. For the most part, however, psychoanalytic scholars believe that defense mechanisms stunt a person's interactions with others and their own work.

RELATIONSHIP TO PSYCHOPATHOLOGY

Freud believed that the various forms of psychopathology resulted from the presence of strong drives or id instincts, which set the stage for the development of unconscious conflicts linked to a particular psychosexual stage. For example, phobias were proposed to be caused by an unresolved Oedipal conflict, with the fear of the father displaced onto some other object or situation. Similarly, obsessive-compulsive disorder was traced to the anal stage, with the urge to soil or to be aggressive transformed by reaction formation into compulsive cleanliness.

In his early writings and lectures Freud postulated that the environmental cause of his patients' hysterical problems was sexual abuse in childhood, typically rape by the father. His views elicited outrage from his colleagues, yet he persisted until 1897, when in a letter to his colleague Wilhelm Fleiss he indicated that he had come to believe that many of his patients' accounts were fantasies. Over the next few years Freud struggled with these competing theories, sometimes favoring one, sometimes the other. But by 1905 the fantasy theory had clearly won out (Masson, 1984).

This change had a profound impact on the development of psychoanalysis, for it directed the search for the causes of psychopathology away from the environment and toward the patient and his or her fantasies. Furthermore, it was crucial to the discovery of the Oedipal conflict, a cornerstone of psychoanalytic thought. So important was this emphasis on fantasy that in a letter to Jeffrey Masson, a well-known critic of psychoanalysis, Anna Freud wrote that without it there would have been no psychoanalysis.

NEO-FREUDIAN PSYCHODYNAMIC PERSPECTIVES

The significance of Freud's theories and clinical work was widely recognized by his contemporaries. Several of them, including Carl Jung and Alfred Adler, met with Freud periodically to discuss psychoanalytic theory and therapy. As often happens when a brilliant leader attracts brilliant followers and colleagues, disagreements arose about many general issues, such as the relative importance of id versus ego and of biological instinctual drives versus sociocultural determinants; the significance of the earliest years of life in contrast with adult experiences; whether sexual urges are at the core of motives and actions that are themselves not obviously sexual; the role of unconscious processes versus conscious ones; and the reflexlike nature of id impulses versus the purposive behavior governed primarily by conscious ego deliberations.

To elaborate on some of these themes we outline the major ideas of three theorists who adapted Freud's ideas in forging approaches of their own. Others who adapted and modified Freud's theories are discussed in Chapter 13 (the object-relations theorists) and Chapter 17 (brief analytic psychotherapy). All continued to embrace Freud's emphasis on human behavior as the product of dynamics within the psyche. For this reason all share with Freud a psychodynamic perspective on mental disorders.

JUNG AND ANALYTICAL PSYCHOLOGY

Carl Gustav Jung (1887–1961), a Swiss psychiatrist originally considered Freud's heir apparent, broke with Freud on many issues in 1914, after a seven-year period of intense correspondence. Jung proposed ideas radically different from Freud's, ultimately establishing **analytical psychology**, a blend of Freudian psychology and humanistic psychology (see p. 505). His theory's similarity to humanistic theories arises from Jung's deemphasis of the importance of biological drives as the main determinants of behavior and his use of the concept of self-realization, a state of fulfillment that occurs

Carl Jung was the founder of analytical psychology, a blending of Freudian and humanistic concepts.

when a person balances and gives expression to all the positive and creative aspects of his or her personality.

Jung hypothesized that in addition to our personal unconscious, which Freud stressed, our **collective unconscious** contains information from the social history of humankind. The collective unconscious is the repository of all the experiences people have had over the centuries and, unlike Freud's unconscious, contains positive and creative forces rather than exclusively sexual and aggressive ones. Jung asserted that each of us has masculine and feminine traits that can be blended and that people's spiritual and religious needs are as basic as their libidinal needs. Jung also catalogued various personality types; perhaps most important among them are extraversion (an orientation toward the external world) versus introversion (an orientation toward the inner, subjective world). Jung wrote at length on religious symbolism and the meaning of life and as a consequence became popular among mystics, novelists, and poets. Finally, whereas Freud regarded current and future behavior as determined primarily by the past, Jung focused on purposiveness, decision making, and goal setting. To understand people, according to Jung, one has to appreciate their dreams and aspirations, not just the effects of their past experiences, as important as those may be (Jung, 1928).

ADLER AND INDIVIDUAL PSYCHOLOGY

Alfred Adler (1870–1937), also an early adherent of Freud's, came to be even less dependent on Freud's views of instincts than was Jung, and Freud remained quite bitter toward Adler after their relationship ended. Adler, who had been a sickly child in Vienna and had had to strive mightily to overcome feelings of inferiority, emphasized striving for superiority, but not in an antisocial sense. Indeed, he regarded people as inextricably tied to their society because he believed that fulfillment was found in doing things for the social good. Like Jung, he stressed the importance of working toward goals, and, also like Jung, much of his theorizing anticipated later developments in humanistic therapy (Adler, 1924).

One central element in Adler's work was his focus on the individual's phenomenology, or **individual psychology**, as the key to understanding that person. Adler worked to help patients change their illogical, mistaken ideas and expectations in the belief that to feel and behave better, one has first to think more rationally, an approach that anticipated contemporary developments in cognitive behavior therapy (p. 46). Finally, Adler's interest in growth and in the prevention of problems and the betterment of society influenced the development of child guidance centers and parent education.

ERIKSON AND PSYCHOSOCIAL STAGES OF DEVELOPMENT

Erik Erikson (1902–1995) is identified as an ego psychologist because he emphasized the independence of the ego from the id and attributed to it a greater role in determining behavior. Whereas Freud believed that development ended early in life, Erikson's major contribution was in a field that has come to be called life-span developmental psychology, which has as a central thesis the idea that people continue to change and differentiate through middle age and into their senior years as they encounter various rites of passage. To get a good sense of the significance of this general viewpoint, consider that "child psychology" used to be synonymous with "developmental psychology." Thanks in large part to Erikson, people now distinguish between the two or, in a more radical vein, suggest that there is only one developmental psychology, which refers to the entire life span.

Erikson proposed eight **psychosocial stages of development** through which people progress, each characterized by a particular challenge or crisis. The resolution of the crisis affects how the individual deals with each subsequent stage (Table 2.1). If an

Alfred Adler was the founder of individual psychology and well-known for his notion of the inferiority complex.

earlier crisis is not adequately handled the resolution of subsequent crises is hampered.

To illustrate, let us look at the fifth stage, perhaps the most important one, in which Erikson intro-

Eric Erikson emphasized the importance of psychosocial development throughout the life-span. He was more optimistic than Freud about people's continuing capacity for growth.

TABLE 2.1   Erikson's Eight Stages of Psychosocial Development

Stage and Approximate Age Range	Psychosocial Crisis	Major Developments
Infancy 0–1	Trust vs. mistrust	In the caregiver–baby relationship, the infant develops a sense of trust or mistrust that basic needs such as nourishment, warmth, cleanliness, and physical contact will be provided.
Early Childhood 1–3	Autonomy vs. shame, doubt	Children learn self-control as a means of being self-sufficient, e.g., toilet training, feeding, walking, or developing shame and doubt about their abilities to be autonomous.
Play Age 3–6	Initiative vs. guilt	Children are anxious to investigate adult activities, but may also have feelings of guilt about trying to be independent and daring.
School Age 7–11	Industry vs. inferiority	Children learn about imagination and curiosity, develop learning skills, or develop feelings of inferiority if they fail—or if they think they fail—to master tasks.
Adolescence 12–20	Identity vs. identity confusion	Adolescents try to figure out who they are, how they are unique, if they want to have a meaningful role in society, how they can establish sexual, ethnic, and career identity. Feelings of confusion can arise over these decisions.
Young Adulthood 20–30	Intimacy vs. isolation	Individuals wish to seek companionship and intimacy with a significant other, or avoid relationships and become isolated.
Adulthood 30–65	Generativity vs. stagnation	Individuals experience the need to be productive—for example, to create products, ideas, or children—or to become stagnant.
Mature Age 65+	Integrity vs. despair	Older adults review and make an effort to make sense of their life, reflecting on completed goals or doubts and despair about unreached goals and desires.

duces a term for which he is famous, **identity crisis**. Erikson's own childhood and adolescence may have contributed to this concept (Hall, Lindzey, &

Erikson believed that an identity crisis occurs during adolescence. Volunteer work may help teenagers develop a clearer sense of their identity and what they value in life.

Manosevitz, 1985). He was born in Germany of Danish parents who separated before his birth. He never knew his biological father and was reared by a German stepfather. He looked Nordic and was taunted as a goy (an uncomplimentary Yiddish term for a non-Jew) by his Jewish peers and as a Jew by his non-Jewish age-mates. He felt out of place in high school and, thinking he might want to become an artist, wandered around Europe making sketches. At age twenty-five he began to teach in Vienna, where he met Freud. Later he enrolled in the Vienna Psychoanalytic Institute and he found his calling as an analyst.

The identity crisis, said to occur between the ages of twelve and twenty, reflects the transition from childhood to adulthood, a period during which we all create a sense of self—the kind of psychological beings we are and the kind of lives we plan to forge for ourselves—much as Erikson did as his period of wandering brought him finally to Vienna and Freud. Although the choice of an occupation, role, or profession is important—physician, lawyer, construction worker, parent, and so on—a person's identity is said to go much deeper. At this psychosocial stage we are concerned with the direction of our lives—what things are going to be important and sought after, what kinds of compromises we are prepared to make to achieve our goals, what kind of person we want to be; in general all the things that go into our sense of self as developing adults who are responsible for themselves and who are ready to make commitments to goals and to other human beings. It is a tumultuous time, considering that young people are simultaneously trying to come to terms with their sexuality.

Like others who adapted Freud's ideas, Erikson was more optimistic than Freud about people's capacity to change and more positive generally about the nature of existence. The resolution of any psychosocial stage could be reversed, Erikson believed, with appropriate psychotherapy (Erikson, 1959).

EVALUATING THE PSYCHOANALYTIC PARADIGM

Perhaps no investigator of human behavior has been so honored and so criticized as Freud. At the time he was first proposing his theory of infantile sexuality he was personally vilified. In turn-of-the-century Vienna sexuality was little discussed. How scandalous, then, to assert that infants and children were also motivated by sexual drives!

Freud's influence on psychoanalytic views of mental disorder has been great, but as we have seen, his theories have been criticized from within the paradigm as well as from without. One of the main criticisms of Freud's theories applies to other psychoanalytic theories as well: because they are based on anecdotal evidence gathered during therapy sessions these theories are not grounded in objectivity and therefore are not scientific. Freud's patients were not only a small sample, they were largely affluent, educated, and Viennese. It is easy to believe that a theory of personality development or structure of the mind based on such a small group of troubled individuals might be limited.

The case reports used by Freud (and his followers) can also be assailed on the grounds of the reliability of Freud's perceptions in those therapy sessions and his ability to recall them accurately (since he did not take careful notes). Freud's own interest in certain topics, such as patients' possible early sexual experiences, might have affected their accounts, causing them to focus on certain experiences and overlook others based not on their own sense of what was of key importance in their lives, but on Freud's emerging views.

It is also important to keep in mind that psychodynamic concepts, such as id, ego, inferiority complex, and the unconscious, though meant to be used as metaphors to describe psychic functions, sometimes were described as though they had an existence of their own and power to act and think. For example, Freud spoke of "immediate and unheeding satisfaction of the instincts, such as the id demands. ... The id knows no solicitude about ensuring survival" (1937).

Even with these substantial criticisms, however, Freud's contribution remains enormous and continues to have an important impact on the field of abnormal psychology. Here are the four areas in which we feel Freud's influence is most evident:

1. Childhood experiences help shape adult personality. Although acknowledging the role of genetics, contemporary researchers still view childhood experience as crucial. They seldom focus on the psychosexual stages that Freud wrote about, but emphasize problematic parent–child relationships in general and how they can influence later adult relationships in negative ways.

2. There are unconscious influences on behavior. In Focus 7.1 we review recent research showing that people can be unaware of the causes of their behavior. However, most current workers do not think of *an* unconscious or view it as a repository of id instincts.

3. People use defense mechanisms to control anxiety or stress. There is a great deal of research on coping with stress (some of it is reviewed in Chapter 8), and defense mechanisms are included in an appendix of DSM-IV. Contemporary research focuses mostly on consciously adopted coping strategies, for example, deliberately trying not to think about some traumatic event. It remains to be demonstrated whether any unconscious method of coping (even repression) actually plays an important role in controlling anxiety.

4. As discussed in greater detail in Chapter 18, Freud and his followers sensitized generations of clinicians and psychopathologists to the nonobviousness of the causes and purposes of human behavior. Psychoanalysis cautions us against being too quick to take everything at face value. A person expressing disdain for another may actually like the other person very much, yet be fearful of admitting positive feelings. This tendency to look under the surface is perhaps the best known legacy of Freud.

Although there are many legitimate concerns about the validity and usefulness of Freud's work, it would be a serious mistake to minimize his importance in psychopathology or, for that matter, in the intellectual history of Western civilization. His work has elicited the kind of critical reaction that helps advance knowledge. He was instrumental in getting people to consider nonbiological explanations for disordered behavior, and his descriptions of abnormal behavior were often extremely perceptive. It is impossible to acquire a good grasp of the field of abnormal psychology without some familiarity with Freud's writings.

PSYCHOANALYTIC THERAPY

Since Freud's time the body of psychoanalytic thinking has changed in important ways, but all treatments purporting to be psychoanalytic have some basic tenets in common. Classical psychoanalysis is based on Freud's second theory of neurotic anxiety, that it is the reaction of the ego when a previously punished and repressed id impulse presses for expression. The unconscious part of the ego, encountering a situation that reminds it of a repressed conflict from childhood—one usually having to do with sexual or aggressive impulses—is overcome by debilitating tension. Psychoanalytic therapy attempts to remove the earlier repression and to help the patient face the childhood conflict and resolve it in the light of adult reality. The repression, occurring so long ago, has prevented the ego from growing in an adult fashion; the lifting of the repression is supposed to enable this relearning to take place.

The essence of psychoanalysis has been captured by Paul Wachtel (1977) in the metaphor of the woolly mammoth. Some of these gigantic creatures, frozen alive eons ago, have been recovered so perfectly preserved that their meat can actually be eaten. Neurotic problems were considered by Freud to be the encapsulated residue of conflicts from long ago. Present adult problems are merely reflections or expressions of these frozen intrapsychic conflicts.

The patient's neurosis is seen as deriving most essentially from his continuing and unsuccessful efforts to deal with internalized residues of his past [the "woolly mammoth"] which, by virtue of being isolated from his adaptive and integrated ego, continue to make primitive demands wholly unresponsive to reality. It is therefore maintained that a fully successful treatment must create conditions whereby these anachronistic inclinations can be experienced consciously and integrated into the ego, so that they can be controlled and modified. (Wachtel, 1977, p. 36)

Analysts employ a number of techniques in their efforts to lift repressions. Perhaps the best known is **free association**. The patient reclines on a couch, facing away from the analyst, who sits near the

In a typical psychoanalytic therapy session, the patient reclines on a couch and the analyst sits out of the patient's view.

patient's head, and is encouraged to give free rein to his or her thoughts, verbalizing whatever comes to mind without the censoring done in everyday life. It is assumed that the patient can gradually learn this skill and that defenses built up over many years can eventually be bypassed. **Dream analysis** is another analytic technique. Psychoanalytic theory holds that in sleep, ego defenses are relaxed, allowing normally repressed material to enter the sleeper's consciousness. Since this material is extremely threatening it usually cannot be allowed into consciousness in its actual form; rather, the repressed material is disguised, and dreams take on heavily symbolic content. For example, a woman concerned about aggressive sexual advances from men may dream of being attacked by savages who throw spears at her; the spears are considered phallic symbols, substituting for an explicit sexual advance.

Another key component of psychoanalytic therapy is the **transference**, which refers to patients' responses to their analysts that are not in keeping with the analyst–patient relationship but seem instead to reflect attitudes and ways of behaving toward important people in the patient's past. For example, a patient may feel that the analyst is generally bored by what he or she is saying and as a result might struggle to be entertaining. Through careful observation of these transferred attitudes the analyst can gain insight into the childhood origin of repressed conflicts. In the example here, the analyst might find that the patient was made to feel boring and unimportant as a child and could only gain the parental attention he or she craved through humor.

Analysis of defenses, long a focus of psychoanalysis, is emphasized by contemporary psychoanalysts, who are sometimes referred to as **ego analysts**. They dispute the relatively weak role that Freud assigned the ego. Defense mechanisms, as we have seen, are the ego's unconscious tools for warding off a confrontation with anxiety. For instance, a man who appears to have trouble with intimacy may look out the window and change the subject whenever anything touches on closeness during the course of a session. The analyst will attempt at some point to interpret the patient's behavior, pointing out its defensive nature in the hope of stimulating the patient to acknowledge that he is in fact avoiding the topic. Psychoanalytic treatment has in the past extended over several years with as many as five sessions per week. It is interesting to note, however, that Freud's own psychoanalyses seldom lasted longer than six months.

Over the past forty or so years the ideas and work of neo-Freudians, such as Karen Horney and Harry Stack Sullivan (see p. 501), and of ego psychologists-analysts, such as Erik Erikson and Heinz Hartman, have blended into psychoanalytically oriented psychotherapy, sometimes called psychodynamic therapy. This approach, developed in part through the work of Alexander and French (1946), advocates a briefer, more present- and future-oriented analytic therapy, informed by such Freudian concepts as defense mechanisms and unconscious motivation. Such therapy is more active and directive than Freudian therapy, focuses more on present problems and relationships than on childhood conflicts, and is briefer and less intensive.

The hope of total personality reconstruction is put aside in favor of dealing with more focal and acute problems, but these therapists feel that their work is enhanced by training in and *sensitivity to psychoanalytic principles*. A large part of the work of current psychoanalysts is in these briefer forms of therapy; few practice standard psychoanalysis exclusively. (Korchin, 1976, p. 335, emphasis added)

To our minds, and in the opinion of specialists in psychodynamic therapy (Henry et al., 1994, p. 498), procedural changes do not reflect important theoret-

ical differences. Session frequency and body position matter less than what the patient does with support from the therapist, namely, slowly examining the true sources of tension and unhappiness by a lifting of repression. Psychoanalysis and related therapies are discussed in greater depth in Chapter 17.

LEARNING PARADIGMS

Psychologists operating on the basis of the **learning (or behavioral) paradigm** view abnormal behavior as responses learned in the same way in which other human behavior is learned. Early twentieth-century psychology was dominated not by learning but by structuralism, which held that the proper subject of study was mental functioning and structure. The goal of psychology, then a very new discipline, was to learn more about what went on in the mind by analyzing its elementary constituents. Experimental psychologists, such as Wilhelm Wundt (1832–1920), who founded the first formal psychological laboratory and the discipline itself in Leipzig in 1879, and Edward Titchener (1867–1927), whose laboratory was at Cornell University, devised elaborate training procedures to teach subjects to report on the most basic aspects of their experiences while being exposed to stimuli. Through painstaking **introspection**, self-observation and reporting of mental processes, subjects attempted to uncover the building blocks of experience and the structure of consciousness. For example, Wundt's subjects listened to a metronome set to click slowly and sometimes to click fast, sometimes sounding only a few times and then many. The subjects looked within themselves and reported that a fast series of clicks made them excited, a slow series relaxed. Just before each click they were conscious of a slight feeling of tension and afterward, slight relief.

THE RISE OF BEHAVIORISM

After some years many in the field began to lose faith in the ability of introspection to obtain useful knowledge about people. The problem was that different laboratories using the introspective method were yielding conflicting data; thus it appeared that introspection was not clarifying the answers to any questions. This dissatisfaction was brought to a head by John B. Watson (1878–1958), who in 1913 revolutionized psychology with his views:

Psychology as the behaviorist views it is a purely objective experimental branch of natural science. Its theoretical goal is the prediction and control of behavior.

Ivan P. Pavlov, Russian psychologist and Nobel Laureate, was responsible for extensive research and theory in classical conditioning. His influence is still very strong in Russian psychology.

John B. Watson. American psychologist, was the major figure in establishing behaviorism, defining psychology as the study of observable behavior rather than an investigation of subjective experience.

Introspection forms no essential part of its methods, nor is the scientific value of its data dependent upon the readiness with which they lend themselves to interpretation in terms of consciousness. (p. 158)

To replace introspection Watson looked to the experimental procedures of the psychologists who were investigating learning in animals. Because of his efforts, the dominant focus of psychology switched to learning from thinking. Finding out which stimuli would elicit which directly observable responses became the task of psychology. With such objective stimulus–response information it was hoped that human behavior could be both predicted and controlled. **Behaviorism** can be defined as an approach that focuses on the study of observable behavior rather than on consciousness. We will look at two types of learning that have attracted the research efforts of psychologists.

CLASSICAL CONDITIONING

One type of learning, **classical conditioning**, had been discovered quite by accident by the Russian physiologist Ivan Pavlov (1849–1936) at the turn of the century. In Pavlov's studies of the digestive system, a dog was given meat powder to make it salivate. Before long Pavlov's laboratory assistants became aware that the dog began salivating when it saw the person who fed it; as the experiment continued the dog began to salivate even earlier, when it heard the footsteps of its feeder. Pavlov was

intrigued by these findings and decided to study the dog's reactions systematically. In the first of many experiments, a bell was rung behind the dog and then the meat powder was placed in its mouth. After this procedure had been repeated a number of times, the dog began salivating as soon as it heard the bell and before it received the meat powder.

In this experiment, because the meat powder automatically elicits salivation with no prior learning, the powder is termed an **unconditioned stimulus** (UCS) and the response of salivation an **unconditioned response** (UCR). When the offering of meat powder is preceded several times by a neutral stimulus, the ringing of a bell, the sound of the bell alone (the **conditioned stimulus**, CS) is able to elicit the salivary response (the **conditioned response**, CR) (see Figure 2.3). The CR usually differs somewhat from the UCR (e.g., Rescorla, 1988), but these subtleties are beyond the needs of this book. As the number of paired presentations of the bell and the meat powder increases, the number of salivations elicited by the bell increases. **Extinction** refers to what happens to the CR when the repeated soundings of the bell are later *not* followed by meat powder; fewer and fewer salivations are elicited, and the CR gradually disappears.

Classical conditioning, it was found, could even instill pathological fear. A famous experiment, questionable from an ethical point of view, was conducted by John Watson and Rosalie Rayner (1920). They introduced a white rat to an eleven-month-old boy, Little Albert, who indicated no fear of the animal and appeared to want to play with it. Whenever the boy reached for the rat, the experimenter made a loud noise (the UCS) by striking a steel bar behind Albert's head, causing him great fright (the UCR). After five such experiences Albert became very

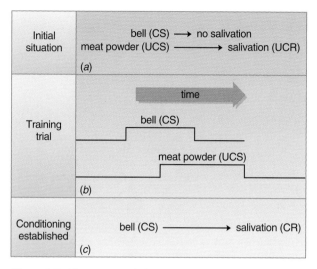

Initial situation	bell (CS) ⟶ no salivation meat powder (UCS) ⟶ salivation (UCR) (a)
Training trial	time bell (CS) meat powder (UCS) (b)
Conditioning established	bell (CS) ⟶ salivation (CR) (c)

Figure 2.3 The process of classical conditioning. (*a*) Before learning, the meat powder (UCS) elicits salivation (UCR), but the bell (CS) does not. (*b*) A training or learning trial consists of presentations of the CS, followed closely by the UCS. (*c*) Classical conditioning has been accomplished when the previously neutral bell elicits salivation (CR).

frightened (the CR) by the sight of the white rat, even when the steel bar was not struck. The fear initially associated with the loud noise had come to be elicited by the previously neutral stimulus, the white rat (now the CS). This study suggests the possible relationship between classical conditioning and the development of certain emotional disorders, in this instance a phobia.

OPERANT CONDITIONING

A second principal type of learning drew primarily on the work of Edward Thorndike (1874–1949) begun in the 1890s. Rather than investigating the association between stimuli, as Pavlov did, Thorndike was interested in the effect of consequences on behavior. He had observed that caged alley cats, in their efforts to escape, would accidentally hit the latch that freed them. Recaged again and again, they would soon come to touch the latch immediately and purposely. Thorndike formulated what was to become an extremely important principle, the **law of effect**: behavior that is followed by consequences satisfying to the organism will be repeated, and behavior that is followed by noxious or unpleasant consequences will be discouraged. Thus the behavior or response that has consequences serves as an instrument, encouraging or discouraging its own repetition. Learning that focuses on consequences was first called *instrumental learning*.

Almost sixty years ago B. F. Skinner (1904–1990) introduced what he called **operant conditioning** because it applied to behavior that operates on the environment. He reformulated the law of effect by shifting the focus from the linking of stimuli and responses—S–R connections—to the relationships between responses and their consequences or contingencies. The distinction is subtle, but it reflects Skinner's contention that stimuli do not so much get connected to responses as they become the occasions for responses to occur, if in the past they have been reinforced. Skinner introduced the concept of **discriminative stimulus** to refer to external events that in effect tell an organism that if it performs a certain behavior a certain consequence will follow.

Renaming the "law of effect" the "principle of reinforcement," Skinner distinguished two types of reinforcement. **Positive reinforcement** refers to the strengthening of a tendency to respond by virtue of the presentation of a pleasant event, called a positive reinforcer. For example, a water-deprived pigeon will tend to repeat behaviors (operants) that are followed by the availability of water. **Negative reinforcement** also strengthens a response, but it does so via the *removal* of an aversive event, such as the cessation of electric shock; Skinner called such consequences negative reinforcers. Extrapolating his extensive work with pigeons to complex human behavior (his book *Walden Two* is one of the better known utopian novels, describing an ideal society governed by his principles of reinforcement), Skinner argued that freedom of choice is a myth and that all behavior is determined by the reinforcers provided by the social environment. The goal of Skinner (1953) and the Skinnerians, like that of their mentor, Watson, is the prediction and con-

B. F. Skinner was responsible for the study of operant behavior and the extension of this approach to education, psychotherapy, and society as a whole.

trol of behavior. These experimenters hope that by analyzing behavior in terms of observable responses and reinforcement, they will be able to determine when certain behavior will occur. The information gathered should then help indicate how behavior is acquired, maintained, changed, and eliminated. In the Skinnerian approach abstract terms and concepts are avoided. For example, references to needs, motivation, and wants are conspicuously absent in Skinnerian writings. To provide an entirely satisfactory account of human behavior Skinner believed that psychology must restrict its attention to directly observable stimuli and responses and to the effects of reinforcement. Psychologists who hold this view do not, as human beings, deny the existence of inner states of mind and emotion. Rather, they urge that investigators not employ such mediators in trying to develop a science of behavior.

In a prototypical operant conditioning experiment a hungry rat might be placed in a box, known as a Skinner box, that has a lever located at one end. The rat will explore its new environment and by chance come close to the lever. The experimenter may then drop a food pellet into the receptacle located near the lever. After a few such rewards the animal will come to spend more and more time in the area around the lever. But now the experimenter may drop a pellet into the receptacle only when the rat happens to touch the lever. After capitalizing on a few chance touches, the rat begins to touch the lever frequently. With lever touching well established, the experimenter can make the criterion for reward more stringent—the animal must now actually press the lever. Thus the desired operant behavior, lever pressing, is gradually achieved by **shaping**, that is, by rewarding a series of responses that

The Skinner box is often used in studies of operant conditioning to demonstrate how a response can be shaped by rewarding it.

Aggressive responses in children are often rewarded, which makes them more likely to occur in the future.

are **successive approximations**, that more and more closely resemble the desired response. The number of lever presses increases as soon as they become the criterion for the release of pellets and decreases, or extinguishes, when the pellet is no longer dropped into the receptacle after a lever press.

As an example of how operant conditioning can be applied to abnormality, let us consider a key feature of conduct disorder, a high frequency of aggressive behavior. Aggression is often rewarded, as when one child beats up another to secure the possession of a toy (getting the toy is the reinforcer). Parents may also unwittingly reinforce aggression by giving in when the child becomes angry or threatens violence to achieve some goal, such as staying up late to watch TV.

MODELING

In real life, learning often goes on even in the absence of reinforcers. We all learn by watching and imitating others, a process called **modeling**. Experimental work has demonstrated that witnessing someone perform certain activities can increase or decrease diverse kinds of behavior, such as sharing, aggression, and fear. For example, Bandura and Menlove (1968) used a modeling treatment to reduce fear of dogs in children. After witnessing a fearless model engage in various activities with a dog, initially fearful children showed a decided increase in their willingness to approach and handle a dog. Similarly, modeling may explain the acquisition of abnormal behavior. Children of parents with phobias or substance-abuse problems may acquire similar behavior patterns, in part through observation.

MEDIATIONAL LEARNING PARADIGMS

Among the learning paradigms, modeling illustrates what is clearly an important issue, namely, the role of mediators in learning and behavior. Consider what happens in the typical modeling experiment. A person watches another do something and immediately shows a change in behavior. No overt responding is necessary for the learning to take place, nor does the observer need to be reinforced. Something is learned before the person makes any observable response. Similar outcomes led some learning theorists of the 1930s and 1940s to infer mediators of various kinds to explain overt behavior.

In the most general terms, a **mediational theory of learning** holds that an environmental stimulus does not initiate an overt response directly; rather, it does so through some intervening process, or **mediator**, such as fear or thinking. The mediator is conceptualized as an internal response. Without divorcing themselves from behaviorism, mediational learning theorists adopt the paradigmatic position that under certain conditions, it is both legitimate and important to go beyond observables.

Consider the mediational learning analysis of anxiety developed by O. Hobart Mowrer (1939) and Neal Miller (1948). In a typical experiment rats were shocked repeatedly in the presence of a neutral stimulus, such as the sound of a buzzer. The shock (UCS) produced a UCR of pain, fear, and flight. After several pairings the fear that was naturally produced by the shock came to be produced by the buzzer. The shock could eventually be omitted, and the animal would continue to react fearfully to the previously neutral stimulus (CS). In addition it was shown that the rat could learn new responses to avoid the CS (e.g., Miller, 1948). The question became how to conceptualize the finding that animals would learn to *avoid* a harmless event. Mowrer (1947) and others suggested that in this, a typical **avoidance conditioning** experiment, two bits of learning were taking place (Figure 2.4): (1) the animal, by means of classical conditioning, learned to fear the CS; and (2) the animal, by means of operant conditioning, learned an overt behavior to remove itself from the CS and thus to reduce the mediating fear response. This came to be known as two-factor theory.

The essential features of this theorizing are that fear or anxiety can be conceived of both as an internal response, which can be learned as observable responses are learned, and as an internal drive, which can motivate avoidance behavior. Anxiety then becomes amenable to the same kind of experimental analysis employed in the investigation of observable behavior. For instance, if we know that

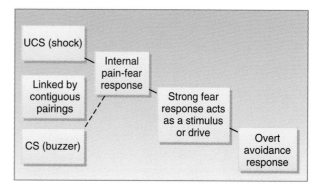

Figure 2.4 Schematic representation of Mowrer's account of avoidance learning. The dashed line indicates that the subject is learning to fear the buzzer, and the solid line that the subject is learning to avoid the shock.

repetition of an overt response without reinforcement leads to the extinction of the response, we can predict that repeated evocation of a fear response while withholding the expected pain or punishment will reduce the fear. This is no trivial prediction, and, as indicated next, treatments based on such reasoning have helped to reduce many irrational fears.

EVALUATING THE LEARNING PARADIGM

The learning view minimizes the importance of biological factors and focuses instead on elucidating the learning processes that may make behavior maladaptive. As we saw in the Langer and Abelson study in Chapter 1, this paradigm reduces the gap between normal and abnormal behavior since both are viewed within the same general framework; thus a bridge is forged between general experimental psychology and the field of abnormal psychology.

One very important advantage of applying a learning view in psychopathology is the increased precision of observation. Stimuli must be accurately observed and controlled; the magnitude and rate of responses and their latency—the rapidity with which they are made—are measured and recorded; and relationships among stimuli, responses, and outcomes are carefully noted. Unobservable processes, such as fear and thought, must be linked to observable behavior.

Although we view these and other features of learning approaches to deviant behavior as advantageous, the learning paradigm of abnormal behavior is in much the same position as the biological paradigm. Just as many pertinent biological malfunctions have not been uncovered, abnormality has not yet been convincingly traced to particular learning experiences. Consider how difficult it would be to show

Relaxation training is the first step in systematic desensitization. Once clients master relaxation, they begin to imagine scenes from the anxiety hierarchy.

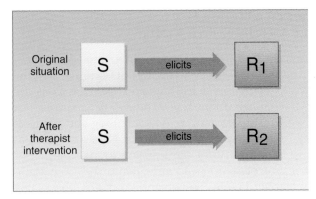

Figure 2.5 Schematic diagram of counterconditioning, whereby an original response (R$_1$) to a given stimulus (S) is eliminated by evoking a new response (R$_2$) to the same stimulus.

that depression results from a particular reinforcement history; a person would have to be observed continually over a period of years while his or her behavior was recorded and occurrences of reinforcement noted. If identical twins reared by their natural parents became schizophrenic later in life, the clinician holding a learning view might assert that they had similar reinforcement histories; whereas if fraternal twins were raised at home and only one became schizophrenic, the learning explanation would be that their reinforcement histories were different. Such explanations are as circular and as unsatisfactory as some psychoanalytic inferences of unconscious processes, a practice deplored by behaviorists.

Although adopting a learning explanation of abnormal behavior has clearly led to many treatment innovations (see the following section on behavior therapy), the fact that a treatment based on learning principles is effective in changing behavior does not show that the behavior was itself learned in a similar way. For example, if the mood of depressed persons is elevated by providing them with rewards for increased activity, this cannot be considered evidence that the depression and apathy were initially produced by an absence of rewards (Rimland, 1964).

BEHAVIOR THERAPY

Behavior therapy focuses on changing specific behaviors rather than on uncovering unconscious conflicts. Several therapeutic techniques have been developed as an outgrowth of the learning para-

digms. The terms **behavior therapy** and **behavior modification** are applied to these techniques because they were initially asserted to be based on the experimentally tested laws of learning formulated by the behaviorists.

Because the learning paradigm assumes that behavior is the result of learning, treatment often involves relearning a new, more adaptive response. **Counterconditioning** is relearning achieved by eliciting a new response in the presence of a particular stimulus. A response (R1) to a given stimulus (S) can be eliminated by eliciting a new response (R2) in the presence of that stimulus, as diagrammed in Figure 2.5. For example, if a child is afraid (R1) of a harmless animal (S), the therapist might attempt to elicit a playful reaction (R2) in the presence of the animal. This counterconditioning, or substitution of a response (R2), can eliminate R1.

The counterconditioning principle is behind one of the most widely used behavior therapy techniques, **systematic desensitization**, developed by Joseph Wolpe (1958). A person who suffers from anxiety works with the therapist to compile a list of feared situations, starting with those that arouse minimal anxiety and progressing to those that are the most frightening. The person is also taught to relax deeply. Step-by-step, while relaxed, the person imagines the graded series of anxiety-provoking situations. The relaxation tends to inhibit any anxiety that might otherwise be elicited by the imagined scenes. The fearful person becomes able to tolerate increasingly more difficult imagined situations as he or she climbs the hierarchy over a number of therapy sessions. This technique is useful in reducing a wide variety of fears.[1]

---

[1]Unreferenced case reports such as this have been drawn from our own clinical files. Identifying features have been altered to protect the confidentiality of the individual.

The thirty-five-year-old substitute mail carrier who consulted us had dropped out of college sixteen years ago because of crippling fears of being criticized. Earlier, his disability had taken the form of extreme tension when faced with tests and speaking up in class. When we saw him he was debilitated by fears of criticism in general and of evaluations of his mail sorting in particular. As a consequence, his everyday activities were severely constricted, and though highly intelligent, he had apparently settled for an occupation that did not promise self-fulfillment.

After the client agreed that a reduction in his unrealistic fears would be beneficial, he was taught over several sessions to relax all the muscles of his body while in a reclining chair. We then created for him a list of anxiety-provoking scenes.

You are saying "Good morning" to your boss.

You are standing in front of your sorting bin in the post office, and your supervisor asks why you are so slow.

You are only halfway through your route, and it is already 2:00 P.M.

As you are delivering Mrs. Mackenzie's mail, she opens her screen door and complains about how late you are.

Your wife criticizes you for bringing home the wrong kind of bread.

The officer at the bridge toll gate appears impatient as you fumble in your pocket for the correct change.

These and other scenes were arranged in an *anxiety hierarchy*, from least to most fear evoking. Desensitization proper began with the client instructed first to relax deeply as he had been taught. Then he was to imagine the easiest item, remaining as relaxed as possible. When he had learned to confront this image without becoming anxious he went on to the next scene, and so on. After ten sessions the man was able to imagine the most distressing scene in the hierarchy without feeling anxious, and gradually his tension in real life became markedly less.

Another behavioral technique is **assertion training**, which teaches and encourages people to speak up and react openly when with others, expressing both positive and negative feelings. In **aversive conditioning**, a stimulus attractive to the patient is paired with an unpleasant event, such as shock to the fingertips, in hopes of endowing it with negative properties. Aversive techniques, somewhat controversial, as might be imagined, have been employed to reduce smoking and drug use and the socially inappropriate attraction that objects have for some people, such as the irresistible appeal a woman's underpants may have for a fetishist.

Several behavioral procedures derive from operant conditioning. For example, children who misbehave in classrooms can be systematically rewarded

In a token economy, changes in patients' behavior are reinforced with chips which can later be exchanged for specific reinforcers.

by the teacher for their socially acceptable behavior, whereas their undesirable behavior is ignored and thus eventually extinguished. Some mental hospitals have established a **token economy** to encourage severely disturbed patients to behave more appropriately. In this operant treatment explicit rules are set up for obtaining rewards in the form of tokens or other moneylike scrip. At predetermined intervals patients can trade in their tokens for specific reinforcers, such as a visit to the canteen or a more desirable sleeping arrangement.

Modeling has also been used in therapeutic interventions. Bandura, Blanchard, and Ritter (1969) were able to help people reduce their phobias of nonpoisonous snakes by having them view both live and filmed close and successful confrontations between people and snakes. In an analogous fashion some behavior therapists use **role-playing** in the consulting room. They demonstrate to patients patterns of behaving that might prove more effective than those in which the patients usually engage and then have the patients practice them. Lazarus (1971), in his **behavior rehearsal** procedures, demonstrates exemplary ways of handling a situation and then encourages patients to imitate them during the therapy session. For example, a student who does not know how to ask a professor for an extension on a term paper might watch the therapist portray a potentially effective way of making the request. The clinician would then help the student practice the new skill in a similar role-playing situation.

THE COGNITIVE PARADIGM

Cognition is a term that groups together the mental processes of perceiving, recognizing, conceiving, judging, and reasoning. The **cognitive paradigm**

focuses on how people (and animals as well!) structure their experiences, how they make sense of them, and how they relate their current experiences to past ones that have been stored in memory.

THE BASICS OF COGNITIVE THEORY

At any given moment we are bombarded by far more stimuli than we can possibly respond to. How do we filter this overwhelming input, put it into words or images, form hypotheses, and arrive at a perception of what is out there? Cognitive psychologists consider the learning process to be much more complex than the passive formation of new stimulus–response associations. Even classical conditioning is viewed by cognitive psychologists as an active process by which organisms learn about relationships among events rather than as an automatic stamping in of associations between stimuli (Rescorla, 1988). Moreover, cognitive psychologists regard the learner as an active interpreter of a situation, with the learner's past knowledge imposing a perceptual funnel on the experience. The learner fits new information into an organized network of already accumulated knowledge, often referred to as a **schema** (Neisser, 1976). New information may fit the schema; if not, the learner reorganizes the schema to fit the information. The cognitive approach may remind you of our earlier discussions of paradigms in science; scientific paradigms are similar in function to a cognitive schema, for they act as filters to our experience of the world.

Contemporary experimental psychology is very much concerned with cognition. The following situation illustrates how a schema, or cognitive set, may alter the way in which information is processed and remembered.

The man stood before the mirror and combed his hair. He checked his face carefully for any places he might have missed shaving and then put on the conservative tie he had decided to wear. At breakfast, he studied the newspaper carefully and, over coffee, discussed the possibility of buying a new washing machine with his wife. Then he made several phone calls. As he was leaving the house he thought about the fact that his children would probably want to go to that private camp again this summer. When the car didn't start, he got out, slammed the door and walked down to the bus stop in a very angry mood. Now he would be late. (Bransford & Johnson, 1973, p. 415)

Now read the excerpt again, but add the word "unemployed" before the word "man." Now read it a third time, substituting "stockbroker" for "man." Notice how differently you understand the passage. Ask yourself what parts of the newspaper these men read. If this query had been posed on a questionnaire, you might have answered "the want ads" for the unemployed man and "the financial pages" for the stockbroker. Since the passage does not specify which part of the paper was read, your answers would have been wrong, but in each instance the error would have been a meaningful, predictable one.

Cognitive psychologists have until recently paid little systematic attention to how their research findings bear on psychopathology or how they might help generate effective therapies. Now cognitive explanations appear more and more often in the search for the causes of abnormality and for new methods of intervention. A widely held view of depression, for example, places the blame on a cognitive set, namely, the individual's overriding sense of hopelessness (see p. 236). Many who are depressed may believe that they have no important effect on their surroundings regardless of what they do. Their destiny seems to them to be out of their hands, and they expect their future to be negative. If depression does develop through a sense of hopelessness, it could have implications for how clinicians treat the disorder.

EVALUATING THE COGNITIVE PARADIGM

The cognitive paradigm is currently the most common paradigm adopted by psychologists, yet some criticisms should be noted. The concepts on which it is based (e.g., schema) are somewhat slippery and not always well-defined. Furthermore, cognitive explanations of psychopathology do not always explain much. That a depressed person has a negative schema tells us that the person thinks gloomy thoughts. But everyone knows that such a pattern of thinking is actually part of the diagnosis of depression. What is distinctive in the cognitive paradigm is that the thoughts are given causal status, that is, the thoughts are regarded as causing the other features of the disorder, such as sadness. Left unanswered is the question of where the negative schema came from in the first place. Cognitive explanations of psychopathology tend to focus on current determinants of disorder and not on its historical antecedents. As a consequence, they have as yet shed little light on the etiology of mental disorders.

COGNITIVE BEHAVIOR THERAPY

The cognitive paradigm has gained widespread attention in behavior therapy. Generally speaking, cognitively oriented behavior therapists attempt to change the thinking processes of their patients in order to influence their emotions and behavior.

Albert Ellis, a cognitive behavior therapist and founder of Rational Emotive Behavior therapy, has focused on the role of irrational beliefs as causes of abnormal behavior.

Aaron Beck developed a cognitive theory of depression and a cognitive therapy for the cognitive biases of depressed people.

A major approach to cognitive therapy stems from the ideas of the prominent cognitive therapist Albert Ellis (1962), who holds that maladaptive feelings and activity are caused by **irrational beliefs**. Through mistaken assumptions people place excessive demands on themselves and others. A man who believes that he must always be perfect in everything he does feels terrible whenever he makes a mistake. A woman may think, "I should be able to win the love and approval of everyone," and then exhaust herself trying to please others. Ellis and his followers, the proponents of **rational-emotive therapy**, help their patients challenge such assumptions and teach them to substitute such ideas as, "Although it would be terrific never to make a mistake, that doesn't mean I *have* to be without fault."

Another leading cognitive therapist is the psychiatrist Aaron Beck (1967, 1976), whose theorizing and research on depression we examine in detail in Chapters 10 and 18. For now it is sufficient to note that Beck's cognitive focus is on how people distort experience. Many depressed individuals selectively abstract from a complex event those features that will maintain their gloomy perspective on life; for example, ignoring all the positive occurrences on a given day and focusing exclusively on negative happenings. Beck's therapy tries to persuade patients to change their opinions of themselves and the way in which they interpret life events. When a

depressed person expresses feelings that nothing ever goes right for him or her during a therapy session, for example, the therapist would offer counterexamples, pointing out how the client had overlooked favorable features of a complex set of events.

LEARNING PARADIGMS AND COGNITIVE PARADIGMS

Is the cognitive point of view basically different and separate from the learning paradigm? Much of what we have just said suggests that it is. But the growing field of cognitive behavior therapy gives us pause, for here workers study the complex interplay of beliefs, expectations, perceptions, and attitudes on the one hand and overt behavior on the other. For example, Albert Bandura (1977), a leading advocate of changing behavior through cognitive means, argues that different therapies produce improvement by increasing people's sense of **self-efficacy**, a belief that they can achieve desired goals (see p. 537). *But*, at the same time, he argues that changing behavior through behavioral techniques is the most powerful way to enhance self-efficacy. Therapists such as Ellis, by way of contrast, emphasize direct alteration of cognitions through argument, persuasion, Socratic dialogue, and the like to bring about improvements in emotion and behavior. Complicating matters still further, Ellis and his followers also place considerable importance on homework assignments that require clients to behave in ways in which they have been unable to behave because they have been hindered by negative thoughts. Ellis even renamed his therapy "rational-emotive behavior therapy" to highlight the importance of overt behavior. Therapists identified with cognitive behavior therapy work at both the cognitive and behavioral levels, and most of those who use cognitive concepts and try to change beliefs with verbal means also use behavioral procedures to alter behavior directly.

This issue is reflected in the terminology used to refer to people such as Beck and Ellis. Are they *cognitive therapists* or cognitive *behavior* therapists? For the most part we will use the latter term because it denotes both that the therapist regards cognitions as major determinants of emotion and behavior and that he or she maintains the focus on overt behavior that has always characterized behavior therapy. Nonetheless, it is important for the reader to know that Beck, even though he assigns many behavioral tasks as part of his therapy, is usually referred to as the founder of cognitive therapy (CT), and that Ellis's rational-emotive therapy (RET) is often spoken of as something separate from behavior therapy.

CONSEQUENCES OF ADOPTING A PARADIGM

The student of abnormal behavior who adopts a particular paradigm necessarily makes a prior decision concerning what kinds of data will be collected and how they will be interpreted. Thus he or she may very well ignore possibilities and overlook other information in advancing what seems to be the most probable explanation. A behaviorist is prone to attribute the high prevalence of schizophrenia in lower-class groups to the paucity of social rewards that these people have received, the assumption being that normal development requires a certain amount and patterning of reinforcement. A biologically oriented theorist will be quick to remind the behaviorist of the many deprived people who do *not* become schizophrenic. The behaviorist will undoubtedly counter with the argument that those who do not become schizophrenic had different reinforcement histories. The biologically oriented theorist will reply that such *post hoc*, or after-the-fact, statements can always be made.

Our biological theorist may suggest that certain biochemical factors that predispose both to schizophrenia and to deficiencies in the intellectual skills necessary to maintain occupational status account for the observed correlation between social class and schizophrenia. The behaviorist will be entirely justified in reminding the biological theorist that these alleged factors have yet to be found, to which the biological theorist might rightfully answer, "Yes, but I'm placing my bets that they are there, and if I adopt *your* behavioral paradigm, I may not look for them." To which the learning theorist may with justification reply, "Yes, but *your* assumption regarding biochemical factors makes it less likely that you will look for and uncover the subtle reinforcement factors that in all likelihood account for both the presence and the absence of schizophrenia."

The fact that our two colleagues are in a sense correct and in another sense incorrect is both exasperating and exciting. They are both correct in asserting that certain data are more likely to be found through work done within a particular paradigm. But they are incorrect to become unduly agitated that each and every social scientist is not assuming that one and the same factor will ultimately be found crucial in the development of all mental disorders. Abnormal behavior is much too diverse to be explained or treated adequately by any one of the current paradigms. It is probably for the best that psychologists do *not* agree on which paradigm is the best. We know far too little to make hard-and-fast decisions on the exclusive superiority of any one paradigm, and there is enough important work to go around. We will often see, too, that a plausible way of looking at the data is to assume multiple causation. A particular disorder may very well develop through an interaction of biological defects and environmental factors, a view we turn to next.

DIATHESIS–STRESS: AN INTEGRATIVE PARADIGM

A paradigm that is more general than the ones we have previously discussed is called **diathesis–stress**. It links biological, psychological, and environmental factors and is not limited to one particular school of thought, such as learning, cognitive, or psychodynamic. This paradigm focuses on the interaction between a predisposition toward disease—the diathesis—and environmental, or life, disturbances—the stress. Diathesis refers most precisely to a constitutional predisposition toward illness, but the term may be extended to any characteristic or set of characteristics of a person that increases his or her chance of developing a disorder. In the realm of biology, for example, a number of problems considered in later chapters appear to have a genetically transmitted diathesis. That is, having a close relative with the disorder and therefore sharing to some degree his or her genetic endowment increases a person's risk for the disor-

Within the diathesis-stress paradigm a stressor activates a predisposition toward illness. Such stressors may range in intensity from relatively minor (such as having too much work to do) to catastrophic (such as living in a city ravaged by war).

der. Although the precise nature of these genetic diatheses is currently unknown (i.e., we don't know exactly what is inherited that makes one person more likely than another to develop schizophrenia), it is clear that a biological predisposition is an important component of many psychopathologies.

Turning to psychological diatheses, the cognitive set already mentioned, the chronic feeling of hopelessness sometimes found in the depressed, may be considered a diathesis for depression. Or, taking a psychodynamic view, an extreme sense of dependency on others, perhaps because of frustrations during one of the psychosexual stages, could also be a diathesis for depression. Other psychological diatheses include the ability to be easily hypnotized, which may be a diathesis for multiple personality disorder, and an intense fear of becoming fat, which predisposes toward eating disorders.

These psychological diatheses can arise for a variety of reasons. Some, such as hypnotizability, are personality characteristics that are in part genetically determined. Others, such as a sense of hopelessness, may result from childhood experiences with harshly critical parents. Sociocultural influences also play an important role; for instance, cultural standards of what is beautiful may lead to an intense fear of being fat and thus to eating disorders. The diathesis–stress paradigm is integrative because it draws on all these diverse sources of information about the causes of diatheses. In later chapters we will see that concepts from the major paradigms we have already discussed are differen-

tially applicable to different disorders. For example, a genetically determined biological diathesis plays a major role in schizophrenia. Cognitive diatheses, in contrast, are more influential in the anxiety disorders and depression. Psychoanalytic concepts figure prominently in theories of hysteria. A diathesis–stress paradigm allows us to draw on concepts from many sources and to make more or less use of them depending on the disorder being considered.

Possessing the diathesis for a disorder increases a person's chance of developing it but does not by any means guarantee that a disorder will develop. The stress part of diathesis–stress is meant to account for how a diathesis may be translated into an actual disorder. In this context stress generally refers to some noxious or unpleasant environmental stimulus that can be either biological or psychological.[2] Examples of biological stressors include oxygen deprivation at birth and poor nutrition during childhood; both may lead to some form of brain dysfunction. Psychological stressors include both major traumatic events (e.g., sexual or physical abuse, death of a spouse) as well as more mundane happenings, which many of us experience (e.g., not achieving goals we have set for ourselves). By

---

[2]*Stress* actually refers to the individual's reaction to a *stressor*, the environmental event that causes stress. For this reason one should probably call this paradigm the diathesis–stressor paradigm, but we adopt the former term because of its general acceptance among psychopathologists. This distinction is discussed more fully in Chapter 8 (p. 180).

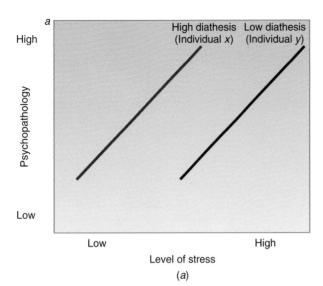

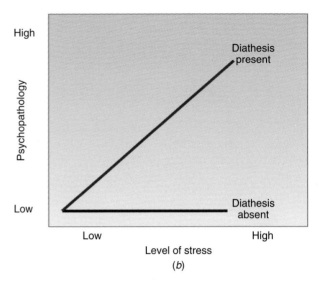

Figure 2.6 Three depictions of diathesis–stress models. (a) An individual with a large dose of the diathesis requires only a moderate amount of stress to develop psychopathology, whereas an individual with a small dose of the diathesis requires a large amount of stress to precipate a breakdown. (b) The diathesis is dichotomous; stress level has no effect on those without the diathesis. (c) The diathesis is continuous; increasing stress increases psychopathology for all people with at least a minimal amount of the diathesis. After Monroe & Simons, 1991.

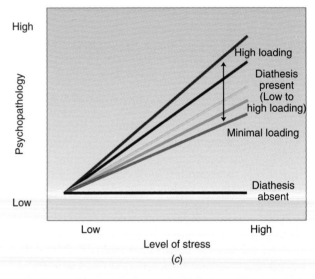

including these environmental events the diathesis–stress model goes beyond the major paradigms we have already discussed.

The key point of the diathesis–stress model is that both diathesis and stress are necessary in the development of disorders (see Figure 2.6). Some people, for example, have inherited a biological predisposition that places them at high risk for schizophrenia (see Chapter 11); given a certain amount of stress, they stand a good chance of becoming schizophrenic. Other people, those at low genetic risk, are not likely to develop schizophrenia, regardless of how difficult their lives are.

Another major feature of the diathesis–stress paradigm is that psychopathology is unlikely to result from the impact of any single factor. A genetically transmitted diathesis may be necessary for some disorders, but it is embedded in a network of multiple factors that also contribute to disorder. These factors could include genetically transmitted diatheses for other personality characteristics; childhood experiences that shape personality, the development of behavioral competencies, and coping strategies; stressors encountered in adulthood; cultural influences; and numerous other factors.

Finally, we should note that within this framework the data gathered by researchers holding different paradigms are not incompatible with each other. It is increasingly common for a researcher who focuses on one area, for example, neurochemistry, to be attentive to data being collected by researchers in another area, for example, the role of psychosocial factors. In this example it would be recognized that stress is needed to activate a predisposition toward a biochemical imbalance. Some of the differences between the paradigms also appear to be more linguistic than substantive. A cognitive theorist may propose that maladaptive cognitions cause depression, whereas a biological theorist may speak of the underactivity of a certain neural pathway. The two positions are not contradictory, but merely reflect different levels of description just as we could describe a table as pieces of wood in a particular configuration or as a collection of atoms.

DIFFERENT PERSPECTIVES ON A CLINICAL PROBLEM

It will now be useful to recall the case of the police officer with which this book began. The information provided is open to a number of interpretations, depending on the paradigm adopted. If you hold a biological point of view you are attentive to the similarity between the man's alternately manic and depressed states and the cyclical swings of mood suffered by his father. You are probably aware of the research (to be reviewed in Chapter 10) that suggests a genetic factor in mood disorders. You do not discount environmental contributions to his problems, but you hypothesize that some inherited, probably biochemical, defect predisposes him to break down under stress. After all, not everyone who experiences a difficult childhood and adolescence develops the kinds of problems Ernest H. has. For treatment you may prescribe lithium carbonate, a drug that is generally helpful in reducing the magnitude of mood swings in manic-depression.

Now suppose that you are committed to a cognitive-behavioral perspective, which encourages you to analyze human behavior in terms of reinforcement patterns as well as cognitive variables. You may focus on Ernest's self-consciousness at college, which seems related to the fact that compared with his fellow students, he grew up with few advantages. Economic insecurity and hardship may have made him unduly sensitive to criticism and rejection. Moreover, he regards his wife as warm and charming, pointing up his own perceived lack of social skills. Alcohol has been his escape from such tensions. But heavy drinking, coupled with persistent doubt about his own worth as a human being, has interfered with sexual functioning, worsening an already deteriorating marital relationship and further undermining his confidence. As a behavior therapist, you may employ systematic desensitization. You teach Ernest to relax deeply as he imagines a hierarchy of situations in which he is being evaluated by others. Or you may decide on rational-emotive therapy to convince Ernest that he need not obtain universal approval for every undertaking. Or, given Ernest's deficiency in social skills, you may choose behavior rehearsal to teach him how to function effectively in social situations in which he has had little experience. You might follow more than one of these strategies.

A psychoanalytic point of view casts Ernest H. in yet another light. Believing that events in early childhood are of great importance in later patterns of adjustment, you may hypothesize that Ernest is still grieving for his mother and has blamed his father for her early death. Such strong anger at the father has been repressed, but Ernest has not been able to regard him as a competent, worthwhile adult and to identify with him. For treatment you may choose dream analysis and free association to help Ernest lift his repressions and deal openly and consciously with his hitherto buried anger toward his father.

ECLECTICISM IN PSYCHOTHERAPY: PRACTICE MAKES IMPERFECT

A final word is needed about paradigms and the activities of therapists. From our presentation of treatment approaches, it may appear that they are practices of separate, nonoverlapping schools of therapy. You may have the impression that a behavior therapist would never listen to a client's report of a dream, nor would a psychoanalyst be caught dead prescribing assertion training to a patient. Such suppositions could not be further from the truth. Most therapists subscribe to **eclecticism**, employing ideas and therapeutic techniques from a variety of schools (Garfield & Kurtz, 1974).

Therapists often behave in ways that are not entirely consistent with the theories they hold. For years practicing behavior therapists have listened empathically to clients, trying to make out their perspectives on events, on the assumption that this understanding would help them plan a better program for changing troublesome behavior. Behavioral theories do not prescribe such a procedure, but on the basis of clinical experience, and perhaps through their own humanity, behavior therapists have realized that empathic listening helps them establish rapport, determine what is really bothering the client, and plan a sensible therapy program. By the same token, Freud himself is said to have been more directive and done far more to change immediate behavior than would be concluded from his writings alone.

In one of Freud's earliest cases, that of Elisabeth von R., he did not restrict himself to the passive and distant analyst's role he recommended in his writings. Though he described his success with this patient in terms of helping her become conscious of certain desires she had repressed—chiefly that of wishing to marry her dead sister's husband—he did so by taking a very active role. Freud not only encouraged his patient to visit her sister's grave and to visit a man she found attractive, he also interacted with her family on her behalf and encouraged them to have more open communication with the patient, even helping them untangle their finances. After the therapy was over Freud secured an invitation for himself to a dance she attended so that he could watch his patient, who had come to him because she had difficulty walking, "whirl past in a lively dance." This extra involvement, a departure from psychoanalytic practice, was as much a part of the therapeutic intervention as was the young woman's time on the couch (from Yalom, 1980).

Today especially psychoanalysts are paying more attention to overt behavior and the relief of symptoms than early analytic theory would prescribe.

Some contemporary writers, such as Paul Wachtel (see p. 549), have proposed that analysts employ behavior therapy techniques, openly acknowledging that behavior therapy has something to offer in the alleviation of behavior pathology.

Treatment is a complex and ultimately highly individual process, and these are weighty issues. The final section of this textbook will give them the attention they need and deserve. The reader should be aware of this complexity at the beginning, however, in order to better appreciate the intricacies and realities of psychotherapy.

SUMMARY

Several major paradigms, or points of view, are current in the study of psychopathology and therapy. The *biological* paradigm assumes that psychopathology is caused by an organic defect. Previous discussions of this point of view have taken the form of arguments, pro and con, about a medical, or disease, model. Because the medical model has one central implication—that psychopathology may be attributed to biological malfunctions and defects—we prefer the term *biological paradigm* to medical model. We described two biological factors relevant to psychopathology—genetics and neurochemistry. Biological therapies attempt to rectify the specific organic defects underlying disorders or to alleviate symptoms of disorders that have not been traced to such defects.

Another paradigm derives from the work of Sigmund Freud. The *psychoanalytic*, or psychodynamic, point of view directs our attention to repressions and other unconscious processes that are traceable to early childhood conflicts that have set in motion certain psychodynamics. Whereas present-day ego analysts who are part of this tradition place greater emphasis on conscious ego functions, the psychoanalytic paradigm has generally searched the unconscious and early life of the patient for the causes of abnormality. Therapeutic interventions based on psychoanalytic theory usually attempt to lift repressions so that the patient can examine the infantile and unfounded nature of his or her fears.

Behavioral, or *learning*, paradigms suggest that aberrant behavior has developed through classical conditioning, operant conditioning, or modeling. Investigators who believe that abnormal behavior may have been learned share a commitment to examine carefully all situations affecting behavior as well as to define concepts carefully. Behavior therapists try to apply learning principles to the direct alteration of overt behavior, thought, and emotion. Less attention is paid to the historical causes of abnormal behavior than to what maintains it, such as the reward and punishment contingencies that encourage problematic response patterns.

More recently, *cognitive* theorists have argued that certain schemata and irrational interpretations are major factors in abnormality. In both practice and theory the cognitive paradigm has usually blended with the behavioral in an approach to intervention that is referred to as cognitive-behavioral.

Because each of these paradigms seems to have something to offer to our understanding of mental disorders, there has recently been a movement to develop more integrative paradigms. The *diathesis–stress* paradigm, which integrates several points of view, assumes that people are predisposed to react adversely to environmental stressors. The diathesis may be biological, as appears to be the case in schizophrenia, or it may be extended to the psychological, for example, the chronic sense of hopelessness that appears to contribute to depression. Diatheses may be caused by early childhood experiences, genetically determined personality traits, or sociocultural influences.

The most important implication of paradigms is that they determine where and how investigators look for answers. Paradigms necessarily limit perceptions of the world, for investigators will interpret data differently according to their points of view. In our opinion it is fortunate that workers are not all operating within the same paradigm, for at this point too little is known about psychopathology and its treatment to settle on any one of them. Indeed, paralleling the current interest in integrative paradigms, most clinicians are eclectic in their approach to intervention, employing techniques that are outside their paradigm but that seem useful in dealing with the complexities of human psychological problems.

KEY TERMS

etiology
biological paradigm
medical (disease) model
genes
behavior genetics
genotype
phenotype
family method
index cases (probands)
twin method
monozygotic (MZ) twins
dizygotic (DZ) twins
concordance
neuron
nerve impulse
synapse
neurotransmitters
reuptake
psychoanalytic
    (psychodynamic)
    paradigm
id
libido
pleasure principle
primary process
ego
secondary process
reality principle
superego
psychodynamics
unconscious
psychosexual stages
oral stage

anal stage
phallic stage
latency period
genital stage
fixation
Oedipus complex
Electra complex
objective (realistic) anxiety
neurotic anxiety
defense mechanism
repression
projection
displacement
reaction formation
regression
rationalization
sublimation
analytical psychology
collective unconscious
individual psychology
psychosocial stages of
    development
identity crisis
free association
dream analysis
transference
analysis of defenses
ego analysts
learning paradigm
introspection
behaviorism
classical conditioning
unconditioned stimulus

unconditioned response
conditioned stimulus
conditioned response
extinction
law of effect
operant conditioning
discriminative stimulus
positive reinforcement
negative reinforcement
shaping
successive approximations
modeling
mediational theory of
    learning
mediator
avoidance conditioning
behavior therapy
behavior modification
counterconditioning
systematic desensitization
assertion training
aversive conditioning
token economy
role-playing
behavior rehearsal
cognition
cognitive paradigm
schema
irrational beliefs
rational-emotive therapy
self-efficacy
diathesis–stress
eclecticism

David Hockney, "David, Celia, Stephen, and Ian, London 1982"

3

CLASSIFICATION AND DIAGNOSIS

Diagnosis is a critical aspect of the field of abnormal psychology. It is essential for professionals to be able to communicate accurately with one another about the types of cases they are treating or studying. Furthermore, to find the causes or best treatments for a disorder, it must first be classified correctly. Only in recent years, however, has diagnosis been accorded the attention it deserves. To beginning students of abnormal psychology, diagnosis can seem tedious because it relies on fine distinctions. For example, anxiety in social situations—being extremely tense around others—is a symptom of both schizotypal and avoidant personality disorders. In a person with schizotypal personality disorder, however, the anxiety does not decrease as the individual becomes more familiar with people, whereas in the person with avoidant personality disorder exposure tends to reduce social anxiety. This fine distinction could certainly be viewed as hairsplitting. However, as we will discuss thoroughly later in the chapter, the decisive factor is whether the distinction is useful in differentiating between the two diagnoses.

In this chapter we focus on the official diagnostic system widely employed by mental health professionals, the **Diagnostic and Statistical Manual of Mental Disorders**, now in its fourth edition, commonly referred to as **DSM-IV**. It is published by the American Psychiatric Association and has an interesting history.

By the end of the nineteenth century medicine had progressed far beyond its practice during the Middle Ages, when bloodletting was at least part of the treatment of virtually all physical problems. Gradually people recognized that different illnesses required different treatments. Diagnostic procedures were improved, diseases classified, and applicable remedies administered. Impressed by the successes that new diagnostic procedures had achieved in the field of medicine, investigators of abnormal behavior also sought to develop classification schemes. Advances in other sciences, such as botany and chemistry, had followed the development of classification systems, reinforcing hope that similar efforts in the field of abnormal behavior might bring progress.

But during the nineteenth century and into the twentieth as well, there was great inconsistency in the classification of abnormal behavior. By the end of the nineteenth century the diversity of classifications was recognized as a serious problem that impeded communication among people in the field. Inconsistency in classification also slows progress in searching for causes and effective treatments. For

example, if one research group finds a successful treatment for depression, but has defined it in an idiosyncratic way, the finding is not likely to be replicated by another group of investigators. In the United Kingdom in 1882 the Statistical Committee of the Royal Medico-Psychological Association produced a classification scheme that, even though revised several times, was never adopted by its members. In Paris in 1889 the Congress of Mental Science adopted a single classification system, but it was never widely used. In the United States the Association of Medical Superintendents of American Institutions for the Insane, a forerunner of the American Psychiatric Association, adopted a somewhat revised version of the British system in 1886. Then, in 1913, this group accepted a new classification, which incorporated some of Emil Kraepelin's ideas (p. 18). Again, consistency was lacking. The New York State Commission on Lunacy, for example, insisted on retaining its own system (Kendell, 1975).

DIAGNOSIS IN THE TWENTIETH CENTURY

More contemporary efforts at achieving uniformity of classification have also not been totally successful. In 1939 the World Health Organization (WHO) added mental disorders to the *International List of Causes of Death*. In 1948 the list was expanded to become the *International Statistical Classification of Diseases, Injuries, and Causes of Death (ICD)*, a comprehensive listing of all diseases, including a classification of abnormal behavior. Although this nomenclature was unanimously adopted at a WHO conference, the mental disorders section failed to be widely accepted. Even though American psychiatrists had played a prominent role in the WHO effort, the American Psychiatric Association published its own *Diagnostic and Statistical Manual (DSM)* in 1952.

In 1969 the WHO published a new classification system, which was more widely accepted. A second version of the American Psychiatric Association's DSM, DSM-II (1968), was similar to the WHO system, and in the United Kingdom a glossary of definitions was produced to accompany it (General Register Office, 1968). But true consensus still eluded the field. The WHO classifications were simply a listing of diagnostic categories; the actual behavior or symptoms that were the bases for the diagnoses were not specified. DSM-II and the British *Glossary* provided this crucial information but did not specify the same symptoms for a given disorder. Thus actual diagnostic practices still varied widely. In 1980 the American Psychiatric Association published an extensively revised diagnostic manual—DSM-III. A somewhat revised version, DSM-IIIR, appeared in 1987.

In 1988 the American Psychiatric Association appointed a task force, chaired by psychiatrist Allen Frances, to begin work on DSM-IV. Working groups, which included many psychologists, were established to review sections of DSM-IIIR, prepare literature reviews, analyze previously collected data, and collect new data if needed. An important change in the process for this edition of the DSM was the adoption of a conservative approach to making changes in the diagnostic criteria—the reasons for changes in diagnoses would be explicitly stated and clearly supported by data. In previous versions of the DSM the reasons for diagnostic changes were not always explicit, so the evidence that led to them was never exposed to public scrutiny.

Despite these improvements some controversy surrounding the new effort surfaced immediately. To some (e.g., Zimmerman, 1988) it appeared that diagnostic revisions had outpaced any real gains in knowledge. The rejoinder to this criticism was that work on DSM-IV followed the publication of DSM-IIIR so quickly because of the expected publication of the tenth version of the *International Classification of Diseases* (ICD-10) in 1993. Many inconsistencies had emerged between the ICD and the DSM, and it was desirable to resolve as many of them as possible.

In 1991 the American Psychiatric Association published the *DSM-IV Options Book*. For each diagnosis the book spelled out problems or controversies and possible solutions. For example, antisocial personality disorder is a DSM diagnosis related to psychopathy, a diagnostic term that does not appear in the DSM but is widely used by researchers. Both antisocial personality and psychopathy describe people who show a general disregard for others and frequently break the law. But the diagnosis of antisocial personality focuses more on antisocial behavior per se, whereas the diagnosis of psychopathy is more oriented toward the psychological characteristics (e.g., no sense of shame) of some of those who act antisocially. Which diagnosis should appear in the DSM? Unfortunately, the scope of such questions far exceeded the ability of the field trials to provide definitive answers; neither the funding nor the time was available. Thus many of the changes that appeared in DSM-IV were based on already-collected data rather than on new information generated by the various working groups.

A draft of DSM-IV became available in March 1993, and the final version was published in 1994. In this chapter we present the major DSM-IV categories in brief summary. We then evaluate classification in general and the DSM in particular. In the next chapter we consider the assessment procedures that provide the data on which diagnostic decisions are based.

THE DIAGNOSTIC SYSTEM OF THE AMERICAN PSYCHIATRIC ASSOCIATION (DSM-IV)

FIVE DIMENSIONS OF CLASSIFICATION

Several major innovations distinguish the third edition and subsequent versions of the DSM. Perhaps the most sweeping change is the use of **multiaxial classification**, whereby each individual is rated on five separate dimensions, or axes (Table 3.1). The multiaxial system, by requiring judgments to be made on each of the five axes, forces the diagnostician to consider a broad range of information. Axis I includes all categories with the exception of the personality disorders and mental retardation, which make up Axis II. Thus Axes I and II constitute the classification of abnormal behavior. Axes I and II are separated to ensure that the presence of long-term disturbances is not overlooked when attention is directed to the current disorder. For example, a heroin addict would be diagnosed on Axis I as having a substance-related disorder; he or she might also have a long-standing antisocial personality disorder, which would be noted on Axis II. A more detailed presentation of the diagnoses of Axes I and II appear inside the front cover of this book.

Although the remaining three axes are not needed to make the actual diagnosis, their inclusion in the DSM indicates recognition that factors other than a person's symptoms should be considered in an assessment. On Axis III the clinician indicates any general medical conditions believed to be relevant to the mental disorder in question. For example, the existence of a heart condition in a person who was also diagnosed with depression would have important implications for treatment; antidepressant drugs would be a poor choice because they could worsen the heart condition. Axis IV codes psychosocial and environmental problems that the person has been experiencing and that may be contributing to the disorder. These include occupational problems, economic problems, interpersonal difficulties with family members, and a variety of problems in other life areas, which may influence psychological functioning. Finally, on Axis V, the clinician indicates the person's current level of adaptive functioning. Life areas considered are social relationships, occupational functioning, and use of leisure time. Ratings of current functioning are supposed to give information about the need for treatment.

DIAGNOSTIC CATEGORIES

In this section we provide a brief description of the major diagnostic categories of Axes I and II. Before presenting the diagnoses we should note that the extensive descriptions in subsequent chapters will focus on instances when the cause of the disorder is not completely known. For many of these diagnoses DSM also includes a provision for indicating that the disorder is due to a medical condition or substance abuse. For example, depression resulting from an endocrine gland dysfunction would be diagnosed in the depression section of the DSM but listed as caused by a medical problem. Clinicians must therefore be sensitive not only to the symptoms of their patients, but also to the possible medical causes of their patients' conditions.

DISORDERS USUALLY FIRST DIAGNOSED IN INFANCY, CHILDHOOD, OR ADOLESCENCE

Within this broad-ranging category are the intellectual, emotional, and physical disorders that usually begin in infancy, childhood, or adolescence. Some of the problems described are *separation anxiety disorder*; *conduct disorder*; *attention deficit/hyperactivity disorder*; *mental retardation* (listed on Axis II); *pervasive developmental disorders* such as *autistic disorder*; and *learning disorders*, which cover delays in the acquisition of speech, reading, arithmetic, and writing skills. These disorders are discussed in Chapter 15.

SUBSTANCE-RELATED DISORDERS

For this diagnosis the ingestion of various substances—alcohol, opiates, cocaine, amphetamines, and so on—has changed behavior enough to impair social or occupational functioning. The individual may become unable to control or discontinue ingestion of the substance and may develop withdrawal symptoms if he or she stops using it. These substances may also cause or contribute to the development of other Axis I disorders, such as those of mood or anxiety. These disorders are examined in Chapter 12.

SCHIZOPHRENIA

For individuals with *schizophrenic disorders* contact with reality has been lost. Their language and communication are disordered, and they may shift from one subject to another in ways that make them impossible to understand. They commonly experience delusions, such as believing that thoughts not their own have been placed in their heads; in addition, they are plagued by hallucinations, in particular, hearing voices that come from outside themselves. Their emotions are blunted, flattened, or inappropriate, and their social relationships and ability to work have markedly deteriorated. These serious mental disorders are discussed in Chapter 11.

MOOD DISORDERS

As the name implies this diagnosis applies to those whose moods are extremely high or low. In *major depressive disorder* the person is deeply sad and discouraged and is also likely to lose weight and energy and to have suicidal thoughts and feelings of self-reproach. The person with *mania* may be described as exceedingly euphoric, irritable, more

Alcohol is the most frequently abused substance.

TABLE 3.1 DSM-IV Multiaxial Classification System

Axis I	Axis II	Axis III
Disorders Usually First Diagnosed in Infancy, Childhood, or Adolescence Delirium, Dementia, Amnestic and other Cognitive Disorders Substance-related Disorders Schizophrenia and Other Psychotic Disorders Mood Disorders Anxiety Disorders Somatoform Disorders Factitious Disorders Dissociative Disorders Sexual and Gender Identity Disorders Eating Disorders Sleeping Disorders Impulse Control Disorders Not Elsewhere Classified Adjustment Disorders	Mental Retardation Personality Disorders	General Medical Conditions

Axis IV
Psychosocial and Environmental Problems

Check:

_____ Problems with primary support group. Specify:

_____ Problems related to the social environment. Specify:

_____ Educational problem. Specify:

_____ Occupational problem. Specify:

_____ Housing problem. Specify:

_____ Economic problem. Specify:

_____ Problems with access to health care services. Specify:

_____ Problems related to interaction with the legal system/crime. Specify:

_____ Other psychosocial and environmental problems. Specify:

Axis V
Global Assessment of Functioning Scale (GAF Scale)

Consider psychological, social, and occupational functioning on a hypothetical continuum of mental health/illness. Do not include impairment in functioning due to physical (or environmental) limitations.

Code

100 | 91	Superior functioning in a wide range of activities, life's problems never seem to get out of hand, is sought out by others because of his many positive qualities. No symptoms.
90 | 81	Absent or minimal symptoms (e.g., mild anxiety before an exam), good functioning in all areas, interested and involved in a wide range of activities, socially effective, generally satisfied with life, no more than everyday problems or concerns (e.g., an occasional argument with family members).
80 | 71	If symptoms are present, they are transient and expectable reactions to psychosocial stressors (e.g., difficulty concentrating after family argument); no more than slight impairment in social, occupational, or school functioning (e.g., temporarily falling behind in school work).
70 | 61	Some mild symptoms (e.g., depressed mood and mild insomnia) OR some difficulty in social, occupational, or school functioning (e.g., occasional truancy, or theft within the household), but generally functioning pretty well, has some meaningful interpersonal relationships.

TABLE 3.1 (continued)	
60 | 51	Moderate symptoms (e.g., flat affect and circumstantial speech, occasional panic attacks) OR moderate difficulty in social, occupational, or school functioning (e.g., no friends, unable to keep a job).
50 | 41	Serious symptoms (e.g., suicidal ideation, severe obsessional rituals, frequent shoplifting) OR any serious impairment in social, occupational or school functioning (e.g., no friends, unable to keep a job).
40 | | 31	Some impairment in reality testing or communication (e.g., speech is at times illogical, obscure, or irrelevant) OR major impairment in several areas, such as work or school, family relations, judgment, thinking, or mood (e.g., depressed man avoids friends, neglects family, and is unable to work; child frequently beats up younger children, is defiant at home, and is failing at school).
30 | 21	Behavior is considerably influenced by delusions or hallucinations OR serious impairment in communication or judgment (e.g., sometimes incoherent, acts grossly inappropriately, suicidal preoccupation) OR inability to function in almost all areas (e.g., stays in bed all day; no job, home, or friends).
20 | 11	Some danger of hurting self or others (e.g., suicide attempts without clear expectation of death, frequently violent, manic excitement) OR occasionally fails to maintain minimal personal hygiene (e.g., smears feces) OR gross impairment in communication (e.g., largely incoherent or mute).
10 | 1	Persistent danger of severely hurting self or others (e.g., recurrent violence) OR persistent inability to maintain minimal personal hygiene OR serious suicidal act with clear expectation of death.
0	Inadequate information.

Note: Reprinted with permission from the DSM-IV, 1994 American Psychiatric Association.

active than usual, distractible, and possessed of unrealistically great self-esteem. *Bipolar disorder* is diagnosed if the person experiences episodes of mania or of both mania and depression. The disorders of mood are surveyed in Chapter 10.

ANXIETY DISORDERS

Anxiety disorders have some form of irrational or overblown fear as the central disturbance. Individuals with a *phobia* fear an object or situation so intensely that they must avoid it, even though they know that their fear is unwarranted and unreasonable and disrupts their lives. In *panic disorder* the person is subject to sudden but brief attacks of intense apprehension, so upsetting that he or she is likely to tremble and shake, feel dizzy, and have trouble breathing. Panic disorder may also be accompanied by *agoraphobia*, when the person is also fearful of leaving familiar surroundings. In people diagnosed with *generalized anxiety disorder*, fear and apprehension are pervasive and persistent. Individuals are jumpy and may have a lump in the throat and a pounding heart. They worry constantly and feel generally on edge. A person with *obsessive-compulsive disorder* is subject to persistent obsessions or compulsions. Obsessions are recurrent thoughts, ideas, and images that uncontrollably

Fear of contamination and excessive handwashing are frequent in obsessive-compulsive disorder.

dominate a person's consciousness. A compulsion is an urge to perform a stereotyped act with the usually impossible purpose of warding off an impending feared situation. Attempts to resist a compulsion create so much tension that the individual usually yields to it.

The anxiety and emotional numbness suffered in the aftermath of a very traumatic event is called *posttraumatic stress disorder*. Individuals have

Agoraphobia, a fear of leaving familiar surroundings, is one of the anxiety disorders and is often accompanied by panic attacks.

painful, intrusive recollections by day and bad dreams at night. They find it difficult to concentrate and feel detached from others and from ongoing affairs. *Acute stress disorder* is similar to posttraumatic stress disorder, but the symptoms do not last as long. The anxiety disorders are reviewed in Chapter 6.

SOMATOFORM DISORDERS

The physical symptoms of somatoform disorders have no known physiological cause but seem to serve a psychological purpose. Persons with *somatization disorder*, or Briquet's syndrome, have a long history of multiple physical complaints for which they have taken medicine or consulted doctors. In *conversion disorder* the person reports the loss of motor or sensory function, such as a paralysis, an anesthesia, or blindness. Individuals with *pain disorder* suffer from severe and prolonged pain. *Hypochondriasis* is the misinterpretation of minor physical sensations as serious illness. People with *body dysmorphic disorder* are preoccupied with an

imagined defect in their appearance. These disorders are covered in Chapter 7.

DISSOCIATIVE DISORDERS

Psychological dissociation is a sudden alteration in consciousness that affects memory and identity. Persons with *dissociative amnesia* may forget their entire past or lose memory for a particular time period. With *dissociative fugue* the individual suddenly and unexpectedly travels to a new locale, starts a new life, and is amnesic for his or her previous identity. The person with *dissociative identity disorder* (formerly called multiple personality disorder) possesses two or more distinct personalities, each complex and dominant one at a time. *Depersonalization disorder* is a severe and disruptive feeling of self-estrangement or unreality. These disorders are examined in Chapter 7.

SEXUAL AND GENDER IDENTITY DISORDERS

The sexual disorders section of DSM-IV lists three principal subcategories. In *paraphilias* the sources of sexual gratification—as in exhibitionism, voyeurism, sadism, and masochism—are unconventional. Persons with *sexual dysfunctions* are unable to complete the usual sexual response cycle. Inability to maintain an erection, premature ejaculation, and inhibition of orgasms are examples of their problems. People with *gender identity disorders* feel extreme discomfort with their anatomical sex and identify themselves as members of the opposite sex. These disorders are studied in Chapter 14.

SLEEP DISORDERS

Two major subcategories of sleep disorders are distinguished in DSM-IV. In the *dyssomnias*, sleep is disturbed in amount (e.g., the person is not able to maintain sleep or sleeps too much), quality (the person does not feel rested after sleep), or timing (e.g., the person experiences inability to sleep during conventional sleep times). In the *parasomnias*, an unusual event occurs during sleep (e.g., nightmares, sleepwalking). These disorders are discussed in Chapter 16.

EATING DISORDERS

In *anorexia nervosa* the person avoids eating and becomes emaciated, usually because of an intense fear of becoming fat. In *bulimia nervosa* there are frequent episodes of binge eating coupled with compensatory activities such as self-induced vomiting and heavy use of laxatives. These disorders are discussed in Chapter 9.

FACTITIOUS DISORDER

This diagnosis is applied to people who intentionally produce or complain of physical or psychological symptoms, apparently because of a psychological need to assume the role of a sick person.

ADJUSTMENT DISORDERS

This diagnosis refers to the development of emotional or behavioral symptoms following the occurrence of a major life stressor. However, the symptoms that ensue do not meet diagnostic criteria for any other Axis I diagnosis.

IMPULSE-CONTROL DISORDERS

This category includes a number of conditions in which the person's behavior is inappropriate and seemingly out of control. In *intermittent explosive disorder* the person has episodes of violent behavior that result in destruction of property or injury to another person. In *kleptomania* the person steals repeatedly but not for the monetary value nor for the use of the object. In *pyromania* the person purposefully sets fires and derives pleasure from doing so. In *pathological gambling* the person is preoccupied with gambling, is unable to stop, and gambles as a way to escape from problems. Finally, *trichotillomania* is diagnosed when the person cannot resist the urge to pluck out his or her hair, often resulting in significant hair loss.

Impulse control disorders include a number of conditions in which the person's behavior is out of control. Pathological gambling is an example.

Antisocial personality disorder begins in adolescence with various delinquent behaviors.

PERSONALITY DISORDERS

Personality disorders are defined as enduring, inflexible, and maladaptive patterns of behavior and inner experience. They are listed on Axis II of the DSM. In *schizoid personality disorder*, for example, the person is aloof, has few friends, and is indifferent to praise and criticism. The individual with a *narcissistic personality* has an overblown sense of self-importance, fantasizes about great successes, requires constant attention, and is likely to exploit others. The *antisocial personality* surfaces before the age of fifteen and is manifested in truancy, running away from home, delinquency, and general belligerence. In adulthood the person with antisocial personality disorder is indifferent about holding a job, being a responsible mate or parent, planning ahead for the future or even for tomorrow, and staying on the right side of the law. Also called psychopaths, antisocial personalities do not feel guilt or shame for transgressing social mores. Chapter 13 covers the personality disorders.

OTHER CONDITIONS THAT MAY BE A FOCUS OF CLINICAL ATTENTION

This all-encompassing category comprises conditions that are not regarded as mental disorders per se but still may be a focus of attention or treatment. This category seems to exist so that anyone entering the mental health system can be categorized, even in the absence of a formally designated mental disorder. If an individual's medical illness appears to be caused, in part, or exacerbated by a psychological condition,

---

FOCUS 3.1 ISSUES AND POSSIBLE CATEGORIES IN NEED OF FURTHER STUDY

One of DSM-IV's appendixes is entitled "Criteria Sets and Axes Provided for Further Study." It contains several proposals for new categories that the DSM-IV task force considers promising but not sufficiently established by data as to merit inclusion in DSM-IV. By listing and describing these categories of disorders, the DSM task force hopes to encourage professionals to consider whether a future DSM should contain any of these syndromes or axes as official ways of classifying mental disorders.

POSSIBLE NEW SYNDROMES

Here is a sampling of the more than two dozen categories mentioned as meriting further study.

CAFFEINE WITHDRAWAL As with withdrawal from other addicting substances, significant distress or impairment in occupational or social functioning must result from not drinking accustomed levels of caffeinated beverages. Symptoms include headache, fatigue, anxiety, depression, nausea, and impaired thinking. Inclusion of caffeine withdrawal as a new category would certainly swell the ranks of the mentally disordered.

PREMENSTRUAL DYSPHORIC DISORDER Written about a good deal in the press and assailed by feminists and sexists alike, this proposed syndrome is marked by depression, anxiety, anger, mood swings, and decreased interest in activities usually engaged in with pleasure, when occurring a week or so before menstruation for most months in a given year. The symptoms are so severe as to interfere with social or occupational functioning. This category is to be distinguished from premen-

strual syndrome, which is experienced by many more women and is not nearly as debilitating.

Feminists may be pleased or displeased with this possible new category. On the plus side, inclusion might alert people to the hormonal bases of monthly mood changes linked to the menstrual cycle and thereby foster more tolerance and less victim-blaming. On the minus side, listing such mood changes in a manual of mental disorders would seem to convey the message that women who suffer these psychological changes are mentally disordered.

MIXED ANXIETY-DEPRESSIVE DISORDER There was a period during the development of DSM-IV when it seemed that this disorder would be formally listed, for clinicians have for many years sometimes found it difficult to decide whether to diagnose a person as having primarily a depressive disorder or primarily an anxiety disorder. Dysphoric mood must have lasted for at least a month and been accompanied by at least four of the following symptoms: concentration or memory problems, disturbances of sleep, fatigue or low energy, irritability, worry, crying easily, hypervigilance, anticipating the worst, pessimism about the future, or feelings of low self-esteem. The person must not be diagnosable as having a major depressive disorder, dysthymic disorder, panic disorder, or generalized anxiety disorder.

PASSIVE-AGGRESSIVE PERSONALITY DISORDER (NEGATIVISTIC PERSONALITY DISORDER) This personality disorder was present in DSM-III and DSM-IIIR but was moved to the appendix in DSM-IV. Not attributable to depression, symptoms include resenting, resisting, and opposing demands and expectations by means of passive activities, such as lateness, pro-

---

the diagnosis is *psychological factors affecting physical condition*. Referred to previously as psychophysiological or psychosomatic disorders, these conditions are reviewed in detail in Chapter 8. Among the other diagnoses in this category are the following:

academic problem (e.g., underachievement)

antisocial behavior (e.g., in professional thieves)

malingering (adopting physical or psychological symptoms to achieve a goal, such as avoiding work)

relational problem (e.g., poor relationship with sibling or spouse)

occupational problem (e.g., dissatisfaction with work)

physical or sexual abuse

bereavement

noncompliance with treatment (e.g., refusing medication)

religious or spiritual problem (e.g., questioning one's faith)

phase-of-life problem (difficulties created by a life transition, such as beginning school)

In this context it is interesting to recall our discussion of the difficulties of defining mental disorder (p. 6–8). Should these life difficulties really be included in a listing of mental disorders? Many of these conditions will not be covered in this book, although malingering is discussed in Chapter 7, therapy for marital problems in Chapter 19, and physical and sexual abuse in Chapters 7 and 14.

crastination, forgetfulness, and intentional inefficiency. The inference is that the person is angry or resentful and is expressing these feelings by *not* doing certain things rather than by more direct expression, such as assertiveness or aggressiveness. Such people often feel mistreated, cheated, or underappreciated.

DEPRESSIVE PERSONALITY DISORDER In lay terms this personality disorder would be applied to people whose general lifestyle is characterized by gloominess, lack of cheer, and a tendency to worry a lot. This (possible) traitlike, long-term disorder may be a precursor to a full-blown dysthymia or major depressive disorder. Indeed, the DSM admits that it is very difficult to distinguish between depressive personality disorder and the main depressive disorders. Another disorder listed in this appendix is *minor depressive disorder*, which may be distinguishable only by virtue of its not being as long-standing as depressive personality disorder.

PROPOSED AXES IN NEED OF FURTHER STUDY

Professionals are being encouraged to consider whether a future axis should include defense mechanisms (equated by DSM with coping styles) and defined as "automatic psychological processes that protect the individual against anxiety and from the awareness of internal or external dangers or stressors" (p. 751). They are divided into groups called "defense levels" and measured by a proposed Defensive Functioning Scale. Some of these coping mechanisms derive from psychoanalytic theory.

There are seven defense levels, each with a set of defense mechanisms. The levels range from "High adaptive level" to "Level of defensive dysregulation." The following examples are among the proposed levels and mechanisms.

HIGH ADAPTIVE LEVEL This most adaptive, "healthy" defense level contains coping efforts that are realistic ways of handling stress and they are conducive to achieving a good balance among conflicting motives. Examples are:

Anticipation—experiencing emotional reactions before a stressful event occurs and considering realistic, alternative courses of action; for example, carefully planning for an upcoming meeting with an employer who is unhappy with your performance.

Sublimation—dealing with a stress by channeling negative feelings into socially acceptable behaviors; for example, working out at a gym.

DISAVOWAL LEVEL This middle level is characterized by defenses that keep troubling stressors or ideas out of conscious awareness.

Denial—refusing to acknowledge a degree of discomfort or threat that is obvious to an observer; for example, maintaining that your marriage is fine despite the obvious and repeated conflicts your friends see.

Projection—falsely attributing to another person one's own unacceptable feelings or thoughts; for example, believing that your professor is angry with you, rather than the reverse.

LEVEL OF DEFENSIVE DYSREGULATION This lowest level is marked by a failure to deal with stress, leading to a break with reality.

Psychotic denial—denial that is so extreme as to be marked by a gross impairment in reality testing; for example, maintaining that the results of all three biopsies showing a cancerous growth are wrong.

DELIRIUM, DEMENTIA, AMNESTIC, AND OTHER COGNITIVE DISORDERS

This category covers disorders in which cognition is seriously disturbed. *Delirium* is a clouding of consciousness, wandering attention, and an incoherent stream of thought. It may be caused by several medical conditions as well as by substance abuse. *Dementia*, a deterioration of mental capacities, especially memory, is associated with Alzheimer's disease and stroke as well as several other medical conditions, and with substance abuse. Delirium and dementia are discussed in detail in Chapter 16, because they are often associated with aging. Amnestic syndrome, an impairment in memory when there is no delirium or dementia, is considered in Chapter 12, because it is often linked to alcohol abuse.

The frequency of Alzheimer's Disease, which severely impairs cognitive functioning, increases with advanced age.

Now that we have briefly described the DSM's diagnostic categories and its axes, we return to the case of Ernest H. with which the book began. Table 3.2 shows how Ernest's diagnosis would look. On Axis I, Ernest is diagnosed with alcohol dependence, which has also created a problem with sexual arousal. His current problems with his marriage are noted, as is his prior history of bipolar disorder. In addition, Ernest is diagnosed on Axis II as having avoidant personality disorder. His feelings of inferiority, his self-consciousness when around others, and his avoidance of activities because of fear of criticism are the basis of this diagnosis. He has no general medical condition relevant to his problems, so he has no diagnosis on Axis III. His problems with his marriage are noted on Axis IV, and his current level of functioning is rated at 55 on the GAF (indicating a moderate level of impairment). Though alcohol may be Ernest's most immediate problem, the multiaxial diagnosis gives clinicians a fairly full picture of the complex of problems that will need to be addressed in treatment.

ISSUES IN THE CLASSIFICATION OF ABNORMAL BEHAVIOR

This review of the major categories of abnormal behavior was brief because they will be examined in more detail throughout this text. On the basis of this overview, however, we will examine here the usefulness of the diagnostic system as it exists today. Among those who are critical of the DSM, one group asserts that classification per se is irrelevant to the field of abnormal behavior; a second group finds specific deficiencies in the manner in which diagnoses are made.

GENERAL CRITICISMS OF CLASSIFICATION

Some critics of diagnosis argue that to classify someone as depressed or anxious results in a loss of information about that person, thereby reducing some of the uniqueness of the person being studied. In evaluating this claim, recall our earlier discussions of paradigms and their effect on how we glean information about our world. It appears to be in the nature of humankind to categorize whenever we perceive and think about anything. Those who argue against classification per se therefore overlook the inevitability of classification and categorization in human thought.

Consider the simple example of casting dice. Any of the numbers one through six may come up on a

TABLE 3.2 DSM-IV Multiaxial Diagnosis of Ernest H.

Axis I	Alcohol Dependence
	Alcohol-Induced Sexual Problem, with Impaired Arousal
	Bipolar I Disorder, Most Recent Episode Manic, In Full Remission
	Partner Relational Problem
Axis II	Avoidant Personality Disorder
Axis III	None
Axis IV	Problem With Primary Support Group
Axis V	GAF=55

given toss of a single die. Let us suppose, however, that we classify each outcome as odd or even. Whenever a one, three, or five comes up on a roll, we call out "odd," and whenever a two, four, or six appears, we say "even." A person listening to our calls will not know whether the call "odd" refers to a one, three, or five or whether "even" refers to a two, four, or six. In classification, some information must inevitably be lost.

What matters is whether the information lost is *relevant*, which in turn depends on the purposes of the classification system. Any classification is designed to group together objects having a common property and to ignore differences in the objects that are not relevant to the purposes at hand. If our intention is merely to count odd and even rolls, it is irrelevant whether a die comes up one, three, or five, or two, four, or six. In judging abnormal behavior, however, we cannot so easily decide what is wheat and what is chaff, for the relevant and irrelevant dimensions of abnormal behavior are uncertain. Thus when we do classify, we may be grouping people together on rather trivial bases while ignoring their extremely important differences.

Classification may also have negative effects on a person. Consider how your life might be changed after being diagnosed as schizophrenic. You might become guarded and suspicious lest someone recognize your disorder. Or you might be chronically on edge, fearing the onset of another episode. The fact that you are a "former mental patient" could have a stigmatizing effect. Friends and loved ones may treat you differently and employment may be difficult to obtain.

There is little doubt that diagnosis can have such negative consequences. It is clear from the existing research that the general public holds a very negative view of mental patients and that patients and their families believe that such stigmatizing effects are common (Rabkin, 1974; Wahl & Harrman, 1989).

Documenting the actual negative consequences of diagnosis, however, has been difficult. Gove and Fain (1973), for example, followed up a large sample of patients one year after discharge from a hospital. The former patients were interviewed about jobs, social relationships, and outside activities. The patients' descriptions of how they were functioning now and how they had functioned in the past were not very different. Thus, although we must recognize and be on guard against the possible social stigma of a diagnosis, this problem may not be as serious as some believe.

THE VALUE OF CLASSIFICATION AND DIAGNOSIS

Assuming that various types of abnormal behavior do differ from one another, classifying them is essential, for these differences may constitute keys to the causes and treatments of the various deviant behaviors. For example, a form of mental retardation, phenylketonuria, is caused by a deficiency in the metabolism of the protein phenylalanine, resulting in the release of incomplete metabolites that injure the brain (see p. 431). A diet drastically reduced in phenylalanine prevents some of this injury. As Mendels (1970) noted, however, "had we taken 100, or even 1000, people with mental deficiency and placed them all on the phenylalanine-free diet, the response would have been insignificant and the diet would have been discarded as a treatment. It was first necessary to recognize a subtype of mental deficiency [retardation], phenylketonuria, and then subject the value of a phenylalanine-free diet to investigation in this specific population, for whom it has been shown to have value in preventing the development of mental deficiency" (p. 35).

Forming categories may thus further knowledge, for once a category is formed, additional information may be ascertained about it. Even though the category is only an asserted, and not a proved, entity, it may still be heuristically[1] useful in that it facilitates the acquisition of new information. Only after a diagnostic category has been formed can people who fit its definition be studied in the hope of uncovering factors responsible for the development of their problems and of devising treatments that may help them.

---

[1]*Heuristic* is a central word and concept in science. It comes from the Greek *heuriskein*, "to discover," or "to find," and is defined in *Webster's* as serving to guide, discover, or reveal, and more specifically as valuable for stimulating or conducting empirical research. The frequent use of this word and its derivatives underlines the importance scientists place on ideas in generating new knowledge.

SPECIFIC CRITICISMS OF DIAGNOSIS

More specific criticisms are commonly made of psychiatric classification, the principal ones concerning whether discrete diagnostic categories are justifiable and whether or not the diagnostic categories are reliable and valid. These criticisms were frequently leveled at DSM-I and DSM-II. At the close of this section we will see how subsequent editions of the DSM have come to grips with them.

DISCRETE ENTITY VERSUS CONTINUUM

The DSM represents a **categorical classification**, a yes–no approach to classification. Is the patient schizophrenic or not? It may be argued that this type of classification, because it postulates discrete diagnostic entities, does not allow continuity between normal and abnormal behavior to be taken into consideration. Those who advance the continuity argument hold that abnormal and normal behavior differ only in intensity or degree, not in kind; therefore, discrete diagnostic categories foster a false impression of discontinuity.

In contrast, in **dimensional classification** the entities or objects being classified must be ranked on a quantitative dimension (e.g., a 1-to-10 scale of anxiety, where 1 represents minimal and 10 extreme). Classification would be accomplished by assessing patients on the relevant dimensions and perhaps plotting the location of the patient in a system of coordinates defined by his or her score on each dimension. A dimensional system can subsume a categorical system by specifying a cutting point, or threshold, on one of the quantitative dimensions. This capability is a potential advantage of the dimensional approach.

Clearly, a dimensional system can be applied to most of the symptoms that constitute the diagnoses of the DSM; anxiety, depression, and the many personality traits that are included in the personality disorders are found in different people in different degrees and thus do not seem to fit well with the DSM categorical model.

The choice between a categorical and a dimensional system of classification, however, is not as simple as it might seem initially. Consider hypertension (high blood pressure), a topic discussed at length in Chapter 8. Blood-pressure measurements form a continuum, which clearly fits a dimensional approach; yet it has proved useful to categorize certain people as having high blood pressure in order to research its causes and possible treatments. A similar situation could exist for the DSM categories. Even though anxiety clearly exists in differing degrees in different people and thus is a dimensional variable, it could prove useful to create a diagnostic category for those people whose anxiety is extreme. There is inevitably a certain arbitrariness to such a categorization (where exactly should the cutoff be?), but it could prove to be fruitful nonetheless.

It is also possible that a variable that on the surface appears dimensional actually represents an underlying categorical or off–on process. This is a complex argument, but some of its flavor can be appreciated by considering a hypothetical single-gene cause for hypertension. Blood pressure might result from a complex interplay between the gene (off or on) and a variety of environmental influences—diet, weight, smoking, stress, and so on. Observed blood pressure is a dimensional variable, but hypertension might result principally from the operation of the single off–on gene, which is a categorical variable. Given that we can observe only the surface variable, how can we tell whether there might be an underlying categorical process? Although well beyond the scope of this book, complex mathematical procedures are being developed to test such questions (e.g., Meehl, 1986), and they have been used to test whether a dimensional or categorical approach is most applicable to several diagnoses (Tykra et al., 1995).

RELIABILITY: THE CORNERSTONE OF A DIAGNOSTIC SYSTEM

The extent to which a classification system, or a test or measurement of any kind, produces the same scientific observation each time it is applied is the measure of its **reliability**. An example of an unreliable measure would be a flexible, elastic-like ruler whose length changed every time it was used. This flawed ruler would yield different values for the height of the same object every time the object was measured. In contrast, a reliable measure such as a standard wooden ruler produces consistent results.

Interrater reliability refers to the extent to which two judges agree about an event. For example, suppose you want to know if a child suspected of having a conduct disorder is aggressive with his or her peers. You could decide to observe the child playing with classmates during recess. To determine whether your observational data were reliable you would want to have at least two people watch the child at play and make independent judgments about the level of aggression. The extent to which the raters agreed would be an index of interrater reliability.

For a classification system to be useful, those applying it must be able to agree on what is and

what is not an instance of a particular category.[2] A person diagnosed as having an anxiety disorder by one clinician should be given the same diagnosis by another clinician as well. Reliability is a primary criterion for judging any classification system. Prior to DSM-III, reliability was not acceptable, mainly because the criteria for making a diagnosis were not presented clearly and methods of assessing the patient's symptoms were not standardized (Ward et al., 1962). As we will see, reliability for most current diagnostic categories is good.

HOW VALID ARE DIAGNOSTIC CATEGORIES?

Whether or not accurate statements and predictions can be made about a category once it has been formed is the test of its **validity**. Validity bears a particular relation to reliability; the less reliable a category, the more difficult it is to make valid statements about that category. If the reliability of diagnosis is not entirely adequate, we can expect that its validity will not be either. For example, if four clinicians all come up with different diagnoses for a patient, their diagnoses will not yield valid predictions about the prognosis or the best treatment for the case.

A diagnosis can have three kinds of validity: etiological, concurrent, and predictive. For a diagnosis to have **etiological validity** the same causal factors must be found in the people who constitute the diagnostic group. Consider the supposition that bipolar disorder is in part genetically determined. According to this theory children of bipolar parents should be more likely than average to develop the disorder themselves. As we shall see in Chapter 10, there is evidence that supports this theory, giving this diagnostic category some etiological validity.

A diagnosis has **concurrent validity** if other symptoms or disordered processes not part of the diagnosis itself are discovered to be characteristic of those diagnosed. Finding that most people with schizophrenia have difficulty in social relationships is an example.

Predictive validity refers to similar future behavior on the part of the disorder or patients suffering from it. The disorder may have a specific prognosis, or outcome; that is, whether recovery is highly likely or whether continuing problems can be expected

---

[2]These two components of reliability—agreeing on who is a member of a class and who is not—are termed *sensitivity* and *specificity*. Sensitivity refers to agreement regarding the presence of a specific diagnosis; specificity refers to agreement concerning the absence of a diagnosis.

may depend on the diagnostic category being considered. Or members of the diagnostic group may be expected to respond in a similar way to a particular treatment. Bipolar patients, for example, tend to respond well to a drug called lithium carbonate. The fact that this drug does not work well for people in most other diagnostic classes supports the predictive validity of the bipolar diagnosis.

We have organized this book around the major DSM diagnostic categories because we believe that they indeed possess some validity. Certain categories have greater validity than others, however; we will discuss these differences in the chapters on each of the major diagnostic categories.

THE DSM AND CRITICISMS OF DIAGNOSIS

Beginning with DSM-III and DSM-IIIR an effort has been made to create more reliable and valid diagnostic categories. The characteristics and symptoms of each diagnostic category in Axes I and II are now described much more extensively than they were in DSM-II. For each disorder there is a description of essential features, then of associated features, such as laboratory findings (e.g., enlarged ventricles in schizophrenia), and results from physical exams

The core symptoms of depression appear to be similiar cross-culturallly. However, guilt is less frequent in Japan than in Western cultures.

(e.g., electrolyte imbalances in people who have eating disorders). Next are statements drawn from the research literature about age of onset, course, prevalence and sex ratio, familial pattern, and differential diagnosis (i.e., how to distinguish one diagnosis from another that is symptomatically similar to it). Much more attention is now paid to how the same disorder may have somewhat different symptoms depending on the culture in which it appears. For example, it is known that the core symptoms of both schizophrenia (e.g., delusions and hallucinations) and depression (e.g., depressed mood and loss of interest or pleasure in activities) are similar cross-culturally (Draguns, 1989). However, guilt is a frequent symptom of depression in Western society but an infrequent symptom in Japan and Iran. Similarly, depression in Latinos appears more likely to involve somatic complaints, such as headaches or "nerves." (Focus 3.2 describes further efforts by the DSM to be more sensitive to the effects of culture.) Finally, specific *diagnostic criteria* for the category—the symptoms and other facts that must be present to justify the diagnosis—are spelled out in a more precise fashion, and the clinical symptoms that constitute a diagnosis are defined in a glossary. Table 3.3 compares the descriptions of a manic episode given in DSM-II with the diagnostic criteria given in DSM-IV. Clearly the bases for making diagnoses are decidedly more detailed and concrete in DSM-IV.

The explicitness of the DSM criteria can be expected to reduce the descriptive inadequacies that were the major source of diagnostic unreliability and thus to lead to improved reliability. Another factor in improved reliability is the use of standardized, reliably scored interviews for collecting the information needed for a diagnosis. (We will describe such interviews in the next chapter.) Results of an extensive evaluation of the reliability of DSM-IIIR are shown in Table 3.4; the reliabilities vary but are quite acceptable for most of the major categories. The relatively low figures for anxiety disorders are higher in other studies that used an assessment interview specifically tailored for them (Dinardo et al., 1993). Although the data are not all in yet, the reliability of DSM-IV diagnoses look comparable to those shown in the table.

Thus far we have described the DSM in positive terms. The attainment of adequate diagnostic reliability is a considerable achievement, but problems remain. It is unclear, for example, whether the rules for making diagnostic decisions are ideal. Examining Table 3.3, we see that for patients to be diagnosed as suffering from mania they must have three symptoms from a list of seven, or four if their mood is irritable. But why require three symptoms

FOCUS 3.2

ETHNIC AND CULTURAL CONSIDERATIONS IN DSM-IV

Previous editions of the DSM were criticized for their lack of attention to cultural and ethnic variations in psychopathology. DSM-IV attempts to enhance its cultural sensitivity in three ways: (1) by including in the main body of the manual a discussion of cultural and ethnic factors for each disorder; (2) by providing in the appendix a general framework for evaluating the role of culture and ethnicity; and (3) by describing culture-bound syndromes in an appendix.

Among the cultural issues of which clinicians need to be aware are language differences between the therapist and the patient and the way in which the patient's culture talks about emotional distress. Many cultures, for example, describe grief or anxiety in physical terms—"I am sick in my heart" or "My heart is heavy" rather than in psychological terms. Individuals also vary in the degree to which they identify with their cultural or ethnic group. Some value assimilation into the majority culture, whereas others wish to maintain close ties to their ethnic background. In general, the clinician is advised to be constantly mindful of how culture and ethnicity influence diagnosis and treatment, a topic discussed in the next chapter.

The DSM also describes "locality-specific patterns of aberrant behavior and troubling experience that may or may not be linked to a particular DSM-IV diagnostic category" (p. 844). The following are some examples that may occur in clinical practices in North America.

amok—a dissociative episode in which there is a period of brooding followed by a violent and sometimes homicidal outburst. The episode tends to be triggered by an insult and is found primarily among men. Persecutory delusions are often present as well. The term is Malaysian and is defined by the dictionary as a murderous frenzy; the reader has probably encountered the phrase "run amok."

brain fag—originally used in West Africa, this term refers to a condition reported by high school and university students in response to academic pressures. Symptoms include fatigue, tightness in the head and neck, and blurring of vision. This syndrome resembles certain anxiety, depressive, and somatoform disorders.

dhat—a term used in India to refer to severe anxiety and hypochondriasis linked to the discharge of semen.

ghost sickness—extreme preoccupation with death and those who have died; found among certain Native American tribes.

koro—reported also in south and east Asia, an episode of intense anxiety about the possibility that the penis or nipples will recede into the body, possibly leading to death.

A therapist must be mindful of the role of cultural differences in the ways that patients describe their problems.

rather than two or five (see Finn, 1982)? Just as there is a degree of arbitrariness to the point at which a person is diagnosed as having high blood pressure, so there is an element of arbitrariness to the DSM's

diagnostic rules. Furthermore, the reliability of Axes I and II may not always be as high in everyday usage, for diagnosticians may not adhere as precisely to the criteria as do those whose work is being

TABLE 3.3   Description of Manic Disorder in DSM-II versus DSM-IV

DSM-II (APA, 1968, p. 36)

Manic-depressive illness, manic type. This disorder consists exclusively of manic episodes. These episodes are characterized by excessive elation, irritability, talkativeness, flight of ideas, and accelerated speech and motor activity. Brief periods of depression sometimes occur, but they are never true depressive episodes.

DSM-IV (APA, 1994)

Diagnostic Criteria for a Manic Episode

A. A distinct period of abnormally and persistently elevated, expansive, or irritable mood, lasting at least 1 week (or any duration if hospitalization is necessary).

B. During the period of mood disturbance, three (or more) of the following symptoms have persisted (four if the mood is only irritable) and have been present to a significant degree:
   (1) inflated self-esteem or grandiosity
   (2) decreased need for sleep (e.g., feels rested after only three hours of sleep)
   (3) more talkative than usual or pressure to keep talking
   (4) flight of ideas or subjective experience that thoughts are racing
   (5) distractibility (i.e., attention too easily drawn to unimportant or irrelevant external stimuli)
   (6) increase in goal-directed activity (either socially, at work or school, or sexually) or psychomotor agitation
   (7) excessive involvement in pleasurable activities that have a high potential for painful consequences (e.g., engaging in unrestrained buying sprees, sexual indiscretions, or foolish business investments)

C. The symptoms do not meet criteria for a Mixed Episode.

D. The mood disturbance is sufficiently severe to cause marked impairment in occupational functioning or in usual social activities or relationships with others, or to necessitate hospitalization to prevent harm to self or others, or there are psychotic features.

E. The symptoms are not due to the direct physiological effects of a substance (e.g., a drug of abuse, a medication, or other treatment) or a general medical condition (e.g., hyperthyroidism).

Note: Manic-like episodes that are clearly caused by somatic antidepressant treatment (e.g., medication, electroconvulsive therapy, light therapy) should not count toward a diagnosis of Bipolar I Disorder. DSM-IV material reprinted with permission from the DSM-IV, 1994, American Psychiatric Association.

TABLE 3.4   Reliability of selected DSM diagnoses (Williams et al., 1992). The numbers in the table are a statistic called kappa, which measures the proportion of agreement over and above what would be expected by chance. Generally, kappas over .70 are considered good.

Diagnosis	Kappa
Bipolar Disorder	.84
Major Depression	.64
Schizophrenia	.65
Alcohol Abuse	.75
Anorexia Nervosa	.75
Bulimia Nervosa	.86
Panic Disorder	.58
Social Phobia	.47

scrutinized in formal studies. And although the improved reliability of the DSM *may* lead to more validity, there is no guarantee that it *will*. The diagnoses made according to it may not reveal anything useful about the patients. Moreover, subjective factors still play a role in evaluations made according to DSM-IV. Consider again the criteria for manic syndrome in Table 3.3. What exactly does it mean to say that the elevated mood must be abnormally and persistently elevated? Or what level of involvement in pleasurable activities with high potential for painful consequences is excessive? As another example, on Axis V the clinician must judge the patient's level of current functioning. The clinician determines what, for the patient, is adaptive and how his or her behavior compares with that of an average person. Such a judgment sets the stage for the insertion of cultural biases as well as the clinician's own personal ideas of what the average person *should* be doing at a given stage of life and in particular circumstances (C. B. Taylor, 1983). A male clinician might have a considerably different take on a single, fifty-year-old female patient than would a female therapist; for example, the female therapist might view this patient's childlessness more negatively than would the male therapist.

Finally, not all the DSM classification changes seem positive. Should a problem such as difficulty in learning arithmetic or reading be considered a psychiatric disorder? By expanding its coverage the DSM seems to have made too many childhood problems into psychiatric disorders, without good justification for doing so.

In sum, although the DSM is continually improving, it is far from perfect. Throughout this book, as we present the literature on various disorders, there will be further opportunities to describe both the strengths and the weaknesses of this effort of health professionals to categorize mental disorders and to consider how DSM-IV may deal with some of the problems that still exist. What is most heartening about the DSM is that its attempts to be explicit about the rules for diagnosis make it easier to detect problems in the diagnostic system. We can expect more changes and refinements over the next several years.

SUMMARY

The recent editions of the *Diagnostic and Statistical Manual of Mental Disorders*, published by the American Psychiatric Association, reflect the continuing efforts by mental health professionals to categorize the various psychopathologies. A novel feature is their multiaxial organization; every time a diagnosis is made the clinician must describe the patient's condition according to each of five axes, or dimensions. Axes I and II make up the mental disorders per se; Axis III lists any physical disorders believed to bear on the mental disorder in question; Axis IV is used to indicate the psychosocial and environmental problems that the person has been experiencing; and Axis V rates the person's current level of adaptive functioning. A multiaxial diagnosis is believed to provide a more multidimensional and useful description of the patient's mental disorder.

Several general and specific issues must be considered when evaluating the classification of abnormality. Because recent versions of the DSM are far more concrete and descriptive than was DSM-II, diagnoses based on these versions are more reliable. Validity—how well the diagnosis predicts other aspects of the disorder, such as prognosis—however, remains an open question. It is too soon to know whether more useful knowledge about psychopathology, its prevention and treatment, will be gained though widespread use of DSM-IV.

KEY TERMS

Diagnostic and Statistical Manual of Mental Disorders (DSM)	categorical classification	validity
	dimensional classification	etiological validity
	reliability	concurrent validity
multiaxial classification	interrater reliability	predictive validity

4

Max Papart,
"Liberty," 1981

CLINICAL ASSESSMENT PROCEDURES

This book began with an account of a police officer who had drinking and marital problems, and the preceding chapter ended with a diagnosis of this man. Yet a DSM diagnosis is only a starting point. Many other questions remain to be answered. Why does Ernest behave as he does? Do his mood swings and violent outbursts constitute a true disorder? Why does he doubt his wife's love for him? What can be done to resolve his marital conflicts? Is his difficulty maintaining an erection caused by physical or psychological factors? Some of both? Has he performed up to his intellectual potential in school and in his career? What type of treatment would be helpful to him? What obstacles might interfere with treatment? Can his marriage be saved? Should it be saved? These are the types of questions that mental health professionals address before therapy begins and as it unfolds, and a clinical assessment helps them to find answers.

All clinical assessment procedures are more or less formal ways of finding out what is wrong with a person, what may have caused a problem or problems, and what steps may be taken to improve the individual's condition. Some of these procedures are also used to evaluate the effects of therapeutic interventions.

In this chapter we describe and discuss the most widely used psychological and biological assessment techniques—and some that are still in the early development phase. We conclude with a look at an important issue that affects all approaches to assessment, that is, the question of whether in the long run, feelings, thoughts, and behavior are consistent or variable. We also discuss a sometimes neglected aspect of assessment, the role of cultural diversity and clinician bias. Throughout the discussion it will be clear that reliability and validity, two concepts first addressed in the discussion of diagnosis in Chapter 3, play a key role in assessment as well.

PSYCHOLOGICAL ASSESSMENT

Psychological assessment techniques are designed to determine cognitive, emotional, personality, and behavioral factors in psychopathological functioning. We will see that beyond the basic interview, which is used in various guises almost universally, many of the assessment techniques stem from the paradigms presented in Chapter 2. We discuss here psychological tests, many of which are psychodynamic in nature, and behavioral and cognitive assessment techniques.

CLINICAL INTERVIEWS

Most of us have probably been interviewed at one time or another, although the conversation may have been so informal that we did not regard it as an interview. To the layperson the word *interview* connotes a formal, highly structured conversation, but we find it useful to construe the term as any interpersonal encounter, conversational in style, in which one person, the interviewer, uses language as the principal means of finding out about another, the interviewee. Thus a Gallup pollster who asks a college student for whom she will vote in an upcoming presidential election is interviewing with the restricted goal of learning which candidate she prefers. A clinical psychologist who asks a patient about the circumstances of his most recent hospitalization is similarly conducting an interview.

One way in which a **clinical interview** is perhaps different from a casual conversation and from a poll is the attention the interviewer pays to *how* the respondent answers questions—or does not answer them. For example, if a client is recounting her marital conflicts, the clinician will generally be attentive to any emotion accompanying her comments. If the woman does not seem upset about a difficult situation, her answers will probably be interpreted differently from how they would be interpreted if she were crying while relating her story.

The paradigm within which an interviewer operates influences the type of information sought, how it is obtained, and how it is interpreted. A psychoanalytically trained clinician can be expected to inquire about the person's childhood history. He or she is also likely to remain skeptical of verbal reports because the analytic paradigm holds that the most significant aspects of a disturbed or normal person's developmental history are repressed into the unconscious. Of course, how the data are interpreted is influenced by the paradigm. By the same token, the behaviorally oriented clinician is likely to focus on current environmental conditions that can be related to changes in the person's behavior, for example, the circumstances under which the person becomes anxious. Thus the clinical interview does not follow a prescribed course, but varies with the paradigm adopted by the interviewer. Like scientists, clinical interviewers in some measure find only the information that they look for.

Great skill is necessary to carry out good clinical interviews, for they are usually conducted with people who are under considerable stress. Clinicians, regardless of their theoretical orientations, recognize the importance of establishing rapport with the client. The interviewer must obtain the trust of the person; it is naive to assume that a client will easily reveal information to another, even to an authority figure with the title "Dr." Even a client who sincerely, perhaps desperately, wants to recount intensely personal problems to a professional may not be able to do so without assistance. Psychodynamic clinicians assume that people entering therapy usually are not even aware of what is truly bothering them. Behavioral clinicians, although they concentrate more on observables, also appreciate the difficulties people have in sorting out the factors responsible for their distress.

Most clinicians empathize with their clients in an effort to draw them out, to encourage them to elaborate on their concerns, and to examine different facets of a problem. Humanistic therapists employ specific empathy techniques (see p. 506) to accomplish these goals. A simple summary statement of what the client has been saying can help sustain the momentum of talk about painful and possibly embarrassing events and feelings, and an accepting attitude toward personal disclosures dispels the fear that revealing "secrets of the heart" (London, 1964) to another human being will have disastrous consequences.

The interview can be a source of considerable information to the clinician. Its importance in abnormal psychology and psychiatry is unquestionable. Whether the information gleaned can always be depended on is not so clear, however. Clinicians often tend to overlook *situational* factors of the interview that may exert strong influences on what the patient says or does. Consider for a moment how a teenager is likely to respond to the question, "How often have you used illegal drugs?" when it is asked by a young, informally dressed psychologist and again when it is asked by a sixty-year-old psychologist in a business suit.

Interviews vary in the degree to which they are structured. In practice, most clinicians probably operate from only the vaguest outlines. Exactly *how* information is collected is left largely up to the particular interviewer and depends, too, on the responsiveness and responses of the interviewee. Through years of clinical experience and both teaching and learning from students and colleagues, each clinician develops ways of asking questions with which he or she is comfortable and that seem to draw out the information that will be of maximum benefit to the client. Thus to the extent that an interview is unstructured, the interviewer must rely on intuition and general experience. As a consequence, reliability for initial clinical interviews is probably low, that is, two interviewers may well reach different conclusions about the same patient. And because the overwhelming majority of clinical interviews are conducted within confidential relationships, it has not been possible to establish their validity through systematic research.

We need to look at the broader picture here to avoid a judgment that may be too harsh. Both reliability and validity may indeed be low for a single clinical interview that is conducted in an unstructured fashion. But clinicians usually do more than one interview with a given patient, and hence a self-corrective process is probably at work. The clinician may regard as valid what a patient said in the first interview, but then at the sixth may recognize it to have been incorrect or only partially correct.

At times mental health professionals need to collect standardized information, particularly for making diagnostic judgments based on the DSM. To meet that need investigators have developed structured interviews, such as the Structured Clinical Interview (SCID) for DSM-IV (Spitzer, Gibbon, & Williams, 1996), which assists researchers and clinicians in making diagnostic decisions. A structured interview is one in which the questions are set out in a booklet for the interviewer. The SCID is a branching interview, that is, the client's response determines the next question. It also contains detailed instructions to the interviewer concerning when to probe in detail and when to go on to questions about another diagnosis. Most symptoms are rated on a three-point scale of severity, with instructions in the interview schedule for directly translating the symptom ratings into diagnoses. The initial questions pertaining to obsessive-compulsive disorder (discussed in Chapter 6) are presented in Figure 4.1. The interviewer begins by asking about obsessions. If the responses elicit a rating of 1 (absent), the interviewer turns to questions about compulsions. If the patient's responses again elicit a rating of 1, the interviewer is instructed to go to the question for posttraumatic stress disorder. On the other hand, if positive responses (2 or 3) are elicited about obsessive-compulsive disorder, the interviewer continues with further questions about that problem. The use of structured interviews such as the SCID is a major factor in the improvement of diagnostic reliability that we described in Chapter 3.

PSYCHOLOGICAL TESTS

Psychological tests are standardized procedures designed to measure a person's performance on a particular task or to assess his or her personality.

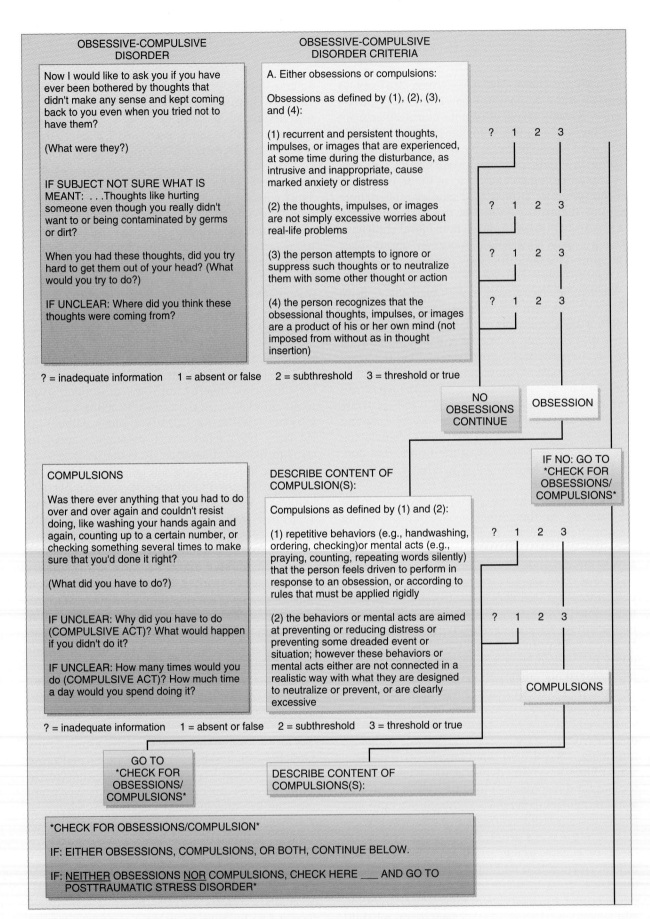

Figure 4.1 Sample item from the SCID. Reprinted by permission of New York State Psychiatric Institute Biometrics Research Division. Copyright © 1996 by the Board of Trustees of the Leland Stanford Junior University. Reprinted by permission of Stanford University Press.

These tests further structure the process of assessment. The same test is administered to many people at different times, and the responses collected are analyzed to indicate how certain kinds of people tend to respond. Statistical norms for the test can thereby be established as soon as sufficient data have been collected. This process is called **standardization**. The responses of a particular patient can then be compared with the statistical norms. We will examine the three basic types of psychological tests: self-report personality inventories, projective personality tests, and tests of intelligence.

PERSONALITY INVENTORIES

In a **personality inventory**, an examinee is asked to complete a self-report questionnaire indicating whether statements assessing habitual tendencies apply to him or her. Perhaps the best known of these tests is the **Minnesota Multiphasic Personality Inventory (MMPI)**, which was developed in the early 1940s by Hathaway and McKinley (1943) and revised in 1989 (Butcher et al., 1989). Intended to serve as an inexpensive means of detecting psychopathology, the MMPI is called *multiphasic* because it was designed to detect a number of psychological problems. Over the years the MMPI has been widely used to screen large groups of people for whom clinical interviews are not feasible.

In developing the test the investigators relied on factual information. First, many clinicians provided statements that they considered indicative of various mental problems. Second, these items were rated as self-descriptive or not by patients already diagnosed as having particular disorders and by a large group of individuals considered normal. Items that discriminated among the patients were retained; that is, items were selected if patients in one clinical group responded to them more often in a certain way than did those in other groups. With additional refinements, sets of these items were established as scales for determining whether a respondent should be diagnosed in a particular way. The ten scales are described in Table 4.1. If the individual answered a large number of the items in a scale in the same way as had a certain diagnostic group, his or her behavior was expected to resemble that of the particular diagnostic group. The scales of the instrument related reasonably well to psychiatric diagnoses, although the original MMPI began to relate less well as the psychiatric classification system changed in the DSM; for example, Winters, Weintraub, and Neale (1981) found that the MMPI did poorly in predicting the DSM-III diagnosis of schizophrenia.

The revised MMPI-2 (Butcher et al., 1989) has several noteworthy changes designed to improve its validity and acceptability. The original sample of fifty years ago lacked representation of racial minorities, including African-Americans and Native Americans; its standardization sample was restricted to white men and women, essentially to rural Minnesotans. The new version was standardized using a sample that was much larger and more similar to 1980 U.S. census figures. Several items containing allusions to sexual adjustment, bowel and bladder functions, and excessive religiosity were removed because they were judged in some testing contexts to be needlessly intrusive and objectionable. Sexist wording was eliminated, along with outmoded idioms. Several new scales deal with substance abuse, Type A behavior (see p. 000), and marital problems. MMPI-2 is otherwise quite similar to the original, having the same format, yielding the same scale scores and profiles (Ben-Porath & Butcher, 1989; Graham, 1988), and in general providing continuity with the vast literature already existing on the original MMPI (Graham, 1990). Items similar to those on the various scales are presented in Table 4.1.

Like many other personality inventories the MMPI can now be administered on computer, and there are several commercial MMPI services that score the test and provide narratives about the respondent. Of course, the validity and usefulness of the printouts are only as good as the program, which in turn is only as good as the competency and experience of the psychologist who wrote it. Figure 4.2 shows a hypothetical profile. Such profiles can be used in conjunction with a therapist's evaluation to help diagnose a client, assess personality functioning and coping style, and identify likely obstacles to treatment.

We may well wonder whether answers that would designate the subject as normal might not be easy to fake. A superficial knowledge of contemporary abnormal psychology would alert even a seriously disturbed person to the fact that in order to be regarded as normal, he or she must not admit to worrying a great deal about germs on doorknobs. There is evidence that these tests *can* be "psyched out." In most testing circumstances, however, people do not *want* to falsify their responses, for they want to be helped. Moreover, as shown in Table 4.1, the test designers have included as part of the MMPI several so-called validity scales designed to detect deliberately faked responses. In one of these, the lie scale, a series of statements sets a trap for the person who is trying to look too good. An item on the lie scale might be, "I read the newspaper editorials every night." The assumption is that few peo-

TABLE 4.1   Typical Clinical Interpretations of Items Similar to Those on the MMPI-2.

Scale[a]	Sample Item	Interpretation
? (cannot say)	This is merely the number of items left unanswered or marked both true and false.	A high score indicates evasiveness, reading difficulties, or other problems that could invalidate the results of the test. A very high score could also suggest severe depression or obsessional tendencies.
L (Lie)	I approve of every person I meet. (True)	Person is trying to look good, to present self as someone with an ideal personality.
F (Infrequency)	Everything tastes sweet. (True)	Person is trying to look abnormal, perhaps to ensure getting special attention from the clinician.
K (Correction)	Things couldn't be going any better for me. (True)	Person is guarded, defensive in taking the test, wishes to avoid appearing incompetent or poorly adjusted.
1. Hs (Hypochondriasis)	I am seldom aware of tingling feelings in my body. (False)	Person is overly sensitive to and concerned about bodily sensations as signs of possible physical illness.
2. D (Depression)	Life usually feels worthwhile to me. (False)	Person is discouraged, pessimistic, sad, self-deprecating, feeling inadequate.
3. Hy (Hysteria)	My muscles often twitch for no apparent reason. (True)	Person has somatic complaints unlikely to be due to physical problems; also tends to be demanding and histrionic.
4. Pd (Psychopathy)	I don't care about what people think of me. (True)	Person expresses little concern for social mores, is irresponsible, has only superficial relationships.
5. Mf (Masculinity–Femininity)	I like taking care of plants and flowers. (True, female)	Person shows non-traditional gender characteristics, e.g., men with high scores tend to be artistic and sensitive; women with high scores tend to be rebellious and assertive.
6. Pa (Paranoia)	If they were not afraid of being caught, most people would lie and cheat. (True)	Person tends to misinterpret the motives of others, is suspicious and jealous, vengeful and brooding.
7. Pt (Psychasthenia)	I am not as competent as most other people I know. (True)	Person is overanxious, full of self-doubts, moralistic, and generally obsessive-compulsive.
8. Sc (Schizophrenia)	I sometimes smell things others don't sense. (True)	Person has bizarre sensory experiences and beliefs, is socially seclusive.
9. Ma (Hypomania)	Sometimes I have a strong impulse to do something that others will find appalling. (True)	Person has overly ambitious aspirations and can be hyperactive, impatient, and irritable.
10. Si (Social Introversion)	Rather than spend time alone, I prefer to be around other people. (False)	Person is very modest and shy, preferring solitary activities.

[a]The first four scales assess the validity of the test; the numbered scales are the clinical or content scales.

Source: S. R. Hathaway and J. C. McKinley (1943); revised Butcher et al. (1989).

ple would be able to endorse such a statement honestly. Thus individuals who endorse a large number of the statements in the lie scale might well be attempting to present themselves in a particularly good light. Their scores on other scales are generally viewed with more than the usual skepticism.

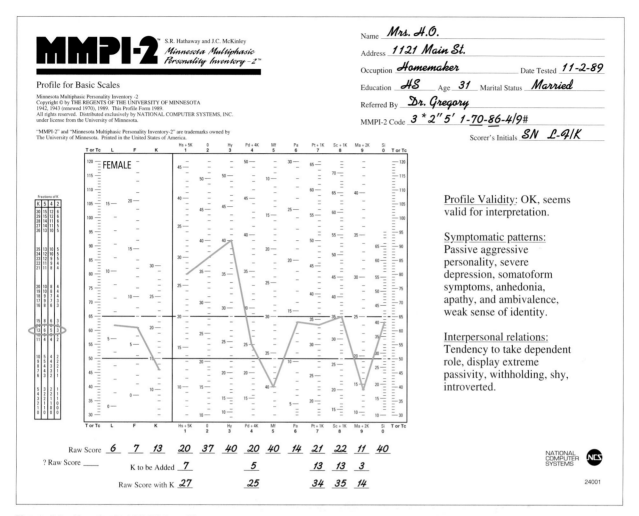

Figure 4.2   Hypothetical MMPI-2 profile.

PROJECTIVE PERSONALITY TESTS

A **projective test** is a psychological assessment device in which a set of standard stimuli—perhaps an inkblot or a drawing—ambiguous enough to allow variation in responses is presented to the individual. The assumption is that because the stimulus materials are unstructured, the patient's responses will be determined primarily by unconscious processes and will reveal his or her true attitudes, motivations, and modes of behavior. This notion is referred to as the **projective hypothesis**. If a patient reports seeing eyes on the Rorschach, for example, the projective hypothesis might be that the patient tends toward paranoia. This technique is derived from the psychoanalytic paradigm. The **Rorschach Inkblot Test** and the **Thematic Apperception Test** are perhaps the best known projective techniques. In the Rorschach test the subject is shown ten inkblots, one at a time, and asked to tell what fig-

ures or objects he or she sees in each of them. Half the inkblots are in black, white, and shades of gray, two also have red splotches, and three are in pastel colors.

In the Thematic Apperception Test (TAT) the examinee is shown a series of black-and-white pictures one by one and asked to tell a story related to each. For example, if a patient, seeing a picture of a prepubescent girl looking at fashionably attired mannequins in a store window, tells a story that contains angry references to the girl's parents, the clinician may through the projective hypothesis infer that the patient harbors resentment toward his or her parents.

The use of projective tests assumes that the respondent would be either unable or unwilling to express his or her true feelings if asked directly. Psychoanalytically oriented clinicians often favor such tests, a tendency that is consistent with the psychoanalytic assumption that people defend

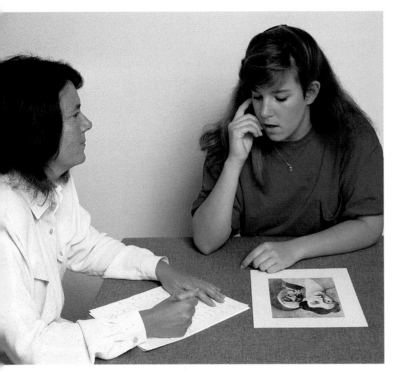

A client relates a story in response to one of the cards from the Thematic Apperception Test. Like the Rorschach, this projective test is designed to reveal unconscious conflicts and concerns.

against unpleasant thoughts and feelings by repressing them into the unconscious. Thus to bypass the defense mechanism of repression and get to the basic causes of distress, the real purposes of a test are best left unclear. Indeed, this has to be the case, for psychoanalytic theory asserts that the factors of greatest importance are unconscious.

The use of the projective hypothesis is not limited to formal tests. A psychoanalytically oriented colleague of ours uses it to form hypotheses about the client during the very first meeting. He sees clients in an office that contains a wide variety and large number of places to sit. When he brings a person into this office for the first time, he makes it a point not to tell the client where to sit. The therapist's belief is that he can learn something useful about the new client from the choice of seating. Being less psychoanalytic in approach, we rejected this tactic outright—until one day one of us had a new client who entered the office and before being shown where to sit, strode resolutely to the author's desk chair! As it turned out, this person was highly resistant to being in therapy and made continual efforts to dominate and control the early sessions.

The preceding discussion of projective tests reflects how they were conceptualized and used originally, that is, as a stimulus to fantasy that was

assumed to bypass ego defenses. The content of the person's responses were viewed as *symbolic* of internal dynamics; for example, a man might be judged to have homosexual interests on the basis of his seeing buttocks in the Rorschach inkblots (Chapman & Chapman, 1969). Other uses of the Rorschach concentrate more on the *form* of the person's responses (Exner, 1978). The test is considered more as a perceptual-cognitive task, and the person's responses are viewed as a sample of how he or she perceptually and cognitively organizes real-life situations (Exner, 1986). For example, Erdberg and Exner (1984) concluded from the research literature that respondents who express a great deal of human movement in their Rorschach responses (e.g., "The man is running to catch a plane.") tend to use inner resources when coping with their needs, whereas those whose Rorschach responses involve color ("The red spot is a kidney.") are more likely to seek interaction with the environment. Rorschach suggested this approach in his original manual, *Psychodiagnostics: A Diagnostic Test Based on Perception* (1921), but he died only eight months after publishing his ten inkblots and his immediate followers devised other methods of interpreting the test.

Though many, perhaps most, clinical practitioners still rely on the projective hypothesis in analyzing Rorschach responses, Exner's work is attracting a good deal of attention from academic researchers (Shontz & Green, 1992), though many of them are critical of both its reliability and its validity (Gann, 1995; Nezworski & Wood, 1995; Wood, Nezworski, & Stejskal, 1996).

The Roberts Apperception Test for Children (1982) illustrates how the use of projective tests has evolved to provide more standardized, objectively

In the Rorschach test the client is shown a series of inkblots and is asked what he or she sees in each of them.

During a ride in the country with his two children, Hermann Rorschach (1884–1922), Swiss psychiatrist, noticed that what they saw in the clouds reflected their personalities. From this observation came the famous inkblot test.

The French psychologist, Alfred Binet, developed the first IQ test to predict how well children would do in school.

scored assessment tools. Similar to the Thematic Apperception Test, in this instrument pictures of children and families are presented to the child, who tells a story about each one. Whereas many scoring approaches to the TAT are impressionistic and nonstandardized, the Roberts test provides objective criteria for scoring, along with normative data to determine whether the child's pattern of responses is abnormal. For example, the response, "The little girl is very sick and she's afraid no one will come to help her," would yield a score on the Anxiety Scale. Scoring on the Depression and Rejection Scales would occur if a child responded, "The mother is sad because the father left home and he's not coming back." A unique aspect of this test is the scales which provide information about a child's coping skills. For example, the response, "The boy asked his mother for help with his homework, and she helped him get started on his story," would be scored for both Reliance on Others and Support from Others.

INTELLIGENCE TESTS

Alfred Binet, a French psychologist, originally constructed mental tests to help the Parisian school board predict which children were in need of special schooling. Intelligence testing has since developed into one of the largest psychological industries. An **intelligence test**, sometimes referred to as an **aptitude test** or an IQ test, is a standardized means of assessing a person's current mental ability. The Scholastic Aptitude Test, the Graduate Record Examination, and individually administered tests such as the Wechsler Adult Intelligence Scale (WAIS) and the Stanford–Binet are all based on the assumption that a detailed sample of an individual's current intellectual functioning can predict how well he or she will perform in school.

These tests have other uses as well: in conjunction with achievement tests, to diagnose learning disabilities and to identify areas of strengths and weaknesses for academic planning; to help determine whether a person is mentally retarded; to identify intellectually gifted children so that appropriate instruction can be provided them in school; and as part of neuropsychological evaluations, for example, periodically testing a person believed to be suffering from a degenerative dementia so that deterioration of mental ability can be followed over time. A Spanish-language version of the WAIS has been available for almost thirty years (Wechsler, 1968) and can be useful in assessing the intellectual functioning of people from Hispanic cultures

(Gomez, Piedmont, & Fleming, 1992; Lopez & Romero, 1988; Lopez & Taussig, 1991).

IQ tests tap several functions asserted to constitute intelligence, including language skills, abstract thinking, nonverbal reasoning, visual-spatial skills, attention and concentration, and speed of processing. Scores on most IQ tests are standardized so that 100 is the mean and 15 or 16 is the standard deviation (a measure of how scores are dispersed above and below the average); thus approximately 65 percent of the population receives scores between 85 and 115. Those with a score below 70 are two standard deviations below the mean of the population and are considered to have "significant subaverage general intellectual functioning." Those with scores above 130 (two standard deviations above the mean) are considered "intellectually gifted." Approximately 2.5 percent of the population falls at each of these extremes. In Chapter 15 we discuss people whose IQ falls at the low end of the distribution.

It is important to keep in mind that, strictly speaking, IQ tests measure only what psychologists consider intelligence to be. The tasks and items on an IQ test were, after all, invented by psychologists—they did not come down to us inscribed on stone tablets. In addition, factors other than what we think of as pure intelligence play an important role in how people will do in school, such as family and personal circumstances, motivation to do well, and the difficulty of the curriculum. Though the correlations between IQ scores and school performance are statistically significant (see p. 110), in technical terms IQ tests explain only a small part of the variance in school performance; much more is unexplained by IQ or aptitude test scores than is explained. Interest has recently been focused on "emotional intelligence," reflected in such abilities as delaying gratification and being sensitive to the needs of others (Goleman, 1995). This aspect of human functioning may be as important to future success as the strictly intellectual achievements measured by traditional IQ tests. Finally, if and when there are major changes in our school systems, we can expect analogous changes in our definition and assessment of intelligence. Some important cross-cultural issues in IQ testing are considered later in this chapter (p. 96).

BEHAVIORAL AND COGNITIVE ASSESSMENT

As part of the continuing development of behavioral and cognitive approaches to the study of psychopathology and treatment, interest has been growing in assessment procedures that differ from the Rorschach Inkblot Test, the TAT, and the MMPI. Chapter 2 described learning researchers and behaviorists as being interested in situational determinants of behavior, that is, in the environmental conditions that precede and follow certain responses. With the growing interest in cognitive explanations we can expect the assessments made by behavioral clinicians to include self-reports as well, since a major method of assessing thought is to ask people to reflect introspectively and report what is on their minds.

Traditional assessment concentrates on measuring underlying personality structures and traits, such as obsessiveness, paranoia, coldness, aggressiveness, and so on. Behavioral and cognitively oriented clinicians, on the other hand, are often guided by a structure that leads them to assess four sets of variables, sometimes referred to by the acronym SORC (Kanfer & Phillips, 1970). The *S* stands for stimuli, the environmental situations that precede the problem. For instance, the clinician will try to ascertain which situations tend to elicit anxiety. The *O* stands for organismic, referring to both physiological and psychological factors assumed to be operating "under the skin." Perhaps the client's fatigue is caused in part by excessive use of alcohol or by a cognitive tendency toward self-deprecation manifested in such statements as "I never do anything right, so what's the point in trying?" The *R* refers to overt responses, which probably receive the most attention from behavioral clinicians, who must determine what behavior is problematic, its frequency, intensity, and form. For example, a client might say that she is forgetful and procrastinates. Does she mean that she does not return phone calls, comes late for appointments, or both? Finally, the *C* refers to consequent variables, events that appear to be reinforcing or punishing the behavior in question. When the client avoids a feared situation, does his spouse offer sympathy and excuses, thereby unwittingly keeping the person from facing up to his fears?

SORC factors are those that a behavioral clinician attempts to specify for a particular client. As might be expected, *O* variables are underplayed by Skinnerians, and *C* variables receive less attention from cognitively oriented behavior therapists than *O* variables.

The information necessary for a behavioral or cognitive assessment is gathered by several methods, including direct observation of behavior in real life as well as in contrived settings, interviews and self-report measures, and various other methods of cognitive assessment. We turn to these now.

DIRECT OBSERVATION OF BEHAVIOR

It is not surprising that behavior therapists have paid considerable attention to careful observation of overt behavior in a variety of settings, but it should not be assumed that they simply go out and *observe*. Like other scientists they try to fit events into a framework consistent with their points of view. The following excerpt from a case report by Gerald Patterson and his colleagues (1969), describing an interaction between a boy named Kevin and his mother, father, and sister Freida, serves as the first part of an example.

> Kevin goes up to father's chair and stands alongside it. Father puts his arms around Kevin's shoulders. Kevin says to mother as Freida looks at Kevin, "Can I go out and play after supper?" Mother does not reply. Kevin raises his voice and repeats the question. Mother says, "You don't have to yell; I can hear you." Father says, "How many times have I told you not to yell at your mother?" Kevin scratches a bruise on his arm while mother tells Freida to get started on the dishes, which Freida does. Kevin continues to rub and scratch his arm while mother and daughter are working at the kitchen sink. (p. 21)

This informal description could probably be provided by any observer. But in formal **behavioral observation**, the observer divides the uninterrupted sequence of behavior into various parts and applies terms that make sense within a learning framework. "Kevin begins the exchange by asking a routine question in a normal tone of voice. This ordinary behavior, however, is not reinforced by the mother's attention; for she does not reply. Because she does not reply, the normal behavior of Kevin ceases and he yells his question. The mother expresses disapproval—punishing her son—by telling him that he does not have to yell. And this punishment is supported by the father's reminding Kevin that he should not yell at his mother." This behavioral rendition acknowledges the consequences of ignoring a child's question. At some point the behavior therapist will undoubtedly advise the parents to attend to Kevin's requests when expressed in an ordinary tone of voice, lest he begin yelling. This example indicates an important aspect of behavioral assessment, namely, its link to *intervention*. The behavioral clinician's way of conceptualizing a situation typically implies a way to try to change it.

It is difficult to observe most behavior as it actually takes place, and little control can be exercised over where and when it may occur. For this reason many therapists contrive artificial situations in their consulting rooms or in a laboratory so that they can

Behavioral assessment often involves direct observation of behavior, as in this case where the observer is behind a one-way mirror.

observe how a client or a family acts under certain conditions. For example, Barkley (1981) had a mother and her hyperactive child spend time together in a laboratory living room, complete with sofas and television set. The mother was given a list of tasks for the child to complete, such as picking up toys or doing arithmetic problems. Observers behind a one-way mirror watched the proceedings and coded the child's reactions to the mother's efforts to control as well as the mother's reactions to the child's compliant or noncompliant responses. These behavioral assessment procedures yielded data that could be used to measure the effects of treatment.

Behavioral observations can also be made by significant others in the client's natural environment. The Conners Teacher Rating Scale (Conners, 1969) enables teachers to provide reliable behavioral assessment data on children in classrooms, noting, for example, whether the child is "constantly fidgeting" or "inattentive, easily distracted"; the Achenbach Child Behavior Checklist (Achenbach & Edelbrock, 1983) allows either parents or teachers to rate children's behavior.

Most of the research just described is conducted within an operant framework that employs no inferential concepts (recall p. 42). But behavioral assessment techniques can also be applied within a framework that makes use of mediators. Gordon Paul (1966) was interested in assessing the anxiety

Behavior Observed	Behavior Observed								
	1	2	3	4	5	6	7	8	Σ
1. Paces									
2. Sways									
3. Shuffles feet									
4. Knees tremble									
5. Extraneous arm and hand movement (swings, scratches, toys, etc.)									
6. Arms rigid									
7. Hands restrained (in pockets, behind back, clasped)									
8. Hand tremors									
9. No eye contact									
10. Face muscles tense (drawn, tics, grimaces)									
11. Face "deadpan"									
12. Face pale									
13. Face flushed (blushes)									
14. Moistens lips									
15. Swallows									
16. Clears throat									
17. Breathes heavily									
18. Perspires (face, hands, armpits)									
19. Voice quivers									
20. Speech blocks or stammers									

Figure 4.3   Paul's (1966) Timed Behavioral Checklist for Performance Anxiety.

of public speakers. He decided to count the frequency of behaviors indicative of this emotional state. One of his principal measures, the Timed Behavioral Checklist for Performance Anxiety, is shown in Figure 4.3. Subjects were asked to deliver a speech before a group, some members of which were raters trained to consider the subject's behavior every thirty seconds and to record the presence or absence of twenty specific behaviors. By summing the scores, Paul arrived at a behavioral index of anxiety. This study provides one example of how observations of overt behavior have been used to infer the presence of an internal state.

In Paul's study people other than the speaker made the observations. For several years behavior therapists and researchers have also asked individuals to observe their own behavior, to keep track of various categories of response. This approach is called **self-monitoring**. An early application of self-monitoring was used in research to reduce smoking. Subjects were provided with booklets in which they recorded the time each cigarette was lighted at baseline, before treatment had been introduced, during treatment, and after (Davison & Rosen, 1968).

Although some research indicates that self-monitoring can provide accurate measurement of such behavior, considerable research indicates that behavior may be altered by the very fact that it is being self-monitored (Haynes & Horn, 1982), that is, the self-consciousness required for self-monitoring affects the behavior. **Reactivity** of behavior is the phenomenon of behavior changing because it is being observed. In general, desirable behavior, such as engaging in social conversation, often increases in frequency when self-monitored (Nelson, Lipinski, & Black, 1976), whereas behavior the subject wishes to reduce, such as cigarette smoking, diminishes (McFall & Hammen, 1971). Such findings suggest that therapeutic interventions can take

Self-monitoring generally leads to increases in desirable behaviors and decreases in undesirable ones. Here the person is monitoring smoking and entering information into a palm-top computer.

advantage of the reactivity that is a natural by-product of self-monitoring. For example, when hyperactive children monitored their own behavior, improvements were noted in time spent working in the classroom (Barkley, Copeland, & Sivage, 1980) and cooperative behavior with peers (Hinshaw, Henker, & Whalen, 1984).

INTERVIEWS AND SELF-REPORT MEASURES

For all their interest in direct observation of behavior, behavioral clinicians still rely very heavily on the interview to assess the needs of their clients. Within a trusting relationship the behavior therapist's job is to determine, by skillful questioning and careful observation of the client's emotional reactions during the interview, the SORC factors that help him or her to conceptualize the client's problem.

Behavior therapists also make use of self-report inventories. For example, McFall and Lillesand (1971) employed a Conflict Resolution Inventory

containing thirty-five items that focused on the ability of the respondent to refuse unreasonable requests. Each item described a specific situation in which a person was asked for something unreasonable. For example, "You are in the thick of studying for exams when a person you know slightly comes into your room and says, 'I'm tired of studying. Mind if I come in and take a break for a while?'" Subjects were asked to indicate the likelihood that they would refuse such a request and how comfortable they would be in doing so. Responses to this self-report inventory were found to be correlated with a variety of direct observational data on social skills (Frisch & Higgins, 1986). This and similar inventories can be used by clinicians and have helped behavioral researchers measure the outcome of clinical interventions as well.

SPECIALIZED APPROACHES TO COGNITIVE ASSESSMENT

Perhaps the most widely employed cognitive assessment methods are self-report questionnaires that tap a wide range of cognitions, such as fear of negative evaluation, tendency to think irrationally, and making negative inferences about life experiences. "When someone criticizes you in class, what thoughts go through your mind?" is a question a client might be asked in an interview or on a paper-and-pencil inventory. When patients are asked about their thoughts in interviews and self-report inventories, they have to reflect backward in time and provide a retrospective and rather general report of their thoughts in certain situations.

As with all kinds of assessment a key feature of contemporary approaches in cognitive assessment is that the development of methods is determined primarily by theory and data as well as by the purposes of the assessment. For example, much research on depression is concerned with cognition—both the things that people consciously and sometimes unconsciously tell themselves, as well as the underlying assumptions or attitudes that can be inferred from their behavior and verbal reports. As we shall examine in greater detail in Chapter 10, one cognitive theory (Beck, 1967) holds that depression is caused primarily by negative ideas that people have about themselves, their world, and their future. For example, people may believe that they are not worth much and that things are never going to get better. These pessimistic attitudes, or schemata, bias the way in which depressed people interpret events around them to the extent that a misstep, such as forgetting to mail a birthday card, which might be taken in stride by a nondepressed person, is construed by a depressed individual as compelling evidence of his or her ineptitude and worthlessness. Researchers employing cognitive assessment set themselves the task of trying to identify these different kinds of cognitions, obtaining their ideas both from clinical reports of practitioners who have firsthand experience with depressed patients and from controlled research that adheres to the methodological principles discussed in the next chapter.

The Dysfunctional Attitude Scale (DAS) contains items such as "People will probably think less of me if I make a mistake" (Weissman & Beck, 1978). Researchers have shown that one can differentiate between depressed and nondepressed people on the basis of their scores on this scale and that scores decrease (that is, improve) after interventions that relieve depression. Furthermore, the DAS relates well to other aspects of cognition in ways consistent with Beck's theory. For example, it correlates with an instrument called the Cognitive Bias Questionnaire (Krantz & Hammen, 1979), which measures the ways in which depressed patients distort information. These and other instruments, most of them self-report questionnaires, both help to test Beck's theory of depression and are validated when certain patterns of scores arise, as when a sample of depressed patients manifests higher levels of cognitive distortion than do controls (an example of what is called construct validity, discussed later). An accumulating body of data is helping to establish both the validity and the reliability of these instruments (Segal & Shaw, 1988).

However, replies of subjects to questions asked by interviewers and to inventories about their thoughts in certain past situations may well be different from what they would report were they able to do so in the immediate circumstance. Researchers have been working on ways to enable subjects to tap into their immediate and ongoing thought processes when confronted with particular circumstances (cf. Parks & Hollon, 1988). Can we show, for example, that a socially anxious person does in fact, as Ellis would predict, view criticism from others as catastrophic, whereas someone who is not socially insecure does not?

The Articulated Thoughts in Simulated Situations (ATSS) method of Davison and his associates (Davison, Robins, & Johnson, 1983) is one way to assess immediate thoughts. In this procedure a person pretends that he or she is a participant in a situation, such as listening to a teaching assistant criticize a term paper. Presented on audiotape, the scene pauses every ten or fifteen seconds. During the ensuing thirty seconds of silence the participant talks aloud about whatever is going through his or her mind in reaction to the words just heard. Then the audiotaped scene continues, stopping after a few moments so that the person can articulate his or her thoughts again. One taped scene in which the participant overhears two pretend acquaintances criticizing him or her includes the following segments.

First acquaintance: He certainly did make a fool of himself over what he said about religion. I just find that kind of opinion very closed-minded and unaware. You have to be blind to the facts of the universe to believe that. [Thirty-second pause for subject's response.]

Second acquaintance: What really bugs me is the way he expresses himself. He never seems to stop and think, but just blurts out the first thing that comes into his head. [Thirty-second pause.]

Participants readily become involved in the pretend situations, regarding them as credible and realistic. Cognitive patterns that have emerged from a few of the studies conducted thus far include the following: socially anxious therapy patients articulated thoughts of greater irrationality (e.g., "Oh God, I wish I were dead. I'm so embarrassed.") than did nonanxious control subjects (Bates, Campbell, & Burgess, 1990; Davison & Zighelboim, 1987); recent ex-smokers who would relapse within three months showed a greater tendency to think of smoking without prompting (Haaga, 1987) and also had fewer negative expectations about the consequences of smoking than did those who would still be abstinent three months later (Haaga, 1988a); men with borderline hypertension achieved significant reductions in anger, as expressed in their articulated thoughts, and experienced decreases in their blood pressure and heart rate following a program of relaxation training and medical information about diet and exercise (Davison, Williams, et al., 1991; see also Chapter 8, p. 201); in a study that directly compared ATSS data with overt behavior (Davison, Haaga, et al., 1991), thoughts of positive self-efficacy were found to be inversely related to behaviorally indexed speech anxiety, that is, the more anxiously subjects behaved on a timed behavioral checklist measure of public-speaking anxiety, the less capable they felt themselves to be while articulating thoughts in a stressful, simulated speech-giving situation.

These and related findings (cf. Davison, Navarre, & Vogel, 1995) indicate that this method ferrets out people's thinking about both inherently bothersome and "objectively" innocuous situations.

Other cognitive assessment methods have also proved useful. In thought listing, for example, the

Cognitive assessment focuses on the person's perception of a situation, realizing that the same event can be perceived differently. For example, moving could be regarded as very stressful or seen in a positive light.

person writes down his or her thoughts prior to or following an event of interest, such as entering a room to talk to a stranger, as a way to determine the cognitive components of social anxiety (Cacioppo, Glass, & Merluzzi, 1979). Open-ended techniques, such as the ATSS just described, may be preferable when investigators know relatively little and want to get general ideas about the cognitive terrain; more focused techniques, such as questionnaires, may be better—and are certainly more easily scored—when investigators have more prior knowledge about the cognitions of interest (Haaga, 1988b). So far the various cognitive assessment techniques correlate poorly with each other (Clark, 1988), an important challenge to researchers and clinicians alike.

The interest in cognitive assessment has recently brought cognitive-behavioral clinicians into contact with literature in experimental cognitive psychology, the branch of psychological research concerned with how people transform environmental input into usable information, how they think and plan, remember, and anticipate. Researchers have developed assessment tools for inferring the existence of several cognitive structures, particularly schemata (Bartlett, 1932). A simple example of a schema would be the idea we carry around in our heads of what a face is—a configuration having two eyes, a nose, a mouth, and two ears. We are able to identify an object as a face even if its configuration is unusual.

Experimental cognitive psychologists have used the schema concept in understanding memory phenomena (see p. 46). Clinical researchers have built on this experimental research and infer schemata from distortions in memory. For example, Nelson and Craighead (1977) wanted to test whether depressed people encounter their world with a failure schema, as posited by Beck. They gave groups of depressed and nondepressed students a task on which they were rewarded or punished 30 percent or 70 percent of the time. In the 70 percent reward condition, the depressed subjects recalled having been reinforced less often than was actually the case. In the 30 percent punishment condition, depressed students recalled having received more punishment. These differences in memory are explained in terms of a schema, or cognitive set; the depressed subject believes something like "I am not competent." In this sense a schema is equivalent to a basic, underlying assumption that people have about themselves and their world and that affects the way they perceive, conceptualize, feel, and act.

BIOLOGICAL ASSESSMENT

For many years researchers and clinicians have attempted to observe directly or make inferences about the functioning of the brain and other parts of the nervous system in their efforts to understand both normal and abnormal psychological functioning (see Focus 4.1). Recall from Chapters 2 and 3

FOCUS 4.1   STRUCTURE AND FUNCTION OF THE HUMAN BRAIN

The brain is located within the protective coating of the skull and is enveloped with three layers of nonneural tissue, membranes referred to as **meninges**. Viewed from the top, the brain is divided by a midline fissure into two mirror-image **cerebral hemispheres**; together they constitute most of the cerebrum. The major connection between the two hemispheres is a band of nerve fibers called the **corpus callosum**. Figure 4.a shows the surface of one of the cerebral hemispheres. The upper, side, and some of the lower surfaces of the hemispheres form the **cerebral cortex**. The cortex consists of six layers of tightly packed neuron cell bodies with many short, unsheathed interconnecting processes. These neurons, estimated to number 10 to 15 billion, make up a thin outer covering, the so-called gray matter of the brain. The cortex is vastly convoluted; the ridges are called **gyri**, and the depressions between them **sulci**, or fissures. Deep fissures divide the cerebral hemispheres into several distinct areas called lobes. The **frontal lobe** lies in front of the central sulcus; the **parietal lobe** is behind it and above the lateral sulcus; the **temporal lobe** is located below the lateral sulcus; and the **occipital lobe** lies behind the parietal and temporal lobes. Different functions tend to be localized in particular areas of the lobes: vision in the occipital; discrimination of sounds in the temporal; reasoning and other higher mental processes plus the regulation of fine voluntary movement in the frontal; initiation of movements of the skeletal musculature in a band in front of the central sulcus; receipt of sensations of touch, pressure, pain, temperature, and body position from skin, muscles, tendons, and joints, in a band behind the central sulcus.

The two hemispheres of the brain have different functions. The left hemisphere, which generally controls the right half of the body by a crossing over of motor and sensory fibers, is responsible for speech and, according to some neuropsychologists, for analytical thinking in right-handed people and in a fair number of left-handed people as well. The right hemisphere controls the left side of the body, discerns spatial relations and patterns, and is involved in emotion and intuition. But analytical thinking cannot be located exclusively in the left hemisphere or intuitive and even creative thinking in the right; the two hemispheres communicate with each other constantly via the corpus callosum. Localization of apparently different modes of thought is probably not as clear-cut as some would have us believe.

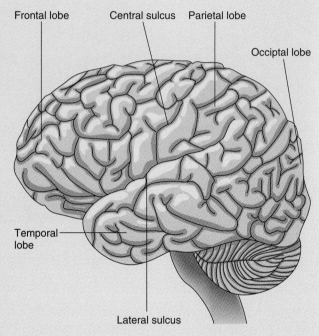

Figure 4.a   Surface of the left cerebral hemisphere, indicating the lobes and the two principal fissures of the cortex

If the brain is sliced in half, separating the two cerebral hemispheres (Figure 4.b), additional important features can be seen. The gray matter of the cerebral cortex does not extend throughout the interior of the brain. Much of the interior is **white matter**, made up of large tracts or bundles of myelinated (sheathed) fibers that connect cell bodies in the cortex with those in the spinal cord and in other centers lower in the brain. These centers are pockets of gray matter, referred to as *nuclei*. The nuclei serve both as way stations, connecting tracts from the cortex with other ascending and descending tracts, and as integrating motor and sensory control centers. Some cortical cells project their long fibers or axons to motor neurons in the spinal cord, but others project them only as far as these clusters of interconnecting neuron cell bodies. Four masses are deep within each hemisphere, called collectively the basal ganglia. Also deep within the brain are cavities called *ventricles*,

that throughout history people interested in psychopathology have assumed, quite reasonably, that some malfunctions of the psyche are likely to be due to or at least reflected in malfunctions of the soma. We turn now to contemporary work in biological assessment.

BRAIN IMAGING: "SEEING" THE BRAIN

Because many behavioral problems can be brought on by brain abnormalities, neurological tests such as checking the reflexes, examining the retina for

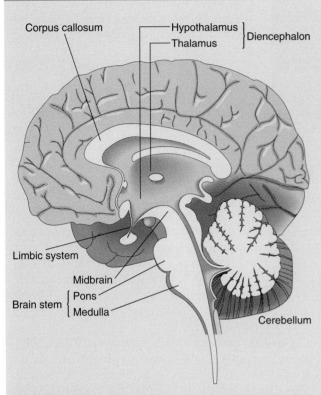

Corpus callosum

Hypothalamus

Thalamus

Diencephalon

Limbic system

Midbrain

Pons

Medulla

Brain stem

Cerebellum

Figure 4.b   Slice of brain through the medial plane, showing the internal structures

which are continuous with the central canal of the spinal cord and are filled with cerebrospinal fluid.

Figure 4.b depicts four important functional areas or structures.

1. The **diencephalon**, connected in front with the hemispheres and behind with the midbrain, contains the *thalamus* and the **hypothalamus**, which consist of groups of nuclei. The thalamus is a relay station for all sensory pathways except the olfactory. The nuclei making up the thalamus receive nearly all impulses arriving from the different sensory areas of the body before passing them on to the cerebrum, where they are interpreted as conscious sensations. The hypothalamus is the highest center of integration for many visceral processes. Its nuclei regulate metabolism, temperature, water balance, sweating, blood pressure, sleeping, and appetite.

2. The **midbrain** is a mass of nerve-fiber tracts connecting

the cerebral cortex with the pons, the medulla oblongata, the cerebellum, and the spinal cord.

3. The **brain stem** comprises the **pons** and the **medulla oblongata** and functions primarily as a neural relay station. The pons contains tracts that connect the cerebellum with the spinal cord and with motor areas of the cerebrum. The medulla oblongata serves as the main line of traffic for tracts ascending from the spinal cord and descending from the higher centers of the brain. At the bottom of the medulla many of the motor fibers cross to the opposite side. The medulla also contains nuclei that maintain the regular life rhythms of the heartbeat, of the rising and falling diaphragm, and of the constricting and dilating blood vessels. In the core of the brain stem is the *reticular formation*, sometimes called the reticular activating system because of the important role it plays in arousal and in the maintenance of alertness. The tracts of the pons and medulla send in fibers to connect with the profusely interconnected cells of the reticular formation, which in turn send fibers to the cortex, the basal ganglia, the hypothalamus, the septal area, and the cerebellum.

4. The **cerebellum**, like the cerebrum, consists primarily of two deeply convoluted hemispheres with an exterior cortex of gray matter and an interior of white tracts. The cerebellum receives sensory nerves from the vestibular apparatus of the ear and from muscles, tendons, and joints. The information received and integrated relates to balance and posture and equilibrium and to the smooth coordination of the body when in motion.

5. A fifth important part of the brain is the **limbic system**, which comprises structures continuous with one another in the lower cerebrum and developed earlier than the mammalian cerebral cortex. The limbic system controls the visceral and physical expressions of emotion—quickened heartbeat and respiration, trembling, sweating, and alterations in facial expressions—and the expression of appetitive and other primary drives, namely, hunger, thirst, mating, defense, attack, and flight. Important structures in the limbic system are the cingulate gyrus, stretching about the corpus callosum; the septal area, which is anterior to the thalamus; the long, tubelike hippocampus, which stretches from the septal area into the temporal lobe; and the amygdala (one of the basal ganglia), which is embedded in the tip of the temporal lobe.

any indication of blood vessel damage, and evaluating motor coordination and perception are useful procedures in diagnosing brain dysfunction.

Computerized axial tomography, the **CT scan**, helps us assess structural brain abnormalities. A moving beam of X rays passes into a horizontal

cross section of the patient's brain, scanning it through 360 degrees; the moving X-ray detector on the other side measures the amount of radioactivity that penetrates, thus detecting subtle differences in tissue density. The computer uses the information to construct a two-dimensional, detailed image of

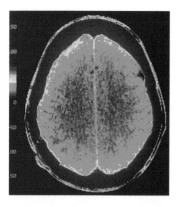 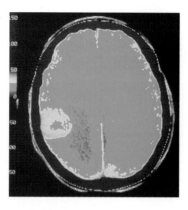

These two CT scans show a horizontal slice through the brain. The one on the left is normal while that on the right has a tumor on the left side.

the cross section, giving it optimal contrasts. Then the patient's head is moved, and the machine scans another cross section of the brain. The resulting images can show the enlargement of ventricles, which signals degeneration of tissue and the locations of tumors and blood clots (see photo).

Newly developed computer-based devices for seeing into the living brain include **magnetic resonance imaging**, also known as MRI, which is superior to a CT scan because it produces pictures of higher quality and does not rely on even the small amount of radiation required by a CT scan. In MRI the person is placed inside a large, circular magnet, which causes the hydrogen atoms in the body to move. When the magnetic force is turned off the atoms return to their original positions and thereby produce an electromagnetic signal. These signals are then read by the computer and translated into pictures of brain tissue. The implications of this technique are enormous. For example, it has allowed physicians to locate and remove delicate brain tumors that would have been considered inoperable without such sophisticated methods of viewing brain structures. More recently, a new modification, called fMRI (functional MRI), has been developed that allows researchers to take MRI

pictures so quickly that blood-flow changes can be measured, providing a picture of the brain at work rather than of its structure alone. Using this technique, a recent study found that there was less activation in the frontal brains of schizophrenic patients as they performed a cognitive task (Yurgelon-Todd et al., 1996).

Positron emission tomography, the **PET scan**, a more expensive and invasive procedure, allows measurement of both brain structure and brain function. A substance used by the brain is labeled with a short-lived radioactive isotope and injected into the bloodstream. The radioactive molecules of the substance emit a particle called a positron, which quickly collides with an electron. A pair of high-energy light particles shoot out from the skull in opposite directions and are detected by the scanner. The computer analyzes millions of such recordings and converts them into a picture of the functioning brain in horizontal cross section, projected onto a television screen. The images are in color; fuzzy spots of lighter and warmer colors are areas in which metabolic rates for the substance are higher (see photo). Visual images of the working brain can indicate sites of epileptic seizures, brain cancers, strokes, and trauma from head injuries, as well

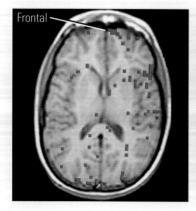 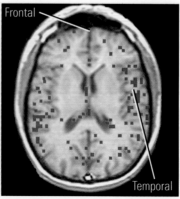

Functional Magnetic Response Images (fMRI) of a schizophrenic patient (right) and a healthy individual (left). The red squares represent activation of the brain during a verbal task compared to baseline. The schizophrenic patient shows less frontal activation and more temporal. (Yurgelun-Todd et al. 1996)

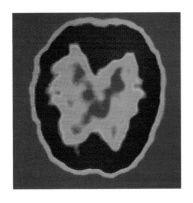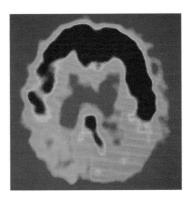

The PET scan on the left is a normal brain; the one on the right shows the brain of a patient with Alzheimer's disease.

as the distribution of psychoactive drugs in the brain. The PET scanner is also being used to study possible abnormal biological processes that underlie disorders, such as the failure of the frontal cortex of schizophrenic patients to become activated while they attempt to perform a cognitive task (see p. 281).

NEUROCHEMICAL ASSESSMENT

It might seem that assessing the amount of a particular neurotransmitter or the quantity of its receptors in the brain would be straightforward. But it is not. Only recently has PET scanning allowed an assessment of receptors in a living brain. Most of the research on neurochemical theories of psychopathology—of increasing importance in recent years—has relied on indirect assessments.

In postmortem studies, the brains of deceased patients are removed and the amount of specific neurotransmitters in particular brain areas can then be directly assayed. Different brain areas can be infused with substances that bind to receptors, and the amount of binding can then be quantified; more binding indicates more receptors.

Another common method of neurochemical assessment involves analyzing the *metabolites* of neurotransmitters that have been broken down by enzymes. A metabolite, typically an acid, is produced when a neurotransmitter is deactivated. For example, the major metabolite of dopamine is homovanillic acid; of serotonin, 5 hydroxyindoleacetic acid. The metabolites can be detected in urine, blood, and cerebrospinal fluid (the fluid in the spinal column and in the brain's ventricles). A high level of a particular metabolite indicates a high level of a transmitter.

All these tools provide startling pictures of and insights into internal organs and permit the gathering of information about living tissue, including the brain. Clinicians and researchers in many disciplines are currently using these techniques both to discover previously undetectable tumors and other organic problems and to conduct inquiries into the neural and chemical bases of thought, emotion, and behavior.

NEUROPSYCHOLOGICAL ASSESSMENT

It is important to note a distinction between neurologists and neuropsychologists, even though both specialists are concerned with the study of the central nervous system. A **neurologist** is a physician who specializes in medical diseases that affect the nervous system, such as muscular dystrophy or cerebral palsy. A **neuropsychologist** is a psychologist who studies how dysfunctions of the brain affect the way we think, feel, and behave. As the term implies, a neuropsychologist is trained as a psychologist and as such is interested in thought, emotion, and behavior, but with a focus on how abnormalities of the brain affect behavior in deleterious ways. Both kinds of specialists contribute much to each other as they work in different ways, often collaboratively, to learn how the nervous system functions and how to ameliorate problems caused by disease or injury to the brain.

One might reasonably assume that neurologists and physicians, with the help of such procedures and technological devices as PET, CT, and MRI scans, can observe the brain and its functions more or less directly and thus assess all brain abnormalities. Many brain abnormalities and injuries, however, involve alterations in structure so subtle or slight in extent that they have thus far eluded direct physical examination.

Neuropsychologists have developed tests to assess behavioral disturbances caused by organic brain dysfunctions. The literature on these tests is extensive and as with most areas of psychology, so, too, is the disagreement about them. The weight of the evidence, however, does indicate that psychological tests have some validity in the assessment of brain damage, and they are often used in conjunction with the brain-scanning techniques just described. They are accordingly called **neuropsychological tests**.

One of these tests is Reitan's modification of a battery or group of tests previously developed by Halstead. The concept of using a battery of tests, each tapping different functions, is critical, for only by studying a person's pattern of performance can an investigator adequately judge whether the person is brain damaged. But the Halstead–Reitan battery can do even more—it can sometimes help to locate the area of the brain that has been affected. The following are four of the tests included in the Halstead–Reitan group.

1. **Tactile Performance Test—Time.**   While blindfolded, the patient tries to fit various shaped blocks into spaces of a form board, first using the preferred hand, then the other, and finally both. The purpose is to measure the person's motor-speed response to the unfamiliar.

2. **Tactile Performance Test—Memory.**   After completing the timed test, the participant is asked to draw the form board from memory, showing the blocks in their proper location. Both this and the timed test are sensitive to damage in the right parietal lobe.

3. **Category Test.**   The patient, seeing an image on a screen that suggests one of the numbers from one to four, presses a button to show which number he or she thinks it is. A bell indicates that the choice is correct, a buzzer that it is incorrect. The patient must keep track of these images and signals in order to figure out the rules for making the correct choices. This test measures problem solving, in particular the ability to abstract a principle from a nonverbal array of events. Impaired performance reflects damage to either of the frontal lobes.

4. **Speech Sounds Perception Test.**   Participants listen to a series of nonsense words, each comprising two consonants with a long *e* sound in the middle. They then select the "word" they heard from a set of alternatives. This test measures left-hemisphere function, especially temporal and parietal areas.

The Luria–Nebraska battery (Golden, Hammeke, & Purisch, 1978), based on the work of the Russian psychologist Aleksandr Luria (1902–1977), is also in widespread use (Adams, 1980; Kane, Parsons, & Goldstein, 1985; Spiers, 1982). A battery of 269 items makes up eleven sections to determine basic and complex motor skills, rhythm and pitch abilities, tactile and kinesthetic skills, verbal and spatial skills, receptive speech ability, expressive speech ability, writing, reading, arithmetic skills, memory, and intellectual processes. The pattern of scores on these sections, as well as on the 32 items found to be the most discriminating and indicative of overall impairment, helps reveal damage to the frontal, temporal, sensorimotor, or parietal-occipital area of the right or left hemisphere.

The Luria–Nebraska battery can be administered in two and a half hours, and research demonstrates that this test can be scored in a highly reliable man-

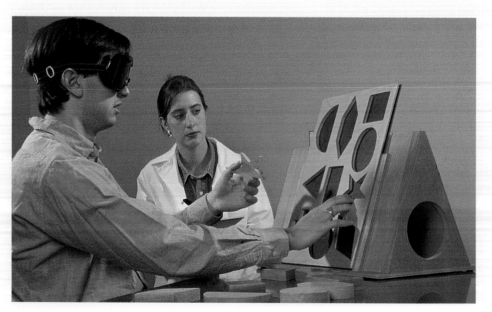

Neuropsychological tests assess various performance deficits in the hope of detecting a specific area of brain malfunction. Shown here is the Tactile Performance Test.

The Children's Luria–Nebraska test is an assessment of possible brain dysfunction or damage. This child is taking a subtest.

ner (Maruish, Sawicki, Franzen, & Golden, 1984; Moses & Schefft, 1984). The Luria–Nebraska is also believed to pick up effects of brain damage that are not (yet) detectable by neurological examination; such deficits are in the cognitive domain rather than in the sensorimotor on which neurological assessments focus (e.g., patellar reflexes) (Moses, 1983). A particular advantage of the Luria–Nebraska tests is that one can control for educational level so that a less-educated person will not receive a lower score solely because of limited educational experience (Brickman, McManus, Grapentine, & Alessi, 1984). Finally, a version (Golden, 1981) for children ages eight to twelve has also been found useful in diagnosing brain damage and in evaluating the educational strengths and weaknesses of children (Sweet, Carr, Rossini, & Kasper, 1986).

A CAUTIONARY NOTE

There is no one-to-one relationship between a score on a given neuropsychological test or a finding on a PET or CAT scan on the one hand and psychological dysfunction on the other. This is especially so with chronic brain damage known or suspected to have been present for some years before the assessment is conducted. The reasons for these sometimes loose relationships have to do with such factors as how the person has, over time, reacted to and coped with the losses brought about by the brain damage. And the success of efforts to cope have, in turn, to do with the social environment in which the individual has lived, for example, how understanding parents and associates have been or how well the school system has provided for the special educational needs of the individual. Therefore, in addition to the imperfect nature of the biological assessment instruments themselves and our incomplete understanding of how the brain actually functions, researchers must consider these experiential factors that operate over time to contribute to the clinical picture.

A final caution to neuropsychological assessors is that they must recognize the simple, yet often unappreciated, fact that in attempting to understand the neurocognitive consequences of any brain-injuring event, one must understand the abilities that the patient has brought to that event (Boll, 1985). This straightforward truth brings to mind the story of the man who, recovering from an accident that has broken all the fingers in both hands, earnestly asks the surgeon whether he will be able to play the piano when his wounds heal. "Yes, I'm sure you will," says the doctor reassuringly. "That's wonderful," exclaims the man, "because I don't even know how to play the piano *now*!"

PSYCHOPHYSIOLOGICAL MEASUREMENT

The discipline of **psychophysiology** is concerned with the bodily changes that accompany psychological events or that are associated with a person's psychological characteristics (Grings & Dawson, 1978). Experimenters have studied such changes as heart rate, tension in the muscles, blood flow in various parts of the body, and brain waves, while subjects are afraid, depressed, asleep, imagining, solving problems, and so on.

The activities of the autonomic nervous system (see Focus 4.2) are frequently assessed by electrical and chemical measurements and analyses in attempts to understand the nature of emotion. One important measure is heart rate. Each heartbeat generates spreading changes in electrical potential, which can be recorded by an electrocardiograph or on a suitably tuned polygraph and graphically depicted in an **electrocardiogram**. Electrodes are usually placed on the chest and lead to an instrument for measuring electric currents. The deflections of this instrument may be seen as waves on a computer

FOCUS 4.2   THE AUTONOMIC NERVOUS SYSTEM

The mammalian nervous system can be divided into two relatively separate functional parts: the **somatic** (or voluntary) **nervous system** and the **autonomic** (or involuntary) **nervous system (ANS)**. Because the autonomic nervous system is especially important in the study of emotional behavior, it will be useful to review its principal characteristics.

Skeletal muscles, such as those that move our limbs, are innervated, or stimulated, by the voluntary nervous system.

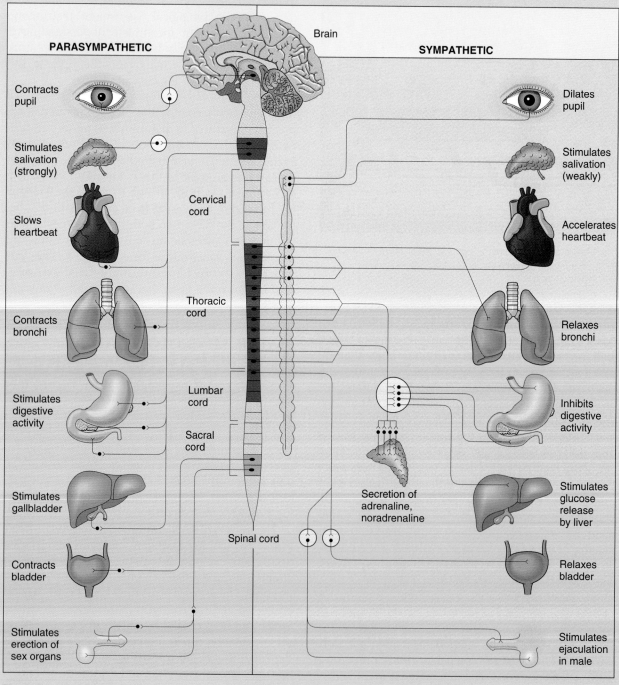

PARASYMPATHETIC

Contracts pupil

Stimulates salivation (strongly)

Slows heartbeat

Contracts bronchi

Stimulates digestive activity

Stimulates gallbladder

Contracts bladder

Stimulates erection of sex organs

Brain

Cervical cord

Thoracic cord

Lumbar cord

Sacral cord

Spinal cord

SYMPATHETIC

Dilates pupil

Stimulates salivation (weakly)

Accelerates heartbeat

Relaxes bronchi

Inhibits digestive activity

Secretion of adrenaline, noradrenaline

Stimulates glucose release by liver

Relaxes bladder

Stimulates ejaculation in male

Figure 4.c   The autonomic nervous system

Much of our behavior, however, is dependent on a nervous system that operates generally without our awareness and has traditionally been viewed as beyond voluntary control, hence the term *autonomic*. However, research on biofeedback has shown that the ANS is under greater voluntary control than previously believed (see p. 200).

The autonomic nervous system innervates the endocrine glands, the heart, and the smooth muscles that are found in the walls of the blood vessels, stomach, intestines, kidneys, and other organs. This nervous system is itself divided into two parts, the **sympathetic nervous system** and the **parasympathetic nervous system** (Figure 4.c), which work sometimes in opposition to each other, sometimes in unison. The sympathetic portion of the ANS, when energized, accelerates the heartbeat, dilates the pupils, inhibits intestinal activity, increases electrodermal activity, and initiates other smooth-muscle and glandular responses that prepare the organism for sudden activity and stress. Some physiologists view the sympathetic nervous system as primarily excitatory, and view the other division, the parasympathetic, as responsible for maintenance functions and more quiescent behavior, such as deceleration of the heartbeat, constriction of the pupils, and acceleration of

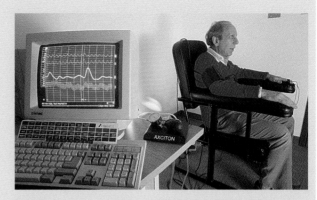

A polygraph is used to assess various features of the functioning of the autonomic nervous system. In this case, electrodermal activity is being recorded and displayed on a computer screen.

intestinal contractions. Division of activities is not quite so clear-cut, however, for the parasympathetic system may be active during situations of stress. Animals, and human beings, to their consternation, may urinate and defecate involuntarily when extremely frightened.

screen, or a pen recorder may register the waves on a continuously moving roll of graph paper. Both types of recordings are called electrocardiograms. Also available is the cardiotachometer, a device that measures the precise elapsed time between two heartbeats and then instantaneously provides the heart rate on a beat-to-beat basis. This technological advance is especially important for experimental psychologists, who are typically interested in bodily changes that occur over short periods of time in response to rapidly shifting circumstances.

A second measure of autonomic nervous system activity is **electrodermal responding**, or skin conductance. Anxiety, fear, anger, and other emotions increase activity in the sympathetic nervous system, which then boosts sweat-gland activity. The electrophysiological processes in the cells of these glands change the electrical conductance of the skin as well as produce sweat. Conductance is typically measured by determining the current that flows through the skin when a known small voltage derived from an external source is passed between two electrodes on the hand. This current shows a pronounced increase after activation of the sweat glands. Since the sweat glands are activated by the sympathetic nervous system, increased sweat-gland activity indicates sympathetic autonomic excitation and is often taken as a measure of emotional arousal. These measures are widely used in research in psychopatholo-

In psychophysiological assessment physical changes in the body are measured. The electrocardiograph is one such assessment.

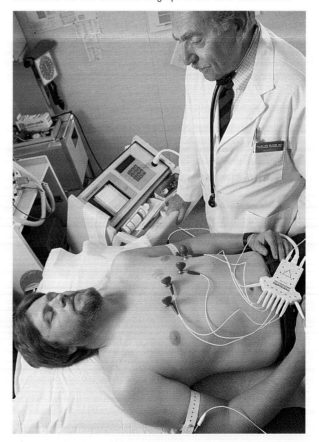

gy. Psychophysiological measures of sexual arousal are described in Chapter 14 (p. 367).

Advances in technology allow researchers to track such things as blood pressure *in vivo*, as the person goes about his or her normal business. The participant wears a portable device that records blood pressure automatically several times during the day. Combined with self-reports recorded by the participant in a specially designed diary, van Egeren and Madarasmi (1987) were able to study how people's thoughts and moods co-vary with increases in blood pressure, data of great interest to psychologically oriented researchers in hypertension (see Chapter 8).

Electroencephalograms, or EEGs, are essential tools for diagnosing epilepsy. Electrodes placed on the scalp record electrical activity in the underlying brain area. Particular abnormal patterns of electrical activity can indicate epilepsy or help in locating brain lesions or tumors.

As is the case with the brain-imaging techniques reviewed earlier, a more complete picture of the human being is obtained by assessing physiological functioning while the person is engaging in some form of behavior or cognitive activity. If experimenters are interested in psychophysiological responding in patients with obsessive-compulsive disorder, for example, they would likely study the patients while presenting stimuli such as dirt that would elicit the problematic behaviors.

Psychophysiological measuring procedures are constantly being improved and are relatively unobtrusive. Once the person has adapted to having electrodes pasted on the arm, for example, measurement of heart rate does not interfere with many experimental tasks, such as listening to a story or solving a mathematical problem.

Inasmuch as psychophysiology employs highly sophisticated electronic machinery and many psychologists aspire to be as scientific as possible, psychologists sometimes believe uncritically in these apparently objective assessment devices without appreciating their real limitations and complications. Many of the measurements do not differentiate clearly among emotional states. Skin conductance, for example, increases with a variety of emotions, among them, happiness, not only anxiety.

RELIABILITY AND VALIDITY IN ASSESSMENT

The concepts of reliability and validity are extremely complex; there are several kinds of each, and an entire subfield of psychology—psychometrics—exists primarily for their study. We provide here a brief and general overview, which supplements our discussion in Chapter 3 and should be sufficient for critically evaluating the wide diversity of clinical assessment procedures.

RELIABILITY

In the most general sense **reliability** refers to consistency of measurement. **Interrater reliability**, discussed in the preceding chapter, refers to the degree to which two independent observers or judges agree. To take an example from baseball, the third-base umpire may or may not agree with the home-plate umpire as to whether a line drive down the left-field line is fair or foul. **Test-retest reliability** measures the extent to which people being observed twice or taking the same test twice, perhaps several weeks or months apart, score in generally the same way. This kind of reliability makes sense only when our theory assumes that people will not change appreciably between testings on the variable being measured; a prime example of when this type of reliability makes sense is in evaluating intelligence tests (see p. 79). Sometimes psychologists use two forms of a test rather than give the same test twice, perhaps when there is concern that people will remember their answers from the first test taking and merely aim to be consistent. This situation enables the tester to determine **alternate-form reliability**. Finally, **internal consistency reliability** assesses whether the items on a test are related to one another. For example, with an anxiety questionnaire containing twenty items we would expect the items to be inter-related, or to correlate with each other, if they are truly tapping anxiety. A person who reports a dry mouth in a threatening situation would be expected to report increases in muscle tension as well.

In each of these types of reliability, a **correlation**, a measure of how closely two variables are related (see p. 109), is calculated between raters or sets of items. The higher the correlation, the better the reliability.

Each of the assessment methods discussed thus far can be evaluated in terms of reliability. More structured, objectively scored tests typically have higher reliability because of the care taken in constructing them. Since personality inventories meet the general requirements of test construction and standardization, it is rare for such a test to lack reliability. Similarly, intelligence tests have demonstrated very good test-retest reliability; students generally receive similar scores on IQ tests taken years apart. And, although unstructured clinical interviews have low interrater reliability (that is, two interviewers are likely to reach different conclusions about the same patient), the structured inter-

Reliability is an essential property of all assessment procedures. One means of determining reliability is to find if different judges agree, as happens when two umpires witness the same event in a baseball game.

views fare much better. The reliability of projective techniques, such as the Rorschach, is more questionable. Regarding test-retest reliability, for example, situational variables have been found to be influential; it has been known for some time that warm versus cold examiners obtain different Rorschach responses (Masling, 1960). Although some scoring methods for projective tests are so inferential that it may not be possible to compare the test results from different examiners, systems such as Exner's Rorschach scoring method, discussed earlier, and the scoring of the Roberts Apperception Test have sometimes demonstrated adequate reliability (e.g., McArthur & Roberts, 1982; Parker, Hanson, & Hunsley, 1988; but see a critical review by Wood et al., 1996, for less sanguine conclusions for the Exner system).

Behavioral and cognitive assessment procedures have generally been developed from empirical research, often in laboratory settings. Thus it is to be expected that workers have been sensitive to whether, for example, behavioral raters agreed with each other when observing subjects (e.g., Paul, 1966) or whether coders of think-aloud data

achieved satisfactory levels of agreement (Davison et al., 1983).

VALIDITY

Validity is the extent to which an assessment procedure is measuring what we intend it to measure. For example, does a paper-and-pencil questionnaire believed to measure anxiety really do so? **Concurrent**, sometimes also called **descriptive, validity** concerns the extent to which scores on an assessment instrument correlate with another measure of a psychological feature that has been assessed at approximately the same point in time. An example of this type of validity would be whether the score on our anxiety questionnaire identifies people who have been designated as being highly anxious when observed interacting with others in a laboratory situation. **Predictive validity** is similar to concurrent validity, except that the measure with which it is to be compared is not available until some time in the future. For example, does our anxiety questionnaire, administered at the beginning of a college semester, predict who will do poorly on final exams because of nervousness?

Finally, perhaps the most subtle and interesting form of validity is **construct validity**. This kind of validity refers to the place of our anxiety questionnaire within a theoretical framework and can be understood only in the context of that framework. Essentially, construct validity refers to whether scores on a test, such as one measuring anxiety, are related in expected ways to a set of other variables. Using anxiety as an example, we would expect it to be related to childhood experiences, to current functioning in school, work, and social relationships, to psychophysiological variables, such as skin conductance, and to other variables that form a comprehensive theory of anxiety. If the pattern of relationships that emerges is generally what the theory predicts, then we have not only provided construct validation for the questionnaire but also support for the underlying theory. Thus construct validation is an important part of theory testing and is understandable only within the context of a theory.

Establishing the validity of assessment techniques is a critical part of justifying their use. As with reliability, since the overwhelming majority of unstructured clinical interviews are conducted within confidential relationships, it has not been possible to establish their validity through systematic research. The MMPI-2 has demonstrated adequate concurrent validity with criteria such as behavioral ratings by spouses and symptom ratings by psychiatrists and psychologists (Graham, 1988). When the Rorschach is scored using the Exner system, its validity has been found to be comparable to that of the MMPI (Parker et al., 1988), though such positive findings have been disputed by other researchers (Gann, 1995). However, many clinicians in practice use scoring systems with less adequate psychometric properties, leading to lower validity for the test in everyday use.

Most of the focus in behavioral and cognitive assessment is on construct validity because experimental research typically involves the testing of hypotheses. Thus a positive correlation between decreases in angry articulated thoughts with decreases in blood pressure both contributed to the construct validity of the articulated thoughts procedure and corroborated a hypothesis about the relationship between anger and hypertension (Davison et al., 1991).

Concurrent validity is very strong for IQ tests. For example, the revised version of the Wechsler Scale readily distinguishes between intellectually gifted and mentally retarded individuals, adults in different occupations, and individuals with different levels of educational attainment (Reynolds, Chastain, Kaufman, & McLean, 1987). Longitudinal studies support the validity of child IQ tests in predicting later occupational success (Terman, 1925; Terman & Oden, 1959) and educational attainment (Brody, 1985), and adult IQ predicts performance ratings and training success in many types of jobs (e.g., Hunter, 1986).

When evaluating the validity of a particular test or other assessment procedure it is important to remember that they are rarely given in isolation. Actual clinical assessments involve the integration of data from a variety of procedures. A self-corrective process occurs in which the practicing clinician develops hypotheses based on some initial assessment data (such as an interview) and then tests those hypotheses by examining additional data. Hypotheses that are confirmed by several sources of assessment data are likely to be given more weight by the clinician in explaining the client's behavior, reaching a diagnosis, or predicting treatment response. Validity for an entire test battery is likely to be superior to that of any one test viewed in isolation. In actual clinical practice, the norm is to use several assessment procedures, not just one.

CULTURAL DIVERSITY AND CLINICAL ASSESSMENT

Recently the reliability and validity of various forms of psychological assessment have been questioned on the grounds that their content and scoring procedures reflect the culture of white European-Americans and so do not accurately assess people from other cultures. But the issue is not a simple one, nor is it clear that such biases make the assessment instruments useless. Controlled studies of bias in testing have demonstrated that mainstream procedures, such as the Wechsler Intelligence Scale for Children—Revised, have equivalent predictive validity for minority and nonminority children (Sattler, 1992); IQ tests predict academic achievement equally well for both groups.

In addition, cultural biases work in different ways—they may cause clinicians to over- or underestimate psychological problems in members of other cultures (Lopez, 1989, 1996). African-American children are overrepresented in special education classes, which may be a result of subtle biases in the tests used to determine such placement (Artiles & Trent, in press). Yet consider the example of an Asian-American man who is very emotionally withdrawn. Should the clinician consider that lower levels of emotional expressiveness in men are viewed positively in Asian cultures as compared with the dominant Euro-American culture? In so doing, the clinician risks overlooking an emotional disorder that he or she would be likely to diagnose

Assessment must take the person's cultural background into account. Believing in possession by spirits is common in some cultures and thus should not always be taken to mean that the believer is psychotic.

if the patient were a white male by attributing the behavior to a cultural difference rather than to a psychological disorder. In short, the effect of cultural bias in clinical assessment works both ways (Lopez, 1989).

How do these biases come about? Cultural differences are many, and they may affect assessment in different ways. Language differences, cultural views of competition, differing spiritual beliefs, as well as the alienation or timidity of members of minority cultures when being assessed by clinicians of the dominant culture—all these factors can play a role. Spanish-speaking people being assessed by English-speaking clinicians may be poorly served by translators (Sabin, 1975). In Puerto Rican cultures a belief that one is surrounded by spirits is common, whereas in other cultures such a belief might be a sign of schizophrenia (Rogler & Hollingshead, 1985). Native Americans, taught by their culture to cooperate with others, are less likely to warm to the task of taking an aptitude test, which is by nature highly individualistic and competitive (O'Conner, 1989).

Although it is important to be aware of the potential of cultural differences to bias clinical assessment, it is not clear that attempting to include cultural differences in one's assessment work necessarily contributes to a helpful diagnosis. Consider the results of a survey of mental health practitioners in California (Lopez & Hernandez, 1986). In an example that echoes that of the emotionally withdrawn Asian-American man just described and that at the same time reflects sensitivity to cultural differences in religious beliefs, one clinician reported attaching less psychopathological significance to the hallucinations of an African-American woman because he believed that hallucinations were more prevalent among African-Americans. This clinician minimized the seriousness of the woman's problems by attributing them to a subcultural norm. As a result, he did not consider a diagnosis of schizophrenia, a decision that may not have been in the woman's best interests.

Cultural biases affect not only who is diagnosed but how the person is diagnosed. One study found that clinicians were more likely to diagnose a patient as schizophrenic if the case summary referred to the person as African-American than if the person were described as white (Blake, 1973). A hospital-based study found that African-American patients were overdiagnosed as schizophrenic and underdiagnosed as mood disordered (Simon et al., 1973). Another study found that based on identical symptoms, lower-class African-American patients were more likely to be diagnosed as alcoholic than

Cultural differences can lead to different results on an aptitude or IQ test. For example, Native American children may lack interest in the individualistic, competitive nature of IQ tests because of the cooperative, group oriented values instilled by their culture.

were white, middle-class patients, a fact that, given the symptoms exhibited, was a disservice to the white patients (Luepnitz, Randolph, & Gutsch, 1982).

Cultural differences cannot be avoided. As we have seen, the cultural biases that can creep into clinical assessment do not necessarily yield to efforts to compensate for them. There is no simple answer. DSM-IV's inclusion of cultural factors in the discussion of every category of disorder may well sensitize clinicians to the issue, a necessary first step. When practitioners were surveyed recently, they overwhelmingly reported taking culture into account in their clinical work (Lopez, 1994), so it appears that the problem, if not the solution, is clearly in focus.

STRATEGIES FOR AVOIDING CULTURAL BIAS IN ASSESSMENT

There are some things that clinicians can—and do—do to minimize the negative effects of cultural biases when assessing patients. Sattler (1982) makes some helpful suggestions that can guide clinicians in the selection and interpretation of tests and other assessment data. First, clinicians should make efforts to learn about the culture of the person being assessed. This knowledge might come from reading, consultation with colleagues, and direct discussion with the client. Second, it is essential for clinicians to determine the client's preferred language and to consider testing in more than one language. Multiple assessments should be conducted to test hypotheses, rather than relying on results from one instrument.

Assessment procedures can also be modified by testing the limits. For example, suppose a Native American child performs poorly on a test measuring psychomotor speed. The examiner's hunch is that the child did not understand the importance of working quickly and was overconcerned with accuracy instead. The test could be administered again after a more thorough explanation of the importance of working quickly without worrying about mistakes. If the child's performance improves, the examiner has gained an important understanding of her and avoids diagnosing "psychomotor speed deficits" when test-taking strategy is more at issue.

Finally, extra effort may be needed to gain rapport when the examiner is of a different ethnic background from the client, in order to obtain the person's best performance. For example, when testing a shy, Hispanic preschooler, one of the authors was unable to obtain a verbal response to test questions. However, the boy was overheard talking in an animated and articulate manner to his mother in the waiting room, leading to a judgment that the test results did not represent a valid assessment of his language skills. When testing was repeated in the child's own home with his mother present, advanced verbal abilities were observed.

As Lopez (1994) points out, however, "the distance between cultural responsiveness and cultural stereotyping can be short" (p. 123). To minimize such problems, clinicians are encouraged to be particularly tentative about drawing conclusions with minority patients, and to make *hypotheses* about the influence of culture on a particular client, entertain alternative hypotheses, and then test those hypotheses. In a case from our files a young man was suspected of having schizophrenia. One prominent symptom he reported was hearing voices. However, he claimed that he heard voices only while meditating and that within his (Buddhist) culture this experience was normative. To test this hypothesis the examiner (with the permission of the client) contacted the family's religious leader. The Buddhist priest indicated that the symptom reported by this young man was very unusual, and it turned out that the religious community to which he belonged was quite concerned about his increasingly bizarre behavior. Thus the hypothesis that his symptom should be attributed to cultural factors was refuted, and an underpathologizing error was avoided.

THE CONSISTENCY AND VARIABILITY OF BEHAVIOR

In this last section we address a critical question that is relevant in any form of clinical assessment: Are people consistent or variable over time? In other words, do we possess personality traits that operate in the same way in a variety of situations or do we behave differently depending on the situation? This question has prompted much debate and research, and it is of concern in any careful consideration of how to assess people and their problems in clinical settings.

Trait theorists believe that human beings can be described as having a certain amount of a characteristic, such as stinginess or obsessiveness, or, in DSM terms, as having a particular disorder. The assumption is that their thoughts, feelings, and behavior in a variety of situations can be predicted reasonably well by the degree to which they possess a particular characteristic. This paradigmatic position implies that people will behave fairly consistently in a variety of situations—a highly aggressive person, for example, will be more aggressive than someone low in aggression at home, at work, and at play.

After reviewing the evidence bearing on this question, Walter Mischel, in *Personality and Assessment* (1968), argued that, except for IQ, personality traits are not very important determinants of behavior. He concluded that the behavior of people is often not very consistent from situation to situation.

Not surprisingly, Mischel's attack on trait theory elicited a heated debate in the literature. For example, the psychodynamic theorist Paul Wachtel (1977) pointed out that the studies Mischel cited were generally done with nonpatients, whose behavior is probably more flexible than that of patients. A hallmark of mental disorder may be rigidity and inflexibility, which is another way of saying that behavior is consistent in a variety of situations. Certainly the personality disorders, discussed in Chapter 13, can be seen as extreme instances of traits that are inflexible and maladaptive. Therefore, by studying basically normal people, Mischel may have concluded that people are more variable than he might had he studied patients.

Wachtel suggested also that differing perceptions can cause people to experience similar situations differently or can render objectively different situations equivalent in their eyes. For example, a person who might be described as paranoid sees threats in routine and innocuous situations. Having one's

The work of the prominent psychologist, Walter Mischel, stimulated the current debate concerning whether traits or situations are the most powerful determinants of behavior.

credit card purchase checked for approval may be seen by an overly suspicious person as questioning his or her integrity and by a truly paranoid person as part of a sinister plot to humiliate and persecute him or her. Insensitivity to circumstances is not the person's problem; rather, this person perceives most if not all situations as containing threats. In addition, people can *elicit* certain kinds of reactions from their surroundings. The paranoid individual may not only perceive people as threatening but may make them so by attacking them first. In effect, he or she transforms different situations into similar and dangerous ones. As a result, the paranoid's own behavior varies little.

Wachtel also proposed that a personality disposition can affect the kinds of situations an individual selects or constructs for himself or herself. A generally optimistic person, for example, may seek out situations that confirm his or her positive outlook, which in turn strengthens the trait tendency to find or to construct similar sanguine situations in the future. There is a constantly reciprocating interaction then, with personality traits influencing situations the person is in and the situations in turn influencing personality. "Consistency over extended periods of time … may be the product of extended histories of choosing situations conducive to one's attitudes, traits, and dispositions" (Snyder, 1983, p. 510). Interestingly enough, Wachtel's psychodynamic speculations are consistent with social psychological research, including that of Bandura (1982), Mischel himself (1977), Snyder (1983), and Emmons and Diener (1986).

In the course of the debate touched off by Mischel's important book, other psychologists suggested that his original position was too extreme. Block (1971) challenged Mischel's conclusions regarding the inconsistency of behavior. In examining the studies Mischel used to support his claim, Block found that most of them had serious flaws. Evidence of consistency and stability of behavior was reported by Epstein (1979), who also criticized the studies used by Mischel to buttress the situationist position. Those studies, noted Epstein, looked only at small bits of behavior, a strategy as inappropriate as it would be to measure IQ by looking at a person's score on a single test item. More appropriate is an *averaging* of behavior from a range of situations. In the studies he conducted Epstein collected and averaged data on a number of occasions and was able to demonstrate marked consistency in behavior. The original views of the famous Harvard psychologist and personality theorist Gordon Allport (1937) on the importance of global traits in understanding complex human behavior are now enjoying a revival of interest as more data are collected that support the importance of personality dispositions (Funder, 1991).

In support of Mischel's concerns and somewhat reflecting Wachtel's point that well-adjusted people adapt their behavior to changing conditions, Bandura (1986) proposed that the heavy reliance of trait theorists on self-report questionnaires colors their conclusions because people may selectively perceive themselves as consistent and respond accordingly on these questionnaires. The questionnaires probe for typical behavior in poorly specified situations, for example, "Do you tend to lose your temper when you get angry?" On the other hand, if people are observed in a variety of different situations their actual behavior will show itself to be much more diverse and sensitive to environmental differences—a conclusion that can be drawn from a vast literature in social and personality psychology.

An intriguing possibility is that a belief in traits conveys predictability and perhaps gives an illusion of control. If Joe is a good guy, then we can rely on him no matter what; and if Dick is a jerk, then that too can be relied on and planned around, even if we wish he were a different sort of person. The culture also fosters a trait orientation to understanding behavior. Most of us grew up with the idea that people can be characterized as nice, good-humored, just, rotten, and so forth. It may also be the case that most of us *value* consistency in our and others' behavior even when, alas, that consistency leads us to conclude that little good is to be expected from a given individual because we judge that person to be lazy or mean.

Bandura (1986) went on to assert that Epstein and other trait theorists neglect the *functionality* of performing behavior X in situation Y, that is, whether it pays off to act a certain way in a particular situation. As a social learning theorist, Bandura focuses more than do trait theorists on the situational determinants of behavior, especially the reinforcements anticipated by the individual. "Aggressive acts by delinquents towards parish priests and rival gang members will correlate poorly, however much averaging one does" (p. 10). Mischel has recently provided data to support this notion, coming up with "if … then" statements about children in a camp setting. For example, Henry exhibits aggressive behavior if warned by adults not to, but he complies when threatened by peers. Thus there is an interaction between a tendency (trait) to be aggressive and the situation in which such behavior may or may not occur. The consequences of expressing a particular tendency, such as aggressiveness, play an important role in whether that trait becomes manifest in a given situation (Shoda, Mischel, & Wright, 1994).

Of course some situations call forth the same behavior from virtually *all* individuals; a situationalist perspective can thus sometimes lead to a traitlike prediction. For example, most people at a beach on a hot summer day are likely to wear few clothes and to swim; and most people in a library are likely to read and to speak only in hushed tones. All well and good, but a complete analysis of behavior would have to include a prediction of whether a given individual would read at the beach, daydream about the beach while sitting in a library, or even be in such a situation at all (Anastasi, 1990)! What is emerging from this sometimes contentious literature on traits versus behavioral variability is an appreciation for how personality factors *interact* with different environments, a paradigmatic perspective that overlaps considerably with the diathesis–stress viewpoint that marks our own study of psychopathology.

SUMMARY

Clinicians rely on several modes of assessment in trying to find out how best to describe a patient, search for the reasons a patient is troubled, and design effective preventive or remedial treatments. Regardless of how unstructured an assessment method may appear, it inevitably reflects the paradigm of the investigator. Our earlier discussion of scientific paradigms in Chapter 2 is important to bear in mind when considering how information is gathered in the clinical context.

The two main approaches to assessment are psychological and biological. Psychological assessments include clinical interviews, structured or relatively unstructured conversations in which the clinician probes the patient for information about his or her problems; psychological tests, which range from the presentation of ambiguous stimuli, as in the Rorschach Inkblot Test and the Thematic Apperception Test, to empirically derived self-report questionnaires, such as the Minnesota Multiphasic Personality Inventory; and intelligence tests, which evaluate a person's intellectual ability and predict how well he or she will do in future academic situations.

In behavioral and cognitive assessment, information is gathered on four sets of factors (SORC): situational determinants, organismic variables, responses, and the consequences of behavior. Whereas traditional assessment seeks to understand people in terms of general traits or personality structure, behavioral and cognitive assessment is concerned more with how people act, feel, and think in particular situations. Specificity is the hallmark of cognitive and behavioral assessment, the assumption being that by operating within this framework it is possible to gather more useful information about people. Critics believe that such data may at times be too narrow to yield conclusions that are meaningful.

Behavioral and cognitive assessment approaches include direct observation of behavior either in natural surroundings or in contrived settings; interviews and self-report measures that are situational in their focus; and specialized, think-aloud cognitive assessment procedures that attempt to uncover beliefs, attitudes, and thinking patterns thought to be important in theories of psychopathology and therapy.

Biological assessments include sophisticated, computer-controlled imaging techniques, such as CT scans, that allow us to actually see various structures of the living brain; neurochemical assays that allow inferences about levels of neurotransmitters; neuropsychological tests, such as the Halstead–Reitan, which base inferences of brain defects on variations in responses to psychological tests; and psychophysiological measurements, such as heart rate and skin conductance.

However clinicians and researchers go about gathering assessment information they must be concerned with both reliability and validity, the former referring to whether measurement is consistent and replicable, the latter to whether our assessments are tapping into what we want to be measuring. The many assessment procedures described in this chapter vary greatly in their reliability and validity.

Cultural and racial factors play a role in clinical assessment. Minority clients may react differently from whites to assessment techniques developed on the basis of research with white populations. Clinicians can have biases when evaluating minority patients, which can lead to minimizing or overdiagnosing a patient's psychopathology. Cultural differences and clinician bias are important for scientific, practical, and ethical reasons.

The stability of human behavior across situations is highly controversial. This issue has been of both theoretical and practical interest to psychologists for years. The answers are far from in, but it appears prudent to say that behavior across situations is probably more variable than was once thought by traditional personality theorists and also more stable than is believed by many of those working in the learning paradigm.

KEY TERMS

clinical interview
psychological tests
standardization
personality inventory
Minnesota Multiphasic
    Personality Inventory
    (MMPI)
projective test
projective hypothesis
Rorschach Inkblot Test
Thematic Apperception Test
intelligence test
aptitude test
behavioral observation
self-monitoring
reactivity (of behavior)
meninges
cerebral hemispheres
corpus callosum
cerebral cortex
gyri

sulci
frontal lobe
parietal lobe
temporal lobe
occipital lobe
white matter
diencephalon
hypothalamus
midbrain
brain stem
pons
medulla oblongata
cerebellum
limbic system
CT scan
magnetic resonance
    imaging (MRI)
PET scan
neurologist
neuropsychologist
neuropsychological tests

psychophysiology
somatic nervous system
autonomic nervous system
    (ANS)
sympathetic nervous system
parasympathetic nervous
    system
electrocardiogram
electrodermal responding
reliability
interrater reliability
test-retest reliability
alternate-form reliability
internal consistency
    reliability
correlation
validity
concurrent (descriptive)
    validity
predictive validity
construct validity

Roy Lichtenstein,
"Magnifying Glass," 1963

RESEARCH METHODS IN THE STUDY OF ABNORMAL BEHAVIOR

Given the different ways of conceptualizing and treating abnormal behavior and the problems in its classification and assessment, it follows that there is also less than total agreement regarding how abnormal behavior ought to be studied. Abnormal behavior has been the subject of theorizing for centuries; the field has a high ratio of speculation to data. Yet it is precisely because facts about mental disorders are hard to come by that it is important to pursue them using the scientific research methods that are applied in contemporary psychopathology. This chapter discusses these methods and should provide a sense of the strengths and limitations of each. We hope, too, that you will gain respect for the information these methods have made available and the discoveries they have made possible.

SCIENCE AND SCIENTIFIC METHODS

In Chapter 1 we described the important role subjective factors play in the collection and interpretation of data, indeed, in the very definition of what constitutes an observation. Although we often read in college textbooks of the scientific method, there is actually no one science or scientific method. In current practice **science** is the pursuit of systematized knowledge through observation. Thus the term, which comes from the Latin *scire*, "to know," refers to a method of systematic acquisition and evaluation of information and to a goal, the development of general theories that explain the information. It is always important for scientific observations and explanations to be testable (open to systematic probes) and reliable. We'll look briefly at the criteria of testability and reliability and in more depth at the key role that theory plays. Then we will examine the major research methods used in studying abnormal psychology.

TESTABILITY AND REPLICATION

A scientific approach requires first that propositions and ideas be stated in a clear and precise way. Only then can scientific claims be exposed to systematic probes and tests, any one of which could negate the scientist's expectations about what will be found. Statements, theories, and assertions, regardless of how plausible they may seem, must be testable in the public arena and subject to disproof. The attitude of the scientist must be a doubting one. It is not enough to assert, for example, that traumatic experiences during childhood may cause psychological maladjustment in adulthood. This is no more than a possibility or proposition. According to a scientific point of view, such a hypothesis must be amenable to systematic testing that could show it to be false.

Closely related to testability is the need for each observation that contributes to a scientific body of knowledge to be reliable. We have discussed the importance of reliability as it relates to diagnosis and assessment. It is equally important in the research process. Whatever is observed must be replicable; it must occur under prescribed circumstances not once, but repeatedly. An event must be reproducible under the circumstances stated, anywhere, anytime. If the event cannot be reproduced, scientists become wary of the legitimacy of the original observation.

THE ROLE OF THEORY

A **theory** is a set of propositions meant to explain a class of phenomena. The paradigms we discussed in Chapters 3 and 4 could also be considered theories of psychopathology. A primary goal of science is to advance theories to account for data, often by proposing cause–effect relationships. The results of empirical research allow the adequacy of theories to be evaluated. Theories themselves can also play an important role in guiding research by suggesting that certain additional data be collected. More specifically, a theory permits the generation of *hypotheses*, expectations about what should occur if a theory is true, to be tested in research. For example, suppose you want to test a classical-conditioning theory of phobias. As a researcher you begin by developing a specific hypothesis based on the theory. For example, if the classical-conditioning theory is valid, people with phobias should be more likely than those in the general population to have had negative experiences with the situations they fear (such as flying). By collecting data on the frequency of negative experiences with phobic stimuli among phobics and comparing this frequency to a similar one from people without phobias, you could determine whether your hypothesis was confirmed, supporting the theory, or disconfirmed, invalidating the theory.

The generation of a theory is perhaps the most challenging part of the scientific enterprise—and one of the least understood. It is sometimes asserted, for example, that a scientist formulates a theory simply by considering data that have been previously collected and then deciding, in a rather straightforward fashion, that a given way of thinking about the data is the most economical and useful.

Although some theory building follows this course, not all does. Aspects too seldom mentioned

FOCUS 5.1 CHAOS THEORY AND LIMITS ON UNDERSTANDING AND PREDICTION

...the Butterfly Effect—the notion that a butterfly stirring the air today in Peking can transform storm systems next month in New York. (Gleick, 1987, p. 8).

This quotation captures the essence of chaos theory, a position that suggests that major events (such as a storm system) may be affected by unexpected and seemingly trivial events (the air turbulence created by a flying butterfly). The chaos theory perspective argues against the ability of scientists to predict with any confidence the long-term outcomes of apparently tiny changes in events (Gleick, 1987). (In our view, chaos theory is more a paradigm than a theory.) The world is almost unfathomably complex, and we are inherently limited in what we can predict and explain. We have all experienced frustration, even annoyance, with weather reports—it is a standing joke to blame the meteorologist for favorable forecasts that turn out to be wrong. But an appreciation of the many factors that enter into the development or movement of a storm system justifies a little more tolerance of the limitations of these prognosticators.

In the human sciences it seems especially appropriate to view our task in terms of chaos theory (e.g., Duke, 1994; Gregerson & Sailer, 1993), or, as some would term it more broadly, complexity studies (Mahoney, 1991; Mahoney & Moes, in press). *Even if* we knew all the variables controlling behavior—and no one would claim that we do—our ability to predict would be limited by many unexpected and uncontrollable factors that are likely to affect a person over a period of time. People do not behave in a social vacuum any more than they can survive in a physical one. We *interact* with others all the time, and so many factors are constantly operating on these other individuals that it becomes very risky indeed to predict the social environment in which a given individual can find himself or herself. Consequently, simple cause–effect statements are exceedingly difficult to construct with confidence.

Choas theory suggests that a major storm like Hurricane Andrew can be influenced by seemingly trivial events such as the air disturbed by a flying butterfly.

As we review the theories and evidence for the causes of abnormal behavior and how to prevent or treat its occurrence we shall often encounter the complexities and shortcomings of efforts to explain and predict. Our discussions of intervention should in particular be informed by the chaos perspective because therapists have limited contact with and control over their patients, even their hospitalized patients, all of whom live their lives moment to moment in exquisitely complex interaction with others who themselves are affected on a moment to moment basis by hundreds of factors that are nigh impossible to anticipate, let alone to influence. This is not an embracing of chaos as a goal—we are not scientific nihilists. Rather, it is to counsel a modicum of humility, even awe, in an enterprise that would presume to try to understand the vagaries of the human condition, especially when things go awry.

---

are the *creativity* of the act and the *excitement* of finding a novel way to conceptualize things. A theory sometimes seems to leap from the scientist's head in a wonderful moment of insight. New ideas suddenly occur and connections previously overlooked are suddenly grasped. What formerly seemed obscure or meaningless makes a new kind of sense within the framework of the new theory.

Theories are *constructions* of scientists. In formulating a theory scientists must often make use of theoretical concepts, unobservable states or processes that are inferred from observable data. Repression is a theoretical concept, as is the mediating fear-response discussed in Chapter 2. Theoretical concepts are inferred from observable data. For example, behaviorists infer a mediating fear-response based on the avoidance of a situation. Similarly, an analyst might infer the presence of a repressed conflict from a patient's continual avoidance of discussing his or her relationship with authority figures.

Several advantages may be gained by using theoretical terms. Theoretical concepts often bridge spatiotemporal relations. For example, in early physics it was noted that a magnet placed close to some iron filings caused some of the filings to move toward it. How does one piece of metal influence another over the spatial distance? The inferred con-

A theoretical concept like acquired fear is useful in accounting for the fact that some earlier experience can have an effect on current behavior.

cept of magnetic fields proved useful in accounting for this phenomenon. Similarly, in abnormal psychology we may want to bridge temporal gaps with theoretical concepts. If a child has had a particularly frightening experience and his or her behavior changes for a lengthy period of time we need to explain how the earlier event exerted an influence over subsequent behavior. The unobservable and inferred concept of *acquired fear* has been very helpful in this regard.

Theoretical concepts may also be used to summarize already observed relationships. We may observe that people who are taking an examination, who expect a momentary electric shock, or who are arguing with a companion all have sweaty palms, trembling hands, and a fast heartbeat. If we ask them how they feel, they all report that they are tense. The relationships can be depicted as shown in Figure 5.1*a*. We could also say that all the situations have made these individuals anxious and that anxiety has in turn caused the reported tension, the sweaty palms, the faster heartbeat, and the trembling hands. Figure 5.1*b* shows anxiety as a theoretical concept explaining what has been observed. The first figure is much more complex than the second, in which the theoretical concept of anxiety becomes a mediator of the relationships.

With these advantages in mind we must consider the criteria to be applied in judging the legitimacy of a theoretical concept. One earlier school of thought, the operationist, proposed that each concept take as its meaning a single observable and measurable operation. In this way each theoretical concept would be nothing more than one particular measurable event. For example, anxiety might be

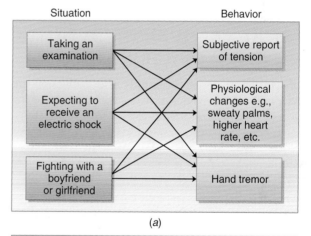

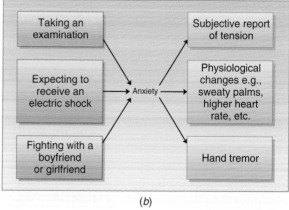

Figure 5.1 An illustration of the advantages of using anxiety as a theoretical concept. The arrows in (*b*) are fewer and more readily understood. After Miller (1959).

identified as *nothing more* than scoring 50 on an anxiety questionnaire. It soon became clear that this approach deprived theoretical concepts of their greatest advantage. If each theoretical concept is *operationalized* in only one way, its generality is lost. If the theoretical concept of learning, for instance, is identified as a *single* operation or effect that can be measured, such as how often a rat presses a bar, other behavior, such as a child performing arithmetic problems or a college student studying this book, cannot also be called learning, and attempts to relate the different phenomena to one another might be discouraged. The early operationistic point of view quickly gave way to the more flexible position that a theoretical concept can be defined by *sets* of operations or effects. In this way the concept may be linked to several different measurements, each of which taps a different facet of the concept. For example, in Figure 5.1*b* a subjective report of tension, physiological changes, and hand trembling are a set of operations defining anxiety. Theoretical concepts are better defined by sets of operations, rather than by a single operation.

THE RESEARCH METHODS OF ABNORMAL PSYCHOLOGY

All empirical research entails the collection of observable data. Sometimes research remains at a purely descriptive level, but often researchers observe several events and try to determine how they are associated or related. In the field of abnormal psychology there is a large descriptive literature concerning the typical symptoms of people who have been diagnosed as having particular disorders. These symptoms can then be related to other characteristics, such as gender or social class; for example, eating disorders are more common in women than in men. But science demands more than descriptions of relationships. We often want to understand the *causes* of the relationships we have observed. For example, we want to know *why* eating disorders are found more often in women than in men.

In this section we describe the most commonly used research methods in the study of abnormal behavior: the case study; epidemiological research; the correlational method; and various types of experiments. The methods vary in the degree to which they permit the collection of adequate descriptive data and the extent to which they allow researchers to infer causal relationships.

THE CASE STUDY

The most familiar and time-honored method of observing others is to study them one at a time and record detailed information about them. A clinician

prepares a **case study** by collecting historical and biographical information on a single individual, often including experiences in therapy. A comprehensive case study would cover family history and background, medical history, educational background, jobs held, marital history, and details concerning development, adjustment, personality, the life course, and the current situation. Important to bear in mind, though, is the role of the clinician's paradigm in determining the kinds of information actually collected and reported in a case study. To take but one example, case studies of psychoanalytically oriented clinicians contain more information about the client's early childhood and conflicts with parents than do reports made by behaviorally oriented practitioners.

Case studies from practicing clinicians may lack the degree of control and objectivity of research using other methods, but these descriptive histories have played an important role in the study of abnormal behavior. Specifically, the case study has been used in the following ways: (1) to provide a detailed description of a rare or unusual phenomenon and of important, often novel, methods or procedures of interviewing, diagnosis, and treatment; (2) to disconfirm allegedly universal aspects of a particular theoretical proposition; and (3) to generate hypotheses that can be tested through controlled research (Davison & Lazarus, 1994).

PROVIDING DETAILED DESCRIPTION

Because it deals with a single individual the case study can include much more detail than other research methods typically include. In a famous case history of multiple personality reported in 1954, two psychiatrists, Thigpen and Cleckley, described a patient, Eve White, who assumed at various times three very distinct personalities. Their description of the case required an entire book, *The Three Faces of Eve*. The following brief summary emphasizes the moments in which new personalities emerged and what the separate selves knew of one another.

Eve White had been seen in psychotherapy for several months because she was experiencing severe headaches accompanied by blackouts. Her therapist described her as a retiring and gently conventional figure. One day during the course of an interview, however, she changed abruptly and in a surprising way.

As if seized by sudden pain, she put both hands to her head. After a tense moment of silence, both hands dropped. There was a quick, reckless smile, and, in a bright voice that sparkled, she said, "Hi there, Doc!" The demure and constrained posture of Eve White had melted into buoyant repose. … This new and apparently carefree girl spoke casually of Eve White and her problems, always using she or her in every reference, always respecting the strict bounds of a separate identity. … When asked her name, she immediately replied, "Oh, I'm Eve Black." (p. 137)

After this rather startling revelation, Eve was observed over a period of fourteen months in a series of interviews that ran to almost a hundred hours. A very important part of Eve White's therapy was to help her learn about Eve Black, her other, infectiously exuberant self, who added seductive and expensive clothing to her wardrobe and lived unremembered episodes of her life. During this period still a third personality, Jane, emerged, while Eve White was recollecting an early incident in which she had been painfully scalded by water from a wash pot.

Jane, who from then on knew all that happened to the two Eves, although they did not share in her existence, was "far more mature, more vivid, more boldly capable, and more interesting than Eve White." She also developed a deep and revering affection for the first Eve, who was considered somewhat of a ninny by Eve Black. Jane knew nothing of Eve White's earlier life, except as she learned of it through Eve's memories.

Some eleven months later, in a calamitous session with all three personalities present at different times, Eve Black emerged and reminisced for a moment about the many good times she had had in the past but then remarked that she did not seem to have real fun anymore. She began to sob, the only time Dr. Thigpen had seen her in tears. She told him that she wanted him to have her red dress to remember her by. All expression left her face and her eyes closed. Eve White opened them. When Jane was summoned a few minutes later, she soon realized that there was no longer any Eve White either and began to experience a terrifying lost event. "No, no! … Oh no, Mother … I can't … Don't make me do it," she cried. Jane, who earlier had known nothing of Eve's childhood, was five years old and at her grandmother's funeral. Her mother was holding her high off the floor and above the coffin and saying that she must touch her grandmother's face. As she felt her hand leave the clammy cheek, the young woman screamed so piercingly that Dr. Cleckley came running from his office across the hall.

The two physicians were not certain who confronted them. In the searing intensity of the remembered moment a new personality had been welded. Their transformed patient did not at first feel herself as apart, and as sharply distinct a person, as had the two Eves and Jane, although she knew a great deal about all of them. When her initial bewilderment lessened, she tended to identify herself with Jane. But the identification was not sure or complete, and she mourned the absence of the two Eves as though they were lost sisters. This new person decided to call herself Mrs. Evelyn White.

The case of Eve White, Eve Black, Jane, and eventually Evelyn constitutes a valuable classic in the literature because it is one of only a few detailed accounts of a rare phenomenon, multiple personality, now known as dissociative identity disorder. Moreover, in addition to illustrating the phenomenon itself, the original report of Thigpen and Cleckley provides valuable details about the interview procedures that they followed and how the treatment progressed in this one case of multiple personality.

However, the validity of the information gathered in a case study is sometimes questionable. Chris Sizemore's book, *I'm Eve* (Sizemore & Pittillo, 1977), indicates the incompleteness of Thigpen and Cleckley's case study. This woman—the real Eve White—claims that following her period of therapy with them her personality continued to fragment. In all, twenty-one separate and distinct strangers came to inhabit her body at one time or another. Contrary to Thigpen and Cleckley's report, Sizemore main-

Chris Sizemore was the woman who was the subject of the famous "three faces of Eve" case. She subsequently claimed to actually have had twenty-one separate personalities.

tains that nine of them existed before Eve Black ever appeared. One set of personalities—they usually came in threes—would weaken and fade, to be replaced by others. Eventually her personality changes were so constant and numerous that she might become her three persons in rapid switches resembling the flipping of television channels. The debilitating round robin of transformations and the fierce battle for dominance among her selves filled her entire life. After resolving what she hoped was her last trio, by realizing finally that her alternate personalities were true aspects of herself rather than strangers from without, Chris Sizemore decided to reveal her story as a means of minimizing the past.

DISCONFIRMING EVIDENCE

Case histories can provide especially telling instances that negate an assumed universal relationship or law. Consider, for example, the proposition that episodes of depression are *always* preceded by an increase in life stress. Finding even a single case in which this is not true would negate the theory or at least force it to be changed to assert that only *some* episodes of depression are triggered by stress.

The case study fares less well in providing evidence *in favor of* a particular theory or proposition. In the presentation of a case study the means for ruling out alternative hypotheses are usually absent. To illustrate this lack of validity, let us consider a clinician who has developed a new treatment for depression, tries it out on a client, and observes that the depression lifts after ten weeks of the therapy. Although it would be tempting to conclude that the therapy worked, such a conclusion cannot be drawn because any of several other factors could also have produced the change. A stressful situation in the patient's life may have resolved itself, or perhaps (and there is evidence for this) episodes of depression are naturally time-limited. Thus there are several plausible rival hypotheses that could account for the clinical improvement. The data yielded by the case study do not allow us to determine the true cause of the change.

GENERATING HYPOTHESES

Although the case study may not play much of a role in confirming hypotheses, it does play a unique and important role in generating them. Through exposure to the life histories of a great number of patients, clinicians gain experience in understanding and interpreting them. Eventually they may notice similarities of circumstances and outcomes

and formulate important hypotheses that could not have been uncovered in a more controlled investigation. For example, in his clinical work with disturbed children Kanner (1943) noticed that some of them showed a similar constellation of symptoms, including failure to develop language and extreme isolation from other people. He therefore proposed the existence of a new diagnosis—infantile autism—which was subsequently confirmed by larger scale research and eventually found its way into the DSM (see Chapter 15).

The case study is an excellent way of examining the behavior of a single individual in great detail and in generating hypotheses that can later be evaluated by controlled research. It is useful in clinical settings, where the focus is on just one person. In the fields of clinical and personality psychology some investigators argue that the essence of psychological studies always lies in the unique characteristics of an individual (e.g., Allport, 1961). The case history is an ideal method of study in such an individualistic context. But when general, universal laws are sought to explain phenomena, the case study is of limited usefulness. Information collected on a single person may *not* reveal principles that are characteristic of people in general. Furthermore, the case study is unable to provide satisfactory evidence concerning cause–effect relationships.

EPIDEMIOLOGICAL RESEARCH

Epidemiology is the study of the frequency and distribution of a disorder in a population. In epidemiological research, data are gathered about the rates of disorder and its possible correlates in a large sample or population. This information can then be used to give a general picture of a disorder, how many people it affects, whether it is more common in men than in women, and whether its occurrence also varies according to social and cultural factors. Epidemiological research focuses on determining the **prevalence** of a disorder, the proportion of a population that has the disorder at a given point or period of time; its **incidence**, the number of new cases of the disorder that occur in some period, usually a year; and **risk factors**, conditions or variables that, if present, increase the likelihood of developing the disorder. Knowledge of risk factors often gives clues to the causes of the disorder being studied. For example, depression is about twice as common in women than in men. Thus gender is a risk factor for depression. In Chapter 10, we will see that knowledge of this risk factor has led to a theory of depression that suggests it is due to a particular

In some epidemiological research, interviewers go to homes in a community, conducting interviews to determine the rates of different disorders.

TABLE 5.1   Lifetime Prevalence Rates (%) of Selected Diagnoses

	Male	Female	Total
Major depressive episode	12.7	21.3	17.1
Manic episode	1.6	1.7	1.6
Dysthymia	4.8	8.0	6.4
Panic disorder	2.0	5.0	3.5
Agoraphobia w/o panic	3.5	7.0	5.3
Social phobia	11.1	15.5	13.3
Simple phobia	6.7	15.7	11.3
Generalized anxiety disorder	3.6	6.6	5.1
Alcohol dependence	20.1	8.2	14.1
Antisocial personality disorder	5.8	1.2	3.5

Source: From data collected in the National Comorbidity Survey (Kessler et al., 1994).

style of coping with stress that is more common in women than in men.

Knowledge of prevalence rates of various mental disorders is important for planning health care facilities and for the allocation of federal grants for their study. Such information was collected in a significant, large-scale, national survey that used structured interviews to collect the information needed to make diagnoses (Kessler et al., 1994). Some data from this study are displayed in Table 5.1. The table presents what are called **lifetime prevalence rates**, the proportion of the sample that had ever experienced a disorder up to the time of the interview. We will make use of the Kessler data throughout this book.

As noted earlier, epidemiological research can also contribute to understanding the causes of illness. A classic example comes from a study by an early epidemiologist, John Snow. During an outbreak of cholera in London, Snow was able to determine how the disease had spread and finally, how to stop it. As he examined cases he learned that most victims drank water from one source, the Broad Street pump. He then hypothesized that cholera was transmitted by contaminated water. He investigated further and showed that rates of the disease were higher in London than in upstream communities where the water was cleaner. Numerous contemporary examples also attest to the importance of epidemiological research in understanding disease. As we will see in Chapter 8, the various risk factors for heart disease (e.g., smoking, high cholesterol) were discovered in large-scale studies comparing rates of disease in persons with and without the risk factor. As another example, schizophrenia is much more frequent in the lowest social class. Again, if the cause of this relationship—it might be stress, poor nutrition, lack of medical attention—were known, it might provide clues to the etiology of the disorder. Similarly, epidemiological research has shown that schizophrenia has a more favorable prognosis in developing than in industrialized countries. This finding could provide clues as to what factors are relevant to improving the prognosis of this very debilitating disorder. Epidemiological research may thus provide empirical results that offer hypotheses to be more thoroughly investigated using other methods.

THE CORRELATIONAL METHOD

A great deal of research in psychopathology relies on the **correlational method**, which establishes whether there is a relationship between or among two or more variables. In correlational research the variables being studied are measured as they exist in nature. This feature distinguishes this method from experimental research, in which variables are actually manipulated and controlled by the researcher. Numerous examples of correlation can be drawn from everyday life. Education correlates with income; the greater the educational level attained, the greater the earning power. Height tends to be positively correlated with weight; taller people are usually heavier.

The correlational method is often employed in epidemiological research as well as in other studies that use smaller samples. Correlational studies address questions of the form "Are variable X and variable Y associated in some way so that they vary together (co-relate)?" In other words, questions are asked concerning relationships; for example, "Is schizophrenia related to social class?" or "Are scores obtained on college examinations related to anxiety?"

MEASURING CORRELATION

The first step in determining a correlation is to obtain pairs of observations of the variables in question, such as height and weight, on each member of a group of subjects (Table 5.2). Once such pairs of observations are obtained the strength of the relationship between the two sets of observations can be computed to determine the **correlation coefficient**, denoted by the symbol r. This statistic may take any value between -1.00 and $+1.00$ and measures both the magnitude and the direction of a relationship. The higher the absolute value of r, the larger or stronger the relationship between the two variables. An r of either $+1.00$ or -1.00 indicates the highest possible, or perfect, relationship, whereas an r of .00 indicates that the variables are unrelated.

If the sign of r is positive, the two variables are said to be *positively related*. In other words, as the values for variable X increase, those for variable Y also tend to increase. The correlation between height and weight, based on the data in Table 5.2, is $+.88$, indicating a very strong positive relationship; as height increases so does weight. Conversely, when the sign of r is negative, variables are said to be negatively related; as scores on one variable increase those for the other tend to decrease. For example, the number of hours spent watching television is negatively correlated with grade point average.

Plotting a relationship graphically often helps make it clearer. Figure 5.2 presents diagrams of positive and negative correlations as well as unrelated variables. In the diagrams each point corresponds to two values determined for the given subject, the value of variable X and that of variable Y. In perfect relationships all the points fall on a straight line; if we know the value of only one of the variables for an individual, we can state with certainty the value of the other variable. Similarly, when the correlation is relatively large there is only a small degree of scatter about the line of perfect correlation. The values tend to scatter increasingly and become dispersed as the correlations become lower. When the correlation reaches .00, knowledge of a person's score on one variable tells us nothing about his or her score on the other.

STATISTICAL SIGNIFICANCE

Thus far we have established that the magnitude of a correlation coefficient tells us the strength of a relationship between two variables. But scientists demand a more rigorous evaluation of the importance of correlations and use the concept of statistical significance for this purpose. Essentially, **statistical significance** refers to the likelihood that the results of an investigation are due to chance. A statistically significant correlation is one that is *not* likely to have occurred by chance.

Traditionally in psychological research a correlation is considered statistically significant if the likelihood is 5 or less in 100 that it is a chance finding. This level of significance is called the .05 level, commonly written as $p \le .05$. In general, as the size of the correlation coefficient increases, the result is more and more likely to be statistically significant. For example, a correlation of .80 is more likely to be significant than one of .40. Whether a correlation attains statistical significance also depends on the number of observations made. The greater the number of observations, the smaller r needs to be in order to reach statistical significance. Thus a corre-

TABLE 5.2 Data for Determining a Correlation[a]

Individuals	Height	Weight, pounds
John	5'10"	170
Asher	5'10"	140
Eve	5'4"	112
Gail	5'3"	105
Jerry	5'10"	177
Gayla	5'2"	100
Steve	5'8"	145
Margy	5'5"	128
Gert	5'6"	143
Sean	5'10"	140
Kathleen	5'4"	116

[a]For these figures $r = +.88$

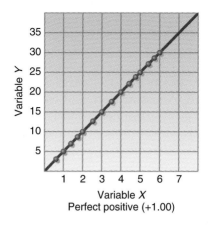

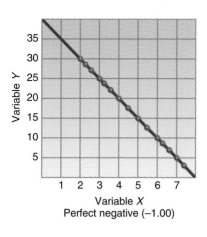

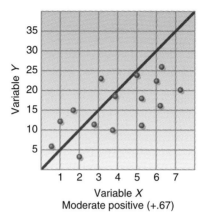

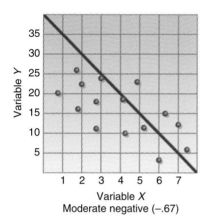

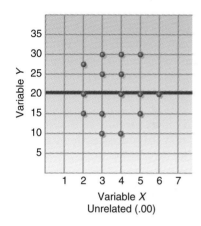

Figure 5.2 Scatter diagrams showing various degrees of correlational relationship.

lation of *r* = .30 is statistically significant when the number of observations is large, for example, 300, although it would not be significant if only 20 observations were made. If the alcohol consumption of 10 depressed and 10 nondepressed men was studied and the correlation between depression and drinking was found to be .32, the correlation would not be statistically significant. However, the same correlation would be significant if two groups of 150 men were studied.

APPLICATIONS TO PSYCHOPATHOLOGY

The correlational method is widely used in the field of abnormal psychology. Whenever we compare people given one diagnosis with those given another or with normal people, the study is correlational. For example, two diagnostic groups may be compared to see how much stress members of each experienced before the onset of their disorders. Or normal people and people with an anxiety disorder may be compared on their physiological reactivity to a stressor administered in the laboratory. When the correlational method is used in research on psychopathology one of the variables is diagnosis, for

example, being diagnosed as having an anxiety disorder or not. To calculate a correlation between this variable and another one, diagnosis is quantified so that having an anxiety disorder is designated by a score of 1 and not having a disorder by 2. The diagnosis variable can then be correlated with another variable, such as the amount of stress that has been recently experienced.

Often such investigations are not recognized as correlational, perhaps because—as is often the case in experiments—subjects come to a laboratory for testing or data are analyzed by comparing the average scores of the groups on each test or measure. But the logic of such studies is correlational; the correlation between two variables—having an anxiety disorder or not and the average score of each group on the physiological measure—is what is being examined. Variables such as having an anxiety disorder or not are called **classificatory variables**. In this case the anxiety disorders were already present before the subjects performed the laboratory task. Other examples of classificatory variables are age, sex, social class, and body build. These variables are naturally occurring patterns and are not manipulated by the researcher, an important requirement for the experimental variables discussed later. Thus, most research on the causes of psychopathology is correlational.

DIRECTIONALITY AND THIRD-VARIABLE PROBLEMS

The correlational method, although often employed in abnormal psychology, has a critical drawback. It does not allow us to determine cause–effect relationships. A sizable correlation between two variables tells us only that they are related or tend to co-vary with each other, but we do not really know which is cause and which is effect. For example, correlations have been found between the diagnosis of schizophrenia and social class; lower-class people are more frequently diagnosed as schizophrenic than are middle- and upper-class people. One possible explanation is that the stresses of living in the lowest social class produce the behavior that is subsequently labeled schizophrenic. But a second and perhaps equally plausible hypothesis has been advanced. It may be that the disorganized behavior patterns of schizophrenic individuals cause them to lose their jobs and thus to become impoverished. The **directionality problem**, as it is sometimes called, is present in many correlational research designs, hence the often-cited dictum "Correlation does not imply causation."

Although correlation does not imply causation, determining whether or not two variables correlate may allow for the disconfirmation of certain causal hypotheses. That is, causation does imply correlation. For example, if an investigator has asserted that cigarette smoking causes lung cancer, he or she implies that lung cancer and smoking will be correlated. Studies of these two variables must show this positive correlation or the theory will be disconfirmed.

One way of overcoming the directionality problem in studying the causes of psychopathology is by using a longitudinal design in which variables of interest are studied before a disorder has developed. In this way the hypothesized cause can be measured before the effect. The most desirable way of collecting information about the development of schizophrenia, for example, would be to select a large sample of babies and follow them for the twenty to forty-five years that are the period of risk for the onset of schizophrenia. But such a method would be prohibitively expensive, for only about one individual in one hundred eventually becomes schizophrenic. The yield of data from such a simple longitudinal study would be small indeed. The **high-risk method** overcomes this problem; only individuals with greater than average risk of becoming schizophrenic in adulthood are selected for study. In most current research using this methodology, individuals who have a schizophrenic parent are selected for study—a schizophrenic parent increases a person's risk for developing schizophrenia. The high-risk method is also used to study several other disorders, and we will examine these findings in subsequent chapters.

Another drawback to interpreting correlational findings is called the **third variable** problem; the correlation may have been produced by a third, unforeseen factor. Consider the following example, which points out an obvious third variable.

One regularly finds a high positive correlation between the number of churches in a city and the number of crimes committed in that city. That is, the more churches a city has, the more crimes are committed in it. Does this mean that religion fosters crime, or does it mean that crime fosters religion? It means neither. The relationship is due to a particular third variable—population. The higher the population of a particular community, the greater … the number of churches and … the frequency of criminal activity (Neale & Liebert, 1980, p. 109).

In psychopathology research there are numerous examples of third variables. Biochemical differences between schizophrenics and normals have frequently been reported. These differences could reflect different diets or the fact that the patients are taking medication for their conditions—the differences do not reveal anything telling about the nature of schizophrenia. Are there any solutions to the third-variable problem? In general, the answer is yes, although the solutions are only partially satisfactory and do not permit unambiguous causal inferences to be made from correlational data.

We have already noted that facts about the causes of abnormal behavior are hard to come by. The issues we have just discussed are major reasons for this state of affairs. The psychopathologist is forced to make heavy use of the correlational method because diagnosis, a classificatory variable, is best suited to this strategy. But the relationships discovered between diagnosis and other variables are then clouded by the third-variable and directionality problems. Searching for the causes of the various psychopathologies will continue to be a challenging enterprise.

THE EXPERIMENT

The factors causing the associations and relationships revealed by correlational research cannot, as we have seen, be determined with absolute certainty. The **experiment** is generally considered to be the most powerful tool for determining causal relationships between events. It involves the manipulation of an independent variable, the measurement of a dependent variable, and the random assignment of subjects to the different conditions being investigated. In the field of psychopathology the experiment is most often used to evaluate the effects of therapies. As an introduction to the basic components of experimental research, let us consider here the major aspects of the design and results of a study of how expressing emotions about past traumatic events is related to health (Pennebaker, Kielcolt-Glaser, & Glaser, 1988). In this experiment, fifty undergraduates participated in a six-week study, one part of which required them to come to a laboratory for four consecutive days. On each of the four days half the students wrote a short essay about a past traumatic event. They were instructed as follows:

During each of the four writing days, I want you to write about the most traumatic and upsetting experiences of your entire life. You can write on different topics each day or on the same topic for all four days. The important thing is that you write about your deepest thoughts and feelings. Ideally, whatever you write about should deal with an event or experience that you have not talked with others about in detail.

The remaining students also came to the laboratory each day but wrote essays describing such things as their daily activities, a recent social event, the shoes they were wearing, and their plans for the rest of the day. Information about how often the participating undergraduates used the university health center was available for the fifteen-week period before the study began and for the six weeks after it had begun. These data are shown in Figure 5.3. Members of the two groups had visited the health center about equally prior to the experiment. After writing the essays, however, the number of

visits declined for students who wrote about traumas and increased for the remaining students. (This increase may have been due to seasonal variation in rates of visits to the health center. The second measure of number of visits was taken in February, just before midterm exams.) From these data the investigators concluded that expressing emotions has a beneficial effect on health.

BASIC FEATURES OF EXPERIMENTAL DESIGN

The foregoing example illustrates many of the basic features of an experiment. The researcher typically begins with an **experimental hypothesis**, what he or she assumes will happen when a particular variable is manipulated. Pennebaker and his colleagues hypothesized that expressing emotion about a past event would improve health. Second, the investigator chooses an **independent variable** that can be manipulated, that is, some factor that will be under the control of the experimenter. In the case of the Pennebaker study, some students wrote about past traumatic events and others about mundane happenings. Third, the researcher arranges for the measurement of a **dependent variable**, which is expected to depend on or vary with manipulations of the independent variable. The dependent variable in this study was the number of visits to the health center. When differences between groups are found to be a function of variations in the independent variable, the researcher is said to have produced an **experimental effect**.

INTERNAL VALIDITY

An important feature of any experimental design is the inclusion of at least one **control group** that does not receive the experimental treatment (the independent variable). A control group is necessary if the effects in an experiment are to be attributed to the manipulation of the independent variable. In the Pennebaker et al. study the control group wrote about mundane happenings. The data from the control group provided a standard against which the effects of expressing emotion could be compared.

To illustrate this point with another example, consider a study of the effectiveness of a particular therapy in modifying some form of abnormal behavior. Let us assume that persons with high anxiety undergo therapy to remedy their condition. Note that there is no control group in this hypothetical study, so it is not an experiment. At the end of six months the patients are reassessed, and it is found that their anxiety has lessened compared with what it was at the beginning of the study. Unfortunately, if there is no control group against

Figure 5.3 Health center illness visits for the periods before and during the experiment. After Pennebaker et al. (1987).

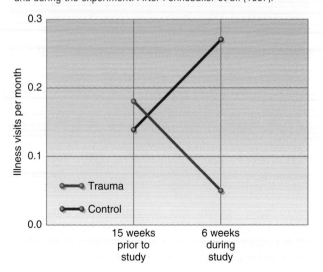

which to compare the improvement, such an investigation would not allow a valid conclusion to be drawn. The improvement in anxiety from the beginning of the treatment to the end could have been brought about by several factors in addition to or instead of the treatment employed. For example, environmental events, such as the resolution of a difficult financial situation occurring within the six months, could have produced the improvement. Or, it may be that people with high anxiety come to feel less tense with the mere passage of time.

Variables such as a change in one's life situation or the passage of time are often called **confounds**; their effects are intermixed with those of the independent variable and, like the third variables in correlational studies, they make the results difficult or impossible to interpret. These confounds and others described in this chapter are widespread in research on the effects of psychotherapy, as is documented often throughout this book. Studies in which the effect obtained cannot be attributed with confidence to the independent variable are called *internally invalid* studies. In contrast, research has **internal validity** when the effect can be confidently attributed to the manipulation of the independent variable.

In the example just outlined internal validity could be improved by the inclusion of a control group. Such a group might consist of individuals with high levels of anxiety who do *not* receive the therapeutic treatment. Changes in anxiety of these control subjects would constitute a standard against which the effects of the independent variable could be assessed. If a change in anxiety is brought about by particular environmental events, quite beyond any therapeutic intervention, the experimental group receiving the treatment and the control group receiving no treatment are equally likely to be affected. On the other hand, if after six months the anxiety level of the treated group has lessened more than that of the untreated control group, we can be relatively confident that this difference is attributable to the treatment.

The inclusion of a control group does not ensure internal validity, however. To illustrate, let us consider another study of therapy, this time the treatment of two hospital wards of psychiatric patients. An investigator may decide to select one ward to receive an experimental treatment and another ward as a control. When the researcher later compares the frequencies of deviant behavior in these two groups, he or she will want to attribute any differences between them to the fact that patients in one ward received treatment and those in the other did not. But the researcher cannot legitimately draw this inference, for there is a competing hypothesis that cannot be disproved—that even before treat-

ment the patients who happened to receive therapy might have had a lower level of deviant behavior than the patients who became the control group. The principle of experimental design disregarded in this defective study is that of **random assignment**, a technique that ensures that every participant in the research has an equal chance of being assigned to any of the groups. For example, in a two-group experiment a coin can be tossed for each participant. If the coin turns up heads, the participant is assigned to one group; if tails, he or she is assigned to the other. This procedure minimizes the likelihood that differences between the groups after treatment will reflect pretreatment differences in the samples rather than true experimental effects. Random assignment was employed in the Pennebaker experiment described earlier.

Even with both a control group and random assignment, the results of the research may still be invalid. An additional source of error is the potential biasing influence of the experimenter or observers (Rosenthal, 1966). The researcher might subtly manipulate the subject to give expected and desired responses. Although the pervasiveness of these effects has been questioned (Barber & Silver, 1968; Kent et al., 1974), experimenters must remain on guard lest their results be influenced by their own expectations. To avoid biases of this type, many studies apply the **double-blind procedure**. For example, in an investigation comparing the treatment effects of two drugs, the person dispensing the pills is kept ignorant (i.e., blind) of their actual content, and the participant is also not informed about the treatment he or she is receiving. With such controls the behavior observed during the course of the treatment is probably not influenced by bias.

Earlier we briefly defined the term *experimental effect*, but we have yet to learn how to decide that an effect is important. To evaluate the importance of experimental results, as with correlations, researchers determine their statistical significance, using the same logic as with correlations.

EXTERNAL VALIDITY

The extent to which the results of any particular piece of research can be generalized beyond the immediate experiment is the measure of **external validity**. If investigators have demonstrated that a particular treatment helps a group of patients, they will undoubtedly want to conclude that this treatment will be effective in ministering to other patients, at other times, and at other places. Pennebaker and his colleagues would hope that their findings would generalize to other instances of emotional expression (e.g., confiding to a close friend), to other situations, and to people other than those who actually participated in the experiment.

Determining the external validity of the results of a psychological experiment is extremely difficult. For example, merely knowing that one is a subject in a psychological experiment often alters behavior, and thus results are produced in the laboratory that may not automatically be produced in the natural environment. In many instances results obtained from investigations with laboratory animals, such as rats, have been generalized to human beings. Such generalizations are risky since there are enormous differences between *Homo sapiens* and *Rattus norvegicus*. Researchers must be alert to the extent to which they claim generalization for findings for there are no entirely adequate ways of dealing with the questions of external validity. The best that can be done is to perform similar studies in new settings with new participants so that the limitations, or the generality, of a finding can be determined.

ANALOGUE EXPERIMENTS

The experimental method is judged to be the most telling way to determine cause–effect relationships. The effectiveness of treatments for psychopathology is usually evaluated by the experimental method, for it has proved a powerful tool for determining whether a therapy reduces suffering. As noted earlier, however, this method has in fact been little used by those seeking the causes of abnormal behavior. Suppose that a researcher has hypothesized that a child's emotionally charged, overdependent relationship with his or her mother causes generalized anxiety disorder. An experimental test of this hypothesis would require assigning infants randomly to either of two groups of mothers! The mothers in one group would undergo an extensive training program to ensure that they would be able to create a highly emotional atmosphere and foster overdependence in children. The mothers in the second group would be trained not to create such a relationship with the children under their care. The researcher would then wait until the subjects in each group reached adulthood and determine how many of them had developed generalized anxiety disorder. Obviously such an experimental design already contains insurmountable practical problems. But practical issues are hardly the principal ones that must concern us. Consider the ethics of such an experiment. Would the potential scientific gain of proving that an overdependent relationship with a person's mother brings on generalized anxiety disorder outweigh the suffering that would surely be imposed on some of the participants? In

almost any person's view it would not. (Ethical issues are considered in detail in Chapter 20.)

In an effort to take advantage of the power of the experimental method, research on the causes of abnormal behavior has sometimes taken the format of an **analogue experiment**. Investigators attempt to bring a *related* phenomenon, that is, an analogue, into the laboratory for more intensive study. Because a true experiment can now be conducted, results can be obtained that are interpretable in cause–effect terms. However, the problem of external validity may be accentuated because the actual phenomenon in which the researchers are interested is not being studied. In one type of analogue study, behavior is rendered temporarily abnormal through experimental manipulations. For example, lactate infusion can elicit a panic attack, hypnotic suggestion can produce blindness, and threats to self-esteem can increase anxiety and depression. If pathology can be experimentally induced by any one of these manipulations, the same process existing in the natural environment *might* well be a cause of the disorder. The key to interpreting such studies lies in the validity of the independent variable as a reflection of some experience one might actually

Harlow's famous analog research examined the effects of early separation from the mother on infant monkeys. Even a cloth surrogate mother is better than isolation for preventing subsequent emotional distress and depression.

have in real life and of the dependent variable as an analogue of a clinical problem. Is a stressor that is encountered in the laboratory fundamentally similar to one that occurs in the natural environment? Are transient increases in anxiety or depression reasonable analogues of their clinical counterparts? Results of such experiments must be interpreted with great caution and generalized with care, but they do provide valuable hypotheses about the origins of psychopathology.

In another type of analogue study, subjects are selected because they are considered similar to patients given certain diagnoses. A large amount of research, for example, has been conducted with college students who were selected for study because they scored high on a questionnaire measure of anxiety or depression. The question is whether these anxious or depressed students are adequate analogues for those with an anxiety disorder or major depression. Some research bearing on this issue is discussed in Chapter 10.

Whether experiments are regarded as analogues depends not on the experiment itself but rather on the use to which it is put. We can very readily study avoidance behavior in a white rat. The data collected from such studies are not analogue data if we limit our discussion to the behavior of rats. They become analogue data only when we draw implications from them and apply them to other domains, such as anxiety in human beings.

Some of the animal experiments we have already examined are analogue in nature. For example, in Chapter 2 we described research on avoidance learning in rats that was very influential in formulating theories of anxiety in humans. It is important to keep in mind that we are arguing by analogy when we attempt to relate fear reactions of white rats to anxiety in people. At the same time, however, we do not agree with those who regard such analogue research as totally and intrinsically worthless for the study of human behavior. Although human beings and other mammals differ on many important dimensions, it does not follow that principles of behavior derived from animal research are necessarily irrelevant to human behavior.

SINGLE-SUBJECT EXPERIMENTAL RESEARCH

Experiments do not always have to be conducted on groups of people. In **single-subject experimental designs** subjects are studied one at a time and experience a manipulated variable.

The strategy of relying on a single subject appears to violate many of the principles of research design that we have discussed. As with the case study, there is no control group to act as a check on a single sub-

ject. Moreover, generalization is difficult because the findings may relate to a unique aspect of the one individual whose behavior has been explored. Hence the study of a single individual would appear unlikely to yield any findings that could possess the slightest degree of internal or external validity. Nevertheless, the experimental study of a single subject *can* be an effective research technique for certain purposes (Hersen & Barlow, 1976).

A method developed by Tate and Baroff (1966) for reducing the self-injurious behavior of a nine-year-old boy, Sam, serves as an example. The child engaged in a wide range of self-injurious behavior, such as banging his head against the floors and walls, slapping his face with his hands, and kicking himself. Despite his self-injurious behavior, Sam was not entirely antisocial. In fact, he obviously enjoyed contact with other people and would cling to them, wrap his arms around them, and sit on their laps. This affectionate behavior gave the investigators the idea for an experimental treatment.[1]

The study ran for twenty days. For a period of time on each of the first five days the frequency of Sam's self-injurious actions was observed and recorded. Then on each of the next five days the two adult experimenters accompanied Sam on a short walk around the campus, during which they talked to him and held his hands continuously. The adults responded to each of Sam's self-injurious actions by immediately jerking their hands away from him and not touching him again until three seconds after such activity had ceased. The frequency of the self-injurious acts was again recorded. During the next part of the experiment, the experimenters reverted to the procedures of the first five days; there were no walks, and Sam's self-afflicting behavior was again merely observed. Then for the last five days the experimenters reinstated their experimental procedure. The dramatic reduction in undesirable behavior induced by the treatment is shown in Figure 5.4. The design of such experiments, usually referred to as a **reversal design** or **ABAB design**, requires that some aspect of the subject's behavior be carefully measured during a given time period, the baseline (A); during a period when a treatment is introduced (B); during a rein-

---

[1]The use of the adjective *experimental* in this context prompts us to distinguish between two different meanings of the word. As applied to the research methods that have been discussed, the adjective refers to the manipulation of a variable that allows drawing conclusions about a cause–effect relationship. Here, however, the word refers to a treatment whose effects are unknown or only poorly understood. Thus, an experimental drug is one about which we know relatively little; however, such a drug might well be used in a correlational design or reported in a case study.

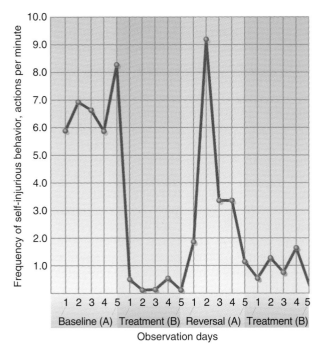

Figure 5.4 Effects of a treatment for self-injurious behavior in an experiment with an ABAB single-subject design. Note the rapid shifts in frequency of problem behavior as treatment is introduced (*B*), withdrawn (*A*), and finally reinstated (*B*). Adapted from Tate and Baroff (1966).

statement of the conditions that prevailed in the baseline period (A); and finally during a reintroduction of the experimental manipulation (B). If behavior in the experimental period is different from that in the baseline period, reverses when the experimentally manipulated conditions are reversed, and re-reverses when the treatment is again introduced, there is little doubt that the manipulation, rather than chance or uncontrolled factors, has produced the change.

The reversal technique cannot always be employed, however, for the initial state of a subject may not be recoverable, as when treatment aims to produce enduring change, the goal of all therapeutic interventions. Moreover, in studies of therapeutic procedures, reinstating the original condition of the subject or patient would generally be considered an unethical practice. Most therapists would be extremely unwilling to act in any way that might bring back the very behavior for which a client has sought help merely to prove that a particular treatment was indeed the effective agent in changing the behavior. Fortunately, other single-subject experimental designs avoid these problems.

As indicated earlier, even though an experiment with a single subject can demonstrate an effect, generalization is usually not possible. The fact that a

treatment works for a single subject does not necessarily imply that it will be universally effective. If the search for more widely applicable treatment is the major focus of an investigation, the single-subject design has a serious drawback. However, it may help investigators to decide whether large-scale research with groups is warranted.

MIXED DESIGNS

The experimental and correlational research techniques can be combined in what is called a mixed design. In a **mixed design** subjects from two or more discrete and typically nonoverlapping populations are assigned to each experimental condition. The two different types of populations, for example, patients with either schizophrenia or a phobia, constitute a classificatory variable; that is, the variables schizophrenia and phobia were neither manipulated nor created by the investigator, and they can only be correlated with the manipulated conditions, which are true experimental variables.

To illustrate how a mixed design is applied, consider an investigation of the effectiveness of three types of therapy (the experimental variable) on patients who were divided into two groups on the basis of the severity of their illnesses (the classificatory variable). The question was whether the effectiveness of the treatments varied with the severity of illness. The hypothetical outcome of such a study is presented in Figure 5.5. Figure 5.5*b* shows the results obtained when the patients were divided into two groups on the basis of the severity of their

Figure 5.5 Effects of three treatments on patients whose symptoms vary in degree of severity. (*a*) When the severity of the illness is not known and the patients are grouped together, treatment number 3 appears to be the best. (*b*) The same data as in (*a*) are reanalyzed, dividing patients by severity. Now treatment 3 is no longer best for any patients.

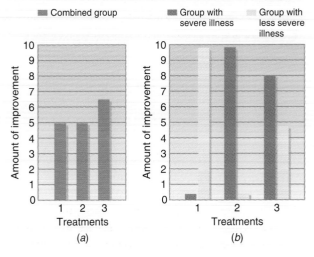

problems. Figure 5.5*a* illustrates the unfortunate conclusions that would be drawn were the patients not divided into those with severe and those with less severe illnesses. When all patients were grouped together, treatment 3 produced the greatest amount of improvement. Therefore, if no information about differential characteristics of the patients were available, treatment 3 would be preferred. When the severity of the patients' difficulties was considered, however, treatment 3 would no longer be the therapy of choice for *any* of the patients. Rather, as seen in Figure 5.5*b*, treatment 1 would be selected for those with less severe illness and treatment 2 for patients with more severe illness. Thus a mixed design can identify which treatment applies best to which group of patients.

In interpreting the results of mixed designs we must be continually aware of the fact that one of the variables (severity of illness in our example) is not manipulated but is instead a classificatory or correlational variable. Therefore the problems we have previously noted in interpreting correlations, especially the possible operation of third variables, arise in interpreting the results of mixed designs as well.

Yet the inclusion of a manipulated variable, particularly one with multiple levels, does offer some advantages. Maher (1974) explains: "With the hypothesis that bulls are characterized by a desire to break Royal Worcester china, we stock a shop exclusively with that item, turn the bulls loose, and watch the ensuing destruction. Our hypothesis is duly confirmed—especially if our control group is composed of mice" (p. 2). Maher goes on to point out that "just as bulls tend to break any kind of china, patient populations tend to do poorly at many tasks." In other words, the demonstration of a simple deficit provides little specific information, because the poor performance could be caused by any number of factors. A differential deficit, however, allows certain rival hypotheses to be ruled out.

We can consider a study that investigated schizophrenic patients' ability to accurately detect facial and vocal displays of emotion. It may be that schizophrenic patients are poor at recognizing emotion, and this could be an important component of their poor social skills. One possibility is that schizophrenic patients have a specific impairment in processing emotional cues. But it is also possible that any deficit in perceiving emotion reflects a more general information-processing deficit.

To address these issues Kerr and Neale (1993) developed tests of the ability to correctly perceive facial and vocal displays of emotion and administered them to schizophrenic patients and normals. As expected the performance of the patients was markedly impaired. To see if this was a specific deficit Kerr and Neale also tested their subjects on their ability to recognize faces (irrespective of any displayed emotion) and speech sounds. Again, the performance of the schizophrenic patients was very poor, as poor as it had been on the tests of emotion perception. Therefore, although schizophrenic patients are indeed impaired in detecting emotion, this deficit is nonspecific and reflects a more generalized impairment.

Our survey of the major research methods of abnormal psychology is now complete. It should be apparent that there is no perfect method that will easily reveal the secrets of psychopathology and therapy. Our task in subsequent chapters will be to attempt to synthesize the information yielded by investigations conducted with varying methodologies and to apply these results to advance knowledge.

SUMMARY

Science represents an agreed-upon problem-solving enterprise, with specific procedures for gathering and interpreting data to build a systematic body of knowledge. Scientific statements must have the following characteristics: they must be testable in the public arena; they must be exposed to tests that could disconfirm them, they must derive from reliable observations; and, although they may contain references to unobservable processes, the concepts inferred must be linked to observable and measurable events or outcomes.

It is important to consider the various methods that scientists employ to collect data and arrive at conclusions. Clinical case studies serve unique and important functions in psychopathology, such as allowing rare phenomena to be studied intensively in all their complexity. Case studies also encourage the formulation of hypotheses that can be tested later through controlled research. However, the data they yield may not be valid, and they are of limited value in providing evidence to favor a theory. Epidemiological research gathers information about the prevalence of disorders and about risk factors that increase the probability of a disorder.

Correlational methods are the most important means of conducting research about the causes of abnormal behavior, for diagnoses are classificatory and not experimentally manipulated variables. In correlational studies statistical procedures allow us to determine the extent to which two or more variables correlate or co-vary. Conclusions drawn from nearly all correlational studies cannot legitimately be interpreted in cause–effect terms, however, although there is great temptation to do so. The third-variable and directionality problems are the source of this difficulty.

The experimental method entails the manipulation of independent variables and the careful measurement of their effects on dependent variables. An experiment begins with a hypothesis to be tested, that manipulation of the independent variable will cause the dependent variable to change in a specific way. Participants are generally assigned to one of at least two groups: an experimental group, which experiences the manipulation of the independent variable; and a control group, which does not. If differences between the experimental and control groups are observed on the dependent variable, we can conclude that the independent variable did have an effect. Since it is important to ensure that experimental and control subjects do not differ from one another before the introduction of the independent variable, they are assigned randomly to groups. Double-blind procedures, in which the experimenter as well as the participant is unaware of who is in the experimental and who is in the control group, help avoid biases resulting from either the behavior of the experimenter or the beliefs and expectations of the participant. If all these conditions are met the experiment has internal validity. The external validity of the findings, whether they can be generalized to situations and people not studied within the experiment, can be assessed only by performing similar experiments in the actual domain of interest with new participants.

Single-subject experimental designs (e.g., the reversal or ABAB design) that expose one person to different treatments over a period of time can provide internally valid results, although the generality of conclusions is typically limited. Mixed designs are combinations of experimental and correlational methods. For example, two different kinds of patients (the classificatory variable) may be exposed to various treatments (the experimental variable).

A science is only as good as its methodology. Students of abnormal psychology must appreciate the strengths and limitations of the research methods of the field if they are to adequately evaluate the research and theories that form the subject matter of the remainder of this book.

KEY TERMS

science	classificatory variables	internal validity
theory	directionality problem	random assignment
case study	high-risk method	double-blind procedure
epidemiology	third-variable problem	external validity
prevalence	experiment	analogue experiment
incidence	experimental hypothesis	single-subject experimental
risk factors	independent variable	design
lifetime prevalence rates	dependent variable	reversal (ABAB) design
correlational method	experimental effect	mixed design
correlation coefficient	control group	
statistical significance	confounds	

PART **2**

PSYCHOLOGICAL DISORDERS

ANXIETY DISORDERS

How would you like to be a tame, somewhat shy and unaggressive little boy of nine, somewhat shorter and thinner than average, and find yourself put three times a week, every Monday, Wednesday, and Friday, as regularly and inexorably as the sun sets and the sky darkens and the globe turns black and dead and spooky with no warm promise that anyone anywhere ever will awaken again, into the somber, iron custody of someone named Forgione, older, broader, and much larger than yourself, a dreadful, powerful, broad-shouldered man who is hairy, hard-muscled, and barrel-chested and wears immaculate tight white or navy-blue T-shirts that seem as firm and unpitying as the figure of flesh and bone they encase like a mold, whose ferocious, dark eyes you never had courage enough to meet and whose assistant's name you did not ask or were not able to remember, and who did not seem to like you or approve of you? He could do whatever he wanted to you. He could do whatever he wanted to me. (Heller, 1966, p. 236)

This excerpt from Joseph Heller's second novel, *Something Happened*, portrays the helplessness of a terrified nine-year-old boy who has to interact every other school day with a burly gym teacher. As described by his equally fearful father, the youngster has an overwhelming anxiety about his gym class, a situation into which he is forced and from which he cannot escape, a situation that makes demands on him that he feels utterly unable to meet. Once again a gifted novelist captures the phenomenology—the direct experience—of an important human emotion in a way that speaks vividly to each of us.

There is perhaps no other single topic in abnormal psychology that touches so many of us as **anxiety**, that unpleasant feeling of fear and apprehension. This emotional state can occur in many psychopathologies and is a principal aspect of the disorders considered in this chapter. Anxiety also plays an important role in the study of the psychology of normal people, for very few of us go through even a week of our lives without experiencing some measure of what we would all agree is the emotion called anxiety or fear. But the briefer periods of anxiety that beset the normal individual are hardly comparable in intensity or duration, nor are they as debilitating, as those suffered by someone with an anxiety disorder.

The specific disorders considered in this chapter and the next were for a considerable period regarded as forms of **neuroses**, a large group of disorders characterized by unrealistic anxiety and other associated problems. They were conceptualized through Freud's clinical work with his patients, and thus the diagnostic category of neurosis was inextricably bound with psychoanalytic theory. In DSM-II the behavior encompassed by the forms of neuroses

varied widely—the fear and avoidance of phobia, the irresistible urge to perform certain acts over and over again found in compulsiveness, the paralyses and other "neurological" symptoms of conversion hysteria. How could such diverse problems be grouped into a single category? Although the observed symptoms differ, all neurotic conditions were assumed, according to the psychoanalytic theory of neuroses, to reflect an underlying problem with repressed anxiety.

Over the years many psychopathologists questioned the viability of the concept of neuroses because it had become so inclusive as to be meaningless as a diagnostic category. Further, no data supported the assumption that all patients labeled *neurotic* shared some common problem or set of symptoms.[1] Beginning in DSM-III and continuing in DSM-IV the old categories of neuroses are distributed among several new, more distinct diagnostic classes: anxiety disorders, the topic of this chapter, and somatoform disorders and dissociative disorders, both of which are covered in Chapter 7.

In all likelihood many people will continue to use the term neurosis as a broad descriptive label when discussing disordered behavior presumed to be due to underlying anxiety; indeed, the term is part of our everyday vocabulary. The important point to remember is that when a precise diagnosis is called for, the term falls short. Thus in this chapter and the next our presentation will be organized according to the newer diagnostic categories.

Anxiety disorders are diagnosed when subjectively experienced feelings of anxiety are clearly present. DSM-IV proposes six principal categories: phobias, panic disorder, generalized anxiety disorder, obsessive-compulsive disorder, posttraumatic stress disorder, and acute stress disorder. Often someone with one anxiety disorder meets the diagnostic criteria for another disorder as well, a situation known as **comorbidity**. Comorbidity among anxiety disorders arises for two reasons. First, symptoms of the various anxiety disorders are not entirely disorder–specific; for example, somatic

---

[1]In many ways the term *neurosis* serves as a nice counter to another broad-based term, *psychosis*, which is also part of our everyday vocabulary and was prominent in DSM-II. Certain diagnoses in DSM-IV—schizophrenic and paranoid disorders and some mood disorders—are recognized as psychoses although they are not generally grouped as such. Individuals with a psychosis typically suffer extreme mental unrest and have lost contact with reality. Their hallucinations and delusions—false perceptions and misguided beliefs that are a jumble of distortions and impossibilities but are firmly accepted by the individual—so engulf them that they are often unable to meet even the most ordinary demands of life.

Fear and avoidance of heights are classified as a specific phobia. Other specific phobias include fears of animals, injections, and enclosed spaces.

signs of anxiety (e.g., sweating, fast heart rate) are among the diagnostic criteria for panic disorder, generalized anxiety disorder, and posttraumatic stress disorder. Second, current ideas about the etiological factors that give rise to various anxiety disorders are applicable to more than one disorder; for example, feeling that you can't control the stressors you encounter has been proposed as relevant to both phobias and generalized anxiety disorder. Therefore comorbidity could reflect the operation of these common mechanisms. As yet theories of anxiety disorders tend to focus exclusively on a single disorder. The development of theories that take comorbidity into account is a challenge for the future.

We turn now to an examination of the defining characteristics, theories of etiology, and therapies for each of the anxiety disorders.

PHOBIAS

Psychopathologists define a **phobia** as a disrupting, fear-mediated avoidance that is out of proportion to the danger posed by a particular object or situation and is recognized by the sufferer as groundless. Extreme fear of heights, closed spaces, snakes, or spiders, provided that there is no objective danger, accompanied by sufficient distress to disrupt one's life, is likely to be labeled a phobia.

Over the years complex terms have been formulated to name these unwarranted avoidance patterns. In each instance the suffix *phobia* is preceded by a Greek word for the feared object or situation. The suffix is derived from the name of the Greek

god Phobos, who frightened his enemies. Some of the more familiar terms are *claustrophobia*, fear of closed spaces; *agoraphobia*, fear of public places; and *acrophobia*, fear of heights. More exotic fears have also been given Greek-derived names, for example, *ergasiophobia*, fear of writing; *pnigophobia*, fear of choking; *taphephobia*, fear of being buried alive, and, believe it or not, *Anglophobia*, fear of England. All too often the impression is conveyed that we understand how a particular problem originated or even

A crowd is one of the situations likely to be very distressing to a person with agoraphobia. The agoraphobic person is often afraid of having a panic attack in a public place.

how to treat it merely because we have an authoritative-sounding name for it. Nothing could be further from the truth. As with so much in the field of abnormal psychology, there are more theories and jargon pertaining to phobias than there are firm findings.

Many specific fears do not cause enough hardship to compel an individual to seek treatment. For example, if a person with an intense fear of snakes lives in a metropolitan area, he or she will probably have little direct contact with the feared object and may therefore not believe that anything is seriously wrong. The term *phobia* usually implies that the person suffers intense distress and social or occupational impairment because of the anxiety.

It is interesting to note that psychologists tend to focus on different aspects of phobias depending on the paradigm they have adopted. Psychoanalysts focus on the *content* of the phobia. They see great significance in the phobic object as a symbol of an important unconscious fear. In a celebrated case reported by Freud, a boy he called Little Hans was afraid of encountering horses if he went outside. Freud paid particular attention to Hans's reference to the "black things around horses' mouths and the things in front of their eyes." The horse was regarded as representing the father, who had a moustache and wore eyeglasses. Freud theorized that fear of the father had become transformed into fear of horses, which Hans then avoided. Countless other such examples might be cited; the principal point is that psychoanalysts believe that the content of phobias has important symbolic value. Behaviorists, on the other hand, tend to ignore the content of the phobia and focus instead on its *function*; for them, fear of snakes and fear of heights are equivalent in the means by which they are acquired, in how they might be reduced, and so on.

With this in mind, let us look now at two types of phobias: specific phobias and social phobias.

SPECIFIC PHOBIAS

Specific phobias are unwarranted fears caused by the presence or anticipation of a specific object or situation. Lifetime prevalence is about 7 percent for men and 16 percent for women. Specific phobias are more common in African-Americans than in whites (Kessler et al., 1994; Magee et al., 1996). DSM-IV subdivides these phobias according to the source of the fear: blood and injections, situations (e.g., planes, elevators, enclosed spaces), animals, and the natural environment (e.g., heights, water). What is feared in a phobia can vary cross-culturally. For example, in China Pa-leng is a fear of the cold in

which the person worries that loss of body heat may be life threatening. This fear appears to be related to the Chinese philosophy of yin and yang; yin refers to the cold, windy, energy-sapping aspects of life. Beliefs that are prevalent in a culture seem to be able to channel what people come to fear.

SOCIAL PHOBIAS

A **social phobia**, sometimes referred to as social anxiety disorder, is a persistent, irrational fear generally linked to the presence of other people. It can be an extremely debilitating condition. The phobic individual usually tries to avoid a particular situation in which he or she might be evaluated and reveal signs of anxiousness or behave in an embarrassing way. Speaking or performing in public, eating in public, using public lavatories, or virtually any other activity that might be carried out in the presence of others can elicit extreme anxiety.

Social phobias can be either generalized or specific, depending on the range of situations that are feared and avoided. People with the generalized type have an earlier age of onset and more depression and alcohol abuse (Mannuzza et al., 1995).

Social phobias are fairly common, with a lifetime prevalence of 11 percent in men and 15 percent in women (Kessler et al., 1994; Magee et al., 1996). Social phobias have a high comorbidity rate with other disorders and often occur in conjunction with

What is feared in a phobia varies cross-culturally. In China, Pa-leng is a fear of loss of body heat as life threatening.

Social phobias typically begin in adolescence and interfere with developing friendships with peers.

generalized anxiety disorder, specific phobias, panic disorder, and avoidant personality disorder (Jansen et al., 1994). As might be expected, onset generally takes place during adolescence, when social awareness and interaction with others are assuming much more importance in a person's life, but as we discuss later (p. 134), such fears are sometimes found in children as well. As with specific phobias, social phobias vary somewhat cross-culturally. For example, in Japan fear of giving offense to others is important, whereas in the United States fear of being negatively evaluated by others is more common.

ETIOLOGY OF PHOBIAS

As is true for virtually all the disorders discussed in this book proposals for the causes of phobias have been made by adherents of the psychoanalytic, behavioral, cognitive, and biological paradigms.

PSYCHOANALYTIC THEORIES

Freud was the first to attempt to account systematically for the development of phobic behavior. According to Freud, phobias are a defense against the anxiety produced by repressed id impulses. This anxiety is displaced from the feared id impulse and moved to an object or situation that has some symbolic connection to it. These objects or situations—for example, elevators or closed spaces—then become the phobic stimuli. By avoiding them the person is able to avoid dealing with repressed

conflicts. As discussed in Chapter 2 (p. 32), the phobia is the ego's way of warding off a confrontation with the real problem, a repressed childhood conflict. For example, Freud thought that Little Hans, mentioned earlier, did not successfully resolve the Oedipal conflict, so that his intense fear of his father was displaced onto horses and he became phobic about leaving his home.

According to another psychoanalytic theory of phobias, proposed by Arieti (1979), the repression is of a particular interpersonal problem of childhood rather than of an id impulse. Arieti theorized that as children, phobics first lived through a period of innocence during which they trusted the people around them to protect them from danger. Later they came to fear that adults, usually parents, were not reliable. This mistrust, or generalized fear of others, was something they could not live with; to be able to trust people again they unconsciously transformed this fear of others into a fear of impersonal objects or situations. The phobia supposedly surfaces when, in adulthood, the person undergoes some sort of stress. As with most psychoanalytic theorizing, evidence in support of these views is restricted for the most part to conclusions drawn from clinical case reports.

BEHAVIORAL THEORIES

The primary assumption of all behavioral accounts of phobias is that such reactions are learned. But the exact learning mechanisms and what is actually learned in the development of a phobia are viewed differently depending on the behavioral theory. We will look at three theories: avoidance conditioning, modeling, and operant conditioning.

THE AVOIDANCE-CONDITIONING MODEL Historically, Watson and Rayner's (1920) demonstration of the apparent conditioning of a fear or phobia in Little Albert (see p. 40) is considered the model of how a phobia may be acquired. A classically conditioned fear of an objectively harmless stimulus forms the basis of an operant avoidance response. This formulation, based on the two-factor theory originally proposed by Mowrer (1947), holds that phobias develop from two related sets of learning (see p. 43): (1) via classical conditioning a person can learn to fear a neutral stimulus (the CS) if it is paired with an intrinsically painful or frightening event (the UCS); (2) then the person can learn to reduce this conditioned fear by escaping from or avoiding the CS. This second kind of learning is assumed to be operant conditioning; the response is maintained by its reinforcing consequences.

Some clinical phobias fit the avoidance-conditioning model rather well, but we will also see that avoidance conditioning does not provide a complete theory of phobias. On the positive side, a phobia of a specific object or situation has sometimes been reported to have developed after a particularly painful experience with that object. Some people become intensely afraid of heights after a bad fall; others develop a phobia of driving after experiencing a panic attack in their car (Munjack, 1984); and social phobics often report traumatic social experiences (Stenberger et al., 1995).

Yet a problem exists in the application of an avoidance-conditioning model for all phobias. The fact that Little Albert's fear was acquired through conditioning can *not* be taken as evidence that *all* fears and phobias are acquired by this means. Rather, the evidence demonstrates only the *possibility* that some fears *may* be acquired in this particular way. Other clinical reports suggest that phobias may develop *without* a prior frightening experience. Many individuals with severe fears of snakes, germs, airplanes, and heights tell clinicians that they have had no particularly unpleasant experiences with any of these objects or situations (Ost, 1987b). That many phobics cannot recall traumatic experiences with their now-feared objects could, however, be the result of distortions of memory. Accounts of traumatic episodes may be questioned on the same grounds. In addition, many people who have had a harrowing automobile accident or a bad fall down stairs do *not* become phobic to automobiles or stairs. For example, 50 percent of people with a severe fear of dogs reported a prior traumat-

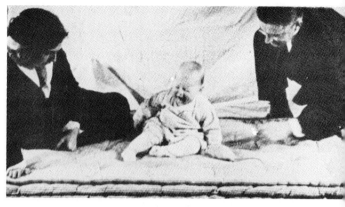

Little Albert, shown here with Watson and Rayner, was classically conditioned to develop a fear of a white rat.

ic experience, yet so did 50 percent of people who were not afraid of dogs (DiNardo et al., 1988).

Attempts to replicate Watson and Rayner's experiment and demonstrate again the acquisition of fear via classical conditioning have for the most part *not* been successful (e.g., English, 1929). Very little experimental evidence supports the contention that human beings can be classically conditioned to fear neutral stimuli even when such stimuli are paired repeatedly with primary aversive stimuli, such as electric shock (e.g., Davison, 1968b; Dawson, Schell, & Banis, 1986). Ethical considerations have restrained most researchers from employing highly aversive stimuli with human beings, but considerable evidence indicates that fear is extinguished rather quickly when the CS is presented a few times without the reinforcement of moderate levels of shock (Bridger & Mandel, 1965; Wickens, Allen, & Hill, 1963). Finally, it is also unclear whether the model itself is an accurate portrayal of a phobia. The essence of phobic behavior is the fear and avoidance elicited by the CS. Yet the avoidance-learning literature reports that an animal's fear of the CS quickly declines, and it has proved difficult (perhaps impossible) to train an animal to avoid a CS (Mineka, 1985).

The avoidance-conditioning view of phobias might be more valid if it were modified to take into account the fact that certain neutral stimuli, called prepared stimuli, are more likely than others to become classically conditioned stimuli. For example, rats readily learn to associate taste with nausea but not taste paired with shock (Garcia, McGowan, & Green, 1972). Phobias may well reflect classical conditioning, but only to stimuli to which an organism is physiologically prepared to be sensitive (Seligman, 1971). Conditioning experiments that show quick extinction of fear may have used CSs that the organism was not prepared to associate with

UCSs. In a related vein, Marks (1969) has pointed out that humans tend to fear only certain objects and events, such as dogs, snakes, and heights, but that few lamb phobics have been found. It is even more remarkable how few people fear electrical outlets, which do present a real danger.

Partial support for this line of reasoning comes from studies that have used different types of stimuli as the CS (Öhman, Erixon, & Loftberg, 1975). During conditioning electric shock is paired with slides of houses, faces, and snakes, and participants acquired a CR to the slides. During extinction the CR to the slides of houses or faces quickly diminished, while those to the snakes remained strong. But in the Öhman study, as well as in subsequent research, the CR to the prepared stimulus (snakes) was not more easily acquired or of greater magnitude; it only extinguished more slowly. Furthermore, as McNally (1987) pointed out, it is not clear if mild shocks actually elicit fear. McNally also argued that the similarities between prepared learning and phobias have been overstated. Specific phobias are fairly easy to extinguish given the right treatment. (The reason they persist without treatment is that the phobic avoids the feared stimulus.) Thus the preparedness hypothesis does not make avoidance conditioning a well-supported model of phobias. It does, however, provide a means of addressing the fact that the feared stimuli are not random.

In sum, the data we have reviewed suggest that not all phobias are learned through avoidance conditioning. Such a process *may* be involved in the etiology of some phobias, but other processes must also be implicated in their development.

MODELING Phobic responses may be learned through imitating the reactions of others. As we have previously noted (see p. 42) a wide range of behavior, including emotional responses, may be learned by witnessing a model. The learning of phobic reactions by observing others is generally referred to as **vicarious learning**. In one study Bandura and Rosenthal (1966) arranged for participants to watch another person, the model (a confederate of the experimenter), in an aversive conditioning situation. The model was hooked up to an impressive-looking array of electrical apparatus. On hearing a buzzer, the model withdrew his hand rapidly from the arm of the chair and feigned pain. The physiological responses of the participants witnessing this behavior were recorded. After the participants had watched the model "suffer" a number of times, they showed an increased frequency of emotional responses when the buzzer sounded. The participants began to react emotionally to a harmless stimulus even though they had had no direct contact with a noxious event.

Vicarious learning may also be accomplished through verbal instructions; that is, phobic reactions can be learned through another's description of what might happen as well as by observing another's fear. As an example from everyday life, a mother may repeatedly warn her child not to engage in some activity lest dire consequences ensue. (We should not assume, however, that such learning is necessarily a product of conditioning.)

The clearest demonstration of the potential importance of observational learning comes from a study by Mineka and her colleagues (1984). Adolescent rhesus monkeys were reared with parents who had an intense fear of snakes. During the observational learning sessions the offspring saw their parents interact fearfully with real and toy snakes as well as nonfearfully with neutral objects. After six sessions, the fear of the adolescent monkeys was indistinguishable from that of the parents. A three-month follow-up showed that the fear remained strong.

In an ingenious follow-up study related to the preparedness concept presented earlier, Cook and Mineka (1989) studied four groups of rhesus monkeys, each of which saw a different videotape. The tapes were created by splicing, so that a monkey exhibiting intense fear appeared to be responding to different stimuli: a toy snake, a toy crocodile, flow-

Mineka's research has shown that when monkeys observe another monkey display fear of a snake, they also acquire the fear. Observational learning may therefore play a role in the etiology of phobias.

ers, or a toy rabbit. Only the monkeys exposed to the tapes showing the toy snake or crocodile acquired fear to the object shown, again demonstrating that not every stimulus is capable of becoming a source of acquired fear.

As with classical conditioning, vicarious-learning experiments fail to provide a complete model for all phobias. First, phobics who seek treatment do not often report that they became frightened after witnessing someone else's distress. Second, many people have been exposed to the bad experiences of others but have not themselves developed phobias.

COGNITIVE THEORIES

Cognitive views of anxiety in general and of phobias in particular emphasize that anxiety is linked to being more likely to attend to negative stimuli and to believe that negative events are more likely to occur in the future (Mathews & MacLeod, 1994). In the DiNardo et al. study mentioned earlier, what differentiated people who had a traumatic experience with dogs and then developed severe fear from those who had a similar experience and did not develop severe fear was that the phobic group focused on and became anxious about the possible occurrence of similar events in the future.

Socially anxious people are more concerned about evaluation than are people who are not socially anxious (Goldfried, Padawer, & Robins, 1984), and they are more aware of the image they present to others (Bates, 1990; Fenigstein, 1979; Fenigstein, Scheier, & Buss, 1975). The study by Davison and Zighelboim (1987) discussed in Chapter 4 provides further evidence for these conclusions. The thoughts of two groups of participants were compared using the Articulated Thoughts During Simulated Situations method as they role-played participation in both a neutral situation and one in which they were being sharply criticized. One group comprised volunteers from an introductory psychology course; the others were undergraduates referred from the student counseling center and identified as shy, withdrawn, and socially anxious. The thoughts articulated by the socially anxious students in both stressful and neutral situations were more negative than were those of the control subjects.

Some of the thoughts expressed by socially anxious students as they imagined themselves being criticized included: "I've been rejected by these people," "I have this very depressed feeling, a feeling of rejection," "There is no place to turn to now," "There is no way to eliminate that feeling I have

inside," "I think I am boring when I talk to people," "I often think I should not talk at all."

Cognitive theories of the origins of phobias are also relevant to another feature of these disorders—the fears actually seem irrational to the person experiencing them. Perhaps this occurs because fear is elicited through early cognitive processes that are not available to conscious awareness. In one study testing this notion people with high levels of fear of either snakes or spiders were presented with pictures of varying content, some expected to elicit fear (snakes and spiders) and some not (flowers and mushrooms). Each picture was followed thirty milliseconds later with another patterned stimulus so that the content of the pictures could not be consciously recognized. Nevertheless, people high in fear of snakes showed increased skin conductance to the snake slides and those high in fear of spiders showed increased skin conductance to the spider slides, indicating that phobic fears may be elicited by stimuli that are not available to consciousness and may therefore appear irrational (Öhman & Soares, 1994).

SOCIAL-SKILLS DEFICITS IN SOCIAL PHOBIAS Another model of social phobia considers inappropriate behavior or a lack of social skills as the cause of social anxiety. According to this view the individual has not learned how to behave so that he or she feels comfortable with others, or the person repeatedly commits faux pas, is awkward and socially inept, and is often criticized by social companions. Support for this model comes from findings that socially anxious people are indeed rated as being low in social skills (Twentyman & McFall, 1975) and that the timing and placement of their responses in a social interaction, such as saying thank you at the right time, are impaired (Fischetti, Curran, & Wessberg, 1977).

PREDISPOSING BIOLOGICAL FACTORS

The theories we have just described look largely to the environment for the cause and maintenance of phobias. But why do some people acquire unrealistic fears when others do not, given similar opportunities for learning? Perhaps those who are adversely affected by stress have a biological malfunction (a diathesis) that somehow predisposes them to develop a phobia following a particular stressful event. Research in two areas seems promising: the autonomic nervous system and genetic factors.

AUTONOMIC NERVOUS SYSTEM One difference in how people react to certain environmental situations is the ease with which their autonomic nervous systems become aroused. Lacey (1967) identified a dimension of autonomic activity that he called stability–lability. Labile, or jumpy, individuals are those whose autonomic systems are readily aroused by a wide range of stimuli. Because of the extent to which the autonomic nervous system is involved in fear and hence in phobic behavior, a dimension such as **autonomic lability** assumes considerable importance. Since there is reason to believe that autonomic lability is to some degree genetically determined (Gabbay, 1992; Lacey, 1967), heredity may very well have a significant role in the development of phobias.

GENETIC FACTORS Several studies have examined whether a genetic factor is involved in phobias. Blood and injection phobia is strongly familial. Sixty-four percent of patients with blood and injection phobia have at least one first-degree relative with the same disorder; its prevalence in the general population is only 3 to 4 percent (Ost, 1992). Similarly, for both social and specific phobias, prevalence is higher than average in first-degree relatives of patients (Fyer et al., 1995).

Related to these findings is the work of Jerome Kagan on the trait of inhibition or shyness (Kagan & Snidman, 1990). Some infants as young as four months become agitated and cry when they are shown toys or other stimuli. This behavior pattern, which may be inherited, may set the stage for the later development of phobias. In one study, for example, inhibited children were greater than five times more likely than uninhibited children to develop a phobia later (Biederman et al., 1990).

The data we have described do not unequivocally implicate genetic factors. Although close relatives share genes, they also have considerable opportunity to observe and influence one another. The fact that a son and his father are both afraid of heights may indicate not a genetic component, but direct modeling of the son's behavior after that of his father (or, both factors could be involved). Although there is some reason to believe that genetic factors may be involved in the etiology of phobias, there has as yet been no clear-cut demonstration of the extent to which they may be important.

THERAPIES FOR PHOBIAS

Most people suffer, sometimes quietly, with their phobias and do not seek treatment (Magee et al., 1996). Many people who could be diagnosed as phobic by a clinician do not regard themselves as having a problem that merits attention. A decision to seek treatment often arises when a change in the person's occupational situation requires exposure that had for years been avoided or minimized.

A thirty-five-year-old industrial engineer consulted us for treatment of his fear of flying in airplanes when a promotion required him to travel frequently. This professional recognition was a result of his having worked with distinction for several years in his firm at a job that kept him at his desk. Family trips were always by car or train, and those close to him worked around his debilitating fear of getting on an airplane. Imagine his mixed feelings at being informed that his excellence was to be rewarded by the promotion! His ambition and self-respect— and encouragement from family and friends—goaded him into seeking assistance.

Throughout the book, after reviewing theories about the causes of the various disorders, we will briefly describe the principal therapies for them. The treatment sections of Chapter 2 were meant to furnish the reader with a context for understanding these discussions of therapy. An in-depth study and evaluation of therapy is reserved for the final section of the book. Here we will look briefly at a number of therapeutic approaches used to treat phobias.

PSYCHOANALYTIC APPROACHES

Just as psychoanalytic theory has many derivations, so, too, does psychoanalytic therapy. In general, however, all psychoanalytic treatments of phobias attempt to uncover the repressed conflicts that are assumed to underlie the extreme fear and avoidance characteristic of these disorders. Because the phobia itself is regarded as symptomatic of underlying conflicts, it is usually not dealt with directly. Indeed, direct attempts to reduce phobic avoidance are contraindicated because the phobia is assumed to protect the person from repressed conflicts that are too painful to confront.

In various combinations the analyst uses the techniques that have been developed within the psychoanalytic tradition to help lift the repression. During free association (see p. 38) the analyst listens carefully to what the patient mentions in connection with any references to the phobia. The analyst also attempts to discover clues to the repressed origins of the phobia in the manifest content of dreams. Exactly what the analyst believes these repressed origins are depends on the particular psychoanalytic theory held. An orthodox analyst will look for conflicts related to sex or aggression, whereas an analyst holding to Arieti's interpersonal theory will encourage patients to examine their generalized fear of other people.

Contemporary ego analysts focus less on historical insights; they encourage the patient to confront the phobia even though they continue to view it as an outgrowth of an earlier problem. Alexander and French in their classic book, *Psychoanalytic Therapy* (1946), spoke of the "corrective emotional experience" in therapy, by which they meant the patient's confrontation with what is so desperately feared. They observed that "Freud himself came to the conclusion that in the treatment of some cases, phobias for example, a time arrives when the analyst must encourage the patient to engage in those activities he avoided in the past" (p. 39). Wachtel (1977) even more boldly recommended that analysts employ the fear-reduction techniques of behavior therapists, such as systematic desensitization.

Many analytically oriented clinicians recognize the importance of exposure to what is feared, although they usually tend to regard any subsequent improvement as merely symptomatic and not as a resolution of the underlying conflict that was assumed to have produced the phobia (Wolitzky & Eagle, 1990).

BEHAVIORAL APPROACHES

A widely used behavioral treatment for phobias is systematic desensitization (see p. 44) (Wolpe, 1958). The phobic individual imagines a series of increasingly frightening scenes while in a state of deep relaxation. Clinical and experimental evidence indicates that this technique is effective in eliminating, or at least reducing, phobias (McGlynn, 1994). Many behavior therapists have come to recognize the critical importance of exposure to real-life phobic situations, sometimes during the period in which a patient is being desensitized in imagination, sometimes instead of the imagery-based procedure (Craske, Rapee, & Barlow, 1992).

Blood and injection phobias have only recently, in DSM-IV, been distinguished from other kinds of severe fears and avoidances because of the distinctive reactions that people with these phobias have to the usual behavioral approach of relaxation paired with exposure (Page, 1994). Relaxation tends to make matters worse for people with a blood and injection phobia. Why? Consider the typical reaction. After the initial fright, associated with dramatic increases in sympathetic nervous system activity, a patient with blood and injection phobia often faints because there is a sudden drop in blood pressure and heart rate after the initial acceleration (McGrady & Bernal, 1986). By trying to relax, patients with blood and injection phobias may well be contributing to their fainting tendencies, increasing their already high levels of fear and avoidance of the entire situation as

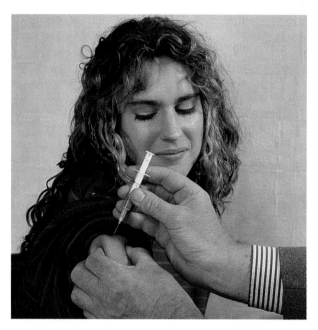

Blood and injection phobias are different from other specific phobias. Patients with this phobia are encouraged not to relax but to tense their muscles when they encounter their feared situation.

well as their embarrassment (Ost, 1992). The upshot of clinical research and observations is that patients with blood and injection phobias are now encouraged to *tense* their muscles instead of relaxing them when confronted by their fearsome situations (Ost, Fellenius, & Sterner, 1991).

Learning social skills can help social phobics who may not know what to do or to say in social situations. Some behavior therapists encourage patients to role-play or rehearse interpersonal encounters in the consulting room or in small therapy groups. Several studies attest to the effectiveness of such an approach (e.g., Heimberg et al., 1989; Turner, Beidel, & Cooley-Quille, 1995). As pointed out recently by Herbert (1995) such practice may also expose the timorous person, even when there is no social-skills deficit, to anxiety-provoking cues, such as being observed by others, so that through real-life exposure extinction of fear takes place (Hope, Heimberg, & Bruch, 1995). This is but one of many examples of how a particular therapeutic technique can work for more than one reason.

Modeling is another technique that exposes fearful clients to filmed or live demonstrations of other people interacting fearlessly with the phobic object, for example, handling snakes or petting dogs. **Flooding** is a therapeutic technique in which the client is exposed to the source of the phobia at full intensity. The extreme discomfort that is an inevitable part of this procedure has tended to discourage therapists from employing it, except perhaps as a last resort when graduated exposure has not worked.

Behavior therapists who favor operant techniques ignore the fear assumed to underlie phobias and attend instead to the overt avoidance of phobic objects and to the approach behavior that must replace it. They treat approach to the feared situation as any other operant and shape it according to the principle of successive approximations. Real-life exposures to the phobic object are gradually achieved, and the client is rewarded for even minimal successes in moving closer to it. Note that exposure is an inevitable aspect of any operant shaping of approach behaviors.

Many behavior therapists attend both to fear and to avoidance, using techniques such as desensitization to reduce fear and operant shaping to encourage approach (Lazarus, Davison, & Polefka, 1965). At the initial stages of treatment, when fear and avoidance are both very great, the therapist concentrates on reducing the fear through relaxation training and graded exposures to the phobic situation. As therapy progresses fear becomes less of an issue and avoidance more. A phobic individual has often over time settled into an existence in which other people cater to his or her incapacities and thus in a way reinforce the person for having a phobia. As the person's anxieties diminish, he or she is able to approach what used to be terrifying; this overt behavior can then be positively reinforced—and avoidance discouraged—by relatives and friends as well as by the therapist.

In the most frequent treatment for phobias, patients are exposed to what they fear most, here an enclosed space.

COGNITIVE APPROACHES

Cognitive treatments for phobias have been viewed with skepticism because of a central defining characteristic. As stated in DSM-IV, the phobic fear is recognized by the individual as excessive or unreasonable. Thus if an otherwise well-functioning person is intensely afraid of something that intellectually he or she acknowledges to be relatively harmless, of what use can it be to alter the person's thoughts about it? Indeed, there is no evidence that eliminating irrational beliefs alone, without exposure to the fearsome situations, reduces phobic avoidance (Turner et al., 1992; Williams & Rappoport, 1983).

With social phobics, on the other hand, such cognitive methods are more promising, especially when combined with social-skills training (Heimberg et al., 1993; Marks, 1995; Mattick & Andrews, 1994). Still, statistically significant differences between a treatment group undergoing, for example, cognitive behavior therapy and a control group does not mean that all or even most of the treatment subjects end up with no social anxiety at all. On the contrary—and this generalization applies to *all* the therapies judged effective that we review in this book—many patients do not respond at all or achieve only a partial reduction of their anxiety as a result of the treatment.

All these various therapies for phobias have a recurrent theme, namely, the need for the patient to desist from customary avoidance of the phobic object or situation and to begin facing what has been deemed too fearsome, too terrifying to face. Although analysts believe that the fear resides in the buried past and therefore delay direct confrontation, eventually they too encourage it (e.g., Zane, 1984). Freud stated: "One can hardly ever master a phobia if one waits until the patient lets the analysis influence him to give it up. One succeeds only when one can induce them to go about alone and to struggle with their anxiety while they make the attempt" (Freud, 1919, p. 400). Thus all these therapies reflect a time-honored bit of folk wisdom, one that tells us that we must face up to what we fear. As an ancient Chinese proverb puts it, "Go straight to the heart of danger, for there you will find safety."

BIOLOGICAL APPROACHES

Drugs that reduce anxiety are referred to as sedatives, tranquilizers, or **anxiolytics** (the suffix *lytic* comes from the Greek word meaning to loosen or dissolve). Barbiturates were the first major category of drugs used to treat anxiety disorders, but because

FOCUS 6.1 CHILDHOOD FEARS AND SOCIAL WITHDRAWAL

Most children experience fears and worries as part of the normal course of development; for fears and worries to be classified as disorders, children's functioning must be impaired. Using this definition it has been estimated that 10 to 15 percent of children and adolescents have an anxiety disorder, making these the most common disorders of childhood (Cohen et al., 1993; Kashani et al., 1989).

SCHOOL PHOBIA

One childhood fear, **school phobia**, has serious academic and social consequences for the youngster and can be extremely disabling. Two types of school phobia have been identified. In the more common, which is associated with separation anxiety, children worry constantly that some harm will befall their parents or themselves when they are away from their parents; when home they shadow one or both of their parents and often try to join them in bed.

Since the beginning of school is often the first circumstance that requires lengthy and frequent separations of children from their parents, separation anxiety is often a principal cause of school phobia. One study found that 75 percent of children who have school refusal caused by separation anxiety have mothers who also refused school in childhood (Last & Strauss, 1990). It has been hypothesized that the child's refusal or extreme reluctance to go to school stems from some difficulty in the mother–child relationship. Perhaps the mother communicates her own separation anxieties and unwittingly reinforces the child's dependent and avoidant behavior.

The second major type of school refusal is that associated with a true phobia of school—either a fear specifically related to school or a more general social phobia. These school phobics generally begin refusing to go to school later in life and have more severe and pervasive avoidance of school. Their fear is more likely to be related to specific aspects of the school environment, such as worries about academic failure or discomfort with peers.

SOCIAL PHOBIA

Most classrooms have in attendance at least one or two children who are extremely quiet and shy. Often these children will play only with family members or familiar peers, avoiding strangers both young and old. Their shyness may prevent them

School phobia is most commonly associated with separation anxiety disorder, an intense fear of being away from parents or other attachment figures.

from acquiring skills and participating in a variety of activities enjoyed by most of their age-mates, for they avoid playgrounds and games played by neighborhood children. Although some youngsters who are shy may simply be slow to warm up, withdrawn children never do, even after prolonged exposure to new people. Extremely shy children may refuse to speak at all in unfamiliar social circumstances; this is called **elective mutism**. In crowded rooms they cling and whisper to their parents, hide behind the furniture, cower in corners, and may even have tantrums. At home they ask their parents endless questions about situations that worry them. Withdrawn children usually have warm and satisfying relationships with family members and family friends, and they do show an eagerness for affection and acceptance. Because the point at which shyness or withdrawal becomes a problem varies, no statistics have been compiled on the frequency of this disorder.

Some children exhibit intense anxiety in specific social situations, showing social phobia similar to that of adults (see

---

they are highly addicting and present great risk of a lethal overdose they were supplanted in the 1950s by two other classes of drugs, propanediols (e.g., Miltown) and benzodiazepines (e.g., Valium and Xanax). The latter are widely used today and are of

demonstrated benefit with some anxiety disorders; however, they are not used much with phobias. One class of drugs commonly used to treat depression (monoamine oxidase inhibitors) fared better in treating social phobia than did a benzodiazepine

p. 127). When such children were asked to keep daily diaries of anxiety-producing events, they reported experiencing anxiety three times more frequently than did a normal control group, with concerns about such activities as reading aloud before a group, writing on the board, and performing in front of others. When faced with these events they reported crying, avoidance, and somatic complaints (Beidel, 1991).

Theories of the etiology of social phobia in children are not well worked out. It has often been suggested that anxiety interferes with social interaction, causing the child to avoid social situations and thus not to get much practice at social skills. Another suggestion is that withdrawn children may simply not have the social know-how that facilitates interaction with their age-mates. The finding that isolated children make fewer attempts to make friends and are less imaginative in their play may indicate a deficiency in social skills. Finally, isolated children may have become so because they have in the past spent most of their time with adults; such children do interact more freely with adults than with other children (Scarlett, 1980).

TREATMENT OF CHILDHOOD PHOBIAS

How are childhood fears overcome? Many simply dissipate with time and maturation. For the most part treatment of such fears is similar to that employed with adults, with suitable modifications to accommodate the different abilities and circumstances of childhood.

Perhaps the most widespread means of helping children overcome fears, employed by millions of parents, is to expose them gradually to the feared object, often while acting simultaneously to inhibit their anxiety. If a little girl fears strangers, a parent takes her by the hand and walks her slowly toward the new person. Mary Cover Jones (see p. 518) was the first psychologist to explain this bit of folk wisdom as a counterconditioning procedure.

Contemporary therapists generally agree that exposure is the most effective way of eliminating baseless fear and avoidance. Modeling has also proved effective, both in laboratory studies (e.g., Bandura, Grusec, & Menlove, 1967) and in countless clinical treatments; for example, having another child, one the fearful child is likely to imitate, demonstrate fearless behavior. In one innovative study youngsters were helped by viewing films in which other isolated children gradually engaged in and came to enjoy play with their peers (O'Connor, 1969). Another group of researchers paired undergraduate volunteers with socially isolated children on the playground during recess (Allen et al., 1976). The goal was to help start group

games that would include the target child and give in vivo feedback to the child about which behaviors promoted or inhibited positive interactions with other children. By the end of the six-month program the volunteers were standing on the sidelines observing the children playing with their peers.

Offering rewards for moving closer to a feared object or situation can also be encouraging to a fearful child. Both modeling and operant treatments involve exposure to what is feared. When the fear and avoidance of a school-phobic child are very great and of long duration, they may require desensitization through direct, graduated exposure plus operant shaping.

In a case already mentioned (Lazarus, Davison, & Polefka, 1965) the therapist began by walking to school with nine-year-old Paul. The boy was then exposed more and more to school with lessening contact with the therapist. On successive days Paul first entered the school yard; next, he entered an empty classroom after school; then he attended the opening morning exercises and left. Later he sat at a desk and spent time in school, first with the therapist beside him, then with the therapist out of sight but still nearby. In the last steps, when anxiety seemed to have lessened, the therapist provided reinforcement for Paul in the form of promises to play the guitar for him at night, comic books, and tokens that would eventually earn him a baseball glove.

As with adults, some new situations may be threatening for children because they lack the knowledge and skills to deal with them. Thus a child's fear of the water may very well be based on a reasonable judgment that danger lurks there because he or she cannot swim. Some shy children lack specific social skills needed for peer interaction. Skills such as asking questions (Ladd, 1981), giving compliments, and starting conversations with age-mates (Michelson et al., 1983) may be taught in small groups or pairs, with interactions videotaped so the child and coach can observe and modify the new behaviors.

Treatment outcome studies suggest that time-limited treatment of children's phobias can be very effective. For example, Hampe et al. (1973) treated sixty-seven phobic children for eight weeks, using either a behavioral or insight-oriented therapy. Sixty percent of the treated children were free of their phobia at the end of the eight-week period and did not experience a relapse or additional emotional problems during the two-year follow-up period. Eighty percent of the sample (those just mentioned plus others who sought further treatment elsewhere) were free of symptoms after two years, with only 7 percent continuing to experience a severe phobia. The authors concluded that although many childhood phobias cease without intervention, treatment greatly hastens recovery.

(Gelernter et al., 1991). Although the risk of lethal overdose is not as great as with barbiturates, benzodiazepines are addicting and produce a severe withdrawal syndrome (Schweizer et al., 1991). The key problem in treating phobias and other anxiety disorders with drugs is that the drugs may be difficult to discontinue and relapse is common if the patient stops taking them (Herbert, 1995). (See Focus 6.1 for a discussion of childhood fears and phobias.)

PANIC DISORDER

In **panic disorder** there is a sudden and often inexplicable attack of a host of jarring symptoms—labored breathing, heart palpitations, nausea, chest pain, feelings of choking and smothering; dizziness, sweating, and trembling; and intense apprehension, terror, and feelings of impending doom. **Depersonalization** and **derealization**—feelings of being outside one's body and of the world's not being real—and fears of losing control, of going crazy, or even of dying may beset and overwhelm the patient. Panic attacks may occur frequently, perhaps once weekly or more often; usually last minutes, rarely hours; and are sometimes linked to specific situations, such as driving a car. When strongly associated with situational triggers, they are referred to as cued panic attacks; when a relationship between a stimulus and an attack is present but not as strong, they are referred to as situationally predisposed attacks. Panic attacks can also occur in seemingly benign states, such as relaxation, in sleep, and in unexpected situations; in these cases they are referred to as uncued attacks. Recurrent uncued attacks are required for the diagnosis of panic disorder; the exclusive presence of cued attacks most likely reflects the presence of a phobia.

The lifetime prevalence of panic disorder is about 2 percent for men and more than 5 percent for women (Kessler et al., 1984). It typically begins in adolescence, and its onset is associated with stressful life experiences (Pollard, Pollard, & Corn, 1989). Panic disorder occurs cross-culturally. In a study conducted in Africa it was diagnosed in about 1 percent of men and 6 percent of women (Hollifield et al., 1990). Disorders that bear some relationship to panic disorder occur in other cultures also. Among the Eskimo of west Greenland, attacks of kayak-angst occur among seal hunters who are alone at sea. It involves intense fear, disorientation, and concerns about drowning. Ataque de nervios was originally identified in Puerto Rico and involves physical symptoms and fears of going crazy in the aftermath of severe stress.

In DSM-IV panic disorder is diagnosed as with or without agoraphobia. **Agoraphobia** (from the Greek *agora*, meaning "marketplace") is a cluster of fears centering on public places and being unable to escape or find help should the individual become incapacitated. Fears of shopping, crowds, and traveling are often present. Many patients with agoraphobia are unable to leave the house or do only with great distress. Patients who have panic disorder typically avoid the situations in which a panic attack could be dangerous or embarrassing. If the avoidance becomes widespread, panic with agora-

Disorders similar to panic attacks occur cross-culturally. Among Eskimos kayak-angst is defined by intense fear among lone hunters.

phobia is the result. (When agoraphobia occurs in the absence of a diagnosable panic disorder the person typically has experienced panic symptoms, but not full-blown attacks. So, in both cases the agoraphobia is linked to a fear of having an attack.) Panic disorder with agoraphobia and agoraphobia without a history of panic disorder are both much more common among women than among men. This situation may reflect an exaggerated extension of the stereotyped female role. Until recently, it has been more socially acceptable for a woman to be housebound (Fodor, 1978).

More than 80 percent of patients diagnosed as having one of the other anxiety disorders also experience panic attacks, although not with the frequency that justifies a diagnosis of panic disorder (Barlow et al., 1985). Coexistence of panic disorder and major depression is also common (Breier et al., 1986), as is comorbidity between panic disorder and generalized anxiety disorder (Sanderson et al., 1990), phobias (Horvath et al., 1995), alcoholism, and personality disorders (Johnson, Weissman, & Klerman, 1990). As with many of the disorders discussed in this book, comorbidity is associated with poor outcomes, probably because there are simply more problems to deal with (Noyes et al., 1990).

ETIOLOGY OF PANIC DISORDER

Panic disorder runs in families (Crowe et al., 1987) and has greater concordance in identical twin pairs than in fraternal twins (Torgersen, 1983); thus a genetic diathesis may be present.

One biological theory suggests that panic is caused by overactivity in the noradrenergic system (neurons that use norepinephrine as a neurotransmitter), particularly in a nucleus in the pons called the locus ceruleus. Stimulation of the locus ceruleus causes monkeys to have what appears to be a panic attack, suggesting that naturally occurring attacks might be based on noradrenergic overactivation (Redmond, 1977). Subsequent research with humans has found that yohimbine, a drug that stimulates activity in the locus ceruleus, can elicit panic attacks in patients with panic disorder (Charney et al., 1987). However, more recent research is not consistent with the theory. Importantly, drugs that block firing in the locus ceruleus have not been found to be very effective in treating panic attacks (McNally, 1994).

Another line of biological inquiry has focused on experimental manipulations that can induce panic attacks. One approach proposes that panic attacks are linked to hyperventilation, or overbreathing (Ley, 1987). Hyperventilation may activate the autonomic nervous system, thus leading to the familiar somatic aspects of a panic episode. Lactate (a product of muscular exertion) can also produce panic, and its level may become elevated in patients with panic disorder because of chronic hyperventilation. Based on the finding that breathing air containing higher than usual amounts of carbon dioxide (CO_2) can generate a panic attack in a laboratory setting, oversensitive CO_2 receptors have also been proposed as a mechanism that could stimulate hyperventilation (Gorman et al., 1988; Klein, 1993). However, more recent research, which monitored patients with panic disorder in their natural environments, found that hyperventilation occurred in only one of twenty-four attacks (Garssen et al., 1996). Therefore this line of biological inquiry has not panned out.

The data indicating that various biological challenges (e.g., carbon dioxide, hyperventilation) can induce panic also show that they do so only in those who have already been diagnosed with the disorder. This could be taken to mean that these stimuli activate some kind of biological abnormality or diathesis in patients with the disorder. However, the physiological responses of people with panic disorder to these biological challenges are very similar to those of people without the disorder. Only the self-reported levels of fear induced by the challenge differentiate the two groups (Margraf, Ehlers, & Roth, 1986). Therefore the results may indicate that it is the psychological reaction to the challenge that is central. Further support for this hypothesis comes from a recent study that found that the effects of carbon dioxide on panic were markedly reduced when experienced in the presence of another person with whom the subject felt safe (Carter et al., 1995).

The principal psychological theory of the agoraphobia that often accompanies panic disorder is the fear-of-fear hypothesis (e.g., Goldstein & Chambless, 1978), which suggests that agoraphobia is not a fear of public places per se but a fear of having a panic attack in public. As to panic disorder itself, one idea is that patients misinterpret physiological sensations in a catastrophic way (Clark, 1986). In this overconcern they may amplify slight physical sensations into signs of impending disaster, which could then spiral into full-blown panic (Holt & Anderson, 1989). For example, a skipped heartbeat may be taken to mean that a heart attack is imminent.

In an important test of this hypothesis Telch and Harrington (in press) studied college students with no history of panic attacks who were divided into two groups (high and low scorers) based on their scores on a questionnaire measure of the extent to which they responded fearfully to their bodily sensations. All participants experienced two trials; on one they breathed room air and on the other air with a higher than usual concentration of carbon dioxide. Half the subjects in each group were told that the carbon dioxide would be relaxing and half were told that it would produce symptoms of high arousal. The frequency of panic attacks in each group is shown in Table 6.1. Note that panic attacks did not occur in subjects when they breathed room air, confirming previous findings. Also, the data

TABLE 6.1 Frequency of panic attacks as a function of breathing room air versus breathing air with carbon dioxide, fear of bodily sensations, and expectations. Students high in fear of bodily sensations who breathed air with a high concentration of carbon dioxide but did not expect its arousing effects had a very high frequency of panic attacks.

Inhale	High Fear of Bodily Sensations		Low Fear of Bodily Sensations	
	Expect Relaxation	Expect Arousal	Expect Relaxation	Expect Arousal
Room air	0	0	0	0
Carbon dioxide	52	17	5	5

show that the frequency of panic attacks was higher in subjects who were high in fear of their own bodily sensations. Finally, and most important, the frequency of panic attacks was strikingly high in subjects who feared their bodily sensations, breathed air containing a high concentration of carbon dioxide, and did not expect it to be arousing. This result is exactly what the theory predicts: unexplained physiological arousal in someone who is fearful of such sensations leads to panic attacks.

The concept of control is also relevant to panic. Patients with the disorder have an extreme fear of losing control, which would happen if they had an attack in public. The importance of control was clearly demonstrated in a study by Sanderson, Rapee, and Barlow (1989). Patients with panic disorder breathed carbon dioxide and were told that when a light turned on they could turn a dial to reduce the concentration of carbon dioxide. For half the subjects the light was on continuously, whereas for the remainder it never came on. Turning the dial actually had no effect on CO_2 levels, so the study was of the effects of *perceived* control on reactions to the challenge. Eighty percent of the group with no control had a panic attack, compared with only 20 percent of the group who thought they could control CO_2 levels. Note that in addition to clearly demonstrating the importance of perceived control in panic disorder, the data again show that it is not the biological challenge per se that elicits panic; rather, a person's psychological reaction is crucial.

THERAPIES FOR PANIC DISORDER AND AGORAPHOBIA

Both antidepressants and anxiolytics, such as the benzodiazepines, have shown some success as biological treatments. The evidence for the effectiveness of alprazolam (Xanax), a benzodiazepine derivative, is particularly compelling as it has been obtained in a large-scale, multinational study (Ballenger et al., 1988). However, drug treatment must be continued indefinitely, for symptoms almost always return if it is stopped (Fyer, Sandberg, & Klein, 1991). Furthermore, the benzodiazapines are addicting, and they produce both cognitive and motor side effects, such as memory lapses and difficulty driving. In their efforts to reduce anxiety many patients use anxiolytics or alcohol on their own; the use and abuse of drugs is common in anxiety-ridden people.

Exposure-based treatments are often useful in reducing agoraphobia. Married patients whose problem is primarily or solely agoraphobia have benefited from family-oriented therapies that involve the nonphobic spouse, who is encouraged to stop catering to his or her partner's avoidance of leaving the home. Barlow's clinical research program has found that successful in vivo exposure treatment, in which the agoraphobic person is encouraged to venture little by little from "safe" domains, is enhanced when the spouse is involved (Cerny et al., 1987). Contrary to the belief that one spouse somehow needs the other to be dependent on him or her (Milton & Hafner, 1979), marital satisfaction tends to improve as the fearful spouse becomes bolder (Craske et al., 1992; Himadi et al., 1986). Thus, while it is understandable that a spouse might become overly solicitous, perhaps from reasonable concern for his or her partner's well-being, perhaps from an inner need to have a spouse who is weak and dependent, the outcome data suggest that relationships improve when the agoraphobic spouse becomes less fearful.

Because treating agoraphobia with exposure does not always reduce panic attacks (Michelson, Mavissakalian, & Marchione, 1985), psychological treatment of panic disorder also takes into account the idea that some panic-disorder patients may become unduly alarmed by noticing sensations from their bodies. One well-validated therapy developed by Barlow and his associates has three principal components: relaxation training; a combination of Ellis- and Beck-type cognitive-behavioral interventions; and, the most novel part, exposure to the internal cues that trigger panic (Barlow, 1988; Barlow & Cerny, 1988; Barlow, Craske, & Klosko, 1989; Klosko et al., 1990). For this third component the client practices in the consulting room behaviors that can elicit feelings associated with panic. For example, a person whose panic attacks begin with hyperventilation is asked to breathe fast for three minutes; someone who gets dizzy might be requested to spin in a chair for several minutes. When sensations such as dizziness, dry mouth, lightheadedness, increased heart rate, and other signs of panic begin to be felt, the client (1) experiences them under safe conditions and (2) applies previously learned cognitive and relaxation coping tactics (which can include breathing from the diaphragm rather than hyperventilating).

With practice and encouragement or persuasion from the therapist, the client learns to reinterpret internal sensations from signals of loss of control and panic to cues that are intrinsically harmless and can be controlled with certain skills. The intentional creation of these signs by the client coupled with success in coping with them reduces their unpredictability and changes their meaning for the client (Craske, Maidenburg, & Bystritsky, 1995). Two-year follow-ups have shown that therapeutic gains from this cognitive and exposure therapy have been maintained to a significant degree and are superior to the use of alprazolam (Craske, Brown, & Barlow, 1992), though many patients are not panic free (Brown & Barlow, 1995). Furthermore, recent comparative reviews of pharmacotherapy and psychotherapy in the treatment of panic disorder (Jacobson and Hollon, 1996; Gorman, 1994) conclude that the kind of cognitive-behavioral treatments pioneered by Barlow are better at long-term follow-up than tricyclics like imipramine (Tofranil), monoamine oxidase inhibitors (another antidepressant, see p. 246, which can have toxic side effects), and benzodiazepines like alprazolam. Also important to take note of is that some people, especially pregnant women, are well-advised to avoid taking medications such as these; other people either tolerate them poorly or do not respond to their therapeutic potential.

GENERALIZED ANXIETY DISORDER

The patient, a twenty-four-year-old mechanic, had been referred for psychotherapy by his physician, whom he had consulted because of dizziness and difficulties in falling asleep. He was quite visibly distressed during the entire initial interview, gulping before he spoke, sweating, and continually fidgeting in his chair. His repeated requests for water to slake a seemingly unquenchable thirst were another indication of his extreme nervousness. Although he first related his physical concerns, a more general picture of pervasive anxiety soon emerged. He reported that he nearly always felt tense. He seemed to worry about anything and everything. He was apprehensive of disasters that could befall him as he worked and interacted with other people. He reported a long history of difficulties in interpersonal relationships, which had led to his being fired from several jobs. As he put it, "I really like people and try to get along with them, but it seems like I fly off the handle too easily. Little things they do upset me too much. I just can't cope unless everything is going exactly right."

The individual with **generalized anxiety disorder (GAD)** is persistently anxious, often about minor things. Chronic, uncontrollable worry about all manner of things is the hallmark of GAD; for example, the individual may be constantly terrified that his or her child will have an accident. So pervasive is this distress that it is sometimes referred to as free-floating anxiety. Somatic complaints—

sweating, flushing, pounding heart, upset stomach, diarrhea, frequent urination, cold, clammy hands, dry mouth, a lump in the throat, shortness of breath—are frequent and reflect hyperactivity of the autonomic nervous system. Pulse and respiration rates, too, may be high. The person may also report disturbances of the skeletal musculature: muscle tension and aches, especially of the neck and shoulders; eyelid and other twitches; trembling; tiring easily; and an inability to relax. He or she is easily startled, fidgety, and restless. The person is generally apprehensive, often imagining and worrying about impending disasters, such as losing control, having a heart attack, or dying. Impatience, irritability, angry outbursts, insomnia, and distractibility are also common, for the person is always on edge.

Although patients with generalized anxiety disorder do not typically seek treatment, the lifetime prevalence of the disorder is fairly high, occurring in about 5 percent of the general population (Wittchen et al., 1994). It typically begins in the person's midteens, though many GAD sufferers report having had the problem all their lives (Barlow et al., 1986). Stressful life events appear to play some role in its onset (Blazer, Hughes, & George, 1987). It is twice as common in women than in men, and it has a high level of comorbidity with other anxiety disorders and mood disorders (Brown, Barlow, & Liebowitz, 1994).

ETIOLOGY OF GENERALIZED ANXIETY DISORDER

PSYCHOANALYTIC VIEW

Psychoanalytic theory regards the source of generalized anxiety as an unconscious conflict between the ego and id impulses. The impulses, usually sexual or aggressive in nature, are struggling for expression, but the ego cannot allow their expression because it unconsciously fears that punishment will follow. Since the source of the anxiety is unconscious, the person experiences apprehension and distress without knowing why. The true source of anxiety, namely, desires associated with previously punished id impulses that are striving for expression, is ever present. In a sense there is no way to evade anxiety; if the person escapes the id he or she is no longer alive. The person feels anxiety nearly all the time. The patient with a phobia may be regarded as more fortunate since, according to psychoanalytic theory, his or her anxiety is displaced onto a specific object or situation, which can then be avoided. The person with generalized anxiety disorder has not developed this type of defense and thus is constantly anxious.

COGNITIVE-BEHAVIORAL VIEWS

In attempting to account for generalized anxiety, learning theorists (e.g., Wolpe, 1958) look to the environment. For example, a person anxious most of his or her waking hours might well be fearful of social contacts. If that individual spends a good deal of time with other people it may be more useful to regard the anxiety as tied to these circumstances rather than to any internal factors. This behavioral model of generalized anxiety is identical to one of the learning views of phobias. The anxiety is regarded as having been classically conditioned to external stimuli, although the range of conditioned stimuli is considerably broader.

The focus of other cognitive and behavioral views of generalized anxiety disorder mesh so closely that we will discuss them in tandem. When people are confronted with painful stimuli over which they have no control, anxiety results. Cognitive theory emphasizes the perception of not being in control as a central characteristic of all views of anxiety (Mandler, 1966). Thus a cognitive-behavioral model of generalized anxiety focuses on control and helplessness.

Studies of humans (including the research on CO_2-induced panic attacks described earlier) have shown that stressful events over which people can exert some control are less anxiety provoking than are events over which they can exercise no control. Research also suggests that in certain circumstances it is sufficient for the control to only be perceived by the subject; control does not need actually to exist (e.g., Geer, Davison, & Gatchel, 1970). Linking these findings to GAD, Barlow (1988) has shown that these patients perceive threatening events as out of their control.

Related to this idea of control is the fact that predictable events produce less anxiety than do unpredictable events (see Mineka, 1992). For example, animals prefer a signaled, and therefore predictable, shock to one that is not signaled (Seligman & Binik, 1977). The absence of the signal can serve as a sign of safety, indicating that no shock is forthcoming and there is no need to worry. Unsignaled and therefore unpredictable aversive stimuli may lead to chronic vigilance and fear, or what in humans we would call worry (Borkovec & Inz, 1990).

In addition to the feeling of being unable to control stressors, several other cognitive processes tend to characterize patients with GAD. These patients often misperceive benign events, such as crossing the street, as involving threats, and their cognitions focus on anticipated future disasters (Beck et al., 1987; Ingram & Kendall, 1987; Kendall & Ingram, 1989). The attention of patients with GAD is easily drawn to stimuli that suggest possible physical harm or social misfortune, such as criticism, embarrassment, or rejection (MacLeod et al., 1986). For example, a person with GAD may be quick to notice that the person with whom he or she is speaking looks around the room from time to time, and thus begins to worry about being rejected. Furthermore, patients with GAD are more inclined to interpret ambiguous stimuli as threatening and to rate ominous events as more likely to occur to them (Butler & Matthews, 1983). The heightened sensitivity of GAD patients to threatening stimuli occurs even when the stimuli cannot be consciously perceived (Bradley et al., 1995).

Another cognitive view has recently been offered by Borkovec, Roemer, and Kinyon (1995). Their focus is on the main symptom of GAD, worry. From a punishment perspective one might wonder why anyone would worry a lot, since worry is thought to be a negative state that should discourage its repetition. Borkovec and his colleagues have marshaled evidence that worry is actually negatively reinforcing; it distracts patients from even more negative emotions.

BIOLOGICAL PERSPECTIVES

Some studies indicate that GAD may have a genetic component. However, although greater prevalence of GAD in the relatives of GAD patients has been reported (Noyes et al., 1992) the results of twin studies are inconsistent (Kendler et al., 1992; Torgerson, 1983). At this time we must conclude that the data are equivocal. The fact that neuroticism, a personality trait linked to all the anxiety disorders, is heritable, indicates that genetic factors should not be ruled out as possible influences.

The most prevalent neurobiological model for generalized anxiety is based on knowledge of the operation of the benzodiazepines, a group of drugs that are often effective in treating anxiety. Researchers have discovered a receptor in the brain for benzodiazepines that is linked to the inhibitory neurotransmitter gamma-aminobutyric acid (GABA) (see p. 28). In normal fear reactions neurons throughout the brain fire and create the experience of anxiety. This neural firing also stimulates the GABA system, which inhibits this activity and thus reduces anxiety. GAD may result from some defect in the GABA system so that anxiety is not brought under control. The benzodiazepines may reduce anxiety by enhancing release of GABA. Similarly, drugs that block or inhibit the GABA system lead to increases in anxiety (Insell, 1986). Much remains to be learned, but this approach seems destined to enhance our understanding of anxiety.

THERAPIES FOR GENERALIZED ANXIETY DISORDER

As they view generalized anxiety disorder as stemming from repressed conflicts, most psychoanalysts work to help patients confront the true sources of their conflicts. Treatment is much the same as that for phobias.

Behavioral clinicians approach generalized anxiety in various ways. If patients can construe the anxiety as a set of responses to identifiable situations, the free-floating anxiety can be reformulated into one or more phobias or cued anxieties, making it easier to treat. For example, a behavior therapist may determine that the generally anxious client seems more specifically afraid of criticizing and of being criticized by others. The anxiety appears free-floating only because the client spends so many hours with other human beings. Systematic desensitization becomes a possible treatment.

However, it can be difficult to find specific causes of the anxiety suffered by such patients. This difficulty has led behavioral clinicians to prescribe more generalized treatment, such as intensive relaxation training, in the hope that learning to relax when beginning to feel tense will keep anxiety from spiraling out of control (Barlow et al., 1984; Borkovec & Mathews, 1988; Ost, 1987). Patients are taught to relax away low-level tensions, responding to incipient anxiety with relaxation rather than with alarm (Goldfried, 1971; Suinn & Richardson, 1971). Recently, this strategy has been found very effective in alleviating GAD (e.g., Borkovec & Roemer, 1994; Borkovec & Whisman, 1996).

If a feeling of helplessness seems to underlie the pervasive anxiety, the cognitively oriented behavior therapist will help the client acquire whatever skills might engender a sense of competence. The skills, including assertiveness, may be taught by verbal instructions, modeling, or operant shaping—and very likely some judicious combination of the three (Goldfried & Davison, 1994). Because chronic worrying is central to GAD it is not surprising that cognitive techniques have been employed in its treatment. Perhaps a person worries needlessly because he or she interprets ambiguous stimuli as threats or overestimates the likelihood that a negative event will occur (Butler & Matthews, 1983). Helping GAD sufferers reappraise a situation may therefore help, and recent evidence suggests that it does (Borkovec & Costello, 1993).

Anxiolytics, such as those mentioned for the treatment of phobias and panic disorder, are probably the most widespread treatment for generalized anxiety disorder. Psychoactive drugs are used because of the disorder's pervasiveness. Once they take effect, they continue to work for several hours in whatever situations are encountered. Unfortunately, many tranquilizing drugs have undesirable side effects, ranging from drowsiness and depression to physical addiction and damage to bodily organs. In addition, when a patient withdraws from these drugs, the gains achieved in treatment are usually lost (Barlow, 1988), perhaps because the person (rightfully) attributes the improvement to an external agent, the medication, rather than to internal changes and his or her own coping efforts (Davison & Valins, 1969) and thus the person continues to believe that the anxiety and the worrisome possibilities remain uncontrollable.

OBSESSIVE-COMPULSIVE DISORDER

Bernice was forty-six when she entered treatment. This was the fourth time she had been in outpatient therapy, and she had previously been hospitalized twice. Her obsessive-compulsive disorder had begun twelve years earlier, shortly after the death of her father. Since then it had waxed and waned and currently was as severe as it had ever been.

Bernice was obsessed with a fear of contamination, a fear she vaguely linked to her father's death from pneumonia. Although she reported that she was afraid of nearly everything, because germs could be anywhere, she was particularly upset by touching wood, "scratchy objects," mail, canned goods, and "silver flecks." By silver flecks Bernice meant silver embossing on a greeting card, eyeglass frames, shiny appliances, and silverware. She was unable to state why these particular objects were sources of possible contamination.

To try to reduce her discomfort Bernice engaged in a variety of compulsive rituals that took up almost all her waking hours. In the morning she spent three to four hours in the bathroom, washing and rewashing herself. Between baths she scraped away the outside layer of her bar of soap so that it would be totally free of germs. Mealtimes also lasted for hours, as Bernice performed her rituals—eating three bites of food at a time, chewing each mouthful 300 times. These steps were meant "magically" to decontaminate her food. Even Bernice's husband was sometimes involved in these mealtime ceremonies, shaking a teakettle and frozen vegetables over her head to remove the germs. Bernice's rituals and fear of contamination had reduced her life to doing almost nothing else. She would not leave the house, do housework, or even talk on the telephone.

Obsessive-compulsive disorder (OCD) is an anxiety disorder in which the mind is flooded with persistent and uncontrollable thoughts or the individual is compelled to repeat certain acts again and again, causing significant distress and interference with everyday functioning. Obsessive-compulsive disorder affects between 2 and 3 percent of the population, more often women than men (Karno & Golding, 1991). It usually begins in early adulthood, often following some stressful event, such as pregnancy, childbirth, family conflict, or difficulties at work (Kringlen, 1970). Early onset is more common among men and is associated with checking compulsions; later onset is more frequent among women and is linked with cleaning compulsions (Noshirvani et al., 1991). During an episode of depression patients occasionally develop obsessive-compulsive disorder, and significant depression is often found in obsessive-compulsive patients (Rachman & Hodgson, 1980). Obsessive-compulsive disorder also shows comorbidity with other anxiety disorders, particularly with panic and phobias (Austin et al., 1990), and with various personality disorders (Baer et al., 1990; Mavissikalian, Hammen, & Jones, 1990).

Obsessions are intrusive and recurring thoughts, impulses, and images that come unbidden to the mind and appear irrational and uncontrollable to the individual experiencing them. Whereas many of us may have similar fleeting experiences, as we saw in the case of Bernice, the obsessive individual has them with such force and frequency that they inter-fere with normal functioning. Clinically, the most frequent obsessions concern fears of contamination, expressing some sexual or aggressive impulse, or hypochondriacal fears of bodily dysfunction (Jenike, Baer, & Minichiello, 1986). Obsessions may also take the form of extreme doubting, procrastination, and indecision.

A **compulsion** is a repetitive behavior or mental act that the person feels driven to perform in order to reduce the distress caused by obsessive thoughts or to prevent some calamity from occurring. The activity is not realistically connected with its apparent purpose or is clearly excessive. Bernice did not need to chew each morsel of food 300 times. Often an individual who continually repeats some action fears dire consequences if the act is not performed. The sheer frequency with which an act is repeated may be staggering. Commonly reported compulsions have to do with cleanliness and orderliness, sometimes achieved only by elaborate ceremonies that take hours and even most of the day; with avoiding particular objects, such as staying away from anything brown; with repetitive, magical, protective practices, such as counting, saying certain numbers, touching a talisman or a particular part of the body; and with checking, going back seven or eight times to verify that already performed acts were actually carried out, for example, that lights, gas jets, or faucets were turned off, windows fastened, doors locked. Sometimes compulsions take the form of performing an act, such as eating, extremely slowly.

This famous scene from *Macbeth* illustrates a compulsion involving handwashing.

We often hear people described as compulsive gamblers, compulsive eaters, and compulsive drinkers. Even though individuals may report an irresistible urge to gamble, eat, and drink, such behavior is not clinically regarded as a compulsion because it is often engaged in with pleasure. A true compulsion is often viewed by the person as somehow foreign to his or her personality. Stern and Cobb (1978) found that 78 percent of a sample of compulsive individuals viewed their rituals as "rather silly or absurd" even though they were unable to stop them.

A frequent consequence of obsessive-compulsive disorder is a negative effect on the individual's relations with other people, especially family members. People saddled with the irresistible need to wash their hands every ten minutes, or touch every doorknob they pass, or count every tile in a bathroom floor are likely to cause concern and even resent-ment in spouses, children, friends, or co-workers. And the antagonistic feelings experienced by these significant others are likely to be tinged with guilt, for at some level they understand that the person cannot really help doing these senseless things. The undesirable effects on others can, in turn, be expected to have additional consequences, engendering feelings of depression and generalized anxiety in the obsessive-compulsive person and setting the stage for even further deterioration of personal relationships. For such reasons family therapists (Hafner, 1982; Hafner et al., 1981) have suggested that obsessive-compulsive disorder is sometimes embedded in marital distress and actually substitutes for overt marital conflict. This speculative hypothesis cautions therapists to consider couples treatment as well as individual therapies.

ETIOLOGY OF OBSESSIVE-COMPULSIVE DISORDER

PSYCHOANALYTIC THEORY

In psychoanalytic theory obsessions and compulsions are viewed as similar, resulting from instinctual forces, sexual or aggressive, that are not under control because of overly harsh toilet training. The person is thus fixated at the anal stage. The symptoms observed represent the outcome of the struggle between the id and the defense mechanisms; sometimes the aggressive instincts of the id predominate, sometimes the defense mechanisms. For example, when obsessive thoughts of killing intrude, the forces of the id are dominant. More often, however, the observed symptoms reflect the partially successful operation of one of the defense mechanisms. For example, an individual fixated at the anal stage may, by reaction formation, resist the urge to soil and become compulsively neat, clean, and orderly.

Alfred Adler (1931) viewed obsessive-compulsive disorder as a result of feelings of incompetence. He believed that when children are kept from developing a sense of competence by doting or excessively dominating parents, they develop an inferiority complex and may unconsciously adopt compulsive rituals in order to carve out a domain in which they exert control and can feel proficient. Adler proposed that the compulsive act allows a person mastery of *something*, even if only the positioning of writing implements on a desk.

BEHAVIORAL AND COGNITIVE THEORIES

Behavioral accounts of obsessions and compulsions consider the disorder to be learned behaviors reinforced by their consequences (Meyer & Chesser,

1970). One set of consequences is the reduction of fear. For example, compulsive hand washing is viewed as an operant escape-response that reduces an obsessional preoccupation with and fear of contamination by dirt or germs. Similarly, compulsive checking may reduce anxiety about whatever disaster the patient anticipates if the checking ritual is not completed. Anxiety as measured by self-report (Hodgson & Rachman, 1972) and psychophysiological responses (Carr, 1971) can indeed be reduced by such compulsive behavior. Research has also shown, however, that not all compulsive acts reduce anxiety to the same degree. Rachman and Hodgson (1980) reported that patients with a cleaning compulsion were more often able to lessen their anxiety than were patients with a checking compulsion. Furthermore, the reduction of anxiety cannot account for obsessions. Indeed, the obsessions of obsessive-compulsive patients usually make them anxious (Rabavilas & Boulougouris, 1974), much as do the somewhat similar intrusive thoughts of normal subjects about stressful stimuli, such as a scary movie (Horowitz, 1975).

A study by Sher, Frost, and Otto (1983) used cognitive tasks to test the idea that college students who scored high on a measure of compulsive checking suffered from a memory deficit for actions performed—Did I turn off the stove?—and for distinguishing between reality and imagination—Maybe I just *imagined* I turned off the stove. (Note that these are two specific kinds of memory problems; the idea is not that patients with OCD have poor memories in general.) In both instances the person would be inclined to reduce uncertainty by checking whether in fact the stove was turned off. The results supported the first hypothesis, that compulsive checkers had poorer recall of prior actions. The second hypothesis was not unequivocally supported, and a more recent investigation also showed that OCD patients were not less accurate than normals in distinguishing previously seen versus previously imagined stimuli (Brown et al., 1994). A replication study, using psychiatric patients as subjects, again showed that high scorers on a measure of compulsive checking were poor at remembering their own recent activities (Sher et al., 1989). These studies are significant in that they construe at least one kind of compulsivity as a problem in a certain kind of memory and test this hypothesis via procedures that derive from basic experimental research in cognition.

How can we account for obsessive thoughts? Most people occasionally experience unwanted ideas that are similar in content to obsessions (Rachman & DeSilva, 1978). These unpleasant thoughts increase when people are subjected to stress (Parkinson & Rachman, 1981). Normal individuals can tolerate or dismiss these cognitions. But for individuals with obsessive-compulsive disorder the thoughts may be particularly vivid and elicit great concern, perhaps because of childhood experiences that have taught them that some thoughts are dangerous or unacceptable. Persons with obsessive-compulsive disorder may try to actively suppress these troubling thoughts, with unfortunate consequences.

Wegner et al. (1987, in press) studied what happens when people are asked to suppress a thought. Two groups of college students were asked either to think about a white bear or not to think about one. One group thought about the white bear and then was told not to; the other group did the reverse. Thoughts were measured by having subjects voice their thoughts and also by having them ring a bell every time they thought about a white bear. Two findings are of particular note. First, attempts to inhibit were not fully successful. Second, the students who first inhibited thoughts of a white bear had more subsequent thoughts about it once the inhibition condition was over. Trying to inhibit a thought may therefore have the paradoxical effect of inducing preoccupation with it. Furthermore, attempts to suppress unpleasant thoughts are typically associated with intense emotional states, resulting in a strong link between the suppressed thought and the emotion. After many attempts at suppression a strong emotion may lead to the return of the thought, accompanied by an increase in negative mood (Wenzlaff, Wegner, & Klein, 1991). The result would be an increase in anxiety.

BIOLOGICAL FACTORS

Encephalitis, head injuries, and brain tumors have all been associated with the development of obsessive-compulsive disorder (Jenike, 1986). Interest has focused on two areas of the brain that could be affected by such trauma, the frontal lobes and the basal ganglia, a set of subcortical nuclei including the caudate, putamen, globus pallidus, and amygdala. PET scan studies have shown increased activation in the frontal lobes of OCD patients, perhaps a reflection of their overconcern with their own thoughts. The focus on the basal ganglia, a system linked to the control of motor behavior, is due to its relevance to compulsions as well as to the relationship between OCD and Tourette's syndrome. Tourette's syndrome is marked by both motor and vocal tics and has been linked to basal ganglia dysfunction. Patients with Tourette's often have OCD as well (Rauch & Jenike, 1993). Providing support for the importance of both brain regions mentioned, Rauch et al. (1994) stimulated OCD symptoms by presenting patients with stimuli specially selected for them, such as a glove contaminated with garbage or an unlocked door. Blood flow in the brain increased in the frontal area and to some of the basal ganglia.

Research on neurochemical factors has focused on serotonin. As we describe later, antidepressants that inhibit the reuptake of serotonin have proved to be useful therapies for OCD (e.g., Pigott et al., 1990). The usual interpretation of this finding would be that because the drugs facilitate synaptic transmission in serotonin neurons, OCD is related to low levels of serotonin or a reduced number of receptors. However, tests of these ideas have not yielded the expected results. For example, research with drugs that stimulate the serotonin receptor indicates that they can exacerbate the symptoms of OCD instead of reducing them (Bastani, Nash, & Meltzer, 1990; Hollander et al., 1992). One possible explanation is that OCD is caused by a neurotransmitter system that is coupled to serotonin; when affected by antidepressants, the serotonin system causes changes in this other system, which is the real location of the therapeutic effect (Barr et al., 1994). Both dopamine and acetylcholine have been proposed as transmitters that are coupled to serotonin and play the more important role in OCD (Rauch & Jenike, 1993).

There is also some evidence for a genetic contribution to OCD (Carey & Gottesman, 1981). High rates of anxiety disorders occur among the first-degree relatives of patients with OCD (McKeen & Murray, 1987). Lenane et al. (1990) found that 30 percent of the first-degree relatives in their study also had OCD. Although it is premature to conclude that biological factors predispose people to OCD, we can expect the search for a biological diathesis to intensify in the coming years.

THERAPIES FOR OBSESSIVE-COMPULSIVE DISORDER

Obsessive-compulsive disorder is one of the most difficult psychological problems to treat. Psychoanalytic treatment for obsessions and compulsions resembles that for phobias and generalized anxiety, namely, lifting repression and allowing the patient to confront what he or she truly fears, that a particular impulse will be gratified. Because the intrusive thoughts and compulsive behavior protect the ego from the repressed conflict, they are difficult targets for therapeutic intervention, and psychoanalytic

procedures have not been effective in treating this disorder. This shortcoming has prompted some analytic clinicians to take a more active, behavioral approach to these disorders and to use analytic understanding more as a way to increase compliance with behavioral procedures (Jenike, 1990). Free association can even feed into the patient's obsessionalism (Salzman, 1980). One psychoanalytic view hypothesizes that the indecision one sees in most obsessive-compulsive patients derives from a need for guaranteed correctness before any action can be taken (Salzman, 1985). Patients therefore must learn to tolerate the uncertainty and anxiety that all people feel as they confront the reality that nothing is certain or absolutely controllable in life.[2] The ultimate focus of the treatment remains insight into the unconscious determinants of the symptoms.

The most widely used and generally accepted behavioral approach to compulsive rituals, pioneered in England by Victor Meyer (1966), combines exposure with response prevention (Rachman & Hodgson, 1980). In this method the person exposes himself or herself to situations that elicit the compulsive act—such as touching a dirty dish—and then refrains from performing the accustomed ritual—hand washing. The assumption is that the ritual is negatively reinforcing because it reduces anxiety that is aroused by some environmental stimulus or event, such as dust on a chair, and that preventing the person from performing the ritual will expose him or her to the anxiety-provoking stimuli, thereby allowing the anxiety to extinguish. Controlled research (e.g., Duggan, Marks, & Richards, 1993; Foa et al., 1985; Stanley & Turner, 1995) suggests that this is at least a partially effective treatment for more than half of OCD sufferers, including children and adolescents (March, 1995).

Sometimes control over obsessive-compulsive rituals is possible only in a hospital. Meyer (1966) created a controlled environment at Middlesex Hospital in London to treat OCD. Staff members were specially trained to restrict the patient's opportunities for engaging in ritualistic acts. Generalization of the treatment to the home required the involvement of family members. Suffice it to say that preparing them for this work

---

[2]The hypothesized need of the obsessive-compulsive person not to err suggests that a rational-emotive approach might also be useful; the person may harbor an irrational belief that he or she must never make a mistake. In a rare clinical trial applying rational-emotive therapy to OCD, Emmelkamp, Visser, and Hoekstra (1988) found that Ellis's therapy achieved results comparable to those of an in vivo response-prevention therapy and was superior to the more strictly behavioral therapy in reducing depressed mood.

was no mean task, requiring skills and care beyond whatever specific behavioral technique was being employed.

In the short term, curtailment is arduous and unpleasant for clients; up to 25 percent of cases refuse treatment (Foa et al., 1985). Refusal to enter treatment and dropping out are generally recognized problems for many interventions for OCD (Jenike & Rauch, 1994). OCD patients tend to procrastinate, to fear changes, and to be overly concerned about others controlling them—characteristics that can be expected to create special problems for avowedly manipulative approaches such as behavior therapy.

Serotonin reuptake inhibitors and the tricyclics, drugs that are more commonly used in treating depression (see Chapter 10), are the biological treatments most often given to obsessive-compulsive patients. Both classes of drugs have yielded some beneficial results (Jenike, 1986). The largest study conducted to date on tricyclics (Clomipramine Collaborative Study Group, 1991) compared clomipramine to a placebo in a double-blind design and found some evidence of effectiveness. However, in a study assessing the role of imipramine in enhancing improvement brought about by response prevention with depressed OCD patients, Foa et al. (1992) failed to find an effect from this antidepressant drug on OCD symptoms, although imipramine did alleviate depression. Patients who received the response-prevention treatment but not imipramine improved on depression as much as those who also received the drug. This finding suggests that depression in OCD patients may be secondary to, or caused by, the OCD symptoms themselves. In another study the benefits of clomipramine on OCD were found to be short-lived; withdrawal from this drug led to a 90 percent relapse rate, much higher than that found with response prevention (Pato et al., 1988).

Research has shown some improvement in OCD patients with serotonin reuptake inhibitors, such as fluoxetine (Prozac). As with the tricyclics, however, treatment gains are modest and symptoms return if the drugs are discontinued (McDougle et al., 1994). It is also not clear whether the drugs work specifically on OCD or on its associated depression (Barr et al., 1994; Tollefson et al., 1994).

A study comparing treatment with fluoxetine and response prevention found that improvement in OCD by *both* treatments was associated with the same changes in brain function, namely, reduced metabolic activity in the right caudate nucleus, overactivity of which has been linked to OCD (Baxter et al., 1992). Only those patients who improved clinically showed this change in brain activity as measured by PET scans. Such findings suggest that markedly different therapies may work for similar reasons, as they are different ways of affecting the same factors in the brain. We should note that in the Baxter et al. study, patients were not randomly assigned to the treatment groups; rather, each patient selected either the drug or the response-prevention treatment. Although this design flaw does not in our view invalidate the findings, comparisons of the two treatments are not quite equivalent for another reason as well: during the posttreatment PET scan the drug subjects were still on medication, whereas the behavior-therapy patients were not and could not be, in any meaningful sense, in treatment, that is, undergoing active response prevention for the rituals.

The desperation of mental health workers, surpassed only by that of the sufferers, explains the occasional use of psychosurgery in treating obsessions and compulsions. The procedure in current use, cingulatomy, involves destroying two to three centimeters of white matter in the cingulum, an area near the corpus callosum. Although some clinical improvement has been reported, for example five of eighteen cases in one trial (Baer et al., 1995), this intervention is rightfully viewed as a treatment of very last resort given its permanence as well as the risks of psychosurgery and the poor understanding of how it works.

Regardless of treatment modality OCD patients are seldom cured. Although a variety of interventions can result in significant improvement, obsessive-compulsive tendencies usually persist to some degree, albeit under greater control and with less obtrusiveness into the conduct of patients' lives (White & Cole, 1990).

POSTTRAUMATIC STRESS DISORDER

A twenty-seven-year-old singer was referred by a friend for evaluation. Eight months before, her boyfriend had been stabbed to death during a mugging from which she escaped unharmed. After a period of mourning she appeared to return to her usual self. She helped the police in their investigation and was generally considered an ideal witness. Nevertheless, shortly after the arrest of a man accused of the murder, the patient began to have recurrent nightmares and vivid memories of the night of the crime. In the dreams she frequently saw blood and imagined herself being pursued by ominous, cloaked figures. During the day, especially when walking somewhere alone, she often drifted off in daydreams, so that she forgot where she was going. Her friends noted that she began to startle easily and seemed to be preoccupied. She left her change or groceries at the store, or when waited on could not remember what she had come to buy. She began to sleep restlessly, and her work suffered because of poor concentration. She gradually withdrew from her friends and began to avoid work. She felt considerable guilt about her boyfriend's murder, although exactly why was not clear. (Spitzer et al., 1981, p. 17)

Posttraumatic stress disorder (PTSD), introduced as a diagnosis in DSM-III (1980), entails an extreme response to a severe stressor, including increased anxiety, avoidance of stimuli associated with the trauma, and a numbing of emotional responses. Although there had been prior awareness that the stresses of combat could produce powerful and adverse effects on soldiers, the aftermath of the Vietnam War spurred the acceptance of the new diagnosis. Like other disorders in the DSM, PTSD is defined by a cluster of symptoms. But unlike the definitions of other psychological disorders, the definition of PTSD includes part of its presumed etiology, namely, a traumatic event or events that the person has directly experienced or witnessed involving actual or threatened death, or serious injury, or a threat to the physical integrity of self or others. The event must have created intense fear, horror, or a sense of helplessness. In previous editions of the DSM the traumatic event was defined as "outside the range of human experience." This definition was too restrictive, as it would have ruled out the diagnosis of PTSD following such events as automobile accidents. The current broadened definition may also be too restrictive, because it focuses on the event's objective characteristics whereas the subjective meaning of the event may be more crucial (King et al., 1995). We shall consider this issue again when we revisit PTSD in Chapter 14 as part of the aftermath of rape.

There is a difference between posttraumatic stress disorder and **acute stress disorder**, a new diagnosis in DSM-IV. Nearly everyone who encounters a trauma experiences stress, sometimes to a considerable degree. This is normal. If the stressor causes a significant impairment in social or occupational functioning, an acute stress disorder is diagnosed. About 60 percent of people recover from an acute stress disorder within a month and go on to lead lives that are not marked by PTSD.

The inclusion in the DSM of severe stress as a significant causal factor of PTSD was meant to reflect a formal recognition that regardless of their history,

Unlike most other diagnoses PTSD includes part of its cause, a traumatic event, in its definition. Rescue workers, such as this man at the Oklahoma City bombing, could be vulnerable to PTSD.

many people may be adversely affected by overwhelming catastrophic stress and that their reactions should be distinguished from other disorders; that is, the cause of PTSD is primarily the event, not the person. Instead of implicitly concluding that the person would be all right were he or she made of sterner stuff, the importance of the traumatizing circumstances is formally acknowledged in this definition (Haley, 1978). Yet the inclusion of this diagnostic criterion is not without controversy. Many people encounter traumatic life events but do not develop PTSD. For example, in one recent study only 25 percent of people who experienced a traumatic event leading to physical injury subsequently developed PTSD (Shalev et al., 1996); thus the event itself cannot be the sole cause of PTSD. Current research has moved in the direction of searching for factors that distinguish between people who do and those who do not develop PTSD after experiencing severe stress.

The symptoms for PTSD are grouped into three major categories. The diagnosis requires that symptoms in each category last longer than one month.

1. **Reexperiencing the traumatic event.** The individual frequently recalls the event and experiences nightmares about it. Intense emotional upset is produced by stimuli that symbolize the event (e.g., thunder, reminding a veteran of the battlefield) or on anniversaries of some specific experience. In a laboratory confirmation of this disturbing symptom, the Stroop test was administered to Vietnam veterans with and without PTSD (McNally et al., 1990). In this test the subject sees a set of words printed in different colors and must name the color of each word as rapidly as possible and not simply say the word. Interference, measured as a slowing of response time, occurs because of the content of some words. Words from several different categories—neutral (e.g., "input"), positive (e.g., "love"), obsessive-compulsive disorder (e.g., "germs"), and PTSD (e.g., "bodybags")—were used in this study. Veterans with PTSD were slower than non-PTSD veterans only on the PTSD words. The same effect has been documented for rape victims (Foa et al., 1991). Similarly, patients with PTSD show better recall for words related to their trauma (Zertlin & McNally, 1991).

   The importance of reexperiencing cannot be underestimated, for it is the likely source of the other categories of symptoms. Some theories of PTSD make reexperiencing the central feature (e.g., Foa, Zinbarg, & Rothbaum, 1992; Horowitz, 1986) by attributing the disorder to an inability to successfully integrate the traumatic event into an existing schema (the person's general beliefs about the world).

2. **Avoidance of stimuli associated with the event or numbing of responsiveness.** The person tries to avoid thinking about the trauma or encountering stimuli that will bring it to mind; there may be amnesia for the event. Numbing refers to decreased interest in others, a sense of estrangement, and an inability to feel positive emotions. These symptoms seem almost contradictory to those in 1. In PTSD there is fluctuation; the person goes back and forth between reexperiencing and numbing.

3. **Symptoms of increased arousal.** These symptoms include difficulties falling or staying asleep, difficulty concentrating, hypervigilance, and an exaggerated startle response. Laboratory studies have confirmed these clinical symptoms by documenting the heightened physiological reactivity of PTSD patients to combat imagery (e.g., Orr et al., 1995) and their high magnitude startle responses (Morgan et al., 1996).

Other problems often associated with PTSD are anxiety, depression, anger, guilt, substance abuse (self-medication to ease the distress), marital problems, and occupational impairment (Bremner et al., 1996; Keane et al., 1992). Suicidal thoughts and plans are common, as are incidents of explosive violence and stress-related psychophysiological problems, such as low back pain, headaches, and gastrointestinal disorders (Hobfoll et al., 1991).

The DSM alerts us to the fact that children can suffer from PTSD but may manifest it differently from adults. Sleep disorders with nightmares about monsters are common, as are behavioral changes, for example, a previously outgoing youngster may become quiet and withdrawn or a previously quiet youngster may become loud and aggressive. Some traumatized children begin to think that they will not live until adulthood. Some children lose already acquired developmental skills, such as speech or

Visiting the Vietnam War Memorial is an emotional experience for veterans.

toilet habits. Finally, young children have much more difficulty talking about their upset than do adults, which is especially important to remember in cases of possible physical or sexual abuse.

PTSD has a prevalence rate of from 1 to 3 percent in the general U.S. population (Helzer, Robins, & McEvoy, 1987), representing over two million people. The rate rises to 3.5 percent among civilians who have been exposed to a physical attack and to 20 percent among those wounded in Vietnam. An even higher percentage of PTSD was found in Rothbaum et al.'s (1992) longitudinal study of rape victims. The women were assessed weekly for twelve weeks following the rape. At the first assessment, 94 percent met the criteria for PTSD;[3] at the end of the study the rate of PTSD had dropped to 47 percent. In a large-scale population study in Detroit, Breslau et al. (1991) found that 39 percent of adults had experienced a traumatic event; of those, 24 percent developed PTSD.

ETIOLOGY OF POSTTRAUMATIC STRESS DISORDER

There are several risk factors for PTSD. In the Breslau et al. study (1991), predictors of PTSD, given exposure to a traumatic event, were being female, early separation from parents, family history of a disorder, and a preexisting disorder (panic disorder, OCD, depression). The likelihood of PTSD increases with the severity of the traumatic event; for example, the greater the exposure to combat, the greater the risk. With a high degree of combat exposure the rates of PTSD are the same in veterans who have family members with other disorders and those who do not. Among those with a family history of disorder even low combat exposure produces a high rate of PTSD (Foy et al., 1987). The initial reaction to the trauma is also predictive. More severe anxiety, depression, and dissociative symptoms (including depersonalization, derealization, amnesia, and out-of-body experiences) all increased the probability of later developing PTSD (Shalev et al., 1996).

Both psychological and biological theories have been proposed to account for PTSD. Learning theorists assume that the disorder arises from a classical conditioning of fear (Fairbank & Brown, 1987; Keane, Zimering, & Caddell, 1985). In the case of a woman who has been raped, for example, she may come to fear walking in a certain neighborhood (the

CS) because of having been assaulted there (the UCS). Based on this classically conditioned fear avoidances are built up, and they are negatively reinforced by the reduction of fear that comes from not being in the presence of the CS. In a sense, PTSD is an example of the two-factor theory of avoidance learning proposed years ago by Mowrer (1947; see p. 43). There is a developing body of evidence in support of this view (Foy et al., 1990) and for related cognitive-behavioral theories that emphasize the loss of control and predictability felt by PTSD sufferers (Chemtob et al., 1988; Foa & Kozak, 1986).

A psychodynamic theory proposed by Horowitz (1986, 1990) posits that memories of the traumatic event occur constantly in the person's mind and are so painful that they are either consciously suppressed (by distraction, for example) or repressed. The person is believed to engage in a kind of internal struggle to integrate the trauma into his or her existing beliefs about himself or herself and the world to make some sense out of it.

On the biological side research on twins shows a possible diathesis for PTSD (True et al., 1993). Furthermore, the trauma may activate the noradrenergic system, raising levels of norepinephrine and thereby making the person startle and express emotion more readily than normal (Krystal et al., 1989; Van der Kolk et al., 1985). Consistent with this view is the finding that levels of norepinephrine were higher in PTSD hospital patients than among those diagnosed as having schizophrenic or mood disorders (Kosten et al., 1987). In addition, stimulating the noradrenergic system induced a panic attack in 70 percent and flashbacks in 40 percent of PTSD patients; none of the control participants had such experiences (Southwick et al., 1993).

As yet theories of PTSD do not fare well in accounting for why only some people develop PTSD in the aftermath of trauma. As mentioned earlier, some hints are now beginning to emerge concerning personal characteristics or diatheses that render a person more vulnerable. These include a preexisting disorder, a family history of disorder, and early separation from parents. In a study of Israeli veterans of the 1982 war with Lebanon, development of PTSD was associated with a tendency to take personal responsibility for failures and to cope with stress by focusing on emotions ("I wish I could change how I feel.") rather than on the problems themselves (Mikhliner & Solomon, 1986; Solomon, Mikulincer, & Flum, 1988). Similarly, a strong sense of commitment and purpose differentiated Gulf War veterans who did not develop PTSD from those who did (Sutker et al., 1995). A high level of social support may lessen the risk for the disorder. Access to social

---

[3]These women could not technically be diagnosed as having PTSD because the DSM specifies that the symptoms must last for at least one month.

Natural disasters such as Hurricane Andrew can trigger PTSD. Social support can reduce the risk of developing the disorder.

support lessened the risk for PTSD in children who had experienced the trauma associated with hurricane Andrew (Vernberg et al., 1996).

THERAPIES FOR POSTTRAUMATIC STRESS DISORDER

As with the other anxieties and phobias examined so far, the key to treating PTSD is exposure to the frightening event, and we shall see this common thread in a variety of treatment approaches for this disorder. However, since the event was by definition traumatic, exposure is almost always in the form of imagery rather than in vivo. Furthermore, before any kind of exposure is attempted, therapists are advised to be sensitive to the typical aftermath of a traumatic experience, regardless of the specific cause (Keane et al., 1994). Common reactions include lack of trust, a frightening belief that the world is a very dangerous and threatening place (Janoff-Bulman, 1992), and maladaptive strategies for coping with the extreme stress, such as substance abuse (Keane & Wolfe, 1990). Educating the patient about the nature of PTSD, in particular about the kinds of symptoms most people experience (sleeplessness, being easily startled, depression, alienation from friends and loved ones, etc.),

can also help. Such knowledge can provide a context for what the patient might be experiencing and reassurance that the patient is not losing his or her mind (Keane et al., 1994).

During World War II "combat-exhausted" soldiers were often treated by narcosynthesis (Grinker & Spiegel, 1945), a procedure that might be considered a drug-assisted catharsis à la Breuer. A soldier was sedated with an intravenous injection of sodium Pentothal, enough to cause extreme drowsiness. The therapist then stated in a matter-of-fact voice that the soldier was on the battlefield, in the front lines, and, if necessary and possible, the therapist mentioned circumstances of the particular battle. The patient usually began to recall, often with intense emotion, sometimes frightening events that had perhaps been forgotten. Many times the actual trauma was relived and even acted out by the patient. As the patient gradually returned to the waking state the therapist continued to encourage discussion of the terrifying events in the hope that the patient would realize that they were in the past and no longer a threat. In this fashion a synthesis, or coming together, of the past horror with the patient's present life was sought (Cameron & Magaret, 1951).

The Veterans Administration, which had served veterans of World War II as well as those of the Korean War, was not prepared at first to address the psychological plight of Vietnam veterans. First of all, many had left the service with bad paper, that is, with less than honorable discharges. Some of the offenses for which a soldier could receive an undesirable discharge included "character and behavior disorders," "alcoholism," and "drug addiction" (Kidder, 1978). It seems likely that some of these veterans were suffering from the trauma of combat. Not until 1979—six years after the truce was signed with North Vietnam—were these sorts of dishonorable discharges upgraded as a result of assistance by the American Civil Liberties Union and the veterans made eligible for treatment through the Veterans Administration (Beck, 1979).

As early as 1971, however, Yale psychiatrist Robert Jay Lifton was approached by antiwar veterans from the New York–New Haven area to work with them in forming rap groups. Initiated by the veterans themselves, these groups had a twofold purpose: a therapeutic goal of healing themselves, and a political goal of forcing the American public to begin to understand the human costs of the war (Lifton, 1976). The rap groups spread outward from New York City until, in 1979, Congress approved a $25 million package establishing Operation Outreach, a network of ninety-one storefront counseling centers for psychologically distressed

Rap groups, like the one shown here, played an important role in treating PTSD among Vietnam veterans.

Vietnam veterans. In 1981 funding was extended for three additional years.

The rap groups focused on the residual guilt and rage felt by the veterans—guilt over what their status as soldiers had called on them to do in fighting a guerrilla war in which enemy and ally were often indistinguishable from one another, and rage at being placed in the predicament of risking their lives in a cause to which they and their country were not fully committed. Discussion extended as well to present-life concerns, such as relationships with women and feelings about masculinity, in particular, the macho view of physical violence. Antidepressant medication was also used, but with equivocal results (Lerer et al., 1987).

Group therapy is discussed in some detail in Chapter 19 (p. 558). For now it suffices to say that in the rap groups—and in the more conventional group-therapy sessions in the 172 Veterans Administration hospitals across the United States—at least two factors probably helped veterans. For perhaps the first time they could partake of the company of returned comrades-in-arms and feel the mutual support of others who had shared their war experiences. They were also able finally to begin confronting, in often emotional discussions, the combat events whose traumatic effects had been suppressed and therefore not examined. As people have known for many, many years, in order for individuals to come to terms with fearsome happenings, to loose themselves from the hold that events can have over them, they must in effect return to the events and expose themselves fully.

There is very little in the way of actual research on the kinds of approaches just described. But controlled research on the treatment of PTSD has accelerated in recent years as more attention has been focused on the aftermath of such traumas as natural disasters, rape, child abuse, and, especially, combat. Recent work in cognitive behavior therapy provides some findings based on studies that employed careful assessment, details of treatment, and appropriate control groups. (Interventions for the PTSD aftermath of child abuse and rape are described in Chapter 14.)

The basic principle of exposure-based behavior therapy is that fears are best reduced or eliminated by having the person confront in some fashion whatever he or she most ardently wishes to avoid. A growing body of evidence indicates that structured exposure to trauma-related events contributes something beyond the benefits of medication, social support, or being in a safe therapeutic environment (Keane, in press).

As part of the diagnosis of PTSD we almost always know what triggered the problem, so the decision is a tactical one, that is, how to expose the frightened patient to what is fearsome. Many techniques have been employed. In one well-designed study from the National Center for Post Traumatic Stress Disorder at the Boston Veterans Administration Medical Center, Terence Keane and his associates compared a no-treatment control group with an imaginal flooding condition in which patients visualized fearsome trauma-related scenes for extended periods of time. The researchers found significantly greater reductions in depression, anxiety, reexperiencing of the trauma, startle reactions, and irritability in PTSD Vietnam veterans in the imaginal procedure (Keane et al., 1989). Case studies such as those of Fairbank, DeGood, and Jenkins (1981) and Muse (1986) demonstrate the clinical efficacy of systematic desensitization with victims of car accidents. Conducting such exposure therapy is difficult for both patient and therapist, however, as it requires detailed review of the traumatizing events. As pointed out by Keane et al. (1992), patients may become temporarily worse in the initial stages of therapy and therapists themselves may become upset when they hear about the horrifying events that their patients experienced.

Another cognitive-behavioral approach conceptualizes PTSD more generally as an extreme stress reaction and therefore as amenable to the kind of multifaceted approach to stress management described in Chapter 8 (p. 203), entailing relaxation, rational-emotive therapy, and training in problem solving. Among the problems addressed within this broader framework is the anger felt by many PTSD sufferers, especially those who have seen combat. Assertion training and couples therapy are often warranted to help patients deal with their anger more appropriately (Keane et al., 1992).

Horowitz's (1988, 1990) psychodynamic approach has much in common with the aforementioned treatment, for he encourages patients to discuss the trauma and otherwise expose themselves to the events that led to the PTSD. But Horowitz emphasizes the manner in which the trauma interacts with a patient's pretrauma personality, and the treatment he proposes has much in common with other psychoanalytic approaches, including discussions of defenses and analysis of transference reactions by the patient. This complex therapy awaits empirical verification.

Finally, a range of psychoactive drugs have been used with PTSD patients, including antidepressants and tranquilizers. Some modest successes have been reported for the former, especially the serotonin reuptake inhibitors (Van der Kolk et al., 1994).

Whatever the specific mode of intervention, PTSD experts agree that social support is critical. Sometimes finding ways to lend support to others can help the giver as well as the receiver (Hobfoll et al., 1991). Belonging to a religious group, having family, friends, or fellow traumatized individuals listen nonjudgmentally to one's fears and recollections of the trauma, and other ways of instilling the belief that one belongs and that others wish to try to help ease the pain may even spell the difference between posttraumatic stress and posttraumatic stress disorder.

SUMMARY

People with anxiety disorders feel an overwhelming apprehension that seems unwarranted. DSM-IV lists six principal diagnoses: phobic disorders, panic disorder, generalized anxiety disorder, obsessive-compulsive disorder, posttraumatic stress disorder, and acute stress disorder.

Phobias are intense, unreasonable fears that disrupt the life of an otherwise normal person. They are relatively common. Social phobia is fear of social situations in which one may be scrutinized by other people. Specific phobias are fears of animals, situations, the natural environment, and blood and injections. The psychoanalytic view of phobias is that they are a defense against repressed conflicts. Behavioral theorists have several ideas of how phobias are acquired—through classical conditioning, the pairing of an innocuous object or situation with an innately painful event; through operant conditioning, whereby a person is rewarded for avoidance; through modeling, imitating the fear and avoidance of others; and through cognition, by making a catastrophe of a social mishap that could be construed in a less negative fashion. But not all people who have such experiences develop a phobia. It may be that a genetically transmitted physiological diathesis, lability of the autonomic nervous system, predisposes certain people to acquire phobias.

A patient suffering from panic disorder has sudden, inexplicable, and periodic attacks of intense anxiety. Panic attacks sometimes lead to the fear of being outside one's home, agoraphobia. A number of laboratory manipulations (e.g., hyperventilation and breathing air with a high concentration of carbon dioxide) can induce panic attacks in those with the disorder. Panic-disorder patients in general ruminate about serious illnesses, both physical and mental; they fear their own physical sensations and then amplify them until they are overwhelmed.

In generalized anxiety disorder, sometimes called free-floating anxiety, the individual's life is beset with virtually constant tension, apprehension, and worry. Psychoanalytic theory regards the source as an unconscious conflict between the ego and id impulses. Some behavioral theorists assume that with adequate assessment, this pervasive anxiety can be pinned down to a finite set of anxiety-provoking circumstances, thereby likening it to a phobia and making it more treatable. A sense of helplessness can also cause people to be anxious in a wide range of situations. Biological approaches focus on the therapeutic effects of the benzodiazepines and their relevance to the neurotransmitter GABA.

People with obsessive-compulsive problems have intrusive, unwanted thoughts and feel pressured to engage in stereotyped rituals lest they be overcome by frightening levels of anxiety. This disorder can become disabling, interfering not only with the life of the person who experiences the difficulties but also with the lives of those close to that person. Psychoanalytic theory posits strong id impulses that are under faulty and inadequate ego control. In behavioral accounts compulsions are considered learned avoidance responses. Obsessions may be related to stress and an attempt to inhibit these unwanted thoughts.

Posttraumatic stress disorder is sometimes the fate of those who have experienced a traumatic event that would evoke extreme distress in most individuals. It is marked by symptoms such as reexperiencing the trauma, increased arousal, and emotional numbing.

There are many therapies for anxiety disorders. Psychoanalytic treatment tries to lift repression so that childhood conflicts can be resolved; direct alleviation of the manifest problems is discouraged. In contrast, behavior therapists employ a range of procedures, such as systematic desensitization and modeling, to encourage exposure to what is feared. Preventing compulsives from performing their rituals is a useful, although initially arduous, technique.

Perhaps the most widely employed treatments are anxiolytic drugs dispensed by medical practitioners. Drugs, however, are subject to abuse, and their long-term use may have untoward and still inadequately understood side effects. Weaning a person from reliance on a chemical that reduces anxiety is problematic because many people become physically dependent on such drugs. Also, gains from using the drugs are usually lost when use is discontinued.

KEY TERMS

anxiety
neuroses
anxiety disorders
comorbidity
phobia
specific phobias
social phobia
vicarious learning
autonomic lability
flooding

anxiolytics
school phobia
elective mutism
panic disorder
depersonalization
derealization
agoraphobia
generalized anxiety
    disorder (GAD)

obsessive-compulsive
    disorder (OCD)
obsessions
compulsion
posttraumatic stress disorder
    (PTSD)
acute stress disorder

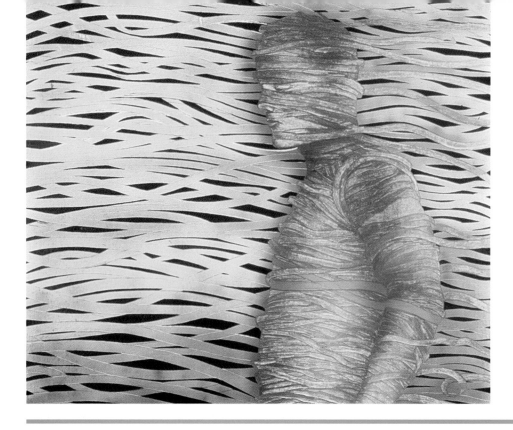

Goodenough,
"Man With
Entanglements," *1982*

SOMATOFORM AND DISSOCIATIVE DISORDERS

A twenty-seven-year-old male was brought to a hospital emergency room after being picked up by the police for lying down in the middle of a busy intersection. He said that he wanted to die and was very depressed. He had no memory of any events prior to being picked up by the police. He didn't know his name nor anything about his life history.

Several neurological tests were administered and revealed no abnormality. After six days in the hospital, hypnosis was begun. Over the first three hypnotic sessions, details of the patient's past life emerged but not his name nor the events that led up to his hospitalization. During the fourth and fifth sessions, the remaining details came forth. The man had just come to town, looking for work. Two men noticed his toolbox, approached him, and asked if he wanted a job. All three then left in a pickup truck, and, after smoking some marijuana, the patient was forced, at gunpoint, to have sex with the other men. (Kaszniak et al., 1988)

Somatoform and dissociative disorders, our focus for this chapter, are related to anxiety disorders in that in early versions of the DSM, all these disorders were subsumed under the heading of neuroses because anxiety was considered the predominant underlying factor in each case. Starting with DSM-III, classification came to be based on observable behavior, not presumed etiology. In the anxiety disorders signs of anxiety are obvious; but anxiety is not necessarily observable in the somatoform and dissociative disorders. In **somatoform disorders**, the individual complains of bodily symptoms that suggest a physical defect or dysfunction—sometimes rather dramatic in nature—but for which no physiological basis can be found. In **dissociative disorders**, the individual experiences disruptions of consciousness, memory, and identity, as illustrated in the opening case. The onset of both classes of disorders is typically related to some stressful experience, and it is not uncommon for these disorders to co-occur. The DSM-IV categories for somatoform and dissociative disorders are listed in Table 7.1. We will examine each of these categories in this chapter, focusing in more depth on those disorders about which more is known. As

before, we will look at symptoms, etiology, and therapies throughout the discussion.

SOMATOFORM DISORDERS

As noted in Chapter 1, *soma* means "body." In somatoform disorders psychological disorders take a physical form. The physical symptoms of somatoform disorders, which have no known physiological explanation and are not under voluntary control, are thought to be linked to psychological factors, presumably anxiety; they are assumed, therefore, to be psychologically caused. In this section we look at two somatoform disorders in depth: conversion disorder and somatization disorder.

DSM-IV includes three additional categories of somatoform disorders about which less information is available. In **pain disorder** the person experiences pain that causes significant distress and impairment; psychological factors are viewed as playing an important role in the onset, maintenance, and severity of the pain. The patient may be unable to work and may become dependent on painkillers or tranquilizers. The pain may have a temporal relation to some conflict or stress, or it may allow the individual to avoid some unpleasant activity and to secure attention and sympathy not otherwise available. Accurate diagnosis is difficult because the subjective experience of pain is always a psychologically influenced phenomenon; that is, pain is not a simple sensory experience, as are vision and hearing. Therefore deciding when a pain becomes a somatoform pain is difficult.

With **body dysmorphic disorder** a person is preoccupied with an imagined or exaggerated defect in appearance, for example, facial wrinkles, excess facial hair, or the shape or size of the nose. Some patients with the disorder may spend hours each day checking on their defect, looking at themselves in mirrors. Others take steps to avoid the defect by eliminating mirrors from their homes. These concerns are distressing and lead to frequent consultations with plastic surgeons. Unfortunately, plastic

TABLE 7.1 Somatoform and Dissociative Disorders	
Somatoform Disorders	*Dissociative Disorders*
Conversion disorder	Dissociative amnesia
Somatization disorder (Briquet's syndrome)	Dissociative fugue
Pain disorder	Depersonalization disorder
Body dysmorphic disorder	Dissociative identity disorder (multiple personality)
Hypochondriasis	

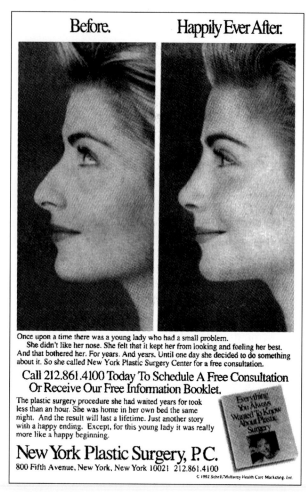

This ad illustrates the type of concern of someone with body dysmorphic disorder.

surgery does little to allay patients' concerns (Phillips et al., 1993).

As with pain disorder, subjective factors and matters of taste play a role. When, for example, does one's vanity become a body dysmorphic disorder? A survey of college students (Fitts et al., 1989) found that 70 percent of the students indicated at least some dissatisfaction with their appearance, with a higher figure for women than for men. Determining when these perceived defects become psychological disorders is difficult indeed. How much distress does the condition have to produce? Social and cultural factors surely play a role in how a person determines whether he or she is attractive, as they do with the eating disorders discussed in Chapter 9.

Although there are some systematic studies of body dysmorphic disorder, it is unclear whether its status as a specific diagnosis is warranted. For example, because of their excessive preoccupation with appearance and frequent checking on their looks, some cases might be diagnosed as obsessive-compulsive. In other cases the belief concerning the defect is

so unrelated to reality as to suggest a delusional disorder (Hollander, Cohen, & Simeon, 1993; McElroy et al., 1993). Preoccupation with imagined defects in physical appearance may therefore not be a disorder itself but a *symptom* that can occur in severe disorders.

Hypochondriasis is a somatoform disorder in which individuals are preoccupied with fears of having a serious disease, which persist despite medical reassurance to the contrary. Patients with this little-used diagnosis are frequent consumers of medical services and are likely to have mood or anxiety disorders (Noyes, 1993). The theory is that they overreact to ordinary physical sensations and minor abnormalities—such as irregular heartbeat, sweating, occasional coughing, a sore spot, stomachache—as evidence for their beliefs. Patients with hyponchondriasis indeed report that they are very sensitive to bodily sensations. However, in one study they were not more accurate than control participants in detecting their own heart rates (Barsky et al., 1995). Hypochondriasis is not very well differentiated from somatization disorder, which is also characterized by a long history of complaints of medical illnesses (Noyes et al., 1994).

We turn now to an in-depth discussion of conversion disorder and somatization disorder.

CONVERSION DISORDER

In **conversion disorder**, sensory or motor symptoms, such as a sudden loss of vision or paralysis, suggest an illness related to neurological damage of some sort, though the bodily organs and nervous system are found to be fine. Individuals may experience partial or complete paralysis of arms or legs; seizures and coordination disturbances; a sensation of prickling, tingling, or creeping on the skin; insensitivity to pain; or the loss or impairment of sensations, called **anesthesias** (see Figure 7.1), although they are physiologically normal people. Vision may be seriously impaired; the person may become partially or completely blind or have tunnel vision, in which the visual field is constricted as it would be if the person were peering through a tube. *Aphonia*, loss of the voice and all but whispered speech and *anosmia*, loss or impairment of the sense of smell are other conversion disorders.

The psychological nature of conversion symptoms is also demonstrated by the fact that they appear suddenly in stressful situations, allowing the individual to avoid some activity or responsibility or to get badly wanted attention. The term *conversion* originally derived from Freud, who thought that the energy of a repressed instinct was diverted into sensory-motor channels and blocked functioning. Thus anxiety and psychological conflict were believed to be *converted* into physical symptoms. Some of the people suffering conversion disorders may in fact seem complacent, even serene, and not particularly eager to part with their symptoms. Nor do they connect their symptoms with whatever stressful situation they may be in.

Hysteria, the term originally used to describe what are now known as conversion disorders, has a long history, dating back to the earliest writings on abnormal behavior. Hippocrates considered it an affliction limited solely to women and brought on by the wandering of the uterus through the body. The Greek word *hystera* means "womb." Presumably the wandering uterus symbolized the longing of the body for the production of a child.

Conversion symptoms usually develop in adolescence or early adulthood. An episode may end abruptly, but sooner or later the disorder is likely to return, either in its original form or with a symptom of a different nature and site. More women than men are diagnosed as having conversion disorders (Viederman, 1986). At one clinic, for example, forty-four of the fifty individuals diagnosed with conversion disorder were women (Folks, Ford, & Regan, 1984). During both world wars, however, a large number of males developed conversion-like difficulties in combat (Ziegler, Imboden, & Meyer, 1960).

In making diagnoses it is important to distinguish a conversion paralysis or sensory dysfunction from similar problems that have a true neurological basis. Sometimes this is an easy task, as when the

Patients with hypochondriasis visit physicians frequently. Despite medical reassurance about their health, they continue to be fearful about having a serious illness.

Figure 7.1 Hysterical anesthesias can be distinguished from neurological dysfunctions. The patterns of neural innervation are shown on the left. Typical areas of anesthesias in hysterical patients are superimposed on the right. The hysterical anesthesias do not make anatomical sense. Adapted from an original painting by Frank H. Netter, M.D. From *The CIBA Collection of Medical Illustrations*, copyright © by CIBA Pharmaceutical Company, Division of CIBA-GEIGY Corporation.

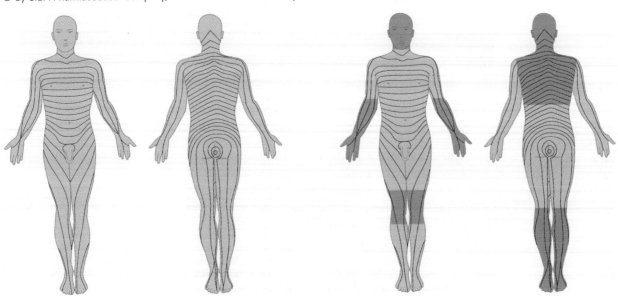

paralysis does not make anatomical sense. A classic example is *glove anesthesia*, a rare syndrome in which the individual experiences little or no sensation in the part of the hand that would be covered by a glove (see Figure 7.1). For years this was the textbook illustration of anatomical nonsense because the nerves here run continuously from the hand up the arm. Yet even in this case it now appears misdiagnosis can occur. A more recently recognized disease, *carpal tunnel syndrome*, can produce symptoms similar to those of glove anesthesia. Nerves in the wrist run through a tunnel formed by the wrist bones and membranes; the tunnel can become swollen and may pinch the nerves, leading to tingling, numbness, and pain in the hand.

Since the majority of paralyses, analgesias, and sensory failures do have biological causes, true neurological problems may sometimes be misdiagnosed as conversion disorders. Slater and Glithero (1965) investigated this disturbing possibility in a follow-up of patients who nine years earlier had been diagnosed as suffering from conversion symptoms. They found that an alarming number—60 percent—of these individuals had either died in the meantime or developed symptoms of physical disease! A high proportion had diseases of the central nervous system. Similarly, Whitlock (1967) compared the incidence of medical diseases in patients earlier diagnosed as having conversion disorder or other Axis I conditions. Medical diseases were found in 62.5 percent of the patients earlier diagnosed as having conversion disorders and in only 5.3 percent of the other groups. The most common problem was head injury, generally found to have occurred about six months before the onset of the conversion symptoms. Other common diseases were stroke, encephalitis, and brain tumors. In subsequent studies both Watson and Buranen (1979) and Fishbain and Goldberg (1991) found that many patients whose symptoms had been considered conversion disorders actually had physical disorders.

These are impressive data, and they suggest that conversion disorder may often be misdiagnosed when the individual actually has a physical disorder. We have already learned that the assessment of physical problems is still far from perfect; it is not always possible to distinguish between psychologically and biologically produced symptoms. It is sobering to contemplate the damage that can result from inappropriate diagnoses. (See Focus 7.1 for other diagnostic issues surrounding the diagnosis.)

SOMATIZATION DISORDER

In 1859 the French physician Pierre Briquet described a syndrome that first bore his name, Briquet's syndrome, and now in DSM-IV is referred to as **somatization disorder**. Recurrent, multiple somatic complaints for which medical attention is sought but that have no apparent physical cause are the basis for this disorder. To meet diagnostic criteria there must be four pain symptoms (e.g., head, back, joint), two gastrointestinal symptoms (e.g., diarrhea, nausea), one sexual symptom other than pain (e.g., indifference to sex, erectile dysfunction), and one pseudoneurological symptom (e.g., those of conversion disorder). DSM-IV notes that the specific symptoms of the disorder may vary across cultures. For example, burning hands or the experience of ants crawling under the skin are more frequent in Asia and Africa than in North America. Furthermore, the disorder is thought to be most frequent in cultures in which the overt display of emotion is deemphasized (Ford, 1995).

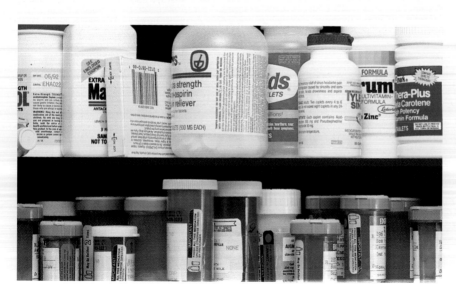

The medicine chest of a patient with a somatization disorder includes many drugs used to treat their numerous medical complaints.

FOCUS 7.1 MALINGERING AND FACTITIOUS DISORDER

One diagnostic problem with conversion disorder is distinguishing it from **malingering**, listed in DSM-IV as a condition that may be a focus of clinical attention (see p. 62). In this condition an individual fakes an incapacity in order to avoid a responsibility such as work or military duty or to achieve some goal such as a large insurance claim. Malingering is diagnosed when the conversion-like symptoms are under voluntary control, which is not thought to be the case in true conversion disorders.

In trying to discriminate conversion reactions from malingering, clinicians may attempt to decide whether the symptoms have been consciously or unconsciously adopted. This means of resolving the issue is at best a dubious one, for it is difficult, if not impossible, to know with any degree of certainty whether behavior is consciously or unconsciously motivated. One aspect of behavior that can sometimes help distinguish the two disorders is known as **la belle indifférence**, which is characterized by a relative lack of concern or a blasé attitude toward the symptoms that is out of keeping with their severity and supposedly long-term consequences. Patients with conversion disorder sometimes demonstrate this behavior; they also appear willing and eager to talk endlessly and dramatically about their symptoms, but often without the concern one might expect. In contrast, malingerers are likely to be more guarded and cautious, perhaps because they consider interviews a challenge or threat to the success of the lie. But this distinction is not foolproof, for only about one-third of people with conversion disorders show la belle indifférence (Stephens & Kamp, 1962). Further, a stoic attitude is sometimes found among patients with verified medical diseases.

Also related to the disorders we have been discussing is another DSM category, **factitious disorder**. In this disorder the person intentionally produces physical symptoms (or sometimes, psychological ones). Patients may make up symptoms, for example, reporting acute pain, or may even inflict injuries on themselves. Unlike malingering the symptoms are less obvi-

Kathleen Bush is taken into custody, charged with child abuse and fraud for deliberately causing her child's illnesses.

ously linked to a recognizable goal; in factitious disorder the motivation for adopting the physical or psychological symptoms is much less clear. Apparently the individual, for some unknown reason, wants to assume the role of patient. Factitious disorder may also involve a parent creating physical illnesses in a child; in this case it is called factitious disorder by proxy. In one extreme case a seven-year-old girl was hospitalized over 150 times and experienced forty surgeries at a cost of over $2 million. Her mother caused her illnesses by using drugs and even contaminating her feeding tube with fecal material (*Time*, April 29, 1996). The motivation in a case such as this appears to be the need to be regarded as an excellent parent and tireless in seeing to the child's needs.

Somatization disorder and conversion disorder share many of the same symptoms, and it is not uncommon for both diagnoses to be applicable to the same patient (e.g., Ford et al., 1984). Visits to physicians, sometimes to several simultaneously, are frequent, as is the use of medication. Hospitalization and even surgery are common (Guze, 1967). Menstrual difficulties and sexual indifference are frequent (Swartz et al., 1986). Patients typically present their complaints in a histrionic, exaggerated fashion or as part of a long and complicated medical history. Many believe that they have been ailing all their lives. The lifetime prevalence of somatization

disorder is estimated at less than 1 percent of the U.S. population (Robins et al., 1984), and in the United States the disorder is much more frequent among women than among men; prevalence among men is higher in some countries, for example, Greece and Puerto Rico (Tomasson, Kent, & Coryell, 1991). In an epidemiological study conducted in Los Angeles, Escobar et al. (1987) found somatization disorder more common among Mexican-American women than among non-Hispanic white women. This difference may reflect the greater intensity of the stressors (e.g., financial strain, social isolation) faced by these Mexican-American women.

Comorbidity is high with anxiety disorders, mood disorders, substance abuse, and a number of personality disorders (Golding, Smith, & Kasher, 1991; Kirmayer, Robbins, & Paris, 1994).

Somatization disorder typically begins in early adulthood and lasts for years (Cloninger et al., 1986). Anxiety and depression are frequently reported, as are a host of behavioral and interpersonal problems, such as truancy, poor work records, and marital difficulties. Somatization disorder also seems to run in families; it is found in about 20 percent of the first-degree relatives of index cases, that is, individuals diagnosed as having somatization disorder (Guze, 1993). The following case illustrates one woman's complaints.

Alice was referred to the psychological clinic by her physician, Joyce Williams. Dr. Williams had been Alice's physician for about six months and in that time period had seen her twenty-three times. Alice had dwelt on a number of rather vague complaints—general aches and pains, bouts of nausea, fatigue, irregular menstruation, and dizziness. But various tests—complete blood workups, X rays, spinal taps, and so on—had not revealed any pathology.

On meeting her therapist Alice immediately let him know that she was a somewhat reluctant client: "I'm here only because I trust Dr. Williams and she urged me to come. I'm physically sick and don't see how a psychologist is going to help." But when Alice was asked to describe the history of her physical problems she quickly warmed to the task. According to Alice, she had always been sick. As a child she had had episodes of high fever, frequent respiratory infections, convulsions, and her first two operations, an appendectomy and a tonsillectomy. As she continued her somewhat loosely organized chronological account of her medical history, Alice's descriptions of her problems became more and more colorful (and probably exaggerated as well): "Yes, when I was in my early twenties I had some problems with vomiting. For weeks at a time I'd vomit up everything I ate. I'd even vomit up liquids, even water. Just the sight of food would make me vomit. The smell of food cooking was absolutely unbearable. I must have been vomiting every ten minutes." During her twenties Alice had gone from one physician to another. She saw several gynecologists for her menstrual irregularity and dyspareunia (pain during intercourse) and had undergone dilatation and curettage (scraping the lining of the uterus). She had been referred to neurologists for her headaches, dizziness, and fainting spells, and they had performed EEGs, spinal taps, and even a CT scan. Other physicians had ordered X rays to look for the possible causes of her abdominal pain and EKGs for her chest pains. Rectal and gallbladder surgery had also been performed.

When the interview finally shifted away from Alice's medical history, it became apparent that she was highly anxious in many situations, particularly those in which she thought she might be evaluated by other people. Indeed, some of her physical complaints could be regarded as consequences of anxiety. Furthermore, her marriage was shaky, and she and her husband were considering divorce. Their marital problems seemed to be linked to sexual difficulties stemming from Alice's dyspareunia and her general indifference toward sex.

ETIOLOGY OF SOMATOFORM DISORDERS

Much of the theorizing in the area of somatoform disorders has been directed solely toward understanding hysteria as originally conceptualized by Freud. With regard to somatization disorder, it has been proposed that patients are more sensitive to physical sensations, overattend to them, or even amplify them somehow (Kirmayer, Robins, & Paris, 1994). A behavioral view of somatization disorder holds that the various aches and pains, discomforts, and dysfunctions are the manifestation of unrealistic anxiety in bodily systems. Perhaps the extreme tension of an individual localizes in stomach muscles, resulting in feelings of nausea or in vomiting. Once normal functioning is disrupted the maladaptive pattern may strengthen because of the attention it receives or the excuses it provides. In a related vein, reports of physical symptoms have been seen as a strategy used to explain poor performance in evaluative situations. Attributing poor performance to illness is psychologically less threatening than attributing it to some personal failing (Smith, Snyder, & Perkins, 1983).

In the next section we shall first examine psychoanalytic views of conversion disorder and then look at what behavioral, cognitive, and biological theorists have to offer.

PSYCHOANALYTIC THEORY

Conversion disorder occupies a central place in psychoanalytic theory, for in the course of treating these cases Freud developed many of the major concepts of psychoanalysis. Conversion disorder offered him a clear opportunity to explore the concept of the unconscious. Consider for a moment how you might try to make sense of a patient's report that she awakened one morning with a paralyzed left arm. Your first reaction might be to give her a series of neurological tests to assess possible biological causes of the paralysis. Let us assume that these tests are negative; no evidence of neurological disorder is present. You are now faced with choosing whether to believe or doubt the patient's communication. On the one hand, she might be lying; she may know that her arm is not paralyzed but has decided to fake paralysis to achieve some end. This would be an example of malingering. But what if you believe the patient? Now you are almost forced to consider that unconscious processes are operating. On a conscious level the patient is telling the truth; she believes and reports that her arm is paralyzed. Only on a level that is not conscious does she know that her arm is actually normal.

In *Studies in Hysteria* (1895), Breuer and Freud proposed that a conversion disorder is caused when a person experiences an event that creates great emotional arousal, but the affect is not expressed and the memory of the event is cut off from conscious experience. They proposed two explanations for why the affect associated with the experience is not expressed. The experience may be so distressing that the person cannot allow it to enter consciousness and therefore represses it; or the experience may occur while the person is in an abnormal psychological state, such as semihypnosis. In both situations, Breuer and Freud proposed, the specific conversion symptoms are causally related to the traumatic event that preceded them.

Anna O. (see p. 19), for example, while watching at the bedside of her seriously ill father, had dropped off into a waking dream with her right arm over the back of her chair. She saw a black snake emerge from the wall and come toward her sick father to bite him. She tried to ward it away, but her right arm had gone to sleep. When she looked at her hand, her fingers turned into little snakes with death's heads. The next day a bent branch recalled her hallucination of the snake, and at once her right arm became rigidly extended. After that her arm responded in the same way whenever some object revived her hallucination. Later, when Anna O. fell into her "absences" and took to her own bed, the contracture of her right arm became chronic and extended to paralysis and anesthesia of her right side.

In his later writings Freud hypothesized that conversion disorder in women is rooted in an early, unresolved Electra complex. The young female child becomes sexually attached to her father, and if her parents' response to these feelings are harsh and disapproving, these early impulses are repressed. The result is both a preoccupation with sex and at the same time an avoidance of it. At a later period of her life sexual excitement or some happenstance reawakens these repressed impulses, creating anxiety. The anxiety is then transformed or converted into physical symptoms. Thus the primary gain from conversion disorder is the avoidance of the unresolved Electra conflict and the previously repressed id impulses. Freud pointed out that there could also be a secondary gain or reinforcement from the symptoms; they might allow the patient to avoid or escape from some currently unpleasant life situation or to obtain attention from others.

A more contemporary psychodynamic interpretation of one form of conversion disorder, hysterical blindness, is based on experimental studies of hysterically blind people whose behavior on visual tests showed that they were influenced by the stimuli even though they explicitly denied seeing them (Sackeim, Nordlie, & Gur, 1979).

Two studies involved cases of teenaged women. The first case, described by Theodor and Mandelcorn (1973), concerned a sixteen-year-old who had experienced a sudden loss of peripheral vision and reported that her visual field had become tubular and constricted. Although a variety of neurological tests had proved negative, the authors wanted to be certain that they were not dealing with a neurological problem, so they arranged a special visual test. A bright, oval target was presented either in the center or in the periphery of the patient's visual field. On each trial there was a time interval bounded by the sounding of a buzzer. A target was illuminated during the intervals or not, and the young woman's task was to report whether a target was present or not.

When the target was presented in the center of the visual field the patient always correctly identified it. This outcome was expected, since she had not reported any loss of peripheral vision. For the peripheral showings of the target, however, the young woman was correct only 30 percent of the time. A person would be expected to be correct 50 percent of the time by chance alone if she were truly blind in her periphery. Therefore, she had performed significantly more poorly than would a person who was indeed blind! The clinicians reasoned that she must have been in some sense aware of the illuminated stimulus and that she wanted, either consciously or unconsciously, to preserve her blindness by performing poorly on the test.

Sackeim et al. also reviewed a seemingly contradictory case reported by Grosz and Zimmerman (1970), in which a hysterically blind adolescent girl showed almost perfect visual performance. Fifteen-year-old Celia's initial symptom was a sudden loss of sight in both eyes, followed thereafter by severe blurring of vision. Celia claimed not to be able to read small or large print. She had set high standards for herself and did very well at school. Her busy parents, continually rushing off to their own many activities, professed concern about their four chil-

Focus 7.2   Cognitive Factors: Awareness, the Unconscious, and Behavior

We are unaware of much that goes on in our minds as we perceive and encode stimuli from our environment. Much of the working of the mind proceeds outside consciousness. Consider an example. When different stimuli are played to each ear and people are asked to attend to one ear only (a common procedure for studying selective attention), they usually report later that they know little or nothing about the sounds that came into the unattended ear. *But further research shows that these unattended stimuli can affect behavior.* In one study people listened to a human voice played into one ear while tone sequences were played in the unattended ear (Wilson, 1975). They reported having heard no tones. Furthermore, in a memory task in which they listened to tone sequences played earlier and others that had not been played, they were unable to distinguish between the two types. Despite this demonstration that the participants did not recognize the tone stimuli played previously, another measure revealed a startling result. When asked to rate how much they liked a series of tone sequences, the ones that had been presented earlier to the unattended ear were preferred to new, unfamiliar sequences. It is known that familiarity affects judgments of tone stimuli similar to those Wilson used. Familiar sequences are liked better than unfamiliar ones. Some aspects of the tone sequences must have been absorbed, even though participants said that they had not heard them and demonstrated that they did not recognize them. At an unconscious level the unattended tones had become familiar.

A similar phenomenon has been observed with vision (Kunst-Wilson & Zajonc, 1980). Participants were presented with different shapes for one millisecond (one-thousandth of a second). Their ability later to recognize the shapes that they had seen was essentially nil, but when they rated how much they liked the shapes they preferred the ones that they had "seen" to new ones that were presented.

A series of studies reported by Nisbett and Wilson (1977) also indicates that awareness as measured by verbal report is not always an accurate indication of the effect of stimuli on behavior. In one study, Nisbett and Wilson had people memorize a list of word pairs. For some participants the pairs of words were specially constructed so that they would be likely to have an effect on their performance in the second part of the study. For example, one of the word pairs these people first memorized was "ocean–moon." This pair was expected to make them more likely to respond "Tide" when they were later asked to name a detergent. The results agreed with expectation; people who had memorized the special word pairs gave double the number of expected associations as people who had not memorized them. Right after the second part of the test, participants were asked why they had given their particular responses. Even though they could still recall the word pairs they almost never mentioned them as bringing their responses to mind. Instead they gave reasons such as "My mother uses Tide" or "Tide is the most popular detergent."

These studies provide laboratory evidence for the operation of unconscious processes. But do they generalize to more naturalistic dependent variables? A study by Bornstein, Leone, and Galley (1987) indicates that the answer is yes. They found that subliminal exposure to a person's face would influence subsequent interactions with that person. Subjects participated with two confederates of the experimenter. They were asked to read ten poems and as a group decide on the gender of the author of each poem. By prior arrangement the two confederates disagreed on seven of the ten, putting the subject in the role of tiebreaker. Prior to judging the poems half the participants viewed, for four milliseconds, five presentations of a slide of one of the confederates. The other half saw a slide of the second confederate. (Pilot data had already shown that exposures

---

dren's education but often left Celia responsible for the three younger children. When Celia's vision blurred so severely, her parents became obliged to read her studies to her. Testing revealed that Celia could readily identify objects of various sizes and shapes and count fingers at a distance of fifteen feet. When three triangles were projected on three display windows of a console, two of the triangles inverted, one of them upright, in 599 trials of 600 she pressed the switch under the upright triangle, the correct response, which then turned off a buzzer for five seconds. We shall return to Celia later in this chapter.

Sackeim et al. proposed a two-stage defensive reaction to account for these conflicting findings:

first, perceptual representations of visual stimuli are blocked from awareness and on this basis people report themselves blind; and second, information is nonetheless extracted from the perceptual representations. If patients feel that they must deny being privy to this information, they perform more poorly than they would by chance on perceptual tasks. If patients do not need to deny having such information, they perform the task well but still maintain that they are blind. Whether hysterically blind people unconsciously need to deny receiving perceptual information is viewed as dependent on personality factors and motivation.

Are the people who claim that they are blind and yet on another level respond to visual stimuli being

such as these could not be discriminated from blank flashes of light.) As in the studies previously discussed, subliminal exposure was expected to increase liking for the confederate whose photograph had been viewed and hence change behavior to favor that confederate. Consistent with the prior work, participants were more likely to agree with the confederate whose slide they had been subliminally exposed to.

These experiments, which are but a small sampling of current research making a similar point, are closely related to the psychoanalytic concept of the unconscious. Contemporary investigators, many of whom would identify themselves as cognitive psychologists, have begun to corroborate Freud's view that some human behavior is determined by unconscious processes. But from a modern cognitive perspective the unconscious processes are understood in a different way. Freud postulated the existence of *the* unconscious, a repository of instinctual energy and repressed conflicts and impulses. Contemporary researchers reject the notions of an energy reservoir and repression, holding more simply that we are not aware of everything going on around us nor of some of our cognitive processes. At the same time these stimuli and processes of which we are unaware can affect behavior powerfully. This recent research suggests that understanding the causes of human behavior will be a difficult task. It will not be sufficient merely to ask someone, "Why did you do that?"

A child participates in a dichotic listening experiment. Although he attends to information presented to only one ear, the information reaching the unattended ear can affect behavior.

truthful? Sackeim and his colleagues reported that some patients with lesions in the visual cortex, rather than damage to the eye, said that they were blind yet performed well on visual tasks. Such patients have vision (sometimes called blindsight), but they do not *know* that they can see. So it is possible for people to claim truthfully that they cannot see and at the same time give evidence that they can. On a more general level a dissociation between awareness and behavior has been reported in many perceptual and cognitive studies (see Focus 7.2).

In a laboratory setting Sackeim and his colleagues tested their assumption that motivation has a bearing on whether an individual will dissociate behavior from awareness. They hypnotized two susceptible participants, gave each a suggestion of total blindness, and then tested them on a visual discrimination task.[1] One was given instructions designed to motivate her to maintain her blindness; she was expected to deny her perceptions and perform more poorly than she would by chance alone

---

[1]Hypnotic susceptibility refers to whether a person will be a good hypnotic subject, that is, able to experience the suggestions of the hypnotist. This characteristic is most often assessed with the Stanford Hypnotic Susceptibility Scales (Weizenhoffer & Hilgard, 1959), in which people are asked to undertake a number of tasks. For example, the hypnotist may suggest that the person's hand is so heavy that it cannot be raised and then ask the person to try to raise it. The good hypnotic subject will not raise his or her arm or will have great difficulty doing so.

on the visual task. The other person was not explicitly urged to maintain her blindness and was expected to do better than expected by chance on the task. A third person was asked to simulate the behavior of someone who had been hypnotized and given a suggestion of total blindness.

The results agreed with the predictions. The participant highly motivated to maintain blindness indeed performed more poorly than she would be expected to by chance, and the less motivated participant performed perfectly, even while reporting that she was blind. The simulator performed at a chance level for the most part; in a postexperimental interview she stated that she had deliberately tried to simulate chance performance. Bryant and McConkey (1989) provide further support of the Sackeim et al. findings. Over a large number of sessions, they tested a man with hysterical blindness, giving different motivational instructions in some sessions. As in the study by Sackeim and his colleagues, motivation was found to influence performance.

As proposed in the psychodynamic view of Sackeim and his colleagues, verbal reports and behavior apparently can be unconsciously separated from one another. Hysterically blind persons are able to say that they cannot see and yet at the same time can be influenced by visual stimuli. The way in which they show signs of being able to see may depend on how much they need to be considered blind.

BEHAVIORAL THEORY

A behavioral account of the development of conversion disorder was proposed by Ullmann and Krasner (1975). They view conversion disorder as similar to malingering in that the person adopts the symptom to secure some end. In their opinion the person with a conversion disorder attempts to behave according to his or her conception of how a person with a disease affecting the motor or sensory abilities would act. This theory raises two questions. Are people capable of such behavior? Under what conditions would it be most likely to occur?

Considerable evidence indicates that the answer to the first question is yes; people can adopt patterns of behavior that match many of the classic conversion symptoms. For example, paralyses, analgesias, and blindness, as we have seen, can be induced in people under hypnosis. Similarly, chemically inert drugs, called placebos, have reduced the pain of patients considered truly ill.

As a partial answer to the second question Ullmann and Krasner specify two conditions that increase the likelihood that motor and sensory dis-

abilities will be imitated. First, the individual must have some experience with the role to be adopted; he or she may have had similar physical problems or may have observed them in others. Second, the enactment of a role must be *rewarded*; an individual will assume a disability only if it can be expected either to reduce stress or to reap other positive consequences.

Although this behavioral interpretation might seem to make sense, the literature does not support it completely. There is some question as to whether the patient is aware of the behavior, that is, whether the behavior is conscious or unconscious. Grosz and Zimmerman's patient Celia, for example, did not act in accordance with Ullmann and Krasner's theory. The very intelligent Celia performed perfectly in the visual discrimination task while still claiming severely blurred vision. Such a pattern of behavior seems a rather clumsy enactment of a role. If you wanted to convince someone that you could not see, would you always correctly identify the upright triangle? Celia's actions seem more consistent with the theorizing offered by Sackeim and his co-workers. On the level of conscious awareness Celia probably saw only blurred images, as she claimed. But during the test the triangles were distinguished on an unconscious level and she could pick out the upright one wherever it appeared. It is interesting to note that Celia's visual problems gained her crucial attention and help from her parents, which is in the nature of conversion disorder as well as of malingering. Three years after the onset of her visual difficulties Celia suddenly and dramatically recovered clear sight while on a cross-country trip with her parents. Earlier in the summer Celia had graduated from high school with grades well above average. The need to receive reinforcement for poor vision had perhaps passed, and her eyesight returned.

SOCIAL AND CULTURAL FACTORS

A possible role for social and cultural factors is suggested by the apparent decrease in the incidence of conversion disorder over the last century. Although Charcot and Freud seemed to have had an abundance of female patients with this sort of difficulty, contemporary clinicians rarely see anyone with such problems. Several hypotheses have been proposed to explain this apparent decrease. For example, therapists with a psychoanalytic bent point out that in the second half of the nineteenth century, when the incidence of conversion reactions was apparently high in France and Austria, repressive sexual attitudes may have contributed to the increased prevalence of the disorder. The decrease in the incidence of conversion reactions, then, may be attributed to a general relaxing of sexual mores and to the greater psychological and medical sophistication of twentieth-century culture, which is more tolerant of anxiety than it is of dysfunctions that do not make physiological sense.

Support for the role of social and cultural factors comes from studies showing that conversion disorder is more common among people from rural areas and people with lower socioeconomic status (Folks et al., 1984). These individuals may be less knowledgeable about medical and psychological concepts. Further evidence derives from studies showing that the diagnosis of hysteria has declined in industrialized societies (e.g., England; Hare, 1969) but has remained more common in undeveloped countries (e.g., Libya; Pu et al., 1986). These data, although consistent, are difficult to interpret. They could mean that increasing sophistication about medical diseases leads to decreased prevalence of conversion disorder. Alternatively, diagnostic practices may vary from country to country, producing the different rates. A cross-national study conducted by diagnosticians trained to follow the same procedures is needed.

BIOLOGICAL FACTORS

Although genetic factors have been proposed as being important in the development of conversion disorder, research does not support this proposal. Slater (1961) investigated concordance rates in twelve identical and twelve fraternal pairs of twins. Probands of each pair had been diagnosed as having the disorder, but none of the co-twins in either of the two groups manifested a conversion reaction. Torgerson (1986) reported the results of a twin study of somatoform disorders that included ten cases of conversion disorder, twelve of somatization disorder, and seven of pain disorder. No co-twin had the same diagnosis as his or her proband! Even the overall concordance for somatoform disorders was no higher in the identical twins than in the fraternal twins. Genetic factors, then, from the studies done so far, seem to be of no importance.

There may be some relationship between brain structure and conversion disorder. Conversion symptoms are more likely to occur on the left side than on the right side of the body (Ford & Folks, 1985; Galin, Diamond, & Braff, 1977; Stern, 1977). In most instances these left-side body functions are controlled by the right hemisphere of the brain. Thus the majority of conversion symptoms may be related to the functioning of the right hemisphere. Research has shown that the right hemisphere can generate emotions, and it is suspected of generating more emotions, particularly unpleasant ones, than are generated by the left hemisphere. Conversion symptoms could in this way be neurophysiologically linked to emotional arousal. Furthermore, this same research indicates that the right hemisphere depends on the neural passageways of the corpus callosum for connection with the left hemisphere's verbal capacity to describe and explain emotions and thereby to gain awareness of them. In conversion disorder it may be that the left hemisphere somehow blocks the impulses carrying painful emotional content from the right hemisphere so that individuals with conversion disorder make no connection between it and their troubling circumstances or their emotional needs. This is an intriguing bit of speculation.

THERAPIES FOR SOMATOFORM DISORDERS

Because somatoform disorders are rarer than other problems that people take to mental health professionals, no significant body of research exists on the relative efficacy of different treatments. Case reports and clinical speculation are for now the only sources of information on how to help people with these puzzling disruptions in bodily functions.

People with somatic complaints as well as those with conversion disorder and pain disorder make many more visits to physicians than to psychiatrists and nonmedical clinicians, such as psychologists, for they define their problems in physical terms. These patients are not open to psychological explanations of their predicaments and therefore resent referrals to "shrinks." Many such people try the patience of their physicians, who often find themselves prescribing one drug or medical treatment after another in the hope of remedying the somatic complaint. One medical intervention that seems to be useful, at least for pain patients, is antidepressant drugs, consistent with the high comorbidity of depression with many of these disorders (Valdes et al., 1989).

The talking cure into which psychoanalysis developed was based on the assumption that a massive repression had forced psychic energy to be transformed or converted into puzzling anesthesias or paralyses. The catharsis as the patient faced up to the infantile origins of the repression was assumed to help, and even today free association and other efforts to lift repression are commonly used to treat somatoform disorder. Psychoanalysis and psychoanalytically oriented psychotherapy have not been demonstrated to be particularly useful with conversion disorder, however, except perhaps to reduce the patient's concern about the disabling problems (Ochitil, 1982).

Behavioral clinicians consider the high levels of anxiety associated with somatization disorder to be linked to specific situations. Alice, the woman described at the beginning of this chapter, revealed that she was extremely anxious about her shaky marriage and about situations in which other people might judge her. Techniques such as exposure or any of the cognitive therapies could address her fears, the reduction of which would help lessen somatic complaints. But it is likely that more treatment would be needed, for a person who has been "sick" for a period of time has grown accustomed to weakness and dependency, to avoiding everyday challenges rather than facing them as an adult. Chances are that people who live with Alice have adjusted to her infirmity and are even unwittingly reinforcing her for her avoidance of normal adult responsibilities. Family therapy could help Alice and the members of her family change the web of relationships in order to support her movement toward greater autonomy. Assertion training and social-skills training—for example, coaching Alice in effective ways to approach and talk to people, to maintain eye contact, to give compliments, to accept criticism, to make requests—could be useful in helping her acquire, or reacquire, means of relating to others and meeting needs that do not begin with the premise "I am a poor, weak, sick person."

In general it seems advisable to shift the focus away from what the patient *cannot* do because of illness and instead to teach the patient how to deal with stress, to encourage greater activity, and to enhance a sense of control, despite the physical limitations or discomfort the patient is experiencing. For patients with pain disorder, pain-management therapy, such as that described in Chapter 18 (p. 538) can be useful (Seligman, 1990).

In vivo exposure was used in the treatment of two patients with psychogenic nausea. The individuals were encouraged to expose themselves to the situations that were making them nauseous, much as a phobic person would confront a particular fear. The authors concluded that the favorable outcomes they achieved were due to extinction of the anxiety underlying the nausea (Lesage & Lamontagne, 1985).

Behavior therapists have applied to somatoform disorders a wide range of techniques intended to make it worthwhile for the patient to give up the symptoms. A case reported by Liebson (1967) provides an example. A man had relinquished his job

Assertion training is sometimes used as a way of reducing anxiety in patients with somatoform disorders.

because of pain and weakness in the legs and attacks of giddiness. Liebson helped the patient return to full-time work by persuading his family to refrain from reinforcing him for his idleness and by arranging for the man to receive a pay increase if he succeeded in getting to work. A reinforcement approach attempts to provide the patient with greater incentives for improvement than for remaining incapacitated.

Another important consideration with any such operant tactic, as noted by Walen, Hauserman, and Lavin (1977), is for the therapist to take measures to ensure that the patient does not lose face when parting with the disorder. The therapist should appreciate the possibility that the patient may feel humiliated at becoming better through treatment that does not deal with the medical (physical) problem.

An excellent, though curious, illustration is provided by Macleod and Hemsley (1985).

A forty-nine-year-old man had developed aphonia, the inability to speak above a whisper, following an injection to his neck.

Although physical examinations were all negative, the patient maintained that his speech difficulty was caused by the injection. Macleod and Hemsley decided not to challenge the patient's attribution and instead to accept it, telling the man that a series of exercises would be necessary to strengthen the damaged muscles. Treatment consisted of having the patient repeat nursery rhymes into a microphone attached to a polygraph that provided constant monitoring and feedback about volume. During each treatment session the patient was required to increase his speech level. Initially, volume increased steadily, but it soon reached a plateau. One day, however, the patient stopped for a beer before his therapy session and on this day his speech returned to normal.

Through a series of unfortunate incidents, however, the treatment gains were not maintained. The patient attributed his cure, in part, to the beer. His wife decided that this was a newsworthy event and informed the local newspaper. The story was picked up by the national press and television, and the manufacturer of the beer the man had drunk began an advertising campaign with him as the focus. The resulting humiliation was too much, and the aphonia returned as well as depressive symptoms that required hospitalization.

DISSOCIATIVE DISORDERS

In this section we examine four dissociative disorders: dissociative amnesia, dissociative fugue, dissociative identity disorder (formerly known as multiple personality disorder), and depersonalization disorder, all of which are characterized by changes in a person's sense of identity, memory, or consciousness. Individuals with these disorders may be unable to recall important personal events or may temporarily forget their identity or even assume a new identity. They may even wander far from their usual surroundings.

High-quality data concerning the prevalence of the dissociative disorders are not available. Perhaps the best study to date found prevalences of 7.0 percent, 2.4 percent, and 0.2 percent for amnesia, depersonalization, and fugue, respectively (Ross, 1991). We will describe this study more fully when considering multiple personality disorder.

Our examination of the four major dissociative disorders will first cover symptoms and then theories of etiology and therapies.

DISSOCIATIVE AMNESIA

The person with **dissociative amnesia** is unable to recall important personal information, usually after some stressful episode, as was the situation in the chapter-opening case. The information is not permanently lost but cannot be retrieved during the episode of amnesia. The holes in memory are too extensive to be explained by ordinary forgetfulness.

Most often the memory loss is for all events during a limited period of time following some traumatic experience, such as witnessing the death of a loved one. More rarely the amnesia is for only selected events during a circumscribed period of distress, is continuous from a traumatic event to the present, or is total, covering the person's entire life (Coons & Milstein, 1992). During the period of

In *Spellbound*, Gregory Peck played a man with amnesia. Dissociative amnesia is typically triggered by a stressful event.

FOCUS 7.3 DISSOCIATIVE IDENTITY DISORDER AND MALINGERING

There has always been some questions as to whether DID is a true disorder rather than a conscious effort to avoid punishment or to achieve gains not otherwise available. Is DID little more than malingering? This issue gained prominence in the early 1980s during the trial of a serial murderer in California who came to be known as the Hillside Strangler. The differing views of several expert witnesses in this highly publicized trial were the subject of three articles in the *International Journal of Clinical and Experimental Hypnosis* (Allison, 1984; Orne, Dinges, & Orne, 1984; Watkins, 1984).

At around the time of the trial a research team (Spanos, Weekes, & Bertrand, 1985) highly skeptical of the reality of DID conducted an ingenious experiment, which added a new perspective to the testimony of Kenneth Bianchi, the man accused of committing these murders. This study supports the possibility that a person may adopt another personality just to avoid punishment. The experimental manipulations were derived from an actual interview with Bianchi while he was supposedly under hypnosis during a pretrial meeting with a mental health professional to determine his legal responsibility for his crimes. The interviewer (I) asked for a second personality to come forward.

I: I've talked a bit to Ken but I think that perhaps there might be another part of Ken that I haven't talked to. And I would like to communicate with that other part. And I would like that other part to come to talk with me…. And when you're here, lift the left hand off the chair to signal to me that you are here. Would you please come, Part, so I can talk to you?… Part, would you come and lift Ken's hand to indicate to me that you are here?… Would you talk to me, Part, by saying "I'm here"? (Schwarz, 1981, pp. 142–143)

Bianchi (B) answered yes to the last question, and then he and the interviewer had the following conversation.

I: Part, are you the same as Ken or are you different in any way…

B: I'm not him.

I: You're not him. Who are you? Do you have a name?

B: I'm not Ken.

I: You're not him? Okay. Who are you? Tell me about yourself. Do you have a name I can call you by?

B: Steve. You can call me Steve. (pp. 139–140)

While speaking as Steve, Bianchi stated that he hated Ken because Ken was nice and that he, Steve, with the help of his cousin, had murdered a number of women. Bianchi's plea in the case became not guilty by reason of insanity; he claimed that he suffered from dissociative identity disorder.

In the Spanos study undergraduate students were told that they would play the role of an accused murderer and that despite much evidence of guilt, a plea of not guilty had been entered. They were also told that they were to participate in a simulated psychiatric interview that might involve hypnosis. Then the students were taken to another room and introduced to the psychiatrist, actually an experimental assistant. After a number of standard questions the interview diverged for students assigned to one of three experimental conditions. Those in the *Bianchi condition* were given a rudimentary hypnotic induction and were then instructed to let a second personality come forward, just as Bianchi's interviewer had done. Students in the *Hidden Part condition* were also hypnotized and given information suggesting that they may have walled off parts of themselves, but these instructions were less explicit than were those given for the first condition. Students in a final condition were not hypnotized and were given even less explicit information about the possible existence of a hidden part.

After the experimental manipulations the possible existence of a second personality was probed directly by the "psychiatrist." In addition, students were asked questions about the facts of the murders. Finally, in a second session, those who

amnesia the person's behavior is otherwise unremarkable, except that the memory loss may bring some disorientation and purposeless wandering. With total amnesia the patient does not recognize relatives and friends but retains the ability to talk, read, and reason and also retains talents and previously acquired knowledge of the world and how to function in it. The amnesic episode may last several hours or as long as several years. It usually disappears as suddenly as it came on, with complete recovery and only a small chance of recurrence.

Memory loss is also common in many organic brain disorders as well as in substance abuse, but amnesia and memory loss caused by a brain disease or substance abuse can be fairly easily distinguished. In degenerative brain disorders memory fails more slowly over time and is not linked to life stress. Memory loss following a brain injury caused by some trauma (e.g., an automobile accident) or substance abuse can be easily linked to the trauma or the substance being abused.

DISSOCIATIVE FUGUE

In **dissociative fugue** the memory loss is more extensive. The person not only becomes totally

the situation demands, people can adopt a second personality. Spanos et al. suggest that some people who present as multiple personalities may have a rich fantasy life and considerable practice imagining that they are other people, especially when, like Bianchi, they find themselves in a situation in which there are inducements and cues to behave as though a previous bad act had been committed by another personality. We should remember, however, that this demonstration illustrates only that such role-playing is possible; it in no way demonstrates that all cases of multiple personality have such origins.

The Spanos study does give us pause. Some professionals still consider dissociative identity disorder nothing more than role-playing. Others consider it a real, though rare, disorder. How can this dispute be resolved? The main method has been to compare cases of multiple personality with people asked to role-play or who are tested while hypnotized or deeply relaxed. The key comparisons are those of the main personality with the alters, and the reality of DID is taken to be reflected by greater differences across the personalities for the clinical cases than for the role players. Physiological measures are frequently used as dependent variables because they are regarded as less subject to conscious control.

Using this type of research strategy Putnam, Zahn, and Post (1990) found greater differences in autonomic nervous system activity across personalities for the cases of DID than for controls, and Miller (1989) found more differences in visual functioning. Do these data unequivocally indicate that DID is more than mere role-playing? Not necessarily. They are interesting, but we must remember that the role players in these studies were considerably less practiced than were the clinical cases in enacting their different personalities. Perhaps with greater practice the differences would lessen.

Returning to the actual trial, Bianchi was found guilty. His insanity plea did not hold up, in part because evidence indicated that his role enactment differed in important ways from how true multiple personalities and deeply hypnotized subjects act (Orne et al., 1984). (For further discussion of DID and the insanity defense see p. 602.)

Ken Bianchi, the Hillside Strangler, attempted an insanity defense for his serial killings but the court decided that he had merely tried to fake a multiple personality.

had acknowledged the presence of another personality were asked to take two personality tests twice—once each for their two personalities. Eighty-one percent of the students in the Bianchi condition adopted a new name, and many of these admitted guilt for the murders. Even the personality test scores of the two personalities differed considerably. Clearly, when

amnesic but suddenly moves away from home and work and assumes a new identity. Sometimes the assumption of the new identity can be quite elaborate, with the person taking on a new name, new home, new job, and even a new set of personality characteristics, and sometimes the person may succeed in establishing a fairly complex social life, all without questioning his or her inability to remember the past. More often, however, the new life does not crystallize to this extent and the fugue is of briefer duration. It consists for the most part of limited, but apparently purposeful, travel, during which social contacts are minimal or absent. Fugues

typically occur after a person has experienced some severe stress, such as marital quarrels, personal rejections, war service, or a natural disaster. Recovery, although it takes varying amounts of time, is usually complete; the individual does not recollect what took place during the flight from his or her usual haunts.

DEPERSONALIZATION DISORDER

Depersonalization disorder, in which the person's perception or experience of the self is disconcertingly and disruptively altered, is also included in

DSM-IV as a dissociative disorder. Its inclusion is controversial, however, because depersonalization disorder involves no disturbance of memory, which is typical of the other dissociative disorders. In a depersonalization episode individuals rather suddenly lose their sense of self. Their limbs may seem drastically changed in size, or they may have the impression that they are outside their bodies, viewing themselves from a distance. Sometimes they feel mechanical, as though they and others are robots, or they move as though in a world that has lost its reality. Similar, but much more intense, episodes sometimes occur in schizophrenia (see Chapter 11). The experience of the patient with schizophrenia, however, does not have the "as if" quality that the person in depersonalization reports; his or her estrangement from the self is real and complete.

DISSOCIATIVE IDENTITY DISORDER

Consider what it would be like to have dissociative identity disorder, as did Chris Sizemore, the woman with the famous three faces of Eve (see p. 106). People tell you about things you have done that seem out of character, events of which you have no memory. You have been waking up each morning with the remains of a cup of tea by your bedside— and you do not like tea. How can you explain these happenings? If you think about seeking treatment, do you not worry whether the psychiatrist or psychologist will believe you? Perhaps the clinician will think you psychotic.

We all have days when we are not quite ourselves. This is assumed to be quite normal and is not what is meant by multiple personality. According to DSM-IV, a proper diagnosis of **dissociative identity disorder (DID)** requires that a person have at least two separate ego states, or alters, different modes of being and feeling and acting that exist independently of each other and that come forth and are in control at different times. Gaps in memory are also common and are produced because at least one alter usually has no contact with the other; that is, alter A has no memory for what alter B is like or even any knowledge of having an alternate state of being. The existence of different alters must also be chronic (long lasting) and severe (causing considerable disruption in one's life); it cannot be a temporary change resulting from the ingestion of a drug, for example.

Each alter may be quite complex, with its own behavior patterns, memories, and relationships; each determines the nature and acts of the individual when it is in command. Usually the personalities are quite different, even opposites of one anoth-

er. They may have different handedness, wear glasses with different prescriptions, and have allergies to different substances. The original and subordinate alters are all aware of lost periods of time, and the voices of the other alters may sometimes echo into their consciousness, even though they do not know to whom these voices belong.

Dissociative identity disorder usually begins in childhood, but it is rarely diagnosed until adolescence. It is more extensive than other dissociative disorders, and recovery may be less complete. It is much more common in women than in men. The presence of other diagnoses—in particular, depression, borderline personality disorder, and somatization disorder—is frequent (Ross et al., 1990). DID is commonly accompanied by headaches, substance abuse, phobias, suicidal ideas, and self-abusive behavior.

Cases of dissociative identity disorder are sometimes mislabeled in the popular press as schizophrenic reactions. This diagnostic category, discussed in greater detail in Chapter 11, derives part of its name from the Greek root *schizo*, which means "splitting away from," hence the confusion. A split in the personality, wherein two or more fairly separate and coherent systems of being exist alternately in the same person, is quite different from any of the recognized symptoms of schizophrenia.

The very existence of dissociative identity disorder has been the subject of much dispute (see Focus 7.3). Although DID is formally recognized in that it is included in the official diagnostic manual, its existence violates a firmly held belief that each body is inhabited by only one person. Its earliest mention occurred in the nineteenth century. In a review of the literature Sutcliffe and Jones (1962) were able to identify a total of 77 cases, most of which were reported in the period between 1890 and 1920. After that period reports of DID declined until the 1970s, when they increased markedly. More formal data on the prevalence of DID were collected on a sample of 454 adults in Winnipeg, Canada (Ross, 1991). Unfortunately, the sample was not representative and the study had other flaws, such as the failure of independent interviewers to confirm diagnoses. Nonetheless, these are the most extensive data available on the prevalence of DID, which was found to be 1.3 percent. Although this figure may not seem high, it is; earlier, prevalence was thought to be about one in one million.

What caused this apparent decline and subsequent reemergence? We cannot be sure whether diagnostic practice changed, whether more people began to adopt the role of a patient with DID, or whether clinicians always saw a similar number of cases but chose to report them only when interest in DID seemed high. It is possible that the decline in diagnoses of DID resulted from the increasing popularity of the concept of schizophrenia. Cases of DID may have been mistakenly diagnosed as cases of schizophrenia (Rosenbaum, 1980). However, the symptoms of the two disorders are actually not very similar; patients with DID do not show the thought disorder and behavioral disorganization of schizophrenia. Another diagnostic issue is that DSM-IIIR did not require that the alters be amnesic for one another, raising the possibility that the diagnosis could be applied to people with high levels of variability in their behavior, as occurs with some personality disorders (Kihlstrom & Tataryn, 1991). Although DSM-IV restored the amnesia component to the diagnosis it is too early to know what effect this will have on prevalence.

Another factor of possible relevance to the increase in DID diagnoses was the publication of *Sybil*, which presented a dramatic case with sixteen personalities. This case attracted a great deal of attention and spawned much public interest in the disorder. It is notable that in the post-*Sybil* era the number of alters in each case has risen dramatically, from two or three in the past to more than twelve at

this point (Goff & Simms, 1993). The increase in the prevalence of DID has been confined largely to the United States and Canada; DID remains rare in England, France, Russia, India, and Japan. Furthermore, a small number of clinicians contribute disproportionately to the diagnosis of DID. A survey in Switzerland found that 66 percent of the diagnoses of DID were made by fewer than 10 percent of the psychiatrists who responded (Modestin, 1992). Couple these facts with data showing that some clinicians ask very leading questions (e.g., directly requesting a part to come out) and conduct interviews while the patient is hypnotized, and it is quite possible that the increase of DID is not real; some cases are being manufactured in the consulting room.

The case of Eve White was at one time the most carefully documented report of DID in the clinical literature. But many other cases have been described. One account appeared in 1976 in the *Journal of Abnormal Psychology*. "The Three Faces of Evelyn" is a detailed history by Robert F. Jeans, the psychiatrist who treated the patient. The therapeutic outcome was an *integration*, or *fusion*, of several of the patient's personalities, not the elimination of all but one of them. Most contemporary workers regard the alters as having a critical function and as important aspects of the whole person, hence the significance of trying to fuse them into a single personality (Ross, 1989).

The film version of *Sybil* depicted this famous case of dissociative identity disorder, played by Sally Field.

Jeans provides the following background on his patient. He was consulted in December 1965 by a Gina Rinaldi, referred to him by her friends. Gina, single and thirty-one years old, lived with another single woman and was at the time working successfully as a writer at a large educational publishing firm. She was considered an efficient, businesslike, and productive person, but her friends had observed that she was becoming forgetful and sometimes acted out of character. The youngest of nine siblings, Gina reported that she had been sleepwalking since her early teens; her present roommate had told her that she sometimes screamed in her sleep.

Gina described her mother, then aged seventy-four, as the most domineering woman she had ever known. She reported that as a child she had been a quite fearful and obedient daughter. At age twenty-six Gina got braces for her teeth, and at age twenty-eight she had an "affair," her first, with a former Jesuit priest, although it was apparently not sexual in nature. Then she became involved with T.C., a married man who assured her he would get a divorce and marry her. She indicated that she had been faithful to him since the start of their relationship. Partly on the basis of analysis of one of her dreams, Jeans concluded that Gina was uncomfortable about being a woman, particularly when a close, sexual relationship with a man might be

FOCUS 7.4   CLASSIFICATION OF CONVERSION DISORDER AND DISSOCIATIVE DISORDERS

Now that both conversion disorder and the dissociative disorders have been described, we return to the manner in which they have been separately classified in DSM-IV—conversion as a somatoform disorder because it involves physical symptoms and the dissociative disorders as a distinct category because they involve disruptions in consciousness. John Kihlstrom, a leading researcher in the field, has argued that this separation is a mistake. He believes that both disorders are disruptions in the normal controlling functions of consciousness. In the dissociative disorders there is a dissociation between explicit and implicit memory. Explicit memory refers to a person's conscious recall of some experience and is what is disrupted in dissociative disorders. Implicit memory refers to behavioral changes elicited by an event that cannot be consciously recalled. Kihlstrom (1994) cites numerous examples of patients with dissociative disorders whose implicit memory remains intact. One woman, for example, became amnesic after being victimized by a practical joke. Although she had no conscious memory of the event, she nonetheless became terrified when passing the location of the incident. It is the dissociation of explicit and implicit memory that is the core of the dissociative disorders.

Kihlstrom argues that the same basic disruption of consciousness is found in conversion disorder, in this case affecting perception. As in the dissociative disorders, stimuli that are not consciously seen, heard, or felt nevertheless affect behavior. (Recall our description of several cases of hysterical blindness that clearly make this point.) So, we might consider conversion disorder as a disruption in explicit perception with unimpaired implicit perception.

As we noted in Chapter 3, beginning with DSM-III the classification of abnormal behavior became behavioral, or symptom based. Kihlstrom's position on conversion and the dissociative disorders illustrates that other principles of classification can be applied to the field. Classification on the basis of what function or mechanism is dysfunctional may be preferable to a behaviorally based system. A behaviorally based system could be misleading when similar behaviors or symptoms have different causes. This box illustrates that a behavioral classification could err by separating disorders that may be caused by similar dysfunctions. The key to the final evaluation of Kihlstrom's position is whether his theory of the similar dysfunctions in conversion and dissociative disorders is correct. As of now there is no conclusive proof, but it remains an interesting idea.

---

expected of her. However, T.C. did not come through with his promised divorce, stopped seeing Gina regularly, and generally fell out of her favor.

After several sessions with Gina, Jeans began to notice a second personality emerging. "Mary Sunshine," as she came to be called by Jeans and Gina, was quite different from Gina. She seemed to be more childlike, more traditionally feminine, ebullient, and seductive. Gina felt that she walked like a coal miner, but Mary certainly did not. Some quite concrete incidents indicated Mary's existence. Sometimes Gina found in the sink cups that had had hot chocolate in them—neither Gina nor her roommate liked hot chocolate. There were large withdrawals from Gina's bank account that she could not remember making. One evening while watching television Gina realized that she was crying and remarked to herself that it was stupid to feel sad about the particular program she was viewing. She even discovered herself ordering a sewing machine on the telephone, although she disliked sewing; some weeks later she arrived at her therapy session wearing a new dress, which Mary had sewn. At work, Gina reported, people were finding her more pleasant to be with, and her colleagues took to consulting her on how to encourage people to work better with one another. All these phenomena were entirely alien to Gina. Jeans and Gina came to realize that sometimes Gina was transformed into Mary.

Then one day T.C. showed up again. Gina was filled with scorn and derision for him, yet she heard herself greeting him warmly with the words, "Gee, I missed you so much! It's good to see you!" (Apparently the psychoanalytically oriented therapy was softening the hitherto impermeable boundaries between the separate ego states of Gina and Mary.) Gina was also surprised to hear T.C. reply on this occasion, "All you ever wanted was to please me. You've done nothing but cater to my every whim, nothing but make me happy." Mary must have been active in the earlier relationship that Gina had had with this man.

More and more often Jeans witnessed Gina turning into Mary in the consulting room. T.C. accompanied Gina to a session during which her posture and demeanor became more relaxed, her tone of voice warmer. When T.C. explained that he really cared for her, Gina, or rather, Mary, said warmly, "Of course, T., I know you do." At another session Mary was upset and, as Jeans put it, chewed off Gina's fingernails. Then the two of them started having conversations with each other in front of Jeans.

A year after the start of therapy an apparent synthesis of Gina and Mary began to emerge. At first it seemed that Gina had taken over entirely, but then Jeans noticed that Gina was not as serious as before, particularly about "getting the job done," that is, working extremely hard on the therapy. Jeans, probably believing that Mary wanted to converse with him, encouraged Gina to have a conversation with Mary. The following is that conversation:

I was lying in bed trying to go to sleep. Someone started to cry about T.C. I was sure that it was Mary. I started to talk to her. The person told me that she didn't have a name. Later she said that Mary called her Evelyn.... I was suspicious at first that it was Mary pretending to be Evelyn. I changed my mind, however, because the person I talked to had too much sense to be Mary. She said that she realized that T.C. was unreliable but she still loved him and was very lonely. She agreed that it would be best to find a reliable man. She told me that she comes out once a day for a very short time to get used to the world. She promised that she will come out to see you [Jeans] sometime when she is stronger. (Jeans, 1976, pp. 254–255)

Throughout January, Evelyn appeared more and more often, and Jeans felt that his patient was improving rapidly. Within a few months she seemed to be Evelyn all the time; soon thereafter this woman married a physician. Now years later, she has had no recurrences of the other personalities.

Severe trauma in childhood is regarded as a major cause of dissociative disorders.

ETIOLOGY OF DISSOCIATIVE DISORDERS

According to psychoanalytic theory all dissociative disorders are instances of a massive repression. The person succeeds in this repression by splitting off an entire part of the personality from awareness (Buss, 1966). When a severe trauma is repressed possible outcomes are amnesia or fugue; the alters in DID are seen as a way of dissociating and thereby protecting the host personality from painful memories (Bryant, 1995).

Although it does not employ the concept of repression the behavioral view of dissociative disorders is somewhat similar to psychoanalytic speculations. Behavioral theorists generally consider dissociation as an avoidance response that protects the person from stressful events and memories of these events. DID may be established in childhood by self-hypnosis as a way of coping with extremely disturbing events (Bliss, 1980). Available data indicate that patients with DID are indeed high in hypnotizability, scoring much higher than controls on the Stanford Hypnotic Susceptibility Scales (Bliss, 1983). A similar high level of hypnotizability may characterize people who develop amnesia after a trauma (Butler et al., 1996).

All the viewpoints just described propose that dissociation is closely linked to extreme stress. Research indicates that the major stress is physical and sexual abuse in childhood. The results from a survey of therapists who work with patients with dissociative identity disorder indicate that 80 per-

cent of these clients reported they had suffered physical abuse in childhood and almost 70 percent had been subjected to incest (Putnam et al., 1983). Other estimates of physical and sexual abuse in childhood are even higher (Kluft, 1984; Ross et al., 1990).

THERAPIES FOR DISSOCIATIVE DISORDERS

Dissociative disorders suggest, perhaps better than any other disorders, the plausibility of Freud's concept of repression. In three—amnesia, fugue, and dissociative identity disorder—people behave in ways that very assuredly indicate they have forgotten earlier parts of their lives. And since these people may at the same time be unaware of having forgotten something, the hypothesis that they have repressed massive portions of their lives is a compelling one.

Consequently, psychoanalytic treatment is perhaps more widespread as a choice of treatment for dissociative disorders than for other psychological problems. The goal of lifting repressions is the order of the day, pursued via the use of basic psychoanalytic techniques.

Focus 7.5

Repressed Memories of Child Sexual Abuse

We have seen in this chapter that a history of abuse in childhood is thought to be an important cause of DID, and in later chapters we will learn that sexual abuse is considered to play a role in several other disorders. Until recently child sexual abuse was thought to be a relatively rare occurrence. Now it is estimated that between 20 and 30 percent of women experienced abuse during childhood (Finkelhor, 1993). Although the data on the frequency of childhood sexual abuse have been derived from the retrospective reports of patients and thus could be distorted, most researchers assume that the reports are fairly accurate.

In this box we focus on the special instance of *recovered memories* of sexual abuse. In these cases the patient had no memory of abuse until it was recovered, typically during psychotherapy. Few issues are more hotly debated in psychology and in the courts than whether these recovered memories are valid. Memory researchers caution against a blanket acceptance of memories of sexual or physical abuse recovered during therapy. It is important to raise these questions; good science requires it, and it is key for court cases when recovered memories may play a major role in convicting a parent or other person of sexual abuse (Pope, 1995).

Recovered memories of childhood sexual abuse have assumed great importance in a series of recent court cases (Earleywine & Gann, 1995; see also p. 625). In a typical scenario a now-adult woman accuses one or both of her parents of having abused her during childhood and brings charges against them. Courts in several states allow plaintiffs to sue for damages within three years of the time they remember the abuse (Wakefield & Underwager, 1994). These cases depend on memories of childhood abuse that were recovered in adulthood,

often during psychotherapy, and were apparently repressed for many years. In the most scientifically accurate study of memories of sexual abuse Williams (1995) was able to interview women whose abuse years earlier had been verified. Fully 38 percent of these women were unable to recall the abuse when they were asked about it almost two decades later.

Williams's data notwithstanding, is it justifiable to assume that recovered memories are *invariably* accurate reports of repressed memories? This is a question of enormous legal as well as scientific importance. Studies have been conducted on women who have reported a history of sexual abuse. The women were asked whether there ever was a time when they could not remember the abuse. Based on these data the frequency of "repression" ranges from 18 to 59 percent (Loftus, 1993). But a simple failure to remember does not mean that repression has occurred. Women could actively try to keep these thoughts out of mind because they are distressing. Or the abuse could have happened before the time of their earliest memories (generally around age three or four). Nor has it been scientifically demonstrated that children repress or even forget traumatic events. One of the hallmarks of posttraumatic stress disorder is frequent reliving of the trauma in one's memory. Numerous studies have shown that rather than repressing negative events, children recall them quite vividly (Earleywine & Gann, 1995).

In some cases allegedly recovered memories may have no basis in fact, but if not, where do they come from? Elizabeth Loftus (1993) suggests several possibilities.

1. **Popular writings.** *The Courage to Heal* (Bass & Davis, 1994) is a guide for victims of childhood sexual abuse and

Combs and Ludwig (1982) have suggested that some patients with rapid-onset amnesia can regain lost memories if the therapist patiently encourages them to tell their life stories as completely as possible, without skipping over difficult-to-remember parts. This recounting of their lives can be combined with a modified free-association technique focusing on remembered events that took place just before the hole in memory. If the patient seems to be jumping forward in time the therapist encourages free association to the event just preceding the memory gap. All the while the therapist should suggest strongly that memory will be regained and should not imply that the patient is deliberately lying or malingering. In some cases, Combs and Ludwig have proposed, all that is necessary is the "tincture of time," a period during which the

patient is separated from stressful surroundings and given support and encouragement.

As discussed in Chapter 1, psychoanalysis had its beginnings in hypnosis, with Mesmer's work in the late eighteenth century and Charcot's work in the nineteenth century. Both men believed that they could eliminate hypnotized patients' various hysterical symptoms by direct suggestion. Then, Breuer and Freud encouraged patients to talk, while hypnotized, about their problems and especially about the earlier origins of them. Though Freud eventually abandoned hypnosis in favor of such techniques as free association, the use of hypnotism did not stop. Through the years practitioners have continued to use hypnosis with patients suffering from dissociative disorders as a means of helping them gain access to hidden portions of the personality—

The validity of recovered memories of childhood sexual abuse has recently been much debated.

widely known in the recovered-memory movement. It repeatedly suggests to readers that they were probably abused and offers as symptoms of abuse low self-esteem, feeling different from others, substance abuse, sexual dysfunction, and depression.

2. **Therapists' suggestions.** By their own accounts some therapists—those who genuinely believe that many adult disorders result from abuse—directly suggest to their clients that childhood sexual abuse is likely, sometimes with the assistance of hypnotic age regression. It is important to bear in mind that one of the defining characteristics of hypnosis is heightened suggestibility. If a therapist believes strongly that sexual abuse has been repressed, it is possible that memories recovered during hypnosis were planted there by the therapist (Kihlstrom, in press; Loftus & Ketchum, 1994).

3. **Research on memory.**   Memory does not function as a tape recorder, and cognitive psychologists have shown that it is possible for people to construct recollections of events that did not happen. For example, Neisser and Harsch (1992) studied people's memories of where they were when they heard about the *Challenger* on January 28, 1986. Participants were interviewed the day after the explosion and again two years later. Despite reporting vivid memories, none of the later accounts was entirely accurate and many were way off the mark. Similarly, an extensive series of studies has shown that it is common to confuse memories of actual happenings with memories of events that have only been imagined (Johnson & Raye, 1982). This last point is clearly relevant to our earlier discussion of the possible role of therapists in planting memories.

There is little doubt that childhood sexual abuse exists and that it may be much more frequent than any of us would like to believe (Finkelhor, 1993). But we must be wary of accepting reports of abuse uncritically. Social scientists, lawyers, and the courts share a heavy responsibility in deciding whether a given recovered memory is in fact a reflection of an actual (and criminal) event. Erring in either direction creates an injustice for either the accused or the accuser.

to a lost identity or to a set of events precipitating or flowing from a trauma.

Some physicians have used sodium Amytal, truth serum, to induce a hypnotic-like state, again assuming that painful repressed memories will be brought forth and remove the need for the dissociative disorder. Dramatic case studies in the clinical literature suggest that both hypnosis and barbiturates, such as sodium Amytal can be helpful, but little can be said about their effectiveness because almost nothing approximating controlled research has been done (see Focus 7.6). When Dysken (1979)

Hypnosis is still used as a treatment for dissociative disorders by trying to restore memory for the traumatic event that led to the dissociation.

FOCUS 7.6   THE SELECTIVE NATURE OF PUBLISHING CASE STUDIES

To illustrate the problem inherent to case studies we offer this personal observation. While working in a mental hospital some years ago, one of the authors encountered on the ward a man suffering from partial amnesia. He did not recognize members of his family when they came to visit him, but he could still recall most other events in his life. Many efforts were made to restore his memory, ranging from hypnotic suggestions to drug therapy. Both sodium Amytal and Methedrine, a powerful stimulant, were administered, Methedrine intravenously. It was hoped that Methedrine would energize his nervous system and dislodge the blocks to memory, much as a drain cleaner is used to open a clogged drain. In all these attempts the patient was cooperative and even eager for a positive outcome, but none of them worked. The unsuccessful treatment was never written up for publication. There is a strong editorial bias against publishing reports of failed clinical treatments, as indeed there is against publishing inconclusive results of experiments. This, a general problem for psychology and psychiatry, is a special detriment when, as for dissociative disorders, there is little in the way of controlled research.

compared the effects on amnesic patients of sodium amobarbital and normal saline acting as a placebo, he failed to find significant differences in the amount of new information remembered.

There seems to be widespread agreement on several principles in the treatment of dissociative identity disorder, whatever the clinician's orientation (Bowers et al., 1971; Caddy, 1985; Kluft, 1985; Ross, 1989):

1. The goal is integration of the several personalities.
2. Each alter has to be helped to understand that he or she is part of one person.
3. The therapist should use the alters' names only for convenience, not as a way to confirm the existence of separate, autonomous personalities who do not share overall responsibility for the actions of the whole person.
4. All alters should be treated with fairness and empathy.
5. The therapist should encourage empathy and cooperation among personalities.
6. Gentleness and supportiveness are needed in consideration of the childhood trauma that probably gave rise to the alters.

The goal of any approach to DID should be to convince the person that forgetting or splitting into different personalities is no longer necessary in order to deal with traumas, either those in the past that triggered the original dissociation or those in the present or yet to be confronted in the future. In addition, assuming that DID and the other dissociative disorders are in some measure an escape response to high levels of stress, treatment can be enhanced by teaching the patient to cope better with challenges.

Because of the rarity of DID and because it has often been misdiagnosed, there are no controlled outcome studies. Nearly all the well-reported outcome data come from the clinical observations of one highly experienced therapist, Richard Kluft (e.g., 1984a). Over a ten-year period Kluft had contact with 171 cases, of which he personally treated 117 and monitored the treatment of 6 others. Of these, 83, or 68 percent, achieved integration of their alters that was stable for at least three months (33 have remained stable for almost two and a half years). The greater the number of personalities, the longer the treatment lasted (Putnam et al., 1986), but in general, therapy took almost two years and upwards of 500 hours per patient. Ross (1989) concluded that therapies following the aforementioned principles can be effective for most DID patients.

Additional information from Kluft (1984b), who has diagnosed some cases of DID in children, suggests that early treatment may be more rapid and more successful than later treatment; that is, the longer the disorder persists, the more resistant it may be to therapy. If this turns out to be true and if improved diagnosis can identify DID at an earlier stage, it may be possible to prevent many cases of DID in adults.

SUMMARY

In somatoform disorders there are physical symptoms for which no biological basis can be found. The sensory and motor dysfunctions of conversion disorder, one of the two principal types of somatoform disorders, suggest neurological impairments, but ones that do not always make anatomical sense; the symptoms do, however, seem to serve some psychological purpose. In somatization disorder multiple physical complaints, not adequately explained by physical disorder or injury, eventuate in frequent visits to physicians, hospitalization, and even unnecessary surgery.

Anxiety plays a role in somatoform disorders, but it is not expressed overtly; instead, it is transformed into physical symptoms. Theory concerning the etiology of these disorders is speculative and focuses primarily on conversion disorder. Psychoanalytic theory proposes that in conversion disorder repressed impulses are converted into physical symptoms. Behavioral theories focus on the conscious and deliberate adoption of the symptoms as a means of obtaining a desired goal. In therapies for somatoform disorder, analysts try to help the client face up to the repressed impulses, and behavioral treatments attempt to reduce anxiety and reinforce behavior that will allow the patient to relinquish the symptoms.

Dissociative disorders are disruptions of consciousness, memory, and identity. An inability to recall important personal information, usually after some traumatic experience, is diagnosed as dissociative amnesia. In dissociative fugue the person moves away, assumes a new identity, and is amnesic for his or her previous life. In depersonalization disorder the person's perception of the self is altered; he or she may experience being outside the body or changes in the size of body parts. The person with dissociative identity disorder has two or more distinct and fully developed personalities, each with unique memories, behavior patterns, and relationships.

Psychoanalytic theory regards dissociative disorders as instances of massive repression of some undesirable event or aspect of the self. In DID the role of abuse in childhood and a high level of hypnotizability are emerging as important. Behavioral theories consider dissociative reactions escape-responses motivated by high levels of anxiety. Both analytic and behavioral clinicians focus their treatment efforts on understanding the anxiety associated with the forgotten memories, since it is viewed as etiologically significant.

KEY TERMS

somatoform disorders	anesthesias	dissociative amnesia
dissociative disorders	hysteria	dissociative fugue
pain disorder	somatization disorder	depersonalization disorder
body dysmorphic disorder	malingering	dissociative identity disorder
hypochondriasis	la belle indifférence	(DID)
conversion disorder	factitious disorder	

8

Ed Paschke,
"Nervosa," *1939*

PSYCHOPHYSIOLOGICAL DISORDERS AND HEALTH PSYCHOLOGY

Mark Howard was thirty-eight. After earning an M.B.A. he had joined the marketing division of a large conglomerate and had worked his way up the corporate ladder. His talent and long hours had recently culminated in a promotion to head of his division. The promotion left him with mixed feelings. On the one hand, it was what he had been working so hard to achieve; but on the other hand, he had never been comfortable giving orders to others and he especially dreaded the staff meetings he would have to run.

Soon after the promotion, during a routine physical checkup, Mark's physician discovered that Mark's blood pressure had moved into the borderline hypertension range. Before implementing any treatment the physician asked Mark to wear a halter monitor for a few days so that his blood pressure could be assessed as he went about his usual routine. The device was programmed to take blood pressure readings twenty times a day. On the first day of monitoring Mark had a staff meeting scheduled for ten o'clock. While he was laying out the marketing plans for a new product, the cuff inflated to take his blood pressure. A couple of minutes later he checked the reading and became visibly pale. It was 195 over 140—not a borderline reading, but seriously high blood pressure. The next day he resigned his managerial role and returned to a less prestigious but, he hoped, a less stressful position.

Psychophysiological disorders, such as asthma, hypertension, headache, and gastritis, are characterized by genuine physical symptoms that are caused by or can be worsened by emotional factors. The term *psychophysiological disorders* is preferred to a former term, which is perhaps better known, **psychosomatic disorders**, although *psychosomatic* connotes quite well the principal feature of these disorders, that the psyche, or mind, is having an untoward effect on the soma, or body.

In contrast to many of the disorders described in Chapter 7 (e.g., hypochondriasis, somatization disorder, and conversion disorder), psychophysiological disorders are real diseases involving damage to the body (see Table 8.1). That such disorders are viewed as being caused by emotional factors does not make the afflictions imaginary. People can just as readily die from psychologically produced high blood pressure or asthma as from similar diseases produced by infection or physical injury.

Psychophysiological disorders as such do not appear in DSM-IV as they did in some earlier versions of the DSM. DSM-IV requires a diagnostic judgment to indicate the presence of **psychological factors affecting medical condition**, and this diagnosis is coded in the broad section that comprises "other conditions that may be a focus of clinical attention." The implication of this placement is that psychophysiological disorders are not a form of mental disorder. Nonetheless, we shall consider them here in some detail because of their historical link to the field of psychopathology.

The new approach to diagnosis is also broader in scope. Formerly, psychophysiological disorders were generally thought to include only a subset of all possible diseases (the classic psychosomatic diseases, such as ulcers, headaches, asthma, and hypertension). The new diagnosis is applicable to any disease, as it is now thought that any disease can be influenced by psychological factors, such as stress. Furthermore, the diagnosis of psychological factors affecting medical conditions includes cases in which the psychological or behavioral factor influences the course or treatment of a disorder, not merely cases in which it influences the onset, again broadening the definition. For example, a person with hypertension may continue to drink alcohol even though he or she knows that alcohol increases blood pressure, or a patient may fail to take prescribed medication regularly. The psychological or behavioral factors include Axis I and II diagnoses; personality traits; coping styles, such as holding anger in rather than expressing it; and lifestyle factors, such as failing to exercise regularly.

What is the evidence for the view that all illness may be in part stress related? For years it has been known that various physical diseases can be produced in laboratory animals by exposure to severe stressors. Usually the diseases produced in such studies were the classic psychophysiological disorders, such as ulcers. More recently, studies have indicated that a broader range of diseases may be related to stress. Sklar and Anisman (1979), for example, induced tumors in mice with a transplant of cancerous tissue and then studied the impact of stress—uncontrollable electric shocks—on growth of the tumors. In animals exposed to electric shock the tumors grew more rapidly, and these animals died earlier.

The fields of **behavioral medicine** and **health psychology** are based on the many demonstrations

TABLE 8.1 Comparing Psychophysiological and Conversion Disorders

Type of Disorder	Organic Bodily Damage	Bodily Function Affected
Conversion	No	Voluntary
Psychophysiological	Yes	Involuntary

of the pervasive role of psychological factors in health. Since the 1970s these areas have dealt with the role of psychological factors in all facets of health and illness. Beyond examining the etiological role that stress can play in illness, workers in these fields study psychological treatments (e.g., biofeedback for hypertension), the maintenance and promotion of healthful behaviors (e.g., dietary change to reduce cholesterol intake and thus lessen the risk of heart attack), and the health care system itself (e.g., how better to deliver services to underserved populations) (Appel et al., 1997; Schwartz & Weiss, 1977; G. Stone, 1982). Many examples of behavioral medicine are discussed throughout this chapter as well as in Chapter 18.

STRESS AND HEALTH

We shall first review general findings on the relationship between stress and health as well as theories about how stress can produce illness. Then we will turn to an in-depth examination of two disorders—cardiovascular disease and asthma. Finally, we will consider psychological interventions.

DIFFICULTIES IN DEFINING THE CONCEPT OF STRESS

We have encountered the term **stress** in earlier chapters, primarily as a concept referring to some environmental condition that triggers psychopathology. Here we shall examine the term more closely and consider the difficulties in its definition.

In 1936, Hans Selye, a physician, introduced the **general adaptation syndrome (GAS)**, a description of the biological reaction to sustained and unrelenting physical stress. There are three phases of the model (see Figure 8.1). During the first phase, the alarm reaction, the autonomic nervous system is activated by the stress. If the stress is too powerful, gastrointestinal ulcers form, the adrenal glands become enlarged, and there is atrophy (wasting away) of the thymus. During the second phase, resistance, the organism adapts to the stress through available coping mechanisms. If the stressor persists or the organism is unable to respond effectively, the third phase, a stage of exhaustion, follows, and the organism dies or suffers irreversible damage (Selye, 1950).

Selye's concept of stress eventually found its way into the psychological literature, but with substantial changes in its definition. Some researchers followed Selye's lead and continued to consider stress a *response* to environmental conditions, defined on

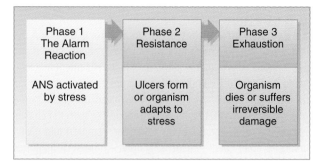

Figure 8.1   Selye's general adaptation syndrome.

the basis of such diverse criteria as emotional upset, deterioration of performance, or physiological changes, such as increased skin conductance or increases in the levels of certain hormones. The problem with these response-based definitions of stress is that the criteria are not clear-cut. Physiological changes in the body can occur in response to a number of stimuli that we would not want to consider stressful (for example, anticipating a pleasurable event).

Other researchers looked on stress as a *stimulus*, often referred to as a **stressor**, and identified with a long list of environmental conditions—electric shock, boredom, uncontrollable stimuli, catastrophic life events, daily hassles, and sleep deprivation. Stimuli that are considered stressors can be major (the death of a loved one), minor (daily hassles, such as being stuck in traffic), acute (failing an exam), or chronic (a persistently unpleasant work environment). For the most part they are experiences that people regard as unpleasant. Like response-based definitions, stimulus-based definitions also are problematic. Stipulating exactly what constitutes a stressor is difficult. It is not merely "negativity," for marriage, generally a positive event, is regarded as a stressor because it requires adaptation. Furthermore, there is wide variation in how people respond to life's challenges. The same event does not create the same amount of stress in different people. For example, a family who has lost its home in a flood but has money enough to rebuild and a strong network of friends nearby to help while rebuilding will experience less stress from this event than will a family that has neither adequate money to rebuild nor a social network to turn to for help and temporary housing.

Some people believe that it is not possible to define objectively what events or situations qualify as psychological stressors (e.g., Lazarus, 1966). They emphasize the cognitive aspects of stress; that is, how we perceive or appraise the environment

According to Richard Lazarus, how a life event is appraised is an important determinant of whether it causes stress. An exam, for example, may be viewed as a challenge or as an event that is extremely stressful.

determines whether or not a stressor is present. When a person determines that the demands of a situation exceed his or her resources, the person experiences stress. A final exam may be merely challenging to one student, yet highly stressful to another who does not feel equipped to take it (whether his or her fears are realistic or not).

Also relevant to individual differences in response to stressful situations is the concept of *coping*, how people try to deal with a problem or handle the emotions it produces. Even among those who appraise a situation as stressful, the effects of the stress may vary depending on how the individual copes with the event. Lazarus and his colleagues have identified two broad dimensions of coping (Lazarus & Folkman, 1984). *Problem-focused coping* includes taking direct action to solve the problem or seeking information that will be relevant to the solution. An example is developing a study schedule to pace assignments over a semester and thereby reduce end-of-semester pressure. *Emotion-focused coping* refers to efforts to reduce the negative emotional reactions to stress, for example, by distracting oneself from the problem, relaxing, or seeking comfort from others.

Effective coping often varies with the situation; distraction may be an effective way of dealing with the emotional upset produced by impending surgery, but it would be a poor way to handle the upset that could be produced by the discovery of a lump on the breast (Lazarus & Folkman, 1984). There is evidence that in general, escape/avoidance coping (such as wishing that the situation would go away or be over with) is the least effective method of coping with life problems (Stanton & Snider, 1993; Suls & Fletcher, 1985).

EFFORTS TO MEASURE STRESS

Given the difficulty of defining stress with precision, it is not surprising that measuring stress is difficult as well. Research on the effects of stress on human health has sought to measure the amount of life stress a person has experienced and then to correlate this measurement with illness. Various scales have been developed to measure life stress. We will examine two in some depth, the Social Readjustment Rating Scale and the Assessment of Daily Experience.

THE SOCIAL READJUSTMENT RATING SCALE

In the 1960s two researchers, Holmes and Rahe (1967), gave a list of life events to a large group of subjects and asked them to rate each item according

Coping can be focused on solving the problem itself or on regulating the negative emotions it has created. Seeking comfort or social support from others is an example of emotion-focused coping.

TABLE 8.2 Social Readjustment Rating Scale

Rank	Life Event	Mean Value
1	Death of spouse	100
2	Divorce	73
3	Marital separation	65
4	Jail term	63
5	Death of close family member	63
6	Personal injury or illness	53
7	Marriage	50[a]
8	Fired from work	47
9	Marital reconciliation	45
10	Retirement	45
11	Change in health of family member	44
12	Pregnancy	40
13	Sex difficulties	39
14	New family member	39
15	Business readjustment	39
16	Change in financial state	38
17	Death of close friend	37
18	Change to different line of work	36
19	Change in number of arguments with spouse	35
20	Mortgage over $10,000	31
21	Foreclosure of mortgage or loan	30
22	Change in responsibilities at work	29
23	Child leaving home	29
24	Trouble with in-laws	29
25	Outstanding personal achievement	28
26	Spouse begins or stops work	26
27	Begin or end school	26
28	Change in living conditions	25
29	Revision of personal habits	24
30	Trouble with boss	23
31	Change in work hours or conditions	20
32	Change in residence	20
33	Change in schools	20
34	Change in recreation	19
35	Change in church activities	19
36	Change in social activities	18
37	Mortgage or loan less than $10,000	17
38	Change in sleeping habits	16
39	Change in number of family get-togethers	15
40	Change in eating habits	15
41	Vacation	13
42	Christmas	12
43	Minor violations of the law	11

Source: From Holmes & Rahe, 1967.

[a] Marriage was arbitrarily assigned a stress value of 500; no event was found to be any more than twice as stressful. Here the values are reduced proportionally and range up to 100.

to its intensity and the amount of time they thought they would need to adjust to it. Marriage was arbitrarily assigned a stress value of 500; all other items were then evaluated using this reference point. For example, an event twice as stressful as marriage would be assigned a value of 1000, and an event one-fifth as stressful as marriage would be assigned a value of 100. The average ratings assigned to the events by the respondents in Holmes and Rahe's study are shown in Table 8.2.

From this study the Social Readjustment Rating Scale (SRRS) emerged. The respondent checks off the life events experienced during the time period in question. Ratings that indicate differential stressfulness of events are then totaled for all the events actually experienced to produce a Life Change Unit (LCU) score, a weighted sum of events. The LCU score has been related to several different illnesses, for example, heart attacks (Rahe & Lind, 1971), fractures (Tollefson, 1972), onset of leukemia (Wold, 1968), and colds and fevers (Holmes & Holmes, 1970).

There is thus some promising information on the relationship between psychological stress and physical illness, but caution is in order before asserting that the relationship is a causal one. For example, illness could cause a high life-change score, as when chronic absenteeism brings dismissal from a job. In addition, reports of stressful events in such studies could be contaminated by knowledge of subsequently occurring illnesses, that is, someone who has experienced many illnesses may try to recall recent stressors to explain these illnesses. Many studies have used a retrospective method, asking participants to recall both the illnesses and the stressful life events that they experienced over some past time period. As we previously mentioned, retrospective reports are subject to considerable distortion and forgetting. Finally, self-reports of illness may not yield a true reflection of disease. Together with the fact that it often takes many years for stress to contribute to illness, the important messages from these criticisms are that research on stress and health must be longitudinal so that changes in stress can be shown to precede changes in health, and care should be taken to minimize retrospective reporting. In selecting research to be discussed in this chapter we have been guided by these methodological points.

ASSESSMENT OF DAILY EXPERIENCE

Consideration of problems with the SRRS led Stone and Neale (1982) to develop a new assessment instrument, the Assessment of Daily Experience (ADE). Rather than relying on retrospective reports,

Experiencing major life events such as marriage (above) or starting school (right) statistically increases risk for illness. Research on the effects of these major stressors assesses them with The Social Readjustment Rating Scale.

which can be inaccurate, the ADE allows individuals to record and rate their daily experiences in prospective investigations. A day was used as the unit of analysis because a thorough characterization of this period should be possible without major retrospective-recall bias. Minor daily events (hassles) may be subjectively important to individuals for reasons not known by the researcher. How events are appraised may be linked to past experience with similar events (e.g., many failures), to more general personality characteristics (an anxious individual faced with a public-speaking engagement), or to the cultural or religious background of the individual (divorce for a strict Catholic). Furthermore, there is now direct evidence that these minor events are related to illness (Jandorf et al., 1986).

The first step in developing the scale was to obtain a sample of daily activities by having people record their experiences in diaries. These events were then reviewed and a list of categories was created and arranged in outline form. Part of the ADE is shown in Figure 8.2.

With an assessment of daily experiences in hand, Stone, Reed, and Neale (1987) began a study of the relationship between life experience and health.

Daily hassles like being stuck in traffic can be emotionally upsetting and also increase risk for illness.

WORK RELATED ACTIVITIES

Concerning Boss, Supervisor, Upper Management, etc.

▶ Praised for a job well done   □ ○ ○ △ 01

▶ Criticism for job performance, lateness, etc.   □ ○ ○ △ 02

Concerning Co-workers, Employees, Supervisees, and/or Clients

▶ Positive emotional interactions and/or happenings with co-workers, employees, supervisees, and/or clients (work related events which were fulfilling, etc.)   □ ○ ○ △ 03

▶ Negative emotional interactions and/or happenings with co-workers, employees, supervisees, and/or clients (work related events which were frustrating, irritating, etc.)   □ ○ ○ △ 04

▶ Firing or disciplining (by Target)   □ ○ ○ △ 05

▶ Socializing with staff, co-workers, employees, supervisees, and/or clients   □ ○ ○ △ 06

General Happenings Concerning Target at Work

▶ Promotion, raise   □ ○ ○ △ 07

▶ Fired, quit, resigned   □ ○ ○ △ 08

▶ Some change in job (different from the above, i.e., new assignment, new boss, etc.)   □ ○ ○ △ 09

▶ Under a lot of pressure at work (impending deadlines, heavy workload, etc.)   □ ○ ○ △ 10

Figure 8.2   Sample page from Stone and Neale's (1982) Assessment of Daily Experience scale. Respondents indicate whether an event occurred by circling the arrows to the left of the list of events. If an event has occurred, it is then rated on the dimensions of desirability, change, meaningfulness, and control using the enclosed spaces to the right.

The goal was to examine the relationship between undesirable and desirable events and the onset of episodes of respiratory illness. Respiratory illness was selected as the criterion variable because it occurs with sufficient frequency to allow it to be analyzed as a distinct category.

After reviewing the participants' data the researchers identified thirty as having episodes of infectious illness. Next, the daily frequency of undesirable and desirable events that occurred from one to ten days before the start of an episode was examined. For each person a set of control days, without an episode, was also selected. The control days matched the others for day of the week to control for the higher frequency of desirable and lower frequency of undesirable events typically reported on weekends; since participants served as their own controls any weekend effects would be the same for days preceding episodes and for control days. The means of desirable events for the days preceding episode starts is shown in Figure 8.3; parallel data for undesirable events are shown in Figure 8.4. It was expected that several days before the onset of the illness episode there would be an increase in undesirable events and a decrease in desirable events relative to control days. The results indeed showed that for desirable events there were significant decreases three and four days prior to episode onset; for undesirable events, there were significant increases at four and five days before the episode onset.

These results, which have subsequently been replicated (Evans & Edgerton, 1990), were the first to show a relationship between life events and health, with both variables measured in a daily, prospective design. Most sources of confounding in prior life-events studies were avoided in this study, and we can now come much closer to asserting that life events play a causal role in increasing vulnerability to episodes of infectious illness. One of the strongest and most interesting aspects of the pattern of events preceding symptom episodes is that there was a peak in undesirable events and a trough in desirable ones several days prior to onset, yet the two days just before onset had average rates of desirable and undesirable events. Speculation that the results were caused by some bias, such as individuals feeling poorly prior to flagrant symptom

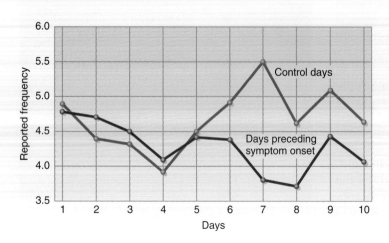

Figure 8.3   Number of desirable events for the ten days preceding an episode of respiratory infection. After Stone, Reed, and Neale (1987).

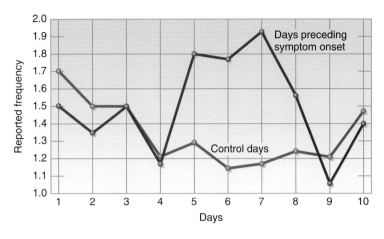

Figure 8.4 Number of undesirable events in the ten days preceding an episode of respiratory infection. After Stone, Reed, and Neale (1987).

onset and thus influencing perception of events, is unlikely to prove true, as most potential biases would produce a change in the frequency of events on days just prior to the onset of symptoms.

ASSESSING COPING

Coping is most often measured by questionnaires, which list a series of coping activities and ask respondents to indicate how much they used each to handle a recent stressor. An example of one such measure, the COPE, is presented in Table 8.3.

As with the effects of stressors, the best way to examine coping is by means of longitudinal study, which can demonstrate that particular ways of coping with stress precede the outcomes in which the researcher is interested. Breast cancer has been

Stone and his colleagues have found that changes in the frequency of daily life events precede the onset of episodes of respiratory infection. The mechanism may be a stress-induced lowering of secretory IgA.

TABLE 8.3 Scales and Sample Items from the COPE

Active Coping
I've been concentrating my efforts on doing something about the situation I'm in.

Suppression of Competing Activities
I've been putting aside other activities in order to concentrate on this.

Planning
I've been trying to come up with a strategy about what to do.

Restraint
I've been making sure not to make matters worse by acting too soon.

Use of Social Support
I've been getting sympathy and understanding from someone.

Positive Reframing
I've been looking for something good in what is happening.

Religion
I've been putting my trust in God.

Acceptance
I've been accepting the reality of the fact that it happened.

Denial
I've been refusing to believe that it has happened.

Behavioral Disengagement
I've been giving up the attempt to cope.

Use of Humor
I've been making jokes about it.

Self-Distraction
I've been going to movies, watching TV, or reading, to think about it less.

Source: From Carver et al., 1993.

investigated in this way. The diagnosis of breast cancer, which strikes about one woman in nine, is a major stressor on many levels. It is a life-threatening illness; surgical interventions are disfiguring and thus have serious implications for psychological well-being; and both radiation therapy and chemotherapy have unpleasant side effects.

Carver et al. (1993) selected women who had just been diagnosed with breast cancer and assessed how they were coping at several times during the following year. Women who accepted their diagnosis and retained a sense of humor had lower levels of distress. Avoidant coping methods, such as denial and behavioral disengagement (see Table 8.3), were related to higher levels of distress. Another longitudinal study of several types of cancer found that avoidant coping ("I try not to think about it." "I try to remove it from my mind.") predicted the extent to which the disease had progressed at a one year follow-up (Epping-Jordan, Compas, & Howell, 1994). These data show that it is not merely the presence of stress, but it is how the person reacts to the stress that is crucial to both its emotional and its physical effects.

MODERATORS OF THE STRESS–ILLNESS LINK

Even with a demonstration that life events are related to the onset of illness important questions remain. We have already noted that the same life experience apparently can have different effects on different people. This situation raises the possibility that other variables moderate or change the general stress–illness relationship. We have described one significant moderator, coping, and we have seen that the use of avoidant coping increases the likelihood of both emotional and physical effects of stress. Another important factor, which can lessen the effects of stress, is social support. There are various types of social support. **Structural social support** refers to a person's basic network of social relationships, for example, marital status and number of friends. **Functional social support** is concerned more with the *quality* of a person's relationships, for example, whether the person believes he or she has friends to call on in a time of need (Cohen & Wills, 1985).

Structural support is a well-established predictor of mortality. Elderly people with few friends or relatives tend to have a higher mortality rate than those with a higher level of structural support (Schoenbach et al., 1986). Similarly, men who have lower levels of structural support are more likely to die after experiencing a myocardial infarction (heart attack) than are those with higher levels of structural support (Ruberman et al., 1984).

A lack of structural support or functional support increases the likelihood of developing an illness. Higher levels of functional support were found to be related to lower rates of atherosclerosis (clogging of the arteries)(Seeman & Syme, 1987) and to the ability of women to adjust to chronic rheumatoid arthritis (Goodenow, Reisine, & Grady, 1990).

How does social support exert its beneficial effects? One possibility is that higher levels of social support increase the occurrence of positive health behaviors, for example, eating a healthy diet, not smoking, and moderating alcohol intake. Alternatively, social support (or lack of it) could have a direct effect on biological processes. For example, low levels of social support are related to an increase in negative emotions (Kessler & McLeod, 1985; see also our earlier discussion of PTSD on p. 149), which may affect some hormone levels and the immune system (Kielcolt-Glaser et al., 1984).

In recent years social support has been studied in the laboratory, where cause and effect can be more readily established than is possible in the naturalistic studies already described. In one such study college-aged women were assigned to high- or low-stress conditions and experienced them with or without a close friend. In one part of the study, stress was created by having the experimenter behave coldly and impersonally, telling participants to improve their performance as they worked on a challenging task. For each woman in the social-support condition, a close friend "silently cheered her on" and sat close to her, placing a hand on her wrist. The dependent variable was blood pressure, measured while participants performed the task. As expected, high stress led to higher blood-pressure levels. But, as Figure 8.5 shows, the high-stress con-

Figure 8.5 Results of a laboratory study of the effects of social support on blood pressure. Stress led to increased blood pressure, but the increase was less pronounced among people who experienced the stressor with a friend. From Kamarck et al. (1995).

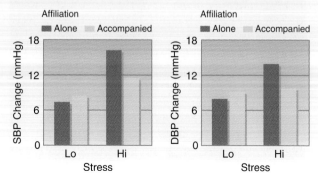

dition produced its effects on blood pressure primarily in those women who experienced the stress alone (Kamarck et al., 1995). Social support was thus shown to have a causal effect on a physiological process.

Not all research has found that social support has positive effects. With very severe stressors the person may be so overwhelmed that support does no good. This point was well made in a study of social support and breast cancer, in which social support did not lead to reduced distress or less physical impairment (Bolger et al., 1996).

THEORIES OF THE STRESS–ILLNESS LINK

In considering the etiology of psychophysiological disorders, we are confronted with three questions: (1) Why does stress produce illness in only some people who are exposed to it? (2) Why does stress sometimes cause an illness and not a psychological disorder? (3) Given that stress produces a psychophysiological disorder, what determines which one of the many disorders it will be? Answers to these questions have been sought by biologically as well as psychologically oriented theorists.

Before reviewing some theories that describe how stress comes to cause or exacerbate physical illness, it is important to note that much of the research in the field has attempted to link stress to *self-reports* of illness. The problem with this approach is that self-reports may not be an accurate reflection of physical illness, as noted in our discussion of the somatoform disorders in Chapter 7. For example, Watson and Pennebaker (1989), after an extensive review of the literature, concluded that an apparent association between negative emotional states and health was actually only a relationship between negative emotions and illness *reporting*. Similarly, Stone and Costa (1990) noted that neuroticism predicted reports of higher numbers of somatic complaints of all kinds (recall our discussion of hypochondriasis and somatization disorder) but did not predict "hard endpoints," such as death or verified coronary artery disease. Perhaps high levels of stress increase vigilance about bodily changes and create a tendency to overreact to these sensations. The result would be an increase in self-reports of illness but not an actual change in health. For this reason, our discussion will focus mainly on research that includes more than self-reports of illness.

In addition, the effects of stress may be indirect, that is, stress may lead to health changes that are not directly due to biological or psychological vari-

Stress may indirectly increase risk for illness by causing lifestyle changes such as increased consumption of alcohol.

ables but are due to changes in health behavior. High stress may result in increased smoking, disrupted sleep, increased alcohol consumption, and altered diet (the opposite of what we saw with social support). These behavioral changes may then increase risk for illness. In this case the stress–illness association would be real but mediated indirectly through changes in health behaviors.

BIOLOGICAL THEORIES

Biological approaches attribute particular psychophysiological disorders to specific weaknesses or overactivity of an individual's organ systems in responding to stress. Genetic factors, prior illnesses, diet, and the like may disrupt a particular organ system, which may then become weak and vulnerable to stress. According to the **somatic-weakness theory**, the connection between stress and a particular psychophysiological disorder is the weakness in a specific bodily organ. For instance, a congenitally weak respiratory system might predispose the individual to asthma.

People have been found to have their own individual patterns of autonomic response to stress. The heart rate of one individual may increase, whereas another person may react with an increased respiration rate but with no change in heart rate (Lacey, 1967). According to the **specific-reaction theory**, individuals respond to stress in their own, idiosyncratic ways, and the body system that is the most responsive may be a likely candidate for the locus of a subsequent psychophysiological disorder. For example, someone reacting to stress with elevated blood pressure may be more susceptible to essential hypertension. Later in this chapter, when we consider specific psychophysiological disorders, evidence in support of both the somatic-weakness and the specific-reaction theory will be presented.

On a general level stressors have multiple effects on various systems of the body—the autonomic nervous system, hormone levels, and brain activity. One major area of current interest is the immune system, which is an important consideration in infectious diseases, cancer, allergies, and autoimmune diseases, such as rheumatoid arthritis, in which the immune system attacks the body. A wide range of stressors have been found to produce changes in the immune system—medical-school examinations, depression and bereavement, marital discord and divorce, job loss, caring for a relative with Alzheimer's disease, and the Three Mile Island nuclear disaster, among others (Cohen & Hebert, 1996). Whether such immune-system changes lead to more negative clinical outcomes, such as early death from cancer or the onset of arthritis, is yet to be determined. That is, it is not yet certain that the changes in the immune system that follow stress are great enough to actually increase risk for disease.

The area of research that comes closest to documenting a role for stress and immune-system changes in actual illness is the study of infectious diseases. To illustrate, we will discuss one aspect of the immune system—secretory immunity—in some detail.

The secretory component of the immune system exists in the tears, saliva, gastrointestinal, vaginal, nasal, and bronchial secretions that bathe the mucosal surfaces of the body. A substance found in these secretions, called immunoglobulin A, or IgA, contains antibodies that serve as the body's first line of defense against invading viruses and bacteria. They prevent the virus or bacterium from binding to mucosal tissues.

A study by Stone et al. (1987) showed that changes in the number of IgA antibodies were linked to changes in mood. Throughout an eight-week study period a group of dental students came to the laboratory three times a week to have their saliva collected and a brief psychological assessment conducted. On days when the students experienced relatively high levels of negative mood, fewer antibodies were present than on days when the students had low levels of negative mood. Similarly, antibody level was higher on days with higher levels of positive mood.

Prior research (e.g., Stone & Neale, 1984) had shown that daily events affect mood. It is therefore quite possible that daily events affect the fluctuations in mood, which in turn suppress synthesis of the secretory IgA antibodies. The process could operate as follows. An increase in undesirable life events coupled with a decrease in desirable life events produces increased negative mood, which in turn depresses antibody levels in secretory IgA. If, during this period, a person is exposed to a virus, he or she will be at increased risk for the virus to infect the body. Bear in mind that the overt symptoms of respiratory illness begin several days following infection.

Two other studies have confirmed the relationship between stress and respiratory infection. In both studies volunteers took nasal drops containing a mild cold virus and also completed a battery of measures concerning recent stress. The advantage of this method was that exposure to the virus was an experimental variable under the investigators' control. Both investigations found that stress was clearly linked to developing a cold (Cohen, Tyrell, & Smith, 1991; Stone et al., 1992). These findings illustrate the complex interplay between psychological and biological variables in the etiology of psychophysiological disorders.

PSYCHOLOGICAL THEORIES

Psychological theories try to account for the development of various disorders by considering such factors as unconscious emotional states, personality traits, cognitive appraisals, and specific styles of coping with stress.

PSYCHOANALYTIC THEORIES

Psychoanalytic theories propose that specific conflicts and their associated negative emotional states give rise to psychophysiological disorders. Franz Alexander (1950) has had perhaps the greatest impact of the psychoanalytic theorists who have studied psychophysiological reactions. In his view the various psychophysiological disorders are products of unconscious emotional states specific to each disorder. For example, undischarged hostile impulses are viewed as creating the chronic emotional state responsible for essential hypertension.

The damming up of ... hostile impulses will continue and will consequently increase in intensity. This will induce the development of stronger defensive measures in order to keep pent-up aggressions in check .... Because of the marked degree of their inhibitions, these patients are less effective in their occupational activities and for that reason tend to fail in competition with others ... envy is stimulated and ... hostile feelings toward more successful, less inhibited competitors are further intensified. (p. 150)

Alexander formulated this unexpressed-anger or **anger-in theory** on the basis of his observations of patients undergoing psychoanalysis. His hypothesis continues to be pursued in present-day studies of the psychological factors in essential hypertension (see p. 192).

COGNITIVE AND BEHAVIORAL FACTORS

Humans perceive more than merely physical threats (Simeons, 1961). We experience regrets about the past and worries about the future. All these perceptions stimulate sympathetic system activity. But negative emotions, such as resentment, regret, and worry, cannot be fought or escaped as readily as can external threats, nor do they easily pass. They may keep the sympathetic system aroused and the body in a continual state of emergency, sometimes for far longer than it can bear. Under these circumstances the necessary balancing of sympathetic and parasympathetic actions is made that much more difficult, and it can go awry. The high level of cognition made possible in humans through evolution also creates the potential for distressed thoughts, which can bring about bodily changes that persist longer than they were meant to and may contribute to an imbalance between sympathetic and parasympathetic activity. Our higher mental capacities, it is theorized, subject our bodies to physical storms that they were not built to withstand.

In our general discussion of stress we saw that the appraisal of a potential stressor is central to how it affects the person. People who continually appraise life experiences as exceeding their resources may be expected to be chronically stressed and at risk for the development of a psychophysiological disorder. How people cope with stress may also be relevant. Later, we describe some findings that show that how people cope with anger is related to hypertension. Personality traits are implicated in several disorders, most notably cardiovascular disease. People with a Type A personality behave in ways that appear to be related to the development of heart problems. Finally, gender is an important variable in health; there are clear differences in the frequency with which men and women experience certain health problems (see Focus 8.1).

Our general overview of theories concerning the etiology of psychophysiological disorders is complete. We turn now to a detailed review of two disorders that have attracted much attention from researchers—cardiovascular disorders and asthma.

CARDIOVASCULAR DISORDERS

Cardiovascular disorders are medical problems involving the heart and blood circulation system. Cardiovascular disease accounts for almost half the deaths in the United States each year (Foreyt, 1990) and affects more than 300 of every 10,000 people (U.S. Census, 1990); its treatment and research consume over $100 billion a year (Weiss, 1986). In this section we focus on two forms of cardiovascular disease that appear to be adversely affected by stress—hypertension and coronary heart disease. Among the cardiovascular diseases, coronary heart disease is the single greatest cause of death. It is generally agreed that many of the deaths resulting from cardiovascular diseases are premature and that they could be prevented by dealing with one or more of the known risk factors (Price, 1982).

ESSENTIAL HYPERTENSION

Hypertension, commonly called high blood pressure, disposes people to atherosclerosis (clogging of the arteries), heart attacks, and strokes; it can also cause death through kidney failure. Yet no more than 10 percent of all cases in the United States are attributable to an identifiable physical cause. Hypertension without an evident organic cause is called **essential** (or sometimes primary) **hypertension**. Recent estimates are that varying degrees of hypertension are found in 15 to 33 percent of the adult population of the United States; it is twice as frequent in African-Americans as in whites. As many as 10 percent of American college students have hypertension; most of them are unaware of their illness. Unless people have their blood pressure checked, they may go for years without knowing that they are hypertensive. Thus this disease is known as the silent killer.

Blood pressure is measured by two numbers; one represents *systolic pressure*, and the other represents *diastolic pressure*. The systolic measure is the amount of arterial pressure when the ventricles contract and the heart is pumping; the diastolic measure is the degree of arterial pressure when the ventricles relax and the heart is resting. A normal blood pressure in a young adult would be 120 (systolic) over 80 (diastolic) (Figure 8.6).

Essential hypertension is viewed as a heterogeneous condition brought on by many possible disturbances in the various systems of the body that are responsible for regulating blood pressure. Blood pressure may be elevated by increased cardiac output, the amount of blood leaving the left ventricle of the heart per minute; by increased resistance to the

FOCUS 8.1   GENDER AND HEALTH

At every age from birth to eighty-five and older, more men die than women. Individual causes of death vary greatly between the sexes. Men are more than twice as likely to die in automobile accidents and of homicides, cirrhosis, heart disease, lung disease, lung cancer, and suicide. In spite of their reduced mortality, women have higher rates of *morbidity*—general poor health or the incidence of several specific diseases. For example, women have higher rates of diabetes, anemia, gastrointestinal problems, and rheumatoid arthritis; they report more visits to physicians, use more prescription drugs, and account for two-thirds of all surgical procedures performed in the United States. In recent years, though, women's mortality advantage has been decreasing; for example, the death rate from cardiovascular disease has declined among men in the last thirty years but stayed about the same in women (Rodin & Ickovics, 1990).

What are some of the possible reasons for the differences in mortality and morbidity rates in women, and why is mortality increasing? From a biological vantage point it might be that women have some mechanism that protects them from life-threatening diseases. The female hormone, estrogen, may offer protection from cardiovascular disease, for example. Several lines of evidence support this idea. Postmenopausal women and those who have had their ovaries removed, in both cases lowering estrogen, have higher rates of cardiovascular disease than do premenopausal women. Hormone-replacement therapy lowers the rate of mortality from cardiovascular disease, per-

haps by maintaining elevated levels of high-density lipoprotein (HDL), the so-called good cholesterol (Matthews et al., 1989).

From a psychological viewpoint, women are less likely than men to be Type A personalities and are also less hostile than men (Waldron, 1976; Weidner & Collins, 1993). Eisler and Blalock (1991) hypothesize that the Type A pattern, discussed more fully later, is part and parcel of a rigid commitment to the traditional masculine gender role, which emphasizes achievement, mastery, competitiveness, not asking for help or emotional support, an excessive need for control, and the tendency to become angry and to express anger when frustrated. They link these attributes to the tendency for men to be more prone to coronary problems and other stress-related health risks, such as hypertension (Harrison, Chin, & Ficarrotto, 1989). As we shall see, both biological and psychological variables play important roles in cardiovascular disease, and they could well be relevant to the lower levels of mortality of women.

Why is the gap between mortality rates in men and women decreasing? In the early twentieth century most deaths were due to epidemics and infection, but now most deaths result from diseases that are affected by lifestyle. One possibility, then, is that lifestyle differences between men and women account for the sex difference in mortality and that these lifestyle differences are decreasing. Men smoke more than women and consume more alcohol. These differences are likely contributors to men's higher mortality from cardiovascular disease and lung cancer. In recent

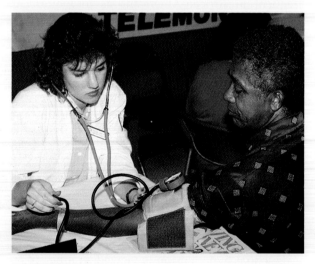

Because high blood pressure is typically not noticeable to the sufferer, regular check-ups are recommended, especially for those at higher than average risk.

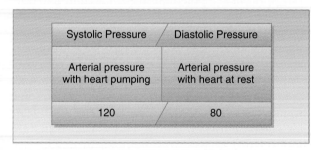

Systolic Pressure	Diastolic Pressure
Arterial pressure with heart pumping	Arterial pressure with heart at rest
120	80

Figure 8.6 Normal young-adult blood pressure.

pressure combine in an extremely complex manner. The autonomic nervous system, hormones, and salt and water metabolism, as well as central nervous system mechanisms, are all involved (Weiner, 1977). Many of these physiological mechanisms can be affected by psychological stress.

STRESS, ANGER, AND BLOOD-PRESSURE INCREASE

Various stressful conditions have been examined to determine their role in the etiology of essential

passage of blood through the arteries, that is, by vasoconstriction; or by both. The physiological mechanisms that contribute to regulation of blood

years women have begun to smoke and drink more, and these changes have been paralleled by increases in instances of lung cancer and the failure of the mortality rate for cardiovascular disease to decrease among women (Rodin & Ickovics, 1990).

Another lifestyle change placing women at greater risk is that more women have entered the workforce in recent years and thus have taken on the stress of filling the dual role of wage earner and homemaker. Frankenhaeuser et al. (1989) studied norepinephrine levels of men and women employed at a Volvo plant in Gothenburg, Sweden. Levels of norepinephrine were similar in both sexes during the day, but those of men declined after work, while those of women rose.

There are several possible explanations for the difference in morbidity of men and women. First, because women live longer than men, they may be more likely to experience several diseases that are associated with aging. Second, women may be more attentive to their health than are men and thus may be more likely to visit physicians and be diagnosed. Finally, women may cope with stress in a way that increases their risk for some illnesses, for example, by focusing their attention on their responses to a negative event (Weidner & Collins, 1993).

The gathering of scientific data on how best to minimize women's risk for a number of disorders has likely been compromised by the tendency to exclude female subjects from studies. Women have been understudied in health research (Rodin & Ickovics, 1990). Future studies need to include equal samples of men and women and also to focus on the special health concerns of women. The Women's Health Initiative represents a promising step in this direction. Since 1993 it has involved more

Women typically have higher rates of illness than do men. One source of stress that may be relevant is that women often must cope with the dual roles of homemaker and wage earner.

than 200,000 women in studies of preventive interventions for osteoporosis, coronary heart disease, and cancer, as well as psychosocial factors that increase risk for these diseases.

hypertension. Stressful interviews, natural disasters, and job stress have all been found to produce short-term elevations in blood pressure. Blood pressure also fluctuates in daily life depending on a person's mood, rising notably during anger (Schwartz, Warren, & Pickering, 1994). Kasl and Cobb (1970) examined the effects of the loss of employment. They studied a group of workers beginning two months before their jobs were to be terminated and for two years subsequent to the loss of employment. A control group, consisting of men in similar occupations who did not lose their jobs, was examined for the same twenty-six-month period. Each participant in the study was visited at home several times by a nurse during six separate periods so that blood pressure could be measured. For the control participants there were no overall changes in blood pressure. In the men who lost their jobs, however, elevated blood pressure was found with anticipation of job loss, after termination of employment, and during the initial probationary period of a new job. Those who had great difficulty finding stable employment suffered the longest periods of high blood pressure. Chronic

Unemployment is one of the stressors that has been well-documented as a cause of increased blood pressure.

psychological stress such as this is widely accepted as an important factor in essential hypertension (Fredrikson & Mathews, 1990).

In another group of studies (Hokanson & Burgess, 1962; Hokanson, Burgess, & Cohen, 1963; Hokanson, Willers, & Koropsak, 1968; Stone & Hokanson, 1969), based in part on psychoanalytic theory, Hokanson and his colleagues attempted to determine whether blood-pressure elevation is associated with the inhibition of aggression. Participants were given a task, but were angered almost immediately by the interruptions of a supposed fellow subject, actually a confederate of the experimenter. Later on, half the participants were given the opportunity to retaliate against their harasser. The results of this classic series of investigations indicate not only that harassment causes blood pressure to rise but also that for men, aggressing against a source of frustration then helps blood pressure to decrease.

Another series of studies examined the effects of stress on blood pressure among paramedics (Shapiro, Jamner, & Goldstein, 1993). In one of these analyses ambulance calls were divided into high- and low-stress types. As expected, the high-stress calls were associated with higher blood pressure. Even more interesting were the results when the paramedics were divided into groups using personality test measures of anger and defensiveness. The groups did not differ in blood pressure during the low-stress calls. However, on the high-stress calls, paramedics high in anger and defensiveness had higher blood pressure.

We should not conclude that negative emotions are the only variables that increase blood pressure. As an illustration we can consider a series of studies by Obrist and his colleagues (e.g., 1978). They used a reaction-time task in which subjects were told they would receive an electric shock if they did not respond quickly enough. Good performance led to a monetary bonus. The reaction-time task yielded significant increases in both heart rate and systolic blood pressure.

For ethical reasons no experimental work has been done with human beings to determine whether short-term increases in blood pressure will develop into prolonged hypertension and structural changes in the organism, but some research has been done on animals. True hypertension has proved elusive in the laboratory. In many studies using electric shock as a stressor, blood pressure increased during the period when the animal was stressed but returned to normal when the stressor was removed. Studies that have used more naturalistic stressors, such as competing with other animals for food (Peters, 1977), have proved somewhat more successful in producing long-term blood pressure elevations. But the overall picture indicates that some predisposing factor or factors, such as the activation of the autonomic nervous system by anger, are required if stress is to bring on essential hypertension.

PREDISPOSING FACTORS

Some people and animals are predisposed to hypertension. Sensitivity to salt, social isolation, becoming angry easily, and cardiovascular reactivity are among the diatheses that make some people more likely than others to develop hypertension in response to stress.

In research with animals several powerful diatheses have been identified—rearing in social isolation (Henry, Ely, & Stephens, 1972), a high level of emotionality (Farris, Yeakel, & Medoff, 1945), and sensitivity to salt (Friedman & Dahl, 1975). In the salt study the researchers worked with two strains of rats who had been bred to be either sensitive or insensitive to the impact of their diet. The sensitive rats developed hypertension and died on a high-salt diet. These salt-sensitive rats were also likely to show sustained blood pressure elevations when placed in an experimentally created conflict situation.

As mentioned earlier, being easily angered could be a psychological diathesis. What isn't clear about the anger variable is whether it is becoming angry easily or becoming angry and not expressing it that is most important. Complicating the picture still further, anger may function differently in men and in women. Expressing anger is related to increased blood pressure reactivity in men, whereas suppressing anger is linked to higher blood pressure reactivity in women (Shapiro, Goldstein, & Jamner, 1995). We return to this issue in our discussion of myocardial infarction.

In the past decade there has been a great deal of interest in cardiovascular reactivity as a biological predisposition to hypertension (and coronary heart disease as well; see p. 195). Cardiovascular reactivity refers to the extent to which blood pressure and heart rate increase in response to stress. The general research strategy is to assess cardiovascular reactivity to a laboratory stressor (e.g., immersing a hand in ice water) among people who are not currently hypertensive and then to follow up the participants some years later to determine whether the reactivity measure (usually the amount of change from a baseline condition to the stressor) predicts blood pressure. Two important points must be demonstrated to ensure the success of this approach. First, reactivity must be reliable if it is going to have predictive power. That is, someone who is high in reactivity must be consistently high. Indications are that it is reliable (e.g., Kasprowicz et al., 1990). Second, the laboratory measure of reactivity must actually relate to what the person's cardiovascular system does during day-to-day activities. Because of what is called white-coat hypertension a person's blood pressure may be high at the clinic or laboratory but normal elsewhere. Though the literature on this issue is somewhat conflicting (see Gerin et al., 1994; Swain & Suls, 1996), studies that have compared laboratory reactivity with reactivity to stressors in the natural environment have shown some relationship (Pollak, 1994).

What are the results of the studies that have tried to predict blood pressure from reactivity? Again, there is some variability, but those from a well-conducted study are positive (Light et al., 1992). Cardiovascular measures were taken while participants were threatened with shock if their responses were slow. A follow-up ten to fifteen years later included both office-based measures of cardiovascular functioning and a day of ambulatory monitoring (for the entire day participants wore a device that obtained several measures of both heart rate and blood pressure every hour). Each of the cardiovascular reactivity measures taken years earlier (heart rate and systolic and diastolic blood pressure) predicted later blood pressure; heart rate reactivity was the strongest predictor. Importantly, these reactivity measures predicted subsequent blood pressure over and above the contribution of standard clinical predictors, such as family history of hypertension.

The focus on reactivity as a predisposing factor in hypertension has led researchers to wonder whether increased cardiac reactivity might be related to the increased risk for the disease found in African-Americans. In the most thorough study to date, a large sample of children were followed from the third to the ninth grade. African-American children were consistently higher in blood-pressure reactivity (Murphy et al., 1995), a fact that may begin to explain the high incidence of hypertension among African-Americans.

Further support for the importance of reactivity comes from high-risk research comparing individuals with and without a positive history for hypertension (e.g., Hastrup et al., 1982). As anticipated, people with a positive family history showed greater blood-pressure reactivity to stress. Coupled with other research showing the heritability of blood-pressure reactivity (Matthews & Rakaczky, 1987) and the heritability of hypertension, blood-pressure reactivity becomes a good candidate for a genetically transmitted diathesis. However, only one study has shown that reactivity actually predicts hypertension in humans, and participants in it were the offspring of hypertensive parents (Falkner et al., 1981).

Furthering our knowledge in this area may require a more fine-grained analysis of blood-pressure reactivity. For example, heightened reactivity could result from either increased sympathetic activation or decreased activation in the parasympathetic system. Knowing which factor has yielded heightened reactivity might relate to the accuracy of prediction (Miller, 1994). Similarly, the laboratory stressors that produce blood-pressure changes vary widely, from physical challenges, such as exposure to cold, to more cognitive ones, such as being harassed or trying to solve difficult arithmetic problems. The type of stressor has implications for the mechanism through which reactivity is produced and therefore may also be an important variable to consider (Sundin et al., 1995). Research is currently proceeding along both these lines.

CORONARY HEART DISEASE

Coronary heart disease (CHD) takes two principal forms, angina pectoris and myocardial infarction, or heart attack.

CHARACTERISTICS OF THE DISEASE

The symptoms of **angina pectoris** are periodic chest pains, usually located behind the sternum and frequently radiating into the left shoulder and arm. The major cause of these severe attacks of pain is an insufficient supply of oxygen to the heart, which in turn is traced to coronary atherosclerosis, a narrowing or plugging of the coronary arteries by deposits of fatty material. Angina is generally precipitated by physical or emotional exertion and is commonly relieved by rest or medication. Serious physical damage to heart muscle rarely results from an angina attack, for blood flow is reduced but not cut off.

Myocardial infarction is a much more serious disorder and is the leading cause of death in the United States today. Like angina pectoris, myocardial infarction is caused by an insufficient supply of oxygen to the heart. The oxygen insufficiency, more extreme than in angina pectoris, results from coronary artery disease, a general curtailment of the heart's blood supply through atherosclerosis, or from coronary occlusion, a sudden obstruction of a large coronary artery by deposits or a blood clot. In both instances parts of the heart muscle die.

The American Heart Association lists seven factors related to increased risk for CHD (Insull, 1973):

age

sex (males are at a greater risk)

cigarette smoking

elevated blood pressure

elevated serum cholesterol

an increase in the size of the left ventricle of the heart as revealed by electrocardiogram

diabetes

The risk for heart disease generally increases with the number and severity of these factors.

STRESS AND MYOCARDIAL INFARCTION

In the short term, physical exertion can trigger a myocardial infarction, as can episodes of anger (Mittleman et al., 1995). More chronic stressors, such as marital conflict and financial worries, are also relevant. Interest has recently focused on depression (Carney et al., 1995; Lesperance, Frasure-Smith, & Talarc, 1996), which commonly co-occurs with a myocardial infarction and also predicts subsequent attacks. One of the most studied stressors is job strain (Karasek, 1979), an employment situation in which the person experiences a high level of demand, too much work and too little time in which to do it, coupled with little authority to make decisions and lack of opportunity to make full use of his or her skills on the job. Many studies have found that a high level of job strain is associated with increased risk for a myocardial infarction (Schall, Landsbergis, & Baker, 1994).

DIATHESES FOR CORONARY HEART DISEASE

The traditional risk factors leave at least half the etiology of coronary heart disease unexplained (Jenkins, 1976). Indeed, people used to pay less attention to contributing causes, such as obesity, poor exercise habits, consumption of fatty foods, and smoking, than they do now, yet in earlier decades the incidence of CHD and related cardiovascular diseases was much lower. Furthermore, in the Midwest, where people's diets are highest in saturated fats and smoking rates are especially high, the incidence of coronary heart disease is low compared with that in more industrialized parts of the United States. Anyone who has visited Paris is aware of the heavy smoking and the fat-rich diets of the French population, yet CHD is relatively low there. Why?

The search for predispositions for coronary heart disease has begun to focus on psychological factors.

Contemporary evidence linking CHD to psychological variables stems from investigations pioneered by two cardiologists, Meyer Friedman and Ray Rosenman (Friedman, 1969; Rosenman et al., 1975). In 1958 they identified a coronary-prone behavior pattern called **Type A behavior pattern**.

The Type A individual has an intense and competitive drive for achievement and advancement, an exaggerated sense of the urgency of passing time and of the need to hurry, and considerable aggressiveness and hostility toward others. Type A persons are overcommitted to their work, often attempt to carry on two activities at once, and believe that to get something done well they must do it themselves. They cannot abide waiting in lines and they play every game to win; even when their opponents are children they are impatient and hostile. Fast-thinking, fast-talking, and abrupt in gesture, they often jiggle their knees, tap their fingers, and blink rapidly. Too busy to notice their surroundings or to be interested in things of beauty, they tabulate success in life in numbers of articles written, projects under way, and material goods acquired. Some theorize that the ongoing struggle to achieve in a visible, tangible fashion is driven by an underlying sense of insecurity and low self-esteem (Price, 1982; Williams et al., 1992).

A second type of behavior pattern is called Type B. The Type B individual is less driven and relatively free of such pressures. Assessment of Type A and Type B individuals was originally done with the Structured Interview (Rosenman et al., 1964), in which questions are asked and inferences made about the intensity of ambitions, competitiveness, the urgency of deadlines, and hostility. Subsequently, self-report measures were also developed. It is now clear, however, that the self-report measures produce results that are not consistent with those of the Structured Interview. Some of the inconsistencies in the Type A literature are likely the result of different assessment devices (Matthews, 1982). For example, the Structured Interview is better than questionnaires at picking up hostility, which is increasingly being viewed as the key factor in contributing to coronary heart disease (Weinstein et al., 1986).

Evidence supporting the idea that the Type A pattern predicts coronary heart disease comes from the classic Western Collaborative Group Study (WCGS) (Rosenman et al., 1975). In this double-blind, prospective investigation, 3524 men aged thirty-nine to fifty-nine were to be followed over a period of eight and a half years. Some 3154 men completed the study. Individuals who had been identified as Type A by the Structured Interview were more than twice as likely to develop CHD as were Type B men. Traditional risk factors, such as high levels of cholesterol, were also found to be related to CHD, but even when these factors were controlled for, Type A individuals were still twice as likely to develop CHD.

More recent studies have not supported the predictive utility of Type A behavior. For example, in several studies Type A failed to predict either mortality or myocardial infarction (Eaker et al., 1992; Orth-Gomer & Unden, 1990; Shekelle et al., 1983). Other research has not found a relationship between Type A and angiographically determined coronary artery disease (Williams, 1987).

There are several reasons for these conflicting results. First, some of the negative findings have come from studies that did not use the Structured Interview to assess Type A. As we have already noted, such assessments probably do not adequately measure Type A. Second, the predictive power of Type A may be limited. One study found that Type A predicted coronary artery disease only among people under the age of fifty (Williams et al., 1986); Type B individuals over age fifty had more severe disease! Thus when studying a population with a broad age range, unless the data are analyzed separately according to age, it is unlikely that a Type A–CHD relationship will be established.

It is also possible that an overall Type A score is not the best measure of coronary-prone behavior. One way of addressing this question is to examine individual items from the Structured Interview to see which are the best predictors of CHD. In the analysis of the interview data from the WCGS done by Matthews and her colleagues (1977), only seven of the whole set of items discriminated between Type A individuals who developed CHD and those who did not. In further analyses of these data, hostility emerged as the major predictor of CHD (Hecker et al., 1988). Hostility is also related to greater blood-pressure reactivity to stress (Weidner et al., 1989), to higher levels of cholesterol (Weidner et al., 1987), and to greater activation of platelets, which play a major role in the formation of clots (Markovitz et al., 1996).

Other findings (e.g., Almada, 1991; Williams et al., 1986) suggest that cynicism is a major factor within the Type A complex. The amount of coronary artery blockage and coronary death were especially high in Type A participants who had earlier endorsed MMPI items reflecting a cynical or hostile attitude (for example, "Most people will use somewhat unfair means to gain profit or advantage, rather than lose it.") An earlier follow-up study of medical students who were healthy when they took

the MMPI twenty-five years earlier found a higher rate of CHD and death in those whose answers had indicated cynicism toward others (Barefoot, Dahlstrom, & Williams, 1983). Other findings concerning cynicism suggest a possible role for it in CHD. It is higher among men than among women and higher among African-Americans than among whites (Barefoot et al., 1991); it is also related to avoidance of seeking social support, a high rate of marital separation, high levels of suppressed anger, greater consumption of alcohol, and obesity (Houston & Vavak, 1991; Miller et al., 1995).

What is not yet clear is the best way to conceptualize these results. Is hostility the critical component? Or is it the cynical attitude that is assessed with the MMPI items? A significant problem is the vague terminology that has been used (anger, hostility, cynicism) and the lack of agreement among measures used to assess these concepts. For example, a recent study followed a large sample of men for two years, using ultrasound to assess the progression of atherosclerosis (Julkunen et al., 1994). Three components of anger and hostility were assessed:

Cognitive: negative beliefs about others

Affective: impatience and irritability

Experience: whether anger is expressed or not

These measures did not correlate well, indicating that just because the terms sound similar they cannot be readily substituted for one another. The affective component did not predict the progression of atherosclerosis, but the other two did. This study is not the last word on the issue, but it does illustrate the complexity of trying to determine whether anger is related to coronary heart disease. Another important issue is identifying the origin of anger and hostility. Research is just beginning on this topic, but indications are that it lies in a high level of family conflict (Matthews et al., 1996).

Research on biological factors has taken a similar course to that of hypertension research, focusing on reactivity. Excessive changes in heart rate and the consequent alterations in the force with which blood is pumped through the arteries may injure them. Heart-rate reactivity has been related to CHD in several research contexts. Manuck, Kaplan, and Clarkson (1983) and Manuck et al. (1989) studied monkeys who were on a special diet designed to promote atherosclerosis. On the basis of a laboratory stress test the animals were divided into high versus low heart-rate reactors. Subsequently, the high heart-rate reactors developed twice as much atherosclerosis as did the low reactors. In a study of

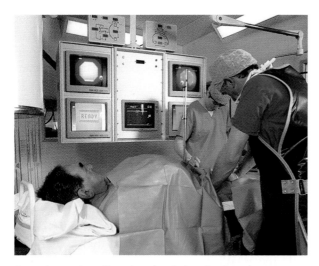

An angiogram is an X-ray based technique for detecting coronary artery disease. A catheter is inserted into a vein in the groin and maneuvered toward the heart. A dye is then released which reveals any blocked arteries.

humans heart-rate reactivity predicted the development of CHD in a twenty-three-year follow-up study (Keys et al., 1971). Thus heart-rate reactivity is a plausible candidate for a biological diathesis, and as we have already seen it is associated with the psychological diathesis of anger and hostility.

ASTHMA

During his childhood Tom had frequent asthma attacks. His asthma was triggered principally by pollen, so that each year he went through a particularly bad period that included several trips to the emergency room of a local hospital. He seemed to get more than his share of colds, which frequently developed into bronchitis. As he reached his teenage years the attacks of asthma mysteriously vanished, and he was symptom free for the next twenty years. But at age thirty-four the attacks returned with a vengeance following a bout of pneumonia. In contrast to his childhood attacks, emotional stress now appeared to be the major precipitant. This hypothesis was confirmed when his physician asked Tom to keep a diary for two weeks in which he recorded how he had been feeling and what had been going on before each attack. He had four attacks over the period, three preceded by unpleasant interactions with his boss at work and one by an argument with his wife over an impending visit by her parents.

Asthma accounts for about $4 billion in health care costs and is the leading cause of school absen-

teeism. In contrast to the situation with most other diseases, the death rate from asthma doubled from 1979 to 1987 and shows no sign of decline in the 1990s. The reason for this increase is unknown (Parker et al., 1989), but air pollution is a real possibility.

In **asthma** the air passages and bronchioles in the lungs are narrowed, causing breathing (particularly exhalation) to be extremely labored and wheezy. This condition reflects a state of dominance of the parasympathetic division of the autonomic nervous system (see p. 92). In addition, there is an inflammation of lung tissue mediated by the immune system, resulting in an increase in mucus secretion and edema (accumulation of fluid in the tissues) (Moran, 1991).

Somewhere between 2 and 5 percent of the population is estimated to have asthma. One-third of asthma sufferers are children, and about two-thirds of these youngsters are boys (Graham et al., 1967; Purcell & Weiss, 1970). By midadolescence the rate of asthma becomes higher in females than males (Sweeting, 1995). Williams and McNicol (1969) studied 30,000 seven-year-old Australian children. They found a high correlation between the age of onset of the symptoms and the length of time the disorder lasted. If onset occurred prior to age one, 80 percent were still wheezing five years later; with ages of onset from three to four, 40 percent were still wheezing five years later; and with an onset age of five or six, only 20 percent were still wheezing five years later. The earlier the disorder begins, the longer it is likely to last.

CHARACTERISTICS OF THE DISEASE

Asthma attacks occur intermittently and vary in severity; the frequency of some patients' attacks may increase seasonally, when certain pollens are present. The airways are not continuously blocked, rather, the respiratory system returns to normal or near normal either spontaneously or after treatment, thus allowing asthma to be differentiated from chronic respiratory problems such as emphysema (Creer, 1982). The major structures of the respiratory system are shown in Figure 8.7.

Most often, asthmatic attacks begin suddenly. The asthmatic individual has a sense of tightness in the chest, wheezes, coughs, and expectorates sputum. A severe attack is a frightening experience and may cause a panic attack (Kinsman et al., 1974). The person has immense difficulty getting air into and out of the lungs and feels as though he or she is suffocating; the raspy, harsh noise of the gasping,

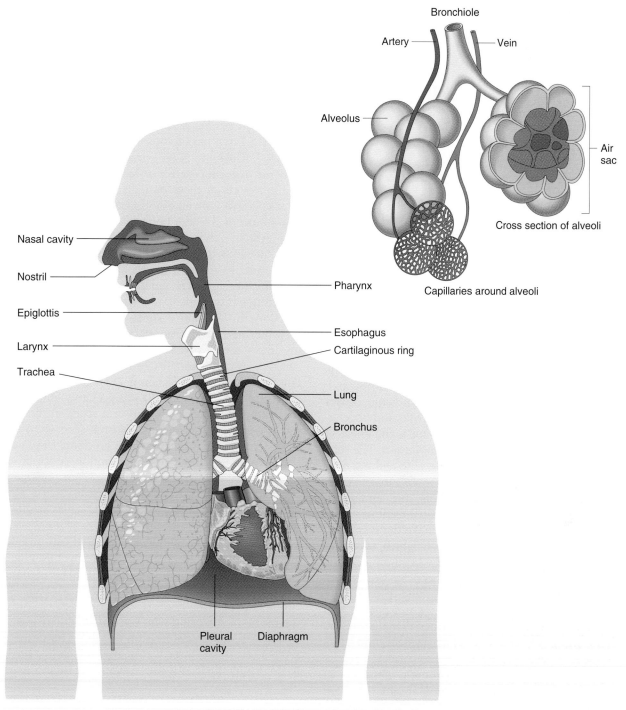

Figure 8.7 Major structures of the respiratory system—trachea, lungs, bronchi, bronchioles, and alveoli—and the ancillary organs. In asthma, the air passages, especially the bronchioles, become constricted and fluid and mucus build up in the lungs.

wheezing, and coughing compounds the terror. The person may become exhausted by the exertion and fall asleep as soon as breathing is more normal.

The asthma sufferer takes a longer time than normal to exhale, and whistling sounds, referred to as rales, can be detected throughout the chest. Symptoms may last an hour or may continue for several hours or sometimes even for days. Between attacks no abnormal signs may be detected when the individual is breathing normally, but forced, heavy expiration often allows the rales to be heard through a stethoscope.

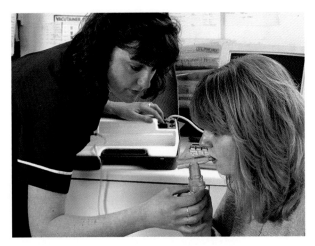

Asthma attacks are often treated by using a nebulizer to spray a fine mist of a bronchodilator into the bronchial tubes.

ETIOLOGY OF ASTHMA

The importance of psychological factors in the development of asthma is a topic of debate. Some believe that emotionality is always implicated. Others have divided the various possible causes into three categories: allergic, infective, and psychological (Rees, 1964). A related factor is the effect of irritants, such as smoke and air pollution. The cells in the respiratory tract of people with asthma may be especially sensitive to one or more substances or allergens, such as pollen, molds, fur, and dust, bringing on asthma. Respiratory infections, most often acute bronchitis, can also make the respiratory system vulnerable to asthma, which seems to have happened in the case at the beginning of this chapter. Anxiety, tension produced by frustration, anger, depression, and anticipated pleasurable excitement are all examples of psychological factors that may, through induced emotionality, disturb the functioning of the respiratory system and thus bring on an asthma attack.

A classic study of 388 asthmatic children in Cardiff, Wales, found that the children could be divided into groups according to the causes of their attacks (Rees, 1964). As shown in Table 8.4, psychological factors were considered a dominant cause in only 37 percent of the cases, and in 30 percent of the cases psychological variables were regarded as totally unimportant—a finding that strongly suggests that asthma is not always psychosomatic.

This study also showed that the different causes of asthma varied in importance depending on the age of the individual. For those asthmatic individuals younger than five years of age, the infective factors predominated. From ages six to sixteen the infective factors still predominated, but psychologi-

cal variables increased in importance. In the range from ages sixteen to sixty-five, psychological factors decreased in importance until about the thirty-fifth year, thereafter becoming more consequential again.

PSYCHOLOGICAL FACTORS IN ASTHMA

Even when asthma is originally induced by an infection or allergy, psychological stress can precipitate attacks. Kleeman (1967) interviewed twenty-six patients over an eighteen-month period. According to the reports of these patients, 69 percent of their attacks began with an emotional disturbance.

Because of the link between the autonomic nervous system (ANS) and the constriction and dilation of the airways, and the connection between the ANS and emotions, most research has focused on emotionality. Research has generally found higher levels of emotionality in people with asthma. Their facial reactions to laboratory stressors are more intense, and they are rated as more hostile and helpless during interviews, as well as more maladjusted. Their self-reports on personality tests reveal high levels of emotionality (Lehrer, Isenberg, & Hochron, 1993).

In interpreting these data it is probably fair to say that some of this emotionality is a reaction to having a chronic disease. But research also shows a clear temporal pattern between emotional arousal and asthma that indicates that emotion does play a role in precipitating attacks (Hyland et al., 1990).

THE ROLE OF THE FAMILY

One source of psychological stress that can initiate asthma or precipitate an attack is parent–child interaction. One investigation looked at 150 pregnant women who had asthma (Klinnert, Mrazek, & Mrazek, 1994). The investigators intended to study the mothers' offspring who were at genetic risk and assess parental characteristics as well. The parents were interviewed three weeks after the child's birth to determine their attitudes toward the infant, their

TABLE 8.4 Relative Importance of Allergic, Infective, and Psychological Factors in the Etiology of Asthma

| Factors | Relative Importance, % | | |
	Dominant	Subsidiary	Unimportant
Allergic	23	13	64
Infective	38	30	32
Psychological	37	33	30

Source. From Rees, 1964.

sensitivity to the infant, their strategy for sharing parenting duties, and the presence of any emotional disturbances. The amount of stress experienced by the mother in the past year was also assessed. The children were closely monitored over the next three years, and the frequency of asthma was then related to the parental characteristics noted earlier. Results showed a high rate of asthma among those children whose mothers had high levels of stress and whose families were rated as having problems (see Figure 8.8). Not all research, however, has found that parent–child relationships figure in asthma (Eiser, Town, & Tripp, 1991). Earlier, Gauthier and his co-workers (1977, 1978) studied young asthmatic children and their mothers through a battery of questionnaires and interviews and by making observations in the home. Most of the children and their mothers were well-adjusted. The children's levels of development were normal for their age, and they were independent and successful at coping with their surroundings.

The research we have reviewed is thus not completely consistent regarding the role that the home life of people with asthma plays in their illness. Even if we allow that family relations are consequential in asthma, we cannot always tell whether the various familial variables are causal agents or maintaining agents. Although certain emotional factors in the home may be important in eliciting early asthmatic attacks in some children, in others the illness may originally develop for nonfamilial reasons and then the children's parents may unwittingly reward various symptoms of the syndrome. For example, parents may cater to asthmatic children and treat them specially because of the asthma.

PHYSIOLOGICAL PREDISPOSITION

Rees (1964) found that 86 percent of the asthmatic individuals had had a respiratory infection before asthma developed. Only 30 percent of his control subjects had been so afflicted. One interpretation of these results could be that infection weakens the lungs, making that organ vulnerable to stress.

Individuals whose asthma is primarily allergic may have an inherited hypersensitivity of the respiratory mucosa, which then overresponds to usually harmless substances such as dust or pollen. That asthma runs in families is consistent with genetic transmission of a diathesis (Konig & Godfrey, 1973). There is also some indication that people with asthma have a less than normally responsive sympathetic nervous system (Mathe & Knapp, 1971; Miklich et al., 1973). Activation of the sympathetic nervous system is known to reduce the intensity of an asthmatic attack. Finally, two studies have found that asthmatic persons, but not normals, respond to gory films with bronchoconstriction (reviewed by Lehrer et al., 1993), suggesting that their respiratory systems respond to stress in a way that may induce an asthma attack.

A diathesis–stress explanation once again seems to fit the data on a psychophysiological disorder. Once the respiratory system is predisposed to asthma, any number of psychological stressors can interact with the diathesis to produce the disease.

THERAPIES FOR PSYCHOPHYSIOLOGICAL DISORDERS

Since psychophysiological disorders are true physical dysfunctions, sound psychotherapeutic practice calls for close consultation with a physician. Whether high blood pressure is biologically caused or, as in essential hypertension, linked to psychological stress, a number of medications can reduce the constriction of the arteries. Asthma attacks can also be alleviated by medications, taken either by inhalation or injection, that dilate the bronchial tubes. The help that drugs provide in ameliorating the damage and discomfort in the particular body systems cannot be underestimated. They are frequently lifesaving. Mental health and medical professionals recognize, however, that most drug interventions treat only the symptoms; they do not deal with the fact that the person is reacting emotionally

Figure 8.8   The effects of parenting problems and prior stress on the number of children with asthma. Children whose mothers had been under a high level of stress and were raised in families with parenting problems had high rates of asthma. From Klinnert, Mrazek, and Mrazek (1994).

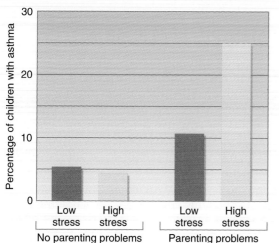

to psychological stress. Although the evidence suggests that the predisposition for a particular organ breakdown is inherited or at least somatically based, the importance of how a person responds psychologically nevertheless indicates that psychotherapeutic interventions are necessary.

Therapists of all persuasions agree that reducing anxiety or anger is the best way to alleviate suffering from psychophysiological disorders. The particular disorder, whether it is essential hypertension, coronary heart disease, or asthma, is considered to be adversely affected by anxiety or anger if not actually caused by these emotions in all cases. Psychoanalytically oriented therapists employ techniques such as free association and dream analysis, as they do with other anxiety sufferers, to help their patients confront the infantile origins of their fears. Ego analysts such as Franz Alexander believe that emotional states underlie the several disorders. Thus they encourage patients with essential hypertension, viewed as laboring under a burden of undischarged anger, to assert themselves and thereby release their anger.

Behavioral and cognitive therapists employ their usual range of procedures for reducing anxiety and anger—systematic desensitization, in vivo exposure, rational-emotive therapy, and assertion training—depending on the source of tension. For example, Lehrer et al. (1994) successfully used relaxation

training to help asthmatic children exhale more fully. Behavior rehearsal and shaping may help people learn to react in difficult situations with less emotional upset.

The field of behavioral medicine, discussed again in Chapter 18, emphasizes treatments that work to lessen habits known to contribute to illness. For example, researchers in behavioral medicine study ways of helping people stop smoking cigarettes, which has been linked to a host of medical problems. Carrying around extra pounds, especially as people grow older, can also contribute to coronary heart disease and hypertension, and behavioral-medicine specialists have devised weight-reduction programs that show some promise, at least in the short term (Brownell & Wadden, 1992). A behavioral procedure designed to help asthma patients is teaching them how better to know when they are having an attack. Many patients who do not recognize their own symptoms and do not respond appropriately can become more attuned to their symptoms and thereby better able to follow a treatment regimen (Creer, Renna, & Chai, 1982).

Biofeedback, in which patients are provided with prompt and exact information, otherwise unavailable, on heart rate, blood pressure, brain waves, skin temperature, and other bodily functions, is also a behavioral-medicine procedure. A particular internal physiological process is detected and amplified by a sensitive electronic recording device. The person knows instantaneously through an auditory or visual signal the rate of the process and whether it is too high or too low or just right. Numerous studies have shown that most people, if given the task, for example, of raising their heart rates or lowering their blood pressure, can do so with the help of biofeedback (Blanchard, 1994; Elmore & Tursky, 1978; Shapiro, Tursky, & Schwartz, 1970). What is not yet clear is whether, through biofeedback, they can achieve results that are clinically significant. Biofeedback will be evaluated in greater depth in Chapter 18.

TREATING HYPERTENSION

Because some antihypertensive drugs have undesirable side effects, such as drowsiness, lightheadedness, and erectile difficulties for men, many investigations have been undertaken on nonpharmacological treatments for borderline essential hypertension. Efforts have been directed at weight reduction, restriction of salt intake, aerobic exercise, and reduction in alcohol consumption. Each of these medical goals involves obvious behavioral-change components, and success in achieving these goals has been mixed (Dubbert, 1995; Foreyt, 1990). For example, dietary changes that lead to less salt

Biofeedback is often used in the treatment of psychophysiological disorders. It can provide accurate information on physiological processes that hopefully will allow the patient to gain better control of them.

intake and to weight loss are useful in reducing blood pressure in hypertensive patients (Jeffrey, 1991). Findings for aerobic exercise are less clear, though promising (e.g., Martin, Dubbert, & Cushman, 1991); a potential—and for practical purposes, welcome—confound is that consistent aerobic exercise raises metabolism and thereby helps people lose weight. An additional health benefit is that losing weight, reducing salt intake, and exercising regularly help reduce harmful levels of cholesterol. Marked reductions in cholesterol via drugs and diet have been observed in the United States since the 1960s and are associated with decreased mortality from cardiovascular diseases (Holme, 1990; Johnson et al., 1993; Weidner & Griffin, 1995).

An interesting and controversial question in this literature is whether lowering levels of cholesterol can have *negative* physical or psychological effects. A recent review by Weidner and Griffin (1995) concludes that there is no evidence for direct negative physical effects of cholesterol lowering, at least by nonpharmacological means. (When it comes to the use of drugs to lower cholesterol and blood pressure, side effects include nausea, abdominal pain, erectile disorder in men, headaches, and dizziness. These unintended consequences are unlikely to enhance the quality of one's daily life.)

But can the behavioral changes necessary to bring about reductions in cholesterol lead to unintended negative psychological effects? Changing one's diet is not easy! Reducing one's fat intake enough to make a healthful difference in cholesterol level can require an enormous change in how one eats. Cutting back on refined sugar and salt is also difficult, for most of us grew up with these condiments within arm's reach on the table. And who among us does not equate rich chocolate desserts with comfort, and then some? Learning to enjoy food that has low amounts of cholesterol can create stress and general disgruntlement.

Fortunately, research shows that lowering cholesterol via low-fat diets *enhances* psychological well-being (Weidner et al., 1992). Provided that the changes are not unreasonable and unreachable, properly designed psychosocial dietary interventions help people feel better about themselves as they reduce their risk of cardiovascular disease. And since the kind of dieting that reduces cholesterol also tends to contribute to weight loss, it is relevant to point out that psychological improvements are also found among people who are dieting to take off unwanted pounds (O'Neil & Jarrell, 1992).

Another psychological approach has been to teach hypertensive individuals to lower sympathetic nervous system arousal, primarily via training in muscle relaxation, occasionally supplemented by biofeedback (Benson, Beary, & Carl, 1974; Blanchard, 1994). Results have been mixed (Kaufmann et al., 1988), and it is unclear how enduring the effects of relaxation treatment are (Patel et al., 1985). The success of this approach probably depends ultimately on whether the person maintains the acquired skill to relax, and that in turn depends on whether the person remains motivated to practice that skill.

DeQuattro and Davison (Lee et al., 1987) found that intensive relaxation, conducted in weekly sessions over two months and using at-home practice with audiotaped instructions, significantly reduced blood pressure immediately following treatment in borderline hypertensive people, more so than did a control condition that included state-of-the-art medical advice and instructions concerning diet, weight loss, and other known risk factors. (The relaxation group also received the same medical information given to the control subjects.) Furthermore, these effects were stronger among those hypertensive subjects previously found to have high sympathetic arousal than among those with lower arousal levels. This result supports the hypothesis of Esler et al. (1977) that there is a subset of hypertensive individuals with relatively high resting levels of sympathetic arousal who may be especially well suited for sympathetic-dampening therapies such as relaxation.

Hypertensive individuals with low levels of sympathetic nervous system arousal may benefit more from a cognitive therapy approach—their hypertension may be sustained by the thoughts they carry in their heads more than by what their sympathetic nervous system is doing. Of course, it could also be the other way around; sympathetic arousal itself might be in part sustained by negative cognitive patterns. In either case, cognitive interventions are one way to reduce this arousal and the consequent hypertension.

Evidence suggesting the importance of cognitive change as well as the role of anger was reported by Davison, Williams, et al. (1991) from the same data set used by Lee et al. Borderline hypertensive patients who achieved significant reductions in anger as expressed in their articulated thoughts had decreased blood pressure—the less angry their articulated thoughts became, the lower their blood pressure became—a finding that is consistent with research linking anger with hypertension.

CHANGING TYPE A BEHAVIOR

Reducing anger and hostility is also the basis for treating those showing Type A behavior. Over the past two to three decades a great deal of research

FOCUS 8.2

COPING WITH CANCER

A growing body of evidence indicates that interventions that alleviate anxiety and depression and foster a fighting spirit can help people cope with cancer (Stolbach et al., 1988; Telch & Telch, 1986) (Focus 15.3 describes such work with children.) A nonpassive attitude may even enhance the capacity to survive cancer (Greer, Morris, & Pettigale, 1979).

An optimistic, upbeat attitude is important in combating illness, even illnesses as serious as cancer (Carver et al., 1993) and HIV-positive status (Taylor et al., 1992). The mechanism by which an optimistic attitude helps people with life-threatening illnesses may be its link to adaptive coping. Optimistic people—like those with high levels of self-efficacy (Bandura, 1986)—may be more likely to engage in risk-reducing health behaviors such as avoidance of risky sex in the case of HIV-prevention or engaging in prescribed regular exercise following coronary bypass surgery (Scheier & Carver, 1987).

A careful review by Anderson (1992) examined the effects of various psychosocial interventions, primarily those aimed at reducing anxiety and stress, on cancers that were grouped according to how life-threatening they were. For cancers with low risk of death (Stage I and Stage II cancers, such as localized breast cancer), treatments led to small reductions in distress and depression. Anderson theorized that such minor effects might be due to the fact that medical treatment is usually successful with these types of cancer, so distress is lessened by this knowledge alone, leaving psychological interventions little to work with. Studies of patients with higher-morbidity-risk cancers show far more powerful effects from psychological interventions. For cancer with highest risk of death, treatment effects are even stronger.

The quality of life and even the survival time of patients with terminal cancer can be improved by psychosocial interventions. Patients with metastatic breast cancer participated in weekly supportive group therapy, where they offered understanding and comfort to each other, openly discussed death and dying, expressed their feelings, and encouraged each other to live life as fully as possible in the face of death. They also came

to have improved communication with family and learned self-hypnosis techniques to control pain and reduce fatigue, anxiety, and depression (Spiegel, Bloom, & Yalom, 1981). A ten-year follow-up found that this one-year supportive-group intervention actually prolonged survival time. Compared with control-group patients, the group-therapy patients lived twice as long (Spiegel, 1990; Spiegel et al., 1989).*

Speculating about these survival findings—which were not expected and were not a discussion topic for the group therapy—Spiegel and his associates suggested that perhaps the therapy helped patients better comply with medical treatment or that it improved their appetite and diet by enhancing their mood. Ability to control pain might also have helped them be more physically active. And, consistent with research reviewed earlier on how stress affects the immune system, the therapy might have improved immune function by reducing stress, with social support a key factor (House, Landis, & Umberson, 1988; Levy et al., 1990).

INTERVENTIONS TO ENCOURAGE PREVENTION

Psychological interventions also focus on preventing cancer by encouraging healthy behaviors and discouraging unhealthy ones. For example, research programs to help people stop smoking are discussed in Chapter 12. Other interventions work to get women to perform breast self-examination (BSE). The

* When surprising, even startling, findings are published in professional journals, the editor sometimes includes an accompanying comment. This was done with the Spiegel et al. (1989) report. Mindful that the results might be regarded as unorthodox, the editor took pains to comment favorably on the methodology and statistical analyses and to suggest that readers adopt an open-minded attitude toward the report, indicating that "the measures described by Spiegel et al. are at least life-enhancing, in stark contrast to the life impoverishment suffered by many terminally ill patients subjected to the vile diets, costly placebos, and exhausting introspections recommended by the more lunatic fringe among alternative practitioners. Other groups should pursue this intellectually honest approach to the psychosocial management of cancer" (Editorial, *The Lancet*, October 14, 1989).

---

has been done to determine whether the behavior patterns associated with Type A can be changed. These studies have generally involved men who have suffered a myocardial infarction, and the focus has been on reducing the likelihood that they will have a second myocardial infarction. We will discuss the techniques used in one of the most comprehensive of these studies, the Recurrent Coronary Prevention Project (Friedman et al., 1982).

In this study participants practiced talking more slowly and listening to others more closely. They attempted to reduce the demands placed on them

so they could relax more, and they watched less television. In addition to the behavioral changes, participants were encouraged to ease up on the demanding beliefs identified as common among Type A's—the tendency to perceive events as direct personal challenges and to believe that the intensity of Type A behavior is essential to success.

This study found that Type A behavior can be changed. After three years of treatment, men who had received Type A counseling had nearly half the risk of a second heart attack. Their risk was 7.2 percent annually, compared with 13.2 percent for Type

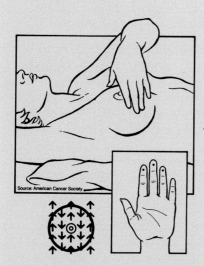

Encouraging women to perform breast self-examination (BSE) can lead to earlier detection of cancer and better treatment outcomes. Shown here is an advertisement from the American Cancer Society demonstrating how to perform BSE.

main hurdle to BSE is that examination significantly raises the probability of an aversive consequence, that is, finding a lump. Logically, it is better to take this risk than not, but the fact is that the fear of learning something unpleasant is a major deterrent to doing the exam (Mahoney, 1977) and many high-risk women (those with first-degree relatives who had breast cancer) do not have regular mammograms (Vogel et al., 1990). In an effort to develop ways to help women perform BSE regularly, Meyerowitz and Chaiken (1987) compared two pamphlets on BSE. One contained persuasive arguments to conduct BSE while emphasizing the negative consequences of not performing BSE; the other emphasized the positive consequences of performing BSE. Both pamphlets contained factual information about breast cancer and instructions about how to do BSE. In the following examples words in parentheses were included in the positive condition, those in brackets in the negative.

By [not] doing BSE now, you (can)[will not] learn what your normal healthy breasts feel like so that you will be (better)[ill] prepared

to notice any small, abnormal changes that might occur as you get older.

Research shows that women who do [not do] BSE have (an increased)[a decreased] chance of finding a tumor in the early, more treatable stage of the disease. (p. 504)

The groups given the different pamphlets did not differ in their attitudes toward BSE immediately after reading the pamphlets. However, four months later, women who had received the negatively framed information were more likely to have engaged in such examination. This effect may have occurred because those who do not engage in regular BSE take an ignorance-is-bliss attitude, but by making the possible negative consequences of not doing BSE more salient, doing the exam became more acceptable. This finding is particularly important because most pamphlets for women doing BSE stress the positive rather than the negative.

The tendency to believe that ignorance is bliss, that not knowing will somehow prevent cancer from occurring, is clearly irrational. Research by Lerman and her colleagues (Lerman & Glanz, 1997) highlights the importance of these *nonrational* factors in whether people engage in practices that can promote health and avoid illness. Women who believe that they are at high risk for ovarian cancer—because of family history of an illness that is known to have inherited components—often have the paradoxical response of *reducing* their adherence to health-promoting practices (Lerman & Schwartz, 1993). Similar findings have been reported for breast-cancer screening (Lerman et al., 1993; Miller, Shoda, & Hurley, 1996). The distress caused by perceptions of high risk can clearly interfere with rational coping, and one means of reducing this distress seems to be minimizing the perceived danger—a strategy of self-deception that can calm nerves in the short run but that can contribute to serious long-term consequences. Psychological treatment in the form of breast-cancer risk counseling can reduce these cognitive distortions and enhance health-promoting behaviors (Lerman et al., 1996) by suggesting, for example, that the knowledge that a first-degree relative has breast cancer can serve as an opportunity to take steps to protect one's own health rather than as a sign of unavoidable impending catastrophe.

A men who received only cardiological counseling (Friedman et al., 1984; Friedman & Ulmer, 1984; Powell et al., 1984; Thoresen et al., 1985). Reductions in hostility may have been particularly important, consistent with its increasing importance in Type A research and in psychophysiological disorders generally (Haaga, 1987b).

STRESS MANAGEMENT

Related to the lessons learned from research on changing Type A behavior is the field of **stress man-** **agement**, a set of varying techniques for reducing stress. The increasing recognition of the role of stress in a variety of medical illnesses, including diseases affected by immune-system dysfunction, has added impetus to stress management as a strategy for reducing stress-related deficits in the functioning of the immune system (Zakowski, Hall, & Baum, 1992; see also the discussion on p. 398 on HIV infection). Stress management has also been used successfully for several other diseases, including tension headaches, cancer, hypertension, and chronic pain.

Stress management encompasses a variety of techniques, and more than one is typically used in any given instance (Davison & Thompson, 1988; Lehrer & Woolfolk, 1993).

- **Arousal reduction.** In arousal reduction the person is trained in muscle relaxation, sometimes assisted by biofeedback. Although the evidence is unclear as to the need to use the complex instrumentation required for proper biofeedback of minute levels of muscle tension or certain patterns of electroencephalographic activity, there is confirmation that teaching people to relax deeply and to apply these skills to real-life stressors can be helpful in lowering their stress levels. There is also some preliminary evidence that immune function can be improved by relaxation training (Jasnoski & Kugler, 1987; Kielcolt-Glaser et al., 1985), although enduring benefits are doubtful unless relaxation is practiced regularly over a long period of time (Davison & Thompson, 1988; Goldfried & Davison, 1994; Zakowski et al., 1992).

- **Cognitive restructuring.** Included under cognitive restructuring are approaches such as those of Ellis (1962) and Beck (1976). The focus is on altering people's belief systems and improving the clarity of their logical interpretations of experience on the assumption that our intellectual capacities can affect how we feel and behave. Providing information to reduce uncertainty and enhance people's sense of control, a theme from Chapter 6, has also been helpful in reducing stress. Promising findings have been reported for various stress-related problems, including genital herpes lesions (McLarnon & Kaloupek, 1988).

- **Behavioral-skills training.** Because it is natural to feel overwhelmed if one lacks the skills to execute a challenging task, stress management often includes instruction and practice in necessary skills as well as in general issues such as time management and effective prioritizing. There is a complex interplay among behavior, emotion, and cognition, and social-skills training can enhance a person's sense of self-efficacy (Bandura, 1986) by improving control over environmental stressors (Rodin, 1986).

- **Environmental-change approaches.** What can be regarded as an environmental approach draws on research mentioned earlier in this chapter (p. 186) on the positive role of social support on health. If social support helps keep people healthy or helps them cope with illnesses, then it is reasonable to assume that enhancing such support can contribute to better functioning (see Focus 8.2 for a closer look at the role of social support with cancer patients).

The work of *community psychologists* is also relevant to stress management. Whereas the individual strategies described aim at helping the person deal with a particular environment, one can also take the position that sometimes the environment is the problem and that change is best directed at altering it. For example, a work environment could be redesigned with partitions to provide some privacy, rather than requiring clerical workers to sit together in a large open area.

Our review of several therapeutic approaches to dealing with psychophysiological disorders, many of which can be subsumed under the rubric of behavioral medicine, illustrates the complex relationships between the *soma* and the *psyche*, the body and the mind. We come full circle to how we began this chapter, namely, an appreciation of the inseparability of bodily and mental processes. Stress is a part of everyone's life. As much as it can pose problems, so too can learning ways to cope with it or manage it promote well-being.

A community psychology approach to stress management focuses on the environment rather than the person. To reduce stress, an office can be redesigned with partitions to provide some privacy for employees.

SUMMARY

Psychophysiological disorders are physical diseases produced in part by psychological factors, primarily stress. Such disorders usually affect organs innervated by the autonomic nervous system, such as those of the respiratory, cardiovascular, gastrointestinal, and endocrine systems. Research has pursued a number of different paths to discover how psychological stress produces a particular psychophysiological disorder. Some researchers have looked at the specifics of the stressor or the psychological characteristics of the person, such as the links between anger and hostility and hypertension and between Type A personality and myocardial infarction. Others have emphasized that psychophysiological disorders occur only when stress interacts with a biological diathesis. Cardiovascular disorders occur in those with a tendency to respond to stress with increases in blood pressure or heart rate. Those with asthma tend to have a respiratory system that overresponds to an allergen or has been weakened by prior infection. Although we have spoken of psychological stress affecting the body, it must be remembered that the *mind* and the *body* are best viewed as two different approaches to the same organism.

Psychophysiological disorders no longer appear as a diagnostic category in the DSM. Instead, the diagnostician can make a diagnosis of psychological factors affecting a medical condition and then note the condition on Axis III. This change reflects the growing realization that life stress is relevant to all diseases and is not limited to those that were previously considered psychophysiological disorders. When events are appraised as stressful, coping efforts are engaged. If coping fails to lessen the amount of stress experienced, the risk of becoming ill increases. Important issues in current work on life stress and health include looking at moderators of the relationship (e.g., social support lessens the effects of stress) and specifying the physiological mechanisms (e.g., the immune system) through which stress can exert its effects.

Psychophysiological disorders represent true physical dysfunctions. As a result, treatment usually includes medication. The general aim of psychotherapies for these disorders is to reduce anxiety or anger. Researchers in the field of behavioral medicine try to find psychological interventions that can improve the patient's physiological state by changing unhealthy behaviors and reducing stress. It has developed ways of helping people relax, smoke less, eat fewer fatty foods, and, using biofeedback, gain control over various autonomic functions, such as heart rate and blood pressure. One study has developed methods by which Type A victims of myocardial infarction can learn to change their angry, hard-driving ways.

The emergent field of stress management helps people without diagnosable problems avail themselves of techniques that allow them to cope with the inevitable stress of everyday life and thereby ameliorate the toll that stress can take on the body.

KEY TERMS

psychophysiological disorders
psychosomatic disorders
psychological factors affecting medical condition
behavioral medicine
health psychology
stressor

stress
general adaptation syndrome (GAS)
structural social support
functional social support
somatic-weakness theory
specific-reaction theory
anger-in theory
cardiovascular disorders

essential hypertension
coronary heart disease (CHD)
angina pectoris
myocardial infarction
Type A behavior pattern
asthma
biofeedback
stress management

EATING DISORDERS

Lynne, twenty-four, was admitted to the psychiatric ward of a general hospital for treatment of anorexia nervosa. Although she didn't really think anything was wrong with her, her husband and parents had consulted with a psychiatrist and the four of them confronted her with a choice of admitting herself or being committed involuntarily.

At the time Lynne had only seventy-eight pounds on her five-foot-five-inch frame. She hadn't menstruated for three years and suffered from a variety of medical problems—hypotension, irregularities in her heartbeat, and abnormally low levels of potassium and calcium.

Lynne had experienced several episodes of dramatic weight loss, beginning at age eighteen when she was going through the dissolution of her first marriage. But none of the prior episodes had been this severe and she had not sought treatment before. She had an intense fear of becoming fat, and although she had never really been overweight she felt that her buttocks and abdomen were far too large. (This belief persisted even when she was at seventy-eight pounds.) During the periods of weight loss she severely restricted food intake and used laxatives heavily. She had occasionally had episodes of binge eating, typically followed by self-induced vomiting so that she would not gain any weight.

Anorexia nervosa can be a life-threatening condition. It is especially prevalent among young women who are under intense pressure to keep their weight low. Gymnast Christy Henrich died from the condition in 1994.

Many cultures are preoccupied with eating; gourmet restaurants abound, and numerous magazines and television shows are devoted to food preparation. At the same time many people are overweight; dieting to lose weight is common and a multimillion-dollar-a-year business. Given this intense interest in food and eating, it is not surprising that this aspect of human behavior is subject to disorder. Although clinical descriptions of eating disorders can be traced back many years, these disorders appeared in the DSM for the first time in 1980 as one subcategory of disorders beginning in childhood or adolescence. With the publication of DSM-IV the eating disorders, anorexia nervosa and bulimia nervosa, became a distinct category reflecting the increased attention they have received from clinicians and researchers over the past two decades.

CLINICAL DESCRIPTION

ANOREXIA NERVOSA

Lynne was suffering from **anorexia nervosa**, one of the two principal eating disorders described in DSM-IV. The term *anorexia* refers to loss of appetite, and *nervosa* indicates for emotional reasons. The term is something of a misnomer because many anorexic patients actually do not lose their appetite or interest in food. To the contrary, while starving themselves many patients with anorexia become preoccupied with food; they may read cookbooks constantly and prepare gourmet meals for their families.

Lynne met all four features required for the diagnosis. First, the person must refuse to maintain a normal body weight; this criterion is usually taken to mean that the person weighs less than 85 percent of what is considered normal for that person's age and height. Weight loss is typically achieved through dieting, although purging (self-induced vomiting, heavy use of laxatives or diuretics) and excessive exercise can also be part of the picture. Second, the person has an intense fear of gaining weight, and the fear is not reduced by weight loss. Third, in females the extreme emaciation often causes amenorrhea, the loss or irregularity of the menstrual period. Fourth, patients with anorexia nervosa have a distorted sense of their body shape.

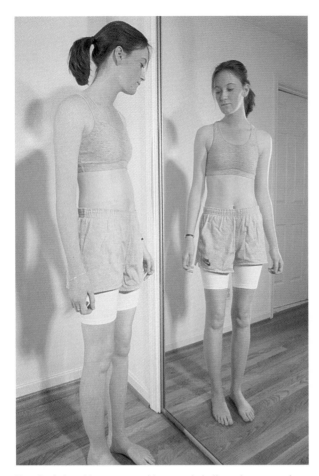

Despite being thin, women with anorexia believe that parts of their bodies are too fat and spend a lot of time critically examining themselves in front of mirrors.

Even when emaciated they maintain that they are overweight or that certain parts of their bodies, particularly the abdomen, buttocks, and thighs, are too fat. When drastically underweight, they usually don't think that anything is wrong. To check on their body size, patients with anorexia typically weigh themselves frequently, measure the size of different parts of the body, and gaze critically at their reflections in mirrors. Their self-esteem is closely linked to maintaining thinness.

The distorted body image that accompanies anorexia has been assessed in several ways. In one type of assessment, patients are shown line drawings of women with varying body weights and asked to pick the one closest to their own and the one that represents their ideal shape (see Figure 9.1). As expected, patients with anorexia overestimate their own body size and choose a thin figure as their ideal.

DSM-IV distinguishes two types of anorexia nervosa. In the *restricting type*, weight loss is due to

food restriction; in the *binge-eating–purging type*, as illustrated in Lynne's case, the person has also regularly engaged in binge eating and purging. Numerous differences between these two subtypes support the validity of this distinction. The binging–purging subtype appears to be more psychopathological; patients exhibit more personality disorders, impulsive behavior, stealing, alcohol and drug abuse, social withdrawal, and suicide attempts than are found in patients with the restricting type (e.g., Da Costa & Halmi, 1992; Dowson, 1992; Pryor, Wiederman & McGilley, 1996).

Anorexia typically begins in the early to middle teenage years, often after an episode of dieting and the occurrence of a life stress such as the separation or divorce of parents. It is about ten times more frequent in women than in men, with an overall prevalence of about 1 percent (Hsu, 1990; Walters & Kendler, 1994). When anorexia does occur in men

Figure 9.1 In this assessment of body image, respondents may indicate their current shape, their ideal shape, and the shape they think is most attractive to the opposite sex. The figure actually rated as most attractive by members of the opposite sex is shown in both panels. Ratings of women who scored high on a measure of distorted attitudes toward eating are shown in (*A*); ratings of women who scored low are shown in (*B*). The high scorers overestimated their current size and ideally would be very thin. From Zellner, Harner, and Adler (1988).

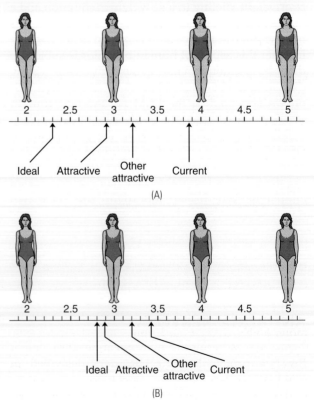

symptomatology and other characteristics, such as reports of family conflict, are generally similar to those reported by women with anorexia (Olivardia et al., 1995). As we discuss more fully later, the gender difference in the prevalence of anorexia most likely reflects the greater emphasis women place on cultural standards of beauty, which have promoted a thin shape as the ideal over the past few decades. Patients with anorexia are frequently diagnosed with depression, obsessive-compulsive disorder, phobias, panic disorder, alcoholism, and various personality disorders (Kennedy & Garfinkel, 1992; Walters & Kendler, 1994) and are likely to show sexual disturbances. In one study 20 percent of a sample of anorexic women with an average age of twenty-four had not had intercourse and more than 50 percent were either inorgasmic or had low sexual desire (Raboch & Faltus, 1991).

ANOREXIA AND DEPRESSION

The strong connection between anorexia and depression has prompted some researchers to consider the possibility that anorexia causes depression (e.g., through the biochemical changes produced by starvation or the feelings of guilt and shame that accompany it); anorexia does not always precede depression, however (Piran et al., 1985). Anorexia and depression may share a common genetic diathesis or environmental causes, such as a disturbed family environment or other life stress. Studies have shown that relatives of anorexics are at high risk for depression (e.g., Hudson et al., 1987). It has also been proposed that depression causes anorexia nervosa or that anorexia is a variant of depression, as there is a symptomatic similarity between depression and anorexia. Weight loss, for example, is a symptom of depression. There are biological similarities as well. For example, both people who are depressed and people with anorexia have low levels of serotonin. All three hypotheses remain plausible explanations of the high comorbidity between anorexia and depression.

PHYSICAL EFFECTS OF ANOREXIA

Self-starvation and use of laxatives produce numerous undesirable biological consequences. Blood pressure often falls, heart rate slows, bone mass declines, the skin dries out, nails become brittle, hormone levels change, and mild anemia may occur. Some patients lose hair from the scalp, and they may develop laguna, a fine, soft hair, on their bodies. As in the case of Lynne, levels of electrolytes, such as potassium and sodium, are altered. Electrolytes, ionized salts present in various body fluids, are essential for the process of neural transmission.

Prognosis in anorexia is not favorable; only about 50 percent of patients recover. As we discuss later, changing anorexic patients' distorted views of themselves is very difficult, particularly in cultures that value thinness. Anorexia is a life-threatening illness; death rates are substantially higher among anorexic patients than among the general population. Death most often results from physical complications of the illness, for example, congestive heart failure, and from suicide (Crisp et al., 1992; Sullivan, 1995).

BULIMIA NERVOSA

Jill was the second child born to her parents. Both she and her brother became intensely involved in athletics at an early age, Jill in gymnastics and Tom in Little League baseball, a sport in which his father was active as well. At age four Jill was enrolled in gymnastics school, where she excelled. By the time she was nine her mother had decided that Jill had outstripped the coaching abilities of the local instructors and began driving her to a nationally recognized coach, several hundred miles distant, several times a week. Over the next few years Jill continued to excel, her trophy case swelled, and aspirations for a place on the Olympic team grew. As she reached puberty her thin frame began to fill out, raising concerns about the effects of her weight gain on her performance as a gymnast. She began to restrict her intake of food, but found that after several days of semistarvation she would lose control and go on an eating binge. This pattern of dieting and binging lasted for several months, during which Jill's fear of becoming fat seemed to increase. At age thirteen, she hit on the solution of self-induced vomiting. She quickly fell into a pattern of episodes of alternating binging and vomiting three or four times per week. Although she maintained this pattern in secret for a while, eventually Jill's parents caught on and initiated treatment for her.

Jill's behavior illustrates well the features of the second eating disorder, **bulimia nervosa**. Bulimia is from a Greek word meaning "ox hunger." This disorder involves episodes of rapid consumption of enormous amounts of food, followed by extreme steps, such as vomiting, fasting, or excessive exercise, to prevent weight gain. The DSM defines a binge as eating an excessive amount of food within less than two hours. Binges typically occur in secret; may be triggered by stress and the negative emotions it arouses, being alone, social eating situations, or concerns about weight gain; and continue until the person is uncomfortably full (Grilo et al., 1994).

During a binge the person feels that he or she cannot control the amount of food that is being consumed. Foods, especially sweets such as ice cream or cake, that can be rapidly consumed are usually part of a binge.

Research shows that during a binge a bulimic patient typically ingests 2000 to 4000 calories (Michell & Pyle, 1985), often more than what a normal person eats in an entire day. Patients are usually ashamed of their binges and try to conceal them. They report that they lose control during a binge, even to the point at which something akin to a dissociative state occurs. After the binge is over, disgust, feelings of discomfort, and fear of weight gain lead to the second step of bulimia nervosa, purging. Patients most often stick fingers down their throats to cause gagging, but after a time many can induce vomiting at will. Laxative and diuretic abuse (which, ironically, do little to reduce caloric intake) as well as fasting and excessive exercise are also used to keep weight down. Although many people binge occasionally—one study found that 50 percent of college students had occasional binges (Mitchell et al., 1982)—and some people also experiment with purging, the diagnosis of bulimia nervosa requires that the episodes of binging and purging occur at least twice a week for three months.

As with patients with anorexia nervosa, those with bulimia nervosa are afraid of gaining weight and their self-esteem depends heavily on maintaining normal weight. They also have a distorted view of their own body size, believing that they are fat even when their weight is relatively normal. Bulimia nervosa is not diagnosed if the binging and purging occur only in the context of anorexia nervosa and its extreme weight loss; the diagnosis in such a case is anorexia nervosa, binge-eating–purging type.

The following case illustrates the severity of bulimia (Oltmanns, Neale, & Davison, 1995).

Gary binged almost every day, sometimes at both lunch and dinner. He typically did not eat anything until lunch. Sometimes he would then go to McDonald's and have a dozen hamburgers, five large orders of fries, several shakes, and apple pie for dessert. Even more appealing were several local restaurants that offered all-you-can-eat lunches. These meals could last for a couple of hours, punctuated by several trips to the bathroom to vomit.

On his way home in the evening Gary regularly stopped at a grocery store to lay in supplies. A typical meal might include ten pounds of potato salad, bowlfuls of green salad, bags of potato chips and pretzels, and bottles of club soda that made eating and vomiting easier.

As with anorexia two subtypes of bulimia nervosa are distinguished: a purging type and a nonpurging type in which the compensatory behaviors are fasting or excessive exercise. As might be expected, nonpurging bulimics tend to be heavier than those who purge; they also binge less frequently and show less psychopathology than do people with purging-type bulimia (Mitchell, 1992).

Bulimia nervosa typically begins in late adolescence or early adulthood; about 90 percent of cases are women. Prevalence among women is thought to be about 1 to 2 percent of the population (Gotesdam & Agras, 1995). Many patients with bulimia nervosa were somewhat overweight before the onset of the disorder, and the binge eating often started during an episode of dieting. Long-term follow-ups of patients with bulimia nervosa reveal that over half recover within five years (Collins & King, 1994).

Bulimia nervosa is associated with numerous other diagnoses, notably depression, personality disorders (especially borderline personality disorder, discussed in Chapter 13), and anxiety disorders (Ames-Frankel et al., 1992; Carroll, Touyz, & Beumont, 1996; Kennedy & Garfinkel 1992; Schwalberg et al., 1992). A twin study has found that bulimia and depression are genetically related (Walters et al., 1992). Somewhat curiously, bulimia is associated with stealing (Rowston & Lacey, 1992). Bulimic patients who steal tend also to be illicit drug users and promiscuous. This combination of behaviors may reflect impulsivity or lack of self-control, characteristics that may be relevant to the behavior of binge eating. Frequent purging can cause potassium depletion. Heavy use of laxatives induces diarrhea, which can also lead to changes in electrolytes. Recurrent vomiting may lead to loss of dental enamel as stomach acids eat away at the teeth, which become ragged. The salivary glands may become swollen. Bulimia nervosa, like anorexia, is a serious disorder with many unfortunate physical consequences.

BINGE EATING DISORDER

DSM-IV includes **binge eating disorder** as a diagnosis in need of further study rather than as a formal diagnosis. Binge eating disorder includes recurrent binges, lack of control during the binging episode, and distress about binging, as well as other characteristics, such as rapid eating and eating alone. It is distinguished from anorexia nervosa by the absence of weight loss and from bulimia nervosa by the absence of purging. Binge eating disorder appears to be more prevalent than either anorexia or bulimia nervosa. In a community sample it was found in 6 percent of successful dieters (those who had kept their weight off for more than one year) and in 19 percent of unsuccessful dieters (Ferguson & Spitzer, 1995). One advantage of including this disorder as a diagnosis is that it would apply to many patients who are now given the vague diagnosis of "eating disorder not otherwise specified" because they do not meet criteria for anorexia or bulimia (Spitzer et al., 1993).

Though it did not meet the higher threshold for including new disorders in DSM-IV (see Fairburn, Welsh, & Hay, 1993), binge eating disorder has several features that support its validity (Spitzer et al., 1993). It occurs more often in women than in men, and is associated with obesity and a history of weight fluctuation. It is linked to impaired work and social functioning, depression, substance abuse, and overconcern with body shape. Binge eating disorder is likely to continue to attract the attention of researchers and to be included in the next DSM.

The diagnoses of anorexia nervosa and bulimia nervosa share several clinical features, most important, an intense fear of overweight. There are some indications that these may not be distinct diagnoses but may be two variants of a single disorder. For example, co-twins of patients diagnosed with anorexia nervosa are themselves more likely than average to have bulimia nervosa (Walters & Kendler, 1994). We will see more similarities and differences between the two diagnoses as we examine theory and research about their etiology and treatment.

ETIOLOGY OF EATING DISORDERS

As with other psychopathologies, a single factor is unlikely to cause an eating disorder. Several areas of current research—genetics, the role of the brain, sociocultural pressures to be thin, the role of the family, and the role of environmental stress—suggest that eating disorders result when several influences converge in a person's life.

BIOLOGICAL FACTORS

GENETICS

Both anorexia nervosa and bulimia nervosa run in families. Female relatives of young women with an eating disorder are about five times more likely than average to have an eating disorder themselves (e.g., Strober et al., 1985; Walters et al., 1992). Twin studies of anorexia nervosa also suggest a genetic influence. Combining the data from several pub-

lished reports, Hsu (1990) calculated a concordance of 47 percent for monozygotic and 10 percent for dizygotic pairs. Hsu reported similar data concerning bulimia nervosa for a small series of MZ and DZ pairs. These data are consistent with the possibility that a genetic diathesis is operating, but more sophisticated adoption studies are needed.

EATING DISORDERS AND THE BRAIN

The hypothalamus is a key brain center in regulating hunger and eating. Research on animals with lesions to the lateral hypothalamus indicates that they lose weight and have no appetite (Hoebel & Teitelbaum, 1966); thus it is not surprising that the hypothalamus has been proposed to play a role in anorexia. The level of some hormones regulated by the hypothalamus, such as cortisol, are indeed abnormal in anorexic patients; rather than causing the disorder, however, these hormonal abnormalities occur as a result of the self-starvation, and levels return to normal following weight gain (Doerr et al., 1980). Furthermore, the weight loss of animals with hypothalamic lesions does not parallel what we know about anorexia; these animals appear to have no hunger and become indifferent to food, whereas patients with anorexia continue to starve themselves despite being hungry. Nor does the hypothalamic model account for body-image disturbance or fear of becoming fat. A dysfunctional hypothalamus thus does not seem highly likely as a factor in anorexia nervosa.

Endogenous opioids are substances produced by the body that reduce pain sensations. Opioids are released during starvation and have been viewed as playing a role in both anorexia and bulimia. Starvation among anorexic patients may increase the levels of endogenous opioids, resulting in a positively reinforcing euphoric state (Marrazzi & Luby, 1986). Hardy and Waller (1988) hypothesized that bulimia is mediated by low levels of endogenous opioids, which are thought to promote craving; a euphoric state is then produced by the ingestion of food, thus reinforcing binging.

Some data support the theory that endogenous opioids play a role in eating disorders, at least in bulimia. For example, both Waller et al. (1986) and Brewerton et al. (1992) found low levels of the endogenous opioid beta-endorphin in bulimic patients. In the Waller study it was also observed that the more severe cases of bulimia had the lowest levels of beta-endorphin.

Finally, research on biological factors in eating disorders has focused on several neurotransmitters related to eating and satiety. Animal research has

Cultural standards regarding the ideal feminine shape have changed over time. In Renoir's time, beautiful women were overweight by today's standards. Even in the 1950s and 1960s, the feminine ideal was considerably heavier than it became in the 1970s, 1980s, and 1990s.

shown that high levels of serotonin promote satiety and that stimulation of the paraventricular nucleus of the thalamus by norepinephrine elicits eating. Researchers have examined levels of these (as well as other) neurotransmitters or their metabolites in bulimic and anorexic patients. Several studies have reported low levels of serotonin in bulimic patients (e.g., Jimerson et al., 1992). This finding fits with the fact that carbohydrate craving is related to low levels of serotonin. Furthermore, the antidepressant drugs that are often effective treatments for bulimia (discussed later) are known to increase serotonin levels. Serotonin could be linked to the impulsive behavior of bulimics (see the discussion of serotonin and impulsivity in Chapter 10, p. 256). Studies have also found evidence for low levels of norepinephrine in both bulimic and anorexic patients (Goldbloom, Garfinkel, & Shaw, 1991). Why levels would be low in both types of patients is still not clear. Though we can expect further biochemical research in the future, it is important to keep in mind that this work focuses exclusively on brain mechanisms relevant to hunger, eating, and satiety and does little to account for other key features of both disorders, in particular, the intense fear of becoming fat. The social and cultural environments appear to play a role in the faulty perceptions and eating habits of those with eating disorders, and it is to these influences we now turn.

SOCIOCULTURAL VARIABLES

"No woman can be too rich or too thin." (Attributed to the duchess of Windsor, per *Bartlett's Familiar Quotations*, 1992)

Throughout history, the standards society has set for the ideal body have varied greatly (especially those

pertaining to the ideal female body). Think of the famous nudes painted by Rubens in the seventeenth century—according to modern standards these women are chubby. In recent times in American culture there has been a steady progression toward increasing thinness as the ideal. *Playboy* centerfolds became thinner between 1959 and 1978 (Garner et al., 1980), although this trend now seems to have leveled off (Wiseman el at., 1992); beauty pageant contestants became thinner through 1988. To achieve the same figure as another ideal, the Barbie doll, the average American woman would have to increase her bust by twelve inches, reduce her waist by ten, and grow to over seven feet in height (Moser, 1989)! We know that this cultural ideal has been internal-

To match the proportions of a Barbie doll, a woman with a normal shape (left) would have to transform her height, waist, and bust to appear like the figure on the right.

As the frequency of eating disorders increased over the past several decades, so too did preoccupation with dieting.

ized by the large percentage of young women who, although of normal weight, perceive themselves as fat. One study of tenth-grade girls found that one-third felt they were overweight although they were not (Killen et al., 1986). As society has become more health and fat conscious, dieting to lose weight has become more common; the number of dieters has increased from 7 percent of men and 14 percent of women in 1950 to 24 percent of men and 40 percent of women in 1993. The diet industry (books, pills, videos, special foods) is valued at more than $30 billion per year. To put this figure in perspective, in 1993 the U.S. government spent about this amount on education, training, employment, and social services combined. Finally, liposuction has become the most common procedure in plastic surgery (Brownell & Rodin, 1994).

There are some indications that this preoccupation with being thin may be on the decline. In the Garner et al. (1980) study mentioned earlier the number of articles on dieting increased steadily during the period when centerfolds were becoming thinner. More recently Nemeroff et al. (1994) analyzed the content of three women's magazines—*Good Housekeeping*, *Cosmopolitan*, and *Ms.*—for the period from 1980 to 1991. The number of articles on weight loss decreased in *Cosmopolitan* and *Ms.* Other studies have found that the intensity of dieting and eating-disordered behaviors has lessened in recent years (Heatherton et al., 1995).

Nemeroff et al. also analyzed the content of several men's magazines and found that the frequency of articles on weight loss, although much less in men's than in women's magazines, actually increased during the time period studied. It would probably be incorrect to assume from these data, however, that we are about to witness an explosion

of eating disorders in men. It is more plausible that the articles focus attention on the masculine ideal of normal body weight or on increased muscle mass (Mishkind et al., 1986).

The sociocultural ideal of thinness shared by most Western industrialized nations is a likely vehicle through which people learn to fear being or even feeling fat. In addition to creating an undesired physical shape, fat has negative connotations such as being unsuccessful and having little self-control. Obese people are viewed by others as less smart and are stereotyped as lonely, shy, and greedy for the affection of others (DeJong & Kleck, 1986).

As society's negative attitude about fat became stronger, the prevalence of eating disorders increased. In an epidemiological study conducted in Switzerland the incidence of anorexia nervosa quadrupled from the 1950s to the 1970s (Willi & Grossman, 1983). Similar increases have been found in other countries (Eagles et al., 1995; Hoek et al., 1995).

Another indication of our society's preoccupation with thinness comes from Miss Universe of 1996, Alicia Machado. After winning the title, and gaining a few pounds, some people became outraged and suggested she give up her crown.

FOCUS 9.1   TO DIET OR NOT TO DIET?

As dieting has become more common and the diet industry has become a multibillion-dollar-a-year business, the incidence of both eating disorders and obesity has increased. Millions of Americans are overweight. Is there a relationship among these facts? As the studies of restrained eaters and bulimics show, dieting can lead to binging, and very "successful" dieters can become anorexic. Is dieting more dangerous than desirable?

People increase the amount of fat in their bodies when they consume more calories than they burn up through metabolism. The body's system for regulating weight requires very fine tuning. For example, consuming a mere 100 calories a day extra, such as two cookies, one beer, or a bowl of chips, will yield about ten extra pounds at the end of a year.

Heredity plays a significant role in obesity. Adoption studies have found that children's weight is more strongly related to the weight of their biological parents than to the weight of their adoptive parents (Price et al., 1987). Similarly, 40 percent of the children of an obese parent will be obese, compared with 7 percent of the children of normal-weight parents. Heredity could produce its effects by regulating metabolic rate, or through the hypothalamus and its impact on insulin level or the production of enzymes that make it easier to store fat and gain weight. Dieting may be of little use to people whose obesity is principally genetically caused. Their metabolic rate may simply slow down to help maintain body weight; when the diet is over the lowered metabolic rate leads to weight gain.

But psychosocial factors are also clearly involved in gaining weight. Stress and its associated negative moods can induce eating in some people (Arnow, Kenardy, & Agras, 1992; Heatherton & Baumeister, 1991). And we are all subject to the continuing impact of advertisements, especially those promoting high-fat, high-calorie products such as snack foods, desserts, and meals at fast-food restaurants.

The motivation to achieve thinness is generally tied to several possible goals.

- Being thin increases personal attractiveness, which in turn can produce both psychological (e.g., increased self-esteem) and social (e.g., advancement in the workplace) benefits.
- Being thin signifies self-discipline; obesity reflects a lack of self-control and failure.
- Thinness is associated with several health benefits; obesity is associated with health problems. For example, obesity is linked to diabetes, hypertension, cardiovascular disease, and several forms of cancer.

Despite this drive to be thin, a backlash against dieting has been emerging (Brownell & Rodin, 1994). Feminist philosophy has challenged the view that women should be defined by their physical characteristics. The National Association to Aid Fat Acceptance defends the rights of obese people against job discrimination and social bias. On an empirical level, we have seen at least one potential danger in dieting—it is often a precursor to eating disorders. It is widely known that although many diets achieve weight loss in the short term (for example, one year), the weight is typically regained later (Garner & Wooley, 1991), suggesting that diets don't work in the long term. Weight fluctuation itself could be a health risk (e.g., for cardiovascular disease). Furthermore, the evidence concerning whether weight loss actually yields health benefits is conflicting. For example, the typical weight loss of fifteen pounds may

GENDER INFLUENCES

The primary reason for the greater prevalence of eating disorders among women than among men is that women appear to have been more heavily influenced by cultural standards reinforcing the desirability of being thin. While these standards have been promoting thinness as the ideal, more and more people have become overweight. The prevalence of obesity has doubled since 1900; currently 20 to 30 percent of Americans are overweight, perhaps because of an abundance of food, and a sedentary lifestyle. Dieting to lose weight, the result of this tendency to be overweight, is especially common among white, upper-socioeconomic-status women—the same group that has the highest rate of eating disorders. Women apparently are more concerned than men about being thin, are more likely to diet, and are thus more

The fear of being fat which is so important in eating disorders, is partly based on society's negative stereotypes about overweight people.

not be sufficient to produce any beneficial effects on health. Finally, it may be that obesity is not the crucial factor that puts people at risk for disease; the distribution of body fat could be

Dieting to lose weight is typically motivated by a desire to become more attractive and to achieve health benefits. Although dieting leads to short term weight loss, the lost pounds are often regained.

more telling. A large concentration of fat around the abdomen is more strongly related to mortality and cardiovascular disease than is a more even distribution of fat or a concentration of fat below the waist (Garner & Wooley, 1991).

In trying to reconcile the competing positions on dieting, Brownell and Rodin (1994) acknowledge that all the data are not in. Nonetheless, they counter some of the points raised by antidieters. They note, for example, that the samples in studies showing the long-term ineffectiveness of dieting typically contained large percentages of binge eaters. Because binge eating is related to a poor prognosis for treating obesity, the data may underestimate the positive effects of dieting. Furthermore, they point to newer studies with more favorable long-term outcomes. In one (Nunn, Newton, & Faucher, 1992), participants with an average weight loss of fifty-five pounds maintained 75 percent of the weight loss at a one-year follow-up and 52 percent at two years. Brownell and Rodin also point out that studies showing an association between weight fluctuation and poor health did not actually study dieting. Therefore, the weight fluctuation that was observed could have been due to other factors, such as alcoholism, stress, or cancer. Finally, they note that returning to prediet weight some time after dieting is not necessarily a bad outcome. Considering a return to baseline as a failure does not take into consideration what the person's weight would have been if no diet had ever been attempted.

Brownell and Rodin suggest that the decision to diet might be more profitably based on individualized risk-to-benefit ratios. Generally these would be expected to become more favorable to dieting in very overweight people. But more individualized applications could also be considered. The benefits of dieting could assume much more importance in someone with a family history of hypertension and cardiovascular disease. Conversely, for someone with a family history of eating disorders, embarking on a diet would have to be viewed as a risky step.

vulnerable to eating disorders. The risk for eating disorders among groups who might be expected to be particularly concerned with their weight, for example, models, dancers, and gymnasts, appears to be especially high (Garner & Garfield, 1980). Furthermore, as the onset of eating disorders is typically preceded by dieting and other concerns about weight (e.g., perceived fatness, fear of weight gain), the role of social standards seems certain (see Focus 9.1) (Killen et al., 1994). This is not to say that everyone who diets will develop an eating disorder; other factors are described in subsequent sections.

CULTURAL INFLUENCES

Eating disorders appear to be far more common in industrialized societies such as the United States, Canada, Japan, Australia, and Europe than in nonin-

dustrialized nations. The wide variation in the prevalence of eating disorders across cultures provides a window on the importance of culture in establishing realistic versus potentially disordered views of one's body. In one study of 369 adolescent girls in Pakistan, none met diagnostic criteria for anorexia nervosa and only one met the criteria for bulimia (Mumford, Whitehouse, & Choudry, 1992). As yet, however, there have been no cross-cultural epidemiological studies employing similar assessments and diagnostic criteria, so it is difficult accurately to compare prevalence rates across cultures. In one study supporting the notion of cross-cultural differences, Ugandan and British college students rated the attractiveness of drawings of nudes ranging from very emaciated to very obese (Furnham & Baguma, 1994). Ugandan students rated the obese female as more attractive than did the British students. Other studies have found that when women from cultures with low prevalence rates of eating disorders move into cultures with higher prevalence rates, their prevalence rate goes up (Yates, 1989). Yet, the cross-cultural variation in prevalence of eating disorders remains a supposition and a sometimes controversial one. For example, Lee (1994) claims that a disorder similar to anorexia exists in several nonindustrialized Asian countries (India, Malaysia, the Philippines). This disorder involves severe emaciation, food refusal, and amenorrhea, but not a fear of becoming fat. Is this a cultural variant of anorexia or a different disorder, such as depression? This question is but one of the challenges that face cross-cultural researchers.

In the United States it has been reported that the incidence of anorexia at one time was eight times greater in white than in nonwhite women (Dolan, 1991). Although this difference may reflect the fact that nonwhite women have less access to health services or utilize them less often, it could also be a real difference. White teenage girls diet more frequently than do African-American teenage girls and are more likely to be dissatisfied with their bodies (Story et al., 1995). Both these factors are related to an increased risk for developing an eating disorder. Recently the emphasis on thinness and dieting has spread beyond white, upper- and middle-class women to women of the lower social classes, and the prevalence of eating disorders has increased among these groups (e.g., Root, 1990).

PSYCHODYNAMIC VIEWS

Early psychoanalytic theories viewed anorexia nervosa as a defense against fears of oral impregnation. Food is avoided because it has been equated symbolically with sex and pregnancy. These concerns increase during adolescence, and the stage is set for the onset of anorexia. Little research has supported this early view. More recently, Hilde Bruch (1982) has proposed that anorexia is an attempt by children who have been raised to feel ineffectual to gain competence and respect and to ward off feelings of helplessness, ineffectiveness, and powerlessness. This sense of ineffectiveness is created by a parenting style in which the parents' wishes are imposed on the child without consideration of the child's needs or wishes. For example, parents may arbitrarily decide when the child is hungry or tired, failing to perceive the child's actual state. Children reared in this way do not learn to identify their own internal states and do not become self-reliant. Facing the demands of adolescence, the child seizes on our societal emphasis on thinness and turns dieting into a means of acquiring control and identity.

Another psychodynamic theory proposes that bulimia nervosa in females stems from a failure to develop an adequate sense of self because of a conflict-ridden mother–daughter relationship. Food becomes a symbol of this failed relationship. The daughter's binging and purging represent the conflict between the need for the mother and the desire to reject her.

Salvador Minuchin and his colleagues have proposed a third influential position, known as family dynamics, which is relevant to both anorexia and bulimia. This position blends elements of psychodynamic theory with a focus on the family. In this view the child is seen as physiologically vulnerable, (although the precise nature of this vulnerability is unspecified), and the child's family has several characteristics that promote the development of an eating disorder. Also, the child's eating disorder plays an important role in helping the family avoid other conflicts. Thus the child's symptoms are a substitute for other conflicts within the family.

According to Minuchin et al. (1975) the families of children with eating disorders exhibit the following characteristics.

1. **Enmeshment.** Families of anorexics often have an extreme form of overinvolvement and intimacy in which parents may speak for their children because they believe they know exactly how they feel.

One theory of bulimia nervosa proposes that it arises from mother-daughter conflict.

2. **Overprotectiveness.** Families of anorexics have an extreme level of concern for each other's welfare.

3. **Rigidity.** These families have a tendency to try to maintain the status quo and avoid dealing effectively with events that require change (for example, the demand that adolescence creates for increased autonomy).

4. **Lack of conflict resolution.** Families of adolescents with eating disorders either avoid conflict or are in a state of chronic conflict.

Evidence for these theoretical positions comes from two sources: studies of personality characteristics of patients with eating disorders and studies of the characteristics of their families. It is difficult to reach definitive conclusions in both areas because the disorder may have resulted in changes in personality or in the patient's family. A study of semistarvation in male conscientious objectors conducted in the late 1940s supports the idea that the personality of eating-disordered patients, particularly patients with anorexia, is affected by their lack of food (Franklin et al., 1948). During the main part of the study the men were given two meals a day totaling 1500 calories, to simulate the meals in a concentration camp. All the men soon became preoccupied with food. They also reported increased fatigue, poor concentration, lack of sexual interest, irritability, moodiness, and insomnia. Four became depressed, and one developed bipolar disorder. This research shows vividly how severe restriction of food intake can have powerful effects on personality and behavior, which we need to keep in mind when evaluating the personalities of patients with anorexia and bulimia.

PERSONALITY AND EATING DISORDERS

In part as a response to the findings just mentioned, some researchers have collected retrospective reports of personality before the onset of an eating disorder. This research describes patients with anorexia as perfectionistic, shy, and compliant. The description of patients with bulimia includes the additional characteristics of histrionic features, affective instability, and an outgoing social disposition (Vitousek & Manke, 1994). It is important to remember, however, that retrospective reports in which subjects and their families recall what the person was like before a disorder was diagnosed can be inaccurate and biased by awareness of the patient's problem.

Studies that have measured the current personality of patients with eating disorders have typically relied on results from established personality questionnaires such as the MMPI. Patients with both anorexia and bulimia are found to be high in neuroticism and anxiety and low in self-esteem. They also score high on a measure of traditionalism, indicating strong endorsement of family and social standards. Some differences emerged between the two groups on the MMPI; patients with anorexia reported depression, social isolation, and anxiety, whereas bulimic patients exhibited more diffuse and serious psychopathology, scoring higher than the anorexics on several of the MMPI scales.

The data are conflicting as to whether anorexic patients are high in perfectionism, perhaps because perfectionism is multidimensional and earlier research has not taken this into account. Perfectionism may be self-oriented (setting high standards for oneself), other oriented (setting high standards for others), or socially oriented (trying to conform to the high standards imposed by others). This last form of perfectionism has been proposed by clinicians as critical in anorexia. A recent laboratory study has confirmed that high scorers on the Eating Attitudes Test did not set higher than normal personal goals, but did maintain unrealistic goals imposed by the experimenter, indicating a high level of conformity with standards imposed by others (Pliner & Hadock, 1996).

Surprisingly, given the clinical findings of an association between bulimia and promiscuity, substance abuse, and theft, no study has found that bulimic patients are high in personality measures of impulsivity (Vitousek & Manke, 1994; Walters & Kendell, 1994).

Prospective studies examine personality characteristics before an eating disorder is present. These studies are just beginning, and the data are not in yet. Research in progress has yielded some interesting information (e.g., Leon et al., 1995). More than 2000 students in a suburban Minneapolis school district completed a variety of tests for each of three consecutive years. Among the measures were assessments of personality characteristics as well as an index of the risk for developing an eating disorder based on the Eating Disorders Inventory. The strongest predictor of risk for eating disorders was a measure of *interoceptive awareness*, the extent to which people can distinguish different biological states of their bodies (see Table 9.1 for items that assess interoceptive awareness).

Data from most studies of the personality of those with eating disorders are somewhat consistent with Bruch's theory of anorexia. Patients with anorexia tend to be compliant, inhibited, and perfectionistic. Leon et al.'s finding that a lack of inte-

TABLE 9.1   Subscales and Illustrative Items from the Eating Disorders Inventory. Responses Use a Six-Point Scale Ranging from Always to Never.

Drive for Thinness	I think about dieting.
	I feel extremely guilty after overeating.
	I am preoccupied with the desire to be thinner.
Bulimia	I stuff myself with food.
	I have gone on eating binges where I have felt that I could not stop.
	I have the thought of trying to vomit in order to lose weight.
Body Dissatisfaction	I think that my thighs are too large.
	I think that my buttocks are too large.
	I think that my hips are too big.
Ineffectiveness	I feel inadequate.
	I have a low opinion of myself.
	I feel empty inside (emotionally).
Perfectionism	Only outstanding performance is good enough in my family.
	As a child, I tried hard to avoid disappointing my parents and teachers.
	I hate being less than best at things.
Interpersonal Distrust	I have trouble expressing my emotions to others.
	I need to keep people at a certain distance (feel uncomfortable if someone tries to get too close).
Interoceptive Awareness	I get confused about what emotion I am feeling.
	I don't know what's going on inside me.
	I get confused as to whether or not I am hungry.
Maturity Fears	I wish that I could return to the security of childhood.
	I feel that people are happiest when they are children.
	The demands of adulthood are too great.

Source: From Garner, Olmsted, & Polivy, 1983.

roceptive awareness predicts risk for eating disorders confirms Bruch's idea that these people are poor at identifying their own internal states.

CHARACTERISTICS OF FAMILIES

Empirical studies of the characteristics of families of patients with eating disorders yield differing results. Some of the variation stems from the different methods used to collect the data and from the sources of the information. For example, the self-reports of patients consistently reveal high levels of conflict in the family (e.g., Kent & Clopton, 1992). However, the reports of parents do not necessarily indicate high levels of family problems. In one study in which the reports of parents of patients with eating disorders did differ from those of controls, parents of patients reported high levels of isolation and lower levels of mutual involvement and support (Humphrey, 1986). Disturbed family relationships do seem to characterize the families of some eating-disordered patients; however, the characteristics

that have been observed, such as low levels of support, have only a loose fit to the psychodynamic theory. And again, these family characteristics could be a result of the eating disorder and not a cause of it.

A study more directly linked to Minuchin's theory assessed both eating-disordered patients and their parents on tests designed to measure rigidity, closeness, emotional overinvolvement, critical comments, and hostility (Dare et al., 1994). Contrary to Minuchin's theory, the families showed considerable variation in enmeshment and were quite low in conflict (low levels of criticism and hostility). Though this latter finding could reflect the conflict-avoiding pattern Minuchin has described, the parents' lack of overinvolvement is clearly inconsistent with his clinical descriptions. Also inconsistent with Minuchin's theory is a family study in which assessments were conducted before and after treatment of the patient (Woodside et al., 1994). Ratings of family functioning improved after treatment, contradicting the idea that improvement in the patient should bring other family conflicts to light.

There is a need to move beyond reports of family functioning and to begin to study these families directly by observational measures. This is not to say that a child's *perception* of his or her family's characteristics is unimportant, but that we need to know how much of family disturbance is perceived and how much is real. In one of the few observational studies conducted thus far, parents of children with eating disorders did not appear to be very different from control parents. The two groups did not differ in the frequency of positive and negative messages given to their children, and the parents of eating-disordered children were more self-disclosing than were the controls. The parents of eating-disordered children did lack some communication skills, however, such as the ability to request clarification of vague statements (Van den Broucke, Vandereycken & Vertommen, 1995). Observational studies such as this, coupled with data on *perceived* family characteristics, would help to settle the issue of whether it is actual or perceived family characteristics that are related to eating disorders.

CHILD ABUSE AND EATING DISORDERS

Some studies have indicated that self-reports of childhood sexual abuse are higher than normal in patients with eating disorders. Since, as discussed in Chapter 7, some data indicate that reports of abuse may be created in therapy, it is notable that this finding was obtained among eating-disordered patients who had not been in treatment as well as those who had (Welch & Fairburn, 1994). However, many attempts to replicate this result have failed (e.g., Rorty, Yager, & Russotto, 1994), so the role of childhood sexual abuse in the etiology of eating disorders remains uncertain. Research has also found higher rates of childhood physical and psychological abuse among eating-disordered patients. These data suggest that future studies should focus on a broad range of abusive experiences, not merely on sexual ones. Furthermore, it has been suggested that the presence or absence of abuse may be too gross a variable. Abuse at a very early age, involving force, and by a family member may bear a stronger relationship to eating disorders (Everill & Waller, 1995).

COGNITIVE-BEHAVIORAL VIEWS

ANOREXIA NERVOSA

Cognitive-behavioral theories of anorexia emphasize the fear of fatness and body-image disturbance as the motivating factors that make self-starvation

and weight loss powerful reinforcers. Behaviors that achieve or maintain thinness are negatively reinforced by the reduction of anxiety. Some theories include personality and sociocultural variables in an attempt to explain how fear of fatness and body-image disturbances develop. For example, perfectionism and a sense of personal inadequacy may lead a person to become especially concerned with his or her appearance, making dieting a potent reinforcer. Similarly, portrayal in the media of thinness as an ideal, being overweight, and a tendency to compare oneself with especially attractive others all contribute to body dissatisfaction (Stormer & Thompson, 1996).

Another important factor in producing a strong drive for thinness is criticism from peers and parents about being overweight (Thompson et al., 1995). In one study supporting this conclusion adolescent girls aged ten to fifteen were evaluated twice, with a three-year interval between assessments. Obesity at the first assessment was related to being teased by peers and at the second assessment was linked to body dissatisfaction. Dissatisfaction was in turn related to symptoms of eating disorder.

It is known that when diets are broken, binging is a frequent result (Polivy & Herman, 1985). The purging following an episode of binge eating can again be seen as being motivated by the fear of weight gain that the binge elicited. Anorexic patients who do not have episodes of binging and purging may have a more intense preoccupation

Being overweight in adolescence often leads to being teased or rejected by peers which, in turn, may produce symptoms of an eating disorder.

with and fear of weight gain (Schlundt & Johnson, 1990) or may be more able to exercise self-control.

BULIMIA NERVOSA

Cognitive-behavioral theories of the etiology of bulimia are similar to those of the binging–purging form of anorexia. Bulimic patients are thought to be overconcerned with weight gain and body appearance, but their attempts at restrictive eating are not maintained, they become anxious, and the binge–purge cycle begins (Fairburn, 1985).

Polivy and Herman (1980) developed the Restraint Scale (see Table 9.2), a questionnaire measure of concerns about dieting and overeating, to study in the laboratory people who are dieting and have distorted attitudes about eating. These studies are generally conducted under the guise of being taste tests. One such study was described as an assessment of the effects of temperature on taste (Polivy, Heatherton, & Herman, 1988). To achieve a "cold" condition, some participants first drank a fifteen-ounce chocolate milk shake (termed a *preload* by the investigators) and were then given three bowls of ice cream to taste and rate for flavor. Participants were told that once they had completed their ratings they could eat as much of the ice cream as they wanted. The dependent variable was the amount of ice cream that was eaten.

In studies following this general design people who scored high on the Restraint Scale ate more than nondieters after a fattening preload, even when the preload was only perceived as fattening but was actually low in calories (e.g. Polivy, 1976) and even when the food was relatively unpalatable (Polivy, Herman, & McFarlane, 1994). Thus dieters who do not have an eating disorder show a pattern similar to that of patients with bulimia nervosa, albeit at a much less intense level. Several addition-al conditions have been found to increase further the eating of restrained eaters following a preload, most notably, various negative mood states, such as anxiety and depression (e.g., Herman et al., 1987). Finally, the increased consumption of dieters is especially pronounced when their self-image is threatened (Heatherton, Herman, & Polivy, 1991) and if they have low self-esteem (Polivy et al., 1988).

The eating pattern of bulimic patients is similar to, but more extreme than, the behavior highlighted by Polivy and her colleagues in their studies of restrained eaters. Bulimic patients typically binge when they encounter stress and experience negative affect. Patients with bulimia nervosa are low in self-esteem (e.g., Garner, Olmsted, & Polivy, 1983). Also, evidence supports the idea that anxiety is relieved by purging. Bulimic patients report increased levels of anxiety when they eat a meal and are not allowed to purge (Leitenberg et al., 1984), and these self-reports have been validated by physiological measures, such as skin conductance (e.g., Williamson et al., 1988). Similarly, anxiety levels decline after purging (Jarrell, Johnson, & Williamson, 1986), again supporting the theory.

TREATMENT OF EATING DISORDERS

It is often difficult to get a patient with an eating disorder into treatment. The patient typically denies that he or she has a problem. For this reason, the majority of patients with eating disorders—up to 90 percent of them—are not in treatment (Fairburn et al., 1996).

To treat patients with anorexia, hospitalization is frequently required so that the patient's ingestion of food can be gradually increased and carefully mon-

---

TABLE 9.2 The Restraint Scale Used to Select Participants for Studies of Factors Controlling Eating in Dieters

1. How often are you dieting? Never; rarely; sometimes; often; always.
2. What is the maximum amount of weight (in pounds) you have ever lost within one month? 0–4; 5–9; 10–14; 15–19; 20+.
3. What is your maximum weight gain within a week? 0–1; 1.1–2; 2.1–3; 3.1–5; 5.1+.
4. In a typical week, how much does your weight fluctuate? 0–1; 1.1–2; 2.1–3; 3.1–5; 5.1+.
5. Would a weight fluctuation of 5 pounds affect the way you live your life? Not at all; slightly; moderately; very much.
6. Do you eat sensibly in front of others and splurge alone? Never; rarely; often; always.
7. Do you give too much time and thought to food? Never; rarely; often; always.
8. Do you have feelings of guilt after overeating? Never; rarely; often; always.
9. How conscious are you of what you are eating? Not at all; slightly; moderately; extremely.
10. How many pounds over your desired weight were you at your maximum weight? 0–1; 1–5; 6–10; 11–20; 21+.

Source: From Polivy & Herman, 1980.

itored. Weight loss can be so severe that intravenous feeding is necessary to save the patient's life. The medical complications of anorexia, such as electrolyte imbalances, also require treatment. For both anorexia and bulimia, both biological and psychological interventions have been employed.

BIOLOGICAL TREATMENTS

Because eating disorders are often comorbid with depression, bulimia nervosa and anorexia nervosa have been treated with a degree of success with various antidepressants. Recent interest has focused on fluoxetine (Prozac) (e.g., Fluoxetine Bulimia Nervosa Study Group, 1992). In a multicenter study 387 bulimic women were treated as outpatients for eight weeks. Fluoxetine was shown to be superior to a placebo in reducing binge eating and vomiting; it also lessened depression and distorted attitudes toward food and eating. Less well controlled studies also suggest that fluoxetine is useful in treating anorexia nervosa (e.g., Kaye et al., 1991). Twenty-nine of 37 anorexics treated with fluoxetine had maintained more normal weight at an eleven-month follow-up.

However, many more patients drop out of drug-treatment conditions in studies on bulimia than drop out of the kind of cognitive-behavioral intervention described later (e.g., Fairburn et al., 1992). In the recent multicenter fluoxetine study, almost one-third of the patients dropped out before the end of the eight-week treatment, primarily because of the side effects of the drug; this figure compares with drop-out rates of under 5 percent with cognitive-behavioral therapy (Agras et al., 1992). Moreover, most patients relapse when the medication is withdrawn (Wilson & Pike, 1993).

TREATMENT OF ANOREXIA

Therapy for anorexia is a two-tiered process. The immediate goal is to help the anorexic patient gain weight in order to avoid medical complications and the possibility of death. The patient is often so weak and physiological functioning so disturbed that hospital treatment, in addition to ensuring that the patient ingest some food, is medically imperative. Behavior therapy programs in which the hospitalized anorexic patient is isolated as much as possible and given mealtime company, then periods of access to a television set, radio, or stereo, walks with a student nurse, mail, and visitors as rewards for eating and gaining weight have been somewhat successful (Hsu, 1991). However, the second goal of treatment, long-term maintenance of gains in body

weight, has not yet been reliably achieved by medical, behavioral, or traditional psychodynamic interventions (Wilson, 1995).

Family therapy is another mode of treatment for anorexia. Like most other treatments family therapy has not yet been sufficiently studied for its long-term effects. One report, however, suggests that as many as 86 percent of fifty anorexic daughters treated with their families were still functioning well when assessed at times ranging from three months to four years after treatment (Rosman, Minuchin, & Liebman, 1976).

Salvador Minuchin and his colleagues, who represent but one of several schools of family therapy, have done considerable work on anorexia nervosa. The treatment they have developed is consistent with Minuchin's psychodynamic theorizing described earlier: the eating-disordered child is viewed as deflecting attention away from underlying conflict in family relationships.

To treat the disorder Minuchin attempts to redefine it as interpersonal rather than individual and to bring the family conflict to the fore. In this way, he theorizes, the symptomatic family member is freed from having to maintain his or her problem, for it no longer deflects attention from the dysfunctional family.

How is this accomplished? At a "family lunch session" families of anorexic patients are seen by the therapist during mealtime, since the conflicts related to anorexia are believed to be most evident then. There are three major goals for these lunch sessions: (1) changing the patient role of the anorexic patient; (2) redefining the eating problem as an interpersonal problem; and (3) preventing the parents from using their child's anorexia as a means of avoiding conflict. One strategy is to instruct each parent to try individually to force the child to eat. The other parent may leave the room. The individual efforts are expected to fail. But through this failure and frustration, the mother and father may now work *together* to persuade the child to eat. Thus rather than being a focus of conflict, the child's eating will produce cooperation and increase parental effectiveness in dealing with the child (Rosman, Minuchin, & Liebman, 1975).

TREATMENT OF BULIMIA

Therapy for bulimia is designed to address several issues. In cognitive behavior therapy the bulimic patient is encouraged to question society's standards for physical attractiveness (such as the adage, You can never be too rich or too thin). Patients must also uncover and then change beliefs that encourage them to starve themselves to avoid becoming overweight; that is, they must be helped to see that normal body weight can be maintained without severe dieting and that unrealistic restriction of food intake can often trigger a binge. They are taught that all is not lost with just one bite of high-calorie food; that snacking does not need to trigger a binge, which is then followed by induced vomiting or laxatives to get rid of the forbidden food as quickly as possible. Altering this all-or-nothing thinking can help patients begin to eat more moderately. Both cognitive-behavioral and interpersonal therapy have achieved some success in ameliorating bulimia. Yet, although they may reduce purges considerably, the overall success rates are less than 50 percent (Wilson, 1995; Wilson & Pike, 1993), indicating that, like anorexia, bulimia is very difficult to treat successfully.

In recent years considerably more research has been done on treating bulimia than on treating anorexia. This research has been almost entirely on the cognitive-behavioral model of Fairburn (1985), who, as indicated earlier, suggests that the bulimic patient's core problem lies with the belief that one's shape and weight are of paramount importance for acceptance by self and by others and must therefore be kept under tight control by strict dieting. This dieting breaks down into binging and then purging to get rid of the ingested food as quickly as possible.

The overall goal of treatment in bulimia nervosa is to develop normal eating patterns. Patients need to learn to eat three meals a day and even to eat some snacks between meals without sliding back into binging and purging. They are encouraged to develop less extreme beliefs about themselves. For example, the therapist may gently but firmly challenge such irrational beliefs as "No one will respect me if I am a few pounds heavier than I am now" or "Eric loves me only because I weigh 112 pounds and would surely reject me if I ballooned [sic] to 120 pounds." A generalized assumption underlying these and related cognitions for female patients might be that a woman has value to a man only if she is a few pounds underweight—a belief that is put forth in the media and advertisements.

Cognitive-behavioral treatments also try to teach the bulimic patient that weight control, which is not an unreasonable goal in a person's life, can be achieved better by eating on a regular basis than by extreme dieting, which usually breaks down into a binge followed by purging. Regular meals control hunger and thereby, it is hoped, the urge to eat enormous amounts of food, the effects of which—being overweight—are counteracted by purging.

This cognitive-behavioral treatment approach has the patient bring small amounts of forbidden food to eat in the session. Relaxation is employed to control the urge to induce vomiting. Unrealistic demands and other cognitive distortions—such as the belief that eating a small amount of high-calorie food means that the patient is an utter failure and doomed never to improve—are continually challenged. The therapist and patient work together to determine events, thoughts, and feelings that trigger an urge to binge and then to learn more adaptive ways to cope with these situations. For example, if the therapist and the patient, usually a young woman, discover that binging often takes place after the patient has been criticized by her boyfriend, therapy could entail any or all of the following: encouraging the patient to assert herself if the criticism is unwarranted; teaching her, à la Ellis, that it is not a catastrophe to make a mistake and it is not necessary to be perfect, even if the boyfriend's criticism is valid; and desensitizing her to social evaluation. The patient, is encouraged to question society's standards for ideal weight and the pressures on women to be thin—not an easy task by any means.

The outcomes of cognitive-behavioral therapies (CBT) are promising, at least in the short term, and there is evidence that they are superior to antidepressant-drug treatments (Agras et al., 1992). Findings from a number of studies indicate that CBT often results in less frequent binging and purging, with reductions ranging from 70 to more than 90 percent; extreme dietary restraint is also reduced significantly, and there is improvement in attitudes toward body shape and weight (Garner et al., 1993; Wilson et al., 1991). However, if we focus on the patients themselves rather than on numbers of binges and purges *across* patients, we find that at least half of those treated with CBT improve very little (Craighead & Agras, 1991; Wilson, 1995; Wilson & Pike, 1993). And if we look at how patients who do improve significantly are doing at six- and twelve-month follow-ups, we find that only about one-third are maintaining their treatment gains (Fairburn et al., 1993). Thus the outcome picture is mixed.

Those who are successful in overcoming their urge to binge and purge also improve in associated problems such as depression and low self-esteem. This result is not surprising: if a person is able to achieve normal eating patterns after viewing bulimia as an uncontrollable problem, the person can be expected to become less depressed and to feel generally better about himself or herself. One last finding from the empirical CBT literature is that self-help groups that follow a manual based on Fairburn's treatment model and are minimally supervised by a mental health professional can achieve significant benefits (Cooper, Coker, & Fleming, 1994).

Is CBT superior to other psychological interventions for the treatment of bulimia? As we often find when comparing different therapies, the answer is unclear. In several studies (e.g., Fairburn et al., 1991; Fairburn et al., 1993), Weissman and Klerman's Interpersonal Therapy (IPT) (p. 243) fared well in comparisons with CBT, though it may not produce results as quickly. The two modes of intervention compare favorably in effecting change across all four of the specific aspects of bulimia, namely, binge eating, purging, dietary restraint, and maladaptive attitudes about body shape and weight (Wilson, 1995). (Similar results were achieved by these two treatment approaches in the large outcome study on depression conducted by the National Institute of Mental Health; see p. 534). It is noteworthy that IPT is effective *at all*, considering that it does not focus, as CBT does, on maladaptive eating patterns, but focuses instead on improving interpersonal functioning. Such success suggests that at least for some patients, disordered eating patterns might be caused by poor interpersonal relationships and their associated negative feelings about oneself and the world.

Although the outcomes from these two leading psychological treatments are superior to those from other modes of intervention, including drugs, a good deal more remains to be learned about how best to treat bulimia—inpatient cognitive-behavioral therapy may, for example, increase effectiveness (Tuschen & Bent, 1995)—and especially anorexia, in which the outcomes are far less sanguine. The fact that at least half of the patients in the controlled studies do not improve in a meaningful way may be due in part to the fact that significant numbers of the patients in these controlled outcome studies have other psychological disorders in addition to eating disorders, such as borderline personality disorder, depression, anxiety, and marital distress (Wilson, 1995). Such patients show less improvement from cognitive-behavioral therapy and from other therapies as well. Gleaves and Eberenz (1994), for example, examined cognitive-behavioral therapy outcomes among 464 bulimic women in a residential-treatment setting and found that those with a history of multiple therapists or hospitalizations, suicide attempts, and sexual abuse derived significantly less benefit from therapy than did those without such backgrounds. The poor therapeutic outcomes could have resulted because such patients simply have more pervasive and more serious psychopathology. Alternatively, the poor prognosis could result from the patients' failure to engage in the therapy, perhaps because of lack of trust in authorities owing to earlier sexual abuse (therapists are authority figures, and if the patient was abused by a parent the ensuing distrust and anger may very well be generalized to a therapist).

People seldom seek therapy for only a single problem, and something as serious as an eating disorder is probably bound up with other psychological problems, such as depression. When we consider that depression itself undoubtedly has multiple causes—person A may be depressed for reasons quite different from those operating with person B—the lesson to be learned is that controlled outcome studies are limited in what they can tell us about how best to deal with a particular patient in a real-life therapy setting. The complexities that practicing clinicians face and try to deal with in individual cases cannot be addressed in comparative outcome studies in which therapists must strive to follow a treatment manual.

SUMMARY

The two main eating disorders are anorexia nervosa and bulimia nervosa. The symptoms of anorexia nervosa include refusal to maintain normal body weight, an intense fear of being fat, a distorted sense of body shape, and, in women, amenorrhea. Anorexia typically begins in the midteens, is ten times more frequent in women than in men, and is comorbid with several other disorders, notably depression. Its course is not favorable, and it can be life threatening. The symptoms of bulimia nervosa include episodes of binge eating followed by purging, fear of being fat, and a distorted body image. Like anorexia, bulimia begins in adolescence, is much more frequent in women than in men, and is comorbid with other diagnoses, such as depression. Prognosis is somewhat more favorable than for anorexia.

Biological research in the eating disorders has examined both genetics and brain mechanisms. Evidence is consistent with a possible genetic diathesis, but adoption studies have not yet been done. Endogenous opioids and serotonin, both of which play a role in mediating hunger and satiety, have been examined in eating disorders. Low levels of both these brain chemicals have been found in patients with eating disorders.

On a psychological level several factors play important roles. As cultural standards changed to favor a thinner shape as the ideal for women, the frequency of eating disorders increased. The prevalence of eating disorders is very high among people who are especially concerned with their weight, such as models, dancers, and athletes. The prevalence of eating disorders is also higher in industrialized countries, where the cultural pressure to be thin is strongest. Psychodynamic theories of eating disorders emphasize parent–child relationships and personality characteristics. Bruch's theory, for example, proposes that the parents of children who later develop eating-disorders impose their wishes on their children without considering the children's needs. Children reared in this way do not learn to identify their own internal states and they become highly dependent on standards imposed by others. Research on characteristics of families with an eating-disordered child have yielded different data depending on how the data were collected. Reports of patients show high levels of conflict, but actual observations of the families do not find them to be especially deviant. Studies of personality have found that patients with eating disorders are high in neuroticism and perfectionism and low in self-esteem.

Cognitive-behavioral theories of eating disorders propose that fear of being fat and body-image distortion make weight loss a powerful reinforcer. Among patients with bulimia nervosa, negative affect and stress precipitate binges that create anxiety, which is then relieved by purging.

The main biological treatment of eating disorders is the use of antidepressants. Although somewhat effective, drop-out rates from drug-treatment programs are high and relapse is common when patients stop taking the medication. Treatment of anorexia often requires hospitalization to reduce the medical complications of the disorder. Providing reinforcers for weight gain, such as visits from friends, has been somewhat successful, but no treatment has yet been shown to produce long-term maintenance of weight gain.

Cognitive-behavioral treatment for bulimia focuses on questioning society's standards for physical attractiveness, challenging beliefs that encourage severe food restriction, and developing normal eating patterns. Outcomes are promising, at least in the short term.

KEY TERMS

| anorexia nervosa | bulimia nervosa | binge eating disorder |

Sherri Silverman, "Blue Woman In Red", 1993

MOOD DISORDERS

Mrs. M., a thirty-eight-year-old factory worker, had been deeply depressed for about two months when she went to see a psychologist. The mother of four children, she had returned to work three years earlier when the worsening economy made it impossible for her family to get by on just her husband's earnings. But seven months before she visited the psychologist she was laid off, and the family's financial situation deteriorated. Ever-present worries about money led to increased arguments with her husband, not only about their finances but also about the children. She began to have difficulty sleeping, and she lost her appetite, resulting in weight loss. She had little energy and no interest in activities that she normally enjoyed. Even though she sat for hours in front of the television, she couldn't get interested in any of the programs that had been her favorites; she didn't even pay attention most of the time. Household chores became impossible for her to do, and her husband began to complain, leading to further arguments. Finally, realizing that something serious had happened to his wife, Mr. M. cajoled her into making a first appointment with a psychologist.

In this chapter we discuss the **mood disorders**. We begin by describing the DSM categories of depression and bipolar disorder. We then present research on biological and psychological factors relevant to these disorders and discuss their treatment. In a final section we examine suicide.

GENERAL CHARACTERISTICS OF DEPRESSION AND MANIA

As illustrated by the case of Mrs. M., **depression** is an emotional state marked by great sadness and apprehension, feelings of worthlessness and guilt, withdrawal from others, loss of sleep, appetite, and sexual desire, or loss of interest and pleasure in usual activities. Just as most of us experience occasional anxiety, so, too, we experience sadness during the course of our lives, although perhaps not to a degree or with a frequency that warrants the diagnosis of depression. Often depression is associated with other psychological problems, such as panic attacks, substance abuse, sexual dysfunction, and personality disorders.

Paying attention is exhausting for people who are depressed. They cannot take in what they read and what other people say to them. Conversation is also a chore; depressed individuals may speak slowly, after long pauses, using few words and a low, monotonous voice. Many prefer to sit alone and remain silent. Others are agitated and cannot sit still. They pace, wring their hands, continually sigh and moan, or complain. When depressed individuals are confronted with a problem, no ideas for its solution occur to them. Every moment has a great heaviness, and their heads fill and reverberate with self-recriminations. Depressed people may neglect personal hygiene and appearance and make numerous hypochondriacal complaints of aches and pains with no apparent physical basis. Utterly dejected and completely without hope and initiative, they may be apprehensive, anxious, and despondent much of the time.

The symptoms and signs of depression vary somewhat across the life span. As we discuss in more detail later (p. 248), depression in children often results in somatic complaints, such as headaches or stomachaches. In older adults depression is often characterized by distractibility and complaints of memory loss (see Chapter 16). Symptoms of depression exhibit some cross-cultural variation, probably resulting from differences in cultural standards of acceptable behavior. For example, complaints of nerves and headaches are more common in Latino culture and reports of weakness and fatigue are more common among Asians. Fortunately most depression, although recurrent, tends to dissipate with time. But an average untreated episode may stretch on for six to eight months or even longer and may seem to be of even greater duration to patients and their families. Depression may become chronic; in such cases the patient does not completely snap back to an earlier level of functioning between bouts.

Mania is an emotional state or mood of intense but unfounded elation accompanied by irritability, hyperactivity, talkativeness, flight of ideas, distractibility, and impractical, grandiose plans. Some people who suffer from episodic periods of depression also at times suddenly become manic. Although there are clinical reports of individuals who experience mania but not depression, this condition is quite rare.

The person in the throes of a manic episode, which may last from several days to several months, is readily recognized by his or her loud and incessant stream of remarks, full of puns, jokes, rhyming, and interjections about nearby objects and happenings that have attracted the speaker's attention. This speech is difficult to interrupt and reveals the manic patient's so-called flight of ideas. Although small bits of talk are coherent, the individual shifts rapidly from topic to topic. The manic patient's need for activity may cause the person to be annoyingly sociable and intrusive, constantly and sometimes purposelessly busy, and, unfortunately, oblivious to the obvious pitfalls of his or her endeavors. Any attempt to curb this momentum can bring quick anger and even rage. Mania usually comes on suddenly over a period of a day or two.

The following description of a case of mania is from our files. The irritability that is often part of this state was not evident in this patient.

Mr. W., a thirty-two-year-old postal worker, had been married for eight years. He and his wife and their two children lived comfortably and happily in a middle-class neighborhood. In retrospect, there appeared to be no warning of what was to happen. On February 12 Mr. W. told his wife that he was bursting with energy and ideas, that his job as a mail carrier was unfulfilling, and that he was just wasting his talent. That night he slept little, spending most of the time at a desk, writing furiously. The next morning he left for work at the usual time but returned home at 11:00 A.M., his car filled to overflowing with aquariums and other equipment for tropical fish. He had quit his job, then withdrawn all the money from the family's savings account and spent it on tropical fish equipment. Mr. W. reported that the previous night he had worked out a way to modify existing equipment so that fish "won't die anymore. We'll be millionaires." After unloading the paraphernalia, Mr. W. set off to canvass the neighborhood for possible buyers, going door-to-door and talking to anyone who would listen.

The following bit of conversation from the period after Mr. W. entered treatment indicates his incorrigible optimism and provocativeness.

Therapist: Well, you seem pretty happy today.

Client: Happy! Happy! You certainly are a master of understatement, you rogue! [Shouting, literally jumping out of his seat.] Why I'm ecstatic. I'm leaving for the West Coast today, on my daughter's bicycle. Only 3100 miles. That's nothing, you know. I could probably walk, but I want to get there by next week. And along the way I plan to contact a lot of people about investing in my fish equipment. I'll get to know more people that way—you know, Doc, "know" in the biblical sense [leering at the therapist seductively]. Oh, God, how good it feels. It's almost like a nonstop orgasm.

FORMAL DIAGNOSTIC LISTINGS

Two major mood disorders are listed in DSM-IV, **major depression**, also referred to as **unipolar depression**, and bipolar disorder. The formal DSM-IV diagnosis of a major depressive episode requires the presence of five of the following symptoms for at least two weeks. Either depressed mood or loss of interest and pleasure must be one of the five symptoms.

- Sad, depressed mood, most of the day, nearly every day.

Patty Duke has experienced episodes of both mania and depression and therefore would be regarded as having bipolar disorder.

- Loss of interest and pleasure in usual activities.
- Difficulties in sleeping (insomnia); not falling asleep initially, not returning to sleep after awakening in the middle of the night, and early morning awakenings; or, in some patients, a desire to sleep a great deal of the time.
- Shift in activity level, becoming either lethargic (psychomotor retardation) or agitated.
- Poor appetite and weight loss, or increased appetite and weight gain.
- Loss of energy, great fatigue.
- Negative self-concept; self-reproach and self-blame; feelings of worthlessness and guilt.
- Complaints or evidence of difficulty in concentrating, such as slowed thinking and indecisiveness.
- Recurrent thoughts of death or suicide.

Major depression is one of the most widespread of the disorders considered in this book, with a lifetime prevalence rate of about 17 percent (Blazer, Kessler, & McGonagle, 1994). It is about twice as common in women as in men; it occurs more frequently among members of the lower socioeconomic classes and most frequently among young adults. It tends to be a recurrent disorder; about 80 percent of those with depression experience another episode within a year (Coryell et al., 1994). In about 15 percent of cases depression becomes a chronic disorder with a duration of more than two years (Lara & Klein, in press).

The prevalence of depression has been increasing steadily over the last fifty years (Klerman, 1988), and at the same time the age of onset has decreased. One possible explanation for this phenomenon lies in the social changes that have occurred over this same period. Today's young people face many challenges, often in the absence of support structures—such as a tightly knit extended family, traditional values and customs, or the church—that were a more central part of society in the past.

Bipolar I disorder is defined by DSM-IV as involving episodes of mania or mixed episodes that include symptoms of both mania and depression. Most individuals with bipolar I disorder also experience episodes of depression. A formal diagnosis of a manic episode requires the presence of elevated or irritable mood plus three additional symptoms (four if the mood is irritable). The symptoms must be sufficiently severe to impair social and occupational functioning.

- Increase in activity level—at work, socially, or sexually.
- Unusual talkativeness, rapid speech.
- Flight of ideas or subjective impression that thoughts are racing.
- Less than the usual amount of sleep needed.
- Inflated self-esteem; belief that one has special talents, powers, and abilities.
- Distractibility; attention easily diverted.
- Excessive involvement in pleasurable activities that are likely to have undesirable consequences, such as reckless spending.

Bipolar disorder occurs less often than major depression, with a lifetime prevalence rate of about 1 percent of the population (Myers et al., 1984). The average age of onset is in the twenties, and it occurs equally often in men and in women. Among women, episodes of depression are more common and episodes of mania less common than among men (Leibenluft, 1996). Like major depression, bipolar disorder tends to recur; over 50 percent of cases have four or more episodes. Notably, some clinicians do not regard euphoria as a core symptom of mania and report that irritable mood and even depressive features are more common (e.g., Goodwin & Jamison, 1990).

BIPOLAR DISORDER AND CREATIVITY

In her book *Touched with Fire: Manic-Depressive Illness and the Artistic Temperament* (1992), Kay Jamison, an expert on bipolar disorder and herself a

Self-portrait by Paul Gauguin. He is but one of the many artists and writers who apparently suffered from a mood disorder.

long-time sufferer of this condition, assembled a vast array of data linking mood disorders, especially bipolar disorder, to artistic creativity. The list of artists, composers, and writers who experienced mood disorders is impressive and includes Michelangelo, Van Gogh, Tchaikovsky, Gauguin, Tennyson, Shelley, and Whitman, among others. Perhaps the manic state fosters creativity through its association with elated mood, increased energy, rapid thoughts, and the ability to make connections among thoughts that normally would remain unrelated. Of course, one could list many creative people who do not have mood disorders as well as many people with mood disorders who are not particularly creative, but mood disorders do seem to play some role in the creative process.

VALIDITY OF THE UNIPOLAR–BIPOLAR DISTINCTION

Whereas a few decades ago distinctions were not typically made among the various mood disorders, it has since become clear that an important distinc-

TABLE 10.1   Differences between Unipolar and Bipolar Depression

Variable	Unipolar	Bipolar
Motor activity	Typically agitated	Typically retarded when depressed
Sleep	Difficulty sleeping	Sleeps more than usual when depressed
Age of onset	Late thirties to early forties	Thirty
Family history	First-degree relatives at high risk for unipolar depression	First-degree relatives at high risk for both unipolar and bipolar depression
Gender	Much more frequent among women	About equal in each gender
Biological treatment	Some response to lithium but better to tricyclics	Best response to lithium

Source: After Depue & Monroe, 1978.

tion can be drawn between bipolar and unipolar disorder (see Table 10.1). These disorders differ on many variables in addition to the presence or absence of manic episodes. For example, when people with bipolar disorder are depressed, they typically sleep more than usual and are lethargic, whereas people with unipolar depression typically have insomnia and are agitated. More relatives of individuals with bipolar disorder have mood disorders than do relatives of those with unipolar depression, suggesting a stronger genetic factor in bipolar than in unipolar depression. Lithium carbonate (see p. 247) is more therapeutic for bipolar patients who are depressed than it is for patients with unipolar depression. All these differences bolster the validity of the bipolar–unipolar distinction (Depue & Monroe, 1978).

Although much of the evidence favors thinking about bipolar and unipolar disorders as distinct, the case is still not airtight. The fly in the ointment comes from research on genetic factors in the two disorders. Relatives of people with unipolar depression are at increased risk for unipolar disorder, whereas relatives of people with bipolar disorder are at increased risk for both unipolar and bipolar disorder, with a higher risk for unipolar disorder (Gershon, 1990). These data can support the argument that unipolar and bipolar disorder are not distinct entities but rather represent different levels of severity of the same disorder, with bipolar disorder the more severe variant (Faraone, Kremen, & Tsuang, 1990). Nonetheless, since most of the literature on the causes of mood disorders treats the two as distinct, we will discuss bipolar and unipolar disorders separately.

HETEROGENEITY WITHIN THE CATEGORIES

A problem in the classification of mood disorders is their great heterogeneity. Some bipolar patients suffer the full range of symptoms of both mania and depression almost every day, termed a *mixed episode*. Other patients have symptoms of only mania or only depression during a clinical episode. So-called bipolar II patients have episodes of major depression accompanied by **hypomania**, a change in behavior and mood that is less extreme than full-blown mania.

Some depressed patients may be diagnosed as psychotic if they are subject to delusions and hallucinations. The presence of delusions appears to be a useful distinction among unipolar depressives (Johnson, Horvath, & Weissman, 1991); depressed patients with delusions do not generally respond well to the usual drug therapies for depression, but they do respond favorably to these drugs when they are combined with the drugs commonly used to treat other psychotic disorders, such as schizophrenia. Furthermore, the course of psychotic depression is more severe than that of depression without delusions and involves more social impairment and less time between episodes (Coryell et al., 1996).

According to DSM-IV some patients with depression may fit a melancholic subtype. They find no pleasure in any activity and are unable to feel better even temporarily when something good happens. Their depressed mood is worse in the morning. They awaken about two hours too early, lose appetite and weight, and are either lethargic or extremely agitated. These individuals had no personality disturbance prior to their first episode of depression and respond well to biological therapies. The validity of the distinction between depressions with or without melancholia has not been well established (Zimmerman et al., 1986), although a recent study found a relationship between this type of depression and poor outcome (Duggan et al., 1991; see Focus 10.1 for discussion of another possible subtype of depression that does not appear in DSM-IV).

Focus 10.1 Anxiety, Depression, and Mixed Anxiety-Depression

In Chapter 6 and in this chapter we have seen that anxiety disorders are frequently comorbid with depression, that is, people can suffer from severe anxiety and clinical depression at the same time. The same phenomenon occurs when anxiety and depression are studied as moods or affects rather than as clinical syndromes; questionnaire measures of anxiety and depression are highly correlated. Can anxiety and depression be better differentiated?

One approach to this question conceptualizes it in terms of three broad dimensions of emotion. High scorers on measures of negative affect experience a high level of distress and negative moods. Both anxious and depressed people score high on measures of negative affect. Anxiety and depression can be distinguished, however, on the next dimension—positive affect, a propensity to experience pleasurable, positive mood states. People who are depressed score lower than those who are anxious. Finally, anxious people score higher than depressed people on the third dimension of emotion—autonomic arousal—reporting more physical signs, such as sweaty palms and high heart rates (Clark, Watson, & Mineka, 1994).

Thus anxiety and depression can be differentiated with the "right" measures. But there may be people who have high levels of negative affect who also score low on positive affect and high on autonomic arousal. These individuals may form a diagnostic category that was considered for inclusion in DSM-IV: mixed anxiety-depression. They do not meet diagnostic criteria for either an anxiety or a mood disorder, but show a mixture of features of both anxiety (worry, anticipating the worst, irritability) and depression (fatigue, hopelessness, low self-esteem). In other words, they are high in negative affect. Although this diagnosis wound up in the DSM appendix, research continues on it and it is a likely addition to the next DSM.

Both manic and depressive episodes may be characterized as having catatonic features, such as motoric immobility or excessive, purposeless activity. Both manic and depressive episodes may also occur within four weeks of childbirth; in this case they are noted to have a postpartum onset.

Finally, DSM-IV states that both bipolar and unipolar disorders can be subdiagnosed as *seasonal* if there is a regular relationship between an episode and a particular time of the year. Most research on the concept of seasonal mood disorder has been done on patients who experienced depression in the winter and mania in the spring or summer (e.g., Rosenthal et al., 1986); the most prevalent explanation is that the mood disorders are linked to changes in the number of daylight hours. Therapy for these winter depressions involves exposing the patients to bright, white light (Blehar & Rosenthal, 1989; Wirz-Justice et al., 1993).

CHRONIC MOOD DISORDERS

DSM-IV lists two long-lasting, or chronic, disorders in which mood disturbances are predominant. Although the symptoms of individuals with either of these disorders must have been evident for at least two years, they are not severe enough to warrant a diagnosis of major depressive or manic episode. In **cyclothymic disorder**, the person has frequent periods of depressed mood and hypomania. These periods may be mixed with, may alternate with, or may be separated by periods of normal mood lasting as long as two months. People with cyclothymic disorder have paired sets of symptoms in their periods of depression and hypomania. During depression they feel inadequate; during hypomania their self-esteem is inflated. They withdraw from people, then seek them out in an uninhibited fashion. They sleep too much and then too little. Depressed cyclothymic patients have trouble concentrating and their verbal productivity decreases; during hypomania their thinking becomes sharp and creative and their productivity increases.

Seasonal depression is one of the subtypes of major depressive disorder. This woman is demonstrating light therapy, which is an effective treatment for patients whose seasonal depression occurs during the winter.

Patients with cyclothymia may also experience full-blown episodes of mania and depression.

The person with **dysthymic disorder** is chronically depressed. Besides feeling blue and losing pleasure in usual activities and pastimes, the person experiences several other signs of depression, such as insomnia or sleeping too much; feelings of inadequacy, ineffectiveness, and lack of energy; pessimism; an inability to concentrate and to think clearly; and a desire to avoid the company of others. Data collected by Klein and his associates (1988) that have validated dysthymia as a form of depression have also indicated that it is a particularly severe form of this disorder. Many dysthymics are chronically depressed and have episodes of major depression as well.

PSYCHOLOGICAL THEORIES OF MOOD DISORDERS

Depression has been studied from several perspectives. We will discuss psychoanalytic views, which emphasize the unconscious conflicts associated with grief and loss; cognitive theories, which focus on the depressed person's self-defeating thought processes; and interpersonal factors, which emphasize how depressed people interact with others. These theories, for the most part, describe different diatheses in a general diathesis–stress theory. The role of stressors in precipitating episodes of depression is well established, although their importance seems to lessen as the number of episodes increases. The theories we discuss are trying to answer the question, What are the psychological characteristics of people who respond to stress with an episode of a mood disorder?

PSYCHOANALYTIC THEORY OF DEPRESSION

In his celebrated paper "Mourning and Melancholia," Freud (1917) theorized that the potential for depression is created early in childhood. During the oral period a child's needs may be insufficiently or oversufficiently gratified, causing the person to become fixated in this stage and dependent on the instinctual gratifications particular to it. With this arrest in psychosexual maturation, this fixation at the oral stage, the person may develop a tendency to be excessively dependent on other people for the maintenance of self-esteem.

From this happenstance of childhood, how can the adult come to suffer from depression? The complex reasoning is based on an analysis of bereavement. Freud hypothesized that after the loss of a loved one, whether by death or, most commonly for a child, separation or withdrawal of affection, the mourner first *introjects*, or incorporates, the lost person; he or she identifies with the lost one, perhaps in a fruitless attempt to undo the loss. Because, Freud asserted, we unconsciously harbor negative feelings toward those we love, the mourner then becomes the object of his or her own hate and anger; in addition, the mourner resents being deserted and feels guilt for real or imagined sins against the lost person.

The period of introjection is followed by the period of *mourning work*, when the mourner recalls memories of the lost one and thereby separates himself or herself from the person who has died or disappointed them and loosens the bonds imposed by introjection.

The grief work can go astray and develop into an ongoing process of self-abuse, self-blame, and depression in overly dependent individuals. These individuals do not loosen their emotional bonds with the person who has been lost; rather, they continue to castigate themselves for the faults and shortcomings perceived in the loved one who has been introjected. The mourner's anger toward the lost one continues to be directed inward. This theorizing is the basis for the widespread psychodynamic view of depression as anger turned against oneself.

Although some research has been generated by psychoanalytic points of view, the little information available does not give strong support to the theory. On the positive side, some depressed people are high in dependency and prone to become depressed following a rejection (Nietzel & Harris, 1990). Dreams and projective tests should theoretically be means of expressing unconscious needs and fears. Beck and Ward (1961) analyzed the dreams of depressed people and found themes of loss and failure, not of anger and hostility. An examination of responses to projective tests established that depressed people identify with the victim and not with the aggressor. Other data are also contradictory. If depression comes from anger turned inward, we would expect depressed people to express little hostility toward others. Yet depressed individuals often express intense anger and hostility toward people close to them (Weissman, Klerman, & Paykel, 1971).

Although Freud cloaked his clinical impressions in theoretical terms that have been rejected by many contemporary writers, we must appreciate that some of his basic suppositions have a continuing influence. For instance, cognitive research (discussed next) has found that depressed people often think in terms of irrational self-statements, such as "It is a dire necessity that I be universally loved and approved of." Such thoughts might be connected to Freud's idea that the oral personality becomes depressed following the loss of a loved one. Similarly, a large body of evidence indicates that depression is precipitated by stressful life events, and these often involve losses, for example, a divorce or job termination (e.g., Brown & Harris, 1978).

Because cognitive theories of depression are those pursued most actively in controlled studies, we now discuss two of them in some detail—Beck's schema theory and the helplessness/hopelessness theory.

COGNITIVE THEORIES OF DEPRESSION

Discussions of the role of cognition in anxiety in Chapter 6 and of Ellis's concept of irrational beliefs in Chapter 2 and elsewhere indicate that cognitive processes play a decisive role in emotional behavior. In some theories of depression, as in some theories of anxiety, thoughts and beliefs are regarded as major factors in causing or influencing the emotional state.

BECK'S THEORY OF DEPRESSION

An important contemporary theory that regards thought processes as causative factors in depression is that of Aaron Beck (1967, 1985, 1987). His central thesis is that depressed individuals feel as they do because their thinking is biased toward negative interpretations. Figure 10.1 illustrates the interactions among three levels of cognitive activity believed by Beck to underlie depression.

According to Beck, in childhood and adolescence depressed individuals acquired a negative schema, a tendency to see the world negatively, through loss of a parent, an unrelenting succession of tragedies, the social rejection of peers, the criticisms of teachers, or the depressive attitude of a parent. (Our later discussion of depression in children will indicate that the acquisition of negative schemata early in life can sometimes lead to depression before adulthood.) All of us have schemata of many kinds; by these perceptual sets, these miniparadigms, we order our lives. The negative schemata or beliefs acquired by depressed persons are activated whenever they encounter new situations that resemble in some way, perhaps only remotely, the conditions in

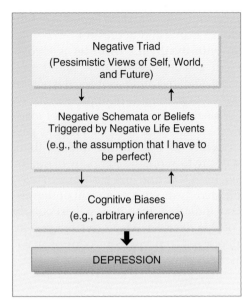

Figure 10.1 The interrelationships among different kinds of cognitions in Beck's theory of depression.

which the schemata were learned. Moreover, the negative schemata of depressed people fuel and are fueled by certain cognitive biases, which lead these people to misperceive reality. Thus an ineptness schema can make depressed individuals expect to fail most of the time, a self-blame schema burdens them with responsibility for all misfortunes, and a negative self-evaluation schema constantly reminds them of their worthlessness.

Being rejected by peers may lead to the development of the negative schema which Beck's theory suggests plays a key role in depression.

The negative schemata, together with cognitive biases or distortions, maintain what Beck called the **negative triad**: negative views of the self, the world, and the future. The world part of Beck's depressive triad refers to the person's judgment that he or she cannot cope with the demands of the environment. It is highly personal—"I cannot possibly cope with all these demands and responsibilities"—and is not a concern for global events that do not implicate the self directly—for example, "The world has been going south since the American League adopted the designated hitter rule" (Haaga et al., 1991, p. 218). The following list describes some of the principal cognitive biases of the depressive individual.

- **Arbitrary inference.** A conclusion drawn in the absence of sufficient evidence or of any evidence at all. For example, a man concludes that he is worthless because it is raining the day he is hosting an outdoor party.
- **Selective abstraction.** A conclusion drawn on the basis of but one of many elements in a situation. A worker feels worthless when a product fails to function, even though she is only one of many people who contributed to its production.
- **Overgeneralization.** An overall sweeping conclusion drawn on the basis of a single, perhaps trivial, event. A student regards his poor performance in a single class on one particular day as final proof of his worthlessness and stupidity.
- **Magnification and minimization.** Exaggerations in evaluating performance. A man, believing that he has completely ruined his car (magnification) when he sees that there is a slight scratch on the rear fender, regards himself as good-for-nothing; or, a woman still believes herself worthless (minimization) in spite of a succession of praiseworthy achievements.

Whereas many theorists see people as victims of their passions, creatures whose intellectual capacities can exert little if any control over feelings—Freud's basic position—in Beck's theory the cause–effect relationship operates in the opposite direction. Our emotional reactions are considered primarily a function of how we construe our world. The interpretations of depressed individuals do not mesh well with the way in which most people view the world. Beck sees such people as victims of their own illogical self-judgments.

EVALUATION At least two points need to be demonstrated when evaluating Beck's theory. The first, that depressed patients, in contrast to nondepressed individuals, judge themselves in the biased ways enumerated by Beck, was initially confirmed by Beck's clinical observations (Beck, 1967).

Further support for this general proposition derives from a number of sources. Questionnaires have been used to assess cognitive biases in reactions to stories describing college students in problematic situations (Krantz & Hammen, 1979) and to allow people to report negative automatic thoughts, ideas that pop into people's minds when they are depressed (Hollon & Kendall, 1980). In general, the responses of depressed individuals to these questionnaires agree with expectations based on Beck's theory (e.g., Dobson & Shaw, 1986). Negative thinking also decreases significantly after treatment to alleviate depression (Simons, Garfield, & Murphy, 1984). As discussed in Chapter 4, a study that used the Articulated Thoughts During Simulated Situations procedure found that the thinking of depressive patients was biased (White et al., 1992). In perceiving and recalling information depressed individuals also have negative schemata; they have been shown to perceive information in more negative terms (Roth & Rehm, 1980), to recall their incorrect answers better than their correct ones (Nelson & Craighead, 1977), and to be more affected by negative words when performing the Stroop test (see p. 148, Segal et al., 1995).

However, another body of research does not support the assertion that cognition is invariably distorted among depressive individuals. For example, depressed people are accurate in their expectations of success, whereas normal people overestimate the likelihood of success (Lobitz & Post, 1979). Thus although depressives are consistently pessimistic, their pessimism does not always reflect cognitive distortion (Layne, 1986). An important task for future research is to try to understand the conditions under which depressive people distort reality and when they seem to perceive it more clearly than do normal people.

Perhaps the greatest challenge for cognitive theories of depression is to demonstrate the second important point, that the negative beliefs of depressed people do not follow their depression but in fact *cause* the depressed mood. Many studies in experimental psychology have shown that a person's mood can be influenced by how he or she construes events. But manipulating affect has also been shown to change thinking (e.g., Isen et al., 1978). Beck and others have found that depression and certain kinds of thinking are *correlated*, but a specific causal relationship cannot be determined from such data; depression could cause negative thoughts, or negative thoughts could cause depression. In our view the relationship in all likelihood works both ways; depression can make thinking more negative, and negative thinking can probably cause and can certainly worsen depression.

Longitudinal studies have begun in which dysfunctional thinking is assessed and participants are followed up some time later to determine who has become depressed. In one such study a large sample of community residents completed a battery of tests that measure cognition and depression (Lewinsohn et al., 1981). At an eight-month follow-up the results of the earlier tests assessing the thinking of people who later became depressed did not indicate a causal role for cognition.

> Prior to becoming depressed, [future depressives] did not subscribe to irrational beliefs, they did not have lower expectancies for positive outcomes or higher expectancies for negative outcomes ... nor did they perceive themselves as having less control over the events in their lives. (p. 218)

A drawback of this study was that the cognitive measures were not a particularly good fit to Beck's theory. A more recent investigation that used a measure of cognition more directly linked to Beck's theory found more positive results (Brown et al., 1995): students with high scores on a measure of depressive thinking who experienced stress reported higher levels of depression subsequently on a questionnaire. However, in this study, clinical diagnoses of

depression were not obtained. More recently, researchers have recognized that the measure of cognition most widely used in studies of Beck's theory (the Dysfunctional Attitudes Scale) is multidimensional, containing subscales that assess different domains of dysfunctional attitudes, for example, a strong need to impress others and a desire to be perfect (Brown et al., 1995). These more specific components of dysfunctional thinking may have more success in predicting the subsequent occurrence of depression when they interact with a stressor specific to them, for example, a personal failure in someone who has a strong need to be perfect (Hewitt, Flett, & Ediger, 1996).

Despite these uncertainties Beck's theory has the advantage of being testable, and it has engendered considerable research on depression. As discussed later in this chapter (p. 244), Beck's work has encouraged therapists to focus directly on the thinking of depressed patients in order to change and alleviate their feelings.

HELPLESSNESS/HOPELESSNESS

In this section we discuss in detail the evolution of an influential cognitive theory of depression—actually, three theories—the original helplessness theory, its subsequent, more cognitive, attributional version, and its transformation into the hopelessness theory (see Figure 10.2 for a summary of the three).

Figure 10.2 The three helplessness theories of depression.

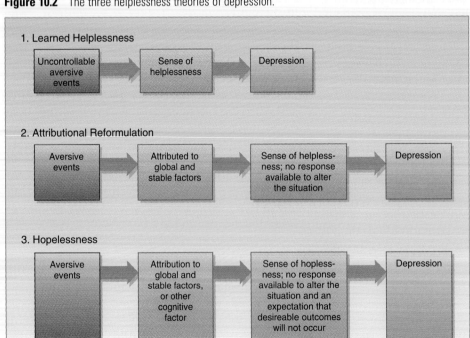

LEARNED HELPLESSNESS The basic premise of the **learned helplessness theory** is that an individual's passivity and sense of being unable to act and control his or her own life is acquired through unpleasant experiences and traumas that the individual tried unsuccessfully to control, bringing on a sense of helplessness, which leads to depression.

This theory began as a mediational learning theory formulated to explain the behavior of dogs who received inescapable electric shocks. Soon after receiving the first shocks the dogs stopped running around in a distressed manner; they seemed to give up and passively accept the painful stimulation. In a subsequent part of the experiment the shocks could be avoided, but the dogs did not acquire the avoidance response as efficiently and effectively as did the control animals; rather, most of them lay down in a corner and whined. On the basis of these observations Seligman (1974) proposed that animals could acquire what might be called a sense of helplessness when confronted with uncontrollable aversive stimulation. This helplessness later tends seriously and deleteriously to affect their performance in stressful situations that *can* be controlled. They appear to lose the ability and motivation to learn to respond in an effective way to painful stimulation.

On the basis of this and other work on the effects of uncontrollable stress, Seligman felt that learned helplessness in animals could provide a model for at least certain forms of human depression. He noted similarities between the manifestations of helplessness observed in laboratory studies of animals and at least some of the symptoms of depression. Like many depressed people the animals appeared passive in the face of stress, failing to initiate action that might allow them to cope. They had difficulty eating or retaining what they ate and lost weight. Further, one of the neurotransmitter chemicals implicated in depression, norepinephrine, was depleted in Seligman's animals (see p. 240).

ATTRIBUTION AND LEARNED HELPLESSNESS After the original research with animals, researchers began to conduct similar studies with humans. By 1978 several inadequacies of the theory and unexplained aspects of depression had become apparent, and a revised version of the learned helplessness model was proposed by Abramson, Seligman, and Teasdale (1978). Some studies with humans, for example, had indicated that helplessness inductions actually led to subsequent facilitation of performance (e.g., see Wortman & Brehm, 1975). In addition, many depressed people hold themselves responsible for their failures. If they regard themselves as helpless, how can they blame themselves? The essence of the revised theory lies in the concept of **attribution**—the explanation a person has for his or her behavior (Weiner et al., 1971)—and in this way it blends cognitive and learning elements. Given a situation in which the individual has experienced failure, he or she will try to attribute the failure to some cause. Table 10.2 applies the Abramson, Seligman, and Teasdale formulation to various ways in which a college student might attribute a low score on the mathematics portion of the Graduate Record Examination (GRE). The formulation is based on answers to three questions: Are the reasons for failure believed to be internal (personal) or external (environmentally caused)? Is the problem believed to be stable or unstable? How global or specific is the inability to succeed perceived to be?

The attributional revision of the helplessness theory postulates that the way in which a person explains failure will determine its subsequent effects. Global attributions ("I never do anything right") increase the generality of the effects of failure; attributions to stable factors ("I never test well") make them long term; attribution of failure to internal characteristics ("I am stupid") is more likely to diminish self-esteem, particularly if the personal fault is also global and persistent.

People become depressed, the theory suggests, when they attribute negative life events to stable and global causes. Whether self-esteem collapses also depends on whether they blame the bad outcome on their own inadequacies. The individual

TABLE 10.2 Attributional Schema of Depression: Why I Failed My GRE Math Exam

| Degree | Internal (Personal) | | External (Environmental) | |
	Stable	Unstable	Stable	Unstable
Global	I lack intelligence.	I am exhausted.	These tests are all unfair.	It's an unlucky day, Friday the thirteenth.
Specific	I lack mathematical ability.	I am fed up with math.	The math tests are unfair.	My math test was numbered "13."

prone to depression is thought to show a "depressive attributional style," a tendency to attribute bad outcomes to personal, global, stable faults of character. When persons with this style (a diathesis) have unhappy, adverse experiences (stressors), they become depressed and their self-esteem is shattered (Peterson & Seligman, 1984).

Where does the depressive attributional style come from? In Chapter 2 we noted that failure to answer such a central question is a problem with most cognitive theories of psychopathology. In general terms the answer to this important question is thought to lie in childhood experiences (a common theme in psychological theories of all kinds), but few data have been collected to support this view. A promising start is the finding that depressive attributional style is related to sexual abuse in childhood as well as to parental overprotectiveness, harsh discipline, and perfectionistic standards (Rose et al., 1994).

Some research gives direct support to the reformulated theory. Seligman and his colleagues (1979) devised the Attributional-Style Questionnaire and as the theory predicted, found that mildly depressed college students did indeed more often attribute failure to personal, global, and persistent inadequacies than did nondepressed students. Metalsky, Halberstadt, and Abramson (1987) conducted a study with college students taking a course in introductory psychology. Early in the semester the students completed the Attributional-Style Questionnaire and a questionnaire pertaining to their grade aspirations. A checklist was used to collect mood information on two occasions before the midterm exam, right after receipt of the exam grades, and again two days later. According to the attributional helplessness theory, a tendency to attribute negative events to global and persistent inadequacies, as determined by the Attributional-Style Questionnaire, should predict a more depressed mood in those students who received a poor grade. A poor grade was defined as a failure to match aspirations; this score was weighted by the importance attached to this negative event by the participants.

The results differed depending on which of the postexam mood assessments was considered. The outcome of the exam was the major determinant of students' initial mood changes; those who did poorly became more depressed. However, two days later, students who had made unstable and specific attributions on the Attributional-Style Questionnaire had recovered, but the stable, global students were still mildly depressed. Following a suggestion by Weiner (1986), Metalsky et al. proposed that a negative event elicits an immediate emotional response that occurs before any attributions are even made. Subsequently, causal interpretations are sought and a pattern of global, stable attributions makes the initial depressive response last longer.

HOPELESSNESS THEORY The latest version of the theory (Abramson, Metalsky, & Alloy, 1989) has moved even further away from the original formulation. Some forms of depression (hopelessness depressions) are now regarded as caused by a state of hopelessness, an expectation that desirable outcomes will not occur or that undesirable ones will occur and that the person has no responses available to change this situation. (The latter part of the definition of hopelessness, of course, refers to helplessness, the central concept of earlier versions of the theory.) As in the attributional reformulation, negative life events (stressors) are seen as interacting with diatheses to yield a state of hopelessness.

One diathesis is the attributional pattern already described—attributing negative events to stable and global factors. However, the theory now considers the possibility that there are other diatheses—low self-esteem and a tendency to infer that negative life events will have severe negative consequences.

Metalsky and his colleagues (1993) conducted the first test of the hopelessness theory in a study similar to his earlier one. Two new features were the direct measurement of hopelessness and the newly proposed diathesis, low self-esteem. As in the earlier study, attributing poor grades to global and stable factors led to more persistent depressed mood. This pattern was found only among students whose self-esteem was low and was mediated by an increase in feelings of hopelessness, thus supporting the theory. A similar study conducted with children in the sixth and seventh grades yielded almost identical results (Robinson, Garber, & Hilsman, 1995). Lewinsohn and his colleagues (1994) also found that depressive attributional style and low self-esteem predicted the onset of depression in adolescents.

An advantage of the hopelessness theory is that it can deal directly with the comorbidity of depression and anxiety disorders. In Chapter 6 we noted that panic disorder, agoraphobia, obsessive-compulsive disorder, and PTSD all occurred frequently with depression. Accounting for this pattern poses a major challenge for many theories, for they deal only with a single diagnosis. Alloy et al. (1990) pointed out several important features of comorbidity. First, cases of anxiety without depression are relatively common, but pure depression is rare.

Second, longitudinal studies reveal that anxiety diagnoses typically precede depression (e.g., Rohde, Lewinsohn, & Seeley, 1991). On the basis of a good deal of prior evidence (e.g., Bowlby, 1980; Mandler, 1972), Alloy and her colleagues proposed that an expectation of helplessness creates anxiety. When the expectation of helplessness becomes certain, a syndrome with elements of both depression and anxiety ensues. Finally, if the perceived probability of the occurrence of negative events becomes certain, hopelessness develops.

ISSUES IN THE HELPLESSNESS/HOPELESSNESS THEORIES

Although these theories are promising, some problems need to be addressed in future work.

1. Which type of depression is being modeled? In his original paper Seligman attempted to document the similarity between learned helplessness and what used to be called reactive depression, depression thought to be brought on by stressful life events. Similarly, Abramson et al. (1989) now talk about a hopelessness depression. Only future research will tell whether these solutions are more than circular statements.

2. Do college-student populations provide good analogues? Although some research on the theories has been done with clinical populations (e.g., Abramson et al., 1978) or has tried to predict the onset of clinical depression, many studies have either examined college students who were selected on the basis of scores on the Beck Depression Inventory (BDI) or have simply tried to predict increases in BDI scores. However, this inventory was not designed to *diagnose* depression, only to allow an assessment of its severity in a clinically diagnosed group. Accumulating evidence indicates that selecting subjects solely on the basis of elevated BDI scores does not yield a group of people who can serve as a good analogue for those with clinical depression. Hammen (1980), for example, found that high scorers, with a mean of 18.37, were down to an average of only 10.87 when retested two to three weeks later. Similarly, the ability of the Attributional-Style Questionnaire to predict BDI scores does not necessarily mean it will do well in predicting the onset of actual clinical depression.

3. Are the findings specific to depression? This issue is raised by the results of a learned helplessness study conducted by Lavelle, Metalsky, and Coyne (1979) with students classified as having high or low test anxiety. The students with high test anxiety performed a task poorly after going through a laboratory situation inducing helplessness. Thus the learned helplessness phenomenon may not be specific to depression. Similarly, the so-called depressive attributional style does not appear to be specific to depression but is related to anxiety as well (Clark, Watson, & Mineka, 1994).

4. Are attributions relevant? At issue here is the underlying assumption that people actively attempt to explain their own behavior to themselves and that the attributions they make have subsequent effects on their behavior. Some research indicates, however, that making attributions is not a process in which everyone engages (Hanusa & Schulz, 1977). Furthermore, in a series of experiments discussed in Chapter 7, Nisbett and Wilson (1977) showed that people are frequently unaware of the causes of their behavior.[1]

    Even if we allow that attributions are relevant and powerful determinants of behavior, we should note that many findings in support of the learned helplessness theory have been gained by giving individuals the Attributional-Style Questionnaire or by determining how they explain laboratory-induced successes or failures. When depressed persons were asked about the five most stressful events of their lives, however, their attributions did not differ from those supplied by normal people (Hammen & Cochran, 1981), and other research shows that the type of dimensional thinking that is forced on people by the Attributional-Style Questionnaire is relatively rare (Anderson et al., 1994).

5. One key assumption of the helplessness/hopelessness theory is that the depressive attributional style is a persistent part of the makeup of depressed people; that is, the depressive attributional style must already be in place when the person encounters some stressor. However, research shows that the depressive attributional style disappears following an episode of depression (Hamilton & Abramson, 1983).

---

[1]The attribution literature makes the basic assumption that people care about what causes their behavior. This central idea is the brainchild of psychologists whose business is to explain behavior. It may be that psychologists have projected their own need to explain behavior onto other people! Laypeople may simply not reflect on why they act and feel as they do to the same extent that psychologists do.

With all its problems, helplessness/hopelessness theory has clearly stimulated a great deal of research and further theorizing about depression. It seems destined to continue to do so for many years to come.

INTERPERSONAL THEORY OF DEPRESSION

In this section we discuss behavioral aspects of depression that generally involve relationships between the depressed person and others. Some of the data we present may be relevant to the etiology of depression, and some to its course.

In Chapter 8 we discussed the role of social support in health. This concept has also been applied to research on depression. Depressed individuals tend to have sparse social networks and to regard them as providing little support. Reduced social support may lessen an individual's ability to handle negative life events and make him or her vulnerable to depression (Billings, Cronkite, & Moos, 1983).

Depressed people may also elicit negative reactions from others (Coyne, 1976). This possibility has been studied in a variety of ways, ranging from conducting telephone conversations with depressed patients, to listening to audiotapes of depressed patients, and even to participating in face-to-face interactions. Data show that the behavior of depressed people elicits rejection from others. For example, the roommates of depressed college students rated social contacts with them as low in enjoyment and reported high levels of aggression toward them; mildly depressed college students were likely to be rejected by their roommates (Joiner, Alfano, & Metalsky, 1989). Not surprisingly given these findings, depression and marital discord frequently co-occur, and the interactions of depressed people and their spouses are characterized by hostility on both sides (Kowalik & Gotlib, 1987). Critical comments of spouses of depressed people are a significant predictor of recurrence of depression (Hooley & Teasdale, 1989). Couples in which one of the partners has a mood disorder report less marital satisfaction than do couples in which neither partner has a history of mood disorder (Beach et al., 1990; Doerfler et al., in press). The relationship between depression and marital discord is explored further in Chapter 19.

Is it simply fate that confronts the depressive person with an inadequate level of social support and rejection by others? Perhaps, but it is also possible that the depressed person plays a role. Several studies have demonstrated that depressed people are low in social skills across a variety of measures—interpersonal problem solving (Gotlib & Asarnow, 1979), speech patterns (speaking very slowly, with silences and hesitations, and more negative self-disclosures), and maintenance of eye contact (Gotlib, 1982; Gotlib & Robinson, 1982). In a longitudinal study of unipolar depressives, Hammen (1991) confirmed that they experience much stress (particularly of an interpersonal nature) and that their own behavior contributes to the high levels of stress that they experience. As an example, Hammen describes the stressors experienced by one woman with unipolar depression in a one-year period:

> [She] had a car accident in which her knee was injured, failed a civil service exam that would have opened job opportunities, moved out of her home after conflict with her husband, had a serious argument with her daughter who remained with the father, divorced the husband, and got into a fight with her ex-husband over her new boyfriend. (p. 559)

Related to this general concept of a social-skills deficit, but somewhat more specific, is the idea that the constant seeking of reassurance is the critical variable in depression (Joiner, 1995; Joiner & Metalsky, 1995). Perhaps as a result of being reared in a cold and rejecting environment (Carnelly, Pietomonaco, & Jaffe, 1994), depressed people seek reassurance that others truly care, but even when reassured they are only temporarily satisfied. Their negative self-concept causes them to doubt the truth of the feedback they have received. Later, they actually seek out negative feedback, which, in a sense, validates their negative self-concept. Rejection ultimately occurs because of the depressed person's inconsistent behavior. Data collected by Joiner and Metalsky on mildly depressed college students have shown that this inconsistent pattern in seeking reassurance predicts increases in depressed mood.

Do any of these interpersonal characteristics of depressed people precede the onset of depression, suggesting a causal relationship? Some research using the high-risk method suggests that the answer is yes. For example, the behavior of elementary-school-age children of depressed parents was rated negatively by both peers and teachers (Weintraub, Liebert, & Neale, 1975; Weintraub, Prinz, & Neale, 1978); low social competence predicted the onset of depression among elementary-school-age children (Cole et al., 1996); and poor interpersonal problem-solving skills predicted increases in depression among adolescents (Davila et al., 1995). Thus social-skills deficits may be a cause of depression as well as a consequence of it. Interpersonal behavior plays a major role in depression.

PSYCHOLOGICAL THEORIES OF BIPOLAR DISORDER

Bipolar disorder has been neglected by psychological theorists and researchers. Theories of the depressive phase of the disorder are similar to theories of unipolar depression. The manic phase of the disorder is seen as a defense against a debilitating psychological state. The specific negative state that is being avoided varies from theory to theory. One of our own cases illustrates why many theorists have concluded that the manic state serves a protective function.

A forty-two-year-old man was experiencing his third manic episode. During each episode he had exhibited the classic pattern of manic symptoms, and much of his manic behavior centered on a grandiose delusion that he was the world's greatest businessman. "Did you know that I've already bought twenty companies today?" he stated at the beginning of a therapy session. "Not even Getty or Rockefeller has anything on me." From sessions between episodes it was apparent that success in business was indeed a central concern to the patient. But he was far from successful. His parents had lent him money to start several companies, but each had gone bankrupt. He was obsessed with matching the business successes of his wealthy father, but as the years passed his opportunities to do so were slipping away. It seemed, therefore, that his manic grandiosity was protecting him from a confrontation with his lack of business success—a realization that would likely have plunged him into a deep depression.

Clinical experience with manic patients as well as studies of their personalities when they are in remission indicate that they appear relatively well-adjusted between episodes. But if mania is a defense, it must be a defense against something, suggesting that the apparently good adjustment of manic people between episodes may not be an accurate reflection of their true state. In an attempt to bypass what may be defensive responding, Winters and Neale (1985) used a specially developed test to examine the notion that manic individuals, even when between episodes, have low self-esteem.

Bipolar patients in remission, unipolar depressive patients, and normal people were given two tests, a self-esteem inventory and a specially constructed memory test. The second test was meant to be a subtle measure of the manic patients' expected low self-esteem. In the memory test participants first read a paragraph describing a series of events, some of which had a positive outcome, others a negative outcome. They were then given a test that appeared to measure their recall of each story. Some items actually assessed recall of facts, but others forced the participants to go beyond the information and draw inferences. For example, one story concerned a man who was currently out of work. The reason for his unemployment was not stated directly, but the story was constructed to allow either of two inferences to be drawn. Participants could infer that the man was unemployed through no fault of his own but because the economy was poor, or that the man's poor work record kept him unemployed. People with low self-esteem were expected to make the second inference.

The results agreed exactly with expectation. On the paper-and-pencil measure of self-esteem, both manic and normal participants scored higher than did those with depression. But on the memory test the manic individuals performed similarly to the depressed participants; both groups drew the inferences that revealed low self-esteem. Thus the self-esteem of manic individuals may be very low. Generally, however, they successfully defend against their feelings of inadequacy without becoming manic.

BIOLOGICAL THEORIES OF MOOD DISORDERS

Since biological processes are known to have considerable effects on moods, it is not surprising that investigators have sought biological causes for depression and mania. Disturbed biological processes must be part of the causal chain if a predisposition for a mood disorder can be genetically transmitted, and evidence that a predisposition for a mood disorder is heritable would provide some support for the view that the disorder has a biological basis. The effectiveness of drug therapies, which increase the levels of certain neurotransmitters, in the treatment of mood disorders also suggests that biological factors are important. In this section we will look at some of the research in the areas of genetics, neurochemistry, and the neuroendocrine system. (There is also a growing literature on structural abnormalities of the brains of patients with mood disorders. Because these abnormalities are similar to those found in schizophrenia, we will discuss them in the next chapter, on page 280.)

THE GENETIC DATA

Research on genetic factors in unipolar depression and bipolar disorder has used the family, twin, and adoption methods discussed in Chapter 2. About 10 to 25 percent of the first-degree relatives of bipolar patients also have experienced an episode of mood disorder (Gershon, 1990). The risk is higher among the relatives of those with early onset of the disorder. These figures are higher than those for the general population. Curiously, among the first-degree relatives of bipolar probands, there are more cases of unipolar depression than of bipolar disorder. For example, James and Chapman (1975) found that the risk estimates for the first-degree relatives of bipolar patients was 6.4 percent for bipolar disorder and 13.2 percent for unipolar depression. Overall, the concordance rate for bipolar disorder in identical twins is about 72 percent and in fraternal twins about 14 percent (Allen, 1976). The evidence thus supports the notion that bipolar disorder has a heritable component.

The information available on unipolar depression indicates that genetic factors, although influential, are not as decisive as they are in bipolar disorder. For example, in one study of depressed individuals relatives were at only slightly higher than normal risk (Kendler et al., 1993). Furthermore, although the relatives of unipolar probands are at somewhat increased risk for unipolar depression, their risk for unipolar depression is less than that among relatives of bipolar probands (Andreasen et al., 1987). Early onset of depression and comorbidity with an anxiety disorder or alcoholism confer greater risk on the relatives (Goldstein et al., 1994; Weissman et al., 1988). A recent study of unipolar depression in twins reported monozygotic concordance of about 46 percent and dizygotic concordance (for same-sex twins) of 20 percent (McGuffin et al., 1996). Several small-scale adoption studies have also supported the idea that both bipolar and unipolar disorder have a heritable component (Cadoret, 1978a; Mendlewicz & Rainer, 1977; Wender et al., 1986).

A recent development in genetic research on mood disorders is the use of what is called **linkage analysis**. The technique involves studying the occurrence of mood disorders over several generations in a family and simultaneously assessing some other characteristic—a genetic marker—for which the genetics are fully understood (e.g., red-green color blindness is known to result from mutations on the X chromosome). When the genes for mood disorder and the genetic marker are linked, that is, when they are sufficiently close together on a chromosome, the family pedigree tends to show that the two traits being examined are inherited together. In a widely reported linkage study of the Old Order Amish, Egeland and her colleagues (1987) found evidence favoring the hypothesis that bipolar disorder results from a dominant gene on

the eleventh chromosome. However, attempts to replicate the Egeland study as well as other apparently successful linkage studies have had mixed success (e.g., Berrittini et al., 1990; Smyth et al., 1996). Research on linkage continues and has broadened to focus on other genes on other chromosomes.

NEUROCHEMISTRY AND MOOD DISORDERS

Over the past several decades researchers have sought to understand the role played by neurotransmitters in mood disorders. Two neurotransmitters have been most studied: norepinephrine and serotonin. The theory involving norepinephrine is most relevant to bipolar disorder and posits that a low level of norepinephrine leads to depression and a high level to mania. The serotonin theory suggests that a low level of serotonin produces depression.

The actions of drugs used to treat depression provided the clues on which both theories are based. In the 1950s two groups of drugs, tricyclics and monoamine oxidase inhibitors, were found effective in relieving depression. **Tricyclic drugs** are a group of antidepressant medications so named because their molecular structure is characterized by three fused rings. They prevent some of the reuptake of both norepinephrine and serotonin by the presynaptic neuron after it has fired, leaving more of the neurotransmitter in the synapse so that transmission of the next nerve impulse is made easier (see Fig. 10.3). **Monoamine oxidase inhibitors** are a group of antidepressant drugs that keep the enzyme monoamine oxidase from deactivating neurotransmitters, thus increasing the levels of both serotonin and norepinephrine; this action produces the same facilitating effect described for tricylics. These drug actions suggest that depression and mania are related to serotonin and norepinephrine. Newer antidepressant drugs such as fluoxetine (Prozac) act more selectively than the older ones, specifically inhibiting the reuptake of serotonin. Because these drugs are effective in treating unipolar depression, a stronger link has been shown between low levels of serotonin and depression.

Two main approaches have been used to evaluate the theories further. The first measures *metabolites* of these neurotransmitters, the by-products of the breakdown of serotonin and norepinephrine as they are found in urine, blood serum, and the cerebrospinal fluid. The problem with such measurements is that they are not direct reflections of levels of either serotonin or norepinephrine in the brain,

Presynaptic
neuron

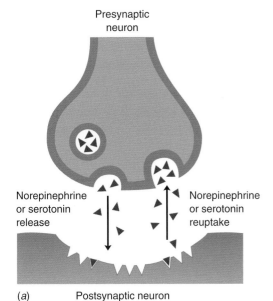

Norepinephrine
or serotonin
release

Norepinephrine
or serotonin
reuptake

(a)   Postsynaptic neuron

Presynaptic
neuron

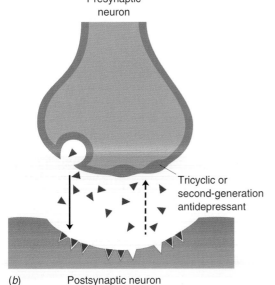

Tricyclic or
second-generation
antidepressant

(b)   Postsynaptic neuron

Figure 10.3   *(a)* When a neuron releases norepinephrine or serotonin from its endings, a pumplike reuptake mechanism immediately begins to recapture some of the neurotransmitter molecules before they are received by the postsynaptic (receptor) neuron. *(b)* Tricyclic drugs block this reuptake process, enabling more norepinephrine or serotonin to reach, and thus fire, the postsynaptic (receptor) neuron. Serotonin reuptake inhibitors act more selectively on serotonin. (Adapted from Snyder, 1986, p. 106.)

increase or to decrease the brain levels of serotonin and norepinephrine. A drug raising the level of serotonin should alleviate depression; one reducing it should deepen depression or induce it in normal subjects. Similarly, a drug that increases norepinephrine might induce a manic episode. This strategy also has its problems, however. Most drugs have multiple effects, making it difficult to choose one that accomplishes a specific purpose without complicating side effects.

These problems notwithstanding, what can be said of the validity of these theories that implicate low levels of norepinephrine or serotonin in depression and high levels of norepinephrine in mania? First, a series of studies conducted by Bunney and Murphy and their colleagues at the National Institute of Mental Health monitored closely the urinary levels of norepinephrine in a group of bipolar patients as they cycled through stages of depression, mania, and normalcy. Urinary levels of norepinephrine decreased as patients became depressed (Bunney et al., 1970) and increased during mania (Bunney, Goodwin, & Murphy, 1972). A problem in interpreting these data is that such changes could result from increases in activity level (increased motor activity in mania can increase norepinephrine activity). Nonetheless, there is evidence that increasing norepinephrine levels can precipitate a manic episode in bipolar patients (Altshular et al., 1995).

The principal metabolite of norepinephrine is 3-methoxy-4-hydroxyphenyl glycol (MHPG). According to the theory, low levels of norepinephrine should be reflected in low levels of MHPG. As expected, depressed bipolar patients have generally been shown to have low levels of urinary MHPG (e.g., Muscettola et al., 1984); further, MHPG levels are higher during a manic than a depressed episode and higher in manic patients than in normal people (Goodwin & Jamison, 1990). As with the studies which directly measured norepinephrine, however, the MHPG results could reflect differences in activity levels.

Studies of serotonin have examined its major metabolite, 5-hydroxyindoleacetic acid (5-HIAA). A fairly consistent body of data indicates that 5-HIAA levels are low in the cerebrospinal fluid of depressed patients (see McNeal & Cimbolic, 1986, for a review). Studies also show that ingestion of L-tryptophan, from which serotonin is subsequently produced, is somewhat effective as a treatment for depression, especially when used in combination with other drugs (Coppen et al., 1972; Mendels et al., 1975). Furthermore, a drug that suppresses serotonin synthesis reduces the therapeutic effect of drugs that usually lessen depression (Shopsin,

since the majority of the neurons that use serotonin are found in the intestines and norepinephrine is also an important neurotransmitter in the peripheral nervous system.

A second strategy is to choose drugs other than the antidepressants that are known either to

Friedman, & Gershon, 1976). Delgado et al. (1988) used a special diet to reduce the level of serotonin in remitted depressed patients by lowering the level of its precursor, tryptophan. They found that 67 percent of patients experienced a return of their symptoms. When their normal diet was resumed a gradual remission followed. Similar results have been found in patients with seasonal depression (Lam et al., 1996). A recent study used this same tryptophan-depletion strategy in normals who had either a positive or a negative family history of depression. Again, as predicted by the low-serotonin theory, those with a positive family history experienced an increase in depressed mood (Benkelfat et al., 1994).

We have indicated that effective antidepressants increase levels of norepinephrine and serotonin and that knowledge of this formed a keystone of the norepinephrine and serotonin theories of depression. It now appears that the explanation of why these drugs work is not as straightforward as it seemed at first; the therapeutic effects of tricyclics and monoamine oxidase inhibitors do *not* depend *solely* on an increase in levels of neurotransmitters. The earlier findings were correct—tricyclics and monoamine oxidase inhibitors do indeed increase levels of norepinephrine and serotonin *when they are first taken*—but after several days the neurotransmitters return to their earlier levels. This information is crucial because it does not fit with data on how much time must pass before antidepressants become effective. Both tricyclics and monoamine oxidase inhibitors take from seven to fourteen days to relieve depression! By that time the neurotransmitter level has already returned to its previous state. It would seem, then, that a simple increase in norepinephrine or serotonin is not a sufficient explanation for why the drugs alleviate depression.

Another key finding that has prompted a move away from the original theories of a simple increase in serotonin and norepinephrine levels comes from studies of new antidepressants. For example, mianserin is an effective antidepressant (Cole, 1986), yet it does not merely increase the amount of norepinephrine or serotonin.

What is the impact of these new findings on the old theories? Researchers are now examining whether tricyclics and monoamine oxidase inhibitors act against depression by altering postsynaptic receptors. Unfortunately, results are contradictory and difficult to interpret. Antidepressants seem to decrease the sensitivity of ß-adrenergic receptors yet increase the sensitivity of serotonin receptors (McNeal & Cimbolic, 1986). This attention to receptors means that new methodologies must be developed to study receptor sensitivity in human beings. Most of our current knowledge of the func-

tioning of receptors was obtained from animal studies. The methods used in human studies have so far been indirect. The next few years of research will undoubtedly see further refinements so that receptor functions can be more thoroughly explored.

Research on bipolar disorder is also moving away from the older norepinephrine theory. One of the major reasons for this shift is that lithium, the most widely used and effective treatment for bipolar disorder, is useful in treating both the manic and the depressive episodes of the disorder, suggesting that it acts by affecting some neurochemical that can either increase or decrease neural activity. Current research is focusing on G-proteins (guanine nucleotide-binding proteins), which are found in postsynaptic cell membranes. They carry information from the presynaptic cell across the postsynaptic cell membrane and amplify the neural signal. High levels of G-proteins have been found in patients with mania, suggesting that the therapeutic effects of lithium may well result from its ability to regulate G-proteins (Manji et al., 1995).

THE NEUROENDOCRINE SYSTEM

The neuroendocrine system may also play a role in depression. The limbic area of the brain is closely linked to emotion and also has effects on the hypothalamus. The hypothalamus in turn controls various endocrine glands and thus the levels of hormones they secrete. Hormones secreted by the hypothalamus also affect the pituitary gland and the hormones it produces. Because of its relevance to the so-called vegetative symptoms of depression, such as disturbances in appetite and sleep, the hypothalamic–pituitary–adrenocortical axis is thought to be overactive in depression.

Various findings support this proposition. Levels of cortisol (an adrenocortical hormone) are high in depressed patients, perhaps because of oversecretion of thyrotropin-releasing hormone by the hypothalamus (Garbutt et al., 1994). The excess secretion of cortisol in depressive persons also causes enlargement of their adrenal glands (Rubun et al., 1995). These high levels of cortisol have even led to the development of a biological test for depression—the dexamethasone suppression test (DST). Dexamethasone suppresses cortisol secretion. When given dexamethasone during an overnight test, some depressed patients, especially those with melancholia, did not experience cortisol suppression (Carroll, 1982). The interpretation is that the failure of dexamethasone to suppress cortisol reflects overactivity in the hypothalamic–pituitary–adrenocortical axis of depressed patients. The failure to show suppression normalizes when the depressive episode ends, indicating that it might be a nonspecific response to stress. Research on a disease called Cushing's syndrome also has linked high levels of cortisol to depression. Abnormal growths on the adrenal cortex lead to oversecretion of cortisol and an ensuing depression. The oversecretion of cortisol in depression may also be associated with the neurotransmitter theories discussed earlier. High levels of cortisol may lower the density of serotonin receptors (Roy et al., 1987) and impair the function of noradrenergic receptors (Price et al., 1986). Finally, the hypothalamic–pituitary–thyroid axis is of possible relevance to bipolar disorder. Disorders of thyroid function are often seen in bipolar patients (Lipowski et al., 1994), and thyroid hormones can induce mania in these patients (Goodwin & Jamison, 1990).

All these data lend some support to theories that mood disorders have biological causes. Does this mean that psychological theories are irrelevant or useless? Not in the least. To assert that behavioral disorders have a basis in biological processes is to state the obvious. No psychogenic theorist would deny that behavior is mediated by some kind of bodily changes. The biological and psychological theories may well be describing the same phenomena, but in different terms (such as learned helplessness versus low serotonin). They should be thought of as complementary, not incompatible.

THERAPIES FOR MOOD DISORDERS

Most episodes of depression lift after a few months, although the time may seem immeasurably longer to the depressed individual and to those close to him or her. That most depressions are self-limiting is fortunate. However, depression is too widespread and too incapacitating, both to the sufferer and to those around him or her, simply to wait for the disorder to go away untreated. Bouts of depression tend to recur (Keller et al., 1982), and as we will see in the last section of this chapter, suicide is a risk for people who are depressed. Thus it is important to treat major depression as well as bipolar disorder. Current therapies are both psychological and biological. Singly or in combination they are somewhat effective.

PSYCHOLOGICAL THERAPIES

PSYCHODYNAMIC THERAPIES

Because depression is considered to be derived from a repressed sense of loss and from anger unconsciously turned inward, psychoanalytic treatment tries to help the patient achieve insight into the repressed conflict and often encourages outward release of the hostility supposedly directed inward. In the most general terms the goal of psychoanalytic therapy is to uncover latent motivations for the patient's depression. A person may, for example, blame himself or herself for his or her parents' lack of affection, but repress this belief because of the anger and pain it causes. The therapist must first guide the patient to confront the fact that he or she feels this way and then help the patient realize that the guilt is unfounded. The recovery of memories of stressful circumstances of the patient's childhood, at which time feelings of inadequacy and loss may have developed, should also bring relief.

Research on the effectiveness of dynamic psychotherapy in alleviating depression is sparse (Craighead, Evans, & Robins, 1992; Klerman, 1988) and characterized by mixed results, in part owing to the high degree of variability among approaches that come under the rubric of psychodynamic or psychoanalytic psychotherapy. For example, early studies found that psychoanalytic therapy combined with tricyclic drugs did not lift mood any more than did the drugs by themselves (Covi et al., 1974; Daneman, 1961). A recent report from the American Psychiatric Association concludes that there are no controlled data attesting to the efficacy of long-term dynamic psychotherapy or psychoanalysis in treating depression (American Psychiatric Association, 1993). However, findings from a well-known large-scale study (Elkin et al., 1989) suggest that a form of psychodynamic therapy that concentrates on present-day interactions between the depressed person and the social environment—Klerman and Weissman's interpersonal therapy (IPT) (Klerman et al., 1984)—is somewhat effective for alleviating unipolar depression as well as for maintaining treatment gains (Frank et al., 1990). The core of the therapy is to help the depressed patient examine the ways in which his or her current interpersonal behavior might interfere with obtaining pleasure from relationships. For example, the patient might be taught how to improve communication with others to meet his or her needs better and to have more satisfying social interactions and support. Additional information on interpersonal therapy is provided in the detailed discussion of the Elkin (1989) study in Chapter 18.

COGNITIVE AND BEHAVIOR THERAPIES

In keeping with their cognitive theory of depression, that the profound sadness and shattered self-esteem of depressed individuals are caused by errors in their thinking, Beck and his associates devised a cognitive therapy aimed at altering maladaptive thought patterns. The therapist tries to persuade the depressed person to change his or her opinions of events and of the self. When a client states that he or she is worthless because "Nothing goes right. Everything I try to do ends in a disaster," the therapist offers examples contrary to this overgeneralization, such as citing abilities that the client is either overlooking or discounting. The therapist also instructs the patient to monitor private monologues and to identify all patterns of thought that contribute to depression. The therapist then teaches the patient to think through negative prevailing beliefs to understand how they prevent making more realistic and positive assumptions.

Although developed independently of Ellis's rational-emotive method described in Chapter 2, Beck's analyses are similar to it in some ways. For example, Beck suggests that depressed people are likely to consider themselves totally inept and incompetent if they make a mistake. This schema can be considered an extension of one of Ellis's irrational beliefs, that the individual must be competent in all things in order to be a worthwhile person.

Beck also includes behavioral components in his treatment of depression. Particularly when patients are severely depressed Beck encourages them to *do* things, such as get out of bed in the morning or go for a walk. He gives his patients activity assignments that will provide them with successful experiences and allow them to think well of themselves. But the overall emphasis is on cognitive restructuring, on persuading the person to think differently. If a change in overt behavior will help in achieving that goal, fine. Behavioral change by itself, however, without altering the negative beliefs and errors in logic that Beck asserts depressed people commit, cannot be expected to alleviate depression in any significant way.

Over the past two decades considerable research has been conducted on Beck's therapy, beginning with a widely cited study by Rush et al. (1977), which indicated that cognitive therapy was more successful than the tricyclic imipramine (Tofranil) in alleviating unipolar depression. The unusually low improvement rate found for the drug in this clinical trial suggests that these patients might have been poorly suited for pharmacotherapy—and that therefore this was not a fair comparison. Nonetheless, the efficacy of Beck's therapy in this study and in a twelve-month follow-up (Kovacs et al., 1981) encouraged many other researchers to conduct additional evaluations, which have confirmed its efficacy (e.g., Hollon et al., 1989; Seligman et al., 1988; Simons et al., 1985; Teasdale et al., 1984),

including data showing that Beck's therapy has a prophylactic effect in preventing subsequent bouts of depression (Blackburn, Eunson, & Bishop, 1986; Evans et al., 1993; Hollon, DeRubeis, & Seligman, 1993).

When we review in detail the large, multisite study comparing cognitive therapy with psychodynamic interpersonal therapy and imipramine drug therapy, we will see that although cognitive therapy fares well, it does not appear to be superior to imipramine or interpersonal therapy; in some ways it is less effective.

Since a key feature of depression is a lack of satisfying experiences with other people, behavioral treatments have also focused on helping the patient improve social interactions. Although there are cognitive components in these approaches—for example, encouraging the depressed patient not to evaluate his or her performance too harshly—evidence supports the effectiveness of a focus on enhancing overt social behaviors by such techniques as assertion and social-skills training (Hersen et al., 1984; Lewinsohn, 1974; Teri & Lewinsohn, 1986). Also, as we describe in the discussion of couples therapy (p. 569), improvement in the kinds of interpersonal conflicts found in a distressed marriage or other intimate relationship also alleviates depression (Jacobson, Holzworth-Monroe, & Schmaling, 1989; O'Leary & Beach, 1990).

Psychological therapies alone also show promise in dealing with many of the interpersonal, cognitive, and emotional problems of bipolar patients. For example, if a patient in a manic phase commits such indiscretions as having an extramarital affair or spending everything in the family bank account, the consequences of these behaviors last much longer than improvements in mood brought about by lithium. Stress is likely to be higher as a result, and stress can trigger a subsequent mood swing. Basco and Rush (1996) have recently published details of a cognitive-behavioral intervention targeted at the thoughts and interpersonal behaviors that go awry during wide mood swings, and preliminary findings of its effectiveness are encouraging.

Determining the best therapy for each individual can be a challenge. For instance, a woman who is disheartened because of the way she is treated by men might be better advised by a feminist therapist, who will encourage her to resist continued subjugation by an overbearing spouse or boss, than by an equally well-intentioned cognitive therapist, who might try to teach her that the treatment she receives from husband or supervisor is not all that bad.

Finally, as with all forms of therapy for a wide range of human problems, the therapist must con-

FOCUS 10.2   AN EXISTENTIAL THEORY OF DEPRESSION AND ITS TREATMENT

In 1959 a remarkable book, *From Death Camp to Existentialism*, was published by Viktor Frankl, an Austrian psychiatrist who spent three horrible years in Nazi concentration camps during World War II. His wife, brother, and parents, imprisoned with him, all lost their lives. Revised since its initial appearance and retitled *Man's Search for Meaning* (1963), Frankl's book vividly describes the humiliation, suffering, and terror experienced by camp prisoners. Frankl tells how he and others managed to survive psychologically in the brutalizing conditions of the death camps.

Frankl concluded that he was sustained emotionally by having succeeded somehow in finding meaning in his suffering and relating it to his spiritual life. The spirit gives the individual freedom to transcend circumstances, and freedom makes the individual responsible for his or her life. Frankl believes that psychopathology, particularly depression, ensues when a person has no purpose in living. From his concentration camp experiences he developed a psychotherapeutic approach called **logotherapy**, after the Greek word *logos*, "meaning."

The task of logotherapy is to restore meaning to the client's life. This is accomplished first by accepting in an empathic way the subjective experience of the client's suffering, rather than conveying the message that suffering is sick and wrong and should therefore not be regarded as normal. The logotherapist then helps the client make some sense out of his or her suffering by placing it within a larger context, a philosophy of life in which the individual assumes responsibility for his or her existence and for pursuing the values inherent in life. As Nietzsche wrote, "He who has a why to live for can bear with almost any how."

It may be useful to relate Frankl's views on depression and its treatment to learned helplessness, for certainly the concentration camp induced helplessness and hopelessness, an utter disbelief that an individual could exert any control over his or her life, and profound depression was commonplace. Logotherapy might be an effective way to reverse the helplessness depressed people experience in contemporary society, under less horrific and brutal conditions. By accepting responsibility for their lives and by seeking some meaning even in trying circumstances, they may achieve a sense of control and competence indispensable for forging an acceptable existence.

---

front the moral and political implications of his or her work, and we shall turn to some of these issues in the last section of this chapter. Should I help the client alter his or her life situation, or should I help the client adjust? Indeed, the very fact that a person is depressed may indicate that he or she is ready for a change in social and personal relations with others (see Focus 10.2).

BIOLOGICAL THERAPIES

There are a variety of biological therapies for depression and mania. The two most common are electroconvulsive shock and various drugs.

ELECTROCONVULSIVE THERAPY

Perhaps the most dramatic, and controversial, treatment for severe depression is **electroconvulsive therapy** (ECT). ECT was originated by two Italian physicians, Cerletti and Bini, in the early twentieth century. Cerletti was interested in epilepsy and was seeking a means by which its seizures could be experimentally induced. The solution became apparent to him during a visit to a slaughterhouse, where he saw animals rendered unconscious by

Electroconvulsive therapy (ECT) is an effective treatment for depression. Using unilateral shock, anesthetics, and muscle relaxants has reduced its undesirable side effects.

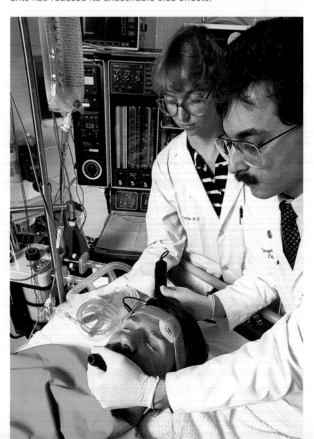

electric shocks administered to the head. Shortly thereafter he found that by applying electric shocks to the sides of the human head, he could produce full epileptic seizures. Then, in Rome in 1938, he used the technique on a schizophrenic patient.

In the decades that followed, ECT was administered to both schizophrenic and severely depressed patients, usually in hospital settings. For the most part its use today is restricted to profoundly depressed individuals. ECT entails the deliberate induction of a seizure and momentary unconsciousness by passing a current of between 70 and 130 volts through the patient's brain. Electrodes were formerly placed on each side of the forehead, allowing the current to pass through both hemispheres, a method known as **bilateral ECT**. Today **unilateral ECT**, in which the current passes through the nondominant (right) cerebral hemisphere only (e.g., Abrams, Swartz, & Vedak, 1991), is more commonly used. In the past the patient was usually awake until the current triggered the seizure and the electric shock often created frightening contortions of the body, sometimes even causing bone fractures. Now the patient is given a short-acting anesthetic, then an injection of a strong muscle relaxant before the current is applied. The convulsive spasms of the body muscles are barely perceptible to onlookers, and the patient awakens a few minutes later remembering nothing about the treatment. The mechanism through which ECT works is unknown. It generally reduces metabolic activity and blood circulation to the brain and may thus inhibit some aberrant brain activity.

Inducing a seizure is still a drastic procedure. Why should anyone in his or her right but depressed mind agree to undergo such radical therapy? How could a parent or a spouse consent to such treatment for a patient judged legally incapable of giving consent? The answer is simple. Although we don't know why, ECT may be the optimal treatment for severe depression (Klerman, 1988). Most professionals acknowledge the risks involved—confusion and memory loss that can be prolonged; however, unilateral ECT to the nondominant hemisphere erases fewer memories than did bilateral ECT, and no detectable changes in brain structure result (Devanand et al., 1994). Clinicians typically resort to ECT only when the depression is unremitting and after less drastic treatments have been tried and found wanting. In considering *any* treatment that has negative side effects, the person making the decision must be aware of the consequences of not providing any treatment at all. Given that suicide is a real possibility among depressed people and given a moral stance that values the preservation of life, the use of ECT, at least after other treatments have failed, is regarded by many as defensible and responsible.

DRUG THERAPY

Drugs are the most commonly used treatments—biological or otherwise—for mood disorders. They do not work for all people, however, and side effects are sometimes serious (see Table 10.3). Determination of proper dosages can also be tricky.

In our earlier discussion of biological research on depression we mentioned three major categories of antidepressant drugs: (1) tricyclics, such as imipramine (Tofranil) and amitriptyline (Elavil); (2) selective serotonin reuptake inhibitors, such as fluoxetine (Prozac); and (3) monoamine oxidase (MAO) inhibitors, such as Parnate. Since the MAO inhibitors have by far the more serious side effects, the other two classes of drugs are more widely used. These medications have been established as effective in a number of double-blind studies with a success rate of 65 to 70 percent among patients who complete a course of treatment (Depression Guideline

TABLE 10.3 Drugs for Treating Mood Disorders

Category	Generic Name	Trade Name	Side Effects
Tricyclic antidepressants	Imipramine Amitriptyline	Tofranil Elavil	Heart attack, stroke, hypotension, blurred vision, anxiety, tiredness, dry mouth, constipation, gastric disorders, erectile failure, weight gain
MAO inhibitors	Tranylcypromine	Parnate	Possibly fatal hypertension, dry mouth, dizziness, nausea, headaches
Selective serotonin reuptake inhibitors	Fluoxetine	Prozac	Nervousness, fatigue, gastrointestinal complaints, dizziness, headaches, insomnia
Lithium	Lithium	Lithium	Tremors, gastric distress, lack of coordination, dizziness, cardiac arrhythmia, blurred vision, fatigue

Panel, 1993). All three types of drugs are believed to work by facilitating neural transmission.

Although the various antidepressants hasten a patient's recovery from an episode of depression, relapse is still common after the drugs are withdrawn. Continuing to take imipramine after remission is of value in preventing recurrence—provided that maintenance doses are as high as the effective treatment doses (instead of lower, as is usually the case) and that the patient was involved during the drug therapy in a psychological treatment, such as Klerman and Weissman's interpersonal therapy (Frank et al., 1990). Antidepressant medication can be and often is used in combination with some kind of psychotherapy. If, for example, a person's depression is (partly) caused by lack of personal satisfaction because of problems or deficits in social skills, it is probably essential for the drug treatment to be supplemented by psychosocial attention to those behavioral deficits (Klerman, 1988, 1990; Weissman et al., 1974). However, the research literature provides no clear answers on the merits of combined treatment (Persons et al., 1996).

Even if a chemical agent manages to alleviate a bout of depression only temporarily, that benefit in itself should not be underestimated given the potential for suicide in depression and given the extreme anguish and suffering borne by the individual and usually by his or her family as well. The judicious use of a drug may make unnecessary an avenue of intervention and control that many regard as very much a last resort, namely, being placed in a mental hospital.

Although some studies suggest that antidepressants should always be used for severely depressed patients, others suggest that cognitive or interpersonal therapy is just as effective, with the added benefit of no drug-produced side effects or relapse when medication is withdrawn (Hollon et al., 1992; Persons, Thase, & Crits-Christoph, 1996). A major controversy on this point is addressed in the discussion in Chapter 18 of the milestone study by Elkin et al.

People with the mood swings of bipolar disorder are often helped by carefully monitored dosages of lithium, an element, taken in a salt form, **lithium carbonate**. Up to 80 percent of bipolar patients experience at least some benefit from taking this drug (Prien & Potter, 1993). Lithium is effective for bipolar patients when they are depressed as well as when they are manic, and it is much more effective for bipolar patients than for unipolar patients—another bit of evidence that these two mood disorders are basically different from each other. Because the effects of lithium occur gradually, therapy typi-

cally begins with both lithium and an antipsychotic such as Haldol, which has an immediate calming effect. Although several hypotheses concerning how lithium works are being pursued (recall our earlier discussion of the effects of lithium on G-proteins, p. 242), conclusive evidence is not yet available.

Because of possibly serious, even fatal, side effects, lithium has to be prescribed and used very carefully. Although it has great value in the elimination of a manic episode, discontinuation of lithium actually increases a person's risk for recurrence (Suppes et al., 1991); thus it is recommended that lithium be used continually.

Two drugs originally used to control seizures offer promise of helping patients with bipolar disorder. Carbamazapine and divalproex sodium (Depakote) are both effective treatments and are tolerated by some patients who are unable to withstand Lithium's side effects (Small et al., 1991).

Although lithium is the treatment of choice for bipolar disorder, the psychological aspects of the disorder also need to be considered, if only to encourage the person to continue taking the medication (Goodwin & Jamison, 1990). A friend of one of the authors put it this way (paraphrased): "Lithium cuts out the highs as well as the lows. I don't miss the lows, but I gotta admit that there were some aspects of the highs that I do miss. It took me a while to accept that I had to give up those highs. Wanting to keep my job and my marriage helped!" A drug alone does not address this kind of concern. For this reason, there is increasing recognition of the importance of psychological interventions in bipolar disorder, usually in combination with lithium. Like any medication, lithium does no good if the patient does not take the prescribed dosage faithfully. Adherence is a major problem; upwards of 40 percent of bipolar patients do not comply with treatment and many drop out of treatment altogether (Basco & Rush, 1996). Psychotherapy of various kinds seems to enhance compliance and thereby increase treatment effectiveness (e.g., Wulsin, Bachop, & Hoffman, 1988).

DEPRESSION IN CHILDHOOD AND ADOLESCENCE

Before ending our discussion of the mood disorders, we shall turn our attention to childhood and adolescence. Considering our typical image of children as happy-go-lucky, it is distressing to observe that major depression and dysthymia occur in children and adolescents as well as in adults. DSM-IV includes mood disorders in children under the adult criteria, while allowing for age-specific features such as irritability and aggressive behavior instead of or in addition to depressed mood.

SYMPTOMS AND PREVALENCE OF CHILDHOOD AND ADOLESCENT DEPRESSION

There are similarities and differences in the symptomatology of children and adults with major depression (Mitchell et al., 1988). Children and adolescents ages seven to seventeen resemble adults in depressed mood, inability to experience pleasure, fatigue, concentration problems, and suicidal ideation. Symptoms that differ are higher rates of suicide attempts and guilt among children and adolescents and more frequent waking up early in the morning, loss of appetite, weight loss, and early morning depression among adults. Cognitive research with depressed children indicates that their outlooks (schemata) are more negative than those of nondepressed children and resemble those of depressed adults (Prieto, Cole, & Tageson, 1992). Such findings provide a possibly useful connection between childhood depression and Beck's theory and research on depressed adults.

As with adults, depression in children is recurrent. Longitudinal studies have demonstrated that both children and adolescents with major depression are likely to continue to exhibit significant depressive symptoms when assessed even four to eight years later (Garber et al., 1988; Hammen et al., 1990; McGee & Williams, 1988).

Estimates of the prevalence of childhood depression vary depending on the age of the child, the country being studied, the type of samples (community based or clinic referred), and the diagnostic criteria (Nottelmann & Jensen, 1995). In general depression occurs in less than 1 percent of preschoolers (Kashani & Carlson, 1987; Kashani, Halcomb, & Orvaschel, 1986) and in 2 to 3 percent of school-age children (Cohen, Cohen, et al., 1993; Costello et al., 1988). In adolescents, rates of depression are comparable to those of adults, with particularly high rates (7–13%) for girls (Angold & Rutter, 1992; Kashani et al., 1987).

One problem complicating the diagnosis of depression in children is frequent comorbidity with other disorders (Hammen & Compas, 1994). Up to 70 percent of depressed children also have an anxiety disorder or significant anxiety symptoms (Anderson et al., 1987; Brady & Kendall, 1992; Kovacs, 1990). Depression is also common in children with conduct disorder and attention deficit disorder (Fleming & Offord, 1990; Kashani et al., 1987; Rohde, Lewinsohn, & Seeley, 1991). Youngsters with both depression and another psychiatric disorder have been found to suffer from more severe depression and to take longer to recover (Keller et al., 1988; Kovacs, Feinberg, Crouse-Novak, Paulauskas, & Finkelstein, 1984; Kovacs, Feinberg, Crouse-Novak, Paulauskas, Pollack, & Finkelstein, 1984).

ETIOLOGY OF DEPRESSION IN CHILDHOOD AND ADOLESCENCE

What causes a young person to become depressed? As with adults, evidence suggests that genetic factors play a role (Puig-Antich et al., 1989; Tsuang & Farone, 1990).

Studies of depression in children have focused also on family and other relationships as sources of stress that might interact with a biological diathesis. Depressed children and their parents have been shown to interact with each other in negative ways, for example, showing less warmth and more hostility toward each other than is the case with nondepressed children and their parents (Chiariello & Orvaschel, 1995; Puig-Antich et al., 1985). Children and adolescents experiencing major depression also have poor social skills and impaired relationships with siblings and friends (Lewinsohn et al., 1994; Puig-Antich et al., 1993). These behavioral patterns are likely to be both a cause and a consequence of depression. Depressed youngsters have fewer and less satisfying contacts with their peers, who often reject them because they are not enjoyable to be around (Kennedy, Spence, & Hensley, 1989); these negative interactions in turn aggravate the negative self-image and sense of worth that the depressed youngster already has (cf. Coyne, 1976). Frequent criticism from parents may be especially harmful to the child's sense of competency and self-worth (Cole & Turner, 1993; Stark et al., in press-b).

Consistent with both Beck's theory (1967) and the learned helplessness theory of depression (Abramson et al., 1988), cognitive distortions and negative attributional styles are associated with depression in children and adolescents in ways similar to what has been found with adults (e.g., Garber et al., 1993; Gotlib et al., 1993; Kaslow et al., 1992). Accumulating evidence indicates that experiences in the home, primarily the manner in which parents deal with their children, *cause* the cognitions and thoughts that can lead to depression (Stark et al., in press-b; see Focus 10.3).

FOCUS 10.3   DEPRESSION IN ADOLESCENTS: THE APPEARANCE OF GENDER DIFFERENCES

Depression occurs about twice as often in women as in men. Research involving both patients in treatment and surveys of community residents consistently yields a female–male ratio of almost 2 to 1. This gender difference does not appear in preadolescent children, however; not until midadolescence does this gender difference emerge consistently. Understanding its cause and its timing may yield some further clues to the etiology of depression.

After reviewing evidence concerning gender differences in depression, Nolen-Hoeksema and Girgus (1994) concluded that girls are more likely than boys to have certain risk factors for depression even before adolescence, but it is only when these risk factors interact with the challenges of adolescence that the gender differences in depression emerge.

What are these risk factors more common to girls than to boys? Nolen-Hoeksema and Girgus discussed three possibilities.

1. Girls are less assertive than boys and score lower than boys on questionnaires that assess leadership abilities.
2. Girls are more likely than boys to engage in what is called ruminative coping. They focus their attention on their depressive symptoms (e.g., "What if I don't get over this?" "What does it mean that I feel this way?"). This coping style is associated with longer and more severe periods of depressive symptoms. Boys and men tend to distract themselves from such introspection by engaging in some physical activity or watching television.
3. Girls are less likely than boys to be physically and verbally aggressive and are less dominant in group interactions.

As adolescence begins, girls are faced with a number of stressors. As their secondary sex characteristics develop, they

The gender difference in depression does not emerge until adolescence. At that time, young women encounter many stressors and tend to ruminate about the negative feelings they create.

may dislike the weight gain and loss of their thin figure. At the same time their risk of physical and sexual abuse increases as do conflicts with parents over issues of independence and gender-appropriate behavior. These stressors, coupled with the risk factors that may result in less effective coping, may be the keys to understanding why women become depressed more frequently than men.

The implications for treatment are clear according to this view. Depressed women—and men—should be encouraged to increase active coping rather than dwelling on their moods and searching for causes of depression. Problem-solving skills and assertiveness should be nurtured. In a preventive vein, Nolen-Hoeksema suggests that parents and other caretakers encourage girls to adopt active behavior in response to negative moods.

TREATMENT OF CHILDHOOD AND ADOLESCENT DEPRESSION

Far less research has been done on therapy with depressed children and adolescents than on therapy with adults (Kaslow & Racusin, 1990). Drug therapies, however, do not seem to be effective; double-blind studies have failed to show reliable differences between placebos and the various types of antidepressant drugs (Puig-Antich et al., 1987; Simeon et al., 1990; Stark et al., 1996).

Most psychosocial interventions are modeled after clinical research with adults. For example, interpersonal therapy (IPT) has been modified for use with depressed adolescents, focusing on issues

of concern to adolescents, such as peer pressure, separation from parents, and authority issues (Moreau et al., 1992; Mufson et al., 1994).

A cognitive-behavioral group intervention involving instruction in coping with depression was found to be effective with depressed adolescents, particularly when parents were involved in treatment (Clarke et al., 1992; Lewinsohn et al., 1990). Fifth and sixth graders showed improvement in depression after a small group role-playing intervention that concentrated on instructions in social skills and social problem solving in stressful situations (Butler et al., 1980). Social-skills training can be expected to help depressed young people by providing them with the behavioral and verbal means to gain access to pleasant, reinforcing environments, such as making friends and getting along with peers (Frame et al., 1982; Stark, Reynolds, & Kaslow, 1987). Better ways of relating to others can also be expected to break into the depression–negative behavior–rejection from others cycle that Coyne (1976) has discussed and that has empirical support in research with young people (e.g., Blechman et al., 1986). However, recent findings from Stark et al. (in press-a) indicate that some depressed children *know* how to relate appropriately to others but are apparently inhibited from doing so by negative thoughts and physiological arousal, suggesting that cognitive interventions and, for some, such procedures as relaxation training could also be useful.

Treatment of children and adolescents for depression may be best accomplished with a broad-spectrum approach that involves not only the child or adolescent but also the family and the school (Stark et al., 1996). Therapy might well have to focus on a depressed parent in addition to the depressed child. Depressed parents probably communicate to their children their own pessimistic views of themselves and the world, and children are influenced strongly by the ideas of their parents. The proposal to include the family and school environments is based on the hypothesis that for young people more than for adults, environmental stressors can be more important than cognitive biases, expectations, and attributions (Cole & Turner, 1993). This approach also points up the importance of teaching the young person ways to cope with interpersonal stress via more effective overt behavior—for example, interacting more effectively with others and being appropriately assertive with overbearing peers—so that the person has alternatives other than the polar extremes of anger or withdrawal.

A case report by Braswell and Kendall (1988) illustrates a cognitive-behavioral therapy with a depressed fifteen-year-old girl.

When initially seen, Sharon was extremely dysphoric, experienced recurrent suicidal ideation, and displayed a number of vegetative signs of depression. ... [After being] placed on antidepressant medication ... she was introduced to a cognitive-behavioral approach to depression. ... She was able to understand how her mood was affected by her thoughts and behavior and was able to engage in behavioral planning to increase the occurrence of pleasure and mastery-oriented events. Sharon manifested extremely high standards for evaluating her performance in a number of areas, and it became clear that her

parents also ascribed to these standards, so that family therapy sessions were held to encourage Sharon and her parents to reevaluate their standards.

Sharon had difficulty with the notion of changing her standards and noted that when she was not depressed she actually valued her perfectionism. At that point she resisted the therapy because she perceived it as trying to change something she valued in herself. With this in mind, we began to explore and identify those situations or domains in which her perfectionism worked for her and when and how it might work against her. She became increasingly comfortable with this perspective and decided she wanted to continue to set high standards regarding her performance in mathematical coursework (which was a clear area of strength), but she did not need to be so demanding of herself regarding art or physical education (p. 194).

SUICIDE

In classical Rome in the period just preceding the Christian era, the quality of life was viewed as far more important than how long one lived. "Living is not good, but living well. The wise man, therefore, lives as well as he should, not as long as he can. ... He will always think of life in terms of quality not quantity," wrote the first-century Roman Stoic philosopher Seneca (cited in Shneidman, 1973, p. 384). Then in its early years, Christianity was a persecuted religion; many early Christians committed suicide as an act of martyrdom (Heyd & Bloch, 1981). Western thought changed radically in the fourth century, when Saint Augustine proclaimed suicide a crime because it violated the Sixth Commandment, Thou shalt not kill. Saint Thomas Aquinas elaborated on this view in the thirteenth century, declaring suicide a mortal sin because it usurped God's power over life and death. So, although neither the Old Testament nor the New explicitly forbids suicide, the Western world came to regard it as a crime and a sin (Shneidman, 1973). The irony is that the Christian injunctions against suicide, deriving from a profound respect for life, contributed to persecution of those who attempted to take their own lives. As late as 1823 anyone in London who committed suicide was buried with a stake pounded through the heart, and not until 1961 did suicide cease to be a criminal offense in the United Kingdom. But what penalty can be imposed on someone who has committed suicide? Some states do categorize suicide attempts as misdemeanors, but these offenses are seldom prosecuted. Most states have laws that make it a crime to encourage or advise suicide (Shneidman, 1987).

Suicide is discussed in this chapter because many depressed persons and persons with bipolar disorder have suicidal thoughts and sometimes make genuine attempts to take their own lives. It is believed that more than half of those who try to kill themselves are depressed and despondent at the time of the act (Frances et al., 1986). A significant number of people who are not depressed, however, make suicidal attempts, some with success. Other disorders are also associated with suicide, especially borderline personality disorder (p. 338) (Linehan & Shearin, 1988). The suicide rate for male alcoholics is much greater than that for the general population of men (Kessel & Grossman, 1961), and it reaches staggering proportions in alcoholic men who are also depressed (Cornelius et al., 1995). Up to 13 percent of schizophrenic individuals commit suicide (Roy, 1982). Our focus here is on issues and factors in suicide that transcend specific diagnoses.

FACTS ABOUT SUICIDE

Self-intentioned death is a complex and multifaceted act (Berman & Jobes, 1991; Fremouw et al., 1990; Hendin, 1982; Holinger, 1987; Moscicki, 1995; National Center for Health Statistics, 1988, 1994; Wright, 1992). No single theory can hope to explain it. Some facts about suicide are listed here; see Focus 10.4 for myths about suicide.

- According to statistics, every twenty minutes someone in the United States kills himself or herself. This figure, translating into more than 30,000 suicides a year, is probably a gross underestimate. The suicide rate in the United States is about 12 per 100,000. It rises in old age; between the ages of seventy-five and eighty-four, the rate reaches 24 per 100,000.

- The ratio of attempted to completed suicides in the United States may be as high as 200 to 1, which means that there are as many as 6 million attempts per year.

- About half of those who commit suicide have made at least one previous attempt, but most attempters never make another attempt. Most do not really intend to die, especially if they are children or adolescents. Some differences between attempters and completers are shown in Table 10.4.

- Men are four to five times more likely than women to kill themselves, although the ratio may be diminishing as women are becoming a higher risk group.

- Three times as many women as men attempt to kill themselves but do not die.

- Being divorced or widowed increases suicide risk by four or five times and may be a risk factor that becomes more influential with age. The importance of marital status may also be one aspect of the role of lack of social support in suicidal risk.

- During spring and summer suicide incidence in the United States is highest.

- Suicide is found at all social and economic levels but is especially common among psychiatrists, physicians, lawyers, and psychologists, even more so if they are women. Also at higher risk are law enforcement officers, musicians, and dentists.

- No other kind of death leaves friends and rela-

TABLE 10.4 Comparison of Suicide Attempters and Completers

Characteristic	Attempters	Completers
Gender	Majority female	Majority male
Age	Predominantly young	Risk increases with age
Method	Low lethality (pills, cutting)	More violent (gun, jumping)
Common diagnoses	Dysthymic disorder	Major mood disorder
	Borderline personality disorder	Alcoholism
	Schizophrenia	
Dominant affect	Depression with anger	Depression with hopelessness
Motivation	Change in situation	Death
	Cry for help	
Hospital course	Quick recovery from dysphoria	
Attitude toward attempt	Relief to have survived	
	Promises not to repeat	

Source: Adapted from Fremouw et al., 1990, p. 24. Reprinted by permission of Simon and Schuster International.

FOCUS 10.4 SOME MYTHS ABOUT SUICIDE

There are many prevalent misconceptions about suicide (Fremouw, Perczel, & Ellis, 1990; Pokorny, 1968; Shneidman, 1973). It is as important to be familiar with them as it is to know the facts.

1. **People who discuss suicide will not commit the act.** Up to three-quarters of those who take their own lives have communicated their intention beforehand, perhaps as a cry for help, perhaps to taunt.

2. **Suicide is committed without warning.** The falseness of this belief is shown by the preceding statement. The person usually gives many warnings, such as saying that the world would be better off without him or her or making unexpected and inexplicable gifts to others, often of his or her most valued possessions.

3. **Only people of a certain class commit suicide.** Suicide is neither the curse of the poor nor the disease of the rich. People in all socioeconomic classes commit suicide.

4. **Membership in a particular religious group is a good predictor that a person will not consider suicide.** It is mistakenly thought that the strong Catholic prohibition against suicide makes the risk that Catholics will take their lives much lower. This belief is not supported by the evidence, perhaps because an individual's formal religious identification is not always an accurate index of true beliefs.

5. **The motives for suicide are easily established.** The truth is that we do not fully understand why people commit suicide. For example, just because a severe reverse in finances precedes a suicide, does not mean that it adequately explains the suicide.

6. **All who commit suicide are depressed.** This fallacy may account for the fact that signs of impending suicide are often overlooked because the person does not act despondently. Many people who take their lives are *not* depressed; some people appear calm and at peace with themselves.

7. **A person with a terminal physical illness is unlikely to commit suicide.** A person's awareness of impending death does not preclude suicide. Perhaps the wish to end their own suffering or that of their loved ones impels many to choose the time of their death.

8. **To commit suicide is psychotic.** Although most suicidal persons are very unhappy, most do appear to be in touch with reality.

9. **Suicide is influenced by cosmic factors such as sunspots and phases of the moon.** No evidence confirms this belief.

10. **Improvement in emotional state means lessened risk of suicide.** Often people, especially those who are depressed, commit suicide after their spirits begin to rise and their energy level improves.

11. **Suicide is a lonely event.** Although the debate whether to commit suicide is waged within the individual's head, deep immersion in a frustrating, hurtful relationship with another person—a spouse, a child, a lover, a colleague—may be a principal cause.

12. **Suicidal people clearly want to die.** Most people who commit suicide appear to be ambivalent about their own deaths; others suffer from depression or alcoholism, which if alleviated, reduces the suicidal desire. For many people the suicidal crisis passes, and they are grateful for having been prevented from self-destruction.

13. **Thinking about suicide is rare.** Estimates from various studies suggest that among nonclinical populations, suicidal ideation runs from 40 percent to as high as 80 percent; that is, these percentages of people have thought about committing suicide at least once in their lives.

14. **Asking a person, especially a depressed one, about suicide will push him or her over the edge and cause a suicidal act that would not otherwise have occurred.** One of the first things clinicians learn in their training is to inquire about suicide in a deeply troubled patient. Asking about it can give the person permission to talk about what he or she might harbor as a terrible, shameful secret, which could otherwise lead to further isolation and depression.

15. **People who attempt suicide by a low-lethal means are not serious about killing themselves.** This statement confuses lethality with intent. Some people are not well-informed about pill dosages or human anatomy. An attempt unlikely to have led to death may nonetheless have been engaged in by someone who really wanted to self-destruct.

tives with long-lasting feelings of distress, shame, guilt, puzzlement, and general disturbance. These survivors are themselves victims, having an especially high mortality rate in the year following the suicide of the loved one.

- Guns are by far the most common means of committing suicide in the United States, accounting for about 60 percent of all suicides. The availability of firearms in U.S. homes increases suicide risk independent of other known risk factors. Men usually choose to shoot or hang themselves; women are more likely to use sleeping pills, which may account for their lower rate of completed suicide.

- Suicide ranks eighth as a cause of death among American adults in general; it ranks third after accidents and homicides among those aged fifteen to twenty-four and second among whites in this age group. It is estimated that each year upwards of 10,000 American college students attempt to kill themselves and as many as 20 percent consider suicide at least once during their college years.

- Suicide rates for white and Native American youths are more than twice those for African-American youths, although in the inner cities the rates among young African-American men are twice as high as those among young white men (a situation similar to the higher incidence of violence and homicide among young, urban African-Americans). The highest rates of suicide in the United States are for white males over age fifty. For African-Americans suicide is most frequent among those aged fifteen to twenty-four.

- The rates of suicide for adolescents and children in the United States are increasing dramatically. As many as 3000 young people between the ages of fifteen and nineteen are believed to kill themselves each year, and attempts are made by children as young as six years old. But the rates are far below those of adults.

- The overwhelming majority of people who commit suicide have diagnosable mental disorders, in particular, mood disorders and alcoholism.[2]

- Physical illness, for example, AIDS and multiple sclerosis, is a contributing factor in as many as half of all suicides (see the later discussion of physician-assisted suicide for the terminally ill).

- Hungary has the highest rate of suicide in the world. The Czech Republic, Finland, Austria, and Switzerland also have high incidences. The countries with the lowest rates are Greece,

Suicide involving violent death, such as jumping off a building, is more common among men than women.

Mexico, the Netherlands, and the United Kingdom. The United States is in the middle range.

- Suicide rates rise during depression years, remain stable during years of prosperity, and decrease during war years.

PERSPECTIVES ON SUICIDE

In imagining a suicide we usually think of a person deliberately performing a dramatic act explicitly chosen to end life almost immediately—the woman sitting in a car in a garage with the motor running, the man with the gun next to his temple, the child with the bottle of a parent's sleeping pills. But suicidologists also regard people as suicidal when they act in self-destructive ways that can cause serious injury or death after a prolonged period of time, such as a diabetic patient who neglects taking insulin or adhering to a dietary regimen or an alcoholic individual who continues to drink and does not seek help despite awareness of the damage being done to his or her body. Sometimes termed *subintentioned death*, these apparent suicides complicate still further the task of understanding and gathering statistics on suicide (Shneidman, 1973).

Ideas about the nature and causes of suicide can be found in many places (Shneidman, 1987). Letters and diaries can provide insights into the phenomenology of people who commit suicide. Novelists,

---

[2]It seems worth pointing out that suicidal thoughts or attempts are one of the characteristics of major depression listed in the DSM. Thus the very definition of depression usually includes suicidality. By the same token, when people with schizophrenia or substance-abuse problems commit suicide they are often diagnosed as also depressed (Roy, 1982; Roy & Linnoila, 1986). It should thus not be surprising that suicidality is widespread among the mentally ill, given that self-destructive behavior is frequently indicated as a feature of several mental disorders.

such as Herman Melville and Leo Tolstoy, have provided insights on suicide, as have writers who have killed themselves, such as Virginia Woolf and Sylvia Plath. Many philosophers have written searchingly on the topic, including Descartes, Voltaire, Kant, as well as existentialists, such as Heidegger and Camus, who grappled with the inherent meaninglessness of life and the individual's need and responsibility to forge some meaning out of what appears to be a dark existence.

Many motives for suicide have been suggested (Mintz, 1968): aggression turned inward; retaliation by inducing guilt in others; efforts to force love from others; efforts to make amends for perceived past wrongs; efforts to rid oneself of unacceptable feelings, such as sexual attraction to members of one's own sex; the desire for reincarnation; the desire to rejoin a dead loved one; and the desire or need to escape from stress, deformity, pain, or emotional vacuum. Many contemporary mental health professionals regard suicide in general as an individual's attempt at problem solving, conducted under considerable stress and marked by consideration of a very narrow range of alternatives of which self-annihilation appears the most viable (Linehan & Shearin, 1988).

A theory about suicide based on work in social and personality psychology holds that some suicides arise from a strong desire to escape from aversive self-awareness, that is, from the painful awareness of shortcomings and lack of success that the person attributes to himself or herself (Baumeister, 1990). This awareness is assumed to produce severe emotional suffering, perhaps depression. Unrealistically high expectations—and therefore the probability of failing to meet these expectations (cf. Beck and Ellis)—play a central role in this perspective on suicide. Of particular importance is a discrepancy between high expectations for intimacy and a reality that falls short, for example, when someone's expectations for intimacy are dashed by a loved one who cannot possibly deliver what the person needs (Stephens, 1985). Oblivion through death can appear more tolerable than a continuation of the painful awareness of one's deficiencies. There is considerable research in support of this hypothesis (Baumeister, 1990).

Media reports of suicide may spark an increase in suicides. This disturbing possibility was discussed by Bandura (1986), who reviewed research by Phillips (1974, 1977, 1985) showing that (1) suicides rose by 12 percent in the month following Marilyn Monroe's death; (2) publicized accounts of self-inflicted deaths of people other than the famous also are followed by significant increases in suicide, suggesting that it is the publicity rather than the

The suicide of Nirvana's lead singer, Kurt Cobain, triggered an increase in suicide among teenagers.

fame of the person who committed suicide that is important; (3) publicized accounts of murder-suicides are followed by increases in automobile and plane crashes in which the driver and others are killed; and finally (4) media reports of natural deaths of famous people are not followed by increases in suicide, suggesting that it is not grief per se that is the influential factor.

We turn now to several other perspectives on suicide, each of which attempts to shed light on this disturbing aspect of humankind.

FREUD'S PSYCHOANALYTIC THEORIES ON SUICIDE

Freud proposed two major hypotheses to account for suicide. One, an extension of his theory of depression, views suicide as murder. When a person loses someone whom he or she has ambivalently loved and hated, and introjects that person, aggression is directed inward. If these feelings are strong enough, the person will commit suicide. The second theory postulates that the death instinct, Thanatos, can turn inward and make a person take his or her life.

DURKHEIM'S SOCIOLOGICAL THEORY OF SUICIDE

Emile Durkheim (1897), a renowned sociologist, analyzed the records of suicide for various countries and during different historical periods and concluded that self-annihilation could be understood in sociological terms. He distinguished three different kinds of suicide. **Egoistic suicide** is committed by people who have few ties to family, society, or community. These people feel alienated from others, cut off from the social supports that are important to keep them functioning adaptively as social beings. **Altruistic suicides** are viewed as responses to societal demands. Some people who commit suicide feel very much a part of a group and sacrifice themselves for what they take to be the good of society. The self-immolations of Buddhist monks and nuns to protest the fighting during the Vietnam War fits into this category. Some altruistic suicides, such as the hara-kiri of the Japanese, are required as the only honorable recourse in certain circumstances. Finally, **anomic suicide** may be triggered by a sudden change in a person's relation to society. A successful executive who suffers severe financial reverses may experience *anomie*, a sense of disorientation, because what he or she believed to be a normal way of living is no longer possible.

Anomie can pervade a society in disequilibrium, making suicide more likely. A recent example of anomic suicide occurred among a rural Brazilian tribe, the Guarani Indians. Their suicide rate in 1995 was 160 per 100,000, markedly higher than it was a

The high suicide rate of the Guarani Indians, who were forced onto crowded reservations, illustrates Durkheim's concept of anomic suicide.

year earlier and dramatically higher than the U.S. rate of about 12 per 100,000. The reason for this high suicide rate may be found in a sudden change in their living conditions. The Guarani have recently lost most of their ancestral lands to industrialization. Communities that used to live by hunting and fishing are now crowded onto reservations too small to support that way of life. Nearby cities tempt the Guarani with consumer goods that they desire and yet can ill afford on their low wages. Because hunting, farming, and family life have religious significance, their demise has significantly affected religious life. Life has lost its meaning for many of the Guarani (Long, 1995).

As with all sociological theorizing Durkheim's hypotheses have difficulty accounting for the differences among individuals in a given society in their reactions to the same demands and conditions. Not all those who unexpectedly lose their money commit suicide, for example. It appears that Durkheim was aware of this problem, for he suggested that individual temperament would interact with any of the social pressures that he found causative.

SHNEIDMAN'S APPROACH TO SUICIDE

While acknowledging that perhaps 90 percent of suicides could be given a DSM diagnosis, Shneidman (1987) reminds us that the overwhelming majority of people with schizophrenia and mood disorders do *not* commit suicide. He suggests also that the *perturbation* of mind that he posits as a key feature of a suicide is not a mental illness.

Shneidman's psychological approach to suicide (1987) is summarized in Table 10.5, which lists the ten most frequent characteristics of suicide, not all of them found in each and every case. His view regards suicide as a conscious effort to seek a solution to a problem that is causing intense suffering. To the sufferer, this solution ends consciousness and unendurable pain—what Melville in *Moby Dick* termed an "insufferable anguish." All hope and sense of constructive action are gone.

Still—and this is of central importance in prevention—most people who contemplate or actually commit suicide are ambivalent. "The prototypical suicidal state is one in which an individual cuts his or her throat, cries for help at the same time, and is genuine in both of these acts. ... Individuals would be happy not to do it, if they didn't have to" (Shneidman, 1987, p. 170). There is a narrowing of the perceived range of options; when not in a highly perturbed suicidal state the person is capable of seeing more choices for dealing with stress. People planning suicide usually communicate their intention, sometimes as a cry for help, sometimes as a

TABLE 10.5 The Ten Commonalities of Suicide
I. The common purpose of suicide is to seek a solution.
II. The common goal of suicide is the cessation of consciousness.
III. The common stimulus in suicide is intolerable psychological pain.
IV. The common stressor in suicide is frustrated psychological needs.
V. The common emotion in suicide is hopelessness–helplessness.
VI. The common cognitive state in suicide is ambivalence.
VII. The common perceptual state in suicide is constriction.
VIII. The common action in suicide is egression.
IX. The common interpersonal act in suicide is communication of intention.
X. The common consistency in suicide is with lifelong coping patterns.

Source: From Shneidman, 1985, p. 167.

withdrawal from others, a search for inviolacy. Typical behaviors include giving away treasured possessions and putting financial affairs in order.

NEUROCHEMISTRY AND SUICIDE

Just as low levels of serotonin appear to be related to depression, research has also established a connection among serotonin, suicide, and impulsivity. Low levels of serotonin's major metabolite, 5-HIAA, have been found in suicide victims in several diagnostic categories—depression, schizophrenia, and various personality disorders (see Brown & Goodwin, 1986; van Praag et al., 1990). Postmortem studies of the brains of people who committed suicide have revealed increased numbers of serotonin receptors (presumably a response to a decreased level of serotonin itself). The link between 5-HIAA levels and suicide is especially compelling in the case of violent and impulsive suicide (Roy, 1994; Traskman et al., 1981; Winchel, Stanley, & Stanley, 1990). Finally, 5-HIAA levels are correlated with questionnaire measures of aggression and impulsivity (Brown & Goodwin, 1986).

PREDICTION OF SUICIDE FROM PSYCHOLOGICAL TESTS

It would be of considerable theoretical and practical value to be able to predict suicide on the basis of psychological tests, and several efforts have been made to do so. Significant correlations have been found between suicide intent and hopelessness.

Especially noteworthy are Aaron Beck's findings, based on prospective data, that hopelessness is a strong predictor of suicide (Beck, 1986b; Beck et al., 1985; Beck et al., 1990), even stronger than is depression (Beck, Kovacs, & Weissman, 1975). The expectation that at some point in the future things will be no better than they are right now—which, to be sure, is part of the phenomenon of depression but can be found among nondepressed people as well—seems to be more instrumental than depression per se in propelling a person to take his or her life. Beck and his group also developed the Suicidal Intent Scale (Beck, Schuyler, & Herman, 1974) and the Scale for Suicide Ideation (Beck, Kovacs, & Weissman, 1979), both of which show promise in helping us understand and predict those at high risk for serious suicide attempts.

Another self-report instrument is Marsha Linehan's Reasons for Living (RFL) Inventory (Ivanoff et al., 1994; Linehan, 1985b; Linehan et al., 1983). Clusters of items tap what is important to the individual, such as responsibility to family and concerns about children. The approach is different from, and possibly more useful than, scales that focus only on negativism and pessimism, because knowing what there is in a person's life that *prevents* him or her from committing suicide has both assessment and intervention value. This instrument can discriminate between suicidal and nonsuicidal individuals and can help the clinician with intervention by identifying reasons the person has for not wanting to die.

Another avenue of research has focused on the cognitive characteristics of people who attempt suicide. It has been suggested that suicidal individuals are more rigid in their approach to problems (e.g., Neuringer, 1964) and less flexible in their thinking (Levenson, 1972). Constricted thinking could account for the apparent inability to seek solutions to life problems other than taking one's own life (Linehan et al., 1987). Research confirms the hypothesis that people who attempt suicide are more rigid than control people, lending support to the clinical observations of Shneidman and others that people who attempt suicide seem almost myopically incapable of thinking of alternative solutions to problems and might therefore tend to settle on suicide as the only way out.

It has proved difficult to predict suicide based on the kind of trait approach that characterizes these research efforts. As we saw in Chapter 4, behavior is influenced a great deal by the environment, and the environment includes stressful events that themselves can be difficult to predict. We can seldom know, for example, whether a given individual is going to lose employment, experience serious marital problems, suffer the loss of a loved one, or be involved in a serious accident. In addition, it is hard to predict with accuracy an infrequent event such as suicide, even with a highly reliable test (Fremouw et al., 1990; Roy, 1995).

PREVENTING SUICIDE

One way to look at the prevention of suicide is to bear in mind that most people who attempt to kill themselves are suffering from a treatable mental disorder such as depression, schizophrenia, substance abuse, or borderline personality disorder. Thus when someone following Beck's cognitive approach successfully lessens a patient's depression, that patient's prior suicidal risk is reduced; likewise for the dialectical behavior therapy of Marsha Linehan (1993b), whose therapy with borderline patients is described in Chapter 13 (p. 352).

The view that efforts to prevent suicide should focus on the underlying psychological disorder is held by many experts in the field (e.g., Moscicki, 1995). But there is another tradition in suicide prevention that downplays mental disorder and concentrates instead on the particular characteristics of suicidal people that transcend mental disorder.

One of the best-known approaches of this nature is that of Edwin Shneidman, a pioneer in the study of suicide and its prevention. We have already reviewed some of his thinking on suicide. His general strategy of suicide prevention (1985, 1987) is threefold: (1) reduce the intense psychological pain and suffering; (2) lift the blinders, that is, expand the constricted view by helping the individual see options other than the extremes of continued suffering or nothingness; and (3) encourage the person to pull back even a little from the self-destructive act. He cites the example of a wealthy college student who was single, pregnant, and suicidal, with a clearly formed plan. The only solution she could think of besides suicide was never to have become pregnant, even to be virginal again.

I took out a sheet of paper and began to widen her blinders. I said something like, "Now, let's see: You could have an abortion here locally." She responded, "I couldn't do that." I continued, "You could go away and have an abortion." "I couldn't do that." "You could bring the baby to term and keep the baby." "I couldn't do that." "You could have the baby and adopt it out." Further options were similarly dismissed. When I said, "You can always commit suicide, but there is obviously no need to do that today," there was no response. "Now," I said, "let's look at this list and rank them in order of your preference, keeping in mind that none of them is optimal." (Shneidman, 1987, p. 171)

Shneidman reports that just drawing up the list had a calming effect. The student's lethality—her drive to kill herself very soon—receded, and she was able to rank the list even though she found something wrong with each item. *But* an important goal had been achieved; she had been pulled back from the brink and was in a frame of mind to consider courses of action other than dying or being a virgin again. "We were then simply 'haggling' about life, a perfectly viable solution" (p. 171).

Suicide prevention centers usually provide round-the-clock consultation to persons who are suicidal. Workers are typically nonprofessional volunteers under professional supervision. They rely heavily on demographic factors to assess risk (Shneidman, Farberow, & Litman, 1970). Workers receiving phone calls from people in suicidal crises have before them a checklist to guide their questioning of each caller. For example, a caller would be regarded as a lethal risk if he were male, middle-aged, divorced, and living alone and had a history of previous suicide attempts. Usually the more detailed and concrete the suicide plan, the higher the risk. More information on suicide prevention centers is provided in Chapter 19 (p. 578).

Studies of suicide notes have found that those who follow through with suicide often leave specific, detailed instructions and that their notes show evidence of more anguish and hostility than do sim-

Community mental health centers often provide a 24-hour-a-day hotline for those people who are considering suicide.

FOCUS 10.5   AN ARGUMENT AGAINST COERCIVE SUICIDE PREVENTION

In a bold and controversial article on coercive suicide prevention Thomas Szasz (1986) argues that it is both impractical and immoral to prevent a person from committing suicide. It is impractical because we cannot really force people to live if they are intent on committing suicide unless—and this is where morality becomes an issue—we are prepared not only to commit them but to enslave them via heavy psychotropic medication or even physical restraints. Even then, hospitalized patients do manage to take their own lives. Szasz asserts further that mental health professionals, in their understandable desire to help their patients, open themselves up to legal liability because, by taking it upon themselves to try to prevent suicide, they assume responsibility for something for which they cannot be responsible. In effect, they are promising more than they can deliver.

Further, Szasz argues that health professionals *should not* assume such responsibility—even if it were practical to do so—because people, including those seriously disturbed, should be accorded freedom to make choices. He allows one exception for what he calls impulsive suicide, when people are temporarily agitated, perhaps truly deranged, and need to be protected for a short while from their uncontrollable impulses. He draws an analogy with patients coming out of general anesthesia, when it is common medical practice to strap them down lest their flailing about involuntarily lead to unintended and preventable harm. But there are limits here as well, including, in our own view, how we can know when we are dealing with an impulsive act rather than an act that the person has been thinking about and planning for a period of time.

Szasz is not against advising a person not to commit suicide or otherwise treating problems, such as depression, that might have a good deal to do with self-destructive thinking. It is forcible prevention that he rails against. Indeed, he believes that if professionals exclude coercive suicide prevention from their intervention options they will be able to be more empathic with their patients and perhaps more helpful. He also suggests a psychiatric will, in which a patient, when not feeling suicidal, agrees ahead of time about how to be treated if later on he or she wishes to commit suicide. If the patient opts for coercive prevention in this will, then it would be all right. This strategy brings to mind the instructions Ulysses gave to his sailors before they were to pass by the coast of the Sirens, sea nymphs whose song compelled hapless mariners to commit suicide by throwing themselves into the sea:

> He filled the ears of his people with wax, and suffered them to bind him with cords firmly to the mast. As they approached the Sirens' island, the sea was calm, and over the waters came the notes of music so ravishing and attractive that Ulysses struggled to get loose, and by cries and signs to his people begged to be released; but they, obedient to his previous orders, sprang forward and bound him still faster. They held on their course, and the music grew fainter till it ceased to be heard, when with joy Ulysses gave his companions the signal to unseal their ears, and they relieved him from his bonds. (*Bulfinch's Mythology*, 1979, p. 243)

Like the other arguments involving freedom and responsibility that Szasz has made over the years (see Chapter 20, p. 598, for a discussion of his seminal writings on mental illness and legal responsibility for crimes), his analysis is radical but worthy of serious consideration. In our view the principal omission in his thesis is that many, if not most, people who somehow

---

ulated suicide notes written by individuals who were not thinking about suicide but who were matched demographically (Ogilvie et al., 1983; Shneidman & Farberow, 1970). Lacking in real suicide notes is the kind of general and philosophical content that characterizes those written by simulators; "Be sure to pay the electric bill" would more likely appear in a real suicide note than "Be good to others" (Baumeister, 1990).

CLINICAL AND ETHICAL ISSUES IN DEALING WITH SUICIDE

Although people are not invariably depressed when they commit suicide or attempt to do so, suicide must always be considered a danger when working with those who are profoundly depressed. The despair and utter hopelessness of their existence may make them see suicide as the only solution, the only exit. Sometimes the sole reason a depressed individual does *not* attempt suicide is that he or she cannot summon the energy to formulate and implement a suicide plan. Thus in working with a seriously depressed individual the clinician must be especially careful as the patient emerges from the low point of depression; at this time the sadness and hopelessness may still be strong enough to make self-annihilation appear the only option, and the person is beginning to have enough energy to do something about it. Because many who commit suicide are depressed, clinicians hope that treatment of depression will reduce the risk of suicide.

Professional organizations such as the American Psychiatric Association, the National Association of Social Workers, and the American Psychological Association all charge their members to protect peo-

weather suicidal crises, including those forcibly prevented from killing themselves, are grateful afterward for another chance at life. It may be that if we were to follow Szasz's urgings we would miss opportunities to save savable lives. Szasz's rejoinder might be that one of the strongest predictors of a suicide attempt is a prior attempt. In other words, many people tend to try more than once to kill themselves. Therefore we would be repeatedly challenged to decide how drastically we were prepared to limit freedom (and sometimes degrade the person by restraints of one kind or another) in the hope of forestalling what may be inevitable. There are no easy answers here, but it is important to raise the questions.

Ulyfses & his Companions after his return from the Shades, escaping the Sirens, & passing between the Rocks Scylla & Charybdis.

The song of the Sirens was resisted by Ulysses, who was lashed to the mast of his ship to prevent his suicide. According to Szasz's views, this would be an acceptable instance of voluntary, coercive suicide prevention.

ple from harming themselves even if doing so requires breaking the confidentiality of the therapist–patient relationship. In Chapter 20 we discuss legal obligations to protect others from the potentially harmful acts of patients (p. 607). The suicide of a therapist's patient is frequently grounds for a malpractice lawsuit, and therapists tend to lose such suits if the patient's agents can prove that there was negligence in making adequate assessments and in taking reasonable precautions according to generally accepted standards of care for suicide prevention (Fremouw, Perczel, & Ellis, 1990; Roy, 1995).

It is not easy to agree about what constitutes reasonable care, particularly when the patient is not hospitalized and therefore not under surveillance and potential restraint. Clinicians must work out their own ethic regarding a person's right to end his or her life. What steps is the professional willing to take to prevent a suicide? Confinement in a hospital? Or, as is more common today, sedation administered against the patient's wishes and strong enough that the person is virtually incapable of taking any action at all? And for how long should extraordinary measures be taken? Clinicians realize that most suicidal crises pass; the suicidal person is likely to be grateful afterward for having been prevented from committing suicide when it seemed the only course. But to what extreme is the professional prepared to go in the interim to prevent a suicide attempt? In Focus 10.5 we discuss some controversial views on this ethical dilemma.

PHYSICIAN-ASSISTED SUICIDE

Physician-assisted suicide is a highly charged current issue. This issue came to the fore in the early

Jack Kervorkian, a Michigan physician, has assisted several patients in taking their own lives. The controversy stimulated by his actions has focused attention on the moral issues surrounding suicide.

1990s when a Michigan physician, Dr. Jack Kevorkian, helped a fifty-four-year-old Oregonian woman with Alzheimer's disease, a degenerative and fatal brain disease (see p. 456), to commit suicide. She pressed a button on a machine designed by Kevorkian to inject a drug that induced unconsciousness and a lethal dose of potassium chloride that stopped her heart (Egan, 1990). Death was painless. Kevorkian was brought to trial several times but was not convicted of murder or professional misconduct. Since that time he has played an active role in assisting upwards of four dozen terminally ill people take their lives, and he has, with steadfast intent, provoked a searching and emotional discussion about the conditions under which a physician may take the life of a dying patient, an issue made all the more heated by widespread knowledge that health professionals every day pull the plug on patients who are brain-dead but who are being kept physically alive by sophisticated medical apparatus.[3]

While Kevorkian was being tried and acquitted in Michigan for having assisted in two suicides,

---

[3] Decisions not to resuscitate terminally ill patients are made every day in hospitals. One informal estimate is that more than half the deaths in hospitals follow a decision to limit or withhold the kinds of life-sustaining equipment currently available. Many people do not consider this practice euthanasia or suicide. Rather than ending life, "they see it as a desire to end dying, to pass gently into the night without tubes running down the nose and a ventilator insistently inflating lungs that have grown weary from the insult" *Newsweek*, 1991, p. 44). Major legal, religious, and ethical issues whirl around decisions about ending dying among the terminally ill. Is this physician-assisted suicide?

TABLE 10.6 Guidelines for Treating Suicidal Clients

General Procedures

1. Talk about suicide openly and matter-of-factly.
2. Avoid prejorative explanations of suicidal behavior or motives.
3. Present a problem-solving theory of suicidal behavior, and maintain the stance that suicide is a maladaptive and/or ineffective solution.
4. Involve significant others, including other therapists.
5. Schedule sessions frequently enough, and maintain session discipline such that at least some therapy time is devoted to long-term treatment goals.
6. Stay aware of the multitude of variables impinging on patients, and avoid omnipotent taking or accepting of responsibility for patient's suicidal behaviors.
7. Maintain professional consultation with a colleague.
8. Maintain occasional contact with persons who reject therapy.

Precrisis Planning Procedures

9. Anticipate and plan for crisis situations.
10. Continually assess the risk of suicide and parasuicide.
11. Be accessible.
12. Use local emergency/crisis/suicide services.
13. Give the patient a crisis card: telephone numbers of therapist, police, emergency, hospital, significant others.
14. Keep telephone numbers and addresses of patients and their significant others with you.
15. Make a short-term antisuicide contract, and keep it up to date.
16. Contact the patient's physician regarding the risks of overprescribing medications.

Therapeutic Maintenance Procedures

17. Do not force the patient to resort to suicidal talk or ideation in order to get your attention.
18. Express your caring openly; provide noncontingent warmth and attention.
19. Clarify and reinforce nonsuicidal responses to problems.
20. Identify to the patient likely therapist responses to the patient's suicidal behaviors (e.g., if the patient dies, the therapist will be sad, but will continue on with life).
21. Ensure that the patient has realistic expectations about the responses of others to future suicidal behaviors.

Source: M. Linehan, 1981, in H. Glazer and J. Clarkin (Eds.), *Depression: Behavioral and directive interpretation strategies* (pp. 229–294), New York: Garland. Copyright © 1981 by Garland.

the Federal Circuit Court for the Ninth District, covering several western states, issued a ruling on March 6, 1996, that *permits* physician-assisted suicide provided that the person is terminally ill and mentally competent (Weinstein, 1996). Writing for the majority of this appeals court, Judge Stephen Reinhardt commented that "a competent, terminally ill adult ... has a strong liberty interest in choosing a dignified and humane death rather than being reduced at the end of his existence to a childlike state of helplessness, diapered, sedated, incompetent. ... There is a constitutionally protected liberty interest in determining the time and manner of one's own death" (quoted in Weinstein, 1996, p. A1). This ruling covers not only physicians who help the person die but others, such as pharmacists and family members, whose help the patient needs in order to commit suicide.

This ruling generated a new spate of passionate arguments pro and con. Right-to-life advocates claim that especially in this era of managed health care, patients will be pressured, albeit subtly, to ask to have their suffering lives terminated in order to spare their families the high costs of medical care. Opponents of the ruling fear that physicians too will lean in this direction, perhaps pressured by insurance companies that want to save money on expensive terminal medical care, and will influence the patient and his or her family to end the person's life. (That health professionals influence goals that patients set for themselves is at the core of an argument regarding sexual reorientation therapy for homosexuals; see p. 624.) Among powerful groups opposing assisted suicide are the American Medical Association and the Catholic Church. Kevorkian's supporters and others, such as the American Civil Liberties Union, who believe that terminally ill people should have the right to end their suffering, have for years objected to the intrusion of the state on what they regard as a person's inalienable right to make such life or death decisions. This ruling was appealed to the U.S. Supreme Court.

Cases such as that of Kevorkian are unusual, though they are likely to become less so as people concentrate more on the quality of life and the right to privacy, which may well include the right to take one's own life. For the most part mental health workers try to prevent suicide, and in that context, they should not hesitate to inquire directly whether a client has thought of suicide. It is important to adopt a phenomenological stance, to view the suicidal person's situation as he or she sees it, and not to convey in any way that the patient is a fool or is crazy to have settled on suicide as a solution to his or her woes. This empathy for suicidal people is sometimes referred to as tuning in by those who work in suicide prevention centers. The clinician treating a suicidal person must be prepared to devote more energy and time than usual even for psychotic patients. Late-night phone calls and visits to the patient's home may be frequent. Finally, the therapist should realize that he or she is likely to become a singularly important figure in the suicidal person's life, and should be prepared both for the extreme dependency of the patient and for the hostility and resentment that sometimes greet efforts to help. Table 10.6 contains general guidelines for dealing with suicidal patients.

SUMMARY

DSM-IV lists two principal kinds of mood disorders. In major, or unipolar, depression a person experiences profound sadness as well as related problems such as sleep and appetite disturbances and loss of energy and self-esteem. In bipolar I disorder a person has episodes of mania alone, episodes of mania and of depression, or mixed episodes, in which both manic and depressive symptoms occur together. With mania, mood is elevated or irritable and the person becomes extremely active, talkative, and distractible. DSM-IV also lists two chronic mood disorders, cyclothymia and dysthymia; both must last for two years. In cyclothymia the person has frequent periods of depressed mood and hypomania; in dysthymia the person is chronically depressed.

Psychological theories of depression have been couched in psychoanalytic, cognitive, and interpersonal terms. Psychoanalytic formulations stress fixation in the oral stage (leading to a high level of dependency) and unconscious identification with a lost loved one whose desertion of the individual has resulted in anger turned inward. Beck's cognitive theory ascribes causal significance to negative schemata and cognitive biases and distortions. According to helplessness/hopelessness theory, early experiences in inescapable, hurtful situations instill a sense of hopelessness that can evolve into depression. Individuals are likely to attribute failures to their own general and persistent inadequacies and faults. Interpersonal theory focuses on the problems depressed people have in relating to others and the negative responses they elicit from others. These same theories are applied to the depressive phase of bipolar disorder. The manic phase is considered a defense against a debilitating psychological state, such as low self-esteem.

Biological theories suggest there may be an inherited predisposition for mood disorders, particularly for bipolar disorder. Linkage analyses may provide information about the chromosome on which the gene is located. Early neurochemical theories related the phenomena of depression to low levels of serotonin and bipolar disorder to norepinephrine (high in mania and low in depression). Recent research has focused on the postsynaptic receptors rather than on the amount of various transmitters. Overactivity of the hypothalamic–pituitary–adrenal axis is also found among depressive patients, indicating that the endocrine system may also influence mood disorders.

Several psychological and somatic therapies are effective for mood disorders and especially for depression. Psychoanalytic treatment tries to give the patient insight into childhood loss and inadequacy and later self-blame. The aim of Beck's cognitive therapy is to uncover negative and illogical patterns of thinking and to teach more realistic ways of viewing events, the self, and adversity.

A range of biological treatments is also available. They are often used in conjunction with psychological treatment and can be very effective. Electroconvulsive shock and several antidepressant drugs (tricyclics, serotonin reuptake inhibitors, and MAO inhibitors) have proved their worth in lifting depression. Patients may avoid the excesses of manic and depressive periods through careful administration of lithium carbonate.

Our exploration of suicide reveals that self-annihilatory tendencies are not restricted to those who are depressed. A good deal of information can be applied to help prevent suicide, although no single theory is likely to account for the wide variety of motives and situations behind it.

Most large communities have suicide prevention centers, and most therapists at one time or another have to deal with patients in suicidal crisis. Suicidal persons need to have their fears and concerns understood but not judged; clinicians must gradually and patiently point out to them that there are alternatives to self-destruction to be explored.

KEY TERMS

mood disorders	learned helplessness theory	bilateral ECT
depression	attribution	unilateral ECT
mania	linkage analysis	lithium carbonate
major (unipolar) depression	tricyclic drugs	egoistic suicide
bipolar I disorder	monoamine oxidase	altruistic suicide
hypomania	inhibitors	anomic suicide
cyclothymic disorder	logotherapy	suicide prevention centers
dysthymic disorder	electroconvulsive therapy	
negative triad	(ECT)	

Gyorgy Kepes, "Eyes," 1941

11

SCHIZOPHRENIA

All of a sudden things weren't going so well. I began to lose control of my life and, most of all, myself. I couldn't concentrate on my schoolwork, I couldn't sleep, and when I did sleep, I had dreams about dying. I was afraid to go to class, imagined that people were talking about me, and on top of that I heard voices. I called my mother in Pittsburgh and asked for her advice. She told me to move off campus into an apartment with my sister.

After I moved in with my sister, things got worse. I was afraid to go outside and when I looked out of the window, it seemed that everyone outside was yelling, "kill her, kill her." My sister forced me to go to school. I would go out of the house until I knew she had gone to work; then I would return home. Things continued to get worse. I imagined that I had a foul body odor and I sometimes took up to six showers a day. I recall going to the grocery store one day, and I imagined that the people in the store were saying, "Get saved, Jesus is the answer." Things worsened—I couldn't remember a thing. I had a notebook full of reminders telling me what to do on that particular day. I couldn't remember my schoolwork, and I would study from 6:00 P.M. until 4:00 A.M. but never had the courage to go to class on the following day. I tried to tell my sister about it, but she didn't understand. She suggested that I see a psychiatrist, but I was afraid to go out of the house to see him.

One day I decided that I couldn't take this trauma anymore, so I took an overdose of thirty-five Darvon pills. At the same moment, a voice inside me said, "What did you do that for? Now you won't go to heaven." At that instant I realized that I really didn't want to die. I wanted to live, and I was afraid. I got on the phone and called the psychiatrist whom my sister had recommended. I told him that I had taken an overdose of Darvon and that I was afraid. He told me to take a taxi to the hospital. When I arrived at the hospital, I began vomiting, but I didn't pass out. Somehow I just couldn't accept the fact that I was really going to see a psychiatrist. I thought that psychiatrists were only for crazy people, and I definitely didn't think I was crazy yet. As a result, I did not admit myself right away. As a matter of fact I left the hospital and ended up meeting my sister on the way home. She told me to turn right back around because I was definitely going to be admitted. We then called my mother, and she said she would fly down on the following day. (O'Neil, 1984, pp. 109–110)

The young woman described in this case study was diagnosed as schizophrenic. Although the diagnosis of schizophrenia has existed now for about a century and the disorder has spawned more research than any other, we are far from understanding this serious mental disorder. **Schizophrenia** is a psychotic disorder characterized by major disturbances in thought, emotion, and behavior—disordered thinking in which ideas are not logically related; faulty perception and attention; bizarre disturbances in motor activity; and flat or inappropriate affect. Schizophrenic patients withdraw from people and reality, often into a fantasy life of delusions and hallucinations. In this chapter we will describe in detail the clinical features of schizophrenia; we will consider the history of the concept and how it has changed over the years; and we will examine research on the etiology of schizophrenia and therapies for the disorder.

CLINICAL SYMPTOMS OF SCHIZOPHRENIA

The symptoms of schizophrenic patients involve disturbances in several major areas—thought, perception, and attention; motor behavior; affect or emotion; and life functioning. The range of problems of people diagnosed as schizophrenic is extensive, although patients typically have only *some* of these problems. The DSM determines for the diagnostician how many problems must be present, and in what degree, to justify the diagnosis. Unlike most of the diagnostic categories we have considered, *no essential* symptom must be present for a diagnosis of schizophrenia. Thus schizophrenic patients differ from one another more than do patients with other disorders. The heterogeneity of schizophrenia suggests that it may be appropriate to subdivide schizophrenic patients into types who manifest particular constellations of problems; we will examine several recognized types later in this chapter.

The major symptoms of schizophrenia derive from the DSM criteria as well as from information collected in a large-scale investigation of schizophrenia, the International Pilot Study of Schizophrenia (IPSS), conducted by the World Health Organization (Sartorius, Shapiro, & Jablonsky, 1974). We present the main symptoms of schizophrenia in two categories, positive and negative, and we also describe some symptoms that do not fit neatly into these two categories. In making a diagnosis the duration of the disorder is regarded as very important in distinguishing schizophrenia from the symptomatically similar schizophreniform disorder and brief psychotic disorder.

POSITIVE SYMPTOMS

Positive symptoms comprise excesses, such as disorganized speech, hallucinations, delusions, and bizarre behavior.

DISORGANIZED SPEECH

Disorganized speech, also known as formal **thought disorder**, refers to problems in the organization of ideas and in speaking so that a listener can understand.

Interviewer: Have you been nervous or tense lately?

Schizophrenic patient: No, I got a head of lettuce.

Interviewer: You got a head of lettuce? I don't understand.

Schizophrenic patient: Well, it's just a head of lettuce.

Interviewer: Tell me about lettuce. What do you mean?

Schizophrenic patient: Well, … lettuce is a transformation of a dead cougar that suffered a relapse on the lion's toe. And he swallowed the lion and something happened. The … see, the … Gloria and Tommy, they're two heads and they're not whales. But they escaped with herds of vomit, and things like that.

Interviewer: Who are Tommy and Gloria?

Schizophrenic patient: Uh, … there's Joe DiMaggio, Tommy Henrich, Bill Dickey, Phil Rizzuto, John Esclavera, Del Crandell, Ted Williams, Mickey Mantle, Roy Mantle, Ray Mantle, Bob Chance …

Interviewer: Who are they? Who are those people?

Schizophrenic patient: Dead people … they want to be fucked … by this outlaw.

Interviewer: What does all that mean?

Schizophrenic patient: Well, you see, I have to leave the hospital. I'm supposed to have an operation on my legs, you know. And it comes to me pretty sickly that I don't want to keep my legs. That's why I wish I could have an operation.

Interviewer: You want to have your legs taken off?

Schizophrenic patient: It's possible, you know.

Interviewer: Why would you want to do that?

Schizophrenic patient: I didn't have any legs to begin with. So I would imagine that if I was a fast runner, I'd be scared to be a wife, because I had a splinter inside of my head of lettuce. (Neale & Oltmanns, 1980, pp. 103–104)

This excerpt illustrates the **incoherence** sometimes found in the conversation of schizophrenic individuals: although the patient may make repeated references to central ideas or a theme, the images and fragments of thought are not connected; it is difficult to understand exactly what the patient is trying to tell the interviewer.

Speech may also be disordered by **loose associations** or **derailment**, in which case the patient may be more successful in communicating with a listener but has difficulty sticking to one topic. He or she seems to drift off on a train of associations evoked by an idea from the past. Schizophrenic patients have themselves provided descriptions of this state.

My thoughts get all jumbled up. I start thinking or talking about something but I never get there. Instead, I wander off in the wrong direction and get caught up with all sorts of different things that may be connected with things I want to say but in a way I can't explain.

People listening to me get more lost than I do…. My trouble is that I've got too many thoughts. You might think about something, let's say that ashtray and just think, oh! yes, that's for putting my cigarette in, but I would think of it and then I would think of a dozen different things connected with it at the same time. (McGhie & Chapman, 1961, p. 108)

Disturbances in speech were at one time regarded as the principal clinical symptom of schizophrenia, and they remain one of the criteria for the diagnosis. But evidence indicates that the speech of many schizophrenic patients is not disorganized, and the presence of disorganized speech does not discriminate well between schizophrenia and other psychoses, such as some mood disorders (Andreasen, 1979). For example, manic patients exhibit loose associations as much as do schizophrenic patients.

DELUSIONS

Deviance in the *content* of thought seems more central to schizophrenia than confusion in speech and in the form of thought. The thoughts of 97 percent of schizophrenic patients in the IPSS were found disordered in a fundamental way: patients lacked insight into their condition. When asked what they thought was wrong or why they had been hospitalized, schizophrenic patients seemed to have no appreciation of their condition and little realization that their behavior was unusual. More recent research has also found that lack of insight is common in schizophrenia (Amador et al., 1994).

No doubt all of us at one time or another have been concerned because we believed that others thought ill of us. Some of the time this belief may be justified. After all, who is universally loved?

Consider, though, what life would be like if you were firmly convinced that many people did not like you, indeed, that they disliked you so much that they were plotting against you. Imagine that your persecutors have sophisticated listening devices that allow them to tune in on your most private conversations and gather evidence in a plot to discredit you. None of those around you, including your loved ones, is able to reassure you that these people are not spying on you. Even your closest friends and confidants are gradually joining your tormentors and becoming members of the persecuting community. You are naturally quite anxious or angry about your situation, and you begin your own counteractions against the imagined persecutors. Any new room you enter must be carefully checked for listening devices. When you meet a person for the first time, you question him or her at great length to determine whether he or she is part of the plot against you.

Kurt Schneider, a German psychiatrist, proposed that particular forms of hallucinations and delusions, which he calls first-rank symptoms, are central to defining schizophrenia.

Such **delusions**, beliefs held contrary to reality, are common positive symptoms of schizophrenia. Persecutory delusions such as those just described were found in 65 percent of the IPSS sample. Delusions may also take several other forms; some of the most important of these were described by the German psychiatrist Kurt Schneider (1959). The following descriptions of these delusions are drawn from Mellor (1970).

- The patient may be the unwilling recipient of bodily sensations imposed by an external agency.

    A twenty-nine-year-old teacher described "X-rays entering the back of my neck, where the skin tingles and feels warm, they pass down the back in a hot tingling strip about six inches wide to the waist. There they disappear into the pelvis which feels numb and cold and solid like a block of ice. They stop me from getting an erection." (p. 16)

- The patient may believe that thoughts that are not his or her own have been placed in his or her mind by an external source.

    A twenty-nine-year-old housewife said, "I look out of the window and I think the garden looks nice and the grass looks cool, but the thoughts of Eamonn Andrews come into my mind. There are no other thoughts there, only his. ... He treats my mind like a screen and flashes his thoughts on it like you flash a picture." (p. 17)

- Patients may believe that their thoughts are broadcast or transmitted, so that others know what they are thinking.

    A twenty-one-year-old student [found that] "As I think, my thoughts leave my head on a type of mental ticker-tape. Everyone around has only to pass the tape through their mind and they know my thoughts." (p. 17)

- Patients may think their thoughts are being stolen from them, suddenly and unexpectedly, by an external force.

    A twenty-two-year-old woman [described such an experience]. "I am thinking about my mother, and suddenly my thoughts are sucked out of my mind by a phrenological vacuum extractor, and there is nothing in my mind, it is empty. ..." (pp. 16–17)

The next three delusions pertain to the patient's experiencing feelings and carrying out actions and impulses imposed on him or her by some external agent.

- Some patients may experience a situation wherein their feelings are controlled by an external force.

    A twenty-three-year-old female patient reported, "I cry, tears roll down my cheeks and I look unhappy, but inside I have a cold anger because they are using me in this way, and it is not me who is unhappy, but they are projecting unhappiness onto my brain. They project upon me laughter, for no reason, and you have no idea how terrible it is to laugh and look happy and know it is not you, but their emotions." (p. 17)

- Some patients believe that their behavior is controlled by an external force.

    A twenty-nine-year-old shorthand typist described her [simplest] actions as follows: "When I reach my hand for the comb it is my hand and arm which move, and my fingers pick up the pen, but I don't control them. ... I sit there watching them move, and they are quite independent, what they do is nothing to do with me. ... I am just a puppet who is manipulated by cosmic strings. When the strings are pulled my body moves and I cannot prevent it." (p. 17)

- Some patients believe that impulses to behave in certain ways are imposed on them by some external force.

    A twenty-nine-year-old engineer [who had] emptied the contents of a urine bottle over the ward dinner trolley [tried to explain the incident]. "The sudden impulse came over me that I must do it. It was not my feeling, it came into me from the X-ray department, that was why I was sent there for implants yesterday. It was nothing to do with me, they wanted it done. So I picked up the bottle and poured it in. It seemed all I could do." (p. 18)

Although delusions are found among more than half of people with schizophrenia, as with speech disorganization they are also found among patients with other diagnoses, notably, mania and delusional depression. The delusions of schizophrenic patients, however, are more bizarre than are those of patients in other diagnostic categories (Juninger, Barker, & Coe, 1992).

HALLUCINATIONS AND OTHER DISORDERS OF PERCEPTION

Schizophrenic patients frequently report that the world seems somehow different or even unreal to them. A patient may mention changes in how his or her body feels, or the patient's body may become so depersonalized that it feels as though it is a machine. As described in the case beginning this chapter, some people report difficulties in attending to what is happening around them.

I can't concentrate on television because I can't watch the screen and listen to what is being said at the same time. I can't seem to take in two things like this at the same time especially when one of them means watching and the other means listening. On the other hand I seem to be always taking in too much at the one time, and then I can't handle it and can't make sense of it. (McGhie & Chapman, 1961, p. 106)

The most dramatic distortions of perception are **hallucinations**, sensory experiences in the absence of any stimulation from the environment. They occur most often in the auditory modality and less often in the visual. Seventy-four percent of the IPSS sample reported having auditory hallucinations.

Some hallucinations are thought to be particularly important diagnostically because they occur more often in schizophrenic patients than in other psychotic patients. Some patients report hearing their own thoughts spoken by another voice:

[The] thirty-two-year-old housewife complained of a man's voice speaking in an intense whisper from a point about two feet above her head. The voice would repeat almost all the patient's goal-directing thinking—even the most banal thoughts. The patient would think, "I must put the kettle on," and after a pause of not more than one second the voice would say, "I must put the kettle on." It would often say the opposite, "Don't put the kettle on." (Mellor, 1970, p. 16)

Other patients claim that they hear voices arguing:

A twenty-four-year-old male patient reported hearing voices coming from the nurse's office. One voice, deep in pitch and roughly spoken, repeatedly said, "G.T. is a bloody paradox," and another higher in pitch said, "He is that, he should be locked up." A female voice occasionally interrupted, saying, "He is not, he is a lovely man." (Mellor, 1970, p. 16)

Still other patients hear voices commenting on their behavior:

A forty-one-year-old housewife heard a voice coming from a house across the road. The voice went on incessantly in a flat monotone describing everything she was doing with an admixture of critical comments. "She is peeling potatoes, got hold of the peeler, she does not want that potato, she is putting it back, because she thinks it has a knobble like a penis, she has a dirty mind, she is peeling potatoes, now she is washing them." (Mellor, 1970, p. 16)

NEGATIVE SYMPTOMS

The **negative symptoms** of schizophrenia consist of behavioral deficits, such as avolition, alogia, anhedonia, and flat affect.

AVOLITION

Avolition, or apathy, refers to a lack of energy and a seeming absence of interest in what are usually routine activities. Patients may be inattentive to grooming and personal hygiene, with uncombed hair, dirty nails, unbrushed teeth, and disheveled clothes. They have difficulty persisting at work, school, or household chores and spend much of their time sitting around doing nothing.

ALOGIA

Alogia is a negative thought disorder that can take several forms. In poverty of speech the amount of speech is greatly reduced. In poverty of content of speech the amount of discourse is adequate but it conveys little information and tends to be vague and repetitive. The following excerpt illustrates poverty of content of speech.

Interviewer: O.K. Why is it, do you think, that people believe in God?

Patient: Well, first of all because, He is the person that, is their personal savior. He walks with me and talks with me. And uh, the understanding that I have, a lot of peoples, they don't really know their personal self. Because they ain't, they all, just don't know their personal self. They don't know that He uh, seems to like me, a lot of them don't understand that He walks and talks with them. And uh, show 'em their way to go. I understand also that, every man and every lady, is not just pointed in the same direction. Some are pointed different. They go in their different ways. The way that

Jesus Christ wanted 'em to go. Myself. I am pointed in the ways of uh, knowing right from wrong, and doing it, I can't do any more, or not less than that. (American Psychiatric Association, 1987, pp. 403–404)

ANHEDONIA

Anhedonia refers to an inability to experience pleasure. It is manifested as a lack of interest in recreational activities, failure to develop close relationships with other people, and lack of interest in sex. Patients are aware of this symptom and report that what are usually considered pleasurable activities are not enjoyable for them.

FLAT OR BLUNTED AFFECT

In patients with **flat affect** virtually no stimulus can elicit an emotional response. The patient may stare vacantly, the muscles of the face flaccid, the eyes lifeless. When spoken to, the patient answers in a flat and toneless voice. Flat affect was found in 66 percent of the IPSS schizophrenic patients.

The concept of flat affect refers only to the outward expression of emotion and not to the patient's inner experience, which may not be impoverished at all. In a study by Kring and Neale (1996), schizophrenic and normal participants watched excerpts from films while their facial reactions and skin conductance were recorded. After each film clip participants self-reported on the moods the films had elicited. As expected, schizophrenic patients were much less facially expressive than were normal people, but they reported about the same amount of emotion and were even more physiologically aroused.

ASOCIALITY

Some schizophrenic patients have severe impairments in social relationships. They have few friends, poor social skills, and little interest in being with other people.

OTHER SYMPTOMS

Several other symptoms of schizophrenia do not fit neatly into the positive–negative scheme we have presented. One of these is *catatonia*, defined by several motor abnormalities. Patients may gesture repeatedly, using peculiar and sometimes complex sequences of finger, hand, and arm movements, which often seem to be purposeful, odd as they may be. Some schizophrenic patients manifest an unusual increase in their overall level of activity, including much excitement, wild flailing of the limbs, and great expenditure of energy similar to that seen in mania. At the other end of the spectrum is **catatonic immobility**: patients adopt unusual postures and maintain them for very long periods of time. A patient may stand on one leg, with the other tucked up toward the buttocks, and remain in this position virtually all day. Catatonic patients may also have **waxy flexibility**—another person can move the patient's limbs into strange positions that the patient will then maintain for long periods of time.

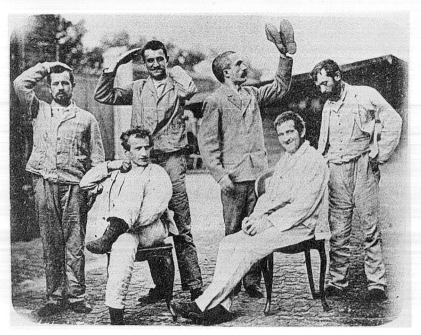

An 1896 photo showing a group of patients with catatonic immobility. These men held these unusual positions for long periods of time.

Some people with schizophrenia have **inappropriate affect**. The emotional responses of these individuals are out of context—the patient may laugh on hearing that his or her mother just died or become enraged when asked a simple question about how a new garment fits. These schizophrenic patients are likely to shift rapidly from one emotional state to another for no discernible reason. Although this symptom is quite rare, when it does appear it is of considerable diagnostic importance. Many patients also exhibit various forms of bizarre behavior. They may talk to themselves in public, hoard food, or collect garbage.

We turn now to a review of the history of the concept of schizophrenia and how ideas of what schizophrenia is have changed over time.

HISTORY OF THE CONCEPT

EARLY DESCRIPTIONS OF SCHIZOPHRENIA

The concept of schizophrenia was initially formulated by two European psychiatrists, Emil Kraepelin and Eugen Bleuler. Kraepelin first presented his notion of **dementia praecox**, the early term for schizophrenia, in 1898. He differentiated two major groups of endogenous, or internally caused, psychoses: manic-depressive illness and dementia praecox. Dementia praecox included several diagnostic concepts—dementia paranoides, catatonia, and hebephrenia—that had been regarded as distinct entities by clinicians in the previous few decades. Although these disorders were *symptomatically* diverse, Kraepelin believed that they shared a common core. His term, *dementia praecox*, reflected what he believed was the common core—an early onset (praecox) and a deteriorating course marked by a progressive intellectual deterioration (dementia). The *dementia* in dementia praecox is not the same as the dementias we discuss in the chapter on aging (Chapter 16). The latter are defined principally by severe memory impairments, whereas Kraepelin's term referred to a general "mental enfeeblement." Among the major symptoms that Kraepelin saw in dementia praecox were hallucinations, delusions, negativism, attentional difficulties, stereotyped behavior, and emotional dysfunction. He focused on both the course and the symptoms in defining the disorder, although he often emphasized the former over the latter.

Kraepelin did not move much beyond a narrow definition of schizophrenia and an emphasis on description. In the eighth edition of his textbook, for

Emil Kraepelin (1856–1926), the German psychiatrist, articulated descriptions of dementia praecox that have proved remarkably durable in the light of contemporary research.

Eugen Bleuler (1857–1939), the Swiss psychiatrist, contributed to our conceptions of schizophrenia and coined the term.

example, he grouped the symptoms of dementia praecox into thirty-six major categories, assigning hundreds of symptoms to each. He made little effort to interrelate these separate symptoms and stated only that they all reflected dementia and a loss of the usual unity in thinking, feeling, and acting. The view of the next major figure, Eugen Bleuler, however, represented both a specific attempt to define the core of the disorder and a move away from

Kraepelin's emphasis on age of onset and course in the definition.

Bleuler broke with Kraepelin on two major points: he believed that the disorder did not necessarily have an early onset, and he believed that it did not inevitably progress toward dementia. Thus the label *dementia praecox* was no longer appropriate, and in 1908 Bleuler proposed his own term, *schizophrenia*, from the Greek words *schizein*, meaning "to split," and *phren*, meaning "mind," to capture what he viewed as the essential nature of the condition.

With age of onset and deteriorating course no longer considered defining features of the disorder, Bleuler faced a conceptual problem. Since the symptoms of schizophrenia could vary widely among patients, he had to provide some justification for putting them into a single diagnostic category. Bleuler therefore tried to specify a common denominator, or essential property, that would link the various disturbances. The metaphorical concept that he adopted for this purpose was the "breaking of associative threads." For Bleuler, associative threads joined not only words but thoughts. Thus goal-directed, efficient thinking and communication were possible only when these hypothetical structures were intact. The notion that associative threads were disrupted in schizophrenic patients could then account for other problems. Bleuler viewed attentional difficulties, for example, as resulting from a loss of purposeful direction in thought, in turn causing passive responses to objects and people in the immediate surroundings. In a similar vein he viewed blocking, an apparently total loss of a train of thought, as a complete disruption of the person's associative threads.

Although Kraepelin recognized that a small percentage of patients who originally manifested symptoms of dementia praecox did not deteriorate, he preferred to limit this diagnostic category to patients who had a poor prognosis. Bleuler's work, in contrast, led to a broader concept of schizophrenia and a more pronounced theoretical emphasis. He diagnosed patients with a good prognosis as schizophrenic, and he also included as schizophrenic many patients who would have received different diagnoses from other clinicians.

THE BROADENED U.S. CONCEPT

Bleuler had a great influence on the concept of schizophrenia as it developed in the United States. Over the first part of the twentieth century the breadth of the diagnosis was extended considerably. At the New York State Psychiatric Institute, for example, about 20 percent of the patients were diagnosed as schizophrenic in the 1930s. The numbers increased through the 1940s and in 1952 peaked at a remarkable 80 percent. In contrast, the European concept of schizophrenia remained narrower. The percentage of patients diagnosed as schizophrenic at the Maudsley Hospital in London stayed relatively constant, at 20 percent, for a forty-year period (Kuriansky, Deming, & Gurland, 1974).

The reasons for the increase in the frequency of diagnoses of schizophrenia in the United States are easily discerned. Several prominent figures in U.S. psychiatry expanded Bleuler's concept of schizophrenia even more. For example, in 1933, Kasanin described nine patients who had been diagnosed with dementia praecox. For all of them, the onset of the disorder had been sudden and recovery relatively rapid. Noting that theirs could be said to be a combination of both schizophrenic and affective symptoms, Kasanin suggested the term *schizoaffective psychosis* to describe the disturbances of these patients. This diagnosis subsequently became part of the U.S. concept of schizophrenia and was listed in DSM-I (1952) and DSM-II (1968).

In the 1960s and 1970s the **process-reactive dimension** was another key means of maintaining the broad concept of schizophrenia in the United States. Once Bleuler had observed that the onset of schizophrenia did not always occur at a young age and that deterioration was not a certain course, clinicians began to note other differences between patients whose onset was later and who sometimes recovered and those whose onset was earlier and who usually deteriorated further. Some schizophrenic patients had been relatively deviant, apathetic individuals for many of their young years, suffering gradual but insidious depletion of thought, emotion, interests, and activity. Others had a rather rapid onset of more severe symptoms, usually later in life. The term *process*, indicating some sort of basic physiological malfunction in the brain, was chosen for insidiously developing schizophrenia, and *reactive* for what appeared suddenly after stress. Since the 1950s the process-reactive dimension has been extensively studied in the United States. Earlier social and sexual adjustment as measured, for example, by the Phillips Scale (1953), became a means of identifying schizophrenic individuals and determining their chances for recovery. People with a *good premorbid* adjustment were more likely to have only an episodic problem and to have a good prognosis. In contrast, process schizophrenia, following an earlier poor adjustment at school, work, and in their sexual and social lives, became equated with Kraepelin's original description of dementia praecox. The inclusion of reactive patients in the definition helped extend the concept.

The concept of schizophrenia was further broadened by two additional diagnostic practices. First, U.S. clinicians tended to diagnose schizophrenia whenever delusions or hallucinations were present. Because these symptoms, particularly delusions, occur in mood disorders, many patients with a DSM-II diagnosis of schizophrenia actually had a mood disorder (Cooper et al., 1972). Second, patients whom we would now diagnose as having a personality disorder (notably schizotypal, schizoid, and paranoid personality disorders; see Chapter 13), were also diagnosed as schizophrenic according to DSM-II criteria.

THE DSM-IV DIAGNOSIS

Beginning in DSM-III, the U.S. concept of schizophrenia has shifted considerably from the former broad definition to a new definition, which narrows the range of patients diagnosed as schizophrenic in four ways. First, the diagnostic criteria are presented in explicit and considerable detail. Second, patients with symptoms of a mood disorder are specifically excluded. Schizophrenia, schizoaffective type, is now listed as *schizoaffective disorder* in a separate section as one of the psychotic disorders. Schizoaffective disorder comprises a mixture of symptoms of schizophrenia and mood disorders.

Third, DSM-IV requires at least six months of disturbance for the diagnosis. The six-month period must include at least one month of the active phase, defined by the presence of at least two of the following: delusions, hallucinations, disorganized speech, grossly disorganized or catatonic behavior, and negative symptoms. (Only one of these symptoms is required if the delusions are bizarre or if the hallucinations consist of voices commenting or arguing.) The remaining time required can be either a prodromal (before the active phase) or a residual (after the active phase) period. Problems during these phases include social withdrawal, impaired role functioning, blunted or inappropriate affect, lack of initiative, vague and circumstantial speech, impairment in hygiene and grooming, odd beliefs or magical thinking, and unusual perceptual experiences. These criteria eliminate patients who have a brief psychotic episode, often stress related, and then recover quickly. DSM-II's acute schizophrenic episode is now diagnosed as either *schizophreniform disorder* or *brief psychotic disorder*, which are also listed in a new section in DSM-IV. The symptoms of schizophreniform disorder are the same as those of schizophrenia but last only from one to six months.

Brief psychotic disorder lasts from one day to one month and is often brought on by extreme stress, such as bereavement. Fourth, what DSM-II regarded as mild forms of schizophrenia are now diagnosed as personality disorders, for example, schizotypal personality disorder.

Finally, DSM-IV differentiates between paranoid schizophrenia, to be discussed shortly, and **delusional disorder**. A person with delusional disorder is troubled by persistent persecutory delusions or by delusional jealousy, the unfounded conviction that a spouse or lover is unfaithful. Other delusions are those of being followed, delusions of erotomania (believing that one is loved by some other person, usually a complete stranger with a higher social status), and somatic delusions (believing that some internal organ is malfunctioning). Unlike the person with paranoid schizophrenia, the person with delusional disorder does not have disorganized speech or hallucinations and his or her delusions are less bizarre. Delusional disorder is quite rare and typically begins later in life than does schizophrenia. In most family studies it appears to be related to schizophrenia, perhaps genetically (Kendler & Diehl, 1993).

Are the DSM-IV diagnostic criteria applicable across cultures? Data bearing on this question have been collected in a World Health Organization study of both industrialized and developing countries (Jablonsky et al., 1992). The symptomatic criteria held up well cross-culturally. However, schizophrenic patients in developing countries have a more acute onset and a more favorable course than those in industrialized societies. The cause of this intriguing finding is unknown (Susser & Wanderling, 1994).

CATEGORIES OF SCHIZOPHRENIA IN DSM-IV

Earlier we mentioned that the heterogeneity of schizophrenic symptoms gave rise to proposals concerning the presence of subtypes of the disorder. Three types of schizophrenic disorders included in DSM-IV—disorganized, catatonic, and paranoid— were initially proposed by Kraepelin many years ago. The present descriptions of Kraepelin's original types provide further information on what schizophrenia is like and on the great diversity of behavior that relates to the diagnosis.

DISORGANIZED SCHIZOPHRENIA

Kraepelin's hebephrenic form of schizophrenia is called **disorganized schizophrenia** in DSM-IV. Speech is disorganized and difficult for a listener to follow. The patient may speak incoherently, stringing together similar-sounding words and even inventing new words, often accompanied by silliness or laughter. He or she may have flat affect or experience constant shifts of emotion, breaking into inexplicable fits of laughter and crying. The patient's behavior is generally disorganized and not goal directed; for example, he or she may tie a ribbon around a big toe or move incessantly, pointing at objects for no apparent reason. The patient sometimes deteriorates to the point of incontinence, voiding anywhere and at any time, and completely neglects his or her appearance, never bathing, brushing teeth, or combing hair.

CATATONIC SCHIZOPHRENIA

The most obvious symptoms of **catatonic schizophrenia** are the catatonic symptoms described earlier. Patients typically alternate between catatonic immobility and wild excitement, but one of these symptoms may predominate. These patients resist instructions and suggestions and often echo (repeat back) the speech of others. The onset of catatonic reactions may be more sudden than the onset of other forms of schizophrenia, although the person is likely to have previously shown some apathy and withdrawal from reality. The limbs of the person with catatonic immobility may become stiff and swollen; in spite of apparent obliviousness, he or she may later relate all that occurred during the stupor. In the excited state the catatonic person may shout and talk continuously and incoherently, all the while pacing with great agitation. This form of schizophrenia is seldom seen today, perhaps because drug therapy works effectively on these bizarre motor processes. Alternatively, Boyle (1991) has argued that the apparent high prevalence of catatonia during the early part of the century reflected misdiagnosis. Specifically, she details similarities between encephalitis lethargica (sleeping sickness) and catatonic schizophrenia and suggests that many cases of the former were misdiagnosed as the latter.

PARANOID SCHIZOPHRENIA

The diagnosis **paranoid schizophrenia** is assigned to a substantial number of incoming patients to mental hospitals. The key to this diagnosis is the presence of prominent delusions. Delusions of persecution are most common, but patients may experience **grandiose delusions**, in which they have an exaggerated sense of their own importance, power, knowledge, or identity. Some patients are plagued by **delusional jealousy**, the unsubstantiated belief

that their sexual partner is unfaithful. The other delusions described earlier may also be evident. Vivid auditory hallucinations may accompany the delusions. Patients with paranoid schizophrenia often develop **ideas of reference**; they incorporate unimportant events within a delusional framework and read personal significance into the trivial activities of others. For instance, they think that overheard segments of conversations are about them, that the frequent appearance of a person on a street where they customarily walk means that they are being watched, and that what they see on television or read in magazines somehow refers to them. Individuals with paranoid schizophrenia are agitated, argumentative, angry, and sometimes violent. But they remain emotionally responsive, although they may be somewhat stilted, formal, and intense with others, and they are more alert and verbal than are patients with other types of schizophrenia. Their language, although filled with references to delusions, is not disorganized.

EVALUATION OF THE SUBTYPES

Although these subtypes form the basis of current diagnostic systems, their usefulness is often questioned. Because diagnosing types of schizophrenia is extremely difficult, diagnostic reliability is dramatically reduced. Furthermore, these subtypes have little predictive validity; that is, the diagnosis of one over another form of schizophrenia provides little information that is helpful either in treating or in predicting the course of the problems. There is also considerable overlap among the types. For example, patients with all forms of schizophrenia may have delusions. Kraepelin's system of subtyping has not proved to be an optimal way of dealing with the variability in schizophrenic behavior.

Supplemental types included in DSM-IV are also flawed. The diagnosis of **undifferentiated schizophrenia** applies to patients who meet the diagnostic criteria for schizophrenia but not for any of the three subtypes. The diagnosis of **residual schizophrenia** is used when the patient no longer meets the full criteria for schizophrenia, but still shows some signs of the illness. Schizophrenia is a disorder with a wide range of possible symptoms. Indeed, Bleuler wrote of the "group of schizophrenias," implying that schizophrenia is not one but a set of disorders, each perhaps with a different etiology.

Because of the symptomatic variability among schizophrenic patients, there is continuing interest in establishing subtypes of symptoms. The system that is currently attracting much attention distinguishes between positive and negative symptoms (Crow,

1980; Strauss, Carpenter, & Bartko, 1974). Andreasen and Olsen (1982) evaluated fifty-two schizophrenic patients and found that sixteen could be regarded as having predominantly negative symptoms, eighteen as having predominantly positive symptoms, and eighteen as having mixed symptoms. Although these data suggest that it is possible to talk about types of schizophrenia, subsequent research has indicated that most schizophrenic patients show mixed symptoms (e.g., Andreasen et al., 1990) and that very few patients fit into the pure positive or pure negative types. More recent analyses of the symptoms of schizophrenia have revealed three dimensions, not two (Lenzenweger, Dworkin, & Wethington, 1991). These studies have shown, in addition to positive and negative symptoms, a disorganized component that includes bizarre behavior and disorganized speech. However, the distinction between positive and negative symptoms (as opposed to types of patients) continues to be used increasingly in research on the etiology of schizophrenia. We will present evidence relevant to the validity of this distinction in the discussion of the possible roles of genetics, dopamine, and brain pathology in the etiology of schizophrenia.

ETIOLOGY OF SCHIZOPHRENIA

We have described how schizophrenic patients differ from normal people in thought, speech, perception, and imagination. What can explain the scattering and disconnection of their thoughts, their inappropriate emotions or lack of emotion, their misguided delusions and bewildering hallucinations? As broad theoretical perspectives, such as psychoanalysis, have not had much of an impact on research in schizophrenia, we look here at major areas of etiological research. For a different approach to schizophrenia, labeling theory, see Focus 11.1.

THE GENETIC DATA

What would you do if you wanted to find an individual who had a very good chance of being diagnosed one day as schizophrenic and you could not consider any behavior patterns or other symptoms? This problem, suggested by Paul Meehl (1962), has one solution with a close-to-even chance of picking a potential schizophrenic: *Find an individual who has a schizophrenic identical twin.* A convincing body of literature indicates that a predisposition for schizophrenia is transmitted genetically. The family, twin, and adoption methods employed in this research, as in other behavior-genetics research projects, have

led researchers to conclude that a predisposition to schizophrenia is inherited. Though most of the major genetic studies of schizophrenia were conducted before the publication of DSM-III, genetic investigators collected extensive descriptive data on their samples, allowing them to be rediagnosed using newer diagnostic criteria. Reanalyses using DSM-III criteria have substantiated the conclusions reached earlier (e.g., Kendler & Gruenberg, 1984).

FAMILY STUDIES

Table 11.1 presents a summary of the risk for schizophrenia in various relatives of schizophrenic index cases. (In evaluating the figures, bear in mind that the risk for schizophrenia in the general population is a little less than 1 percent.) Quite clearly, relatives of schizophrenic patients are at increased risk, and the risk increases as the genetic relationship between proband and relative becomes closer. More recent data confirm what is shown in Table 11.1 and also indicate that risk for schizophrenia is particularly high in the families of female and early-onset probands (Sham et al., 1994). The data gathered by the family method thus support the notion that a predisposition for schizophrenia can be transmitted genetically. Yet relatives of a schizophrenic proband share not only genes but also common experiences. The behavior of a schizophrenic parent could be very disturbing to a developing child. The influence of the environment cannot be discounted as a rival explanation for the higher morbidity risks.

TWIN STUDIES

Concordance rates for MZ and DZ twins are also given in Table 11.1. Concordance for identical twins (44.3%), although greater than that for fraternal

TABLE 11.1 Summary of Major European Family and Twin Studies of the Genetics of Schizophrenia

Relation to Proband	Percentage Schizophrenic
Spouse	1.00
Grandchildren	2.84
Nieces/nephews	2.65
Children	9.35
Siblings	7.30
DZ twins	12.08
MZ twins	44.30

Source: After Gottesman, McGufflin, & Farmer, 1987.

FOCUS 11.1 LABELING THEORY

In a radical departure from the traditional conceptualization of schizophrenia, Scheff (1966) argues that the disorder is a learned social role. This position, also known as **labeling theory**, is essentially unconcerned with etiology. According to Scheff, the crucial factor in schizophrenia is the act of assigning a diagnostic label to the individual. Presumably this label influences the manner in which the person will continue to behave, based on stereotypic notions of mental illness, and at the same time determines the reactions of other people to the individual's behavior. The social role, therefore, *is* the disorder, and it is determined by the labeling process. Without the diagnosis, Scheff argues, deviant behavior—or, to use his term, residual rule breaking—would not become stabilized. It would presumably be both transient and relatively inconsequential.

By residual rules, Scheff means the rules that are left over after all the formal and obvious ones, about stealing and violence and fairness, have been laid down. The examples are endless. "Do not stand still staring vacantly in the middle of a busy sidewalk." "Do not talk to the neon beer sign in the delicatessen window." "Do not spit on the piano." Scheff believes that one-time violations of residual rules are fairly common. Normal people, through poor judgment or bad luck, may be caught violating a rule and may then be diagnosed as mentally ill. Once so judged, these people are likely to accept this social role and to find it difficult to rejoin the sane. They will be denied employment, and other people will know about their pasts. In the hospital they will receive attention and sympathy and be free of all responsibilities. So, once hospitalized, they actually perceive themselves as mentally ill and settle into acting as they are expected to do—crazy.

Scheff's theory has some intuitive appeal. Most people who have worked for any amount of time at a psychiatric facility have witnessed abuses of the diagnostic process. Patients are sometimes assigned labels that are poorly justified.

The theory has a number of serious problems, however, indicating that it is at most of secondary importance to our understanding of schizophrenia. First, Scheff refers to deviance as residual rule breaking, and in his description it is indeed merely that. However, calling schizophrenia residual rule breaking trivializes a serious disorder. Second, very little evidence indicates that unlabeled norm violations are indeed transient, as Scheff implies. Third, information regarding the detrimental effects of the social stigma associated with mental illness is inconclusive (Gove, 1970).

An important correlate of the labeling position is the notion of cultural relativism, according to which definitions of abnormality should be very different in cultures different from our own because of the wide variation in social norms and rules. As an example, proponents of labeling theory might argue that the visions of a shaman are the same as the hallucinations of a schizophrenic but that cultural differences allow a favorable response to shamans.

---

twins (12.08%), is less than 100 percent. This finding is important; if genetic transmission alone accounted for schizophrenia and one twin was schizophrenic, the other twin would also be schizophrenic because MZ twins are genetically identical. Consistent with a genetic interpretation of these data, concordance among MZ twins does increase when the proband is more severely ill (Gottesman & Shields, 1972).

Questions have been raised about the interpretation of data collected on twins. Some have argued that the experience of being an identical twin may itself predispose toward schizophrenia. If schizophrenia is considered an identity problem, it might be argued that being a member of an identical pair of twins could be particularly stressful. But schizophrenia occurs about as frequently in single births as in twin births. If the hypothesis were correct, simply being a twin would have to increase the likelihood of becoming schizophrenic, and it does not (Rosenthal, 1970).

The most critical problem of interpretation remains. A common deviant environment rather than common genetic factors could account for the concordance rates. By common environment we mean not only similar child-rearing practices but also a more similar intrauterine environment, for MZ twins are more likely than DZ twins to share a single blood supply. A clever analysis supporting a genetic interpretation of the high concordance rates found for identical twins was performed by Fischer (1971). She reasoned that if these rates indeed reflected a genetic effect, the children of even the discordant, or nonschizophrenic, identical co-twins of schizophrenics should be at high risk for schizophrenia. These nonschizophrenic twins would presumably have the genotype for schizophrenia, even though it was not expressed behaviorally, and thus might pass along an increased risk for the disorder to their children. In agreement with this line of reasoning, the rate of schizophrenia and schizophrenic-like psychoses in the children of nonschizophrenic co-twins of schizophrenic probands was 9.4 percent. The rate among the children of the schizophrenic probands themselves was only slightly and

Some writers have held that visions of shamans are the same as the hallucinations of schizophrenics. Murphy's research, however, finds that the behavior of shamans is clearly distinguished from psychopathology.

This and several other questions were addressed by Murphy (1976) in a report of her investigations of Eskimo and Yoruba. Contrary to the labeling view, both cultures have a concept of being crazy that is quite similar to our definition of schizophrenia. The Eskimo's *nuthkavihak* includes talking to oneself, refusing to talk, delusional beliefs, and bizarre behavior. The Yoruba's *were* encompasses similar symptoms. Notably, both cultures also have shamans but draw a clear distinction between their behavior and that of crazy people.

A final perspective on labeling theory is found in an anecdote related by colleagues of Paul Meehl, the famous schizophrenia theorist. Meehl was giving a lecture on genetics and schizophrenia when someone in the audience interrupted him to point out that he thought that schizophrenic patients behaved in a crazy way because others had labeled them schizophrenic. Meehl had the following reaction:

> I just stood there and didn't know what to say. I was thinking of a patient I had seen on a ward who kept his finger up his ass "to keep his thoughts from running out," while with his other hand he tried to tear out his hair because it really "belonged to his father." And here was this man telling me that he was doing these things because someone had called him a schizophrenic. What could I say to him? (Kimble, Garmezy, & Zigler, 1980, p. 453)

In sum, the labeling position does not have much support. The view that schizophrenia is role taking reinforced by the attitudes of diagnosticians and mental hospital staff is without substantiating evidence.

nonsignificantly higher, 12.3 percent. Both rates are substantially higher than those found in an unselected population.

Dworkin and his colleagues reevaluated the major twin studies according to the positive–negative symptom distinction discussed earlier (Dworkin et al., 1987; Dworkin & Lenzenweger, 1984). Ratings of positive and negative symptoms were compiled from published case histories of the twins and compared for probands of concordant and discordant pairs. No differences emerged for positive symptoms, but probands from concordant pairs were higher in negative symptoms than were probands from discordant pairs. These data suggest that negative symptoms have a stronger genetic component than positive ones.

ADOPTION STUDIES

The study of children of schizophrenic mothers who were reared from early infancy by nonschizophrenic adoptive parents has provided more con-

clusive information on the role of genes in schizophrenia by eliminating the possible effects of a deviant environment. Heston (1966) was able to follow up forty-seven people who had been born between 1915 and 1945 to schizophrenic mothers in a state mental hospital. The infants were separated from their mothers at birth and raised by foster or adoptive parents. Fifty control subjects were selected from the same foundling homes that had placed the children of schizophrenic mothers.

The follow-up assessment, conducted in 1964, consisted of an interview, the MMPI, an IQ test, social class ratings, and so on. A dossier on each subject was rated independently by two psychiatrists, and a third evaluation was made by Heston. Ratings were made on a 0 to 100 scale of overall disability, and whenever possible, diagnoses were offered. The control participants were rated as less disabled than the children of schizophrenic mothers. Thirty-one of the forty-seven children of schizophrenic mothers (66 percent) but only nine of the fifty controls (18 percent) were given a diagnosis. None of the con-

TABLE 11.2 Participants Separated from Their Mothers in Early Infancy

Assessment	Offspring of Schizophrenic Mothers	Control Offspring
Number of participants	47	50
Mean age at follow-up	35.8	36.3
Overall ratings of disability (low score indicates more pathology)	65.2	80.1
Number diagnosed schizophrenic	5	0
Number diagnosed mentally defective	4	0
Number diagnosed psychopathic	9	2
Number diagnosed neurotic	13	7

Source: From Heston, 1966.

trols was diagnosed as schizophrenic, but 16.6 percent of the offspring of schizophrenic mothers were so diagnosed.[1] Children of schizophrenic mothers were also more likely to be diagnosed as mentally defective, psychopathic, and neurotic (Table 11.2). They had been involved more frequently in criminal activity, had spent more time in penal institutions, and had more often been discharged from the armed services for psychiatric reasons. Heston's study clearly supports the importance of genetic factors in the development of schizophrenia. Children reared without contact with their so-called pathogenic mothers were still more likely to become schizophrenic than were the controls.

A study similar to Heston's was carried out in Denmark under Kety's direction (Kety et al., 1976, 1994). The starting point for the investigation was a culling of the records of children who had been adopted at a young age. All adoptees who had later been admitted to a psychiatric facility and diagnosed as schizophrenic were selected as the index cases. From the remaining cases the investigators chose a control group of people who had no psychiatric history and who were matched to the index group on such variables as sex and age. Both the adoptive and the biological parents and the siblings and half-siblings of the two groups were then identified, and a search was made to determine who among them had a psychiatric history. As might be expected if genetic factors figure in schizophrenia, the biological relatives of the index cases were diag-

nosed as schizophrenic more often than were members of the general population; the adoptive relatives were not.

EVALUATION OF THE GENETIC DATA

The data collected so far indicate that genetic factors play an important role in the development of schizophrenia. Early twin and family studies were criticized because they did not separate the effects of genes and environment. However, more recent studies of children of schizophrenic parents who were reared in foster and adoptive homes, plus the follow-up of relatives of adopted schizophrenic children, have virtually removed the potential influence of the environment.

Despite this evidence, we cannot conclude that schizophrenia is a disorder completely determined by genetic transmission, for we must always keep in mind the distinction between phenotype and genotype (see p. 26). The diathesis–stress model introduced in Chapter 2 seems appropriate for guiding theory and research into the etiology of schizophrenia. Genetic factors can only be predisposers for schizophrenia. Some kind of stress is required to render this predisposition an observable pathology.

The genetic research in schizophrenia has some further limitations as well. First, it has not been possible to specify exactly how a predisposition for schizophrenia is transmitted. Is it by a single gene (and, if so, dominant or recessive) or by a collection of genes? This point is critically relevant to linkage analysis (see p. 240), in which family pedigrees are studied to try to determine on which chromosome the schizophrenia gene is located. Although positive results have been reported with this method, most recently linking schizophrenia to chromosome 6 (Buckley et al., 1996), such results have a history of

---

[1]The figure of 16.6 percent figure was *age corrected*. By this process raw data are corrected to take into account the age of the participants. If a person in Heston's sample was twenty-four years old at the time of the assessment, he or she might still have become schizophrenic at some point later in life. The age-correction procedure attempts to account for this possibility.

not being replicated (Kendler & Diehl, 1993), possibly because the success of the method requires that the predisposition be transmitted by a single gene or small set of genes and this assumption may be faulty.

Second, the nature of the inherited diathesis remains unknown. What exactly is inherited that puts some people at risk for schizophrenia? One way of addressing this question is to study relatives of schizophrenic patients. Although not necessarily disordered, these individuals, who are genetically at risk for schizophrenia, may reveal signs of the genetic predisposition. A major area of research is the study of how well the eyes track a moving target such as a pendulum. Schizophrenic patients do poorly on this task, as do about 50 percent of their first-degree relatives (Holzman et al., 1984). The importance of eye tracking is supported by data showing that it is influenced by genetic factors (Iacono et al., 1992). Deficient eye tracking may reflect a problem in the frontal lobes of the brain.

Despite the problems and loose ends in the genetic data, it would be a mistake to dismiss them. Many of the criticisms raised here could also be leveled at the genetic studies of other disorders. The strong positive correlation between genetic relatedness and the prevalence of schizophrenia remain one of the strongest links in the chain of information about the causes of schizophrenia.

BIOCHEMICAL FACTORS[2]

The demonstrated role of genetic factors in schizophrenia suggests that biochemicals should be investigated, for it is through the body chemistry and biological processes that heredity may have an effect. However, the search for possible biochemical causes faces a key difficulty. An aberrant biochemical found in schizophrenic patients and not in control subjects may be produced by a third variable rather than by the disorder. Most schizophrenic patients take psychoactive medication. Although the effects of such drugs on behavior diminish quite rapidly once they are discontinued, traces may remain in the bloodstream for several weeks, making it difficult to attribute a biochemical difference between schizophrenic and control participants to the disorder. Prolonged drug therapy may also lead to changes in the very process of neural transmission. Institutionalized patients may smoke more,

---

[2]This section is necessarily technical and may be difficult to follow for readers who have not studied biochemistry. For those who have this background we want to provide details; for those who lack it, we hope at least to convey the logic and general trends in the research on biochemical factors.

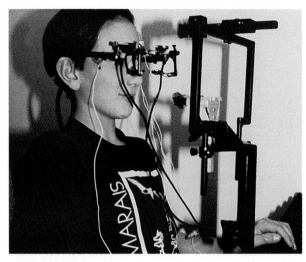

Apparatus used to assess a person's ability to track a moving target. This ability is impaired in both schizophrenic patients and their relatives, suggesting that eye-tracking is a genetic marker for the disorder.

drink more coffee, and have a less nutritionally adequate diet than do various control groups, and they may be relatively inactive. All these variables can conspire to produce biochemical differences between schizophrenic patients and controls that confound attempts to seek deviant biochemicals as causes of schizophrenia.

Nonetheless, the search for biochemical causes of schizophrenia proceeds at a rapid rate. Improved technology now allows a much greater understanding of the relation between biochemistry and behavior. Present research is examining several different neurotransmitters, such as norepinephrine and serotonin. No biochemical theory has unequivocal support, but because of the great amount of effort that continues to be spent in the search for biochemical causes of schizophrenia, we shall review one of the best researched factors, dopamine.

DOPAMINE ACTIVITY

The theory that schizophrenia is related to activity of the neurotransmitter dopamine is based principally on the knowledge that drugs effective in treating schizophrenia alter dopamine activity. The phenothiazines (see p. 287), in addition to being useful in treating some symptoms of schizophrenia, produce side effects resembling the symptoms of Parkinson's disease. Parkinsonism is known to be caused in part by low levels of dopamine in a particular nerve tract of the brain. It is therefore supposed that phenothiazines lower dopamine activity. Because of their structural similarities to the

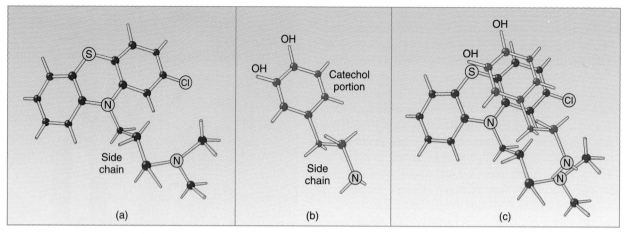

Figure 11.1 Conformation of (*a*) chlorpromazine, a phenothiazine, and (*b*) dopamine, and (*c*) their superimposition, determined by X-ray crystallographic analysis. Chlorpromazine blocks impulse transmission by dopamine by fitting into its receptor sites. Adapted from Horn and Snyder (1971).

dopamine molecule (Figure 11.1), phenothiazine molecules fit into and thereby block postsynaptic receptors in dopamine tracts. From this speculation about the action of the drugs that help schizophrenic patients, it is but a short inductive leap to view schizophrenia as resulting from excess activity in dopamine nerve tracts.

Further indirect support for the **dopamine activity theory** of schizophrenia comes from the literature on amphetamine psychosis. Amphetamines can produce a state that closely resembles paranoid schizophrenia, and they can exacerbate the symptomatology of patients with schizophrenia (Angrist, Lee, & Gershon, 1974). The amphetamines cause the release of catecholamines into the synaptic cleft and prevent their inactivation. We can be relatively confident that the psychosis-inducing effects of amphetamines are a result of their impact on dopamine rather than on norepinephrine, because phenothiazines are antidotes to amphetamine psychosis.

Based on the data just reviewed, researchers at first assumed that schizophrenia was caused by an excess of dopamine. But as other studies progressed, this assumption did not gain support. For example, the major metabolite of dopamine, homovanillic acid (HVA), was *not* found in greater amounts in schizophrenic patients (Bowers, 1974).

Such data, plus improved technologies for studying neurochemical variables in humans, led researchers to propose excess or oversensitive dopamine *receptors*, rather than a high level of dopamine, as factors in schizophrenia. Research on the phenothiazines' mode of action suggests that the dopaminergic receptors are a more likely locus of disorder than the level of dopamine itself. Some postmortem studies of brains of schizophrenic

patients as well as PET scans of schizophrenic patients have revealed that dopamine receptors may increase in number or become hyperactive in some people with schizophrenia (Hietala et al., 1994; Tune et al., 1993; Wong et al., 1986).

Excess dopamine receptors may not be responsible for all the symptoms of schizophrenia; they appear to be related mainly to positive symptoms. Some studies have shown, for example, that amphetamines do not worsen the symptoms of all patients (e.g., Kornetsky, 1976); one study has reported that symptoms lessen after an amphetamine has been administered (Kammen et al., 1977). Furthermore, phenothiazines have been shown to benefit only a subgroup of patients. These divergent results are related to the positive–negative symptom distinction noted earlier. Amphetamines worsen positive symptoms and lessen negative ones. Phenothiazines lessen positive symptoms but their effect on negative symptoms is less clear; some studies show no benefit (e.g., Haracz, 1982), and others show a positive effect (e.g., vanKammen et al., 1987).

More recent developments in the dopamine theory (e.g., Davis et al., 1991) have expanded its scope. The key change involves the recognition of differences among the neural pathways that use dopamine as a transmitter. The excess dopamine activity that is thought to be most relevant to schizophrenia is localized in the mesolimbic pathway (see Figure 11.2), and the therapeutic effects of phenothiazines on positive symptoms occur by blocking dopamine receptors there. The mesocortical dopamine pathway begins in the same brain region as the mesolimbic but projects to the prefrontal cortex. The prefrontal cortex also projects to limbic areas that are innervated by dopamine. These dopamine neurons in the

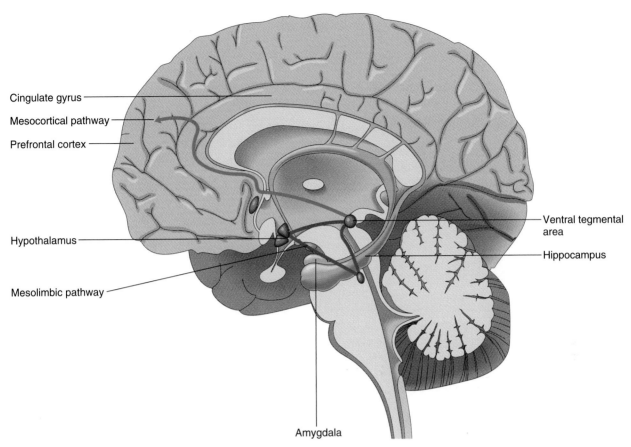

Figure 11.2 The brain and schizophrenia. The mesocortical pathway begins in the ventral tegmental area and projects to the prefrontal cortex. The mesolimbic pathway also begins in the ventral tegmental area but projects to the hypothalamus, amygdala, hippocampus, and nucleus accumbens.

prefrontal cortex may be underactive and thus fail to exert inhibitory control over the dopamine neurons in the limbic area. The underactivity of the dopamine neurons in the prefrontal cortex may also be the cause of the negative symptoms of schizophrenia (see Figure 11.3). This proposal has the advantage of allowing the simultaneous presence of positive and negative symptoms in a schizophrenic patient. Furthermore, because phenothiazines do not have major effects on the dopamine neurons in the prefrontal cortex, we would expect them to be relatively ineffective as treatments for negative symptoms, and they are. When we examine research on structural abnormalities in the brains of schizophrenic patients, we will see some close connections between these two domains.

EVALUATION OF THE BIOCHEMICAL AREA

Despite favorable developments, the dopamine theory does not explain some other information about treatment. For example, phenothiazines gradually lessen positive schizophrenic symptoms over a

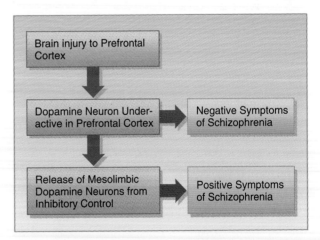

Figure 11.3 Dopamine theory of schizophrenia.

period of several weeks but rapidly block dopamine receptors, so that after several weeks tolerance should develop (Davis, 1978). This disjunction between the behavioral and pharmacological effects of phenothiazines is difficult to understand within the context of the theory.

It is also puzzling that to be therapeutically effective, phenothiazines must reduce dopamine levels or receptor activity to *below normal*, producing Parkinsonian side effects. According to the theory, reducing dopamine levels or receptor activity to normal should be sufficient for a therapeutic effect.

Furthermore, as we describe later, newer drugs used in treating schizophrenia implicate other neurotransmitters, such as serotonin, in the disorder. Dopamine neurons generally function to modulate the activity of other neural systems; for example, in the prefrontal cortex they regulate GABA neurons. Similarly, serotonin neurons regulate dopamine neurons in the mesolimbic pathway. Thus dopamine may be only one piece in a much more complicated jigsaw puzzle.

Glutamate, a transmitter that is widespread in the human brain, may also play a role. Low levels of glutamate have been found in cerebrospinal fluid of schizophrenic patients, and postmortem studies have revealed low levels of the enzyme needed to produce glutamate (Tsai et al., 1995). The street drug PCP can induce a psychotic state that is very similar to schizophrenia and this effect is produced by interfering with one of glutamate's receptors.

Although dopamine remains the most actively researched biochemical position, it is not likely to provide a complete explanation of the biochemistry of schizophrenia. Schizophrenia is a disorder with widespread symptoms covering perception, cognition, motor activity, and social behavior. It is unlikely that a single neurotransmitter, such as dopamine, could account for all of them. Schizophrenia researchers are starting to cast a broader biochemical net, moving away from the heavy emphasis on dopamine. Glutamate and serotonin may well be at the forefront of these inquiries.

THE BRAIN AND SCHIZOPHRENIA

The search for a brain abnormality that causes schizophrenia began as early as the syndrome was identified, but the research did not prove promising, as studies did not yield the same findings. Interest gradually waned over the years. In the last two decades, however, spurred by a number of methodological advances, the field has reawakened and yielded some promising evidence. Some schizophrenic patients have been found to have observable brain pathology.

Postmortem analysis of the brains of schizophrenic patients is one source of evidence. Such studies consistently reveal abnormalities in the brains of schizophrenic patients, although the specific problems reported vary from study to study (Weinberger et al., 1983). The most consistent findings indicate structural problems in temporal–limbic areas, such as the hippocampus and amygdala, and in the prefrontal cortex (Benes et al., 1992).

Even more impressive are the images obtained in CT scan and MRI studies. Researchers were quick to apply these new tools to the living brains of schizophrenic patients. Thus far these images of living brain tissue have most consistently revealed that some schizophrenic patients, especially males (Andreasen et al., 1990), have enlarged lateral ventricles and reduced volume in limbic structures (Chua & McKenna, 1995; Gur & Pearlson, 1993), suggesting deterioration or atrophy of brain tissue.[3] Large ventricles are correlated with impaired performance on neuropsychological tests, poor premorbid adjustment, and poor response to drug treatment (Andreasen et al., 1982; Weinberger et al., 1980). The extent to which the ventricles are enlarged, however, is modest, and many schizophrenic patients do not differ from normals in this respect. Furthermore, enlarged ventricles are not specific to schizophrenia, as they are also evident in

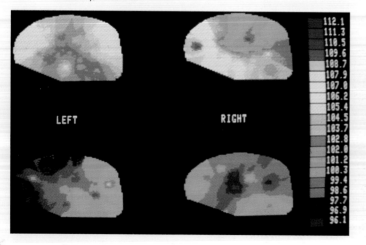

Differences in regional cerebral blood flow between schizophrenics (bottom) and normals (top) for each hemisphere. The values shown were scored as the percentage change in cerebral blood flow from a control task to the Wisconsin Card Sort, which was expected to activate prefrontal cortex. The normals showed greater prefrontal cortical activation as indexed by the "hotter" color of this brain region. *Source*: Weinberger, Berman, & Illowsky, 1988.

---

[3]This difference between male and female schizophrenic patients prompts us to mention that there are other gender effects as well. For example, schizophrenic men have an earlier age of onset and are more likely to express negative symptoms and to have a more deteriorating course than women (Goldstein et al., 1990; Haas et al., 1990).

FOCUS 11.2   PSYCHOTIC MOOD DISORDERS AND SCHIZOPHRENIA

As we have mentioned, enlarged ventricles are not specific to schizophrenia; other psychotic patients, notably those with mood disorders, show ventricular enlargement almost as great as that seen in schizophrenia (Elkis et al., 1995). Similarly, increased density of dopamine receptors has been reported among psychotic patients with bipolar disorder (Pearlson et al., 1995). The phenothiazines, used most often to treat schizophrenia, are also effective with manic patients and with patients with psychotic depression. Finally, the twin literature reports a set of identical triplets, two with bipolar disorder and one with schizophrenia.

These data suggest that the diagnostic categories of schizophrenia and psychotic mood disorders may *not* be totally separate entities. They share some common symptoms (notably delusions) and some possible etiological factors (increased dopamine activity), and they respond similarly to biological treatments. An important implication is that researchers would be well served to focus some of their efforts on psychotic symptoms across diagnostic groups, rather than just on the diagnosis of schizophrenia.

---

the CT scans of patients with other psychoses, such as mania (Rieder et al., 1983). (See Focus 11.2.)

Further evidence concerning large ventricles comes from an MRI study of fifteen pairs of MZ twins who were discordant for schizophrenia (Suddath et al., 1990). For twelve of the fifteen pairs the schizophrenic twin could be identified by simple visual inspection of the scan. Because the twins were genetically identical, these data also suggest that the origin of these brain abnormalities may not be genetic.

A variety of data suggest that the prefrontal cortex is of particular importance. In studies of the sulci (the shallow furrows in the cerebral cortex), prefrontal rather than general atrophy has been found (Doran et al., 1985). In applications of PET scanning in which glucose metabolism is studied in various brain regions while patients perform psychological tests, schizophrenic patients have shown low metabolic rates in the prefrontal cortex (Buchsbaum et al., 1984). Similarly, when performing the Wisconsin Card Sorting Task (a measure of

prefrontal function), schizophrenic patients do poorly and also fail to show activation in the prefrontal region as measured by the amount of blood flowing to this area (Rubin et al., 1992; Weinberger, Berman, & Illowsky, 1988). The frontal hypoactivation is less pronounced in the nonschizophrenic twin of discordant MZ pairs, again suggesting that this brain dysfunction may not have a genetic origin (Torrey et al., 1994).[4] The findings regarding the importance of the prefrontal area and limbic system parallel the work on dopamine already discussed.

---

[4]The Torrey et al. study of discordant MZ twins consistently found that the well twin was indistinguishable from normals on both structural and functional measures of the brain. The authors viewed this finding as evidence that these abnormalities are not genetically determined. However, the small number of participants in the study makes it difficult to statistically differentiate between groups. Furthermore, a large body of evidence has found neuropsychological impairments in the first-degree relatives of people with schizophrenia (e.g., Cannon et al., 1993). Therefore it would be unwise to conclude that genes play no role in the brain dysfunction of schizophrenia.

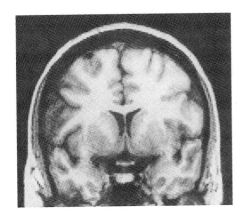 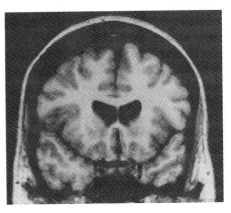

MRI of the brains of a woman with schizophrenia (right) and a normal woman (left). Enlarged ventricles (see dark spaces at center of photos) are one of the best validated biological features of schizophrenia.

A possible interpretation of these brain abnormalities is that they result from infection by a virus that invades the brain and damages it during fetal development (Mednick et al., 1988; 1994). During a five-week period in 1957 Helsinki experienced an epidemic of influenza virus. Researchers examined rates of schizophrenia among adults who had likely been exposed during their mothers' pregnancies. People who had been exposed to the virus during the second trimester of pregnancy had much higher rates than those who had been exposed in either of the other trimesters or in nonexposed controls. This finding is intriguing, especially since cortical development is in a critical stage of growth during the second trimester. During this period neurons are being produced in the rudimentary brain called the neural tube. These neurons then have to move to their appropriate location, passing through layers of cells as they do so. Perhaps this process of cell migration is disrupted in people who later develop schizophrenia. Consistent with this speculation, postmortem analyses of neurons in the brains of schizophrenic individuals have shown reduced numbers of cells in the outer layers of the cortex in both the prefrontal and the temporal areas (Akbarian et al., 1995; Benes, 1991). Similarly, a widespread thinning of the cortex of schizophrenic patients has been reported, apparently resulting from loss of dendrites and axons (Selemon, Rajkowska, & Goldman-Rakic, 1995).

If the brains of people with schizophrenia are damaged early in their development, why does the disorder begin in adolescence or early adulthood? Weinberger (1987) proposed one answer to this question. He hypothesized that the brain injury interacts with normal brain development and that the prefrontal cortex is a brain structure that matures late, typically in adolescence. Thus an injury to this area may remain silent until the period of development when the prefrontal cortex begins to play a larger role in behavior. Notably, dopamine activity also peaks in adolescence, which may further set the stage for the onset of schizophrenic symptoms. Further work on the relationship of the brain and schizophrenia is proceeding at a rapid rate and will no doubt lead to more insights about this disorder over the next several years.

PSYCHOLOGICAL STRESS AND SCHIZOPHRENIA

Thus far we have discussed several possible diatheses for schizophrenia. We now turn to the role of stressors. Data show that, as with many of the disorders we have discussed, increases in life stress can precipitate a relapse of schizophrenia (Brown & Birley, 1968; Ventura & Neuchterlein, 1989).

Two stressors that have played an important role in schizophrenia research are social class and the family. These are psychological stressors, to be contrasted with the biological stressor of exposure to a virus just discussed.

SOCIAL CLASS AND SCHIZOPHRENIA

For many years we have known that the highest rates of schizophrenia are found in central city areas inhabited by people in the lowest socioeconomic classes (e.g., Hollingshead & Redlich, 1958; Srole et al., 1962). The relationship between social class and schizophrenia does not show a continuous progression of higher rates of schizophrenia as the social class becomes lower. Rather, there is a decidedly sharp difference between the number of people with schizophrenia in the lowest social class and the number in other social classes. In the classic ten-year Hollingshead and Redlich study of social class and mental illness in New Haven, Connecticut, the rate of schizophrenia was found to be twice as high in the lowest social class as in the next to the lowest class. These findings have been confirmed cross-culturally by similar community studies carried out in countries such as Denmark, Norway, and England (Kohn, 1968).

The correlations between social class and schizophrenia are consistent, but they are difficult to interpret in causal terms. Some people believe that being in a low social class may cause schizophrenia—the **sociogenic hypothesis**. The degrading treatment a person receives from others, the low level of education, and the lack of both rewards and opportunity taken together may make membership in the lowest social class such a stressful experience that an individual develops schizophrenia. Alternatively, the stressors encountered by those in the lowest social class could be biological; for example, the children of mothers whose nutrition during pregnancy was poor are at increased risk for schizophrenia (Susser et al., 1996).

Another explanation of the correlation between schizophrenia and low social class is the **social-selection theory**. During the course of their developing psychosis, people with schizophrenia may drift into the poverty-ridden areas of the city. The growing cognitive and motivational problems besetting these individuals may so impair their earning capabilities that they cannot afford to live elsewhere. Or, they may choose to move to areas where little social pressure will be brought to bear on them and where they can escape intense social relationships.

The prevalence of schizophrenia is highest among people in the lowest social class.

One way of resolving the conflict between these differing theories is to study the social mobility of schizophrenic people. Three studies (Lystad, 1957; Schwartz, 1946; Turner & Wagonfeld, 1967) found that schizophrenic people are downwardly mobile in occupational status. But an equal number of studies have shown that schizophrenic people are *not* downwardly mobile (Clausen & Kohn, 1959; Dunham, 1965; Hollingshead & Redlich, 1958). Kohn (1968) suggested another way of examining this question: Are the fathers of schizophrenic patients also from the lowest social class? If they are, this could be considered evidence in favor of the hypothesis that lower-class status is conducive to schizophrenia, for class would be shown to *precede* schizophrenia. If the fathers are from a higher social class, the social-selection hypothesis would be the better explanation.

Goldberg and Morrison (1963) conducted such a study in England and Wales. They reported that the occupations of male schizophrenic patients were less remunerative and prestigious than those of their fathers. Turner and Wagonfeld (1967) conducted a similar study in the United States and found evidence for both the sociogenic and social-selection hypotheses. Fathers of schizophrenic patients were more frequently from the lowest social class, supporting the sociogenic hypothesis. At the same time, many of the schizophrenic patients were lower in occupational prestige than their fathers, supporting the social-selection hypothesis.

A more recent study relevant to the two theories employed a new methodology, simultaneously investigating both social class and ethnic background (Dohrenwend et al., 1992). The rates of schizophrenia were examined in Israeli Jews of European ethnic background and in more recent immigrants to Israel from North Africa and the Middle East. The latter group experiences considerable racial prejudice and discrimination. The sociogenic hypothesis would predict that because they experience high levels of stress in all social classes, the members of the disadvantaged ethnic group should have consistently higher rates of schizophrenia in all social classes. However, this pattern did not emerge. Thus some, but not all, of the relationship between social class and schizophrenia can be accounted for by the selection hypothesis. Social class does appear to play a role as a stressor, but the exact way in which the stresses associated with it exert their effect remains unknown.

THE FAMILY AND SCHIZOPHRENIA

Early theorists regarded family relationships, especially those between a mother and her son, as crucial in the development of schizophrenia. At one time the view was so prevalent that the term **schizophrenogenic mother** was coined for the supposedly cold and dominant, conflict-inducing parent who was said to produce schizophrenia in her offspring (Fromm-Reichmann, 1948). These mothers were characterized as rejecting, overprotective, self-sacrificing, impervious to the feelings of others, rigid and moralistic about sex, and fearful of intimacy.

Controlled studies evaluating the schizophrenogenic mother theory have not yielded supporting data. Studies of families of schizophrenic individuals have, however, revealed that they differ in some ways from normal families, for example, by showing vague patterns of communication and high levels of conflict. It is plausible, though, that the conflict and unclear communication are a response to having a young schizophrenic member of the family.

Some findings do suggest, however, that the faulty communications of parents may play a role in the etiology of schizophrenia. One type of communication deviance that has been studied is illustrated in the following example.

Daughter (complainingly): Nobody will listen to me. Everybody is trying to kill me.

Mother: Nobody wants to kill you.

Father: If you're going to associate with intellectual people, you're going to have to remember that still is a noun and not a verb. (Wynne & Singer, 1963, p. 195)

In an important study of communication deviance, adolescents with behavior problems were studied intensively along with their families. A five-year follow-up revealed that a number of the young people had developed schizophrenia or schizophrenia-related disorders. The investigators were then able to relate these disorders discovered at follow-up to any deviance in the communications of parents that had been evident five years earlier (Goldstein & Rodnick, 1975). Communication deviancies in the families were indeed found to predict the later onset of schizophrenia in their offspring, supporting its significance (Norton, 1982). However, it does not appear that communication deviance is a *specific* etiological factor for schizophrenia, since parents of manic patients are equally high on this variable (Miklowitz, 1985).

Further evidence favoring some role for the family comes from a substantial adoption study by Tienari and his colleagues (1991) that is under way in Finland. A large sample of adopted offspring of schizophrenic mothers is being studied along with a control group. As of 1991, 144 children of schizophrenic mothers and 178 controls had been assessed. Unlike Heston's adoption study, extensive data were collected on various aspects of family life in the adoptive families. Data on the adjustment of the children were related to data collected on their adoptive families. The families were categorized into levels of maladjustment based on material from clinical interviews as well as psychological tests. More serious psychopathology was found among the adoptees if they were reared in a disturbed family environment; children of schizophrenic parents showed a greater increase in psychopathology than did the controls if they were reared in a disturbed family environment. Although it is tempting to conclude that both a genetic predisposition and a noxious environment are necessary to increase risk for psychopathology, a problem in interpretation remains. The disturbed family environment could be a response to a disturbed child. Thus we can only tentatively say that an etiological role for the family has been established.

A series of studies initiated in London indicate that the family can have an important impact on the adjustment of patients *after* they leave the hospital. Brown and his colleagues (1966) conducted a nine-month follow-up study of a sample of schizophrenic patients who returned to live with their families after being discharged from the hospital. Interviews were conducted with parents or spouses before discharge and rated for the number of critical comments made about the patient and for expressions of hostility toward or emotional overinvolvement with him or her. On the basis of this variable, called **expressed emotion (EE)**, families were divided into those revealing a great deal, high-EE families, and those revealing little, low-EE families. At the end of the follow-up period 10 percent of the patients returning to low-EE homes had relapsed. In marked contrast, in the same period 58 percent of the patients returning to high-EE homes had gone back to the hospital!

This research, which has since been replicated (Koenigsberg & Hadley, 1976; Leff, 1976; MacMillan et al., 1981; Vaughn & Leff, 1986), indicates that the environment to which patients are discharged has great bearing on whether they are rehospitalized. What is not yet clear is exactly how to interpret the effects of EE. Is EE causal, or do these attitudes reflect a reaction to the patients' behavior? For example, if the condition of a schizophrenic patient begins to deteriorate, family concern and involvement may be increased. Indeed, bizarre or dangerous behavior by the schizophrenic individual might seem to warrant limit setting and other familial efforts that could increase the level of expressed emotion (Kanter, Lamb, & Loeper, 1987).

Research indicates that both interpretations of the operation of EE may be correct (Rosenfarb et al., 1995). Recently discharged schizophrenic patients and their high- or low-EE families were observed as they engaged in a discussion of a family problem. Two key findings emerged.

1. The expression of unusual thoughts by the patients ("If that kid bites you, you'll get rabies.") elicited higher levels of critical comments by family members who had previously been characterized as high in EE.

2. In high-EE families critical comments by family members led to increased expression of unusual thoughts.

Thus this study found a bidirectional relationship: critical comments by family members elicited higher levels of unusual thoughts by patients; and unusual thoughts expressed by the patients led to increased critical comments.

HIGH-RISK STUDIES OF SCHIZOPHRENIA

How does schizophrenia develop? We know that the clinical symptoms begin in adolescence and early adulthood, somewhat earlier for men than for women. But what are these individuals like before their symptoms begin? An early method of answering this question was to construct developmental histories by examining the childhood records of those who had later become schizophrenic. Such research revealed that individuals who became schizophrenic were different from their contemporaries even before any serious problems were noted in their behavior. In the 1960s Albee and Lane and their colleagues repeatedly found that preschizophrenic individuals had lower IQs than did members of various control groups, usually comprising siblings and neighborhood peers (Albee, Lane, & Reuter, 1964; Lane & Albee, 1965). Investigations of the social behavior of preschizophrenic patients yielded some interesting findings as well. For example, teachers described preschizophrenic boys as disagreeable in childhood and preschizophrenic girls as passive (Watt, 1974; Watt et al., 1970). Both men and women were described as delinquent and withdrawn in childhood (Berry, 1967).

Researchers have also examined home movies taken before the onset of schizophrenia (Walker, Savoie, & Davis, 1994; Walker et al., 1993). Compared with their siblings who did not later become schizophrenic, preschizophrenic children showed poorer motor skills and more expressions of negative affect.

The major limitation of such developmental research is that the data on which it relies were not originally collected with the intention of describing preschizophrenic patients or of predicting the development of schizophrenia from childhood behavior. More specific information is required if developmental histories are to be a source of new hypotheses.

The high-risk method, described in Chapter 5, can yield this information. The first such study of schizophrenia was begun in the 1960s by Sarnoff Mednick and Fini Schulsinger (Mednick & Schulsinger, 1968). They chose Denmark because the Danish registries of all people make it possible to keep track of them for long periods of time. Mednick and Schulsinger selected as their high-risk subjects 207 young people whose mothers had chronic schizophrenia and had had poor premorbid adjustment. The researchers decided that the mother should be the parent suffering the disorder because paternity is not always easy to determine. Then, 104 low-risk subjects, individuals whose mothers were not schizophrenic, were matched to the high-risk subjects on variables such as sex, age, father's occupation, rural–urban residence, years of education, and institutional upbringing versus rearing by the family.

In 1972 the now-grown men and women were followed up with a number of measures, including a diagnostic battery. Fifteen of the high-risk subjects were diagnosed as schizophrenic; none of the control men and women was so diagnosed. Looking back to the information collected on the subjects when they were children, the investigators found that several circumstances predicted the later onset of schizophrenia.

Sarnoff Mednick is a psychologist at the University of Southern California who pioneered the use of the high-risk method for studying schizophrenia. He has also contributed to the hypothesis that a viral infection is implicated in this disorder.

These data, albeit from a small study, seem to suggest that the etiology of schizophrenia may differ for positive- and negative-symptom patients. In the most recent analysis of the data, the schizophrenic patients were divided into two groups, those with predominantly positive and those with predominantly negative symptoms (Cannon, Mednick, & Farnas, 1990). Variables predicting schizophrenia were different for the two groups. Negative-symptom schizophrenia was preceded by a history of pregnancy and birth complications and by a failure to show electrodermal responses to simple stimuli. Positive-symptom schizophrenia was preceded by a history of family instability, such as separation from parents and placement in foster homes or institutions for periods of time.

In the wake of Mednick and Schulsinger's pioneering study several other high-risk investigations were undertaken, some of which have also yielded information concerning the prediction of adult psychopathology. The New York High-Risk Study found that a composite measure of attentional dysfunction predicted behavioral disturbance at follow-up (Cornblatt & Erlenmeyer-Kimling, 1985). Furthermore, low IQ was a characteristic of the first high-risk children to be hospitalized (Erlenmeyer-Kimling & Cornblatt, 1987). In an Israeli study, poor neurobehavioral functioning (poor concentration, poor verbal ability, lack of motor control and coordination) predicted schizophrenia-like outcomes, as did earlier interpersonal problems (Marcus et al., 1987). As participants in other high-risk studies mature we will gain further glimpses of the development of this debilitating disorder.

THERAPIES FOR SCHIZOPHRENIA

The puzzling, often frightening array of symptoms displayed by people with schizophrenia makes treatment difficult. The history of psychopathology, reviewed in Chapter 1, is in many respects a history of humankind's efforts, often brutal and unenlightened, to deal with schizophrenia, arguably the most serious of the disorders described in this book. Although some of the profoundly disturbed people confined centuries ago in foul asylums may have suffered from problems as prosaic as syphilis (see p. 18), there seems little doubt that many, if examined now, would carry a diagnosis of schizophrenia. Today we know a good deal about the nature and etiology of schizophrenia and we can treat its symptoms somewhat effectively, yet a cure remains elusive.

For the most part clinical research indicates that traditional hospital care does little to effect meaningful, enduring changes in the majority of patients with mental disorders (we described mental hospitals in Chapter 1, p. 16). The overwhelming body of evidence shows rehospitalization rates of 40 to 50 percent after one year and upwards of 75 percent after two years (Anthony et al., 1986; Paul & Menditto, 1992). Studies specifically designed to follow schizophrenic patients show generally poor outcomes as well (Breier et al., 1991; Carone, Harrow, & Westermeyer, 1991).

A problem with *any* kind of treatment for schizophrenia is that many schizophrenic patients lack insight into their impaired condition and refuse any treatment at all. As they don't see anything wrong with themselves, they don't see the need for professional intervention, particularly when it includes hospitalization or drugs. This is especially true of those with paranoid schizophrenia, who may regard any therapy as a threatening intrusion from hostile outside forces. Family members therefore face a major challenge in getting their schizophrenic relatives into treatment, which is one reason they sometimes turn to involuntary hospitalization via civil commitment (p. 603) as a last resort.

We will now take a closer look at the treatment of schizophrenia, most of which is hospital based.

BIOLOGICAL TREATMENTS

SHOCK AND PSYCHOSURGERY

The general warehousing of patients in mental hospitals earlier in this century, coupled with the shortage of professional staff, created a climate that allowed, perhaps even subtly encouraged, experimentation with radical biological interventions. In the early 1930s inducing a coma with large dosages of insulin was introduced by Sakel (1938), who claimed that up to three-quarters of the schizophrenic patients he treated showed significant improvement. Later findings by others were less encouraging, and insulin-coma therapy, which presented serious risks to health, including irreversible coma and death, was gradually abandoned. As discussed in Chapter 10, electroconvulsive therapy (ECT) was also used after its development in 1938 by Cerletti and Bini; it, too, proved to be only minimally effective.

In 1935, Moñiz, a Portuguese psychiatrist, introduced the **prefrontal lobotomy**, a surgical procedure that destroys the tracts connecting the frontal lobes to lower centers of the brain. His initial reports claimed high rates of success (Moñiz, 1936), and for twenty years thereafter thousands of mental patients—not only those diagnosed as schizophrenic—underwent variations of psychosurgery. The procedure was used especially for those whose behavior was violent. Many patients did indeed quiet down and could even be discharged from hospitals. During the 1950s, however, this intervention fell into disrepute for several reasons. After surgery many patients became dull and listless and suffered serious losses in their cognitive capacities, for example, becoming unable to carry on a coherent conversation with another person—which is not surprising given the destruction of parts of their brains believed responsible for thought. The principal reason for its abandonment, however, was the introduction of drugs that seemed to reduce the behavioral and emotional excesses of many patients.

One Flew Over the Cuckoo's Nest provides a compelling illustration of the horrors of older mental hospitals and the treatments then in use.

DRUG THERAPIES

Without question the most important development in the treatment of the schizophrenia disorders was the advent in the 1950s of several drugs collectively referred to as antipsychotic medications, also referred to as neuroleptics because they produce side effects similar to the symptoms of a neurological disease. One of the more frequently prescribed **antipsychotic drugs**, *phenothiazine*, was first produced by a German chemist in the late nineteenth century and used to treat parasitic worm infections of the digestive system of animals. Not until the discovery of the antihistamines, which have a phenothiazine nucleus, in the 1940s did phenothiazines receive any attention. Reaching beyond their use to treat the common cold and asthma, the French surgeon Laborit pioneered the use of antihistamines to reduce surgical shock. He noticed that they made his patients somewhat sleepy and less fearful about the impending operation. Laborit's work encouraged pharmaceutical companies to reexamine antihistamines in light of their tranquilizing effects. Shortly thereafter a French chemist, Charpentier, prepared a new phenothiazine derivative, which he called chlorpromazine. This drug proved very effective in calming schizophrenic patients. As already mentioned, phenothiazines derive their therapeutic properties by blocking dopamine receptors in the brain.

Chlorpromazine (trade name Thorazine) was first used therapeutically in the United States in 1954 and rapidly became the preferred treatment for schizophrenia. By 1970 more than 85 percent of all patients in state mental hospitals were receiving chlorpromazine or another phenothiazine. Other antipsychotics that have been used for years to treat schizophrenia include the *butyrophenones* (e.g., haloperidol, Haldol) and the *thioxanthenes* (e.g., navane, Taractan). Both types seem generally as effective as the phenothiazines. These classes of drugs seem able to reduce positive schizophrenic symptoms but have much less effect on the negative ones.

Although phenothiazines reduce positive symptoms of schizophrenia so that many patients can be released from the hospital, they are not a cure. About 30 percent of schizophrenic patients do not respond favorably, although these patients may respond to some newer antipsychotic drugs (e.g., Clozaril and Risperidal, discussed later), or may be treated with lithium, antidepressants, anticonvulsants, or benzodiazepines. Antidepressants are particularly effective with patients who become depressed after a psychotic episode (Hogarty et al., 1995; Siris et al., 1994). However, because of the side effects of the whole range of antipsychotic drugs—such as dizziness, muscle stiffness, blurred vision, restlessness, and sexual dysfunction—about half the patients who take them quit after one year and up to three-quarters quit after two years (*The Harvard Mental Health Letter*, July 1995). For this reason patients are frequently treated with long-lasting antipsychotics (for example, fluphenazine decanoate, Prolixin), which require an injection every two weeks.

Even patients who respond positively to the phenothiazines are kept on so-called *maintenance doses* of the drug, just enough to continue the therapeutic effect. They take their medication and return to the hospital or clinic on occasion for adjustment of the dose level. Released patients who are maintained on phenothiazine medication may make only marginal adjustment to the community. For example, they may be unable to live unsupervised or to hold down the kind of job for which they would otherwise be qualified. Their social relationships are likely to be sparse. And again, although the phenothiazines keep positive symptoms from returning, they have little effect on negative symptoms such as flat affect. Reinstitutionalization is frequent. The phenothiazines have significantly reduced long-term institutionalization, but they have also initiated the revolving-door pattern seen in some patients of admission, discharge, and readmission.

In addition to the side effects already mentioned is a group of particularly disturbing ones, termed *extrapyramidal side effects*. These stem from dysfunctions of the nerve tracts that descend from the brain to spinal motor neurons. Extrapyramidal side effects resemble symptoms of neurological diseases; they most closely resemble the symptoms of Parkinson's disease. People taking phenothiazines have tremors of the fingers, a shuffling gait, muscular rigidity, and drooling. Other side effects include dystonia, a state of muscular rigidity, and dyskinesia, an abnormal motion of voluntary and involuntary muscles, producing chewing movements as well as other movements of the lips, fingers, and legs. Together they cause arching of the back and a twisted posture of the neck and body. Akasthesia is an inability to remain still; people pace constantly and fidget. These perturbing symptoms can be treated by drugs used with patients who have Parkinson's disease. In a muscular disturbance of older patients, called tardive dyskinesia, the mouth muscles involuntarily make sucking, lip-smacking, and chin-wagging motions. This syndrome affects about 10 to 20 percent of patients treated with phenothiazines for a long period of time and is not responsive to any treatment at this time (Kane et al., 1986; Sweet et al., 1995).

Because of these serious side effects some clinicians believe it is unwise to take high doses of phenothiazines for extended periods of time. Current clinical practice calls for treating patients with the smallest possible doses of drugs. The clinician is put in a bind by this situation: if medication is reduced, the chance of relapse increases; but if medication is continued, serious and untreatable side effects may develop. One possible solution is to keep medication levels low but monitor patients closely so that when symptoms worsen, medication can be increased. Unfortunately, this strategy has not yet been shown to be effective (Marder et al., 1994).

Recent research indicates that two new drugs, clozapine (Clozaril) and risperidone (Risperidal), can produce therapeutic gains in schizophrenic patients who do not respond positively to phenothiazines (Kane et al., 1988; Marder & Merbach, 1994). These drugs also generate fewer motor side effects and may alleviate negative symptoms to a greater extent than do traditional antipsychotics. Although the precise mechanism of the therapeutic effects of both drugs is not yet known, both have an impact on serotonin and dopamine. Clozapine can impair the functioning of the immune system, making patients vulnerable to infection, and it can produce seizures and other side effects, among them, dizziness, fatigue, drooling, and weight gain (Meltzer et al., 1993).

Despite these difficulties, antipsychotic drugs are an indispensable part of treatment for schizophrenia and will undoubtedly continue to be the primary intervention until something better is discovered. They are surely preferable to the straitjackets formerly used to restrain patients. Furthermore, the recent success of clozapine and risperidone has stimulated a major effort to find new and more effective drug therapies for schizophrenia. Two new drugs were given FDA approval in 1996. One of these is called olanzapine (Zyprexa); like risperidone it affects a number of neurotransmitters and produces fewer side-effects than traditional antipsychotics. A large number of other drugs are currently being evaluated, so that we may be on the verge of a new era in the treatment of schizophrenia.

PSYCHOLOGICAL TREATMENTS

Although Freud did not advocate psychoanalysis as a treatment for schizophrenia, others have proposed adaptations, some of which we review here. We will also examine recent family and behavioral therapies for schizophrenia and will suggest at the end of this section that it is best to combine biological and psychological treatments in an integrated approach to this debilitating disorder.

PSYCHODYNAMIC THERAPY

Freud did little, either in his clinical practice or through his writings, to adapt psychoanalysis to the treatment of schizophrenic patients. He believed that they were incapable of establishing the close interpersonal relationship essential for analysis. It was Harry Stack Sullivan, the American psychiatrist, who pioneered the use of psychotherapy with schizophrenic hospital patients. Sullivan established a ward at the Sheppard and Enoch Pratt Hospital in Towson, Maryland, in 1923 and developed a psychoanalytic treatment reported to be markedly successful. He held that schizophrenia reflects a return to early childhood forms of communication. The fragile ego of the schizophrenic individual, unable to handle the extreme stress of interpersonal challenges, regresses. Therapy therefore requires the patient to learn adult forms of communication and to achieve insight into the role that the past has played in current problems. Sullivan advised the very gradual, nonthreatening development of a trusting relationship. For example, he recommended that the therapist sit somewhat to the side of the patient in order not to force eye contact, which is deemed too frightening in the early stages of treatment. After many sessions, and

Freida Fromm Reichman played an important role in adapting psychoanalytic procedures for the treatment of schizophrenia.

with the establishment of greater trust and support, the analyst begins to encourage the patient to examine his or her interpersonal relationships.

A similar ego-analytic approach was proposed by Frieda Fromm-Reichmann (1889–1957), a German psychiatrist who emigrated to the United States and worked for a period of time with Sullivan at Chestnut Lodge, a private mental hospital in Rockville, Maryland. Fromm-Reichmann was sensitive to the symbolic and unconscious meaning of behavior, attributing the aloofness of schizophrenic patients to a wish to avoid the rebuffs suffered in childhood and thereafter judged inevitable. She treated them with great patience and optimism, making it clear that they need not take her into their world or give up their sickness until they were completely ready to do so. Along with Sullivan, Fromm-Reichmann (1952) helped establish a variant of psychoanalysis as a major treatment for schizophrenia.

The overall evaluation of analytically oriented psychotherapy with schizophrenic patients justifies little enthusiasm for applying it with these severely disturbed people (Feinsilver & Gunderson, 1972; Stanton et al., 1984). Results from a long-term follow-up of patients bearing a diagnosis of schizophrenia and discharged after treatment between 1963 and 1976 at the New York State Psychiatric Institute confirm the lack of success (Stone, 1986). It may be, as Stone hypothesized, that gaining psychoanalytic insight into one's problems and illness may even worsen a schizophrenic patient's psychological condition. Such treatment may in itself be too intrusive and too intense for some schizophrenic patients to handle. Earlier, great claims of success were made for the analyses done by Sullivan and Fromm-Reichmann, but a close consideration of the patients they saw indicates that many were only mildly disturbed and might not even have been diagnosed as schizophrenic by the strict DSM-IV criteria for the disorder.

FAMILY THERAPY AND EXPRESSED EMOTION

Many schizophrenic patients discharged from mental hospitals go home to their families of origin. Earlier we discussed research showing that high levels of expressed emotion (EE) within the family (including being hostile, hypercritical, and overprotective) have been linked to relapse and rehospitalization. Based on these findings a family therapy team at the University of Southern California decided to try to lower, through cognitive and behavioral means, the emotional intensity of the households to which schizophrenic patients returned (Falloon et al., 1982, 1985).

Family therapy sessions took place in the patients' homes, with family and patient participating together. The focus was on teaching the family ways to express both positive and negative feelings in a constructive, empathic, nondemanding manner rather than in a finger-pointing, critical, or overprotective way and to defuse tense, personal conflicts by working together to solve them. The therapists encouraged family members to lower their expectations of their schizophrenic kin as a way to reduce their criticism of them. They made clear to family and patient alike that schizophrenia is primarily a biochemical illness and that proper medication and the kind of therapy they were receiving could reduce stress on the patient and prevent deterioration. They also stressed the importance of the patient's taking his or her medication regularly. Treatment extended over the first nine months after the patient returned home, when the danger of relapse is especially great.

This family treatment, aimed at calming the home life of the patient, was compared with an individual therapy in which the patient was seen alone at a clinic, with supportive discussions centering on problems in daily living and on developing a social network. Family members of patients in the control group were seldom seen; when they were seen, it was not in home sessions with the patients. The control patients received the typical, individual, supportive management in widespread use in aftercare programs for schizophrenic patients.

Ongoing assessments were made of the patient's symptomatology, with special attention to signs of relapse, such as delusions of control and hallucinations. Family members were evaluated for their problem-solving skills and for the emotions they expressed toward the patient. All patients, including the controls, were maintained on antipsychotic medication, primarily Thorazine, which was monitored and adjusted throughout the project by a psychiatrist unaware of which patients were receiving family therapy and which individual therapy.

In all, thirty-six patients were treated over a two-year period, half in each group. Those receiving family therapy fared much better. Only one person in this group had a major clinical relapse, compared with eight in the control group. Further, of the schizophrenic episodes that occurred in the control group, two-thirds were considered major, whereas only one-third in the family-therapy group were so categorized. Finally, hospital readmission rates were consistently different; nine of the eighteen control patients were returned to the hospital, whereas only two of the eighteen family-therapy patients had to return.

In interpreting their results the investigators were properly mindful of the possibility that the patients in family therapy may have improved more than the controls because they took their medications more faithfully; family-therapy subjects complied better with their medication regimens. However, results from other studies have shown that drugs alone do not prevent deterioration in such patients. The conclusion is that this kind of family therapy, geared toward lowering the emotional intensity of the atmosphere at home, was of major importance in the patients' improvement.

Falloon's findings were replicated to some extent by a larger-scale study by Hogarty et al. (1986). After one year, a patient-focused social-skills treatment achieved low relapse results just as good as those of the Falloon family therapy. Furthermore, *no* patient whose family EE diminished had to return to the hospital—including a handful of patients in the control group, which received only maintenance medication and nonspecific support from a nurse practitioner. Conversely, among households that remained high on EE, relapse rates were similar regardless of treatment conditions. In a treatment group that combined family therapy with patient-focused social-skills training, there were no relapses whatsoever after a year.

After two years of treatment, however, the pattern of results changed. Relapse rates no longer differed between groups (Hogarty et al., 1991). Finally, it is also important to bear in mind when interpreting the Hogarty study as well as all others that the actual real-life adjustment of the nonrelapsing patients remained marginal (Hogarty, 1993). Prevention or delay of rehospitalization is a worthwhile goal, but these patients do not as a rule become fully functioning members of society; they continue to require care and treatment.

BEHAVIOR THERAPY

We briefly described a major behavior therapy for hospitalized schizophrenic patients, the token economy, in Chapter 2 and will return to it in more depth in Chapter 18. Here we discuss social-skills training which is used to deal directly with some of the interpersonal deficits and problems of schizophrenic patients. This application is important for at least two reasons: (1) as noted, antipsychotic drugs work primarily on positive symptoms such as delusions, not on negative symptoms such as social withdrawal and lack of social skills; (2) the use of these drugs allows many more patients to live outside mental hospitals; as a result, they must cope with the demands of life outside an institution.

Programs led by Bellack (e.g., Bellack & Mueser, 1993) and Liberman (e.g., Liberman, 1994) demonstrate the effectiveness of teaching patients, via role-playing and reinforcement for appropriate behaviors, how to fill out job applications, behave in interviews, shop in supermarkets, and make themselves otherwise presentable for everyday social intercourse. In a two-year evaluation, social skills-training was found to be superior to supportive therapy in improving social adjustment (Marder et al., 1996). The cognitive deficits of many schizophrenic patients, however, may limit the extent of positive changes. For this reason, cognitive rehabilitation, involving direct training on attentional and cognitive tests, might improve the effectiveness of social-skills training (Penn & Mueser, 1996). These programs and related behavioral techniques have also been employed in mental hospitals and are discussed in greater detail in Chapter 18.

At the present time it is generally acknowledged among mental health professionals that therapy programs with a learning framework are the most effective psychological procedures for helping schizophrenic patients function better. But the changes brought about by behavior therapy are seldom so extensive as to allow us to speak of curing schizophrenia. Behavioral interventions do, however, reverse somewhat the effects of institutionalization, fostering such social skills as assertiveness in people who have been reinforced by hospital staff for passiveness and compliance.

GENERAL TRENDS IN TREATMENT

Only a generation ago many, if not most, mental health professionals and laypeople believed the primary culprit in the etiology of schizophrenia was the child's psychological environment, most especially, the family. The thinking now is that biological factors predispose a person to become schizophrenic and that stressors, principally of a psychological nature, trigger the illness in a predisposed individual. The most promising contemporary approaches to treatment make good use of this increased understanding and emphasize the importance of both pharmacological and psychosocial interventions.

- Families and patients are now given realistic and scientifically sound information about schizophrenia as a disability that can be controlled but that is probably lifelong. They learn that, as with many other chronic disabilities, medication is necessary to maintain control and allow the patient to perform daily activities.

What is *not* necessary, and is even counterproductive, is the guilt of family members, especially parents, who may have been led to believe that something in the patient's upbringing initiated the problem. Considerable effort is devoted in many treatment programs to dispelling this sense of culpability while encouraging a focus on the biological diathesis and the associated need for medication.

- Medication is only part of the whole treatment picture. Family-oriented treatment aims to reduce the stress experienced by the patient after discharge from the hospital by reducing hostility, overinvolvement, intrusiveness, and criticality in the family (EE).

- It is also important to teach the patient social skills so that he or she can function more normally outside the hospital and probably reduce the EE encountered both inside and outside the home.

- Families affected by schizophrenia are encouraged to join support groups and formal organizations, such as the Alliance for the Mentally Ill, to reduce the isolation and stigma associated with having a family member who is schizophrenic (Greenberg et al., 1988).

ONGOING ISSUES IN THE CARE OF SCHIZOPHRENIC PATIENTS

As schizophrenic patients grow older they are less likely to be living with their families. The transition to living arrangements outside the parents' home is fraught with risk. As described later in greater detail (p. 580), aftercare is one of society's thorniest social problems. Though only about 5 to 15 percent of homeless people in the U.S. are mentally ill, many people with schizophrenia are among those without residences. The downward spiral in functioning is difficult to reverse. Social Security benefits are available to those with schizophrenia, but many do not receive all to which they are entitled because of inadequately staffed federal and state bureaucracies. And many schizophrenic patients have lost contact with their posthospital treatment programs.

Obtaining employment poses a major challenge because of bias against those who have been in mental hospitals. Although the Americans with Disabilities Act of 1990 prohibits employers from asking applicants if they have a history of serious mental illness, former mental hospital patients still have a difficult time obtaining regular employment because of negative biases and fear on the part of employers.

There are some positive signs, however. Twenty or thirty years after first developing schizophrenic symptoms, about half of schizophrenic patients can be found looking after themselves and participating meaningfully in society at large. Some continue to take medications, but many do not and still function well enough to stay out of hospital (*The Harvard Mental Health Letter*, July 1995). The United States Department of Housing and Urban Development has recently begun providing rent subsidies to former mental patients to help them live in their own apartments, where they are occasionally checked on by mental health workers.

Preventing substance abuse among schizophrenic patients is a largely unmet challenge. The lifetime prevalence rate for substance abuse among those with schizophrenia is an astounding 47 percent; the rate is even higher among the homeless mentally ill. Programs for treating substance abuse usually exclude the seriously mentally ill, and programs for treating the seriously mentally ill usually exclude substance abusers; in both instances the reason is that the comorbid condition is considered disruptive to the treatment (Mueser, Bellack, & Blanchard, 1992). Additional problems arise because schizophrenic substance abusers often do not continue to take their antipsychotic medication.

SUMMARY

The symptoms of schizophrenia are typically divided into positive and negative types. Positive symptoms refer to behavioral excesses, such as delusions, hallucinations, and disorganized speech. Negative symptoms refer to behavioral deficits, such as flat affect, avolition, alogia, and anhedonia. Schizophrenic individuals also show deterioration in functioning in occupational and social roles. The diagnosis requires that symptoms be present for at least one month and that a prodromal or residual phase, in which some symptoms persist but at a lower level of severity, last for at least five months. Schizophrenia is typically divided into subtypes, such as paranoid, catatonic, and disorganized. These subtypes are based on the prominence of particular symptoms (e.g., delusions in the paranoid subtype) and reflect the considerable variations in behavior found among people diagnosed as schizophrenic.

The concept of schizophrenia arose from the pioneering efforts of Kraepelin and Bleuler. Kraepelin's work fostered a descriptive approach and a narrow definition, whereas Bleuler's theoretical emphasis led to a broad diagnostic category. Bleuler had a great influence on the U.S. concept of schizophrenia, making it extremely broad. By the middle of the twentieth century the differences in how schizophrenia was diagnosed in the United States and Europe were vast. Subsequent to the publication of DSM-III, the U.S. concept of schizophrenia has become narrower and more similar to the European view.

Research has tried to determine the etiological role of specific biological variables, such as genetic and biochemical factors and brain pathology, as well as that of stressors, such as low social class and the family. The data on genetic transmission are impressive. Adoption studies, which are relatively free from most of the criticisms leveled at family or twin studies, show a strong relationship between having a schizophrenic parent and the likelihood of developing the disorder. Perhaps the genetic predisposition has biochemical correlates, although research in this area permits only tentative conclusions. At this point it appears that increased sensitivity of dopamine receptors in the limbic area of the brain is related to the positive symptoms of schizophrenia. The negative symptoms may be due to dopamine underactivity in the prefrontal cortex. The brains of schizophrenic patients, especially those with negative symptoms, have enlarged lateral ventricles and prefrontal atrophies, as well as reduced metabolism and structural abnormalities in the temporal and limbic areas. Some of these structural abnormalities could result from maternal viral infection during the second trimester of pregnancy.

The diagnosis of schizophrenia is most frequently applied to members of the lowest social class. Available information indicates that this is so in part because the stresses of lower-class existence are great and in part because the disorder keeps people with it from achieving higher social status. Vague communications and conflicts are evident in the family life of schizophrenic patients and probably contribute to their disorder. The level of expressed emotion (EE) in families has been shown to be an important determinant of relapse.

Much of the available information is consistent with a diathesis–stress view of schizophrenia. Investigators have turned to the high-risk method, studying children who are particularly vulnerable to schizophrenia by virtue of having a schizophrenic parent. Mednick and Schulsinger found that circumstances predicting maladjustment in adulthood differ depending on whether positive or negative symptoms are most prominent.

There are both biological and psychological therapies for schizophrenia. Insulin and electroconvulsive treatments and even surgery were in vogue earlier in the century, but they are no longer much used, primarily because of the availability of antipsychotic drugs, in particular the phenothiazines. In numerous studies these medications have been found to have a major beneficial impact on the disordered lives of schizophrenic patients. They have also been a factor in the deinstitutionalization of hospital patients. Drugs alone are not a completely effective treatment, though, as schizophrenic patients need to be taught or retaught ways of dealing with the challenges of everyday life.

Psychoanalytic theory assumes that schizophrenia represents a retreat from the pain of childhood rejection and mistreatment; the relationship gradually and patiently established by the analyst offers the patient a safe haven in which to explore repressed traumas. Good evidence for the efficacy of analytic treatments is not plentiful, although case studies of dramatic cures are many in both the professional and the popular literature. Family therapy, aimed at reducing high levels of expressed emotion, has been shown to be valuable in preventing relapse. More recently, behavioral treatments such as social skills training have helped patients discharged from mental hospitals meet the inevitable stresses of family and community living, and, when discharge is not possible, lead more ordered and constructive lives within an institution. The most effective treatments for schizophrenia are likely to involve both biological and psychological components.

KEY TERMS

schizophrenia
positive symptoms
disorganized speech
   (thought disorder)
incoherence
loose associations
   (derailment)
delusions
hallucinations
negative symptoms
avolition
alogia
anhedonia

flat affect
catatonic immobility
waxy flexibility
inappropriate affect
dementia praecox
process-reactive dimension
delusional disorder
disorganized schizophrenia
catatonic schizophrenia
paranoid schizophrenia
grandiose delusions
delusional jealousy
ideas of reference

delusions of persecution
delusions of grandiosity
undifferentiated
   schizophrenia
residual schizophrenia
labeling theory
dopamine activity theory
sociogenic hypothesis
social-selection theory
schizophrenogenic mother
expressed emotion (EE)
prefrontal lobotomy
antipsychotic medication

*Henri de Toulouse-Lautrec,
"A La Buvette"*

12

SUBSTANCE-RELATED DISORDERS

Alice was fifty-four years old when her family finally persuaded her to check into an alcohol rehabilitation clinic. She had taken a bad fall down her bedroom steps while drunk, and it may have been this event that finally got her to admit that something was wrong. Her drinking had been out of control for several years. She began each day with a drink, continued through the morning, and was totally intoxicated by the afternoon. She seldom had any memory for events after noon of any day. Since early adulthood she had drunk regularly, but rarely during the day and never to the point of drunkenness. The sudden death of her husband in an automobile accident two years earlier had triggered a quick increase in her drinking, and within six months she had slipped into a pattern of severe alcohol abuse. She had little desire to go out of her house and had cut back on social activities with family and friends. Repeated efforts by her family to get her to curtail her intake of alcohol had only led to angry confrontations.

From prehistoric times humankind has used various substances in the hope of reducing physical pain or altering states of consciousness. Almost all peoples have discovered some intoxicant that affects the central nervous system, relieving physical and mental anguish or producing euphoria. Despite the often devastating consequences of taking such substances into the body, their initial effects are usually pleasing, a factor that is perhaps at the root of substance abuse. In this chapter we will examine both the effects of various drugs and the psychological and biological causes of abuse.

The United States is a drug culture. Americans use drugs to wake up (coffee or tea) and stay alert throughout the day (cigarettes, soft drinks), as a way to relax (alcohol) and to reduce pain (aspirin). The widespread availability and frequent use of various drugs sets the stage for the potential abuse of drugs, the topic of this chapter. The most recent data on the frequency of use of several drugs, both legal and illegal, are presented in Table 12.1. These figures do not represent the frequency of abuse (figures on abuse are presented in the discussion of individual drugs), but simply provide an indication of how pervasive drug use is in the United States.

The pathological use of substances falls into two categories: substance abuse and substance dependence. Together these constitute the major DSM-IV category substance-related disorders.

Substance dependence is characterized by DSM-IV as the presence of at least three of the following criteria:

- The person develops **tolerance**, indicated by either (a) larger doses of the substance being needed to produce the desired effect; or (b) the effects of the drug becoming markedly less if the usual amount is taken.

- **Withdrawal** symptoms, negative physical and psychological effects, develop when the person stops taking the substance or reduces the amount. The person may also use the substance to relieve or avoid withdrawal symptoms.

- The person uses more of the substance or uses it for a longer time than intended.

- The person recognizes excessive use of the substance; he or she may have tried to reduce usage but has been unable to do so.

- Much of the person's time is spent in efforts to obtain the substance or recover from its effects.

- Substance use continues despite psychological or physical problems caused or exacerbated by the drug (e.g., smoking despite knowledge that it increases the risk for cancer and cardiovascular disease).

- The person gives up or cuts back participation in many activities (work, recreation, socializing) because of the use of the substance.

Substance dependence is diagnosed as accompanied by physiological dependence (also called addiction) if either tolerance or withdrawal is present.

For the diagnosis of **substance abuse** the person must experience one of the following as a result of recurrent use of the drug:

- Failure to fulfill major obligations, for example, absences from work or neglect of children.

- Exposure to physical dangers, such as operating machinery or driving while intoxicated.

- Legal problems, such as arrests for disorderly conduct or traffic violations.

TABLE 12.1 Percentage of U.S. Population Reporting Drug Use in the Past Month (1995)

Substance	Percentage Reporting Use
Alcohol	52.2
Cigarettes	28.8
Marijuana	4.7
Cocaine	0.7
Hallucinogens	0.7
Inhalants	0.4
Crack	0.2
Heroin	0.1

Source: National Institute on Drug Abuse, 1996.

- Persistent social or interpersonal problems, such as arguments with a spouse.

The DSM-IV section on substance-related disorders includes several other diagnoses. Substance intoxication is diagnosed when the ingestion of a substance affects the central nervous system and produces maladaptive cognitive and behavioral effects. If a person who is addicted to a drug is denied it and then experiences withdrawal, that person receives a diagnosis of both substance dependence and substance withdrawal. An example of a diagnosis of substance withdrawal is alcohol withdrawal delirium, commonly known as the DTs. Furthermore, drugs can cause dementia and the symptoms of other Axis I disorders.

We turn now to an overview of the major substance-related disorders, considering problem drinking, nicotine and cigarette smoking, marijuana, sedatives and stimulants, and the hallucinogens. We will then look at etiological factors suspected in substance abuse and dependence and conclude with an examination of the therapies available for these serious disorders.

ALCOHOL ABUSE AND DEPENDENCE

The term *alcoholic* is familiar to most people, yet it does not have a precise meaning. To some it implies a person slumped against a building, to others an abusive husband or co-worker and to still others a man or woman sneaking drinks during the day. All these images are to some extent accurate, yet none provides a full or useful definition. DSM-IV distinguishes between *alcohol dependence* and *alcohol abuse*. This distinction is not always made in the research literature. The term *abuse* is often used to refer to both aspects of the excessive and harmful use of alcohol.

Alcohol dependence may include tolerance or withdrawal reactions. People who begin drinking early in life develop their first withdrawal symptoms in their thirties or forties. The effects of the abrupt withdrawal of alcohol from a chronic, heavy user may be rather dramatic because the body has become accustomed to the drug. Subjectively, the patient is often anxious, depressed, weak, restless, and unable to sleep. Tremors of the muscles, especially of the small musculatures of the fingers, face, eyelids, lips, and tongue, may be marked, and there is an elevation of pulse, blood pressure, and temperature. In relatively rare cases a person who has been drinking heavily for a number of years may also suffer from **delirium tremens (DTs)** when the level of alcohol in the blood drops suddenly. The person becomes delirious as well as tremulous and suffers from hallucinations that are primarily visual but may be tactile as well. Unpleasant and very active creatures—snakes, cockroaches, spiders, and the like—may appear to be crawling up the wall or over the person's body or they may fill the room. Feverish, disoriented, and terrified, the person may

An etching displaying the vivid portrayal of a delirium tremens scene in a play.

claw frantically at his or her skin to get rid of the vermin or may cower in the corner to escape an advancing army of fantastic animals. The delirium and physiological paroxysms caused by withdrawal of alcohol indicate that the drug is addictive.

Increased tolerance is evident following heavy, prolonged drinking. Some alcohol abusers can drink a quart of bourbon a day without showing signs of drunkenness (Mello & Mendelson, 1970). Moreover, levels of alcohol in the blood of such people are unexpectedly low after what is usually viewed as excessive drinking, suggesting that the body adapts to the drug and becomes able to process it more efficiently. Although changes in the liver enzymes that metabolize alcohol can account to a small extent for tolerance, most researchers now believe that the central nervous system is implicated. None of the areas being pursued has unequivocal support, but some research suggests that tolerance results from changes in the number or sensitivity of GABA receptors (see p. 140).

The drinking pattern of people who are alcohol dependent indicates that their drinking is out of control. They need to drink daily and are unable to stop or cut down despite repeated efforts to abstain completely or to restrict drinking to certain periods of the day. They may go on occasional binges, remaining intoxicated for two, three, or more days. Sometimes they consume a fifth of alcohol at a time. They may suffer blackouts for the events that took place during a bout of intoxication; their craving may be so overpowering that they are forced to ingest alcohol in a nonbeverage form, such as hair tonic. Such drinking, of course, causes social and occupational difficulties, quarrels with family or friends, sometimes violence when intoxicated, frequent absences from work, possibly loss of job, and arrest for intoxication or traffic accidents.

The alcohol abuser experiences negative social and occupational effects from the drug but does not show tolerance, withdrawal, or the compulsive pattern of abuse seen in the alcohol-dependent person.

Alcohol abuse or dependence is often part of **polydrug abuse**, using or abusing more than one drug at a time. Nicotine dependence is especially common in association with heavy drinking, as any visit to a cocktail lounge will confirm (though we do not mean to imply that all those in cocktail lounges are alcoholics). Polydrug abuse can create serious health problems because the effects of some drugs when taken together are synergistic, that is, the effects of each combine to produce an especially strong reaction. For example, mixing alcohol and barbiturates is a common means of suicide, intentional or accidental. Alcohol is also believed to have

Polysubstance abuse involves the use of multiple drugs. Alcohol and nicotine are a frequent combination, although most people who smoke and drink in social situations do not become substance abusers.

contributed to deaths from heroin, for it can reduce the amount of the narcotic needed to make a dose lethal.

PREVALENCE OF ALCOHOL ABUSE

Following World War II alcohol consumption rose in the United States and in most other countries. By 1970, 68 percent of the U.S. population drank and 9 percent were problem drinkers (Caddy, 1983). As of 1985, 86 percent of the U.S. population reported having consumed alcohol and about 12 percent reported using it twenty or more days each month (National Institute on Drug Abuse [NIDA], 1988). Problem drinking began to decline in the late 1980s.

In the large U.S. epidemiological study described on page 109, lifetime prevalence rates for alcohol dependence defined by DSM criteria were greater than 20 percent for men and just over 8 percent for women (Kessler et al., 1994). The prevalence of alcohol abuse declines with advancing age, both because of early death among long-term abusers and because of achievement of stable abstinence from alcohol among others (Vaillant, 1996). Among young women, rates of problem drinking are approaching those of men. The rates of alcohol abuse or dependence among whites and Latinos are highest in those aged eighteen to twenty-nine. For African-Americans the highest rate is among thirty to forty-four year olds. Alcohol abuse is common in some Native American tribes and is associated with 40 percent of deaths and virtually all crimes committed by Native Americans (Yetman, 1994). Problem drinking is comorbid with antisocial personality disorder, mania, other drug use, schizophrenia, and panic disorder (Robins et al., 1988).

Alcohol use is especially frequent among college-aged adults. A nationwide survey revealed that 50 percent of men and 40 percent of women engaged in binge drinking, defined as having five drinks in a row for men and four for women (Wechsler, 1994).

COURSE OF THE DISORDER

For some time the life histories of alcohol abusers were thought to have a common, downhill progression. On the basis of an extensive survey of 2000 members of Alcoholics Anonymous, Jellinek (1952) described the male alcohol abuser as passing through four stages, beginning with social drinking and progressing to a stage at which the person lives only to drink. Although Jellinek's description has been widely cited, the available evidence does not always corroborate it. The histories of alcohol-dependent people do indeed show a progression from alcohol abuse to alcohol dependence (Langenbucher & Chung, 1995); however, data reveal considerable fluctuation in the drinking patterns of many drinkers, from heavy drinking for some periods of time to abstinence or lighter drinking at others (Vaillant, 1996). Furthermore, patterns of maladaptive use of alcohol are more variable than Jellinek implied. Heavy use of the drug may be restricted to weekends, or long periods of abstinence may be interspersed with binges of continual drinking for several weeks (Robins et al., 1988). There is no single pattern of alcohol abuse.

Evidence also indicates that Jellinek's account does not apply to women. Difficulties with alcohol usually begin at a later age in women than in men and often after an inordinately stressful experience, such as the death of a husband or a serious family crisis, as in Alice's case. For women the time interval between the onset of heavy drinking and alcohol abuse is briefer than for men (Mezzich et al., 1994). Women with drinking problems tend more than men to be steady drinkers and to drink alone; they are also less likely to engage in binge drinking (Hill, 1980; Wolin, 1980).

COSTS OF ALCOHOL DEPENDENCE

Although most people who have a drinking problem do not seek professional help, people who abuse alcohol constitute a large proportion of new

Alcohol is often implicated in vehicular accidents. The driver of this New York subway train, which derailed killing 5 and injuring over 100, was intoxicated.

admissions to mental and general hospitals. Problem drinkers use health services four times more than do nonabusers, and their medical expenses are twice as high as those of nondrinkers (*The Harvard Medical School Mental Health Letter*, 1987). As mentioned earlier (p. 253), the suicide rate of alcohol abusers is much higher than that of the general population. Alcohol is a contributing cause in one-third of all suicides. Moreover, some people estimate that alcohol is implicated in about half the total number of highway deaths each year. A California study found that 70 percent of driving fatalities had alcohol in their blood (Stinson & De Bakey, 1992). Alcohol may be a factor in airplane crashes, industrial accidents, and mishaps in the home. Alcohol also presents law-enforcement problems; about one-third of all arrests in the United States are for public drunkenness. Homicide is an alcohol-related crime—it is believed that over half of all murders are committed under its influence—and so too are rapes, assaults, and family violence (Murdoch, Pihl, & Ross, 1990).

The overall cost of problem drinking in the United States—from absenteeism to damaged health—was estimated in 1990 at more than $125 billion. The human costs, in terms of broken lives and losses to society, are incalculable.

SHORT-TERM EFFECTS OF ALCOHOL

After being swallowed and reaching the stomach alcohol begins to be metabolized by enzymes. Most of it goes into the small intestines and from there is absorbed into the blood. It is then broken down, primarily in the liver, which can metabolize about one ounce of 100 proof (that is, 50 percent alcohol) whiskey per hour. Quantities in excess of this amount remain in the bloodstream. Whereas absorption of alcohol can be very rapid, removal is always slow. The effects of alcohol vary with the level of concentration of the drug in the bloodstream, which in turn depends on the amount ingested in a particular period of time, the presence or absence of food in the stomach to retain the alcohol and reduce its absorption rate, the size of the individual's body, and the efficiency of the liver. Two ounces of alcohol will have different effects on a 180-pound man who has just eaten and on a 110-pound woman with an empty stomach.

Because drinking alcoholic beverages is accepted in most societies, alcohol is rarely regarded as a drug, especially by those who drink. But it is indeed a drug and has what is referred to as a *biphasic* effect. The initial effect of alcohol is stimulating; the drinker experiences an expansive feeling of sociability and well-being as his or her blood-alcohol level rises. But after the blood-alcohol level peaks and begins to decline, alcohol acts as a depressant, and the person may experience increases in negative emotions. Large amounts of alcohol interfere with complex thought processes; motor coordination, balance, speech, and vision are also impaired. At this stage of intoxication some individuals become depressed and withdrawn. Alcohol is capable of blunting pain and in larger doses, of inducing sedation and sleep.

Alcohol produces its effects through its interactions with several neural systems in the brain. It stimulates GABA receptors, which may be responsible for its ability to reduce tension. (GABA is a major inhibitory neurotransmitter; the benzodiazepines, such as Valium, have an effect on the GABA receptor similar to that of alcohol.) Alcohol also increases levels of serotonin and dopamine, and these effects may be the source of its capacity to serve as a potent reinforcer. Finally, alcohol inhibits glutamate receptors, which may cause the cognitive effects of alcohol intoxication, such as slurred speech and memory loss (U.S. Public Health Service [USPHS], 1994).

There are many beliefs about the effects of alcohol; it is thought to reduce anxiety, increase sociability, relax inhibitions, and the like. But it appears that some of the short-term effects of ingesting small amounts of alcohol are as strongly related to the drinker's expectations about the effects of the drug as they are to its chemical action on the body. For example, alcohol is commonly thought to stimulate aggression and increase sexual responsiveness. Research has shown, however, that these reactions may not be caused by alcohol itself but by the drinker's beliefs about alcohol's effects. In experiments demonstrating these points, participants are told that they are consuming a quantity of alcohol when they are actually given an alcohol-free beverage with its taste disguised. They subsequently become more aggressive (Lang et al., 1975) and report increased sexual arousal (Wilson & Lawson, 1976). People who actually drink alcohol also report increased sexual arousal, even though alcohol makes them less aroused physiologically (Farkas & Wilson, 1976). Once again, cognitions have a demonstrably powerful effect on behavior. We shall see later that beliefs about the effects of drugs are importantly related to their abuse.

LONG-TERM EFFECTS OF PROLONGED ALCOHOL ABUSE

The possible long-term effects of prolonged drinking are vividly illustrated in the following case history. This case is a good example of the course of the disorder, the toll it takes on family relationships, and how difficult it is to quit drinking.

At the time of his first admission to a state hospital at the age of twenty-four, the patient, an unmarried and unemployed laborer, already had a long history of antisocial behavior, promiscuity and addiction to alcohol and other drugs. ... There had been eight brief admissions to private sanatoria for alcoholics, a number of arrests for public intoxication and drunken driving, and two jail terms for assault.

The patient had been born into a wealthy and respected family in a small town. The patient's father, a successful and popular businessman, drank excessively and his death at the age of fifty-seven was partly due to alcoholism. The mother also drank to excess. The parents exercised little control over the patient as a child, and he was cared for by nursemaids. His father taught him to pour drinks for guests of the family when he was very young and he reported that he began to drain the glasses at parties in his home before he was six; by the time he was twelve he drank almost a pint of liquor every weekend and by seventeen was drinking up to three bottles every day. His father provided him with money to buy liquor and shielded him from punishment for drunken driving and other consequences of his drinking.

The patient was expelled from high school his freshman year for striking a teacher. He then attended a private school until the eleventh grade, when he changed the date on his birth certificate and joined the Army paratroops. After discharge, he was unemployed for six months; he drank heavily and needed repeated care at a sanatorium. When a job was obtained for him he quit within a month. On his third arrest for drunken driving he was jailed. His father bailed him out with the warning that no more money would be forthcoming. The patient left town and worked as an unskilled laborer—he had never acquired any useful skills—but returned home when his father died. During the next few years he was jailed for intoxication, for blackening his mother's eyes when he found a male friend visiting her, and for violating probation by getting drunk. He assaulted and badly hurt a prison guard in an escape attempt and was sentenced to two additional years in prison. When released, he began to use a variety of stimulant, sedative and narcotic drugs as well as alcohol. (Rosen, Fox, & Gregory, 1972, p. 312)

Chronic drinking creates severe biological damage in addition to psychological deterioration. Almost every tissue and organ of the body is adversely affected by prolonged consumption of alcohol. Malnutrition may be severe. Because alcohol provides calories—a pint of 80 proof spirits supplies about half a day's caloric requirements—heavy drinkers often reduce their intake of food. But the calories provided by alcohol are empty; they do not supply the nutrients essential for health. Alcohol also contributes directly to malnutrition by impairing the digestion of food and absorption of vitamins. In older chronic alcohol abusers, a deficiency of B-complex vitamins can cause *amnestic syndrome*, a severe loss of memory for both recent and long-past events. These memory gaps are often filled in by reporting imaginary events (confabulation) that are highly improbable.

Prolonged alcohol use plus reduction in the intake of protein contribute to the development of cirrhosis of the liver, a disease in which some liver cells become engorged with fat and protein, impeding their function; some cells die, triggering an inflammatory process. When scar tissue develops, blood flow is obstructed. Cirrhosis ranks ninth among causes of death in the United States (U.S. Department of Health and Human Services [USDHHS], 1990); paralleling the decrease in drinking in the late 1980s, this figure represents a decline in deaths from cirrhosis, which peaked at over 14 per 100,000 in the 1970s. Other common physiological changes include damage to the endocrine glands and pancreas, heart failure, hypertension, stroke, and capillary hemorrhages, which are responsible for the swelling and redness in the face, and especially of the nose, of chronic alcohol abusers. Prolonged use of alcohol appears to damage brain cells, especially those in the frontal lobes, causing

cortical atrophy and other changes in structure (Parsons, 1975). Alcohol also reduces the effectiveness of the immune system, resulting in increased susceptibility to infection and cancer.

Heavy alcohol consumption during pregnancy is the leading known cause of mental retardation. The growth of the fetus is slowed, and cranial, facial, and limb anomalies are produced. The condition is known as **fetal alcohol syndrome**. Even moderate drinking can produce less severe but undesirable effects on the fetus, leading the National Institute on Alcohol Abuse and Alcoholism to counsel total abstention during pregnancy as the safest course (*Alcohol, Drug Abuse and Mental Health Administration News*, May 2, 1980).

Although it is appropriate and accurate to concentrate on the deleterious effects of alcohol, tantalizing evidence suggests positive health benefits for some people. Light drinking (fewer than three drinks a day), especially of wine, has been related to decreased risk for coronary heart disease in both men and women (Stampfer et al., 1988). Not all researchers, however, accept this finding at face value. Some people who abstain may have done so for health reasons, for example, because of hypertension. Comparing these abstainers to light drinkers could result in misleading conclusions. If alcohol does have a beneficial effect, it could be either physiological (for example, acetate, a metabolite of alcohol, increases coronary blood flow) or psychological (a less driven lifestyle and decreased

Heavy drinking during pregnancy causes fetal alcohol syndrome. Such children have facial abnormalities as well as mental retardation.

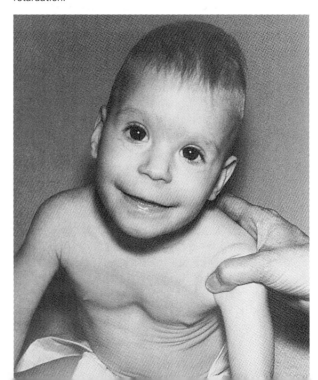

levels of hostility). Research on the topic we have been describing was stimulated by the so-called French paradox—despite diets rich in saturated fats, the French have relatively low cholesterol levels. Some hypothesize that the French may be offsetting their cholesterol levels by consuming low to moderate amounts of red wine. (Of course, the French lifestyle has other characteristics that may result in lower risk of heart disease, such as eating more fresh foods and getting more daily exercise, for example, walking instead of driving to work.) Nevertheless, promoting alcohol in the U.S. diet may set the stage for a dangerous flirtation with potential alcohol abuse.

The psychological, biological, and social consequences of prolonged consumption of alcohol are extremely serious. Because the alcohol abuser's own functioning is so severely disrupted, the people with whom he or she interacts are also deeply affected and hurt by this conduct. Society, too, suffers, for the alcohol abuser is unlikely to be able to hold a job. As mentioned earlier, the accumulated costs—money spent on liquor, lost work efficiency, damage caused by traffic accidents, expense of physicians and psychologists—run to well over $125 billion dollars each year. The human tragedy, much more devastating, is virtually incalculable.

NICOTINE AND CIGARETTE SMOKING

The history of tobacco smoking bears much similarity to that of other addictive drugs (Brecher, 1972). It was not long after Columbus's first commerce with Native Americans that sailors and merchants began to imitate the Native Americans' smoking of rolled leaves of tobacco and experienced, as they did, the increasing craving for it. When not smoked, tobacco was—and is—chewed or ground into small pieces and inhaled as snuff.

Nicotine, the principal alkaloid of tobacco, is its addicting agent. It stimulates receptors, called nicotinic receptors, in the pleasure centers of the brain. Some idea of the addictive qualities of tobacco can be appreciated by considering how much people have sacrificed to maintain their supplies. In sixteenth-century England, for example, tobacco was exchanged for silver ounce for ounce. Poor people squandered their meager resources for their several daily pipefuls. Even the public tortures and executions engineered as punishment by Sultan Murad IV of Turkey during the seventeenth century could not dissuade those of his subjects who were addicted to the weed.

PREVALENCE AND HEALTH CONSEQUENCES OF SMOKING

The threat to health posed by smoking has been documented convincingly by the surgeon general of the United States in a series of reports since 1964. It is estimated that more than 430,000 American tobacco users die prematurely each year (Schultz, 1991). Cigarette smoking is responsible in some way for 1 of every 6 deaths in the United States, killing more than 1100 people each day. It remains the single most preventable cause of premature death. Tobacco kills more Americans each year than AIDS, car accidents, cocaine, crack, heroin, homicide, and suicide *combined*. Children of smokers are more likely to suffer from upper respiratory infections, bronchitis, and inner ear infections than are their peers whose parents do not smoke. The health risks of smoking are significantly less for cigar and pipe smokers because they seldom inhale the smoke into their lungs, but cancers of the mouth are increased by such consumption.

Among the medical problems associated with, and almost certainly caused or exacerbated by, long-term cigarette smoking are lung cancer, emphysema, cancer of the larynx and of the esophagus, and a number of cardiovascular diseases. The most probable harmful components in the smoke from burning tobacco are nicotine, carbon monoxide, and tar; the latter consists primarily of certain hydrocarbons, many of which are known carcinogens (Jaffe, 1985).

The twentieth and twenty-first surgeon general's reports, published in 1989 and 1990 (USDHHS, 1989, 1990), a report from the Centers for Disease Control (Cimons, 1992), and other publications (Cherner, 1990; Jansen et al., 1996; Type, 1991) draw several conclusions from over twenty-five years' experience in focused federal government efforts to discourage cigarette smoking.

- The prevalence of habitual smoking among American adults decreased from a little over 40 percent in 1965 to about 25 percent in 1990, a hefty 25 percent decrease; almost half of all living adults who ever smoked quit. But 45 million Americans still smoke, and smoking rates are higher still in Asia and South America. The rate of quitting since 1987 more than doubled that between 1965 and 1985. However, rates of smoking have been increasing among teenagers since 1991.

- Prevalence remains high among Native Americans, African-Americans, blue-collar workers, and less educated individuals, though some sharp declines have occurred in prevalence among African-American men in recent years. Prevalence is lowest among college graduates and those over the age of 75.

- Prevalence has declined much less among women than among men; more women are taking up the habit, often as a means of losing weight.

- People begin to smoke primarily in childhood and adolescence; the age at which smoking begins is decreasing, especially among young women.

- Of the approximately 1000 children and adolescents who begin smoking every day, 750 will die prematurely from a preventable, smoking-related disease.

Health risks decline dramatically over a period of five to ten years after quitting, to levels only slightly above those of nonsmokers, although the destruction of lung tissue is not reversible (Jaffe, 1985). As with alcohol, the socioeconomic cost of smoking is considerable; each year smokers compile in excess of an additional 80 million lost days of work and 145 million days of disability over their nonsmoking peers. This loss of productivity coupled with the health care costs associated with smoking run to more than $65 billion annually in the United States. Another way to understand this figure is to realize that it amounts to $178 million a day—enough money to feed 19,000 children for a year or to build a major urban teaching hospital.

A recent development has been the creation of ad campaigns to recruit young people to low-nicotine cigarettes. Young women find these cigarettes easier to get used to because the low level of nicotine is less likely to induce unpleasant side effects such as nausea; thus experimenting with smoking becomes more likely (Silverstein, Feld, & Kozlowski, 1980). Concern about teenage smoking is also relevant to the current controversy over cigarette-vending machines. Many states prohibit the sale of cigarettes to minors, yet these vending machines are an easy way to circumvent the law and have therefore become a target of antismoking groups.

CONSEQUENCES OF SECONDHAND SMOKE

As we have known for many years the health hazards of smoking are not restricted to those who smoke. The smoke coming from the burning end of a cigarette, so-called secondhand smoke, or environmental tobacco smoke (ETS), contains higher concentrations of ammonia, carbon monoxide, nicotine, and tar than does the smoke actually inhaled by the

Environmental tobacco smoke can damage the lungs of nonsmokers and increase their risk for respiratory infections.

smoker. Nonsmokers can suffer lung damage, possibly permanent, from extended exposure to cigarette smoke. Many nonsmokers greatly dislike the smell of smoke from burning tobacco, and some have allergic reactions to it. Environmental tobacco smoke is blamed for more than 50,000 U.S. deaths a year,[1] and in 1993 the Environmental Protection Agency classified ETS as a hazard as dangerous as asbestos and radon. Babies of women who smoke during pregnancy are more likely to be born prematurely, to have lower birth weights, and to have birth defects.

In recent years various local governments have passed ordinances regulating cigarette smoking in public places and work settings. Smoking is banned in many supermarkets, buses, hospitals, government buildings, and on all domestic U.S. airline flights. Restaurants must often post signs indicating whether they have an area for nonsmokers, and many restaurants ban smoking altogether. Workplaces with more than fifty employees must either ban smoking on the premises or restrict it to designated areas. One of the most talked-about bans is in a well-known indoor sports arena, where not only smoking but also smoking advertisements are forbidden. Many nonsmokers express enthusiastic approval of such measures, but pressure from smokers and from the tobacco industry sometimes defeats efforts to enact laws. Some smokers object strongly to what they view as undue infringement on their rights.

---

[1]To get some perspective on this statistic, U.S. fatalities from the Vietnam War totaled about 58,000.

MARIJUANA

Marijuana consists of the dried and crushed leaves and flowering tops of the hemp plant, *Cannabis sativa*. It is most often smoked, but it may be chewed, prepared as a tea, or eaten in baked goods. **Hashish**, much stronger than marijuana, is produced by removing and drying the resin exudate of the tops of high-quality cannabis plants. Originally, the plant was extensively cultivated in the United States not for smoking, but for its fibers (hemp), which were used in the manufacture of cloth and rope. By the nineteenth century the medicinal properties of cannabis resin were noted, and it was marketed by several drug companies as a treatment for rheumatism, gout, depression, cholera, and neuralgia. It was also smoked for pleasure though little seen in the United States until 1920, when the passage of the Eighteenth Amendment prohibiting the sale of alcohol prompted some people to begin smoking marijuana brought across the border from Mexico. Unfavorable reports in the press attributing crimes to marijuana use led to the enactment of a federal law against the sale of the drug in 1937. Today marijuana use is illegal in most countries, many of them bound by a United Nations treaty prohibiting its sale (Goodwin & Guze, 1984).

PREVALENCE OF MARIJUANA USE

Periodically the National Institute of Drug Abuse (NIDA), a federal agency charged to investigate drug use in the United States, publishes the results of surveys taken of youths, ages twelve to seven-

Early recreational use of hashish occurred in a fashionable apartment in New York City. An 1876 issue of the *Illustrated Police News* carried this picture with the title "Secret Dissipation of New York Belles: Interior of a Hasheesh Hell on Fifth Avenue."

teen; young adults, eighteen to twenty-five; and people over twenty-six years old. The participants are questioned about current drug use, past use, frequency of use, range of drugs used, and so forth. Trends over the past twenty years suggest that the use of marijuana peaked in 1979, then declined for the next decade, and is on the rise again. The following percentages of respondents between the ages of twelve and seventeen reported having used marijuana at least once: 14 percent in 1972, 31 percent in 1979, 24 percent in 1985, and 13 percent in 1991 (Kozel & Adams, 1986; *Marijuana Research Findings*, 1980; *National Survey on Drug Abuse*, 1979, 1982, 1991). As with tobacco, marijuana use has increased markedly since 1991 (Cimons, 1995 Greenberg, 1996; Kipke, Montgomery, & MacKenzie, 1993).

EFFECTS OF MARIJUANA

Like most other drugs marijuana is not without its risks. Science has generally found that the more we learn about a drug, the less benign it turns out to be. Marijuana is no exception (see Focus 12.1).

PSYCHOLOGICAL EFFECTS

The intoxicating effects of marijuana, as of most drugs, depend in part on its potency and the size of the dose. Smokers of marijuana find it makes them feel relaxed and sociable. Large doses have been reported to bring rapid shifts in emotion, to dull attention, to fragment thoughts, and to impair memory. Time seems to move more slowly. Extremely heavy doses have sometimes been found to induce hallucinations and other effects similar to those of LSD, including extreme panic, sometimes arising from the belief that the frightening experience will never end. Dosage can be difficult to regulate because it may take up to half an hour after smoking marijuana for its effects to appear; many users thus get themselves much higher than intended. People with psychological problems are generally believed to be at highest risk for negative reactions to marijuana or any other psychoactive drug. Contrary to popular belief, marijuana does show some association with violent behavior (Spunt et al., 1994), although the mechanisms are unclear (Sussman et al., in press).

The major active chemical in marijuana has been isolated and named delta-9-tetrahydrocannabinol (THC). The amount of THC in marijuana is variable, but in general marijuana is more potent now than it was a decade ago (Zimmer & Morgan, 1995). In the late 1980s cannabis receptors were discovered

FOCUS 12.1   THE STEPPING-STONE THEORY—FROM MARIJUANA TO HARD DRUGS

A concern prevalent for some time is expressed in the so-called stepping-stone theory of marijuana use. According to this view, marijuana is dangerous not only in itself but also because it is a first step that can lead young people to become addicted to other drugs such as heroin. In the late 1960s when information on the harmfulness of marijuana was scant, the issue was basically political and generational. People in their teens and college years believed that the older generation, lacking scientific data to discourage marijuana use, had concocted the stepping-stone theory, which itself lacked empirical support, to justify harsh legal penalties for the use and sale of marijuana. Since there was little doubt that hard drugs were very harmful, marijuana was said to be so too because it was a first step to a career of abusing these drugs.

Studies done in the last twenty years have established several specific dangers from using marijuana, as described in the text. But is marijuana a stepping-stone to more serious substance abuse? The question may not be so difficult to answer. About 40 percent of regular marijuana users do *not* go on to use such drugs as heroin and cocaine (Stephens, Roffman, & Simpson, 1993). So if by stepping-stone we mean that there is an inevitability of escalating to a more serious drug, then marijuana is not a stepping-stone. On the other hand, we do know that many, but far from all, who abuse heroin and cocaine began their drug experimentation with marijuana. At least in the United States, users of marijuana are more likely than nonusers to experiment later with heroin and cocaine (Kandel, 1984). (We also know that cigarette smokers are more likely to use marijuana than are nonsmokers, one of the arguments made by President Clinton in August 1996 to justify restrictions on promoting tobacco use among minors.) Furthermore, the single best predictor of cocaine use in adulthood is heavy use of marijuana during adolescence (Kandel, Murphy, & Karus, 1985; Kozel & Adams, 1986). Perhaps a third variable can link all such

Most people who use marijuana do not go on to use other drugs such as heroin, but many heroin abusers did begin their drug use with marijuana.

drugs, including the legal drug alcohol. There is growing evidence that users of even legal drugs are at higher risk for using illegal drugs. It is likely that the use of either illegal or legal substances exposes users to environmental cues that increase the probability of drug use.

Thus, better than a stepping-stone theory might be a network theory. *Network* implies a complex set of relationships in which cause and effect are virtually impossible to isolate but some degree of association among many variables is acknowledged. Some regular users of heroin and cocaine, for example, turn to marijuana as a safer substitute, or lesser evil (Sussman et al., in press). Marijuana is part of the picture, but only one of many contributing factors to involvement in harmful substance use.

in the brain; shortly thereafter it was found that the body produces its own cannabis-like substance, anandamide, named for the Sanskrit word for bliss (Sussman et al., in press).

An abundance of scientific evidence indicates that marijuana interferes with a wide range of cognitive functions. Laboratory studies conducted for the most part in the late 1960s found that a number of tests—substituting symbols for numbers, reaction-time tests, repeating series of digits forward and backward, arithmetic calculations, reading comprehension and speech tests—all revealed intellectual impairment in those under the influence of

marijuana *(Marijuana Research Findings: 1980).* Of special significance are findings that show loss of short-term memory. It appears that the many high school students who use marijuana regularly may be seriously hindering their learning.

Several studies have demonstrated that being high on marijuana impairs complex psychomotor skills necessary for driving. Highway fatality and driver-arrest figures indicate that marijuana plays a role in a significant proportion of accidents and arrests (Brookoff et al., 1994). Marijuana has similarly been found to impair manipulation of flight simulators. Some performance decrements measurable after smoking one or two marijuana cigarettes containing 2 percent THC can persist for up to eight hours after a person believes he or she is no longer high, creating the very real danger that people will attempt to drive or to fly when they are not functioning adequately.

Does chronic use of marijuana affect intellectual functioning even when the person is not using the drug? Studies of memory and problem solving conducted in Egypt and India in the late 1970s indicated some deterioration in users compared with nonusers (Soueif, 1976; Wig & Varma, 1977). A more recent U.S. study found memory impairment but not a general intellectual inefficiency (Millsaps, Azrin, & Mittenberg, 1994). It is impossible to know whether these problems existed before heavy drug use.

Survey findings suggest that heavy use of marijuana during teenage years may well contribute to psychological problems in adulthood. Kandel et al. (1986) interviewed 1004 adults in their midtwenties who had been part of an earlier New York public high school survey of drug use. Those who reported using marijuana in high school tended to have higher rates of separation or divorce, more delinquency, increased tendencies to consult mental health professionals, and, among women, less stable employment patterns. The authors caution, however, that the specific effects of a single drug such as marijuana are very difficult to disentangle from the effects of other drugs that marijuana smokers sometimes use, in particular, alcohol and cocaine.

SOMATIC EFFECTS

The short-term effects of marijuana include bloodshot and itchy eyes, dry mouth and throat, increased appetite, reduced pressure within the eye, and somewhat raised blood pressure. There is no evidence that smoking marijuana has untoward effects on a normal heart. The drug apparently poses a danger to people with already abnormal heart functioning, however, for it elevates heart rate, sometimes dramatically. As a NIDA report suggests, this effect may be of particular concern as present smokers grow older. The relatively healthy thirty-year-old marijuana users of today are the fifty-year-olds of tomorrow, with a statistically greater chance of having a cardiovascular system impaired for other reasons, such as atherosclerosis. If they are still using the drug then, their hearts will be more vulnerable to its effects. It is also possible that long-term use of marijuana, like the chronic use of tobacco, may be harmful in ways that cannot be predicted from the short-term effects studied so far (Jones, 1980).

Long-term use of marijuana seriously impairs lung structure and function (Grinspoon & Bakalar, 1995). Even though marijuana users smoke far fewer cigarettes than do tobacco smokers, most inhale marijuana smoke more deeply and retain it in their lungs for much longer periods of time. Since marijuana has some of the same carcinogens found in tobacco cigarettes, its harmful effects are much greater than would be expected were only the absolute number of cigarettes or pipefuls considered. For example, one joint is the equivalent of five tobacco cigarettes in carbon monoxide intake, four in tar intake, and ten in terms of damage to cells lining the airways (Sussman et al., in press). Marijuana also impairs immune function (Swan, 1994).

Finally, marijuana may be harmful to reproduction. Two studies of chronic male users found lower sperm counts and less motility of the spermatozoa, suggesting that fertility might be decreased (Hembree, Nahas, & Huang, 1979; Issidorides, 1979). Similarly, female marijuana users fail to ovulate normally (Vardaris et al., 1976).

Is marijuana addictive? Contrary to widespread earlier belief, it may be. The development of tolerance began to be suspected when U.S. service personnel returned from Vietnam accustomed to concentrations of THC that would be toxic to domestic users. Controlled observations have confirmed that habitual use of marijuana does produce tolerance (Compton, Dewey, & Martin, 1990; Nowlan & Cohen, 1977). Whether long-term users suffer physical withdrawal when accustomed amounts of marijuana are not available is less clear (Johnson, 1991). If people do develop a physical dependency on marijuana, it is far less serious than what we know to be the case with nicotine, cocaine, and alcohol.

The question of physical addiction to marijuana is complicated by *reverse tolerance*. Experienced smokers need only a few hits or puffs to become high from a marijuana cigarette, whereas less experienced users puff many times to reach a similar state of intoxication. Reverse tolerance is the direct opposite of tolerance for an addicting drug such as heroin. The substance THC, after being rapidly metabolized, is stored in the body's fatty tissue and then released very slowly, over as long a period as a month, which may explain reverse tolerance for it.

THERAPEUTIC EFFECTS

In a seeming irony, therapeutic uses of marijuana came to light just as the negative effects of regular and heavy usage of the drug were being uncovered.

In the 1970s several double-blind studies (e.g., Salan, Zinberg, & Frei, 1975) showed that THC and related drugs can reduce the nausea and loss of appetite that accompany chemotherapy for some cancer patients. Recent findings confirm this (Grinspoon & Bakalar, 1995). Marijuana often appears to reduce nausea when other antinausea agents fail. Marijuana is also a treatment for the discomfort of AIDS and for glaucoma, a disease in which outflow of fluid from the eyeball is obstructed (Sussman et al., in press).

However, the therapeutic use of marijuana is controversial. Some AIDS patients have derived relief from smoking the drug—it stimulates the appetite, eases nausea, and helps them get to sleep—yet a federal program that supplied marijuana to about two dozen terminal patients was canceled in 1992, ostensibly because marijuana is bad for one's health (Klein, 1992). THC is still available in pill form (Nahos & Manger, 1995), but many sick patients cannot take it without vomiting. These pills also do not seem to be as helpful to AIDS patients and to others who benefited from smoking the drug.

SEDATIVES AND STIMULANTS

Addiction to drugs was disapproved of but tolerated in the United States until 1914, when the Harrison Narcotics Act made the unauthorized use of various drugs illegal and those addicted to them criminals. The drugs we discuss here, not all of which are illegal, may be divided into two general categories: sedatives and stimulants.

SEDATIVES

The major **sedatives**, often called downers, slow the activities of the body and reduce its responsiveness. This group of drugs includes the opiates—opium and its derivatives morphine, heroin, and codeine—and the synthetic barbiturates and tranquilizers, such as secobarbital (Seconal).

OPIATES

Opiates represent a group of addictive sedatives that in moderate doses relieve pain and induce sleep. Foremost among them is **opium**, originally the principal drug of illegal international traffic and known to the people of the Sumerian civilization dating as far back as 7000 B.C. They gave the poppy that supplied this drug the name by which it is still known, meaning "the plant of joy." Opium is a mix-

ture of about eighteen alkaloids, but until 1806 people had no knowledge of these substances to which so many natural drugs owe their potency.

In that year the alkaloid **morphine**, named after Morpheus, the Greek god of dreams, was separated out from raw opium. This bitter-tasting powder proved to be a powerful sedative and pain reliever. Before its addictive properties were noted, it was commonly used in patent medicines. In the middle of the nineteenth century when the hypodermic needle was introduced in the United States, morphine began to be injected directly into the veins to relieve pain. Many soldiers wounded in battle and those suffering from dysentery during the Civil War were treated with morphine and returned home addicted to the drug.

Concerned about administering a drug that could disturb the later lives of patients, scientists began studying morphine. In 1874 they found that morphine could be converted into another powerful pain-relieving drug, which they named **heroin**. Used initially as a cure for morphine addiction, heroin was substituted for morphine in cough syrups and other patent medicines. So many maladies were treated with heroin that it came to be known as G.O.M., or "God's own medicine" (Brecher, 1972). However, heroin proved to be even more addictive and more potent than morphine, acting more quickly and with greater intensity. In 1909, President Theodore Roosevelt called for an international investigation of opium and the opiates.

An opium poppy. Opium is harvested by slitting the seed capsule, which allows the raw opium to seep out.

Heroin was synthesized from opium in 1874 and was soon being added to a variety of medicines that could be purchased without prescription. This ad shows a teething remedy containing heroin. It probably worked.

PSYCHOLOGICAL AND PHYSICAL EFFECTS Opium and its derivatives morphine and heroin produce euphoria, drowsiness, reverie, and sometimes a lack of coordination. Heroin has an additional initial effect, the rush, a feeling of warm, suffusing ecstasy immediately following an intravenous injection. The addict sheds worries and fears and has great self-confidence for four to six hours, but then experiences letdown, bordering on stupor. Opiates produce their effects by stimulating neural receptors of the body's own opioid system. The body produces opioids, called endorphins and enkephalins, and opium and its derivatives fit into their receptors and stimulate them. Opiates are clearly addicting in the physiological sense, for users show both increased tolerance of the drugs and withdrawal symptoms when they are unable to obtain another dose.

Reactions to not having a dose of heroin may begin within eight hours of the last injection, at least after high tolerance has built up. During the next few hours the individual typically has muscle pain, sneezes, sweats, becomes tearful, and yawns a great deal. The symptoms resemble those of influenza. Within thirty-six hours the withdrawal symptoms become more severe. There may be uncontrollable muscle twitching, cramps, chills alternating with excessive flushing and sweating, and a rise in heart rate and blood pressure. The addict is unable to sleep, vomits, and has diarrhea. These symptoms typically persist for about seventy-two hours and then diminish gradually over a five- to ten-day period.

In spite of enormous difficulties in gathering data, the considered opinion is that there are more than a million heroin addicts in the United States (Goldstein, 1994). For many years dependence has been many times higher among physicians and nurses than in any other group with a comparable educational background. This problem is believed to arise from a combination of the relative availability of opiates in medical settings and the stresses under which people often work in such environments (Jaffe, 1985). Heroin used to be confined to poor neighborhoods and the inner city. In recent years it has started to become the cool drug for middle- and upper-middle-class college students and young professionals, and it is beginning to vie with cocaine for popularity among these groups. One statistic makes this clear: in 1988, 1250 people went to emergency rooms after smoking or snorting heroin; in 1994 this figure increased more than 2000 percent, to 27,300. Drug rehabilitation centers have seen commensurate increases in traffic (Corwin, 1996).

Some of these increases in drug casualties are due to the nature of the heroin that is now available. Fifteen years ago the heroin sold in southern California, for example, was in powder form that was less than 5 percent pure. Today heroin ranges from 25 to 50 percent pure and is sold in a gummy form that is difficult to dilute, or step down, making it more likely that users, especially the less experienced, will overdose (Corwin, 1996).

Opiates present a serious set of problems for the abuser. In a twenty-four-year follow-up of 500 heroin addicts, about 28 percent had died by age forty; half of these deaths were from homicide, suicide, or accident and one-third were from overdose (Hser, Anglin, & Powers, 1993). Equally serious are the social consequences of using an illegal drug. The drug and obtaining it become the center of the abuser's existence, governing all activities and social relationships. The high cost of the drugs—addicts must often spend upwards of $200 per day for their opiates—means that they must either have great wealth or acquire money through illegal activities, such as prostitution or selling drugs. The correlation between opiate addiction and criminal activities is thus rather high, undoubtedly contributing to the popular notion that drug addiction per se causes crime. An additional problem now associated with intravenous drug use is exposure, through sharing needles, to the human immunodeficiency virus (HIV) and AIDS (see p. 395).

SYNTHETIC SEDATIVES

Barbiturates, a major type of sedative, were synthesized as aids for sleeping and relaxation. The first barbiturate was produced in 1903, and since then hundreds of derivatives of barbituric acid have been made. These drugs were initially considered highly desirable and prescribed frequently. In the 1940s a campaign was mounted against them because they were discovered to be addicting, and physicians began to prescribe barbiturates less frequently. Today, the benzodiazepines, such as Valium, are more commonly used and abused. In the United States sedatives are manufactured in vast quantities, enough, it is estimated, to supply each man, woman, and child with fifty pills per year. Many are shipped legally to Mexico and then brought back into the United States and trafficked illegally. Many polydrug abusers choose a barbiturate or other sedative as one of their drugs, sometimes to come down from a stimulant or to reduce withdrawal effects.

Sedatives relax the muscles, reduce anxiety, and in small doses produce a mildly euphoric state. As with alcohol, they are thought to produce these psychological effects by stimulating the GABA system.[2] With excessive doses, however, speech becomes slurred and gait unsteady. Judgment, concentration, and ability to work may be extremely impaired. The user loses emotional control and may become irritable and combative before falling into a deep sleep. Very large doses can be fatal because the diaphragm muscles relax to such an extent that the individual suffocates. As indicated in Chapter 10, sedatives are frequently chosen as a means of suicide. However, many users accidentally kill themselves by drinking alcohol, which potentiates, or magnifies, the depressant effects of sedatives. With prolonged excessive use the brain can become damaged and personality deteriorates.

Increased tolerance follows prolonged use of sedatives, and the withdrawal reactions after abrupt termination are particularly severe and long lasting and can cause sudden death. The delirium, convulsions, and other symptoms resemble those following abrupt withdrawal of alcohol.

Three types of abusers can be distinguished. The first group fits the stereotype of the illicit drug abuser: adolescents and young adults, usually male and often antisocial, who use the drugs to alter their moods and consciousness, sometimes mixing them with other drugs. The second group consists of middle-aged, middle-class individuals who begin their use of sedatives under a physician's orders, to alleviate sleeplessness and anxiety, and then come to use larger and larger doses until they are addicted. These people rely less on street purchases because

they are generally able to obtain refills of their drug prescriptions whenever they wish, sometimes changing physicians so as not to raise suspicion. The third group comprises health professionals, physicians and nurses who have easy access to these drugs and often use them to self-medicate for anxiety-related problems (Liskow, 1982).

STIMULANTS

Stimulants, or uppers, such as cocaine, act on the brain and the sympathetic nervous system to increase alertness and motor activity. The amphetamines, such as Benzedrine, are synthetic stimulants; cocaine is a natural stimulant extracted from the coca leaf. Focus 12.2 discusses a less risky and more prevalent stimulant, caffeine.

AMPHETAMINES

Seeking a treatment for asthma, the Chinese-American pharmacologist Chen studied ancient Chinese descriptions of drugs. He found a desert shrub called mahuang commended again and again as an effective remedy. After systematic effort Chen was able to isolate an alkaloid from this plant belonging to the genus *Ephedra*, and ephedrine did indeed prove highly successful in treating asthma. But relying on the shrub for the drug was not viewed as efficient, and so efforts to develop a synthetic substitute began. **Amphetamines** were the result of these efforts (Snyder, 1974).

The first amphetamine, Benzedrine, was synthesized in 1927. Almost as soon as it became commercially available in the early 1930s as an inhalant to relieve stuffy noses, the public discovered its stimulating effects. Physicians thereafter prescribed it and the other amphetamines soon synthesized to control mild depression and appetite. During World War II soldiers on both sides were supplied with the drugs to ward off fatigue; today amphetamines are sometimes used to treat hyperactive children (see p. 412).

Amphetamines, such as Benzedrine, Dexedrine, and Methedrine, produce their effects by causing the release of norepinephrine and dopamine and blocking the reuptake of these neurotransmitters. They are taken orally or intravenously and can be addicting. Wakefulness is heightened, intestinal functions are inhibited, and appetite is reduced—hence their use in dieting. The heart rate quickens, and blood vessels in the skin and mucous membranes constrict. The individual becomes alert, euphoric, and outgoing and is possessed with seemingly boundless energy and self-confidence. Larger doses can make a person nervous, agitated, and confused, subjecting him or her to palpitations,

---

[2]Methaqualone, a sedative sold under the trade names Quaalude and Sopor, is similar in effect to barbiturates and has become a popular street drug. Besides being addictive it brings other dangers—internal bleeding, coma, and even death from overdose.

FOCUS 12.2   OUR TASTIEST ADDICTION—CAFFEINE

What may be the world's most popular drug is seldom viewed as a drug at all, and yet it has strong effects, produces tolerance in people, and even subjects habitual users to withdrawal (Hughes et al., 1991). Users and nonusers alike joke about it, and most readers of this book have probably had some this very day. We are, of course, referring to caffeine, a substance found in coffee, tea, cocoa, cola and other soft drinks, some cold remedies, and some diet pills.

Two cups of coffee, containing between 150 and 300 milligrams of caffeine, affect most people within half an hour. Metabolism, body temperature, and blood pressure all increase; urine production goes up, as most of us will attest; there may be hand tremors, appetite can diminish, and, most familiar of all, sleepiness is warded off. Panic disorder can be exacerbated by caffeine, not surprising in light of the heightened sympathetic nervous system arousal occasioned by the drug. Extremely large doses of caffeine can cause headache, diarrhea, nervousness, severe agitation, even convulsions and death. Death, though, is virtually impossible unless the individual grossly overuses

tablets containing caffeine, because the drug is excreted by the kidneys without any appreciable accumulation.

Although it has long been recognized that drinkers of very large amounts of caffeinated coffee daily can experience withdrawal symptoms when consumption ceases, people who drink no more than two cups of regular coffee a day can suffer from clinically significant headaches, fatigue, and anxiety if caffeine is withdrawn from their daily diet (Silverman et al., 1992), and these symptoms can markedly interfere with social and occupational functioning. These findings are disturbing because more than three-quarters of Americans consume a little more than two cups of caffeinated coffee a day (Roan, 1992). And although parents usually deny their children access to coffee and tea, they often do allow their children to imbibe caffeine-laden cola drinks, hot chocolate, and cocoa and to eat chocolate candy and coffee and chocolate ice cream. Thus our addiction to caffeine can begin to develop as early as six months of age, the form of it changing as we move from childhood to adulthood.

---

headaches, dizziness, and sleeplessness. Sometimes the heavy user becomes so suspicious and hostile that he or she can be dangerous to others. Large doses taken over a period of time can induce a state quite similar to paranoid schizophrenia, including its delusions.

Tolerance to amphetamines develops rapidly so that more and more of the drug is required to produce the stimulating effect. As tolerance increases the user may stop taking pills and inject Methedrine, the strongest of the amphetamines, directly into the veins. The so-called speed freaks give themselves repeated injections of the drug and maintain intense and euphoric activity for a few days, without eating or sleeping (a run), after which they are exhausted and depressed and sleep, or crash, for several days. Then the cycle starts again. After several repetitions of this pattern the physical and social functioning of the individual deteriorates considerably. Behavior is erratic and hostile, and the speed freak may become a danger to self and to others.

Amphetamine use in the workplace has been increasing. Under time pressure to produce—the saying of the nineties is to do more with less—many white-collar workers are turning to speed to stay awake, be more productive, and in general feel more energized, even euphoric. In some instances supervisors have encouraged use, even supplying the drug to an already motivated employee. While this

may work in the short run, over time extreme irritability sets in, and more and more of the addicting substance is taken to combat the angry feelings. Sometimes alcohol is used in the evening to help the person wind down. The emotional and physical costs are steep as the addict's personal relationships begin to deteriorate along with his or her job performance. In 1994 and 1995, 35 percent of admissions to California drug treatment centers were for amphetamine abuse, compared with 27 percent for heroin and 24 percent for cocaine. Emergency admissions to California hospitals for amphetamine abuse have also skyrocketed in recent years (Marsh, 1996).

The problem is apparently more serious in California than elsewhere in the United States because of the high concentration there of clandestine laboratories that manufacture this easily made and inexpensive drug. Chemicals for manufacturing amphetamines are readily available, but highly volatile and dangerous to breathe. Danger inheres in frequent explosions and fires; the hazardous chemicals cause damage ranging from eye irritation and nausea to coma and death.

COCAINE

The natives of the Andean uplands, to which the coca shrubs are native, chew the leaves, but Europeans, introduced to coca by the Spanish con-

A coca plant. The leaves contain about one percent cocaine.

quistadors, chose to brew them instead in beverages. The alkaloid **cocaine** was extracted from the leaves of the coca plant in 1844 and has been used since then as a local anesthetic. In 1884, while still a young neurologist, Sigmund Freud began using cocaine to combat his depression. Convinced of its wondrous effects, he prescribed it to a friend with a painful disease and published one of the first papers on the drug, "Song of Praise," which was an enthusiastic endorsement of the exhilarating effects he had experienced. Freud subsequently lost his enthusiasm for cocaine after nursing a physician friend to whom he had recommended the drug through a night-long psychotic state brought on by it. Perhaps the most famous fictional cocaine addict was Sherlock Holmes.

In addition to reducing pain, cocaine acts rapidly on the brain, blocking the reuptake of dopamine and thereby heightening sensory awareness and inducing a state of euphoria. Sexual desire is accentuated, and feelings of self-confidence, well-being, and indefatigability are increased. An overdose may bring on chills, nausea, and insomnia, as well as a paranoid breakdown and terrifying hallucinations of insects crawling beneath the skin. Chronic use often leads to changes in personality that include heightened irritability, impaired social relationships, paranoid thinking, and disturbances in eating and sleeping (*Scientific Perspectives on Cocaine Abuse*, 1987).

Cocaine is a vasoconstrictor, causing the blood vessels to narrow. As users take larger and larger doses of the purer forms of cocaine now available, they are more often rushed to emergency rooms and may die of an overdose, often from a myocardial infarction (Kozel, Crider, & Adams, 1982). Because of its strong vasoconstricting properties cocaine poses special dangers in pregnancy, for the blood supply to the developing fetus may be compromised.

Cocaine can be sniffed (snorted), smoked in pipes or cigarettes, swallowed, or even injected into the veins as is heroin; some heroin addicts mix the two drugs in combination. In the 1970s cocaine users in the United States began to separate, or free, the most potent component of cocaine by heating it with ether. When purified by this chemical process the cocaine base—or freebase—is extremely powerful. It is usually smoked in a water pipe or sprinkled on a tobacco or marijuana cigarette. It is rapidly absorbed into the lungs and carried to the brain in a few seconds and induces an intense two-minute high, followed by restlessness and discomfort. Some freebase smokers go on marathon binges lasting up to four days (Goodwin & Guze, 1984). The freebasing process is hazardous, however, because ether is flammable. Comedian Richard Pryor nearly died from the burns he suffered when the ether he was using ignited.

Cocaine freebase is produced by heating cocaine with ether. Richard Pryor was severely burned when the ether he was using caught fire.

In the mid-1980s a new form of freebase, called crack, appeared on the streets. The presence of crack brought about an increase in freebasing and in casualties. Because it was available in small, relatively inexpensive doses ($10 dollars for about 100 milligrams versus the $100 per gram that users formerly had to shell out to obtain cocaine), younger and less-affluent buyers began to experiment with the drug and to become addicted (Kozel & Adams, 1986). Many public health and police officials regard crack as the most dangerous illicit drug in society today.

Cocaine use soared in the 1970s and 1980s, increasing by more than 260 percent between 1974 and 1985. More recently use of cocaine has dramatically decreased. The number of users declined to 2.9 million in 1988 and to 1.6 million in 1990 (*HHS News*, 1990). The frequency of use of crack has not followed suit, however. Figures for crack use in the past month in 1991 were about 0.3 percent for young (ages eighteen to thirty-four) people (NIDA, 1991), but in 1996 have increased to 0.8 percent (NIDA, 1996).

The economics of cocaine provides staggering figures for money spent by heavy users. In 1985 people snorting cocaine once a day spent more than $1500 a week for the drug. People using it more often reported spending much more, and were able to support their expensive habit because they sold the drug or were independently wealthy (Siegel, 1982). In the early 1980s cocaine cost $2000 an ounce, making it approximately five times more expensive than gold.

Ceasing cocaine use appears to cause a severe withdrawal syndrome. Cocaine can take hold of people with as much tenacity as that demonstrated for years with the established addictive drugs. As with alcohol, developing fetuses are markedly and negatively affected in the womb by the mother's use of cocaine during pregnancy, and many babies are born addicted to the drug.

LSD AND OTHER HALLUCINOGENS

In 1943 a Swiss chemist, Albert Hofmann, recorded a description of an illness he had seemingly contracted.

Last Friday ... I had to interrupt my laboratory work ... I was seized with a feeling of great restlessness and mild dizziness. At home, I lay down and sank into a not unpleasant delirium, which was characterized by extremely exciting fantasies. In a semiconscious state with my eyes closed ... fantastic visions of extraordinary realness and with an intense kaleidoscopic play of colors assaulted me. (cited in Cashman, 1966, p. 31)

Earlier in the day Hofmann had manufactured a few milligrams of *d*-lysergic acid diethylamide, a drug that he had first synthesized in 1938. Reasoning that he might have unknowingly ingested some and that this was the cause of his unusual experience, he deliberately took a dose and confirmed his hypothesis.

After Hofmann's experiences with **LSD** in 1943, the drug was referred to as psychotomimetic because it was thought to produce effects similar to the symptoms of a psychosis. Then the term *psychedelic*, from the Greek words for "soul" and "to make manifest," was applied to emphasize the subjectively experienced expansions of consciousness reported by users of LSD. The term in current use is **hallucinogen**, which describes one of the main effects of such drugs, producing hallucinations. Unlike hallucinations in schizophrenia, however, these are usually recognized by the person as being caused by the drug.

Four other important hallucinogens are mescaline, psilocybin, and the synthetic compounds MDA and MDMA. In 1896 **mescaline**, an alkaloid and the active ingredient of peyote, was isolated from small, disklike growths of the top of the peyote cactus. The drug has been used for centuries in the religious rites of Indian peoples living in the Southwest and northern Mexico. **Psilocybin** is a crystalline powder that Hofmann isolated from the mushroom *Psilocybe mexicana* in 1958. The early Aztec and Mexican cultures called the sacred mushrooms "god's flesh," and the Indians of Mexico still use them in their worship. Each of these substances is structurally similar to several neurotransmitters, but their effects are thought to be due to stimulating serotonin receptors.

During the 1950s, LSD, mescaline, and psilocybin were given in research settings to study what were thought to be psychotic experiences. In 1960, Timothy Leary and Richard Alpert of Harvard University began an investigation of the effects of psilocybin on institutionalized prisoners. The early results, although subject to several confounds, were encouraging: released prisoners who had a psilocybin trip proved less likely to be rearrested. At the same time the investigators started taking trips themselves and soon had gathered around them a group of people interested in experimenting with psychedelic drugs. By 1962 their activities had attracted the attention of law-enforcement agencies. As the investigation continued, it became a scandal, culminating in Leary's and Alpert's departures

In the 1960s Timothy Leary was one of the leading proponents of the use of hallucinogens to expand consciousness.

from Harvard.[3] The affair seemed to give tremendous impetus to the use of the hallucinogens, particularly since the manufacture of LSD and the extraction of mescaline and psilocybin were found to be relatively easy and inexpensive. In 1966 the use of these substances was banned by Congress. Since then, little research has been done on their effects in humans.

The use of LSD and other hallucinogens peaked in the 1960s; by the 1980s only 1 or 2 percent of people could be classified as regular users. Even those who use hallucinogens do not indulge more than once or twice every two weeks (*HHS News*, 1990; *National Survey on Drug Abuse: Main Findings*, 1982,

---

[3]Like many of the old-timers in the psychedelic drug revolution, Alpert went on to espouse an Eastern meditation philosophy that urged people to forsake drugs and work instead on creating their own meaningful trips without the aid of chemical agents. Known as Baba Ram Dass, he has lectured and written eloquently about the possibility of cultivating expanded states of consciousness. Those who would devote the necessary time and energy to meditation techniques will be open to such experiences, according to Ram Dass. Most recently Ram Dass seems to have rediscovered his Jewish roots and is exploring the possibilities of integrating Judaism with the teachings of Eastern mystics.

1983). LSD use has increased somewhat in the 1990s. There is no evidence of withdrawal symptoms during abstinence, but tolerance appears to develop rapidly (McKim, 1991).

A new hallucinogen joined the ranks of illegal drugs on July 1, 1985. **Ecstasy**, which refers to two closely similar synthetic compounds, MDA (methylenedioxyamphetamine) and MDMA (methylenedioxymethamphetamine), is chemically similar to mescaline and the amphetamines and is the psychoactive agent in nutmeg. MDA was first synthesized in 1910, but it was not until the 1960s that its psychedelic properties came to the attention of the drug-using, consciousness-expanding generation of the sixties. Today it is popular on some college campuses. Users report that the drug enhances intimacy and insight, improves interpersonal relationships, elevates mood, and promotes aesthetic awareness. It can also cause muscle tension, rapid eye movements, nausea, faintness, chills or sweating, and anxiety, depression, and confusion. The Drug Enforcement Administration considers the use of Ecstasy and other so-called designer drugs unsafe and a serious threat to health. Several deaths have been reported from accidental overdose (Climko et al., 1987). (See Focus 12.3 on nitrous oxide.)

EFFECTS OF HALLUCINOGENS

The typical dose of LSD is extremely small, from about 100 to 350 micrograms, administered as a liquid absorbed in sugar cubes or as capsules or tablets; for psilocybin the usual dose is about 30,000 micrograms; and for mescaline the usual dose is between 350,000 and 500,000 micrograms. The effects of LSD and mescaline usually last about twelve hours and those of psilocybin about six hours.

The following description is of the general effects of LSD, but it also applies to the other hallucinogens.

Synesthesias, the overflow from one sensory modality to another, may occur. Colors are heard and sounds may be seen. Subjective time is also seriously altered, so that clock time seems to pass extremely slowly. The loss of boundaries [between one's sense of self and one's environment] and the fear of fragmentation create a need for a structuring or supporting environment; and in the sense that they create a need for experienced companions and an explanatory system, these drugs are "cultogenic." During the "trip," thoughts and memories can vividly emerge under self-guidance or unexpectedly, to the user's distress. Mood may be labile, shifting from depression to gaiety, from elation to fear. Tension and anxiety may mount and reach panic proportions. After about 4 to 5 hours, if a major panic episode does not

FOCUS 12.3 NITROUS OXIDE—NOT A LAUGHING MATTER*

Nitrous oxide is a colorless gas that has been available since the nineteenth century. Within seconds it induces light-headedness and a state of euphoria in most people; for some, important insights seem to flood the mind. Clinical reports and some controlled research (e.g., Devine et al., 1974) confirm that this gaseous mixture raises pain thresholds, perhaps by an induction of positive feelings that dull sensations that would normally be experienced as noxious. Many people find otherwise mundane events and thoughts irresistibly funny, hence the nickname laughing gas.

Perhaps readers of this book have had nitrous oxide at a dentist's office to facilitate relaxation and otherwise make a potentially uncomfortable and intimidating dental procedure more palatable (and to make it easier for the dentist to work on the patient). A major advantage of nitrous oxide over other analgesics and relaxants is that the patient can return to the normal waking state within minutes of breathing enriched oxygen or normal air. An additional advantage is that patients can be taught to control how deep they go by taking a few breaths of regular air through the mouth (the gas is administered through a small mask that covers only the nose; otherwise the dentist could not work on the person's teeth). The health professional can easily make continuing adjustments based on experienced judgment of the patient's level of intoxication.

Since it first became available nitrous oxide has been used recreationally, although it has been illegal for many years in most states. As with the other mind-altering drugs examined in this chapter, illegality has not prevented unsupervised use. Illicit use is not a priority for police, perhaps because there is no evidence that nitrous oxide is physically addicting. And because nitrous oxide is legally available for refilling aerosol canisters and souping up race-car engines, its use is not (yet) associated with crime, as is the use of heroin and cocaine. Nor does nitrous oxide directly provoke violent behavior, as does phencyclidine (PCP). It does, however, carry serious risk.

An important difference between the way in which dentists use nitrous oxide and the way in which it is used casually is that in the dental office, the air mixture is seldom more than 80 percent nitrous oxide (the rest is oxygen). This mixture allows for the safe and effective use of the gas. Such was not the case for three men who were found dead in the closed cab of a pick-up truck in the early morning hours of March 6, 1992. They had apparently been asphyxiated from the nitrous oxide in an eighty-pound industrial-sized canister that was lying across their laps. Evidence at the scene suggested that they had been filling balloons with the gas and, perhaps inadvertently, allowed the gas to escape freely into the sealed cab. With little air from outside, the men had been breathing pure nitrous oxide and their own exhaled carbon dioxide—and very little oxygen. They were not the first victims. In 1988 four young adults met a similar death in a dental storage room in Cedar City, Utah. And in Birmingham, Alabama, a party host was charged with manslaughter in 1990 for allegedly giving the gas to a teenager who died after inhaling it.

Sometimes called hippie crack, nitrous oxide balloons are often supplemented with the use of Ecstasy and other designer drugs in a psychedelic atmosphere of bright laser lights and loud dance music. The illegal use of nitrous oxide appears to be on the increase, and promoters of some of these rave parties make a great deal of money selling nitrous oxide and Ecstasy. Police fear that gangs and organized crime are moving into this arena as has happened with other illicit drugs.

---

*Some of this material was taken from two *Los Angeles Times* articles, Connelly (1992) and Romero (1992).

---

occur, there may be a sense of detachment and the conviction that one is magically in control.… The user may be greatly impressed with the drug experience and feel a greater sensitivity for art, music, human feelings, and the harmony of the universe. (Jaffe, 1985, p. 564)

The effects of the hallucinogens depend on a number of psychological variables in addition to the dose itself. A subject's set, that is, attitudes, expectancies, and motivations with regard to taking drugs, is widely held to be an important determinant of his or her reactions to hallucinogens. The setting in which the drug is experienced is also important. Among the most prominent dangers of taking LSD is the possibility of experiencing a bad trip, which can sometimes develop into a full-blown panic attack and is far more likely to occur if some aspect of taking the drug creates anxiety. Often the specific fear is of going crazy. These panics are usually short-lived and subside as the drug is metabolized. A minority of people, however, go into a psychotic state that can require hospitalization and extended treatment. **Flashbacks**, a recurrence of psychedelic experiences after the physiological effects of the drug have worn off, also sometimes occur, most frequently in times of stress, illness, or fatigue (Kaplan & Sadock, 1991). Flashbacks are not believed to be caused by drug-produced physical changes in the nervous system, in part because only

15 to 30 percent of users of hallucinogenic drugs are estimated ever to have flashbacks (e.g., Stanton & Bardoni, 1972). Moreover, there is no independent evidence of measurable neurological changes in these drug users. Flashbacks seem to have a force of their own and may come to haunt people weeks and months after they have taken the drug; they are very upsetting for those who experience them.

A drug not easy to classify is PCP, phencyclidine. Developed as a tranquilizer for horses and other large animals, it generally causes serious negative reactions, including severe paranoia and violence. Coma and death are also possible. Though often as terrifying to the user as to observers, its use in the 1990s has been increasing.

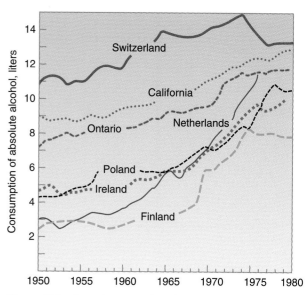

Figure 12.1 Annual consumption of alcoholic beverages (in liters of absolute alcohol per person) among people aged 15 years and over in countries studied in ISACE, from 1950–1980. After Mäkelä et al., 1981.

ETIOLOGY OF SUBSTANCE ABUSE AND DEPENDENCE

In trying to understand the causes of substance abuse and dependence disorders, researchers have generally distinguished the variables that lead someone to begin using the substance, then to use it heavily, and finally to abuse or become dependent on it. The general idea is that after prolonged heavy use the person becomes ensnared by the biological processes of tolerance and withdrawal.

Although applicable in many cases, this model does not account for all of them. For example, there are documented cases of heavy use of both tobacco and heroin that did not eventuate in addiction. Nevertheless, guided by this general model, most research has examined variables related to initial use and its subsequent escalation. As we discuss sociocultural, psychological, and biological variables it is important to keep in mind that they are likely to be differentially related to different substances. Genetics, for example, may play some role in alcoholism but be irrelevant to crack abuse.

SOCIOCULTURAL VARIABLES

Sociocultural variables can play a widely varying role in drug abuse. From the effect of one's peers and parents to the influence of the media and what is considered acceptable behavior in one's culture, the social world can affect people's interest in and access to drugs. At the broadest level, for example, there is great cross-national variation in alcohol consumption. The data in Figure 12.1 from a large-scale longitudinal study illustrate that in addition to great differences in consumption among countries and, consequently, cultures, there are also commonalities. First, over the study period (1950–1980) alco-

hol consumption rose greatly in each country. Second, the differences in consumption decreased with the passage of time. Other research has found striking cross-national differences in alcohol consumption, some of them even greater than those shown here. For example, the highest consumption rates have typically been found in wine-drinking societies, such as those of France, Spain, and Italy, where drinking alcohol regularly is widely accepted (deLint, 1978). Cultural attitudes and patterns of drinking thus influence the likelihood of drinking heavily and therefore of abusing alcohol.

Turning to sociocultural studies within the population of a single country (the United States), there is considerable variation in the use of substances. For example, high levels of drinking are found among sailors, railroad workers, and people in the drink trade—restaurant owners, bartenders, waiters, and liquor dealers (Fillmor & Caetano, 1980). In all these occupations heavy drinking is normative, that is, almost expected as part of the job, and alcohol is readily available.

Family variables are also important sociocultural influences. For example, if both parents smoke, a child is four times more likely to do so than if no other family member smokes. Similarly, exposure to alcohol use by parents increases children's likelihood of drinking (Cloninger et al., 1981). Psychiatric, marital, or legal problems in the family are related to drug abuse, and a lack of emotional support from parents is linked to increased use of

Alcoholism is higher in countries in which alcohol use is heavy, such as vinicultural societies. Everyone is drinking wine in this French bar.

cigarettes, cannabis, and alcohol (Cadoret et al., 1995; Wills, DuHamel, & Vaccaro, 1995). Finally, a longitudinal study has shown that a lack of parental monitoring leads to increased association with drug-abusing peers and subsequent higher use of drugs (Chassin et al., 1996).

The social milieu in which a person operates can also affect substance abuse. Tobacco use among high school students is highest in identifiable subgroups—those with poor grades, behavior problems, and a taste for heavy metal music (Sussman et al., 1990), and those with little adult supervision after school (Richardson et al., 1989). In longitudinal studies peer-group identification in the seventh grade predicted smoking in the eighth (Sussman et al., 1994), and in a three-year study it predicted increased drug use in general (Chassin et al., 1996). Peer influences are also important in promoting alcohol and marijuana use (Kandel & Andrews, 1987; Sussman et al., 1995). Thus peer influence is important in the decisions adolescents make about using substances, but those who have a high sense of self-efficacy (Bandura, 1997) to resist social pressure—"I can imagine refusing to use tobacco with students my age and still have them like me" (Stacy et al., 1992, p. 166)—are influenced less by their peers. Heroin and crack abuse is most common in ghettos, and marijuana and hallucinogen use was linked to social activism and other characteristics of the late 1960s. In all these cases, members of a subcultural group are likely to be exposed to multiple exemplars of drug use, peer pressure to conform, and substances that are readily available.

Another variable to be considered in this context is the media. We are bombarded with TV commercials in which beer is associated with athletic-looking males, bikini-clad women, and good times, and billboards equating cigarettes with excitement, relaxation, or being in style. Supporting the role of advertising in promoting alcohol use is an analysis of consumption in seventeen countries between 1970 and 1983. Those countries that banned ads for spirits had 16 percent less consumption than those that did not (Saffer, 1991). As another example we can consider the Marlboro Man, a clear attempt to present smoking as a macho activity.[4]

More recent, and particularly pernicious, is the Old Joe Camel campaign for Camel cigarettes. With the number of smokers declining, the tobacco industry's profitability depends on recruiting new smokers to replace those who are quitting. The obvious target—elementary and high school students. Camel launched its campaign in 1988 with the Joe Camel character modeled after James Bond or the character played by Don Johnson in *Miami Vice*. Prior to the campaign (1976–1988) Camels were the preferred brand of less than 0.5 percent of seventh through twelfth graders. By 1991 Camel's share of this *illegal* market had increased to 33 percent (Di Franza et al., 1991)! In March 1992, the surgeon general as well as the American Medical Association (AMA) asked R. J. Reynolds, the manufacturer of Camel cigarettes, to drop Old Joe Camel from its ads because of this

---

[4]The actor who portrayed the Marlboro Man in the mid-1970s was diagnosed with lung cancer in 1991 and died soon thereafter.

F.T.C. Charges Joe Camel Ad Illegally Takes Aim at Minors

Linda Rosier for The New York Times

Internal Documents of R. J. Reynolds Are Cited by Agency

By JOHN M. BRODER

WASHINGTON, May 28 — In another blow to an industry under siege, the Federal Trade Commission charged today that the R. J. Reynolds Tobacco Company illegally aimed its Joe Camel advertising campaign at minors.

The agency asserted in an administrative complaint that the company violated Federal fair trade practice laws by promoting a lethal and addictive product to children and adolescents who could not legally purchase or use it.

This is the first time that the commission has accused the tobacco industry of peddling its products to minors. The complaint will be supported, agency officials said, by extensive citations from internal company documents.

The Government says it believes that R. J. Reynolds papers will prove that the company deliberately designed its cartoon-based advertising campaign in the mid-1980's to increase its shrinking market share among young smokers.

The complaint amounts to a civil indictment of a company commission officials ...

Advertising is an important sociocultural variable in stimulating drug use. The Joe Camel campaign greatly increased Camel's share of the market among elementary and high school students.

apparent appeal to youngsters. Billboard companies and print media were also requested to stop running the ads. The response from R. J. Reynolds? "We have no reason to believe that this campaign is causing anyone to begin smoking. If we thought it was causing young people to smoke, we'd pull it" (spokesperson for the company, quoted in Horovitz, 1992).

The days of Joe Camel and other cartoon characters that appeal to young people may be numbered. On March 13, 1996, the Liggett Group, manufacturers of cigarettes, agreed to stop using such advertising tools and to take other steps to discourage smoking among minors. These actions were part of a settlement in a class action lawsuit against the U.S. cigarette industry that charged companies with manipulating nicotine levels to keep smokers addicted.

PSYCHOLOGICAL VARIABLES

We examine next two classes of psychological variables. The first class comprises primarily the effects of alcohol on mood, the situations in which a ten-

sion-reducing effect occurs, and the role of cognition in this process. The second includes the personality traits that may make it more likely for some people to use drugs heavily.

MOOD ALTERATION

Many studies suggest that one of the principal psychological motives for using drugs is to alter mood. Drug use is therefore reinforcing, either by enhancing positive mood states or by diminishing negative ones. Most of the research in this area has focused on the tension-reducing properties of alcohol. Early animal experiments (Conger, 1950) showed that alcohol impairs avoidance learning, which is usually regarded as mediated by anxiety. Some later experiments with humans (e.g., Sher & Levenson, 1982) also indicated that alcohol reduces tension in people who are not yet alcoholic, but some conflicting findings emerged as well (e.g., Thyer & Curtis, 1984).

Subsequent research to examine the reasons for these inconsistent results has focused on the situation in which alcohol is consumed. Findings indicate that alcohol may produce its tension-reducing effect by altering cognition and perception (Steele & Joseph, 1988, 1990). Alcohol impairs cognitive processing and narrows attention to the most immediately available cues, resulting in what the authors term *alcohol myopia*; the intoxicated person has less cognitive capacity to distribute between ongoing activity and worry. If a distracting activity is available, attention will be diverted to it rather than focusing on worrisome thoughts, with a resultant decrease in anxiety. However, in some situations alcohol could increase tension, for example, when no distractors are present and an intoxicated person therefore focuses all his or her limited processing capacity on unpleasant thoughts. In this case the discouraged person broods and can become even more depressed while drinking.

Another situational variable that influences the tension-reducing effects of alcohol is the relationship of alcohol consumption to stress, that is, whether alcohol consumption precedes or follows stress. The notion most people have about alcohol and tension reduction is that an increase in tension (for example, because of a bad day at the office) leads to increased consumption to reduce the effects of the earlier stressor. Empirical support for this idea comes from studies showing that increases in life stress precede relapses in reformed alcoholics (e.g., Brown et al., 1990). However, experimental research on the tension-reducing properties of alcohol has typically reversed the order of the two variables, having subjects drink and then encounter a stressor. One study compared alcohol's effects in both orders (stress–alcohol vs. alcohol–stress) and found tension reduction only in the alcohol–stress sequence (Sayette & Wilson, 1991). Based on these results, alcohol may not be a potent tension reducer in many life situations when it is consumed after stress.

If it is true that alcohol does not reduce stress when consumed after the fact, why do so many people who drink believe that it helps them unwind? Returning to a concept introduced earlier in this chapter (p. 299), it may be that people use alcohol after stress not because it reduces distress directly but because they *expect* it to reduce their tension. In support of this idea studies have shown that people who expect alcohol to reduce stress and anxiety are those likely to be frequent users (Rather et al., 1992; Sher et al., 1991). Furthermore, positive expectancies about alcohol and drinking appear to influence each other. The expectation that drinking will reduce anxiety increases drinking, which in turn makes the positive expectancies even stronger (Smith et al., 1995). Other research has also shown that positive expectancies about a drug's effects predict increased drug use in general (Stacy, Newcomb, & Bentler, 1991).

Another psychological variable related to drug use is the extent to which a person believes a drug is harmful. For example, use of marijuana peaked in 1978, when almost 11 percent of high school seniors reported daily use. At that time only 12 percent of seniors believed there was risk associated with occasional use and 35 percent believed there was risk with regular use. Compare this with 1985, when daily use had plummeted to 5 percent; 25 percent of high school seniors believed marijuana was harmful if used occasionally, and 70 percent believed it was harmful if used on a regular basis (Kozel & Adams, 1986). As beliefs changed, so did behavior. The dramatic increase in marijuana use in the 1990s was mainly among those adolescents who considered marijuana harmless (USDHHS, 1994).

Tension reduction is only one aspect of the possible effects of drugs on mood. Some people may use drugs to reduce negative affect, whereas others use drugs when they are bored or underaroused to increase positive affect (Cooper et al., 1995). In both cases drug use reflects a failure of other means of coping with emotional states. But in the former case, a high level of negative affect plus expecting drugs to reduce tension leads to increased drug use, while in the latter a high need for stimulation plus expectancies that drugs will promote increased positive affect are predictive. This line of reasoning has been confirmed among alcohol and cocaine abusers (Ball, Carroll, & Rounsaville, 1994; Cooper et al., 1995).

PERSONALITY AND DRUG USE

Neither sociocultural factors nor mood alteration theories can completely account for individual differences in drug use. Not all members of a particular culture or subculture are heavy users, nor do all who experience stress increase drug usage. Personality variables attempt to explain why certain people are drawn to substance abuse.

Consistently high levels of negative affect and an enduring desire for arousal and increased positive affect are two personality traits that have been studied in this context. An association has been found between drug use in general and antisocial personality disorder (Ball et al., 1994). Drug abuse may be part of the thrill-seeking behavior of the psychopath, to be discussed in Chapter 13. We might also expect opiates and tranquilizers to be used by anxious individuals to reduce their distress.

Hyperactivity in childhood, which is highly correlated with antisocial behavior, is also related to drug abuse, probably for reasons similar to those noted for antisocial personalities. For example, in a prospective study spanning more than ten years, hyperactivity was an important predictor of later alcohol abuse (Hechtman, Weiss, & Perlman, 1984). Hyperactivity has also been associated with tobacco and cannabis use (Wills, DuHamel, & Vaccaro, 1995) and with cocaine abuse (Ball, Carroll, & Rounsaville, 1994).

One longitudinal study spanning the years from preschool to age eighteen investigated personality characteristics that predict frequent marijuana use (Shadler & Block, 1990). Those who later became heavy users were described at age seven as not getting along well with others, unconcerned with moral fairness, and showing physical symptoms of stress. They were also described as indecisive, not trustworthy or dependable, unable to admit to negative feelings, and lacking confidence and self-esteem. At age eleven they appeared more emotionally labile, inattentive and unable to concentrate, less involved in activities, and stubborn as compared with their peers who later experimented with the drug but did not become frequent users.

BIOLOGICAL VARIABLES

Most of the research on biological factors in substance abuse has addressed the possibility that a genetically transmitted alteration in some biological process serves as a predisposition for problem drinking. We will focus primarily on these data in our consideration of the biological variables that contribute to substance use.

Evidence for a genetic predisposition for alcohol abuse is found in studies in which animals have been bred that greatly prefer alcohol to other beverages (Li et al., 1981). Data also indicate that problem drinking in human beings runs in families, suggesting a genetic component. Several studies have shown that relatives and children of problem drinkers have higher than expected rates of alcohol abuse or dependence (e.g., Shu et al., 1991). Twin studies have revealed greater concordance for alcohol abuse (e.g., McGue, Pickens, & Suikis, 1992) and caffeine, nicotine, and opiate use (Look & Gurling, 1988) in identical twins than in fraternal twins, pointing again toward a possible role of heredity. Although these findings are consistent with the genetic transmission of a predisposition, these individuals might also have become substance users through exposure to their parents' drug-related behavior or to other features of the parenting styles of alcohol-abusing parents.

Adoption studies add further support for the importance of a genetic diathesis in both alcohol and drug abuse (Cadoret et al., 1995; Goodwin et al., 1973). Large-scale adoptee research conducted in Sweden has raised the possibility that there are subtypes of alcohol abuse with different genetic bases (Cloninger et al., 1981). The investigators divided their sample of adopted children who were problem drinkers into two groups. Type I problem drinking occurred in both men and women and was not too severe. It was associated with mild, adult-onset problem drinking in the biological parents and exposure to alcohol abuse in the adoptive home. Thus both genes and the environment seemed to play a role. In contrast, Type II alcohol abuse or dependence was found only in men, had an early age of onset, was associated with antisocial behavior in the adoptees, and was linked only to alcohol abuse in biological parents. Although other research has not replicated all of these results, an early age of onset of alcohol abuse in men seems to be the crucial factor in this type of alcohol abuse (Fils-Aime et al., 1996). Linking these findings to the different effects of alcohol on mood would suggest that Type I drinkers may consume alcohol to reduce tension, whereas Type IIs may drink to increase pleasure (recall that drinking to increase pleasure is associated with antisocial behavior, as is the Type II category).

The ability to tolerate alcohol may be what is inherited as a diathesis for alcohol abuse or dependence (Goodwin, 1979). To become a problem drinker a person first has to be able to drink a lot, in other words a person must be able to tolerate large quantities of alcohol. Some ethnic groups, such as Asians, may have a low rate of alcohol abuse because of their physiological intolerance, which is caused by an inherited deficiency in an enzyme that

metabolizes alcohol. About three-quarters of Asians experience unpleasant effects from small quantities of alcohol. Noxious effects of the drug may then protect a person from alcohol abuse.

This hypothesis focuses on short-term effects, possibly on how alcohol is metabolized or on how the central nervous system responds to alcohol. Animal research indicates that genetic components are at work in both these processes (Schuckit, 1983). Corroborating this notion are recent findings from research using the high-risk method. These studies have compared young, nonalcoholic adults with a first-degree alcohol-abusing relative to similar individuals without a positive family history for the disorder. Two variables were able to predict the development of alcohol abuse in men in a ten-year follow-up (Schuckit, 1994; Schuckit & Smith, 1996): self-report of a low level of intoxication after a dose of alcohol; and less body sway (a measure of steadiness while standing) after drinking. Both findings indicate that alcohol abuse is more likely to occur in those in whom alcohol has little effect. Notably, these variables predict alcohol abuse among men with and without an alcohol-abusing father.

The smaller response of the later alcohol abusers may at first seem puzzling, but it fits with the notion that you have to drink a lot to become a problem drinker. A small response to alcohol may set the stage for heavier than normal drinking. The size of the response to alcohol is also related to our earlier discussion of alcohol's biphasic effects (p. 299). In the research we have just discussed, the largest differences between sons of problem drinkers and controls occurred when their blood levels of alcohol were declining. Therefore, sons of alcohol abusers may experience fewer of the negative, depressing effects of alcohol. Other research indicates that sons of alcohol abusers experience greater effects of alcohol, for example, more tension reduction, as their blood-alcohol levels are on the rise. Thus these genetically predisposed individuals receive more reinforcement and less punishment from the drug (Newlin & Thompson, 1990).

Having reviewed the nature and possible causes of the several kinds of substance-related disorders, we turn now to their treatment and prevention.

THERAPY FOR ALCOHOL ABUSE AND DEPENDENCE

The havoc created by problem drinking, both for the drinker and for his or her family, friends, employer, and community, makes this problem a serious public health issue in the United States and many other countries. Consequently, a great deal of research and clinical effort has gone into the design and evaluation of various treatments.

The treatment of alcohol abuse is difficult not only because of the addictive nature of the drug, but also because many other psychological problems are likely to be present. Alcohol abusers often suffer from depression, anxiety, and severe disruptions in their social and occupational functioning. As indicated in Chapter 10, the risk of suicide is also very high (Galanter & Castenada, 1985). Although some of these problems may have preceded and even contributed to the abuse of alcohol, by the time an abuser is treated it is seldom possible to know what is cause and what is effect. What *is* certain is that the person's life is usually a shambles, and any treatment worth attempting has to address more than merely the excessive drinking. Interventions for problem drinking are both biological and psychological, yet whatever the kind of intervention, the first step is for the person to admit the problem and decide to do something about it.

ADMITTING THE PROBLEM

To admit that one has a serious drinking problem may sound straightforward to someone who has never had a drinking problem or has never known someone who did. However, substance abusers of all kinds are adept at denying that they have a problem and may react angrily to any suggestion that they do. Moreover, because patterns of problem drinking are highly variable—someone truly dependent on alcohol, for example, does not always drink uncontrollably—the need for intervention is not always recognized by friends or even by health professionals. Enabling the drinker to take the first step to betterment—what has been called the contemplation stage (Prochaska, DiClimente, & Norcross, 1992)—can be achieved through questions that somewhat indirectly get to the issue.

Do you sometimes feel uncomfortable when alcohol is not available?

Do you drink more heavily than usual when you are under pressure?

Are you in more of a hurry to get to the first drink than you used to be?

Do you sometimes feel guilty about your drinking?

Are you annoyed when people talk about your drinking?

When drinking socially, do you try to sneak in some extra drinks?

Are you constantly making rules for yourself about what and when to drink?

(*Harvard Mental Health Letter*, 1996a, pp. 1–2)

Once the alcohol abuser recognizes that he or she has a problem, there are many ways to try to deal with it.

TRADITIONAL HOSPITAL TREATMENT

Public and private hospitals worldwide have for many years provided retreats for alcohol abusers, sanctums where individuals can dry out and avail themselves of a variety of individual and group therapies. The withdrawal from alcohol, **detoxification,** can be difficult, both physically and psychologically, and usually takes about one month. Tranquilizers are sometimes given to ease the anxiety and general discomfort of withdrawal. Because many alcohol abusers misuse tranquilizers, some clinics try a gradual tapering off without tranquilizers rather than a sudden cutoff of alcohol. This non-drug-assisted withdrawal works for most problem drinkers (Wartenburg et al., 1990). To help get through withdrawal, alcohol abusers also need carbohydrate solutions, B vitamins, and, sometimes, anticonvulsants.

The number of for-profit hospitals treating alcohol abuse increased almost fourfold from 1978 to 1984, fueled in part because such treatment is covered in large measure by both private insurance companies and the federal government (Holder et al., 1991). Annual costs run in the billions. Because inpatient treatment is much more expensive than outpatient treatment, its cost-effectiveness must be questioned. Is it worth the expense? From the available data Miller and Hester (1986b) found that the higher costs of inpatient treatment were not matched by higher degrees of effectiveness. For one thing, detoxification can be safely managed on an outpatient basis for most people. Further, in general, the therapeutic results of hospital treatment are not superior to those of outpatient treatment.

BIOLOGICAL TREATMENTS

Some problem drinkers who are in treatment, whether inpatient or outpatient, take disulfiram, or **Antabuse,** a drug that discourages drinking by causing violent vomiting if alcohol is ingested. It blocks the metabolism of alcohol so that noxious by-products are created. As one can imagine, adherence to an Antabuse regimen can be a problem. The drinker must already be committed to change.

Indeed, *if* an alcohol abuser is able or willing to take the drug every morning as prescribed, the chances are good that drinking will lessen because of the negative consequences of imbibing (Sisson & Azrin, 1989). However, in a large, multicenter study with placebo controls, Antabuse was not shown to have any specific benefit, and drop-out rates were as high as 80 percent (Fuller, 1988; Fuller et al., 1986). Antabuse can also cause serious side effects, such as inflammation of nerve tissue (Moss, 1990).

Biological treatments are best viewed as adjunctive, that is, they may offer some benefit when combined with a psychological intervention. For example, the Food and Drug Administration approved in 1995 the opiate antagonist naltrexone, which blocks the activity of endorphins that are stimulated by alcohol, thus reducing the craving for it. Naltrexone adds to overall treatment effectiveness when combined with cognitive-behavioral therapy (Volpicelli et al., 1995). Like many other drug treatments we have discussed, the benefits of naltrexone alone are short-lived (O'Malley et al., 1996). The serotonin agonist, buspirone, is also of some therapeutic value (Kranzler et al., 1994). Clonidine, which reduces noradrenergic activity in the brain, also has some value in reducing withdrawal effects from several drugs, including alcohol, opiates, and nicotine (Baumgartner & Rowen, 1987).

Though not specifically targeted to excessive drinking, certain psychoactive drugs are used to treat problems associated with drinking, for example, antidepressants for depression and tranquilizers for anxiety, and via general improvement in the patient's mental state, can have a beneficial impact on problem drinking.

The use of drugs to treat alcohol-abusing patients carries some risk because liver function is often impaired and therefore the metabolism of the prescribed drug in the liver can be adversely affected, leading to undesirable side effects (Klerman et al., 1994).

ALCOHOLICS ANONYMOUS

The largest and most widely known self-help group in the world is Alcoholics Anonymous (AA), founded in 1935 by two recovered alcoholics. It currently has 70,000 chapters and membership numbering more than two million people in the United States and more than 100 other countries throughout the world. An AA chapter runs regular and frequent meetings at which newcomers rise to announce that they are alcoholics, and older, sober members give testimonials, relating the stories of their problem drinking and indicating how their lives are better

now. The group provides emotional support, understanding, and close counseling for the problem drinker as well as a social life to relieve isolation. Members are urged to call on one another around-the-clock when they need companionship and encouragement not to relapse into drink. About 70 percent of Americans who have ever been treated for alcohol abuse have attended at least one AA meeting. Programs modeled after AA are available for other substance abusers, for example, Cocaine Anonymous and Marijuana Anonymous. There are even twelve-step programs called Overeaters Anonymous and Gamblers Anonymous.

The belief is instilled in each AA member that alcohol abuse is a disease that can never be cured, that continuing vigilance is necessary to resist taking even a single drink lest uncontrollable drinking begin all over again. The basic tenet of AA was vividly articulated in the classic film *Lost Weekend*, for which Ray Milland won an Oscar for best actor. In a scene in which he is confronted with his denial of the seriousness of his drinking problem, his brother remonstrates, "Don't you ever learn that with you it's like stepping off a roof and expecting to fall just one floor?"

The spiritual aspect of AA is apparent in the twelve steps of AA shown in Table 12.2, and there is evidence that belief in this philosophy is important

Alcoholics Anonymous is the largest self-help group in the world. At their regular meetings, newcomers rise to announce their addiction and receive advice and support from others.

TABLE 12.2 Twelve Suggested Steps of Alcoholics Anonymous

1. We admitted we were powerless over alcohol—that our lives had become unmanageable.
2. Came to believe that a power greater than ourselves could restore us to sanity.
3. Made a decision to turn our will and our lives over to the care of God *as we understood Him.*
4. Made a searching and fearless moral inventory of ourselves.
5. Admitted to God, to ourselves, and to another human being the exact nature of our wrongs.
6. Were entirely ready to have God remove all these defects of character.
7. Humbly asked Him to remove our shortcomings.
8. Made a list of all persons we had harmed, and became willing to make amends to them all.
9. Made direct amends to such people wherever possible, except when to do so would injure them or others.
10. Continued to take personal inventory and, when we were wrong, promptly admitted it.
11. Sought through prayer and meditation to improve our conscious contact with God *as we understood Him,* praying only for knowledge of His will for us and the power to carry that out.
12. Having had a spiritual awakening as the result of these steps, we tried to carry this message to alcoholics and to practice these principles in all our affairs.

Source: The Twelve Steps and Twelve Traditions. Copyright © 1952 by Alcoholics Anonymous World Services, Inc. Reprinted with permission of Alcoholics Anonymous World Services, Inc.

for achieving abstinence (Gilbert, 1991). Two related self-help groups have developed from AA. The relatives of problem drinkers meet in Al-Anon Family Groups for mutual support in dealing with their family members and in realizing that they cannot *make* them change their ways. Similarly, Alateen is for the children of alcohol abusers, who also require support and understanding to help them overcome the sense that they are in some way responsible for their parents' problems and responsible also for changing them. Other self-help groups do not have the religious overtones of AA, relying instead on social support, reassurance, encouragement, and suggestions for leading a life without alcohol. People often see mental health professionals while attending self-help meetings.

The claims made by AA about the effectiveness of its treatment have begun to be subjected to scientific scrutiny (USPHS, 1993). A recent study has demonstrated significant benefit from AA (Ouimette, Finney & Moos, 1997). However, AA has high drop-out rates, and the dropouts are not always factored into the results. In addition, there is only limited long-term follow-up of AA clients. Results from the best controlled study to date are mixed (Walsh et al., 1991). It does appear that many people who choose AA and stay with it for more than three months—a select group, to be sure—remain abstinent for at least a few years (Emerick et al., 1993). The needs of such people seem to be met by the fellowship, support, and religious overtones of AA. For them it becomes a way of life; members often attend meetings regularly for many years, even when they are out of town. As with other forms of intervention, it remains to be determined for whom this particular mode is best suited.

COUPLES THERAPY

Although many severe problem drinkers have had their lives so disrupted by alcohol that they live fairly solitary lives, many remain married or in other close relationships. It is not surprising, then, that efforts have been made to use various kinds of couples therapy to help the drinker abstain or control his or her excessive drinking. Described in more detail in Chapter 19, marital or couples therapy has been found to achieve some reductions in problem drinking as well as some improvement in couples' distress generally (e.g., McGrady et al., 1991; McGrady et al., in press). The importance of a partner's support in the problem drinker's effort to deal with life's inevitable stresses is not to be underestimated. But also not to be underestimated is the difficulty of maintaining moderate drinking or abstinence at one- and two-year follow-ups, regardless of the mode of marital intervention (Alexander et al., 1994).

COGNITIVE AND BEHAVIORAL TREATMENTS

Behavioral and cognitive-behavioral researchers have been studying the treatment of alcohol abuse for many years—one of the earliest articles on behavior therapy concerned aversive conditioning of alcoholism (Kantorovich, 1930).

AVERSION THERAPY

In aversion therapy a problem drinker is shocked or made nauseous while looking at, reaching for, or beginning to drink alcohol. In one procedure, called

covert sensitization (Cautela, 1966), a hierarchy of scenes designed to extinguish the desire to drink is established and the problem drinker is instructed to imagine being made violently and disgustingly sick by his or her drinking.

Despite some evidence that aversion therapy may slightly enhance the effectiveness of inpatient treatment (Smith et al., 1991), some well-known behavior therapists discourage its use because it lacks empirical support and causes great discomfort (e.g., Wilson, 1991). Aversion therapy, if used at all, seems best implemented in the context of broadly based programs that attend to the patient's particular life circumstances, for example, marital conflict, social fears, and other factors often associated with problem drinking (Tucker, Vuchinich, & Downey, 1992).

CONTINGENCY MANAGEMENT

Contingency-management therapy (a term often used interchangeably with operant conditioning) for alcohol abuse involves teaching patients and those close to them to reinforce behaviors inconsistent with drinking, for example, taking Antabuse. This therapy also includes teaching job-hunting and social skills as well as assertiveness training for refusing drinks. This community reinforcement approach has generated promising results (Azrin et al., 1982; Keane et al., 1984; Sisson & Azrin, 1989).

A strategy sometimes termed *behavioral self-control training* (Tucker et al., 1992) builds on this work. This approach emphasizes patient control and includes one or more of the following: (1) stimulus control, whereby patients narrow the situations in which they allow themselves to drink, for example, with others on a special occasion; (2) modification of the topography of drinking, for example, having only mixed drinks and taking small sips rather than gulps; and (3) reinforcing abstinence, for example, patients allow themselves a nonalcoholic treat if they resist the urge to drink.

A central issue not formally addressed by advocates of behavioral self-control training is getting the person to abide by restrictions and conditions that if implemented, will reduce or eliminate drinking (see p. 546 on the limits of self-control in a behavioral paradigm). In other words, the challenge with such therapies seems not so much to discover the means necessary to control drinking as to get the alcohol abuser to employ these tools without constant external supervision and control. There is evidence for the general effectiveness of this approach (Hester & Miller, 1989), some of it in the context of controlled-drinking programs, to which we turn now.

MODERATION IN DRINKING

Until recently it was generally agreed that alcohol abusers had to abstain completely if they were to be cured, for they were believed to have no control over imbibing once they had taken that first drink. Although this continues to be the belief of Alcoholics Anonymous, research mentioned earlier, indicating that drinkers' *beliefs* about themselves and alcohol may be as important as the physiological addiction to the drug itself, has called this assumption into question. Considering the difficulty in society of avoiding alcohol altogether, it may even be *preferable* to teach the problem drinker, at least the person who does not abuse alcohol in an extreme fashion, to imbibe with moderation. A drinker's self-esteem will certainly benefit from being able to control a problem and from feeling in charge of his or her life.

Controlled drinking refers to a pattern of alcohol consumption that is moderate, avoiding the extremes of total abstinence and inebriation. Findings of one well-known treatment program suggested that at least some alcohol abusers can learn to control their drinking and improve other aspects of their lives as well (Sobell & Sobell, 1976, 1978). Problem drinkers attempting to control their drinking were given shocks when they chose straight liquor rather than mixed drinks, gulped their drinks down too fast, or took large swallows rather than sips. They also received problem-solving and assertiveness training, watched videotapes of themselves inebriated, and identified the situations that precipitated their drinking so that they could settle on a less self-destructive course of action. Their improvement was greater than that of alcohol abusers who tried for total abstinence and were given shocks for any drinking at all.

In contemporary controlled-drinking treatment programs patients are taught to respond adaptively to situations in which they might otherwise drink excessively. They learn various social skills to help them resist pressures to drink; they receive assertiveness, relaxation, and stress-management training, sometimes including biofeedback and meditation; and they are encouraged to exercise and maintain a healthy diet.

Patients are also taught that a lapse will not inevitably precipitate a total relapse and should be regarded as a learning experience rather than as a sign that the battle is lost, a marked contrast from the AA perspective (Marlatt & Gordon, 1985). This noncatastrophizing approach to relapse after therapy—falling off the wagon—is important because the overwhelming majority of problem drinkers who become abstinent do experience a relapse over a four-year period (Polich et al., 1980). In this therapy alcohol abusers examine sources of stress in their work, family, and relationships so that they can become active and responsible in anticipating and resisting situations that might tempt excesses (Marlatt, 1983; Sobell et al., 1990).

The Sobells' current approach to teaching moderation to problem drinkers is primarily cognitive (Sobell & Sobell, 1993). Their basic assumption is that people have more potential control over their excessive drinking than they typically believe and that heightened awareness of the costs of drinking to excess as well as of the benefits of abstaining or cutting down can be of material help. Termed *guided self-change,* this outpatient approach emphasizes personal responsibility and control. Patients are encouraged to view themselves as basically healthy people who have been making unwise, often self-destructive choices about how to deal with life's inevitable stresses, rather than as victims of an addictive disease.

The therapist is empathic and supportive while he or she makes salient to the problem drinker the negative aspects of excessive drinking that the person may have been overlooking. For example, most problem drinkers don't calculate the expense of drinking to excess (the cost of drinking at home can easily run to more than $2000 a year; the cost of drinking in a bar or restaurant is double or triple that amount) or the amount of weight gain attributable to alcohol. They also seldom try to identify seemingly minor behavioral changes that can help them drink less, such as finding a new route home that does not take them by a bar they have been frequenting. Sometimes getting the person to delay twenty minutes before taking a second or third drink can help him or her reflect on the costs versus the benefits of drinking to excess. Evidence supports the effectiveness of this approach in helping problem drinkers moderate their intake and otherwise improve their lives (Sobell & Sobell, 1993).

Whether abstinence or controlled drinking should be the goal of treatment is controversial. This issue pits influential forces, such as AA, that uphold abstinence as the *only* proper goal for problem drinkers, against more recent researchers, such as the Sobells and those adopting their general approach, who have shown that moderation can work for many patients, including those with severe drinking problems. If the therapeutic means of achieving the goal of moderate drinking are available—and research strongly suggests that they are—then controlled drinking may be a more realistic goal even for an addicted person. Controlled drinking is currently much more widely accepted in Canada and Europe than it is in the United States.

CLINICAL CONSIDERATIONS IN TREATING ALCOHOL ABUSE

Many attempts to treat problem drinking are impeded by the therapist's often unstated assumption that all people who drink to excess do so for the same reasons. From what we have examined thus far in this chapter, we know that this assumption is unlikely to be correct.

A comprehensive clinical assessment considers what place drinking occupies in the person's life (Tucker et al., 1992). A woman in a desperately unhappy marriage, with time on her hands now that her children are in school and no longer need her constant attention, may seek the numbing effects of alcohol to help pass the time and avoid facing life's dilemmas. Making the taste of alcohol unpleasant for this patient by pairing it with shock or an emetic seems neither sensible nor adequate. The therapist should concentrate on the marital and family problems and try to reduce the psychological pain that permeates the patient's existence. She will also need help in tolerating the withdrawal symptoms that come with reduced consumption. Without alcohol as a reliable anesthetic, she will need to mobilize other resources to confront her hitherto-avoided problems. Social-skills training may help her do so.

Problem drinking is sometimes associated with other mental disorders, in particular with mood disorders and psychopathy (Goodwin, 1982). Therapists of all orientations have to recognize that depression is often comorbid with alcohol abuse and that suicide is also a risk. The clinician must therefore conduct a broad-spectrum assessment of the patient's problem, for if heavy drinking stems from the desperation of deep depression, a regimen of Antabuse or any other treatment focused on alcohol alone is unlikely to be of lasting value.

Alcohol researchers have been aware for some time that different treatment approaches are most likely appropriate for different kinds of drinkers (Mattson et al., 1994). The issue is *what* factors in the drinkers are important to align with *what* factors in treatment. Client–treatment matching, or what in the psychotherapy literature is coming to be known as aptitude-treatment interaction (ATI), has been cited by the Institute of Medicine (1990) as a critical issue in the development of better interventions for problem drinking. A large-scale effort to address the question is Project Match, a multisite clinical trial designed to test the hypothesis that certain kinds of treatments are good matches for certain kinds of problem drinkers. The three treatments studied were one that encouraged involvement in AA; cognitive behavior therapy that focused on teaching skills for coping without drinking; and a motivational enhancement treatment that encouraged the drinker to use his or her personal resources to cut down on drinking. While all three treatments worked equally well (see Chapter 18, p. 550 for details), the study failed to demonstrate the predicted interactions (Project Match Research Group, 1997).

Researchers have so far directed little attention to treating polydrug abuse (Sobell et al., 1990). It is known, for example, that up to 95 percent of problem drinkers also smoke cigarettes regularly and thus are probably addicted to both alcohol and nicotine (Istvan & Matarrazo, 1984). Should a therapist try to wean someone from alcohol and cigarettes simultaneously or sequentially (Kozlowski et al., 1989)? Should no attempt at all be made to discourage the use of both drugs, on the assumption that the patient somehow needs to be reliant on at least one of them? Should both dependencies be treated, on the assumption that cigarettes have become so closely associated with drinking that an alcohol abuser trying to remain dry will be drawn to drinking if he or she smokes? These are important and unanswered questions.

Even with the many treatment programs available, it has been estimated that no more than 10 percent of people with drinking problems are ever in professional treatment and that upwards of 40 percent cure themselves. How does such recovery take place? Among the apparent factors are a new marriage, new job, religious or spiritual experience or conversion, a near-fatal auto accident while driving drunk, and being shaken by a serious illness. It is not known, however, why some people can stop drinking after a serious crisis while others react by seeking the solace of the bottle (Valliant, 1983).

It is doubtful that a single event, even a dramatic one, can bring about the kind of profound changes necessary to wean a person from an addiction. It is more probable that successful abstinence, whether resulting from treatment or not, relies on a confluence of many life events and forces that can support the recovering alcoholic's efforts to lead a life without substance abuse. Whatever combination of factors helps problem drinkers become abstinent or controlled drinkers, a key element is social support for their efforts from family, friends, work, or self-help groups, such as AA (McCrady, 1985).

THERAPY FOR THE USE OF ILLICIT DRUGS

Some factors involved in treatment for alcohol abuse are relevant also to treatment for addiction to illegal drugs. We focus here on issues and data that have special relevance for those who abuse illicit drugs.

Central to the treatment of people who use addicting drugs, such as heroin and cocaine, is detoxification, withdrawal from the drug itself. Heroin-withdrawal reactions range from relatively mild bouts of anxiety, nausea, and restlessness for several days to more severe and frightening bouts of delirium and panic anxiety, depending primarily on the purity of the heroin that the individual has been using. Someone high on amphetamines can be brought down by appropriate dosages of one of the phenothiazines, a class of drugs more commonly used to treat schizophrenia (see p. 287), although it is important to remember that the speed freak may also have been using other drugs in conjunction with amphetamines. Withdrawal reactions from barbiturates are especially severe, even life threatening; they begin about twenty-four hours after the last dose and peak two or three days later. They usually abate by the end of the first week but may last for a month if large doses were taken. Withdrawal from barbiturates is best undertaken gradually, not cold turkey (a term that derives from the goosebumps that occur during withdrawal, making the person's skin resemble that of a plucked turkey), and should take place under close medical supervision (Honigfeld & Howard, 1978).

Detoxification is the first way in which therapists try to help an addict or drug abuser, and it may be the easiest part of the rehabilitation process. Enabling the drug user to function without drugs is an arduous task that promises more disappointment and sadness than success for both helper and client. A variety of approaches to this task are available.

BIOLOGICAL TREATMENTS

Two widely used drug-therapy programs for heroin addiction involve the administration of **heroin substitutes**, drugs chemically similar to heroin that can replace the body's craving for it, or **heroin antagonists**, drugs that prevent the user from experiencing the heroin high. The first category includes **methadone** and methadyl acetate, synthetic narcotics designed to take the place of heroin. Since these drugs are themselves addicting, successful treatment merely converts the heroin addict into a methadone addict. This conversion occurs because methadone is **cross-dependent** with heroin; that is, by acting on the same central nervous system receptors, methadone becomes a substitute for the original dependency.

Abrupt discontinuation of methadone results in its own pattern of withdrawal reactions. Because these reactions are less severe than those of heroin,

Methadone is a synthetic narcotic substitute. Former heroin addicts come to clinics each day and swallow their dose.

methadone has potential therapeutic properties for weaning the addict altogether from drug dependence (Jaffe, 1985).

For this treatment the addict must go to a clinic and swallow the drug in the presence of a staff member, once a day for methadone and three times a week for methadyl acetate. Some methadone users are able to hold jobs, commit no crimes, and refrain from using other illicit drugs (Cooper et al., 1983), but many others are unable to do so (Condell et al., 1991). The effectiveness of methadone treatment is improved if combined with regular psychological counseling (Ball & Ross, 1991).

Preexisting behavioral patterns and life circumstances play a role in how the individual will react to methadone treatment. Since methadone does not provide a euphoric high, many addicts will return to heroin if it becomes available to them. Many people drop out of methadone programs in part because of side effects, such as insomnia, constipation, excessive sweating, and diminished sexual functioning. Yet in this era of AIDS and the transmission of the human immunodeficiency virus through shared needles (p. 396), this treatment has a big advantage because methadone *can* be swallowed.

In treatment with the opiate antagonists, cyclazocine and naloxone, addicts are first gradually weaned from heroin. They then receive increasing dosages of one of these drugs, which prevent them from experiencing any high should they later take heroin. These drugs have great affinity for the receptors to which opiates usually bind; their mole-

cules occupy the receptors without stimulating them, and heroin molecules have no place to go. The antagonist changes the whole nature of heroin so that heroin simply does not produce the euphoric effect that the addict seeks. As with methadone, however, addicts must make frequent and regular visits to a clinic, which requires motivation and responsibility on their part. In addition, addicts do not lose the craving for heroin for some time. Thus patient compliance with therapy involving opiate antagonists is very poor, and the overall outcomes are only fair (Ginzburg, 1986; Goldstein, 1994).

Cocaine is now the focus of a search for drugs that will ease the symptoms of withdrawal and perhaps also attack the physical basis of the addiction. Although some favorable results with antidepressants were reported earlier, findings from two more recent and better-controlled studies were decidedly less positive. In two similarly conducted double-blind experiments, use of desipramine by cocaine abusers did not lead to decreased use of cocaine as compared with a placebo at the end of eight weeks of treatment (Kosten et al., 1992), and cocaine use was significantly *greater* than that of placebo patients at three- and six-month follow-ups after a twelve-week treatment period (Arndt et al., 1992). On the other hand, desipramine fared better in a more recent study, which will be discussed shortly (Carroll et al., 1994).

Clonidine, an antihypertensive medication, may ease withdrawal from a variety of addicting drugs, including cocaine (Baumgartner & Rowen, 1987). Bromocriptine also shows some promise in reducing craving, perhaps by reversing the depletion of dopamine that is believed to underlie cocaine's addicting properties (Dackis & Gold, 1986; Moss, 1990).

PSYCHOLOGICAL TREATMENTS

People turn to drugs for many reasons, and even though in most instances drug use becomes controlled primarily by a physical addiction, the entire pattern of an addict's existence is bound to be affected by the drug and must therefore be addressed in any treatment. One of the chief difficulties of maintaining abstinence is the negative influence of many stimuli on the recovering addict. The presence of needles, neighborhoods, and people with whom a person used to take drugs can elicit a craving for the substance (Wikler, 1980). Alcoholics and cigarette smokers have similar experiences.

Drug abuse is treated in the consulting rooms of psychiatrists, psychologists, and other mental health workers. Several kinds of psychotherapy are applied to drug-use disorders as they are to other human maladjustments, often in combination with biological treatments aimed at reducing the physical dependence.

In the first direct comparison in a controlled study, the tricyclic antidepressant desipramine and a cognitive-behavioral treatment were found to be somewhat effective in reducing cocaine use as well as in improving abusers' family, social, and general psychological functioning. In a twelve-week study by Carroll et al. (1994a, 1995), desipramine was better than a placebo for patients with a low degree of dependence on cocaine whereas the cognitive treatment was better for more dependent patients. This finding illustrates the significance of the psychological aspects of substance abuse.

Patients receiving cognitive treatment learned how to avoid high-risk situations (e.g., being around people using cocaine), recognize the lure of the drug for them and develop alternatives to using cocaine (e.g., recreational activities with nonusers). Cocaine abusers in this study also learned strategies for coping with the craving other than by using the drug, and for resisting the tendency to regard a slip as a catastrophe ("relapse prevention training," per Marlatt & Gordon, 1985). The more depressed the patient, the more favorable the outcome from both the drug and the cognitive therapy. Overall, the results for the psychosocial treatment were superior to those for the antidepressant drug, and this pattern was maintained at a one-year follow-up (Carroll et al., 1994b). The authors of the study take pains to point out that different treatments are probably necessary for different kinds of patients, a theme that is increasingly evident in the therapy literature.

Self-help residential homes or communes are the most widespread psychological approach to dealing with heroin addiction and other drug abuse. Modeled after Synanon, a therapeutic community of former drug addicts founded by Charles Dederich in Santa Monica, California, in 1958, these residences are designed to restructure radically the addict's outlook on life so that illicit drugs no longer have a place. Daytop Village, Phoenix House, Odyssey House, and other drug-rehabilitation homes share the following features:

- Separation of addicts from previous social contacts, on the assumption that these relationships have been instrumental in fostering the addictive lifestyle.

- A comprehensive environment in which drugs are not available and continuing support is offered to ease the transition from regular drug use to a drug-free existence.

- The presence of charismatic role models, former addicts who appear to be meeting life's challenges without drugs.

- Direct, often brutal confrontation in group therapy, in which addicts are goaded into accepting responsibility for their problems and for their drug habits and are urged to take charge of their lives.

- A setting in which addicts are respected as human beings rather than stigmatized as failures or criminals.

There are several obstacles to evaluating the efficacy of residential drug-treatment programs. Since entrance is voluntary, only a small minority of dependent users enter such settings. Furthermore, because the drop-out rate is high, those who remain cannot be regarded as representative of the population of people addicted to illicit drugs; their motivation to go straight is probably much stronger than that of the average addict. Any improvement participants in these programs make may reflect more their uncommonly strong desire to rid themselves of the habit rather than the specific qualities of the treatment program. Such self-regulating residential communities do, however, appear to help a large number of those who remain in them for a year or so (Institute of Medicine, 1990; Jaffe, 1985).

TREATMENT OF CIGARETTE SMOKING

Of the more than forty million smokers who have quit since 1964, it is believed that 90 percent did so without professional help (National Cancer Institute, 1977; USDHHS, 1982, 1989). Each year more than 30 percent of cigarette smokers try to quit with minimal outside assistance, but fewer than 10 percent succeed even in the short run (Fiore et al., 1990). Research is ongoing on smokers' use of self-help methods outside the framework of formal smoking-cessation programs (DiClemente, 1993; Orleans et al., 1991).

Some smokers attend smoking clinics or consult with professionals for specialized smoking-reduction programs. The American Cancer Society, the American Lung Association, and the Church of the Seventh Day Adventists have been especially active in offering programs to help large groups of people stop smoking. The numerous laws that prohibit smoking in restaurants, trains, airplanes, and public buildings are part of a social context that provides more incentive and support to stop smoking than existed in 1964 when the surgeon general first warned of the serious health hazards associated with cigarette smoking. It is estimated that 2.1 million smoking-related deaths will be postponed or avoided between 1986 and 2000 owing to the publicity from the surgeon general's reports and associated programs to discourage the habit (Foreyt, 1990). Even so, it is estimated that only about half those who go through smoking-cessation programs succeed in abstaining by the time the program is over; only about one-third of those who have succeeded in the short term actually remain nonsmoking after a year (Hunt & Bespalec, 1974; Schwartz, 1987).

PSYCHOLOGICAL TREATMENTS

Many other efforts have been made to reduce or eliminate cigarette smoking. Although short-term results are often very encouraging—some programs (e.g., Etringer, Gregory, & Lando, 1984) have reported as many as 95 percent of smokers abstinent by the end of treatment—longer-term results are far less positive. Regardless of how well things look when an intervention ends, most smokers return to their drug dependence within a year (DiClemente, 1993). This evidence does not belie the fact that a substantial minority of smokers can be helped; as with other efforts to change behavior, though, the task is not easy.

Many techniques have been tried. The idea behind some of them is to make smoking unpleasant, even nauseating. For a while in the 1970s, there was considerable interest in *rapid-smoking treatment*, in which a smoker sits in a poorly ventilated room and puffs much faster than normal, perhaps as often as every six seconds (e.g., Lando, 1977). Newer variations include *rapid puffing* (rapid smoking without inhaling), *focused smoking* (smoking for a long period of time but at a normal rate), and *smoke holding* (retaining smoke in the mouth for several minutes but without inhaling). Although such treatments reduce smoking and foster abstinence more than no-treatment control conditions, they usually do not differ from each other or from other credible interventions and, as noted, show high rates of relapse at follow-ups of several months to a year (Schwartz, 1987; Sobell et al., 1990).

Cognitively oriented investigators have tried to encourage more control in people who smoke with treatments that have them develop and utilize various coping skills, such as relaxation and positive self-talk, when confronted with tempting situations, for example, following a meal or sitting down to read a book. Results are not very promising (Hill, Rigdon, & Johnson, 1993).

As reviewed recently by Williams et al. (in press), scheduled smoking shows real promise. The strategy is to reduce nicotine intake gradually over a period of a few weeks by getting the smoker to agree to increase the time intervals between cigarettes. In this way, smoking cigarettes is controlled by the passage of time rather than by urges, mood states, or situations. Breaking this link—assuming the smoker is able to stay with the agreed upon schedule—has led to 44 percent abstinence after one year, a very impressive outcome (Cinciripini et al., 1994; Cinciripini et al., 1995). Another approach, in the spirit of tailoring treatment to characteristics of the person, is applying cognitive therapy to depressed mood in certain smokers; early results are encouraging (Hall, Munoz, & Reus, 1994; Hall et al., 1996).

Probably the most widespread intervention is advice or direction from a physician to stop smoking. Each year millions of smokers are given this counsel—because of hypertension, heart disease, lung disease, diabetes, or on general grounds of preserving or improving health. There is some evidence that a physician's advice can get some people to stop smoking, at least for a while, especially when the patients also chew nicotine gum (Law & Tang, 1995; Russell et al., 1983). But much more needs to be learned about the nature of the advice, the manner in which it is given, its timing, and other factors that must surely play a role in determining whether an addicted individual is prepared and able to alter his or her behavior primarily on a physician's say-so.

As with other addictions, psychological factors may make it difficult for smokers to quit. As these factors may vary significantly among addicts, one treatment package cannot be expected to help all smokers! People have trouble quitting for many different reasons and diverse methods need to be developed to help them. Yet in their zeal to make an impact on the smoking problem, clinicians have until recently put smokers in standardized programs.

BIOLOGICAL TREATMENTS

Nicotine gum and nicotine patches are the two chief biological treatments used to reduce a smoker's craving for nicotine. There is some evidence for their effectiveness (Fiore et al., 1994).

Each of the hundreds of hits a smoker takes each day during the consumption of a pack or two of cigarettes delivers nicotine to the brain in seven seconds. Available in the United States since 1984 by doctor's prescription and recently over the counter, gum containing nicotine may help smokers endure

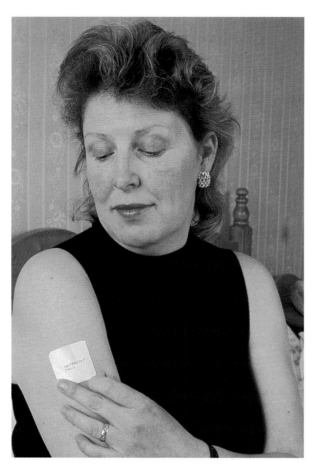

Nicotine patches are now available over the counter to help relieve withdrawal symptoms.

the nicotine withdrawal that accompanies any effort to stop smoking. The nicotine in gum is absorbed much more slowly and steadily than that in tobacco. The rationale for providing the addicting drug in gum is that it unlinks the act of smoking from the nicotine hit; at the same time, cessation of smoking is disconnected from the nicotine fit, or withdrawal. The long-term goal is for the former smoker to be able to cut back on the use of the gum as well, eventually eliminating reliance on nicotine altogether.

Ex-smokers can become dependent on this gum. Moreover, in doses that deliver an amount of nicotine equivalent to smoking one cigarette an hour, the occurrence of cardiovascular changes, such as increased blood pressure, can be dangerous to people with cardiovascular diseases. Nevertheless, some experts believe that even prolonged continued use of the gum is healthier than obtaining nicotine by smoking, because at least the poisons in the smoke are avoided. A recent review indicates that nicotine gum is useful in a limited way even with-

out a structured psychological therapy as part of the treatment package (Hughes, 1995).

Nicotine gum does not duplicate the effects of an inhaled cigarette. It does not produce the peak in plasma nicotine produced by an average cigarette, nor does it raise nicotine blood levels as high (Russell, Feyerabend, & Cole, 1976). These differences probably account for the limited, though significant, benefits of the gum in reducing withdrawal once a smoker abstains—smokers prefer to get their nicotine from a cigarette! On the other hand, these differences are an integral part of the process of weaning the nicotine addict from the drug. The best results are obtained when the gum is combined with a behaviorally oriented treatment (Hughes, 1995; Killen et al., 1990).

Hughes (1995) points out that although nicotine replacement alleviates withdrawal symptoms, which justifies its use in gum and in the nicotine patches to be described next (Hughes et al., 1990), the severity of withdrawal is only minimally related to success in stopping smoking (Hughes & Hatsukami, 1992). Thus the logic of employing nicotine replacement to help people stop smoking appears a bit shaky.

Nicotine patches first became available in December 1991 with a doctor's prescription and in 1996 over the counter. A polyethylene patch taped to the arm serves as a transdermal (through the skin) nicotine delivery system that slowly and steadily releases the drug into the bloodstream and thence to the brain. An advantage of the patch over nicotine gum is that the person needs only to apply the patch each day and not remove it, making compliance easier. A program of treatment usually lasts ten to twelve weeks, with smaller and smaller patches used as treatment progresses. A drawback is that a person who continues smoking while wearing the patch risks increasing the amount of nicotine in the body to dangerous levels.

Recent evidence suggests that the nicotine patch is superior to the use of a placebo patch in terms of abstinence as well as subjective craving (see Hughes, 1995). However, as with nicotine gum, the patch is not a panacea. Abstinence rates are less than 40 percent immediately following the termination of treatment, and at nine-month follow-ups differences between the drug and a placebo disappear. The manufacturers state that the patch is to be used only as part of a psychological smoking-cessation program and then for not more than three months at a time.

The patch is probably helpful for some smokers in temporarily easing discomfort from smoking cessation or tapering off; but again, the person's commitment, will, and use of behavior-change procedures are necessary for breaking one of the most stubborn of addictions.

RELAPSE PREVENTION

Mark Twain quipped that stopping smoking was easy—he'd done it hundreds of times. Indeed, it is maintaining abstinence that is difficult. Most smokers relapse within a year of stopping, regardless of the means used to stop. Attention has to focus on helping ex-smokers maintain their gains. This challenge is proving difficult. Data (and common sense) tell us that ex-smokers who do not live with a smoker do better at follow-up than do those who do live with a smoker (McIntyre-Kingsolver, Lichtenstein, & Mermelstein, 1986). So-called booster or maintenance sessions help, but in a very real sense they represent a continuation of treatment; when they stop, relapse is the rule (Brandon, Zelman, & Baker, 1987). However, at least in the United States, there is considerably more social support for not smoking than there was just ten years ago. Perhaps as time goes on, societal sanctions against smoking will help those who have succeeded in quitting remain abstinent.

Another approach to the relapse problem is to change the cognitions of ex-smokers (Baer & Lichtenstein, 1988). Using the articulated thoughts paradigm (Davison et al., 1983; see p. 84), Haaga (1989) found that recent ex-smokers who tended to think of smoking without prompting relapsed more readily three months later. However, if they learned some effective ways of countering these smoking-related thoughts, such as distracting themselves, their abstinence was better months later. Using a questionnaire measure, Haaga found that ex-smokers' self-efficacy in their most difficult challenge situation—their Achilles' heel—was a good predictor of abstinence a year later (Haaga, 1990). These and related studies indicate that the prediction of maintenance or relapse in smoking cessation is enhanced by measuring the cognitions of ex-smokers. Such information may help therapists design programs that will improve the ability of a person to remain a nonsmoker (Williams et al., in press).

PREVENTION OF SUBSTANCE ABUSE

From all that is known about the etiology of substance abuse, discouraging people from beginning to abuse drugs makes the most sense. It is difficult—and for many, impossible—to loose oneself from substances that create both psychological and physical dependency. We turn our attention next to prevention efforts in the realm of alcohol abuse, illicit drug abuse, and cigarette smoking.

Many prevention efforts have been aimed at adolescents because substance abuse in adulthood often follows experimentation in the teens and earlier. Programs, usually conducted in schools, have been directed at enhancing the young adolescent's self-esteem, teaching social skills, and encouraging the young person to say no to peer pressure. The results are mixed (Hansen, 1993; Jansen, Glynn, & Howard, 1996). Self-esteem enhancement, sometimes called affective education, has not demonstrated its effectiveness. In contrast, social-skills training and resistance training (learning to say no) have shown some positive results, particularly with girls. A highly publicized program, Project DARE (Drug Abuse Resistance Education), which combines affective education and resistance training and is delivered by police officers in fifth- and sixth-grade classrooms, has shown disappointing results (Clayton et al., 1991; Ringwalt et al., 1991).

Other preventive efforts, yet to be adequately evaluated, include parental involvement in school programs for their children; warning labels on containers of alcoholic beverages (mandated by law in 1989: telling consumers that drinking alcohol during pregnancy can cause birth defects in the fetus and that alcohol impairs driving a car and operating machinery); cautionary announcements in the media about stiff legal penalties for driving under the influence and exhortations to arrange for designated drivers before imbibing at social occasions; and testing for alcohol and drugs in the workplace.

In recent years we have seen well-known sports and entertainment figures urge audiences not to experiment with illicit drugs, especially cocaine. The message in the 1960s and the 1970s was often that certain drugs—especially the hallucinogens—would help people realize their potential or at least provide an escape from the humdrum and the stressful. The message in the 1990s, however, is that mind-altering drugs interfere with psychological functioning and the achievement of one's personal best and that above all, these drugs are harmful to the body and can cause unexpected death. "Just say no" has replaced "Turn on, tune in, drop out."

Also better appreciated are the relationships among drug-usage patterns. As mentioned earlier, it now appears that marijuana may be one factor in subsequent, more serious drug abuse, a hypothesis that in the 1960s was ridiculed by young people for whom marijuana was as much a form of political and social protest as a mind-altering excursion.

Developing ways of discouraging young people from experimenting with tobacco has become a top priority among health researchers and politicians, with encouragement from the surgeon general and funding from the National Cancer Institute, one of the National Institutes of Health.

The measures that hold promise for persuading young people to resist smoking may be useful also in dissuading them from trying illicit drugs and alcohol. Many people apparently do fear disastrous consequences later in life and try to cut down on cigarettes, yet both young and old smokers seem able to discount the possibility that they are at higher risk for coronary heart disease or lung cancer—the "It won't happen to me" syndrome. Although heavy smokers are eleven times more likely than nonsmokers to develop lung cancer, many heavy smokers do live long and healthy lives. In addition, it is the nature of young people to have a limited time perspective. Teenagers would seem to be more concerned with next Saturday evening's festivities or Friday's math exam than with their life situation at age sixty.

Recent years have seen scores of school-based programs aimed at preventing the onset of tobacco use by young people. By and large such programs have succeeded in delaying the onset of smoking (Sussman et al., 1996). These programs share some common components (Hansen 1992; Hansen et al., 1988; Sussman, 1996):

1. **Peer-pressure resistance training.** Students learn about the nature of peer pressure and ways to say no. For example, specially prepared films portray teenagers resisting appeals from friends to try smoking (Evans et al., 1981), not an easy matter for young people for whom peer approval and acceptance are acutely important. Sixth graders who learned assertive refusal skills smoked less two years later than a control group that received only attention and information about the harmful effects of smoking (Schinke & Gilchrist, 1985). Refusal-skills training is much more effective for girls than for boys (Graham et al., 1990).

2. **Correction of normative expectations.** Many young people believe that cigarette smoking is more prevalent (and by implication, more okay) than it actually is. Changing beliefs about the prevalence of smoking has been shown to be an effective strategy, perhaps because of the sensitivity young people have to what others their age do and believe. Establishing that it is *not* standard behavior to smoke cigarettes (or drink alcohol or use marijuana) appears to be

significantly more effective than resistance training (Hansen & Graham, 1991).

3. **Inoculation against mass-media messages.** Some prevention programs try to counter the positive images of smokers that are put forth in the media, for example, the Joe Camel ads mentioned earlier. For several years television and radio have not carried cigarette ads, and print ads have had to contain explicit warnings about the dangers of smoking.

4. **Information about parental and other adult influences.** Since it is known that parental smoking is strongly correlated with and most probably contributes to smoking by their children, some programs point out this fact and argue that this aspect of one's parents' behavior does not have to be imitated.

5. **Peer leadership.** Most smoking and other drug-prevention programs involve peers of recognized status to enhance the impact of the anti-use messages being conveyed.

6. **Affective education, self-image enhancement.** Several programs focus on the idea that intrapsychic factors, such as poor self-image and inability to cope with stress, underlie the onset of smoking in young people. However, there are indications that such programs may actually *increase* drug use, perhaps because their focus on drugs as a poor way to resolve self-esteem issues unintentionally suggests drug experimentation as a way to deal with life stress.

7. **Other components.** Additional features of preventive programs include information about the harmful effects of smoking or of drug use (a common element in adult smoking-cessation programs) and efforts to produce a public commitment not to smoke, such as making a commitment on videotape.

Beginning in August 1995 the Clinton administration, and especially the Food and Drug Administration, began to focus public attention on the addictive nature of nicotine and in particular on the need to discourage young people from taking up the habit. Cigarettes were described as "nicotine delivery systems," despite denials from the heads of major tobacco companies that nicotine is addictive[5]. A year later President Clinton took action to give the FDA regulatory control over tobacco products, suggesting that since nicotine is a drug, and an

---

[5]In March 1997, Liggett broke ranks with the other cigarette companies and admitted that nicotine is in fact addictive.

addicting one at that, its promotion and sale should be under the purview of the FDA.

The implications of this action are enormous. President Clinton announced a variety of measures designed to make it more difficult for people under age eighteen—90 percent of adult smokers began their habit before that age—to obtain cigarettes on their own, including a ban on cigarette vending machines in places where people under age eighteen could access them.

The federal government is increasing its pressure on the tobacco industry, but it remains to be seen whether these strict regulations will have the intended effect or whether, as some people predict, young people will only see the use of tobacco as more cool because the adult establishment makes it more difficult for them to obtain the product (Stolberg, 1996a).

SUMMARY

Using substances to alter mood and consciousness is virtually a human characteristic and so also is the tendency to abuse them. DSM-IV distinguishes between substance dependence and substance abuse. Dependence refers to a compulsive pattern of substance use and consequent serious psychological and physical impairments. It can involve physiological dependence, or addiction, when tolerance and withdrawal are present. In substance abuse, drug use leads to failure to meet obligations and to interpersonal and legal problems.

Alcohol has a variety of short-term and long-term effects on human beings. Many of these effects are tragic in nature, ranging from poor judgment and motor coordination and their dire consequences for the alcohol-abusing person and society, to addiction, which makes an ordinary, productive life impossible and is extremely difficult to overcome. As with other addicting drugs, people come to rely on alcohol less because of how good it makes them feel and more because it provides an escape from feeling bad.

Less prevalent but more notorious, perhaps because of their illegality, are the opiates, which include heroin; the barbiturates, which are sedatives; and the amphetamines and cocaine, which are stimulants. All these substances are addicting, and cocaine, including crack, is especially so. Heroin has been the focus of concern in recent years because usage is up and stronger varieties have become available. Barbiturates have for some time been implicated in both intentional and accidental suicides; they are particularly lethal when taken with alcohol.

Nicotine, especially when taken into the body via the inhaled smoke from a cigarette, has worked its addictive power on humankind for centuries, and despite somberly phrased warnings from public health officials it continues in widespread use. Smoking by school-aged youngsters and teenagers is a notable concern. Each year the government and private individuals spend millions of dollars to dissuade people from beginning the habit or to help those already addicted to stop smoking.

Marijuana is smoked by a large number of young Americans. Its use declined in the 1980s, but increased in the 1990s. Arguments for deregulation of marijuana have stressed its supposed safety in comparison with the known harm caused by the habitual use of alcohol, which is a legal and integral part of our culture. But currently available evidence indicates that marijuana, when used regularly, is not benign; it can damage the lungs and cardiovascular system and lead to cognitive impairments. There is also evidence that constituents of marijuana may adversely affect fetal development, heart function in people who already have coronary problems, and pulmonary function. Further, marijuana appears to be addicting. Ironically, just as the possible dangers of marijuana began to be uncovered, it was found to ease the nausea of cancer patients undergoing chemotherapy and to reduce the excessive intraocular pressure of glaucoma patients.

The hallucinogens, LSD, mescaline, and psilocybin, are taken to alter or expand consciousness. Their use reflects humankind's desire not only to escape from unpleasant realities but also to explore inner space.

Several factors are related to the etiology of substance abuse and dependence. Social attitudes and culture can play a role in encouraging the abuse of drugs, alcohol, and cigarettes. Sociocultural variables such as attitudes toward the substance, peer pressure, and how the substance is portrayed by the media are all related to how frequently a substance is used. Many substances are used to alter mood (for example, to reduce tension or increase positive affect), and people with certain personality traits, such as those high in negative affect or psychopathy, are especially likely to use drugs. Cognitive variables, such as the expectation that the drug will yield positive effects, are also important. Finally, biological factors, most notably a genetic predisposition or diathesis, appear to play a role in the use of some substances, particularly alcohol.

Therapies of all kinds have been used to help people refrain from the use of both legal (e.g., alcohol and nicotine) and illegal drugs (e.g., heroin and cocaine). As all the drugs discussed in this chapter are addictive, biological treatments have attempted to release users from their physiological dependency. Some benefits have been observed for treatments using such drugs as clonidine, naltrexone, and methadone. Recently nicotine replacement via gum or patches has met with some success in reducing cigarette smoking. None of these somatic approaches appears to lead to enduring change unless accompanied by psychological treatments with such goals as helping patients resist pressures to indulge, cope with normal life stress, control emotions without relying on chemicals, and make use of social supports, such as Alcoholics Anonymous.

Health professionals recognize that substance abuse is a multifaceted problem, requiring a broad range of interventions, and that different people use and abuse drugs for different reasons, making it necessary to assess carefully those factors of particular importance for a given individual. Since it is far easier never to begin using drugs than to stop using them, considerable effort has been expended in recent years to prevent substance abuse by implementing educational and social programs to equip young people to develop their lives without a reliance on drugs.

KEY TERMS

substance dependence	opium	nitrous oxide
substance abuse	morphine	flashback
tolerance	heroin	detoxification
withdrawal	barbiturates	Antabuse
delirium tremens (DTs)	stimulants	covert sensitization
polydrug abuse	amphetamines	controlled drinking
fetal alcohol syndrome	cocaine	heroin substitutes
nicotine	LSD	heroin antagonists
marijuana	hallucinogen	methadone
hashish	mescaline	cross-dependent
sedatives	psilocybin	clonidine
opiates	Ecstasy	

Bette Alexande, "Heads," 1991

PERSONALITY DISORDERS

Mary was twenty-six years old at the time of her first admission to a psychiatric hospital. She had been in outpatient treatment with a psychologist for several months when her persistent thoughts of suicide and preoccupation with inflicting pain on herself (by cutting or burning) led her therapist to conclude that she could no longer be managed as an outpatient.

Mary's first experience with some form of psychological therapy had occurred when she was an adolescent. Her grades declined sharply in the eleventh grade, and her parents suspected she was using drugs. She began to miss curfews and even failed to come home at all on a few occasions. She was frequently truant. Family therapy was undertaken, and it seemed to go well at first. Mary was enthusiastic about her therapist and asked for additional, private sessions with him.

During the family sessions her parents' fears were confirmed as Mary revealed an extensive history of drug use, including "everything I can get my hands on." She had been promiscuous and had prostituted herself several times to get drug money. Her relationships with her peers were changeable, to say the least. The pattern was a constant parade of new friends, at first thought to be the greatest ever, but who soon disappointed Mary somehow and were cast aside, often in a very unpleasant way. Except for the one person with whom she was currently enamored, Mary had no other friends. She reported that she stayed away from others for fear that they would harm her in some way. She claimed to be totally uninterested in school and bored with everything but the altered states that drugs produced in her.

After several weeks of therapy Mary's parents noticed that her relationship with the therapist had cooled appreciably. The sessions were marked by Mary's angry and abusive outbursts toward the therapist. After several more weeks had passed, Mary refused to attend any more sessions. In a subsequent conversation with the therapist, Mary's father learned that Mary had behaved seductively toward the therapist during their private sessions and that her changed attitude toward him coincided with the rejection of her advances despite the therapist's attempt to mix firmness with warmth and empathy.

Mary managed to graduate from high school and enrolled in a local community college, but the old patterns returned. Poor grades, cutting classes, continuing drug use, and lack of interest in her studies finally led her to quit in the middle of the first semester of her second year. After leaving school Mary held a series of clerical jobs. Most of them didn't last long, as some dispute with her co-workers typically led to her dismissal. Her relationships with co-workers paralleled her relationships with her peers in high school. When Mary started a new job she would find someone she really liked a lot, but something would come between them and the relationship would end angrily. Mary was frequently suspicious of her co-workers and reported that she often heard them talking about her, plotting how to prevent her from getting ahead on the job. She was quick to find hidden meanings in their behavior, as when she interpreted being the last person asked to sign a birthday card to mean that

she was the least liked person in the office. She indicated that she "received vibrations" from others and could tell when they really didn't like her even in the absence of any direct evidence.

Mary's behavior includes many characteristic symptoms of several personality disorders, in particular borderline personality disorder. Her frequent mood swings, with periods of depression and extreme irritability (diagnosable as bipolar disorder on Axis I), led her to seek therapy several times. But after initial enthusiasm her relationship with her therapist always deteriorated, resulting in premature termination of therapy. The therapist she was seeing just before her hospitalization was her sixth.

Personality disorders are a heterogeneous group of disorders, coded on Axis II of the DSM and regarded as long-standing, pervasive, and inflexible patterns of behavior and inner experience that deviate from the expectations of a person's culture and that impair social and occupational functioning. Some, but not all, can cause emotional distress.

As we examine the personality disorders, some may seem to fit people we know, not to mention ourselves! This seems a good point to remind readers about the medical student syndrome, so called because medical students (and psychology students) have a tendency to see themselves or their family and friends in descriptions of disorders they study. However, although the symptoms of the personality disorders come close to describing characteristics that we all possess from time to time and in varying degrees, an actual personality disorder is defined by the *extremes* of several traits. The personality each of us develops over the years reflects a persistent means of dealing with life's challenges, a certain *style* of relating to other people. One person is overly dependent; another is challenging and aggressive; another is shy and avoids social contact; and still another is concerned more with appearance and bolstering his or her vulnerable ego than with relating honestly and on a deep level with others. These individuals would not be diagnosed as having personality disorders unless the patterns of behavior were long-standing, pervasive, and dysfunctional. For example, on entering a crowded room and shortly thereafter hearing a loud burst of laughter, you might feel that you are the target of some joke and that people are talking about you. Such concerns become symptoms of paranoid personality disorder only if they occur frequently and intensely and prevent the development of close personal relationships.

One final prefatory comment. In addition to being viewed as clinical syndromes in their own right, personality disorders are often comorbid with an Axis I disorder. Personality disorders can serve as a *context* for Axis I problems, shaping them in different ways (Millon, 1996). A person diagnosed with an anxiety disorder on Axis I and avoidant personality disorder on Axis II will be withdrawn and anxious, whereas an anxiety-disordered person who is diagnosed as histrionic on Axis II will make his or her anxiety highly visible. An analogy might be viewing the same photograph through different-colored lenses or listening to the same song played on a piano or performed by a full orchestra. As Millon put it:

> [a] unipolar depression [for example] will be experienced and reacted to differently in an individual with an avoidant personality disorder than in one with a narcissistic personality. … [Different personality disorders] will … evoke contrasting ways of perceiving and coping with [an individual's Axis I disorder]. For these and other reasons, we believe that clinicians should be oriented to the "context of personality" when they deal with … all forms of psychiatric [Axis I] disorders. (1996, p. vii)

In this chapter we will look first at how we classify personality disorders and at the problems associated with classification. Then we will turn to the personality disorders themselves, theory and research on their etiology, and therapies for dealing with them.

CLASSIFYING PERSONALITY DISORDERS: CLUSTERS, CATEGORIES, AND PROBLEMS

Because personality disorders are indicated on a separate axis, Axis II, their presence or absence is considered whenever a diagnosis is made. They were placed on a separate axis to ensure that diagnosticians would pay attention to their possible presence. Although a diagnostic interview sometimes points directly to the presence of a personality disorder, more often a person arrives at a clinic with an Axis I disorder (such as panic disorder), which, quite naturally, is the primary focus of attention. Placing the personality disorders on Axis II is meant to guide the clinician to consider whether a personality disorder is also present.

In the past, personality disorders had little diagnostic reliability, in spite of attempts to improve the clarity of their definitions. One clinician might diagnose a flamboyant patient as narcissistic while another might consider him or her psychopathic. These low reliabilities may have been caused by the lack of a good assessment device. More recent work with structured interviews specially designed for assessing personality disorders indicates that good reliabilities can be achieved, even across cultures (Loranger et al., 1987; Widiger et al., 1988). Consider the results of a study that was conducted in nine countries of North America, Europe, Asia, and Africa using a newly developed structured interview. The interrater reliabilities presented in Table 13.1 compare favorably with reliabilities of Axis I disorders (Chapter 3, p. 66). Thus by using these structured interviews, reliable diagnoses of personality disorders can be achieved.

Because personality disorders consist of maladaptive personality traits presumed to be stable over time, test-retest reliability—a comparison of whether patients receive the same diagnosis when they are assessed twice with some time interval separating the two assessments—is also an important factor in their evaluation. A summary of test-retest reliability is given in Table 13.1 (Zimmerman, 1994). Note the wide variability of the figures. Antisocial

TABLE 13.1 Interrater and Test-Retest Reliability for the Personality Disorders		
Diagnosis	*Interrater Reliability*	*Test-Retest Reliability*
Paranoid	.75	.57
Schizoid	.83	—
Schizotypal	.82	.11
Borderline	.89	.56
Histrionic	.81	.40
Narcissistic	.83	.32
Antisocial	.88	.84
Dependent	.89	.15
Avoidant	.82	.41
Obsessive-compulsive	.82	.52

Source: Figures for interrater reliability are from the Loranger et al. (1994) cross-national study and reflect the amount of agreement above chance. Test-retest figures are rates of agreement from Zimmerman's (1994) summary of longer (generally more than a year) studies.

personality disorder has a high test-retest reliability, indicating that it is a stable diagnosis—a patient given the diagnosis at one time is very likely to receive the same diagnosis when evaluated later. The figures for schizotypal and dependent personality disorders, on the other hand, are very low, indicating that the symptoms of people with these latter two diagnoses are not stable over time. Thus it appears that many of the personality disorders are not as enduring as implied by the DSM.

Another major problem with the category of personality disorders is that it is often difficult to diagnose a single, specific personality disorder because many disordered people exhibit a wide range of traits that make several diagnoses applicable. Mary, described in the case opening this chapter, met the diagnostic criteria not only for borderline personality disorder but also for paranoid personality disorder, and she came close to meeting the criteria for schizotypal disorder as well. One study found that 55 percent of patients with borderline personality disorder also met the diagnostic criteria for schizotypal personality disorder, 47 percent for antisocial personality disorder, and 57 percent for histrionic personality disorder (Widiger, Frances, & Trull, 1987). Such data are particularly discouraging when we try to interpret the results of research that compares patients who have a specific personality disorder with some control group. If, for example, we find that people with borderline disorder differ from normal people, is what we have learned specific to borderline personality disorder or related to personality disorders in general or perhaps even applicable to another diagnosis? Because the changes in diagnostic criteria from DSM-III and DSM-IIIR to DSM-IV are relatively minor, it is unlikely that the problem of comorbidity has been solved.

These problems suggest that the categorical diagnostic system of DSM-IV may not be ideal for classifying personality disorders. The personality traits that constitute the data for classification form a continuum; that is, most of the relevant characteristics are present in varying degrees in most people. When people with a personality disorder take a general personality inventory, it reveals a personality with a structure similar to that of normals, but more extreme (Livesley & Schroeder, 1993). The personality disorders can be construed as the extremes of characteristics we all possess. A dimensional approach to classification of personality disorders (see Chapter 3, p. 65), then, may be more appropriate. A dimensional system was considered for inclusion in both DSM-IIIR and DSM-IV, but consensus could not be reached on which dimensions to include. A promising effort to develop a dimensional classification system will be described later (Focus 13.1, p. 348).

Despite severe problems with their diagnosis, we should not dismiss the personality disorders. These disorders are prevalent, and they cause severe impairment in peoples' lives. They have been the subject of serious research for a much shorter time than have most of the other diagnoses considered in this book. As research continues, the diagnostic categories will most likely be refined, perhaps with a dimensional system, and many of these problems may be solved.

Personality disorders are grouped into three clusters in DSM-IV. Individuals in cluster A (paranoid, schizoid, and schizotypal) seem odd or eccentric; those in cluster B (antisocial, borderline, histrionic, and narcissistic) seem dramatic, emotional, or erratic; and those in cluster C (avoidant, dependent, and obsessive-compulsive) appear anxious or fearful. Although the empirical evidence on the validity of these clusters is mixed, they form a useful organizational framework for this chapter.

ODD/ECCENTRIC CLUSTER

This cluster comprises three diagnoses—paranoid, schizoid, and schizotypal personality disorders. The symptoms of these disorders bear some similarity to the symptoms of schizophrenia, especially its prodromal and residual phases.

PARANOID PERSONALITY DISORDER

The **paranoid personality** is suspicious of people. He or she expects to be mistreated or exploited by others and thus is secretive and continually on the lookout for possible signs of trickery and abuse. He or she is often hostile and reacts angrily to perceived insults. Such individuals are reluctant to confide in others and tend to blame others and hold grudges even when they themselves are at fault. They are extremely jealous and may unjustifiably question the fidelity of a spouse or lover.

Patients with paranoid personality disorder are preoccupied with unjustified doubts about the loyalty or trustworthiness of others. They may read hidden messages into events, for example, believing that a neighbor's dog deliberately barks in the early morning to disturb them. Paranoid personality disorder occurs most frequently in men and co-occurs most frequently with schizotypal, borderline, and avoidant personality disorders (Bernstein,

1994; Morey, 1988). Its prevalence is about 1 percent (Weissman, 1993).

SCHIZOID PERSONALITY DISORDER

The patient with **schizoid personality** disorder does not desire or enjoy social relationships and usually has no close friends. He or she appears dull, bland, and aloof and has no warm, tender feelings for other people. These patients rarely report strong emotions, are not interested in sex, and experience few pleasurable activities. Indifferent to praise, criticism, and the sentiments of others, individuals with this disorder are loners and pursue solitary interests. The prevalence of schizoid personality disorder is reported to be less than 1 percent. It is slightly less common among women than among men (Weissman, 1993).

Comorbidity is highest for schizotypal, avoidant, and paranoid personality disorders, most likely because of the similar diagnostic criteria in the four categories. The diagnostic criteria for schizoid personality disorder are also similar to some of the symptoms of the prodromal and residual phases of schizophrenia.

SCHIZOTYPAL PERSONALITY DISORDER

The modern concept of the **schizotypal personality** grew out of Danish studies of the adopted children of schizophrenic parents (Kety et al., 1968). Although some of these children developed full-blown schizophrenia as adults, an even larger number developed what seemed to be an attenuated form of schizophrenia. The diagnostic criteria for schizotypal personality disorder were devised by Spitzer, Endicott, and Gibbon (1979) to describe these individuals. These criteria were incorporated in DSM-III and were narrowed somewhat in DSM-IIIR and DSM-IV.

Patients with schizotypal personality disorder usually have the interpersonal difficulties of the schizoid personality and excessive social anxiety that does not diminish with familiarity. Several additional, more eccentric symptoms occur in schizotypal personality disorder. Not severe enough to warrant a diagnosis of schizophrenia (see Chapter 11), these symptoms are essentially those that define the prodromal and residual phases of that disorder. Patients with schizotypal personality disorder may have *odd beliefs* or *magical thinking*—superstitiousness, beliefs that they are clairvoyant and telepathic—and recurrent *illusions*—they may sense the presence of a force or a person not actually there. Their speech may use words in an unusual

and unclear fashion, for example, "I'm not a very talkable person." Their behavior and appearance may also be eccentric—they may talk to themselves or wear dirty and disheveled clothing, for example. Also common are ideas of reference (the belief that events have a particular and unusual meaning for the person), suspiciousness, and paranoid ideation. Affect appears to be constricted and flat. In a study of the relative importance of these symptoms for diagnosis, Widiger, Frances, and Trull (1987) found that paranoid ideation, ideas of reference, and illusions were most telling. The prevalence of schizotypal personality disorder is estimated at about 3 percent, and it is slightly more frequent among men than among women (Zimmerman & Coryel, 1989).

The biggest problem in the diagnosis of schizotypal personality disorder is its overlap with the diagnoses of other personality disorders. Morey (1988) found that 33 percent of people diagnosed with schizotypal personality according to DSM-IIIR criteria also met the diagnostic criteria for borderline personality disorder, 33 percent for narcissistic personality disorder, 59 percent for avoidant personality disorder, 59 percent for paranoid personality disorder, and 44 percent for schizoid personality disorder. Clearly these figures are unsatisfactory figures if we want to consider schizotypal personality disorder a discrete diagnostic entity.

ETIOLOGY OF THE ODD/ECCENTRIC CLUSTER

What causes the odd, sometimes paranoid thinking, bizarre behavior, and interpersonal difficulties that appear in this cluster of personality disorders? The search for causes of these disorders has been guided by the idea that they are genetically linked to schizophrenia, perhaps as less severe variants of this Axis I disorder. The evidence for this idea varies depending on which of the odd/eccentric disorders is considered. Family studies have consistently shown that the relatives of schizophrenic patients are at increased risk for schizotypal personality disorder (Nigg & Goldsmith, 1994). However, increased rates of schizotypal personality disorder have also been found in the first-degree relatives of patients with unipolar depression, suggesting that schizotypal personality disorder is related to disorders other than schizophrenia (Squires-Wheeler et al., 1993). Family studies of paranoid personality disorder for the most part find higher than average rates in the relatives of patients with schizophrenia or delusional disorder (Bernstein, Useda, & Siever, 1993). A clear pattern has not emerged from behavior genetic research on schizoid personality disorder.

Thus family studies provide at least some evidence that personality disorders of the odd/eccentric cluster are related to schizophrenia. For schizotypal personality disorder there is also further evidence on this point. Such patients have deficits in cognitive and neuropsychological functioning (Siever et al., 1993) and some structural brain abnormalities (Cannon et al., 1994) that are similar to those seen in schizophrenia.

DRAMATIC/ERRATIC CLUSTER

The diagnoses in this cluster—borderline, histrionic, narcissistic, and antisocial personality disorders—include patients with a wide variety of symptoms, ranging from highly variable behavior to inflated self-esteem, exaggerated emotional displays, and antisocial behavior.

BORDERLINE PERSONALITY DISORDER

This disorder was adopted by the DSM as an official diagnosis in 1980. The person diagnosed as a **borderline personality** has instability in relationships, mood, and self-image. For example, attitudes and feelings toward other people may vary considerably and inexplicably over short periods of time. Emotions are erratic and can shift abruptly, particularly from passionate idealization to contemptuous anger. Patients with borderline personality disorder are argumentative, irritable, sarcastic, quick to take

The character played by Glenn Close in the film *Fatal Attraction* had many characteristics of the borderline personality.

offense, and altogether very hard to live with. Their unpredictable and impulsive behavior, which may include gambling, spending, sex, and eating sprees, is potentially self-damaging. These individuals have not developed a clear and coherent sense of self and remain uncertain about their values, loyalties, and career choices. They cannot bear to be alone, have fears of abandonment, and demand attention. They tend to have a series of intense one-on-one relationships that are usually stormy and transient, alternating between idealization and devaluation; one moment they lavish praise on someone, the next, they scornfully demean them. Subject to chronic feelings of depression and emptiness, they often attempt suicide and engage in self-mutilating behavior, such as slicing into the legs with a razor blade. Paranoid ideation and dissociative symptoms may appear during periods of high stress. Of all these varied symptoms, unstable and intense interpersonal relationships appear as a critical feature (Modestin, 1987).[1]

Clinicians and researchers have used the term *borderline personality* for some time, but they have given it many meanings. Originally the term implied that the patient was on the borderline between neurosis and schizophrenia. The DSM concept of borderline personality no longer has this connotation. The current conceptualization of borderline personality derives from several sources. After reviewing the available research literature and interview studies of borderline personalities, Gunderson, Kolb, and Austin (1981) proposed a set of specific diagnostic criteria similar to those that ultimately appeared in DSM-III. The DSM-III criteria for borderline personality were established through a study done by Spitzer, Endicott, and Gibbon (1979). They identified schizotypal personality disorder as a cluster of traits related to schizophrenia. They also identified another syndrome, which became DSM-III's borderline personality disorder. DSM-IV maintains these distinctions.

Borderline personality disorder begins in adolescence, has a prevalence of 1 to 2 percent, and is more common in women than in men (Swartz et al., 1990). Borderline patients are likely to have an Axis I mood disorder (Manos, Vasilopoulou, & Sotorou, 1988), and their relatives are more likely than average to have mood disorders (Zanarini et al., 1988).

---

[1]Patients with both borderline and schizotypal personality disorders would probably have been diagnosed as schizophrenic using DSM-II criteria. Designating the behavior of these people as the criteria for these two personality disorders is one way in which DSM-IIIR and DSM-IV narrowed the schizophrenia diagnosis (see Chapter 11).

The depression of patients with borderline personality disorder appears to be somewhat different from the usual unipolar mood disorder; somatic complaints, guilt, helplessness, and boredom are less apparent (Rogers, Widiger, & Krupp, 1995). Comorbidity is found with substance abuse (Clarkin, Marziali, & Munroe-Blum, 1992) as well as with histrionic, narcissistic, dependent, avoidant, and paranoid personality disorders (Morey, 1988).

A good sense of this disorder can be obtained from a colorful account written by Jonathan Kellerman, a clinical psychologist turned successful mystery writer.

The borderline patient is a therapist's nightmare … because borderlines never really get better. The best you can do is help them coast, without getting sucked into their pathology. … They're the chronically depressed, the determinedly addictive, the compulsively divorced, living from one emotional disaster to the next. Bed hoppers, stomach pumpers, freeway jumpers, and sad-eyed bench-sitters with arms stitched up like footballs and psychic wounds that can never be sutured. Their egos are as fragile as spun sugar, their psyches irretrievably fragmented, like a jigsaw puzzle with crucial pieces missing. They play roles with alacrity, excel at being anyone but themselves, crave intimacy but repel it when they find it. Some of them gravitate toward stage or screen; others do their acting in more subtle ways. …

Borderlines go from therapist to therapist, hoping to find a magic bullet for the crushing feelings of emptiness. They turn to chemical bullets, gobble tranquilizers and antidepressants, alcohol and cocaine. Embrace gurus and heaven-hucksters, any charismatic creep promising a quick fix of the pain. And they end up taking temporary vacations in psychiatric wards and prison cells, emerge looking good, raising everyone's hopes. Until the next letdown, real or imagined, the next excursion into self damage.

What they don't do is change. (Kellerman, 1989, pp. 113–114)

ETIOLOGY OF BORDERLINE PERSONALITY DISORDER

Object relations theory, an important variant of psychoanalytic theory, concerns itself with the way children incorporate (or introject) the values and images of important people, such as their parents. In other words, the focus is on the manner in which children identify with people to whom they have strong emotional attachments. These introjected objects (object representations) become part of the person's ego, but they can come into conflict with the wishes, goals, and ideals of the developing adult, for example, when a college-age woman who has adopted her mother's notion of the proper role of a woman in society finds herself drawn to the more modern ideals of feminism. Object relations theorists hypothesize that people react to their world through the perspectives of important people from their past, primarily their parents or primary caregivers. Sometimes these perspectives conflict with the person's own wishes and interests. The two leading object relations theorists are Heinz Kohut, whose views on narcissism will be discussed later, and Otto Kernberg, who has written extensively about the borderline personality.

Kernberg (1985) proposes that adverse childhood experiences, for example, having parents who inconsistently provide love and attention, perhaps praising achievements but unable to offer emotional support and warmth, cause children to develop insecure egos, a major feature of borderline personality disorder. Although borderlines have weak egos and need constant reassuring, they retain the capacity to test reality. As a result, borderline patients are in touch with reality, but frequently engage in a defense mechanism called *splitting*, dichotomizing objects into all good or all bad and failing to integrate positive and negative aspects of another person into a whole. This inability to make sense of contradictory aspects of others or the self causes extreme difficulty in regulating emotions because the borderline patient sees the world, including himself or herself, in black-and-white terms. Somehow this defense protects the borderline patient's weak ego from intolerable anxiety.

A number of studies have yielded data relevant to Kernberg's theory. As expected, borderlines report a low level of care by their mothers (Patrick, Hobson, & Dastia, 1994). They view their families as emotionally unexpressive, low in cohesion, and high in conflict. They also frequently report childhood sexual and physical abuse (Silk et al., 1995) and have often experienced separation from parents during childhood (Paris, Zweig, & Guzder, 1994). There is speculation that borderline personality may be a part of posttraumatic stress disorder or dissociative identity disorder arising from severe, traumatizing abuse in childhood.

Borderline personality disorder runs in families, suggesting that it may have a genetic component (Baron et al., 1985). Borderline patients are also high in neuroticism, a trait known to be heritable (Nigg & Goldsmith, 1994). Some data suggest that functioning of the frontal lobes, which are often thought to play a role in impulsive behavior, is impaired. For example, borderline patients' performance on neurological tests of frontal functioning is poor, and they show low levels of glucose metabolism in the frontal lobes (Goyer et al., 1994; Van Ruckum et al., 1993). Also relevant to impulsivity is the neurotransmitter serotonin. Consistent with the idea that low levels of serotonin are associated with impulsivity, when borderline patients were administered a drug to increase serotonin levels, their level of anger decreased (Hollander et al., 1993). Thus biological research on borderline personality disorder has yielded some promising leads concerning their impulsive behavior.

HISTRIONIC PERSONALITY DISORDER

The diagnosis of **histrionic personality**, formerly called hysterical personality, is applied to people who are overly dramatic and attention–seeking. They often use features of their physical appearance, such as unusual clothes, makeup, or hair color, to draw attention to themselves. These individuals, although displaying emotion extravagantly, are thought to be emotionally shallow. They are self-centered, overly concerned with their physical attractiveness, and uncomfortable when not at the center of attention. They can be inappropriately sexually provocative and seductive and are easily influenced by others. Their speech is often impressionistic and lacking in detail. For example, they may state a strong opinion yet be unable to give any supporting information.

This diagnosis has a prevalence of 2 to 3 percent and is more common among women than among men (Corbitt & Widiger, 1995). The prevalence of histrionic personality disorder is higher among separated and divorced people, and it is associated with high rates of depression and poor physical health (Nestadt et al., 1990). Comorbidity with borderline personality disorder is high.

ETIOLOGY OF HISTRIONIC PERSONALITY DISORDER

Little research has been conducted on this personality disorder. Psychoanalytic theory predominates and proposes that the histrionic's emotionality and seductiveness were encouraged by parental seductiveness, especially father to daughter. Histrionic patients are thought to have been raised in a family environment in which parents talked about sex as something dirty yet behaved as though it was exciting and desirable. This upbringing may explain the preoccupation with sex, coupled with a fear of actually behaving sexually. The exaggerated displays of emotion on the part of histrionic persons are seen as symptoms of such underlying conflicts, and their need to be the center of attention is seen as a way of defending against their true feelings of low self-esteem (Apt & Hurlbert, 1994; Stone, 1993).

NARCISSISTIC PERSONALITY DISORDER

People with a **narcissistic personality** have a grandiose view of their own uniqueness and abilities; they are preoccupied with fantasies of great success. To say that they are self-centered is an understatement. They require almost constant attention and excessive admiration and believe they can be understood only by special or high-status people. Their interpersonal relationships are disturbed by their lack of empathy, feelings of envy, arrogance, and taking advantage of others as well as by their feelings of entitlement—they expect others to do special, not-to-be-reciprocated favors for them. Most of these characteristics, with the exception of lack of empathy and extreme reactions to criticism, have been validated as aspects of narcissistic personality disorder in empirical studies (Ronningston & Gunderson, 1990). The prevalence of narcissistic personality disorder is less than 1 percent. It most often co-occurs with borderline personality disorder (Morey, 1988).

Narcissistic personality disorder draws its name from Narcissus of Greek mythology. He fell in love with his own reflection, was consumed by his own desire, and was then transformed into a flower.

ETIOLOGY OF NARCISSISTIC PERSONALITY DISORDER

The diagnosis of narcissistic personality disorder is rooted in modern psychoanalytic writings. Many psychoanalytically oriented clinicians have regarded it as a product of our times and our system of values. On the surface the narcissistic personality has a remarkable sense of self-importance, complete self-absorption, and fantasies of limitless success, but these characteristics mask a very fragile self-esteem. Constantly seeking attention and adulation, narcissistic personalities are, underneath, extremely sensitive to criticism and deeply fearful of failure. Sometimes they seek out others whom they can idealize because they are disappointed in themselves, but they generally do not allow anyone to be genuinely close to them. Their personal relationships are few and shallow; when people inevitably fall short of their unrealistic expectations they become angry and rejecting. The inner lives of narcissists are similarly impoverished because despite their self-aggrandizement, they actually think very little of themselves.

At the center of contemporary interest in narcissism is Heinz Kohut, whose two books, *The Analysis of the Self* (1971) and *The Restoration of the Self* (1977), have established a variant of psychoanalysis known as self-psychology. According to Kohut, the self emerges early in life as a bipolar structure with an immature grandiosity at one pole and a dependent, overidealizaton of other people at the other. A failure to develop healthy self-esteem occurs when parents do not respond to their children's displays of competency by expressing approval; that is, the child is not valued for his or her own self-worth but is valued as a means to foster the parents' self-esteem. When parents respond to a child with respect, warmth, and empathy, they endow the youngster with a normal sense of self-worth, a healthy self-esteem. But when parents further their own needs rather than directly approve of their children, the result, according to Kohut, may be a narcissistic personality:

> A little girl comes home from school, eager to tell her mother about some great successes. But this mother, instead of listening with pride, deflects the conversation from the child to herself [and] begins to talk about her own successes which overshadow those of her little daughter. (Kohut & Wolf, 1978, p. 418)

Children neglected in this way do not develop an internalized, healthy self-esteem and have trouble accepting their own shortcomings. They develop into narcissistic personalities, striving to bolster their sense of self through unending quests for love and approval from others.

Heinz Kohut has played a major role in conceptualizing narcissistic personality disorder.

ANTISOCIAL PERSONALITY DISORDER AND PSYCHOPATHY

In current usage the terms *antisocial personality disorder* and *psychopathy* (sometimes referred to as sociopathy) are often used interchangeably, although there are important differences between the two. Antisocial behavior, such as breaking laws, is an important component of both terms.

The attempt to regard certain antisocial behavior as reflecting psychological abnormality has an interesting history. At the beginning of the nineteenth century Philippe Pinel conceived of *manie sans délire*. Pinel chose this term to describe a violently insane (*manie*) person who did not show other cognitive symptoms (*sans délire*) common among the insane. In 1835, James Prichard, an English psychiatrist, described the disorder "moral insanity" in an attempt to account for antisocial behavior so far outside the usual ethical and legal codes that it seemed a form of lunacy. The man whose nature prompted Prichard's term was an easily angered aristocrat who had whipped a horse, kicked a dog to death, and thrown a peasant woman into a well. In both these examples, the antisocial behavior had a quality of depravity and

The character played by Anthony Hopkins in *The Silence of the Lambs* displayed many of the characteristics of the psychopath, especially his total lack of regard for the rights of others.

bizarreness that seemed to set it apart from most criminal or aggressive acts.

The current DSM-IV concept of antisocial personality disorder (APD) involves two major components. The first refers to the presence of a conduct disorder (described in Chapter 15) before the age of fifteen. Truancy, running away from home, frequent lying, theft, arson, and deliberate destruction of property are major symptoms of conduct disorder. The second major component refers to the continuation of this pattern of antisocial behavior in adulthood. Thus DSM reserves the diagnosis not only for certain patterns of antisocial behavior but to patterns that began in childhood. The adult with **antisocial personality** disorder shows irresponsible and antisocial behavior by working only inconsistently, breaking laws, being irritable and physically aggressive, defaulting on debts, and being reckless. He or she is impulsive and fails to plan ahead and is completely aware of lies and misdeeds but shows neither regard for truth nor remorse.

It is estimated that about 3 percent of adult American men and 1 percent of women are antisocial personalities (Robins et al., 1984). Rates are much higher among younger than among older adults, and the disorder is more common among people of low socioeconomic status. Antisocial per-

sonality disorder is comorbid with a number of other diagnoses, most notably, substance abuse.

The concept of **psychopathy** is closely linked to the writings of Hervey Cleckley and his classic book, *The Mask of Sanity* (1976). On the basis of his vast clinical experience Cleckley formulated a set of criteria by which to recognize the disorder. Unlike the DSM criteria for antisocial personality disorder, Cleckley's criteria for psychopathy refer less to antisocial behavior per se and more to the psychopath's thoughts and feelings. One of the key characteristics of the psychopath is poverty of emotions, both positive and negative. Psychopaths have no sense of shame, and even their seemingly positive feelings for others are merely an act. The psychopath is superficially charming and manipulates others for personal gain. The lack of negative emotions may make it impossible for psychopaths to learn from their mistakes, and the lack of positive emotions leads them to behave irresponsibly toward others. Another key point in Cleckley's description is that the antisocial behavior of the psychopath is inadequately motivated; that is, antisocial behavior does not arise for a reason such as a need for money, but instead is performed impulsively, as much for thrills as for anything else.

Most researchers diagnose psychopathy using a checklist developed by Hare and his associates (Hare et al., 1990). The checklist identifies two major clusters of psychopathic behaviors. The first, referred to as *emotional detachment*, describes a selfish, remorseless individual with inflated self-esteem who exploits others. The second characterizes an antisocial lifestyle marked by impulsivity and irresponsibility. Among Axis I diagnoses, psychopathy is frequently comorbid with abuse of alcohol and other drugs (Smith & Newman, 1990).

Thus we have two related but not identical diagnoses—antisocial personality disorder and psychopathy. Hare, Hart, and Harpur (1991) have criticized the DSM diagnosis of antisocial personality disorder because it requires accurate reports of events that took place many years earlier by people who are habitual liars (recall the onset-in-childhood criterion). Furthermore, a diagnostic concept in the field of psychopathology should not be synonymous with criminality, but 75 to 80 percent of convicted felons meet the criteria for antisocial personality disorder. In contrast, only 15 to 25 percent of convicted felons meet the criteria for psychopathy (Hart & Hare, 1989). Therefore the concept of psychopathy seems to have some distinct advantages. As we review the research in this area it is important to keep in mind that it has been conducted on individuals diagnosed in different ways—some as antisocial personalities and some as psychopaths—which makes integrating these findings somewhat difficult.

Before considering current research on psychopathy, we will examine an excerpt from a case history. This case illustrates the classic characteristics of the psychopath but is unusual in that the person described was neither a criminal nor in psychiatric treatment at the time the data for the study were collected. This is an important point, for the majority of psychopaths who are the subjects of research studies have broken the law and been caught for doing so. Only rarely do we have the opportunity to examine in detail the behavior of an individual who fits the diagnostic definition yet has managed not to break the law or at least has not been convicted of a crime.

THE CASE OF DAN

This case history was compiled by a psychologist, Elton McNeil (1967), a personal friend of Dan's.

Dan was a wealthy actor and disc jockey who lived in an expensive house in an exclusive suburb and generally played his role as a personality to the hilt. One evening, when he and McNeil were out for dinner, Dan made a great fuss over the condition of the shrimp de Johnge he had ordered. McNeil thought that Dan deliberately contrived the whole scene for the effect it might produce, and he said to his companion:

"I have a sneaking suspicion this whole scene came about just because you weren't really hungry." Dan laughed loudly in agreement and said, "What the hell, they'll be on their toes next time." "Was that the only reason for this display?"…

"No," he replied, "I wanted to show you how gutless the rest of the world is. If you shove a little they all jump. Next time I come in, they'll be all over me to make sure everything is exactly as I want it. That's the only way they can tell the difference between class and plain ordinary. When I travel I go first class."

"Yes,…but how do you feel about you as a person—as a fellow human being?"

"Who cares?" he laughed. "If they were on top they would do the same to me. The more you walk on them, the more they like it. It's like royalty in the old days. It makes them nervous if everyone is equal to everyone else. Watch. When we leave I'll put my arm around that waitress, ask her if she still loves me, pat her on the fanny, and she'll be ready to roll over any time I wiggle my little finger." (McNeil, 1967, p. 85)

Another incident occurred when a friend of Dan's committed suicide. Most of the other friends whom Dan and McNeil had in common were concerned and called McNeil to see whether he could provide any information about why the man had taken his life. Dan did not. Later, when McNeil mentioned the suicide to Dan, all he could say was, "That's the way the ball bounces." In his public behavior, however, Dan's attitude toward the incident appeared quite different. He was the one who collected money and presented it personally to the widow. In keeping with his character, however, Dan remarked that the widow had a sexy body that really interested him.

These two incidents convey the flavor of Dan's behavior. McNeil had witnessed a long succession of similar events, which led him to conclude:

[the incidents] painted a grisly picture of lifelong abuse of people for Dan's amusement and profit. He was adept at office politics and told me casually of an unbelievable set of deceptive ways to deal with the opposition. Character assassination, rumor mongering, modest blackmail, seduction, and barefaced lying were the least of his talents. He was a jackal in the entertainment jungle, a jackal who feasted on the bodies of those he had slaughtered professionally. (p. 91)

In his conversations with Dan, McNeil was also able to inquire into Dan's life history. One early and potentially important event was related by Dan.

I can remember the first time in my life when I began to suspect I was a little different from most people. When I was in high school my best friend got leukemia and died and I went to his funeral. Everybody else was crying and feeling sorry for themselves and as they were praying to get him into heaven I suddenly realized that I wasn't feeling anything at all. He was a nice guy but what the hell. That night I thought about it some more and found that I wouldn't miss my mother and father if they died and that I wasn't too nuts about my brothers and sisters for that matter. I figured there wasn't anybody I really cared for but, then, I didn't need any of them anyway so I rolled over and went to sleep. (p. 87)

(Copyright © 1967. Adapted by permission of Prentice-Hall.)

The moral depravity described long ago by Pinel and Prichard clearly marks Dan's behavior. A person may be otherwise quite rational and show no loss of contact with reality and yet behave in a habitually and exceedingly unethical manner. The final excerpt illustrated Dan's complete lack of feeling for others, a characteristic that will later be shown to have considerable relevance in explaining the behavior of the psychopath.

RESEARCH AND THEORY ON THE ETIOLOGY OF PSYCHOPATHY

We now turn to research and theory on the etiology of psychopathy. We will examine genetics as well as the psychological factors that operate in the family and in emotions. A final section on response modulation and impulsivity ties together several of the individual research domains. We note again that most research has been conducted on psychopaths who have already been convicted as criminals. Thus the available literature may not allow generalization to the behavior of psychopaths who elude arrest.

GENETIC CORRELATES OF PSYCHOPATHIC BEHAVIOR
Research suggests that both criminality and antisocial personality disorder have heritable components, but behavior genetic research has not been conducted on the concept of psychopathy developed by Cleckley and Hare. Twin studies, including those of twins reared apart, and adoption research indicate that genetic factors play a significant role in the likelihood that a person will commit a criminal act (Gottesman & Goldsmith, 1994; Grove et al., 1990; Mednick, Gabrielli, & Hutchings, 1984). For antisocial personality disorder, twin studies show higher concordance for MZ than for DZ pairs (Lyons et al., 1995); adoption studies reveal higher than normal prevalence of antisocial behavior in adopted children of biological parents with antisocial personality disorder (Cadoret et al., 1995).

Both twin and adoption studies also show that the *environment* plays a substantial role in antisocial personality disorder. For example, in Cadoret et al.'s adoption study, an adverse environment in the adoptive home (such as marital problems and substance abuse) was related to the development of antisocial personality disorder, irrespective of whether the adoptive parents had antisocial personality disorder. Furthermore, high levels of conflict and negativity and low levels of parental warmth predicted antisocial behavior in a twin study by Reiss et al. (1995).

THE ROLE OF THE FAMILY
Since much psychopathic behavior violates social norms, it is not surprising that many investigators have focused on the primary agent of socialization, the family, in their search for the explanation of such behavior. McCord and McCord (1964) concluded, on the basis of a classic review of the literature, that lack of affection and severe parental rejection were the primary causes of psychopathic behavior. Several other studies have related psychopathic behavior to parents' inconsistencies in disciplining their children and in teaching them responsibility toward others (Bennett, 1960). Furthermore, the fathers of psychopaths are likely to be antisocial in their behavior.

Such data on early rearing must be interpreted cautiously as they were gathered by means of retrospective reports—individual recollections of past events. We have seen (see p. 182) that information obtained in this way cannot be accepted uncritically. When people are asked to recollect early events in the life of someone now known to be psychopathic, their knowledge of the person's adult status

may well affect what they remember or report about childhood events. They may be more likely to recall deviant incidents, whereas more typical or normal events that do not fit with the person's current behavior may be overlooked. Moreover, the retrospective reports of psychopaths themselves are to be considered unreliable.

The problems of retrospective data can be avoided by conducting a follow-up study in adulthood of individuals who as children were seen at child-guidance clinics. In one such study detailed records had been kept on the children, including the type of problem that had brought them to the clinic and considerable information relating to the family (Robins, 1966). Ninety percent of an initial sample of 584 cases were located thirty years after their referral to the clinic.[2] In addition, 100 control subjects who had lived in the same geographic area served by the clinic but who had not been referred to it were also interviewed in adulthood.

By interviewing the now-adult subjects in the two samples, the investigators were able to diagnose and describe any maladjustments of these individuals. They then related the adult problems to the characteristics that these people had had as children to find out which of them predicted psychopathic behavior in adulthood. Robins's summary brings to mind the category of conduct disorder, which is introduced in the discussion of antisocial behavior in juveniles in Chapter 15:

> If one wishes to choose the most likely candidate for a later diagnosis of [psychopathy] from among children appearing in a child guidance clinic, the best choice appears to be a boy referred for theft or aggression who has shown a diversity of antisocial behavior in many episodes, at least one of which could be grounds for Juvenile Court appearance, and whose antisocial behavior involves him with strangers and organizations as well as with teachers and parents. ... More than half of the boys appearing at the clinic [with these characteristics were later] diagnosed sociopathic personality. Such boys had a history of truancy, theft, staying out late, and refusing to obey parents. They lied gratuitously, and showed little guilt over their behavior. They were generally irresponsible about being where they were supposed to be or taking care of money. (p. 157)

In addition to these characteristics several aspects of family life were again found to be consequential; both inconsistent discipline and no discipline at all predicted psychopathic behavior in adulthood, as did antisocial behavior of the father.

---

[2]It should be appreciated that tracking down this large a percentage of individuals thirty years after their contact with the clinic is an incredible feat.

However, many individuals who come from what appear to be similarly disturbed social backgrounds do not become psychopaths or develop any other behavior disorders. This point is important; adults may have no problems whatsoever in spite of the inconsistent and otherwise undesirable manner of their upbringing. Thus although family experience is probably a significant factor in the development of psychopathic behavior, it is not the sole factor.

EMOTION AND PSYCHOPATHY In defining the psychopathic syndrome Cleckley pointed out the inability of such persons to profit from experience or even from punishment; they seem to be unable to avoid the negative consequences of social misbehavior. Many are chronic lawbreakers despite their experiences with jail sentences. They seem immune to the anxiety or pangs of conscience that help keep most of us from breaking the law or lying to or injuring others, and they have difficulty curbing their impulses.

From these clinical observations Lykken (1957) deduced that psychopaths may have few inhibitions about committing antisocial acts because they experience so little anxiety. He performed several tests to determine whether psychopaths do indeed have low levels of anxiety. One of these tests involved avoidance learning.

In this study a group of male psychopaths, defined according to Cleckley's criteria, were selected from a penitentiary population. Their performance on an avoidance-learning task was compared with that of nonpsychopathic penitentiary inmates and college students. It is critical in such a case to test only avoidance and not learning mediated by other possible rewards. For example, if a person perceives that the task is to learn to avoid pain, he or she may be motivated not only by the desire to avoid the pain but also by a desire to demonstrate his or her cleverness to the investigator. To ensure that no other motives would come into play, Lykken made the avoidance-learning task seem *incidental*, an apparently secondary aspect of the test. He used the following apparatus. On a panel in front of the subject there were four red lights in a horizontal array, four green lights below the red ones, and a lever below each column, as illustrated in Figure 13.1. The participant's task was to learn a sequence of twenty correct lever presses; for each sequence he first had to determine by trial and error which of the four alternatives was correct. The correct lever turned on a green light. Two of the remaining three incorrect levers turned on red lights, indicating an error. The third incorrect lever delivered an electric shock. The location of the correct lever was not always the same. The participants

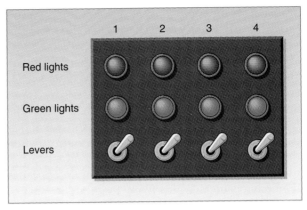

Figure 13.1 Lykken (1957) devised this apparatus for his study of avoidance learning in psychopaths. For the first lever press assume that lever 3 is correct, that is, that pressing it lights the green bulb; that levers 1 and 4 are incorrect, lighting red bulbs; and that pressing lever 2 lights a red bulb and gives the participant a shock. For the second lever press the meaning of the levers may change entirely; for example, lever 2 may be correct, levers 3 and 4 incorrect, and lever 1 may give the shock. The participants had to learn a sequence of twenty correct lever presses.

were told to figure out and to learn the series of twenty correct lever presses. They were not informed that avoiding shock was desirable or possible, only that shock was randomly administered as a stimulant to make them do well.

In overall number of errors made in learning the sequence there were no significant differences among the groups in Lykken's study. The college students, however, made fewer errors that resulted in shock. The psychopaths made the most shocked errors. From these results Lykken concluded that because the psychopaths did not avoid the shocks as often, they operate under lower levels of anxiety than do normal individuals.

Studies of the activity of the autonomic nervous system are also consistent with the idea that psychopaths respond less anxiously to fear-eliciting stimuli. In resting situations psychopaths have lower-than-normal levels of skin conductance, and their skin conductance is less reactive when they are confronted with intense or aversive stimuli or when they anticipate an aversive stimulus (Harpur & Hare, 1990). A different picture emerges, however, when heart rate is examined. The heart rate of psychopaths is normal under resting conditions and remains normal when neutral stimuli are presented. But in situations in which psychopaths anticipate a stressful stimulus, their hearts beat faster than those of normal people anticipating stress.

These physiological reactions indicate that the psychopath cannot be regarded as simply underaroused, for measurements of skin conductance and heart rate are inconsistent. Basing his theorizing in part on Lacey's work (1967), Hare (1978) focused on the *pattern* of psychophysiological responses of psychopaths. Faster heartbeats are viewed as a concomitant of gating out or reducing sensory input and thus lowering cortical arousal. Thus the increased heart rate of psychopaths who are anticipating an aversive stimulus would indicate that they are tuning it out. Their skin conductance is then less reactive to an aversive stimulus because they have been able effectively to ignore it. That is, with skin conductance considered an index of anxiety, that of psychopaths does not increase to any extent after expected aversive stimulation because they have already dealt with it by screening it out. This interpretation of the physiological reactions of psychopaths is plausible and consistent with Lykken's study on avoidance learning; it has also been directly confirmed in subsequent research (Ogloff & Wong, 1990). Further research by Hare and his associates has confirmed that in both their behavior and their biological response (Jutai & Hare, 1983) psychopaths are particularly adept at ignoring stimuli and focusing their attention on what interests them (Forth & Hare, 1989).

Research using other methods of assessing emotion has also confirmed Lykken's original result. One of these methods involves the measurement of the eye-blink component of the startle response, currently considered the best nonverbal indicator of whether a person is in a positive or negative emotional state. Participants are shown a series of slides of varying content—some positive (e.g., opposite-sex nudes), some negative (e.g., burn victims), and some neutral. While watching the slides they sometimes hear a blast of loud noise, which elicits a startle response. The magnitude of the startle response varies depending on the emotional state a subject is in when the noise occurs. A negative emotional state causes the startle reflex to increase, whereas a positive emotional state causes it to decrease.

A startle-response study was conducted on four groups of penitentiary inmates selected using the Hare checklist: nonpsychopaths (low on both antisocial behavior and emotional detachment), detached offenders (high only on emotional detachment), antisocial offenders (high only on antisocial behavior), and psychopaths (high on both components). Participants were first exposed to a baseline condition in which a simple visual cue was presented, sometimes with a blast of loud noise. Next they experienced a situation in which they again saw the visual cue and were told that when it disappeared the loud noise would occur.

During the second phase of the study marked differences emerged among the groups in the magnitude of their startle responses. Both the psychopaths and the detached offenders showed much smaller increases in their startle responses, indicating that less fear had been aroused. The pattern of results is important because it suggests that it is the emotional deficits of psychopaths, not their antisocial behavior, that is linked to emotional detachment (Patrick, 1994).

RESPONSE MODULATION AND PSYCHOPATHY An important addition to our current thinking about the causes of psychopathy might be the inclusion of something that would stimulate or push for antisocial behavior. Similarities between aspects of psychopathy and the behavior of animals who have had parts of their brains destroyed in a neural system including the septum, hippocampus, and prefrontal cortex, have led some researchers to propose that a key element of psychopathy is heightened impulsivity and the inability to sustain goal-directed activity (Gorenstein & Newman, 1980). For example, these lesioned animals show deficits in avoidance learning as well as impulsive responding to immediate rewards. The idea that a key feature of psychopathy is impulsivity is also supported by studies of their brain waves, which reveal slow waves and spikes in the temporal area. These are often linked to impulsivity (Syndulko, 1978).

This impulsivity shows up when psychopaths are presented with a task designed to test their ability to modify their responses depending on success or failure (Patterson & Newman, 1993). In one study demonstrating this phenomenon participants viewed playing cards on a computer-generated video display (Newman, Kosson, & Patterson, 1987). If a face card appeared the participant won five cents; if a nonface card appeared he lost five cents. After each trial the participant had the opportunity to continue or end the game. The probability of losing was controlled by the experimenter and started at 10 percent. Thereafter the probability of losing increased by 10 percent for every ten cards played until it reached 100 percent. Psychopaths continued to play the game much longer than nonpsychopaths. Nine of twelve psychopaths never quit even though they had lost money on nineteen of the last twenty trials. They were unable to alter their maladaptive responses.

The same game was played again with one procedural variation—a five-second waiting period was imposed after feedback, thus delaying the decision about whether to play again. This manipulation dramatically reduced the number of trials for which psychopaths played the game. Enforcing a delay may therefore force psychopaths to reflect on the feedback they have received and thus behave less impulsively.

It may be that the cognitive representations of events that are not immediately present in the environment are weak in psychopaths (Gorenstein, 1991). Thus behavior often is not directed toward long-term goals but instead is governed to an inordinate extent by stimuli that are immediately present.

The studies we have reviewed show that psychopaths do not react as most of us do. In particular, they have almost no anxiety, so it can have little deterrent effect. Because psychopaths are in greater control of their negative emotional reactions, they actually seek arousal; and because psychopaths are deficient in planning and in inhibition, they behave impulsively. These are possible reasons for the psychopath's misconduct without regret and thrill seeking without regard for society's rules.

ANXIOUS/FEARFUL CLUSTER

This cluster comprises three personality disorders. Avoidant personality disorder applies to people who are fearful in social situations; dependent personality disorder refers to those who lack self-reliance and are overly dependent on others; and obsessive-compulsive personality disorder applies to those who have a perfectionistic approach to life.

AVOIDANT PERSONALITY DISORDER

The diagnosis of **avoidant personality** disorder applies to people who are keenly sensitive to the possibility of criticism, rejection, or disapproval and are therefore reluctant to enter into relationships unless they are sure they will be liked. If others express liking for them, avoidant personalities are apt to doubt their sincerity. In social situations they are restrained because of an extreme fear of saying something foolish or of being embarrassed by blushing or other signs of anxiety. They believe they are incompetent and inferior to others and typically exaggerate the risks, dangers, or difficulties in doing something outside their usual routine.

The prevalence of avoidant personality disorder is about 1 percent (Weissman, 1993), and it is comorbid with dependent personality disorder (Trull, Widiger, & Frances, 1987) and borderline personality disorder (Morey, 1988). The diagnostic criteria are also strik-

ingly similar to those of generalized social phobia, which accounts for the high comorbidity between these two conditions (Hoffmann et al., 1995).

DEPENDENT PERSONALITY DISORDER

Patients with the **dependent personality** disorder lacks self-confidence and self-reliance. These individuals passively allow their spouses or partners to assume responsibility for deciding where they should live, what jobs they should hold, with whom they should be friendly. Because they fear losing approval, they agree with others even when they know the others are wrong, and they have difficulty initiating any activities or making decisions on their own. Their intense need to be taken care of often leads them to feel uncomfortable when alone, and they may be preoccupied with fears of being left alone to take care of themselves. They are unable to make demands on others, and they subordinate their own needs to ensure that they do not break up the protective relationships they have established. When a close relationship ends, they urgently seek another relationship to replace the old one.

The prevalence of dependent personality disorder is a little over 1.5 percent, and it occurs more frequently among women than among men, perhaps

Children normally go through a phase in which separation from a parent is distressing. People with dependent personality disorder may be experiencing a similiar phenomenon in their adult relationships.

FOCUS 13.1 A DIMENSIONAL APPROACH TO PERSONALITY DISORDERS

Earlier in this chapter we noted that a dimensional approach to diagnosis seems to provide a better fit for the personality disorders. Now that we have described the discrete entity system in current use, it is time to return to this issue.

The most promising dimensional approach to personality disorders considers that they represent extremes of personality traits that are found in everyone. Although literally hundreds of traits could be considered, contemporary research in personality focuses on a model of personality called the Five Factor Model (McCrae & Costa, 1990). The five factors, or major dimensions, of personality are neuroticism, extraversion/introversion, openness to experience, agreeableness/antagonism, and conscientiousness. Table 13.2 presents questionnaire items that assess each of these dimensions. By reading the table carefully you can acquire a sense of what each dimension refers to.

Widiger and Costa (1994) have summarized the results of several studies linking these personality traits to schizoid, borderline, and avoidant personality disorders. Both patients with schizoid and those with avoidant personality disorder are high in introversion. Thus the Five Factor Model would predict that these two disorders would be hard to differentiate, and this has indeed been found to be true. There is some differentiation between the two disorders, however, on the neuroticism dimension; patients with avoidant personality disorder are higher than those with schizoid personality disorder. Rather than forcing each patient into a discrete category and encountering problems in distinguishing between these two disorders, the dimensional approach would simply describe patients on their levels of neuroticism and introversion.

Borderline personality disorder is most strongly related to neuroticism and antagonism. Because high scores on neuroticism are found in many personality disorders and Axis I disorders as well, it is not surprising that borderline personality is comorbid with numerous personality disorders and Axis I conditions. Borderline patients also score high on antagonism, which allows them to be discriminated from patients with avoidant personality disorder. High scores on antagonism are also found in patients with paranoid and antisocial disorders, so comorbidity with these disorders would be expected. Again, the dimensional approach doesn't force patients into discrete categories but simply describes their scores on the five factors.

A dimensional model thus appears to have several distinct advantages. First and foremost, it handles the comorbidity problem, because comorbidity is a difficulty only in a categorical classification system. The dimensional system also forges a link between normal and abnormal personality so that the findings on personality development in general become relevant to the personality disorders. For example, most of the traits of the Five Factor Model have been studied by behavior genetic researchers and found to be heritable (Bouchard et al., 1990). Genetic factors, therefore, become plausible as variables related to the causes of personality disorders. Similarly, because there are sex differences in scores on the five factors, the model becomes relevant to sex differences in the prevalence of the personality disorders. For example, women score higher than men on neuroticism, agreeableness, and extraversion (Costa & McRae, 1988). Thus it would be expected that women would also be more likely than men to experience histrionic personality disorder (high scores on extraversion and neuroticism), dependent personality disorder (high scores on agreeableness and neuroticism), and borderline personality disorder (high scores on neuroticism). Conversely, antisocial personality disorder (low scores on agreeableness) should be more frequent in men. Data confirm these expectations.

---

because of different childhood socialization experiences of men and women (Corbitt & Widiger, 1995; Weissman, 1993). The causes of the disorder may also differ in men and in women. Reich (1990) found that relatives of men with dependent personality disorder showed a high rate of depression, whereas relatives of women with the disorder had a high rate of panic disorder. Dependent personality disorder co-occurs frequently with borderline and avoidant personality disorders (Morey, 1988) and is linked to several Axis I diagnoses as well as poor physical health.

OBSESSIVE-COMPULSIVE PERSONALITY DISORDER

The **obsessive-compulsive personality** is a perfectionist, preoccupied with details, rules, schedules, and the like. These people often pay so much attention to detail that they never finish projects. They are work rather than pleasure oriented and have inordinate difficulty making decisions (lest they err) and allocating time (lest they focus on the wrong thing). Their interpersonal relationships are often poor because they are stubborn and demand that everything be done their way. They are generally serious, rigid, formal, and inflexible, especially regarding moral issues. They are unable to discard worn-out and useless objects, even those with no sentimental value, and are likely to be miserly and stingy. This dysfunctional attention to work and productivity is found more often in men than in women.

Obsessive-compulsive personality disorder is quite different from obsessive-compulsive disorder;

TABLE 13.2 Sample Items from the Revised NEO Personality Inventory Assessing the Five Factor Model

Neuroticism	I am not a worrier (−)
	I am not easily frightened (−)
	I rarely feel fearful or anxious (−)
	I often feel tense or jittery (+)
Extraversion/introversion	I really like most people I meet (+)
	I don't get much pleasure from chatting with people (−)
	I'm known as a warm and friendly person (+)
	Many people think of me as somewhat cold and distant (−)
Openness to experience	I have a very active imagination (+)
	I try to keep my thoughts directed along realistic lines and avoid flights of fancy (−)
	I have an active fantasy life (+)
	I don't like to waste my time daydreaming (−)
Agreeableness/antagonism	I tend to be cynical and skeptical of other's intentions (−)
	I believe that other people are well intentioned (+)
	I believe that most people will take advantage of you if you let them (−)
	I think most people I deal with are honest and trustworthy (+)
Conscientiousness	I am known for my prudence and common sense (+)
	I don't take civic duties like voting very seriously (−)
	I keep myself informed and usually make intelligent decisions (+)
	I often come into situations without being prepared (−)

Source: Costa & McCrae, 1992.

Note: Agreeing with an item marked with a + increases your score on that factor; agreeing with an item marked − decreases it.

The Five Factor Model is not the only system for describing personality; other models are currently under consideration. However, the trend in all this research is clear—personality disorders are better described dimensionally than categorically.

People with obsessive-compulsive personality disorder are often workaholics. Their excessive work may be a defense against a fear of losing control.

it does not include the obsessions and compulsions that define the latter. Although the use of the two similar terms suggests that the two disorders are related, it is not clear that they are; obsessive-compulsive personality disorder is found in only a minority of OCD cases (Baer & Jenike, 1992). Obsessive-compulsive personality disorder is most highly comorbid with avoidant personality disorder and has a prevalence of about 1 percent (Lassano, del Bueno, & Latapano, 1993).

ETIOLOGY OF THE ANXIOUS/FEARFUL CLUSTER

Few data exist on the causes of the personality disorders in this cluster. Speculation as to their causes has focused on parent–child relationships.

The DSM-IV diagnosis of dependent personality disorder contains two types of symptoms: those describing dependent behavior and those describing what can be referred to as attachment problems (Livesley, Schroeder, & Jackson, 1990). Attachment has been studied by developmental psychologists and is regarded as important for personality development. The basic idea is that the young infant becomes attached to an adult and uses the adult as a secure base from which to explore and pursue other goals. Separation from the adult leads to anger and distress. As development proceeds, the child becomes less dependent on the attachment figure for security. It is possible that the abnormal attachment behaviors seen in dependent personalities reflect a failure in the usual developmental process arising from a disruption in the early parent–child relationship caused by death, neglect, rejection, or overprotectiveness. Persons with dependent personality disorder engage in a number of tactics, originally established to maintain their relationship with their parents, to keep their relationships with other people at any cost, for example, always agreeing with them (Stone, 1993).

Much like the fears and phobias discussed in Chapter 6, avoidant personality disorder may reflect the influence of an environment in which the child is taught to fear people and situations that most of us regard as harmless. For example, one of the child's parents may have similar fears, which are transmitted by modeling.

Obsessive-compulsive personality traits were originally viewed by Freud as caused by fixation at the anal stage of psychosexual development. More contemporary psychodynamic theories emphasize a fear of loss of control, which is handled by overcompensation. For example, the man who is a compulsive workaholic may fear that his life will fall apart if he allows himself to relax and have fun.[3]

THERAPIES FOR PERSONALITY DISORDERS

There is not much research-based information on treating personality disorders. There is, though, a lively and burgeoning clinical case literature on therapies for many of these disorders. Though the ideas outlined here are for the most part based solely on the clinical experiences of a small number of mental health professionals and not on studies that contain suitable controls, these therapeutic guidelines are almost all that is available on treating personality disorders. It is important to bear in mind that a therapist working with such patients is typically also concerned with Axis I disorders—most patients with personality disorders enter treatment because of an Axis I disorder rather than a personality disorder. For example, a person with antisocial personality is likely to have substance-abuse problems; a person with avoidant personality disorder may seek treatment for a social phobia; and an obsessive-compulsive personality may be seen for depression.

Psychoactive drugs are often used to treat the various personality disorders; the choice is determined by the Axis I problem that the personality disorder resembles. For example, patients with avoidant personality disorder can be prescribed minor tranquilizers such as the benzodiazepine Xanax in hopes of reducing their social anxieties and phobias. When depression is present in an Axis II disorder, antidepressant medication, such as fluoxetine (Prozac) can be helpful.

Psychodynamic therapists aim to correct the childhood problems assumed to underlie a personality disorder. For example, they may guide a compulsive personality to the realization that the childhood quest to win the love of his or her parents by being perfect need not be carried into adulthood—that he or she does not need to be perfect to win the approval of others, that it is possible to take risks and make mistakes without being abandoned by those whose love and caring is sought.

Behavior and cognitive therapists, in keeping with their attention to situations rather than to traits, have had little to say until recently about specific treatments for the personality disorders designated by the DSM (Howes & Vallis, 1996). These therapists analyze the individual problems that taken together reflect a personality disorder. For example, a person diagnosed as having a paranoid or an avoidant personality is extremely sensitive to criticism. This sensitivity may be treated by systematic desensitization or rational-emotive therapy (see Chapter 2, p. 47). The paranoid personality's argumentativeness and hostility when disagreeing with other people pushes others away and provokes counterattacks from them. The behavior therapist may help the paranoid individual learn more adaptive ways of disagreeing with other people. Social-skills training in a support group might be suggested to encourage avoidant personalities to be more

---

[3]DSM-IIIR proposed diagnostic criteria for two additional personality disorders that were not formal diagnoses but "categories in need of further study." The most controversial of these was self-defeating personality disorder; the other proposed personality disorder was sadistic personality disorder, These two diagnoses were dropped entirely from DSM-IV. Passive-aggressive personality disorder, which was previously a formal diagnosis, was demoted in DSM-IV to a category in need of further study.

assertive with other people. Such an approach, perhaps combined with rational-emotive therapy, may help them cope when efforts to reach out do not succeed, as is bound to happen at times (Millon, 1996; Turkat & Maisto, 1985).

In looking at cognitive therapy for personality disorders, Beck and his associates (1990) apply the same kind of analysis as that found promising in the treatment of depression (cf. Chapter 10, p. 243, and Chapter 18, p. 530). Each disorder is analyzed in terms of logical errors and dysfunctional schemata. For example, cognitive therapy with an obsessive-compulsive personality entails first persuading the patient to accept the essence of the cognitive model, that feelings and behaviors are primarily a function of thoughts. Errors in logic are then explored, such as when the patient concludes that he or she cannot do anything right because of failing in one particular endeavor (an example of overgeneralization). The therapist also looks for dysfunctional assumptions or schemata that might underlie the person's thoughts and feelings, for example, the belief that it is critical for every decision to be correct (adherents of Ellis's methods would also take this step). A review of the clinical details makes it clear that Beck's approach to personality disorders represents a combination of a variety of behavioral and cognitive-behavioral techniques, all designed to address the particular, longstanding, and pervasive difficulties presented by patients. Beck's approach to borderline personality disorder and antisocial personality disorder is described in the sections that follow.

THERAPY FOR THE BORDERLINE PERSONALITY

Whatever the intervention modality, one thing is certain: few patients pose a greater challenge to treatment than a borderline personality. The problems that borderline personalities have with other people are replicated in the consulting room. For the borderline patient, trust is inordinately difficult to create and sustain, thus handicapping the therapeutic relationship. The patient alternately idealizes and vilifies the therapist, demanding special attention and consideration one moment—such as therapy sessions at odd hours—and refusing to keep appointments the next; imploring for understanding and support but insisting that certain topics are off-limits. Suicide is always a serious risk, but it is often difficult for the therapist to judge whether a frantic phone call at 2:00 A.M. is a call for help or a manipulative gesture designed to see how special the patient is to the therapist and to what lengths the therapist will go to meet the patient's needs at

the moment. As happened in the case presented at the beginning of this chapter, hospitalization is often necessary when the behavior of the patient becomes unmanageable on an outpatient basis or when the threat of suicide cannot be managed without the greater supervision possible only in the controlled setting of a mental hospital. Seeing such patients is so stressful that it is common practice for therapists to have regular consultations with another therapist, sometimes for support and advice, sometimes for professional help in dealing with their own emotions as they try to cope with the extraordinary challenges of helping borderline patients. (In psychoanalytic terms, these feelings of the therapist are called countertransference, discussed on p. 498.) In her own cognitive-behavioral approach to therapy with borderlines (discussed later), Linehan makes this kind of ongoing consultation an integral part of the treatment.

A number of drugs have been tried in the pharmacotherapy of borderline personality disorder, most notably antidepressants and antipsychotic medications. There is little to recommend antidepressants, but antipsychotics show some modest effects on borderline patients' anxiety, suicidality, and psychotic symptoms (Gitlin, 1993). Because such patients often abuse drugs and are suicide risks, extreme caution must be used in any drug therapy regimen (Waldenger & Frank, 1989).

OBJECT RELATIONS PSYCHOTHERAPY

The two leading, contemporary object relations theorists, Heinz Kohut, whose views on narcissism were discussed earlier, and Otto Kernberg, who has written extensively about the borderline personality, have developed a therapeutic strategy for borderline patients. As noted earlier (p. 339), Kernberg (1985) operates from the basic assumption that borderline personalities have weak egos and therefore inordinate difficulty tolerating the probing of childhood conflicts that occurs in psychoanalytic treatment. The weak ego fears being flooded by primitive primary-process thinking. Kernberg's modified analytic treatment has the overall goal of strengthening the patient's weak ego so that he or she does not fall prey to splitting, or dichotomizing, into all good or all bad rather than accepting that people and events have both positive and negative qualities. Splitting is regarded as resulting from an inability to form complex ideas (object representations) that do not fit a simple good–bad dichotomy. For example, the patient may see the therapist as a godlike genius only to be crushed and furious when the therapist later mentions that the patient is behind in therapy payments. The techniques

Otto Kernberg, one of the leading object relations therapists, has been very influential in the study of borderline personality disorder.

employed are basically interpretive, that is, the therapist points out how the patient is allowing his or her emotions and behavior to be regulated by such defenses as splitting.

The borderline patient must also be helped to test reality (it is not clear in what way this step differs from the overall psychoanalytic goal of helping patients discriminate between irrational childhood-based fears and adult reality). Kernberg's approach is more directive than that of most analysts; in addition to interpreting defensive behavior, he gives the patient concrete suggestions for behaving more adaptively and he will hospitalize a patient whose behavior becomes dangerous to the self or others. Kernberg's opinion that such patients are inappropriate for classical psychoanalysis because of their weak egos is consistent with a long-term study conducted at the world-famous analytically oriented Menninger Clinic (Stone, 1987).

DIALECTICAL BEHAVIOR THERAPY

An approach that combines client-centered empathy with cognitive-behavioral problem solving and social-skills training was introduced by Marsha Linehan (1987). What she calls **dialectical behavior therapy** (DBT) centers on the therapist's full acceptance of borderline personalities with all their contradictions and acting out, empathically validating their (distorted) beliefs with a matter-of-fact attitude toward their suicidal and other dysfunctional behavior. The cognitive-behavioral aspect of the treatment, conducted both individually and in groups, involves helping patients learn to solve problems, to acquire more effective and socially acceptable ways of handling their daily living problems and controlling their emotions. Work is also done on improving their interpersonal skills and controlling their anger and anxieties. After many months of intensive treatment, limits are set on their behavior, consistent with what Kernberg advocates.

Linehan and her associates have published the results of the first randomized, controlled study of a psychological intervention for borderline personality disorder (Linehan et al., 1991). Patients were randomly assigned either to dialectical behavior therapy or to treatment as usual, meaning any therapy available in the community (Seattle, Washington). At the end of one year of treatment and again six and twelve months later patients in the two groups were compared on a variety of measures (Linehan, Heard, & Armstrong, 1992). The findings immediately after treatment revealed highly significant superiority of DBT on the following measures: intentional self-injurious behavior, including sui-

Marsha Linehan created dialectical behavior therapy, which combines cognitive behavior therapy with Zen and Rogerian notions of acceptance.

FOCUS 13.2 ACCEPTANCE IN DIALECTICAL BEHAVIOR THERAPY

Marsha Linehan's (1987, 1993a, 1993b) notion of acceptance within the framework of her dialectical behavior therapy is subtle, hence some elaboration is warranted. In a Zenlike way, Linehan argues that a therapist working with a borderline personality has to adopt what to the Western mind is an inconsistent posture. The therapist must be clear with the patient about limits and work for change while at the same time accepting the person as client-centered therapists would, which means accepting the real possibility that no changes are going to occur. Linehan's reasoning is that the borderline personality is so exquisitely sensitive to rejection and criticism as well as so emotionally unstable that even gentle encouragement to behave or think differently can lead to high levels of emotional arousal and subsequent misinterpretation of suggestions as a serious rebuke. The therapist who a moment earlier was revered is now vilified and spurned. Thus, while observing limits—"I would be very sad if you killed yourself so I hope very much that you won't"—the therapist must convey to the borderline patient that he or she is fully accepted even while threatening suicide and making everyone else's life, including the therapist's, miserable! (Recall Kellerman's vivid description of this syndrome, p. 339.)

This complete acceptance of the patient does not mean that the therapist *approves* of everything the patient is doing, only that the therapist accepts the situation for what it is. Indeed, argues Linehan, the therapist must truly accept the patient as he or she is; acceptance should not be in the service of change, an indirect way of encouraging the patient to behave differently. Linehan's concept of acceptance is not a means to an end. "Acceptance can transform but if you accept in order to transform, it is not acceptance. It is like loving. Love seeks no reward but when given freely comes back a hundredfold. He who loses his life finds it. He who accepts, changes" (M. M. Linehan, personal communication, November 16, 1992). For a more instrumental view of acceptance as a way of encouraging change see p. 570.

Full and thoroughgoing acceptance does not, in Linehan's view, preclude change. She proposes that it is the refusal to accept that prevents change. She puts it this way when talking to her patients:

If you hate the color purple, move into a house that is painted purple, and then refuse to rush out and buy paint to repaint it. The person who immediately accepts that the house is painted purple—without excess ado or distortion or denial or outrage at the fact of the color or one's own preferences—will probably get it repainted the quickest. (personal communication, September 18, 1992)

cide attempts; dropping out of treatment; and inpatient hospital days. At the follow-ups superiority was maintained, and, additionally, DBT patients had better work histories, reported less anger, and were judged as overall better adjusted than the comparison therapy patients. As a result of this study and a book and manual on dialectical behavior therapy (Linehan, 1993a, 1993b), there is widespread interest in this approach to borderline personality disorder (Focus 13.2).

DYNAMIC-COGNITIVE-BEHAVIOR THERAPY

Turner's dynamic-cognitive-behavior therapy is directed primarily at the impulsivity and anger components of borderline personality (Turner, 1993, 1994). Turner blends cognitive and interpretative procedures to make clear to patients how they are resisting the therapist's attempts to help them change. The therapist tries to teach the patient better ways to handle stress, solve life's inevitable problems, and establish less stormy and more rewarding interpersonal relationships. Initial research evaluations confirm that this approach has a positive impact on patients with borderline personality.

COGNITIVE THERAPY

Cognitive approaches also emphasize the difficulties in establishing trust with borderline personalities; their tendency to test the reliability of the therapist with threats and other demands; their low tolerance for intimacy and yet exquisite sensitivity to rejection; and the presence in each session of constantly emergent crises that make it hard to focus on a limited number of themes and goals. Beck and his colleagues (1990) even borrowed a basic tenet of object relations, cautioning about *transference reactions* by the borderline patient. An example provided by Beck is a patient who was convinced that people in authority were manipulative and controlling, a residue of her past dealings with her parents. Suggestions for specific behavioral changes from the therapist were met with anger and resistance because these efforts reminded the patient of sensitizing experiences from childhood. The therapist dealt with these transference reactions by taking care again and again to point out clearly and patiently what the reasons for the various suggestions were and what they were not.

Beck and his associates theorize that borderline personalities operate with one or more of the following three negative schemata: (1) the world is dangerous and malevolent; (2) they themselves are vulnerable and powerless; and (3) they are unacceptable to others. The very specific and goal-oriented nature of Beck's cognitive therapy makes it a challenge to adapt it to the tumultuous, conflicted, and confusing picture commonly found in borderline patients. A general guideline is for the therapist to be more flexible than he or she would be with other kinds of patients, adapting techniques and foci to the idiosyncrasies of the patient. For example, in collecting information about negative thoughts (cf. p. 233) the therapist is advised to solicit the patient's suggestions for doing so rather than to use a standard thought-listing procedure commonly found in the clinical and research literature on cognitive therapy. The kind of directiveness and certainty that can be reassuring to a depressed patient by imposing such structure can be threatening and anger-provoking to a borderline patient, who is likely to see the therapist as rejecting and overly critical.

The splitting, or dichotomous thinking, referred to earlier is a familiar therapeutic target for the cognitive therapist. The general strategy is to show (gently) the borderline patient that he or she is, in fact, thinking in a dichotomous fashion and then to persuade the patient that it would be in his or her best interest to experiment with looking at the world in terms of shades of gray rather than black and white. As thinking becomes less dichotomous, the rapid and extreme emotional fluctuations typical of borderline personalities also tend to moderate. The explanation of exactly how this cognitive change is effected is exceedingly subtle and difficult and beyond the scope of this book; suffice it to say that such cognitive shifts are not achieved easily or quickly. Whereas many depressed patients can be helped by cognitive therapy in fewer than twenty sessions, borderline personalities may need up to two years of weekly sessions.

FROM DISORDER TO STYLE: A COMMENT ON GOALS

The traits that characterize the personality disorders are probably too ingrained to change thoroughly. Instead, the therapist—regardless of theoretical orientation—may find it more realistic to change a disorder into a style, a problem into a general and adaptive but particular way of approaching life (Millon, 1996):

> If all goes well, avoidant personality disorder becomes avoidant personality style: discreet, reserved, sensitive to what others think, comfortable with familiar routines; close to family and a few friends but not gregarious. Dependent personality disorder becomes dependent personality style: polite, agreeable, and thoughtful; respectful of authority and the opinions of others, strongly committed to friends and romantic partners, disliking solitude and preferring teamwork in a subordinate role. Obsessive personality disorder becomes obsessive personality style: thrifty, cautious, orderly, morally principled, proud of doing jobs right, and careful to weigh all alternatives before making decisions. (*Harvard Mental Health Letter*, 1996c, p. 3)

THERAPY FOR PSYCHOPATHY

As for the treatment of psychopathy, there is unusual—and unfortunate—agreement among therapists of varying theoretical persuasions: psychopathy is virtually impossible to treat (Cleckley, 1976; McCord & McCord, 1964; Palmer, 1984).

It may be that people with the classic symptoms listed by Cleckley are by their very natures incapable of benefiting from any form of psychotherapy. In fact, it is unlikely that psychopaths would even *want* to be in therapy! The primary reason for their unsuitability for psychotherapy is that they are unable and unmotivated to form any sort of trusting, honest relationship with a therapist. People who lie almost without knowing it, who care little for the feelings of others and understand their own even less, who appear not to realize that what they are doing is morally wrong, who lack any motivation to obey society's laws and mores, and who, living only for the present, have no concern for the future are, all in all, extremely poor candidates for therapy. One clinician experienced in working with psychopaths has suggested three general principles for therapists working with these patients:

> First, the therapist must be continually vigilant with regard to manipulation on the part of the patient. Second, he must assume, until proven otherwise, that information given him by the patient contains distortions and fabrications. Third, he must recognize that a working alliance develops, if ever, exceedingly late in any therapeutic relationship with a psychopath. (Lion, 1978, p. 286)

Many valiant attempts have been made to establish tenable connections with psychopaths, but both the published literature and informal communications among mental health professionals support the conclusion that true psychopathy cannot be

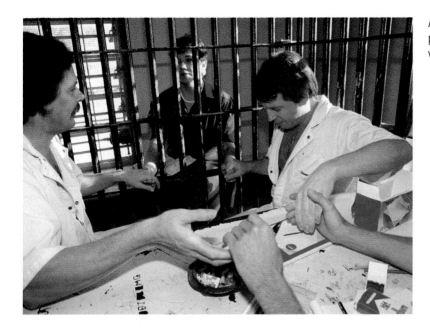

Although therapy is sometimes offered to prison inmates, its results have not been very encouraging.

reached through psychological efforts. Similar negative conclusions may be drawn about somatic methods—electroconvulsive shock; drugs such as Dilantin, stimulants, and sedatives; and psychosurgery. There is, however, some evidence that large doses of antianxiety agents can reduce hostility in psychopaths (Kellner, 1982), and there is some tentative evidence that psychopaths who had attention-deficit disorder (see Chapter 15, p. 409) as children might benefit from the drug Ritalin, which has had some positive effects with hyperactive youngsters (Stringer & Josef, 1983).

Beck and associates (1990) proposed conceptualizing psychopathy in terms of particular kinds of thoughts and assumptions.

[They have] self-serving beliefs that emphasize immediate, personal satisfactions and minimize future consequences. The underlying belief that they are always right makes it unlikely that they will question their actions. … Instead of evaluating the potential helpfulness of [guidance and counseling from others, such] patients tend to dismiss input from others as irrelevant to their purposes. … Antisocial patients' lack of concern for future outcomes might be placed on the opposite end of a continuum from obsessive-compulsive patients' excessive striving toward perfectionistic future goals. (p. 154)

Specific beliefs are said to include justification (merely wanting something justifies any actions to attain it), personal infallibility (believing that one always makes good choices), the impotence of others (what others think doesn't matter), and low-impact consequences (negative outcomes may happen, but they will not matter). The general goal of cognitive therapy is to challenge such beliefs and to try to bring the patient's ideas and behaviors in line with those of a lawful society in which people respect the rights and sensibilities of others and in which their behavior is responsive to social controls. Efforts should be made to demonstrate to the patient that his or her goals can be more readily achieved by altering behavior so that it is less impulsive and more empathic and in general better conforms to societal standards. Considering the feelings of others might be more advantageous to the psychopathic patient than continuing to ignore others' feelings. It remains to be seen whether this cognitive-behavioral conceptualization will generate interventions any more successful than others that have been tried in vain.

Since many psychopaths spend time in prison for committing crimes, the discouraging results of imprisonment as rehabilitation are traced at least in part to the inability to modify psychopathic behavior. As criminologists have stated repeatedly, our prison system seems to operate more as a school for crime than as a place where criminals, and psychopaths, can be rehabilitated.

An interesting argument in favor of incarceration is that psychopaths often settle down in middle age and thereafter (Craft, 1969). Whether through biological changes, eventual insight into their self-defeating natures, or simply becoming worn out and unable to continue in their finagling, often violent ways, many psychopaths grow less disruptive as they approach age forty. Prison therefore protects society from the antisocial behavior of active psychopaths, with release considered more plausible when the prisoner enters a stage of life in which the excesses of the disorder are less in evidence.

SUMMARY

Coded on Axis II in DSM-IV, personality disorders are defined as enduring patterns of behavior and inner experience that disrupt social and occupational functioning. They are usually codiagnosed with such Axis I disorders as depression and anxiety disorders. Although these diagnoses have become reliable in recent years, they overlap considerably, and it is usual for a person to meet diagnostic criteria for more than one. This high comorbidity, coupled with the fact that personality disorders are seen as the extremes of continuously distributed personality traits, has led to proposals to develop a dimensional rather than a categorical means of classifying these disorders.

Personality disorders are grouped into three clusters in DSM-IV. Specific diagnoses in the first cluster, odd/eccentric, include paranoid, schizotypal, and schizoid. These disorders are usually considered to be less severe variants of schizophrenia, and their symptoms are similar to those of the prodromal or residual phases of schizophrenia. Behavior genetic research gives some support to this assumption, especially for schizotypal personality disorder.

The dramatic/erratic cluster includes borderline, histrionic, narcissistic, and antisocial personality disorders. The major symptom of borderline personality disorder is unstable, highly changeable emotions and behavior; for histrionic personality disorder, exaggerated emotional displays; for narcissistic personality disorder, highly inflated self-esteem; and for antisocial personality disorder, antisocial behavior. Theories of the etiology of the first three of these diagnoses focus on early parent–child relationships. For example, object relations theorists, such as Kernberg and Kohut, have detailed proposals concerning borderline and narcissistic personality disorders.

More is known about antisocial personality disorder or psychopathy than about other disorders in this cluster. Though they overlap a great deal the two diagnoses are not exactly equivalent. Antisocial personality focuses on antisocial behavior, whereas psychopathy, influenced by the writings of Cleckley, emphasizes emotional deficits, such as a lack of fear, regret, or shame. Psychopaths are thought to be unable to learn from experience, to have no sense of responsibility, and to be unable to establish genuine emotional relationships with other people. Research on their families indicates that psychopaths tend to have fathers who themselves were antisocial and that discipline during their childhoods was either absent or inconsistent. Genetic studies, particularly those using the adoption method, suggest that a predisposition to psychopathy is inherited. The core problem of the psychopath may be that impending punishment creates no inhibitions about committing antisocial acts. A good deal of overlapping evidence supports this view: (1) psychopaths are slow to learn to avoid shock, and they show small startle responses; (2) psychopaths, according to their electrodermal responses, show little anxiety, but as indicated by their faster heart rates, they seem more able than normal people to tune out aversive stimuli; and (3) psychopaths have difficulty altering their responses, even when their behavior is not producing desirable consequences.

The anxious/fearful cluster includes avoidant, dependent, and obsessive compulsive personality disorders. The major symptom of avoidant personality disorder is fear of rejection or criticism; for dependent personality disorder, low self-confidence and overreliance on others; and for obsessive-compulsive personality disorder, a perfectionistic, detail-oriented style. Theories of etiology focus on early experience. Avoidant personality disorder may result from the transmission of fear from parent to child via modeling. Dependent personality may be caused by disruptions of the parent–child relationship (e.g., through separation or loss) that leads the person to fear losing other relationships in adulthood.

Little is known about effective therapy for the various personality disorders for several reasons. The high level of comorbidity among the diagnoses make it difficult to evaluate reports of therapy. Some promising evidence is emerging, however, for the utility of dialectical behavior therapy for borderline personality disorder. This approach combines client-centered acceptance with a cognitive-behavioral focus on making specific changes in thought, emotion, and behavior. Psychotherapy for psychopathy is rarely successful. In addition to the pervasiveness and apparent intractability of an uncaring and manipulative lifestyle, the antisocial personality is by nature a poor candidate for therapy. People who habitually lie and lack insight into their own or others' feelings—and have no inclination to examine emotions—will not readily establish a trusting and open working relationship with a therapist.

KEY TERMS

personality disorders
paranoid personality
schizoid personality
schizotypal personality
borderline personality

histrionic personality
narcissistic personality
antisocial personality
psychopathy
avoidant personality

dependent personality
obsessive-compulsive
   personality
dialectical behavior therapy

Henri Matisse,
"The Conversation," *1909*

SEXUAL AND GENDER IDENTITY DISORDERS

William V. is a twenty-eight-year-old computer programmer who currently lives alone. He grew up in a rural area within a conservative family with strong religious values. He has two younger brothers and an older sister. William began to masturbate at age fifteen; his first masturbatory experience took place while he watched his sister urinate in an outdoor toilet. Despite considerable feelings of guilt, he continued to masturbate two or three times a week while having voyeuristic fantasies. ...

On a summer evening at about 11:30 P.M. William was arrested for climbing a ladder and peeping into the bedroom of a suburban home. Just before this incident he had been drinking heavily at a cocktail lounge featuring a topless dancer. ... Feeling lonely and depressed [after leaving the bar], he had begun to drive slowly through a nearby suburban neighborhood, where he noticed a lighted upstairs window. With little premeditation, he had parked his car, erected a ladder he found lying near the house, and climbed up to peep. The householders, who were alerted by the sounds, called the police, and William was arrested. Although this was his first arrest, William had committed similar acts on two previous occasions. ...

[In therapy] William described a lonely and insecure life. ... Six months before the arrest, he had been rejected in a long-term relationship. ... As an unassertive and timid individual, he had responded by withdrawing from social relationships, and increasing his use of alcohol. His voyeuristic fantasies, which were present to begin with, became progressively more urgent as William's self-esteem deteriorated. His arrest had come as a great personal shock, although he recognized that his behavior was both irrational and self-destructive. (Rosen & Rosen, 1981, pp. 452–453. Reprinted by permission of McGraw-Hill Book Company.)

Sexuality is one of the most personal—and generally private—areas of an individual's life. Each of us is a sexual being with preferences and fantasies that may surprise or even shock us from time to time. These are part of normal sexual functioning. But when our fantasies or desires begin to affect us or others in unwanted or harmful ways, as with William's peeping, they begin to qualify as abnormal. This chapter considers the full range of human sexual thoughts, feelings, and actions that are generally regarded as abnormal and dysfunctional and are listed in DSM-IV as **sexual and gender identity disorders** (Table 14.1).

Our study of these disorders is divided into four major sections. First we examine theory and research in gender identity disorders. Next we consider the paraphilias, including some critical discussion of homosexuality. Though no longer listed as a sexual disorder in the DSM, the history of controversy regarding the status of homosexuality war-

rants our consideration here. Included also in this section is rape, which, although not a separate listing in DSM-IV, merits examination in an abnormal psychology textbook. The third major section of the chapter addresses sexual dysfunctions, disruptions in normal sexual functioning found in many people who are in otherwise reasonably sound psychological health. A final section of the chapter deals with AIDS, a topic that is associated with certain patterns of behavior, a principal one being sexual.

GENDER IDENTITY DISORDERS

"Are you a boy or a girl?" "Are you a man or a woman?" For virtually all people—even those with serious mental disorders such as schizophrenia—the answer to such questions is immediate and obvious. And others would also agree unequivocally with the answer. Our sense of ourselves as male or female, our **gender identity**, is so deeply ingrained from earliest childhood that whatever

---

TABLE 14.1 Sexual and Gender Identity Disorders

A. Gender Identity Disorders
B. Paraphilias
1. Fetishism
2. Transvestic fetishism
3. Pedophilia
4. Exhibitionism
5. Voyeurism
6. Sexual masochism
7. Sexual sadism
8. Frotteurism
9. Paraphilias not otherwise specified (e.g., coprophilia, necrophilia)
C. Sexual Dysfunctions
1. Sexual desire disorders
   a. Hypoactive sexual desire disorder
   b. Sexual aversion disorder
2. Sexual arousal disorders
   a. Female sexual arousal disorder
   b. Male erectile disorder
3. Orgasmic disorders
   a. Female orgasmic disorder (inhibited female orgasm)
   b. Male orgasmic disorder (inhibited male orgasm)
   c. Premature ejaculation
4. Sexual pain disorders
   a. Dyspareunia
   b. Vaginismus

Source: From DSM-IV (1994).

stress is suffered at one time or another, the vast majority of people are certain beyond a doubt of their gender. (Note: Sexual identity or sexual orientation is the preference we have for the sex of a partner. A man may be attracted to men without believing that he is a woman, and similarly for women.)

Some people, more often men than women, feel deep within themselves from early childhood that they are of the opposite sex. The evidence of their anatomy—normal genitals and the usual secondary sex characteristics, such as beard growth for men and developed breasts for women—does not persuade them that they are what others see them to be. A man can look at himself in a mirror, see a biological man, and yet announce to himself that he is a woman. Furthermore, he may try to convince the medical profession to bring his body in line with his gender identity.

We look first at gender identity disorder (GID) in adults, sometimes called transsexualism, then at gender identity disorder as it is first evidenced in childhood.

GENDER IDENTITY DISORDER

The DSM-IV category of gender identity disorder includes people who are gender dysphoric—those unhappy with their anatomical sex who wish to be of the opposite sex. Among these are people who try to pass as members of the opposite sex and people who wish to alter themselves surgically, as described later. These latter people, the extremes of GID, are sometimes referred to as **transsexuals**. A further subclassification specifies whether the person is a child (discussed next), adolescent, or adult. Excluded from GID are people with schizophrenia who on very rare occasions claim to be of the other sex, as well as hermaphrodites, so-called intersexed individuals who have both male and female reproductive organs. GID is also differentiated from transvestism, which is one of the paraphilias discussed later in this chapter. Although they often dress in opposite sex clothing, transvestites do not identify themselves as of the opposite sex.

People with gender identity disorder generally suffer from anxiety and depression, not surprising in light of their psychological predicament. Moreover, a male with GID experiences his sexual interest in men as a conventional heterosexual preference, given that he considers himself really a woman. Predictably, those with GID often arouse the disapproval of others and often suffer discrimination in employment when they choose to cross-dress in clothing of the other sex. Cross-dressing is less of a problem for women with GID because con-

temporary fashions allow women to wear clothing very similar to that worn by men. The prevalence rates for GID are slight, one in about 30,000 for men and one in 100,000 to 150,000 in women (American Psychiatric Association [APA], 1994).

CAUSES OF GID

The long-standing and apparently unchangeable nature of disorders in gender identity has led researchers to speculate that transsexuals are hormonally different from those with normal gender identity. Perhaps a woman who believes that she is a man has an excess of androgens, such as testosterone and androsterone, hormones known to promote the development and maintenance of male secondary sex characteristics. In a review of several such investigations, Gladue (1987) found few if any differences in hormone levels among men with GID, male heterosexuals, and male homosexuals. In another survey Meyer-Bahlburg (1979) found equivocal results: some women with GID had elevated levels of male hormones, but most of them did not. Differences, when found, are difficult to interpret because many with GID use sex hormones in an effort to alter their bodies in the direction of the sex to which they believe they belong. Even though a researcher may study only transsexuals who have not taken such exogenous hormones for a few months, relatively little is known at present about the long-term effects of earlier hormonal treatment. Therefore, the available data do not

A transsexual or person with gender identity disorder experiences great discomfort with their gender and often has sex-reassignment surgery to become as much as possible like someone of the opposite sex. The transsexual shown here was elected "Miss Transsexual" in Italy.

clearly support an explanation of adult transsexualism in terms of hormones. Even less conclusive is the research on possible chromosomal abnormalities, and efforts to find differences in brain structure between transsexuals and control subjects have likewise been negative (Emory et al., 1991).

GENDER IDENTITY DISORDER IN CHILDHOOD

We know that most adults with GID who have been studied by sex researchers report a history of profound cross-gender behavior in childhood—femininity in boys and masculinity in girls (Green, 1969; Tsoi, 1990). An examination of **gender identity disorder in childhood** might therefore provide clues to the etiology of GID.

Children diagnosed with GID are profoundly feminine boys and profoundly masculine girls, youngsters whose behavior, likes, and dislikes do not fit our culture's ideas of what is appropriate for the two sexes. Thus a boy may dislike rough-and-tumble play, prefer the company of little girls, dress up in women's clothing, and insist that he will grow up to be a girl. He may even claim that his penis and testes are disgusting. Many gender-disordered children harbor the belief that as they grow, their genitalia will somehow change into those of the opposite sex, a belief that can be construed as a child's version of the adult transsexual's wish for sex-reassignment surgery. Green and Blanchard (1994) report that parents usually detect cross-gender behavior in their children before age three. GID in children is more prevalent than in adults (about 3% for boys and 1% for girls).

CAUSES OF GID IN CHILDREN

The categorization of boys and girls as having their own masculine and feminine ways is so heavily laden with value judgments and stereotyping that considering cross-gender behavioral patterns abnormal may seem unjustified. But some evidence suggests tentatively that these patterns can come from a physical disturbance. Human and other primate offspring of mothers who have taken sex hormones during pregnancy frequently behave like members of the opposite sex *and* have anatomical abnormalities. For example, girls whose mothers took synthetic progestins, which are precursors to male sex hormones, to prevent uterine bleeding during pregnancy were found to be tomboyish during their preschool years (Ehrhardt & Money, 1967). Young boys whose mothers ingested female hormones when pregnant were found to be less athlet-

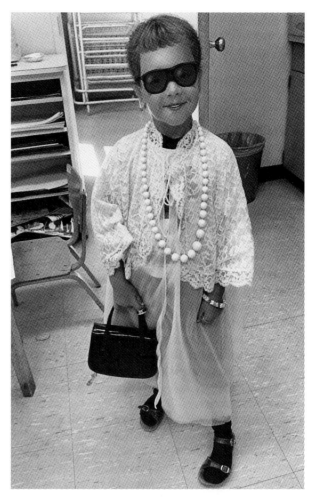

Although dressing up is normal in childhood, most transsexuals trace their gender identity disturbance to childhood and report dressing in gender-inappropriate clothes.

ic as young children and to engage less in rough-and-tumble play than their male peers (Yalom, Green, & Fisk, 1973). Although such children were not necessarily abnormal in their gender identity, the mother's ingestion of prenatal sex hormones did apparently give them higher than usual levels of cross-gender interests and behavior.

Many, perhaps most, young children engage in cross-gender behavior now and then. In some homes such behavior may receive too much attention and reinforcement from parents and other relatives. Interviews with the parents of children who show signs of GID frequently reveal that they did not discourage, and in many instances clearly encouraged, cross-dressing behavior in their atypical children. This holds true especially for feminine boys. Many mothers, aunts, and grandmothers found it cute when the boys dressed in Mommy's old dresses and high-heeled shoes, and very often they instructed the youngsters on how to apply makeup. Family albums typically contain photographs of the young boys attired in women's clothing. Such reactions on the part of the family to an atypical child probably contribute in a major way to the conflict between his or her anatomical sex and the acquired gender identity (Green, 1974, 1987; Zuckerman & Green, 1993). Richard Green's noteworthy prospective, longitudinal study of feminine boys and tomboys[1] revealed that compared with a control group of nontomboys, tomboys were more likely to choose their fathers as a favored parent (and presumably to regard their fathers rather than their mothers as a role model); they were also more likely to have mothers who themselves were tomboys as children and who were more accepting of their daughters' masculine behavior. The possible modeling and operant shaping of more masculine behavior within the family may be supplemented by the positive reinforcement these girls might experience from their male peer groups as a result of their tomboyish behavior (Williams, Goodman, & Green, 1985). It should be borne in mind that most children with gender identity disorder do not grow up to be disordered in adulthood, *even without professional intervention* (Zucker et al., 1984), although many demonstrate a homosexual orientation (Coates & Person, 1985; Green, 1985).

A novel hypothesis is that feminine behavior in boys is encouraged by mothers who, prior to the child's birth, wanted very much to have a girl. This hypothesis was not confirmed, however, in a recent study; mothers whose sons did not have a childhood feminine identity reported that they had had the same level of interest in having a girl as mothers whose sons did manifest a feminine identification (Zucker et al., 1994).

Investigators working in this field are very much aware of the culture-relative aspects of masculinity and femininity and of the difference between enjoying activities more typical of the opposite sex and actually believing that one *is* of the opposite sex. The vast majority of little boys engage in varying amounts of feminine play and little girls in varying amounts of masculine play with no identity conflicts whatsoever (Green, 1976). This is not to say

that feminine boys are not subject to considerable stress. Our society has a low tolerance for boys who act like girls, whereas girls can be tomboys and still conform to acceptable standards of behavior for girls (Williams, Goodman, & Green, 1985). Gender identity disorder in both childhood and adulthood is far less prevalent than would be indicated by the numbers of little boys who play with dolls and little girls who engage in contact sports.

THERAPIES FOR GENDER IDENTITY DISORDERS

We turn now to the interventions available to help people with gender identity disorders. These interventions are of two main types: one attempts to alter the body to suit the person's psychology; the other is designed to alter the psychology to match the person's body.

SEX-REASSIGNMENT SURGERY

Innovations in surgical procedures, coupled with advances in hormonal treatments and a sociocultural atmosphere that permits their implementation, have allowed many individuals with GID to pursue their wish to become in some respects a member of the opposite sex. **Sex-reassignment surgery** is an operation in which the existing genitalia are removed and replaced by a constructed substitute for the genitals of the opposite sex. The first sex-reassignment operation took place in Europe in 1930, but the surgery that attracted worldwide attention was performed on an ex-soldier, Christine (originally George) Jorgensen, in Copenhagen in 1952.

For male-to-female reassignment surgery, the male genitalia are almost entirely removed, with some of the tissue retained to form an artificial vagina. At least a year before the operation, appropriate female hormones are given to develop the breasts, soften the skin, and change the body in other ways; hormones have to be taken indefinitely after the surgery (Green & Money, 1969). Most male-to-female transsexuals have to undergo extensive and costly electrolysis to remove beard and body hair and receive training to raise the pitch of their voices, as the female hormones prescribed do not make hair distribution and the voice less masculine. Some male-to-female transsexuals also have plastic surgery on their chin, nose, and Adam's apple to rid them of masculine largeness. At the same time the sex-change patient begins to live as a female member of society in order to experience as fully as possible what it is like. The genital surgery itself is usually not done until a one- or two-year trial period

---

[1]What is a tomboy? This study defined a tomboy as a girl who was regarded as one by her parents and had the following characteristics: "(1) a peer group which was at least half male; (2) a preference for traditionally masculine attire such as a baseball jacket and cap; (3) a low interest in dress-up dolls (e.g., Barbie); (4) a preference for male roles when engaging in make-believe games; (5) a stronger interest in sports than most same-age girls; and (6) a more than rarely expressed desire to be a boy" (Williams et al., 1985, p. 722). The data described here were collected on Long Island, New York, during the mid-1970s.

James Morris (in a 1960 picture), after sex-change surgery, became Jan Morris (in a 1974 photograph).

has been completed. Conventional heterosexual intercourse is possible for male-to-female transsexuals, although pregnancy is out of the question since only the external genitalia are altered.

For female-to-male reassignment surgery the process is more arduous. The penis that can be constructed is small and not capable of normal erection; artificial supports are therefore needed for conventional sexual intercourse. An operation now available extends the urethra into the newly constructed penis to allow the person the social comfort of being able to use public urinals. Less cosmetic follow-up is needed than for male-to-female transsexuals because the male hormones prescribed to women seeking sexual reassignment drastically alter fat distribution and stimulate the growth of beard and body hair. The relatively greater ease of the female-to-male change may be due in part to our society's lesser focus on the physical attributes of men. A small, soft-spoken man with a relatively high-pitched voice may be more acceptable to society than a deep-voiced woman of large stature. Sex-reassignment surgery is an option much more frequently exercised by men than by women.

HOW BENEFICIAL IS SEX-REASSIGNMENT SURGERY? Over the years controversy has existed over the benefits of sex-reassignment surgery. One of the first outcome studies (Meyer & Reter, 1979) found no advantage to the individual "in terms of social rehabilitation" (p. 1015). The findings of this study led to the termination of the Johns Hopkins University School of Medicine sex-reassignment program, the largest such program in the United States. However, other researchers criticized the Meyer–Reter findings. A review of twenty years of research indicated an overall improvement in social-adaptation rates as a result of sex-reassignment surgery, with female-to-male transsexuals showing somewhat greater success than male-to-female transsexuals (Abramovitz, 1986).

A more recent review by Green and Fleming (1990) of reasonably controlled outcome studies published between 1979 and 1989 with at least a one-year follow-up drew even more favorable conclusions. Of 130 female-to-male surgeries, about 97 percent could be judged satisfactory; of 220 male-to-female surgeries, 87 percent were satisfactory. Preoperative factors that seemed to predict favorable postsurgery adjustment were (1) reasonable emotional stability, (2) successful adaptation in the new role for at least one year, (3) adequate understanding of the actual limitations and consequences of the surgery, and (4) psychotherapy in the context of an established gender identity program. The authors caution, however, that satisfactory ratings meant only that the patients reported that they did not regret having had the surgery. Such patient reports may be an overly generous criterion for favorable outcome, especially since they follow the investment of considerable time, money, and energy for an outcome that is, for the most part, irreversible. An even more recent report from the University of Pennsylvania indicates that sexual responsiveness and sexual satisfaction increase dramatically in both male-to-female and female-to-male transsexuals, with an overall high level of satisfaction with the results of the surgery (Lief & Hubschman, 1993).

Sex-reassignment programs continue in many medical-psychological settings. It is estimated that each year in the United States upwards of 1000 transsexuals are surgically altered to the opposite sex. And yet the long-term effectiveness, or even wisdom, of sex-reassignment surgery is still difficult to evaluate. Given that people who go to great lengths to have this surgery performed claim that their future happiness depends on the change, should this surgery be evaluated in terms of how happy such people are afterward? If so, it can probably be said that most GID patients who have crossed over anatomically are generally better off, although some are not. But if a surgically altered transsexual becomes dismally unhappy, is the surgery to be indicted as antitherapeutic? Consider this: those who undergo these procedures often cut their ties to former friends and family members and to aspects of their previous lives—"Was it *I* who played tailback on the football team?" Considerable stress is the lot of those who choose to divorce themselves from the past, for the past contributes to our sense of ourselves as people, as much as do the present and the future. A person who has sex-reassignment surgery confronts challenges few others have occasion to face, and this adjustment may well have to be made without the social support of family and friends.

All experienced therapists, whatever their theoretical persuasion, are wary of a client who says, "If only. …" The variations are legion: "If only I were not so fat …," "If only I were not so nervous …," "If only I had not left school before graduation. …" Following each "if only" clause is some statement indicating that life would be far better, even wonderful … if only. Most of the time the hopes expressed are an illusion. Things are seldom so simple. Those focusing on the discrepancy between their gender identity and biological makeup tend to blame present dissatisfactions on the horrible trick nature has played on them. But these people usually find that sex reassignment falls short of solving life's problems. It may handle this one set of them, but it usually leaves untouched other difficulties to which all human beings are subject, such as conflicts at work, with intimates, and even within oneself.

ALTERATIONS OF GENDER IDENTITY

Is sex reassignment the only option? Surgery and associated hormone administration used to be considered the only viable treatment for gender identity disorders because psychological attempts to shift gender identity had consistently failed. Gender identity was assumed to be too deep-seated to alter. Some successful procedures for altering gender identity through behavior therapy have been reported, however. One apparently successful case was reported by Rekers and Lovaas (1974). The patient was a five-year-old boy who had been cross-dressing since the age of two. The parents were instructed to encourage masculine behavior, such as playing with traditionally male toys, and to discourage such behavior as playing with dolls. A two-year follow-up showed no signs of cross-gender behavior. Though this case has been criticized for reinforcing cultural stereotypes (Winkler, 1977), the parents were concerned enough about the social ridicule the youngster was encountering to seek professional treatment.

A similar case was reported by Barlow, Reynolds, and Agras (1973). The patient was a seventeen-year-old male who wanted to change his gender identity rather than—the choice of most transsexuals—change his anatomy to fit his feminine gender identity. The treatment involved shaping of various specific behaviors, such as mannerisms and interpersonal behavior—how to talk to young women, for instance—but it also included attention to cognitive components, such as fantasies. One technique paired slides of women with slides of men, the idea being that the sexual arousal from the latter might be transferred, or classically conditioned to, the former. This positive approach to changing the arousal properties of images and fantasies was complemented by aversion therapy to reduce the attractiveness of men. After half a year of intensive treatment the young man was thinking of himself as a man, not as a woman, and was finding women sexually attractive. At a five-year follow-up these changes were still present (Barlow, Abel, & Blanchard, 1979). Two additional cases treated in the same way were reported by Barlow et al. Two men in their mid-twenties were on the route to sex-reassignment surgery, but had second thoughts. The behavioral retraining succeeded in altering their gender identity but not their attraction to men; that is, their sexual orientation remained homosexual.

This work demonstrates that cross-gender identity may be amenable to change. But as the researchers point out, their clients might have been different from others with GID because they consented to participate in a therapy program aimed at changing gender identity. Most transsexuals refuse such treatment. For them, sex-reassignment surgery is the only legitimate goal. But if the surgery option did not exist, would more professional energy be expended on developing psychological procedures for altering gender identity? And if that involved teaching men to be more traditionally masculine and women more traditionally feminine, would that be desirable or ethically defensible? These are but two of the ethical conundrums associated with treating disorders of gender identity. Ethical issues are part and parcel of *any* therapeutic effort, especially when pressures are brought to bear on people to feel uncomfortable with the way they are. We address some of the ethical issues in the treatment of homosexuality later in this chapter (p. 382) and in the final chapter of the book (p. 624).

THE PARAPHILIAS

In DSM-IV the **paraphilias** are a group of disorders in which sexual attraction is to unusual objects or sexual activities are unusual in nature. In other words, there is a deviation (*para*) in what the person is attracted to (*-philia*). This attraction has to be intense and last at least six months. The diagnosis is made only if the person has acted on these urges or experiences significant distress from them. A person can have the same fantasies and urges that a person with a paraphilia has (such as fantasizing about exhibiting the genitals to an unsuspecting stranger) but not be diagnosed if the fantasies are not recurrent and intense and if he or she has never acted on the urges *or is not markedly distressed by them.*

People often exhibit more than one paraphilia, and such patterns can be an aspect of other mental disorders, such as schizophrenia or one of the personality disorders. Prevalence statistics indicate that people with paraphilias, of whatever sexual orientation, are almost always men; even with masochism, which does occur with noticeable numbers of women, men affected outnumber women by a ratio of twenty to one. Paraphilic behavior declines after age twenty-five. As some persons with paraphilias seek nonconsenting partners, these disorders often have legal consequences.

FETISHISM

Whether it is legs or a derriere shaped a certain way, most people find particular body parts sexually arousing. **Fetishism**, however, involves a reliance on an inanimate object for sexual arousal. The fetishist, almost always a male, has recurrent and intense sexual urges toward nonliving objects, called fetishes (e.g., women's shoes), and the presence of the fetish is strongly preferred or even necessary for sexual arousal to occur.

Beautiful shoes, sheer stockings, gloves, toilet articles, fur garments, and, especially, underpants are common sources of arousal for fetishists. An unusual fetishistic attraction was reported by King (1990), who described a twenty-six-year-old man who was aroused by other people sneezing. Some can carry on their fetishism by themselves in secret by fondling, kissing, smelling, sucking, placing in their rectum, or merely gazing at the adored object as they masturbate. Others need their partner to don the fetish as a stimulant for intercourse. Fetishists sometimes become primarily interested in making a collection of the desired objects, and they may commit burglary week after week to add to their hoard.

The attraction felt by the fetishist toward the object is involuntary and irresistible. It is the degree of the erotic focalization—the exclusive and very special status the object occupies as a sexual stimulant—that distinguishes fetishisms from the ordinary attraction that, for example, high heels and sheer stockings may hold for heterosexual men in western cultures. The boot fetishist *must* see or touch a boot to become aroused, and when the fetish is present, the arousal is overwhelmingly strong. The disorder usually begins by adolescence, although the fetish may have acquired special significance even earlier, during childhood.

TRANSVESTIC FETISHISM

When a man is sexually aroused by dressing in women's clothing, although he still regards himself as a man, the term **transvestic fetishism**, or transvestism, applies. A transvestite may enjoy appearing socially as a woman; some female impersonators become performers in nightclubs, catering to the delight that many sexually conventional people take in skilled cross-dressing. Unless the cross-dressing is associated with sexual arousal, however, these impersonators are not considered transvestic. Transvestism should not be confused with the cross-dressing associated with GID or with the cross-dressing preferences of some homosexuals.

Transvestic fetishism or transvestism is diagnosed when the person produces sexual arousal by dressing in opposite sex clothing. This transvestite is attending a fund raiser for AIDS at the Waldorf Astoria in New York.

Transvestites are heterosexual, always males, and by and large cross-dress episodically rather than on a regular basis. Some wear female panties under their conventional clothing. They tend to be otherwise masculine in appearance, demeanor, and sexual preference. Many are married. Cross-dressing usually takes place in private and in secret and is known to few members of the family. The urge to cross-dress may become more frequent over time but only rarely develops to a change in gender identity, that is, to the man's believing that he is actually a woman. Some transvestites do report *feeling* like a woman when they are cross-dressing. Transvestism usually begins with partial cross-dressing in childhood and adolescence (APA, 1994).

PEDOPHILIA AND INCEST

Pedophiles (*pedos*, Greek for "child") are adults, usually men as far as police records indicate, who derive sexual gratification through physical and often sexual contact with prepubertal children unrelated to them. DSM-IV requires that the offender be at least sixteen years old and at least five years older than the child. The pedophile can be heterosexual or homosexual. Violence is seldom a part of the molestation—although it can be, as occasionally comes to people's attention through lurid stories in the media. But even if most pedophiles do not physically injure their victims, some frighten the child by, for example, killing a pet and threatening further harm if the youngster tells his or her parents. Sometimes the pedophile is content to stroke the child's hair, but he may also manipulate the child's genitalia, encourage the child to manipulate his, and, less often, attempt intromission. The molestations may be repeated over a period of weeks, months, or years if they are not discovered by other adults or if the child does not protest. A minority of pedophiles, who might also be classified as sexual sadists or antisocial (psychopathic) personalities, inflict serious bodily harm on the object of their passion. Such individuals, whether psychopathic or not, are perhaps best viewed as child rapists and are fundamentally different from pedophiles by virtue of their wish to hurt the child physically at least as much as to obtain sexual gratification (Groth et al., 1982).

Incest refers to sexual relations between close relatives for whom marriage is forbidden. The taboo against incest seems virtually universal in human societies (Ford & Beach, 1951), with a notable exception in the marriages of Egyptian pharaohs to their sisters or other females of their immediate families. In Egypt it was believed that the royal blood should not be contaminated by that of outsiders. Some anthropologists consider the prohibition against incest to have served the important function of forcing more widely spread social ties and consequently greater social harmony than would have been likely had family members chosen their mates only from among their own. The incest taboo makes sense according to present-day scientific knowledge. The offspring from a father-daughter or a brother-sister union has a greater probability of inheriting a pair of recessive genes, one from each parent. For the most part, recessive genes have negative biological effects, such as serious birth defects. The incest taboo, then, has adaptive evolutionary significance (Geer, Heiman, & Leitenberg, 1984). Incest is listed in DSM-IV as a subtype of pedophilia. It is most common between brother and sister. The next most common form, which is considered more pathological, is between father and daughter.

Two major distinctions are drawn between incest and pedophilia. First, incest is by definition between members of the same family. Second, and more important, most incest victims tend to be older than the object of a pedophile's desires. It is more often the case that a father becomes interested in his daughter when she begins to mature physically, whereas the pedophile is interested in the youngster precisely because he or she is sexually immature. Data from penile plethysmography studies (see Figure 14.1 for an explanation of these measures) confirm that men who molest children unrelated to them are sexually aroused from photographs of nude children, whereas men who molest children within their families show greater penile arousal to adult heterosexual cues (Marshall,

Figure 14.1 Behavioral researchers use two genital devices for measuring sexual arousal. Both are sensitive indicators of vasocongestion of the genitalia, that is, the flooding of the veins with blood, a key physiological process in sexual arousal; both provide specific measurements of sexual excitement (e.g., Adams et al., 1992; Barlow et al., 1970; Geer, Morokoff, & Greenwood, 1974; Heiman et al., 1991). (a) For men, the penile plethysmograph measures changes in the circumference of the penis by means of a strain gauge, consisting of a very thin rubber tube filled with mercury. As the penis is engorged with blood, the tube stretches, changing its electrical resistance, which can then be measured by a suitably configured polygraph. (b) For women, sexual arousal can be measured by a vaginal plethysmograph, such as the device invented by Sintchak and Geer (1975). Shaped like a menstrual tampon, this apparatus can be inserted into the vagina to provide direct measurement of the increased blood flow characteristic of female sexual arousal.

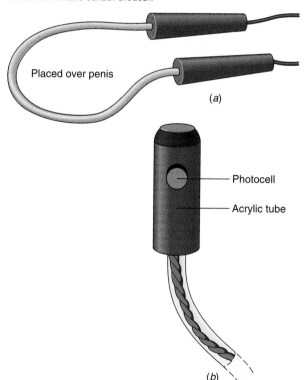

Placed over penis

(a)

Photocell

Acrylic tube

(b)

Barabee, & Christophe, 1986). In defining pedophilia, state laws vary on a prescribed upper age limit for those considered children.

Men who are otherwise conventional in their sexual interests and behavior can be sexually aroused by pedophilic stimuli. In a study using both self-report and penile plethysmographic measures, one-quarter of people drawn from a community sample showed or reported pedophilic arousal (Hall et al., 1993). The investigators found that this abnormal arousal was correlated with conventional arousal, that is, the more aroused the people were to adult heterosexual pictures, the more aroused they were to the pedophilic pictures. Although this finding might be disturbing to us, it highlights the importance of the distinction made by the DSM and health professionals in general between fantasy and behavior.

Recent evidence suggests that child molesters have sexual fantasies about children when their mood is negative, perhaps as a way to cope with their dysphoria; however, it appears also that having the pedophilic fantasy enhances the negative affect. Perhaps this downward spiral leads at some point to the person's acting on the impulse to molest a child (Looman, 1995).

It is sometimes alleged that child pornography is a critical ingredient in motivating child molestation in some people, but a recent clinical study of eleven male pedophiles indicates that such materials may not even be necessary. These men were arousable by media materials widely available, such as television ads and clothing catalogues picturing young children in underwear. In other words, rather than using explicitly pornographic materials, these men appeared to construct their own sexually stimulating material from sources generally viewed as innocuous (Howitt, 1995).

Pedophiles and perpetrators of incest are often rigidly religious and moralistic (Gebhard et al., 1965).[2] As in most paraphilias, a strong subjective attraction impels the behavior. According to Gebhard and his colleagues, pedophiles generally know the children they molest; they are neighbors or friends of the family. Clinical observations suggest that pedophiles are low in social maturity, self-esteem, impulse control, and social skills (Finkelhor & Araji, 1986), views that have been confirmed in

[2]The association that has been reported between strong religious beliefs and the disorders of incest and pedophilia should not be taken to mean that being religious, even rigidly so, predisposes one to these sexual disorders. It may be that some people, overcome by the intensity of their attraction to their own or others' children, seek solace and forgiveness in religion. The data are correlational and hence are open to different interpretations.

recent research (Kalichman, 1991; Overholser & Beck, 1986). Most older heterosexual pedophiles are or have been married at some time in their lives.

There is evidence that the structure of families in which incest occurs is unusually patriarchal and traditional, especially with respect to the subservient position of women relative to men (Alexander & Lupfer, 1987). Parents in these families also tend to neglect and remain emotionally distant from their children (Madonna, VanScoyk, & Jones, 1991). Furthermore, it is believed that incest is more prevalent when the mother is absent or disabled (Finkelhor, 1979), as mothers otherwise usually protect their daughters from intrafamilial sexual abuse.

It has only recently been recognized that up to half of all child molestations, including those that take place within the same family, are committed by adolescent males (Becker et al., 1986; Morenz & Becker, 1995). Many adult offenders began their illegal behavior in their early teens, presumably because of the chaotic and negative character of their family lives. Their homes often lack structure and positive support (Blaske et al., 1989). Many of these teenagers were themselves abused as children (Worling, 1996). Those who engage in child molestation are more socially isolated and have poorer social skills than peers who are in trouble with the law for nonsexual crimes (Awad & Saunders, 1989). Academic problems are also common (Blaske et al., 1989). In general these young males (females are much less often found among the ranks of sex offenders) are what one would call juvenile delinquents, in frequent trouble with the police for a wide variety of lawbreaking. Not surprisingly, conduct disorder is a frequent diagnosis made of these young men (see p. 413). Somewhat more surprisingly, depression is also a common feature (Becker et al., 1991); perhaps behind their calloused exploitation of young children, these people are profoundly unhappy with their lives.

Because overt physical force is seldom used in incest or pedophilia, the child molester often denies that he is actually forcing himself on his victim. But it is disingenuous to assume that there is no coercion. The older child or man takes advantage of the naivete of the victim and of the imbalanced power relationship that exists between an adult and a child (e.g., scoutmaster and one of the boys in his troop, the camp counselor and one of the children in his bunk). Sometimes the molester rationalizes that he is doing something good for the child, unaware of the betrayal of trust that is inherent in child sexual abuse and unaware as well of the serious negative psychological consequences that often befall the victim some years later (Focus 14.1).

Both incest and pedophilia occur much more often than was formerly assumed. A study of 796 college students found that an astounding 19 percent of the women and 8.6 percent of the men had been sexually victimized as children. Of the victimized women, 28 percent had had incestuous relations; of the men, 23 percent had (Finkelhor, 1979). More recent survey data confirm these findings (Siegel et al., 1987). When states pass more effective legislation on reporting molestation, such as requiring health care professionals and teachers to report child abuse if they suspect it, confirmed cases increase 50 to 500 percent.

VOYEURISM (PEEPING)

Now and then a man may by chance happen to see a nude woman without her knowing he is watching her. If his sex life is primarily conventional, his act is voyeuristic, but he would not generally be considered a voyeur. **Voyeurism** is a marked preference for obtaining sexual gratification by watching others in a state of undress or having sexual relations. As in the case of William at the beginning of this chapter, the looking, often called peeping, is what helps the individual become sexually aroused and is sometimes essential for arousal. The voyeur's orgasm is achieved by masturbation, either while watching or later, remembering what he saw. Sometimes the voyeur fantasizes about having sexual contact with the observed person, but it remains a fantasy; in voyeurism, there is seldom contact between the observer and the observed.

A true voyeur, almost always a man, does not find it particularly exciting to watch a woman who is undressing for his special benefit. The element of risk seems important, for the voyeur is excited by the anticipation of how the woman would react if she knew he was watching. Some voyeurs derive special pleasure from secretly observing couples having sexual relations. As with all categories of behavior that are against the law, frequencies of occurrence are difficult to assess, since the majority of *all* illegal activities go unnoticed by the police.

Voyeurs tend to be young, single, submissive, and fearful of more direct sexual encounters with others. Their peeping serves as a substitute gratification and possibly gives them a sense of power over those watched. They do not seem to be otherwise disturbed, however.

After all restrictions against the sale of pornographic materials to adults had been lifted in Denmark, one of the few observed effects of this liberalization was a significant reduction in peeping, at least as reported to the police (Kutchinsky, 1970). It may be that the increased availability of completely frank pictorial and written material, typically used in masturbation, satisfies the needs that earlier made voyeurs of some men without other outlets.

EXHIBITIONISM

Exhibitionism is a recurrent, marked preference for obtaining sexual gratification by exposing one's genitals to an unwilling stranger. As with voyeurism there is seldom an attempt to have actual contact with the stranger. Sexual arousal comes from fantasizing that one is exposing himself or from actually doing so, and the exhibitionist masturbates either while fantasizing or even during the actual exposure. In most cases there is a desire to shock or embarrass the observer.

Voyeurism and exhibitionism together account for close to a majority of all sexual offenses that come to the attention of the police. The frequency of exhibitionism is much greater among men, who are often arrested for what is legally termed *indecent exposure*.

The urge to expose seems overwhelming and virtually uncontrollable to the exhibitionist, or flasher, and is apparently triggered by anxiety and restlessness as well as by sexual arousal. One exhibitionist persisted in his practices even after suffering a spinal cord injury that left him without sensation or movement from the waist down (DeFazio et al., 1987). Because of the compulsive nature of the urge, the exposures may be repeated rather frequently and even in the same place and at the same time of day. Apparently exhibitionists are so strongly driven that at the time of the act, they are usually oblivious to the social and legal consequences of what they are doing (Stevenson & Jones, 1972). In the desperation and tension of the moment, they may suffer headaches and palpitations and have a sense of unreality. Afterward they flee in trembling and remorse (Bond & Hutchison, 1960). Like voyeurs, exhibitionists only rarely seek physical contact with their unwilling observers; even less often is there danger of a more violent sexual offense, such as rape (Rooth, 1973). Generally, exhibitionists are immature in their approaches to the opposite sex and have difficulty in interpersonal relationships. Over half of all exhibitionists are married, but their sexual relationships with their spouses are not satisfactory (Mohr, Turner, & Jerry, 1964).

The penile plethysmograph was used in a study of male exhibitionists in an effort to determine whether they were sexually aroused by stimuli that do not arouse nonexhibitionists (Fedora, Reddon, & Yeudall, 1986). Compared with normal subjects and with sex offenders who had committed violent assaults, the exhibitionists showed significantly greater arousal to slides of fully clothed women in nonsexual situations, such as riding on an escalator or sitting in a park, but they showed *similar* levels of sexual interest to erotic and sexually explicit slides. These results are consistent with the hypothesis that exhibitionists misread cues in the courtship phase of sexual contact, in the sense that they construe certain situations to be sexual that are judged to be nonerotic by nonexhibitionists. In this same study measures indicated that exhibitionists were *less* aroused than either control group by slides that depicted violence. This would seem to undermine the widespread concern that exhibitionists might be physically threatening.

SEXUAL SADISM AND SEXUAL MASOCHISM

A marked preference for obtaining or increasing sexual gratification by inflicting pain or psychological suffering (such as humiliation) is the key characteristic of **sexual sadism**. A marked preference for obtaining or increasing sexual gratification through subjection to pain or humiliation is the key characteristic of **sexual masochism**. Both these disorders are found in heterosexual and homosexual relationships, though it is estimated that upwards of 85 percent of people with these disorders are exclusively or predominantly heterosexual (Moser & Levitt, 1987). Some sadists and masochists are women. The disorders seem to begin by early adulthood, and most sadists and masochists are relatively comfortable with their unconventional sexual practices (Spengler, 1977).

The majority of sadists establish relationships with masochists to derive mutual sexual gratification. Moser and Levitt (1987) estimate that millions of Americans engage in sexual practices that involve the infliction of pain or humiliation (though far fewer engage in such practices often or intensively enough to be diagnosed as sadists or masochists). The majority of sadists and masochists lead otherwise conventional lives, and there is some evidence that they are above average in income and educational status (Moser & Levitt, 1987; Spengler, 1977). The sadist may derive full orgasmic pleasure by inflicting pain on his or her partner, and the masochist may be completely gratified by being subjected to pain. For other partners the sadistic and masochistic practices, such as spanking, are a prelude to or aspect of sexual intercourse.

Although a great many are switchable, that is, able to take both dominant and submissive roles,

Focus 14.1   Child Sexual Abuse: Effects on the Victim and Modes of Intervention

Both pedophilia and incest are forms of **child sexual abuse** (CSA), and should be distinguished from nonsexual child abuse. Both can have very negative consequences, and sometimes they co-occur. Nonsexual child abuse may include neglecting the child's physical and mental welfare, for example, punishing the child unfairly; belittling the child; intentionally withholding suitable shelter, food, and medical care; and striking or otherwise inflicting physical pain and injury. Parents often engage in nonsexual abuse of their children when no sexual abuse is involved. Both types of abuse are reportable offenses.

Child sexual abuse generally refers to such physical contact as penetration of the child's vagina or anus with the perpetrator's penis, finger, or other object; fellatio, cunnilingus, or anilingus; and fondling or caressing. The term also extends to exhibitionism and child pornography, which may not involve actual sexual activity between an adult and a child (Wolfe, 1990).

PREVALENCE

Accurate figures are notoriously difficult to determine, but it is estimated that from 15 percent to 33 percent of women have been sexually abused (Finkelhor et al., 1990). Among women in therapy the rate is as high as 75 percent (Polunsy & Follette, 1995). For men the estimates are much lower but far from negligible: up to 16 percent in the general population and 23 percent of those in therapy (Finkelhor et al., 1990; Jacobson & Herald, 1990). Another way to state the prevalence of child abuse is that more than 156,000 children in the United States are reported each year to child protective agencies and the police as having been abused, most of them many times (National Center for Child Abuse and Neglect, 1988); and these figures are probably underestimates (Finkelhor et al., 1990).

EFFECTS ON THE VICTIM

A growing body of evidence attests to the long-term adverse effects of incest and pedophilia (Felitti, 1991). Many of these long-term consequences can qualify the aftermath of CSA as a form of posttraumatic stress disorder. DSM-IV lists sexual assault as one of the stressors that can be traumatic: "For children, sexually traumatic events may include developmentally inappropriate experiences" (APA, 1994, p. 424). However, the DSM also lists sexual abuse of children under "Other Conditions That May Be a Focus of Clinical Attention." Regardless of how child sexual abuse may be categorized in the official nosology, it is obviously regarded as serious and potentially traumatic.

Recent reviews of both short-term and long-term consequences of CSA conclude that sexually abused children report more general psychological distress and higher rates of a wide range of Axis I and Axis II disorders than are reported by nonabused children (Polusny & Follette, 1995; Trickett & Putnam, 1993). Within a year following their being abused, many children experience anxiety, depression, low self-esteem, learning disorders, conduct disorder, and self-mutilation. In adulthood, anxiety and depression continue as problems while substance abuse, binge eating, somatization disorders, and suicidal behaviors occur as well. It has been hypothesized that the higher prevalence of depression in adult women is partially due to the higher incidence of CSA among female children (Culter & Nolen-Hoeksema, 1991). Former abuse victims also report poorer social and interpersonal functioning, including more sexual dissatisfaction and dysfunction as well as higher levels of high-risk sexual behavior. People who have been sexually victimized early in life also have a greater tendency as adults to be victimized sexually and to be the object of physical violence from their partners.

In our opinion, an important and generalized long-term outcome of CSA appears to be a diminished sense of self-respect and self-worth, which may occur because the adult survivor has not been helped to recognize that he or she is not to blame for what happened and is not a bad person for having been molested as a child. Adult survivors of CSA may also experience a sense of powerlessness and incompetence (Trickett & Putnam, 1993).

In addition to the act of sexual abuse, certain aspects of a child's home life may contribute to some of the later psychological problems. For example, the high frequency of domination by the father in incestuous homes might contribute to a sense of helplessness that, apart from the sexual abuse, could result in making these women more vulnerable to depression (cf. p. 235). Research has found that prostitution, sexual promiscuity, substance abuse, anxiety disorders, and sexual dysfunctions are often a part of CSA's aftermath (Burnam et al., 1988). As indicated previously, sexual abuse in childhood is implicated in multiple personality disorder (p. 173) and borderline personality disorder (p. 339) (Saunders, 1991). One study found that a long-term effect of child sexual abuse is an increased vulnerability to subsequent sexual assault. "The actual occurrence of abuse, regardless of perpetrator, appeared to [play a role] ... in instilling an expectation of victimization" (Alexander & Lupfer, 1987, p. 244). Although it is important to emphasize that this interpretation is not equivalent to a degrading "she asked for it," it does point to the possibility that victims of sexual abuse are adversely affected in their adult years by not having learned to deal assertively with unwanted sexual advances.

A molester is usually *not* a stranger. He may be an uncle, a brother, a teacher, a coach, a neighbor, or even a cleric. This fact is very difficult to discuss with a child, difficult also to confront for ourselves, but the child molester is often a male adult

whether the children are able to translate what they have learned into *overt behavior* and whether such changes reduce the problem (Wolfe, 1990). At the very least these programs seem to legitimize discussion of the problem at home (Wurtele & Miller-Perrin, 1987) and might therefore achieve one important goal, namely, to increase the *reporting* of the crime by encouraging and empowering children to tell their parents or guardians that an adult has made a sexual overture to them.

DEALING WITH THE PROBLEM

When they suspect that something is awry parents must learn to raise the issue with their children; many adults are uncomfortable doing so. Physicians also need to be sensitized to signs of sexual abuse, both physical and psychological. In most states licensed health professionals and teachers are *required* to report sexual abuse (as well as nonsexual child abuse) to child protection agencies or the police when they become aware of it. In California, licensed psychologists must take a day-long course on the subject to ensure that they are at least minimally knowledgeable about it and aware of their legal responsibilities to report child sexual abuse.

For a child, reporting sexual abuse can be extremely difficult. We tend to forget how helpless and dependent a youngster feels and how frightening it can be to tell parents that he or she has been fondled by a brother or grandfather. Even more threatening are advances from Daddy himself, for the child is likely to be torn by allegiance to and love for his or her father on the one hand and by fear and revulsion on the other, coupled with the knowledge that what is happening is wrong. And when, as sometimes is the case, the mother suspects what is happening to her child and yet allows it to continue, the victim's complaints to the mother can be met with lack of support, with disbelief, and even with hostility.

Great skill is required in questioning a child about possible sexual abuse to ensure that the report is accurate, to avoid biasing the youngster one way or the other, and to minimize the stress that is inevitable in recounting a disturbing experience, especially if a decision is made to prosecute. Some jurisdictions use innovative procedures that can reduce the stress on the child while protecting the rights of the accused, for example, videotaped testimony, closed-courtroom trials, closed-circuit televised testimony, and special assistants and coaching sessions to explain courtroom etiquette and what to expect (Wolfe, 1990). Having the child play with anatomically correct dolls can be useful in getting at the truth, but it should be but one part of an assessment, because many nonabused children portray such dolls having sexual intercourse (Jampole & Weber, 1987). While doing everything possible to enable an abused child to reveal what has happened to him or her, care must be taken not to lead the child to report abuse that did not take place. All things considered, it is little wonder that many, perhaps most, occurrences of child molestation within families go unreported

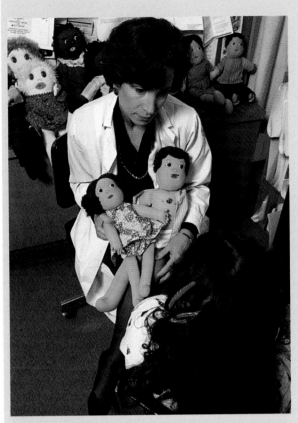

Great sensitivity is required when interviewing a child about the possibility of sexual abuse. Anatomically correct dolls are often used to facilitate the process.

whom the child knows and probably also trusts. The betrayal of this trust makes the crime more abhorrent than it would be if no prior relationship existed between perpetrator and victim.

PREVENTION

An important goal of any prevention program (in Chapter 19 we discuss prevention as a key aspect of what is called community psychology; p. 575) is to reduce the incidence, prevalence, and severity of a particular problem. For CSA, prevention efforts have focused on elementary schools. Content varies from program to program, but common elements include teaching children how to recognize inappropriate adult behavior, to resist inducements, to leave the situation quickly, and to report the incident to an appropriate adult (Wolfe, 1990). Children are taught to say no in a firm, assertive way when an adult talks to or touches them in a way that makes them feel uncomfortable. Instructors may use comic books, films, and descriptions of risky situations to try to teach about the nature of sexual abuse and how children can protect themselves. Evaluations of school programs tend to support the notion that they increase awareness of sexual abuse among children, but less is known about

and become a developing adult's terrible secret that can lower self-esteem, distort what could otherwise be positive relationships, and even contribute to serious mental disorders.

Parents go through their own crisis when they become aware that someone has been molesting their child. If incest is involved, it is a true family crisis; and if it is the father, then there is often conflict about what to do, for he is frequently the dominant figure in the family and is feared as well as loved. Shame and guilt abound within the home, and the family may well be struggling with other serious problems, such as alcoholism in one or both parents. Decisions have to be made about how to protect the youngster from further sexual abuse or vindictive threats or actions from a frightened, angry perpetrator. The incest victim's mother is in a particularly difficult situation, sometimes torn between her husband and her child, sometimes facing financial uncertainty should the father leave the home or be arrested. It is impossible to know what percentage of incest cases are not reported to the police, but it is safe to say that it is sizable, perhaps the great majority (Finkelhor, 1983). Pedophilic offenses, when the perpetrator is not a member of the family, are more frequently reported to police and prosecuted in court.

Parents also need help in knowing how to respond to the child's allegations. A parent's strong emotional reaction, although understandable, is likely to make the child feel worse, yet the complaints must be taken seriously. It is important to remember that children construe things differently than adults, and although molestation of any kind is serious, pre-school-aged children may well not understand the exact nature of what has been done to them. Still, they must be protected and sometimes treated for physical injuries.

After the immediate crisis is past, many children may need continued professional attention (Wolfe, 1990). Like adult victims of rape (p. 378)—and in a very real sense molested children are often rape victims—posttraumatic stress disorder can be a consequence. Many interventions are similar to those used for PTSD in adults; the emphasis is on exposure to memories of the trauma through discussion in a safe and supportive therapeutic atmosphere (Johnson, 1987). Also important is learning that healthy human sexuality is not about power and fear, that it can be a bolstering part of one's personality as one continues to mature (McCarthy, 1986). Inhibitions about body contact can be addressed in group therapy settings via structured, nonsexual hand-holding and back rubs (Wolfe, 1990). As with rape, it is important to externalize the blame for what happened, changing the victim's attribution of responsibility from an "I was bad" self-concept to "He/she was bad." Intervention varies with the subject's age—a fourteen-year-old does not need dolls to recount what was done, and a three-year-old is not an appropriate candidate for group therapy. As yet there has been no controlled research on these various and complex interventions, but clinical reports are encouraging.

The sexual sadist obtains sexual gratification from inflicting pain or humiliation on another person, often a sexual masochist, who is aroused by being dominated or humiliated.

masochists outnumber sadists. For this reason bondage-and-discipline services may constitute a considerable portion of the business of a house of prostitution. The manifestations of sexual masochism are varied. Examples include restraint (physical bondage), blindfolding (sensory bondage), spanking, whipping, electrical shocks, cutting, and humiliation (e.g., being urinated or defecated on, being forced to bark like a dog, or being subjected to verbal abuse). The term *infantilism* refers to a desire to be treated as a helpless infant and clothed in diapers. One particularly dangerous form of masochism, called hypoxyphilia, involves sexual arousal by oxygen deprivation, which can be achieved using a noose, a plastic bag, chest compression, or a chemical that produces a temporary decrease in brain oxygenation by peripheral vasodilation (APA, 1994).

The shared activities of a sadist and a masochist are heavily scripted (Gagnon & Simon, 1977). Pain, humiliation and domination, or both take place as part of a story that the two agree to act out together. Themes of submission–domination appear to be as important as inflicting physical pain. The activities of the sadist and masochist assume for both parties a certain fictional *meaning* that heightens sexual arousal. The masochist, for example, may be a mischievous child who must be punished by a discipline-minded teacher, or a slave from ancient times, recently sold to a powerful sultan.

Some sadists do occasionally murder and mutilate and are among sex offenders who are imprisoned for torturing victims, mostly strangers, and deriving sexual satisfaction from doing so (Dietz, Hazelwood, & Warren, 1990). When sadists aggress against people, the pattern of their offenses differs from that of nonsadistic sex offenders; sadistic offenders seem more often to impersonate police officers, commit serial murders, tie up their victims, and conceal the corpse (Gratzer & Bradford, 1995). Fortunately, however, sadism and masochism are usually restricted to fantasies and are not then regarded as disorders according to the DSM, unless the person is "markedly distressed by them." This is a constant theme in DSM-IV, that is, that it is okay to have very unconventional fantasies provided that one does not act on them or that one is not bothered by them. If the social milieu supports creativity, at least in fantasies, we can expect more people not to be bothered by the stories they tell themselves and the pictures they generate in their minds while having sex. The result may be more sadistic and/or masochistic fantasies but less diagnosable sadism and masochism.

ETIOLOGY OF THE PARAPHILIAS

Of the many theories and hypotheses about the etiology of the paraphilias, the principal ones come from psychodynamic and behavioral perspectives; others are from the biological perspective.

PSYCHODYNAMIC PERSPECTIVES

The paraphilias are viewed by psychodynamic theorists as defensive in nature, guarding the ego from dealing with repressed fears and memories and representing fixations at pregenital stages of psychosexual development. The person with a paraphilia is seen as someone who is fearful of conventional heterosexual relationships, even of hetero*social* relationships that do not involve sex. His (less often, her) social and sexual development is immature, stunted, and overall inadequate for both social and heterosexual intercourse with the adult world (Lanyon, 1986).[3]

---

[3]It is interesting to note that psychoanalytic views of sexual problems often implicate nonsexual factors such as those just mentioned, whereas analytic theorizing about nonsexual disorders usually implicates sexual urges.

For example, the fetishist and the pedophile are viewed as men whose castration anxiety makes heterosexual sex with other adults too threatening. Castration anxiety leads the exhibitionist to reassure himself of his masculinity by showing his manhood (his genitals) to others; it results in the sadist's dominating others, sometimes to the extent of harming them.

The voyeur prefers to spy on unaware women rather than to have direct contact with them. If the woman the voyeur is watching surreptitiously should become aware of him, he might conclude that she has some interest in him, which, because of his insecurity as a man and a lover, would be extremely threatening and thereby less sexually arousing to him. It may be then that a man engages in voyeurism not because the risk of being discovered is titillating; rather, undiscovered peeping, because it protects the voyeur from a possible relationship with a woman, may be the least frightening way for him to have some kind of contact with her.

BEHAVIORAL AND COGNITIVE PERSPECTIVES

Theorists operating within a behavioral paradigm often hold the view that the paraphilias arise from classical conditioning that by chance has linked sexual arousal with classes of stimuli deemed by the culture to be inappropriate causes of sexual arousal (Kinsey et al., 1948; Kinsey et al., 1954). A young man may—for whatever reasons—masturbate to pictures or images of women dressed in black leather boots. According to this theory, repetitions of these experiences endow boots with properties of sexual arousal. Similar proposals have been made for transvestism, pedophilia, voyeurism, and exhibitionism. Although there is some minor support from clinical case studies (e.g., McGuire, Carlisle, & Young, 1965) and controlled experimentation (e.g., Rachman, 1966), this orgasm-conditioning hypothesis enjoys very little empirical support (O'Donohue & Plaud, 1994). However, as described later, some innovative therapeutic strategies have been developed based on this etiological speculation.

Another behavioral hypothesis focuses on anxiety or frustration that prevents the person with a paraphilia from approaching and interacting with people in conventional ways. It has been suggested that fathers who commit incest may do so because of serious marital problems (although to be sure, the overwhelming majority of maritally distressed men do *not* commit incest). According to this theory, feeling constrained by religious prohibitions against extramarital affairs or contacts with prostitutes, the man seeks sexual and emotional gratification from his daughter, keeping things "in the family," as it were (Frude, 1982; Lang et al., 1990). One wonders, though, how having sex with one's daughter is more acceptable within *any* religious framework than having sex with a mature adult outside the family.

From an operant conditioning perspective, many paraphilias are considered an outcome of inadequate social skills or reinforcement of unconventionality by parents or relatives. For example, case histories of transvestites often refer to childhood incidents in which the little boy was praised and fussed over for looking cute in his mother's dresses.

Hypotheses that focus on cognitions sometimes sound psychoanalytic in nature. For example, some clinicians of a cognitive-behavioral perspective and some of a psychodynamic persuasion regard transvestism as a beleaguered male's refuge from responsibilities he sees himself saddled with solely by virtue of being a man. Women's clothing, then, is believed to have a particular *meaning* for the male transvestite beyond any sexual arousal that is elicited by donning it. Perhaps less rigid gender roles will alter the meaning that women's clothes have for such men. (Interestingly, in recent years men's clothing, including underwear, has been available in silky fabrics formerly reserved for women's clothing.)

BIOLOGICAL PERSPECTIVES

As the overwhelming majority of people with paraphilias are male, there has been speculation that androgen, the principal male hormone, plays a role. Because the human fetus begins as a female, with maleness emerging from later hormonal influences, perhaps something can go wrong during fetal development. Findings of hormonal differences between normal people and people with paraphilias are inconclusive, however. If biology turns out to be important, it most likely will be but one factor in a complex network of causes that includes experience as a major, if not *the* major, player (Meyer, 1995).

THERAPIES FOR THE PARAPHILIAS

A prevalent psychoanalytic view of the paraphilias is that they arise from a character disorder, an older term for personality disorder, and that they are therefore exceedingly difficult to treat with any reasonable expectation of success. This perspective is probably also held by the courts and by the lay public (Lanyon, 1986). Although psychoanalytic views have had an impact on views of causation, they have made few contributions to effective therapy for these disorders.

Behavior therapists have been less interested in presumed deep-seated personality defects among people with paraphilias and have focused more on the particular pattern of unconventional sexuality. Consequently, they have tried to develop therapeutic procedures for changing only the sexual aspect of the individual's makeup. Some successes have been achieved, especially when a variety of techniques are used in a broad-spectrum, multifaceted treatment (Becker, 1990; Maletsky, 1991; Marshall et al., 1991).

In the earliest years of behavior therapy, paraphilias were narrowly viewed as attractions to inappropriate objects and activities. Looking to experimental psychology for ways to reduce these attractions, workers fixed on aversion therapy. Thus a boot fetishist would be given shock (on the hands or feet) or an emetic when looking at a boot, a transvestite when cross-dressing, a pedophile when gazing at a photograph of a nude child, and so on. It was soon recognized that many of these individuals related poorly to others in ordinary social situations, such as making small talk, and even more poorly, if at all, through conventional sexual activity. Aversive treatments, therefore, were supplemented by social-skills training. There is reason to believe that aversion therapy, especially when combined with skills training, can have some beneficial effects on pedophilia, transvestism, exhibitionism, and fetishism (Brownell, Hayes, & Barlow, 1977; Marks & Gelder, 1967; Marks, Gelder, & Bancroft, 1970; Marshall & Barabee, 1990). Although aversion therapy may not completely eliminate the attraction, in some cases it provides the patient with a greater measure of control over the overt behavior (McConaghy, 1990, 1994).

Patients with one of the paraphilias also need help increasing their arousal to conventional stimuli. **Orgasmic reorientation** is a behavioral technique used to enhance sexual arousal to particular classes of stimuli (Brownell et al., 1977). In this procedure patients (again, most of whom are men) are confronted with a conventionally arousing stimulus, such as a photograph of a woman, while they are responding sexually for other, undesirable reasons. In the first clinical demonstration of this technique, Davison (1968a) instructed a young man troubled by sadistic fantasies to masturbate at home in the following manner:

When assured of privacy in his dormitory room … he was first to obtain an erection by whatever means possible—undoubtedly with a sadistic fantasy, as he indicated. He was then to begin to masturbate while looking at a picture of a sexy, nude woman (the "target" sexual stimulus). … If he began losing his erection, he was to switch back to his sadistic fantasy until he could begin masturbating effectively again. Concentrating again on the ... picture, he was to continue masturbating, using the fantasy only to regain the erection. As orgasm was approaching, he was at all costs to focus on the ... picture. (p. 84)

The client was able to follow these instructions and over a period of weeks began to find conventional pictures, ideas, and images sexually arousing. However, the therapist had to complement the orgasmic procedure with some aversion therapy (Cautela, 1966) for the sadistic imaginings. The follow-up after a year and a half found the client capable of conventional arousal, although he apparently reverted to his sadistic fantasies every now and again. This dubious outcome has been reported for other instances of orgasmic reorientation, but behavior therapists continue to explore its possibilities, and some behavior therapists believe it to be the treatment of choice for increasing conventional sexual arousal in persons with paraphilias (Abel, Mittelman, & Becker, 1985).

As mentioned at the beginning of this chapter, most paraphilias are illegal, and some of them, such as child molestation, pose dangers to others. Thus many child molesters and rapists (discussed later) are imprisoned or committed to mental hospitals (see Chapter 20). Treatment outcomes for incarcerated sex offenders are highly variable; published success rates range from more than 90 percent to as low as 30 percent (Marshall et al., 1991). Published data are hard to interpret for several reasons. Some programs select the most problematic prisoners for treatment, whereas others treat those with the most promising prognoses, for example, first offenders. Some programs do not have follow-up sessions after release, while others do. Recidivism increases as the years go by, especially when two years have passed since termination of treatment (Marshall & Barabee, 1990).

As we have seen with substance abusers, sex offenders often lack motivation to try to change their illegal behavior. Undermining their motivation for treatment are such factors as denial of their problem, minimizing the seriousness of their problem, a belief that their victims will not be credible witnesses, and the confidence that they can control their behavior without professional assistance. For these reasons they are frequently judged to be inappropriate for treatment programs (Dougher, 1988) and, when they do become involved, to drop out (Knopp, 1984). Methods are available to enhance their motivation (Miller & Rollnick, 1991). For example, the therapist can empathize with the person's reluctance to admit that he is an offender,

thereby reducing the defensiveness and hostility; point out to him the treatments available that might help him control his behavior better; emphasize the negative consequences of refusing treatment (e.g., transfer to a less attractive incarceration setting if the person is already in custody) and of offending again (e.g., stiffer legal penalties); having elaborated on the possible benefits of treatment, implement a paradoxical intervention (see p. 542) by expressing doubt that the person is motivated to enter into or continue in treatment, thereby challenging him to prove wrong the therapist whom he has been resisting; and explain that there will be a psychophysiological assessment of his sexual arousal, the implication being that this can reveal his sexual proclivities without his admitting to them (Garland & Dougher, 1991).

The doubtful outcomes of efforts to rehabilitate sex offenders, which result in the release from prison of rapists and child molesters who commit these crimes again, have led to public pressure to forbid such offenders from returning where they were arrested. A further trend is exemplified in recent laws that allow police to publicize the whereabouts of registered sex offenders if they are considered by the police to be a potential danger. The law also permits citizens to use police computers to determine whether such individuals are living in their neighborhoods. Referred to by some as Megan's Law, this statute and others like it across the country arose from public outrage at the brutal murder of a second grader in New Jersey who was kidnapped while walking home from school. The person convicted of this crime was a twice-convicted child molester. The law applies to sex offenders who have harmed adults or children (Ingram, 1996). Tracking offenders will be facilitated by a national computer network created by President Clinton in August 1996, which allows police to monitor these people anywhere in the country (Kempster, 1996).

An unintended consequence of Megan's law is that people who were arrested many years ago for consensual gay sex are now being contacted by police departments with the demand that they be certain that they have registered as sex offenders so that their presence in their community can be generally known, even though the laws under which they were originally arrested are no longer on the books, and even though the current concern is to protect people from sexual predators, not those who were involved long ago in consensual homosexual sex with another adult. The means of notification can often be indiscreet. One ninety-year-old man who pled guilty to a charge of lewd conduct in 1944 after police found him touching another man's knee in a car parked in a secluded area was recently notified by police that he had to register as a sex offender or else be arrested. The letter came to his home in an envelope stamped "SEX CRIME" in red ink, and his wife, who did not know of his arrest more than fifty years earlier, opened it before he had a chance to (Riccardo & Leeds, 1997).

A variety of medical interventions have also been tried on sex offenders. Castration, or removal of the testes, was used a great deal in western Europe a generation ago, with some apparent efficacy in terms of reducing the incidence of paraphiliac behavior (e.g., Langeluddeke, 1963). However, those operated on were a heterogeneous group; among them were homosexuals involved in *noncoercive* sex with other adults (Marshall et al., 1991). It is unclear how many were offenders whose crimes harmed innocent others, that is, child molesters and rapists. The lack of clarity of outcome, coupled with major ethical concerns, has led to infrequent use of castration today though there are trends to use chemical means as described next.

Biological efforts to control illegal and socially disapproved paraphiliac behavior among sex offenders have more recently involved the use of drugs. Treatment has employed medroxyprogesterone acetate (MPA, trade name Depo-Provera), which lowers testosterone levels in men. By reducing the frequency of erections and ejaculations, use of this drug presumably inhibits unconventional sexual arousal and consequent disapproved behavior. Results so far are mixed. In an early study Berlin and Meinecke (1981) found that after periods of MPA administration ranging from five to twenty years, seventeen of twenty sex offenders did not engage in paraphiliac behaviors; however, when the drug was discontinued, most reverted to their forbidden ways. More favorable results have also been reported, however (Green, 1992; McConaghy et al., 1988). If this sexual appetite suppressant has to be taken indefinitely, many ethical issues are raised, including the sometimes serious side effects of long-term use, such as infertility and diabetes (Gunn, 1993).

A sensible program of treatment must always consider the multifaceted nature of a particular disorder. An exhibitionist, for example, may experience a great deal of tension in connection with the urge to expose himself; it would therefore make sense to desensitize him to women who cause sexual arousal in him. After imagining them in a succession of street and other public scenes until they no longer make him anxious, he may be more relaxed when he encounters these types of women in public places and so may not feel the urge to expose (Bond

& Hutchison, 1960). Other people with paraphilias might be questioned about social situations and aspects of relating to women that cause them undue discomfort. They could be desensitized to these situations in the hope of becoming generally less anxious. Social-skills training and sex education are often warranted to address deficits that are commonly found among such individuals. Finally, the availability of an adult sexual partner strengthens the potential for long-term improvement.

There is a call for a multifaceted approach in the treatment of incest, a problem that is increasingly viewed as involving an entire family—the victim, the spouse, and siblings. A **family systems approach** is advocated, whereby the entire family is involved in therapy sessions that are primarily insight oriented, aimed at helping all members understand why the father (in most instances) turns to a daughter for emotional support and sexual gratification (Lanyon, 1986).

In general, cognitive-behavioral approaches have become more sophisticated and broader in scope since the 1960s, when the paraphilias were addressed almost exclusively in terms of sexual attraction to inappropriate environmental stimuli. In many instances therapy is modeled on the approach of Masters and Johnson (1970; cf. p. 392), under the assumption that some paraphilias develop or are maintained by unsatisfactory sexual relationships with consenting adults (Marshall & Barabee, 1990). Overall, both institution-based and outpatient programs that follow a cognitive-behavioral model with sex offenders reduce recidivism more than what would be expected were no treatment at all attempted. These outcomes are much better for child molesters than for rapists. Although sex offenders generally evoke disgust and fear more than genuine interest from people, society often overlooks the fact that efforts to treat such people, even if only minimally effective, are not only cost-effective but stand the chance of protecting others when the person is released from prison (Prentky & Burgess, 1990).

As mentioned earlier, a problem in any treatment of sex offenders is the pattern of denial and refusal to take responsibility for the offense. Many child molesters and rapists do not regard their behavior as problematic. Some blame the victim—even a child—for being overly seductive. Many rapists assert that their victims really enjoyed the experience and that their "no" really meant "yes." Still others blame their unhappy childhoods or deprived social circumstances. Whatever the reasons, treatment is virtually impossible unless the person sees that he has a problem worthy of professional intervention. The need for the offender to acknowledge the problem, however, conflicts with the situation in which society typically places him—treatment is usually *required* of the offender, even if he has served time in prison for his offense. Furthermore, therapists are required to reveal any concerns that arise during treatment that the person may again cause harm (Morenz & Becker, 1995). With all the difficulties associated with treatment, and since incarceration alone has little if any impact on sex offenders, we face a challenging situation indeed.

We have mentioned rape several times in our discussion of the paraphilias, especially in connection with pedophilia and incest; yet forced sexual contact occurs far more often between adults than between an adult and a child. We turn now to an examination of the important topic of rape.

RAPE

Few other antisocial acts are viewed with more revulsion and anger by most people than is **forced rape**, sexual intercourse with an unwilling partner. A second category of rape, **statutory rape**, refers to sexual intercourse between a male and a female minor, someone under the age of consent. The age of consent is decided by state statutes and is typically eighteen, although in recent years people have suggested lowering the age. It is assumed that a person younger than the age of consent should not be held responsible for her sexual activity. A charge of statutory rape can be made even if it is proved that the girl entered into the situation knowingly and willingly. Thus statutory rape need not involve force, only a consummated intercourse with a female minor that was reported to the police. We focus in this section on forced rape.

THE CRIME

In what is sometimes termed *sadistic rape*, the rapist severely injures the victim's body, for example, by inserting foreign objects into the vagina or pulling and burning her breasts. We are all too familiar with the fact that some rapists murder and mutilate (Holmstrom & Burgess, 1980). Little wonder then that rape is considered as much an act of violence, aggression, and domination as an act of sex. In many jurisdictions the definition of rape includes oral and anal entry as well as vaginal penetration. Focusing on the victim's reactions—the helplessness, fear, and humiliation—rather than on the specifics of the perpetrator's acts, Calhoun and Atkeson (1991) con-

strue *any* act of sexual domination as rape. This expanded definition may be useful for purposes of helping victims, but it differs from legal definitions. Although men can be victims of sexual assault—especially by other men in prison—our discussion focuses on women because rape is primarily an act committed by men against women.

As many as 25 percent of American women will be raped during their lifetimes (Kilpatrick & Best, 1990), and it is likely that more than 80 percent of sexual assaults are not reported. If we consider coerced sexual activity that stops short of rape, findings show that as many as 75 percent of female college students have been subjected to this type of unwanted sexual activity (Koss, 1985).

THE VICTIM, THE ATTACK, AND THE AFTERMATH

A prevalent belief is that all women who are raped are young and attractive. This is a myth; although many victims do fit this description, many others do not. Age and physical appearance are no barriers to some rapists; they may choose children as young as one year old and women in their eighties.

Rape victims are usually traumatized by the attack, both physically and mentally (Calhoun, Atkeson, & Resick, 1982; Resick et al., 1986; Resick, 1993; Rothbaum et al., 1992). In the minutes or seconds preceding rape, the woman begins to recognize her dangerous situation but can scarcely believe what is about to happen to her. During the assault she is first and foremost in great fear for her life. The physical violation of her body and the ripping away of her freedom of choice are enraging, but the victim also feels her vulnerability in not being able to fight off her typically stronger attacker. Moreover, the attacker usually has the element of surprise and sometimes a weapon to intimidate and coerce. Resistance is seriously compromised by terror. For weeks or months following the rape many victims feel extremely tense and deeply humiliated; they feel guilt that they were unable to fight harder and may have angry thoughts of revenge. Many have nightmares about the rape. Depression and loss of self-esteem are common. Some victims of rape develop phobias about being outdoors or indoors or in the dark, depending on where the rape took place. They may also fear being alone or in crowds or having anyone behind them. Unfortunately, some of these reactions are exacerbated by insensitivity on the part of police and even friends and loved ones, some of whom may question the victim's complicity in what happened (more on this later). Sometimes an unwanted pregnancy results from a rape, and justifiable concern about sexually transmitted diseases, including AIDS (p. 394), adds to the trauma of the attack. For good reason DSM-IV mentions rape as one of the traumas that can give rise to posttraumatic stress disorder (p. 149).

Many women who have been raped subsequently develop a negative attitude toward sex and experience difficulty in their relationships with their husbands or lovers (Becker et al., 1986). So certain are Calhoun and Atkeson (1991), two experienced clinical researchers on rape, that sexual problems are a frequent long-term consequence of untreated rape trauma that they urge clinicians to consider the possibility that rape or sexual assault has occurred in women who come to therapy for many of the sexual dysfunctions discussed later in this chapter. For some women, even though frequency of sex and of orgasms may not be diminished, satisfaction with sex can be reduced for years (Feldman-Summers, Gordon, & Mengler, 1979).

Without intervention, symptoms of anxiety and depression—and in some cases, full-blown PTSD—can persist in some women for many years following an assault (Calhoun & Atkeson, 1991; Resick, 1993). Suicidal risk is also high for many victims (Cohen & Roth, 1987; Kilpatrick et al., 1985; Kilpatrick et al., 1992), as is substance abuse (Burnam et al., 1988), which might have begun as an attempt to self-medicate to reduce anxiety and general dysphoria. Moreover, consistent with research on the effects of stress on physical health, rape victims can suffer a variety of somatic problems and their use of medical services tends to increase (Phelps, Wallace, & Waigant, 1989).

The nature and duration of what some call rape trauma syndrome (Burgess & Holstrom, 1974) depend a great deal on what the victim's life is like both prior to and following the attack. Factors that can mitigate the negative aftermath of rape include a supportive spouse and friends as well as the kind of crisis intervention described later (Atkeson et al., 1982; Ruch & Leon, 1983). Research is inconclusive, however, as to whether the negative emotional consequences of rape correlate with the violence of the assault, the setting, or the familiarity of the rapist (Resick, 1993). These complexities led Calhoun and Atkeson (1991) to conclude that the aftermath is more a function of how the victim appraises the events than of the circumstances themselves. Again we see the apparent importance of how people *construe* events.

Many jurisdictions allow the very existence of rape trauma syndrome in a victim, which may include depression, anxiety, and sleep disturbances, to be admitted as evidence supporting an allegation of rape. The existence of the syndrome may also explain behavior on the part of the victim that might otherwise be considered an indication of consent, for example, delays in reporting the crime, memory loss, and making inconsistent statements (Block, 1990).

THE RAPIST

The vast majority of rapes are almost surely planned; it is inaccurate to say that rape is the spontaneous act of a man whose sexual impulses have gone out of control. The rapist may have a sadistic streak, but unlike the sadist, he often does not know the victim beforehand and attacks someone who is unwilling; moreover, a sadist usually has an established, ongoing relationship with a masochist that involves voluntary mutual exchange of sexually pleasurable pain. In many cases, a pattern of repeated rape is part of a psychopathic lifestyle.

Many rapists do not reach orgasm during the attack, and some may not even attain or maintain an erection. In one study of 170 men convicted of sexual assault, one-third of the subjects had experienced erectile failure as well as premature and retarded ejaculation during the criminal act although almost none reported having had these problems in consenting sexual relations. Only one-fourth of the men gave no evidence of sexual dysfunction during rape (Groth & Burgess, 1977). Rapists often abuse alcohol, so the frequency of erectile failure might be due in part to the inhibitory effects of alcohol on sexual arousal (Wilson & Lawson, 1976). Also, the violence that is intrinsic to rape may arise from the *disinhibitory* effects of alcohol on aggression (Barabee, Marshall, & Yates, 1983).

As documented some years ago in a classic book on the politics of rape, that men with their generally superior strength can usually overpower women buttresses the view that rape has served in the past and still serves to control and intimidate women (Brownmiller, 1975). The Crusaders raped their way across Europe on their holy pilgrimages in the eleventh through the thirteenth centuries to free Jerusalem from the Muslims; the Germans raped as they rampaged through Belgium in World War I; U.S. forces raped Vietnamese women and girls as they searched and destroyed; Iraqi soldiers raped and brutalized women as they occupied Kuwait in 1990; and most recently, some male soldiers in U.S. Army training bases have been found to have raped female soldiers under their command. Brownmiller contends that rape is actually *expected* in war. In her view membership in the most exclusive males-only clubs in the world—the fighting forces of most nations—encourages a perverse sense of masculine superiority and creates a climate in which rape is acceptable (1975).

In June 1996 a United Nations tribunal announced the indictment of eight Bosnian-Serb soldiers and police for the rape of Muslim women during the Bosnian war in 1992–1993. What is noteworthy about this action is that it is the first time that sexual assault has been treated separately as a war crime. Previously, as in the Nuremberg trials that judged Nazi war crimes during World War II, rape was not mentioned specifically. Rape during war will now occupy the attention of the international community, making it less likely that it will be tacitly condoned or regarded as an inevitable part of one nation or group waging war against another (Simons, 1996).

Who is the rapist? Is he primarily the psychopath who seeks the thrill of dominating and humiliating a woman through intimidation and often brutal assault? Is he an ordinarily unassertive man with a fragile ego who, feeling inadequate after disappointment and rejection in work or love, takes out his frustrations on an unwilling stranger? Is he an otherwise respectable, even honored, man in authority who takes advantage of his position of power over a woman? Or is he the teenager, provoked by a seductive and apparently available young woman who, it turns out, was not as interested as he in sexual intimacy? Is he a man whose inhibitions against expressing anger have been dissolved by alcohol? The best answer is that the rapist is all these men, often operating under a combination of several of these circumstances.

What many rapists probably have in common is unusually high hostility toward women, arising from beliefs of having been betrayed, deceived, or demeaned by them (Duke & Durham, 1990). Reports from rapists indicate that the urge to rape is heightened by feelings of loneliness, anger, humiliation, inadequacy, and rejection (McKibben, Proulx, & Lusignan, 1994). From a sociological perspective, the more a society accepts interpersonal violence as a way to handle conflict and solve problems, the higher the frequency of rape (Sanday, 1981). It seems worth noting that in a controlled experiment male college students who stated that they regarded rape as unacceptable were aroused by video portrayals of rape if the woman was depicted as having an orgasm during the assault (Malamuth & Check, 1983). This research suggests that rape may be encouraged by pornography that depicts women enjoying coerced sexual relations.

Rape occurs also on dates, so-called **acquaintance rape**, or **date rape**. Rapes of this kind outnumber rapes by strangers by as much as three to one (Kilpatrick & Best, 1990). Date rape victims tend to be blamed for the rape and tend to blame themselves more than do women who are raped by

Rape victims of the war in Bosnia. Rape occurs frequently during war but only recently has sexual assault been considered a war crime.

strangers—after all, date rape victims associated willingly with the men who raped them. This viewpoint has been strongly challenged, however, for it overlooks the right of the weaker party, usually the woman, to say no at any time. Willingness to have dinner, even to embrace and kiss, is not tantamount to consenting to anything more intimate.

A recent development with regard to date rape is the use of the tranquilizer Rohypnol. This drug is

This famous scene from *Gone with the Wind* illustrates one of the myths about rape—that despite initial resistance women like to be "taken."

odorless and tasteless and can be easily slipped into a drink; if ingested, it causes the person to pass out and have little if any memory of what happens. Men have used Rohypnol to enable them to rape women when on a date. In August 1996 a federal law was passed making it possible to add up to twenty years to a sentence for conviction of rape or other violent crimes if Rohypnol has been used. What is particularly significant is that this is the first U.S. law that makes the use of a drug in a criminal offense grounds for increasing the penalty for that crime (Associated Press, 1996).

Studies of rape and of other patterns of unconventional sexual behavior indicate that sexuality can serve many purposes. An act labeled sexual because it involves the genitalia may sometimes be better understood in nonsexual terms. The classic study of sex offenders (Gebhard et al., 1965) concluded that up to 33 percent of rapists carried out the act to express aggression rather than to gain sexual satisfaction.

Many feminist groups object to the classification of rape as a *sexual* crime at all, lest this terminology mask the basically assaultive and typically brutal nature of the act and create an atmosphere in which the sexual motives of the *victim* are questioned. Although a person who is beaten and robbed without being sexually abused is hardly suspected of secretly wanting to be attacked, by cruel irony the victim of rape must often prove her moral purity to husbands, friends, police—even to herself. What did *she* do that might have contributed to the incident? After all, she must have done something, especially if the rapist is not a complete stranger. There are indications that the stigma of rape is being lessened by more enlightened views.

THERAPY FOR RAPISTS AND RAPE VICTIMS

Unlike most of the disorders discussed in this book, rape has the dubious distinction of presenting two different challenges to the mental health professional: treating the man who has committed the act and treating the woman who has been the victim.

Therapists who try to help men who rape have to consider a wide range of causes that might underlie the problem—loneliness, deficient social skills (Overholser & Beck, 1986), fear of dealing with women in conventional ways, hatred of women, inability or unwillingness to delay gratification, especially after excessive drinking, and exaggerated conceptions of masculinity that relegate women to an inferior status.

A number of therapy programs have been developed to reduce the tendency of men to rape. In some prisons confrontational group therapy has been employed in efforts to goad convicted rapists, in direct and unmistakable terms, to take responsibility for their violence toward women and to explore more decent ways of handling their anger and relating to the opposite sex. They are encouraged to feel empathy for rape victims, an approach consistent with advice sometimes given to women should they find themselves in a rape situation, that is, to personalize themselves, for example, by talking about their children, friends, or job. But the effectiveness of these programs has not been adequately studied. Most rapists assault many times in their lives, and prison terms have limited effect on reducing the future incidence of rape.

Biological interventions, such as surgical castration and the chemical lowering of testosterone, rest on the assumption that rape is primarily a sexual act. However, as mentioned earlier, having an erection is not necessary for rape. These drastic medical measures do not fully address the violent, aggressive aspects of this act (Geer, Heiman, & Leitenberg, 1984). Moreover, there are still questions about the effectiveness of castration as a means of lowering the sex drive in adult human beings.

Efforts to counsel rape victims have expanded considerably in recent years. Rape crisis centers and telephone hot lines have been established throughout the United States. Some are associated with hospitals and clinics; others operate on their own. Staffed both by professionals and by female volunteers who may themselves have been rape victims, these centers offer support and advice within a crisis intervention framework. They focus on normalizing the victim's emotional reactions—"Everyone goes through this emotional turmoil after an assault"—encouraging her to talk about her feelings, and helping her meet immediate needs such as arranging for child care or improving the security arrangements in her home. In short, the goal is to help the victim solve problems and cope with the immediate aftermath of the traumatic event (Calhoun & Atkeson, 1991; Sorenson & Brown, 1990). Discouraging self-blame is also important (Frazier, 1990), especially when the rapist was someone the woman knew (Stewart et al., 1987).

Rape counselors urge the woman not to withdraw or become inactive. Women from the crisis center often accompany the rape victim to the hospital and to the police station, where they help her with the legal procedures and with recounting the events of the attack. They may later arrange for examinations for pregnancy and venereal diseases and for professional therapy if necessary. The possibility of HIV infection also has to be addressed. Empathic companions from the crisis center help the victim begin to express her feelings about the ordeal, and they urge her to continue venting with her own relatives and friends. If the attacker or attackers have been apprehended, women from the center support the victim in her decision to go through with prosecuting the rapist. They attend both her meetings with the district attorney and the trial itself.

If the victim sees a mental health professional, that person typically focuses attention on the woman's ongoing relationships, which may be disrupted or negatively affected by the rape. Friends and family, especially spouses and lovers, will need help handling their own emotional turmoil so that they can provide the kind of nonjudgmental support that rape victims need. Much of the therapy for rape has a great deal in common with the treatment of PTSD (Keane et al., 1989). The victim is asked to relive the fearsome events of the attack by discussing them with the therapist, perhaps also imagining them in vivid detail. Such repeated exposure to the trauma is designed to extinguish the fear (or, in psychoanalytic terms, work it through) (Calhoun & Atkeson, 1991; Calhoun & Resick, 1993; Rothbaum & Foa, 1992). As is the case with other kinds of anxieties, it is no easy task to encourage the person to reflect on her fears, because denial and avoidance are the typical coping methods used by rape victims—for the most part unsuccessfully. Depression can be addressed by helping the woman reevaluate her role in the rape, as many victims tend to see themselves as (at least partially) responsible. A little-researched topic is the anger and rage many victims have toward their assailants; women are often afraid of expressing or socialized not to express such feelings (Calhoun & Atkeson, 1991).

A cognitive-behavioral intervention that is beginning to be empirically validated is the cognitive processing therapy of Resick (1992; Resick & Schnicke, 1992). This therapy combines the exposure to memories of the trauma that is found in other anxiety-reduction interventions with the kind of cognitive restructuring found in the work of Ellis and Beck. For example, the rape victim is encouraged to dispute any tendency to attribute the blame to herself and to consider fully those aspects of the attack that were beyond her control.

Social attitudes and support systems encourage the victim to report rape and pursue the prosecution of the alleged rapist, but the legal situation is still problematic. Interviews with half a million women indicated three reasons for reluctance to report rape: considering the rape a private matter, fearing reprisals from the rapist or his family or friends, and believing that the police would be inefficient, ineffective, or insensitive (Wright, 1991). Estimates are that only a very small percentage of rapists are ultimately convicted of their crimes. Furthermore, there is no denying that going to trial is very stressful; any familiarity of the victim with her assailant argues strongly against conviction, and the victim's role in her own assault is almost always examined by defense attorneys. Finally, even though many rapists rape hundreds of times, they are only occasionally imprisoned for an offense. Society must be attentive and active to ensure that the victim's rights are defended by the legal system.

Before closing the discussion of the paraphilias, we present in Focus 14.2 a brief discussion of a sexual variation that used to be considered abnormal—homosexuality.

SEXUAL DYSFUNCTIONS

Robert S. was a highly intelligent and accomplished twenty-five-year-old graduate student in physics at a leading East Coast university who consulted us for what he called "sexual diffidence." He was engaged to a young woman whom he said he loved very much and with whom he felt compatible in every conceivable way except in bed. There, try as he might, and with apparent understanding from his fiancée, he found himself interested very little either in initiating sexual contact or in responding to it when initiated by her. Both parties believed for the two years of their friendship and later engagement that academic pressures on the man lay at the root of the problem, but an early discussion with the therapist revealed that the client had had little interest in sex—either with men or with women—for as far back as he could remember, and that his desire for sex did not increase when pressures from other obligations lessened. He asserted that he found his fiancée very attractive and appealing, but, as with other young women he had known, his feelings were not passionate.

He had masturbated very infrequently in adolescence and did not begin dating until late in college, though he had had many female acquaintances. His general approach to life, including sex, was analytical and intellectual, and he described his problems in a very dispassionate way to the therapist. He freely admitted that he would not have contacted a therapist at all were it not for the quietly stated wishes of his fiancée, who worried that his disinterest in sex would interfere with their future marital relationship.

After a few individual sessions the therapist asked the young man to invite his fiancée to a therapy session, which the client readily agreed to do. During a conjoint session the couple appeared to be very much in love and looking forward to a life together, though the woman expressed concern about her fiancée's lack of interest in her sexually.

FOCUS 14.2 SOME COMMENTS ON HOMOSEXUALITY

Although homosexuality does not appear in DSM-IV as a clearly definable category, we believe that sufficient controversy remains about these patterns of emotion and behavior—among both laypeople and health professionals—to warrant consideration of the topic. A historical overview will provide perspective on some of the many issues surrounding the ways in which we view those whose sexual preferences include or are restricted to members of their own sex.

HOMOSEXUALITY AND THE DSM

From the publication of DSM-II in 1968 until 1973, **homosexuality**, sexual desire or activity directed toward a member of one's own sex, was listed as one of the sexual deviations. In 1973 the Nomenclature Committee of the American Psychiatric Association, under pressure from many professionals and from gay activist groups, recommended to the general membership the elimination of the category homosexuality and the substitution of *sexual orientation disturbance*. This new diagnosis was to be applied to gay men and women who are "disturbed by, in conflict with, or wish to change their sexual orientation." The members of the psychiatric association voted on the issue, and the change was approved, but not without vehement protests from several renowned psychiatrists who remained convinced that homosexuality reflects a fixation at an early stage of psychosexual development and is therefore inherently abnormal.

The controversy continued among mental health professionals, but as DSM-III was being developed during the late 1970s it became increasingly clear that the new nomenclature would maintain the tolerant stance toward homosexuality that had become evident in 1973. The new DSM-III category **ego-dystonic homosexuality** referred to a person who is homosexually aroused, finds this arousal a persistent source of distress, and wishes to become heterosexual. DSM-III, in our view, thereby took an inconsistent position: a homosexual is abnormal if he or she has been persuaded by a prejudiced society that his or her sexual orientation is inherently deviant; at the same time, according to DSM-III, homosexuality is not in itself abnormal!

In the years following publication of DSM-III in 1980, very little use was made by mental health professionals of the diagnosis of ego-dystonic homosexuality. Was this because homosexuals in therapy were no longer asking for sexual reorientation? Did the greater tolerance of homosexuality—despite the AIDS crisis (p. 394) and the erroneous allegation that AIDS was a homosexual problem and maybe even God's punishment for their sins—enable gay people to seek therapy for problems unrelated to their sexual orientation? Perhaps some gay people, as gay activists had been urging for twenty years, were no longer willing to tolerate the prejudice against their sexual orientation and were seeking assistance in resisting societal biases. Perhaps clinicians began to focus more on such problems as anxiety and depression in their gay clients without seeing these problems as necessarily connected with a wish to become heterosexual. It is impossible to establish the exact reasons, but it is clear that by the time the American Psychiatric Association was ready in 1987 to publish DSM-IIIR, it had decided that even the watered-down diagnosis of ego-dystonic homosexuality should not be included. Instead, the catchall category of sexual disorder not otherwise specified referred to "persistent and marked distress about one's sexual orientation" (p. 296); this category is also included in DSM-IV. DSM-IIIR and DSM-IV contain no specific mention of homosexuality as a disorder in its own right.

It is noteworthy that the new category does not specify a sexual orientation. Although the door is still open for a diagnosis of ego-dystonic homosexuality, the psychiatric nosology now appears to allow as well for ego-dystonic *hetero*sexuality. Our own expectation is that *neither* diagnosis is going to be made very often.

HOMOPHOBIA: A DEFENSE AGAINST LATENT HOMOSEXUALITY?

One of the arguments gay activists have made over the years is that antagonism toward homosexuality reflects not a rational analysis but an irrational fear of or aversion to homosexuality—what has been called homophobia. Some writers have alleged that homophobia is an unconscious defensive reaction against a person's unacknowledged homosexual interests or inclinations, a sort of reaction formation.

That homophobic men may be defending against their own homosexuality has been a psychoanalytic hypothesis for many years (e.g., West, 1977). Some recent data from an ingenious experiment lend support to this hitherto theoretical and political position. Adams, Wright, and Lohr (1996) demonstrated that homophobia may be related to unacknowledged—repressed?—homosexual inclinations (latent homosexuality). Undergraduate, male, heterosexual college students, categorized as either homophobic or nonhomophobic via a questionnaire, viewed videotapes explicitly depicting heterosexual, male homosexual, and lesbian acts. Sexual arousal was assessed with a penile plethysmograph and by self-report. The plethysmograph findings showed that, whereas both groups of participants were sexually aroused by the heterosexual and lesbian videos (a common finding among heterosexual men), only the homophobic men were sexually aroused by the male homosexual portrayals, although to a much lesser extent than they were aroused by the heterosexual and lesbian videos. The self-reports of sexual arousal indicated no differences between the two groups, which is consistent with the notion that homophobic men deny their homosexual interests.

Having discussed the unconventional patterns of sexual behavior of a small minority of the population, we turn now to sexual problems that interfere with conventional sexual enjoyment during the course of many people's lives. Our concern here is with **sexual dysfunctions**, the range of sexual problems that are usually considered to represent inhibitions in the normal sexual response cycle.

What is defined as normal and desirable in human sexual behavior varies with time and place. The contemporary view that *inhibitions* of sexual expression underlie abnormality can be contrasted with views held during the nineteenth and early twentieth centuries in the Western world, when *excess* was regarded as the culprit. It is well to keep these varying temporal and cultural norms in mind as we study human sexual dysfunctions.

A psychological problem has consequences not only for the individual who experiences them but also for those with whom he or she is involved. People who are unable to interact socially with others are inevitably cut off from many opportunities in life and often have low opinions of themselves. Such people can be a source of frustration and guilt for a spouse, a child, or a friend. This aspect of human emotional problems is especially important in our consideration of sexual dysfunctions, which usually occur in the context of intimate personal relationships. A marriage is bound to suffer if one or both of the partners fear sex. And most of us, for better or for worse, base part of our self-concept on our sexuality. Do we please the people we love, do we gratify ourselves, or, more simply, are we able to

enjoy the fulfillment and relaxation that can come from a pleasurable sexual experience? Sexual dysfunctions can be so severe that tenderness itself is lost, let alone the more intense satisfaction of sexual activity.

We will look first at the human sexual response cycle as it normally functions and with that as context, the several sexual dysfunctions. Then we will discuss etiologies and therapies for these problems.

SEXUAL DYSFUNCTIONS AND THE HUMAN SEXUAL RESPONSE CYCLE

As indicated in Table 14.1 (p. 359), DSM-IV divides sexual dysfunctions into four principal categories: sexual desire disorders, sexual arousal disorders, orgasm disorders, and sexual pain disorders. The difficulty should be persistent and recurrent, a clinical judgment acknowledged in the DSM to entail a degree of subjectivity. The requirement that the disturbance cause marked distress or interpersonal problems is new in DSM-IV and allows the person's *own* reactions to, say, having no interest in sex, play a role in whether he or she should be diagnosed. A diagnosis of sexual dysfunction is not to be made if the disorder is believed to be due entirely to a medical illness (such as advanced diabetes, which can cause erectile problems in men) or if it is believed to be due to another Axis I disorder (such as major depression).

Most contemporary conceptualizations of the sexual response cycle are a distillation of proposals by Masters and Johnson (1966) and Kaplan (1974).

In DSM-II, homosexuality was listed as one of several sexual deviations. In subsequent editions of the DSM, homosexuality was gradually dropped as a mental disorder, in part due to pressure from gay rights groups.

The work of Masters and Johnson more than thirty years ago signaled a revolution in the nature and intensity of research in and clinical attention to human sexuality. These researchers extended the earlier interview-based breakthroughs of the Kinsey group (Kinsey et al., 1948, 1953) by making direct observations and physiological measurements of people masturbating and having sexual intercourse. Four phases in the human sexual response cycle are typically identified; they are considered quite similar in men and women.

1. **Appetitive.** Introduced by Kaplan (1974), this stage refers to sexual interest or desire, often associated with sexually arousing fantasies.[4]

2. **Excitement.** Masters and Johnson's original first stage, a subjective experience of sexual pleasure associated with physiological changes brought about by increased blood flow to the genitalia and, in women, to the breasts. This **tumescence**, the flow of blood into tissues, shows up in men as erection of the penis and in women as enlargement of the breasts and changes in the vagina, such as increased lubrication.

3. **Orgasm.** In this phase sexual pleasure peaks in ways that have fascinated poets and the rest of us ordinary people for thousands of years. In men, ejaculation feels inevitable and indeed almost always occurs (in rare instances some men can have an orgasm without ejaculating and vice versa). In women, the walls of the outer third of the vagina contract. In both sexes there is general muscle tension and involuntary pelvic thrusting.

4. **Resolution.** This last of Masters and Johnson's stages refers to the relaxation and sense of well-being that usually follow an orgasm. In men there is an associated refractory period, during which further erection and arousal are not possible, but for varying periods of time across individuals and even within the same person across occasions. Women are often able to respond again with sexual excitement almost immediately, an ability that permits multiple orgasms.

It is important to note that this rendition of the human sexual response cycle is a *construct*, that is, a

The pioneering work of the sex therapists William H. Masters and Virginia Johnson helped launch a candid and scientific appraisal of human sexuality.

Helen Singer Kaplan is the noted sex therapist who introduced the appetitive phase to the sexual response cycle.

---

[4]Masters and Johnson omitted this stage because, we believe, they used well-functioning volunteers in their landmark laboratory work; the issue of desire or readiness to be sexual did not arise. This is a good example of how the nature of knowledge-gathering techniques—in this case the kinds of subjects studied—constrains the kinds of information obtained.

scientific creation, a way of conceptualizing into different stages what is really a continuous set of thoughts, feelings, behaviors, and biological reactions. There have been various other proposals. Havelock Ellis (1906), for example, spoke only of tumescence and **detumescence**, the flow of blood out of tissue. The four-stage view just described is one of many conceivable inventions or conceptual schemes created by scientists as a way to organize and discuss a body of information (Gagnon, 1977; Kuhn, 1962). We are about to see how the DSM uses this scheme to describe sexual dysfunctions.

DESCRIPTIONS AND ETIOLOGY OF SEXUAL DYSFUNCTIONS

The prevalence of occasional disturbances in sexual functioning is believed to be so great that a person should not assume a need for treatment if he or she sometimes experiences one or more of the problems described in this section. In the diagnostic criteria for each sexual dysfunction the phrase "persistent or recurrent" is used to underscore the fact that a problem must be serious indeed for the diagnosis to be made. In addition, there is a fair amount of comorbidity among the sexual dysfunctions. For example, almost half of both men and women diagnosed with hypoactive sexual disorder (low sexual desire) also have at least one other dysfunction (Segraves & Segraves, 1991). As we review the various disorders, their interconnectedness will become evident.

SEXUAL DESIRE DISORDERS

DSM-IV distinguishes two kinds of sexual desire disorders. **Hypoactive sexual desire disorder** refers to deficient or absent sexual fantasies and urges; **sexual aversion disorder** represents a more extreme form of the disorder, in which the person actively avoids nearly all genital contact with another. About 20 percent of the general adult population may have hypoactive sexual desire disorder, although accurate estimates are difficult to come by because of definitional problems. Among people seeking treatment for sexual dysfunctions, more than half complain of low desire. In general, hypoactive sexual desire increased in clinical samples for both men and women from the 1970s to the 1990s (Beck, 1995).

Of all the DSM-IV diagnoses, what is colloquially referred to as low sex drive (as illustrated in the case that opened this section) seems the most problematic. How frequently *should* a person want sex? The reason a person goes to a clinician in the first place and ends up with this diagnosis is probably

that *someone else* is dissatisfied with that person's interest in sex *with him or her*. The hypoactive desire category appeared for the first time in DSM-III in 1980, under the title of inhibited sexual desire,[5] and may owe its existence to the high expectations people in our time and culture have about being sexual. It is striking that entire books, for example, Leiblum and Rosen (1988), have been written about a disorder that twenty-five years ago was hardly mentioned in professional sexology circles. Data attest to the significance of subjective factors in the extent to which a person believes he or she has a low sex drive; for example, hypoactive sexual desire disorder was reported more often by American men than by British (Hawton et al., 1986) or German men (Arentewicz & Schmidt, 1983).

We know little about the causes of either hypoactive sexual desire or sexual aversion disorder. Among the causes of low sex drive in people seen clinically are religious orthodoxy, trying to have sex with a partner of the nonpreferred sex, fear of loss of control, fear of pregnancy, depression, side effects from such medications as antihypertensives and tranquilizers, interpersonal tensions (as in marital or couples conflicts), and lack of attraction resulting from such factors as poor personal hygiene in the partner (LoPiccolo & Friedman, 1988). Other possible causes include a past history of sexual trauma, such as rape or child sexual abuse (Stuart & Greer, 1984), and fears of contracting sexually transmitted diseases, such as AIDS (Katz et al., 1989). Two empirical studies indicate that anger is a major factor in reducing sexual desire in both men and women, though it has a smaller role for women (Beck & Bozman, 1995; Bozman & Beck, 1991). Sexual desire is lower when people complain of high levels of everyday stress, or hassles (Morokoff & Gilliland, 1993). There are also data pointing to the importance of testosterone levels in men—the lower the levels, the lower the sexual desire (Bancroft, 1988).

SEXUAL AROUSAL DISORDERS

Some people have little or no trouble experiencing sexual desire but do have difficulty attaining or maintaining sexual arousal, the next stage of the sexual response cycle described by Masters and Johnson. The two subcategories of arousal disorders are **female sexual arousal disorder** and **male erec-**

---

[5]The DSM-III term *inhibited* was deemed by those who produced DSM-IIIR to suggest psychodynamic causality. In DSM-IIIR and DSM-IV preference was given to the more descriptive term *hypoactive* (Lief, 1988).

tile disorder. The former used to be called frigidity, and the latter, impotence.

Replacement of the words *impotence* and *frigidity* by the phrase *sexual arousal disorder* can be considered an advance. Impotence implies that the man is not potent, in control, or truly masculine, and negatively supports the macho conception of masculinity that many people today challenge. Frigidity implies that the woman is emotionally cold, distant, unsympathetic, and unfeeling. Both terms are derogatory and encourage a search for causes *within* the person, rather than focusing attention on the relationship, a domain that many contemporary investigators explore for answers and solutions.

The diagnosis of arousal disorder is made for a woman when there is consistently inadequate vaginal lubrication for comfortable completion of intercourse and for a man when there is persistent failure to attain or maintain an erection through completion of the sexual activity. Prevalence rates for female sexual arousal disorder range from 11 percent (Levine & Yost, 1976) to as high as 48 percent (Frank, Anderson, & Rubenstein, 1978); the actual figure is probably closer to 20 percent (Laumann et al., 1994). For male erectile disorder prevalence is estimated at between 3 and 9 percent (e.g., Ard, 1977; Frank et al., 1978) and increases greatly in older adults (Feldman et al., 1994; Kinsey et al., 1948). Arousal problems account for about half the complaints of men and women who seek help with sexual dysfunctions (Frank et al., 1976; Renshaw, 1988).

In addition to the fear of performance and the spectator role (observing the sexual interaction rather than just "going with the flow"), discussed later as general causes of sexual dysfunctions, some specific causes are believed to underlie female arousal problems. A woman may not have learned adequately what she finds sexually arousing and may even lack knowledge about her own anatomy. Coupled with a shyness about communicating her needs, she may find the behavior of her partner unstimulating and even aversive.

Helen Singer Kaplan (1974) outlined a wide range of erectile problems for men. Some get an erection easily but lose it as they enter the woman's vagina. Others are flaccid when intercourse is imminent but maintain an erection easily during fellatio. Some men are erect when the partner dominates the situation, others when they themselves are in control. An obvious aspect of the problem is that it is in fact obvious. A woman can go through the motions of lovemaking, but sexual intercourse is usually stalemated if the man is not erect. A great deal is at stake for both the man and his partner if the penis becomes flaccid when it "should" be erect.

Recent reviews (e.g., LoPiccolo, 1992a, in press; Mohr & Beutler, 1990) suggest that as many as two-thirds of erectile problems have some biological basis, usually combined with psychological factors. In general, any disease or hormonal imbalance that can affect the nerve pathways or blood supply to the penis (Geer, Heiman, & Leitenberg, 1984) can contribute to erectile problems; examples are certain drugs, such as Mellaril, Prozac, and some antihypertensive medications, and illnesses, such as diabetes and chronic alcoholism. But it is probably a mistake to think in terms of *either–or*, for somatic and psychological factors usually interact to produce and maintain erectile difficulties.

ORGASMIC DISORDERS

Three kinds of orgasmic disorders are described in DSM-IV, one found in women and two in men. **Female orgasmic disorder**, formerly called **inhibited female orgasm**, refers to absence of orgasm after a period of normal sexual excitement. Stimulation can come either from masturbation or from having sex with a partner.

The published prevalence rates for female orgasmic disorder vary widely. The classic Kinsey study reported that 10 percent of all women said they had never experienced an orgasm (Kinsey et al., 1953); a quarter of a century later Levine and Yost (1976) found that only 5 percent of woman were nonorgasmic over their lifetime. If low frequency of orgasm is included, however, the rates jump to 20 percent (Spector & Carey, 1990), and it seems that women from lower socioeconomic strata have higher prevalence rates for this disorder (Levine & Yost, 1976). Whatever the true prevalence rate, this is the problem that most often brings women into therapy (Kaplan, 1974; Spector & Carey, 1990).

We can make a distinction between problems a woman may have in becoming sexually aroused and those she may have in reaching an orgasm. Although as many as 10 percent of adult women have never experienced an orgasm (Anderson, 1983), far fewer are believed to remain unaroused during lovemaking. Kaplan (1974) argued that this distinction is important, for "as a general rule, women who suffer from orgasmic dysfunction [female orgasm disorder] are responsive sexually. They may fall in love, experience erotic feelings, lubricate copiously, and also show genital swelling" (p. 343). Kaplan argued that failure to have orgasms should not be regarded as a disorder at all, but as a normal variation of female sexuality.

Numerous reasons have been put forward to explain the problem. Perhaps many women, unlike men, have to *learn* to become orgasmic; that is, the capacity to have an orgasm may not be innate in females as it is in males. In men, ejaculation, which almost always is accompanied by orgasm, is necessary for reproduction. Survey findings indicate that women who masturbated little or not at all before they began to have intercourse were much more likely to be nonorgasmic than were those who had masturbated to orgasm before becoming sexually active with a partner (Hite, 1976; Hoon & Hoon, 1978; Kinsey et al., 1953). These are, of course, correlational data; some third factor may be responsible both for infrequent masturbation and for diminished ability to have orgasms. Lack of sexual knowledge also appears to play a role according to clinical data; many nonorgasmic women, as well as those who experience little excitement during sexual stimulation, are unaware of their own genital anatomy and therefore have trouble knowing what their needs are and communicating them to a partner. Chronic use of alcohol may be a somatic factor in orgasmic dysfunction in women (Wilsnak, 1984).

Women have different thresholds for orgasm. Although some have orgasms quickly and without much clitoral stimulation, others seem to need intense and prolonged stimulation during foreplay or intercourse. Because a man may conclude that he and his penis are inadequate if the female asks for manual stimulation of her clitoris during intercourse, the reaction of a woman's partner can contribute to the problem.

Another factor may be fear of losing control. The French have an expression for orgasm, *la petite mort*, "the little death." Some women fear that they will scream uncontrollably, make fools of themselves, or faint. A related source of inhibition is a belief, perhaps poorly articulated, that to let go and allow the body to take over from the conscious, controlling mind is somehow unseemly. The state of a relationship is important as well. Although some women can enjoy making love to a person they are angry with, or even despise, most hold back under such circumstances. The nonsexual feelings each partner has for the other play a role.

Male orgasmic disorder and premature ejaculation are the two orgasm disorders of men in DSM-IV. **Male orgasmic disorder** or difficulty in ejaculating, is relatively rare, occurring in 3 to 8 percent of patients in treatment (Spector & Carey, 1990). Causes that have been put forth include fear of impregnating a female partner, withholding love, expressing hostility, and, as with female orgasm problems, fear of letting go. In some instances the problem may be traced to a physical source, such as spinal cord injury or certain tranquilizers (Rosen, 1991).

Premature ejaculation is probably the most prevalent sexual dysfunction among males; it is a problem for as many as 40 percent of men at some time in their lives (Laumann et al., 1994; St. Lawrence & Madakasira, 1992). There is some laboratory-based evidence that men who have such problems ejaculate at lower levels of sexual arousal and that they have longer periods of abstinence from climactic sex than do men who are not premature ejaculators (Spiess, Geer, & O'Donohue, 1984). Premature ejaculation is generally associated with considerable anxiety. Sometimes the man ejaculates even before he penetrates the vagina, but more usually within a few seconds of intromission.

Concern about ejaculating too soon may be a natural result of an overemphasis on intercourse in sexual behavior. The problem for couples who prize conventional sexual intercourse above all other sexual activities is that because the man's erection is slowly lost after an ejaculation, his partner may be deprived of her own orgasm. If lovemaking stops when the penis is no longer hard, ejaculation may indeed be premature. But if, as sex therapists advise, couples expand their repertoire of activities to include techniques not requiring an engorged penis, such as oral or manual manipulation, gratification of the partner is eminently possible after the man has climaxed. When the focus on penile-vaginal or anal intercourse is removed, a couple's anxieties about sex usually diminish sufficiently to permit greater ejaculatory control in the male and sexual intercourse of longer duration. It will be interesting to observe whether shifts in sexual expectations and practices alter the concept of premature ejaculation.

SEXUAL PAIN DISORDERS

Two pain disorders associated with sex are listed in the DSM, dyspareunia and vaginismus. **Dyspareunia** is diagnosed when there is persistent or recurrent pain before, during, or after sexual intercourse. In women the diagnosis should not be made when the pain is believed to be due to lack of vaginal lubrication (when presumably female sexual arousal disorder would be diagnosed); nor should it be made when it is judged to be a function of the second pain disorder, **vaginismus**, which is marked by involuntary spasms of the outer third of the vagina to a degree that makes intercourse impossible. Prevalence rates for dyspareunia in women range from 8 percent (Schover, 1981) to 15 percent (Laumann et al., 1994); it is generally accepted that the disorder is far less often found in men, perhaps in as few as 1 percent (Bancroft, 1989). Estimates for vaginismus range from 12 to 17 percent of women seeking sex therapy (Rosen & Leiblum, 1995).

Genital pain associated with intercourse is almost always caused by a medical problem, such as an infection of the vagina or uterus or of the glans of the penis. Vaginismus, though defined by DSM-IV as a sexual problem, can occasionally be observed during pelvic examinations by a physician.

One theory regarding the source of vaginismus supposes that the woman wishes, perhaps unconsciously, to deny herself, her partner, or both the pleasures of sexual intimacy. As plausible as this idea may seem, no evidence supports it. Women with vaginismus can often have orgasms through clitoral stimulation. Fear of pregnancy and negative attitudes toward sex in general may play a role in vaginismus. Negative attitudes often are traceable to molestation in childhood or rape (LoPiccolo & Stock, 1987). Masters and Johnson found that for a number of couples the man's inability to maintain an erection preceded the development of vaginismus in his partner. For some women, then, the sexual problems of their partners may be so anxiety-provoking as to result in the development of vaginismus.

GENERAL THEORIES OF SEXUAL DYSFUNCTIONS

Having reviewed descriptions of the sexual dysfunctions and some of the causes believed to underlie each, we turn now to a consideration of general theoretical perspectives.

Prior to modern scientific theorizing, sexual dysfunctions were generally viewed as a result of moral degeneracy. As recently reviewed by LoPiccolo (in press), excessive masturbation in childhood was widely believed to lead to sexual problems in adulthood. Von Krafft-Ebing (1902) and Havelock Ellis (1910) postulated that such early masturbation damaged the sexual organs and exhausted a finite reservoir of sexual energy, resulting in lessened abilities to function sexually in adulthood. Even in adulthood excessive sexual activity was thought to underlie such problems as erectile failure. The general Victorian view was that dangerous sexual appetite had to be restrained. To discourage handling of the genitals by children, metal mittens were promoted; and to distract adults from too much sex, outdoor exercise and a bland diet were recommended. In fact, Kellogg's Corn Flakes and graham crackers were developed as foods that would lessen sexual interest. They didn't.

Psychoanalytic views have assumed that sexual dysfunctions are symptoms of underlying repressed conflicts. The analyst considers the symbolic meaning of the symptom both to understand its etiology and to guide treatment. Since sexual dysfunctions bring discomfort and psychological pain to the individual and to his or her partner, and since unimpaired sexuality is inherently pleasurable, the theme of repressed anger and aggression competing with the gratification of sexual needs pervades psychoanalytic writings. Thus a man who ejaculates so quickly that he frustrates his female partner may be expressing repressed hostility toward women who remind him unconsciously of his mother. A woman with vaginismus may be expressing her hostility toward men, perhaps as a result of childhood sexual abuse, or more directly because of her husband's overbearing manner. Many contemporary psychoanalysts now supplement their therapy with cognitive-behavioral techniques (LoPiccolo, 1977). The spirit of rapprochement has also affected cognitive-behavioral approaches to the treatment of sexual dysfunctions, as these therapists are coming to appreciate the role of psychodynamic themes in what used to be straightforward behavioral treatments (cf. p. 390).

Based on uncontrolled case studies, the most comprehensive account of the etiology of human sexual dysfunctions was offered by Masters and Johnson in their widely acclaimed book *Human Sexual Inadequacy* (1970). We will first examine their suggestions and then consider modifications and extensions of their ideas that have been proposed more recently.

THE THEORETICAL MODEL OF MASTERS AND JOHNSON

Masters and Johnson (1970) used a two-tier model of current and historical causes to conceptualize the etiology of human sexual inadequacy (Figure 14.2). Current variables can be distilled down to two, **fears of performance** and the adoption of a **spectator role**. Both involve a pattern of behavior in which the individual's focus on and concern for sexual performance impedes his or her natural sexual responses. As the authors put it, "fear of inadequacy is the greatest known deterrent to effective sexual functioning, simply because it so completely distracts the fearful individual from his or her natural responsivity by blocking reception of sexual stimuli" (Masters & Johnson, 1970, pp. 12–13).

Viewed as the *current* or proximal reasons for sexual dysfunctions, performance fears and the spectator role were hypothesized to have one or more *historical* antecedents:

- **Religious orthodoxy.** Some conservative religious upbringing looks askance at sexuality for

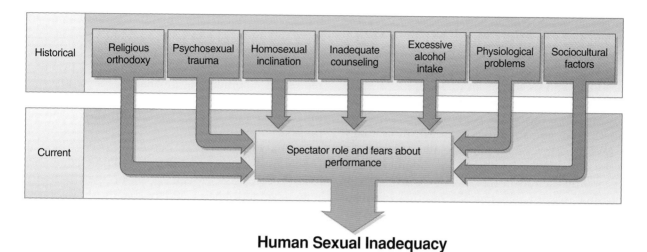

Figure 14.2 Historical and current causes of human sexual inadequacies, according to Masters and Johnson.

the sake of pleasure per se, particularly outside marriage. Masters and Johnson found that many of their sexually dysfunctional patients had negative views of sexuality as a consequence. One female patient, for example, had been taught as she was growing up not to look at herself naked in the mirror and that intercourse was reserved for marriage and then only to be endured for purposes of having children.

- **Psychosexual trauma.** Some dysfunctions can be traced to rape or other degrading encounters. One young male patient of Masters and Johnson was told by a prostitute that he would never be able to "get the job done" with other women if he didn't "get it done here and now with a pro."

- **Homosexual inclination.** Sexual enjoyment is understandably less if a person with homosexual inclinations tries to engage in heterosexual sex. Though not discussed in their early books, an analogous result can be expected for heterosexuals in homosexual situations.

- **Inadequate counseling.** This phrase is a euphemism for comments made by professionals that are incorrect and destructive, such as a health care worker's telling a healthy sixty-five-year-old man to forget about sex, or a cleric's saying that erectile dysfunction is God's punishment for sins.

- **Excessive intake of alcohol.** As Shakespeare wrote in *Macbeth*, "It provokes the desire but it takes away the performance" (Act II, Scene 3). If an inebriated man cannot achieve or maintain an erection, he may begin to fear that his erectile problem will recur rather than attribute the problem to alcohol. Because he becomes preoccupied with the possibility of not maintaining

an erection, he begins to assume the spectator role. Empathy from his partner may then be interpreted as a threat to his masculinity and overall sexual attractiveness. The relationship suffers, and the originally alcohol-induced erectile problem becomes pervasive and serious.

- **Biological causes.** Masters and Johnson alerted us back in 1970 to somatic factors contributing to sexual dysfunction; now even more is known about such factors. For example, long-term diabetes reduces peripheral blood flow; since the engorgement of tissues with blood is intrinsic to sexual arousal in both sexes, diabetes is rightly viewed as a cause of some sexual dysfunctions. Such drugs as the selective serotonin reputake inhibitors (SSRIs; e.g., Prozac) and antihypertension medications can also reduce sexual interest and arousal (this is a principal reason that compliance to such drug regimens is problematic).

- **Sociocultural factors.** Expectations and concerns differ between women and men and as a function of social class. For example, men have the blessing, even demand, of society to develop sexual expressiveness and to take the initiative, whereas, despite the changes that have resulted from the feminist movement of the past thirty years, it remains questionable whether this holds as strongly for women.

OTHER CONTEMPORARY VIEWS

Masters and Johnson considered sexual dysfunctions as problems in and of themselves that could be treated directly, rather than as symptoms of other intrapsychic or nonsexual interpersonal difficulties. The couples whose treatment formed the basis of their second book, *Human Sexual Inadequacy* (1970), had marriages that in spite of sexual problems, were marked by caring and closeness. But as the Masters and Johnson therapy techniques became widespread and as the social milieu became such that more people felt comfortable seeking help, sex therapists were seeing people whose relationships were seriously impaired. It is not difficult to imagine why a marriage or other relationship might deteriorate when the couple has not had intercourse for years. By the time a therapist is consulted, it is impossible to know whether the hostility between the two people caused the sexual problem or vice versa. The working assumption of most contemporary sex therapists is that sexually dysfunctional couples have both sexual and interpersonal problems (Rosen & Leiblum, 1995). It is unrealistic to expect a satisfying sexual encounter when, for example, the man is angry with the woman for spending more and more time outside the home, or when the woman resents the man's insensitive dealings with their children. Such negative thoughts and emotions can intrude into the sexual situation and thereby inhibit whatever arousal and pleasure might otherwise be found.

Though cognitive-behavioral in theoretical orientation, Joseph LoPiccolo (in press), a leading sex therapist, offers some psychodynamic reasons for the *meaning* a sexual problem might have in a person's life or within a relationship, which may not be immediately apparent:

> For some patients, sexual dysfunction is a way of resolving negative feelings about their sexuality. … Sexual dysfunction may ward off depression about some highly distressing life situation, by simply giving the patient another problem upon which to focus. A man with erectile failure who is very unhappy in his marriage but who finds divorce too threatening an idea to process, exemplifies this issue. … Other patients may find that during intercourse [with an adult partner], deviant fantasies such as sex with a child occur. In such cases, sexual dysfunction fosters repression of unacceptable sexual impulses, allows maintenance of one's self image as a decent, moral person. … Sexual dysfunction may almost be a psychic necessity to maintain self esteem.

Also, a couple's sexual difficulties may serve a purpose not immediately obvious to the therapist or even to the couple themselves. Such hidden benefits—known in the psychoanalytic paradigm as **secondary gain**—may underlie the occasional sabotaging therapists encounter when a therapy seems to be proceeding well. For example, a man who is angry with his wife may derive satisfaction from knowing that his erectile problems interfere with her sexual gratification. As the kind of direct sex

therapy described later in this chapter begins to show the intended effect, the man finds reasons not to attend therapy session or "forgets" appointments. The secondary gain of the sexual problem represents a familiar psychoanalytic theme that has recently begun to be recognized in the largely cognitive-behavioral field of sex therapy (LoPiccolo, in press).

As mentioned earlier, people who have sexual problems are often found to lack knowledge and skill (LoPiccolo & Hogan, 1979); or, their partners may have deficiencies—the husbands of nonorgasmic women are often reported to be awkward lovers (Kaplan, 1974; LoPiccolo, 1977). Simply caring for the partner may not be enough to establish a mutually satisfying sexual relationship. In fact, Kaplan (1974) suggested that inhibiting anxiety can arise when one partner wants *too much* to please the other; he or she may feel in the spotlight, resulting in a kind of performance anxiety. Another proposed cause of sexual dysfunction is response anxiety, that is, anxiety about not being aroused (Apfelbaum, 1989).

Poor communication between partners also contributes to sexual dysfunction. For any number of reasons—embarrassment, distrust, dislike, resentment, depression, to name but a few—one lover may not inform the other of his or her preferences, likes, and dislikes and then may misinterpret the failure of the partner to anticipate or mind–read as a sign of not really caring. Although communication about sexual matters is frequently inadequate in distressed marriages and is therefore addressed in couples therapy (see p. 565), it can also be poor in people who are otherwise compatible. Open discussions of sex by partners, among friends, in the media, and even in professional training programs are, after all, relatively recent phenomena.

Concerns about contracting a venereal disease have probably long been a distractor and hence an inhibitor of deriving pleasure from sex with a partner. The spread of acquired immunodeficiency syndrome among sexually active individuals is no doubt now yet another reason behind many sexual dysfunctions. We will discuss the critical topic of AIDS at the end of this chapter.

In considering these hypothesized etiological factors it is important to keep two things in mind. First, many people have unsatisfying episodes in their sex lives, perhaps after a bruising argument with their partner or when preoccupied with problems at work. Usually these periods pass and the sexual relationship returns to normal. Second, many people who have past histories or present lives that include one or more of the pathogenic factors discussed do *not* develop persistent sexual dysfunctions. Although to date there is little real understanding of this phenomenon, there is speculation that other variables, such as an unusually supportive network of friends or a particularly understanding sexual partner, must be operating in these people's present lives to mitigate the putative negative effects of the pathogenic factors.

THERAPIES FOR SEXUAL DYSFUNCTIONS

Perhaps in no area of psychotherapy have behavioral and cognitive therapies been more notably successful than in treating sexual dysfunctions (e.g., D'Amicis et al., 1985; LoPiccolo et al., 1985). The overall success rates for the kind of direct cognitive-behavioral approaches described here are far from perfect, however.

The pioneering work of Masters and Johnson (1970) in the treatment of sexual dysfunctions is described in Focus 14.3. Over the past thirty years therapists and researchers have elaborated on this early report and added to the armamentarium of clinicians who seek to improve the sexual lives of dysfunctional patients. We will describe several strategies and procedures that extend the Masters and Johnson work. A therapist may choose only one technique for a given case, but the complex and multifaceted nature of sexual dysfunctions usually demands several.

ANXIETY REDUCTION

Well before the publication of the Masters and Johnson therapy program, behavior therapists appreciated that their dysfunctional clients needed gradual and systematic exposure to anxiety-provoking aspects of the sexual situation. Wolpe's systematic desensitization and in vivo desensitization (desensitization by real-life encounters) have been employed with high degrees of success (Andersen, 1983; Hogan, 1978), especially when combined with skills training. In vivo desensitization would appear to be the principal technique of the Masters and Johnson program, although additional components probably contribute to its overall effectiveness.

PROCEDURES TO CHANGE ATTITUDES AND THOUGHTS

In what are called **sensory-awareness procedures**, clients are encouraged to tune in to the pleasant sensations that accompany even incipient sexual arousal. The sensate-focus exercises described in Focus 14.3, for example, are a way of opening the

individual to truly sensual and sexual feelings. Rational-emotive therapy tries to substitute less self-demanding thoughts for "musturbation," the "I must" thoughts that often cause problems for people with sexual dysfunctions.

SKILLS AND COMMUNICATION TRAINING

To improve sexual skills and communication, therapists assign written materials, show clients videotapes and films demonstrating explicit sexual techniques, and discuss techniques (McMullen & Rosen, 1979). Of particular importance for a range of sexual dysfunctions is encouraging partners to communicate their likes and dislikes to each other (Hawton et al., 1992; Rosen et al., 1994). Taken together, skills and communication training also expose patients to anxiety-provoking material—such as seeing one's partner naked—which allows for a desensitizing effect. Telling one's partner one's preferences in sex is often made more difficult by tensions that go beyond the sexual relationship, which leads us to the next strategy.

COUPLES THERAPY

Sexual dysfunctions are often embedded in a distressed marital or other close relationship, and troubled couples usually need special training in nonsexual communications skills. As noted earlier (p. 390), recent writings on sex therapy emphasize the need for a systems perspective, that is, for the therapist to appreciate that a sexual problem is embedded in a complex network of factors and that the problem sometimes works for the couple, as when a man's erectile problems relieve the woman of her concern about satisfying his sexual desires. Sometimes a therapy that focuses on nonsexual issues, such as difficulties with in-laws or with childrearing, is necessary and appropriate—either in addition to or instead of a Masters and Johnson type of sex therapy. Couples therapy is discussed in more detail in Chapter 19.

PSYCHODYNAMIC TECHNIQUES AND PERSPECTIVES

A man may not at first admit that he cannot have an erection, in which case the therapist must listen for clues in what he says. A woman may be reluctant to initiate sexual encounters because, although she may not verbalize it to the therapist, she considers such assertiveness unseemly and inappropriate to her traditional female role. In such instances the general psychodynamic view that clients are often unable to express clearly to their therapists what

FOCUS 14.3 MASTERS AND JOHNSON'S THERAPY FOR SEXUAL DYSFUNCTIONS

In 1970 the publication of Masters and Johnson's *Human Sexual Inadequacy* generated an excitement in the mental health community that is seldom encountered. This book reported on a therapy program carried out with close to 800 sexually dysfunctional people. Each couple had traveled to St. Louis and spent two weeks attending the Reproductive Biology Research Foundation for intensive therapy during the day and doing sexual homework in a motel at night. Away from home, they were free of domestic distractions and able to make their stay a sort of second honeymoon.

Many of the Masters and Johnson techniques had been used by therapists for some time, and although some methodological problems have been uncovered by close examination of their report (Zilbergeld & Evans, 1980), other therapists using their techniques have had the same high rates of success (Andersen, 1983; LoPiccolo, in press; Mohr & Beutler, 1990). Masters and Johnson virtually created the sex therapy movement, and their work therefore deserves a detailed description. With some variations, such as not using a dual-sex therapy team or meeting weekly instead of daily, their approach is still followed by most practitioners conducting therapy for sexual dysfunctions (LoPiccolo, in press).

The overall aim of Masters and Johnson was to reduce or eliminate fears of performance and to take the participants out of the maladaptive spectator role. They hoped that these steps would enable the couple to enjoy sex freely and spontaneously.

Each day the couple met with a dual-sex therapy team, under the assumption that men best understand men and women best understand women. For the first several days the experiences of all couples were the same, regardless of their specific problem. An important stipulation in those early days was that sexual activity between the two partners was expressly forbidden. A complete social and sexual history was obtained during the first two days, and physical examinations were conducted to determine whether there were biological factors that needed specific medical attention.

The assessment interviews placed considerable focus on the so-called **sexual value system**, the ideas of each partner about what was acceptable and needed in a sexual relationship. Sometimes the sexual value system of one or both partners had to be changed before sexual functioning could improve. For example, if one partner regarded sexuality as ugly and unacceptable, it is doubtful whether even the most powerful therapy could help that person and the partner enjoy sex.

On the third day the therapists began to offer interpretations about why problems had arisen and why they were continuing. In all cases the emphasis was on the problems in the relationship, not on individual difficulties of either partner. A basic premise of the Masters and Johnson therapy was that "there is no such thing as an uninvolved partner in any marriage in which there is some form of sexual inadequacy" (1970, p. 2). Whatever the problem, the couple was encouraged to see it as their mutual responsibility. At this time the clients were introduced to the idea of the spectator role. They were told, for example, that a male with erectile problems—and often his partner as well—usually worries about how well or poorly he is doing rather than participating freely and that this pattern of observing the state of the erection, although totally understandable in context, blocks his natural responses and greatly interferes with sexual enjoyment.

At the end of the third day an all-important assignment was given to the couple, namely, to engage in **sensate focus**. The couple was instructed to choose a time when they felt "a natural sense of warmth, unit compatibility ... or even a shared sense of gamesmanship" (Masters & Johnson, 1970, p. 71). They were to undress and give each other pleasure by touching each other's bodies. The cotherapists appointed one marital partner to do the first pleasuring, or giving; the partner who was "getting" was simply to be allowed to enjoy being touched. The one being touched was *not* required to feel a sexual response and was responsible for immediately telling the partner if something became distracting or uncomfortable. Then the roles were to be switched. Attempts at intercourse were still forbidden. To Masters and Johnson this approach was a way of breaking up the frantic groping common among these couples. The sensate-focus assignment usually promoted

truly bothers them can help in proper assessment and planning for behavioral treatment (Kaplan, 1974). No doubt elements of nonbehavioral therapy are to be found in the actual practices of sex therapists, even if they are usually not made explicit by these workers when discussing their techniques in journals or with colleagues. Our earlier discussion of eclecticism in therapy (p. 51) may serve as a reminder of the complexity of the therapeutic enterprise. Rapprochement between psychodynamic and cognitive behavior therapies is also discussed in Chapter 18.

MEDICAL AND PHYSICAL PROCEDURES

As more discoveries are made about biological factors in sexual dysfunctions, it becomes increasingly important for therapists to consider whether under-

contact where none had existed for years, constituting a first step toward gradually reestablishing sexual intimacy.

Although sensate focus may uncover deep, hidden animosities, most of the time partners began to realize that encounters in bed could be intimate and pleasurable without necessarily being a prelude to sexual intercourse. On the second evening the partner being pleasured was instructed to give specific encouragement and direction by placing his or her hand on the hand of the giving partner in order to regulate pressure and rate of stroking. The touching of genitals and breasts was now allowed. Still, however, there was no mention of orgasm, and the prohibition on intercourse remained in effect. The partners were shown diagrams if they were ignorant of or uncertain about basic female and male anatomy, as they often were. After this second day of sensate focusing, treatment branched out according to the specific problem or problems of the couple. To illustrate the process, we will outline the therapy for female orgasmic disorder.

After the sensate-focus exercises made the couple more comfortable with each other in bed, the woman was encouraged to focus on maximizing her own sexual stimulation without trying to have an orgasm. As a result, her own sexual excitement usually increased. The therapists gave her partner explicit instructions about generally effective means of manually stroking the female genital area, although ultimate decisions were to be made by the female partner, who was encouraged to make her wishes clear to the man moment by moment. In the treatment of this dysfunction, as in the treatment of others, it was emphasized that at this stage having orgasms was not the focus of interaction between partners.

After the woman began to enjoy being pleasured by manual stimulation, the next step was to move the source of sensate pleasure from the man's hand on her body to his penis inside her vagina. She was told to place herself on top of the man, gently insert the penis, and simply tune in to her feelings. When she felt inclined, she could begin slowly to move her pelvis. She was encouraged to regard the penis as something for her to play with, something that could provide her with pleasure. The male could also begin to thrust slowly. At all times, however, the woman was to decide what should happen next and when. When the couple was able to maintain this containment for minutes at a time, without the man thrusting forcefully toward

orgasm, a major change had usually taken place in their sexual interactions: for perhaps the first time the woman was allowed to feel and think sexually, and indeed selfishly, about her own pleasure. In their subsequent encounters most couples began to have mutually satisfying intercourse.

Clinicians had to be extremely sensitive in presenting these various treatment procedures to a couple whose problems may have stretched back many years. Sometimes the couple discussed sex for the very first time at the Masters and Johnson clinic. The calm and open manner of the therapists put the couple at ease, encouraging in them both a commitment to follow certain instructions and a more open attitude toward sex and the activities in which people may engage together when making love. Although behavioral prescriptions were specific, the therapists could never lose sight of the atmosphere that had to be maintained in the consulting room and, it was hoped, transferred over to the privacy of the bedroom, where much of the *actual* therapy took place. As in other forms of behavior therapy, there was a strong emphasis on technique, but interpersonal factors set the stage for behavior to change.

A caveat about sensate focus is in order. As LoPiccolo (1992a) pointed out, more and more people are aware that not getting an erection from sensate focus is at the same time expected and not expected! That is, although the instruction from the therapist is not to feel sexual, even a moderately knowledgeable man knows that *at some point* he is supposed to get an erection from this nonsexual situation (which, after all, is not really nonsexual at all, involving as it does two nude people who care for each other enough to be spending time and money to feel more sexual toward each other). Thus rather than reducing performance anxiety and the spectator role, sensate focus may create in some men what can be called metaperformance anxiety, taking the form of self-statements such as, "Okay, I don't have any pressure to get an erection and have intercourse. Right. So now ten minutes have passed, there's no pressure to perform, but I don't have an erection yet. When am I going to get an erection? And if I do, will I be able to maintain it long enough to insert it?" The sensate-focus stage of treatment, and indeed other aspects of Masters and Johnson's sex therapy, have elements of a very subtle approach to intervention known as paradoxical therapy, which we discuss in Chapter 18 (p. 542).

lying somatic problems are contributing to the dysfunction (LoPiccolo, 1992b; Rosen & Leiblum, 1995). Consideration of possible somatic factors is especially important for the disorders of dyspareunia and complete erectile dysfunction. Dyspareunia can be ameliorated in postmenopausal women by estrogen treatments, which can reduce the thinning of vaginal tissue and improve vaginal lubrication (Masters, Johnson, & Kolodny, 1988; Walling, Anderson, &

Johnson, 1990). When depression is part of the clinical picture along with severely diminished sex drive, antidepressant drugs can be helpful. Tranquilizers are also used as an adjunct to anxiety-reduction techniques. However, a complicating factor is that some of these psychoactive drugs themselves interfere with sexual responsiveness.

Surgical procedures are also available; a semirigid silicone rod can be implanted in a chronically flaccid penis, or an inflatable device can allow the man to pump up his penis on demand. However, long-term follow-ups of men who have had such operations indicate that poor sexual functioning continues in many cases (Tiefer, Pedersen, & Melman, 1988). If the psychological components of the problem are not addressed, men with rod implants may continue to have sexual problems, but with a penis that is never flaccid (with a rod, sexual interest and arousal are not necessary for intercourse, and this situation is usually not favorable for long-term psychological adjustment). Vascular surgery involves correction of problems with blood inflow via arteries or outflow via veins in the penis. Results are mixed at best (Melman & Rossman, 1989), but the possibility exists for restoration of normal functioning because, unlike the case with implants, erection will occur only with desire and arousal (Wincze & Carey, 1991).

Recently, the drug yohimbine hydrochloride taken orally has been used with some success with male patients in whom biological factors are suspected (Sonda, Mazo, & Chancellor, 1990); it is believed to work by increasing blood flow into the penis and reducing outflow from it (Meyer, 1988). There is some mixed evidence that injection of the drug papaverine or another vasoactive (encouraging blood flow) into the spongy portion of the penis improves erections in some men (Montorsi et al., 1994), though for many the continuing existence of interpersonal conflicts negates whatever improvement in erectile capacity is achieved. Dependency on the injections and serious side effects, such as liver problems, also seem to be significant problems with this mode of treatment (Turner et al., 1989).

In all instances of medical intervention, consideration of psychosocial factors remains important, for sexual dysfunctions are almost always embedded in a complex set of interpersonal and intrapsychic conflicts. The current trend toward medicalizing or "biologizing" sexual dysfunctions may divert the attention of therapists and patients from the inherently interpersonal nature of these problems, giving rise to a quick-fix mentality that is probably ill-advised (Rosen & Leiblum, 1995).

In our discussion of sexual dysfunctions we have alluded to inhibitions about sexual relations that arise from a concern about sexually transmitted diseases. Put simply, it can be distracting and anxiety provoking to be worried about contracting or spreading a venereal disease while having sex. But when it comes to AIDS, the topic to which we now turn, it is appropriate to say that it should be anxiety provoking *not* to be concerned about this particular disease when having sex.

AIDS: A CHALLENGE FOR THE BEHAVIORAL SCIENCES

There is no greater public health threat today than **AIDS (acquired immunodeficiency syndrome)**. This invariably fatal illness has three unique, interrelated characteristics that make it appropriate for discussion in an abnormal psychology textbook: (1) it usually arises from behavior that is apparently irrational and certainly self-defeating; (2) it is not presently curable or preventable by medical means; and (3) it *is* usually preventable by psychological means.[6]

SCOPE OF THE PROBLEM

First identified in 1981, AIDS has emerged as the most serious infectious epidemic of modern times. Statistics on incidence and prevalence are updated periodically by the Centers for Disease Control and Prevention, a federal agency, as well as by the United Nations Program on HIV/AIDS. The numbers are getting more and more grim. In the United States 1 in every 300 people over the age of thirteen is infected with the human immunodeficiency virus (HIV)—or as many as 1,000,000 Americans. Each year about 40,000 Americans become HIV positive. In 1994, 55,000 Americans died of AIDS-related illnesses—almost as many as died during the entire Vietnam War—bringing the total since the epidemic was formally identified in 1981 to more than 325,000.

Yet figures from other countries dwarf these statistics. It is estimated that about 21 million people worldwide, including 1 million children, are HIV positive; 90 percent of these people live in underdeveloped countries. About 8500 new cases of HIV are diagnosed daily, 1400 of them in children. The worst statistics are from Africa, south of the Sahara Desert, where 63 percent of the world's HIV-positive population and 80 percent of its HIV-positive women live. Incidence is rising sharply in Asia, especially in India and China; most of these new

---

[6]The reader should not conclude from this discussion of HIV and AIDS in a chapter on sexual disorders, that unsafe sex is the only risk factor. It is not. But unsafe sex is the most important of the risk factors in terms of numbers of people affected, accounting in the United States for about 60 percent of HIV transmission, of which about ten percent is from heterosexual contacts. The other factors are the sharing of needles by intravenous drug users (20 percent); having a transfusion of tainted blood, as happened years ago, especially with hemophiliacs (3 percent); and transmission from mother to fetus during pregnancy and to infant during delivery or, after birth, from breast feeding (about 5 percent). The causes for remaining cases are undetermined (Kalichman, 1995).

cases result from heterosexual activity. Drug abuse is the principal cause in the Ukraine, Spain, and Vietnam. About 4.5 million people around the world have AIDS, and more than 4 million have died from it (Kalichman, 1995; Maugh, 1996a, 1996b).

For some, HIV infection appears to be a form of suicide. The disintegration of the Soviet Union brought far-reaching social and economic dislocation, creating what Durkheim termed *anomie* (p. 255). The consumption of vodka has been rising, and now poppy straw, an inexpensive liquid opiate brewed from poppy plants in many areas of the Ukraine, Russia, and Belarus, is cheaper than vodka. To escape boredom and a profound sense of meaninglessness, many young people in these regions have become addicts and think nothing of sharing needles, even when they know the risks. Consider this comment from an addict in Belarus: "Younger people don't care. ... Someone will say, 'I've got HIV; I'm not going to give you my syringe.' But the younger addict will say, 'Shoot me up anyway.' They don't see the point of living" (Boudreaux, 1996, p. A14).

Originally neglected in the study and discussion of AIDS, statistics on women are now attracting the attention of researchers and clinicians. And with good reason. Worldwide, about 42 percent of AIDS victims are female, and predictions are that by the year 2000 most new infections will be among women. In the United States, African-American and Hispanic women are seventeen times more likely than Anglo women to become infected. Since it is women who bear children and since many babies born of HIV-positive mothers inherit the disease from them, the problem is all the more alarming. Although incidence in the United States is decreasing somewhat, the picture in less-developed countries is much more negative. For example, in Thailand, women tend to have less premarital and extramarital sex, except prostitutes, who are frequented by married men; unprotected sex and the relatively high prevalence of HIV among prostitutes spread the infection to the men and thence to their wives, who lack power in the marital relationship to insist on safer sex (Maugh, 1996b, 1996c).

AIDS was first proclaimed in this country to be a disease of homosexuals. But AIDS never was a homosexual disease, and there are indications that the disease is increasing among heterosexuals, both men and women. In Africa and parts of Latin America, AIDS is found primarily among heterosexuals, and throughout the world infected women are giving birth to babies who are HIV positive. Even in parts of the world in which AIDS is not yet a significant health problem, it is likely to become one.

DESCRIPTION OF THE DISEASE

Although the medical complexities of AIDS are beyond the scope of this book, it is important to understand a few fundamentals. AIDS is a disease in which the body's immune system is severely compromised by HIV, putting the individual at high risk for opportunistic and fatal diseases, such as Kaposi's sarcoma, rare forms of lymph cancer, and a wide range of dangerous fungal, viral, and bacterial infections. (The term *opportunistic* is used because these illnesses are seldom found in people with healthy immune systems. We can say that these diseases take advantage of the opportunity afforded by a weakened immune system [Kalichman, 1996].) Medical authorities suspect AIDS when an otherwise healthy person presents with an illness that he or she would not likely have with a properly functioning immune system. People who have had an organ transplant, for example, are at risk for such opportunistic diseases because they are given drugs to suppress the immune system so that the body will not reject the new organ. In a sense, the AIDS patient is someone who presents similarly without having taken antirejection, immunosuppressant medication. The big difference, of course, is that the transplant patient is kept in an antiseptic, intensive-care hospital environment while his or her immune system is being *artificially*—and *temporarily*—compromised. Strictly speaking, people do not die of AIDS as much as they die of fatal infectious and other diseases to which AIDS makes them vulnerable.

SPREAD OF THE DISEASE

The AIDS crisis has been exacerbated because many untested HIV-positive people feel healthy and are unaware of their illness. HIV-positive individuals can infect others and contribute to what some have called a ticking time bomb in the health of the human race. Efforts to control transmission of HIV are hindered because the most widely employed tests for HIV detect antibodies to infection and these antibodies do not appear in most people until several months following infection (McCutchan, 1990). Thus even if an antibody test is negative, a person recently exposed to an infected individual may have HIV. Newer tests may make possible direct and earlier measurement of the concentration of HIV in the blood.

The core of the problem is risky sexual practices, not sexual orientation. HIV is present only in blood, semen, and vaginal secretions and can be transmitted only when infected liquids get into the bloodstream. AIDS cannot be caught through casual social contact or even by living with a person who has AIDS or is HIV positive, provided that reasonable care is taken to avoid contact with his or her blood. Unprotected receptive anal intercourse (i.e., having a penis inserted into one's anus) is the riskiest of sexual practices (Kingsley et al., 1987). Considerably less risky but still chancy is vaginal intercourse without a condom, and probably also unprotected oral-genital contact and finger or hand insertion into the anus or vagina. The other category of risky behavior occurs among *intravenous drug users who share unsterilized needles* and thus can introduce HIV-carrying blood into the bloodstream of another. Perhaps the most tragic victims are infants born to HIV-positive mothers, for the virus can cross the placental barrier and infect the developing fetus. The virus can also be transmitted through breast-feeding.

Preventing the spread of AIDS is turning out to be more difficult than people originally expected. In the 1980s, when prevention efforts focused on encouraging the use of condoms during every sexual contact, new cases of HIV dropped in many large cities, from an annual infection rate among gays of around 10 percent or more to 1 or 2 percent. But there are disturbing indications from the Centers for Disease Control that younger gay men in the mid-1990s are engaging in more unprotected penetrative sexual behaviors than are older gays (Boxall, 1995).

Why might this be happening? Perhaps young gay men do not see as many of their age cohort infected as do older homosexuals, and so they fail to see AIDS as much of a threat for themselves as for others. It has also been suggested that in the 1990s some people sensed that a medical cure for AIDS was just around the corner, so that engaging in unsafe sex might no longer seem so life threatening. Yet even with the promising advances of just the past few years, safer sex has to become a lifelong commitment—and for all people, not just for male homosexuals. Among the many support groups there are new groups for HIV-negative gay men to provide encouragement for hewing to the safer sex line (Boxall, 1995).

Any decisions about safer sex have to be made with the sobering understanding that people are most infectious in the months immediately following HIV infection, and this is when it is most difficult to get valid laboratory findings on HIV.

DRUG TREATMENT OF HIV AND AIDS

In the past few years encouraging findings have been reported for the drug treatment of HIV and AIDS. In November 1995 an advisory panel of the Food and Drug Administration recommended approval of the first in a new line of anti-AIDS compounds (Cimons, 1995). The generic name of this new drug is saquinavir, marketed under the brand name Invirase. A protease inhibitor, saquinavir works differently from the other class of drugs that have been used in the fight against AIDS, the so-called nucleoside analogues, such as AZT. These latter drugs can control HIV for short periods of time by preventing the virus from copying its own genetic material. The problem is that the human immunodeficiency virus develops resistance to such medications. The newer agents such as saquinavir operate by attacking an enzyme that is crucial to the reproduction of HIV. Used in combination (the so-called "cocktail"), these two kinds of drugs are believed to hold promise in delaying the onset of full-blown AIDS by interfering with the replication of HIV.

Just nine months after the FDA action, a combination of protease inhibitors and AZT-like drugs was shown to be very effective in suppressing the replication of HIV, even in patients with full-blown AIDS. The result is that many people are managing to live with AIDS—if they can afford these expensive new drugs (Maugh, 1996a, 1996b; Richman, 1996).

PREVENTION OF THE DISEASE

Despite these promising advances in drug treatment, the primary focus in prevention of sexually transmitted AIDS is on changing sexual *practices*. Exposure can be eliminated by being in a monogamous relationship with a partner who tests negative for HIV. However, monogamous relationships are very rare among young people and are not invariably found among married people or those in other committed relationships. Prevention is best directed at encouraging sexually active people to use condoms, which are about 90 percent effective in preventing HIV infection. Employing sophisticated probability modeling techniques, Reiss and Leik (1989) demonstrated that risk is far more significantly reduced by using condoms—even though they are less than 100 percent effective—than by reducing the number of partners with whom a person has sex. Avoiding sex after using alcohol or drugs is also prudent because use of these substances increases the tendency to engage in risky sex (Stall et al., 1986). The safest strategy is to use condoms in a monogamous relationship, yet this approach is probably unrealistic and is contrary to the strictures of some religious groups (since condoms are a form of birth control). The approach prevalent in the public health arena is advocacy of monogamous relationships, a proposition based more on morality than on data.

Does rationality always prevail in a committed relationship? Apparently not. In a study of gay male couples who had been in their relationship at least six months (the average length was almost four years), Appleby (1995) found that engaging in risky sex symbolized trust, love, and commitment, whereas safer sex was seen negatively by partners and could threaten the closeness of a committed relationship. Further, indications by a partner that safer sex should be practiced were viewed with suspicion, as a sign of infidelity. There is no reason to expect the views of heterosexual couples to be any different.

This rationalizing of risk poses health hazards because HIV tests can produce false negatives and because monogamous relationships, both gay and straight, may not be as monogamous as the parties believe (Peplau & Cochran, 1988). In Appleby's sample, 62 percent of the men in committed same-sex relationships reported having had sex with someone else at some time during the relationship, and 84 percent of these reported that his partner knew. In some instances the unfaithful partner in an ostensibly monogamous relationship had unprotected sex with someone else, did not tell his partner, and later had unprotected sex with the partner.

Prevention efforts also include advising people to explore the pleasures of low-risk sex, such as mutual masturbation and frottage (body rubbing without insertion of the penis into the vagina, mouth, or anus of the partner). For the most part this advice holds for same- or opposite-sexed partners. Prevention for intravenous drug users should include, in addition to these measures, the use of new or sterilized needles, though the best precaution would be to get off drugs altogether.

Ironically, in cities in which AIDS is less of a problem than it is in such centers as New York and San Francisco, high-risk behavior is much more common. Perhaps there is a (mistaken) sense of personal invulnerability when there is not an epidemic in one's immediate vicinity (St. Lawrence et al., 1988). This certainly seems to be the case for young heterosexuals (both male and female), among whom infection is spreading particularly fast through unprotected sex (Centers for Disease Control, 1994). These young people apparently continue to view AIDS as limited mostly to gays and drug users; they may also wish to distance themselves from a disease that bears the social stigma of those whom it affects the most at the present time. High-risk sexual behavior among heterosexual

African-Americans and Hispanics has not changed as much as it has among homosexuals (Thomas, Gilliam, & Iwrey, 1989). Adolescents in general see AIDS as less of a personal threat than do people in their twenties and beyond (Strunin & Hingson, 1987). These facts pose a serious problem because the most prudent judgment for people to make—regardless of sexual orientation—when they consider having sexual relations, especially with a new partner, is that their partner could be HIV positive.

How can changes be brought about, especially (at least for heterosexuals) in a generation of sexually active people for whom the pill marked a welcome release from the need to use condoms? Also daunting is the challenge of changing the attitudes and practices of adults for whom the 1960s ushered in a period of sexual liberation, restrained by the danger of herpes and other venereal diseases but not by the certainty of dying. Social psychological and behavior-therapy theory and research suggest strategies that can form the basis of effective interventions (Kalichman, 1995; Kelly, 1995; Kelly & St. Lawrence, 1988a, 1988b). Educational messages should:

- **Provide accurate information about HIV transmission** (readily available via pamphlets from the Centers for Disease Control and from local AIDS organizations as well as from commercially available guides in question-and-answer format, e.g., Kalichman, 1996)

- **Explain clearly what the person's risks are** (e.g., people with many sexual partners are at higher risk, and heterosexuals, though at lower risk than gays and needle-using drug users, are still at risk)

- **Identify cues to high-risk situations** (e.g., drinking alcohol in a sexually provocative situation is associated with higher risk sexual behavior)

- **Provide instruction in condom use** (and, as appropriate, needle cleaning)

- **Explain in detail how certain changes in behavior reduce risk** (e.g., that a condom usually prevents semen from entering a partner's vagina, anus, or mouth)

- **Provide social-skills training that includes sexual assertive skills** (e.g., insisting that safer sex be practiced, and other communication skills that can help preserve relationships while insisting on HIV risk reduction)

Interventions implementing these principles lead to reductions in unprotected anal intercourse and increased use of condoms in gay and bisexual men

Promoting the use of condoms by distributing them at no charge. Condom use helps prevent the spread of the disease.

(Kelly et al., 1989; Kelly et al., 1990), inner-city women, African-American adolescent men, and chronically mentally ill adults (Kelly et al., 1993). Such efforts are having a positive impact in reducing the spread of HIV infection among gays, and they can be expected to be effective with heterosexuals as well.

VALUES AS A FOCUS IN BEHAVIOR CHANGE

Any approach to prevention might benefit from some social-psychological research inspired by Milton Rokeach's work on values (1973; Ball-Rokeach & Rokeach, 1984). Rokeach held that human behavior is controlled in important ways by values, for example, involvement in civil rights is associated with a person's valuing equality more than freedom of choice. Using a technique he called **value self-confrontation**, Rokeach and others showed that if one confronts an individual with a discrepancy between the values held by those whom the person wishes to emulate and the values the person currently holds, one can influence the individual to change his or her behavior in an enduring fashion.

A recently completed survey study lays the groundwork for such an intervention. In a sample of undergraduates of both sexes and diverse sexual orientations, Chernoff and Davison (1997) found that those who engaged in the highest-risk sexual behavior endorsed values favoring immediate gratification ("an exciting life") and were less inclined

toward values favoring delayed gratification ("wisdom" and "mature love"). The next step is to use these contrasting value orientations in a value self-confrontation intervention that presents to high-risk people who want to lower their HIV exposure the value patterns of those whom they would like to emulate, that is, low-risk people. If Rokeach is right, such a communication may encourage them to change their own values and thereby regard their sexuality in a way that promotes more healthful, less risky behavior in the interests of a long-term benefit. Research inspired by Rokeach (e.g., Schwarz & Inbar-Saban, 1988) would seem to be of particular importance to social scientists concerned with behavioral risk reduction with relation to AIDS, because to be meaningful, any behavioral changes effected need to be enduring. Cognitive change aimed at a deep level, such as a change in values, is likely to be superior to a more superficial change.

THERAPY FOR HIV-POSITIVE AND AIDS PATIENTS

What can mental health professionals offer HIV-positive people and those afflicted with AIDS? Common among them are high levels of stress, anxiety, and depression, as well as a sense of outrage that Nature has perpetrated such a sick joke on humankind.

In the chapter on psychophysiological disorders we discussed a growing body of evidence that psychological stress can have a negative impact on the immune system (p. 188) and that alleviating such stress can have positive benefits (Kielcolt-Glaser et al., 1986). This kind of work is being applied to therapy for HIV-positive and AIDS patients because the infection results in a suppression of the immune system. There is some promising evidence that in the early stages of HIV infection, aerobic exercise can increase T-4 cell levels (these cells are the core of the body's immune system) and reduce anxiety and depression (Antoni et al., 1990). Antoni et al. (1991) implemented a cognitive-behavioral intervention for gay men *prior to* their notification of test results. This treatment included relaxation training, cognitive restructuring of stressful events à la Beck and Ellis, and expansion of social networks. The result was a reduction in post–test-notification depression and an enhanced sense of personal control.

A cognitive-behavioral stress-management program developed by Chesney and Folkman (1994) reduced depression and enhanced morale in HIV-positive homosexual men. In general the strategies already reviewed for prevention of HIV, for exam-

As with other stressful situations, patients with AIDS can benefit from the support they receive from joining a group.

ple, instruction in condom use, are relevant to any therapeutic interventions with people who are seropositive, that is, whose blood has HIV.

Lifestyle changes are an important focus of therapy with both AIDS and HIV-positive patients. For example, helping patients stop smoking is important so as not to worsen an already serious health picture. So, too, is helping the person make social contacts that will provide support and encouragement.

A challenge for patients who are not yet visibly ill is whether and how to inform others of their health status. Notification can raise serious issues if it is tantamount to the person's having been unfaithful in an exclusive relationship, and there are also issues surrounding notification of employers and colleagues (especially if the patient works in a health-care setting, such as a hospital). There are no easy and pat answers on how best to proceed, but an understanding therapist can help the person problem solve around these and related disclosure issues.

Because most of the attention relative to AIDS has focused on gay men, there is a need for a better appreciation among health professionals of the particular effects of AIDS on women. For example, in spite of feminist advances the double standard in sexuality still exists, especially among some minority groups, and the social stigma against HIV infection is probably greater for women than it is for men (even when it is their husbands who have infected them). Moreover, women sometimes learn of their seropositive status during prenatal screening and decisions about treatment are thus complicated by the fact that they are responsible not only for their own health but for the well-being of the fetus growing within them (Kalichman, 1995).

In Chapter 20 we discuss the Tarasoff decision, which requires health professionals to protect oth-

ers from danger from their patients (p. 607). This consideration can arise when a therapist's HIV-positive patient has not disclosed his or her seropositive status to a partner and continues to engage in unsafe sex with that person. Where do the therapist's responsibilities lie? Emerging guidelines from professional associations such as the American Psychiatric Association support the therapist's breaking confidentiality as mandated by Tarasoff if the therapist is not successful in convincing the patient to disclose his or her status or engage in safer sexual behavior (American Psychiatric Association, 1992). This position is consistent with long-standing professional rules that require physicians to notify others of a patient's infectious disease so as to protect the public. Once again, the likelihood that the person is seropositive because of infidelity makes such actions fraught with difficulty for the patient's relationship with loved ones.

What also seems to be emerging in the clinical literature is the appropriateness of an existential approach that encourages examination of the meaning of one's life and impending death and the importance of achieving some manner of resolution, including making out a will, saying good-bye, and in general doing what has long been believed to be useful and meaningful as a person confronts his or her mortality and obligations to those who will be left behind. No doubt a religious belief in an afterlife can bring comfort both to the patient and to his or her loved ones. Since many terminal AIDS patients have been estranged from their families because of their sexual orientation, drug use, or family members' fears of contagion, concerted efforts are needed to effect what can be remarkable and bolstering reconciliations (McCutchan, 1990).

As happens in terminal illnesses (p. 260), however, many AIDS patients commit suicide, some of them with professional assistance. For years an underground network of physicians in San Francisco have provided lethal doses of opiates or barbiturates for terminal AIDS sufferers to take at the time and in the manner they choose to exit this world. Though operating in gray areas of legality, morality, and professional responsibility, there is a corps of physicians whose private code of ethics permits them to provide the chemical means for terminally ill patients who are close to death to commit suicide. This assisted-suicide underground includes a former Catholic priest who runs a non-profit organization dedicated to "enhancing life near death," according to his brochure. He conducts ten-week programs that teach terminally ill patients, primarily people with AIDS, what he calls the "practical aspects of dying wisely and well." The group sessions discuss such topics as spirituality, intimacy, and legal concerns, such as estate plan-ning. Many participants in these groups report that knowing that they can take their own lives in a painless fashion allows them to forget about the disease and focus on living.

The planned suicide of one such patient was described in the following way by a journalist:

> The California sunlight will stream through his bay window, bathing his apartment in a warm glow. He will be surrounded by his paintings and his music; the crescendos and quiet strains of Richard Straus' "An Alpine Symphony" will fill the room. ... His cat, a 12-year-old Abyssinian named Cruiser, will be curled up beside him. A few friends will be on hand. His physician will have written him a prescription for barbiturates. The 55-year-old artist and former gardener will say a few short goodbyes, then slip himself a lethal dose of the pills and drift off into a numbing, everlasting sleep. (Stolberg, 1996b, p. A1)

SUMMARY

The gender identity disorders (GID) involve the deep and persistent convictions of individuals that their anatomic sexual makeup and psychological sense of self as man, woman, boy, or girl are discrepant. Thus a man with GID is physically male but considers himself a woman and desires to live as a woman. Child-rearing practices may have encouraged the young child to believe that he or she was of the opposite sex. These disorders are of significant theoretical as well as practical importance for they illustrate a degree of plasticity in our beliefs about ourselves as males or females. For a time the only kind of help available to such individuals was sex-reassignment surgery to bring certain bodily features into line with their gender identity. Now, however, there is preliminary evidence that behavior therapy can help bring gender identity into line with anatomy.

In the paraphilias unusual imagery and acts are persistent and necessary for sexual excitement or gratification. The principal paraphilias are fetishism, reliance on inanimate objects for sexual arousal; transvestic fetishism, sometimes called transvestism, the practice of dressing in the clothing of the opposite sex, usually for the purpose of sexual arousal but without the gender identity confusion of a person with GID; pedophilia and incest, marked preferences for sexual contact with minors and in the case of incest, for members of one's own family; voyeurism, which is a marked preference for watching others undressed or in sexual situations; exhibitionism, obtaining sexual gratification by exposing oneself to unwilling strangers; sexual sadism, a reliance on inflicting pain on another person to obtain or increase sexual gratification; and sexual masochism, obtaining or enhancing sexual gratification through being subjected to pain, usually from a sadist.

Many hypotheses have been put forward to account for the several paraphilias. Psychoanalytic theories generally hold that they are defensive in nature, protecting the person from repressed conflicts and representing fixations at immature stages of psychosexual development. According to this perspective, the person with a paraphilia is basically fearful of conventional heterosexual relationships. Fetishists and pedophiles, for example, are hypothesized to suffer from castration anxiety that makes conventional sex with adults too threatening to engage in. Behavioral and cognitive theorists focus more directly on the sexual behavior itself. A widely held view is that a fetishistic attraction to objects like boots arises from accidental classical conditioning of sexual arousal. Another behavioral hypothesis posits deficiencies in social skills that make it difficult for the person to interact normally with other adults. Efforts have also been made to detect hormonal anomalies in people with paraphilia, but the findings are inconclusive at this time.

Rape, although it is not separately diagnosed in DSM-IV, is a pattern of behavior that results in considerable social and psychological trauma for the victim. The inclusion of rape in a discussion of human sexuality is a matter of some controversy, as many theorists regard rape as an act of aggression and violence rather than of sex.

The most promising treatments for the paraphilias are behavior therapies, such as training in social skills to help the person have ordinary relations with members of the opposite sex. Treatment for rape victims involves social support and frank discussion of the traumatic event.

Like DSM-IIIR, DSM-IV does not contain any specific mention of homosexuality, continuing a process of liberalization that began in 1973 when DSM-II introduced a variation of the diagnosis that was to be applied only to those homosexuals disturbed by their sexual orientation. The current nomenclature alludes to those distressed by their sexual orientation without specifying whether that orientation is heterosexual or homosexual.

Few emotional problems are of greater interest to people than the sexual dysfunctions. These disruptions in the normal sexual response cycle are often caused by inhibitions, and they rob many people of sexual enjoyment. DSM-IV categorizes these disturbances in four groups: sexual desire disorders, sexual arousal disorders, orgasmic disorders, and sexual pain disorders. The disorders can vary in severity, chronicity, and pervasiveness, occurring generally or only with certain partners and in particular situations. In no instance should a person believe that he or she has a sexual dysfunction unless the difficulty is persistent and recurrent; most people normally experience sexual problems on an intermittent basis throughout their lives.

Although biological factors must be considered, especially for dyspareunia and complete erectile failure, the etiology of the disorders usually lies in a combination of unfavorable attitudes, difficult early experiences, fears of performance, assumption of a spectator role, relationship problems, and lack of specific knowledge and skills. Sex-role stereotypes may play a part in some dysfunctions—a man who has trouble maintaining his erection is often called impotent, with the implication that he is not much of a man; and a woman who does not have orgasms with regularity is often termed frigid, with the implication that she is generally cold and unresponsive. The problems of females in particular appear to be linked to cultural prejudices against their sexuality, ironic in light of laboratory data indicating that women are capable of more frequent sexual enjoyment than men.

Information on the causes of sexual dysfunctions derives almost entirely from uncontrolled case studies and must therefore be viewed with caution. The absence of solid data on etiology, however, has not deterred therapists from devising effective interventions, many of them cognitive and behavioral in nature, often blended with psychodynamic perspectives and techniques. Direct sex therapy, aimed at reversing old habits and teaching new skills, was propelled into public consciousness by the Masters and Johnson book *Human Sexual Inadequacy* in 1970. Their method hinges on gradual, nonthreatening exposure to increasingly intimate sexual encounters and the sanctioning of sexuality by credible and sensitive therapists. Other means applied by sex therapists include educating patients in sexual anatomy and physiology; reducing anxiety; teaching communication skills; and working to change patients' attitudes and thoughts about sex and their own sexuality. Couples therapy is appropriate when the sexual problem is embedded, as it often is, in a snarled relationship. Medical and other physical procedures may also be used, especially when the sexual dysfunction is primarily physical rather than psychological in nature, as in dyspareunia. Controlled data are just beginning to appear, but there is good reason to be optimistic about the ultimate ability of the mental health professions to help many people achieve at least some relief from sexual problems.

Acquired immunodeficiency syndrome (AIDS) has created a worldwide health crisis. Behavioral scientists have attempted to help people reduce their chances of contracting AIDS by changing from risky to safer sexual practices.

KEY TERMS

sexual and gender identity disorders
gender identity
transsexual
gender identity disorder of childhood
sex-reassignment surgery
paraphilias
fetishism
transvestic fetishism
pedophilia
incest
child sexual abuse
voyeurism
exhibitionism
sexual sadism
sexual masochism

orgasmic reorientation
family systems approach
forced rape
statutory rape
acquaintance (date) rape
homosexuality
ego-dystonic homosexuality
sexual dysfunctions
tumescence
detumescence
hypoactive sexual desire disorder
sexual aversion disorder
female sexual arousal disorder
male erectile disorder

female orgasmic disorder (inhibited female orgasm)
male orgasmic disorder
premature ejaculation
dyspareunia
vaginismus
fears of performance
spectator role
secondary gain
sexual value system
sensate focus
sensory-awareness procedures
AIDS (acquired immunodeficiency syndrome)
value self-confrontation

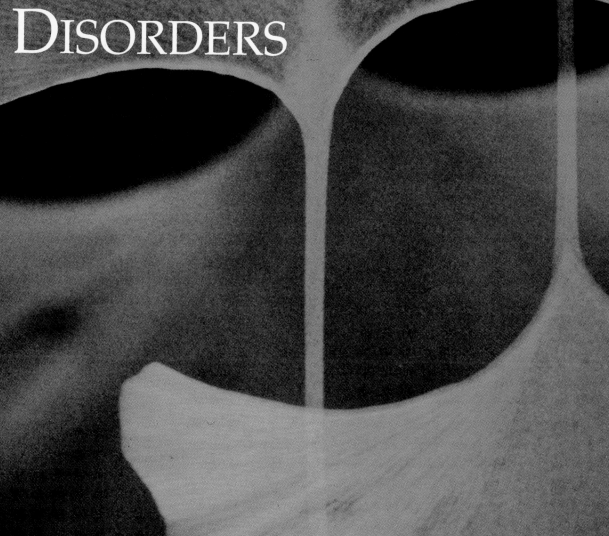

PART 3

LIFE-SPAN DEVELOPMENTAL DISORDERS

15

Elizabeth Barakah Hodges,
"The Way Home," 1994

DISORDERS OF CHILDHOOD

"**E**ric. Eric? Eric!!" His teacher's voice and the laughter of his classmates roused the boy from his reverie. Glancing at the book of the girl sitting next to him, he noticed that the class was pages ahead of him. He was supposed to be answering a question about the Declaration of Independence, but had been lost in thought about what seats he and his father would have for the baseball game they'd be attending that evening. A tall, lanky, twelve-year-old, Eric had just begun seventh grade. His history teacher had already warned him about being late to class and not paying attention, but Eric just couldn't seem to get from one class to the next without stopping for drinks of water or to investigate an altercation between classmates. In class, he was rarely prepared to answer when the teacher called on him, and he usually forgot to write down the homework assignment. He already had a reputation among his peers as a "space cadet."

Eric's relief at the sound of the bell was quickly replaced by anxiety as he reached the playground for physical education. Despite his speed and physical strength, Eric was always picked last for baseball teams. His team was up to bat first, and Eric sat down to wait his turn. Absorbed in studying a pile of pebbles at his feet, he failed to notice his team's third out and missed the change of innings. The other team had already come in from the outfield before Eric noticed that his team was out in the field—too late to avoid the irate yells of his P.E. teacher to take his place at third base. Resolved to watch for his chance to field the ball, Eric nonetheless found himself without his glove on when a sharply hit ball rocketed his way; he had taken it off to toss it in the air in the middle of the pitch.

At home, Eric's father told him he had to finish his homework before they could go to the Dodgers game. He had only one page of math problems and was determined to finish them quickly. Thirty minutes later, his father emerged from the shower to find Eric building an elaborate Lego structure on the floor of his room; the math homework was half done. In exasperation, Eric's father left for the game without him.

By bedtime, frustrated and discouraged, Eric was unable to sleep. He often lay awake for what seemed like hours, reviewing the disappointments of the day and berating himself for his failures. On this night, he ruminated about his lack of friends, the frustration of his teachers, and his parents' exhortations to pay attention and "get with the program." Feeling hopeless to do better despite his daily resolve, Eric's thoughts often turned to suicide. Tonight he reviewed his fantasy of wandering out into the street in front of a passing car. Although Eric had never acted on his suicidal thoughts, he frequently replayed in his mind his parents' sorrow and remorse, his classmates' irritation with him, and the concern of his teachers.

Eric's difficulty in focusing his attention is characteristic of attention deficit/hyperactivity disorder—just one of the disorders clinicians encounter when they work with children. The clinical problems loosely characterized as disorders of childhood cover a wide range of difficulties, from an attentional problem like that suffered by Eric, to the sometimes serious intellectual deficits found in mental retardation, the gross and sometimes callous disregard for the rights of others found in conduct disorder, depression, fear, and the social isolation of autistic disorder. Children typically have access to fewer social, financial, and psychological resources than do adults in dealing with such problems. The extreme dependency of troubled children on their parents and guardians adds to the sense of responsibility these people feel, and to their guilt, justified or not. Whether such children receive professional attention at all usually depends on the adults in their lives—parents, teachers, school counselors.

Most psychodynamic, behavioral, cognitive, and even biological theories consider childhood experience and development critically important to adult mental health. Most theories also regard children as better able to change than adults and thus as particularly suitable for treatment. Although earlier research devoted little attention to childhood disorders, recent years have brought a dramatic increase in professional interest in the nature, etiology, prevention, and treatment of child psychopathology.

In this chapter we discuss several of the emotional and behavioral disorders that are most likely to arise in childhood and adolescence. We consider disorders in which the acquisition of cognitive, language, motor, or social skills is disturbed, including learning disabilities and the most severe of developmental disorders, mental retardation and pervasive developmental disorders (especially autism), which are usually chronic and often persist into adulthood.

Classification of Childhood Disorders

To classify abnormal behavior in children, diagnosticians must first consider what is normal for a particular age. The diagnosis for a child who lies on the floor kicking and screaming when he or she doesn't get his or her way, must take into account whether the child is two years old or seven. The field of *developmental psychopathology* studies disorders of childhood within the context of normal life-span development, enabling us to identify behaviors that are appropriate at one stage but considered disturbed at another.

Table 15.1 outlines the principal childhood disorders included in DSM-IV. Some childhood disor-

TABLE 15.1 Disorders of Childhood and Adolescence in DSM-IV

I. DISORDERS USUALLY FIRST DIAGNOSED IN INFANCY, CHILDHOOD, OR ADOLESCENCE

Mental retardation: Intellectual functioning that is significantly below average, accompanied by concurrent deficits in adaptive functioning, and noticeable before age 18.

Learning disorders: Academic achievement in reading, mathematics, or written expression substantially below that expected for age, schooling, and level of intelligence.

Motor skills disorder: Problems in motor coordination.

Communication disorders: Problems in expressing and/or understanding speech.

Pervasive developmental disorders: Severe and pervasive impairment in several areas of development, including interacting and communicating with others, and exhibiting stereotyped behavior.

Attention-deficit/hyperactivity disorder: A persistent pattern of inattention and/or hyperactivity-impulsivity that is more frequent or severe than is typically observed in individuals at a comparable level of development. Symptoms must be present before age 7 and interfere with functioning in at least two settings.

Conduct disorder: A repetitive and persistent pattern of seriously antisocial behavior, usually criminal in nature.

Oppositional defiant disorder: A recurrent pattern of defiant, disobedient, and hostile behavior toward authority figures.

Feeding and eating disorders of infancy or early childhood: Persistent feeding and eating disorders, such as eating nonnutritive substances (pica), repeated regurgitation and rechewing of food (rumination disorder), or persistent failure to eat adequately, as reflected in significant weight loss or failure to gain weight (feeding disorder of infancy or early childhood).

Tic disorders (e.g., Tourette's): Characterized by sudden, rapid, recurrent, nonrhythmic, stereotyped motor movements or vocalizations.

Elimination disorders: Repeated defecation in inappropriate places after age 4 (encopresis), or voiding of urine in bed or clothes after age 5 (enuresis).

Separation anxiety disorder: Excessive anxiety concerning separation from the home or from those to whom the person is attached, to the extent that it causes distress or impairs functioning.

Selective mutism: Persistent failure to speak in specific social situations (e.g., at school), despite speaking in other situations (e.g., with parents).

Reactive attachment disorder of infancy or early childhood: Markedly disturbed and developmentally inappropriate social relatedness in most contexts that begins before age 5 and is associated with grossly pathological care by parents or other caregivers.

II. DIAGNOSES THAT MAY BE APPLIED TO ADULTS, ADOLESCENTS OR CHILDREN

Substance-related disorders: See Chapter 12

Schizophrenia: See Chapter 11

Mood disorders: See Chapter 10

Anxiety disorders, such as **specific phobia, social phobia, obsessive-compulsive disorder, posttraumatic stress disorder, generalized anxiety disorder**: See Chapter 6; for aftermath of child sexual abuse, see Chapter 14

Somatoform disorders: See Chapter 7

Dissociative disorders: See Chapter 7

Gender identity disorders: See Chapter 14

Eating disorders, such as **anorexia nervosa** and **bulimia nervosa**: See Chapter 9

Parasomnias: Abnormal behavioral or physiological events occurring in association with sleep. For example, **nightmare disorder, sleep terror disorder**, and **sleepwalking disorder**.

Source: Adapted from DSM-IV.

ders, such as separation anxiety disorder, are unique to children, whereas others, such as depression, are subsumed under the criteria used for adults. Still others, such as attention-deficit/hyperactivity disorder, have been conceptualized primarily as childhood disorders, but may nonetheless continue into adulthood. Eric, the distressed boy described at the beginning of this chapter, might be given the following multiaxial DSM-IV diagnosis:

Axis I: Attention-deficit/hyperactivity disorder, predominantly inattentive type; dysthymic disorder, early onset

Axis II: No diagnosis on Axis II

Axis III: No general medical conditions

Axis IV: Educational problems: discord with teacher and classmates

Axis V: Global assessment of functioning = 50

FOCUS 15.1 THE ROLE OF CULTURE IN CHILDHOOD PROBLEMS OF SELF-CONTROL

The values and mores of a culture play a role in whether a certain pattern of child behavior develops or is considered a problem. One study found that in Thailand, children with problems of overcontrol, such as fearfulness, were most likely to be seen in clinics, whereas in the United States, those with problems of undercontrol, such as aggressiveness and hyperactivity, were more commonly seen (Weisz et al., 1987). The researchers attributed these differences to Thailand's widely practiced Buddhism, which disapproves of and discourages aggression.

Child-rearing practices in Thailand reflect parental intolerance of undercontrolled behavior, such as disrespect and aggression. The additional finding that problems of overcontrol were reported more often for adolescents than for children may have resulted because Buddhist strictures are especially strong in the teen years, when young men may serve as novices in the temples, an activity that demands strong discipline and self-control.

The underlying assumption of this study is that because undercontrol is actively discouraged in Thai culture and religion, children, virtually by default, are more likely than American children to develop problems of overcontrol. Could it could be, though, that adults in Thailand have a lower tolerance for problems of undercontrol? Further research suggests that, compared with Americans, Thai parents and teachers have a *higher* tolerance for *both* undercontrolled *and* overcontrolled behavior. Consistent with Buddhist teachings, adults in Thailand perceive children's problems as transient and likely to change for the better (Weisz et al., 1988). The finding that Thai children are more likely to be referred for problems of overcontrol probably reflects the actual higher prevalence of these problems in Thailand, although it may be that Thai parents are too embarrassed to seek help for their children's undercontrolled behavior because they are reluctant to reveal to outsiders that their children are aggressive or disobedient.

(suicidal ideation; no friends; behind in schoolwork)

Childhood disorders may be conceptualized by a dimensional model rather than a categorical model as represented by the DSM. A dimensional model portrays dysfunctional behavior as existing on a continuum. One dimension is the degree to which behavior is controlled. At one end of the continuum of control, undercontrolled behavior is characterized by excess, such as extreme aggressiveness; at the other end of the continuum children are overcontrolled, and show emotional inhibitions such as school phobia (Achenbach & Edelbrock, 1978). A distinction sometimes drawn between these two extremes is whether the child creates a problem primarily for others (undercontrolled) or primarily for the self (overcontrolled). Children and adolescents may exhibit symptoms from both extremes, as Eric did.

There is considerable controversy about categorical versus dimensional systems (Kazdin & Kagan, 1994), and while we organize our discussion of childhood psychopathology partially in dimensional terms—problems lying on a continuum ranging from undercontrol to overcontrol—we also follow the DSM in its categorical approach, that is, discrete diagnostic categories into which a person fits or does not fit. As Kazdin and Kagan put it:

Nature often comes to us in discrete units: a tree, a branch, a bird, and a beak. One must blur that scene seriously in order to produce an apparent continuum of color, light, and forms. Our models, therefore, should consider both continuous psychological dimensions as well as categories of people (p. 39).

Overcontrolled and undercontrolled behavior are prevalent across many countries, including England (Collins, Maxwell, & Cameron, 1962), Japan (Hayashi, Toyama, & Quay, 1976), Greece, Finland, and Iran (Quay & Parskeuopoulos, 1972). Undercontrol problems are found more often among boys and overcontrol among girls consistently across cultures (Weisz et al., 1987). Focus 15.1 discusses the possible role of culture in the degree of prevalence of undercontrolled and overcontrolled behavior problems in children.

Problems of overcontrol include childhood depression and anxiety disorders and are discussed in the chapters devoted to these disorders (Chapters 10 and 6, respectively). Here we discuss disorders of undercontrolled behavior, followed by an examination of learning disabilities, mental retardation, and autism.

DISORDERS OF UNDERCONTROLLED BEHAVIOR

The child who is undercontrolled does not behave in a given setting in a way that is expected and is appropriate to his or her age. Eric, for example, should be able to follow his teacher's lessons as well as his team's progress at bat. The undercontrolled child is therefore frequently an annoyance to adults and peers. Two general categories of undercontrolled behavior are typically differentiated: attention-deficit/hyperactivity disorder and conduct disorder.

Problems of undercontrol are defined by the type, form, and frequency of the behavior. The high frequency of some problem behavior, such as fidgeting in class, in the general population of children, brings into question whether isolated incidents should be considered abnormal. Other behavior, such as assaulting a teacher, is considered abnormal by most people.

ATTENTION-DEFICIT/HYPERACTIVITY DISORDER

The term *hyperactive* is familiar to most people, especially parents and teachers. The child who is constantly in motion, tapping fingers, jiggling legs, poking others for no apparent reason, talking out of turn, and fidgeting is often called hyperactive. This is the child who, in colloquial terms, drives parents and teachers nuts. The DSM has shifted its focus from hyperactivity to the child's difficulty in concentrating on the task at hand for an appropriate period of time and involvement in non-goal-directed overactivity. The current diagnostic term is **attention-deficit/hyperactivity disorder** (ADHD).

ADHD is typically diagnosed when children encounter a school environment that requires them to conform to the rules of the classroom.

These inattentive children seem to have particular difficulty controlling their activity in situations that call for sitting still, such as in the classroom or at mealtimes. When required to be quiet, they appear unable to stop moving or talking. They are disorganized, erratic, tactless, obstinate, and bossy. Their activities and movements seem haphazard. They quickly wear out their shoes and clothing, smash their toys, and exhaust their family and teachers. They are difficult, however, to distinguish from normals during free play, when there are fewer restrictions placed on a child's behavior.

Many hyperactive children have inordinate difficulty getting along with peers and establishing friendships (Whalen & Henker, 1985), probably because their behavior is often aggressive and generally annoying to others. Although these children are usually friendly and talkative, they often miss subtle social cues, such as noticing when playmates are tiring of their constant jiggling. They also frequently misinterpret the wishes and intentions of their peers and make inadvertent social mistakes, such as insisting on staying uninvited at a friend's house for dinner when a normal child would understand that it was time to go home. (Such cognitive misattributions are also found in some conduct-disordered children.) ADHD children can know what the socially correct action is in hypothetical situations but be unable to translate this knowledge into appropriate behavior in real-life social interactions (Whalen & Henker, 1985).

About 20 to 25 percent of children with ADHD have a learning disability (see p. 420) in math, reading, or spelling (Barkley, DuPaul, & McMurray, 1990), and many more ADHD children are placed in special educational programs because of their difficulty in adjusting to a typical classroom environment.

The ADHD diagnosis does not properly apply to youngsters who are rambunctious, active, or slightly distractible, for in the early school years children are often so (Whalen, 1983). To use the label simply because a child is more lively and more difficult to control than a parent or teacher would like represents a misuse of the term. The diagnosis of ADHD is reserved for truly extreme and persistent cases.

Because the symptoms of ADHD are varied, DSM-IV has three subcategories: (1) children whose problems are primarily those of poor attention; (2) children whose difficulties result primarily from hyperactive-impulsive behavior; and (3) children who have both sets of problems. The third subcategory comprises the majority of ADHD children. Children with attentional problems *and* hyperactivity are more likely to develop conduct problems and oppositional behavior, to be placed in special classes for behavior-disordered children, and to have peer difficulties (Barkley, DuPaul, & McMurray, 1990). Children with attentional problems but with normal activity levels appear to have more problems with focused attention or speed of information processing (Barkley, Grodzinsky, & DuPaul, 1990), believed to stem from some problem in the right frontal lobe (Posner, 1992). Studies suggest that it may be best to think of two separate disorders (Barkley, 1990); however, most of the theory and research does not make this distinction.

A difficult differential diagnosis is between ADHD and conduct disorder, which as we shall see shortly, involves gross violation of social norms. An overlap of 30 to 90 percent between the two categories (Hinshaw, 1987) has caused some researchers to assert that the two types of undercontrolled behavior are actually the same disorder (Quay, 1979). There are differences, however. Hyperactivity is associated more with off-task behavior in school, cognitive and achievement deficits, and a better long-term prognosis. Children with conduct disorder act out in school and elsewhere and are likely to be much more aggressive and to have antisocial parents; their home life is also marked by family hostility and low socioeconomic status, and they are much more at risk for delinquency and substance abuse in adolescence (Hinshaw, 1987; Loney, Langhorne, & Paternite, 1978). When these two disorders occur in the same youngster, the worst features of each are manifest; such children exhibit the most serious antisocial behavior and have the poorest prognosis (Biederman, Newcorn, & Sprich, 1991; Cadoret & Stewart, 1991; Moffitt, 1990). In fact, it has recently been suggested that comorbid ADHD/CD children form a distinct subtype that is highly likely to progress to the adult psychopathic patterns of antisocial personality disorder (Lynam, 1996). One way this might operate is that ADHD comes first, with the child's aggravating behavior eliciting hostile reactions from peers and adults. There is then an escalation into more and more extreme attacks and counterattacks, the result being the aggressive behaviors characteristic, as we shall see, of conduct disorder. In concluding a careful review of the literature comparing the two disorders, Hinshaw (1987) recommended continuing to view hyperactivity and conduct disorder as separate but related disorders. Unfortunately, much of the research on hyperactive children confounds ADHD with conduct problems and aggressiveness, making the findings about hyperactivity less clear.

The prevalence of ADHD has been difficult to establish because of varied definitions of the disorder over time and differences in the populations sampled. Estimates vary from 1 to 20 percent (DuPaul, 1991; Ross & Ross, 1982, Szatmari et al., 1989), with a consensus that about 3 to 5 percent of children currently have ADHD (American Psychiatric Association, 1994). It is usually believed that the disorder is more common in boys than in girls, but exact figures depend on whether the sample is taken from clinic referrals (boys are more likely to be referred because of a higher likelihood of aggressive behavior in addition to ADHD symptoms) or from the general population. Some epidemiological studies have failed to find differences in the prevalence of ADHD among boys and among girls. Some studies have been conducted of girls with ADHD, but few differences have been found between girls with ADHD and boys with ADHD (Breen, 1989; Horn, Wagner, & Ialongo, 1989; McGee, Williams, & Silva, 1987).

Although many preschoolers are considered inattentive and overactive by their parents and teachers, the majority of these youngsters are going through a normal developmental stage that will not become a persistent pattern of ADHD (Campbell, 1990). On the other hand, most children who *do* develop ADHD exhibit excessive activity and temperamental behavior quite early in life. Their insatiable curiosity and vigorous play make childproofing a necessity to avoid such tragedies as accidental poisoning, tumbling downstairs, and falling out windows. Although the preschool years are stressful for parents whose children have ADHD, the problems become salient when the children enter school and are suddenly expected to sit in their seats for longer periods of time, complete assignments independently, and negotiate with peers on the playground.

At one time it was thought that hyperactivity simply went away by adolescence. However, this belief has been challenged by several longitudinal studies completed during the 1980s (Barkley et al., 1990; Gittelman et al., 1985; Mannuzza et al., 1991; Weiss & Hechtman, 1986). In one study more than 70 percent of children with ADHD still met criteria for the disorder in adolescence (Barkley et al., 1990). Table 15.2 provides a catalog of behaviors that are found more often among ADHD than among normal adolescents. In addition to these fidgety, distractible, impulsive behaviors, adolescents with ADHD are far more likely to drop out of high school than are their peers. In adulthood, although most are employed and financially independent, these individuals generally reach a lower level of socioeconomic status and change jobs more frequently than would normally be expected.

TABLE 15.2 Prevalence of Symptoms in ADHD and Normal Adolescents

Symptom	ADHD, %	Normal, %
Fidgets	73.2	10.6
Difficulty remaining seated	60.2	3.0
Easily distracted	82.1	15.2
Difficulty waiting turn	48.0	4.5
Blurts out answers	65.0	10.6
Difficulty following instructions	83.7	12.1
Difficulty sustaining attention	79.7	16.7
Shifts from one uncompleted task to another	77.2	16.7
Difficulty playing quietly	39.8	7.6
Talks excessively	43.9	6.1
Interrupts others	65.9	10.6
Doesn't seem to listen	80.5	15.2
Loses things needed for tasks	62.6	12.1
Engages in physically dangerous activities	37.4	3.0

Source: Adapted from Barkley et al., 1990.

Although most adults with a history of ADHD continue to exhibit some symptoms of the disorder, most also learn to adapt to these symptoms, perhaps by finding a niche for themselves in the working world.

BIOLOGICAL THEORIES OF ADHD

The search for causes of ADHD is complicated by the heterogeneity of children given this diagnosis; any factor found to be associated with the syndrome is perhaps linked with only some of those carrying the diagnosis.

GENETIC FACTORS. A predisposition toward ADHD is probably inherited. In a study of 238 twin pairs, Goodman and Stevenson (1989) found concordance for clinically diagnosed hyperactivity in 51 percent of identical twins and 33 percent of fraternal twins. Exactly what is inherited is as yet unknown, but recent studies suggest some differences in brain function. Brain metabolism was lower than normal in ADHD adolescent females, but not in males (Ernst et al., 1994), though this might have been due to the greater severity of the disorder in the young women studied (the participants were drawn from an ADHD organization). In an important ten-year study at the National Institute of Mental Health, Catellanos et al. (1996) compared MRI scans (cf. p. 88) in ADHD and normal boys and found smaller frontal lobes in boys with the disorder. Evidence from other research that shows poorer performance of ADHD children on neuropsychological tests of frontal lobe functioning (such as inhibiting behavioral responses) provides further support for the theory that a basic deficit in this part of the brain may be related to the disorder (Barkley, 1997; Chelune et al., 1986; Heilman, Voeller, & Nadeau, 1991).

ENVIRONMENTAL TOXINS. Popular theories of ADHD over the years have involved the role of environmental toxins in the development of hyperactivity. A biochemical theory of hyperactivity put forth by Feingold (1973) enjoyed much attention in the popular press for many years. He proposed that food additives upset the central nervous systems of hyperactive children, and he prescribed a diet free of them. It is unlikely, though, that more than a small percentage of cases of hyperactivity are caused by sensitivity to food additives. Well-controlled studies of the Feingold diet have found that very few children respond positively to it (Goyette & Conners, 1977). Similarly, the popular view that refined sugar can cause ADHD (Smith, 1975) has not been supported by careful research (Gross, 1984; Wolraich et al., 1985). Although some evidence suggests that lead poisoning may be associated to a small degree with symptoms of hyperactivity and attentional problems (Thompson et al., 1989), most children with ADHD do not show elevated levels of lead in the blood.

Nicotine, specifically, maternal smoking, is an environmental toxin that may play a role in the development of ADHD. Milberger et al. (1996) recently reported that 22 percent of mothers of chil-

Smoking cigarettes during pregnancy has recently been linked to increased risk for ADHD.

dren with ADHD reported smoking a pack of cigarettes per day during pregnancy, compared with 8 percent of control mothers. Further, animal studies indicate that chronic exposure to nicotine increases dopamine release in the brain and causes hyperactivity (Fung & Lau, 1989; Johns et al., 1982). On the basis of these data, Milberger and his associates hypothesize that maternal smoking can affect the dopaminergic system of the developing fetus, resulting in behavioral disinhibition and ADHD.

PSYCHOLOGICAL THEORIES OF ADHD

The child psychoanalyst Bruno Bettelheim (1973) proposed a diathesis–stress theory, suggesting that hyperactivity develops when a predisposition to the disorder is coupled with authoritarian upbringing by parents. If a child with a disposition toward overactivity and moodiness is stressed by a mother who easily becomes impatient and resentful, he or she may be unable to cope with the mother's demands for obedience. As the mother becomes more and more negative and disapproving, the mother–child relationship ends up a battleground. With a disruptive and disobedient pattern estab-

lished, the child cannot handle the demands of school, and his or her behavior is often in conflict with the rules of the classroom.

Learning may figure in hyperactivity as well. Hyperactivity could be reinforced by the attention it elicits, thereby increasing in frequency or intensity. Or, as Ross and Ross (1982) have suggested, hyperactivity may be modeled on the behavior of parents and siblings.

The parent–child relationship is bidirectional. Just as parents of hyperactive children give them more commands and have negative interactions with them, so hyperactive children have been found to be less compliant and more negative in interactions with their parents (Barkley, Karlsson, & Pollard, 1985; Tallmadge & Barkley, 1983). As we will describe shortly, stimulant medication has been shown to reduce hyperactivity and increase compliance in ADHD children. Significantly, when such medication is used, the parents' commands and negative behavior also decrease (see Barkley, 1990), suggesting that it is, at least in part, the child's behavior that affects the parents negatively rather than only the reverse.

TREATMENT OF ADHD

Stimulant drugs, in particular methylphenidate, or Ritalin, have been prescribed for ADHD since the early 1960s (Sprague & Gadow, 1976). The stimulating effects of these drugs calm ADHD children and improve their ability to concentrate. One survey found that 6 percent of elementary schoolchildren and 25 percent of those in special education classrooms were receiving stimulant medication (Safer & Krager, 1988). The prescription of these medications has sometimes continued into adolescence and even adulthood in light of the accumulating evidence that the symptoms of ADHD do not often disappear with the passage of time.

Does Ritalin work? Several controlled studies comparing stimulants with placebos in double-blind designs have shown dramatic short-term improvements in concentration, goal-directed activity, classroom behavior, and fine motor activity and reductions in aggressiveness and impulsivity in many ADHD children (Hinshaw, 1991; Weiss, 1983). One ingenious study demonstrated that Ritalin helped children playing softball to assume the ready position in the outfield and keep track of the status of the game, whereas children given placebos frequently threw or kicked their gloves while the pitch was in progress (Pelham et al., 1990).

However, research indicates that such drugs may not improve academic achievement over the long haul (Whalen and Henker, 1991), or improve batting and throwing skills, for that matter! Further, stimulant medication has side effects. In addition to transient loss of appetite and sleep problems, a risky side effect of the widespread prescription of stimulants has emerged: *Newsweek* reported that children are beginning to use Ritalin and other stimulants obtained from their siblings or friends as recreational drugs (Leland, 1995).

Treatments of ADHD children based on operant conditioning have demonstrated at least short-term success in improving both social and academic behavior. In these treatments children's behavior is monitored at home and in school, and they are reinforced for behaving appropriately, for example, for remaining in their seats and working on assignments. Point systems and star charts are typical components of these programs. Youngsters earn points and younger children earn stars for behaving in certain ways; the children can then spend their earnings for rewards. The focus of these operant programs is on improving academic work, completing household tasks, or learning specific social skills, rather than on reducing signs of hyperactivity, such as running around and jiggling (O'Leary et al., 1976). The therapists who devised these interventions conceptualize hyperactivity as a deficit in certain skills rather than as an excess of disruptive behavior. Although hyperactive children have proved responsive to these programs, the optimal treatment for the disorder may require the use of both stimulants and behavior therapy (Barkley, 1990; Gittelman et al., 1980; Pelham et al., 1993).

CONDUCT DISORDER

The term **conduct disorder** encompasses a wide variety of undercontrolled behavior. DSM-IV focuses on behaviors that violate the basic rights of others and major societal norms. Nearly all such behavior is also illegal. The types of behavior considered symptomatic of conduct disorder include aggression toward people or animals, damaging property, lying, and stealing. Conduct disorder denotes a frequency and severity of acts that go beyond the mischief and pranks common among children and adolescents. Often the behavior is marked by callousness, viciousness, and lack of remorse, making conduct disorder one of the criteria for antisocial personality disorder or psychopathy (p. 342).

A lesser known related category in the DSM is **oppositional defiant disorder** (ODD). There is a debate as to whether it is distinct from conduct disorder, a precursor to it, or merely an earlier manifestation of it (Loeber, Lahey, & Thomas, 1991). The

Point systems and star charts, which are common in classrooms, are particularly useful in the treatment of attention deficit/hyperactivity disorder.

diagnosis of ODD is made if a child does not meet the criteria for conduct disorder—most especially extreme physical aggressiveness—but exhibits such behaviors as losing his temper, arguing with adults, repeatedly refusing to comply with requests from adults, deliberately doing things to annoy others, and being angry, spiteful, touchy, or vindictive. The DSM also mentions that such children, most of them boys, seldom see their conflicts with others as their fault; they justify their oppositional behavior

Conduct disorder is diagnosed among those who are aggressive, steal, lie, and vandalize property.

FOCUS 15.2 BEHAVIORAL PEDIATRICS

An earlier discussion of behavioral medicine (see p. 200) enumerated several applications of psychological knowledge to the prevention and treatment of physical disease, for example, altering the Type A behavior pattern as a way of reducing the incidence of later coronary heart disease. This type of attention has been paid to childhood and adolescent diseases as well.

Russo and Varni (1982) proposed a normal person–abnormal situation (NPAS) model as a way of conceptualizing **behavioral pediatrics**, a branch of behavioral medicine concerned with the psychological aspects of childhood medical problems. An acutely or chronically ill child is a young person who may have psychological problems because he or she has been placed by illness in a complex and stressful predicament. Many sick children suffer considerable pain and sometimes defacement and have to spend long periods of time in a hospital, away from parents, siblings, and the comforting surroundings of their homes and neighborhoods.

Behavioral pediatrics is an interdisciplinary effort that combines behavior therapy and pediatrics to manage disease in children. It is concerned with parent–child, school–child, and medical team–child relations (Varni & Dietrich, 1981). Some specific examples will convey the scope and aims of this field (Kellerman & Varni, 1982).

In recent years many forms of childhood cancer, such as acute lymphoblastic leukemia, have become treatable; some types can be treated so effectively that they go into remission and the children are alive five years after the onset of cancer. With such improvement, however, come new problems of a psychological nature for both patients and families—learning to live with the disease and its treatment.

Concealing from a youngster the true nature of his or her illness and how life threatening it is increases rather than decreases anxiety (e.g., Spinetta, 1980). Open communication with the child is advocated. Research advises maintaining the child in his or her regular school as much as possible (Katz, 1980). Because cancer and its treatment can bring physical disfigurement, such as hair loss, the child should be taught to handle the teasing that often awaits any youngster who looks different; assertion training and learning to ignore the hurtful remarks can be helpful.

Pain accompanies both the diagnosis and the treatment of childhood cancer. A child with leukemia must undergo frequent and regular bone-marrow aspiration. The doctor inserts a long needle into the middle of the thigh bone and extracts some marrow. It hurts. And it is not the kind of pain to which the individual readily habituates (Katz, Kellerman, & Siegel, 1980). The experience takes a toll on the young patient and on the parents as well. Specialists in behavioral pediatrics have developed multicomponent cognitive-behavioral interventions that include filmed modeling, breathing exercises, positive reinforcement, imagery/distraction, and behavioral rehearsal to reduce distress related to painful procedures (Jay et al., 1991). Such interventions appear to be most successful when combined with pain medications (Varni et al., in press).

Children who develop anticipatory anxiety before undergoing other painful medical procedures have been helped by viewing films of a coping model (Jay et al., 1982). Systematic desensitization to situations associated with the pain, such as entering the hospital and sitting in the waiting room, can reduce the level of anxiety with which a patient comes to the medical procedure and thus alleviate the pain. Reducing anxiety can be of more general importance also. An extremely anxious child, for example, may avoid the medical procedure or may begin to lose weight. Weight loss decreases the chances of surviving cancer (Dewys et al., 1980).

Certain kinds of reading matter may also help children and their parents deal with the trauma of a terminal illness in a youngster. A recent example is an illustrated children's book by David Saltzman, published posthumously (1995). Saltzman, who died of Hodgkin's disease in 1990, 11 days before his 23rd birthday, worked single-mindedly to finish his book, *The Jester Has Lost His Jingle*, before his death. *The Jester* charmingly describes how a sick child learns the benefits of laughter in dealing with serious illness.

Children and adolescents with other medical problems have also been helped by behavioral pediatrics. Chronic arthritic pain in the joints is a serious problem for hemophiliacs, people whose blood lacks a critical clotting factor. Varni (1981) successfully treated such pain by hypnotic imagery techniques, teaching his patients both to relax and to increase blood flow to the affected joint. A higher surface temperature about the joint diminishes the need for pain medications, many of which have the undesirable side effect of inhibiting platelet aggregation, thus worsening an already bad blood-clotting condition. Varni's subsequent work in pain management for children with

---

by claiming that unreasonable demands are being placed on them. Common comorbid problems are ADHD, learning disorders, and communication disorders, but ODD is different from ADHD in that the defiant behavior is not deemed to arise from attentional deficits or sheer impulsiveness. One

way to appreciate the difference is that ODD children are more planful in their obstreperousness than ADHD children. (An operant theorist would see ODD behavior as more instrumental in nature than that of an ADHD child.) Interesting to mention is the observation in the DSM that mothers with a

"Sometimes I feel like crying too,"
the Jester whispered in her ear.
"But instead of letting teardrops fall,
I make them disappear.

Whenever I feel like crying,
I smile hard instead!
I turn my sadness upside down
and stand it on its head!

When I get sad or lonesome,
or when I get depressed,
that's when I sing my loudest
and dance my very best!"

"So won't you try it, little girl?
Won't you laugh with me?
We'll start off very slowly
with a tiny Tee-Hee-Hee."

In David Salzman's *The Jester Has Lost his Jingle*, the Jester, with Pharley, his talking scepter, discovers that he can lighten the emotional load of others, even sick children, by helping them discover the laughter within them even under the direst of circumstances. (The Jester & Pharley are registered trademarks of The Jester Co., Inc. Excerpts from *The Jester Has Lost His Jingle*. Story and Pictures by David Saltzman ©&™ 1995 by The Jester Co., Inc. reprinted with permission. All Rights Reserved.)

rheumatoid arthritis exemplifies the kind of research-based behavioral medicine that is having a positive impact on helping children and their families cope with serious medical illnesses (Varni & Bernstein, 1991; Walco, Varni, & Ilowite, 1992).

Obesity in children is highly predictive of obesity in adulthood, a major risk factor for such diseases as hypertension, heart disease, and diabetes. Childhood obesity has also been associated with low social competence, behavior problems, and poor self-concept (Banis et al., 1988). Behavioral investigators have been working to help overweight youngsters alter their eating habits, exercise practices, and other aspects of their lifestyles that appear to contribute to the caloric intake and how it is or is not burned off (Epstein, Masek, & Marshall, 1978). For example, obese children, like obese adults, eat faster, take bigger bites, and chew their food less than do age peers of normal weight (Drabman et al., 1979). When their parents are also involved in treatment, weight loss is maintained better (Coates, Killen, & Slinkard, 1982; Epstein et al., 1987).

Another topic in behavioral pediatrics (and in behavioral medicine generally) is known as *therapeutic compliance*. How can we get people to do the things that are necessary to prevent or manage an illness (Varni & Wallander, 1984)? Juvenile diabetes serves as a good example of the challenge facing the youngsters

and families affected. Urine must be tested several times a day to determine glucose (sugar) levels so that food intake and the amount of insulin can be adjusted. Diet poses a major challenge to these youngsters. They must learn to resist candy and other sweets. Their meals need to be timed to coincide with the peak action of an insulin injection so that the insulin does not lower glucose levels abnormally. Activity and exercise must also become part of the regimen, for they exert their own natural, insulin-like effect of utilizing glucose in the cells (Hobbs, Beck, & Wansley, 1984). With no cure for diabetes in sight, diabetics need to accept both their condition and the required regulation of some of the most basic of human drives. The complex set of self-care skills that a young person needs to cope with this serious but treatable disease has benefited from clinical research in behavioral pediatrics (Epstein et al., 1981). For example, psychologists are beginning to explore the factors associated with the control of blood-sugar levels, including family support, knowledge about the disease, and the patient's developmental level vis-à-vis the physician's presentation of prescriptions and directions (Johnson, 1995). In one study parents of diabetic children were taught relaxation techniques for use with their children; the result was improved control over the children's metabolism and hence the diabetes (Guthrie et al., 1990).

depressive disorder are more likely to have such children; less clear, the manual goes on to say, is whether the depression contributes to or is caused by the child's behavior (APA, 1994). In everyday language, some would use the word "brat" for such a child. Because of ODD's questionable status, our

attention is focused here on the more serious diagnosis of conduct disorder.

Perhaps more than any other childhood disorder, conduct disorder is defined by the impact of the child's behavior on people and surroundings. Schools, parents, peers, and the criminal justice system usually determine which undercontrolled behavior constitutes unacceptable conduct. Preadolescents and adolescents are often identified as conduct problems by legal authorities, in which case they might be considered juvenile delinquents, a legal, not a psychological, term.

Many children with conduct disorder display other problems as well. We have noted the high degree of overlap between conduct disorder and attention-deficit/hyperactivity disorder. Substance abuse also commonly co-occurs with conduct problems. Investigators from the Pittsburgh Youth Study, a longitudinal study of conduct problems in boys, found a strong association between substance use and delinquent acts (Van Kammen, Loeber, & Stouthamer-Loeber, 1991). For example, among seventh graders who reported having tried marijuana, more than 30 percent had attacked someone with a weapon and 43 percent admitted breaking and entering; fewer than 5 percent of children who reported no substance use had committed these acts.

Anxiety and depression are common among children with conduct disorder, with comorbidity estimates varying from 15 to 45 percent (Loeber & Keenan, 1994). There is some evidence that conduct-disordered boys with a comorbid anxiety disorder are less antisocial than those with conduct disorder alone (Walker et al., 1991).

Population-based studies indicate that conduct disorder is common. A study of more than 2500 children in Ontario, Canada, found that 8 percent of boys and about 3 percent of girls aged four to sixteen met the DSM criteria for conduct disorder (Offord, Boyle, et al., 1987). Burglary and violent crime like forcible rape and aggravated assault are largely crimes of male adolescents. As shown in Figure 15.1, both the incidence and prevalence of serious law-breaking peak sharply at around age 17 and drop precipitously in young adulthood (Moffitt, 1993). Most criminals of this physically violent kind are teenagers; by the late twenties, most of these former juvenile delinquents have stopped offending (Blumstein & Cohen, 1987). To some extent, the pattern is similar for young women as well. However, these are police data, which often fail to include crimes by youngsters not yet in their teens. In fact, antisocial behavior begins its steep incline at age 7 (Loeber et al., 1989). While not all these criminal acts are marked by the viciousness and callousness that are often a part of conduct disorder, these data do help illustrate the problem of antisociality in children and adolescents.

The prognosis for children diagnosed as having conduct disorder is mixed. Robins (1978) summarized several longitudinal studies that examined antisocial behavior in a number of cohorts from the

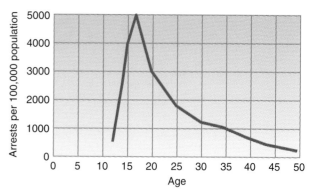

Figure 15.1   Arrest rates across ages for the crimes of homicide, forcible rape, robbery, aggravated assault, and auto theft. From "Criminal Career Research: Its Value for Criminology," by A. Blumstein, J. Cohen, and D. P. Farrington, 1988. *Criminology: 26*, p. 11. Copyright 1988 by the American Society of Criminology. Adapted by permission.

1920s to the 1970s, with follow-ups over as long as thirty years. She concluded that the vast majority of highly antisocial adults had also been highly antisocial as children. However, more than half the conduct-disordered children did *not* go on to become antisocial adults. Thus conduct problems may be a necessary but not a sufficient condition for antisocial behavior in adulthood. DSM-IV makes clearer than previous editions that the earlier the onset of conduct problems, the more likely the adult outcome will be antisocial personality disorder.

Moffitt (1993) has theorized that two different courses of conduct problems should be distinguished. Some individuals seem to show a "life-course-persistent" pattern of antisocial behavior, beginning their conduct problems by age three and continuing serious transgressions in adulthood. Others are "adolescence-limited." These people had normal childhoods, engaged in high levels of antisocial behavior during adolescence, and returned to nonproblematic lifestyles in adulthood. Moffitt proposes that the temporary form of antisocial behavior is the result of a "maturity gap" between the adolescent's physical maturation and his or her opportunity to assume adult responsibilities and obtain the rewards usually accorded such behavior.

Although almost all research in this area has been conducted with males, one study followed for several years fifty-five hospitalized adolescent girls with conduct disorder (Zoccolillo & Rogers, 1991). As with boys, the majority of these girls had a history of substance use and most also met diagnostic criteria for depression or an anxiety disorder. The outcome for these girls paralleled the poor prognosis found in boys; 88 percent of the sample had problems such as premature death (6 percent), dropping out of school (41 percent), encounters with the legal system (50 percent), running away (48 percent), pregnancy before age seventeen (32 percent), and suicide attempts (22 percent).

ETIOLOGY OF CONDUCT DISORDER

Numerous ideas have been put forward for the etiology of conduct disorder. Data showing a high prevalence of antisocial personality disorder in both mothers and fathers of children with conduct disorder suggest familial, perhaps (but not necessarily) genetic, transmission (Lahey et al., 1988). Since adoptive parents of conduct-disordered children have *not* been found to have antisocial problems or alcoholism (Jary & Stewart, 1985), the connection between parents' and childrens' conduct problems may be at least partly genetic. Twin studies have shown higher concordance rates for antisocial behavior in identical pairs than in fraternal pairs (Eysenck, 1975). The effects of upbringing are indicated by findings that families of these children frequently lack cohesiveness (Craig & Glick, 1963) and have experienced the stresses of marital discord and divorce (Emery & O'Leary, 1979; Rutter, 1971). Neuropsychological deficits have been implicated in the childhood profiles of children with conduct disorder (Moffitt, Lynam, & Sylva, 1994; Moffitt, 1993). These deficits include poor verbal skills, difficulty with "executive functioning" (that is, the ability to anticipate, plan, use self-control, and problem-solve), and problems with memory.

An important part of normal child development is the growth of moral awareness, acquiring a sense of what is right and wrong and the ability, even desire, to abide by rules and norms. Most people refrain from hurting others, not only because it is illegal but because it would make them feel guilty to do otherwise. Conduct-disordered children, like the psychopaths discussed in Chapter 13, seem often to be deficient in this moral awareness, viewing antisocial acts as exciting and rewarding, as central to their very self-concept (Ryall, 1974). Research into the backgrounds of conduct-disordered youngsters has shown a pattern of family life lacking in factors believed to be central to the development of a strong moral sense. Parents who are affectionate with their children and each other, who clearly express moral principles and demand that their children uphold them, who use punishment justly and consistently, and who use reasoning and explanations with the child generally do not raise conduct-disordered children (Herbert, 1982; Hoffman, 1970; Wright, 1971).

A good deal of evidence indicates that modeling is involved in increasing aggressiveness. Viewing televised violence is one way in which this can occur.

As these findings also suggest, learning theories that look to both modeling and operant conditioning provide useful explanations of the development and maintenance of conduct problems. Bandura and Walters (1963) were among the first researchers to appreciate the significance of the fact that children can learn aggressiveness from parents who behave aggressively. Children may also imitate aggressive acts seen from other sources, such as on television (Huesmann & Miller, 1994; Liebert, Neale, & Davidson, 1973). Since aggression is an effective, albeit unpleasant, means of achieving a goal, it is likely to be reinforced. Thus once imitated, aggressive acts will probably be maintained. This social mimicry may at least partially explain the dramatic surge in delinquent behavior in adolescence among children who had not previously shown conduct problems. Moffitt (1993) proposed that these adolescents imitate the behavior of persistently antisocial peers because they see them as enjoying high-status possessions and sexual opportunities.

A cognitive perspective on aggressive behavior (and by extension, conduct disorder) comes from the work of Kenneth Dodge and his associates. In one of his early studies (Dodge & Frame, 1982), the cognitive processes of aggressive children were found to have a particular bias: these youngsters interpreted ambiguous acts like being bumped in line as evidence of hostile intent on the part of the other child. This perception may lead such boys to retaliate aggressively to actions that may not have been intended as provocative. Subsequently, their peers, remembering these aggressive behaviors, may tend to aggress more often against them, further angering the already aggressive children and continuing a cycle of rejection and aggression. Dodge has gone on to construct a social-information processing theory of child behavior which focuses on the ways children process information about their world and how these cognitions markedly affect their behavior (Crick & Dodge, 1994).

Any discussion of conduct disorder and delinquency must recognize the work of sociologists. Social class and urban living are related to the incidence of delinquency. High unemployment, poor educational facilities, disrupted family life, and a subculture that deems delinquency acceptable have all been found to be contributing factors (Gibbons, 1975). Any comprehensive theory of delinquency and conduct disorders needs to include these consistent sociological findings. Patterson's recent research suggests that the combination of early antisocial behavior in the child and socioeconomic disadvantage in the family predict early criminal arrests (Patterson, Crosby, & Vuchinich, 1992).

TREATMENT OF CONDUCT DISORDER

The management of conduct disorder poses a formidable challenge to contemporary society. Sociologists and politicians as well as community psychologists, working on the assumption that poor economic conditions create most of the problem, argue for a fairer distribution of income and for job programs and other large-scale efforts to alleviate the material deprivation of the lower classes, among which delinquency is often found. Although sociological considerations may play some role in planning treatments, we emphasize here psychological methods aimed at the particular individuals and their families.

As mentioned, some of the young people with conduct disorder are the psychopaths of tomorrow. Just as precious little in the way of effective psychological treatment has been found for psychopathy, reaching young people who commit violent and antisocial acts with little remorse or emotional involvement is extraordinarily difficult. Incarceration, release, and recidivism are the rule. One of society's most enduring problems is how to deal with people whose social consciences appear grossly underdeveloped. Simply jailing juvenile delinquents will not reduce crime. A longitudinal study demonstrated that punitive discipline, such as juvenile incarceration, leads to lower job stability and more adult crime. Thus harsh discipline, whether imposed by the state or by the parents, appears to contribute in a major way to further delinquency and criminal activity in adulthood (Laub & Sampson, 1995).

Some of the most promising approaches to treating conduct disorder involve intervening with the parents or families of the antisocial child. Gerald Patterson and his colleagues have worked for over three decades developing and testing a behavioral program of parent management training, in which parents are taught to modify their responses to their children so that prosocial rather than antisocial behavior is consistently rewarded. Parents are taught to use techniques such as positive reinforcement when the child exhibits positive behaviors and time-out and loss of privileges for aggressive or antisocial behavior. Sessions include practicing the techniques and a discussion of difficulties the parents may encounter when applying the methods to an antisocial child. Both parents' and teachers' reports of children's behavior and direct observation of behavior at home and at school support the program's effectiveness (Patterson, 1982). Parent management training has even been shown to improve the behavior of siblings and reduce depression in mothers involved in the program (Kazdin, 1985). A recent study of chronic adolescent offenders by Patterson's group (Bank et al., 1991) found that both parent training and court-provided family treatment reduced rates of criminal offense. The parent-training approach, which included teaching parents to monitor their adolescents more closely and use age-appropriate rewards and consequences, led to more rapid improvement.

A new and promising treatment for serious juvenile offenders has demonstrated reductions in arrests four years following treatment (Borduin et al., 1995). Henggeler's multisystemic treatment involves delivering comprehensive therapy services, targeting the adolescent, the family, the school, and in some cases the peer group. The intervention is based on a family systems approach (described earlier in the treatment of anorexia nervosa, p. 221), which views the conduct problem as enmeshed in family relationships and therefore treatable only by involving the entire family. The treatment uses behavioral techniques, encouraging changes in behavior, particularly in interactions among all members of the family and also the community system. Treatment is provided in "ecologically valid" settings, such as the home, school, or local recreational center, to maximize generalization of therapeutic changes. In comparison to a control group that received an equivalent number of sessions (about twenty-five) of traditional individual therapy in an office setting, adolescents in the multisystemic-treatment group showed reduced behavior problems and far fewer arrests over the following four years. For example, whereas more than 70 percent of adolescents receiving traditional therapy were arrested in the four years following treatment, only 22 percent of those in the multisystemic-treatment group were arrested. In addition, assessment of other family members indicated that parents who were involved in multisystemic treatments showed reductions in psychiatric symptomatology, and families showed improved supportiveness and decreased conflict and hostility in videotaped interactions. Families of the adolescents receiving traditional individual therapy deteriorated in the quality of their interactions following treatment. Even the adolescents in the multisystemic group who dropped out of treatment after about four sessions demonstrated significantly reduced arrest rates compared with adolescents who completed the full course of traditional individual therapy.

Although research by Patterson's and Henggeler's groups suggests that intervention with parents and families is a critical component of success, such treatment is expensive and time-consuming, and some families may not be able or willing to become involved in it. Thus it is noteworthy that other research indicates that cognitive therapy with conduct-disordered children can improve their behavior even without the involvement of the family. For example, teaching children cognitive skills to control their anger shows real promise in helping them reduce their aggressive behavior. In anger-control training aggressive children are taught self-control in anger-provoking situations. Hinshaw, Henker, and Whalen (1984) helped children learn to withstand verbal attacks without responding aggressively, by using distracting techniques such as humming a tune, saying calming things to themselves, or turning away. The children then applied these self-control methods while a peer provoked and insulted them.

Another strategy is to focus on the deficient moral development of conduct-disordered children. Teaching moral reasoning skills to groups of behavior-disordered adolescents in school has achieved far-reaching success (Arbuthnot & Gordon, 1986). Adolescents who were nominated by their teachers as having behavior problems (such as aggressiveness, stealing, and vandalism) participated for four to five months in weekly groups at school aimed at encouraging higher levels of moral reasoning. Group sessions included discussion of vignettes such as the following:

Sharon and her best friend, Jill, are shopping in a boutique. Jill finds a blouse she wants but cannot afford. She takes it into a fitting room and puts it on underneath her jacket. She shows it to Sharon and, despite Sharon's protests, leaves the store. Sharon is stopped by a security guard. The manager searches Sharon's bag, but finding nothing, concludes that Jill shoplifted the blouse. The manager asks Sharon for Jill's name, threatening to call both Sharon's parents and the police if she doesn't tell. Sharon's dilemma is whether or not to tell on her best friend.

Members were encouraged to debate with one another the merits of alternative perspectives and the rights and responsibilities of characters in the dilemmas as well as other people and society.

Compared with a control group of nominated students who received no intervention, adolescents participating in the groups showed improvement in moral reasoning skills and school grades, as well as reductions in tardiness, referrals to the principal for behavior problems, and contacts with police or juvenile courts. Follow-ups in the next school year showed increased differences between the two groups, with the adolescents who had received the intervention showing continued advances in moral reasoning and further reductions in behavior problems.

This improvement is impressive, even many months after treatment was terminated, but other research cautions that behavioral changes produced by altering cognitive patterns may yield only short-term gains, improvements which may be lost when the youngsters return to their familiar "bad" neighborhoods. Environmental contingencies—the communities in which people live—need to be considered when dealing with the complexities of aggression (Guerra & Slaby, 1990).

LEARNING DISABILITIES

Several years ago a young man enrolled in one of our undergraduate courses showed an unusual pattern of strengths and difficulties. His oral comments in class were exemplary, but his handwriting and spelling were sometimes indecipherable. After the instructor had noted these problems on the student's midterm examination, the undergraduate came to see him and explained that he was dyslexic and that it took him longer to complete the weekly reading assignments and to write papers and exams. The instructor decided to accord him additional time for preparing written work. The student was obviously of superior intelligence and highly motivated to excel. Excel he did, earning an A in the seminar and on graduation being admitted to a leading law school.

Learning disabilities signify inadequate development in a specific area of academic, language, speech, or motor skills, which is not due to mental retardation, autism, a demonstrable physical or neurological disorder,[1] or deficient educational opportunities. People with these disorders are usually of average or above-average intelligence but as children, have difficulty learning some specific skill (e.g., arithmetic or reading), and thus their progress in school is impeded.

The term *learning disabilities* is not used by DSM-IV, but is used by most health professionals to group together three disorders that do appear in the DSM: learning disorders, communication disorders, and motor skills disorder. Any of these disorders may apply to a child who fails to develop to the degree expected by his or her intellectual level in a specific academic or language or motor skill area. Learning disabilities are usually identified and treated within the school system rather than through mental health clinics. Although they are widely believed to be far more common in males than in females, evidence from population-based studies (which avoid the problem of referral biases), indicate that as with ADHD, the disorders are only slightly more common in males (e.g., Shaywitz et al., 1990). Though individuals with learning disabilities usually find ways to cope with their problems, their academic and social development is nonetheless affected, sometimes quite seriously.

LEARNING DISORDERS

DSM-IV divides **learning disorders** into three categories: reading disorder, mathematics disorder, and disorder of written expression. None of these diagnoses is appropriate if the disability can be accounted for by a sensory deficit such as visual or auditory problems.

Children with **reading disorder**, better known as **dyslexia**, have significant difficulty with word recognition, reading comprehension, and typically with written spelling as well. When reading orally they omit, add, or distort the pronunciation of words to an unusual extent for their age. In adulthood, problems with fluent oral reading, comprehension, and written spelling persist (Bruck, 1987). This disorder, present in 2 to 8 percent of school-age children, does not preclude great achievements. Like the college student described at the opening of this section, it is widely known that Nelson Rockefeller, former governor of New York and former vice president of the United States, suffered from dyslexia.

[1]Physical bases for one or more learning disabilities may be uncovered by future research. Evidence is now emerging for a biological basis for one of the learning disabilities, dyslexia.

In **mathematics disorder**, the child may have difficulty recognizing numerical symbols, remembering to add in carried numbers, and counting objects or following sequences of mathematical steps. Poor achievement in mathematics is at least as common as poor achievement in reading and spelling, and often people suffer from all three (Badian, 1983; Rourke & Finlayson, 1978).

Disorder of written expression describes an impairment in the ability to compose the written word (including spelling errors, errors in grammar or punctuation, or very poor handwriting) that is serious enough to interfere significantly with academic achievement or daily activities that require writing skills. Few systematic data have yet been collected on the prevalence of this disorder, which our college student had in addition to his dyslexia.

COMMUNICATION DISORDERS

In **expressive language disorder**, the child has difficulty expressing himself or herself in speech. The youngster may seem eager to communicate but have inordinate difficulty finding the right words; for example, he or she may be unable to come up with the word car when pointing to a car passing by on the street. By age four, this child speaks only in short phrases. Old words are forgotten when new ones are learned, and the use of grammatical structures is considerably below age level.

Unlike children who have trouble finding words, youngsters with **phonological disorder** comprehend and are able to use a substantial vocabulary, but their speech sounds like baby talk. *Blue* comes out *bu*, and *rabbit* sounds like *wabbit*, for example. They have not learned articulation of the later-acquired speech sounds, such as *r, sh, th, f, z, l,* and *ch*. With speech therapy complete recovery occurs in almost all cases, and milder cases may recover spontaneously by age eight.

A third communication disorder is **stuttering**, a disturbance in verbal fluency that is characterized by one or more of the following speech patterns: frequent repetitions or prolongations of sounds, long pauses between words, substituting easy words for those that present difficulty in articulating (like words beginning with certain consonants), and repeating whole words (like saying "go-go-go-go-" instead of just a single "go"). Sometimes bodily twitching and eye blinking accompany the verbal dysfluencies. Not surprisingly, stuttering can interfere with academic, social, and occupational functioning and can prevent otherwise capable persons from fulfilling their potential. Stuttering is frequently worse when the person is nervous and often improves or even disappears when the person

A speech therapist works with a child with phonological disorder by having him practice the sounds he finds difficult.

sings. The stuttering of a friend of ours would disappear almost completely when he performed in plays even though being on stage was somewhat anxiety-provoking for him. He would tell us that it was much easier to verbalize the words from a script than to speak on his own, consistent with the improvement often seen in stutterers when they read aloud. About three times as many males than females have the problem, which usually shows up at around age 5 and almost always before the age of 10. The DSM estimates that up to 80 percent of people recover, most of them without professional intervention, before the age of 16.

MOTOR SKILLS DISORDER

In **motor skills disorder**, also referred to as developmental coordination disorder, children show marked impairment in the development of motor coordination that is not explainable by mental retardation or a known physical disorder such as cerebral palsy. The young child may have difficulty tying shoelaces and buttoning shirts and when older, with model building, playing ball, and printing or handwriting. The diagnosis is made only if the impairment interferes significantly with academic achievement or with the activities of daily living.

ETIOLOGY OF LEARNING DISABILITIES

Most of the research on learning disabilities concerns dyslexia, perhaps because it is the most prevalent and debilitating of this group of disorders.

Family and twin studies confirm that there is a heritable component to dyslexia (Pennington, 1995), possibly controlled by chromosome 6 (Cardon et al., 1994; Grigorenko et al., in press). Other evidence

suggests that brain abnormalities, possibly heritable, may be responsible for dyslexia. Autopsies of the brains of right-handed individuals with childhood dyslexia have revealed microscopic abnormalities in the location, number, and organization of neurons on the left side of the brain in what is called the posterior language area of the cortex (Galaburda, 1989, 1993). PET scans made of dyslexic and normal children while performing a variety of cognitive tasks revealed differences in how another part of the cortex functions. During a test that required children to detect rhymes, the left temporoparietal cortex of the normal children was activated, but not that of the dyslexic children. This finding is important because what is called phonological awareness is believed to be critical to the development of reading skills (Rumsey, Anderson, et al., 1992; Rumsey, Zametkin, et al., 1994).

Past psychological theories have focused on visual perceptual deficits as the basis for dyslexia. One popular hypothesis suggested that children with reading problems *perceive* letters in reverse order or mirror image, mistaking, for example, a *d* for a *b*. No relationship has been found between letter confusions at age five or six and subsequent reading ability, however (Calfee, Fisk, & Piont-kowski, 1985), nor does a person need to be able to *see* to have reading problems—blind people may have difficulty learning to read Braille (McGuiness, 1981).

More recent research sheds further light on the complexity and subtle nature of visual-perceptual deficits in dyslexic individuals. These people have been found to process visual stimuli more slowly than do normal people and to be less likely to notice minor contrasts between stimuli (Martin & Lovegrove, 1984). For example, dyslexic children do not perform as well as normal children on visual tasks that require rapid processing, such as determining how many dots are presented on a screen in a series of presentations (Eden et al., 1995).

Other research points to one or more problems in language processing that might underlie dyslexia, including perception of speech and analysis of the sounds of spoken language and their relation to printed words (Mann & Brady, 1988). A series of longitudinal studies suggests that some early language problems can predict later dyslexia. Children who have difficulty recognizing rhyme and alliteration at age four (Bradley & Bryant, 1985) or who have problems rapidly naming familiar objects at age five (Scarborough, 1990; Wolf, Bally, & Morris, 1986), as well as those with delays in learning syntactic rules at age two and a half (Scarborough, 1990), are all more likely than peers without these difficulties to develop dyslexia. These language-processing difficulties and the visual-processing deficits noted earli-

FOCUS 15.3 ENURESIS

It is well-known that infants have no bladder or bowel control. As they become older, the inevitable toilet training begins. Some children learn toileting at eighteen months, others at thirty months, and so on. When is it no longer normal to be unable to control the bladder? The answer, determined by cultural norms and statistics, is fairly arbitrary.

DSM-IV and other classification systems distinguish among children who wet during sleep—nocturnal **enuresis**—those who wet while awake—diurnal enuresis—and those who wet both days and nights. Daytime continence is established earlier because bladder control is a much simpler matter when one is awake. When a child falls behind in bladder control, it is usually for the nighttime hours. DSM-IV estimates that at age five, 7 percent of boys and 3 percent of girls are enuretic; at age ten, 3 percent of boys and 2 percent of girls; and at age eighteen, 1 percent of young men and less for young women.

In the United States nocturnal enuresis is not diagnosed, according to DSM-IV, until the child is five years old. Primary enuretics, who represent two-thirds of all enuretics (Starfield, 1972), have wet the bed from infancy, whereas secondary enuretics were once able to remain dry at night but have apparently lost the capacity.

CAUSES OF ENURESIS

One consistent finding about enuresis is that the likelihood of an enuretic having a first-degree relative who also wets is very high, approximately 75 percent (Bakwin, 1973). A recent Danish study provides the first direct genetic link for bed-wetting; a segment of chromosome 13 apparently holds the gene for nocturnal enuresis (Eiberg, Berendt, & Mohr, 1995).

As many as 10 percent of all cases of enuresis are caused by purely medical conditions. The most common of the known physical causes is urinary tract infection. Approximately one in ten female and one in twenty male enuretics have such an infection (Stansfield, 1973). Treatment of the infection stops the enuresis in about 40 percent of cases (Schmidt, 1982). Other infrequent but known physical causes are chronic renal or kidney disease, tumors, diabetes, and seizures (Kolvin, MacKeith, & Meadow, 1973). Because of the substantial incidence of physical causes of enuresis, most professionals refer enuretics to physicians before beginning psychological treatment.

Some psychoanalytic theorists have suggested that enuresis serves as a symbol for other conflicts. Enuresis has been hypothesized to be both symbolic masturbation and a disguised means of expressing anger toward parents (Mowrer, 1950). A related notion considers enuresis a symptom of a more general psychological disorder, such as anxiety. Many investigators argue, however, that such problems are a reaction to the embarrassment and guilt of wetting, rather than causes of enuresis.

Children will lose self-esteem if their peers tease them and their parents become angry and rejecting. When bladder control is gained, most of the correlated problems are also likely to disappear (Moffatt, Kato, & Pless, 1987; Starfield, 1972). On the other hand, those who begin bed-wetting after an extended period of continence have been found to have experienced more stressful events, suggesting that emotional factors are influential in some cases of enuresis (Jarvelin et al., 1990).

Bladder control, the inhibition of a natural reflex until voluntary voiding can take place, is a skill of considerable complexity. Medical evidence regarding activity of the pelvic floor muscles provides support for the idea that children who wet the bed fail to spontaneously contract these muscles at night (Norgaard, 1989a, 1989b).

Learning theorists propose that children wet when toilet training begins at too early an age (when the body is simply not ready), when training is lax and insufficient reinforcement is given for proper toileting, and more specifically when children do not learn to awaken as a conditioned response to a full bladder or to inhibit sufficiently relaxation of the sphincter muscle that controls urination (Baller, 1975; Mowrer & Mowrer, 1938; Young, 1965).

Some preliminary research suggests another biological theory to account for nocturnal enuresis. Danish researchers found that adolescents with enuresis had a nighttime deficiency of antidiuretic hormone (ADH) (Rittig et al., 1989). In normal children ADH concentrates the urine more during sleep than during the waking hours. Someone deficient in ADH at night will have nighttime urine that exceeds ordinary bladder capacity. Alternative theories, such as the idea that enuretic children have sleep and arousal problems or an abnormally small functional bladder capacity, have not been supported by research (Barclay & Houts, 1995).

TREATMENT OF ENURESIS

Home remedies for bed-wetting have run the gamut from restricting fluids to making children sleep on golf balls or hanging the incriminating evidence—wet sheets—out the window (Houts, 1991). Most such strategies have been ineffective. Similarly, waiting for the child to grow out of the problem has not been satisfactory. Only about 15 percent of enuretics between ages five and nineteen show spontaneous remission within a year (Forsythe & Redmond, 1974).

The two most widely used treatments prescribed by professionals involve either medication or urine alarm systems. The latter first came on the scene in 1938, when Mowrer and Mowrer introduced the bell and pad. (Recall from Chapter 2 that O. H. Mowrer was a leading researcher and theoretician whose work was important in laying the foundations for behavioral approaches to psychopathology and intervention.) Over the years this treatment has proved markedly successful in reducing or eliminating bed-wetting. It is estimated that 75 percent of enuretic children will learn to stay dry through the night with the help of this remarkably simple device.

A bell and a battery are wired to a pad composed of two metallic foil sheets, the top one perforated, separated by a layer of absorbent cloth (Figure 15.2). The pad is inserted into a pillowcase and placed beneath the child at bedtime. When the first drops of urine, which act as an electrolyte, reach the cloth, the electric circuit is completed between the two foil sheets. The completed circuit sets off the bell, which awakens the child immediately or soon after beginning to wet. The child then typically stops urinating, turns off the device, and goes to the bathroom.

Mowrer and Mowrer (1938) viewed the bell and pad as a classical-conditioning procedure wherein an unconditioned stimulus, the bell, wakes the child, the unconditioned response. The bell is paired with the sensations of a full bladder so that these sensations eventually become a conditioned stimulus that produces the conditioned response of awakening before the bell sounds. Others have questioned the classical-conditioning theory, suggesting, in operant-conditioning terms, that the bell, by waking the child, serves as a punisher and thus reduces the undesirable behavior of wetting. In actual practice the bell usu-

ally wakes the child's parents too; their reactions may serve as an additional incentive for the child to remain dry. Other methods that use an operant-conditioning approach without the help of the urine-alarm have not been nearly as successful (Houts, Berman, & Abramson, 1994). On the other hand, greater success may be achieved by additions to the basic urine-alarm procedure, such as drinking increasing amounts of fluid on successive nights before bedtime (to get the child used to retaining fluid in the bladder without wetting the bed) and making sure that the child awakens and changes sheets each time the alarm rings (to add another negative consequence to bed-wetting) (Barclay & Houts, 1995). Newer urine alarms are worn on the body and are more reliable than the original mattress pad.

Pharmacological treatment is another approach; about one-third of enuretics who seek professional help are prescribed medications, such as the antidepressant imipramine (Tofranil) and, more recently, desmopressin, which is a synthetic version of ADH, the hormone mentioned earlier. Such medications work either by changing the reactivity of the muscles involved in urinating (imipramine) or by concentrating urine in the bladder (desmopressin). Although an immediate positive effect is usually seen, in the vast majority of cases children relapse as soon as the medication is stopped (Houts, 1991). Treatments combining medication with the behavioral approach described earlier are promising (Sukhai, Mol, & Harris, 1989).

Figure 15.2 The bell-and-pad apparatus for halting bed-wetting, devised by O. H. Mowrer and W. M. Mowrer.

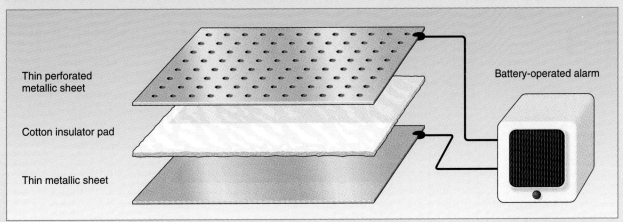

er may arise from the same neurological problem, namely, a deficit in the brain structures that are used to process stimuli rapidly (Eden & Zeffiro, 1996)

TREATMENT OF LEARNING DISABILITIES

The anxiety of parents whose otherwise normal child lags behind in reading or cannot speak effec-

tively and normally for his or her age cannot be underestimated. Professional attempts to remedy learning disabilities have been subject to somatic, educational, and psychological fads—from the use of stimulants and tranquilizers to training the child in motor activities, such as crawling, believed to have been inadequately mastered at a younger age, in the hope of reorganizing neuronal connections in the brain.

Several methods are currently being used to treat learning disabilities. Traditional linguistic approaches, used primarily in cases of reading and writing difficulties, focus on instruction in listening, speaking, reading, and writing skills in a logical, sequential, and multisensory manner, such as reading out loud under close supervision (Lyon & Moats, 1988). In young children, readiness skills, such as letter discrimination, phonetic analysis, and learning letter–sound correspondences, may need to be taught before explicit instruction in reading is attempted. As in the case described at the beginning of this section, dyslexic individuals often can succeed in college with the aid of instructional supports, such as tape-recorded lectures, tutors, writing editors, and untimed tests (Bruck, 1987). Most colleges have special services to help such students.

Recently there has been an exciting development in treating language disorders (Merzenich et al., 1996; Tallal, Miller, et al., 1996). Based on previous findings that such children have difficulty discriminating hard consonants such as *b* and *d*, the researchers developed special computer games and audiotapes that slow speech sounds. After intensive training with these modified speech stimuli for one month, children with severe language disorders were able to improve their language skills by approximately two years, to the point at which they were functioning as normal children do. Similar training using unmodified speech stimuli resulted in very little progress. Although the number of participants in these initial studies was small, the remarkable gains suggest a promising new approach that will surely be investigated further. The researchers speculate that this training method may even help prevent dyslexia, since many reading-disordered children had difficulties understanding language as young children.

Most children with learning disabilities have probably experienced a great deal of frustration and failure that erode their motivation and confidence. Whatever their design, treatment programs should be structured to provide opportunities for children to experience feelings of mastery and self-efficacy. Rewarding small steps can be helpful in increasing the child's motivation, focusing attention on the learning task, and reducing behavioral problems caused by frustration.

MENTAL RETARDATION

Mental retardation, an Axis II disorder, is defined in DSM-IV as (1) significantly subaverage intellectual functioning along with (2) deficits in adaptive behavior and (3) occurring prior to age eighteen. We examine first these traditional criteria and discuss later some newer perspectives from the American Association of Mental Retardation.

TRADITIONAL CRITERIA FOR MENTAL RETARDATION

INTELLIGENCE-TEST SCORES AS A CRITERION

The first component of the DSM definition requires a judgment of intelligence. As discussed in Chapter 4 (p. 80), approximately two-thirds of the population achieves IQ (intelligent quotient) test scores between 85 and 115. Those with a score below 70 to 75, two standard deviations below the mean of the population, are considered to have "significant subaverage general intellectual functioning" and are therefore classified as mentally retarded. Approximately 3 percent of the population falls into this category.

The determination of IQ should be based on tests administered to an individual by a competent, well-trained professional. Interpretation of scores must take into account cultural, linguistic, and sensory or motor limitations that may affect performance. For example, when testing a child with cerebral palsy who has limited use of his or her hands, the examiner might select IQ tests that require verbal responses or simple gestural responses, rather than the traditional intellectual tests, which include a nonverbal or performance component requiring fairly complex and rapid motor movements. Similarly, a child who speaks Farsi at home and English at school cannot be tested in a valid way using only English-language measures (American Association of Mental Retardation [AAMR], 1992).

ADAPTIVE FUNCTIONING AS A CRITERION

Adaptive functioning refers to childhood skills such as toileting and dressing; understanding the concepts of time and money; being able to use tools, to shop, and to travel by public transportation; and becoming socially responsive. An adolescent is expected to be able to apply academic skills, reasoning, and judgment to daily living and to participate in group activities. An adult is expected to be self-supporting and to assume social responsibilities.

Several tests have been constructed to assess adaptive behavior. Best known are the American Association of Mental Deficiency Adaptive Behavior Scale (ABS) (Nihira et al., 1974) and the Vineland Adaptive Behavior Scales (Sparrow, Balla, & Cicchetti, 1984; see Table 15.3).

TABLE 15.3 Sample Items from the Vineland Adaptive Behavior Scales

Age, Years	Adaptive Ability
2	Says at least fifty recognizable words.
	Removes front-opening coat, sweater, or shirt without assistance.
5	Tells popular story, fairy tale, lengthy joke, or plot of television program.
	Ties shoelaces into a bow without assistance.
8	Keeps secrets or confidences for more than one day.
	Orders own meal in a restaurant.
11	Uses the telephone for all kinds of calls without assistance.
	Watches television or listens to radio for information about a particular area of interest.
16	Looks after own health.
	Responds to hints or indirect cues in conversation.

Source: From Sparrow, Balla, & Cicchetti, 1984.

Although impairments in adaptive functioning have long been included in the definition of mental retardation, only recently have the tests been ade-quately standardized with firmly established norms. One problem with many assessments of adaptive behavior, however, is that they fail to consider the environment to which the person must adapt. A person who lives in a small rural community where everyone is acquainted may not need skills as complex as those needed by someone who lives in New York City. Youngsters who are competent working at farm chores, walking to school, and shopping at the local general store, when transported to a city may be considered deficient in adaptive behavior if they are not able to ride the subway to school or buy groceries at a store where a foreign language is spoken. By the same token, city children may find themselves at a loss with some of the activities expected of youngsters living on a farm. An effective and valid assessment of adaptive behavior should therefore consider the interaction between the child and the surroundings in which he or she must function.

TIME OF ONSET AS A CRITERION

A final definitional criterion is that mental retardation be manifest before age eighteen, to rule out classifying as mental retardation any deficits in intelligence and adaptive behavior from traumatic accidents or illnesses occurring later in life. Children with severe impairments are often diagnosed during infancy. Most children considered mentally retarded, however, are not identified as

When assessing normal adaptive behavior, the environment must be considered. A person living in a rural community may not need the same skills as those needed by someone living in New York City.

such until they enter school. These children have no obvious physiological, neurological, or physical manifestations, and their problems become apparent only when they are unable to keep up with their peers in school.

CLASSIFICATION OF MENTAL RETARDATION

Four levels of mental retardation are recognized by DSM-IV, each corresponding to a specific subaverage range on the far left of the normal distribution curve of measured intelligence. Again, the IQ ranges are not the sole basis of diagnosis; deficiencies in adaptive behavior are also a criterion of mental retardation. Some persons falling in the mildly retarded range based on IQ may have no deficits in adaptive behavior and thus would not be considered mentally retarded. Usually the IQ criterion is applied only after deficits in adaptive behavior have been identified. The following is a brief summary of characteristics of people at each level of mental retardation (American Psychiatric Association, 1994; Robinson & Robinson, 1976).

- **Mild Mental Retardation (50–55 to 70 IQ).** About 85 percent of all those who have IQs less than 70 are classified as having **mild mental retardation**. They are not always distinguishable from normal youngsters before they enter school. By their late teens they can usually learn academic skills at about a sixth-grade level. As adults they are likely to be able to maintain themselves in unskilled jobs or in sheltered workshops, although they may need help with social and financial problems. They may marry and have children of their own.

- **Moderate Mental Retardation (35–40 to 50–55 IQ).** About 10 percent of those with IQs less than 70 are classified as having **moderate mental retardation**. Brain damage and other pathologies are frequent. Moderately retarded people may have physical defects and neurological dysfunctions that hinder fine motor skills, such as grasping and coloring within lines, and gross motor skills, such as running and climbing. They may learn to travel alone in a familiar locality. Many are institutionalized, but most live dependently within the family or in supervised group homes.

- **Severe Mental Retardation (20–25 to 35–40 IQ).** Of those with IQs less than 70, about 3 to 4 percent come under the category of **severe mental retardation**. These people commonly have congenital physical abnormalities and

limited sensorimotor control. Most are institutionalized and require constant aid and supervision. Severely retarded adults may be friendly but can usually communicate only briefly on a very concrete level. They engage in little independent activity and are often lethargic, for their severe brain damage leaves them relatively passive and the circumstances of their lives allow them little stimulation. They may be able to perform very simple work under close supervision.

- **Profound Mental Retardation (below 20–25 IQ).** One to two percent of retarded people are classified as having **profound mental retardation**, requiring total supervision and often nursing care all their lives. Most have severe physical deformities as well as neurological damage and cannot get around on their own. The profoundly mentally retarded have a very high mortality rate during childhood.

We turn now to an approach to mental retardation that is being followed by increasing numbers of professionals.

THE APPROACH OF THE AMERICAN ASSOCIATION OF MENTAL RETARDATION

In the ninth edition of its classification system, the American Association of Mental Retardation (AAMR, 1992) shifted its focus from establishing IQ scores for identifying severity of disability to determining what remedial supports are necessary to facilitate higher functioning. Professionals are now encouraged to identify an individual's strengths and weaknesses on psychological, physical, and environmental dimensions with a view toward determining the kinds and intensities of environmental supports needed to enhance a person's functioning in different domains.

As an example of this approach, consider Roger, a twenty-four-year-old man with an IQ of 45 who has attended a special program for mentally retarded children since he was six. According to the DSM, he would be considered moderately mentally retarded. Based on this diagnosis he would not be expected to be able to live independently, get around on his own, or progress beyond second grade. The AAMR classification system, however, would emphasize what is needed to maximize Roger's functioning. Thus, a clinician might discover that Roger can use the bus system if he takes a route familiar to him, and thus he might be able to go to a movie by himself from time to time. And although he cannot prepare complicated meals, he may be taught to prepare frozen entrees in a microwave oven. The assumption is that by concentrating and building on what he *can* do, Roger will make more progress.

In the schools, an individualized placement is based on the person's strengths and weaknesses and on the amount of instruction needed. A student who needs considerable one-on-one instruction because of deficient intellectual functioning may be placed in the same classroom with a child who needs intensive instruction because of emotional problems or physical disabilities. Students are identified by the classroom environment they are judged to need. This approach can lessen the stigmatizing effects of being considered retarded and may also encourage a focus on what can be done to improve the student's learning rather than on how to label the child.

DEFICIENCIES IN SKILLS AND COGNITIVE ABILITIES IN MENTAL RETARDATION

Figure 15.3 shows three rings or levels that can help organize our thinking about the deficiencies characteristic of mental retardation.

DEFICIENCIES IN ADAPTIVE SKILLS

As pictured in the outer ring of Figure 15.3, a retarded person is generally limited at least to some extent in six skills needed for daily living—communication, social skills, functional academics, self-care, home living, community use, self-direction, health and safety, and work skills.

COMMUNICATION Although most children spontaneously develop the ability to speak and communicate, children with mental retardation may need help to achieve effective communication. Those with mild disabilities may require only minimal support, such as a speech class to help them learn to articulate words so that they can be understood by others. Children with more severe disabilities may need years of intensive language training in order to express effectively their basic needs and feelings.

SOCIAL SKILLS It is not uncommon for children who are mildly retarded to have difficulty making and keeping friends. More seriously retarded children show little awareness of social conventions. Many such youngsters seem overly friendly, wanting to be held and hugged by people whom they have just met, or they may appear to be unaware of those

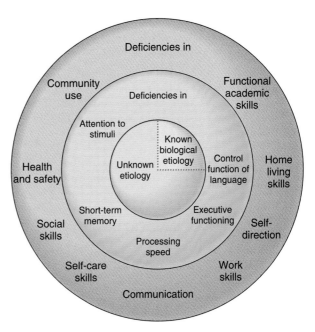

Figure 15.3 The nature and causes of mental retardation and the adaptive skills and general cognitive abilities that people with mental retardation lack.

who approach them. Lack of expressive social behavior does not mean that the person is not responding to social events; it may be that the individual is experiencing more emotion than he or she is able to express.

FUNCTIONAL ACADEMIC SKILLS Mastering reading, writing, and mathematics poses difficult problems for children with even mild mental disabilities. However, many can learn enough arithmetic to shop effectively, balance checkbooks, and budget money. They may also competently read recipes, how-to manuals, or just-for-fun books. Few teachers attempt to teach these skills, in their usual sense, to children with severe disabilities. But with adequate instruction many of these children can learn functional academics, for example, how to read signs and labels frequently found on their daily route or use a calculator at a store.

SELF-CARE SKILLS These are skills exercised in the routine activities of daily living—bathing, dressing, eating, toileting. Many children with retardation have all these skills. Children with profound retardation often require extensive, arduous training and supervision to perform these basic tasks. Many of these children also have physical disabilities—a movement that is simple for a nondisabled person may pose a real challenge for someone with a limited range of motion.

HOME LIVING SKILLS For adults with mental retardation, skills such as housekeeping, property maintenance, shopping for and preparing food, and daily scheduling may be difficult. Although some retarded individuals are able to master many of these tasks, others need help, ranging from being taught specific steps in cooking simple meals to having all their meals prepared and delivered.

COMMUNITY USE A person requiring limited support in this area might be able to ride the bus without assistance but not to drive, to attend religious services without assistance and to pick up groceries paid for by another through a credit system. An individual requiring pervasive support may need a one-on-one staff person to take them on outings in the community.

SELF-DIRECTION Skills related to initiating activities, asking for help when needed, following a schedule, and solving problems in new situations determine the extent to which a person with mental retardation can live and work independently. An adult with mild mental retardation might work successfully at a clearly defined job in the community for many years, yet need help in finding a new job when laid off due to downsizing.

HEALTH AND SAFETY Determining what to do about a bout of influenza or how to handle a minor cut, protecting oneself by wearing a seatbelt, interacting appropriately with strangers, and using birth control are all skills that make a difference in being able to live independently.

WORK SKILLS One goal of education is to prepare children for a vocation. By the time most youngsters with mild mental retardation have finished school, they have acquired most of the skills needed to support themselves with a job in a competitive marketplace. Mild disabilities readily apparent in an academic setting may not be apparent in the world of work. People with moderate mental retardation may also acquire some work skills, and many gain employment, usually in simple jobs, structured and supervised, in sheltered workshops or family businesses.

Some people with mental retardation do clerical, maintenance, and laundry work; packaging; electronic and other light assembly; metal cutting, drilling, and other machine work; farming; gardening; and carpentry. They also work in domestic and food services. Some are taught to participate in the care and training of those more disabled than themselves and benefit greatly from the experience. Many retarded workers are persistent, accurate, and punctual employees.

Training in vocational skills is an important component of the education of the mentally retarded. Even children with moderate retardation can acquire skills which sometimes allow them to work with those more retarded than themselves.

DEFICIENCIES IN GENERAL COGNITIVE ABILITIES

The middle ring of Figure 15.3 consists of general cognitive abilities that people with mental retardation lack to some extent. These abilities underlie the adaptive skills in the outer ring.

ATTENTION TO STIMULI Persons with mental retardation attend to different dimensions of a stimulus than do non-mentally-disabled people (Zeaman & Hanley, 1983). For example, individuals with mental retardation attend more readily to the position of an object than to its other dimensions, such as color or shape, and can thus be at a disadvantage in solving problems that require flexibility in point of view.

SHORT-TERM MEMORY Although the long-term memories of children with and without mild mental retardation have been found to be the same, individuals with mental retardation have much poorer short-term memory than do others. This deficit may be due to a failure to mentally rehearse items in short-term memory tasks, which normal individuals do spontaneously, for example, when asked to remember a series of seven digits (Detterman, 1979). When instructed and helped with recall, the short-term memory of people with mental retardation can improve, although the amount of improvement is limited (Ellis, Deacon, & Wooldridge, 1985).

PROCESSING SPEED Most individuals with mental retardation process information slowly; for example, they take much more time than normals to accurately identify which of two lines in a visual array is longer (Nettelbeck, 1985).

EXECUTIVE FUNCTIONING Such cognitive skills include knowing how to plan, monitor one's progress, and check the outcomes of one's efforts for completeness and accuracy. Retarded people show general deficits in this area (Butterfield & Belmont, 1977).

CONTROL FUNCTION OF LANGUAGE Lev Semenovich Vygotsky (1896–1934), a Russian neuropsychologist, emphasized the importance of so-called private speech in controlling one's behavior. A child's behavior is first controlled or regulated by instructions from other people. Then the child imitates these instructions aloud, and they serve as a cue or guide to behavior. The process is completed when the child's formerly spoken words become internalized, when they become inner speech (Vygotsky, 1978). This connection between language and action may fail to develop in retarded children, leading to deficits in self-regulation (Whitman, 1990).

ETIOLOGY OF MENTAL RETARDATION

As portrayed in the innermost circle in Figure 15.3, in only 25 percent of the mentally retarded population can the primary cause be specifically identified at this time.

NO IDENTIFIABLE ETIOLOGY

In contrast to persons with severe or profound mental retardation, those with less severe mental retardation do not, as far as is known at this time, have an identifiable organic brain defect. Whereas persons whose mental retardation is associated with identifiable organic impairments are found in much the same percentages throughout all socioeconomic, ethnic, and racial groups, those with mild or moderate mental retardation are overrepresented in the lower socioeconomic classes, suggesting that certain social conditions of deprivation are major factors in retarding their intellectual and behavioral development.

One theory, proposed by Yale psychologist Edmund Zigler (1967), stresses the importance of motivational factors in the milder forms of mental retardation. The theory holds that the social deprivation common in institutions for the retarded, the history of task failures, and the lesser importance of reinforcers such as being told one is correct can lead some individuals with mental retardation to have lower motivation than normal children for performing cognitive tasks. Strengthening those motivational variables therefore should improve the performance of children with mild retardation. There is

some empirical support for this view, though the improvement that can be achieved is limited (Weiss, Weisz, & Bromfield, 1986; Weisz & Yeates, 1981).

More recent theories expand on Zigler's view by positing interactions between biological and environmental factors. Baumeister, Kupstas, and Klindworth (1992) suggested several classes of variables that might act in concert to produce milder forms of mental retardation. These include predisposing variables (diatheses) such as undetermined genetic factors, and resource variables such as educational and health care resources. Consider two persons with the same biological brain impairment, so subtle as to be undetectable by the neurological methods currently available. One youngster comes from an upper-socioeconomic level, the other from a lower level. The first individual's slight deficit could be compensated for by the enriched social and educational environment made possible by the family's financial resources. In contrast, the second individual's deficit might be exaggerated by impoverished circumstances. To show signs of retardation, a socially advantaged person would have to have more extensive damage, which is less responsive to or even impervious to help from an enriched upbringing.

KNOWN BIOLOGICAL ETIOLOGY

The approximately 25 percent of people whose mental retardation has a known biological cause inflates the incidence of retardation in the population over what would be statistically expected were no abnormal conditions present. These individuals create what is referred to as a bump at the bottom end of the normal curve (Figure 15.4). Genetic conditions, infectious diseases, accidents, and environmental hazards are four categories of causes of impairment.

Figure 15.4 Normal curve showing the theoretical distribution of IQ scores. The bump on the left represents the actual frequency of severe and profound retardation with biological causes.

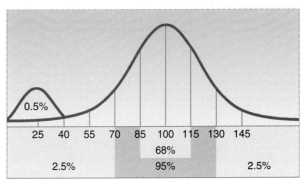

GENETIC OR CHROMOSOMAL ANOMALIES Just under 5 percent of all recognized pregnancies have chromosomal abnormalities. The majority of these pregnancies end in spontaneous abortions or miscarriages. About one-half of 1 percent of the babies who are born have a chromosomal abnormality (Smith, Bierman, & Robinson, 1978). A significant proportion of these infants die soon after birth. Of the babies that survive, the majority have **Down syndrome**, or **trisomy 21**.

People with Down syndrome have moderate to severe retardation as well as several distinctive physical signs of the syndrome, such as short and stocky stature; oval, upward-slanting eyes; a prolongation of the fold of the upper eyelid over the inner corner of the eye; sparse, fine, straight hair; a wide and flat nasal bridge; square-shaped ears; a large, furrowed tongue, which protrudes because the mouth is small and its roof low; and short, broad hands with stubby fingers.

Perhaps 40 percent of children with Down syndrome have heart problems; a small minority may have blockages of the upper intestinal tract; and about one in six dies during the first year. Mortality after age forty is high; at autopsy brain tissue generally shows deterioration similar to that in Alzheimer's disease (p. 456). Despite their mental retardation some of these children learn to read, write, and do arithmetic.

Down syndrome is named after the British physician Langdon Down, who first described its clinical signs in 1866. In 1959 the French geneticist Jerome Lejeune and his colleagues identified its genetic basis. Human beings usually possess forty-six chromosomes, inheriting twenty-three from each parent. Individuals with Down syndrome almost always have forty-seven chromosomes instead of forty-six. During maturation of the egg, the two chromosomes of pair 21, the smallest ones, fail to separate. If the egg is fertilized, uniting with a sperm, there will be three of chromosome 21; thus the technical term *trisomy 21*. Down syndrome is found in approximately one in 800 to 1200 live births.

Another chromosomal disease that causes mental retardation is **fragile X syndrome**. In certain individuals the X chromosome may break in two. Physical symptoms associated with fragile X include facial features such as large, underdeveloped ears, a long, thin face, and a broad nasal root, and enlarged testicles in males. Recent studies using DNA testing of individuals with the fragile X genotype have provided evidence for a spectrum of dysfunction in individuals with different forms of fragile X (Hagerman, 1995). Although many such individuals exhibit mental retardation and behavior problems, others have normal IQ but evidence problems such as learning disabilities, difficulties with frontal-lobe and right-hemisphere tasks, and mood lability. It is believed that some cases of autistic disorder (p. 436) are caused by a form of fragile X. Some individuals with fragile X have very few

Left: The normal complement of chromosomes is 23 pairs. Right: In Down syndrome there is a trisomy of chromosome 21.

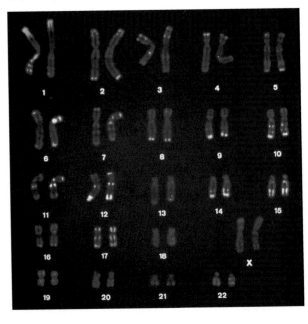

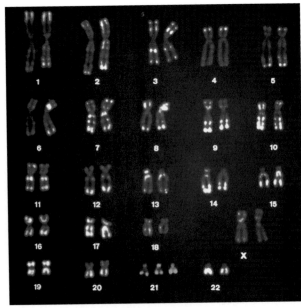

problems, although they have been found to have social difficulties such as shyness or poor eye contact. Fragile X is the second leading cause of mental retardation with a chromosomal basis, after Down syndrome (Dykens et al., 1988).

RECESSIVE-GENE DISEASES When a pair of defective recessive genes misdirects the formation of an enzyme, metabolic processes are disturbed. The problem may affect development of the embryo in the uterus or become important only much later in life.

In **phenylketonuria (PKU)** the infant, born normal, soon suffers from a deficiency of liver enzyme, phenylalanine hydroxylase. This enzyme is needed to convert phenylalanine, an amino acid contained in protein, to tyrosine, an amino acid that is essential for the development of such hormones as epinephrine. Because of this enzyme deficiency, phenylalanine and its derivative phenylpyruvic acid are not broken down and instead build up in the body fluids, eventually causing irreversible brain damage. The unmetabolized amino acid interferes with the process of myelination, the sheathing of neuron axons, which is essential for the rapid transmittal of impulses and thus of information. As the neurons of the frontal lobes, the site of many important mental functions, such as rational decision making, are particularly affected, mental retardation is profound.

Although PKU is rare, with an incidence of about one in 14,000 live births, it is estimated that one person in seventy is a carrier of the recessive gene. There is a blood test for prospective parents who have reason to suspect that they might be carriers. Also, after the PKU newborn has consumed milk for several days, an excess amount of unconverted phenylalanine can be detected in the blood, and state laws require testing. If the test is positive, the parents are urged to provide the infant a diet low in phenylalanine. Although early guidelines suggested restricting the diets of children from three months to six years of age (Collaborative Study of Children Treated for Phenylketonuria, 1975), parents are now encouraged to introduce the special diet as early as possible and to maintain it indefinitely. This regimen is especially important for pregnant women so that the fetus will not be exposed to toxic levels of phenylalanine (Baumeister & Baumeister, 1995). Recent studies have indicated that children whose dietary restrictions stop at age five to seven begin to show subtle declines in functioning, particularly in IQ, reading, and spelling (Fishler et al., 1987; Legido et al., 1993). Even among children with PKU who maintain the

diet, deficits in visual-perceptual skills and arithmetic may emerge over time.

Several hundred other recessive-gene diseases have been identified, and many of them cause mental retardation. Only a very small percentage of cases of mental retardation are accounted for by any *single* disease. Genetic counseling can help future parents determine whether their backgrounds suggest that they are at risk for carrying certain of these recessive genes.

INFECTIOUS DISEASES While in utero the fetus is at increased risk of mental retardation resulting from maternal infectious diseases such as rubella (German measles). The consequences of these diseases are most serious during the first trimester of pregnancy, when the fetus has no detectable immunological response. Cytomegalovirus, toxoplasmosis, rubella, herpes simplex, and syphilis are all maternal infections that may cause both physical deformities and mental retardation of the fetus. The mother may experience slight or no symptoms from the infection, but the effects on the developing fetus can be devastating. Pregnant women who go to prenatal clinics are given a blood test for syphilis. Women today can also have their blood tested to determine whether they are immune to rubella; nearly 85 percent of American women are. Women who are not immune should be vaccinated at least six months before becoming pregnant. If a fetus contracts rubella from its mother, the child is likely to be born with brain lesions that cause mental retardation.

HIV infection has become a significant cause of mental retardation. An HIV-positive woman passes on the virus to the developing fetus about one-third of the time, and about half of these infected infants develop mental retardation. Some develop normally at first but decline in their cognitive and motor functioning as their HIV condition worsens; some remain HIV infected for many years without any impairment in intelligence.

Infectious diseases can affect a child's developing brain after birth also. Encephalitis and meningococcal meningitis may cause irreversible brain damage and even death if contracted in infancy or early childhood. These infections in adulthood are usually far less serious, probably because the brain is largely developed by about the age of six. There are several forms of childhood meningitis, a disease in which the protective membranes of the brain are acutely inflamed and fever is very high. Some children who survive without severe retardation may become mildly to moderately retarded. Other disabling aftereffects are deafness, paralysis, and epilepsy.

ACCIDENTS In the United States accidents are the leading cause of severe disability and death in children over one year of age. Falls and automobile accidents are among the most common mishaps in early childhood and may cause varying degrees of head injuries and mental retardation. The institution of laws mandating that children riding in automobiles wear seat belts may play a major role in reducing the incidence of mental retardation in young children.

ENVIRONMENTAL HAZARDS Several environmental pollutants can cause poisoning and mental retardation, including mercury, which may be transmitted through affected fish, and lead, which is found in lead-based paints, smog, and the exhaust from automobiles that burn leaded gasoline. Lead poisoning can cause kidney and brain damage as well as anemia, mental retardation, seizures, and death. Lead-based paint is now prohibited in the United States, but it is still found in older homes, where it may be flaking.

Although lead-based paint is now illegal, it can still be found in older homes. Eating chips of it can cause lead poisoning and mental retardation.

PREVENTION AND TREATMENT OF MENTAL RETARDATION

In the early part of this century many large institutions were built to house retarded individuals apart from the rest of the population. Most were no more than warehouses for anyone unfortunate enough to do poorly on newly constructed intelligence tests (Blatt, 1966). The majority of residents were recently arrived immigrants, members of racial minorities, children with physical disabilities, and indigents.

Although forced segregation reduced the number of children born to couples with one partner of questionable intelligence, it did not stop couples within institutions from bearing children. In Indiana in 1907 the first mandatory sterilization law for women with mental retardation was passed. By 1930 twenty-eight states had these laws. Although their constitutionality was questioned, forced sterilization—especially for undereducated minority and immigrant groups—continued to be practiced in many institutions through the 1950s. In the 1960s safeguards were passed to protect the rights of mentally retarded individuals to marry and bear children. Current workers in the field promote the right of mentally retarded adults to freedom of sexual expression as well as to marry and have children.

The warehousing of children with mental retardation can still be found in many parts of the world, for example, in Russia, where the Soviet ideal of "perfect children" continues to encourage parents to give up their disabled children to the care—actually neglect—of state-run institutions (Bennett, 1997).

Prevention of mental retardation depends on understanding its causes. The field of medical genetics is not yet equipped to prevent the more severe genetic causes of mental retardation, but startling advances in genetics may change this situation in the not-too-distant future. When the causes of mental retardation are unknown, prevention is not possible, but treatment to improve the person's ability to live on his or her own is an option. When an impoverished environment is the source of mild retardation, enrichment programs can prevent further deficits and sometimes even overcome them.

ENVIRONMENTAL INTERVENTIONS AND ENRICHMENT PROGRAMS

Those whose lack of a stimulating environment is believed to underlie their mild to moderate retardation can participate in such programs as Head Start, a federally funded program whose goal is to prepare children socially and culturally to succeed in the regular school setting by giving them experiences that they are missing at home. The impetus for Head Start came during the 1960s, when national attention was directed to problems of hunger and civil rights.

The core of the Head Start program is community-based preschool education, focusing on the development of early cognitive and social skills. Head Start contracts with professionals in the community to provide children with health and dental services, including vaccinations, hearing and vision testing, medical treatment, and nutrition informa-

Early intervention, as illustrated by Head Start programs, is a way of counteracting the impoverished environments of retarded children.

tion (North, 1979). Mental health services are another important component of these programs. Psychologists may identify children with psychological problems and consult with teachers and staff to help make the preschool environment sensitive to psychological issues, for example, by sharing knowledge of child development, consulting on an individual case, or helping staff address parents' concerns (Cohen, Solnit, & Wohlford, 1979). Social workers can serve as advocates for the child's family, linking families with needed social services and encouraging parents to get involved with their children's education (Lazar, 1979).

A comparison of Head Start children with other disadvantaged children who attended either a different preschool or no preschool showed that Head Start children improved significantly more than both control groups on social-cognitive ability and motor impulsivity; the relative improvement was strongest for African-American children, particularly those with initial ability below average. Although the Head Start program succeeded in enhancing the functioning of the neediest children, these children were still behind their peers in terms of absolute cognitive levels after one year in the program (Lee, Brooks-Gunn, & Schnur, 1988). Other reports confirm the value of Head Start in helping poor youngsters improve their intellectual functioning (e.g., Cronan et al., 1996; Perkins, 1995; Schleifer, 1995). (Focus 15.4)

RESIDENTIAL TREATMENT

Since the 1960s, there have been serious and systematic attempts to educate retarded children as fully as possible. Most people with mental retarda-

tion can acquire the competence needed to function effectively in the community. The trend has been to provide these individuals with educational and community services rather than largely custodial care in big mental hospitals. Since 1975, individuals with mental retardation have a right to appropriate treatment in the least restrictive residential setting. Ideally, moderately retarded people live in small-to-medium-sized homelike residences that are integrated into the community. A transition period gradually prepares the individual to move from an institution to a community home. Medical care is

Individuals with mental retardation have the right to treatment in the least restrictive environment. Moderately retarded people often live in community residences under supervision by trained aides.

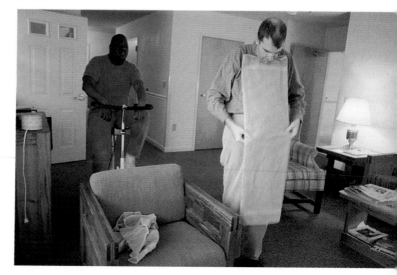

FOCUS 15.4   MAINSTREAMING

In 1975 the United States Congress passed Public Law 94-142, the Education for All Handicapped Children Act. Passage of this law represented substantial gains for the educational rights of children with disabilities and secured their integration into the community. The law guarantees children between the ages of three and twenty-one a free, appropriate public education in "the least restrictive environment." Such an environment is one that allows the student with a disability to develop mentally, physically, and socially with the fewest barriers yet provides necessary support. The goals for each child are set forth in an individual educational program (IEP) that is evaluated annually. To some, the least restrictive environment means that the children are educated at the same schools as normally achieving youngsters and are mainstreamed, that is, integrated, into some of their classrooms. Others would say that a segregated school provides the best resources and intensive training required by children with disabilities.

Mainstreaming received a big push when Public Law 99-457 was passed in 1986. This law extended the earlier statute by requiring that all public schools serve disabled preschoolers by 1991 or lose their federal funding. Both laws apply to all children with exceptional needs, including those with mental retardation, autism, and learning disabilities, as well as children with speech, hearing, motor, or visual impairments, gifted and talented children,* and children with serious emotional disturbances that interfere with their school progress.

Mainstreaming is not without its problems, however. For example, African-Americans have been overrepresented among children diagnosed as mentally retarded. Since scores on standardized intelligence tests are central in deciding on such placement, there is some concern that African-Americans may be unfairly stigmatized and otherwise disadvantaged by being assigned to special education classes, even though the classes are in public schools (Heller, Holtzman, & Messick, 1982). The reasons for the disproportionately large numbers of African-Americans in such classes are complex; they include historical patterns of discrimination that can lead to poor economic conditions, disrupted home lives, malnutrition, poor-quality school instruction, and other disadvantages that contribute to low test scores and poor school performance. Personal biases of teachers and administrators may also play a role in whether a child is placed in a special class. Our heterogeneous society has

Disabled students are now often mainstreamed, educated in the same classrooms as non-disabled students.

been grappling with these weighty social issues for well over a hundred years.

Generally, programs that are sensitive to the problems inherent in mainstreaming appear likely to yield positive results for students with and without disabilities (Gottlieb, 1990; Zigler, Hodapp, & Edison, 1990). Normal children can learn early in life that there is tremendous diversity among human beings and that a child may be different in some very important ways and yet be worthy of respect and friendship. With support from parents and teachers, normal children may reach adulthood without the burden of the prejudice of earlier generations. Such an eventuality would benefit both normal children and their emotionally or cognitively disadvantaged age-mates.

---

*It may seem odd that gifted and talented children are covered by this law, apparently designed for those with serious disabilities. Surely being uncommonly bright or talented in an area such as music or art is not a disability! True. But parents of such children know that the public schools sometimes do damage to gifted youngsters by not challenging them sufficiently and sometimes by discouraging, even disparaging, their abilities and interests. Such young people also have special educational needs; but it is understandable that when budgets are tight, resources are directed toward those who are mentally retarded and otherwise intellectually or physically compromised.

---

provided, and trained, live-in supervisors and aides attend to the residents' special needs around the clock. Residents are encouraged to participate in the household routines to the best of their abilities. Severely retarded children may live at home or in foster-care homes provided with educational and

psychological services. Many mildly retarded persons who have jobs and are able to live independently have their own apartments. Others live semi-independently in apartment housing of three to four retarded adults, with the aid of a counselor generally provided in the evening. Only people with severe and profound retardation and with physical disabilities tend to remain in institutions (Cunningham & Mueller, 1991).

BEHAVIORAL INTERVENTIONS BASED ON OPERANT CONDITIONING

Whereas programs such as Head Start can help prevent mild mental retardation in disadvantaged children, other early-intervention programs using cognitive and behavioral techniques have been developed to improve the level of functioning of individuals with more serious retardation. Several pilot projects have intervened with children with Down syndrome during infancy and early childhood to attempt to improve their functioning. These programs typically include systematic home- and treatment-center-based instruction in language skills, fine and gross motor skills, self-care, and social development. Specific behavioral objectives are defined, and in an operant fashion, children are taught skills in small, sequential steps (e.g., Clunies-Ross, 1979).

Severely retarded children usually need intensive instruction to be able to feed, toilet, and groom themselves. To teach a severely retarded child a particular routine, the therapist usually begins by analyzing and dividing the targeted behavior, such as eating, into smaller components: pick up spoon, scoop food from plate onto spoon, bring spoon to mouth, remove food with lips, chew and swallow food. Operant-conditioning principles are then applied to teach the child these components of eating. For example, the child may be reinforced for successive approximations to picking up the spoon until he or she is able to do so.

This operant approach, sometimes called **applied behavior analysis**,[2] is also used to reduce inappropriate and self-injurious behavior. Children with severe and profound mental impairment who live in institutions are especially prone to stereotyped behaviors performed in isolation—repetitive, rhythmic, self-stimulatory motions, such as rocking back and forth, swaying, rolling the head—and to aggression against the self or toward other children and staff. These maladaptive movements and injurious actions can often be reduced by reinforcing substitute responses.

Studies of these programs indicate consistent improvements in fine motor skills, social acceptance, and self-help skills. However, the programs

appear to have little effect on gross motor skills and linguistic abilities, and long-term improvements in IQ and school performance have not been demonstrated. It is not yet clear whether the benefits of the programs are greater than what parents can provide in the home without special training (Gibson & Harris, 1988).

The significance of learning self-care and of reducing stereotyped and injurious actions in people with severe or profound retardation must not be underestimated. Toilet-trained children, for example, are more comfortable, are liked better by the staff, and can leave the ward for other rooms and leave the building to play on the grounds. Mastering toilet training and learning to feed and dress themselves may even mean that severely retarded children can live at home. Most retarded people face discrimination from others, based in part on violations of norms. Being able to act more normally increases their chances of interacting meaningfully with others. Moreover, the self-esteem that comes from learning to take better care of oneself is extremely bolstering.

COGNITIVE INTERVENTIONS

As indicated earlier, retarded children fail to use strategies in solving problems and when they do have strategies, they often do not apply them effectively. **Self-instructional training**, based on Vygotsky's work, described earlier (p. 429), teaches retarded children to guide their problem-solving efforts through speech. Meichenbaum and Goodman (1971) outlined a five-step procedure. First the teacher performs the task, speaking instructions aloud to himself or herself while the child watches and listens. Then the child listens and performs the task while the teacher says instructions to the child. The child repeats the task twice again, first giving himself or herself instructions aloud, then whispering them. Finally, the child is ready to perform the task while uttering instructions to himself or herself.

Self-instructional training has been employed to teach retarded children self-control and how to pay attention as well as how to master academic tasks. Johnston and her colleagues (1980) found that self-instruction was effective for teaching metacognitive skills in helping mildly retarded children learn to add and subtract. The children ask themselves, "How do I begin?" and "What kind of math problem is this?" They are also given answers to these questions. For example, "It's an add problem. I can tell by the sign." To self-instruct in specific arithmetic techniques for carrying and borrowing, the

---

[2]In the behavioral literature on mental retardation, this term is used more frequently than operant conditioning, but the two terms refer to the same kinds of assessments and interventions.

children may learn to say, "I start with the top number in the one column. Since it has two numbers, I have to carry." A question designed to foster monitoring or checking skills might be, "Is the answer right? I need to check it." Finally, the children learn to reinforce themselves for correct answers. "I got it right. I'm doing very well."

COMPUTER-ASSISTED INSTRUCTION

Computer-assisted instruction is increasingly found in educational settings of all kinds; it may be especially well suited to the education of individuals with mental retardation. The visual and auditory components of computers maintain the attention of distractible students; the level of the material can be geared to the individual, ensuring successful experiences; and the computer can meet the need for numerous repetitions of material without becoming bored or impatient as a human teacher might. Computer-assisted instruction programs have been shown to be superior to traditional methods for teaching people with mental retardation spelling, money handling, arithmetic, text reading, word recognition, handwriting, and visual discrimination (Conners, Caruso, & Detterman, 1986).

AUTISTIC DISORDER

Imagine that you are walking into a special education classroom for children. You are taking a course on child disabilities and one of the requirements is to volunteer some time in this class. As several of the children rise to greet you, you become aware of some minor or major physical signs. One child has slanted eyes and a flat nose, characteristic of Down syndrome. Another makes spastic movements, which you recognize as a sign of cerebral palsy. A third child may call to you from a wheelchair with grunting noises and communicate with a combination of hand gestures and pictures. So far the children are as you expected from your readings.

Finally, you notice a fourth child in the room. He is standing in front of the fish tank. As you approach him, you notice his graceful, deft movements, the dreamy, remote look in his eyes. You wonder if he is a visitor to the class or a sibling of one of the students. You start talking to him about the fish. Instead of acknowledging your comment, or even your presence, he begins rocking back and forth while continuing to smile, as if enjoying a private joke. When the teacher enters the room, your first question is about the boy at the fish tank. She tells you that he is autistic.

Computer-assisted instruction is well suited for applications in the field of mental retardation.

DESCRIPTIVE CHARACTERISTICS OF AUTISTIC DISORDER

From the time it was first distinguished, **autistic disorder** has had a somewhat mystical aura. The syndrome was first identified in 1943 by a psychiatrist at Harvard, Leo Kanner, who noticed that eleven disturbed children behaved in ways that were not common in children with mental retardation or schizophrenia. He named the syndrome *early infantile autism*, because he observed that "there is from the start an *extreme autistic aloneness* that, whenever possible, disregards, ignores, shuts out anything that comes to the child from the outside" (Kanner, 1943). Kanner considered autistic aloneness the most fundamental symptom, and he also found that these eleven children had been unable *from the beginning of life* to relate to people in the ordinary way. They were also severely limited in language and had a strong obsessive desire for everything about them to remain exactly the same. Despite its early description by Kanner and others (e.g., Rimland, 1964), the disorder was not accepted into official diagnostic nomenclature until the publication of DSM-III in 1980.

There has been a good deal of confusion in the classification of serious disorders that begin in childhood. DSM-II used the diagnosis of childhood schizophrenia for these conditions, implying that autism was simply an early-onset form of adult schizophrenia, but the available evidence indicates that childhood-onset schizophrenia and autism are separate disorders (Frith, 1989; Rutter & Schopler, 1987). Although the social withdrawal and inappropriate affect seen in autistic children may appear similar to the negative symptoms of schizophrenia, autistic children do not exhibit hallucinations and delusions and do not grow up to become schizophrenic adults (Wing & Attwood, 1987). Further, people with autism do not have a higher prevalence of schizophrenia in their families, as do children and adults with schizophrenia. Other features associated with autism but not with schizophrenia include a higher male–female ratio (more boys than girls have autism), onset in infancy or very early childhood, and co-occurrence of mental retardation and epileptic seizures.

In part to clarify the differentiation of autism from schizophrenia, DSM-III introduced (and DSM-IIIR and DSM-IV have retained) the term **pervasive developmental disorders**. This term emphasized that autism involves a serious abnormality in the developmental process itself and thus differs from the mental disorders that originate in adulthood. In DSM-IV autistic disorder is but one of several pervasive developmental disorders; the others are Rett's disorder, child disintegrative disorder, and Asperger's disorder. The description of Asperger's disorder suggests a mild form of autism; social relationships are poor but language and intelligence are often intact. Because these newly included categories have not been researched much, our focus here is on autism.

Autistic disorder begins in early childhood and can be evident in the first weeks of life. It occurs infrequently in the general population, in 2 to 5 infants in 10,000, or 0.05 percent of births. To put this in perspective, recall that the prevalance of schizophrenia is estimated at a little less than 1 percent, almost twenty times greater. Studies show that about four times more boys than girls have autism. Autism is found in all socioeconomic classes and in all ethnic and racial groups.

AUTISM AND MENTAL RETARDATION

Approximately 80 percent of autistic children score below 70 on standardized intelligence tests. Because of the significant number of autistic children who are also mentally retarded, it is sometimes difficult to differentiate the two disabilities.

There are important differences, however. Although retarded children usually score consistently poorly on all parts of an intelligence test, the scores of autistic children may have a differentiated pattern. In general, autistic children do worse on tasks requiring abstract thought, symbolism, or

sequential logic, all of which may be associated with their language deficits. They usually obtain better scores on items requiring visual-spatial skills, such as matching designs in block design tests and putting together disassembled objects (DeMyer, 1975; Rutter, 1983). In addition, as described in Focus 15.5, they may have isolated skills that reflect great talent, such as the ability to multiply two four-digit numbers rapidly in their heads. They may also have exceptional long-term memory, being able to recall the exact words of a song heard years earlier. Sensorimotor development is the area of greatest relative strength among autistic children. Retarded children are also much more delayed in areas of gross motor development, such as learning to walk, whereas autistic children, who may show severe and profound deficits in cognitive abilities, can be quite graceful and adept at swinging, climbing, or balancing.

EXTREME AUTISTIC ALONENESS

In a sense autistic children do not withdraw from society—they never joined it to begin with. Table 15.4 shows how such children have been described by their parents. Note that there is much variability in the autistic signs observed.

Normally, infants show signs of attachment, usually to their mothers, as early as three months of age. In autistic children this early attachment is virtually absent. They do not smile, reach out, or look at their mothers or caregivers when being fed. Autistic infants may reject parents' affection by refusing to be held or cuddled, arching their backs when they are picked up to minimize the contact that normal infants—and parents—love. Although normal babies often coo, cry, or fret to attract parental attention, autistic children seldom initiate contact with their caregivers except when hungry or wet. Such children are often described as good babies because they make few demands. Autistic infants are usually content to sit quietly in their playpens, completely self-absorbed, never noticing the comings, goings, and doings of other people. These children are so unresponsive that their parents may believe that they are deaf. By age two or three many autistic children do form some emotional attachment to their parents or to other caregivers, though it is still considerably weaker than that of normal toddlers.

Impaired attachment to parents is only one manifestation of the autistic child's poor social development. Autistic children rarely approach others and may look through or past people or turn their backs on others. When play is initiated by someone else,

FOCUS 15.5 THE IDIOT OR AUTISTIC SAVANT

A classic case reported by Scheerer, Rothman, and Goldstein (1945) set forth a syndrome called idiot savant, referring to a mentally retarded person with superior functioning in one narrow area of intellectual activity. In recent years the term *autistic savant* has also been applied, under the assumption that some of these individuals are autistic. The autism is believed to discourage these individuals from using their intact intellectual abilities for normal pursuits, instead channeling their attention, efforts, and abilities into internal mental games that occupy their time and focus their concentration. This may be analogous on the mental level to self-stimulation and twirling on the psychomotor level, two other characteristics of autistic children.

In *The Man Who Mistook His Wife for a Hat*, a wonderfully written book about people suffering from a wide range of neuropsychological disorders, the physician Oliver Sacks (1985) describes twins John and Michael, twenty-six years old at the time he met them. They had been hospitalized since age seven, diagnosed at various times as autistic, psychotic, or severely retarded. They had been on television many times because of their ability to say immediately on what day of the week a date far in the past or future had fallen or would fall.

Their memory for digits is remarkable—and possibly unlimited. They will repeat a number of three digits, of thirty digits, of three hundred digits, with equal ease. ... But when one comes to test their ability to calculate—the typical forte of arithmetical prodigies and "mental calculators"—they do astonishingly badly, as badly as their IQs of sixty might lead one to think. They cannot do simple addition or subtraction with any accuracy, and cannot even comprehend what multiplication or division means. ...

And yet, even in some of their performances, their "tricks," there is a quality that takes one aback. They can tell one the weather, and the events, of any day in their lives—any day from about their fourth year on. Their way of talking ... is at once childlike, detailed, without emotion. Give them a date, and their eyes roll for a moment, and then fixate, and in a flat, monotonous voice they tell you of the weather, the bare political events they would have heard of, and the events of their own lives—this last often including the painful or poignant anguish of childhood, the contempt, the jeers, the mortifications they endured, but all delivered in an even and unvarying tone, without the least hint of any personal inflection or emotion. (pp. 197–198)

When Sacks met the twins, they were in the hospital where they lived. The following scene is reminiscent of an incident in the movie *Rain Man*, starring Dustin Hoffman.

A box of matches on their table fell, and discharged its contents on the floor: "111," they both cried simultaneously; and then, in a murmur, John said "37." Michael repeated this, John said it a third

time and stopped. I counted the matches—it took me some time—and there were 111.

"How could you count the matches so quickly?" I asked. "We didn't count," they said. "We *saw* the 111." ...

"And why did you murmur '37,' and repeat it three times?" I asked the twins. They said in unison, "37, 37, 37, 111." And this, if possible, I found even more puzzling. That they should *see* 111—"111-ness"—in a flash was extraordinary. ... But they had then gone on to "factor" the number 111—without having any method, without even "knowing" (in the ordinary way) what factors meant. ...

"How did you work that out?" I said, rather hotly. They indicated, as best they could, in poor, insufficient terms—but perhaps there are no words to correspond to such things—that they did not "work it out," but just "saw" it, in a flash. John made a gesture with two outstretched fingers and his thumb, which seemed to suggest that they had spontaneously *trisected* the number, or that it "came apart" of its own accord, into these three equal parts, by a sort of spontaneous, numerical "fission." They seemed surprised at my surprise—as if *I* were somehow blind; and John's gesture conveyed an extraordinary sense of immediate, *felt* reality. ...

[Another time I saw the twins], they were seated in a corner together, with a mysterious, secret smile on their faces, a smile I had never seen before, enjoying the strange pleasure and peace they now seemed to have. I crept up quietly, so as not to disturb them. They seemed to be locked in a singular, purely numerical, converse. John would say a number—a six-figure number. Michael would catch the number, nod, smile, and seem to savour it. Then he, in turn, would say another six-figure number, and now it was John who received, and appreciated it richly. They looked, at first, like two connoisseurs wine-tasting, sharing rare tastes, rare appreciations. I sat still, unseen by them, mesmerized, bewildered. *What* were they doing? What on earth was going on? I could make nothing of it. It was perhaps a sort of game, but it had a gravity and an intensity, a sort of serene and meditative and almost holy intensity, which I had never seen in any ordinary game before, and which I certainly had never seen before in the usually agitated and distracted twins. I contented myself with noting down the numbers they uttered—the numbers that manifestly gave them such delight, and which they "contemplated," savoured, shared, in communion.

Had the numbers any meaning, I wondered on the way home. ... As soon as I got home I pulled out tables of powers, factors, logarithms and primes—mementos and relics of an odd, isolated period in my own childhood. ... I already had a hunch—and now I confirmed it. *All the numbers, the six-figure numbers, which the twins had exchanged were primes*—i.e., numbers that could be evenly divided by no other whole number than itself or one. Had they somehow seen or possessed such a book as mine—or were they, in some unimaginable way, themselves "seeing" primes, in somewhat the same way they had "seen" 111-ness, or triple 37-ness? Certainly they could not be *calculating* them—they could calculate nothing.

I returned to the ward the next day, carrying the precious book of primes with me. I again found them closeted in their numerical communion, but this time, without saying anything, I quietly joined them. They were taken aback at first, but when I made no interruption, they resumed their "game" of six-figure primes. After a few minutes I decided to join in, and ventured a number, an eight-figure prime. They both turned towards me, then suddenly became still, with a look of intense concentration and perhaps wonder on their faces. There was a long pause—the longest I had ever known them to make, it must have lasted a half-minute or more—and then suddenly, simultaneously, they both broke into smiles.

They had, after some unimaginable internal process of testing, suddenly seen my own eight-digit number as a prime—and this was manifestly a great joy, a double joy, to them; first because I had introduced a delightful new plaything, a prime of an order they had never previously encountered; and, secondly, because it was evident that I had seen what they were doing, that I liked it, that I admired it, and that I could join in myself.

They drew apart slightly, making room for me, a new number playmate, a third in their world. Then John, who always took the lead, thought for a very long time—it must have been at least five minutes, though I dared not move, and scarcely breathed—and brought out a nine-figure number; and after a similar time his twin, Michael, responded with a similar one. And then I, in my turn, after a surreptitious look in my book, added my own rather dishonest contribution, a ten-figure prime I found in my book.

There was again, and for even longer, a wondering, still silence; and then John, after a prodigious internal contemplation, brought out a twelve-figure number. I had no way of checking this, and could not respond, because my own book … did not go beyond ten-figure primes. But Michael was up to it, though it took him five minutes—and an hour later the twins were swapping twenty-figure primes, at least I assume this was so, for I had no way of checking it. (pp. 199–203)

however, autistic children may be compliant and engage in the selected activity for a period of time. Physical play, such as tickling and wrestling, may appear to be enjoyable to autistic children. Observations of their spontaneous play in an unstructured setting reveal that children with autism spend much less of their time engaged in symbolic play, such as making a doll drive to the store or pretending that a block is a car, than do either mentally retarded or normal children of comparable mental age (Sigman et al., 1987); autistic children are more likely to twirl a favorite block continually for hours on end.

Few autistic children initiate play with other children, and they are usually unresponsive to any who may approach them. Autistic infants may avert

TABLE 15.4 Parental Report of Social Relatedness in Autistic Children before Age 6

Relatedness Measure	Percentage of Responses				
	Never	Rarely	Often	Very Often	Almost Always
1. Ignored people	0	4	22	29	45
2. Emotionally distant	0	8	23	19	50
3. Avoided eye contact	2	4	20	16	58
4. No affection or interest when held	11	11	35	26	17
5. Going limp when held	30	33	17	17	2
6. Stiff/rigid when held	33	24	7	18	18
7. Ignored affection	6	30	34	11	19
8. Withdrew from affection	12	33	29	10	15
9. Cuddling when held	26	24	29	10	15
10. Accept/return affection	30	34	26	4	6
11. Looked through people	4	10	22	22	41
12. Seemed not to need mother	12	20	32	8	28
13. Responsive smile to mother	14	30	30	14	12
14. Unaware of mother's absence	17	25	25	14	19

Source: Adapted from F. R. Volkmar, D. J. Cohen, & R. Paul, 1986. "An Evaluation of DSM-III Criteria for Infantile Autism," *Journal of the American Academy of Child Psychiatry, 25,* p. 193. Copyright © 1986 by the American Academy of Child Psychiatry. Adapted by permission.

their gaze if parents try to communicate with them, and they are described as engaging in less eye contact than do their peers. The sheer amount of gazing may sometimes be relatively normal, but not the way in which it is used. Normal children gaze to gain someone's attention or to direct the other person's attention to an object; the autistic child generally does not (Mirenda, Donnellan, & Yoder, 1983).

Some autistic children appear not to recognize or distinguish one person from another. They become preoccupied with and form strong attachments to inanimate objects—such as keys, rocks, a wire-mesh basket, light switches, a large blanket—and to mechanical objects—such as refrigerators and vacuum cleaners. If the object is something they can carry, they may walk around with it in their hands, thus preventing them from learning to do more useful things.

It may be that the autistic child's social isolation is the source of his or her retarded development in other areas, such as language (Kanner, 1943). Children with Down syndrome do not show the kinds of social aloofness present in even high-functioning autistic children (Fein et al., 1986). On the other hand, it is possible that the core deficit is an inability to process certain kinds of sensory input, leaving the child helpless to understand and respond to the world around him or her (Ornitz, 1989; Rimland, 1964).

COMMUNICATION DEFICITS

Even before they acquire language autistic children show deficits in communication. Babbling, a descriptive term for the utterances of infants before they actually begin to use words, is less frequent in infants with autism and conveys less information than it does in other infants (Ricks, 1973).

By two years of age, most normally developing children use words to represent objects in their surroundings and construct one- and two-word sentences to express more complex thoughts, such as "Mommy go" or "Me juice." About 50 percent of all autistic children never learn to speak at all (Paul, 1987; Rutter, 1966). The speech of those who do learn includes peculiarities, such as **echolalia**, in which the child echoes, usually with remarkable fidelity and in a high-pitched monotone, what he or she has heard another person say. The teacher may ask an autistic child, "Do you want a cookie?" The child's response may be "Do you want a cookie?" This is immediate echolalia. In delayed echolalia the child may be in a room with the television on and with others conversing and appear to be complete-

ly uninterested. Several hours later or even the next day, the child may echo a word or phrase from the conversation or television program. Mute autistic children who later acquire some functional speech through training usually first pass through a stage of echolalia.

In the past most educators and researchers believed that echolalia served no functional purpose. Echolalia may, however, be an attempt to communicate (Prizant, 1983). The child who was offered a cookie may decide later that he or she does want one. The child will approach the teacher and ask, "Do you want a cookie?" Although the child may not know what each individual word means, he or she has learned that the phrase is connected with getting a cookie.

Another abnormality common in the speech of autistic children is **pronoun reversal**. The children refer to themselves as "he," or "you," or by their own proper names. Pronoun reversal is closely linked to echolalia. Since autistic children often use echolalic speech, they will refer to themselves as they have heard others speak of them and misapply pronouns. For example:

Parent: What are you doing, Johnny?
Child: He's here.
Parent: Are you having a good time?
Child: He knows it.

If speech continues to develop more normally, this pronoun reversal might be expected to disappear. In most instances, however, it is highly resistant to change (Tramontana & Stimbert, 1970); some children have required very extensive training even after they have stopped parroting the phrases of other people.

Neologisms, made-up words or words used with other than their usual meaning, are another characteristic of the speech of autistic children. A two-year-old autistic child might refer to milk as "moyee" and continue to do so well beyond the time when a normal child has learned to say "milk."

Children with autism are very literal in their use of words. If a father provided positive reinforcement by putting the child on his shoulders when he or she learned to say the word yes, then the child might say yes to mean that he or she wants to be lifted onto the father's shoulders. Or the child may say, "Do not drop the cat" to mean "no," because his or her mother had used these emphatic words when the child was about to drop the family kitten.

These communication deficiencies may be the source of the social retardation in children with autism rather than the other way around. Such a causal relationship is made plausible by the often spontaneous appearance of affectionate and dependent behavior in these children after they have been trained to speak (Churchill, 1969; Hewett, 1965). Even after they learn to speak, however, people with autism often lack verbal spontaneity and are sparse in their verbal expression and less than entirely appropriate in their use of language (Paul, 1987).

OBSESSIVE-COMPULSIVE AND RITUALISTIC ACTS

Autistic children become extremely upset over changes in their daily routine and surroundings. An offer of milk in a different drinking cup or a rearrangement of furniture may make them cry or precipitate a temper tantrum. One child had to be greeted with the set phrase "Good morning, Lily, I am very, very glad to see you." If any word, even one "very," was omitted, or another added, the child would begin to scream (Diamond, Baldwin, & Diamond, 1963).

An obsessional quality pervades the behavior of autistic children in other ways. In their play they may continually line up toys or construct intricate patterns with household objects. As they grow older, they may become preoccupied with train schedules, subway routes, and number sequences.

Autistic children are also given to stereotypical behavior, peculiar ritualistic hand movements, and other rhythmic movements, such as endless body rocking, hand flapping, and walking on tiptoe.

Autistic children frequently engage in stereotypical behavior, such as ritualistic hand movements.

They spin and twirl string, crayons, sticks, and plates, twiddle their fingers in front of their eyes, and stare at fans and spinning things. These are often described as self-stimulatory activities. They may become preoccupied with manipulating a mechanical object and may become very upset when interrupted.

PROGNOSIS IN AUTISTIC DISORDER

What happens to such severely disturbed children when they reach adulthood? Kanner (1973) reported on the adult status of nine of the eleven children whom he had described in his original paper on autism. Two developed epileptic seizures, one of them died, and the other was in a state mental hospital. Four others had spent most of their lives in institutions. Of the remaining three, one was still mute but was working on a farm and as an orderly in a nursing home. The other two had made satisfactory recoveries. Although both still lived with their parents and had little social life, they were gainfully employed and had developed some recreational interests.

Other follow-up studies corroborate this generally gloomy picture of adult autistics (e.g., Lotter, 1974; Rutter, 1967; Treffert, McAndrew, & Dreifuerst, 1973). From his review of all published studies, Lotter (1978) concluded that only 5 to 17 percent of autistic children had made a relatively good adjustment in adulthood, leading independent lives but with some residual problems, such as social awkwardness. Most of the others led limited lives, and about half were institutionalized.

Similar outcomes have been found in more recent population-based follow-up studies (Gillberg, 1991; Gillberg & Steffenburg, 1987). Generally, children with higher IQs and development of communicative speech before age six have the best outcome, and a few of these function nearly normally in adulthood. Follow-up studies focusing on non-mentally-retarded, high-functioning autistic individuals have indicated that most do not require residential care and some are able to attend college and support themselves through employment (Yirmiya & Sigman, 1991). Still, many independently functioning adults with autism continue to show impairment in social relationships. Focus 15.6 describes an autistic woman whose adult life is remarkable for its professional distinction blended with autistic social and emotional deficits.

Prior to the passage of the Developmentally Disabled Assistance and Bill of Rights Act in 1975 (p. 434), autistic children were often excluded

FOCUS 15.6 THE STORY OF A HIGH-FUNCTIONING AUTISTIC WOMAN

Temple Grandin is an autistic woman. She also has a Ph.D. in animal science, runs her own business designing machinery for use with farm animals, and is an assistant professor at Colorado State University. Two autobiographical books (Grandin, 1986, 1995) and a profile by neurologist Oliver Sacks (1995) provide a moving and revealing portrait of the perplexities of autism. Lacking understanding of the complexities and subtleties of human social intercourse, deficient in ability to empathize with others, Grandin sums up her relationship to the nonautistic world saying: "Much of the time … I feel like an anthropologist on Mars" (Sacks, 1995, p. 259). Because of her high level of intellectual functioning, the diagnosis of Asperger's syndrome might be applicable. Controversy exists, however, as to whether this should be a separate diagnostic entity or viewed as a less severe form of autism.

Dr. Grandin recalls from her childhood growing up on a farm sudden impulsive behavior and violent rages, as well as a hyperfocus of attention, "a selectivity … so intense that it could create a world of its own, a place of calm and order in the chaos and tumult" (Sacks, 1995, p. 254). She describes "sensations heightened, sometimes to an excruciating degree … [and] she speaks of her ears, at the age of 2 or 3, as helpless microphones, transmitting everything, irrespective of relevance, at full, overwhelming volume" (Sacks, 1995, p. 254).

Diagnosed with autism at age three, Temple had no speech at all, and doctors predicted that institutionalization would be her fate. With the help of a therapeutic nursery school and speech therapy and with the support of her family, she learned to speak by age six and began to make more contact with others. Still, as an adolescent observing other children interact, Grandin "sometimes … wondered if they were all telepathic" (Sacks, 1995, p. 272), so mysterious did she find the ability of normal youngsters to understand each other's needs and wishes, to empathize, to communicate.

Visiting her one day at her university, Sacks made several observations that convey the autistic flavor of this uncommon person.

She sat me down [in her office] with little ceremony, no preliminaries, no social niceties, no small talk about my trip or how I liked Colorado. … She plunged straight into talking of her work, speaking of her early interests in psychology and animal behavior, how they were connected with self-observation and a sense of her own needs

Despite being diagnosed with autism in early childhood, Temple Grandin, Ph.D., has had a successful academic career.

as an autistic person, and how this had joined with the [highly developed] visualizing and engineering part of her mind to point her towards the special field she had made her own: the design of farms, feedlots, corrals, slaughterhouses—systems of many sorts for animal management. …

She spoke well and clearly, but with a certain unstoppable impetus and fixity. A sentence, a paragraph, once started, had to be completed; nothing left implicit, hanging in the air. (pp. 256–257)

Having traveled all day, missing lunch, feeling hungry and thirsty, Sacks hoped in vain for Dr. Grandin to notice his fatigued and needy state and offer him something to drink or suggest they go somewhere for a bite, but after an hour, realizing that this was not going to happen, he asked for some coffee.

There was no "I'm sorry, I should have offered you some before," no intermediacy, no social junction. Instead she immediately took me to a coffeepot that was kept brewing in the secretaries' office upstairs. She introduced me to the secretaries in a somewhat brusque manner, giving me the feeling, once again, of someone who

from educational programs in the public schools. Thus most of the autistic children followed into adulthood had not had the benefit of intensive educational interventions or the kind of intensive behavioral program described later (p. 446). New

follow-up studies are needed to determine whether the prognosis for autism will remain as universally devastating as it was before the training and education of people with autism were taken seriously by society.

had learned, roughly, "how to behave" in such situations without having much personal perception of how other people felt—the nuances, the social subtleties involved. (p. 257)

In her own writings Grandin points out that many autistic people are great fans of *Star Trek*, and especially of Spock and Data, the former a member of the Vulcan race, characterized by a purely intellectual, logical approach that eschews any consideration of the emotional side of life, the latter an android, a highly sophisticated computer housed in human form and, like Spock, lacking in affective experience. (One of the dramatic themes in both characters was, of course, their flirtation with the experience of human emotion, portrayed with particular poignancy by Data. This is a theme in Grandin's life as well.) As she wrote at age forty-seven:

All my life I have been an observer, and I have always felt like someone who watches from the outside. I could not participate in the social interactions of high school life. ...
Even today, personal relationships are something I don't really understand. ... I've remained celibate because doing so helps me avoid the many complicated situations that are too difficult for me to handle. ... [M]en who want to date often don't understand how to relate to a woman. They [and I myself] remind me of Data, the android on *Star Trek*. In one episode, Data's attempts at dating were a disaster. When he tried to be romantic [by effecting a change in a subroutine of his computer program], he complimented his date by using scientific terminology. Even very able adults with autism have such problems. (Grandin, 1995, pp. 132–133)

Some of the deficiencies of people with autism make them charmingly honest and trustworthy. "Lying," wrote Grandin, "is very anxiety-provoking because it requires rapid interpretations of subtle social cues [of which I am incapable] to determine whether the other person is really being deceived" (1995, p. 135).

Grandin's professional career is impressive. She uses her remarkable powers of visualization and her empathy for farm animals to design machines such as a chute leading cows to slaughter that takes them on a circular route, protecting them from awareness of their fate until the moment of death.

She has also designed and built a "squeeze machine," a device that provides comforting hugs without the need for human contact. It has "two heavy, slanting wooden sides, perhaps four by three feet each, pleasantly upholstered with a thick, soft padding. They [are] joined by hinges to a long, narrow bottom board to create a V-shaped, body-sized trough.

There [is] a complex control box at one end, with heavy-duty tubes leading off to another device, in a closet. ... [An] industrial compressor 'exerts a firm but comfortable pressure on the body, from the shoulders to the knees'" (Sacks, 1995, pp. 262–263). Her explanation of the rationale behind this contraption is that as a little girl she longed to be hugged but was also very fearful of any physical contact with another person. When a favorite, large-bodied aunt hugged her, she felt both overwhelmed and comforted. Terror comingled with pleasure.

She started to have daydreams—she was just five at the time—of a magic machine that could squeeze her powerfully but gently, in a huglike way, and in a way entirely commanded and controlled by her. Years later, as an adolescent, she had seen a picture of a squeeze chute designed to hold or restrain calves and realized that that was it: a little modification to make it suitable for human use, and it could be her magic machine. (Sacks, 1995, p. 263)

After watching her demonstrate the machine and trying it himself, Sacks observed:

It is not just pleasure or relaxation that Temple gets from the machine but, she maintains, a feeling for others. As she lies in her machine, she says, her thoughts often turn to her mother, her favorite aunt, her teachers. She feels their love for her, and hers for them. She feels that the machine opens a door into an otherwise closed emotional world and allows her, almost teaches her, to feel empathy for others. (p. 264)

Sacks has great admiration for Grandin's professional success and for the interesting and productive life she has made for herself, but when it comes to human interactions it is clear that she does not get it. "I was struck by the enormous difference, the gulf, between Temple's immediate, intuitive recognition of animal moods and signs and her extraordinary difficulties understanding human beings, their codes and signals, the way they conduct themselves" (p. 269).

Accounts such as those of Grandin and Sacks can provide insights into ways of adapting to idiosyncrasies, using the sometimes peculiar gifts that one has been given and working around the deficiencies with which one has been saddled. "Autism, while it may be ... pathologized as a syndrome, must also be seen as a whole mode of being, a deeply different mode or identity, one that needs to be conscious (and proud) of itself," wrote Sacks (p. 277). "At a recent lecture, Temple ended by saying, 'If I could snap my fingers and be nonautistic, I would not—because then I wouldn't be me. Autism is part of who I am'" (p. 291).

ETIOLOGY OF AUTISTIC DISORDER

The earliest theorizing about the etiology of autism was that it was psychogenic, that is, that psychological factors were responsible for its development. This narrow perspective has been replaced in recent years by speculation about and evidence supporting the importance of biological factors, some of them genetic, in the etiology of this puzzling syndrome.

PSYCHOLOGICAL BASES

Some of the same reasons that led Kanner to believe that autistic children were of average intelligence—their normal appearance and apparently normal physiological functioning—led early theorists to discount the importance of biological factors. People may have tacitly assumed that for a biological cause to underlie something as devastating as autism, it would have other obvious signs, such as the physical stigmata of Down syndrome. Thus the early focus was on psychological factors, primarily family influences very early in life.

One of the best known of the psychological theories was formulated by Bruno Bettelheim (1967), who worked extensively with autistic children. His basic supposition was that autism closely resembles the apathy and hopelessness found among inmates of German concentration camps during World War II and that therefore something very negative must take place in early childhood. Bettelheim hypothesized that the young infant has rejecting parents and is able to perceive their negative feelings. The infant finds that his or her own actions have little impact on the parents' unresponsiveness. The child thus comes to believe "that [his or her] own efforts have no power to influence the world, because of the earlier conviction that the world is insensitive to [his or her] reactions" (p. 46). The autistic child never really enters the world but builds the "empty fortress" of autism against pain and disappointment.

Some behavioral theorists, like those who are psychoanalytically oriented, have postulated that certain childhood learning experiences cause autism. In an extremely influential article, Ferster (1961) suggested that the inattention of the parents, especially of the mother, prevents establishment of the associations that make human beings social reinforcers. Because the parents have not become reinforcers, they cannot control the child's behavior, and the result is autistic disorder.

Both Bettelheim and Ferster, as well as others, have stated that parents play the crucial role in the etiology of autism. Many investigators have therefore studied the characteristics of these parents; for a psychogenic theory of a childhood disorder to have any plausibility at all, something very unusual and damaging about the parents' treatment of their children would have to be demonstrated.

In his early papers Kanner described the parents of autistic children as cold, insensitive, meticulous, introverted, distant, and highly intellectual (Kanner & Eisenberg, 1955). Singer and Wynne (1963) described several means by which these parents "disaffiliate" themselves from their children. Some are cynical about all interpersonal relations and are emotionally cold; others are passive and apathetic; and still others maintain an obsessive, intellectual distance from people.

Systematic investigations, however, have failed to confirm these clinical impressions. For example, Cox and his colleagues (1975) compared the parents of autistic children with those of children with receptive aphasia (a disorder in understanding speech). The two groups did *not* differ in warmth, emotional demonstrativeness, responsiveness, and sociability. This and other studies (e.g., Cantwell, Baker, & Rutter, 1978) provide no evidence that there is anything remarkable about the parents of autistic children. In fact, such parents raise other perfectly normal and healthy siblings.

Even if we were to ignore these findings, the direction of a possible correlation between parental characteristics and autism is not easily determined. As noted earlier in the discussion of ADHD (p. 412) and many other disorders, any deviant parental behavior could be a reaction to the child's abnormality rather than the other way around. There is no evidence that any kind of emotional maltreatment, deprivation, or neglect can produce behavior that resembles the dramatically pathological symptoms of autism (Ornitz, 1973; Wing, 1976).

The early popularity of psychogenic hypotheses may have had an unintended negative consequence (Rimland, 1964). Consider, for a moment, what your feelings might be if a psychiatrist or psychologist were to tell you that your unconscious hostility has caused your child to be mute at the age of six. Or how would you feel if you were told that your commitment to professional activities had brought about the autistic behavior patterns of your child? The truth of such allegations has never been demonstrated, and as we have seen, considerable information contradicts these views. Nonetheless, over the years a tremendous emotional burden has been placed on parents who have been told that they are at fault.

BIOLOGICAL BASES

The very early onset of autism, along with an accumulation of neurological and genetic evidence that we turn to now, strongly implicates a biological basis for this puzzling disorder.

GENETIC FACTORS Genetic studies of autism are difficult to conduct because the disorder is so rare. The family method presents special problems because autistic persons almost never marry. Nonetheless, emerging evidence strongly suggests a genetic basis for autistic disorder.

For example, the risk of autism in the siblings of people with the disorder is about seventy-five times greater than it is if the index case does not have autistic disorder (McBride, Anderson, & Shapiro, 1996).

Stronger evidence for genetic transmission of autism comes from twin studies, which have found 60 to 91 percent concordance for autism between identical twins, compared with concordance rates of under 20 percent in fraternal twins (Bailey et al., 1995; Steffenberg et al., 1989).

A series of studies following twins and families with an autistic member suggest that autism is linked genetically to a broader spectrum of deficits in communicative and social areas (Bailey et al., 1995; Bolton et al., 1994; Folstein & Rutter, 1977a, 1977b). For example, almost all the nonautistic identical twins of autistic adults were unable to live independently, have stable employment, or maintain a confiding relationship. In addition, most of the nonautistic identical twins evidenced communication deficits, such as language delays or reading impairments. Taken together, the evidence from family and twin studies strongly supports a genetic basis for autistic disorder.

NEUROLOGICAL FACTORS Early EEG studies of autistic children indicated that many had abnormal brain-wave patterns (e.g., Hutt et al., 1964). Other types of neurological examination also revealed signs of damage in many autistic children (e.g., Campbell et al., 1982; Gillberg & Svendsen, 1983). For example, a recent study using magnetic resonance imaging (MRI) to compare brain size in autistic and normal young men found enlargement of the brain in autistic subjects (Piven et al., 1995). Further evidence supporting the possibility of brain dysfunction derives from another MRI study, which found that portions of the cerebellum were underdeveloped in autistic children (Courchesne et al., 1988). This abnormality was present in fourteen of eighteen autistic subjects.

In adolescence 30 percent of those who had severe autistic symptoms as children begin having epileptic seizures, another sign that a brain defect is involved in the disorder. The prevalence of autism in children whose mothers had rubella during the prenatal period is approximately ten times higher than that in the general population of children, and we know that rubella in the mother during pregnancy can harm the developing fetus's brain. A syndrome similar to autism sometimes follows in the aftermath of meningitis, encephalitis, fragile-X, and tuberous sclerosis, all of which may affect central nervous system functioning. These findings, together with the degree of mental retardation, seem to link autism and brain damage (Courchesne et al., 1988).

TREATMENT OF AUTISTIC DISORDER

Because their isolation is so moving and their symptoms so pronounced, a great deal of attention has been given to trying to improve the condition of children with autism. As with theories of etiology, the earliest efforts were psychological in nature, and some of them have shown considerable promise. More recently various psychopharmacotherapies have been studied as well, with mixed results. Treatments for autistic children usually try to reduce their unusual behavior and improve their communication and social skills. Sometimes an eagerly sought-after goal for a family is simply to be able to take their autistic child to a restaurant or market without attracting negative attention.

SPECIAL PROBLEMS IN TREATING AUTISTIC CHILDREN

Autistic children have several problems that make teaching them difficult, however. First, they do not adjust well to changes in routine, and the very nature and purpose of treatment involves change. Second, their isolation and self-stimulatory movements may interfere with effective teaching. Although the similar behavior of children with other disabilities may intrude on the teacher's efforts, it does not do so with the same frequency and severity.

Third, it is particularly difficult to find ways to motivate autistic children. For reinforcers to be effective with autistic children, they must be explicit, concrete, and highly salient. A widely used method of increasing the range of reinforcers to which autistic children respond is to pair social reinforcement, such as praise, with primary reinforcers, such as a highly desired food.

A further problem that often interferes with the learning of autistic children is their overselectivity of attention; when the child's attention becomes focused on one particular aspect of a task or situation, other properties, including relevant ones, may not even be noticed (Lovaas et al., 1971). The overselective nature of these children's attention makes it especially difficult for them to generalize or apply their learning to other areas. For example, the child who has learned several words by watching the instructor's lip movements may not comprehend the same words spoken by another person with less pronounced lip movements.

In spite of these problems, educational programs for students with autism have achieved some positive results, and we turn to these now.

BEHAVIORAL TREATMENT OF AUTISTIC CHILDREN

Using modeling and operant conditioning, behavior therapists have taught autistic children to talk (Hewett, 1965), modified their echolalic speech (Carr, Schreibman, & Lovaas, 1975), encouraged them to play with other children (Romanczyk et al., 1975), and helped them become more generally responsive to adults (Davison, 1964).

Ivar Lovaas, a leading clinical researcher at the University of California at Los Angeles, conducted an intensive operant program with very young (under four years old) autistic children (Lovaas, 1987). Therapy encompassed all aspects of the children's lives for more than forty hours a week over more than two years. Parents were trained extensively so that treatment could continue during almost all the children's waking hours. Nineteen youngsters receiving this intensive treatment were compared with forty controls who received a similar treatment for less than ten hours per week. All children were rewarded for being less aggressive, more compliant, and more socially appropriate, for example, talking and playing with other children. The goal of the program was to mainstream the children, the assumption being that autistic children, as they improve, benefit more from being

Ivar Lovaas, a behavior therapist, is noted for his operant-conditioning treatment of autistic children.

with normal peers than by remaining by themselves or with other seriously disturbed children.

The results were dramatic and encouraging for the intensive therapy group. Their measured IQs averaged 83 in first grade (after about two years in the intensive therapy) compared with about 55 for the controls; twelve of the nineteen reached the normal range, compared with only two (of forty) in the control group. Furthermore, nine of the nineteen in the intensive therapy group were promoted to second grade in a regular public school, whereas only one of the much larger control group achieved this level of normal functioning. A follow-up of these children four years later indicated that the children's intensive treatment group maintained their gains in IQ, adaptive behavior, and grade promotions in school (McEachin, Smith, & Lovaas, 1993). Although critics have pointed out weaknesses in the study's methodology and outcome measures (Schopler, Short, & Mesibov, 1989), this ambitious program confirms the benefits of heavy involvement of both professionals and parents in dealing with the extreme challenge of autistic disorder.

There is reason to believe that the education provided by parents is more beneficial to the child than is clinic- or hospital-based treatment. In work similar to that of Lovaas, Koegel and his colleagues (1982) demonstrated that after only 25 to 30 hours of parent training, autistic children's improvements on standardized tests and behavioral measures were similar to those achieved after more than 200 hours of direct clinic treatment. Koegel concluded that parent training is superior in generalizing learning because parents are present in many different situations, and when training their children they may actually spend more time with them in recreational and leisure activities.

It must be clearly understood, however, that some autistic and other severely disturbed children can be adequately cared for only in a hospital or in a group home staffed by mental health professionals. Moreover, the circumstances of some families preclude the home care of a seriously disturbed child. That effective treatments can be implemented by parents does not mean that this is the appropriate course for all families.

PSYCHODYNAMIC TREATMENT OF AUTISTIC CHILDREN

Because he viewed attachment difficulties and emotional deprivation as the sources of autism, Bruno Bettelheim (1967, 1974) argued that a warm, loving atmosphere must be created to encourage the child to enter the world. Patience and what Rogerians would call unconditional positive regard were believed to be necessary for the child to begin to trust others and to take chances in establishing relationships. At his Orthogenic School at the University of Chicago, Bettelheim and his colleagues reported many instances of success, but the uncontrolled nature of their observations makes it difficult to evaluate their claims. Furthermore, the accuracy of Bettelheim's reports on the procedures used and the successes achieved with the students at his school have recently been called into question, casting serious doubt on the validity of his claims (Gardner, 1997; Pollak, 1997).

DRUG TREATMENT OF AUTISTIC CHILDREN

The most commonly used medication for treating autistic behaviors is probably haloperidol (brand name Haldol), an antipsychotic medication. A few controlled studies have shown that this drug reduces social withdrawal, stereotyped motor behavior, and maladaptive behavior, such as self-mutilation (Anderson et al., 1989; McBride et al., 1996; Perry et al., 1989). Many autistic children do not respond positively to this drug, however, and it has not shown any positive effects on other aspects of autistic disorder, such as abnormal interpersonal relationships and language impairment (Holm & Varley, 1989). Haloperidol also has potentially serious side effects (p. 287).

Evidence that autistic children may have elevated blood levels of serotonin (Anderson & Hoshino, 1987) had encouraged research on medications that reduce the action of serotonin. In the early 1980s a large, multisite study was conducted in twenty medical centers to examine the effectiveness of fenfluramine, a drug known to lower serotonin levels in rats and monkeys. After an initial flurry of enthusiastic claims that the drug effected dramatic improvement in the behavior and thought processes of autistic children (Ritvo et al., 1983), later studies delivered much more modest findings. Although fenfluramine may have some modest positive effects in some autistic children by improving social adjustment, attention span, activity level, and stereotypic behavior, no consistent effect has been shown on cognitive measures such as IQ or language functioning. Recent reviews concur that the effects of fenfluramine are at best subtle and the drug certainly does not represent a cure for autism (Aman & Kern, 1989; Campbell, Anderson, & Small, 1990; duVerglas, Banks, & Guyer, 1988).

Researchers have also studied an opioid receptor antagonist, naltrexone, and found that this drug reduces hyperactivity in autistic children (Campbell et al., 1993); a recent controlled study suggested mild improvements in initiation of communication as well (Kolmen et al., 1995). Although more studies need to be conducted to determine whether naltrexone is useful in reducing self-injurious behavior, the drug does not appear to affect the core symptoms of autism.

As we concluded in our section on the treatment of schizophrenia (p. 290), it would appear that effective intervention for the complex and serious disorder that we call autism will depend on interdisciplinary work by people of both a psychological and biological bent. Searching for a magic bullet is unlikely to lead to success.

SUMMARY

Attention-deficit/hyperactivity disorder and conduct disorder are marked by undercontrolled behavior. ADHD is a persistent pattern of inattention and/or impulsivity that is judged to be more frequent and more severe than what is typically observed in youngsters of a given age. There is growing evidence for genetic and neurological factors in its etiology, but the reactions of parents to the child's behavior are also important, at least in the course of the disorder over time. Stimulant drugs, such as Ritalin, and reinforcement for staying on task have some effectiveness in reducing the intensity of ADHD.

Conduct disorder is often a precursor to antisocial personality disorder in adulthood, though many children carrying the diagnosis do not progress to that extreme. It is characterized by high and widespread levels of aggression, lying, theft, vandalism, and other acts that violate laws and social norms. Among the apparent etiological factors are a genetic predisposition, inadequate learning of moral awareness, modeling and direct reinforcement of antisocial behavior, and living in impoverished and crime-ridden areas. Of some help in controlling conduct-disordered young people are parental reinforcement of prosocial behavior and lack of involvement in the criminal justice system if at all possible.

Learning disorders are diagnosed when a child fails to develop to the degree expected by his or her intellectual level in a specific academic, language, or motor skill area. These disorders are usually identified and treated within the school system rather than through mental health clinics. There is mounting evidence that the most widely studied of the learning disorders, dyslexia, has genetic and other biological components. The most widespread interventions for dyslexia, however, are educational.

The diagnostic criteria for mental retardation are subaverage intellectual functioning and deficits in adaptive behavior, with onset before the age of eighteen. Many contemporary treatments focus more on the strengths of individuals with mental retardation rather than on their assignment to a particular level of severity. This shift in emphasis is associated with increased efforts to design psychological and educational interventions that make the most of individuals' abilities.

The more severe forms of mental retardation have a biological basis, such as the chromosomal trisomy that causes Down syndrome. Certain infectious diseases in the pregnant mother, such as HIV and AIDS, rubella, and syphilis, and illnesses that affect the child directly, for example, encephalitis, can stunt cognitive and social development, as can malnutrition, severe falls, and automobile accidents that injure the brain. Environmental factors are considered the principal causes of mild retardation. Thus far no brain damage has been detected in people with mild retardation, who often are from lower-class homes, living in an environment of social and educational deprivation.

Researchers try to prevent mild retardation by giving children at risk through impoverished circumstances special preschool training and social opportunities. The best-known and largest of these programs is Project Head Start, which has been shown to be helpful in equipping children to benefit from school. Many children with mental retardation who would formerly have been institutionalized are now being educated in the public schools under the mainstreaming provisions of Public Law 94-142. In addition, using applied behavioral analysis, self-instructional training, and modeling, behavior therapists have been able to treat successfully many of the behavioral problems of retarded individuals and to improve their intellectual functioning.

Autistic disorder, one of the pervasive developmental disorders, begins before the age of two and a half. The major symptoms are extreme autistic aloneness, a failure to relate to other people; communication problems, consisting of either a failure to learn any language or speech irregularities, such as echolalia and pronoun reversal; and preservation of sameness, an obsessive desire to keep daily routines and surroundings exactly the same. Originally the disorder was believed to be the result of coldness and aloofness in parents and their rejection of their children, but recent research gives no credence to such notions. Although no certain biological basis of autism has been found, a biological cause is suspected for a number of reasons: its onset is very early; family and twin studies give evidence of a genetic predisposition; abnormalities have been found in the brains of autistic children; a syndrome similar to autism can develop following meningitis and encephalitis; and many autistic children have the low intelligence associated with brain dysfunctions.

The most promising psychological treatments of autism are those employing procedures that rely on modeling and operant conditioning. Although the prognosis for autistic children remains poor in general—except for some startling cases such as that described in Focus 15.6—recent work suggests that intensive behavioral treatment involving the parents as their children's therapists may allow some of these children to participate meaningfully in normal social intercourse. Recent drug treatments, in particular those that lower serotonin, show little promise.

KEY TERMS

attention deficit/
  hyperactivity disorder
behavioral pediatrics
conduct disorder
oppositional defiant
  disorder
enuresis
learning disabilities
learning disorders
reading disorder (dyslexia)
mathematics disorder
disorder of written
  expression

expressive language
  disorder
phonological disorder
stuttering
motor skills disorder
mild mental retardation
moderate mental
  retardation
severe mental retardation
profound mental
  retardation

Down syndrome
  (trisomy 21)
fragile X syndrome
phenylketonuria (PKU)
applied behavior analysis
self-instructional training
autistic disorder
pervasive developmental
  disorders
echolalia
pronoun reversal

George Tooker,
"Mirror II," 1963

AGING AND PSYCHOLOGICAL DISORDERS

T he patient is a fifty-six-year-old right-handed businessman who had entered the hospital for cervical disk surgery. Because of his busy schedule and his anxiety relating to surgery, he had canceled his admission on two previous occasions. The patient was a fairly heavy social drinker but not to the point of interfering in any way with his business performance. The surgery was uneventful and there were no immediate complications of the procedure. The patient was greatly relieved and seemed to be making a normal recovery until the third postoperative night. During that night he became quite restless and found it difficult to sleep. The next day he was visibly fatigued but otherwise normal. The following night his restlessness became more pronounced, and he became fearful and anxious. As the night progressed, he thought that he saw people hiding in his room, and shortly before dawn he reported to the nurse that he saw some strange little animals running over his bed and up the drapes. At the time of morning rounds, the patient was very anxious and frightened. He was lethargic, distractible, and quite incoherent when he tried to discuss the events of the night before. He knew who he was and where he was but did not know the date or when he had had his surgery. During that day his mental status fluctuated, but by nightfall he had become grossly disoriented and agitated. At this point, psychiatric consultation was obtained.

The consultant's diagnosis was acute postoperative confusional state [delirium]. The cause was probably due to a combination of factors: withdrawal from alcohol, fear of surgery, use of strong analgesics, stress of the operation, pain, and the sleepless nights in an unfamiliar room. The treatment consisted of a reduction in medications for pain, partial illumination of the room at night, and a family member in attendance at all times. These simple changes in conjunction with 50 mg of chlorpromazine (Thorazine) three times daily and 500 mg of chloral hydrate at bedtime reversed his confusional state within two days, and he was able to return home in a week with no residual evidence of abnormal behavior. To date there has been no recurrence of these problems. (Strub & Black, 1981, pp. 89–90)

The more fortunate readers of this book will grow old one day. As you do, physiological changes are inevitable, and there may be many emotional and mental changes as well. Are the aged at higher risk for mental disorders than the young? Are earlier emotional problems of anxiety and depression likely to become worse in old age? Do these emotional problems develop in people who did not have them when younger?

Most segments of society in the United States tend to have certain assumptions about old age. We fear that we will become doddering and befuddled. We worry that our sex lives will become unsatisfy-ing. This chapter examines such issues and questions and considers whether some therapies are better suited than others to deal with the psychological problems of older adults. We shall consider also whether, as life expectancy extends into the seventies and beyond, society is devoting enough intellectual and monetary resources to studying aging and helping elderly people.

In contrast to the esteem in which they are held in most Asian countries, elderly adults are generally not treated very well in the United States. The process of growing old, although inevitable for us all, is abhorred by many, even resented. Perhaps the lack of regard for senior citizens stems from our own deep-seated fear of and misconceptions about growing old. The old person with serious infirmities is an unwelcome reminder that some of us may one day walk with a less steady gait, see less clearly, taste food less keenly, enjoy sex with less intensity, and fall victim to some of the many diseases and maladies that are the lot of many old people.

The psychological problems of aging may be especially severe for women. Even with the consciousness raising of the past three decades, our society does not readily accept in women the wrinkles and sagging that become more and more prominent with advancing years. Although gray hair at the temples and even a bald head are often considered distinguished in a man, signs of aging in women are not valued in our society. The cosmetics and plastic-surgery industries make billions of dollars each year exploiting the fear inculcated in women about looking their age.

Elderly individuals from minority ethnic groups experience a double jeopardy; African-American and Mexican-American elders have considerably lower incomes and poorer health, as well as less life satisfaction, than their white counterparts (Dowd & Bengston, 1978; Gerber, 1983). Societal biases against women contribute to what some consider triple jeopardy, with elderly minority women running the greatest risk of economic dependency and associated problems (Blau, Oser, & Stephens, 1979). On the other hand, as explored in Focus 16.1, some observers see benefits in being female and/or a member of a minority group.

The physical realities of aging are complicated by **ageism**, which can be defined as discrimination against any person, young or old, based on chronological age. Ageism can be seen when a professor in her sixties is considered too old to continue teaching at a university as well as when a person older than seventy-five is ignored in a social gathering on the assumption that he has nothing to contribute to the conversation. Like any prejudice, ageism

FOCUS 16.1 GENDER ROLE FLEXIBILITY, COPING, AND THE TRANSITION TO OLD AGE IN WOMEN*

Although they suffer from disadvantages as elders, it appears that women deal better with certain aspects of aging *because* they have usually occupied roles that are more marginal and less valued in society compared with those of men, despite the advances of the women's liberation movement and increased awareness of feminist issues. For one thing, women have more roles in society than do men. Whereas most men enter retirement having served in the roles of primary breadwinner and sometimes also parent, though seldom as primary parental caregiver, women frequently have had several roles—mother, spouse, homemaker, employee, widow, and sometimes caregiver to an infirm parent. Women have also adjusted to changing roles, for example, when children leave home the role of mother gives way to that of someone presiding over an empty nest (Sinnott, 1986). This diversity and inconstancy—what some call gender role flexibility—may contribute to women's greater resilience in old age; they have had more practice navigating major role changes throughout their lives. And this larger variation in social roles may reduce stress and play some role in women's generally longer life expectancy.

As men have not developed and practiced this degree of role flexibility, they face a more difficult and stressful adjustment when the reduction in traditional male role demands and privileges takes place in retirement. This negative aspect of retirement sometimes detracts from the positive features of this stage of life. Indeed, the ability to become involved in multiple social roles in old age, for example, becoming a student after spending years as a boss, is associated with fewer depressive symptoms, greater life satisfaction, and higher levels of perceived self-efficacy in both women and men (Adelmann, 1994; Turk-Charles, Rose, & Gatz, 1996).

Women may also come to old age—and the negative ageism of our society—better equipped than men because they have had more practice coping with discrimination (Canetto, 1992). In a similar way, the oppression that gays and lesbians deal with across their life spans may prepare them to cope with ageism and with the loss in status that is frequently associated with being old. And this strength through adversity may be particularly significant for minority elderly women, who face triple jeopardy—discrimination from three sources (Stoller & Gibson, 1994). On the other hand, problems associated with limited financial means, such as poor health care and poorer overall health, may override any advantages that accrue to someone who has had to cope with high levels of stress and challenge throughout life.

Suicide rates among those over sixty-five are the highest of any age group. This high rate is due to a steady rise among men over sixty-five, particularly white men. Rates among women, especially minority women, *decrease* after age fifty (McIntosh, 1995; McIntosh et al., 1994). Similarly, widows are less likely than widowers to commit suicide even though after age sixty-five women are more than three times more likely than men to be widowed (Canetto, 1992). One reason for this difference between the sexes may be that men are more dependent than women on their spouses for the satisfaction of their emotional and interpersonal needs (Spacapan & Oskamp, 1989); this may also account in part for the higher rate of remarriage among widowed men.

*This material is based on an unpublished manuscript by E. H. Davison (1996).

---

ignores the *diversity* among people in favor of employing stereotypes (Gatz & Pearson, 1988).

Mental health professionals have until recently paid little attention to the psychological problems of elderly people. Many operate under the popular misconceptions that intellectual deterioration is prevalent and inevitable, that depression among old people is widespread and untreatable, that sex is a lost cause. Although those who provide mental health services are probably not extremely ageist (Gatz & Pearson, 1988), their attitudes and practices merit special attention because of the influence they have on policies that affect the lives of older adults. Since the 1980s many schools and universities that prepare people for the health professions have added research and training in gerontology into their curricula, yet there is still a dearth of profes-

sionals primarily committed to serving the needs of older adults (Gatz & Smyer, 1992; Knight, 1996).

In any discussion of the differences between those who are elderly and those not yet old, the elderly are usually defined as those over the age of sixty-five. The decision to use this age was set largely by social policies, not because age sixty-five is some critical point at which the physiological and psychological processes of aging suddenly begin. To have some rough demarcation points for better describing the diversity of the elderly population, gerontologists usually divide those over age sixty-five into three groups: the young-old, those aged sixty-five to seventy-four; the old-old, those aged seventy-five to eighty-four; and the oldest-old, those over age eighty-five. The health of these groups differs in important ways.

Ageism refers to discrimination against someone because of his or her age. In one form of ageism, countermyth, we especially applaud achievements of the elderly, as in former President Bush's parachute jump.

It is estimated that Americans over age sixty-five will number 52 million by the year 2020, an increase of more than 20 million since the late 1980s (Spencer, 1989). And the oldest-old, those above age eighty-five, are expected to grow to at least 24 million by the year 2040, up from 3.8 million in the mid-1990s. Thus it is important to examine what we know about the psychological and neuropsychological problems of older adults and to expose some of our misconceptions about aging. In this chapter we review some general concepts and issues critical to the study of aging. We look next at brain disorders of old age. Then we examine psychological disorders—most of which were discussed earlier—with a particular focus on how these disorders are manifest in old age. Finally, we discuss general issues of treatment and care for older adults.

ISSUES, CONCEPTS, AND METHODS IN THE STUDY OF OLDER ADULTS

Theory and research bearing on older adults require an understanding of several rather specialized issues.

DIVERSITY IN OLDER ADULTS

The word *diversity* is well suited to the older population. Not only are older people different from one another, but they are more different from one another than are individuals in any other age group! People tend to become less alike as they grow older. That all old people are alike is a prejudice held by many younger people, but to know that a person is sixty-seven years old is actually to know very little about him or her. Yet a moment's honest reflection may reveal that certain traits come to mind when we hear that a person is age sixty-seven. The many *differences* in people who are sixty-five and older will become increasingly evident in the course of reading this chapter.

AGE, COHORT, AND TIME-OF-MEASUREMENT EFFECTS

Chronological age is not as simple a variable in psychological research as it might seem. Because other factors associated with age may be at work, we must be cautious when we attribute differences in age groups solely to the effects of aging. Being age seventy in 1994 is different from having been seventy in 1964. In the field of aging, as in studies of earlier development, including childhood, a distinction is made among the contributions of what are called **age effects**, the consequences of being a given chronological age; **cohort effects**, the consequences of having been born in a given year and having grown up during a particular time period with its own unique pressures, problems, challenges, and opportunities; and **time-of-measurement effects**, confounds that arise because events at a particular point in time can have a specific effect on a variable that is being studied over time (Schaie & Hertzog, 1982). The two major research designs used to assess developmental change, the cross-sectional and the longitudinal, clarify these terms.

In **cross-sectional studies** the investigator compares different age groups at the same moment in time on the variable of interest. Suppose that in 1985 we took a poll and found that many interviewees over age seventy spoke with a European accent, whereas those in their thirties and forties did not. Could we conclude that as people grow older, they develop European accents? Hardly! Cross-sectional studies do not examine the same people over time; thus they allow us to make statements only about age effects in a particular study or experiment, not about age changes over time. In our hypothetical study, many people in the older sample, or cohort, came to the United States from abroad.

Cohort effects refer to the fact that people of the same chronological age may differ considerably depending on when they were born.

In **longitudinal studies**, the researcher selects one cohort, say, the class of 1999, and periodically retests it using the same measure over a number of years. This design allows us to trace individual patterns of consistency or change over time—cohort effects—and to analyze how behavior in early life relates to behavior in old age.

However, because each cohort is unique, conclusions drawn from longitudinal studies are restricted to the particular cohort chosen. For example, if members of a cohort studied from 1956 to 1996 are found to decline in sexual activity as they enter their sixties, we cannot conclude that the sexuality of those in a cohort studied from 1996 to 2036 will decline when they reach the same age. Improvements over time in health care and changes in other variables such as social mores might enhance the sexual activity of the younger cohort, a time-of-measurement effect. An additional problem that arises with longitudinal studies is that participants often drop out as the studies proceed, creating a source of bias commonly called **selective mortality**. The least able people are the most likely to drop out from a study; the nonrepresentative people who remain are usually healthier than the general population. Thus findings based on longitudinal studies may be overly optimistic concerning the rate of decline of a variable such as sexual activity over the life span.

DIAGNOSING PSYCHOPATHOLOGY IN LATER LIFE

The DSM criteria for older adults are basically the same as those for younger adults. The nature and manifestations of mental disorders are usually assumed to be the same in adulthood and old age, even though little research supports this assumption (Gatz, Kasl-Godley, & Karel, 1996; LaRue, Dessonville, & Jarvik, 1985). We often do not know what certain symptoms in older adults mean because we have few specifics about psychopathology in the elderly (Zarit, Eiler, & Hassinger, 1985). For example, somatic symptoms are generally more prevalent in late life, but these symptoms are also evident in depression in older adults. Are the somatic symptoms of a depressed older adult necessarily a part of depression, or might they (also) reflect physical changes?

RANGE OF PROBLEMS

We know that mental health may be tied to the physical and social problems in a person's life. As a group, no other people have more of these problems than the aged. They have them all—physical decline and disabilities, sensory and neurological deficits, loss of loved ones, the cumulative effects of a lifetime of many unfortunate experiences and social stresses. However, it is important to remember that in addition to a lifetime of exposure to losses and to other stressors, both expected and unexpected, older adults have many positive life experiences, coping mechanisms, and wisdom on which to draw. Moreover, some cultural and ethnic factors appear to mitigate the negative effects of aging, as suggested in Focus 16.1. Finally, older adults who belong to groups that provide meaningful, strong roles for the elderly seem to have an easier time adjusting to growing old than do those who are not allowed such input into the family or society (Amoss & Harrell, 1981; Keith, 1982).

OLD AGE AND BRAIN DISORDERS

Although the majority of older people do not have brain disorders, these problems account for more admissions and hospital inpatient days than any other condition of geriatric adults (Christie, 1982).

We will examine two principal types of brain disorders, dementia and delirium.

DEMENTIA

Dementia, what laypeople call senility, is a gradual deterioration of intellectual abilities to the point at which social and occupational functioning are impaired. Difficulty remembering things, especially recent events, is the most prominent symptom of dementia. People may leave tasks unfinished because they forget to return to them after an interruption. The person who had started to fill a teapot at the sink leaves the water running; a parent is unable to remember the name of a daughter or son and later may not even recall that he or she has children or recognize them when they come to visit. Hygiene may be poor and appearance slovenly because the person forgets to bathe or how to dress adequately. Patients with dementia also get lost, even in familiar surroundings.

Judgment may become faulty, and the person may have difficulty comprehending situations and making plans or decisions. People with dementia relinquish their standards and lose control of their impulses; they may use coarse language, tell inappropriate jokes, shoplift, and make sexual advances to strangers. The ability to deal with abstract ideas deteriorates, and disturbances in emotions are common, including symptoms of depression, flatness of affect, and sporadic emotional outbursts. Patients with dementia are likely to show language disturbances as well, such as vague patterns of speech and an inability to name familiar objects. They may be unable to carry out motor activities, such as those involved in brushing the teeth, waving goodbye, or dressing themselves. Episodes of delirium, a state of great mental confusion (discussed in detail later), may occur.

The course of dementia may be progressive, static, or remitting, depending on the cause. Many people with progressive dementia eventually become withdrawn and apathetic. In the terminal phase of the illness, the personality loses its sparkle and integrity. Relatives and friends say that the person is just not himself or herself anymore. Social involvement with others keeps narrowing. Finally, the person is oblivious to his or her surroundings.

The prevalence of dementia increases with advancing age. One study found a prevalence of 1 percent in people sixty-five to seventy-four, 4 percent in those aged seventy-five to eighty-four, and 10 percent in those over eighty-four (George et al., 1991). These figures may well be underestimates because they do not include individuals who have died from some causes of dementia (see following discussion of Alzheimer's disease); data on annual incidence (the number of new cases developing in a year) show an 8.5 percent figure for those over age eighty-five (Paykel et al., 1994).

CAUSES OF DEMENTIA

A number of diseases can cause dementia, some of them progressive and terminal, others reversible.

ALZHEIMER'S DISEASE Alzheimer's disease accounts for 50 percent of dementia in elderly patients. A definitive diagnosis can be made only by microscopic examination of the brain tissue after death. When the person is alive a diagnosis of Alzheimer's, usually referred to as dementia of the Alzheimer's type (DAT), is made by exclusion, that is, by ruling out other possible causes of the person's cognitive and behavioral symptoms. These clinically based diagnoses are fairly accurate. Research may soon lead to more direct tests for the disease in living patients (Meschino & Lennon, 1994; Post, 1994).

In **Alzheimer's disease** the brain tissue irreversibly deteriorates, and death usually occurs ten or twelve years after the onset of symptoms. About 100,000 Americans die each year from this disease. Alzheimer's was initially described by the German neurologist Alois Alzheimer in 1860. The person may at first have difficulties only in concentration and in memory for newly learned material, and

appears absentminded and irritable, shortcomings that may be overlooked for several years but that soon interfere with daily living. The person often blames others for personal failings and may have delusions of being persecuted. Memory continues to deteriorate, and the individual becomes increasingly disoriented and agitated. Depression is common, occurring in up to 30 percent of DAT cases (Strauss & Ogrocki, 1996).

The main physiological change in the brain, evident at autopsy, is an atrophy (wasting away) of the cerebral cortex (especially the enterorhinal cortex), hippocampus, and other brain areas as neurons are lost, primarily axons and dendrites rather than the cell bodies themselves (Kowall & Beal, 1988). The fissures widen and the ridges become narrower and flatter. The ventricles also become enlarged. **Plaques**—small, round areas comprising the remnants of the lost neurons and β[beta]-amyloid, a waxy protein deposit—are scattered throughout the cortex. Tangled abnormal protein filaments, **neurofibrillary tangles**, accumulate within the cell bodies of neurons. These plaques and tangles are present throughout the cerebral cortex and the hippocampus. The cerebellum, spinal cord, and sensory areas of the cortex are less affected, which is why Alzheimer's patients do not appear to have anything physically wrong with them until late in the disease process. For some time patients are able to walk around normally and their overlearned habits, such as making small talk, remain intact, so that in

In this photograph of brain tissue from a patient with Alzheimer's Disease, the waxy amyloid shows up as areas of dark pink. On the right are computer generated images of a brain of a patient with Alzheimer's and a normal brain. Note that the patient's brain (left) has shrunk considerably due to the loss of nerve cells.

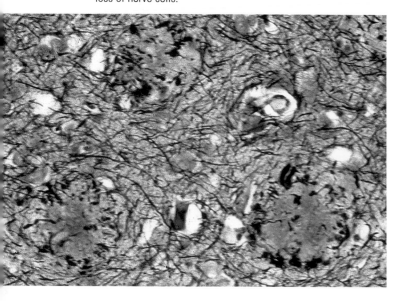
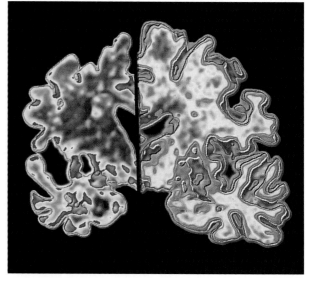

short encounters, strangers may not notice anything amiss.

There is currently a lively controversy over the relative importance of the amyloid deposits and the neurofibrillary tangles in Alzheimer's disease (Wischik, 1994). Both substances can disrupt brain function. When amyloid builds up in a cell, the cell dies. Neurofibrillary tangles are associated with changes in tau proteins, which are crucial for maintaining the transport of essential components of neural function (such as synaptic vesicles) from the axon to the synaptic terminal. Evidence favoring the importance of amyloid comes primarily from genetic studies (discussed later). However, as an increase in amyloid is found in normal aging, it is not unique to Alzheimer's disease. The tangles, in contrast, are more specific to Alzheimer's and thus may be more important in its etiology. Furthermore, when amyloid and tangles are correlated with cognitive deficits, tangles show a stronger association (Nagy et al., 1995). These substances continue to be the subject of much research.

Although neural pathways using other transmitters (e.g., serotonin, norepinephrine) deteriorate (Lawlor et al., 1989; Wester et al., 1988), those using acetylcholine are of particular importance. There is evidence that anticholinergic drugs can produce memory impairments in normal subjects similar to those found in Alzheimer's patients. There are fewer acetylcholine terminals in the brains of DAT patients (Strong et al., 1991), and levels of the major metabolite of acetylcholine are also low and are negatively related to the extent of the patient's mental deterioration (Wester et al., 1988).

The risk for Alzheimer's is increased in first-degree relatives of afflicted individuals (Silverman et al., 1994), and among some families the pattern of inheritance suggests the operation of a single dominant gene. Because people with Down syndrome invariably develop Alzheimer's if they survive until middle age, interest has focused on chromosome 21, which is aberrant in Down syndrome (see Chapter 15). A gene controlling the protein responsible for the formation of β–amyloid was found to be on the long arm of chromosome 21, and linkage studies have demonstrated an association between this gene and the expression of the disease (e.g.,Tanzi et al., 1987). A genetic study that did not confirm these results (Schellenberg et al., 1988) involved much younger patients. Therefore, early and late-onset Alzheimer's may have different etiologies (Nyth et al., 1991; Raskind, Carta, & Bravi, 1995; Small et al., 1989), and only a subset of cases of DAT may be genetically linked to chromosome 21. Other genes, on chromosome 14 for early-onset cases and on chromosome 19 for late-onset cases, are also being investigated (Clark & Goate, 1993; van Broeckhoven, 1995).

The amyloid found in the brains of patients with DAT is also present in diseases in which the immune system plays a significant role, so the immune system may be involved in Alzheimer's. Furthermore, some researchers have reported finding a novel antigen in the brains of DAT patients that could be attacking the brain (Bisette et al., 1991).

Finally, the environment is likely to play some role in Alzheimer's, as demonstrated by reports of long-lived MZ twins who are discordant for the disorder. However, the only well-documented risk factors are the occurrence of a head injury earlier in life (Rasmussen et al., 1995) and depression (Devanand et al., 1996). Although animal research shows that aluminum can induce lesions similar to those of Alzheimer's, the results of human studies of exposure to aluminum are not conclusive (Heston & White, 1991).

We are still far from understanding the causes of Alzheimer's disease, but it remains an active focus of research.

CAUSES OF OTHER DEMENTIAS Alzheimer's is almost always a disease of old age, but other kinds of dementing diseases exist, some of which afflict much younger people.

A number of infectious diseases can produce irreversible dementia. *Encephalitis*, a generic term for any inflammation of brain tissue, is caused by viruses that enter the brain either from other parts of the body (e.g., the sinuses or ears) or from the bites of mosquitoes or ticks. *Meningitis*, an inflammation of the membranes covering the outer brain, is usually caused by a bacterial infection. The organism (*Treponema pallidum*) that produces the venereal disease syphilis can invade the brain and cause dementia. Several rare viral illnesses (Creutzfeld-Jacob disease, kuru, and Gerstmann-Straussler syndrome) are also causes.

HIV and AIDS can cause irreversible dementia. Although this kind of dementia is so far primarily a problem of younger people, cases have been reported of AIDS-related dementia in older adults (Rosenzweig & Fillit, 1992; Weiler, Mungas, & Pomerantz, 1988). These same authors have cautioned that HIV- and AIDS-related symptoms in the elderly may be misdiagnosed as Alzheimer's or other, more common forms of dementia. There is a need for increased awareness of the growing numbers of HIV and AIDS cases among older adults, at least in the United States (Catania et al., 1989).

Neurological diseases, such as *Huntington's chorea*, can also produce dementia. Huntington's is caused by a single dominant gene located on chromosome 4 and is diagnosed principally by the presence of writhing (choreiform) movements. Perhaps the best-known victim of this disease was folksong writer and singer Woody Guthrie. Similarly, *Parkinson's disease*, which Muhammed Ali has, is marked by muscle tremors, muscular rigidity, and akinesia (an inability to initiate movement), and can lead to dementia. Dementia is common also in Pick's disease, a degenerative disease affecting the frontal lobes.

Several other medical conditions can cause dementia. In *normal pressure hydrocephalus*, an impairment in the circulation of the cerebrospinal fluid leads to its accumulation in the brain's ventricles ("water on the brain"). Pressure builds and creates dementia as well as difficulty standing and walking. The condition is reversible with surgery to restore normal circulation of cerebrospinal fluid. Head traumas, brain tumors, nutritional deficiencies (especially of B-complex vitamins), kidney or liver failure, and endocrine gland problems such as hyperthyroidism can result in dementia. Exposure to toxins, such as lead or mercury, and chronic use of drugs, including alcohol, are additional causes.

Vascular dementias are diagnosed when a patient with dementia has neurological signs such as weakness in an arm or abnormal reflexes, or when brain scans show evidence of cerebrovascular disease. Most commonly, the patient has suffered a series of strokes in which a clot formed, impairing circulation and causing cell death. Vascular dementias are believed to be the next most common dementias after Alzheimer's (Rorsman, Hagnell, & Lanke, 1986).

TREATMENT OF DEMENTIA

If the dementia has a reversible cause, appropriate medical treatment can be beneficial, such as correcting a hormonal imbalance. To date no clinically significant treatment has been found that can halt or reverse Alzheimer's disease, despite numerous investigations, although some drugs, as described here, show promise in improving some cognitive functions.

BIOLOGICAL TREATMENTS Because DAT involves the death of brain cells that secrete acetylcholine, various studies have attempted to increase the levels of this neurotransmitter. Research using choline (a precursor of the enzyme that catalyzes the reaction that produces acetylcholine) and physostigmine (a drug that prevents the breakdown of acetylcholine)

has been disappointing. Tetrahydroaminoacridine (THA), which inhibits the enzyme that breaks down acetylcholine, has yielded positive effects on short-term memory, but whether any longer-term benefits will be produced is not known (Heston & White, 1991). THA cannot be used in high doses because it has severe side effects; for example, it is toxic to the liver. In March 1993 the Food and Drug Administration approved the marketing of the drug, also known as tacrine and sold under the brand name Cognex, in recognition of the lack of promising alternatives to the treatment of this fatal disease.

Long-term strategies focus on slowing the progression of the disease. Operating on the hypothesis that the buildup of β–amyloid is the crucial factor in Alzheimer's, a great deal of current research is focusing on ways of blocking the creation of amyloid from its precursor protein (Whyte, Beyreuther, & Masters, 1994). Recent findings also indicate that vitamin E may be useful in slowing the progression of the disease in people already afflicted with it (Sano et al., 1997). Management of other symptoms of DAT includes many of the drugs previously discussed, for example, phenothiazines for paranoia, antidepressants for depression, benzodiazepines for anxiety, and sedatives for sleep difficulties.

There is recent promising evidence that the female hormone estrogen may improve the memory, thinking, and attentional capacities of Alzheimer's patients. At the 1996 meeting of the Society for Neuroscience, Asthana et al. (1996) reported their finding that estrogen, known from earlier research (Matsumoto, Murakami, & Arai, 1988; Toran-Allerand, 1976) to promote the growth of brain cells and to facilitate connections among them, had led to a significant improvement in memory in five elderly women with Alzheimer's disease. Estrogen was administered through a skin patch (similar to the transdermal administration of nicotine to help people stop smoking, cf. p. 328) in doses similar to those used successfully to counteract some of the undesirable effects of menopause, such as bone loss. Within one week these patients doubled their memory and tripled their concentration as measured by neuropsychological tests; five patients who were given placebos showed no such changes. The improvements were maintained to some degree up to five weeks following the termination of treatment, suggesting some long-term benefits of the drug even when patients are no longer taking it. Taken with evidence that postmenopausal decreases in estrogen may cause forgetfulness and decreased attention in people who do not have Alzheimer's, a growing body of research is confirming the importance of this hormone in human cognitive abilities. If data are confirmed in subsequent studies, use of estrogen could mark an important breakthrough in at least the symptomatic treatment of Alzheimer's disease.

PSYCHOSOCIAL TREATMENTS FOR PATIENT AND FAMILY

Although effective treatment for Alzheimer's is not yet available, patients and their families can be helped to deal with the effects of the disease. The general psychological approach is supportive with the overall goal of minimizing the disruption caused by the patient's behavioral changes. This goal is achieved by allowing the person and the family the opportunity to discuss the illness and its consequences, providing accurate information about the illness, helping family members care for the patient in the home, and encouraging a problem solving rather than a catastrophizing attitude in dealing with the many specific issues and challenges that this brain disorder presents (Knight, 1996; Zarit, 1980).

Counseling the impaired person is difficult. Because of their cognitive losses, counseling provides little long-term benefit for those with severe deterioration. However, some patients seem to enjoy and be reassured by occasional conversations with professionals and with others not directly involved in their lives. In contrast to what we have seen in dealing with virtually all other psychological problems, it may be desirable not to make an effort to get patients to admit to their problems, for their denial may be the most effective coping mechanism available (Zarit, 1980).

The cognitive limitations of senile persons should always be treated with gentleness. Others should not consider them nonbeings, talking about their disabilities in their presence, making fun of their occasional antics and forgetfulness, discounting their paranoid suspicions about others. Older people, even those with no biological disorder, are often infantilized or ignored by their juniors, a sign of disrespect that demeans not only the elderly person but the person showing the discourtesy.

For every individual with a severely disabling dementia living in an institution, there are at least two living in the community, usually supported by a spouse, daughter, or other family member. As the care of the elderly person with dementia generally falls on family members, psychosocial treatment concerns not only the individual, but the family as well. Family caregivers and friends, faced with taxing demands on their time, energies, and emotions, can become depressed. Caregivers need support and encouragement, opportunities to vent their feelings of guilt and resentment. Some may need permission to take time off or to feel that they will be able to should the pressure become too great.

Caring for a person with Alzheimer's disease has been shown to be extremely stressful (Anthony-Bergstone, Zarit, & Gatz, 1988; Gwynther & George, 1986; Zarit, Todd, & Zarit, 1986). Two studies (Dura, Stukenberg, & Kielcolt-Glaser, 1991; Schulz & Williamson, 1991) have documented unusually high levels of clinical depression and anxiety in adult children and spouses caring for their demented parents or spouses as compared with noncaregiver controls. Other studies have found more physical illness (Haley et al., 1987; Potashnik & Pruchno, 1988) and decreased immune functioning (Kielcolt-Glaser et al., 1991) among such caregivers. In many instances the disorders seem to be attributable to the stresses of caregiving; prior to these challenges the families of caregivers usually did not experience psychological difficulties (Gatz, Bengston, & Blum, 1990). Factors that increase depression and anxiety among caregivers include the severity of the patient's problem behaviors, perceived unavailability of social support, and concerns about financial resources to handle expenses during the long, debilitating, and often expensive illness.

Researchers have begun to examine cognitive factors that affect caregivers (e.g., Gatz, Bengston, & Blum, 1990; Pearlin et al., 1990; Zarit, 1989). For example, it may be that less distressed caregivers adopt a fatalistic attitude toward the patient's behavior—"There's nothing I can do to change the situation, so let me just resign myself to it"—rather than a more active coping approach, which is more suitable to dealing with challenges that are amenable to modification (Fiore, Becker, & Coppel, 1983; Folkman & Lazarus, 1985). In a study by Knight, Lutzky, and Olshevski (1992), efforts to help distressed caregivers solve problems and accept responsibility actually *increased* their stress as measured by cardiovascular reactivity. Knight et al. speculate that problem-solving training may reinforce the view that the caregiver is responsible for the patient's problem behaviors.[1]

Families can be taught, however, how to cope better with the stress of having a family member with Alzheimer's and at the same time help their dementing relatives cope with lost functions. One element

---

[1]This brings to mind our observations in the previous chapter (p. 444) on the pernicious nature of psychogenic theories of psychopathology. Those who are entrusted with the care of children as well as demented older adults are often subtly encouraged to accept responsibility and hence blame for the predicament of their charges. We do not wish to advocate inaction and neglect, rather only to place a caregiver's responsibilities in proper perspective.

of support is accurate information on the nature of the patient's problems. For example, because people with Alzheimer's have great difficulty placing new information into memory, they can engage in a reasonable conversation but forget a few minutes later what has been discussed. A caregiver may become impatient unless he or she understands that this impairment is to be expected because of the underlying brain damage. Substituting recognition for recall in daily situations may help patients and families better manage their lives. Families can be taught to ask questions that embed the answer. It is much easier to respond to "Was the person you just spoke to on the phone Harry or Tom?" than to "Who just called?" Labels on drawers, appliances, and rooms help orient a person. If the individual has lost the ability to read, pictures instead of verbal labels can be used. Prominent calendars, clocks, and strategic notes, as well as an automatic dialer on a telephone, can all help (Zarit, 1980).

It is useful for caregivers to understand that patients do not always appreciate their limitations and may attempt to engage in activities beyond their abilities, sometimes dangerously so. Although it is not advisable to coddle patients, it is important to set limits in light of their obliviousness to their own problems and impairments. Sometimes the caregiver's reactions to the patient's problems require attention. In one case, the daughter-in-law of a woman was offended by the woman's color combinations in clothing and wished to take over responsibility for coordinating her wardrobe, even though the patient was capable of dressing herself in an adequate, although not aesthetically pleasing fashion. The caregiver was urged not to impose her standards and taste on the patient, and to understand that the patient's ability to dress herself and to take responsibility for her clothes was more important than adherence to conventional appearance (Zarit, 1980).

Some of the tensions between caregiver and patient may well have their roots in aspects of the relationship that predate the onset of the dementia. There is a tendency to consider the most obvious facet of a situation, in this case the impairments of a sick person, as the cause of all difficulties. Counseling directed toward long-standing problems may be needed.

Perhaps the most wrenching decision is whether to institutionalize the person with dementia. At some point the patient's nursing needs may become so onerous and mental state so deteriorated that placement in a nursing home is the only realistic option for the benefit of the person and of the family. The conflicts people face when making this decision are considerable. The counselor can be a source of information about nearby facilities as well as a source of support for making and implementing a decision (Zarit, 1980).

DELIRIUM

The term **delirium** is derived from the Latin words *de*, meaning "from" or "out of," and *lira*, meaning "furrow" or "track." The term implies being off track or deviating from the usual state (Wells & Duncan, 1980). As illustrated in the case that opened this chapter, delirium is typically described as a clouded state of consciousness. The patient, sometimes rather suddenly, has great trouble concentrating and focusing attention and cannot maintain a coherent and directed stream of thought. In the early stages of delirium the person is frequently restless, particularly at night. The sleep–waking cycle becomes disturbed so that the person is drowsy during the day and awake, restless, and agitated during the night. The individual is generally worse during sleepless nights and in the dark. Vivid dreams and nightmares are common.

Delirious patients may be impossible to engage in conversation because of their wandering attention and fragmented thinking. In severe delirium speech is rambling and incoherent. Bewildered and confused, some delirious individuals may become disoriented for time, place, and sometimes for person. Sometimes they are so inattentive that they cannot be questioned about orientation. Memory impairment, especially for recent events, is com-

Providing memory aids is one way of combating memory loss.

mon. In the course of a twenty-four-hour period, however, delirious people have lucid intervals and become alert and coherent. These daily fluctuations help distinguish delirium from other syndromes, especially dementia.

Perceptual disturbances are frequent. Individuals mistake the unfamiliar for the familiar; for example, they may state that they are at home instead of in a hospital. Although illusions and hallucinations are common, particularly visual and mixed visual-auditory ones, they are not always present. Paranoid delusions have been noted in 40 to 70 percent of delirious older adults. These delusions tend to be poorly worked out, fleeting, and changeable.

Accompanying disordered thoughts and perceptions are swings in activity and mood. Delirious people can be erratic, ripping their clothes one moment and sitting lethargically the next. They are in great emotional turmoil and may shift rapidly from one emotion to another—depression, anxiety, fright, anger, euphoria, and irritability. Fever, flushed face, dilated pupils, rapid tremors, rapid heartbeat, elevated blood pressure, and incontinence of urine and feces are common. If the delirium proceeds, the person will completely lose touch with reality and may become stuporous (Lipowski, 1980, 1983; Strub & Black, 1981).

Although delirium is one of the most frequent biological mental disorders in older adults, it has been neglected in research and like dementia, is often misdiagnosed (Knight, 1996). Progress in diagnosis has been impeded by terminological chaos. The literature reveals thirty or more synonyms signifying delirium (Liston, 1982); acute confusional state and acute brain syndrome are the two most common.

People of any age are subject to delirium, but it is more common in children and older adults. Investigators have reported that 10 to 15 percent of older general-surgery patients become delirious after their operations (Miller, 1981). A review of the literature on delirium concluded that between one-third and one-half of all hospitalized elderly patients are likely to be delirious at some point during their stay, and it is common for those with dementia to experience episodes of delirium (Lipowski, 1983). Although the rates vary widely, even the lowest figures indicate that delirium is a serious health problem for older adults. The mortality rate for delirium is extremely high; approximately 40 percent of patients die, either from the underlying condition or from exhaustion (Rabins & Folstein, 1982). When fatality rates for dementia and delirium are compared over a one-year period, the rates are higher for delirium than for dementia, 37.5 compared with 16 percent.

Although the accurate diagnosis of delirium and its differentiation from conditions that resemble it are critical to the welfare of older persons, the disorder often goes unrecognized. For example, an elderly woman found in a filthy apartment with no food was believed by a poorly informed physician to be demented and was given routine custodial care in a nursing home. Fortunately, a professional knowledgeable about delirium learned that she had become depressed over the loss of a loved one and had neglected her diet. Once this was recognized, appropriate attention was given to her nutritional deficiencies, and her condition improved such that she was discharged to her own home after one month (Zarit, 1980).

Unfortunately, this case is fairly typical. Cameron et al. (1987) assessed 133 consecutive admissions to an acute medical ward. They found fifteen cases of delirium, only one of which had been detected by the admitting physician. Older adults are frequently mistaken for senile and therefore beyond hope. Long-term institutional care is all too often viewed as the only option even though the person may have a reversible condition. The older adult who has cognitive impairment must be examined thoroughly for all possible reversible causes of the disorder, such as drug intoxications, infections, fever, malnutrition, and head trauma, and then treated accordingly.

Knight (1996) offers a useful suggestion for distinguishing delirium from dementia:

> The clinical "feel" of talking with a person with delirium is rather like talking to someone who is acutely intoxicated or in an acute psychotic episode. Whereas the demented patient may not remember the name of the place where she or he is, the delirious patient may believe it is a different sort of place altogether, perhaps mistaking a psychiatric ward for a used car lot. ... Hallucinations, especially visual hallucinations, are common in delirium, but are rarely seen in demented patients until the very late stages of the disease. (pp. 96–97)

CAUSES OF DELIRIUM

The causes of delirium in the aged can be grouped into several general classes: drug intoxications and drug-withdrawal reactions, metabolic and nutritional imbalances (as in uncontrolled diabetes and thyroid dysfunction), infections or fevers, neurological disorders, and the stress of a change in the person's surroundings (Knight, 1996). Delirium may also occur following major surgery, most commonly, hip surgery (Gustafson et al., 1988); during withdrawal from psychoactive substances; and following head trauma or seizures. Common physical illnesses that cause delirium in this age group include congestive heart failure, pneumonia, urinary tract infection, cancer, kidney or liver failure, malnutrition, and cerebrovascular accidents or strokes. Probably the single most frequent cause of delirium in elderly people is intoxication with prescription drugs (Besdine, 1980; Lipowski, 1983). However, as in the case at the start of this chapter, delirium most often has more than one cause (Sloane, 1980).

Although delirium usually develops swiftly, within a matter of hours or days, the exact mode of onset depends on the underlying cause. Delirium resulting from a toxic reaction or concussion has an abrupt onset; when infection or metabolic disturbance underlies delirium, the onset of symptoms is somewhat more gradual.

Why are older adults especially vulnerable to delirium? Many explanations have been offered: the physical declines of aging, the increased general susceptibility to chronic diseases, the many medications prescribed for older patients, the greater sensitivity to drugs, and vulnerability to stress. One other factor, brain damage, increases the risk of delirium. Elderly individuals with dementing disorders appear to be the most susceptible to delirium of all. A retrospective review of 100 hospital admissions of people of all ages who had a diagnosis of delirium revealed that 44 percent of them had delirium superimposed on another brain condition (Purdie, Honigman, & Rosen, 1981).

TREATMENT OF DELIRIUM

Complete recovery from delirium is possible if the syndrome is correctly identified and the underlying cause promptly and effectively treated. It generally takes one to four weeks for the condition to clear; it takes longer in the elderly than in the young. If the underlying causative condition is not treated, however, the brain can be permanently damaged and the patient may die.

One often neglected aspect of the management of delirium is educating the family of a senile parent to recognize the symptoms of delirium and its reversible nature. They may interpret the onset of delirium as a new stage of a progressive dementing condition. For example, a patient with Alzheimer's disease may run a high fever from an infection and begin to hallucinate and otherwise act bizarrely. These new symptoms, superimposed on the intellectual deterioration to which members of the family have become accustomed, may alarm them into concluding that the patient is losing ground fast and irreversibly. They may be rushed into a premature

decision to institutionalize the patient. With proper diagnosis and treatment, however, the person can usually return to the earlier state, which, although problematic, can be coped with in the home.

OLD AGE AND PSYCHOLOGICAL DISORDERS

We tend to attribute all the ups and downs of older adults to their advanced years. The most obvious characteristic of a seventy-five-year-old man is that he is old. If he is cranky, it is because he is old. If he is depressed, it is because he is old. Even when he is happy, it is often assumed to be because of his age. Moreover, the old-age explanation is generally a somatic one, even if this is not made explicit. Some ill-defined physical deterioration is assumed to underlie not only the physical problems of old people but their psychological problems as well.

Although a psychological disorder at any age may have at least a partial physical explanation, this explanation can be misleading because for older adults much psychopathology found in the aged has *not* been directly linked to the physiological processes of aging. Rather, maladaptive personality traits and inadequate coping skills that the person brings into old age play a role in psychological disturbances, as do health, genetic predisposition, and life stressors.

We look first at the prevalence of mental disorders in late life and then survey a number of them, paying specific attention to how they are manifest in elderly people.

OVERALL PREVALENCE OF MENTAL DISORDERS IN LATE LIFE

Is age itself a contributing factor to emotional and mental malfunction? Do more old people than young people have mental disorders? Whether mental disorders become more prevalent with age is not clear, partly because of the methodological and conceptual difficulties that we have already discussed. The extensive cross-sectional study conducted by the National Institute of Mental Health (NIMH) yielded valuable data on mental disorders in all age groups, including the elderly.

Current prevalence data indicate that persons over age sixty-five have the lowest overall rates of all age groups when the various mental disorders are grouped together. The primary problem of old age was found to be *cognitive impairment*, not a separate DSM category but an important characteristic of more than one disorder (e.g., depression, dementia, delirium). Rates for mild cognitive impairment were about 14 percent for elderly males and females; for severe cognitive impairment rates were 5.5 percent for elderly men and 4.7 percent for elderly women (Myers et al., 1984). These rates tell us only the overall prevalence of cognitive impairment in the aged, not whether the causes were reversible or irreversible.

The majority of persons sixty-five years of age and older are free from serious psychopathology, but 10 to 20 percent do have psychological problems severe enough to warrant professional attention (Gatz et al., 1996; Gurland, 1991).

DEPRESSION

According to NIMH and other data, mood disorders are less prevalent in older adults than in younger adults —under 3 percent as compared to as high as 20 percent among younger people (Eaton et al., 1989; Myers et al., 1984; Regier et al., 1988), but they are estimated to account for nearly half the admissions of older adults to acute psychiatric care (Gurland & Cross, 1982; Wattis, 1990). Moreover, there may be a cohort effect: younger cohorts of older adults are showing *higher* rates of depressive disorder (Lewinsohn et al., 1993).

Unipolar depressions are much more common than are bipolar depressions among elderly patients (Post, 1978; Regier et al., 1988). The onset of bipolar disorder after the age of sixty-five is believed to be rare (Jamison, 1979; Shulman, 1993); Regier et al. found almost no person aged sixty-five or older who met diagnostic criteria for mania. Our discussion therefore addresses unipolar depression in older adults.

Women have more periods of depression than men for most of their lives, except possibly when they reach old-old age (Wolfe et al., 1996). As many as 40 percent of older individuals who have chronic health problems or are confined in hospitals are depressed (Rapp, Parisi, & Walsh, 1988). Moreover, people with a dementing disorder such as Alzheimer's may also be depressed; in addition to the 30 percent of those with dementia of the Alzheimer's type who are estimated to have a superimposed major depressive disorder, many more have some symptoms of depression that interfere with their lives (Burns, 1991).

CHARACTERISTICS OF DEPRESSION IN OLDER VERSUS YOUNGER ADULTS

Worry, feelings of uselessness, sadness, pessimism, fatigue, inability to sleep, and difficulties getting things done are common symptoms of depression in older adults (Blazer, 1982), as in other age groups. But there are also some interesting differences (Blazer, 1982; Small et al., 1986). Feelings of guilt are less common and somatic complaints are more common in the depressed elderly. Furthermore, older depressed patients show greater motor retardation, more weight loss, more of a general physical decline, less hostility, and less suicidal ideation than younger depressed patients (Musetti et al., 1989). The difference in suicidal ideation contrasts with our knowledge that actual suicide attempts and successes increase as men enter old age (see p. 473). Finally, memory complaints—not necessarily actual memory problems—are more common in older than in younger depressed individuals (O'Connor et al., 1990).

DEPRESSION VERSUS DEMENTIA

As noted earlier, a number of case histories and research studies have documented that symptoms of elderly individuals, seemingly of dementia, remit spontaneously or improve when they are treated for depression (LaRue, 1992). On the other hand, cases of depression are often misdiagnosed as a dementing disorder because of the cognitive impairment often found in depressed people. This is an important issue in differential diagnosis because depression is generally reversible, whereas dementia usually is not.

Depressed patients may be absentminded, leading their loved ones to suspect dementia. But whereas depressed persons may complain of forgetfulness (Kahn et al., 1975; Raskin & Rae, 1981), those with dementia may forget that they forget! Moreover, depressed patients tend to underestimate their abilities and to be preoccupied with negative feedback (Weingartner & Silberman, 1982). Depressed older adults, although they complain more than nondepressed controls about memory problems, do not perform less well than controls on laboratory memory tests (O'Connor et al., 1990); their performance on memory tests is above average or superior even if they complain about memory deficits (Williams et al., 1987). This discrepancy between memory complaints and actual memory deficits among elderly depressed people is found among younger people also and probably reflects self-deprecating evaluations in the clinical syndrome of depression.

Another difference between those who are depressed and those who suffer from dementia is that depressed people tend to have more errors of omission; they may not answer a question because it is just too much effort for them or because they expect to make mistakes. People with dementia, on the other hand, tend to make random or confabulatory errors (Spar & LaRue, 1990). (Confabulation refers to filling in gaps in memory with contrived and often improbable stories that the person accepts as true.) Patients can suffer from both dementia and depression. For example, an Alzheimer's patient can become depressed over his or her growing physical and cognitive limitations (Reifler et al., 1982; Teri & Reifler, 1987).

CAUSES OF DEPRESSION IN OLDER ADULTS

Many aged patients in poor physical health are depressed. A survey of 900 elderly people living in the community found that 44 percent of people with depressive symptoms were medically ill (Blazer & Williams, 1980). In a recent study of hospitalized medical patients who were elderly, about 15 percent were found to be clinically depressed (Reifler, 1994). Older men who have their first onset of depression in late life are likely to have undergone surgery before their episode of depression, to have unusually high rates of chronic illness, and to have suffered from more medical conditions than have other persons (Roth & Kay, 1956). Many physicians who care for elderly medical patients are insensitive to the likelihood of depression coexisting with physical illnesses and more often than not fail to diagnose and therefore to treat the psychological condition (Rapp et al., 1988; Rapp, Parisi, & Walsh, 1988). This oversight can worsen not only the depression, but also the medical problem itself (Wolfe et al., 1996).

Physical illness and depression are linked for reasons other than the disheartening aspects of an illness. A genetic diathesis for depression may also play a role. A higher prevalence of depression is found among the relatives of DAT patients who became depressed after the onset of DAT (Strauss & Ogrocki, 1996). Medications prescribed to treat a chronic condition can aggravate a depression that already exists, cause a depression to start, or produce symptoms that resemble the disorder but are not in fact a true depression (Klerman, 1983). The drugs most likely to have these effects are antihypertensive medications; other possibilities include hormones, corticosteroids, and antiparkinsonism medications (Spar & LaRue, 1990). On the other side of the coin, longitudinal and retrospective studies have pointed out that individuals who are depressed may be predisposed to develop physical illness (Vaillant, 1979; Wigdor & Morris, 1977). And because of their discouraged and lethargic state of mind, they may not seek appropriate medical treatment for symptoms they are experiencing, for example, weakness in the limbs or unpredictable bouts of nausea, which could be signals of serious cardiovascular problems.

As we grow older we almost inevitably experience a number of life events that could cause depression. Various studies have documented higher rates of illness and death among the widowed (Clayton, 1973; Parkes & Brown, 1972), and bereavement has been hypothesized to be a common precipitating factor for depressions that hospitalize elderly patients (Turner & Sternberg, 1978). However, studies have found relatively low rates of depression in the bereaved (Musetti et al., 1989), and it has been concluded that the symptoms of depression in bereft individuals are generally less severe and fewer than those in individuals institutionalized for depression (Bornstein et al., 1973; Gallagher et al., 1982). Few older people, then, appear to develop a disabling depressive illness following an expected loss of a loved one.

As with younger adults, psychological stress plays a role in depression in older adults, but a

Although many elderly people experience the loss of a spouse, they do not typically develop a severe depression.

stressor that might trigger or exacerbate a depressive episode in a younger person may not do so in an older adult (George, 1994). For example, social isolation is not as strongly linked to depression in old age as it is in middle age (Musetti et al., 1989). The importance of race and socioeconomic factors seems secondary to such variables as medical problems; that is, older adults of a racial minority may suffer from more serious medical problems or have poorer health care and it seems it is these factors, rather than racial prejudice or financial pressures, that contribute to depression (Blazer et al., 1991). Many people over the age of sixty-five—and of course younger people as well—deal with the stress of looking after disabled parents and relatives, especially those with Alzheimer's disease, and several studies have revealed high levels of depression (as well as anxiety) among these caregivers (e.g., Hannappel et al., 1993).

Although retirement has been assumed to have negative consequences, research does not generally support this assumption (Atchley, 1980; George, 1980). Any ill effects of retirement may have to do with the poor health and low incomes of some retirees, not with retirement per se (Pahkala, 1990). For many older adults, retirement often ushers in a satisfying period of life (Wolfe et al., 1996).

Each older person brings to late life a developmental history that makes his or her reactions to common problems unique. Their coping skills and personality determine how effectively they will respond to new life events (Butler & Lewis, 1982). It would be well to assume that adaptation rather than depression is the common reaction to losses and stress in late life.

TREATMENT OF DEPRESSION

Although clinical lore holds that depressions in elderly patients are more resistant to treatment, these claims are not substantiated (Small & Jarvik, 1982). Rather, there is considerable evidence that depressed older adults can be helped by both psychological and pharmacological interventions.

Gallagher and Thompson (1982, 1983) compared cognitive, behavioral, and brief psychodynamic psychotherapies for older depressed individuals. All three were found equally effective, and in subsequent studies (Gallagher-Thompson & Thompson, 1995a, 1995b; Thompson, Gallagher, & Breckenridge, 1987) about three-quarters of the patients were judged either completely cured or markedly improved. These rates compare very favorably with the outcomes of psychotherapy in younger depressed people. Another notable finding

is that untreated control patients did not improve, as younger untreated depressed patients often do, suggesting that older adults are less likely than younger patients to recover without treatment.

Research on the use of drugs to treat depression is not as extensive for older adults as it is for younger adults, but emerging evidence suggests that certain antidepressants can be useful, particularly selective serotonin reuptake inhibitors such as fluoxetine (Prozac) (Hale, 1993). However, the use of antidepressant drugs with older adults is complicated by side effects, such as postural hypotension (a fall in blood pressure when standing up), which causes some patients treated with tricyclic antidepressants to become dizzy when they stand up and then to fall. These drugs also pose a risk to the cardiovascular system, with the danger of a heart attack. Moreover, older people generally are at high risk for toxic reactions to medications. For these reasons, nonpharmacological approaches to depression in the elderly are particularly important (Bressler, 1987; Scogin & McElrath, 1994). Electroconvulsive therapy (p. 245) is back in favor among many geriatric psychiatrists (Hay, 1991), particularly for patients who had an earlier favorable response to it (Janicak et al., 1993).

ANXIETY DISORDERS

Among elderly adults, anxiety disorders are more prevalent than depression (Gatz et al., 1996; Regier et al., 1988). However, less research has been done on anxiety disorders. Anxiety disorders in old age can be a continuation or reemergence from problems earlier in life, or they can develop for the first time in the senior years. Like depression, DSM-defined anxiety disorders appear to be less prevalent among older than among younger adults (Kessler et al., 1994). As nearly all the available data are cross-sectional, however, it is wise to be cautious about this conclusion. It may be that younger cohorts of older adults are exhibiting higher rates of these disorders than are older cohorts; thus although anxiety disorders may decrease with age, those becoming old in the 1990s may experience an upward trend in prevalence. A further complicating factor in determining prevalence is that, as with younger people, *symptoms* of anxiety among older adults are more predominant than diagnosable anxiety disorders, indicating that unwarranted anxiety among seniors is fairly common (Gurian & Miner, 1991). The quality of a person's life can be compromised by symptoms that, although not severe, frequent, or enduring enough to warrant a formal DSM diagnosis, could still justify professional concern and intervention (Fisher & Noll, 1996). In general, symptoms of anxiety disorders do not differ as people enter old age.

Causes of anxiety disorders reflect some of the circumstances of getting older (Fisher & Noll, 1996). Anxiety problems are often associated with medical illness (Heidrich, 1993) and can be a reaction to worries about being sick and becoming infirm. Sometimes an older person's anxieties can be a reaction to medication, for example, antidepressants or antiparkinsonism drugs, or part of the delirium that frequently accompanies medical illness in the aged (Lipowski, 1990). Signs of extreme distress, sometimes aggression, are seen in people suffering from dementias, such as Alzheimer's, and probably reflect anxiety arising from confusion and frustration when they are unable to deal with seemingly minor tasks such as putting on a coat (Fisher et al., 1994, cited in Fisher & Noll, 1996). Many other medical diseases can create anxiety symptoms that are not properly considered part of an anxiety disorder but that warrant professional attention. Some of these are found in all adults, but most of them are more often suffered by elderly adults. Metabolic conditions, such as hypoglycemia and anemia; endocrine disorders, such as hyperthyroidism; cardiovascular conditions, such as angina and congestive heart failure; and excessive caffeine consumption all may cause such symptoms as a faster heart rate, which are also symptoms of anxiety (Fisher & Noll, 1996). Age-related deterioration in the vestibular system (inner-ear control of one's sense of balance) can account for panic symptoms such as severe dizziness (Raj, Corvea, & Dagon, 1993).

Anxiety problems in the elderly seem to respond to the same kinds of psychological treatments found useful with younger adults (cf. Chapter 6), but controlled research is in its infancy (Stanley, Beck, & Glassco, 1997). Because it is the medical doctor who usually hears the psychological complaints of older adults—at least for current cohorts of elders—psychoactive medications are in widespread use (see the later discussion of the *abuse* of such drugs by older patients), but potentially dangerous interactions with other drugs that older adults frequently take, along with their increased sensitivity to *any* drug, make antianxiety medication a risky intervention (Fisher & Noll, 1996; Hersen & Van Hasselt, 1992).

A concluding comment by Fisher and Noll (1996) in their review of anxiety disorders in the elderly could be applied to other psychological disorders as well:

Although old age naturally presents the challenges of physical and emotional losses that may seem overwhelming to the young, the ability to competently cope with these losses [and challenges] is indeed probably the most remarkable aspect of the relationship between aging and anxiety. Perhaps through the study of the means by which the majority of older adults rise to the challenges associated with aging, researchers will better inform the treatment of anxiety across the lifespan. (p. 323)

DELUSIONAL (PARANOID) DISORDERS

A sixty-six-year-old married woman reluctantly agreed to a clinical evaluation. She [had] a six-week history of bizarre delusions and hallucinations of her husband spraying the house with a fluid that smelled like "burned food." She complained that he sprayed the substance everywhere around the house, including draperies and furniture, although she had never seen him do it. She could smell the substance almost constantly, and it affected her head, chest, and rectum. She also complained that someone in the neighborhood had been throwing bricks and rocks at her house. In addition, she suspected her husband of having affairs with other women, whose footprints she claimed to have seen near home. ...

Interviews revealed a sullen woman who was extremely hostile toward her husband. She focused on the delusion that he was spraying an unusual substance in an attempt to upset her; other issues in the relationship seemed secondary. She looked very sad at times and would occasionally wipe away a tear; but her predominant affect was extreme hostility and consternation about her husband's alleged behavior. (Varner & Gaitz, 1982, p. 108)

In addition to the distress experienced by the patient, paranoia may have a disturbing and immediate impact on others, often bringing angry reactions and contributing to a decision to institutionalize the older adult (Berger & Zarit, 1978). Paranoid symptomatology is found in many elderly psychiatric patients (Heston, 1987; Pfeiffer, 1977).

Clinicians report an interesting difference that is sometimes found between the paranoid delusions of older people and those of younger individuals. The suspicions of older adults are often more down-to-earth, concerned with persons in their immediate surroundings—neighbors, sons and daughters, people in stores, and the like. In contrast, the persecutors of younger paranoid patients are often located far away, in the CIA, the FBI, or even in outer space. Some younger paranoid patients are given to more grandiosity than are older ones (Post, 1987). Moreover, older patients are more likely to be women who are in good health except for problems with vision and, as we will see, hearing.

CAUSES OF PARANOIA

Paranoia in elderly patients may be the continuation of a disorder that began earlier in life, or it may accompany brain diseases, such as delirium and dementia. Paranoia may even serve a function for demented patients, filling in the gaps caused by memory loss. Instead of admitting, "I can't remember where I left my keys," they think, "Someone must have come in and taken my keys" (Zarit, 1980).

Paranoid ideation has been linked to sensory losses, in particular to loss of hearing. Some believe that older people with severe paranoid disorders tend to have long-standing hearing loss in both ears, which makes them socially deaf (Eastwood et al., 1985; Pearlson & Rabins, 1988; Post, 1980). An older person who is deaf may believe that other people are whispering about him or her so that he or she cannot hear what is being said. The person's paranoid reactions may be an attempt to fill in the blanks caused by sensory loss (Pfeiffer, 1977; see Focus 16.2). By explaining bewildering events, delusions are in a sense adaptive and understandable. There is, however, conflicting evidence about this presumed link between hearing problems and delusional disorder. Whereas some researchers report that hearing loss precedes the onset of paranoid symptoms, others report that such sensory losses are not common among people with delusional disorder (Jeste et al., 1988).

Since those who become paranoid also have poor social adjustment, the onset of their symptoms may follow a period in which they have become increasingly isolated (Gurland, 1991). This isolation itself limits the person's opportunities to check his or her suspicions about the world, making it easier for delusions to take hold. The individual builds a pseudocommunity—a private world of his or her own—rather than social relations based on good communication and mutual trust (Cameron, 1959).

Older people are especially vulnerable to all kinds of abuse from others. Others may talk about them behind their backs, or even to their faces, as though they were not present, and people take advantage of the elderly in many ways. The complaint of persecution from an older person that is blithely dismissed as a sign of late-life paranoia may be justified. An older client of one of the authors complained bitterly about being followed by a detective hired by her evil husband. Inquiry revealed that the husband was worried that she was having an affair and had indeed hired someone to follow her! It should always be determined whether suspicions have any bases in reality before they are attributed to paranoia.

TREATMENT OF PARANOIA

The treatment of paranoia is much the same for older adults as for younger adults. Although controlled data are lacking, clinicians suggest that a patient, supportive approach is best, the therapist providing empathic understanding of the person's concerns. Directly challenging the paranoid delusion or attempting to reason the person out of his or her beliefs is seldom effective. By the time the patient sees a health professional, many others—family, friends, the police—have probably tried this approach. Nonjudgmental recognition of the distress caused by the paranoia is more likely to promote a therapeutic relationship with the patient. When the patient trusts and feels safe with the therapist, the delusions can gradually be questioned.

If a hearing or visual problem is present, a hearing aid or corrective lenses may alleviate some of the paranoid symptoms. If the individual is socially isolated, efforts can be made to increase his or her activities and contacts. Regular supportive therapy may help the patient in reestablishing relations with family members and friends. Positive reinforcement can be provided for appropriate behavior, for example, the therapist may pay special attention to comments by the patient that are not paranoid in nature. Even if these straightforward measures do not relieve paranoia, they may be beneficial in other areas of the person's life.

Studies of therapy outcomes indicate that delusions in elderly patients can be treated with some success with phenothiazines (Schneider, 1996), although paranoid individuals are generally suspicious of the motives of those who give them drugs. Toxicity from medications must also be considered, given the particular sensitivity of older people to drugs. Institutionalization, best considered as a last resort, may do little good. In practice, this decision depends more on the level of tolerance in the person's social environment than on the severity and disruptiveness of the paranoid beliefs.

SCHIZOPHRENIA

As discussed in Chapter 11, the symptoms of schizophrenia include, in addition to delusions, cognitive impairment, hallucinations, and negative symptoms such as flat affect. Does schizophrenia ever appear for the first time in old age? Debate on this question has raged for years. Even Kraepelin had doubts that it was always appropriate to use the adjective *praecox*, meaning early onset, to describe schizophrenia. When schizophrenia does make a rare appearance for the first time in older adults, it is often called **paraphrenia** (Howard, 1993;

FOCUS 16.2 PARTIAL DEAFNESS, GROWING OLD, AND PARANOIA

A possible relationship between hearing problems in old age and the development of paranoid thinking was noted many years ago by Emil Kraepelin and has been supported since by careful laboratory studies (Cooper et al., 1974). The connection appears to be specific to paranoia, for the relationship between difficulties in hearing and depression in older individuals is not as great. Since, according to some research, hearing losses appear to predate the onset of paranoid delusions, this may be a cause–effect relationship of some importance.

Stanford psychologist Philip Zimbardo and his associates conducted an ingenious experiment to study the relation of poor hearing to paranoia. They reasoned that loss of hearing acuity might set the stage for the development of paranoia if the person does not acknowledge, or is unaware of, the hearing problem (Zimbardo, Andersen, & Kabat, 1981). The scenario goes something like this: If I have trouble hearing people around me, which makes them seem to be whispering, I may conclude that they are whispering *about me*, and that what they say is unfavorable. I will think this way, however, only if I am unaware of my hearing problem. If I know that I am partially deaf, I will appreciate that I do not hear them well because of my deafness and will not think that they are whispering. A hard-of-hearing grandfather may eventually challenge the light-voiced, gesturing grandchildren he believes are whispering about him; and they will deny that they are. A tense cycle of allegations, denials, and further accusations will isolate the increasingly hostile and suspicious grandfather from the company of his grandchildren.

The experiment done by Zimbardo and his group examined the initial stage of this hypothesized development of paranoia. College students, previously determined to be easily hypnotized

and capable of responding to a posthypnotic suggestion of partial deafness, participated in what they believed to be a study of the effects of various hypnotic procedures on creative problem solving. Each student sat in a room with two others who were confederates of the experimenter. The trio were provided a task to perform either cooperatively or by themselves; they were to make up a story concerning a Thematic Apperception Test (TAT) picture. First the word *focus* was shown on a screen, then the picture was projected. The confederates, as planned, began to joke with each other as they made decisions about the story, inviting the student to join them in the cooperative venture. After the story was completed, the person was left alone to fill out the questionnaires, among them MMPI measures of paranoia and an adjective checklist to assess mood.

As described so far, there is nothing particularly notable about this experiment. The actual manipulations had taken place earlier, *before* the TAT picture was presented. Each student had been hypnotized and given one of the three following posthypnotic suggestions.

1. *Induced partial deafness without awareness.* Members of this group were told that when they saw the word *focus* projected on a screen in the next room, they would have trouble hearing noises and what other people were saying, that the others would seem to be whispering, and that they would be concerned about not being able to hear. They were also instructed that they would not be aware of this suggestion until an experimenter removed the amnesia by touching their shoulder.

2. *Induced partial deafness with awareness.* Students in the

---

Roth, 1955). Symptoms differ from those seen in early-onset schizophrenia; paraphrenia typically involves more hallucinations and paranoid delusions (Howard et al., 1993; Jeste et al., 1988). Patients tend to be unmarried, live in isolation, have few surviving relatives, experience hearing losses, have a family history of schizophrenia, and belong to the lower socioeconomic classes (Harris & Jeste, 1988; Post, 1987).

In the United States the term *paraphrenia* has been inconsistently used (Berger & Zarit, 1978; Bridge & Wyatt, 1980; Howard, 1993). Some researchers believe that a number of the older patients diagnosed as having paraphrenia actually have a mood disorder (Cooper, Garside, & Kay, 1976; Kay et al., 1976), for in many with prominent symptoms, cognition and overall functioning are preserved, that is, their lives are not marked by the deterioration and upheaval common in schizophrenia. In a study of

patients who appeared to have become schizophrenic for the first time after age sixty-five, roughly two-thirds were actually suffering from dementia or from a mood disorder (Leuchter, 1985).

With older adults, biological factors that have little if anything to do with mental disturbance per se have to be considered with special care in making a diagnosis of a mental illness such as paraphrenia. For example, several reversible medical and surgical problems can produce signs and symptoms that mimic schizophrenia (Marengo & Westermeyer, 1996), including hyperthyroidism, hypothyroidism, Addison's disease, Cushing's disease, Parkinson's disease, Alzheimer's disease, and vitamin deficiencies (Jeste et al., 1991).

For the treatment of schizophrenia in older adults antipsychotic medication, such as the phenothiazines discussed earlier (p. 287), are effective (Jeste et al., 1993), though side effects and interactions

second group, the control group, were given the same partial-deafness suggestion, but they were instructed to remember that their hearing difficulty was by posthypnotic suggestion.

3. *Posthypnotic-suggestion control.* Participants in the third group, controls for the effects of posthypnotic suggestion, were instructed to react to the word *focus* by experiencing an itchiness in the left earlobe, with amnesia for this suggestion until touched on the left shoulder by the experimenter.

After being given their posthypnotic suggestions, all participants were awakened from the hypnotic state and ushered into the next room, where the experiment proceeded with the TAT picture, as described. It can now be appreciated that participants who had deafness without awareness might perceive the joking of the confederates as directed toward them, for they would have trouble hearing what was being said and would be unlikely to attribute this difficulty to any hearing problem of their own. Those who had deafness with awareness would have the same problem hearing the joking, but they would know that they had a temporary decrement in hearing through hypnotic suggestion. The other control students would have no hearing problems, just itchy earlobes. At the completion of the study all were informed about the purposes of the experiment, and steps were taken to ensure that the posthypnotic suggestions of partial deafness and itchy earlobes had been lifted.

The results were fascinating. The experience of being partially deaf without awareness showed up significantly on cognitive, emotional, and behavioral measures. Compared with members of the two control groups, these students scored more paranoid on the MMPI scales and described themselves as more irritated, agitated, and hostile. The two confederates who were in the same room with these students rated them as more hostile than they rated the controls. (The confederates were not aware of which group a given participant was in.) When the confederates invited each person to work with them in concocting the TAT story, only one of six in the deafness-without-awareness group accepted the overture, although most of the controls agreed. At the end of the study, just before the debriefing, all were asked whether they would like to participate in a future experiment with the same partners; none of the deafness-without-awareness participants responded affirmatively, but most of the controls did.

The overall reaction of those who had trouble hearing and had no ready explanation for it other than that others were whispering was suspicion, hostility, agitation, and unwillingness to affiliate with these people. This pattern is similar to what Zimbardo hypothesized to be the earliest stage of the development of some paranoid delusions. The creation of this "analogue incipient paranoia" in the laboratory by inducing deafness without awareness of the deafness is consistent with the view that when people's hearing becomes poor in old age, some of them are susceptible to paranoia *if*, for whatever reasons, they do not acknowledge their deafness.

In subsequent research, Zimbardo strengthened these findings by inducing physiological arousal via hypnotic suggestion and then suggesting amnesia for the true source of the arousal. Unexplained arousal was experienced as significantly more distressing than arousal that could be attributed to the hypnosis (Zimbardo, LaBerge, & Butler, 1993). Other studies indicate that if people look to the actions of others to understand the reasons for their unexplained arousal, they become more paranoid than people whose search for the causes of the arousal is guided into other domains, for example, something in the physical environment (P. Zimbardo, personal communication, September 29, 1992).

with other drugs being taken by the patient can pose a challenge to the prescribing physician. A supportive therapeutic relationship also appears to be helpful and bolstering (Marengo & Westermeyer, 1996).

SUBSTANCE-RELATED DISORDERS

Substance abuse is less prevalent in today's cohorts of older adults than among younger adults, but it is a problem nonetheless. One reason for the lower prevalence may be increased mortality among those who have abused drugs in the past or are doing so in their elder years.

ALCOHOL ABUSE AND DEPENDENCE

Alcohol abuse is generally believed to be less prevalent in the elderly than in younger cohorts, yet the problem is not trivial. Prevalence rates for DSM-defined alcohol abuse or dependence are 3.1 percent for elderly men and 0.46 percent for elderly women (Helzer, Burnam, & McEvoy, 1991; Myers et al., 1984); averaging out to less than 2 percent. This rate is much lower than the rates that have been determined for the general adult population (p. 297). If figures include people who consume at least a dozen drinks a week, about 8 percent of older adults are heavy drinkers (Molgaard et al., 1990). It should be noted that a given amount of alcohol has a stronger effect on the average older adult than on a younger person—the ratio of body water to body mass decreases as one ages, resulting in higher blood-alcohol concentration per unit of alcohol imbibed (Morse, 1988). For this reason alone, a sizable percentage of older adults who are heavy drinkers can be considered alcohol abusers. From a longitudinal perspective, it appears that heavy drinkers tend to drink less as they enter old age (Fillmore, 1987). However, the significantly higher prevalence of alcohol abuse and dependence—as well as abuse of other drugs—in current cohorts who are yet to reach their senior stages of life portends a much greater problem in the future. (Recall the earlier methodological discussion of cohort effects in research that compares people of different ages at the same point in time, p. 453.)

Many alcohol abusers do not survive to old age. The peak years for death from cirrhosis are between fifty-five and sixty-four years of age. Mortality from cardiovascular problems is also higher (Shaper, 1990).

It might be assumed that problem drinking in an older adult is always a continuation of a pattern established earlier in life, but this is not the case. Many problem drinkers begin having alcohol-related problems after the age of sixty, so-called late-onset alcoholism. Estimates vary widely, but a recent review of the literature concluded that between one-third and one-half of those who have drinking problems in old age began their problem drinking after the age of sixty (Liberto et al., 1996).

As people age their tolerance for alcohol is reduced, for they metabolize alcohol more slowly. Thus the drug may cause greater changes in brain chemistry and may more readily bring on toxic effects, such as delirium, in older people. Several neuropsychological studies have shown that cognitive deficits associated with alcohol abuse, such as memory problems, are likely to be more pronounced in the aged alcoholic than in younger individuals with comparable drinking histories (Brandt et al., 1983). Although some intellectual functioning is recovered with abstinence, residual effects may remain long after the older person has stopped drinking.

Clinicians may be less likely to look for alcohol abuse in older people than in younger patients and may instead attribute symptoms such as poor motor coordination and impaired memory to a medical problem or to late-life depression. Indeed, alcohol problems often are comorbid with major depression and brain damage (Liberto et al., 1996). Whether there is comorbidity or not, if alcohol abuse goes unrecognized, treatment of the patient will be severely compromised. Controlled research on intervention is scant.

ILLEGAL DRUG ABUSE

The current older population abuses illegal drugs infrequently compared with other age groups. In the previously cited NIMH survey (Regier et al., 1988), none of those aged sixty-five and older, and

only 0.1 percent of those between forty-five and sixty-four years of age, had a drug abuse or dependency disorder, compared with much higher rates for younger age groups. Studies of older narcotics abusers indicate that they began their habit early in life and reduced their drug intake as they grew older (Ball & Chambers, 1970). Many experts believe, however, that the abuse of illegal drugs is higher than these formal estimates indicate.

MEDICATION MISUSE

The misuse of prescription and over-the-counter medicines is a much greater problem than drug or alcohol abuse in the aged population (LaRue, Dessonville, & Jarvik, 1985). The elderly have a higher overall rate of legal drug intake than any other group; although they constitute only 13 percent of the population, they consume about one-third of all prescribed medications (Weber, 1996). Some of these prescriptions reflect serious drug abuse.

Abuse of prescription or legal drugs can be deliberate or inadvertent. Some people may seek drugs to abuse, obtaining medications from a number of sources, for example, by going to more than one physician, filling their prescriptions at different pharmacies, and paying cash instead of using credit cards to reduce the chances of their multiple pre-

Medication misuse, whether deliberate or inadvertent, can be a serious problem among the aged and can cause delirium.

scriptions being discovered (Weber, 1996). One study of 141 well-functioning middle-class elderly people living in their own homes found that almost half reported having misused prescription or over-the-counter drugs at least once over a period of six months (Folkman, Bernstein, & Lazarus, 1987).

Often prescribed years earlier to deal with post-operative pain or the grief and anxiety of losing a loved one, many tranquilizers, antidepressants, and sleep aids create physical as well as psychological dependency in older adults, who, because they tend not to go to work regularly or even sometimes be seen in public for days or weeks at a time, can hide their abuse for years. The slurred speech and memory problems caused by drugs may be attributed to old age and senility (LaRue, Dessonville, & Jarvik, 1985), another example of how popular stereotypes can interfere with proper diagnosis and treatment. Said one addiction specialist, "They're not like a 25-year-old mixing it up [using drugs and alcohol] to get high. … They're trying to make a lonely, miserable life less miserable" (quoted in Weber, 1996, p. A36). A former Valium addict and now a leader of Pills Anonymous groups in California stated the problem this way: "Closet junkies, that's what we call them here. They're at home. They're alone. They're afraid. They're just hiding. Their drug pusher is their doctor" (quoted in Weber, 1996, p. A36).

With the growth of health plans that compensate physicians for the number of patients they look after rather than for the time they spend with each, it is increasingly difficult for doctors to take the time to find out what is really bothering an older patient and thus many just write out a prescription that may reduce the verbal complaints. Furthermore, as most psychoactive drugs are tested on younger people, gauging the dosage appropriate for the less efficient kidneys and liver of the older person represents a difficult challenge for the medical practitioner.

Since the current cohort of older adults is not as acculturated as are younger people to seeking help for psychological problems, including drug problems, many make unsupervised efforts to abstain, sometimes going cold turkey. Doing so can be very dangerous, even life threatening, because withdrawal reactions place great demands on the cardiovascular system. When people now in middle age reach their seventies and beyond, the prevalence of prescription-drug abuse may be even greater, exacerbated by the "take a pill for your ills" mentality they have acquired and by the likely availability of even more medications designed to affect mood and ease discomfort.

Some elderly addicts end up in places where one doesn't expect to find an older adult:

Her skin itched as if an invisible case of hives were creeping across her flesh. She would shiver, then sweat. She felt suffocated by despair.

She was 65, a doctor's wife, a proud grandma with a purseful of photographs. But there she was, curled in a ball like any other junkie at the … drug treatment center, sobbing as her body withdrew from a diet of painkillers and tranquilizers.

She couldn't believe it had come to this.

People her age, the woman said, "don't associate themselves with the lowlifes [who] sneak into doorways to shoot up. No, they sneak into the bathroom for a pill." (Weber, 1996, p. A1).

HYPOCHONDRIASIS

Older adults complain of a multitude of physical problems, among them sore feet and backs, poor digestion, constipation, labored breathing, and cold extremities. All are to be taken seriously by responsible health professionals. However, some elderly people believe they are ill and complain unendingly about aches and pains for which there are no plausible physical causes. It has been widely believed that hypochondriasis is especially common in the elderly population, but the prevalence of hypochondriasis may not be any greater among older adults than among others (Siegler & Costa, 1985). Taken as a group, older adults tend to *under*report somatic symptoms rather than overreport them and often fail to seek help for serious illnesses (Besdine, 1980), perhaps because of concern for health care costs or a belief—probably true—that aches and pains are an inevitable part of aging and may not reflect a specific medical problem.

Longitudinal survey data indicate that concerns about health do not increase with age but remain fairly stable over the life span. Since actual health *problems* do increase with age without accompanying increases in *concerns* about health, such data do not support the idea that people become more hypochondriacal as they get older (Costa et al., 1987). Those older persons who have many physical complaints have long-standing personality traits that predict such complaining (Siegler and Costa, 1985). Their excessive somatic complaints appear to be associated with neuroticism or poor adjustment, which are *not* associated with age. In addition, the NIMH study (Regier et al., 1988) found only 0.1 percent of those aged sixty-five years or older to have somatization disorder, the same rate as in younger age groups.

No controlled studies of the treatment of hypochondriasis in older adults have been done. Clinicians generally agree that reassuring the person that he or she is healthy is generally useless, for these people are not swayed by negative laboratory tests or authoritative pronouncements from official sources. Some tentative evidence suggests that ignoring the somatic complaints and concentrating instead on more positive aspects of existence can be helpful (Goldstein & Birnbom, 1976). "I know that you're feeling bad and that your feet really hurt, but let's take a walk in Palisades Park anyway." Diverting activities may allow these individuals to function in the face of their perceived medical ills and perhaps obtain some positive satisfaction from life.

SLEEP DISORDERS

Insomnia is a frequent complaint among elderly people. One national survey found insomnia in 25 percent of respondents aged sixty-five to seventy-nine, as compared with 14 percent in the eighteen to thirty-four age group; another 20 percent had less serious but still problematic insomnia (Mellinger, Balter, & Uhlenhuth, 1985).

The most common sleep problems experienced by the elderly are waking often at night, frequent early-morning awakenings, difficulty falling asleep, and daytime fatigue (Miles & Dement, 1980). These complaints parallel the physiological changes that occur normally as people enter old age (Bootzin, Engle-Friedman, & Hazelwood, 1983). Elderly adults sleep somewhat less or the same amount of time as do younger adults, but their sleep is also more often spontaneously interrupted; and they take longer to fall back asleep after awakening (Webb & Campbell, 1980). Thus older people generally sleep less in relation to the total time they spend in bed at nighttime; they tend to make up for this loss with daytime naps. Elderly people also spend less absolute time in a phase known as rapid eye movement (REM) sleep, and stage 4 sleep, the deepest, is virtually absent. Sleep disturbances represent extremes of what is basically a normal pattern. Elderly men generally experience more disturbances of their sleep than do elderly women, a difference found to a lesser extent in young adults (Dement, Laughton, & Carskadon, 1981).

CAUSES OF SLEEP DISORDERS

In addition to the changes associated with aging, various illnesses, medications, caffeine, stress, anxiety, depression, lack of activity, and poor sleep habits may make insomniacs of older adults. Depressed mood—even in the absence of a full-blown mood disorder—has been shown to be related to sleep disturbances in older adults, especially early-morning awakening (Rodin, McAvay, & Timko, 1988). Since

the prevalence of insomnia greatly exceeds the prevalence of depression in old age, however, all geriatric sleep problems should not be attributed to an underlying depression (Morgan, 1992).

Pain, particularly that of arthritis, is a principal disrupter of sleep for older adults (Prinz & Raskin, 1978), and sleep problems are also associated with Alzheimer's disease.

Whatever the cause of insomnia at any age, it is worsened by self-defeating actions such as ruminating over it and counting the number of hours slept and those spent waiting to fall asleep. Sleeping problems can also be worsened by medications that are taken to deal with them.

Sleep apnea is a respiratory disorder in which breathing ceases repeatedly for a period of ten seconds or more throughout the night. It seriously disrupts normal sleep and can lead to fatigue, muscle aches, and elevation in blood pressure over a period of time. The disruption in normal breathing is usually due to markedly reduced airflow caused by an obstruction from excess tissue at the back of the throat. These interruptions in breathing can occur upwards of twenty times an hour. It is rare for the person to become aware of the problem unless his or her bed partner complains about snoring, a typical accompaniment to most apnea problems. Sometimes the partner is aware of the person's ceasing to breathe and then loudly gasping for breath. Apneic episodes can be frightening to the observer. Both snoring (which may or may not be linked to obstructive sleep apnea) and sleep apnea increase as people get older (Bliwise et al., 1984). Reliable diagnosis of sleep apnea requires the person to spend a night in a sleep lab, where various parameters of sleep (e.g., eye movements, respiration, muscle tension) are monitored on a polygraph.

TREATMENT OF SLEEP DISORDERS

Over-the-counter medications and prescription drugs are taken by many older people with insomnia. The little bottle of sleeping pills is a familiar companion to the many medications that sit on the night table. The elderly are major consumers of sleep aids; more than 60 percent of users of prescription sleep drugs are over the age of fifty (Mellinger et al., 1985). Yet sleep drugs rapidly lose their effectiveness and with continuous use may even make sleep light and fragmented. REM rebound sleep, an increase in REM sleep after prolonged reliance on drugs, is fitful (Bootzin et al., 1996). Medications can even bring about what is called a drug-dependent insomnia. These so-called aids can also give people drug hangovers and increase respiratory difficulties, which in the elderly is a great hazard, given the increased prevalence of sleep apnea. Side effects of tranquilizers such as the benzodiazepines (e.g., Valium) include problems in learning new information—anterograde amnesia—and serious difficulties in thinking clearly the following day (Ghoneim & Mewaldt, 1990; Schatzberg, 1991).

There is now considerable evidence that sleep medication is not the appropriate treatment for the patient of any age with chronic insomnia, and particularly not for the elderly patient with insomnia. Nonetheless, sleep medications are prescribed for most nursing home residents, and in many instances they are administered daily even without evidence of a sleep disturbance (Bootzin et al., 1996; Cohen et al., 1983).

Jokes have been told for years about taking a little nip of alcohol to help get to sleep. As a central nervous system depressant, alcohol does induce relaxation and drowsiness in most people. But like nearly all other drugs, alcohol has negative effects on what is called the architecture of sleep, namely, the presence of certain stages of sleep, such as rapid eye movement (REM) sleep, which is associated with dreaming. Alcohol markedly reduces REM sleep, resulting in such problems as fatigue and difficulty thinking clearly the next day. Furthermore, since tolerance develops with alcohol use, the person drinks more in an effort to obtain the same effect. People with sleep disturbances, including older adults, sometimes mix alcohol with sedatives or tranquilizers. These combinations—which we have seen can lead to unintended death—can be particularly dangerous for older adults because of their greater sensitivity to biochemicals. Finally, alcohol exacerbates sleep apnea.

Intervention for sleep apnea usually entails the person's wearing a nasal mask attached to a device that increases airflow, thereby relieving the obstruction at the back of the throat. This treatment is generally quite effective and also virtually eliminates loud snoring, a bonus that can improve interpersonal relations between the patient and his or her bed partner! Surgery is sometimes used to widen the airways at the back of the throat, but evidence for its effectiveness is less certain than for the airflow treatment (Bootzin et al., 1996).

Nonpharmacological treatment of sleep disorders in elderly adults has not been investigated much, perhaps because researchers have assumed that the normal age-related changes in sleep patterns noted earlier preclude effective intervention (Bootzin & Engle-Friedman, 1987). Nonetheless, improvement is possible (Bootzin et al., 1996). Explaining the nature of sleep and the changes that take place as a normal part of the aging process can reduce the worry that older persons have about their sleep patterns, concern that itself can interfere with sleep. The therapist can also reassure patients that going without sleep from time to time is not a calamity; it will not cause irreversible brain damage or insanity, as some people fear. Worrying less about sleeping usually helps one sleep. As with people of any age, attending to any psychopathogical condition underlying the sleep disturbance, such as anxiety or depression, can lead to improvement in sleep.

Some individuals are given relaxation training to help them fall asleep and instructions to help them develop good sleep habits—rising at the same time every day; avoiding activities at bedtime that are inconsistent with falling asleep; and lying down only when sleepy, and, if unable to go to sleep, getting up and going into another room. Regular exercise can also help (Stevenson & Topp, 1990). All these tactics can loosen the grip of insomnia on adults of all ages (Bootzin et al., 1996; Morin & Azrin, 1988).

SUICIDE

Several factors put people in general at especially high risk for suicide: serious physical illness, feelings of hopelessness, social isolation, loss of loved ones, dire financial circumstances, and depression (see Chapter 10). Because these problems are widespread among the elderly, it should not be surprising that suicide rates for people over age sixty-five are high, perhaps three times greater than the rate for younger individuals (McIntosh, 1995).

However, an examination of cross-sectional data indicates that the relationship between suicide rates and age is not as straightforward as it appears initially. The suicide rate for males rises from youth and increases in a linear fashion with age (Atchley, 1982). Older white men are more likely to commit suicide than are members of any other group; the peak ages for committing suicide are from eighty to eighty-four (Conwell, 1994). The rate for white women peaks before they reach the age of fifty and declines steadily thereafter, perhaps because they tend to find it easier to adjust to life without a spouse than do men (recall Focus 16.1, p. 452). Thus rates of suicide in white men increase sharply during old age, and rates for white women decline somewhat. Throughout the life span, men have higher suicide rates than women, but the difference is most notable in the old-old, with men over age eighty having the highest rates of any group (McIntosh et al., 1994). Marked increases have also recently been noted among nonwhite men (Manton, Blazer, & Woodbury, 1987). As more and more people survive longer, the number of suicides in people over age sixty-five could double over the next forty years (Blazer, Bachar, & Manton, 1986).

Older persons communicate their intentions to commit suicide less often than do the young and make fewer attempts. When they do make an attempt they are more often successful (McIntosh et al., 1994). Suicide attempts by people younger than thirty-five fail more often than they succeed, but those of people over age fifty are more likely to be lethal. Once people are past age sixty-five their attempts rarely fail (Butler & Lewis, 1982). Furthermore, the statistics are probably underestimates; older adults have many opportunities to give up on themselves by neglecting their diet or medications, thus killing themselves in a more passive fashion.

Butler and Lewis (1982) argued that the suicide of older adults may more often be a rational or philosophical decision than is that of younger people. Consider, for example, the elderly person who faces the intractable pain of a terminal illness and knows that with each passing day the cost of medical care is using up more and more of the money that might otherwise be left to his or her family. Recall also our earlier discussions of how some older people with Alzheimer's and other debilitating diseases have arranged to take their own lives. The issue of physician-assisted suicide (p. 259) is likely to focus increasing attention on suicide among elders.

Intervention to prevent the suicide of an older person is similar to that discussed in Chapter 10. In general, the therapist tries to persuade the person to regard his or her problems in less desperate terms. Mental health professionals, who are usually younger and healthier, may unwittingly try less hard to prevent an older person's suicide attempt. But even an older person, once the crisis has passed, is usually grateful to have another chance at life.

SEXUALITY AND AGING

People tend to expect both men and women to lose interest in and capacity for sex once they reach their senior years. Some believe that old people are unable to enjoy anything more passionate than an affectionate hug and a kiss on the cheek. In contrast to the strong sexual value placed on them when young, older women are no longer considered especially sexual (Steuer, 1982). Furthermore, their capacity for sexual arousal is often confused with their postmenopausal inability to procreate.

In contrast to such beliefs, most older people have considerable sexual interest and capacity (Deacon, Minichiello, & Plummer, 1995; Hodson & Skeen, 1994). This holds true even for many healthy eighty- to one-hundred-year-old individuals, among whom the preferred activities tend to be caressing and masturbation, with some occasions of sexual intercourse

Contrary to the stereotypes, many older people maintain an active interest in sex. Studies indicate that the frequency of sexual activity among those in their 70s is as high as among middle-aged people.

(Bretschneider & McCoy, 1988). As we review the data, it is important to bear in mind that sexual interest and activity vary greatly in younger adults; disinterest or infrequent sex on the part of an older person should not be taken as evidence that older people are inherently asexual. The sixty-eight-year-old man who has no sex life may well have had little if any interest at age twenty-eight. Whether the person is twenty-eight or sixty-eight, one of the best predictors of continued sexual activity is past sexual enjoyment and frequency (Antonovsky, Sadowsky, & Maoz, 1990).

Early studies of the frequencies of sexual activity, such as the famous Kinsey reports (Kinsey, Pomeroy, & Martin, 1948; Kinsey et al., 1953) and the Duke Longitudinal Studies (George & Weiler, 1980; Pfeiffer, Verwoerdt, & Wang, 1968, 1969), noted a decline in heterosexual activity, masturbation, and homosexual intercourse beginning around age thirty and continuing across the life span. The belief that sex necessarily becomes less important to people in their middle years and in old age was not substantiated by later research, however. The second Duke study (George & Weiler, 1980), which covered the years 1968 through 1974, indicated no decline in the sexual activity of people between ages forty-six and seventy-one, and it further indicated that 15 percent of older persons increased their sexual activity as they aged. Other studies have shown that about half those between the ages of sixty and seventy-one have regular and frequent intercourse (Comfort, 1980; Turner & Adams, 1988). A later study of cognitively unimpaired men living in nursing homes confirmed high levels of sexual interest and when partners were available, sexual intercourse and other forms of sexual activity (Mulligan & Palguta, 1991).

These facts can be interpreted in several ways. Clearly older people can be sexually active; even the earlier surveys indicated that. But it is noteworthy that the second Duke study did not reveal the decline of the first. The older people surveyed in the second study may have had to contend with less negative stereotyping and they may have been healthier—both cohort effects. They may also have been more willing to discuss their sexual interests and activities with researchers because the cultural atmosphere had become more supportive—a time-of-measurement effect. Historical factors and sexual attitudes in society at large may affect sexuality among older adults. In one study seventy- and eighty-year-olds reported rates of intercourse similar to those that Kinsey found in forty-year-olds in the 1940s and 1950s (Starr & Weiner, 1981). Perhaps the amount of sexual activity in the elderly will continue to rise as today's young grow older, which would be a cohort effect.

PHYSIOLOGICAL CHANGES IN SEXUAL RESPONSE WITH AGING

Among the volunteer subjects studied by Masters and Johnson (1966) were a number of older adults. We know a great deal about heterosexual sexuality in older adults both from their physiological research and from later work (Comfort, 1984; O'Donohue; 1987; Segraves & Segraves, 1995; Weg, 1983). What is true of both sexes is that there are wide individual differences in sexual capacity and behavior among older adults, as indeed is the case for other areas in the lives of seniors. Some of the differences between older and younger adults are discussed next.

MEN Older men take longer to have an erection, even when they are being stimulated in a way they like. They can maintain an erection longer before ejaculating than younger men, however, and the feeling that ejaculation is inevitable may disappear. It is not known whether physiological changes or control learned over the years explains this. During the orgasm phase contractions are less intense and fewer in number, and less seminal fluid is expelled under less pressure. Once orgasm has occurred, erection is lost more rapidly in older men, and the capacity for another erection cannot be regained as quickly as in younger men. The refractory period actually begins to lengthen in men in their twenties (Rosen & Hall, 1984).

Older men are capable of the same pattern of sexual activity as younger men, the major difference being that things take longer to happen, and when they do, there is less urgency. How men and their partners view normal, age-related physiological changes may contribute to sexual dysfunction. If, for example, a man or his partner reacts with alarm to a slow buildup of sexual arousal, the stage is set for performance fears, a principal reason for sexual dysfunction (p. 388). Changes that occur with aging are often misinterpreted as evidence that older men are becoming impotent (LoPiccolo, 1991; Sbrocco, Weisberg, & Barlow, 1995). Yet older men do not lose their capacity for erection and ejaculation unless physical or emotional illness interferes (Badeau, 1995; Kaiser et al., 1988).

WOMEN A number of age-related differences have been found in older women, but again none of them justifies the conclusion that older women are incapable of a satisfactory sex life (Morokoff, 1988; Sherwin, 1991). Like younger women, older women are capable of at least as much sexual activity as are men. Some women become orgasmic for the first time in their lives at age eighty. Older women need more time to become sexually aroused, which may dovetail nicely with the slowdown in men's arousal patterns. Vaginal lubrication is slower and reduced because estrogen levels are lower, and there may be vaginal itching and burning. Hormone replacement therapy can reduce many of these symptoms. Vaginal contractions during orgasm are fewer in number compared with those of younger women. Spastic contractions of the vagina and uterus, rather than the rhythmic ones of orgasm in younger women, can cause discomfort and even pain in the lower abdomen and legs. Estrogen deficiency, which can be corrected, can change skin sensitivity such that caressing the breast and having a penis inside the vagina may not feel as pleasurable as it did when the woman was younger (Morokoff, 1988). Older women return more quickly to a less-aroused state. There is some evidence that these physical changes are not as extensive in women who have been sexually stimulated on a regular basis once or twice a week throughout their sexual lives.

AGE-RELATED PROBLEMS

Physical illness can interfere with sex in older people as it can in younger people. Because elderly people have more chronic ailments, however, the potential for interference from illness and medications is greater (Badeau, 1995; Mulligan et al., 1988), especially for men, as any disease that disrupts male hormone balance, the nerve pathways to the pelvic area, or blood supply to the penis can prevent erection. Diabetes is one such disease; it affects men and women similarly in terms of nerve damage and reduction of blood supply to the genitalia, but older women seem to complain less than do older men about its negative effects on their sexuality. It may be that the current cohorts of older women, raised at a time when female sexuality was downplayed and even denigrated, suffer as much from diabetes-related reduction in vaginal lubrication as men do from erectile difficulties, but they do not tell their partners and physicians and may use a lubricant to reduce vaginal pain during intercourse (LoPiccolo, 1991).

Tranquilizers and antihypertensive drugs can bring about sexual dysfunction, as can fatigue and excessive drinking and eating (Segraves & Segraves, 1995). Older adults are sometimes challenged as well by having to adjust to disease-related changes in their bodies, such as alterations in the genitalia from treatment of urological cancer (Anderson & Wolf, 1986).

Fears of resuming sexual activities after a heart attack or coronary bypass surgery have inhibited older adults and their lovers, but for most of them the fears are exaggerated (Friedman, 1978); heart rate, for example, is frequently higher during such activities as climbing stairs than it is during intercourse. Physicians often fail to provide accurate information to these patients. The situation for patients with congestive heart failure, in which the heart is unable to maintain an adequate circulation of blood in the tissues of the body or to pump out venous blood returned by the venous circulation, does create for some a risk in intercourse, but less strenuous sexual activity is usually not a problem (Kaiser et al., 1988).

Although women experience fewer physical problems than men, they are subject to many myths about aging women's sexuality (Deacon et al., 1995; Gatz, Pearson, & Fuentes, 1984). Also, a heterosexual woman's sexual activity typically centers on having a partner and on whether he is well (Caven, 1973). Thus older women are less sexually active than are older men, perhaps because they lack a partner or because if they are married, their husbands tend to be older and to have significant health problems. Women live longer than men and therefore are more likely to have lost a spouse. Divorced or widowed men tend to remarry women younger than they, sometimes considerably so; elderly widowers have a remarriage rate seven times that of elderly widows (U.S. Bureau of the Census, 1986).

TREATMENT OF SEXUAL DYSFUNCTION

Making the facts of sexuality in old age available to the general public and to the professionals who look after their medical and mental health needs is likely to benefit many older people (Hodson & Skeen, 1994). As with younger adults, a degree of permission giving is useful—it is okay to have sex and to enjoy it when you are past age sixty-five—especially in light of widespread societal stereotypes of the asexuality of seniors. Physicians have been guilty of telling older patients to forget about sex or of not raising the issue when discussing the patient's adjustment, perhaps because of their own discomfort, lack of knowledge, or ageism (LoPiccolo, 1991). Clinicians need to bear in mind that the current cohort of people over age sixty-five was socialized into sexuality at a time when the open discussion of sex was in no way as prevalent as it has been since the 1960s. Nursing homes are often intolerant of sexuality among their residents; a married couple residing in the same nursing home may not be allowed to share a room (Ballard, 1995; Comfort, 1984; Deacon et al., 1995). The situation for homosexuals is even worse. The authors have witnessed nurses in geriatric wards caution residents against stimulating themselves in public but fail to provide them with privacy.

Some older people prefer not to be sexually active, but older adults who are experiencing and are troubled by sexual dysfunctions are likely to be good candidates for the type of sex therapy devised by Masters and Johnson (Berman & Lief, 1976) and Kaplan (1991). Providing these people with information about normal age-related changes in sexual functioning is particularly important. As today's older adults acquired their attitudes toward sex at a time when, for example, genital foreplay was not emphasized, and indeed was often discouraged, clinicians have to be tactful about asking an older patient to fondle his or her partner in order to provide the tactile stimulation older people often need to become aroused (LoPiccolo, 1991).

With older adults greater attention must be paid to physical condition than is usual with younger adults, including creative and open discussion of sexual techniques and positions that take into consideration physical limitations resulting from such illnesses as arthritis (Deacon et al., 1995; Zeiss, Zeiss, & Dornbrand, 1988).

This focus on sexuality should not blind us to the links between sexual satisfaction and the nonsexual aspects of a relationship between adults, especially if the people are married or in an otherwise committed relationship. As with younger adults, nonsexual distress in a couple can be both a cause and an effect of sexual problems. The situation can be particularly complex with older partners, who must deal with such transitions as retirement and illness. Many couples who have been together for decades encounter distress in their relationship for the first time in their senior years. One particularly daunting challenge arises when one of the partners is cast in the role of caregiver for the other, especially when the ill spouse has a deteriorative disorder such as Alzheimer's disease. Communication and problem-solving training of the kind discussed in Chapter 19 may be of value in such cases (p. 572) (Smyer et al., 1990).

TREATMENT AND CARE OF THE ELDERLY

Older adults often go to mental health centers or seek private psychotherapy through referrals. Yet older people are less likely than younger adults to be referred (Ginsburg & Goldstein, 1974; Knight, 1996; Kucharski, White, & Schratz, 1979). General practitioners, for example, usually fail to detect depression in older patients (Bowers et al., 1990). This situation may be due in part to inadequate geriatric training for medical professionals. The reimbursement system used by many health care providers may pose some problems as well, for it is biased toward inpatient care and pays less for outpatient therapy, especially for mental health services.

Clinicians tend to expect to treat elderly patients less successfully than they treat young patients (Knight, 1996; Settin, 1982). In one study, older patients were rated by therapists as having more severe psychopathology, less motivation for treatment, a poorer prognosis, and less insight than younger patients (Karasu, Stein, & Charles, 1979). Yet, research does not show that psychotherapy is less successful for elderly patients (Gallagher-Thompson & Thompson, 1995a, 1995b; Knight, 1996; Knight, Kelly, & Gatz, 1992; Scogin & McElreath, 1994). If elderly patients are viewed as having limited possibilities for improvement, they may not be treated. On the other hand, a therapist may lack the knowledge necessary to give good treatment to older people, which would keep them from improving.

There is an irony in questioning whether psychotherapy is appropriate for older adults. With increasing years come increasing reflectiveness and a tendency to be philosophical about life (Neugarten, 1977). Running counter to earlier pessimism about the capacity for older people to change, both of these traits augur well for the suitability of older adults for psychotherapeutic interventions, and, indeed, this suitability is borne out by data already reviewed as well as data described later.

Admissions of older adults to state and county mental hospitals and to psychiatric wards of city hospitals have substantially decreased in recent years. Most older people needing mental health treatment now live in nursing homes or receive community-based care.

NURSING HOMES

The prevalent myth regarding nursing homes is that families dump their older relatives into these institutions at the first sign of frailty. However, families usually explore all their alternatives and exhaust their own resources before they institutionalize an older relative. Thus the decision to institutionalize comes as a last resort, not as a first choice. Institutionalization can sometimes have a negative impact on family relations, for there can be heated disagreement, anger, and feelings of guilt arising from discussions of whether to place the parent in a nursing home. One study, however, found that for a large number of families, moving the parent to a nursing home strengthened family ties and brought a renewed closeness between the parent and the child who was the primary caregiver. The care provided by the nursing home alleviated the strain and pressure caused by the multiple physical or mental problems of the parent. In only about 10 percent of the families were relations worsened by the move (Smith & Bengston, 1979).

Nursing homes are now the major locus for institutional care for the elderly with severe chronic illnesses and mental disorders (Gatz & Smyer, 1992; Horgas, Wahl, & Baltes, 1996). Given projected future needs, it does not appear that enough people are being trained to provide mental health services within these nursing homes.[2] This is a matter of concern, particularly since a minority of the nation's approximately 15,000 nursing homes offer counseling as a routine service, and the great majority of patients have diagnosed mental disorders (including dementia) (National Center for Health Statistics, 1989; Rovner et al., 1986). Worse still, recent nursing home reforms aim to exclude from such settings older adults with mental disorders, a step that is likely to place further strains on state and private psychiatric hospitals as well as on general hospitals with psychiatric units (Gatz & Smyer, 1992; Smyer & Gatz, 1995), and it is unlikely that care in these settings will be any better.

---

[2]Especially in large urban centers, nursing homes often have nonprofessional staff who do not speak English and who take care of residents who speak only English. A related problem is the non-English-speaking resident who is dependent for care on staff who do not speak his or her language.

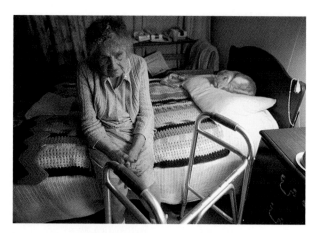

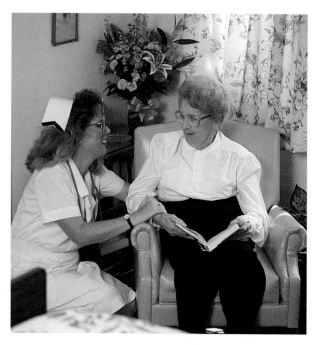

Nursing homes play a major role in the institutional care of the aged, providing for people with a variety of physical and psychological needs. They have often been severely criticized for the poor care they provide. While conditions and care can differ widely across different homes, advances in knowledge about the processes of aging have aided many homes in better meeting the needs of all their residents.

Even a good nursing home—and not all of them are run well—may have unintended negative consequences on some residents. This caution is based on a classic study by Blenker (1967). Elderly people who went to a family service center were *randomly* assigned to one of three treatments: intensive, intermediate, and minimal. Intensive treatment involved the services of a nurse and a social worker; intermediate treatment involved somewhat less professional attention; minimal treatment consisted of information and referral to community-based services. One might expect intensive treatment to have been the most effective, but after half a year the death rate of members of the intensive-care group was four times that of people in the minimal-care group! The intermediate-care group was better off than the intensive-care group; the death rate of its members was "only" twice that of the minimal-care group. What happened? It turned out that the major factor was being placed in an institution such as a nursing home. A person was much more likely to be institutionalized if a nurse and social worker were intensively involved in planning his or her care, and the excessive death rates were found in institutionalized patients. Since people had been assigned randomly to the three treatments, it is unlikely that the death rates were related to differences existing before treatment began.

What is it about nursing homes that contributes to such decline? First, relocation to a new setting is in itself stressful and is believed to play a role in increased mortality (Schulz & Brenner, 1977). Once in the nursing home, the extent and nature of care discourage rehabilitation and even maintenance of

whatever self-care skills and autonomous activities the resident may be capable of. For example, a resident able to feed himself or herself, but slowly and with occasional spills, will be assisted, or even fed like a child at mealtimes to shorten the time devoted to serving meals and minimize messes on the floor and stains on the patient's clothing. The resident then no longer thinks of himself or herself as able to eat without help, which is likely to lead to still more loss of function and lowered morale. Muscles weaken and deteriorate through disuse (DeVries, 1975). Relatives, anxious to know that they have made the right decision and that their loved one is being well cared for, are pleased by the tidiness and orderliness that are the result of excessive staff involvement in all details of living.

We know that depression is found in some older people, especially those in nursing homes. The type of intervention employed is usually a drug, and the psychoactive drug prescribed is more likely to be a tranquilizer than an antidepressant; a less agitated, relatively inactive patient is easier to handle. Psychological interventions are virtually unheard of, for the staff either is untrained in their implementation or operates under the widely held assumption that such therapy is inappropriate for an old person (Zarit, 1980).

In sum, all the problems of institutionalization are in bold and exaggerated relief in nursing homes. Independence is inadvertently, but with sad consequences, discouraged, and both physical and mental deterioration, because they are expected, occur (see Focus 16.3).

FOCUS 16.3 LOSS OF CONTROL AND MINDLESSNESS IN NURSING HOMES

Is the loss of control over his or her own life that results when a person comes to reside in a nursing home actually damaging to the person's physical and mental health? Ellen Langer and Judith Rodin believe that it is. Since we know that a perceived or actual lack of control leads to deterioration in adaptive behavior, at least some of what we regard as senility—the inactivity of elderly people and their poor adjustment to changing circumstances—may be caused by loss of control rather than by progressive brain disease (Langer, 1981). Residents of nursing homes, even if they are able to do so, are not permitted to cook, do their laundry, buy groceries, or tend the yard. This diminution in a sense of self-efficacy and control appears to have especially negative effects in the elderly (Langer & Rodin, 1976b; Rodin, 1986).

In our eagerness to help older people we end up preventing them from making decisions that they are most likely able to make. In our concern to protect them from physical harm we arrange environments that require little effort to control, reducing their opportunities to operate independently. And for most occupations we set ages for compulsory retirement, overlooking the large individual differences of old people. These practices, especially in a society that values competence and activity, do much to destroy an elderly person's belief that he or she is still worthwhile.

Langer and Rodin's research indicates that giving elderly nursing home residents control and responsibility can improve their health. In one study, patients were assigned a particular fifteen-minute period during which the nurse would be on call specifically for them, thus increasing each individual's control over his or her own caretaking. The health of these patients improved more than that of the control group, and they were more sociable (Rodin, 1980).

In another study Langer and Rodin (1976a) told one group of residents that they would be given a variety of decisions to make, instead of the staff's making decisions for them; they were also given plants to take care of. A control group was told how eager the staff was to take care of them; the plants they were given would be looked after by the staff. Although initially matched on variables such as health, these two groups of elderly residents differed three weeks later on several measures of alertness, happiness, and general well-being. Members of the group given enhanced responsibility—and presumably a sense of greater control—tested superior on these measures. Even more impressive was the finding eighteen months later that only half as many of the experimental group as of the control group had died, seven of forty-seven, compared with thirteen of forty-four. Moreover, the group given responsibilities continued to show better psychological and physical health (Rodin & Langer, 1977). In a subsequent study Rodin (1983) found that nursing home residents who were taught coping skills manifested lower stress in self-reports, on

physiological measures, and on physicians' judgments of health. Rodin's presumption is that the skills training enhanced both their perceived and their actual control over problems that commonly arise in nursing homes. Other research has generally shown that people who feel in greater control actually do more things that enhance their health, such as complying with medical regimens, losing weight, and engaging in other self-care behaviors (Rodin, 1986).

Increased control is not positive under all circumstances and for all individuals, however, as Rodin concluded after a review of work in diverse areas on control (Rodin, 1986). With increased control comes more responsibility, and some people may convert this into self-blame when such an internal attribution is not warranted, for example, in the case of a dementing illness caused by factors beyond the patient's control. And if the actual environment is not supportive of increased efforts to exert control and assume responsibility, people are likely to feel worse. For example, if nursing home staff discourage independence, a patient's efforts to become less dependent on staff might lead to arguments rather than to encouragement. With this caveat in mind, Rodin concludes that health professionals as well as family members should look for ways to enhance control in older adults, including those in institutional settings such as nursing homes.

Not only may our treatment of old people engender in them a sense of powerlessness, but their repetitious, unchallenging environments—especially the surroundings of those who are hospital patients or live in nursing homes—may encourage a mode of cognitive functioning that Langer terms *mindlessness* (Langer, 1989). Mindlessness is a kind of automatic information processing studied by cognitive psychologists, a mode of thinking that is adaptive when people are in situations that recur frequently, for example, remembering a familiar sequence such as tying one's shoes. Attending to such overlearned activities—making the information processing conscious, not mindless—can actually *interfere* with performance; but when a situation is novel and requires our attention, we want to operate *mindfully*.

What are the clinical implications of too much mindlessness, this mode of mental functioning that entails little cognitive effort? Elderly patients may be afforded too few opportunities to be thoughtful and to maintain an alert state of mind. Because of the restricted mobility of nursing home residents and hospital patients and because little is demanded of them, their experiences tend to be repetitious and boring. The Langer and Rodin nursing home research may well demonstrate that conscious *thinking* as well as perceived control are essential in maintaining emotional and physical well-being. Lack of control and mindlessness are probably related, for what is there really to think about when people believe that they have lost control over the events in their lives?

COMMUNITY-BASED CARE

At any given time 95 percent of elderly persons reside in the community. Traditional individual, family, and marital counseling, pet therapy,[3] and peer counseling have all been shown effective to some degree in relieving depression, anxiety, and loneliness; most of these therapies are described elsewhere.

The frail elderly also have an urgent need for help with their daily living arrangements. Some communities are organized to provide telephone reassurance, daily phone calls to old persons living alone to check that they are all right; home services, such as Meals on Wheels, which bring a hot meal each day to the person's door, visits from volunteers who cook meals and do household chores, shopping help from young people, and light repair work by volunteers; a community center for older people, which may also serve a hot lunch and provide help with state and federal forms; sheltered housing, apartments in which several old people may live together semi-independently; home visits by health professionals and social workers, who can assess the actual needs of old people and treat them; and regular social visits from community neighbors. A range of available services allows a true match with the needs of the older person so that he or she will not have too much or too little help. Some research indicates that such community psychology projects can enhance the quality of life of elderly people and reduce their dependency on institutional care (e.g., Knight, 1983; Nocks et al., 1986). However, current incentives provided in insurance coverage encourage more expensive inpatient care or refraining from seeking mental health services altogether (Gatz & Smyer, 1992).

Mere availability of services is not enough. Services must be coordinated, and they are not in most localities. All too often an older person and his or her family are shuffled from one agency to another, getting lost in Kafkaesque bureaucracies. Even professionals who have experience with the system often have difficulty working through it to get needed services for their clients. Frustrating rules can interfere with the very goals for which programs were instituted. In California, for example, Medicare does not always pay for rehabilitation services, such as physical therapy after a broken hip has healed. As a consequence, many older people do not regain as much function as they might; thus they may suffer additional physical and emotional deterioration, exacerbations that require more expensive services.

One of the main difficulties when it comes to health care for the elderly is that the chronic health problems of old people are not appealing to physicians because they seldom diminish. Many, if not most, of the maladies of old people—such as hearing loss, visual impairments, loss of mobility, aches and pains, especially in the feet (Pearson & Gatz, 1982), and a steadily declining cardiovascular system—are unlikely to get better and must somehow be adjusted to. Elderly persons rely heavily on their relationships with health care providers, but these providers may become impatient with them

---

[3]Pet therapy builds on age-old observations that people who have pets to care for benefit from the companionship of their animals. The dependence of a domesticated animal on a human being can help the person physically and emotionally, by keeping him or her active and feeling useful. A pet's acceptance is more nearly unconditional than that given by people. Sheer physical contact with an animal is also beneficial. We do not argue that older adults, or anyone else, are better off taking care of household pets than having human companions. But the responsibility and pleasure of taking care of a cat, dog, or bird enhances simple daily living, fosters healthful thoughts and actions (Brickel, 1984), and improves the morale of those living alone (Goldmeier, 1988).

Among community-based services are day care centers where the aged participate in various activities such as exercise classes.

because, as Zarit (1980) suggested, the illnesses of older people are often incurable and therefore violate a "law" that most of the medical profession lives by. Furthermore, older people do not always take medication as instructed, and even when they do, adverse drug reactions are not uncommon (Leach & Roy, 1986). Relations with family members who must look after them are likely to suffer. Ailing elderly patients are sometimes torn both by feelings of guilt for needing so much from others and by anger toward these younger people whom they have spent so many years looking after and sacrificing for. The sons and daughters also have feelings of guilt and anger (Zarit, 1980). Focus 16.4 describes the kind of interdisciplinary team effort that can serve the needs of older adults.

Being able to use a computer and access the Internet is one way the elderly can now increase their social contacts.

ISSUES SPECIFIC TO THERAPY WITH OLDER ADULTS

As mentioned throughout this chapter, discussing a group of people who have only chronological age in common runs the risk of overlooking important differences in their backgrounds, developmental histories, and personalities (Smyer, Zarit, & Qualls, 1990). Although adults over age sixty-five do share physical and psychological characteristics that make them different from younger adults, they are nonetheless *individuals*, each of whom has lived a long time and experienced unique joys and sorrows. In spite of this uniqueness, there are a few general issues important to consider in the conduct of therapy with older people. They can be divided into issues of content and issues of process (Zarit, 1980).

CONTENT OF THERAPY WITH OLDER ADULTS

The incidence of brain disorders increases with age, but as we have seen, other mental health problems of older adults are not that different from those experienced earlier in life. Although clinicians appreciate how physical incapacities and medications may intensify psychological problems, consistency and continuity from earlier decades of the older person's life are also to be noted.

The emotional distress of older adults may be a realistic reaction to problems in living. Medical illnesses can create irreversible difficulties in walking, seeing, and hearing. Finances may be a problem. Therapists treating psychological distress in the elderly must bear in mind that much of it is an understandable response to real-life challenges rather than a sign of psychopathology. Professional intervention, however, may still be helpful.

Therapy with elderly persons must take into account the social contexts in which they live, which cannot be done merely by reading in the professional literature. The therapist who, for example, urges a lonely widower to seek companionship in a neighborhood senior recreation center may be misguided if the nature of that center does not suit the particular patient (Knight, 1996); such an experience may make the patient feel even lonelier. All social organizations, even those as loosely structured as a senior center, develop their own local mores and practices, or what social scientists have come to call social ecology. Some may be tolerant of physical frailty, others not. Some may be frequented primarily by elders who used to be well-paid professionals, others may have primarily former state mental hospital patients as regulars. Mental health care workers need to know and understand the social environments in which their older patients live. We take this need for granted when dealing with younger patients but, Knight points out, often neglect to consider it with older adults.

Elderly patients often have a different set of social needs from those of younger people as well. Widespread concern that old people are socially isolated and that they need to be encouraged to interact more with others, as perhaps they did when younger, appears to be ill founded. There is no relationship between level of social activity and psychological well-being among the elderly (Carstensen, 1996). As we age, our interests shift away from new social interactions to cultivating those few social relationships that really matter to us, such as spending time with family and with

FOCUS 16.4 INTERDISCIPLINARY TEAMWORK IN GERIATRIC HEALTH CARE

The health problems of older adults—including those involving their psychological functioning—are often more complex and longer standing (chronic) than those of younger adults and of children (Birren & Schaie, 1996). Thus the guiding principle that organizes the thinking and the work of gerontological practitioners is *interdisciplinary* (Zeiss & Steffen, 1996). Although we have sounded this theme before (see especially our discussion of the broad-spectrum treatment of schizophrenia, p. 290), there is a particular need for professionals from several disciplines to work collaboratively in helping older adults deal with psychological difficulties. The Venn diagram in Figure 16.1 graphically illustrates interdisciplinary roles in a hospital-based home-care team devoted to serving geriatric patients who are being discharged to live at home with a caregiver (Zeiss & Steffen, 1996).

What this diagram portrays is a complex set of disciplinary responsibilities and resources that operate both separately (the nonoverlapping areas of the Venn diagram) and collaboratively (the overlapping areas) so that the respective expertise of the several groups of professionals can be brought to bear in a fruitful way to assess, plan, and intervene on behalf of a particular patient. For example, although the medical doctor serves as the primary care physician, the cognitive screening (how well the patient remembers and thinks about things) can be done by the physician, by the psychologist, or both.

It is no easy matter to assemble or participate in such an interdisciplinary team, for the ethos in graduate training in all these health-related disciplines is still discipline centered, even when the subject matter is not. In the Venn diagram, while overlapping areas indicate domains of collaboration, they also show where turf battles can erupt. The care of older adults constitutes an arena in which these tensions are being put aside for the ultimate benefit of the consumer. (There are other examples, of course. In Chapter 8, we discussed how psychologists collaborate with physicians in the new field called behavioral medicine.)

Not all geriatric problems require such an approach, but as Zeiss and Steffen (1996) argue, even a seemingly straightforward health problem in an older adult can benefit from an interdisciplinary approach. They give an example of an eighty-year-old woman with bronchitis. Can she be adequately treated by a physician alone? Maybe not.

It may be essential to know that she is a caregiver for a demented husband, what other medications she is taking, what her immune status is, and other issues pertinent to her physical and emotional well-being. Social work, pharmacy, psychology, psychiatry, or other team members may be essential in planning not only acute treatment for her bronchitis but also backup care for her demented husband. (p. 430)

It may seem that coordinating the efforts of all these professionals represents an unnecessary expense, but consider what would happen if medication were prescribed for the woman but then not taken by her because its side effects interfered with her ability to care for her infirm husband. Such noncompliance—a serious problem with *all* medications across all ages—would result in a failed medical intervention and possibly a *worsening* of the patient's medical condition, and this could result in even more expensive intervention down the line, including hospitalization and its associated risks. And while in the hospital, the care of the husband would become an acute and salient problem. Many other complicated and problematic scenarios are possible.

Interdisciplinary teams are committed to the idea that patients will be best served when their care is coordinated and provided by team members who learn from each other, rely on each other, and are willing to challenge each other when appropriate. Interdisciplinary teams require the wise and creative integration of diverse viewpoints and function best when team members value diversity, remain cohesive when viewpoints conflict, and negotiate agreement to which all team members are committed (Zeiss & Steffen, 1996, p. 450).

---

close friends and associates. What some therapists see as psychologically harmful social withdrawal is really social *selectivity*. Having less time ahead of us we tend to place a higher value on emotional intimacy than on learning more about the world. This preference applies not just to older people but to younger people who see themselves as having limited time, such as when they are preparing to move far away from those to whom they feel closest (Frederickson & Carstensen, 1990) or if they have AIDS. When we can't see a future without end, we prefer to interact less with casual acquaintances—like those one might meet in a recreation center for older adults—and to be more selective about with whom we spend our limited time.

Women may suffer doubly as psychotherapy patients, as not only ageist but also sexist attitudes can negatively influence the direction of psychotherapy (Steuer, 1982). For example, stress in an older couple can increase when the husband retires. A common therapeutic goal is to help the woman accommodate to the husband's loss of status and

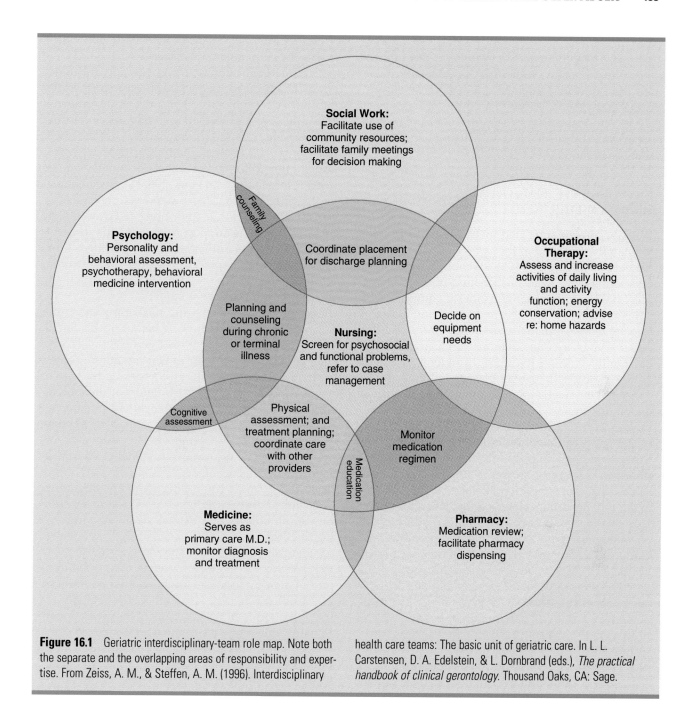

Figure 16.1 Geriatric interdisciplinary-team role map. Note both the separate and the overlapping areas of responsibility and expertise. From Zeiss, A. M., & Steffen, A. M. (1996). Interdisciplinary health care teams: The basic unit of geriatric care. In L. L. Carstensen, D. A. Edelstein, & L. Dornbrand (eds.), *The practical handbook of clinical gerontology*. Thousand Oaks, CA: Sage.

learn to spend more time with him each day rather than to help the husband make accommodations.

The expectations and values that present-day cohorts of older adults place on marriage can be quite different from those of people in their fifties and younger. Most readers of this book probably expect a marriage to provide happiness and personal fulfillment. This expectation cannot be readily assumed for people who are currently in their seventies and older (Knight, 1996). When a therapist comes to believe that some of an older patient's clin-ical problems are due to a distressed marriage, he or she has to consider the patient's viewpoint.

Death and dying figure prominently in therapy with older patients. They may need help dealing with the fear of facing death or a debilitating illness that requires life support. Older clients may be counseled to examine their lives from a philosophical or a religious perspective. Leo Tolstoy was but one of many people who become increasingly religious as they grow old. Philosophical and religious perspectives can help the client transcend the limitations that aging imposes on human existence. When the person is dying, discussions of the meaning of the individual's life can facilitate self-disclosure and enhance his or her sense of well-being and personal growth (see the discussion of life review that follows). The loved ones, who will experience the inevitable loss, will also benefit from such discussions.

PROCESS OF THERAPY WITH OLDER ADULTS

We have already indicated that traditional individual, family, and marital therapies are effective with the elderly (Gatz et al., 1985). Some clinicians make adaptations and focus on here-and-now problems. They hold that therapy with elderly patients needs to be more active and directive, providing information, taking the initiative in seeking out agencies for necessary services, and helping the client and his or her family through the maze of federal and local laws and offices that are in place to help them.

Some characteristics of aging, such as the tendency for certain kinds of thinking simply to take longer as well as some diminution in working memory—the number of things that can be held in mind at any one time—may mean that therapy will proceed differently (Knight, 1996; Light, 1990). Therapists may find that it helps to move with greater deliberation when seeing an older adult. Explanations may have to be more elaborate and conversation more extended. Therapists need to avoid the common tendency, when another person seems not to be following the thread of the conversation, to become nervous and speak faster or louder—this latter reaction can arise from the stereotyped notion that impaired hearing in the older person is causing the communication problem.

In a historical overview of psychotherapy with older adults, Knight, Kelly, and Gatz (1992) discuss life review, proposed by Butler (1963) as a psychotherapeutic approach uniquely suitable for older adults. This approach reflects the influence of Erik Erikson's (1950, 1968) life-span developmental theory, which postulated stages of conflict and growth extending well into the senior years (p. 35). Life review facilitates what appears to be a natural tendency of older adults to reflect on their lives and to try to make sense of what has happened to them. In Eriksonian terms, it helps the person address the conflict between ego integrity and despair. Methods include having the patient bring in old photographs, travel to a childhood home, and write an autobiography. As one might imagine, people can feel worse as well as better from this kind of therapy; it takes considerable skill on the part of the therapist to guide the patient to a positive view of life and to the coming end of existence.

Psychoanalytically oriented therapy for older adults has been studied in recent years, especially the shorter-term therapy that concentrates more on strengthening ego functions than on exploring childhood repressions through analysis of the transference (p. 498) (Kahana, 1987). A previously mentioned effort (p. 465) by Gallagher and Thompson (1982, 1983; Thompson et al., 1987) showed equivalent improvement in depressed older patients from cognitive, behavioral, and brief psychodynamic therapies, lending support to the idea that present-oriented dynamic intervention (described more fully in the next chapter) can be effective with older adults. Other research also provides promising results (Smyer et al., 1990).

The very process of being in therapy can foster dependency. Older adults, whether institutionalized or living at home with caregivers, often receive much more social reinforcement (attention, praise) for dependent behaviors, such as asking for help or being concerned about the opinion of their therapist, than for instances of independent functioning (Baltes, 1988). The growing specialization of behavioral gerontology (Nemeroff & Karoly, 1991) emphasizes helping seniors to enhance their self-esteem by focusing on specific, deceptively minor behaviors such as controlling their toileting better (Whitehead, Burgio, & Engel, 1985), increasing self-care and mobility (Burgio et al., 1986), and improving their telephone conversational skills as a way to enhance social contacts (Praderas & MacDonald, 1986). A very recent development, though hardly a formal therapy, involves teaching older adults computer skills so that they can access the Internet and make the kinds of social contacts that were inconceivable only a few years ago (Cody et al., 1997).

No matter what their theoretical orientation, all therapists must be able to interpret the facial expressions of their patients as an aid to understanding the meaning of what they are saying and otherwise to appreciate their phenomenological experience of the world. Research on emotional changes over the life span suggests real potential for error when a therapist younger than his or her patient is working with an older adult (Knight, 1996). Because of their more varied and more extensive life experiences, older people's emotions can be more complex and subtle than those of younger adults (Schulz, 1982). This sets the stage for the facial expressions of seniors to reflect several feelings at once, and it turns out that younger people commit more errors when trying to identify emotions in photographs of older adults than they do with people closer to them in age (Malatesta &

Izard, 1984). All this adds to the challenge of working therapeutically with older adults.

Another aspect of psychotherapy, regardless of theoretical orientation, that is highlighted by working with elders is reminiscent of the analytic concept of countertransference. Therapists, usually many years younger than these patients, can be troubled by the patients' problems, for these difficulties can touch on sensitive personal areas of their own, such as unresolved conflicts with their own parents, worries about their own aging process, and a reluctance to deal with issues of death and dying. As Knight et al. (1992) speculated, "the perception that therapy is different with older adults is now thought to be due more to the emotional impact on the therapists of working with the elderly than to actual differences in technique, process, or likelihood of success. … [Working with older adults] will challenge therapists intellectually and emotionally to reach a maturity beyond their years (pp. 540, 546)."

SUMMARY

Until recently the psychological problems of older people were neglected by mental health professionals. As the proportion of people who live beyond age sixty-five continues to grow, it will become ever more important to learn about the disorders suffered by some older people and the most effective means of preventing or ameliorating them. Although physical deterioration is an obvious aspect of growing old, it appears that some of the emotional distress to which old people are prone is psychologically produced.

Serious brain disorders affect a very small minority of older people, fewer than 10 percent. Two principal disorders have been distinguished, dementia and delirium. In dementia the person's intellectual functioning declines; memory, abstract thinking, and judgment deteriorate. If the dementia is progressive, as most are, the individual seems another person altogether and is in the end oblivious to his or her surroundings. A variety of diseases can cause this deterioration; the most important is Alzheimer's disease in which cortical cells waste away. In delirium there is sudden clouding of consciousness and other problems in thinking, feeling, and behaving—fragmented and undirected thought, incoherent speech, inability to sustain attention, hallucinations, illusions, disorientation, lethargy or hyperactivity, and mood swings. The condition is reversible, provided that the underlying cause is self-limiting or adequately treated. Brain cells malfunction but are not necessarily destroyed. Causes include overmedication, infection of brain tissue, high fevers, malnutrition, dehydration, endocrine disorders, head trauma, and cerebrovascular problems.

The treatments of these two disorders are quite different from each other. If delirium is suspected, there should be a search for the cause, for example, nutritional deficiencies or a toxic reaction to medication so that is can be rectified. Progressive dementia usually cannot be treated, but the person and the family affected by the disease can be counseled on how to make the remaining time tolerable and even rewarding. If adequate support is given to caregivers, many dementia patients can be looked after at home. There usually comes a time, however, when the burden of care impels most families to place the person in a nursing home or hospital.

Older people suffer from the entire spectrum of psychological disorders, in many instances brought with them from their earlier years. Yet it appears that, overall, the prevalence of depression and anxiety is lower among older adults than among those younger than sixty-five. The newer cognitive behavior therapies as well as various psychodynamic therapies are being applied to depression in elderly patients, and results so far are encouraging.

Although not as widespread as depression, paranoia is a problem for older people and for those who have a relationship with them. In contrast to the persecutors often found in younger paranoid patients (distant agencies such as the FBI and aliens from outer space), those of older individuals usually live closer to home (the neighbor who opens the person's mail, the ungrateful child who is conniving to steal his or her elderly parent's money, the physician who prescribes drugs that pollute the mind). Paranoia is sometimes brought on by brain damage in dementia, but it can be caused by psychological factors. Paranoia may be a reaction to hearing difficulties—If I cannot hear what they are saying (especially if I do not acknowledge my hearing problem) perhaps it is because they are whispering nasty things about me. Isolation can be a factor as well; when a person has little social intercourse, it is difficult to verify impressions and suspicions, setting the stage for the development of delusions. Other psychological disorders experienced in old age include rare cases of schizophrenia (sometimes called paraphrenia); hypochondriasis; substance abuse, in particular the misuse of medication; and sleep disorders. All are treatable.

More of the suicide attempts of old people result in death than do those of younger people. Mental health professionals, most of them younger than age sixty-five, may assume that people who are old and debilitated have nothing to live for. This attitude may reflect their own fear of growing old.

Considerable mythology has surrounded sexuality and aging, the principal assumption being that at the age of sixty-five sex becomes improper, unsatisfying, and even impossible. Evidence indicates otherwise. Barring serious physical disability, older people, even well into their eighties and older, are capable of deriving enjoyment from sexual intercourse and other kinds of lovemaking. The principal difference as people age is that it takes longer to become aroused and the orgasm is less intense. Dissemination of accurate information about sexual capacity in old age would probably prevent much unnecessary sexual dysfunction and disinterest.

Nursing homes and other extended-care facilities often do little to encourage residents to maintain or enhance whatever skills and capacities they still have; both physical and mental deterioration are the rule. Today, care is provided in the community whenever possible. Comprehensive services, such as Meals on Wheels, regular home visits by health professionals, and support for caregivers seem to be beneficial when they are available and coordinated so that people do not have to confront a bureaucratic maze. All intervention should be minimal so that older people remain as independent as their circumstances permit.

Many older people can benefit from psychotherapy, but several issues specific to treating the older adult need to be kept in mind. The emotional distress of the elderly is often realistic in content. They have often suffered irreplaceable losses and face real medical and financial problems; it is unwise always to attribute their complaints to a psychopathological condition. Death is a more immediate issue as well. As for the process of therapy, clinicians should sometimes be active and directive, providing information and seeking out the agencies that give the social services needed by their clients. Therapy should also foster a sense of control, self-efficacy, and hope, and should help the older person elucidate a sense of meaning as he or she approaches the end of life.

KEY TERMS

ageism	longitudinal studies	neurofibrillary tangles
age effects	selective mortality	delirium
cohort effects	dementia	paraphrenia
time-of-measurement effects	Alzheimer's disease	sleep apnea
cross-sectional studies	plaques	

PART 4

INTERVENTION AND LEGAL AND ETHICAL ISSUES

17

Rene Magritte,
"The Human Condition,"
1934

INSIGHT THERAPIES

In ordinary conversation, you usually try to keep a connecting thread running through your remarks, excluding any intrusive ideas or side issues so as not to wander too far from the point, and rightly so. But in this case you must talk differently. As you talk, various thoughts will occur to you which you like to ignore because of certain criticisms and objections. You will be tempted to think, "That is irrelevant or unimportant or nonsensical," and to avoid saying it. Do not give in to such criticism. Report such thoughts in spite of your wish not to do so. Later, the reason for this injunction, the only one you have to follow, will become clear. Report whatever goes through your mind. Pretend that you are a traveler, describing to someone beside you the changing views which you see outside the train window. (Ford & Urban, 1963, p. 168)

WHAT IS PSYCHOTHERAPY?

Throughout our account of the various psychopathologies we have considered the ways in which therapists attempt to prevent, lessen, and even eliminate mental and emotional suffering. Our descriptions in Chapter 2 of the several paradigms of treatment—biological, psychoanalytic, learning, and cognitive—laid the groundwork for a variety of ways in which to approach the task. In Chapters 6 through 16 we learned that some forms of intervention are more appropriate than others for particular problems. For example, because of advances in our understanding of biological processes, new parents now have means to halt or at least reduce certain forms of genetically transmitted mental retardation. And through better understanding of the process of learning, children with mental retardation now acquire more cognitive, social, and self-care skills than was earlier thought possible. Psychoanalytic theory helps therapists treat dissociative disorders, for it alerts them to the possibility that an amnesic patient, for example, cannot remember because the pain of certain past events forced them to be massively repressed. Humanistic and existential therapies help clients explore the depth and causes of their psychological pain and encourage them to take action, make choices, and assume responsibility for bettering their lives.

It is time now to take a closer, more intensive look at therapy, to consider issues of general importance, to explore controversies, and to make comparisons. What we have studied so far of psychopathology and treatment should enable us to do so with some sophistication and perspective.

Shorn of its theoretical complexities, any **psychotherapy** is a social interaction in which a trained professional tries to help another person, the client or patient, behave and feel differently. The therapist follows procedures that are to a greater or lesser extent prescribed by a certain theory or school of thought. The basic assumption is that particular kinds of verbal and nonverbal exchanges in a trusting relationship can achieve goals such as reducing anxiety and eliminating self-defeating or dangerous behavior.

Basic as this explanation may seem, there is little general agreement about what really constitutes psychotherapy. A person's next-door neighbor might utter the same words of comfort as a clinical psychologist, but should we regard this as psychotherapy? In what way is psychotherapy different from such nonprofessional reassurance? Is the distinction made on the straightforward basis of whether the dispenser of reassurance has a particular academic degree or license? Does it relate to whether the giver of information has a theory that dictates or at least guides what he or she says? Does it depend on how sound the basic assumptions of the theory are? These are difficult questions, and as in other areas of abnormal psychology, there is less than complete agreement among professionals.

It is important to note at the outset that the people who seek or are sent for *professional* help have probably tried nonprofessional avenues to feeling better and have failed to obtain relief. Before most individuals go to a therapist they have confided in friends or in a spouse, perhaps spoken to the family doctor, consulted with a member of the clergy, and maybe tried several of the vast number of self-help books and programs that are so popular. For most people in psychological distress, one or more of these options provide enough relief, and they seek no further help (Bergin, 1971). But for others these attempts fall short, and individuals are left feeling helpless, often hopeless. These are the people who go to mental health clinics, university counseling centers, and the private offices of independent practitioners.

Theories and psychotherapies are great in number. There are scores, perhaps hundreds, each with its enthusiastic supporters. We present in this and the following two chapters a close look at the more prominent theories of intervention and the research that supports them. Our intent is to provide enough detail about the major approaches to allow a grasp of the basic issues and an overall perspective on the therapeutic enterprise. We hope, too, that this will provide the reader with the means to evaluate critically new therapies that arise, or at the very least to know the questions to ask in order to evaluate them effectively.

Evaluation of the effectiveness of psychotherapy has become a significant issue because of the

Troubled people may talk about their problems with friends or seek professional therapy. Therapy is typically sought by those for whom the advice and support of friends have not provided relief.

increasing demand and responsibility that is being placed on psychotherapists by insurance companies (Johnson, 1995). Consonant with the health care restructuring movement, insurance companies want psychotherapists to restrict themselves to the most effective and efficient treatments. Professional organizations are becoming involved as well. For example, the clinical division of the American Psychological Association has been spearheading efforts to reach consensus on which treatments are supported by enough controlled data to be regarded as "empirically supported therapies" (Chambless et al., 1996; Task Force, 1995).

Our principal concern in this chapter and the next is individual therapy, that is, therapy conducted by a clinician with one patient or client. Nearly everything discussed in these two chapters is relevant also for therapy in groups, one of three principal topics in Chapter 19.

London (1964, 1986) categorized psychotherapies as *insight* or *action* (behavioral) therapies. Behavior therapy, as well as cognitive behavior therapy, is discussed in Chapter 18. **Insight therapy**, discussed in depth in this chapter, assumes that behavior, emotions, and thoughts become disordered because people do not adequately understand what motivates them, especially when their needs and drives conflict. Insight therapy tries to help people discover the true reasons for behaving, feeling, and thinking as they do. The premise is that greater awareness of motivations will yield greater control over and subsequent improvement in thought, emotion, and behavior.

Of course *insight* is not exclusive to the insight therapies. The action therapies bring insight to the individual as well, and the newer cognitive therapies can be seen as a blend of insight and behavioral therapies. It is a matter of emphasis, a matter of

focus. In the behavioral therapies the focus is on changing behavior; insight is often a peripheral benefit. In the insight therapies the focus is less on changing people's behavior directly than on enhancing their understanding of their motives, fears, and conflicts. To facilitate such insights, therapists of different theoretical persuasions have employed a variety of techniques, ranging from the free association of psychoanalysis to the reflection of feelings practiced in client-centered therapy.

GENERAL ISSUES IN EVALUATING PSYCHOTHERAPY RESEARCH

Before we examine several insight therapies we consider a few general issues that will inform our understanding and appreciation of research in psychotherapy.

THE PLACEBO EFFECT

Any study of the effects of psychotherapy—whether insight or action oriented—should include a consideration of the **placebo effect**. This term refers to an improvement in physical or psychological condition that is attributable to a patient's expectations of help rather than to any specific active ingredient in a treatment. Frank (1973, 1978) related placebo effects to faith healing in prescientific or nonscientific societies. For centuries, suffering human beings have made pilgrimages to sanctified places and ingested sometimes foul-smelling concoctions in the belief that these efforts would improve their condition. Sometimes they did.

Many people dismiss placebo reactions as not real or as second-best to benefits of actual treatments. After all, if a person has a tension headache, what possible benefit can he or she hope to get from a pill that is totally devoid of chemical action or direct physiological effect? The fact is, however, that the effects of placebos are sometimes significant and even long lasting. Frank (1973, 1978) furnished extensive evidence attesting to improvement in a variety of physical and mental problems after ingestion of placebo sugar pills and from exposure to other ministrations that in themselves could not possibly account for this relief. This placebo effect is commonly found and universally accepted in drug research.

It is not a simple matter, however, to extend the findings of research on chemical placebos directly to research on psychological placebos. In psychotherapy the mere expectation of being helped can be an active ingredient! Why? If the theory adopted by the therapist holds that positive expectancy of improvement is an active ingredient, then improvement arising from the expectancy would by definition *not* be considered a placebo effect. Lambert, Shapiro, and Bergin (1986) argued that "placebo factors" should be replaced with the concept of "common factors" in the study of the effects of psychotherapy. They reiterated Rosenthal and Frank's (1956) early caveat that a placebo as something therapeutically inert can be understood only from the standpoint of a particular *theory* of change. They defined common factors as

> those dimensions of the treatment setting … that are not specific to a particular technique. Those factors that are common to most therapies (such as expectation for improvement, persuasion, warmth and attention, understanding, encouragement, etc.) should not be viewed as theoretically *inert* nor as *trivial*; they are central to psychological treatments and play an active role in patient improvement. (Lambert et al., 1986, p. 163)

In research evaluating the effects of psychotherapy, patients in so-called placebo control groups, as Lambert et al. (1986) pointed out, generally improve more than patients in no-treatment groups—though often not as much as patients in treatment groups. The issue of common factors is important in the movement toward psychotherapy integration, a topic examined in Chapter 18 after our review of both insight and action therapies.

The place of placebo control groups in psychotherapy research is an often-debated and complex topic, the intricacies of which are beyond the scope of this book. We should note, though, that a study that compares a particular therapy to no treatment at all and finds that therapy brings about more improvement does suggest that being treated is better than receiving no treatment. This is not a trivial finding. But a given therapy usually tries to create improvement in a particular way—by removing the person's defenses, by easing the individual's way to self-actualization, by enhancing responsible choices, by extinguishing fears, and so forth. To determine whether these *processes* are at work and are effective, a study needs, at the very least, a control group of patients who are instilled with expectancies of help, who believe that something worthwhile and beneficial is being done for them. *All* therapies derive at least some of their power from the faith people have in the healer and from their profound desire to get better.

THERAPY AS RESEARCHED AND THERAPY AS PRACTICED

The use of therapist manuals—detailed guides on how to conduct a particular therapy, often stipulating specific procedures to be followed at different stages of treatment—has become the norm in psychotherapy research (e.g., Addis, 1997; Wilson, 1996). It is impossible nowadays to obtain funding to conduct a study of the outcome of psychotherapy without first explicitly defining the independent variables (p. 113) via a manual that the therapists in the study must follow as closely as possible. This standard is widely touted as an important advance in the scientific study of psychotherapy. It allows someone reading a psychotherapy study to *know* what happened to patients in a given experimental condition.

Earlier research, primarily involving the insight therapies discussed in this chapter, made this knowledge much more elusive. To read in an article that patients "received psychodynamic psychotherapy" or "client-centered therapy" (or, for that matter, "behavior therapy") conveyed some information but did not specify what the therapy was actually like and, most important, whether patients in a given condition who happened to receive therapy from Dr. X had the same or reasonably similar experiences as those whose therapist in the same experimental condition was Dr. Y.

Using manuals, training therapist-experimenters in their use, and monitoring what those therapists actually *did* in their sessions with patients came into play only in the 1960s. The first manual-based study comparing different treatment modalities was Paul's (1966) study, which compared systematic desensitization to an insight therapy (p. 519), and it heralded a major change in psychotherapy research.

All well and good, but a moment's reflection suggests a problem. While the use of manuals buys us greater internal validity (p. 113)—results obtained can be attributed with some confidence to the action of the independent variable—what of *external* validity, that is, do the results obtained from manual-based studies generalize to the actual practice of psychotherapy outside the constraints of a controlled study? There is perhaps no more important and more hotly debated topic in psychotherapy than this (Goldfried & Davison, 1994; Persons, 1989).

Here's a way to look at the issue. The oft-documented fact that most therapists describe themselves as eclectic (e.g., Jensen, Bergin, & Greaves, 1990; Smith, 1982; recall our earlier discussion of "practice makes imperfect," p. 51) indicates that controlled studies of specific techniques (e.g., desensitization) or approaches (e.g., client-centered therapy) are limited in what they can tell us about the nature and outcomes of therapy *as actually practiced* (Lambert & Bergin, 1994). That is, we know that most therapists seldom behave strictly in line with a particular theoretical orientation—whether psychoanalytic, client centered, or behavioral. Therefore the kinds of controlled studies emphasized in this chapter and the following two are limited in what they can tell us about the effectiveness of the psychotherapy available to patients who are not participants in research studies. This situation is ironic, for it is these controlled studies that provide the evidence that proponents of particular techniques or general theoretical approaches look to for support of their respective positions!

Other common characteristics of today's controlled studies are the exclusion of people on such grounds as their having more problems than the one being studied (the comorbidity issue), and the reliance on people who are willing to be seen in a highly structured treatment protocol rather than on those who see therapists for a host of reasons unrelated to the motivation of people who volunteer for such studies. In other words, the patients who volunteer and are accepted as participants in controlled studies are different from many—and perhaps from the vast majority—of patients in psychotherapy. This situation may make it risky to generalize from controlled studies to the actual practice of psychotherapy.

Another related attribute of controlled studies is the widespread use of a DSM diagnosis to define patients as homogeneous. For example, the large-scale NIMH study of depression that we examine in Chapter 18 (p. 534) followed the DSM criteria in defining people as having major depression and then randomly assigned them to different experimental conditions. But as we have seen many times, people are depressed, anxious, or dependent on alcohol or cigarettes for many different reasons.

What is not possible in such studies is an *idiographic* analysis of a person, that is, an analysis of the unique features of a single case, to determine what factors are most important in making him or her feel, think, and behave in a certain way (Beutler, 1997; Goldfried & Davison, 1994). Controlled outcome studies generally treat patients deemed depressed, for example, as alike, and then randomly assign them to treatment conditions so that, in the best tradition of experimental research, the studies will have good internal validity (recall the earlier discussion of the importance of random assignment of subjects, p. 114).

Psychotherapy researchers have recently been distinguishing between efficacy and effectiveness. The *efficacy* of an intervention is what we determine from a controlled outcome study, typically conducted in an academic research setting. The *effectiveness* of an intervention refers to what is offered to and received by people in the everyday world when they go to therapists whose adherence to a treatment manual does not define their actions as practitioners. Whereas the elimination of observable, well-defined problems, such as how far an agoraphobic can venture from his or her home, is the usual focus of efficacy studies, effectiveness is usually judged by patients themselves on the basis of more global and subjective criteria, such as the level of satisfaction people have with their therapy, how much they believe they have been helped, and whether they believe that the quality of their life has improved (cf. Consumer Reports, 1995; Seligman, 1995, 1996).

PROCESS AND OUTCOME

A basic distinction can be made between research that tells us how well a given intervention works—**outcome research**—and research that tells us how a given outcome occurs, that is, that elucidates the processes believed to underlie therapeutic change—**process research**. Generally, outcome research precedes process research. After all, if intervention X doesn't have a positive effect on people, why bother to study how it works?

NO-TREATMENT CONTROLS

In examining psychotherapy research we will encounter many studies that demonstrate improvement in patients after a regime of one or another psychotherapy and that claim that these data constitute evidence for the effectiveness (or efficacy) of the psychotherapy. Such claims possess some validity—after all, before treatment the patients were unhappy but after treatment, they were better. What is being overlooked, however (a point made in Chapter 5, p. 114), is that we cannot know from such treatment outcome data what would have happened with the mere passage of time. People live their lives all the time, and events happen that can change a person's life for good or for ill (see the following discussion on chaos theory). A no-treatment control is a basic and minimum criterion in a therapy outcome study, yet it is lacking surprisingly often.

CHAOS THEORY AND LIFE

In Chapter 5 we discussed chaos theory and its implications for our understanding of the complexities of psychopathology and therapy (p. 104). So many unpredictable and sometimes uncontrollable factors impinge on people every moment of their lives that our understanding of human behavior and our ability to predict and alter it are bound to be limited. How does this relate to the study of psychotherapy?

Some people in no-treatment control groups, who are receiving none of the putative benefits of a professional treatment, get better. Why? For one thing, they are living their lives every moment, encountering events that can affect them favorably, such as meeting someone special or getting a promotion at work. Researchers studying psychotherapy outcomes can only hope that such events occur about equally often to subjects in each condition of an experiment. Partly because of such events, conclusions are not drawn based on a small number of patients and patients are randomly assigned to conditions. Of course, participants in a therapy study, whether in control or therapy groups, can also have negative experiences, which leave them worse off.

A compelling hypothesis for some of the improvement in treatment research was put forward by Robyn Dawes (1994), one of the severest critics of psychotherapy that lacks empirical validation. Nonprofessional "therapists," such as teachers, can sometimes be as successful as professionals in delivering effective treatment (Berman & Norton, 1985; Christensen & Jacobson, 1993).[1] Dawes specu-

lated that when people become involved in even a nonprofessional counseling relationship, they are motivated to institute changes in their lives even if the therapy may not itself be efficacious and even if the changes are unrelated to what they are working on with the therapist. The therapist, however, tends to attribute these positive changes—good "spillovers"—to his or her ministrations. To be sure, control groups in efficacy studies such as those we examine in this book permit us to evaluate such alternative interpretations, yet it remains important to be aware of how much is *unexplained* and *unexamined* in any kind of psychotherapy research. The points we have reviewed here—especially the distinction between efficacy and effectiveness studies—underscore the need for modesty in scientific theorizing and conclusions (see Focus 17.1).

PSYCHOANALYTIC THERAPIES

Psychoanalysis and its many offshoots are an important force in psychiatry and clinical psychology. We outlined the main features in Chapter 2. In this section we describe in greater detail and evaluate the important elements of classical (Freudian) psychoanalysis, ego analysis, and interpersonal therapies.

BASIC TECHNIQUES AND CONCEPTS IN CLASSICAL PSYCHOANALYSIS

At the heart of classical **psychoanalysis** is the therapeutic attempt to remove repressions that have prevented the ego from helping the individual grow into a healthy adult. Psychopathology is assumed to develop when people remain unaware of their true motivations and fears. They can be restored to healthy functioning only by becoming conscious of what has been repressed. When people can understand *what* is motivating their actions, they have a greater number of choices. Where id is, let there ego be, to paraphrase a maxim of psychoanalysis. The ego—the primarily conscious, deliberating, choosing portion of the personality—can better guide the individual in rational, realistic directions if repressions are minimal.

Wachtel's (1977) woolly mammoth (see p. 38) is an apt metaphor for the unresolved, buried conflicts that psychoanalytic theory assumes underlie psychological problems. The proper focus of therapy, then, is not on the presenting problem, such as fears of being rejected, but on unconscious childhood conflicts that exist in the psyche. Only by lifting the

---

[1]These conclusions have not gone unchallenged. To counter the claim that professional experience and credentials do not matter in how effective a therapy is, Peterson (1995) argues that the data used to support these claims come from what he calls "conversational counseling," or unstructured conversations between a sympathetic listener and a person *whose problems are not serious*. He asserts that this is different enough from therapy-as-actually-practiced to constitute a fragile foundation on which to make such claims. One can expect this particular debate to rage, especially given the advent of managed health care and the increased scrutiny being exercised by business-minded managers in deciding what kinds of treatments will be eligible for insurance coverage.

repression can the person confront the underlying problem and reevaluate it in the context of his or her adult life.

FREE ASSOCIATION

Psychoanalysts use several techniques to help their patients recover repressed conflicts. Perhaps the best known and most important is **free association**, in which the patient, reclining on a couch, is encouraged to give free rein to thoughts and feelings and to verbalize whatever comes to mind. The quotation at the start of this chapter is an example of instructions that might be given to a patient to free-associate. It is assumed that, with enough practice, free association will facilitate the uncovering of unconscious material.

The adjective *free* does not mean uncaused, only free from conscious censorship and control. "As an avowed determinist, Freud believed that unconscious mechanisms governed by psychological laws produced the flow of free associations. Free associations are thus not truly free" (Morse, 1982, p. 215). Indeed, it is the assumption that associations are *not* free that makes this technique important in psychoanalysis.

In therapy the patient must follow the fundamental rule of reporting thoughts and feelings as accurately as possible, without screening out the elements that might seem unimportant or shameful. Freud assumed that thoughts and memories occurred in associative chains and that recent ones reported first would ultimately trace back to earlier, crucial ones. To get to these earlier events the therapist must be careful not to guide or direct the patient's thinking; thus the therapist usually sits behind the patient to minimize any influence.

RESISTANCE

Blocks to free association arise, however, virtually thrusting themselves across the thoughts supposedly given free rein. Patients may suddenly change the subject or be unable to remember how a long-ago event ended. They may try any tactic to interrupt the session—remaining silent, getting up from the couch, looking out the window, making jokes and personal remarks to the analyst. Patients may arrive late or "forget" sessions altogether. Freud accorded great significance to such obstacles to free association, called **resistances**, and they contributed to the development of his concept of repression. According to Freud, interference with free association can be traced to unconscious control over sensitive areas, precisely areas that psychoanalytic therapists want to probe. In some respects resistances provide the analyst with the most critical information about the patient.

ANALYSIS OF DREAMS

Akin to free association, **dream analysis** is a classic analytic technique in which the therapist guides the patient in remembering and later analyzing his or her dreams. Freud assumed that during sleep the ego defenses are lowered, allowing repressed material to come forth, usually in disguised form. Concerns of the patient are often expressed in symbols (**latent content**) to help protect the conscious ego from the true significance of dream material. The **manifest content** of dreams, what is immediately apparent, may be regarded as a compromise between repression of true meaning and a full expression of unconscious material. The cutting down of a tall tree (manifest content) might symbolize the patient's anger toward his or her father (latent content). The content of dreams, then, is distorted by unconscious defensive structures, which, never completely abandoned, even in sleep, continue their fight to protect the ego from repressed impulses.

INTERPRETATION AND DENIAL

As unconscious material begins to appear in therapy, **interpretation** comes into play. This technique helps the person finally face the emotionally loaded conflict that was previously repressed. At the right time the analyst begins to point out the patient's defenses and the underlying meaning of his or her dreams, feelings, thoughts, and actions. The analyst must be careful not to offer this interpretation too soon, lest the patient totally reject it and leave treatment. To be effective, the analyst's interpretations should reflect insights that the patient is on the verge of making; the patient can then regard these insights as his or her own, rather than viewing them as coming from the analyst. Presumably an interpretation that a patient attributes to himself or herself will be more readily accepted and thereby have a stronger therapeutic effect.

Interpretation is the analyst's principal weapon against the continued use of defense mechanisms. The analyst may point out how certain of the patient's verbalizations relate to repressed unconscious material or suggest what the manifest content of dreams *truly* means. If the interpretation is timed correctly, the patient will begin to examine the repressed impulse in the light of present-day reality; in other words, the patient will begin to real-

FOCUS 17.1 META-ANALYSIS AND THE EFFECTS OF PSYCHOTHERAPY

A development in psychotherapy research that has attracted enormous attention in recent years is **meta-analysis**. Devised by Smith, Glass, and Miller (1980), meta-analysis is:

a quantitative method for averaging ... standardized results of a large number of different studies. The unit of analysis is the effect size (ES), a quantitative index of the size of the effect of therapy ... arrived at] by subtracting the mean of the control group from the mean of the treatment group and dividing that difference by the standard deviation of the control group. ... The larger the ES, the greater the effect of therapy.

The basis of comparison need not be therapy A versus therapy B, rather, one can compare on dimensions such as type of patients and settings in which therapy was administered. The independent variables, in other words, can be any factors considered influential in the outcome of an intervention. The great advantage of meta-analysis is that it provides a common metric across studies conducted in diverse settings by different investigators at different times (Kazdin, 1986).

In their original and oft-cited report, Smith et al. (1980) meta-analyzed 475 psychotherapy outcome studies involving more than 25,000 patients and 1700 effect sizes and came to two conclusions that have attracted considerable attention and created some controversy. First, they concluded that a wide range of therapies produce larger effect sizes than no treatment. Specifically, treated patients were found to be better off than almost 80 percent of untreated patients. Subsequent meta-analyses by other authors have confirmed these early findings (Lambert & Bergin, 1994). Second, Smith et al. contended that effect sizes across diverse modes of intervention do not differ from each other.

The psychotherapy research literature is full of references to and use of meta-analysis in an effort to sort through scores of studies and bring a sense of order and fairness to the task of making comparative statements on the merits of contrasting kinds of therapy. Indeed, the *Handbook of Psychotherapy and Behavior Change* (Garfield & Bergin, 1994), a standard in the field, relies heavily on literature reviews using meta-analysis. As part of a growing trend toward eclecticism in psychotherapy, reviewers have relied increasingly on meta-analysis as an evaluative and comparative tool. In this spirit, Lambert et al. (1986) drew several conclusions about psychotherapy *in gener-*

al, that is, without explicit consideration of *differences among* theoretical orientations. Although this tactic runs the risk of comparing the proverbial apples and oranges, their conclusions are nonetheless useful in our broad-gauged study of this field.

1. Lambert et al. (1986) went beyond the findings of Smith et al. (1980) as well as others and found that many psychotherapeutic interventions were more effective than a number of so-called attention-placebo control groups. They concluded that psychotherapists are more than "placebologists" (p. 163). By the same token, what Lambert et al. call "common factors" (see p. 553), rather than placebo factors, namely, warmth, trust, and encouragement, may themselves effect significant and even lasting improvement in a broad range of anxiety and mood disorders.

2. They found that the positive effects of psychotherapy tend to be maintained for many months following termination. Lambert et al. (1986) based this sanguine conclusion on a meta-analysis of sixty-seven outcome studies by Nicholson and Berman (1983), mostly behavioral in nature, with patients other than those diagnosed as psychotic, brain-disordered, antisocial personality, or addictive-disordered. Posttreatment status correlated well with follow-up status, and in general group differences at follow-up were similar to those immediately following termination of therapy. This finding is obviously important to the client and to the individual therapist (who hopes that patients will continue to do well once they stop coming for regular sessions). It is important as well to psychotherapy researchers, who often have to undertake expensive and arduous follow-up measures to convince their colleagues that the effects of a given treatment are enduring. Yet Lambert et al. (1986) remind us that some disorders probably need to be followed up more than others, for example, depression, which is known to be recurrent.

3. There is considerable variability among participants in a given treatment condition. Although treatment group X may on average show significant improvement, there are often patients in that group who get worse. This deterioration effect is discussed in greater detail in Focus 19.1.

ize that he or she no longer has to fear the awareness of the impulse.

Wolitzky (1995) suggests that the optimal interpretation is one that reveals the similarity between the patient's past and present behaviors. For example, the therapist might say: "What you are doing

with me now [e.g., not listening closely when I suggest a different way of behaving] may be similar to what you did with your mother. And it might also have something to do with how frustrated your wife sometimes gets with you." The purpose of this interpretation would be to help the patient recog-

4. Recent meta-analytic studies comparing insight therapy with the cognitive and behavioral interventions reviewed in the next chapter show a slight but consistent advantage to the latter, although there is criticism by proponents of insight therapy that behavioral and cognitive therapies focus on milder disorders.*

However, meta-analysis has been criticized by a number of psychotherapy researchers for the following reasons:

1. The behavioral researchers Wilson and Rachman (Rachman & Wilson, 1980; Wilson & Rachman, 1983) point out that many behavior-therapy studies, in particular those employing single-subject designs (see p. 116), were omitted in the Smith et al. (1980) review. They claim that the exclusion of these studies weakens the case for behavior therapy.

2. A more general problem is the quality control of studies that are included in a meta-analysis. Therapy studies differ in their internal and external validity *as judged by particular researchers*. By giving equal weight to all studies, the meta-analyses of Smith et al. created a situation in which a poorly controlled outcome study received as much attention as a well-controlled one. When Smith et al. attempted to address this problem by comparing effect sizes of good versus poor studies and found no differences, they were further criticized for the criteria they employed in separating the good from the not so good (Rachman & Wilson, 1980)! O'Leary and Wilson (1987) considered other critiques as well and concluded that the ultimate problem is that *someone* has to make a judgment of good versus poor quality in psychotherapy research and that *others* can find fault with that judgment.

   This seems an insoluble problem, one that has existed for years in reviews of therapy outcome research. There are times when a scholar has no choice but to make his or her own judgment about the validity of a piece of research and to decide whether or not to ignore it. Perhaps Mintz (1983) was correct in saying that the move toward meta-analysis in this field has at least sensitized us to the subjectivity that is inherent in passing judgment on research and has also encouraged greater explicitness in the criteria used to accept or to reject the findings of a given outcome study. Moreover, meta-analysis has uncovered deficiencies in some published research, for example, inadequate reporting of means and standard deviations and the collection of outcome data by persons who were aware of the treatment condition to which subjects were assigned (Shapiro & Shapiro, 1983). A long-term beneficial effect of meta-analysis may be an improvement in research practices and a tightening of publication standards (Kazdin, 1986).

3. The overwhelming majority of outcome studies employ more than one dependent measure. In their original work Smith et al. (1980) computed effect sizes separately for each measure in each study; this led to greater weight being given to studies with larger numbers of outcome measures. Efforts to correct this inequity (e.g., Landman & Dawes, 1980; Prioleau, Murdock, & Brody, 1983) included combining separate measures to come up with a single effect size estimate for each study. At first blush this seems a good and fair solution, but as O'Leary and Wilson (1987) pointed out, it obscures the different information that disparate measures can provide and also overlooks the fact that different measures may change at different rates from a given intervention. They pointed out, for example, that rapid-weight-reduction programs can lead to quick weight loss *but* to an increase in depression (Stunkard & Rush, 1974). If one statistically combines these two measures into a single one, a finding of no significant effect emerges, thus concealing a clinically important outcome.

4. Insight-oriented therapists claim that there is a bias against them because most of the therapy outcome research has been done by cognitive and behavioral therapists (Lambert et al., 1986). This claim is troublesome because Smith et al. (1980) found larger effect sizes for those techniques to which the investigator had a prior allegiance.

A continuing challenge, then, is the seemingly inescapable role of the investigator's own paradigm in judging the merits of another's meta-analysis. We have noted this aspect of science many times already.

---

*As one might expect, charges of bias go back and forth between proponents of diverse approaches. Dispassionate, paradigm-free interpretations of data are no less difficult to come by in therapy research than in psychopathology.

nize repetitive and problematic patterns of relating to others.

The analyst's interpretations may also help establish the meaning of the resistances that disturb the patient's free association. The analyst may, for example, point out that the patient tends to avoid a particular topic. It is common for the patient to deny such interpretations. This **denial** is sometimes taken as a sign that the analyst's interpretation is correct rather than as a sign that it is incorrect. In the slow process of working through the disturbing conflicts, of confronting them again and again, the patient gradually faces up to the validity of the analyst's interpretations, often with great emotion. Feeling safe in the accepting and nonjudgmental conditions arranged by the analyst, the patient should uncover more and more repressed material.

Determining when a patient's denial of an interpretation means that it is correct is one of the thorniest problems in psychoanalysis, a truly daunting epistemological[2] challenge. When is it appropriate to consider that a no is really a yes? It would seem a scenario ripe for mistakes. But the analyst, like any clinician, does not judge in a vacuum. He or she formulates hypotheses over time about the patient, noticing how one problem area relates to others. The analyst searches for clues in a slowly developing picture, and every statement, every gesture of the patient, is viewed within this scheme. A patient's no is considered a yes only in the *context* of other ideas already formed by the analyst. And the analyst bases that judgment, in part, on how vigorously the patient denies an interpretation, generally regarding as defensive a denial expressed in an excessive manner. As Queen Gertrude in Shakespeare's *Hamlet* commented, "The lady doth protest too much, methinks" (act III, scene 2).

TRANSFERENCE

The core of psychoanalytic therapy is the **transference neurosis**. Freud noted that his patients sometimes acted toward him in an emotion-charged and unrealistic way. For example, a patient much older than Freud would behave in a childish manner during a therapy session. Although these reactions were often positive and loving, they could also be quite negative and hostile. Since these feelings seemed out of character with the ongoing therapy relationship, Freud assumed that they were relics of attitudes *transferred* to him from those held in the past toward important people in the patient's childhood, most often parents. That is, Freud felt that patients responded to him *as though* he were one of the important people in their past. Freud used this transference of attitudes, which he came to consider an inevitable aspect of psychoanalysis, as a means of explaining to patients the childhood origin of many of their concerns and fears. This revelation and explanation tended also to help lift repressions and allow the confrontation of buried

impulses. In psychoanalysis, transference is regarded as essential to a complete cure. It is precisely when analysts notice transference developing that they take hope that the important repressed conflict from childhood is getting closer to the surface.

Analysts encourage the development of transference by intentionally remaining shadowy figures, generally sitting behind the patient while the patient free-associates and serving as relatively blank screens on which important persons in the repressed conflicts can be projected. They take pains to reveal as little as possible of their own personal lives or of their feelings during the session (in marked contrast to the humanistic and existential therapies). They try to demonstrate a caring attitude, which may remind the patient of attributes, real or hoped for, in his or her parents. Because the therapy setting is so different from the childhood situation, analysts can readily point out to patients the irrational nature of their fears and concerns (see Focus 17.2).

COUNTERTRANSFERENCE

Related to transference is **countertransference**, the feelings of the analyst toward the patient. One writer on psychoanalysis calls countertransference "empathy gone awry" (Wolinsky, 1995, p. 36). The analyst must be careful not to allow his or her own emotional vulnerabilities to affect the relationship with the patient. The analyst's own needs and fears must be recognized for what they are; the analyst should have enough understanding of his or her own motivations to be able to see the client clearly, without distortion. The problem is well articulated in the following discussion of therapy with depressed people, during which countertransference is a continuing challenge to a therapist.

Depressed patients bring their hopelessness and despair into therapy, and the therapist may be affected. If the depression improves slowly, or not at all, the therapist may feel guilty, angry, and/or helpless. After seeing several severely depressed patients in a day, the therapist may feel quite drained and eventually may become unwilling to work in the future with similar patients. Suicidal patients can evoke particularly difficult countertransferences. …

One safeguard against such difficulties is the therapist's continuing awareness of these feelings and their relation to his or her own psychodynamics. A suffering patient may mobilize the therapist's fantasy of being able to heal and earn gratitude, deftly and single-handedly; or may stir up the therapist's anger at the existence of suffering. An abiding awareness of these reactions will help the therapist maintain the patience and satisfaction with small gains that are necessary for conducting psychotherapy with severely depressed patients. At

---

[2]Epistemology, from the Greek *epistanai*, "to know" or "to understand," is the branch of philosophy concerned with how we decide that we know something. As we discussed in Chapter 1, inherent to any scientific paradigm is a particular epistemology, a set of rules and standards that determine when we can say that we have acquired some knowledge.

FOCUS 17.2 EXCERPT FROM A PSYCHOANALYTIC SESSION—AN ILLUSTRATION OF TRANSFERENCE

Patient (a fifty-year-old male business executive) I really don't feel like talking today.

Analyst (Remains silent for several minutes, then) Perhaps you'd like to talk about why you don't feel like talking.

Patient There you go again, making demands on me, insisting I do what I just don't feel up to doing. (Pause) Do I always have to talk here, when I don't feel like it? (Voice becomes angry and petulant) Can't you just get off my back? You don't really give a damn how I feel, do you?

Analyst I wonder why you feel I don't care.

Patient Because you're always pressuring me to do what I feel I can't do.

This excerpt must be viewed in context. The patient had been in therapy for about a year, complaining of depression and anxiety. Although extremely successful in the eyes of his family and associates, he felt weak and incompetent. Through many sessions of free association and dream analysis the analyst had begun to suspect that the patient's feelings of failure stemmed from his childhood experiences with an extremely punitive and critical father, a man even more successful than the client, who seemed never to be satisfied with his son's efforts. The exchange quoted here was later interpreted by the analyst as an expression of resentment by the patient of his *father's* pressures on him; hence it had little to do with the analyst himself. The patient's tone of voice (petulant), as well as his overreaction to the analyst's gentle suggestion that he talk about his feelings of not wanting to talk, indicated that the patient was angry not at his analyst but at his father. The therapist viewed the expression of such feelings, that is, the patient's transferring the feelings from his father to his analyst, as significant, and built on this inference in subsequent sessions to help the patient reevaluate his childhood fears of expressing aggression toward his father.

---

the same time, the therapist must avoid overstepping his/her role and trying to do all the work for an apparently weak patient. (Jacobson & McKinney, 1982, p. 215)

Because of issues of countertransference, a training analysis, or *Lehranalyse*, wherein the trainee is psychoanalyzed by a senior analyst, is a formal part of the education of an analyst. Although many therapists of different theoretical persuasions consider it useful to have been in therapy themselves, therapy is *required* in analytic training institutes. It is essential that analysts reduce to a minimum the frequency and intensity of countertransference toward their clients.

DETACHMENT

The analyst must *not* become actively involved in helping the patient deal with everyday problems. He or she carefully avoids any intervention, such as a direct suggestion about how to behave in a troublesome situation, as short-term relief might deflect the patient's efforts to uncover the repressed conflicts. Freud was emphatic on this point, writing in 1918 that the analyst must take care not to make the patient's life so comfortable that he or she would no longer be motivated to delve into the unconscious, and he criticized nonanalytic therapists for not adhering to this principle.

Their one aim is to make everything as pleasant as possible for the patient, so that he may feel well there and be glad to take refuge there again from the trials of life. In so doing, they make no attempt to give him more strength for facing life and more capacity for carrying out his actual tasks in it. In analytic treatment, all such spoiling must be avoided. As far as his relations with the physician are concerned, the patient must be left with unfulfilled wishes in abundance. It is expedient to deny him precisely those satisfactions which he desires most intensely and expresses most importunately. (1955, p. 164)[3]

The detachment of the analyst has often been ridiculed or misinterpreted, which does an injustice both to analytic theory and to the people who apply it. When a person is in pain and is needy, the initial impulse is, figuratively, to take the sufferer into one's arms and comfort him or her, providing reassurance that all will be well, that the patient will be taken care of. But the analyst has a different perspective: when a patient enters therapy it is likely that others have tried to provide solace, and if sympathy and support were going to help they probably already would have done so. Thus, the analyst must work hard to resist showing concern through expressions of support as well as with concrete advice. Acting in a directive fashion will interfere with transference, because the therapist necessarily

---

[3]Recall, however, other reports of Freud being more active and directive than statements like this would suggest. He would certainly not be the only therapist whose actual behavior sometimes diverged from his theory.

becomes less of a blank screen if he or she expresses opinions, voices objections, and gives advice and direction. By keeping a distance from the patient the analyst intends to help the patient. This stratagem is consistent with analytic theory and is faithfully applied by the more orthodox psychoanalysts.

PSYCHOANALYSIS AND BEHAVIOR THERAPY

Classical psychoanalysis is directly opposite in thrust to cognitive and behavior therapy. Practitioners of the latter are unconcerned with factors that analysts presume are buried in the unconscious, and they concentrate precisely on what analysts ignore, helping patients change their attitudes, feelings, and overt behavior in concrete, current life situations. What the analyst, and to a large degree the ego analyst, terms *supportive therapy*, the cognitive behavior therapist regards as the essence of therapy. By the same token, what the behavior therapist sees as unnecessary and even detrimental to the client—digging into the repressed past and withholding advice on how to make specific changes in the here and now—is judged by the analyst to be essential to complete psychotherapeutic treatment.

CONTEMPORARY ANALYTIC THERAPIES

Current analytic therapies include ego analysis, brief psychodynamic therapy, and interpersonal psychodynamic therapy.

EGO ANALYSIS

After Freud's death a group of practitioners generally referred to as ego analysts introduced some important modifications to psychoanalytic theory. Their approach is sometimes described as psychodynamic rather than psychoanalytic. The major figures in this loosely formed movement include Karen Horney (1942), Anna Freud (1946), Erik Erikson (1950), David Rapaport (1951), and Heinz Hartmann (1958). Although Freud did not ignore the interactions of the organism with the environment, his view was essentially a push model, in which people are driven by intrapsychic urges. Those who subscribe to **ego analysis** place greater emphasis on a person's ability to control the environment and to select the time and the means for satisfying certain instinctual drives. Their basic contention is that the individual is as much ego as id. In addition, they focus more on current living conditions than did Freud, although they sometimes

advocate delving deeply into the historical causes of an individual's behavior.

Important for the ego analysts is a set of ego functions that are primarily conscious, capable of controlling both id instincts and the external environment, and that, significantly, do not depend on the id for their energy. Ego analysts assume that these functions and capabilities are present at birth and then develop through experience. Underemphasized by Freud, ego functions have energies and gratifications of their own, usually separate from the reduction of id impulses. And whereas in Freud's view society was essentially a negative inhibition against the unfettered gratification of libidinal impulses, the ego analysts hold that an individual's social interactions can provide their own special kind of gratification.

BRIEF PSYCHODYNAMIC THERAPY

Although many laypeople assume that patients usually spend many months, even years, in psychodynamic psychotherapy, most courses of therapy last fewer than ten sessions (Garfield, 1978). Actually, Freud originally conceived of psychoanalysis as relatively short term. He thought that the analyst should focus on specific problems, make it clear to the patient that therapy would not exceed a certain number of sessions, and structure sessions in a directive fashion. Freud thus envisioned a more active psychoanalysis than what eventually developed. The early pioneers in brief therapy were the psychoanalysts Ferenczi (1920) and Alexander and French (1946). Among the many reasons for the short duration of therapy is that people today are less likely to consider the ambitious examination of the past as the best way to deal better with today's realities—the essence of classical analytic treatment. Indeed, most patients expect therapy to be fairly short-term and targeted to specific problems in their everyday lives. These expectations contributed to the design of briefer forms of dynamic therapy.

Insurance companies have also played a role both in shortening the duration of treatment and in encouraging analytically oriented workers to adapt their ideas to time-limited psychotherapy, called **brief therapy**. These insurance companies have become increasingly reluctant to cover more than a limited number, say, twenty-five psychotherapy sessions in a given calendar year and have set limits as well on reimbursement amounts. Moreover, the cognitive and behavioral therapies that have emerged since the 1960s focus on discrete problems and eschew long-term therapy, as explained in greater detail in the next chapter.

Another strand in the history of brief psychodynamic therapy can be found in the challenges faced by mental health professionals to respond to psychological emergencies (Koss & Shiang, 1994). Shell-shock emergencies in World War II led to Grinker and Spiegel's (1944) classic short-term analytic treatment of what is now called posttraumatic stress disorder (p. 147). A related contribution came from Eric Lindemann's (1944) crisis intervention with the survivors of the famous Cocoanut Grove nightclub fire in 1943.

All these factors, combined with the growing acceptability of psychotherapy in the population at large, have set the stage for a stronger focus on time-limited psychodynamic therapy. Brief therapies share several common elements (Koss & Shiang, 1994):

- Assessment tends to be rapid and early.
- It is made clear right away that therapy will be limited and that improvement is expected within a small number of sessions, from six to twenty-five.
- Goals are concrete and focused on the amelioration of the patient's worst symptoms, on helping the patient understand what is going on in his or her life, and on enabling the patient to cope better in the future.
- Interpretations are directed more toward present life circumstances and patient behavior than on the historical significance of feelings.
- Development of a transference neurosis is not encouraged, but some positive transference to the therapist is fostered to encourage the patient to follow the therapist's suggestions and advice.
- There is a general understanding that psychotherapy does not cure, but that it can help troubled individuals learn to deal better with life's inevitable stressors.

INTERPERSONAL PSYCHODYNAMIC THERAPY

A variant of brief psychodynamic therapy, often referred to as interpersonal therapy, is found in a group of psychodynamic therapies that emphasize the interactions between a patient and his or her social environment. A pioneer in the development of this approach was the American psychiatrist Harry Stack Sullivan. Sometimes called a neo-Freudian, Sullivan held that the basic difficulty of patients is misperceptions of reality stemming from disorganization in the interpersonal relations of childhood, primarily those between child and parents.

Over 400 lives were lost in the fire at the Cocoanut Grove nightclub in 1942. The crisis intervention work that followed was an influence in the development of brief psychodynamic therapy.

Sullivan departed from Freud in his conception of the analyst as a "participant observer" in the therapy process. In contrast with the classical or even ego-analytical view of the therapist as a blank

Harry Stack Sullivan modified the traditional psychoanalytic concept of transference and instead proposed that the therapist was a participant observer.

screen for the transference neurosis, Sullivan argued that the therapist, like the scientist, is inevitably a part of the process he or she is studying. An analyst does not see patients without at the same time affecting them.

In a searching critique of transference Wachtel (1977) placed even greater emphasis on the interpersonal nature of therapy. Opposing the orthodox psychoanalytic view that a shadowy therapist enables transference to develop, Wachtel hypothesized that such unvarying behavior on the part of the therapist frustrates the client, who may be seeking some indication of how the therapist feels about what he or she is doing and saying. The sometimes childish reactions assumed to be part of the transference neurosis Wachtel regarded, in part, as the normal reactions of an adult who is thwarted. The troubled client sees the analyst as a professional person who remains distant and noncommittal in the face of his or her increasing expression of emotion. Thus, rather than an unfolding of the client's personality, transference may actually be in some measure the client's extreme frustration with minimal feedback. Moreover, because the analyst restricts his or her own behavior so severely in the consulting room and intentionally limits the setting to which the client is exposed, the analyst can sample only a limited range of the client's behavior, attitudes, and feelings. Wachtel's blend of psychoanalytic and behavioral viewpoints is further explored in the later discussion of developments toward a rapprochement between these major paradigms (p. 548).

A contemporary example of a brief psychodynamic therapy is the **Interpersonal Therapy (IPT)** of Klerman and Weissman (Klerman et al., 1984). This therapy was described earlier (p. 243) as an effective treatment of depression. In Chapter 18 we will review a major study that compared IPT with Beck's cognitive therapy and with imipramine (Tofranil), a widely used antidepressant medication. IPT concentrates on current interpersonal difficulties and on discussing with the patient—even teaching the patient directly—better ways of relating to others. The kind of major personality change sought by classical psychoanalysis is not a goal of IPT.

IPT includes strategies from both psychodynamic and cognitive-behavioral therapies. Its focus is on here-and-now problems rather than on childhood or developmental issues (Weissman & Markowitz, 1994), an emphasis in stark contrast to that of traditional psychoanalytic theory. Although IPT incorporates some psychodynamic ideas, it is quite distinct, especially from traditional forms of psychoanalysis. In particular, IPT diverges from traditional psychoanalysis in the role of the therapist, which is that of

an active patient advocate rather than a neutral blank screen (Frank & Spanier, 1995; Weissman, 1995). In *Mastering Depression: The Patient's Guide to Therapy*, the following section appears in the description of IPT:

> The IPT therapist will not: 1) Interpret your dreams; 2) Have treatment go on indefinitely; 3) Delve into your early childhood; 4) Encourage you to free associate; 5) Make you feel very dependent on the treatment or the therapist. (Weissman, 1995, pp. 11–12)

Although IPT was initially developed for the treatment of depression in mid-life (and the efficacy data bear primarily on this application), Klerman and Weissman (1993) advocate IPT for older and younger patients, HIV patients, people with eating disorders, and patients with dysthymic disorder and bipolar disorder. Efficacy data on these new applications are just beginning to appear in the literature. In addition, IPT has a maintenance version, in which the goal of therapy is to prevent recurrence of depressive episodes in patients who are remitted (Frank et al., 1991).

A CONCLUDING WORD ON BRIEF THERAPY

Although there can be confusion about what is considered brief psychotherapy, the term almost always refers to the ego-analytical and interpersonal approaches described here. A defining characteristic seems to be that psychoanalytic ideas and practices are adapted for short-term use. Sometimes, however, the term has been applied to therapies based on other paradigms, for example, Wolpe's desensitization and related techniques, Ellis's rational-emotive therapy, and Beck's cognitive therapy; the common characteristic in this case is the typically short-term nature of these interventions (Koss & Shiang, 1994). As the latter categorization would include *any* intervention that happens to involve a patient in fewer than two dozen sessions, such as electroconvulsive therapy, many drug therapies, and even psychosurgery, our discussion has assumed the more substantive definition of brief therapy as equivalent to some variation of psychoanalysis that is designed for short-term application.

EVALUATION OF ANALYTIC THERAPIES

Paradigmatic differences bear on any evaluation of the effectiveness of psychoanalysis, in all its various forms. What are the criteria for improvement? A principal criterion is the lifting of repressions, making the unconscious conscious. But how is that to be demonstrated? Attempts to assess outcome have sometimes relied on projective tests, such as the Rorschach, which in turn rely on the concept of the unconscious (Cook, Blatt, & Ford, 1995). For those who reject the very concept of an unconscious, data from projective tests are not very convincing, however.

The central concept of insight has also been questioned. Rather than accept insight as the recognition by the client of some important, externally valid, historical connection or relationship, several writers (e.g., Bandura, 1969; London, 1964) have proposed that the development of insight is better understood as a *social conversion process* whereby the patient comes to accept the belief system of his or her therapist. Marmor (1962), a noted psychoanalytic scholar, suggested that insight means different things depending on the school of therapy; a patient treated by a proponent of any one of the various schools develops insights along the lines of its particular theoretical predilections. Freudians tend to elicit insights regarding Oedipal dilemmas, Sullivanians insights regarding interpersonal relationships, and so forth.

If an insight is part of a social conversion process, do we need to be concerned with its truth? We encounter this question again in our examination of cognitive behavior therapy, especially Ellis's rational-emotive therapy, in the next chapter. Therapists who encourage clients to look at things differently—as do all the therapists discussed in this chapter and the cognitive behavior therapists of the next—believe that an insight may help the client change, whether or not the insight is true. Because of the immense complexity of human lives, it is impossible to know with any degree of certainty whether an event really happened, and if it did, whether it caused the current problem.

This issue has other ramifications. In our discussion of ethics in therapy in Chapter 20, we examine the proposal that psychotherapy is inherently, ultimately, a moral enterprise. That is, therapists, sometimes unwittingly, convey to clients messages about how they *ought* to live their lives. Therapists assume the role of secular priest (London, 1964, 1986). In this framework the usefulness of a given insight depends on whether it helps the client lead a life more consonant with a particular set of shoulds and oughts.

As noted recently by several leading researchers in analytic therapy (Henry et al., 1994), it is difficult to distinguish between classical psychoanalysis and psychodynamic psychotherapy *in practice*. It is generally held that most classical psychoanalysts act in a fairly passive way, in contrast to those who practice psychodynamic psychotherapy, especially brief therapy. As noted in Chapter 2 (p. 51), however, Freud seems to have been a good deal less remote and more directive than the classical analysts who have followed him. In a report of a large psychotherapy project from the famous Menninger Foundation, a psychoanalytic clinical and research center in Topeka, Kansas, Wallerstein (1989) downplayed clear distinctions between psychoanalysis and forms of treatment based on Freud's thinking but containing greater amounts of direct support and direction from the therapist: "Real treatments in actual practice are intermingled blends of expressive-interpretive and supportive-stabilizing elements; all treatments (including even pure psychoanalyses) carry many more supportive components than they are usually credited with" (p. 205).

With all these cautions in mind, let us consider the efforts researchers have made to evaluate the efficacy of classical psychoanalytic, ego-analytic, and interpersonal therapies.

RESEARCH ON CLASSICAL PSYCHOANALYSIS

As Bachrach et al. (1991) have pointed out, there are only four outcome studies of long-term psychoanalytic treatment. Each of these studies suffers from methodological problems, the most limiting of which is the lack of a no-treatment control group. Although some people argue that the inclusion of a control group may be unethical (Wolitzky, 1995), it is difficult to make a substantive case for the efficacy of any therapy given such an omission. What would have happened to the patients' problems if no professional treatment at all had been provided? The study that perhaps came closest to a sufficient design was the Menninger Foundation Psychotherapy Research Project, which began in the mid-1960s. In this study forty-two patients were seen in either psychoanalysis (twenty-two) or short-term psychodynamic psychotherapy (twenty). In both groups about 60 percent of the patients improved; there were no significant differences between the two groups (Wallerstein, 1986).

An earlier review of research on classical psychoanalysis led to the following generalizations (Luborsky & Spence, 1978):

- Patients with severe psychopathology (e.g., schizophrenia) do not do as well as those with anxiety disorders. This result is understandable in view of Freud's admitted emphasis on neurosis rather than on psychosis and the heavy reliance of psychoanalysis on rationality and verbal abilities.

- The more education a patient has, the better he or she does in analysis, probably because of the heavy emphasis on verbal interaction.

- There is conflicting evidence as to whether the outcome of psychoanalysis is any better than what would be achieved through the mere passage of time or by engaging other professional help, such as a family doctor (Bergin, 1971). This is *not* to say that psychoanalysis does no good, only that clear evidence is as yet lacking. Given the great diversity in the characteristics of both patients and therapists and in the severity of patients' problems, the question is probably too complex to yield a single, scientifically acceptable answer.

RESEARCH ON EGO-ANALYTIC, BRIEF, AND INTERPERSONAL THERAPIES

We look first at outcome research and then at research aimed at elucidating the processes by which favorable outcomes might be achieved.

OUTCOME RESEARCH The picture emerging from outcome studies on brief psychodynamic therapy is inconsistent but generally positive. Koss and Butcher (1986) reached the conclusion that brief therapy is no less effective than time-unlimited psychoanalysis, perhaps because both patient and therapist work harder and focus on goals that are more specific and manageable than a major restructuring of the personality. Two other reviews indicate either no superiority (Crits-Christoph, 1992) or modest superiority (Svartberg & Stiles, 1991), as compared to nonpsychotherapeutic interventions such as self-help groups. In their review, Goldfried, Greenberg, and Marmar (1990) concluded that brief dynamic therapy is effective in treating stress and bereavement (Marmar & Horowitz, 1988), late-life depression (Thompson, Gallagher, & Breckenridge, 1987), and mood and personality disorders (Marziali, 1984). Other literature reviews have found that brief psychodynamic therapy is useful with job-related distress and a variety of anxiety disorders (Koss & Shiang, 1994), including posttraumatic stress disorder (Horowitz, 1988). The NIMH Treatment of Depression Collaborative Research Program, described in detail in the next chapter, provides additional evidence that interpersonal psychotherapy (IPT) is effective in treating depression, confirming some earlier research by Weissman, Klerman, and associates (DiMascio et al., 1979).

Another study assessed the maintenance of treatment gains from IPT three years following termination of therapy for depression (Frank et al., 1990).

This study was a randomized controlled trial complete with all the methodological rigor needed to establish efficacy. The conclusions point to the potential of IPT to bring about long-term improvement (Frank & Kupfer, 1994). Thus IPT may be successful in relapse prevention, which is always a concern in the arena of psychotherapy effectiveness.

One especially interesting outcome study pitted IPT against cognitive and behavioral therapies in the treatment of the eating disorder bulimia. IPT was as effective as the other therapies in the treatment of this disorder immediately after treatment (see p. 223) (Fairburn et al., 1991) and had surpassed the other therapies in some assessment areas at a one-year follow-up (Fairburn et al., 1993), with the caveat that only one-third of the patients had maintained their treatment gains. IPT showed these positive effects even with no discussion at all of eating behaviors or body image. Frank and Spanier (1995) suggested that this study may indicate the centrality of interpersonal conflict in the development of a variety of psychological conditions.

PROCESS RESEARCH The Fairburn et al. study on bulimia provocatively raises the question of what may be the active ingredients in IPT. Frank and Spanier (1995) summarized the hypothesis in this way: IPT perhaps exerts its therapeutic effect by improving the quality of attachment, enhancing social support, and decreasing adversity and/or improving the patient's ability to cope with hardship. However, process studies are needed to illuminate fully the mechanism of effect. In this connection, Frank and Spanier related a conversation with the late Daniel Freedman, a leading academic psychiatrist, on the subject of IPT's active ingredient(s). Freedman suggested the possibility that IPT may work through what it does *not* do rather than through what it does; specifically, the focus on current and future issues may preclude the patient's preoccupation with the past, thereby preventing the individual's rumination on past events that cannot be changed.

Process research in brief therapy has improved since 1980, with more careful delineation of therapeutic procedures, the use of manuals, and more operational measurement of concepts such as the working alliance developed between therapist and patient (Hartley & Strupp, 1983; Howard & Orlinsky 1989). The term *therapeutic* or *working alliance* refers here to rapport and trust and to a sense that the therapist and the patient are working together to achieve mutually agreed upon goals. A study by Kolden (1991) found that the better this bond, the more favorable the outcome after an average of twenty-five sessions. Reviews of other studies confirm that the stronger the therapeutic relationship, or alliance, the better the outcome (Howard et al., 1991; Luborsky et al., 1988, 1990).

There are different views on *how* a good working alliance works (Henry et al., 1994). It might have a direct therapeutic effect (Henry & Strupp, 1994) or it might make interpretations more effective, thus having an indirect effect. It may be that a strong working alliance is the result, rather than the cause, of therapeutic change; that is, patients might feel better about their relationship with their therapist if they have improved. However the alliance works, it seems to be an important factor for any therapeutic approach, not only for psychodynamic approaches.

A tentative conclusion that can be drawn from recent studies of interpretations of the transference relationship is that higher frequencies of interpretations may be related to poorer outcome (Henry et al., 1994). Frequent interpretations may get in the way of the therapeutic alliance, perhaps by making the patient feel criticized and defensive if not in agreement with the therapist's views.[4] Findings such as these—with the proviso that they arise from correlational studies having methodological problems—tend to confirm the wisdom of briefer forms of dynamic and cognitive-behavioral therapies, which discourage the development and interpretation of transference.

HUMANISTIC AND EXISTENTIAL THERAPIES

Sometimes called experiential therapies, **humanistic** and **existential therapies**, like psychoanalytic therapies, are insight focused, based on the assumption that disordered behavior can best be treated by increasing the individual's awareness of motivations and needs. But there are useful contrasts between psychoanalysis and its offshoots on the one hand and humanistic and existential approaches on the other. The psychoanalytic paradigm assumes that human nature, the id, is something in need of restraint, that effective socialization requires the ego to mediate between the environ-

ment and the basically antisocial, at best, asocial, impulses stemming from biological urges. (As we have seen, though, ego-analytic theorizing deemphasized these features of classical Freudian thought and introduced concepts that bring contemporary psychoanalytic thinking closer to humanistic and existential approaches.)

Humanistic and existential therapies place greater emphasis on the person's freedom of choice, regarding free will as the person's most important characteristic. Yet free will is a double-edged sword, for it not only offers fulfillment and pleasure but also threatens acute pain and suffering. It is an innately provided gift that *must* be used and that requires special courage to use. Not everyone can meet this challenge; those who cannot are regarded as candidates for client-centered, existential, and Gestalt therapies.

CARL ROGERS'S CLIENT-CENTERED THERAPY

Carl Rogers was an American psychologist whose theorizing about psychotherapy grew slowly out of years of intensive clinical experience. After teaching at the university level in the 1940s and 1950s, he helped organize the Center for Studies of the Person in La Jolla, California. Rogers's **client-centered therapy** is based on several assumptions about human nature and the means by which we can try to understand it (Ford & Urban, 1963; Rogers, 1951, 1961).

- People can be understood only from the vantage point of their own perceptions and feelings, that is, from their phenomenological world. To understand individuals we must look at the way they experience events rather than

Carl Rogers, a humanistic therapist, proposed that the key ingredient in therapy is the attitude and style of the therapist rather than specific techniques.

---

[4]Of course, if the patient finds no validity in the therapist's interpretation and disagrees with it, it may be that the interpretation is wrong. At the least, it is not very useful. As Henry et al. (1994) put it, "Piper, Azim, Joyce, and McCallum (1991) noted that high levels of interpretations may make patients feel criticized and cause them to 'shut down.' [W]ith given patients, certain interpretations might be perceived as irrelevant or intrusive and traumatizing" (p. 477).

at the events themselves, for each person's phenomenological world is the major determinant of behavior and makes that person unique.

- Healthy people are aware of their behavior. In this sense Rogers's system is similar to psychoanalysis and ego analysis, for it emphasizes the desirability of being aware of motives.

- Healthy people are innately good and effective; they become ineffective and disturbed only when faulty learning intervenes.

- Healthy people are purposive and goal directed. They do not respond passively to the influence of their environment or to their inner drives. They are self-directed. In this assumption Rogers is closer to ego analysis than to orthodox Freudian psychoanalysis.

- Therapists should not attempt to manipulate events for the individual; rather, they should create conditions that will facilitate independent decision making by the client. When people are not concerned with the evaluations, demands, and preferences of others, their lives are guided by an innate tendency for *self-actualization*.

THERAPEUTIC INTERVENTION

Assuming that a mature and well-adjusted person makes judgments based on what is intrinsically satisfying and actualizing, Rogers avoided imposing goals on the client during therapy. According to Rogers, the client is to take the lead and direct the course of the conversation and of the session. The therapist's job is to create conditions so that during their hour together the client can return once again to his or her basic nature and judge which course of life is intrinsically gratifying. Because of his very positive view of people, Rogers assumed that their decisions would not only make them happy with themselves but also turn them into good, civilized people. The road to these good decisions is not easy, however.

According to Rogers and other humanistic and existential therapists, people must take responsibility for themselves, even when they are troubled. It is often difficult for a therapist to refrain from giving advice, from taking charge of a client's life, especially when the client appears incapable of making his or her own decisions. But Rogerians hold steadfastly to the rule that an individual's innate capacity for growth and self-direction will assert itself provided that the therapeutic atmosphere is warm, attentive, and receptive. They believe that if the therapist steps in, the process of growth and self-actualization will

only be thwarted, that whatever short-term relief might come from the therapist's intervening will interfere with long-term growth. The therapist must not become yet another person whose wishes the client strives to satisfy.

Rogers's thinking evolved from a clear specification of techniques (Rogers, 1942) to an emphasis on the attitude and emotional style of the therapist and a deemphasis of specific procedures (Rogers, 1951). The therapist should have three core qualities: genuineness, unconditional positive regard, and empathic understanding.

Genuineness, sometimes called congruence, encompasses spontaneity, openness, and authenticity. The therapist has no phoniness and no professional facade and discloses his or her feelings and thoughts informally and candidly to the client. In a sense the therapist, through honest self-disclosure, provides a model for what the client can become by being in touch with feelings and being able to express them and to accept responsibility for doing so. The therapist has the courage to present himself or herself to others as he or she really is. (Note the contrast with psychoanalysis.)

The second attribute of the successful therapist, according to Rogers, is the ability to extend **unconditional positive regard**. Other people set what Rogers called "conditions of worth"—"I will love you if…" The client-centered therapist prizes clients as they are and conveys unpossessive warmth for them, even if he or she does not approve of their behavior. People have value merely for being people, and the therapist must care deeply for and respect a client for the simple reason that he or she is another human being engaged in the struggle of growing and being alive.

The third quality, **accurate empathic understanding**, is the ability to see the world through the eyes of clients from moment to moment, to understand the feelings of clients both from their own phenomenological vantage point, which is known to them, and from perspectives of which they may be only dimly aware.

EMPATHY

Empathy is probably the most important and yet poorly understood aspect of Rogers's theorizing. Empathy is the recognition and acceptance of another person's feelings and it is one of the few techniques of Rogerian therapy. Within the context of a warm therapeutic relationship the therapist encourages the client to talk about his or her most deeply felt concerns and attempts to restate the emotional aspects, and not merely the content, of what the

FOCUS 17.3   EXCERPT FROM A CLIENT-CENTERED THERAPY SESSION

Client (an eighteen-year-old female college student) My parents really bug me. First it was Arthur they didn't like, now it's Peter. I'm just fed up with all their meddling.

Therapist You really are angry at your folks.

Client Well, how do you expect me to feel? Here I am with a 3.5 GPA, and providing all sorts of other goodies, and they claim the right to pass on how appropriate my boyfriend is. (Begins to sob.)

Therapist It strikes me that you're not just angry with them. (Pause) Maybe you're worried about disappointing them.

Client (Crying even more) I've tried all my life to please them. Sure their approval is important to me. They're really pleased when I get A's, but why do they have to pass judgment on my social life as well?

Although the emotion expressed initially was anger, the therapist believed that the client actually was fearful of criticism from her parents. The therapist therefore made an advanced empathic statement in an effort to explore with the client what was implied but not expressed. Previous sessions had suggested that the client worked hard academically primarily to please her parents and to avoid their censure. She had always been able to win their approval by getting good grades, but more recently the critical eye of her mother and father was directed at the young men she was dating. The client was beginning to realize that she had to arrange her social life to please her parents. Her fear of disapproval from her parents became the focus in therapy after the therapist had helped her see beyond her anger.

---

client says. This reflection of feelings to the client is meant gradually to remove the emotional conflicts that block self-actualization. Because feelings are mirrored without judgment or disapproval, the client can look at them, clarify them, and acknowledge and accept them. Feared thoughts and emotions that were previously too threatening to enter awareness can become part of the self-concept. If therapeutic conditions allowing self-acceptance are established, clients begin to talk in a more honest and emotional way about themselves. Rogers assumed that such talk in itself is primarily responsible for changing behavior.

In this approach the therapist is not being truly nondirective, a term often applied to Rogers, for he or she selectively attends to evaluative statements and feelings expressed by the client. The therapist believes that these are the matters the client should be helped to examine.

Rogers's application of empathy is sometimes assumed to be an easy, straightforward matter, but it requires much subtlety and constitutes strong medicine indeed. The therapist does not always restrict himself or herself to finding words for the emotional aspects of what the client says, but in what one writer called **advanced accurate empathy** (Egan, 1975), he or she goes beyond to what he or she believes *lies behind* the client's observable behavior and most obvious thoughts and feelings (see Focus 17.3). The therapist makes an inference about what is troubling the client and interprets what the client has said in a way that seems different from the client's actual statements.

In our view, advanced empathy represents theory building on the part of the therapist. After considering over a number of sessions what the client has been saying and how he or she has been saying it, the therapist generates a hypothesis about what may be the true source of distress and yet remains hidden from the client.[5] The following example illustrates the difference between primary and advanced empathy.

Client: I don't know what's going on. I study hard, but I just don't get good marks. I think I study as hard as anyone else, but all of my efforts seem to go down the drain. I don't know what else I can do.

Counselor A: You feel frustrated because even when you try hard you fail [primary empathy].

Counselor B: It's depressing to put in as much effort as those who pass and still fail. It gets you down and maybe even makes you feel a little sorry for yourself [advanced empathy]. (Egan, 1975, p. 135)

In **primary empathy** the therapist tries to restate the client's thoughts, feelings, and experiences *from the client's own point of view*. This work occurs at the phenomenological level—the therapist views the client's world from the client's perspective and then communicates to the client that this frame of reference is understood and appreciated. In advanced empathy the therapist generates a view that takes

---

[5] Whether an advanced empathy statement by the therapist should be regarded as *accurate* is another question. These interpretations by client-centered therapists can never be known for sure to be true. Rather, like scientific theories and insights into the past, they may be more or less *useful*.

the client's world into account but conceptualizes things in what is hoped to be a more constructive way. *The therapist presents to the client a way of considering himself or herself that may be quite different from the client's accustomed perspective.*

To understand this important distinction, bear in mind that therapists operating within the client-centered framework assume that the client views things in an unproductive way, as evidenced by the psychological distress that has brought the client into therapy. At the primary empathic level the therapist accepts this view, understands it, and communicates to the client that it is appreciated. But at the advanced or interpretive level, the therapist offers something new, a perspective that he or she hopes is better and more productive and implies new modes of action. Advanced empathizing builds on the information provided over a number of sessions in which the therapist concentrated on making primary-level empathic statements.

The client-centered therapist, operating within a phenomenological philosophy, *must* have as the goal the movement of a client from his or her present phenomenological world to another one, hence the importance of the advanced-empathy stage. Since people's emotions and actions are determined by how they construe themselves and their surroundings, by their phenomenology, those who are dysfunctional or otherwise dissatisfied with their present mode of living are in need of a *new* phenomenology. From the very outset then, client-centered therapy—and all other phenomenological therapies—concentrates on clients' adopting frameworks different from what they had upon beginning treatment. Merely to reflect back to clients their current phenomenology cannot in itself bring therapeutic change. A new phenomenology must be acquired.

EVALUATION

Largely because of Rogers's insistence that the outcome and process of therapy be carefully scrutinized and empirically validated, efforts have been made to evaluate client-centered therapy. Rogers can be credited with originating the field of psychotherapy research. He and his students deserve the distinction for removing the mystique and excessive privacy of the consulting room. For example, they pioneered the tape recording of therapy sessions for subsequent analysis by researchers.

Most research on Rogerian therapy has been process rather than outcome oriented, focused principally on relating outcome to the personal qualities of therapists. Results have been inconsistent, casting doubt on the widely held assumption that posi-

tive outcome is strongly related to the therapist's empathy and genuineness (Beutler, Crago, & Arizmendi, 1986; Greenberg, Elliott, & Lietaer, 1994; Lambert et al., 1986). It probably makes sense to continue emphasizing these qualities in the training of clinicians, however, as such qualities are likely to help create an atmosphere of trust and safety within which the client can reveal the deep inner workings of the self (Bohart & Greenberg, 1997). But it is not justifiable, from a research perspective, to assert that these qualities by themselves are sufficient to help clients change.

In keeping with Rogers's phenomenological approach, self-reports by clients have been the usual measures of the outcome of therapy. The basic data have been the individual's own phenomenological evaluation of and reaction to the self and events in his or her world. The overt behavior believed to follow from these perceptions, that is, how patients actually *behave* following therapy, until recently has not typically been the focus of study by client-centered therapy researchers.

Rogers's emphasis on subjective experience raises epistemological problems, for the therapist must be able to make accurate and incisive inferences about what the client is feeling or thinking. Validity is a real issue. Rogers relied on what the client said, yet he also asserted that clients can be unaware of their true feelings; it is this lack of awareness that brings most of them into therapy in the first place. As with psychoanalysis, we must ask how a therapist is to make an inference about internal processes of which a client is seemingly unaware and then by what procedures the usefulness or validity of that inference is to be evaluated.

The early use of self-descriptive measures of outcome from client-centered therapy has given way to more direct and theoretically neutral measures that tap into the patient's daily functioning in life, such as the adequate performance of social roles. An associated trend is the use of multiple methods of assessing therapeutic change (Beutler, 1983; Lambert et al., 1986) as investigators have come increasingly to appreciate the complex nature of behavior and the need to assess it along many dimensions. For example, physiological measures can be supplemented with self-reports from the patients as well as with reports from significant others (e.g., spouses). A meta-analysis of studies on client-centered therapy from 1978 to 1992 revealed only eight that had a control group and concluded that after such intervention clients were better off than about 80 percent of comparable people who had not received any professional therapy (Greenberg et al., 1994). Although not bad, this outcome is no better than that achieved by comparison therapies, such as brief psychodynamic treatment, with people who are not severely disturbed.

Rogers may be criticized for assuming that self-actualization is the principal human motivation. He inferred this motive from his observation that people seek out situations offering fulfillment, but then he proposed the self-actualization tendency as an *explanation* of the search for these situations.

Finally, Rogers assumed both that the psychologically healthy person makes choices to satisfy self-actualizing tendencies and that people are by their very natures good. But some social philosophers have taken a less optimistic view of human nature. Thomas Hobbes, for example, stated that life is "nasty, brutish, and short." How do we explain a person who behaves in a brutish fashion and yet asserts that this behavior is intrinsically gratifying and self-actualizing?

It may be that the problem of extreme unreasonableness was not adequately addressed by Rogers because he and his colleagues concentrated on people who were only mildly disturbed. As a way to help unhappy but not severely disturbed people understand themselves better (and *perhaps* even to behave differently), client-centered therapy may be appropriate and effective. This humanistic approach remains popular in the encounter group movement (see p. 560), but Rogerian therapy may not be appropriate for a severe psychological disorder, as Rogers himself warned.

EXISTENTIAL THERAPY

Together with the humanistic perspective, the existential approach constituted in the 1950s what Abraham Maslow (1968) termed a *third force* in psychology (psychoanalysis and behaviorism being the other two forces). Humanism and existentialism have much in common, but the humanistic work of Americans such as Rogers can be contrasted with the more European existential approach that derives from the writings of such philosophers as Sartre, Kierkegaard, and Heidegger and such psychiatrists as Binswanger and Boss of Switzerland and Viktor Frankl of Austria, whose logotherapy and views on depression were discussed earlier (p. 245). In an influential book on existential psychotherapy, Stanford University psychiatrist Irvin Yalom portrayed well the differences between these approaches.

The existential tradition in Europe has always emphasized human limitations and the tragic dimensions of existence. Perhaps it has done so because Europeans have had a greater familiarity with geographic and ethnic confinement, with war, death, and uncertain existence. The United States (and the humanistic

The existential approach to therapy draws heavily on the writings of existential philosophers such as Sartre.

psychology it spawned) bathed in a Zeitgeist of expansiveness, optimism, limitless horizons, and pragmatism. Accordingly, the imported form of existential thought has been systematically altered [as American humanistic psychology has absorbed some of European existentialism].... The European focus is on limits, on facing and taking into oneself the anxiety of uncertainty and nonbeing. The humanistic psychologists, on the other hand, speak less of limits and contingency than of development of potential, less of acceptance than of awareness, less of anxiety than of peak experiences and oceanic oneness, less of life meaning than of self-realization [and self-actualization], less of apartness and basic aloneness than of I-thou and encounter. (1980, p. 19)

The existential point of view, like humanism, emphasizes personal growth. There are, though, some important distinctions. Humanism, exemplified by Rogers's views, stresses the goodness of human nature. It holds that if unfettered by ground-

Humanistic therapist Abraham Maslow made Carl Jung's self-actualization a central factor in his psychology.

less fears and societal restrictions, human beings will develop normally, even exceptionally, much as a flower will sprout from a seed if given enough light, air, and water. Existentialism is gloomier; it contains a strain of darkness. Although it embraces free will and responsibility, existentialism stresses the anxiety that is inevitable in making important choices, the existential choices on which existence depends, such as staying or not staying with a spouse, with a job, or even with this world. Hamlet's famous soliloquy beginning "To be, or not to be, that is the question" (act III, scene 1) is a classic existential statement. To be truly alive is to confront the anxiety that comes with existential choices. Existential anxiety comes from several sources (Tillich, 1952):

- We are all aware that one day we shall die; when we honestly confront this inescapable reality, we face existential anxiety.
- We are also aware of our helplessness against chance circumstances that can forever change our lives, such as a crippling automobile accident.
- We are aware that we must ultimately make decisions, act, and live with the consequences.
- We must ourselves create the meaning of our lives; the ultimate responsibility for endowing our world and our lives with substance and purpose rests with each of us.
- We know that we are ultimately alone.

To avoid choices, to pretend that they do not have to be made, may protect people from anxiety, but it also deprives them of living a life with meaning and is at the core of psychopathology. Thus whereas the humanistic message is upbeat, almost ecstatic, the existential is tinged with sadness and anxiety, but not despair, unless the exercise of free will and the assumption of responsibility that accompanies it are avoided.

THE GOALS OF THERAPY

So oftentimes it happens that we live our lives in chains, and we never even know we have the key. (Jack Tempchin and Robb Strandlund, "Already Gone," 1973, 1975)

According to existentialism, we are the sum of the choices we make. Difficulties in making choices can be understood only by exploring experience. A goal of the existential therapist is to offer support and empathy through the adoption of the individual's phenomenological frame of reference; the therapist then helps the individual explore his or

her behavior, feelings, relationships, and what life means. The therapist encourages the client to confront and clarify past and present choices. Present choices and their implications for behavior are considered the most important. The person must at some point during therapy begin to behave differently, both toward the therapist and toward the outside world, in order to change his or her own existential condition.

Another goal of the existential therapist is to help the individual relate *authentically* to others, a tenet borrowed and greatly elaborated by the encounter-group movement. People are assumed to define their identity and existence in terms of their personal relationships; a person is threatened with nonbeing—or alienation—if isolated from others. Even though the person may be effective in dealing with people and the world, he or she can become anxious if deprived of open and frank relationships. Hence, although the existential view is highly subjective, it strongly emphasizes *relating to others* in an open, honest, spontaneous, and loving manner. At the same time each of us is ultimately and basically *alone*; the paradox of life is that we are inherently separate from others, that we came into the world alone and must create our own existence in the world alone.

The existential therapist strives to make the therapeutic relationship an authentic encounter between two human beings so that the patient has some practice in relating to another individual in a straightforward fashion. The therapist, through honesty and self-disclosure, helps the client learn authenticity. The therapist may do so by openly disagreeing with what the client is doing—but without rejecting the client as a worthwhile human being.

The ultimate goal of existential therapy is to make the patient more aware of his or her own potential for choice and growth. In the existential view, people create their existence anew at each moment. The potential for disorder as well as for growth is ever present. Individuals must be encouraged to accept the responsibility for their own existence and to realize that, within certain limits, they can redefine themselves at any moment and behave and feel differently within their own social environment.

This freedom to choose and the responsibility that comes with it are not easy for humans to accept and work with. Many people are afraid of this freedom, and as they begin to make choices they realize that fulfillment is a *process*, that they must constantly choose and accept responsibility if they are to be truly human and fulfill their potential. Their prospects then are not cheery; with greater awareness of their freedom to choose comes more existential anxiety. One of the goals of therapy is to bolster their resolve and ability to cope with this inescapable anxiety and to continue growing.

The existential writers are vague about what therapeutic techniques will help the client grow. A reliance on technique may even be seen as an objectifying process in which the therapist acts on the client as though he or she were a thing to be manipulated (Prochaska, 1984). The existential approach is best understood as a general *attitude* taken by certain therapists toward human nature rather than as a set of therapeutic techniques.

EVALUATION

Existential therapy lacks the definable, concrete operations on which scientific research can be conducted. Thus, although existential therapists have published numerous case reports relating successes with a variety of clinical problems, no research has been done. Moreover, existential therapists tend to see contemporary science as dehumanizing and hence to be avoided. They believe that applying science to individuals denies their unique humanness.

Many of the criticisms of client-centered therapy apply as well to existential treatment. Since by definition a person's subjective experience is unique, how can the therapist know that he or she is truly understanding a patient's world as it appears to the patient? Yet attention to subjective impressions is not necessarily unproductive. Paying heed to our freedom to choose and ability to change at any time may be an important means of improving behavior. The message implicit in existentialism, that our existence is constantly being reaffirmed and that we are not prisoners of our past mistakes and misfortunes, might well be incorporated into *any* therapy.

GESTALT THERAPY

A therapy that has both humanistic and existential elements, **Gestalt therapy** derives from the work of Frederich S. (Fritz) Perls. After receiving a medical degree in Germany in 1921, Perls became a psychoanalyst. He was rejected years later by European analysts because he challenged some of the basic precepts of psychoanalytic theory, particularly the important place accorded to the libido and its various transformations in the development of neurosis (Perls, 1947). He emigrated to the Netherlands in 1933, shortly after Hitler came to power, because he was opposed to totalitarianism, and to South Africa in 1934, as the country's first teaching analyst. There he developed the basis of Gestalt therapy. Perls took up residence in the United States in 1946 and even-

tually settled at Esalen, a center for humanistic-existential therapy in Big Sur, California. There his ideas and techniques of therapy underwent impressive growth, especially as applied in groups (Perls, 1970; Perls, Hefferline, & Goodman, 1951). During his lifetime Perls had a near cultlike following (see Focus 17.4).

BASIC CONCEPTS OF GESTALT THERAPY

Like Rogers, Perls held that people have an innate goodness and that this basic nature should be allowed to express itself. Psychological problems originate in frustrations and denials of this inborn virtue. Gestalt therapists, along with other humanistic therapists, emphasize the creative and expressive aspects of people, rather than the problematic and distorted features on which psychoanalysts often seem to concentrate.

A central goal of Gestalt therapy is to help patients understand and accept their needs, desires, and fears and to enhance their awareness of how they block themselves from reaching their goals and satisfying their needs. A basic assumption is that all of us bring our needs and wants to any situation. We do not merely perceive situations as they are; instead, we engage our social environment by projecting our needs, fears, or desires onto what is out there. Thus if I am talking to a stranger, I do not merely react to the person as that person exists; I react to the stranger in the context of my needs. Sometimes unfinished business with a significant person from the past can affect how we deal with someone in the present.

Perls and his followers have concentrated on the here and now and on the individual as an actor, as a being who is responsible for his or her own behavior and who is capable of playing a central role in bringing about beneficial changes.

Gestalt therapy draws from Gestalt psychology, a branch of psychology concerned primarily with perception. Their closest similarity may be in the attention to *wholes*. Perls wanted to make individuals whole by increasing their awareness of unacknowledged feelings and having them reclaim the parts of their personality that had been denied or disowned.

GESTALT THERAPY TECHNIQUES

Gestalt therapists focus on what a client is doing in the consulting room here and now, without delving into the past, for the most important event in the client's life is what is happening at this moment. In Gestalt therapy all that exists is the now. If the past

FOCUS 17.4   A GLIMPSE OF FRITZ PERLS

As Joe got on the elevator, he hardly noticed the short, gray-bearded man standing against the wall. Then recognition hit him. "Uh, Dr. Perls, I'm, uh, honored to meet you. I've read your work, and it's such—such an honor to meet—to be in your presence. ..." Joe's stammering speech trailed away with no effect. The old man did not move.

The elevator slowed and Joe, realizing that an opportunity was slipping away, heard himself say, hopelessly, "I'm really nervous." Perls turned and smiled at him. As the doors opened, he took Joe's arm and said, "Now let us talk." (Gaines, 1974)

Frederich (Fritz) Perls (1893-1970) was the colorful founder of Gestalt therapy.

is bothersome, it is brought into the present. Questions of why are discouraged, because searching after causes in the past is considered an attempt to escape responsibility for making choices in the present, a familiar existential theme. Clients are exhorted, cajoled, sometimes even coerced into

Gestalt therapists use the empty-chair technique to help clients confront their feelings more directly.

awareness of what is happening now. Awareness is an immediate and direct thinking and sensing. Individuals must know what is going on about them, what they think and fantasize, want and feel, what they are doing at the moment, and they must also sense posture, facial expressions, muscular tensions, and gestures, the words they use, the sound of their voice. Perls believed that awareness is curative. People have only to be moved away from their generalized, abstract ideas about themselves to an awareness of what they are feeling and doing at this exact moment.

Gestalt therapy is noted for its emphasis on techniques, in contrast to their paucity in the humanistic and existential therapies discussed so far. At its core, however, Gestalt therapy is not merely a collection of techniques; rather, it is a set of *attitudes* about the nature of humankind, a philosophy that values creativity and openness to experience. The Gestalt therapist aims to help the patient be as creative and open as the therapist is, to encounter the world on an immediate, nonjudgmental, nonreflective basis. The means to this end are the many techniques for which this approach is well-known, some of which have been taken over and adapted by therapists of other theoretical persuasions. We describe here a small sample of current Gestalt practices.

- **I-language.** To help patients bear responsibility for their present and future lives, the therapist instructs them to change "it" language into "I" language.

  Therapist: What do you hear in your voice?

  Patient: My voice sounds like it is crying.

  Therapist: Can you take responsibility for that by saying, I am crying? (Levitsky & Perls, 1970, p. 142)

  This simple change in language, besides encouraging the patient to assume responsibility for feelings and behavior, reduces the sense of being alienated from aspects of his or her very being. It helps the patient see the self as active rather than passive, as an open and searching person rather than as someone whose behavior is determined entirely by external events.

- **The empty chair.** In the empty-chair technique, a client projects and then talks to the projection of a feeling, or of a person, object, or situation. For example, if a patient is crying, the Gestalt therapist might ask the patient to regard the tears as being in an empty chair opposite him or her and to speak *to* the tears. This tactic often seems to help people confront their feelings. Indeed, to ask a person to talk *about* his or her tears is assumed to encourage the person to establish an even greater distance from his or her feelings—which Gestalt therapists assert interferes with psychological well-being.

- **Projection of feelings.** Gestalt therapists working with groups sometimes have people pair off, close their eyes, and imagine the face of an individual to whom they have a strong emotional attachment. They are encouraged to concentrate on the feelings they have about that person. Then all open their eyes and look at their partner. After a few moments they are instructed to close their eyes again and think of something neutral, such as an arithmetic problem. They then open their eyes again and look a second time at their partner. Finally, they are asked whether there was an important difference in the way they felt about their partner in the two situations. This exercise is designed to exaggerate what is assumed to be inevitable in all our social interactions, namely, the intrusion of our feelings into whatever is happening at any particular moment.

- **Reversal.** This technique involves having the person behave opposite to the way he or she feels. Someone who is excessively timid might be asked during the therapy session to behave like an outgoing person. Perls assumed that the opposite side of the coin actually lies within the being of the person and that acting out feelings not usually expressed allows the person to become aware of a part of the self that had been submerged.

- **Attending to nonverbal cues.** All therapists pay attention to nonverbal and paralinguistic cues given by the client. Nonverbal cues are body movements, facial expressions, gestures, and the like; paralinguistic cues are the tone of voice, the rapidity with which words are spoken, and other audible components of speech beyond its content. People can negate with their hands or their eyes what they are saying with the larynx. Perls placed special emphasis on these nonlinguistic signals, closely observing them to determine what clients might really be feeling. "What we say is mostly lies or bullshit. But the voice is there, the gesture, the posture, the facial expression, the psychosomatic language" (Perls, 1969, p. 54).

- **The use of metaphor.** During the therapy session Gestalt therapists often create unusual scenarios to externalize, to make more vivid and understandable, a problem they believe a client is having. For example, the following scene occurred in a session we observed:

A husband and wife sat together on a sofa, bickering about the woman's mother. The husband seemed very angry with his mother-in-law, and the therapist surmised that she was getting in the way of his relationship with his wife. The therapist wanted to demonstrate to the couple how frustrating this must be for both of them, and he also wished to goad both of them to do something about it. Without warning, he rose from his chair and wedged himself between the couple. Not a word was said. The husband looked puzzled, then hurt, and gradually became angry at the therapist. He asked him to move so that he could sit next to his wife again. The therapist shook his head. When the husband repeated his request, the therapist removed his jacket and placed it over the wife's head so that the husband could not even see her. A long silence followed, during which the husband grew more and more agitated. The wife meanwhile was sitting quietly, covered by the therapist's coat. Suddenly the husband stood up, walked past the therapist, and angrily removed the coat; then he pushed the therapist off the sofa. The therapist exploded in good-natured laughter. "I wondered how long it would take you to do something!" he roared.

This staged scene drove several points home in a way that mere words might not have. The husband, having been trained already by the therapist to get in better touch with his feelings and to express them without fear or embarrassment, reported tearfully that he had felt cut off from his wife by the therapist, in much the same way that he felt alienated from her by her mother. The mother was intruding, and he was not doing anything about it. He did not trust himself to assert his needs and to take action to satisfy them. The fact that he was able to remove the coat and the therapist as well made him wonder whether he might not behave similarly toward his mother-in-law. As he spoke, his wife began to sob; she confided to her husband that all along she had been wanting him to take charge of the problem with her mother. So far so good. But then the therapist turned to the woman and asked her why she had not removed the coat herself! The husband grinned as the therapist gently chided the wife for being unduly passive about her marital problems. By the end of the session, the clients, although emotionally drained, felt in better contact with each other and expressed their resolve to work together actively to alter their relationship with her mother.

- **Dream work.**   The interpretation of dreams is another important part of Gestalt therapy. In contrast to psychoanalytic approaches, Gestalt therapy does not consider the dream a rich source of symbolism relating to unconscious processes.

> Every image in the dream, whether human, animal, vegetable, or mineral, is taken to represent an alienated portion of the self. By reexperiencing and retelling the dream over and over again in the present tense, from the standpoint of each image, the patient can begin to reclaim these alienated fragments, and accept them, live with them and express them more appropriately. (Enright, 1970, p. 121)

For example, a woman in Gestalt therapy dreamed of walking down a crooked path among tall, straight trees. The therapist asked her to *become* one of the trees, and this made her feel serene and more deeply rooted. She then expressed her desire for such security. When she was asked to become the crooked path, tears welled as she confronted the deviousness of the way in which she lived. Once again the Gestalt therapist helped the client externalize feelings customarily avoided, so that she could become aware of them, acknowl-

edge them as her own, and then perhaps decide to change them.

Whether these interpretations actually reflect the real meaning of the dream is not of concern to the Gestalt therapist. Consistent with their phenomenological approach, Gestalt therapists encourage clients to recount, with emotion, the meaning that the dream has for them *at that very moment*. Even though the therapist may have a hypothesis about what a particular dream means to the client, the therapist takes care not to impose that meaning on the dreamer, for it is the dreamer's dream. The only significance it has for the dreamer is the meaning it holds as it is discussed in the session. In this sense Gestalt therapy does not have a theory of dreams. It is concerned with dream *work*, the analysis of dreams by the client with support from the therapist. Since only the phenomenal world has importance for each client, his or her immediate experience is the one thing worth focusing on. The same dream could have a different meaning for the client five minutes later.

EVALUATION

Gestalt therapists spend much or most of their time urging clients to be more expressive, spontaneous, and responsive to their own needs. Perls described this activity as making the person more attentive to emerging gestalts. Therapy also attempts to make the person whole by encouraging a reclamation of parts of the personality until now denied. Gestalt therapy is therefore aligned with the experimental findings of Gestalt psychology. It is open to question, however, whether Perls's description is the most accurate or parsimonious way of talking about the techniques, and, more important, whether such concepts assist in the effective training of good therapists.

Gestalt therapy forcefully conveys the existential message that a person is not a prisoner of the past, that he or she can at any time make the existential choice to be different, and that the therapist will not tolerate stagnation. No doubt this optimistic view helps many people change. If the person does not know how to behave differently, however, considerable damage can be done to an already miserable individual. For example, if a socially inhibited patient never learned *how* to talk assertively to others, it would do little good only to have the person become more aware of this nonassertiveness and to encourage him or her to become more expressive. Lacking social skills, the person would probably behave awkwardly and ineffectually with others and could end up feeling even worse about himself or herself than before.

Perls's emphasis on responsibility is not to be confused with commitment or obligation to others. Even as a therapist Perls did not present himself as a person who assumed responsibility for others, and he did not urge this on his patients either. The individual has the responsibility to take care of himself or herself, to meet his or her *own* needs as they arise. This apparent egocentrism may be troubling for people with a social conscience and for those who have in the past made commitments to others. Perls believed that such commitments should never be made (Prochaska, 1984).

According to humanists such as Perls and Rogers, people are by their very nature good, purposive, and resourceful. If this is true, it would be reasonable to trust this intrinsic good nature and to encourage direct expression of needs. But are people always good? Sometimes clients—especially those who are psychologically troubled—feel they must do something that in the judgment of the professional is not in their own best interest. Suppose that a client feels the need to murder someone or to engage in other behavior that to outside observers is undesirable. What is the therapist's responsibility? At what point does the therapist intervene and impose his or her judgment? When patients threaten to act in destructive ways, few therapists stand by and do nothing. As seen in the discussion of the Tarasoff ruling in Chapter 20, therapists now have no choice *but* to take action in such circumstances, even against the wishes of the patient. But even apart from this legal constraint, Gestalt therapists do *not* abdicate all decisions to their clients and they *do* exert considerable influence on them, if only by virtue of the models they provide. As we have indi-

cated, Perls was a charismatic figure. Most people probably adopt the values of their therapist, regardless of theoretical orientation (Pentony, 1966; Rosenthal, 1955), and it seems preferable to us to admit this social influence so that it can be addressed, rather than to deny that such influence exists and perhaps allow for even greater tyranny of therapists over patients.

A few studies have attempted to examine aspects of Gestalt therapy, in particular, the empty-chair technique. In an analogue study with college undergraduates, Conoley and his colleagues (1983) found that self-rated anger was reduced after a twenty-minute empty-chair exercise. Greenberg and Rice (1981) reported that the technique increases awareness and emotional expression, and Clarke and Greenberg (1986) found it superior to problem solving in helping people make decisions.

All therapies are subject to abuse. Gestalt is no exception, and it may indeed present special problems. It is not difficult, even for trainees with a minimum of experience, to induce clients to express their feelings. Some Gestalt techniques may be so powerful in opening people up that clients can be harmed unintentionally. The forcefulness of Perls's personality and his confrontational style have led some therapists to mimic him without the thoughtfulness, skill, and caring he appeared to possess in unusual abundance. The responsible Gestalt therapist is a professional who keeps the client's interests at the forefront and who understands that the expression of strong emotion for its own sake is seldom enough to ease an individual's suffering. The nature of Gestalt therapy and the fact that a cult has grown up around the memory of Fritz Perls are reasons that practicing Gestalt therapists should strive for an extra measure of caution and humility.

SUMMARY

Research on the various forms of psychotherapy has been conducted for many decades, with sometimes complicated and inconsistent results. The evaluation of the effects of psychotherapy has grown in significance as increased demands for accountability are being imposed by health insurance companies. Several general issues were reviewed to provide a context for the study of psychotherapeutic interventions in this and the next two chapters. These issues included the placebo effect, which refers to improvement brought about by expectations rather than specific action of the treatment; differences between therapy as researched and therapy as practiced, as when, for example, research studies employ treatment manuals that bear only a remote resemblance to therapy conducted by clinicians outside of the constraints of a research project; the absence of no treatment controls in much psychotherapy research, rendering it impossible to compare therapy outcomes with what would have happened without professional intervention;

and the implications of chaos theory for the limits of understanding how patients are going to change as a result of the many unpredictable and uncontrollable forces in life.

Insight therapies share the basic assumption that behavior is disordered because the person is not aware of what motivates his or her actions. Psychoanalysis emphasizes factors from the past, whereas most humanistic and existential approaches, such as those of Rogers and Perls, emphasize the current determinants of behavior. A concern with present-day factors in the patient's life is also found in many contemporary variants of classical psychoanalysis, such as ego analysis and brief psychodynamic interpersonal therapy.

Classical psychoanalysis tries to uncover childhood repressions so that infantile fears of libidinal expression can be examined by the adult ego in the light of present-day realities. Brief psychodynamic therapy puts more emphasis on the need and ability of the patient to achieve greater control over the environment and over instinctual gratification. It is a time-limited therapy, in which expectations are set for fewer than two dozen sessions. There is a focus on concrete goals and learning ways to cope with life's inevitable stressors, forsaking the goal of psychoanalysis to obtain a personality overhaul through analysis of the transference neurosis.

Rogers trusted the basic goodness of the drive to self-actualize, and he proposed the creation of nonjudgmental conditions in therapy. Through empathy and unconditional positive regard for their clients, Rogerian therapists help them view themselves more accurately and trust their own instincts for self-actualization. Existential therapists, influenced primarily by European existential philosophy, similarly regard people as having the innate ability to realize their potential; people also have the freedom to decide at any given moment to become different. Both Rogerians and existentialists assume that the only reality is the one experienced by the individual. Thus the therapist must try to view the world from the client's phenomenological frame of reference, rather than from his or her own.

The Gestalt therapy of Perls stresses living in the now, and the many techniques he and his followers have introduced are designed to help clients experience their current needs and feel comfortable about satisfying them as they emerge.

A growing body of research supports the efficacy of some of the insight therapies. Some of this research is process oriented, that is, it examines the factors responsible for improvement. The working alliance between therapist and patient is emerging as an important variable. Psychotherapy research, though, is exceedingly complex and difficult, and scientifically based conclusions are not as available as strongly held unsubstantiated beliefs about how to help people change.

KEY TERMS

psychotherapy
insight therapy
placebo effect
outcome research
process research
meta-analysis
psychoanalysis
free association
resistances
dream analysis

latent content
manifest content
interpretation
denial
transference neurosis
countertransference
ego analysis
brief therapy
interpersonal therapy (IPT)

humanistic and existential
  therapies
client-centered therapy
genuineness
unconditional positive regard
accurate empathic
  understanding
advanced accurate empathy
primary empathy
Gestalt therapy

18

Alfredo Castañeda,
"When the Mirror Dreams
With Another Image,"
1988

COGNITIVE AND BEHAVIOR THERAPIES

A middle-aged construction worker sought help for his depression. He was having trouble getting out of bed in the morning and viewed his job and life in general with dread and foreboding. Careful assessment revealed that the man was inordinately concerned whether the men working under him liked and approved of him. His depression had set in after he had been promoted to foreman, a position that required him to issue orders and monitor and criticize the activities of other workers. His men would occasionally object to his instructions and comments, and the client found their resentful stares and sullen silences very upsetting. He agreed with the therapist that he was unduly anxious when criticized or rejected. The reduction in job-related anxiety that followed treatment by systematic desensitization succeeded in lifting his depression. (adapted from Goldfried & Davison, 1994, p. 114)

A new way of treating psychopathology, called **behavior therapy**, emerged in the 1950s. In its initial form this therapy applied procedures based on classical and operant conditioning to alter clinical problems. Sometimes the term *behavior modification* is used as well, and therapists who employ operant conditioning as a means of treatment often prefer that term. Although there has been considerable ferment over how to define the field (e.g., Fishman, Rotgers, & Franks, 1988; Mahoney, 1993), behavior therapy today is characterized more by its epistemological stance—its search for rigorous standards of proof—than by allegiance to any particular set of concepts. Behavior therapy is an attempt to change abnormal behavior, thoughts, and feelings by applying in a clinical context the methods used and the discoveries made by experimental psychologists in their study of both normal and abnormal behavior.

That the most effective clinical procedures will be developed through science is an *assumption* (Beutler & E. H. Davison, 1995). There is nothing inherent in the scientific method that guarantees victories for those studying human behavior according to its principles. Because we have reached the moon, Mars, and beyond by playing the science game does not mean that the same set of rules should be applied to human behavior. The existentialists, who emphasize free will, assume that the nature of humankind cannot be meaningfully probed by following the rules favored by the authors of this textbook. Although we are placing our bets on the scientific work described in this chapter, it nonetheless remains an article of faith that behavior therapy will prove the best means of treating disordered behavior, cognition, and affect.

Exactly when behavior therapy first began to be developed is difficult to know, but it did not begin when some social scientist woke up one morning and proclaimed that from this day forward people with psychological problems should be treated with techniques suggested by experimental findings. Rather, over a number of years people in the clinical field began to formulate a new set of assumptions about dealing with the problems they were encountering. Although there are areas of overlap, we have found it helpful to distinguish four theoretical approaches in behavior therapy—counterconditioning, operant conditioning, modeling, and cognitive behavior therapy. We review these approaches, then discuss behavioral medicine, a new specialization that blends behavioral and biomedical knowledge to enhance physical health and lessen physical illness. Then we consider how gains made in therapy can be generalized to real life and be effectively maintained. We go on to examine some important problems and issues as they pertain to cognitive and behavior therapies. Finally, we consider the growing interest in eclecticism and theoretical integration in psychotherapy, examining both the advantages and pitfalls in any such effort.

COUNTERCONDITIONING

In counterconditioning, illustrated in Figure 2.5 (p. 44), a response (R1) to a given stimulus (S) is eliminated by eliciting different behavior (R2) in the presence of that stimulus. For example, if an individual is afraid (R1) of being in an enclosed space (S), the therapist attempts to help the person have a calm reaction (R2) when he or she is in such a space. Evidence shows that unrealistic fears can be eliminated in this way. An early and now famous clinical demonstration of counterconditioning was reported by Mary Cover Jones (1924). She successfully eliminated a little boy's fear of rabbits by feeding him in the presence of a rabbit. The animal was at first kept several feet away and then gradually moved closer on successive occasions. In this fashion the fear (R1) produced by the rabbit (S) was "crowded out" by the stronger positive feelings associated with eating (R2). Systematic desensitization and aversion therapy are two behavioral techniques assumed to be effective because of counterconditioning.

SYSTEMATIC DESENSITIZATION

Joseph Wolpe (1958) created a therapy technique for fearful adults similar to the procedures used by Jones three decades earlier. He found that many of

Joseph Wolpe, one of the pioneers in behavior therapy, is known particularly for systematic desensitization, a widely applied behavioral technique.

his patients could be encouraged to expose themselves gradually to the situation or object they feared if they were at the same time engaging in behavior that inhibited anxiety. Rather than have his patients eat, however, Wolpe taught these adults deep muscle relaxation. His training procedures were adapted from earlier work by Edmond Jacobson (1929), who had shown that strong emotional states such as anxiety could be markedly inhibited if a person were in a state of deep relaxation.

Many of the fears felt by Wolpe's patients were so abstract—for example, fear of criticism and fear of failure—that it was impractical to confront them with real-life situations that would evoke these fears. Consistent with earlier proposals by Salter (1949), Wolpe reasoned that he might have fearful adults *imagine* what they feared. Thus he formulated a new technique that he called **systematic desensitization**, in which imagery that reflects the person's fears is paired with a state of deep relaxation. As documented by Wolpe and many other clinicians, the ability to tolerate stressful imagery is generally followed by a reduction of anxiety in related real-life situations. The case study in Chapter 2 (p. 45) illustrates the application of this technique.

Between therapy sessions patients are usually instructed to place themselves in progressively more frightening real-life situations. These homework assignments help move their adjustment from imagination to reality. As noted in Chapter 6 (p. 132), exposure to feared real-life situations has long been known to be an important means of reducing unwarranted anxieties.

Clinicians have treated many different anxiety-related problems by systematic desensitization. The technique appears deceptively simple. However, as with any therapy for people in emotional distress, its proper application is a complicated affair. The clinician must first determine, by means of a comprehensive behavioral assessment, that the situations eliciting the patient's anxious reactions do not warrant such reactions. If a person is anxious because he or she lacks the skills to deal with a given set of circumstances—for example, if a person is anxious about piloting an airplane because he or she doesn't know how to operate an aircraft—desensitization is inappropriate. Desensitization is appropriate, however, if a person seems to be inhibited by anxiety from behaving in customary and known ways. Sometimes the technique can be used when the patient does not appear obviously anxious, as in the case that opened this chapter. As with all the techniques we describe, this one is very rarely used exclusively. A person fearful of social interactions might well be given training in conversational and other social skills in addition to desensitization. In the most general sense the applicability of desensitization depends largely on the therapist's ingenuity in discovering the source of the anxiety underlying a patient's problems (Goldfried & Davison, 1994).

Researchers became interested in studying desensitization because clinical reports indicated that the technique was effective. Scores of controlled studies have lent credence to the prior clinical claims, beginning with the earliest experiments in the 1960s (e.g., Davison, 1968b; Lang & Lazovik, 1963; Paul, 1966).

A recent technological innovation used in treating unrealistic fears is the virtual reality (VR) device.

VR integrates real-time computer graphics, body tracking devices, visual displays, and other sensory input devices to immerse a participant in a computer-generated virtual environment (VE; Kalawsky, 1993). Participants usually wear a head-mounted display fitted with an electromagnetic sensor. The user is presented with a computer-generated view of a virtual world that changes in a natural way with head and body motion. For some environments, users may also hold a second position sensor in their hand that allows them to manipulate a virtual hand to interact with the environment, for example, push an elevator button and ascend. (Rothbaum et al., 1995a, p. 548)

These complex computer-driven apparatuses permit the therapist to expose a fearful patient *in the consulting room* to a vivid rendition of what he or she fears in real life. This process is less time-consuming and more controllable than, for example, taking an acrophobic person to the top of a building and encouraging him or her to remain there, perhaps relaxing at the same time to control or countercondition the fear. Virtual reality devices may produce images that are more realistic than those the patient might generate during systematic desensitization, and their use would certainly make sense for fearful individuals who are unable to generate realistic images. Evidence abounds that VR does generate very realistic experiences for people (e.g., Hodges et al., 1994, cited in Rothbaum et al., 1995b).

The first published case report (Rothbaum et al., 1995a) and controlled study (Rothbaum et al., 1995b) of the successful use of VR in treating an anxiety disorder (acrophobia) involved a treatment the authors dubbed "virtual reality graded exposure" (VRGE). The therapy consisted of five sessions of less than an hour's duration each over a period of three weeks. Exposures involved the person's being encouraged to look out and down from each of several virtual floors in an ascending glass elevator. The VR display showed views from the same elevator in a high-rise (forty-nine floors) hotel that had been used in vivo to assess pretreatment fear and was employed at posttreatment as well. Self-reported distress and avoidance of heights decreased markedly as a result of the VR treatment. Similar success was reported by the same clinical research group in the case of a woman fearful of flying (Rothbaum et al., 1996). We can expect increasing use of VR in psychotherapy, though its superiority to standard desensitization based on imagery is yet to be evaluated. Current VR technology does not permit exposure to more complex situations like interacting with another person.

Like researchers in the insight therapies, behavioral researchers are interested not only in whether a given technique works—the outcome question—but also in why—the process question. Wolpe hypothesized that counterconditioning underlies the efficacy of desensitization: a state or response antagonistic to anxiety is substituted for anxiety as the person is exposed gradually to stronger and stronger doses of what he or she fears. Some experiments (e.g., Davison, 1968b) suggest that counterconditioning underlies the efficacy of the technique, but a number of other explanations are possible. Most contemporary theorists attach importance to exposure per se to what the person fears; relaxation is then considered merely a useful way to encourage a frightened individual to confront what he or she fears (Wilson & Davison, 1971).

AVERSION THERAPY

The literature on classical aversive conditioning of animals (i.e., pairing a neutral or positive stimulus with an unpleasant unconditioned stimulus such as shock) led therapists to believe that negative reactions could be conditioned in human beings, and they formulated treatment programs that pair negative stimuli with stimuli that are considered inappropriately attractive, with the intent of making the latter less appealing.[1] The method called **aversion therapy**, is similar to desensitization but has the opposite goal, since the new response of anxiety, or an aversion reaction, is to be substituted for a positive response. Among the problems treated with aversion therapy are excessive drinking, smoking, transvestism, exhibitionism, and overeating (McConaghy, 1994; Miller, 1995). For example, a problem drinker who wishes to be discouraged from drinking is asked to taste, see, or smell alcohol and is then made uncomfortable while doing so. In addition to employing painful but not harmful shock to the hands as the unconditioned stimulus, some therapists have adopted the use of emetics, drugs that make the client nauseous when presented with the undesirable stimulus.

Consistent with animal research on conditioned taste aversion (Chambers & Bernstein, 1995), investigations of chemical aversion with alcoholism and nicotine dependence lend some support to the proposition that nausea paired with the taste of alcohol or with inhaling a cigarette can produce stable conditioned aversions and subsequent abstinence from alcohol or tobacco (e.g., Baker & Brandon, 1988; Cannon et al., 1986).

Aversion therapy has been controversial for ethical reasons. A great outcry has been raised about inflicting pain and discomfort on people, even when they ask for it. Perhaps the greatest ethical concern has been voiced by gay liberation organizations that have suggested that homosexuals who

---

[1]Some commentators (e.g., Sandler, 1986) consider aversion therapy a form of punishment and place it under the general rubric of operant conditioning. Our preference is otherwise, though we accept the widely held assumption in learning theory that all classical conditioning procedures have operant elements and that all operant conditioning procedures have Pavlovian features. The issue appears to be whether, as in classical conditioning, the therapist or experimenter attempts to pair a *stimulus* with an aversive event, regardless of what the person is doing, or, as in operant conditioning, the therapist attempts to pair a *response* with an aversive event. In practice there is more overlap than the conceptual scheme implies.

request painful treatment to help them shift sexual preference are actually seeking to punish themselves for behavior that a prejudiced society has convinced them is dirty. These groups have accused behavior therapists of impeding the acceptance of homosexuality as a legitimate lifestyle when they accede to such requests (Silverstein, 1972). We explore this issue in another chapter (Focus 20.5).

Behavior therapists who choose aversive procedures seldom use them exclusively. More positive techniques are also instituted to teach new behavior to replace maladaptive responses, for example, teaching a problem drinker to cope with stress by learning new skills rather than escaping from unpleasant feelings through the anesthetizing effects of alcohol. Even if the effects of aversion therapy are short-lived, the temporary reduction in undesirable behavior can allow for the learning of new responses judged by the person or the culture to be more appropriate. When aversion therapy is employed, it is generally chosen as a last resort.

Time-out is an operant procedure wherein the consequence for misbehavior is removal to an environment with no positive reinforcers.

OPERANT CONDITIONING

In the 1950s a number of investigators suggested that therapists should try to shape overt behavior in humans through rewards and punishments (Skinner, 1953). In the belief that they could through operant conditioning exercise some control over the complex, puzzling, often frenetic behavior of hospitalized patients, some psychologists set about the task of bringing practical order into the chaos of institutions for the severely disturbed.

In addition to the familiar positive reinforcers of praise, tokens, and food and negative reinforcers of verbal or physical punishment, operant researchers have developed other reinforcers. The *Premack principle* (Premack, 1959) holds that in a given situation a more probable behavior can serve as a reinforcer for a less probable behavior. For example, if you know that John would rather watch a football game than do the laundry, you can make the former contingent on the latter; allowing John to watch football can function as a positive reinforcer for washing the clothes. Most of us have applied this principle to our own behavior many times, resolving not to reward ourselves with going to a movie unless we first complete a task that holds less appeal for us.

Another operant tool is *time-out*, which refers to removing a person from an environment in which he or she can earn positive reinforcers. For example, rather than just ignoring undesirable behavior—the typical extinction method—one banishes the person for a stated period of time to a dreary location where positive reinforcers are unavailable. *Overcorrection* is a punisher that requires the person not only to restore an environment he or she has sullied but also to improve on its original condition (e.g., Azrin, Sneed, & Foxx, 1973). Thus if a destructive child tears the sheets off the bed instead of making it, the therapist requires the child to make not only that bed but others as well. Generally speaking, operant treatments work best in situations in which considerable control can be exercised by the therapist. We look first at the token economy and then at operant procedures with children.

THE TOKEN ECONOMY

An early example of work within the operant tradition is the **token economy**, a procedure in which tokens (such as poker chips or stickers) are given for desired behavior and can later be exchanged for desirable items and activities. On the basis of research that Staats and Staats (1963) conducted with children, Ayllon and Azrin (1968) set aside an entire ward of a mental hospital for a series of experiments in which rewards were provided for activities such as making beds and combing hair and were not given when behavior was withdrawn or bizarre. The forty-five female patients, who averaged sixteen years of hospitalization, were systematically rewarded for their ward work and self-care with plastic tokens that could later be exchanged for special privileges, such as listening to records, going to the movies, renting a private room, or enjoying extra visits to the canteen. The life of each patient was as much as possible controlled by this regime.

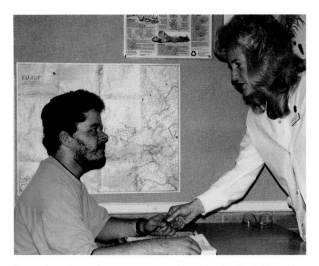

Shown here is a token economy conducted by the Social-Learning Program at Fulton State Hospital, Fulton, Missouri. The patient is receiving a token and verbal praise from the staff member for actively participating in an academic class.

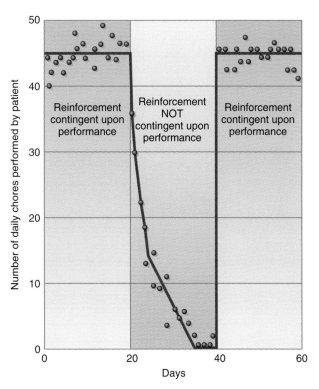

Figure 18.1 When they received tokens, patients on a ward spent more time grooming themselves and doing chores than when they were given no reward. Adapted from Ayllon and Azrin (1965).

The rules of a token economy—the medium of exchange, the chores and self-care rewarded and by what number of tokens, the items and privileges that can be purchased and for how many tokens—are carefully established and usually posted. These regimes have demonstrated how even markedly regressed adult hospital patients can be significantly affected by systematic manipulation of reinforcement contingencies, that is, rewarding some behavior to increase its frequency or ignoring other behavior to reduce its frequency. Ayllon, Azrin, and others demonstrated in this way the effect of contingencies on the behavior of their ward patients. Figure 18.1 indicates that conduct such as brushing teeth and making beds markedly decreased when rewards were withdrawn but became more frequent again when rewards were reinstated.

Since the publication of these early studies of the token economy, several similar programs have been instituted throughout the United States (Paul, Stuve, & Menditto, in press). We have already cited (p. 17) the most impressive of these, reported by Gordon Paul and Robert Lentz (1977). The long-term, regressed, and chronic schizophrenic patients in their program are the most severely debilitated institutionalized adults ever studied systematically. Some of these patients screamed for long periods, some were mute; many were incontinent, a few assaultive. Most of them no longer used silverware, and some buried their faces in their food. The patients were matched for age, sex, socioeconomic background, symptoms, and length of hospitalization and then assigned to one of three wards—

social learning (behavioral), milieu therapy, and routine hospital management. Each ward had twenty-eight residents. The two treatment wards shared ambitious objectives: to teach self-care, housekeeping, communication, and vocational skills; to reduce symptomatic behavior; and to release patients to the community.

- **Social-learning ward.** Located in a new mental health center, the social-learning ward operated on a token economy that embraced all aspects of the residents' lives. Their appearance had to pass muster in eleven specific ways each morning to earn a token. Well-made beds, good behavior at mealtime, classroom participation, and socializing during free periods were other means of earning tokens. Residents learned through modeling, shaping, prompting, and instructions. They were also taught to communicate better with one another, and they participated in problem-solving groups. Tokens were a necessity, for they purchased meals as well as small luxuries. In addition to living by the rules of the token economy, individuals received behavioral treatments tailored to their needs.

Residents were kept busy 85 percent of their waking hours learning to behave better.

- **Milieu-therapy ward.**   This ward in the new center operated according to the principles of Jones's (1953) therapeutic community, an approach reminiscent of Pinel's moral treatment of the late eighteenth century (p. 14). These residents, too, were kept busy 85 percent of their waking hours. Both individually and as a group they were expected to act responsibly and to participate in decisions about how the ward was to function. In general, they were treated more as normal individuals than as incompetent mental patients. Staff members impressed on the residents their positive expectations and praised them for doing well. When patients behaved symptomatically, staff members stayed with them, making clear the expectation that they would soon behave more appropriately.

- **Routine hospital management.**   These patients continued their accustomed hospital existence in an older state institution, receiving custodial care and heavy antipsychotic medication. Except for the 5 percent of their waking hours occupied by occasional activity, and recreational, occupational, and individual and group therapies, these people were on their own.

Gordon L. Paul, whose innovative research and evaluation of behavioral therapy for hospitalized patients has pointed the way to effective non-pharmacological treatment for schizophrenia.

Before the program began the staffs of the two treatment wards were carefully trained to adhere to detailed instructions in therapy manuals; regular observations confirmed that they were implementing the principles of a social-learning or a milieu-therapy program. Over the four and a half years of hospitalization and the one and a half years of follow-up, the patients were carefully evaluated at regular six-month intervals by structured interviews and by meticulous, direct, behavioral observations.

The results? Both the social-learning and the milieu therapy reduced positive and negative symptoms, with the social-learning ward achieving better results than the milieu ward on a number of measures. The residents also acquired self-care, housekeeping, social, and vocational skills. The behavior of members of these two groups within the institution was superior to that of the residents of the hospital ward, and by the end of treatment, more of them had been discharged—over 10 percent of the social-learning patients left the center for independent living; 7 percent of the milieu patients achieved this goal; and none of the hospital treatment patients did.

An interesting finding emerged on medication usage. About 90 percent of the patients in all three groups were receiving antipsychotic drugs at the outset of the study. Over time, use among the routine-hospital-management group increased to 100 percent, while in the other two groups the percentage of patients on drugs dropped dramatically, to 18 percent in the milieu group and 11 percent in the social-learning ward. In addition, many patients from all three groups were discharged to community placements, such as boarding homes and halfway houses, where there was supervision but also considerably less restraint than they had experienced for an average of seventeen years. Members of the social-learning group did significantly better at remaining in these community residences than did patients in the other two groups.

Considering how poorly these patients were functioning before this treatment project, these results are remarkable. That the social-learning program was superior to the milieu program is also significant, for milieu treatment is used in many mental hospitals. As implemented by Paul's team of clinicians, it provided patients with more attention than those on the social-learning ward received. This greater amount of attention would appear to control well for the placebo effect of the social-learning therapy.

These results, though, should not be accepted as confirming the usefulness of token economies per se, for the social-learning therapy contained elements that went beyond operant conditioning of overt motor behavior. Staff provided information to residents about appropriate behavior and attempted verbally to clarify misconceptions. Paul (personal communication, 1981) relegated the token economy to a secondary, although not trivial, role. He saw it as a useful device for getting the attention of severely regressed patients in the initial stages of treatment. The token economy created the opportunity for his patients to acquire new information, or, in Paul's informal phrase, to "get good things into their heads."

Paul and Lentz never claimed that any one of these patients was cured. Although they were able to live outside the hospital, most continued to manifest many signs of mental disorder, and few of them had gainful employment or participated in the social activities that most people take for granted. (The aftercare aspects of the Paul and Lentz project are discussed in detail in Chapter 19, p. 581.) The outcome, though, is not to be underestimated: chronic mental patients, those typically shut away on back wards and forgotten by society, can be resocialized and taught self-care. They can learn to behave normally enough to be discharged from mental institutions. This is a major achievement in mental health care. Reports published since the Paul and Lentz study support the effectiveness of social-learning programs (see reviews by Mueser & Liberman, 1995, and Paul & Menditto, 1992; Paul, Stuve, & Cross, in press).

OPERANT WORK WITH CHILDREN

Some of the best operant-conditioning behavior therapy has been done with children, perhaps because much of their behavior is subject to the control of others. Children, after all, tend more than adults to be under continual supervision. At school their behavior is scrutinized by teachers, and at home, parents frequently oversee their play and other social activities. In most instances the behavior therapist works with the parents and teachers in an effort to change the ways in which they reward and punish the children for whom they have responsibility. It is assumed that altering the reinforcement practices of the adults in a child's life will ultimately change the child's behavior.

The range of childhood problems dealt with through operant conditioning is broad, including bed-wetting, thumb sucking, nail biting, aggression, tantrums, hyperactivity, disruptive classroom behavior, poor school performance, language deficiency, extreme social withdrawal, and asthmatic attacks (Kazdin, 1994; Nemeroff & Karoly, 1991). Self-mutilation has also been effectively treated with punishment procedures, sometimes involving

the response-contingent application of painful electric shock to the hands or feet. Such extreme measures are used only when less drastic interventions are ineffective and when the problem behaviors are health or life threatening (Sandler, 1991). Gender identity also appears susceptible to operant procedures (see p. 364). Rates of improvement for these several problems are generally superior to those reported for traditional forms of therapy (Franks et al., 1990).

Before applying these techniques the therapist must determine that the problem behavior is an operant, that it is under the control of a contingent reinforcer. A child who is crying because of physical pain, for example, should be attended to. Encouraging results have been achieved by applying operant techniques to therapy with children with mental retardation and autism (see Chapter 15). Many therapists who apply operant-conditioning techniques have challenged assumptions about the limited trainability of such children, much to the benefit of the children and their families.

MODELING

Modeling is the third theoretical approach employed by behavior therapists. The importance of modeling and imitation in behavior is self-evident, for children as well as adults are able to acquire complex responses and eliminate emotional inhibitions merely by watching how others handle themselves. We look first at the variety of problems that can be treated by modeling and then at the role of cognition in modeling.

PROBLEMS TREATED BY MODELING

The effectiveness of modeling in clinical work was shown in an early study by Bandura, Blanchard, and Ritter (1969) in which they were attempting to help people overcome snake phobias. The researchers had fearful adults view both live and filmed confrontations of people gradually approaching and handling snakes. The fears of the patients were decidedly reduced. The pioneering work of Ivar Lovaas mentioned in Chapter 15 has from its inception employed modeling to teach complex skills, such as speech, to autistic children (Lovaas et al., 1966). Sex-therapy researchers have found that inhibited adults can become more comfortable with their sexuality if shown tastefully designed explicit films of people touching themselves, masturbating, and having intercourse (McMullen & Rosen, 1979; Nemetz, Craig, & Reith,

1978). Other films or slide presentations have significantly reduced children's fears of dogs (Hill, Liebert, & Mott, 1968), of hospitalization (Roberts et al., 1981), of surgery (Melamed & Siegel, 1975), and of dental work (Melamed et al., 1975). Using modeling films to reduce children's fears of medical treatments can be considered a behavioral-medicine or health-psychology procedure (see p. 200). Modelling is also a component of assertion training, which is described in Focus 18.1.

Some of the clinical work of Arnold Lazarus, one of the earliest behavior therapists, is also regarded as modeling treatment. As indicated in Chapter 2 (p. 45), in *behavior rehearsal* Lazarus (1971) demonstrates for a client a better way to handle a difficult interpersonal problem. The client observes the therapist's exemplary performance and then attempts to imitate it during the therapy session. By continual practice and observation the client can frequently acquire entire repertoires of more effective and more satisfying behavior. Videotape equipment can be creatively used to facilitate such modeling and imitation.

In their review of cognitive-behavioral interventions with children, Braswell and Kendall (1988) indicate that nearly all such efforts entail a model, usually an adult, providing exemplars of desired performance. For example, in an early report Meichenbaum (1971) found that having a model verbalize his or her thoughts while solving a problem—"Let's see, if I can't get anywhere, I'll try another way altogether"—led to greater improvement than when the model merely solved the problem without thinking aloud. Kendall and Braswell (1985) also encourage child behavior therapists to use naturally occurring events as modeling opportunities, for example, thinking out loud while trying to find a suitable room for the therapy session or figuring out when to schedule the next meeting. Children learn a great deal from observing others, both adults and peers; this work indicates that patterns of thought can be acquired as readily as overt behavior (Kendall, 1990).

Behavior therapy programs for hospitalized patients also make use of modeling. In an early demonstration Bellack, Hersen, and Turner (1976) contrived social situations for three chronic schizophrenic patients and then observed whether they behaved appropriately. For instance, a patient was told to pretend that he had just returned home from a weekend trip to find that his lawn had been mowed. As he gets out of the car, his next-door neighbor approaches him and says that he has cut the patient's grass because he was already cutting his own. The patient must then respond to the situation. As expected, patients were initially not very good at making a socially appropriate response, which in this instance might have been some sort of thank-you. Training followed. The therapist encouraged the patients to respond, commenting helpfully on their efforts. If necessary, the therapist also modeled appropriate behavior so that the patients could observe and then try to imitate it. This combination of role-playing, modeling, and positive reinforcement effected significant improvement in all three patients. There was even generalization to social situations that had not been worked on during the training. This study and others like it (e.g., Wallace et al., 1985) indicate that severely disturbed patients can be taught new social behavior that may help them function better, though generalization to life outside the hospital is far from a reliable finding (Hayes, Halford, & Varghese, 1995).

THE ROLE OF COGNITION

How is the observation of a model translated into changes in overt behavior? In their original writings on modeling Bandura and Walters (1963) asserted that an observer could somehow learn new behavior by watching others. Given the emphasis that much of experimental psychology places on learning through doing, this attention to learning *without* doing was important. But it left out the processes that could be operating. A moment's reflection on the typical modeling experiment suggests the direction that theory and research have taken in recent years. The observer, a child, sits in a chair and watches a film of another child making a number of movements, such as hitting a large, inflated, plastic doll in a highly stereotyped manner, and hears the child in the film uttering peculiar sounds. An hour later the youngster is given the opportunity to imitate what was earlier seen and heard. The child is able to do so, as common sense and folk wisdom would predict. How can we understand what happened? Since the observer did not *do* anything of interest in any motoric way while watching the film, except perhaps fidget in the chair, it would not be fruitful to look at overt behavior for a clue. Obviously, the child's cognitive processes were engaged, including the ability to remember later on what had happened.

Bandura (1986, 1997) has written extensively on the cognitive factors involved in modeling, which he defines as a process by which a person rather efficiently acquires rules for the generation of behavior. This interest led Bandura to formulate a social cognitive theory of behavior, in which the person's symbolic, cognitive processes play a key role. For exam-

FOCUS 18.1 ASSERTION TRAINING

"Children should be seen and not heard." "Keep a stiff upper lip." "He's the strong silent type." Our society does not generally value the open expression of beliefs and feelings, and yet people often pay an emotional price for concealing their thoughts and suppressing their feelings. People's wants and needs may not be met if they shy away from stating them clearly. Poor communication between sexual partners is one of the major factors contributing to an unsatisfying sexual relationship. Therapists of all persuasions spend a good deal of time encouraging clients to discover what their desires and needs are and then to take responsibility for meeting them. If patients have trouble expressing their feelings and wishes to others, assertion training, conducted individually or in groups (see p. 563) may be able to help them.

Andrew Salter, in his book *Conditioned Reflex Therapy* (1949), was the first behavior therapist to set assertiveness as a positive goal for people. Using Pavlovian, classical-conditioning terms, Salter wrote that much human psychological suffering is caused by an excess of cortical inhibition; therefore, greater excitation is warranted. He encouraged socially inhibited people to express their feelings to others in an open, spontaneous way. They should do so verbally, telling people when they are happy or sad, angry or resolute, and nonverbally, with smiles and frowns, what Salter called facial talk. They should also contradict people with whom they disagree, with appropriate feeling; use the pronoun I as often as possible; express agreement with those who praise them; and improvise, that is, respond intuitively in the moment without ruminating. In helping patients to assert themselves, behavior therapists, whether they acknowledge it or not, are doing therapeutic work with goals similar to those of humanistic therapists, who also regard expression of positive and negative feelings as a necessary component of effective living.

How are we to define assertion? Might it not be inconsiderate to put ourselves forward and express our beliefs and feelings to others? What if we hurt someone else's feelings in

Andrew Salter, one of the founders of behavior therapy.

doing so? Much effort has gone into articulating the differences between assertive behavior and aggressive behavior. The following useful distinction was made some years ago by Lange and Jakubowski (1976):

> [Assertion involves] expressing thoughts, feelings, and beliefs in direct, honest, and appropriate ways which respect the rights of other people. In contrast, aggression involves self-expression which is characterized by violating others' rights and demeaning others in an attempt to achieve one's own objectives. (pp. 38–39)

ple, Bandura, Jeffrey, and Bachica (1974), drawing on experimental cognitive research, showed that having a code by which to summarize information helps a person retain it better. In addition, they found that the use of such a code helped observers pattern their actions on what they had seen modeled. Other theories about memory storage and retrieval may shed light on how people acquire new and complex patterns of behavior "simply" by watching others. The word *simply* is placed in quotation marks because the process is not simple at all. The literature on

modeling, which at first offered straightforward, commonsensical, social-learning explanations, now regards modeling interventions as a type of cognitive behavior therapy.

COGNITIVE BEHAVIOR THERAPY

In the therapies discussed thus far the emphasis has been on the direct manipulation of overt behavior and occasionally of covert behavior. Relatively little

People may be unassertive for any number of reasons. The specific therapy procedures used depend on the reasons believed to be causing the individual's unassertiveness. Assertion training is actually a set of techniques having in common the goal of enhancing assertiveness, or what Lazarus (1971) calls "emotional freedom." Goldfried and Davison (1994) suggested several possible causes of unassertiveness—one or more of which may be found in a given individual—as well as related therapy techniques.

- The patient may not know what to say. Some unassertive people lack information on what to say in situations that call for expressiveness. The therapist should supply this information.

- Patients may not know how to behave assertively. They may not assume the tone and volume of voice, the fluency of speech, the facial expression and eye contact, and the body posture necessary for assertiveness. Modeling and role-playing can help these people acquire the signals of firmness and directness.

- Patients may fear that something terrible will happen if they assert themselves. Systematic desensitization may reduce this anticipatory anxiety. Or assertiveness may be blocked by negative self-statements, such as "If I assert myself and am rejected, that would be a catastrophe" (Schwartz & Gottman, 1976). These people may profit from rational-emotive behavior therapy.

- The patient may not feel that it is proper or right to be assertive. The value systems of some people preclude or discourage assertiveness. For example, some of the problems of a Catholic nun undergoing therapy seemed to relate to her unassertiveness, but through discussion it became clear that she would violate her vows were she more expressive and outspoken. By mutual agreement assertion training was not undertaken; instead, therapy focused on helping her work within her chosen profession in ways that were more personally satisfying and yet not more assertive.

Assertion training may begin with conversations in which the therapist tries to get the person to distinguish between assertiveness and aggression. For people who are submissive, even making a reasonable request or refusing a presumptuous one may cause them to feel that they are being hostile. Therapists then usually give patients sample situations that require that they stand up for their rights, their time, and their energies, such that if the person is unable to handle the situation, he or she feels put-upon:

> You have been studying very hard for weeks, taking no time off at all for relaxation. But now a new film, which will play for only a few days, interests you and you have decided to take a few hours and go late this evening to see it. On the way to an afternoon class, your very good friend tells you that she has free tickets to a concert this evening and asks you to go with her. How do you say no?

Behavior rehearsal is a useful technique in assertion training. The therapist discusses and models appropriate assertiveness and then has the patient role-play situations. Improvement is rewarded by praise from the therapist or from other members of an assertion-training group. Graded homework assignments, such as asking the mechanic to explain the latest bill for repairs, then telling a relative that his or her constant criticisms are resented, are given as soon as the client has acquired some degree of assertiveness through session work.

Assertion training raises several ethical issues. To encourage assertiveness in people who, like the nun mentioned earlier, believe that self-denial is a greater good than self-expression would violate their value system and could generate an unfavorable ripple effect in other areas of their life. Drawing a distinction between assertion and aggression is also an ethical issue. Behavior considered assertive by one person may be seen by another as aggressive. If we adopt the distinction made by Lange and Jakubowski that assertion respects the rights of others whereas aggression does not, we still have to make a judgment about what the rights of others are. Thus assertion training touches on moral aspects of social living, namely, the definition of other people's rights and the proper means of standing up for one's own rights.

attention has been paid to direct alteration of the thinking and reasoning processes of the client. Perhaps it was in reaction to insight therapy that behavior therapists initially discounted the importance of cognition, regarding any appeal to thinking as a return to the mentalism to which John Watson had vigorously objected in the early part of the twentieth century (p. 39).

If behavior therapy is to be taken seriously as applied experimental psychology, however, it will have to incorporate theory and research on cognitive processes. For a number of years behavior therapists have paid attention to private events—thoughts, perceptions, judgments, self-statements, and even tacit (unconscious) assumptions—and have studied and manipulated these processes in their attempts to understand and modify overt and covert disturbed behavior (Mahoney, 1974), the latter being thoughts and feelings construed as internal behaviors (recall the discussion of mediational learning paradigms, p. 43). **Cognitive restructuring** is a general term for changing a pattern of thought that is presumed to be causing a disturbed emotion or behavior. It is implemented in several ways by cognitive behavior therapists.[2]

ELLIS'S RATIONAL-EMOTIVE BEHAVIOR THERAPY

The principal thesis of Ellis's rational-emotive therapy (RET), recently renamed **rational-emotive behavior therapy (REBT)** (Ellis, 1993a, 1995), is that sustained emotional reactions are caused by internal sentences that people repeat to themselves and these self-statements reflect sometimes unspoken assumptions—irrational beliefs—about what is necessary to lead a meaningful life. The aim of this therapy is to eliminate self-defeating beliefs through a rational examination of them. As indicated earlier, anxious persons may create their own problems by making unrealistic demands on themselves or others, such as, "I must win the love of everyone." Or a depressed person may say several times a day, "What a worthless jerk I am." Ellis proposes that people interpret what is happening around them, that sometimes these interpretations can cause emotional turmoil, and that a therapist's attention should be focused on these beliefs rather than on historical causes or, indeed, overt behavior (Ellis, 1962, 1984).

Ellis used to list a number of irrational beliefs that people can harbor. One very common notion was that people must be thoroughly competent in everything they do. Ellis suggested that many people actually believe this untenable assumption and evaluate every event within this context. Thus if a person makes an error, it becomes a catastrophe because it violates the deeply held conviction that he or she must be perfect. It sometimes comes as a shock to clients to realize that they actually believe such strictures and as a consequence run their lives so that it is virtually impossible to live comfortably or productively.

More recently, Ellis (1991; Kendall et al., 1995) has shifted from a cataloguing of specific beliefs to the more general concept of "demandingness," that is, musts or shoulds that people impose on themselves and others. Thus, instead of wanting for something to be a certain way, feeling disappointed, and then perhaps engaging in some behavior that might bring about the desired outcome, the person demands that it be so; it is this unrealistic, unproductive demand, Ellis hypothesizes, that creates the kind of emotional distress and behavioral dysfunction that bring people to therapists.

CLINICAL IMPLEMENTATION

After becoming familiar with the client's problems the therapist presents the basic theory of rational-emotive behavior therapy so that the client can understand and accept it.[3] The following transcript is from a session with a young man who had inordinate fears about speaking in front of groups. The therapist guides the client to view his inferiority complex in terms of the unreasonable things he may be telling himself. The therapist's thoughts during the interview are indicated in italics.

Client: My primary difficulty is that I become very uptight when I have to speak in front of a group of people. I guess it's just my own inferiority complex.

Therapist: [*I don't want to get sidetracked at this point by talking about that conceptualization of his problem. I'll just try to finesse it and make a smooth transition to something else.*] I don't know if I would call it an inferiority complex but I do believe that people can, in a sense, bring on their own upset and anxiety in certain kinds of situations. When you're in a particular situation, your anxiety is often not the result of the situation itself, but rather the way in which you *interpret* the situation—what you tell yourself about the situation. For example, look at this pen. Does this pen make you nervous?

Client: No.

Therapist: Why not?

Client: It's just an object. It's just a pen.

Therapist: It can't hurt you?

Client: No …

Therapist: It's really not the object that creates emotional upset in people, but rather what you think about the object. [*Hopefully, this Socratic-like dialogue will eventually bring him to the conclusion that self-statements can mediate emotional arousal.*] Now this holds true for … situations where emotional upset is caused by what a

---

[2]There is a terminological issue here. As mentioned in Chapters 2 and 10 and discussed further in this chapter, Aaron Beck's therapy is called cognitive therapy; the word *behavior* is not included. Ellis's rational-emotive behavior therapy is regarded as one of the cognitive behavior therapies. Both approaches reserve an important place for overt behavior while emphasizing the cognitive component of therapy. The recent addition of the word *behavior* to Ellis's system reflects the focus he has always had on this aspect of the human condition. Here we follow general practice by regarding both Beck's cognitive therapy (CT) and Ellis's REBT as cognitive behavior therapies. More generally we find that people today use "cognitive therapy" and "cognitive behavior therapy" interchangeably.

[3]We said in Chapter 17 that the usefulness of an empathy statement or insight into the past does not depend on whether it is true. Nor does the usefulness of rational-emotive behavior therapy. Ellis's views may be only partially correct, or even entirely wrong, and yet it may be helpful for a client to act as though they are true.

person tells himself about the situation. Take, for example, two people who are about to attend the same social gathering. Both of them may know exactly the same number of people at the party, but one person can be optimistic and relaxed about the situation, whereas the other one can be worried about how he will appear, and consequently be very anxious. [*I'll try to get him to verbalize the basic assumption that attitude or perception is most important here.*] So, when these two people walk into the place where the party is given, are their emotional reactions at all associated with the physical arrangements at the party?

Client: No, obviously not.

Therapist: What determines their reactions, then?

Client: They obviously have different attitudes toward the party.

Therapist: Exactly, and their attitudes—the ways in which they approach the situation—greatly influence their emotional reactions. (Goldfried & Davison, 1994, pp. 163–165)

Having persuaded the client that his or her emotional problems will benefit from rational examination, the therapist proceeds to teach the person to substitute for irrational self-statements an internal dialogue meant to ease the emotional turmoil. At the present time therapists who implement Ellis's ideas differ greatly on how they persuade clients to change their self-talk. Some therapists, like Ellis himself, argue with clients, cajoling and teasing them, sometimes in very blunt language. Others, believing that social influence should be more subtle and that individuals should participate more in changing themselves, encourage clients to discuss their own irrational thinking and then gently lead them to discover more rational ways of regarding the world (Goldfried & Davison, 1994).

Once a client verbalizes a different belief or self-statement during a therapy session it must be made part of everyday thinking. Ellis and his followers provide patients with homework assignments designed to afford opportunities for the client to experiment with the new self-talk and to experience the positive consequences of viewing life in less catastrophic ways. Ellis emphasizes the importance of getting the patient to *behave* differently, both to test out new beliefs and to learn to cope with life's disappointments.

Ellis (1993b) has recently begun to emphasize self-actualization, encouraging clients to experiment with and ultimately select their own self-actualizing path. This shift in focus accords considerable autonomy to the client in facilitating his or her own recovery and is reminiscent of Rogers's emphasis on self-actualization. However, REBT still encourages the therapist to be quite directive.

EVALUATION OF RATIONAL-EMOTIVE BEHAVIOR THERAPY

Although the outcome research on REBT is not without its problems (Haaga & Davison, 1993), several conclusions can be offered (Haaga & Davison, 1989; Kendall et al., 1995).

- REBT reduces self-reports of general anxiety, speech anxiety, and test anxiety.

- REBT effects improvements both in self-report and in behavior for social anxiety, though it may be less effective than systematic desensitization.

- REBT is inferior to exposure-based treatments for agoraphobia.

- Preliminary evidence suggests that REBT may be useful in treating excessive anger, depression, and antisocial behavior.

- REBT is useful only as part of more comprehensive behavioral programs for sexual dysfunction.

- As described in Chapter 8, REBT shows promise in reducing the Type A behavior pattern, but as with other psychological interventions, it has not yet shown its utility in preventing coronary heart disease (Haaga, 1987).

- There is some preliminary evidence that REBT may be useful in a preventive fashion for untroubled people, that is, to help emotionally healthy people cope better with everyday stress.

- Rational-emotive education, whereby teachers explain to children in classrooms the principles of REBT and how they can be applied to the children's everyday lives, has been used in the hope of forestalling full-blown emotional problems later in life. Evidence suggests that this education can improve self-concept (Cangelosi, Gressard, & Mines, 1980) and reduce test anxiety (Knaus & Bokor, 1975).

- There is only some tentative evidence (e.g., Smith, 1983) that REBT achieves its effects through a reduction in the irrationality of thought. The importance of the support REBT gives patients to confront what they fear and to take risks with new, more adaptive behavior should not be underestimated. In other words, analogous to the role that relaxation might play in systematic desensitization (p. 520), some of the fear-reducing effects of REBT might derive from its encouraging people to expose themselves to what they fear.

As with most other clinical procedures, the relevance of REBT to a given problem depends in part on how the clinician *conceptualizes* the patient's predicament. Thus, if a therapist is trying to help an overweight person lose pounds, he or she might conceptualize eating as a way of reducing anxiety; in turn, the anxiety might be viewed as the result of social distress that is caused by extreme fear of rejection arising from an irrational need to please everyone and never make a mistake. The REBT therapist would direct his or her efforts to the irrational beliefs about pleasing others and being perfect, with the rationale that this will alleviate the patient's distress and ultimately the overeating. Such analysis into underlying causes is discussed at the end of this chapter.

DEFINING IRRATIONALITY AND THE ISSUE OF ETHICS IN REBT

Like other therapists, Ellis preaches an ethical system; this becomes clear when we try to define irrational or rational thinking. If we say that irrational thinking is what creates psychological distress, the definition is unsatisfyingly circular. If we regard as irrational any thought that is not objective and rigorous, then we would have to conclude that much of the thinking of *nondistressed* people is irrational, for considerable research indicates that the stories people tell themselves in order to live (Didion, 1979) frequently have illusory elements (e.g., Geer et al., 1970; Taylor & Brown, 1988). It is possible that, in order to achieve something unique or outstanding, one sometimes *has* to harbor beliefs that might be seen by those not committed to a cause as unrealistic. Albert Bandura put it this way:

> Visionaries and unshakable optimists, whose misbeliefs foster hope and sustain their efforts in endeavors beset with immense obstacles, do not flock to psychotherapists. ... Similarly, the efforts of social reformers rest on illusions about the amount of social change their collective actions will accomplish. Although their fondest hopes are likely to be unrealized during their lifetime, nevertheless their concerted efforts achieve some progress and strengthen the perceived efficacy of others to carry on the struggle. For those leading impoverished, oppressed lives, realism can breed despair. ... Clearly the relationship between illusion and psychological functioning is a complex one. (1986, p. 516)

We do not believe that a definition of irrational thinking can be constructed on empirical or scientific grounds. Ultimately, REBT therapists—*and their patients*—decide that it would be more useful or satisfying to think about the world in certain ways. As Ellis has recently acknowledged (Ellis, 1995), this decision is based on what one believes is functional or ethical, not necessarily on what is strictly objective or rational.

BECK'S COGNITIVE THERAPY[4]

Beck holds that numerous disorders, particularly depression, are caused by negative beliefs that individuals have about themselves, the world, and the future (see p. 232, Figure 10.1). These dysfunctional beliefs, or negative schemata, are maintained by one or more biases or errors in logic, such as arbitrary inference or selective abstraction. The overall goal of Beck's **cognitive therapy (CT)** is to provide the client with experiences, both in and outside the consulting room, that will alter the negative schemata in a favorable way. Thus a client who, through an ineptness schema, bemoans his or her witlessness for burning a roast, is encouraged to view the failure as regrettable but not to overgeneralize (one of the cognitive biases) and conclude, through a hopelessness schema, that he or she can do no good on future occasions. The therapist tries to break into the vicious cycle of a negative schema fueling an illogicality, which in turn fuels the negative schema.

CLINICAL IMPLEMENTATION

Attempts to change negative thinking are made at both the behavioral and the cognitive levels. One behavioral technique, useful for patients who are convinced that they are depressed all the time and who become still more deeply depressed because of this belief, is to have them record their moods at regular intervals during the day. If it turns out that these reports show some variability, as indeed often happens even with very depressed people, this information can serve to challenge their general belief that life is always miserable. This change in thinking can then serve as the basis for a change in behavior, such as getting out of bed in the morning, doing a few chores, or even going to work.

Similarly, depressed people often do very little because tasks seem insurmountable and they believe they can accomplish nothing. To test this belief, or schema, of insurmountableness, the therapist breaks down a particular task into small steps and encourages the patient to focus on just one step at a time. If this tactic is skillfully handled—and a good therapeutic relationship is obviously important—the patient finds that he or she can, in fact, accomplish *something*. These accomplishments are then discussed with the therapist as inconsistent with the notion that tasks are beyond the patient's

---

[4]Some of this section is based on Haaga and Davison (1991).

capabilities. As the view of the self begins to change, tasks of greater difficulty appear less forbidding, and success can build on success, with still further beneficial changes in the person's beliefs about the self and his or her world.

Collaborative empiricism is inherent to Beck's therapy. Therapist and patient work as co-investigators to uncover and examine any maladaptive interpretations of the world that may be aggravating the depression. They try to uncover both automatic thoughts and dysfunctional assumptions. Automatic thoughts are the things we tell or picture to ourselves as we go about our daily business, the running dialogue we have with ourselves as we drive to school, listen to a friend, or watch others crossing the street. Patients usually need practice in taking note of such thoughts and images, especially the ones that are associated with depressed mood. For example, a parent hears a child say that he or she failed a test at school and thinks, "What a lousy parent I am." Thereafter the parent feels blue. The therapist helps the patient monitor such thoughts, and together they examine their validity. Why should your child's problems at school mean that you are a bad parent? What else affects your youngster and determines whether he or she does well at school? In this fashion the therapist teaches the patient to check his or her thoughts against the available information and to entertain hypotheses that might attribute the child's failure on the test to factors other than having a bad parent.

This phase of identifying and modifying automatic thoughts is followed by a more subtle phase, the identification of underlying dysfunctional assumptions, schemata, or beliefs. These can be likened to a leitmotiv in music, a dominant, recurring theme. The parent may come to realize that he or she has taken on responsibility for the happiness and welfare of the entire family, including the child's performance in school. The therapist can examine with the patient the implications of the worst possible case, that the evidence does indeed indicate that he or she is not an omnipotent parent. Is this something to be clinically depressed about? To be sure, concern and desire to do something about the child's problems are understandable, but these reactions can energize a person to new action, rather than plunge him or her into despair.

How can the therapist help the individual alter his or her dysfunctional assumptions? In addition to verbal persuasion, the therapist may encourage the client to behave in a way inconsistent with these assumptions. For example, a person who believes that he or she must please everyone at the office can decline the next unreasonable request made and see

In cognitive therapy, the therapist often helps the client discover automatic thoughts such as "what a bad parent I am" in response to a child's poor report card.

whether, as he or she has been assuming, the sky falls. If the situation has been properly analyzed ahead of time by patient and therapist, clearly a necessary step, the person can experience what happens when he or she acts against this absolutist belief.

Beck's therapy, like others that alter thinking, is *difficult*! Clients would probably not be depressed if they were readily convinced by mastery experiences that they were worthwhile individuals. Our brief account is only an outline; the implementation is invariably less systematic, less unidirectional, and certainly more arduous than the description implies.

EVALUATION OF COGNITIVE THERAPY

The effectiveness of Beck's approach is under intensive study. A number of experiments with depressed patients lent early support to it (Rush et al., 1977; Shaw, 1977; Wilson, Goldin, & Charbonneau-Powis, 1983). Moreover, CT may have a preventive effect relative to drug treatment, a consideration of major importance in light of the oft-observed tendency for depressive episodes to recur (Blackburn, Eunson, & Bishop, 1986; Hollon, DeRubeis, & Evans, 1996). Perhaps cognitive therapy patients acquire some useful cognitive behavior skills that they are able to use following termination of therapy. As seen in Chapter 16, because older patients can be extremely sensitive to medications and can also suffer from medical problems that contraindicate prescribing psychoactive drugs, nonpharmacological interventions are especially appropriate for them.

A meta-analysis of outcome studies of diverse therapies concluded that Beck's therapy achieves greater short-term improvement than wait-list controls, drug therapies, noncognitive-behavioral treatments, and a heterogeneous group of other psychotherapies (Dobson, 1989). Such research laid the foundations for the widely publicized comparative outcome study sponsored by the National Institute of Mental Health (Elkin et al., 1985), a study that did *not* find CT superior to a drug therapy or to interpersonal psychotherapy (IPT) but nonetheless supported the utility of Beck's approach to the treatment of depression (see Focus 18.2).

Freeman and Reinecke (1995) recently reviewed the literature and concluded that relapse rates after cognitive therapy are lower than with antidepressants. Their review also indicated that cognitive therapy could be used effectively in conjunction with medications. Seligman (1994) conducted a review of efficacy studies that passed standards of methodological rigor, concluding that cognitive therapy is an effective treatment for panic disorder and that cognitive therapy is successful in the treatment of bulimia, faring better than medications alone.

Data are becoming available indicating that when cognitive therapy works, it does so because it helps patients change their cognitions. Predictable changes in cognitions do occur in cognitive therapy (Hollon & Beck, 1994; Hollon et al., 1996)—*but* they are found as well in successful treatment of depression by drugs (e.g., Rush et al., 1982). Cognitive change may be the *consequence* of change produced by other means (Jacobson et al., 1996). Or, at least with depression (the disorder in which cognitive therapy has been most researched), cognitive change may be the mediator of therapeutic improvement brought about by *any* therapy, whether Beck's cognitive therapy, interpersonal therapy, or drugs.

SOME COMPARISONS BETWEEN THE THERAPIES OF BECK AND ELLIS

The views and techniques of Ellis and Beck are widely used by therapists today. With the inevitable changes that inventive clinicians make as they apply the work of others, and with the evolution in the thinking of the theorists themselves, the differences between the two therapies can sometimes be difficult to discern. They do contrast, however, in interesting and important ways (Haaga & Davison, 1991, 1992).

To the parent who became depressed on learning that his or her child had failed a test at school, Ellis would say immediately, in essence, "So what if you are an inadequate parent? It is irrational to be depressed about that." Beck, in contrast, would first examine the evidence for the conclusion. His is a more empirical approach. "What evidence is there for thinking that you are an inadequate parent?" If proof is lacking, this discovery in itself will be therapeutic. Ellis regards his own type of solution as more thoroughgoing. *Even if* the person is wanting as a parent, the world will not end, for a person does not have to be competent in everything he or she does. Beck will also eventually question with the patient whether one has to be competent in everything to feel good about oneself, but perhaps not until accumulated evidence suggests that the person is an inadequate parent.

The therapist adopting Beck's approach certainly has preconceptions about negative schemata and especially about the forms that maladaptive, illogical, or biased thinking takes, such as overgeneralization. But working with a depressed individual is a collaborative, *inductive* procedure by which patient and therapist attempt to discover the *particular* dysfunctional assumptions underlying the person's negative thoughts. Rational-emotive behavior therapists, by contrast, are *deductive*. They are confident that a distressed person subscribes to one or more of a predetermined list of irrational beliefs or that they make unrealistic demands of themselves or others.

Beck's therapy and standard rational-emotive practices differ in style on this inductive–deductive basis. Beck suggests that the therapist should avoid being overly didactic, but Ellis often uses minilectures and didactic speeches. Beck proposes calling negative thoughts "unproductive ideas" to promote rapport. He does not favor adjectives such as irrational or nutty, which might be heard—with supportive humor, it must be pointed out—from Ellis. Finally, Beck recommends that the therapist begin by acknowledging the patient's frame of reference and asking for an elaboration of it. Having had a chance to present his or her case and feel understood, the person may be more willing to go through the collaborative process of undermining beliefs. Ellis, on the other hand, supposes that quite forceful interventions are necessary to disrupt a well-learned maladaptive pattern of thinking; he will therefore directly confront the patient's irrational beliefs, sometimes within minutes in the first session.

Both approaches have one thing in common, and this factor makes Beck and Ellis soul mates of the experiential (humanistic and existential) therapies reviewed in Chapter 17. They both convey the message that people can change their psychological predicaments by thinking differently. They emphasize that how a person construes himself or herself and the world is a major determinant of the kind of person he or she will be—and that people have *choice* in how they construe things. They assert that people can, sometimes with great effort, choose to behave differently. However, unlike behavior therapists who are not cognitive, but like the humanists and existentialists, Beck and Ellis believe that new behavior is important primarily for the evidence it can provide about how the person looks at himself or herself and the world. Thus the focus remains on the cognitive dimension of humankind and on the abiding belief that people's minds can be set free and that their thinking can provide the key to positive psychological change.

SOCIAL PROBLEM SOLVING

Some psychological distress can be regarded as a reaction to problems for which people believe they have no solution. I am late with a term paper and am upset about it. Shall I approach the professor, or is it better to deal at least initially with the teaching assistant? Should I request an incomplete, or will it look bad on my transcript, which is going to be sent out soon to the graduate programs I am applying to? But isn't an incomplete better than a C? Students caught in such a predicament can be helped by knowing how to solve a problem in the most effective, efficient manner.

Therapists have devised an approach known as **social problem solving (SPS)** (D'Zurilla & Goldfried, 1971; Goldfried & D'Zurilla, 1969; Kanfer & Busenmeyer, 1982; Nezu et al., 1996). Training clients in SPS consists of a number of steps. They are first taught to regard their distress as a reaction to unsolved problems and even to regard problems as challenges or opportunities rather than as threats (D'Zurilla, 1986). They are then taught to identify what the problems might be; to brainstorm, to generate as many alternative solutions as possible without evaluating their feasibility or possible effectiveness; to assess the likely consequences of each solution; and to implement a decision and evaluate its effectiveness for achieving their particular goals.

Some clinical research finds SPS training useful, at least in the short term. For example, depressed older adults in a nursing home improved more after such training than did patients given a more behaviorally based treatment (Hussian & Lawrence, 1981). Similarly good outcomes were achieved by Nezu (1986), who found greater reductions in depression among patients who received the entire SPS package compared with a control condition

whose group discussions about problems did not contain systematic procedures for solving them and evaluating the effectiveness of the solutions. In another study, school-age children acquired problem-solving skills that generalized to situations different from those considered in the SPS training (Weissberg et al., 1981); other work (e.g., Elias & Clabby, 1989) has applied the approach to entire elementary school curricula. SPS training has been found useful for enhancing social skills in psychiatric patients (Bedell, Archer, & Marlow, 1980), for treating alcohol abuse (Chaney, O'Leary, & Marlatt, 1978), and for reducing stress and improving academic competence in college students (D'Zurilla & Sheedy, 1991, 1992). In the best of all possible worlds, patients learn a general attitude and set of skills that they can apply to a wide range of future situations, thereby enhancing their general well-being.

Metacognition, that is, what people know about knowing (Meichenbaum & Asarnow, 1979), is also applied in solving social problems. If I come to a new city, I am likely to get lost without a map. But once I obtain a street map, granted that I have earlier learned the general skill of map reading, I am well able to find my way around. At the metacognitive level I know that to locate streets and areas in a new city, I should get a city map and then read it.

The SPS approach may be criticized for conveying the message that people *should* always strive to take effective action against any frustration or problem in order to gain control over it (e.g., Goldfried, 1980). To view one's world as full of challenges to be overcome might encourage the development of a Type A personality. In reaction to this implicit theme in SPS, D'Zurilla (1986, 1990) expanded the social problem-solving perspective to include "emotion-focused solutions," adapted from Richard Lazarus's (Lazarus & Folkman, 1984) classic work on cognition and stress. According to this view, if a situation is judged unchangeable or uncontrollable, a sensible approach to solving the problem is to change one's emotional reaction to it (by relaxing, for example) and thereby to adapt to the difficult environmental situation.

MULTIMODAL THERAPY

Multimodal therapy is a cognitive-behavioral approach proposed by Rutgers University psychologist Arnold Lazarus (1989, 1997). Lazarus broke with Wolpe in the late 1960s out of dissatisfaction with what he viewed as undue constraints that the behavioral paradigm placed on assessment and on the design of maximally effective psychotherapeu-

FOCUS 18.2 NIMH TREATMENT OF DEPRESSION COLLABORATIVE RESEARCH PROGRAM

In 1977 the National Institute of Mental Health (NIMH) undertook a large, complex, and expensive three-site study of Beck's cognitive therapy (CT), comparing it with interpersonal psychotherapy (IPT) and pharmacotherapy (Elkin et al., 1985). Called the Treatment of Depression Collaborative Research Program (TDCRP), this was the first multisite coordinated study initiated by the NIMH in the field of psychotherapy (the NIMH had fruitfully conducted such research in pharmacology).

SELECTION OF THERAPIES

Three criteria were employed in selecting a psychotherapy to compare with Beck's. The therapy had to have been developed for treating depression, it had to be explicit and standardized enough to allow for instructing other therapists (preferably using a manual), and it had to have empirically shown some efficacy with depressed patients. Further, there should be little overlap with Beck's cognitive therapy.

The NIMH team selected Gerald Klerman's interpersonal psychotherapy, which, as we saw in Chapter 17, is a brief, psychodynamic, Sullivanian, insight-oriented approach that focuses on current problems and interpersonal relationships and has demonstrated effectiveness for depression (Klerman et al., 1984; Weissman et al., 1979). This therapy is not as much intrapsychic as it is interpersonal, however; it emphasizes better understanding of the interpersonal problems assumed to give rise to depression and aims at improving relationships with others. As such, the focus is on better communication, reality testing, developing effective social skills, and meeting present social-role requirements. Actual techniques include somewhat nondirective discussion of interpersonal problems, exploration of and encouragement to express unacknowledged negative feelings, improvement of both verbal and nonverbal communications, and problem solving.*

A pharmacological therapy, imipramine (Tofranil), a well-tested tricyclic drug widely regarded as a standard therapy for depression, was used as a reference against which to evaluate the two psychotherapies. Dosages were adjusted according to predetermined guidelines that were flexible enough to allow for some clinical judgment of the psychiatrist in the context of clinical management, that is, in a warm, supportive atmosphere (Fawcett et al., 1987). Elkin et al. (1985) regarded this almost as a drug-plus-supportive-therapy condition, *supportive* referring

to the nature of the doctor–patient relationship, not to the application of any explicit psychotherapeutic techniques.

A fourth and final condition was a placebo–clinical management group against which to judge the efficacy of imipramine. It was also conceived of as a partial control for the two psychotherapies because of the presence of strong support and encouragement. In a double-blind design similar to that used in the imipramine condition, patients in this group received a placebo that they believed might be an effective antidepressant medication; they were also given direct advice when considered necessary. As placebo conditions go, this was a very strong one, that is, it included much more psychological support and even intervention than do most placebo control groups in both the psychotherapy and the pharmacotherapy literatures. Clinical management—support and advice—was common to both this and the imipramine group.

All treatments lasted sixteen weeks, with slight differences in numbers of sessions, depending on the treatment manuals. For example, cognitive therapy patients received twelve sessions during the first eight weeks, followed by weekly sessions during the second half of the study. These twenty sessions exceeded the sixteen for interpersonal therapy, which, however, could number as many as twenty at the therapist's discretion. Throughout all therapies patients were closely monitored, and professional safeguards were employed to minimize risk, for example, excluding imminently suicidal patients and maintaining close and regular contact during the study. These considerations were particularly important in the placebo condition.

SELECTION AND TRAINING OF THERAPISTS

An important feature of this study was the care and thoroughness of therapist selection and training at each of the treatment sites. This phase took almost two years, beginning with careful screening of recruits for general clinical competence and some experience in one of the three modalities under study. Altogether twenty-eight therapists were selected—ten each for interpersonal therapy and drug therapy and eight for cognitive therapy.

This was not a random selection of therapists, for they had to seek participation, be accepted after rigorous screening, and agree to adhere to an established treatment protocol, as well as have each of their therapy sessions videotaped for concurrent as well as subsequent scrutiny to ensure adherence to the respective therapy protocol. Training took months and was rigorous, involving 119 patients. This selection and training phase itself constituted an achievement in psychotherapy research and was reported on by those involved in instruction and supervision (Rounsaville, Chevron, & Weissman, 1984; Shaw, 1984; Waskow, 1984). This lengthy procedure was undertaken to ensure the

---

*Differences in techniques have been noted between the therapies of Beck and Klerman (DeRubeis et al., 1982). In the study under discussion CT and IPT therapists adhered well to the procedures required of their respective therapies (Hill, O'Grady, & Elkin, 1992). Nonetheless, there is considerable overlap, for both emphasize improving accuracy in perception as well as efficacy in social behavior. The reader may want to consider this factor when the results of this milestone study are described.

integrity of the independent variable, the therapy each subject received; and the training and supervision efforts were successful (Hill et al., 1992). Only recently have psychotherapy outcome studies devoted suitable attention to the training and monitoring of therapist-experimenters to ensure that the independent variables are being manipulated in the study.

SELECTION OF PATIENT SUBJECTS

The overall design of the study called for 240 outpatients, 60 in each of the four conditions. They had to meet the criteria for major depressive disorder but could not be imminently suicidal, have medical contraindications for the use of imipramine (in case they were assigned to the drug condition), or be bipolar or psychotic. A good deal more information was gathered on the patients so that it could later be related to treatment outcome (e.g., is melancholia a negative factor in cognitive therapy? Do minority patients drop out of therapy more often than others?). Seventy percent of the patients were female (which corresponds well to the 2:1 ratio of women to men with this disorder), and patients were on average moderately to severely depressed for an outpatient sample. Of those who began treatment, 162, or 68 percent, completed at least fifteen weeks and twelve sessions; although more patients in the placebo condition dropped out of treatment, their number was not statistically greater than that for the other three groups.

TYPES OF ASSESSMENTS

A wide range and large number of assessments were made at pre- and postreatment, as well as three times during treatment and again at six-, twelve-, and eighteen-month follow-ups. Measures included some that might provide answers to questions about processes of change. For example, do interpersonal-therapy patients learn to relate better to others during therapy, and if so, is this improvement correlated with clinical outcome? Do cognitive-therapy patients manifest less cognitive distortion during the later sessions than at the beginning of treatment, and if so, is this shift associated with better clinical outcome? Various assessment instruments tapped the perspectives of the patient, the therapist, an independent clinical evaluator blind to treatment condition, and whenever possible, a significant other from the patient's life, for example, a spouse. Three domains of change were assessed: depressive symptomatology, overall symptomatology and life functioning, and functioning related to particular treatment approaches (e.g., the Dysfunctional Attitudes Scale of Weissman and Beck [1978], to assess cognitive change).

RESULTS

Analyses of the data suggest variations among research sites, between those who completed treatment and the total sample (including dropouts), and among assessments with different perspectives (e.g., patient versus clinical evaluator judgments). Some of the complex findings thus far published are summarized here (Elkin et al., 1986; Elkin et al., 1989; Elkin et al., 1996; Imber et al., 1990; Shea et al., 1990; Shea et al., 1992).

- At termination and without distinguishing patients according to severity of depression, there were no significant differences in reduction of depression or improvement in overall functioning between cognitive therapy (CT) and interpersonal therapy (IPT) or between either of them and imipramine plus clinical management. In general the three active treatments achieved significant *and equivalent* degrees of success and were, for the most part, superior to the placebo group. The placebo-plus-clinical-management subjects also showed significant improvement. (Note: Several other controlled studies have found cognitive therapy superior to other treatments and to placebo conditions, cf. Persons, Thase, & Crits-Christoph, 1996. There are inconsistencies in the psychotherapy outcome literature!)

- Imipramine was faster than the other treatments in reducing depressive symptoms during treatment. By the end of sixteen weeks of therapy, however, the two psychotherapies had caught up with the drug.

- On some measures the less severely depressed placebo patients were doing as well at termination as were the less depressed people in the three active treatment conditions.

- Severely depressed patients in the placebo condition did not fare as well as did those in the three active treatments.

- There was some evidence that IPT was more effective than CT with the more severely depressed patients, most notably in terms of recovery rates.

- There was some evidence that particular treatments effected change in expected domains. For example, IPT patients showed more improvements in social functioning than imipramine or CT patients, and CT reduced certain types of dysfunctional attitudes more than did the other treatments.

- For IPT and pharmacotherapy, but not for CT, patients diagnosed with personality disorders were more likely to have residual depressive symptoms after therapy than those without these Axis II diagnoses.

- A follow-up study eighteen months after the end of treatment found that the active treatment conditions did *not* differ significantly, and of those patients across the four conditions who had markedly improved immediately at the end of treatment, only between 20 and 30 percent remained completely without depression.

Particular controversy swirls around the relative effectiveness of the imipramine condition versus the two psychosocial therapies. Recent reanalyses of the TDCRP data confirm the original finding that at least in the short term, imipramine was superior to CT across a wide range of measures (Elkin et al., 1995; Klein & Ross, 1993). Yet Jacobson and Hollon (1996) have pointed out that the TDCRP study is the only one that shows such superiority of pharmacotherapy over CT for even severely depressed patients. They point out also that differences between imipramine and both of the psychotherapy groups were not consistent across the three treatment sites. For example, in one site, CT did as well with severely depressed patients as did imipramine, and at another site, IPT did as well with these patients as did the drug. Finally, Jacobson and Hollon also noted that, although better than a pill placebo, 33 percent of the imipramine subjects dropped out before completing treatment; of those remaining, half did not recover immediately after treatment ended, and of those who did recover, half relapsed within months after medication was withdrawn.

Complex situation! To make matters even more complex, Donald Klein (1996), a renowned drug researcher, as well as some of the TDCRP investigators themselves (Elkin et al., 1996), read the very same TDCRP data and came to the opposite conclusion, namely, that imipramine in this study was significantly more effective for severe depression than was either cognitive or interpersonal therapy. Furthermore, Klein questions the adequacy of the imipramine condition itself because of the number of dropouts and notes that imipramine treatment for depression is not synonymous with pharmacotherapy for depression. The newer selective serotonin reuptake inhibitors, such as Prozac (p. 246), have fewer side effects and may well be more effective than tricyclics such as imipramine.

Much remains to be learned about effecting even short-term improvement in depressed patients. Even less is known about how to maintain over the long haul any benefits that are evident right after treatment ends. Certainly there is little in the many findings from this milestone study of comparative outcome that can gladden the hearts of proponents of any of the interventions.

---

tic interventions. Lazarus's basic premise is that people are a composite of seven dimensions, according to the acronym BASIC IB: Behavior, Affective processes, Sensations, Images, Cognitions, Interpersonal relationships, and Biological functions. Effective therapy must designate problems in all or in some subset of these areas, decide the order in which problems should be treated, and then apply to each problem area the techniques that are best suited to it.

If, for example, a patient's duress seems to be triggered by aberrant thought processes, attention should focus on the C, for cognition, and procedures that clinical and experimental research has suggested are well suited to altering how people think about things should be applied. However, the first B, behavior, might be problematic as well, and although set in motion by an aberrant thought, might require specific attention in and of itself, for example, when a person has learned to act in ways that are not reinforced by his or her present environment.

For each patient Lazarus draws up a modality profile, which helps him and the patient to see the areas that merit attention. This scheme is similar to (and preceded by several years) the multiaxial system of the DSM in that it is designed to draw attention to domains that are worthy of attention, basically *forcing* the clinician to focus on particular categories or areas. But the BASIC IB approach goes further in that Lazarus attempts to outline for each of the seven areas a range of procedures that can be effective.

Lazarus's approach as described thus far fits easily into a general cognitive-behavioral framework. But he goes on to argue that the decision to use a given technique should be guided not by theoretical approach or school affiliation, but by an open-minded consideration of the data. For example, given what the therapist believes he or she knows about how to change cognitions, what techniques might be used to change the maladaptive beliefs of this particular client? If a technique from Gestalt therapy could be useful, then use it, Lazarus suggests. In this sense Lazarus was one of the early principal figures in the psychotherapy integration movement (discussed later).

REFLECTIONS ON COGNITIVE BEHAVIOR THERAPY

As we indicated earlier in this book (p. 44), behavior therapy initially aligned itself with the study of classical and operant conditioning, under the assumption that principles and procedures derived from conditioning experiments could be applied to lessen psychological suffering. This orientation came from behaviorists, such as Watson and Skinner, who had become dissatisfied with the work done on the contents of the mind and consciousness in Wundt's and Titchener's laboratories and with the use of introspection in their studies. What developed into cognitive behavior therapy (or cognitive therapy) may appear to be a radical and novel departure, given the earlier focus of behavior therapists on classical and operant conditioning, but in a historical sense it represents a return to the cognitive foci of the earliest period of experimental psychology. Many experimental psychologists have continued through the years to do research into cognition—into the mental processes of perceiving, recognizing, conceiving, judging, and reasoning, of problem solving, imagining, and other symbolizing activities.

Ellis and Beck try to change cognitive processes directly in order to relieve psychological distress. From the beginning, however, behavior therapists have relied heavily on the human being's capacity to symbolize, to process information, to represent the world in words and images. Wolpe's systematic desensitization is a clear example. This technique, believed by Wolpe to rest on conditioning principles, is inherently a cognitive procedure, for the patient *imagines* what is fearful. The most exciting overt behavioral event during a regimen of desensitization is the person's occasional signaling of anxiety by raising an index finger. If anything important is happening, it is surely going on under the skin, and some of this activity is surely cognitive.

As behavior therapy goes cognitive, however, it is important to bear in mind that many contemporary researchers continue to believe that behavioral *procedures* are more powerful than strictly verbal ones in affecting cognitive *processes* (Bandura, 1977). That is, they favor behavioral techniques while maintaining that it is important to alter a person's beliefs in order to effect an enduring change in behavior and emotion. Bandura suggests that all therapeutic procedures, to the extent that they are effective, work their improvement by giving the person a sense of mastery, of self-efficacy (Bandura, 1997). At the same time he finds that the most effective way to gain a sense of self-efficacy, if one is lacking, is by changing behavior. Whether or not we believe self-efficacy is as important as Bandura does, a distinction can be made between processes that underlie improvement and *procedures* that set these processes in motion.

Cognitive behavior therapists continue to be behavioral in their use of performance-based procedures and in their commitment to behavioral change (Dobson & Jackman-Cram, 1996; Jacobson et al., 1996), but they are cognitive in the sense that they believe that cognitive change (e.g., enhanced self-efficacy) is an important mechanism that accounts for the effectiveness of at least some behavioral procedures. Cognition and behavior continually and reciprocally influence each other— new behavior can alter thinking, and that new mode of thinking can in turn facilitate the new behavior. In addition, the environment influences both thought and action and is influenced by them. This model, termed **triadic reciprocality** by Bandura (1986), highlights the close interrelatedness of thinking, behaving, and the environment.

As Salovey and Singer (1991) have pointed out, though, Bandura's triadic reciprocality underemphasizes the concept of emotion. People have many cognitions that are affect–laden—sometimes referred to as "hot cognitions"—and these tend to relate to the self (Cantor et al., 1986), to one's dreams and fantasies, fondest hopes and direst fears, what Singer (1984) called the private personality. "The therapist must be alert to emotions that color the maladaptive cognitions that are traditionally the focus of treatment. Even though feelings often also arise as a consequence of cognition, it may still be possible to alter maladaptive cognitions by first assessing and then intervening at the level of feelings" (Salovey & Singer, 1991, p. 366). Both clinical observations (Greenberg & Safran, 1984) and experimental findings (e.g., Snyder & White, 1982) point to the importance of emotion in personality and suggest that it should be included more systematically in cognitive-behavioral conceptions of disorder and treatment.

All cognitive behavior therapists heed the mental processes of their patients in another way. They pay attention to the world as it is perceived by the patient. It is not what impinges on us from the outside that controls our behavior, the assumption that has guided behavioral psychology for decades. Rather, our feelings and behavior are determined by how we view the world. The Greek philosopher Epictetus stated in the first century: "[People] are disturbed not by things, but by the view they take of them." And Shakespeare put it this way: "There is nothing either good or bad, but thinking makes it so" (*Hamlet*, act II, scene 2). Cognitive behavior therapy is being brought closer to the humanistic and existential therapies reviewed in Chapter 17. A central thesis of experiential therapists, such as Rogers and Perls, is that clients must be understood from their own frame of reference, from their phenomenological world, for it is this experience of the world that controls life and behavior.

From a philosophical point of view such assumptions on the part of those who would understand people and try to help them are profoundly important. Experimentally minded clinicians and researchers are intrigued by how much the new field of cognitive behavior therapy has in common with the experientialists and their attention to the phenomenological world of their patients. To be sure, the *techniques* used by cognitive behavior therapists are usually quite different from those of the followers of Rogers and Perls. But as students of psychotherapy and of human nature, these surface differences should not blind us to the links between the two approaches. Further discussion of integration among diverse therapeutic modalities is found at the end of this chapter.

BEHAVIORAL MEDICINE

Behavioral medicine is "the interdisciplinary field concerned with the development of behavioral and biomedical science, knowledge, and techniques relevant to the understanding of health and illness, and the application of this knowledge and these techniques to prevention, diagnosis, treatment, and rehabilitation" (Society of Behavioral Medicine, 1989, p. 1). What is noteworthy about this definition—and what clearly reflects the nature of the field—is that the approach is *interdisciplinary*. It draws on the knowledge and skills of a variety of researchers and practitioners, including psychologists, psychiatrists, nonpsychiatric physicians, nurses, and social workers, who bring to the analysis and treatment of health-related behaviors their own particular perspectives and expertise and often collaborate with one another on such diseases as essential hypertension and coronary heart disease (Chapter 8), the problems of seriously ill children (Chapter 15), substance abuse (Chapter 12), AIDS (Chapter 14), and many of the problems of older adults (Figure 16.1, page 483). In the 1980s and 1990s the U. S. government has increasingly recognized that illnesses formerly regarded as strictly medical have important psychological components and that a key to addressing the medical health crisis in the United States and elsewhere lies in altering people's thoughts and behaviors relevant to maintaining health and treating illness (Department of Health and Human Services, 1990).

Behavioral medicine, often referred to as health psychology, is not restricted to a set of techniques or particular principles of changing behavior. Clinicians in this field employ a wide variety of procedures—from contingency management through operant conditioning, to desensitization through counterconditioning, and a variety of cognitive-behavioral approaches—all of which have in common the goal of altering bad living habits, distressed psychological states, and aberrant physiological processes in order to have a beneficial impact on a person's physical condition. A sampling of three important areas of behavioral medicine—the management of pain, chronic diseases and lifestyle, and biofeedback—will convey an even better sense of the scope of this emerging multidisciplinary field of research and treatment.

THE MANAGEMENT OF PAIN[5]

Like anxiety, pain can be adaptive. People with congenital inability to feel pain are at an extreme disadvantage, indeed, are at serious risk for injury. Imagine how dangerous it would be if you could not feel pain from contact with a hot stove or a sharp knife. Our concern here is with pain that is *mal*adaptive, pain that is out of proportion to the situation and unduly restricts a person's capacity for meaningful and productive living.

We know enough about pain to appreciate the fact that there is no one-to-one relationship between a stimulus that is capable of triggering the experience of pain, referred to as nociceptive stimulation, and the actual sensation of pain. Soldiers in combat can be wounded by a bullet and yet be so involved in their efforts to survive and inflict harm on the enemy that they do not feel any pain until later. This well-known fact tells us something important about pain even as it hints at ways of controlling it: if one is *distracted* from a nociceptive stimulus, one may not experience pain or at least not as much of it as when one attends to the stimulation (Turk, 1996). The importance of distraction in controlling pain, both acute and chronic, is consistent with research in experimental cognitive psychology. Each person has only a limited supply of attentional resources such that attention to one channel of input blocks the processing of input in other channels (Kahneman, 1973). This human limitation can thus be seen as a positive benefit when it comes to the experience of pain. In addition to distraction, other factors that reduce pain are lowered anxiety, feelings of optimism and control (Geer et al., 1970), and a sense that what one is engaged in has meaning and purpose (Gatchel et al., 1989; Gendlin, 1962).

Psychologists have contributed to our understanding of both acute and chronic pain. Acute pain is linked to nociception. Chronic pain can evolve from acute pain and refers to pain that is experienced after the time for healing has passed, when there is little reason to assume that nociception is still present.

ACUTE PAIN

The importance of a sense of personal control in dealing with acute pain is readily seen in situations in which patients are allowed to administer their own painkillers (with a preset upper limit). Patients who control the administration of the medication experience greater relief from pain and even use

---

[5]Some of this section is based on Davison and Darke (1991).

In the midst of the Olympics, Kerry Strug was able to complete her performance, despite an injury and pain which might have been totally debilitating in another situation.

less analgesic medication than patients who have to ask a nurse for pain medication, which is the more common hospital situation (White, 1986). It is significant that this patient-controlled analgesia reduces pain even though it requires focusing on the pain, a finding that goes against the well- docu-

Patients allowed to administer their own pain killers use less medication and experience more relief from pain.

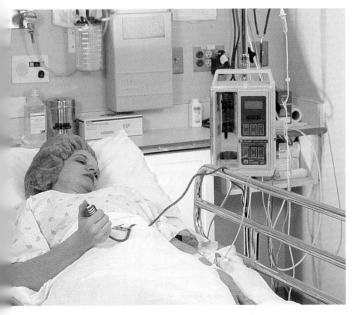

mented benefits of distraction. Apparently the positive effects of control outweigh the negative consequences of focusing on the pain.

Relying on a nurse to administer pain medication also requires the patient to attend to the pain, though, perhaps even more so than when the patient administers the drug. For with nurse-administered analgesia the patient learns to wait until the pain is substantial before requesting medication; after making the request, the patient then usually waits until the nurse has time to fulfill it. This system obviously does not enhance distraction from the pain!

CHRONIC PAIN

Chronic pain is the lot of millions of Americans, accounting for billions of dollars of lost work time and incalculable personal and familial suffering (Turk, 1996). Traditional medical treatments seldom help with this kind of pain. To understand chronic pain it is useful to distinguish between pain per se, that is, the perception of nociceptive stimulation (as in acute pain) and *suffering* and *pain behaviors*. Suffering refers to the emotional response to nociception and can be present even in the absence of pain, as when a loved one leaves a person. Pain behaviors—chronic pain—refer to observable behaviors associated with pain or suffering; examples include moaning, clenching teeth, irritability, and avoidance of activity (Turk, Wack, & Kerns, 1985). The treatment of chronic pain focuses on suffering and pain behaviors rather than on whether the person is actually experiencing pain. The emphasis is on toughing it out, working through the pain rather than allowing oneself to be incapacitated by it. If handled properly, the result is often increased activity and function that can sometimes even reduce the actual experience of pain.

A well-researched example of chronic pain is lower back pain caused by severe muscle spasms. Initially the person is unable to engage in activity any more vigorous than getting in and out of bed. In the acute phase this is sensible behavior. As the spasms ease, and if no other damage has occurred, such as to the disks between the vertebrae, the patient should begin moving more normally, stretching, and eventually attempting exercises to strengthen the muscles that went into spasm. In their classic work on pain Fordyce and his colleagues (Fordyce et al., 1986; Fordyce, 1994) have shown the superiority of a behavioral over a traditional medical program for management of back pain. In the traditional program patients exercised and otherwise moved about only until they felt pain, whereas the behavioral management program encouraged them to exercise at a predetermined intensity for a predetermined period of time, even if they experienced pain. Low-back-pain patients have also been given relaxation training and encouraged to relabel their pain as numbness or tickling (Rybstein-Blinchik, 1979), a cognitive-restructuring procedure. Obviously care must be taken not to push patients beyond what their bodies can actually handle. The implicit message seems to be that traditional medical practice has underestimated the capabilities of chronic-pain patients (Keefe & Gil, 1986). A frequent outcome of these studies is that increased activity improves muscle tone, which can reduce nociception over time and even reduce the likelihood of future recurrences of muscle spasms. In a review of studies on the treatment of chronic pain, Blanchard (1994) concluded that both strictly behavioral (operant conditioning) and cognitive-behavioral approaches are important for effective treatment.

CHRONIC DISEASES AND LIFESTYLE

Behavioral medicine is concerned not only with alleviation of illness and pain but with their prevention; when it has this purpose it is usually called **health psychology**. At the beginning of the twentieth century the leading cause of death was infectious diseases, such as influenza and tuberculosis. In the 1980s, with these illnesses largely under medical control, Americans succumbed most often to heart diseases, cancer, cerebrovascular diseases, such as stroke, and accidents. For all of these diseases the behavior of people over their lifetimes—their lifestyles—is implicated. Of all the strategies

directed at preventing and controlling hypertension (high blood pressure), for example, reducing weight, restricting sodium and alcohol use, and increasing physical activity are the most successful (Dubbert, 1995). However, there is some inconsistency and failure to replicate positive effects for many of the so-called stress-management and exercise strategies (Blanchard, 1994).

Physicians have for years been dispensing sound advice about diet, exercise, and smoking, usually with little effect on lifestyle. Getting people to do what is in the best interest of their health is a challenge! Merely telling a sedentary accountant to exercise for at least fifteen minutes three times a week at 70 percent of maximum heart rate will probably not rouse him or her to adhere to such a schedule.

In one study (Epstein et al., 1980) female college students agreed to run one to two miles a day for five weeks; they paid a substantial deposit, which was returned to them a dollar at a time as they complied. These young women ran more consistently than those in a control group who had no contingency. A number of similar programs for encouraging regular exercise have also been reported. Of particular interest was the posting of a cartoon at the base of a public stairway and escalator (Brownwell, Stunkard, & Albaum, 1980). It portrayed a glum, unhealthy-looking heart taking the escalator, next to a robust, happy heart bounding up a flight of stairs; the caption read, "Your heart needs exercise … here's your chance." Simple and inexpensive, the cartoon effected a dramatic change in people passing that way; three times as many used the stairs as had been observed earlier. Stairs are of course far more available than aerobic exercise sessions, and climbing them is easier than instituting a jogging regimen. Regular stair use is known to be a healthful cardiovascular exercise for people throughout their lives.

Many industries and corporations maintain their own health and fitness programs, screening their employees for such illnesses as hypertension and providing facilities and incentives for taking regular exercise, even during work hours. More than magnanimity is operating here; such programs often reduce absenteeism and improve health generally, making them cost-effective for the companies.

BIOFEEDBACK

A visit to the commercial exhibit area of any psychological or psychiatric convention will reveal a plentiful display of complex biofeedback apparatuses, touted as an efficient, even miraculous, means of helping people control one or another

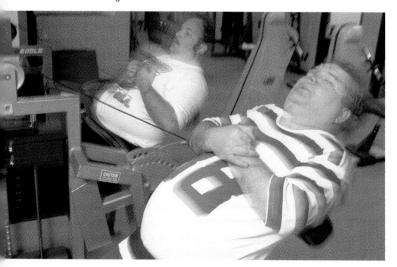

Exercise is an important aspect of lifestyle that is related to health. The application of contingencies can yield lifestyle changes.

bodily-mental state. By using sensitive instrumentation, **biofeedback** gives a person prompt and exact information, otherwise unavailable, on muscle activity, brain waves, skin temperature, heart rate, blood pressure, and other bodily functions. It is assumed that a person can achieve greater voluntary control over these phenomena—most of which were once considered to be under involuntary control only—if he or she knows immediately, through an auditory or visual signal, whether a somatic activity is increasing or decreasing. Because anxiety has generally been viewed as a state involving the autonomic (involuntary) nervous system, and because psychophysiological disorders often afflict organs innervated by this system, it is obvious why researchers and clinicians became intrigued with biofeedback. For a time, biofeedback was virtually synonymous with behavioral medicine.

In a series of classic studies at Harvard Medical School, Shapiro, Tursky, and Schwartz (1970; Schwartz, 1973) demonstrated that human volunteers could achieve significant short-term changes in blood pressure and in heart rate. They found that some people could even be trained to increase their heart rate while decreasing blood pressure. Achievement of this fine-grained control lent impetus to biofeedback work with human beings and awakened hope that certain clinical disorders might be alleviated in this new way.

In the move from laboratory analogue to the more challenging world of the clinic, at least four questions must be asked. First, can persons whose systems are *malfunctioning* achieve the same biofeedback control over bodily events that normal people can acquire? Second, if actual patients can achieve some degree of control, will it be enough to make a significant difference in their problems? Third, can the control achieved by patients hooked up to and receiving immediate feedback from a remarkable apparatus be carried over to real-life situations in which they will have no special devices to inform them of the state of the bodily functions that they have learned to control? And fourth, does biofeedback add anything beyond training in relaxation, a strategy usually followed when biofeedback is taught to people with psychophysiological disorders?

Research with patients suffering from essential hypertension has been somewhat encouraging, but results have not been certain enough to establish biofeedback as a standard treatment for the problem (Blanchard, 1994). Moreover, several investigators believe that relaxation training, which is often given along with biofeedback, does more than the biofeedback to reduce blood pressure (Blanchard et al., 1979; Emmelkamp, 1986; Reed, Katkin, and Goldband, 1986).

Tension headaches, believed to be caused by excessive and persistent tension in the frontalis muscles of the forehead and in the muscles of the neck, have also been handled within this framework; the standard treatment entails feedback of tension in the frontalis muscles. Although such biofeedback has indeed been shown to be effective (e.g., Birbaumer, 1977), some studies suggest that cognitive factors may play a role. For example, Holroyd et al. (1984) found that *believing* that one was reducing frontalis tension via biofeedback was associated with reductions in tension headaches, whether or not such reductions were actually being achieved. Enhanced feelings of self-efficacy and internal control appear to have inherent stress-reducing properties, a theme encountered in the discussion of control and anxiety in Chapter 6. Biofeedback may strengthen the sense of control, thus reducing general anxiety levels and ultimately tension headaches. Other studies (e.g., Blanchard et al., 1982; Cox, Freundlich, & Meyer, 1975) suggest that relaxation per se is the critical variable, similar to the nondrug treatment of essential hypertension.

There is only limited evidence that biofeedback has any specific effects other than distraction, relaxation, and instilling a beneficial sense of control. In addition, clinicians must remain mindful of the complexities of human problems. A person with high blood pressure, for example, might have to alter a tense, driven lifestyle before he or she can significantly reduce blood pressure through biofeedback. It is unwise, and a sign of naive clinical practice, to assume that one technique focused on a specific malfunction or problem will invariably cure the patient.

GENERALIZATION AND MAINTENANCE OF TREATMENT EFFECTS

Generalizing to real life and maintaining whatever gains have been achieved in therapy is a problem common to all treatments. Insight therapists assume that therapeutic effects are made more general through restructuring of the personality. Looking a good deal to the environment for factors that affect people, behavior therapists wonder how therapeutic changes can be made to persist once clients return to their everyday situations, which are often assumed to have been a factor in creating their problems in the first place! This challenge has been addressed in several ways.

Focus 18.3 You're Changed If You Do and Changed If You Don't

Have you ever tried to persuade a friend to do something by asking him or her not to do it? Intuition tells us that this sneaky ploy might be effective when a person is spiteful or doesn't like to be controlled by others. The thinking of such an individual might be: "So, he wants me to continue arriving late, huh? I'll show him—I'll start arriving *early*!"

Since the publication of *Pragmatics of Human Communication*, a book by Watzlawick, Beavin, and Jackson (1967) on complex communication and interaction, a small but committed number of psychotherapists have been drawn to what have come to be called **paradoxical interventions**. These attempts to effect change have in common a request or prescription by the therapist for the patient to continue the problem or to increase its severity or frequency. If a person cannot go to sleep, he or she is asked to *remain awake*. If a patient cannot stop thinking of a disturbing event, he or she is asked to think of it *more often*. If he or she becomes anxious for no apparent reason, the request is made to *make himself or herself anxious*. Clinical reports from enthusiasts of the approach suggest that at least some patients benefit from such counterintuitive efforts (e.g., Frankl, 1967; Seltzer, 1986; Shoham-Salomon & Rosenthal, 1987), but only recently have paradoxical interventions been studied experimentally (e.g., Akillas & Efron, 1995; Asher & Turner, 1979).

We examine here some research by Shoham-Salomon and her co-workers. They postulate two mechanisms that could account for the beneficial changes reported clinically for some patients: reactance and increases in self-efficacy. Reactance refers to a motivational state aroused when people perceive that their range of freedom is being limited—they make efforts to restore their freedom (Brehm & Brehm, 1981). A reactant person, when asked by the therapist to become more anxious, will see this symptom prescription as an infringement of freedom and will protect himself or herself from this perceived threat by

becoming *less* anxious. The second mechanism proposed by Shoham-Salomon, which underlies the response of *non*reactant patients to a paradoxical directive, is Bandura's (1986) concept of self-efficacy, the sense that one is capable of performing a desired behavior. In the context of psychotherapy this entails the person's gaining control over the problem and reducing its intensity or frequency. Bandura's research suggests that self-efficacy is enhanced when people have successful experiences. Thus, when a nonreactant patient follows a paradoxical directive, for example, and increases his or her anxiety, the short-term outcome is not symptom reduction, as with the reactant person, but cognitive change, namely, a belief that he or she is not helpless and can exert some control over the previously uncontrollable problem (even if the control leads to something that is opposite to what the person really wants). The implication is promising: if patients can make themselves worse, then maybe they can make themselves better.

Both kinds of individuals are expected to change in positive ways from paradoxical treatment, but for different reasons and at different times. The reactant person is expected to change rather quickly because he or she is defying the therapist's directive. The nonreactant client is expected not to change right away, but the groundwork is laid for later behavioral change via an increase in self-efficacy. This nonreactant person will not improve in the short term, but will construe his or her symptomatic behavior as more controllable and may improve later on.

These predictions were confirmed in two studies of college students suffering from procrastination, as reported in an article (part of the title of which is used as the title of this box) by Shoham-Salomon, Avner, and Neeman (1989). Participants were divided into reactant and nonreactant groups, using procedures that detected spitefulness in tone of voice. The experimenters had them undergo one of two treatments, each conducted for two weekly sessions. In the *paradoxical intervention*,

INTERMITTENT AND NATURALISTIC REINFORCEMENT

Because laboratory findings indicate that intermittent reinforcement—rewarding a response only a portion of the times it appears—makes new behavior more enduring, many operant programs take care to move away from continuous schedules of reinforcement once desired behavior is occurring with satisfactory regularity. For example, if a teacher has succeeded in helping a disruptive child spend more time sitting down by praising the child generously for each arithmetic problem finished while seated, the teacher will gradually reward the child for every other success, and ultimately only infrequently.

Another strategy is to move from artificial reinforcers to those that occur naturally in the social environment. A token program might be maintained only long enough to encourage certain desired behavior, after which the person is weaned to natural reinforcers, such as praise from peers.

ENVIRONMENTAL MODIFICATION

Another approach to bringing about generalization takes the therapist into the province of community psychology, which is discussed in the next chapter. Behavior therapists manipulate surroundings, or attempt to do so, to support changes brought about

the therapist explained that they needed to understand their procrastination problem better and become more aware of it. To this end they were to observe the problem carefully by trying to procrastinate deliberately. Students were instructed to gather all their study materials on their desks but not to study for half an hour, to resist any impulse to study, and to concentrate on procrastinating, for example, by ruminating about the problem as they usually did when procrastination occurred normally. *Studying at these times was not permitted.* If they succeeded in this unusual observation task for six days, on the seventh day they could either study or not study, as they wished and whenever they wished. At the second therapy session participants discussed this assignment. Those who were able to do it were congratulated and reminded that their not studying had allowed them to better understand their problem and therefore to begin to deal with it. If a student reported having studied *more*, he or she was not praised; in fact, the therapist voiced skepticism and suggested that the change was probably only temporary. If they did not schedule procrastination time, the therapist exhorted them to try it again in the coming week.* Above all, participants were not encouraged to procrastinate less or study more.

The contrasting intervention was one of *self-control.* Students were told that procrastination was a learned habit and that they needed to develop new behaviors incompatible with procrastination. They were directed to select a place in which they could study more effectively and to try to study as much as possible there, the idea being that these new stimulus conditions would become associated with improved study habits. Any reported successes were praised by the therapist.

Results showed that study time as well as self-efficacy were improved via both treatments, but the really interesting results concern interactions between reactance and treatment modality, an issue addressed in Focus 18.5. Higher reactance was correlated with improvement in study habits (less procrastination) in the paradoxical but not in the self-control group, as expected. That is, students who were motivated to restore freedom that they viewed as being threatened engaged in

behavior that went against the instructions of the therapist— told to study less, they studied more. This contrariness was not found among reactant students in the self-control condition. Increases in self-efficacy were correlated with better studying in the self-control condition, consistent with many findings that show a link between behavioral improvement and self-efficacy (Bandura, 1986). However, this link was not found in the paradoxical-treatment group, for which increases in self-efficacy were associated with *lack of behavioral change*, as predicted. The findings from this mixed-design study (reactance was a correlational variable embedded in an experimental design; cf. p. 117) were replicated in a second experiment.

Further research with more clinically disturbed patients and with long follow-ups needs to be conducted, and Shoham-Salomon and her colleagues are engaged in such efforts (for example, with insomnia [Shoham et al., 1995]). But these two analogue experiments provide strong empirical support for the idea that for some people, telling them *not* to change their problematic behaviors may be more effective than encouraging them to work directly on making those behavioral changes.

Several important issues are raised by the success of paradoxical interventions. Do some treatments or therapists arouse more reactance in patients than others? Is reactance fairly stable and traitlike in people (Beutler, 1979), or is it more situational, aroused by particular social influences (Brehm & Brehm, 1981)? Are changes brought about by paradoxical maneuvers as stable as those effected by less indirect procedures? Does trust in the therapist suffer if the patient comes to realize that the therapist is saying one thing but intending another? Can the problems that all therapies have with compliance be addressed more effectively by studying therapeutic paradoxes?

---

*An interesting problem arises in paradoxical therapy when a reactant patient defies the therapist's directive to exacerbate a problem behavior. One might label this "meta-defiance." If one is not careful, one can get caught in an infinite regress!

---

in treatment. For example, Lovaas and his colleagues (1987; McEachin et al., 1993) found that the gains painstakingly achieved in therapy for autistic children were sustained only when their parents continued to reinforce their good behavior.

ELIMINATING SECONDARY GAIN

Most behavior therapists assign their clients homework tasks to do between sessions. Patients may be asked to listen to audiotapes containing relaxation-training instructions, for example. They sometimes fail to follow through in a consistent fashion, however, complaining of not having enough quiet time

at home to listen to the tapes or saying that they forgot about the assignment. Many patients are so resistant to doing on their own what they consciously and rationally agree is in their best interest that therapists often invoke as an explanation the psychoanalytic concept of secondary gain, that the patient derives benefit from his or her problem. For complex and poorly understood reasons people sometimes act as though they unconsciously wish to keep their symptoms. Therapists, whatever their persuasion, may have to examine the client's interpersonal relationships for clues as to why a person who is suffering directly from a problem seems to prefer to hold on to it (see Focus 18.3).

RELAPSE PREVENTION

Marlatt (1985) proposed the "abstinence violation effect" as a focus of concern in relapse prevention. His research on alcoholism sensitized him to the generally negative effects of a slip, as when a former drinker, after a successful period of abstinence, imbibes to a stupor after taking a single drink. Marlatt suggested that the manner in which the person reacts cognitively to the slip determines whether he or she will overcome the setback and stay on the wagon or relapse and resume drinking to excess. The consequences of the slip are hypothesized to be worse if the person attributes it to internal, stable, and global factors believed to be uncontrollable—in much the same way that Abramson, Seligman, and Teasdale (1978) theorized about helplessness and depression (see p. 235). An example would be a belief, prevalent in Alcoholics Anonymous (p. 320), that the lapse was caused by an uncontrollable disease process that overwhelms the person once a single drink is taken. In contrast, relapse is assumed to be less likely if the individual attributes the slip to causes that are external, unstable, specific, and controllable, such as an unexpectedly stressful life event. In essence, the person is encouraged to distinguish between a lapse and relapse. Cognitive behavior therapists attempt to minimize the abstinence violation effect by encouraging attributions to external, unstable, and specific factors *and* by teaching strategies for coping with life stressors.

ATTRIBUTION TO SELF

The concept of attribution may also offer insight on how to maintain treatment gains once therapy is over. How people explain to themselves why they are behaving or have behaved in a particular way presumably helps determine their subsequent actions. A person who has terminated therapy might attribute improvement in behavior to an external cause, the therapist, and therefore lose ground, even relapse, once that attributed factor is no longer present.

In an early analogue demonstration of this effect (Davison & Valins, 1969), college undergraduates were shocked on their fingertips to determine how much they could bear. Then they took a "fast-acting vitamin compound" (actually an inert placebo) and were told that they would be able to endure greater amounts of shock. Indeed they were, at least in their own minds. The experimenters had surreptitiously lowered the voltage levels to create this belief. Half the participants were then told that the capsule ingested was only a placebo, the others that its pain-reducing effects would soon wear off. Those who believed that they had taken a placebo attributed to themselves a greater ability to withstand discomfort and endured higher levels of shock on the third test. Those who believed that they had been given a real analgesic drug that was no longer effective were in the third round able to endure only lesser amounts of shock, mirroring findings with most psychoactive drugs.

In an experiment with a similar design, conducted with people who were having trouble falling asleep, Davison, Tsujimoto, and Glaros (1973) obtained comparable results, indicating that real problems may be treated by helping patients attribute improvements to themselves. Individuals attempting to reduce smoking (Chambliss & Murray, 1979; Colletti & Kopel, 1979) and lose weight (Jeffrey, 1974) have similarly benefited from attributing gains to their own efforts and changes in attitudes rather than to external forces. In a series of non-behavior-therapy outcome studies from the Johns Hopkins Psychotherapy Research Unit, patients who attributed their gains to a drug did not maintain their improvement as much as did those who construed their changes as arising from their own efforts (Frank, 1976).

What are the implications of attribution research? Since in behavior therapy much improvement seems to be controlled by environmental forces, especially therapy relying on operant manipulation, it might be wise for behavior therapists to help their clients feel more responsible. By encouraging an "I did it" attitude, perhaps by motivating them to practice new skills and to expose themselves to challenging situations, therapists may help their clients depend less on therapy and therapist and better maintain their treatment gains. Insight therapies have always emphasized the desirability of patients' assuming primary responsibility for their improvement. Behavior therapists have begun to realize that they must come to grips with the issue. On a more general level, the question of attributing improvement underscores the importance of cognitive processes in behavior therapy.

Finally, when patients maintain their improvement, it is often assumed that they are continuing to apply after termination of treatment specific skills that they acquired during treatment. A recent controlled comparative outcome study, discussed in Chapter 12 (p. 326), on the treatment of cocaine dependence (Carroll et al., 1994a, 1994b) found two important instances of generalization at a one-year follow-up: patients treated with the drug desipramine maintained their treatment-produced gains; and patients in the cognitive-behavior-therapy condition not only maintained their improvement but showed signs of even further improvement, or what the authors called "delayed emergence of effects"

(Carroll et al., 1994b, p. 995). That the drug-produced effects were maintained at one-year follow-up is a welcome exception to the general finding of relapse following drug withdrawal. That the cognitive-behavioral treatment gains were actually *greater* at one-year follow-up prompted the investigators to speculate that CBT had taught patients coping skills that they were able to implement long after formal therapy had ended, something lacking in the drug-therapy group (see Focus 18.4).

Since one purpose of professional intervention is to make the professional helper superfluous, we can expect increasing formal attention to be focused on what it is that patients take away from treatment that can help them maintain and enhance their gains as well as deal with the new challenges that await them in their day-to-day lives (or, as the lyricist-satirist Tom Lehrer put it, as they "go sliding down the razorblade of life").

BASIC ISSUES IN COGNITIVE AND BEHAVIOR THERAPIES

Cognitive and behavior therapies are expanding each year; with such a proliferation of activity, everyone concerned should remain aware of problems and issues that transcend particular experimental findings. The following considerations, many alluded to earlier, need to be kept in mind.

INTERNAL BEHAVIOR AND COGNITION

In Chapter 5 we demonstrated that the inference of intervening processes and other explanatory fictions is useful in interpreting data and generating fruitful hypotheses. Behavior therapists are sometimes thought to hold only the radical behavioristic positions of Watson and Skinner, that it is not useful or legitimate to make inferences about internal processes of the organism.

Our position is that behavior therapy, as applied experimental psychology, is legitimately concerned with internal as well as external events, provided that the internal mediators are securely anchored to observable stimuli or responses. The cognitive therapies certainly illustrate this situation.

UNCONSCIOUS FACTORS AND UNDERLYING CAUSES

With the growing interest in cognitive factors, cognitive therapists have begun to focus their assessments and interventions on internal mediators that lie outside the patient's awareness, that is, that are unconscious (Bowers & Meichenbaum, 1984; Mahoney, 1993). Ellis, for example, assumes that people are distressed by one or more beliefs that he designates irrational—even though a patient seldom states the problem in such terms. Based on what the patient says and how the patient says it, and working from rational-emotive theory, Ellis may infer the operation of a belief such as "It is a dire necessity that I be perfect in everything I do." He then persuades the patient to accept the notion that this belief underlies the problems. Therapy is directed at altering that belief, of which the patient may well have been unaware earlier. Although he tends to work more slowly and inductively than Ellis, Beck infers similar beliefs, which he calls negative schemata or dysfunctional assumptions.

This is an interesting turn of events for an approach that developed in the 1950s out of a rejection of conceptualizations that relied on the notion of unconscious motivation and thought! Yet it is consistent with decades of research by experimental cognitive psychologists, who infer sets, beliefs, attitudes, and other abstract cognitive concepts of which the person is often unaware. To be sure, appreciation of factors of which a person may be unaware does not make any of the cognitive therapies equivalent to psychoanalysis, but it does demonstrate the wisdom of some of Freud's clinical insights and is reflected in the kinds of rapprochements we explore later.

Cognitive behavior therapists, like their analytic counterparts, have come to believe generally that there is more to the patient than immediately meets the eye (Goldfried & Davison, 1976). Guidano and Liotti (1983) spoke of the "protective belt" behind which one must search for core beliefs, which themselves are generally related to one's idea of oneself, such as a negative self-image. According to Mahoney (1982, 1990), core, central cognitions may be extremely difficult to change, even when uncovered, because they stem from one's earlier developmental history. And well before the popularity of cognitive behavior therapy, George Kelly distinguished between "core constructs" and "peripheral constructs," the former relating to the person's basic sense of self or identity (Kelly, 1955).

Although changing core beliefs is not a simple matter for either patient or therapist, it is believed by many contemporary researchers to be essential to cognitive therapy if the positive effects of therapy are to be enduring. The subtlety in assessing variables that are not immediately apparent is similar to that of advanced accurate empathy, discussed in Chapter 17 (p. 507), as illustrated in the following case from Safran et al. (1986).

FOCUS 18.4   SELF-CONTROL—OUTSIDE A BEHAVIORAL PARADIGM?

Operant research and theory seem to assume that the human being is a relatively passive recipient of stimulation from the environment. Given this apparent dependence on the external world, how can we account for behavior that appears to be autonomous, willed, and often contrary to what might be expected in a particular situation? How, for example, do we account for the fact that a person on a diet refrains from eating a luscious piece of chocolate cake even when hungry?

Psychoanalytic writers, including ego analysts, posit some kind of agent within the person. Many ego analysts assert that the ego can operate on its own power, making deliberate decisions for the entire psychic system, including decisions that go against the wishes of the id. Behaviorists, especially Skinner (1953), have objected to this explanation, regarding it as simply a relabeling of the phenomenon. Perhaps the most widely accepted behavioral view of self-control is Skinner's—an individual engages in self-control when he or she arranges the environment so that only certain controlling stimuli are present. A person wishing to lose weight rids the house of fattening foods and avoids passing restaurants when hungry. Behavior remains a function of the surroundings, but the surroundings are controlled by the individual.

A related behavioral conception of self-control is reflected in Bandura's (1969) explanation of aversive conditioning. Rather than being passively conditioned to feel distaste for stimuli that have been paired with shock, a person learns a skill of aversive self-stimulation, which he or she *deliberately* applies in real life. According to this view, a person resists a temptation by *deliberately* recalling the earlier aversive experience of being shocked or nauseated during therapy. The individual is said to create symbolic stimuli that control behavior.

A familiar means of exercising self-control, also discussed in the behavior therapy literature, is setting standards for oneself and denying oneself reinforcement unless they are met (Bandura & Perloff, 1967). One such tactic is often employed by the authors of this book—I will not check my E-mail until I have finished writing this page. When a person sets goals, makes a contract with himself or herself about achieving them before enjoying a reward, and then keeps to the contract without obvious external constraints, that person is said to have exercised self-control.

Self-control can be applied with *any* therapy technique. The only stipulation is that the person must implement the procedure on his or her own, after receiving instructions from the therapist. For example, a patient who was being desensitized decided to imagine some of the hierarchical scenes while relaxing in a warm tub. He felt that he understood the rationale of desensitization well enough and had enough control over the processes of his imagination to meet the procedural requirements of the technique. Consequently, after achieving what he felt to be a state of deep relaxation in the bathtub, he closed his eyes and carried out the scene presentation and termination as he had been taught by the behavior therapist. When he was with the therapist later, they were able to skip the items to which he had desensitized himself in the tub and proceed more rapidly through the anxiety hierarchy.

Implicit in all concepts of self-control are three criteria: (1) there are *few external controls* that can explain the behavior; (2) control of self is difficult enough that the person has to *put*

A client who failed an exam … accessed the automatic thought: "I can't handle university." At this point the therapist could have challenged this belief or encouraged the client to examine evidence relevant to this belief. Instead she decided to engage in a process of vertical exploration. In response to the therapist's probes a constellation of automatic thoughts emerged that revolved around the client's beliefs that he was not smart enough. The client at this point spontaneously recalled two memories of situations in which he had felt humiliated and worthless because he felt he had "been stupid" at the time. As he recounted these memories he became visibly more emotional. Further exploration revealed that these feelings of intellectual inferiority and associated feelings of worthlessness cut across a number of problem situations for the client. It also emerged that he believed that his value as a person was completely dependent upon his intellectual performance. In this situation had the therapist intervened when the first automatic thought emerged, she may not have accessed the entire chain of self-evaluative cognitions and higher level constructs that underlay the client's distress. (p. 515)

BROAD-SPECTRUM TREATMENT

Our review of the cognitive and behavior therapies has necessarily been fragmented because we have dealt with separate techniques one at a time. In clinical practice, however, several procedures are usually employed at once or sequentially in an attempt to deal with all the important controlling variables; this approach is generally referred to as *broad-spectrum behavior therapy* (Lazarus, 1971). For example, a patient fearful of leaving home might well undergo in vivo desensitization by walking out the door and gradually engaging in activities that take him or her farther from that safe haven. Over the years, however, the person may also have built up a dependent

Self-control, as illustrated by dieting, is difficult to explain within a behavioral paradigm.

forth some effort; and (3) the behavior is engaged in with *conscious deliberation and choice*. The individual actively decides to exercise self-control either by performing some action or by keeping himself or herself from doing something, such as overeating. The person does not do this automatically and is not forced by someone else to take action.

To illustrate these criteria, let us take the example of a male jogger. If an army sergeant is goading the jogger along, the first criterion is not met; the running is not an instance of self-control even though considerable effort is probably required to maintain it.

If the jogger finds running pleasurable, so that he would rather jog than engage in other activities, the running cannot be considered an instance of self-control. Self-control may be seen in the *earliest* stages of a jogging regime, when the person may

indeed be exerting great effort—he groans as he dons his Nikes, looks at his watch after only a few minutes of running to see how long this torture has been going on, and collapses in relief after half a mile, glad that the ordeal is over.

The third criterion, acting with conscious deliberation and choice, distinguishes self-control from actions people perform in a mindless way. It is probably a good thing that much of our everyday behavior is mindless, for imagine how fatiguing (and boring) it would be to mull over and make specific decisions to do such things as tie our shoelaces. But these very acts would be categorized as instances of self-control if, on a given occasion, we had to decide whether to engage in them. Eating would require self-control if we were on a strict diet and had agreed, with our partner, or doctor, or self, to reduce caloric intake.

The concept of self-control places a strain on the behaviorist paradigm, for people are described as acting independently, putting forth effort, deliberating and choosing. Each of these verbs supposes the person to be an *initiator* of action, the place where control *begins*. Ardent behaviorists may counter by asserting with Skinner that the view of the person as an initiator only indicates ignorance of the external forces that ultimately control behavior. Thus the person who denies himself or herself an extra dessert is not really controlling the self; rather, this self-denial is controlled by some subtle reward unappreciated by the observer, or by a distant reinforcer, such as the potential to wear clothes of a smaller size. The flaw in this line of reasoning is that it is purely *post hoc* and irrefutable. We can *always* assert that at some later date the reinforcer that sustains the behavior will arrive. Such an explanation should be as unsatisfactory to the behaviorist as the psychoanalyst's *post hoc* invocation of an unconscious defense mechanism to account for an action.

relationship with his or her spouse. As the person becomes bolder in venturing forth, this change in behavior may disrupt the equilibrium of the relationship that the couple has worked out over the years. To attend only to the fear of leaving home would be incomplete (Lazarus, 1965) and might even lead to replacement of the agoraphobia with another difficulty that would serve to keep the person at home—a problem frequently called symptom substitution.

In a related vein, therapists do not invariably focus only on the patient's complaint as stated during the first interview. A clinical graduate student was desensitizing an undergraduate for test anxiety. The person made good progress up the hierarchy of imagined situations but was not improving at all in the real world of test taking. The supervisor of the graduate student suggested that the therapist find

out whether the patient was studying for the tests. It turned out that he was not; worry about the health of his mother was markedly interfering with his attempts to study. Thus the goal of making the person nonchalant about taking tests was inappropriate, for he was approaching the tests themselves without adequate preparation. On the basis of additional assessment, the therapy shifted away from desensitization to a discussion of how the client could deal with his realistic fears about his mother's possible death.

RELATIONSHIP FACTORS

A good relationship between patient and therapist is important for many reasons and regardless of the particular theoretical orientation. As discussed in Chapter 4, it seems doubtful that people will reveal deeply personal information if they do not trust or respect their therapists. Furthermore, since therapy can seldom be imposed on an unwilling client, a therapist must obtain the cooperation of the person if the techniques are to have their desired effect. In desensitization, for example, a patient could readily sabotage the best efforts of the therapist by not imagining a particular scene, by not signaling anxiety appropriately, and by not practicing relaxation. And in virtually all other cognitive and behavior therapy procedures clients are able to, and sometimes will, work against the therapist if relationship factors are neglected (Davison, 1973; Patterson & Chamberlain, 1992).

The importance of the therapeutic relationship has most recently been highlighted by Linehan (1993b) in her dialectical behavior therapy (p. 352). She argues that it is essential to create an atmosphere of acceptance and empathy within which specific cognitive-behavioral techniques can be implemented with patients suffering from borderline personality disorder. Although behavior therapists seldom use the term *therapeutic alliance*, the strongly affective interpersonal bond between therapist and patient is increasingly recognized as a necessary condition for implementing cognitive and behavioral procedures (Goldfried & Davison, 1994).

FLESH ON THE THEORETICAL SKELETON

A challenge faced by any therapist is the move from a general principle to a concrete clinical intervention. To illustrate, consider an early study in which undergraduates were trained to analyze the behavior of severely disturbed children in operant-conditioning terms (Davison, 1964). The students were encouraged to *assume* that the important determinants of the children's behavior were the consequences of that behavior. Armed with M & M candies as reinforcers, these student-therapists attempted to bring the behavior of the severely disturbed children under their control. Eventually, one child appeared to be losing interest in earning the candies. Working within a framework that required an effective reinforcer, the therapist looked around for another incentive. He noticed that each time the child passed a window, she would pause for a moment to look at her reflection. In an implementation of the Premack principle mentioned earlier (p. 521), the therapist obtained a mirror and was subsequently able to make peeking into the mirror the reinforcer for desired behavior; the peeks into the mirror were used in the same *functional* way as

the M & M candies. Thus, *although guided by a general principle, the therapist had to rely on improvisation and inventiveness as demanded by the clinical situation.*

Devising interventions along behavioral lines requires ingenuity and creativity. As with any therapy, the application of a general principle to a particular case is not a simple matter. Although a given theoretical framework helps guide the clinician's thinking, it is by no means sufficient.

> The clinician in fact approaches his work with a given set, a framework for ordering the complex data that are his domain. But frameworks are insufficient. The clinician, like any other applied scientist, must fill out the theoretical skeleton. Individual cases present problems that always call for knowledge beyond basic psychological principles. (Lazarus & Davison, 1971, p. 203)

The preceding quotation from two behavior therapists is very similar to the following one from two experimental social psychologists.

> In any experiment, the investigator chooses a procedure which he intuitively feels is an empirical realization of his conceptual variable. All experimental procedures are "contrived" in the sense that they are invented. Indeed, it can be said that the art of experimentation rests primarily on the skill of the investigator to judge the procedure which is the most accurate realization of his conceptual variable and has the greatest impact and the most credibility for the subject. (Aronson & Carlsmith, 1968, p. 25)

Behavior therapists face the same kinds of decision-making challenges faced by their experimental colleagues. There are no easy solutions in dealing with human problems (see Focus 18.5).

PSYCHOANALYSIS AND BEHAVIOR THERAPY—A RAPPROCHEMENT?

Is contemporary psychoanalysis compatible with behavior therapy? This question has been discussed for many years, and few professionals are optimistic about a meaningful rapprochement, arguing that these two points of view are incompatible paradigms. But Paul Wachtel, in his work on just such an integration (1977, 1982, 1993, 1997), offers a scheme that holds considerable promise, at least for establishing a dialogue between psychoanalytically oriented therapists and behavior therapists.

As indicated in Chapter 17, ego analysts place much more emphasis on current ego functioning than did Freud. Sullivan, for example, suggested that patients would feel better about themselves and function more effectively if they focused on problems in their current interpersonal behavior.

But Sullivan appears to have been ambivalent about the wisdom of working directly on how people act and feel in the present if doing so meant that they would not recover memories of repressed infantile conflicts. Wachtel, however, suggests that therapists, including those working within a psychoanalytic paradigm, *should* help the client change current behavior, not only so that he or she can feel better in the here and now, but indeed so that he or she can *change* those fears from the past.

Wachtel bases his principal position on Horney (1939), Sullivan (1953), and Erikson (1950) and calls it "cyclical psychodynamics" (1982). He believes that people maintain repressed problems by their current behavior and the feedback it brings from their social relations. Although their problems were set in motion by repressed past events, people keep acting in ways that maintain these problems. For example, consider a young man who has repressed his extreme rage at his mother for having mistreated his father years ago, during his childhood. As a youngster, to control this rage, he developed defenses that took the form of overpoliteness and deference to women. Today this solicitude and unassertiveness encourage some women to take advantage of him, but he also misperceives situations in which women are genuinely nice to him. By misinterpreting friendly overtures as condescending insults, he has come to resent women even more and to retreat still further. This young man's submissiveness, originating in his "woolly mammoth" (p. 38)—his buried problem of long ago—is creating personal problems in the present and has revived his repressed rage. It is as though his adult ego is saying, unconsciously, "You see, women, like my mother, really are bitchy. They're not to be trusted. They're hurtful and sadistic." This present-day confirmation of his belief from childhood turns back on the buried conflict and keeps it alive. The cycle continues, with the young man's own behavior and misconceptions confirming the nastiness of women.

Wachtel's approach suggests that therapy should attempt to alter current behavioral patterns both for their own sake, which is the behavior therapist's credo, and for the purpose of uncovering and changing the underlying psychodynamics. By pointing out that a direct alteration of behavior may help patients attain a more realistic understanding of their repressed past conflicts, traditionally the goal of psychoanalysis, Wachtel hopes to interest his analytic colleagues in the techniques employed by behavior therapists. He would probably give the deferential young man some assertion training in the hope of breaking into the vicious cycle by changing his here-and-now relations with women.

After repeated disconfirmation of the belief that all women want to take advantage of him, the young man could begin to understand the repressed conflict of love–hate with his mother.

Wachtel also holds that behavior therapists can learn much from their analytic colleagues, especially concerning the *kinds* of problems people tend to develop. For example, psychoanalytic theory tells us that children have strong and usually ambivalent feelings about their parents, some of which are so unpleasant that they are repressed, or at least are difficult to focus on and talk about openly.

To a behavior therapist the deferential young man might initially appear fearful of heterosexual relationships. Taking these fears at face value, the therapist would work to help the client reduce them, perhaps by a combination of desensitization, rational-emotive behavior therapy, and social-skills training. But the therapist would fail to explore the possibility, suggested by the psychoanalytic literature, that the young man is basically *angry* at women. Wachtel would advise the behavior therapist to be sensitive to the childhood conflicts on which analysts focus and to question the young man about his relationship with his mother. The patient's reply or manner might give a hint of resentment. The therapist would then *see* the deferential young man differently and hypothesize that he is not fearful of women but angry at them, because he associates them with a mother who has been the object of both hate and love from early childhood. This additional information would presumably suggest a different behavioral intervention, one aimed at the patient's anger at women, not his apparent fear of them.

Wachtel also wants behavior therapists to appreciate that reinforcers can be *subtle* and that a patient may deny that he or she really wants something and may well be unaware of this denial. In other words, therapists should be attuned to unconscious motivation, to the possibility that a person may be motivated or reinforced by a set of events of which he or she is unaware. Focus 17.3 (p. 507) described a college student whose expressed anger at her parents masked a deep-seated need to obtain their approval.

Contemporary psychoanalytic thought may help behavior therapists become aware of the *meaning* that a particular intervention has for a patient. Consider the case of a young woman with whom a behavior therapist decided to do assertion training. As the therapist began to describe role-playing procedures, she stiffened in her chair and then began to sob. To proceed with the training without dealing with her reaction to its description would have been

FOCUS 18.5 MATCHING PATIENT TO TREATMENT—PROJECT MATCH

For many years both practitioners and researchers have understood the importance of employing treatments that are suitable for particular patients. This notion goes beyond the question of the kind of therapy best suited for a particular kind of problem (which we addressed in the therapy sections of Chapters 6 through 16). Rather, what is called **aptitude-treatment interaction** (ATI) focuses on characteristics of patients with the same disorders that might make them more suitable for one generally effective treatment than for another.

To see how ATI comes into play, consider the technique of systematic desensitization, which relies on ability to imagine oneself in a fearsome situation and to become anxious from this image. *The procedure requires that an image stand in the place of the actual event.* If patients cannot conjure up an image that makes them anxious, then there is no point in going through a time-consuming procedure that has as its aim imagining a frightening situation without becoming anxious! Focus 18.3 described how paradoxical interventions were expected to have different effects on more- or less-reactant patients—another example of ATI.

The results of a large, eight-year, multisite study on aptitude-treatment interaction in the treatment of alcohol abuse, Project Match, have recently been published (Project Match Research Group, 1997). (We alluded briefly to these findings in the discussion of therapy for alcoholism on page 323.) This study is becoming controversial in professional circles because of its failure to find what it was looking for, namely, a way to match particular kinds of alcoholic patients with specific interventions.

Ten matching variables, among them severity of alcohol dependency, severity of cognitive impairment, motivation to change, severity of psychological disturbance (referred to as "psychiatric severity"), support from one's social milieu for drinking, and sociopathic tendencies, were chosen because they had been found in previous research to be associated with outcome of intervention. There were three treatments. The twelve-step-facilitation treatment (TSF) was designed to convert patients to the AA view of alcoholism as an incurable but manageable disease and to encourage their involvement in AA; the motivational enhancement therapy (MET), based on William Miller's approach (Miller et al., 1992), attempted to mobilize the person's own resources to reduce drinking. Finally, a cognitive-behavioral coping skills therapy (CBT) presented to patients the idea that drinking is functionally related to problems in a person's life; it taught them skills to cope with situations that trigger drinking or, if the person had abstained for a while, to prevent relapse. Some of the predicted interactions were that drinkers under heavy pressure to stop would do best with the twelve-step-facilitation therapy; those with psychological problems would do best with the cognitive therapy; and those with low motivation to change would do best with the motivational enhancement therapy.

All treatments were carefully administered in individual sessions by trained therapists over a twelve-week period, following treatment manuals prepared for this study. Exclusionary criteria were used in selecting patients; they could not be dependent on other drugs and otherwise had to have pretty stable lives. As in other efficacy studies (cf. p. 493), internal validity was quite good, but external validity—the generalizability of the findings to therapy as actually practiced—was apparently low. However, this seems a defensible strategy when posing complex theoretical questions such as those posed in this study. Sound research strategy calls for optimizing the chances of getting significant results before looking for subtleties.

The principal dependent (outcome) measures were percentage of days abstinent and drinks per drinking day during a one-

insensitive and poor clinical practice. An awareness of psychoanalytic theories had sensitized the therapist to the possibility that assertion *symbolized* something to the woman. The therapist gently encouraged her to talk freely, to free-associate about the idea of assertion training. She recalled a series of incidents from childhood in which her parents had criticized the way she acted with her friends, without providing support and constructive suggestions about other ways to behave. Without initially being aware of it herself, the patient was reminded of this pain from the past when the therapist suggested that she learn more assertive ways of dealing with others. The psychologist was able to explain to her

the current enterprise, assertion training, and to distinguish it from the unhelpful and negative criticisms made in the past and thereby persuade the young woman to try role-playing. This incident also reflected the patient's unresolved problems with her parents and with authority figures in general.

In a related vein Wachtel argues that psychoanalysts are more likely than behavior therapists to consider the nonnormative or unusual concerns, wishes, and fears of their patients. Guided by the view that emotional problems derive from the repression of id conflicts, they consider psychological difficulties to be reflections of infantile wishes and fears, dark mysteries of primary-process think-

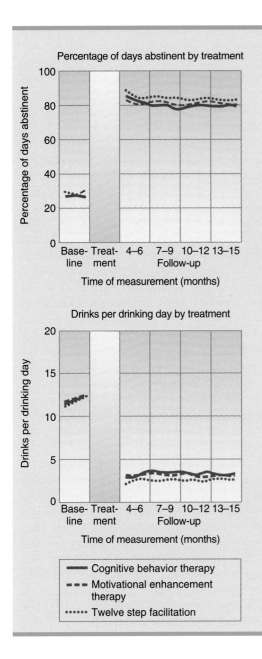

Cognitive behavior therapy

Motivational enhancement therapy

Twelve step facilitation

year posttreatment assessment period. Figure 18.2 portrays the main results of this study. Significant within-group improvement was observed—all treatments were very helpful on average, consistent with a subsequent study by Ouimette et al. (1997). But as noted at the outset of this discussion, interactions between treatments and matching variables—the main purpose of the study—were not found except for psychiatric severity; patients in better psychological shape had more abstinent days after the twelve-step facilitation program than did patients in the cognitive-behavioral condition, although patients in worse psychological condition did not fare differently across the three treatments. Future articles will report additional analyses of the huge data set generated by this study. For now, the researchers have concluded:

> The lack of other robust matching effects suggests that, aside from psychiatric severity, providers need not take [the] client characteristics [that were studied] into account when triaging clients to one or the other of these three individually administered treatment approaches, despite their different treatment philosophies. (Project March Research Group, 1997, p. 7)

There is a long way to go before statements can be made with confidence about the kinds of patients who will benefit from particular *generally effective* treatments.

Figure 18.2   Monthly percentage of days abstinent and drinks per drinking day (DDD) for baseline (averaged over 3 months prior to treatment) and for each month of the posttreatment period (months 1 – 15). If a person was abstinent during a given month, the DDD score was zero.

ing, such as feeling hostility toward a loved one. Behavior therapists tend to have a more straightforward, perhaps more prosaic, view of their patients' problems.

In our view as clinical psychologists who have taught and practiced in a cognitive-behavioral framework for many years, the actual practice of experienced behavioral clinicians often reflects the kind of subtlety characteristic of psychodynamic clinicians such as Wachtel. What is unclear to us, and we believe to Wachtel, is the degree to which sophisticated practice can be derived from the theories that constitute contemporary cognitive and behavior therapy. The disjunction between theory

and practice lies at the core of Wachtel's critical discussion of behavior therapy and the ways in which psychoanalysis might enrich both behavioral theory and practice. We turn now to some general issues in eclecticism and psychotherapy integration.

ECLECTICISM AND THEORETICAL INTEGRATION IN PSYCHOTHERAPY

Wachtel's efforts at rapprochement are part of a long tradition in the field of psychotherapy (e.g., Dollard & Miller, 1950; Frank, 1971; Goldfried &

Davison, 1976; Marmor, 1971). A new periodical, *Journal of Psychotherapy Integration*, is devoted to this topic. More than three decades ago, Perry London put the issue this way:

> There is a quiet blending of techniques by artful therapists of either school, a blending that takes account of the fact that people are considerably simpler than the Insight schools give them credit for, but that they are also more complicated than the Action [behavior] therapists would like to believe. (London, 1964, p. 39)

THE LAZARUS–MESSER DEBATE

Some of the issues surrounding eclecticism and integration were explored in an article by two leading figures, Arnold Lazarus and Stanley Messer, colleagues at Rutgers University (Lazarus & Messer, 1991). The article's point–counterpoint framework mirrors a debate that took place at the 1990 convention of the Society for the Exploration of Psychotherapy Integration. This organization, founded in 1983, is noted for annual meetings that involve lively and spirited exchanges among theorists and clinicians who might in other times never have attended the same convention.

The core epistemological question is one that we have addressed many times in this book: Is it possible to make theory-free observations; that is, in our complex world, can we speak of objective facts outside a particular paradigm or theory? The answer one gives to this very abstract question about the nature of knowledge and reality influences one's

Arnold Lazarus, Rutgers psychologist and master clinician, who developed multimodal therapy.

view of the challenge of integrating diverse forms of psychotherapy.

For many years Lazarus, trained as a behavior therapist by Wolpe in the late 1950s in South Africa, advocated what he called "technical eclecticism," a willingness to use whatever techniques work best for a particular patient or disorder without regard to the theoretical approach from which they are drawn. As we will see, though, the technique is incorporated into the therapist's theoretical framework. This view is elaborated in his own approach to psychotherapy, multimodal therapy (cf. p. 533). Lazarus argues not only that this empirically based eclecticism at the technique level will be of most benefit to the most patients, but that to attempt rapprochement or integration at the theoretical level— for example, seeking a way, as Wachtel does, to blend psychoanalytic and behavioral theory—is fruitless, a waste of time, and impossible. Recent moves toward theoretical integration, instead of facilitating dialogue and rapprochement, are, in Lazarus's view, creating even more chaos.

Before getting into the particulars of the Lazarus–Messer debate, it will be useful to distinguish among three modes of psychotherapy integration (Arkowitz, 1989): technical eclecticism,[6] common factorism, and theoretical integration. In the first mode, exemplified in Lazarus's multimodal approach and in Beutler's prescriptive psychotherapy (Beutler & Harwood, 1995), the therapist works within a particular theoretical framework, for example, cognitive behavior therapy, but sometimes imports from other orientations techniques deemed effective *without subscribing to the theories that spawned them*. Use whatever works is the operating principle of the technical eclectic, but rationalize the use of a technique from one's own framework. For example, Lazarus sometimes uses the Gestalt empty chair as a method of behavioral rehearsal rather than as a way to help the patient reclaim disowned parts of his or her personality, which is how the technique is conceived in Gestalt therapy.

---

[6]As discussed in Chapter 2 (p. 51), eclecticism per se refers to "a largely pragmatic approach in which the therapist uses whatever techniques he or she believes are likely to be effective, with little or no underlying theory to guide these choices" (Arkowitz, 1992, p. 262). This strategy is regarded with skepticism by many mental health professionals, including Lazarus and the authors of this book, for it lacks a rationale for determining which technique to use and under what circumstances. Without theoretical guidelines to help the therapist conceptualize the client's problem and the processes of therapeutic change, eclecticism is equivalent to chaos, in which choices are made on whim, on the basis of what feels right, or for any number of other reasons that make for neither good science nor sound practice.

Common factorism (e.g., Frank, 1961, 1982; Goldfried, 1980, 1991; Schofield, 1964) seeks strategies that all therapy schools might share. For example, informing a patient how he or she affects others is a strategy employed by many different kinds of therapists and believed by many (e.g., Brady et al., 1980) to be an important component of effective psychotherapy.

The third approach, theoretical integration, tries to synthesize not only techniques but theories. Wachtel's efforts to justify and make sense of assertion training within a modified psychoanalytic framework is a prime example of an effort toward theoretical integration. The resulting theory is itself something different because of the blending of psychoanalytic and behavioral elements.

It is theoretical integration against which Lazarus inveighs, in part because most theories of psychotherapy are epistemologically incompatible. For example, the definition of a fact in psychoanalysis differs from the definition of a fact in behavior therapy. Different standards of evidence prevail. The argument is that one cannot integrate two theories that do not share the same definition of reality. Our earlier discussion of Kuhn and paradigms in science bears directly on this discussion (cf. p. 21).

But, Lazarus asks rhetorically, can one not use a "disembodied technique" (Strupp, 1989)? His answer is yes, one can borrow techniques without buying into the theories that gave rise to them. Thus he uses the empty chair as one way to implement behavior rehearsal within his cognitive-behavioral framework. Lazarus believes that having the patient imagine that a significant other, such as a parent, is in an empty chair makes the role-play more vivid and realistic. Apparently there is something about the person's talking to an empty chair that helps bring the parent into the consulting room, perhaps better than having the therapist pretend to be the patient's parent. Lazarus argues that one can employ the procedure without adopting the Gestalt conceptual framework in which it was developed.

Lazarus's technical eclecticism is not a mishmash based on personal preferences or ignorance; it is, he asserts, based solely and simply on *data*, on information about what works under certain conditions. And this information is for the most part theory-free; one can determine what is true or not true without subscribing to a particular theory. As he puts it: "Observations simply reflect empirical data without offering explanations. 'Adolescents tend to imitate the behavior of peers whom they respect,' is an observation. 'They do so unconsciously due

to inadequate parental introjects,' is a theory" (Lazarus & Messer, 1991, p. 147).

In response, Messer suggests that Lazarus's dissatisfaction with theoretical integration stems in part from a belief that an all-encompassing theory of psychotherapy is lurking in the wings, waiting to be discovered, and that until this happy uncovering it is best to eschew attempts to integrate theories in favor of using whatever techniques work (technical eclecticism). In contrast, Messer's view, sometimes described as social constructionist (cf. Davison, 1991; Gergen, 1982; Mahoney, 1991), sometimes as hermeneutic (cf. Messer, Sass, & Woolfolk, 1988), holds that we *invent* our theories—something Lazarus would not dispute—*and that we view the world through the prisms that our theories or paradigms provide*—a notion that we espouse and that Lazarus does not fully embrace. That is, there is no such thing as an objective observation, an objective fact; rather, we understand reality only within the context of a particular theory or paradigm. As Messer puts it, there is no such thing as an "immaculate perception."

This perspective leads Messer to criticize Lazarus's technical eclecticism. When Lazarus borrows a technique and uses it within his own cognitive-behavioral framework, that technique becomes something different from what it was in its original theoretical framework. The Gestalt empty chair that Lazarus uses is different from that used by Perls. Messer credits Lazarus for making creative use of this technique, but notes that in doing so it becomes something else, something other than the Gestalt empty chair. Both in theory and in practice the empty chair in Lazarus's hands is different from what it is in Gestalt therapy. In the latter, the technique is designed to put the client in better touch with unacknowledged feelings and conflicting parts of the self. In contrast, Lazarus uses it to help the client relate differently to a significant person in his or her life, in a form of behavior rehearsal, a strategy aimed at improving how the person behaves toward another.

Consider now Lazarus's criterion for importing a technique—it has to be demonstrably effective. Herein lies a serious problem, according to Messer, for any evidence that the Gestalt literature provides on the effectiveness of the empty chair is not relevant to the cognitive-behavioral context in which Lazarus works. Again, simply put, the empty chair that Lazarus uses is not the empty chair that the Gestalt therapist uses. To support his argument that he uses only empirically validated techniques, Lazarus must look for evidence in experiments that evaluate the empty chair as a behavior-rehearsal procedure, which Gestalt therapists have not bothered with (nor have behaviorally oriented researchers).

Messer critiques Lazarus's assertion that "Adolescents tend to imitate the behavior of peers whom they respect" is an objective, verifiable, theory-free observation. No, says Messer, it is replete with theory. Adolescents may imitate their peers for a host of other reasons; that they do so out of respect is a theoretical explanation of their imitative behavior. Further, the very phrase "imitate the behavior of peers whom they respect" is not a theory-free statement, for there are other ways to refer to such behavior, for example, "act in ways similar to the behavior of people of the same age whose social status they envy."[7]

In conclusion Messer suggests a fourth mode of integration: evolutionary or assimilative integration (which we regard as equivalent to theoretical integration). By this he means that "techniques and concepts from one therapy ... find their way into another, and get incorporated within its slowly evolving theory and mode of practice" (Lazarus & Messer, 1991, p. 153). As in technical eclecticism, a technique is imported into a new framework, but then that framework begins to change as it incorporates theoretical elements from the imported technique's framework. In this way one's original theory evolves, becoming something different and presumably more comprehensive and useful. Wachtel's cyclical psychodynamics is an example, for it evolved from its psychoanalytic source by incorporating techniques and ideas from behavior therapy. It is a blend of the two approaches. As Messer wrote: "I would not claim, as does Lazarus, that I am merely importing an observation or technique shorn of excess theoretical baggage. Rather, I am incorporating an attitude, perspective, or approach that is transformed in its new context even while retaining something of value from its point of origin" (Lazarus & Messer, 1991, p. 153).

ARGUMENTS AGAINST PREMATURE INTEGRATION

In contemplating efforts at theoretical integration, we have wondered whether a grand, all-encompassing theory or approach is necessarily desirable or even possible. We believe not, and our own use of different paradigms in the study of both psychopathology and intervention aligns us more with the views of Garfield and Bergin.

A comprehensive conception of how the body works does not demand that every system or organ of the body operate according to the same principles. Thus, our view of how the circulatory system works is quite different from our view of the nervous system. The forces and actions of the human heart operate according to the principles of fluid mechanics, whereas the principles of electrochemistry apply to the transmission of nerve impulses through the neuron; yet these two quite different processes occur in the same human body and are coordinated harmoniously despite their apparently disparate functions.

Similarly, human personality may operate in accordance with a complex interaction of seemingly disparate processes that act together, though each differently and in its own sphere. Thus, it is conceivable that the same individual may suffer at one time from a repressed conflict, a conditioned response, an incongruent self-image, and irrational cognitions; and that each of these dysfunctions may operate in semi-independent systems of psychic action that are amenable to rather different interventions, each of which is compatible with the "system" to which it is being applied. Diagnosis and therapy might then become concerned with the locus of the disorder or with which portion or portions of the multisystem psyche is involved. (1986, p. 10)

Indeed, not all those interested in psychotherapy integration agree with the overall notion that the more blurring between conceptual frameworks, the better. In an article entitled "Disappearing Differences Do Not Always Reflect Healthy Integration," Haaga and Davison (1991) pointed out several ways in which Ellis's REBT and Beck's CT have begun to merge. For example, Beck originally focused almost entirely on cognitive biases and how they might distort a person's analysis of a situation. Thus a depressed person who complains that he or she has no friends is encouraged, like a scientist, to determine whether in fact this is true. In contrast, Ellis emphasized the belief or assumption under which a person operates, for example, "I must be perfect in everything I do." Now, however, Beck devotes at least as much time talking about "dysfunctional schemata," which can look a great deal like Ellis's "irrational beliefs." And Ellis does not ignore social realities, for even at the beginning (Ellis, 1962) he advocated teaching someone without social skills how better to interact with others, with the goal of improving relationships (rather than just encouraging the person to care little about turning people off).

---

[7]In fairness to Lazarus, Messer's argument here is almost tantamount to saying that whenever we use language, we are not theory neutral. "Imitative behavior" seems as free of theorizing as can reasonably be expected; it is certainly less theory–laden than a phrase such as "identify with," which assumes a psychodynamic process. But perhaps that is the essence of the constructionist thesis.

From an integrative point of view this might be seen as progress, but Haaga and Davison caution that such optimism may be ill-advised. They suggest that we may lose something by blurring such distinctions,[8] especially if integration is not based on research (and they argue that it isn't). If we preserve the uniqueness of these two therapies, we might then construct a more integrative therapy that uses the particular strengths of each. For example, perhaps for certain people under certain circumstances it is best to focus on changing social realities, whereas other circumstances might call for changing people's interpretations of an unchanging and perhaps unchangeable social reality. Creating this kind of integration requires (1) holding on to at least some of the original distinctions between REBT and CT and, most importantly, (2) constructing or utilizing a superordinate theory that can subsume both REBT and CT and specify when a particular aspect of one is suitable and when a feature of the other is appropriate. The intricacies of this process are beyond our purposes; suffice it to say that science sometimes moves forward more readily when rapprochement among divergent theories is *not* encouraged.

---

[8]A former student used a salad metaphor to describe what is lost when one blurs distinctions between elements that are best combined without blending them. "One may want to initially grow and chop the vegetables of a salad separately because it is quicker, cleaner, and more organized. Later you might put them into a large tossing bowl to have all of the individual vegetables (or paradigms) readily available for your guests (therapists) to choose from. When each guest takes from the bowl, he takes what will fit together the best, what tastes the best. You wouldn't want a salad full of onion-carrot hybrids" (C. J. Getty, personal communication, December 1994).

SUMMARY

The cognitive and behavior therapies attempt to apply the methodologies and principles of experimental psychology to the alleviation of psychological distress.

Through counterconditioning, a substitute desirable response is elicited in the presence of a stimulus that has evoked an undesired response. Systematic desensitization is believed by some to be effective because of counterconditioning, but it may be that relaxation, rather than being a substitute response for fear, functions to encourage frightened patients to expose themselves to what they fear. Desensitization has been useful for a wide range of anxiety-related problems.

In operant conditioning, desired responses are taught and undesired ones discouraged by applying the contingencies of reward and punishment. The token economy is a prime example of the clinical application of operant conditioning to improve the functioning of schizophrenic patients in mental hospitals. Other operant techniques are also useful with many different childhood disorders.

Modeling, helping the person to acquire new responses and unlearn old ones by observing models, has been used effectively to eliminate fears and to teach new patterns of complex behavior.

Cognitive therapies, such as Ellis's rational-emotive behavior therapy and Beck's cognitive therapy, alter the thoughts that are believed to underlie emotional disorders. They reflect the increasing importance of cognition in experimentally based psychological interventions. Self-control presents some interesting challenges to the behavioral paradigm: an active and conscious human being by autonomous and deliberate choice acts independently of environmental influences.

Behavioral medicine attempts by psychological procedures to alter bad living habits, distressed psychological states, and aberrant physiological processes in order to prevent and to treat medical illnesses. Paradoxical therapy is a mode of intervention that directs the person not to change or to make worse the problems for which he or she is seeking help.

Several strategies are employed to maintain gains once a patient is no longer in regular contact with the therapist, such as eliminating sources of secondary gain and encouraging the person to attribute improvement more to his or her own efforts than to the expertise of the therapist.

Current important issues in cognitive and behavior therapy include the role of mediational variables, unconscious influences, relationship factors, and the possibility of rapprochement, such as integrating some parts of psychoanalytic theorizing into behavior therapy. Three main approaches to integration are technical eclecticism, common factors, and theoretical integration. There seem to be both advantages and disadvantages to blurring the differences between theoretical approaches in psychotherapy.

KEY TERMS

behavior therapy
systematic desensitization
aversion therapy
token economy
cognitive restructuring
rational-emotive behavior
   therapy (REBT)

cognitive therapy (CT)
social problem solving (SPS)
metacognition
multimodal therapy
triadic reciprocality
behavioral medicine

health psychology
biofeedback
paradoxical interventions
aptitude-treatment
   interaction

Marisol Escobar, "The Family," 1962

GROUP, COUPLES AND FAMILY THERAPY, AND COMMUNITY PSYCHOLOGY

A couple with a marriage of twenty years' duration sought treatment for the male's problem of total inability to have an erection. This had been a problem for over nineteen of their twenty years of marriage. Successful intercourse had only taken place in the first few months of the marriage. The woman in this couple was also unable to reach an orgasm, and indeed had never had an orgasm from any form of stimulation, in her entire life. However, she reported that she greatly enjoyed sex and was extremely frustrated by her husband's inability to have an erection.

In treating this couple, through techniques [based on those of Masters and Johnson], very rapid progress was made. The husband very quickly began to have erections in response to his wife's manual stimulation of his genitals.

She also learned to have orgasm, first through her own masturbation and then through her husband's manual and oral stimulation of her genitals. By session 10 of weekly therapy, the couple was able to engage in normal intercourse with both of them having orgasm. Thus, the case was essentially "cured" within ten sessions.

However, at this point, something rather peculiar happened. Rather than continuing intercourse after this success, the couple discontinued all sexual activity for the next several weeks. Upon careful exploration by the therapist a rather interesting picture emerged. First, it became clear that the husband had a great need to remain distant and aloof from his wife. He had great fears of being overwhelmed and controlled by her, and found closeness to be very uncomfortable. He himself had had a rather disturbed relationship with his mother, with her being extremely controlling, manipulating, and intrusive in his life, well into his adulthood. For him, the inability to have an erection served to keep his wife distant from him, and to maintain his need for privacy, separateness, and autonomy in the relationship.

In exploring the situation with the wife, [the therapist found] in contrast to her overt statements … an extremely ambivalent attitude toward sex. She had been raised in a very anti-sexual family. While she claimed to have rejected these anti-sexual teachings in her own late adolescence and adulthood, in point of fact this rejection had occurred only at a superficial intellectual level. Emotionally, she still had a great deal of difficulty in accepting her sexual feelings. She had fears of being overwhelmed by uncontrollable sexual urges if she allowed herself to enjoy sex. Thus, her husband's erectile problems served to protect her from her own fears about sex. Furthermore, over the nineteen years of her husband being unable to attain an erection, she had come to have a very powerful position in the relationship. She very often reminded her husband that he owed her a lot because of her sexual frustration. Thus, she was essentially able to win all arguments with him, and to get him to do anything that she wanted.

For this couple, the rapid resolution of their sexual dysfunction threatened elements in both their own personalities, and in the way their relationship was structured. In exploring their inability to continue having intercourse, once they had succeeded, they came to realize the [link] between their sexual problems and the structure of their [marriage]. With several additional weeks of therapy focused on resolving these individual and relationship factors, they were able to resume sexual activity successfully. (LoPiccolo & Friedman, 1985, pp. 465–466)

In this chapter we review four modes of therapeutic intervention. Although different from one another in many important ways, they are similar in that they make far more efficient use of professional time and are more economical than the one-to-one therapies reviewed in the preceding two chapters. However, economy is not the primary reason any of these is chosen. Each treatment has developed from a particular rationale for providing effective help. In **group therapy** a professional treats a number of patients simultaneously; in **couples (marital) therapy** and **family therapy**, committed partners and sometimes children are seen together in conjoint sessions; **community psychology** seeks to prevent the initial onset of disorders and behavior problems by intervening in various segments of the community; and **community mental health** provides inpatient and outpatient mental health care in a way that is more accessible and economical to less affluent people.

Group Therapy

The first group psychotherapy was conducted in the United States in 1905 by an internist named Joseph H. Pratt, who led a group consisting of patients with tuberculosis. Pratt's use of group therapy to provide psychological support was in response to the epidemic proportions of tuberculosis and the corresponding ostracism of these patients from the community. He treated debilitated patients who could not afford individual care. Pratt's approach made more efficient use of health care resources and was soon applied to institutionalized mental patients. By 1925, group psychotherapy was also being used with noninstitutionalized patients.

The development of group therapy accelerated in the 1930s, perhaps because of the Great Depression and the leadership of President Franklin Roosevelt, whose New Deal approach emphasized the utility of collective action. Short of money, people tried to find solutions in group endeavor. In 1948, Samuel Slavson founded the American Group

Psychotherapy Association, which is considered to have had the most influence on the growth of group psychotherapy today (Wong, 1995). As psychotherapists experimented with therapy in groups, they concluded that for many patients, it was as good as individual therapy (Wolf & Kutash, 1990).

Vinogradov and Yalom (1989) refer to the writings of Harry Stack Sullivan (see Chapter 17) to underscore the general utility they see in group therapy. Sullivan held that personality is almost entirely the product of interactions with others and that psychopathology develops when these interactions and the person's perceptions of them are distorted. The implication of this view is that treatment should be directed toward the correction of interpersonal distortions. Extrapolating from Sullivan's notion of individual psychotherapy, Vinogradov and Yalom prefer the group setting for treatment, reasoning that interpersonal distortions and relationships can be more powerfully affected in the "interpersonal arena" afforded by group therapy.

Most group therapists regard their form of treatment as uniquely appropriate for accomplishing certain goals. Group members can learn vicariously when attention is focused on another participant. Social pressures can be surprisingly strong in groups. If a therapist tells an individual client that his or her behavior seems hostile even when hostility is not intended, the message may be rejected; however, if three or four other people agree with the interpretation, the person may find it much more difficult to dismiss. Further, many people derive comfort and support solely from the knowledge that others have problems similar to their own, as in Pratt's original groups.

Many of the techniques employed in individual therapy have been or can be used for treating people in groups. Thus there are psychoanalytic groups (Slavson, 1950; Wolf, 1949), Gestalt groups (Perls, 1969), client-centered groups (Rogers, 1970), behavior therapy groups (Heimberg & Juster, 1994; Lazarus, 1968a; Paul & Shannon, 1966), and countless other groups. Some researchers argue that it is hazardous to build a group therapy on the basis of a theory of individual psychotherapy (Bednar & Kaul, 1994), as extrapolation from a model of individual therapy overlooks the uniqueness of a group setting. For example, the group setting involves complex interactions among people who are fellow patients, whereas in the individual setting the only interaction is between client and therapist. In addition, theories about individual therapy tend to be biased toward intrapsychic rather than interpersonal processes. These differences between individual-intrapsychic and interpersonal approaches play a

central role in couples and family therapy, which is addressed later.

BASIC FEATURES OF GROUP THERAPY

Several considerations must be taken into account in forming any group for therapy purposes (Wong, 1995).

- *Selecting Patients* It is easier to identify people for whom group therapy is *in*appropriate than those for whom it is appropriate. Generally patients with acute psychosis or depression, psychopathy, or substance-abuse problems are poor candidates for this type of therapy, although specialized groups may be of some benefit to them. Inpatient settings provide little flexibility in terms of group membership because usually all patients are put in groups. Outpatient settings provide the therapist with more control over who becomes a group member.

- *Preparing Patients* Most group therapists get to know individual participants at least minimally before having them become part of a group. In addition to helping with selection, this step helps the therapist prepare participants for the group process, for example, by informing them of ground rules, such as maintaining confidentiality about what is discussed in group and refraining from aggressive behavior. Preparation of members is associated with lower drop-out rates, fewer nonconstructive silences, and better outcomes, and may be one of the most important factors in creating successful treatment groups (Bednar & Kaul, 1994).

- *Frequency and Duration of Sessions* Groups generally meet once per week for one to two hours at a time. Inpatient groups tend to be of shorter duration because hospitalized patients are generally more disturbed than are outpatients and cannot handle longer sessions.

- *Cohesion* It is widely assumed that when there is group cohesion—members feel committed to the group or feel a sense of loyalty to it—they participate more freely and fully and are more amenable to the therapeutic interventions (Bednar and Kaul, 1994). However, empirical investigations on the efficacy of cohesion have yielded mixed results.

- *Termination* Ideally, a group terminates when all members have reached their therapeutic goals, but this rarely occurs. Extratherapeutic factors—limitations imposed by health insurance, insufficient funds, members moving out of the area, therapist–trainees graduating or moving to another rotation in the clinical setting—often play a key role in when a particular group disbands. Termination may induce a wide variety of emotions, ranging from happiness to abandonment, and these feelings typically become topics for group discussion.

- *Inpatient Versus Outpatient Setting* Most of the preceding points pertain to outpatient groups. Inpatient groups differ from outpatient groups in several respects. Typically, patients are assigned to a group that meets every day; the groups have rapid turnover and are more heterogeneous than are outpatient groups. Patients tend to be more ambivalent than are outpatients because attendance is mandatory. Inpatients are much more disordered than outpatients; when their antipsychotic or antidepressant medication is not working, their ability to participate meaningfully is markedly reduced. The therapeutic focus of inpatient groups is to help the patients regain their previous level of functioning and prepare them for discharge and outpatient treatment. But often discussion centers on problems that arise on the ward, such as misbehavior on the part of some patients or difficulty getting an appointment with the ward psychiatrist or psychologist. Group leaders generally take a more active role and encourage participation more than do leaders of outpatient groups. Finally, unlike the situation with outpatient groups, contact among the patients when outside the group is common because they live together (Sultenfuss & Geczy, 1994).

Group therapies have been used with children and their parents, with adolescents, with patients suffering from a host of medical illnesses, with elderly adults and their caregivers, with abusive parents, with delinquents, with homosexuals, and with hospitalized mental patients (Lubin, 1983). We examine next a few group psychotherapies, in the hope of imparting some idea of the range of theories and procedures, and review the evidence bearing on their effectiveness.

INSIGHT-ORIENTED GROUP THERAPY

PSYCHOANALYTIC GROUP THERAPY

At the annual meeting of the American Group Psychotherapy Association in 1957, a discussion took place between the well-known psychoanalytic

theoretician Lawrence Kubie and two pioneering group therapists who were working within a psychoanalytic framework, Foulkes and Grotjahn. Kubie's assertion, as published a year later in the *International Journal of Group Psychotherapy*, was that psychoanalysis in groups could not be effective because the transference to the therapist would be diluted. Debating against this view were Foulkes and Grotjahn, whose psychoanalytic work on group therapy derives from Alexander Wolf, considered to have begun the practice of psychoanalysis in groups in 1938. Foulkes and Grotjahn's arguments are believed by some to have "dealt a blow to the invincibility of individual psychoanalysis to be the only really effective method of psychotherapy" (Sager, 1990, p. xi).[1] Since then, analytically oriented therapists have adapted some of the concepts and methods of individual psychoanalysis and psychodynamic therapy to the group setting.

Psychoanalytic group therapists employ such Freudian concepts and methods as transference, free association, dream analysis, resistance, the unconscious, and the importance of past history, all in an effort to move patients toward an understanding of intrapsychic processes. Some therapists (e.g., Wolf & Kutash, 1990) concentrate on the psychodynamics of each individual group member, whereas others (e.g., Bion, 1959; Foulkes, 1964) conceive of the group itself as having a collective set of psychodynamics, manifested in such things as a group transference to the therapist. Sometimes the therapist sees each of the group members for many sessions of individual psychoanalysis or psychoanalytically oriented therapy prior to group therapy. Interpretations of what members say are offered not only by the therapist but by other members of the group. What all psychoanalytic approaches have in common is the belief that increased self-understanding and deep emotional change can take place in the individual within the context of a group and that the group itself can facilitate these curative psychoanalytic processes. Psychodynamic group therapy modeled after the individual brief dynamic therapy described in Chapter 17 is also widely employed.

SENSITIVITY TRAINING AND ENCOUNTER GROUPS

Some years ago Aronson (1972) proposed a distinction between the **sensitivity training** or **T-group** (T, for training) and the more radical **encounter group**,

---

[1]Also during this same period individual psychotherapy was broadened to include the various behavioral and cognitive-behavioral approaches described in Chapter 18, as well as the several humanistic and existential approaches presented in Chapter 17.

which was popular primarily on the West Coast at such places as the Esalen Institute, where Perls was in residence in the 1960s. T-groups tend to rely more on verbal procedures and to avoid the physical contact, touching exercises, and unrestrained expressions of emotion that are employed by many encounter groups.

Aronson's distinction was not accepted by all workers. For example, Rogers (1970) traced the development of encounter groups to his training of counselors at the University of Chicago in 1946, in which he emphasized personal growth and improved interpersonal communication. We agree with Rogers's judgment that T-groups and encounter groups are usually impossible to distinguish from one another today.

Throughout the turbulent sixties, when public attacks on perceived hypocrisies and on the Establishment were becoming commonplace, more and more people—including those who would be unlikely to carry a DSM diagnosis—sought to understand themselves better and to learn to relate openly and honestly to each other. Ideas from Gestalt therapy and other approaches were also introduced into T-groups. These groups are not usually regarded as therapy groups in the strictest sense of the word, for people with known psychiatric problems tend to be screened out. Extremely popular in the 1960s and 1970s, they are less common today. However, we present them here because elements of these groups are present in most therapy groups. Moreover, their principles and ideas have been adopted in various religious and secular retreats, which frequently focus on issues relating to human distress (Wong, 1995).

The T-group was originally conceived in 1947, and the National Training Laboratory was established through conferences on small-group dynamics held in Bethel, Maine. The impetus came from colleagues of Kurt Lewin, a famous social psychologist at the Massachusetts Institute of Technology (Lubin, 1983). The original groups comprised people in industry, and the goal was to increase efficiency in business practices at the highest levels of management by making executives more aware of their impact on other people and of their own feelings about others. Since that time, millions of people have participated in such groups, including no doubt some readers of this book. Attention has shifted over the years from group dynamics to individual growth and the attainment of one's full human potential.

Typically, members are encouraged to focus on their here-and-now relationships with one another. Individuals are often drawn to encounter or T-groups because, even though their lives are not full of problems, they feel that they are missing something, that they are existing without intensity and intimacy. Some people also participate in such groups in hopes of preventing a psychological problem that they fear might develop in the future, especially one that is interpersonal in nature, such as a couples or marital problem.

In the most general terms, T-groups and encounter groups provide a setting in which people are encouraged to behave in an unguarded, honest fashion. They are then helped to receive and give feedback, to see how they come across to and affect others, and to examine how they feel about their behavior and that of others. They are expected to become more aware and accepting of themselves and of other group members.

LEVELS OF COMMUNICATION Figure 19.1 is a schematic representation of a dyadic, or two-person, interaction (Aronson, 1972). In our everyday lives we usu-

Encounter groups can be distinguished from T-groups by their greater use of touching exercises and emphasis on emotional expression.

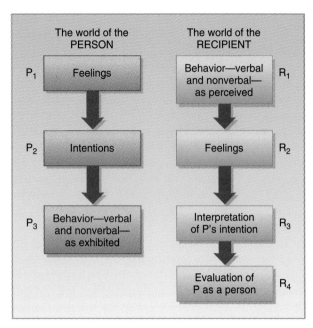

Figure 19.1 Schematic representation of the different levels of communication possible in a two-person interaction. After Aronson (1972).

ally operate at level P_3, behaving in some verbal or nonverbal way toward another person. Usually the recipient of our P_3 behavior responds at level R_4, evaluating us. Misjudgments can occur at many points. For example, at level R_3 the recipient may misinterpret P's intention. Even though the person

Synanon was among the earliest residential treatment centers for drug addicts. Direct and often brutal confrontation is used to help addicts confront their problems honestly.

may feel warmly (P_1) toward his or her friend, the recipient, the person may have difficulty expressing warmth and therefore show sarcasm at P_3. The recipient then interprets P's intention as a wish to hurt (R_3), rather than as a desire to express warm feelings. Without the open discussion that is encouraged in a T-group, the recipient can reject (R_4) the person as a nasty individual and never come to understand that the person really feels warmly (P_1) but has not learned to express those feelings (P_3) appropriately. A properly run T-group encourages the participants to break down their personal communications and reactions into all the various components so that they can examine their true feelings toward other persons and their perceptions of what they are receiving from them. This theme will be encountered again in our discussion of couples therapy.

Experienced and competent group leaders watch for undue coercion and direct the stream of conversation away from an individual when they sense excessive probing into the person's private feelings. They make every effort not to impose their will and ideas on the other participants, but they are aware of the very powerful position they occupy in the group. It seems likely that some of the unfortunate abuses of encounter and T-groups can be attributed to the all-too-human tendency of some trainers to wield this power unwisely.

VARIATIONS Sensitivity and encounter groups may vary in a number of ways. Rogerian groups tend to operate according to individual client-centered therapy, outlined in Chapter 17. The leader tries to clarify the feelings of group members on the assumption that growth can occur as people confront their emotions with honesty. The group leader—sometimes referred to as a facilitator in the spirit of the "nondirectiveness" of Rogerian therapy—tends to be less active than the leaders in the T-groups Aronson describes. Some groups may meet for hours at a time, perhaps over a weekend, with little if any sleep allowed. Such marathons (Bach, 1966; Mintz, 1967; Stoller, 1968) rely on fatigue and extended exposure to a particular set of social conditions to weaken defenses and help the participants become more open and presumably more authentic. A particularly direct, and sometimes brutal, variation of encounter groups is the type of meeting pioneered at Synanon and other residential drug-abuse treatment centers (p. 326), where the assumption is that vigorous and speedy stripping away of defenses and cop-outs is necessary to help substance abusers confront their problems and take responsibility for their lives (Casriel, 1971).

BEHAVIOR-THERAPY GROUPS

INDIVIDUALIZED BEHAVIOR THERAPY IN GROUPS

Arnold Lazarus (1968a), a pioneer in group behavior therapy, pointed out years ago that behavior therapists may, primarily for reasons of efficiency, choose to treat several people suffering from the same kind of problem by seeing them in a group rather than individually. The emphasis remains, as in one-to-one therapy, on interactions between the therapist and each individual patient or client (Figure 19.2a).[2] This focus on the group as a more efficient way to conduct what is basically individual therapy was affirmed more recently by Rose (1991).

Group desensitization (Lazarus, 1961) is a good example of this individualized approach. A single therapist can teach deep muscle relaxation and present a hierarchy to the members of the group simultaneously, thus saving therapist time. (Of course group members have to have the same fear.) Fears handled in this manner include test anxiety (Nawas, Fishman, & Pucel, 1970), snake phobias (Ritter, 1968), anxiety about public speaking (Paul & Shannon, 1966), and social anxiety (Wright, 1976).

Groups using behavioral techniques to help individual members lose weight (Wollersheim, 1970), stop smoking (Koenig & Masters, 1965), and control anger (J. Rose, 1996) have also been successful, as have groups that reinforce conversational efforts by hospitalized patients with chronic schizophrenia (Liberman, 1972). Whether this should be considered group therapy is open to question. The members of these special-purpose groups do seem to provide valuable encouragement and social support for one another, however.

SOCIAL-SKILLS TRAINING GROUPS

Social skills are taught to groups of people who have similar deficits in relating to others, for example, in job-interview skills or conversational and dating skills (Rose, 1991). Efforts are usually made to treat people with comparable levels of deficiency so that an appropriate pace can be maintained for all group members (Bartzokis, Liberman, & Hierholzer, 1990; Kelly, 1985). Participants rehearse together the skills they are learning and thus provide one another unique and appropriate help in changing behavior. Because members interact, the lines of communication are among all participants,

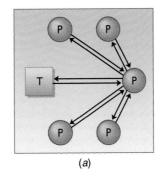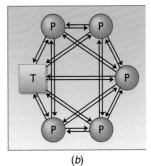

(a)   (b)

Figure 19.2   Distinction between (a) individualized group therapy and (b) group therapy in which interactions among all the members are regarded as important. Arrows indicate lines of communication and influences; T stands for therapist, P for patient.

not just between therapist and participant (Figure 19.2b). Groups of depressed people, for example, have learned social skills that are likely to bring them more reinforcement from others (Lewinsohn, Weinstein, & Alper, 1970; Teri & Lewinsohn, 1986); and social-skills training groups have helped schizophrenic and seriously mood-disordered patients learn to cope with the interpersonal challenges they are likely to face when discharged from a mental hospital (Hayes et al., 1995; Liberman, DeRisi, & Mueser, 1989).

ASSERTION-TRAINING GROUPS

A particularly important social skill is assertiveness (see p. 526). Lazarus conducts assertion training groups composed of about ten people of the same sex. At the first meeting he describes the general goals of the therapy group, commenting particularly on the problems that unassertiveness can create for individuals in society. He also suggests that the therapy group can provide a good setting for cooperative problem-solving. Like Rogers, he calls for honesty and acceptance within the group and prescribes constructive criticism and the diligent practice of new skills.[3] Members introduce themselves briefly, and the others are encouraged to comment on the manner of each person's presentation, especially if he or she was apologetic.

Members of the group are then given a situation that calls for an assertive response. The therapist

---

[2]Gestalt therapy groups generally operate in this fashion as well. The therapist works with one group member at a time; often the individual sits in a particular chair or on a particular pillow, referred to as the hot seat.

[3]Because assertion training involves awareness and encouragement of feelings, it should come as no surprise that commonalities have been noted between this kind of behavioral group and those run along humanistic lines (Lazarus, 1971). This is another sign of the rapprochement among therapy orientations discussed in Chapter 18 (p. 551).

turns the situation into a skit and demonstrates being assertive. Group members, in pairs or larger groupings, take turns playing out the skit. The therapist and other members tell the persons practicing assertiveness what they are doing that might or might not lead to a desired outcome. Assertiveness is rehearsed again and again in this fashion. Of particular importance are assignments carried out by the members between sessions. People are encouraged to describe both successful and unsuccessful attempts at assertive behavior in their everyday activities, and they often role-play within the group to help them improve on their assertion in past or anticipated situations. A sensitive and skillful therapist can create an atmosphere in which group members begin to trust themselves to express criticism without fearing that they are hurting other people's feelings. Assertion groups may even be effective in reducing the compliant, withdrawn behavior of chronic schizophrenic patients (Bloomfield, 1973).

There are some similarities between Lazarus's assertion-training groups and the sensitivity-training groups described earlier, but an important difference is the attention Lazarus pays to between-session activities. People are trained within the group to make specific changes later, outside the group therapy setting. Although T-groups are similarly concerned with helping people change their everyday lives, much less systematic attention is paid to what clients do between group sessions.

COGNITIVE-BEHAVIORAL GROUPS

The cognitive-behavioral approaches of Ellis and of Beck have been adapted for group use and combined with social skills training in the treatment of such disorders as panic (Neron, Lacroix, & Chaput, 1995), the posttraumatic aftermath of child sexual abuse (Sinclair et al., 1995), obsessive-compulsive disorder (Kobak, Rock, & Greist, 1995), social phobia (Albano et al., 1995; Heimberg & Juster, 1994), and risky sexual behavior in adolescents (St. Lawrence et al., 1994). REBT group therapy has also been employed in treating juvenile sex offenders (Whitford & Parr, 1995) and, since the early 1970s, in feminist-oriented groups to help women with issues such as depression, sexual dysfunctions, concerns about aging, dependency, authority, and risk-taking (Wolfe, 1995). Integrative therapy approaches that combine elements of cognitive behavior therapy and psychodynamic therapy have been described in work with men who have physically abused their wives (Pressman & Sheps, 1994).

Social problem-solving (p. 533) has also been employed in group settings. For example, Rose

(1986) described problem-solving groups on college campuses in which members helped each other generate possible solutions to each other's life challenges. Some group leaders introduce what is termed *problem-solving the group*—challenging group members to deal with a particular problem, such as a few people doing all the talking. The group process itself thus becomes material for the honing of problem-solving skills. This general approach has been followed for many years in sensitivity training and encounter groups.

EVALUATION OF GROUP THERAPY

Like other therapies, group therapy has its share of glowing testimonials.

I have known individuals for whom the encounter experience has meant almost miraculous change in the depth of their communication with spouse and children. Sometimes for the first time real feelings are shared. ... I have seen teachers who have transformed their classroom ... into a personal, caring, trusting, learning group, where students participate fully and openly in forming the curriculum and all the other aspects of their education. Tough business executives who described a particular business relationship as hopeless have gone home and changed it into a constructive one. (Rogers, 1970, p. 71)

Such observations, especially by a highly skilled and respected clinician, contribute to the faith many people have in encounter groups. Comments of this nature do not, however, satisfy most behavioral scientists.

Some critics have suggested that those who participate in T-groups learn only how to participate in T-groups. They are not able to transfer to real-life situations the insights and skills that have been acquired in a group (Houts & Serber, 1972, in a book with the provocative title *After the Turn-on, What?*). Transfer of learning is a difficult problem, for whether we like it or not, the world is not set up to encourage openness and frankness in most social interactions. Those who are not operating by the rules of a T-group may be offended by the open and honest expression of feelings. Indeed, as Aronson (1972) notes, if someone insists that others be totally open when they do not want to be, he or she is being insensitive to their feelings and so really has *not* learned some of the essentials from what might have seemed a good T-group experience. This is not to say that T-group experiences can never transfer to the real world. Knowledge of how a person feels about others and comes across to them may be extremely useful in everyday activities, even though the overt behavior encouraged in a T-group or encounter group is not continued.

COUPLES AND FAMILY THERAPY   **565**

In reviews appearing in three editions of a widely cited handbook, Bednar and Kaul (1978, 1986, 1994) found few studies of group therapy that met basic standards of psychological research, for example, random assignment of patients to different treatments. Even when research designs are good, independent variables (p. 113) are often described so vaguely that it is difficult to know what was studied. We know little when told only that a group intervention was nondirective simply because the therapist was trained in the Rogerian tradition, or that a behavior therapy group was conducted. Nevertheless, several tentative conclusions can be drawn from these careful reviews of research as well as from the considered opinions of others.

- In general, group therapies of different kinds appear to have beneficial effects on a wide variety of clients, and in some instances these favorable outcomes endure at several months' follow-up. However, there have seldom been appropriate attention-placebo controls for non-specific factors.

- Pregroup training, that is, teaching general skills about participating in group therapy and instilling positive attitudes toward the experience, can help people get more out of group therapy experiences.

- Dependent people appear to do better in a highly structured group, whereas independent, better-functioning individuals improve to a greater extent in groups that have less structure and offer more opportunities for self-expression.

- Different factors are more or less important at different stages of group development. For example, Kivlighan and Mullison (1988) found that in the earliest sessions, universality—the sense that one's problems are not unique to oneself—is important, whereas interpersonal learning—discovering how one does and can relate to others—has relatively greater influence in later sessions. Other variables believed to be significant include feelings of belonging and inculcation of hope (Yalom, 1985). It is likely that factors differ depending on the needs and character of the group members. Of all the factors believed to be active ingredients for positive change, probably none is as operative as group cohesiveness (though findings would be more persuasive if the dependent measures relied less on self-report by the participants about the benefits derived from the group).

- Marathon groups may have no particular advantage over similarly constituted groups that meet for shorter periods of time; in fact, concentrating group hours in a few marathon sessions may accomplish less than spreading them over more sessions.

- Casualties of therapy—people who become worse in the course of treatment—are very few, with most studies finding rates of less than 3 percent. But the problem is not to be ignored. Members who do become worse are usually particularly disturbed or lacking in self-esteem. Those responsible for selecting group members try to screen out people who might need more individual attention or for whom the stress of confrontation and open sharing of feelings with others might be too great. Particular styles of leadership, such as a challenging, authoritative attitude that pushes group members to deal more with feelings, especially anger, than they are ready for, may be harmful (Lieberman, Yalom, & Miles, 1973; see Focus 19.1).

- Except for Heimberg's cognitive-behavioral group therapy for social phobia (Heimberg & Juster, 1994), no body of evidence supports the superiority of one kind of group therapy over another. Although one theoretical approach may be more suitable than another for treating a particular problem, research has only begun to address such questions.

- It has long been assumed that progress in group therapy is facilitated by feedback, by candid comments made by one person to another about the feelings he or she arouses, the impressions made, "how you're comin' across." Evidence indicates that feedback is indeed useful, especially when negative feedback—"You sound imperious when you ask things of people"—is accompanied by positive feedback—"I like the way you said that" (Jacobs et al., 1973).

COUPLES AND FAMILY THERAPY

Many married couples who seek or who are referred for therapy to deal with problems in their relationship have children. Sometimes the problems that parents have with a child arise from conflicts in the marriage; other times a child's behavior creates distress in an otherwise well-functioning couple. The line between marital therapy and family therapy is often blurred, and professionals who specialize in working with couples often find themselves working with children as well. For these reasons we have elected to discuss couples and family therapy together, distinguishing between the two when useful.

FOCUS 19.1 THERAPY, FOR BETTER OR FOR WORSE

In 1966, Bergin applied the term *deterioration effect* to the harm that can come to someone from being a therapy patient. Several reviews of the literature since his initial report (Bergin, 1971; Bergin & Lambert, 1978; Lambert & Bergin, 1994; Lambert, Bergin, & Collins, 1977; Strupp, Hadley, & Gomes-Schwartz, 1977) indicate an unpleasant fact of life: although individual psychotherapy benefits many people, some are hurt by the experience. Group therapy (Yalom & Lieberman, 1971) and couples and family treatment (Gurman, Kniskern, & Pinsoff, 1986) also have casualties. Risk of being harmed is of course not peculiar to psychological intervention. Patients have been made worse by a wide range of medical procedures as well, including electroconvulsive therapy (Elmore & Sugerman, 1975) and the prescription of psychoactive drugs (Shader & DiMascio, 1970), both of which aim at psychological change. Some people who do *not* seek treatment also deteriorate. Avoiding contact with a mental health professional—indeed, *any* health professional—is no guarantee against getting worse.

Several noted behavior therapists examined the studies on which Bergin and others based their claim of a deterioration effect (Mays & Franks, 1980; Rachman & Wilson, 1980). They suggested that the evidence was far weaker than assumed. It is proving as difficult to show that therapy can sometimes harm as it has been to show that it can help! One problem is insufficient information on spontaneous deterioration, that is, on the rate at which people who receive no therapy at all become worse. We know that some disturbed and untreated people do get worse. But therapy outcome studies have thus far failed to analyze this deterioration adequately. Thus certain people who deteriorate while in therapy may do so not because of the therapy itself, but because of factors outside the consulting room, beyond the control of the therapist. Even so, some patients clearly worsen during therapy, which raises serious empirical and ethical questions.

What are the factors that might be responsible for the deterioration effect? Highly disturbed people and those with great expectations and a need to improve are among those often harmed. Another factor is the therapist's failure to structure sessions properly, inadequately focusing on important issues and allowing the patient to ramble. Other factors relating to the therapist include failure to deal with the patient's negative attitudes toward therapy or the therapist, dealing inadequately with patient resistance, and timing interpretations poorly (Sachs, 1983). Evidence indicates that there are therapists whose work is associated with a disproportionate number of therapy casualties as well as therapists who seldom have patients get worse and who generally help their patients (Lambert et al., 1986).

The therapist bears ultimate responsibility for harm to the client. Lieberman, Yalom, and Miles (1973) found casualties in encounter groups that were led by an "aggressive stimulator," a challenging, authoritative person who insisted on self-disclosure and catharsis of group participants even when they were not willing or ready for it. Any therapy can be abused by a practitioner who follows it foolishly, without tailoring it to the needs of the client. Some clients, desperate for support, reassurance, and advice and lacking in interpersonal skills, may become worse if a client-centered therapist unflinchingly declines to provide some guidance. Other clients, already overly dependent on others, may not be able to make choices and grow if a behavior therapist does not recognize this as a need and instead takes total charge of their lives.

Any therapist or community worker can err when assessing the patient's problem, thereby embarking on treatment that cannot help him or her. And, therapists, after all, are only human beings! Their training and experience do not qualify them as superpeople in mental health. Their own needs and personal problems, even though therapists know they should not allow them to intrude, can blind them to the needs of the client and can otherwise reduce their ability and willingness to work on the client's behalf. Sadly, some therapists are unethical as well. A few go so far as to claim that clients (always the more attractive ones) can profit from a sexual encounter with the therapist; these clinicians sometimes initiate or permit sexual intimacies. Licensing laws and codes of ethics do not themselves ensure that therapists will always act wisely and humanely. Most do, and the vast majority of clients are *not* hurt by them. But the deterioration effect has been observed too often to be disregarded or underestimated.

Changing mores prompt us sometimes to use the term *couples therapy* rather than marital therapy because of the growing numbers of couples who live together in a committed relationship and are not married. These include both heterosexual and homosexual couples, and, again, children are sometimes part of the therapeutic picture. Couples or family therapy, therefore, may involve adult partners who are unmarried or of the same sex.

THE NORMALITY OF CONFLICT

There is almost universal agreement among couples therapists and researchers, regardless of theoretical orientation, that conflict is inevitable in a marriage or in any other long-term relationship. The aura of the honeymoon passes when the couple makes unromantic decisions about where to live, where to seek employment, how to budget money, what kind of meals to prepare and the sharing of that responsibility, when to visit in-laws, if and when to have children, and whether to experiment with novel sexual techniques. Today, in addition, couples have the changed nature of gender roles to negotiate. For example, if both spouses work, will their place of residence be determined by the husband's employment or by the wife's? These sources of conflict must be handled by any two people living together, whether they are married or not, whether they are of the opposite sex or not. Authorities agree that it is how couples deal with such inherent conflicts that determines the quality and duration of their cohabitation relationship (e.g., Schwartz & Schwartz, 1980).

A strategy some couples adopt, deliberately or unconsciously, is to avoid acknowledging disagreements and conflicts. Because they believe in the reality of the fairy-tale ending, "And they lived happily ever after," any sign that their relationship is not going smoothly is threatening and must be ignored. Such patterns may keep peace in the short term at the expense of contributing to serious dysfunction in the long term (Gottman & Krokoff, 1989). Dissatisfaction and resentment usually develop and begin to take their toll as time goes by. Because the partners do not quarrel they may appear to be a perfect couple to observers, but without opening the lines of communication they may drift apart emotionally. Conversely, whereas disagreement and even the expression of anger are related to unhappiness in couples in the short term, they actually are predictive of more satisfaction over time (Gottman & Krokoff, 1989).

FROM INDIVIDUAL TO CONJOINT THERAPY

The terms *family therapy* and *couples therapy* do not denote a set procedure. They tell us that therapeutic focus is on at least two people in a relationship, but they leave undefined such issues as how the therapist views the nature and causes of the problem, what techniques are chosen to alleviate it, how often clients are seen, and whether children and even grandparents are included.

Couples and family therapy share some theoretical frameworks with individual therapy. Psychoanalytic marital therapists, for example, focus on how a person seeks or avoids a partner who resembles, to his or her unconscious, the opposite-sexed parent (Segraves, 1990). Frustrated and unsatisfied by his love-seeking attempts as a child, the adult man may unconsciously seek maternal nurturance from his wife and make excessive, even infantile,

demands of her. Much of the discussion in this kind of couples therapy centers on the conflicts he is having with his wife and, presumably, the repressed striving for maternal love that underlies his immature ways of relating to her. These unconscious forces are plumbed, with the wife assisting and possibly revealing some of her own unresolved yearnings for her father. Transference is explored, but in analytic couples therapy it is the transference between the two partners rather than between the client and the therapist that is usually the focus. The overall goal is to help each partner see the other as he or she actually is rather than as a symbolic parent (Fitzgerald, 1973). Each partner can be seen separately by different therapists (Martin & Bird, 1953), separately by the same therapist (Greene, 1960), or conjointly by the same therapist (Ackerman, 1966).

Wachtel's interpersonal psychoanalytic views have been applied to couples and family therapy (Wachtel & Wachtel, 1986). Because of their concern with interactions among people, the Wachtels bring families together in the consulting room so that interactions can be directly observed, commented on to all family members, and altered by gentle prodding, encouragement, and reinforcement. Although this approach sounds similar to cognitive-behavioral methods, the difference lies in the assumptions made by the therapists of the importance of the clients' unconscious wishes and fears, along the lines of the individual therapy that Wachtel (1977) advocates.

Ellis's rational-emotive behavior therapy has also been applied to family conflict. Again, the perspective is individualistic or intrapsychic. The therapist assumes that something going on within one or both of the partners is causing the distress in the relationship. The wife, for example, may harbor the irrational belief that her husband must constantly adore her, that his devotion must never falter. She is likely then to overreact when at a social gathering he enjoys himself away from her side, talking to other men and women.

Early sex therapy treated a sexual problem of one or both partners directly, expecting that whatever other difficulties the couple might have—anger, resentment—would dissipate thereafter. This pattern undoubtedly holds for many sexually distressed couples. But, as mentioned in Chapter 14, the increasing popularity of sex therapy since the publication of Masters and Johnson's *Human Sexual Inadequacy* in 1970 has brought to the attention of sex therapists many troubled couples for whom the sexual problem is but one aspect of a more complex *system* (Friedman & Hogan, 1985; Heiman & Verhulst, 1990). Couples and family therapy examine these

Couples therapy deals with relationship problems. It can take a number of forms ranging from psychoanalytic to behavioral.

systems. The case history that opened this chapter illustrates how a sexual dysfunction can serve a *useful* purpose in maintaining a couple's relationship and how its apparently successful treatment can actually worsen their overall connection and cut short their newfound sexual enjoyment.

With this as background to the shift from individual to conjoint therapies, we describe now some of the details of conjoint therapy. Some are common to all couples and family therapies, whereas others differ according to theoretical orientation.

THE ESSENTIALS OF CONJOINT THERAPY

THE MENTAL RESEARCH INSTITUTE TRADITION

As an overall approach, family and couples therapy seems to have begun with the efforts of John Bell (1961, 1975), a psychologist working in the 1950s at the Mental Research Institute (MRI) in Palo Alto, California. Since the mid-1950s, an increasing number of mental health professionals have devoted their professional lives to this kind of work. During the 1960s the efforts of Virginia Satir (1967), a social worker, and Donald Jackson, a psychiatrist, also at MRI, provided the field with fresh impetus.

The MRI people targeted for intervention faulty communication patterns, uneasy relationships, and inflexibility. Members of the family were shown how their behavior affected their relations with others. They were then persuaded to make specific changes, such as making their needs and dislikes

more clearly known to others. Few family therapists who identify themselves with the MRI approach are concerned with past history. Their focus is on how current problems are being maintained and how they might be changed (a viewpoint consistent with cognitive behavior therapy).

Until recently, few believed that working with only one member of the family could be fruitful, but current proponents of the MRI model do not eschew individual treatment when they believe it will further the goals of the couples or family relationship (Shoham, Rohrbaugh, & Patterson, 1995). Whatever the clinical problem, the family therapist takes a **family systems approach**, a general view of etiology and treatment that focuses on the complex interrelationships within families. The legacy of the MRI group is less a body of techniques than a general way of thinking about the complexities and constant interactive patterns in couples and family conflict.

COGNITIVE-BEHAVIORAL APPROACHES

Distressed couples do not react very positively toward each other, and this antagonism is usually evident in the very first session. It is not uncommon for one partner to feel coerced into attending conjoint therapy, even for an initial session. In an early treatise on behavioral marital therapy, Jacobson and Margolin (1979) recommended attending to this problem of antagonism as a first step in helping partners improve their marriage. One strategy is the "caring days" idea of Richard Stuart (1976), which applies an operant strategy to couples conflict. The husband, for example, is cajoled into agreeing to devote himself to doing nice things for his wife all day on a given day, without expecting anything in return. The agreement is that the wife will do the same for him the next day. If successful, this strategy accomplishes at least two important things: first, it breaks the cycle of distance, suspicion, and aversive control of each other; and second, it shows the giving partner that he or she is able to affect the spouse in a positive way. This enhanced sense of positive control is achieved simply by pleasing the partner. The giving can later be more reciprocal; each partner may agree to please the other in certain specific ways, in anticipation of the partner's reciprocating. For example, one partner may agree to prepare dinner on Tuesdays, and on that day the other contracts to stop at the supermarket on the way home from work and do the weekly shopping. The improved atmosphere that develops as a consequence of each partner's doing nice things for the other and having nice things done for him or her in return helps each become motivated to please the other person on future occasions.

Behavioral couples therapists generally adopt Thibaut and Kelley's (1959) exchange theory of interaction. According to this view of human relationships, people value others if they receive a high ratio of benefits to costs, that is, if they see themselves getting at least as much from the other person as they give. Furthermore, people are assumed to be more disposed to continue a given relationship if other alternatives are less attractive to them, promising fewer benefits and costing more. Therapists therefore try to encourage a mutual dispensing of rewards by partner A and partner B.

Behavioral marital or couples therapy has in common with other approaches, such as the MRI approach, a focus on enhancing communication skills between the partners. But the emphasis is more on increasing the ability of each partner to please the other; the core assumption is that "the relative rates of pleasant and unpleasant interactions determine the subjective quality of the relationship" (Wood & Jacobson, 1985). Indeed, behavioral couples therapists consider this more than an assumption, for they can point to data supporting the view that distressed couples differ from nondistressed couples in that they report lower frequencies of positive exchanges and higher frequencies of unsatisfying exchanges. Also, as Camper et al. (1988) found, spouses in distressed marriages view negative behavior on the part of their partners as global and stable, whereas they construe positive behavior as less so. These and related findings suggest that

distressed spouses are highly reactive to immediate or recent events in their relationship, while happy couples tend to maintain their satisfaction independently of recent events (Jacobson, Waldron, and Moore, 1980; Margolin, 1981). ... They are also more likely to reciprocate negative or punishing behaviors initiated by their partners (Billings, 1979; Gottman, 1979; Margolin and Wampold, 1981). In contrast, nondistressed marriages are relatively resilient, even in the face of unpleasant events, and less vulnerable to the impact of negative interchange. While happy couples also respond to variability in the quality of day-to-day interactions, their degree of affective reactivity is much lower than that of distressed couples. (Wood & Jacobson, 1985, p. 345)

Thus behavioral couples therapy concentrates on increasing positive exchanges in the hope not only of increasing short-term satisfaction, but also of laying a foundation for long-term trust and positive feelings, qualities that the aforementioned research shows to be characteristic of nondistressed relationships. Cognitive change is also seen as important,

for couples often need training in problem-solving and encouragement to acknowledge when positive changes are occurring (distressed couples often *perceive* inaccurately the ratio of positive to negative exchanges, tending to overlook the former and fixate on the latter).

Many operant behavior therapists follow Gerald Patterson's (1974a) practice of working with the parents to alter reinforcement of a child whose behavior is a problem. The child has few direct contacts with the therapist. An improvement in the child's behavior often reduces much distress between husband and wife. But sometimes a child's aberrant behavior can be traced to the marital distress; although the child may be the identified patient, his or her problems may better be regarded as reflecting marital conflict. In such instances family-marital therapists usually decide to intervene in the marital relationship, hoping that the child's difficulties will diminish if the parents learn to get along better. There is little decisive information on when it is best to intervene. Some research by K. D. O'Leary's Stony Brook group has suggested that altering the child's problematic behavior can improve the marital relationship (Oltmanns, Broderick, & O'Leary, 1976); other research by the same group has indicated that successful marital treatment has a favorable impact on children's problems (Turkewitz & O'Leary, 1977).

Behavioral couples therapists have become increasingly interested in cognitive components of relationships and relationship distress, a reflection of the cognitive trend in behavior therapy as a whole (Baucom, Epstein, & Rankin, 1995). The interest in cognition in couples therapy can also be traced to the influence of attribution theory in social psychology (the study of how people explain the reasons for their own and others' behavior) and the overlap between marital distress and depression (see p. 238). As a result of adding this cognitive component and broadening its treatment strategies many people now refer to behavioral marital therapy as cognitive-behavioral marital therapy (CBMT).

Baucom, Epstein, Sayers, and Sher (1989) propose five types of cognitions that influence a couples' relationship: selective attention (what people attend to in a relationship affecting how they feel about the relationship), attributions (who they decide is responsible or blameworthy for an event), expectancies (how they expect a relationship will progress in the future), assumptions (their beliefs regarding how the relationship is actually functioning currently), and standards (how they think a relationship should be functioning). Therapy involves increasing the partners' awareness of their

FOCUS 19.2 ACCEPTANCE IN BEHAVIORAL COUPLES THERAPY

An interesting development in behavioral couples therapy (BCT); a term that seems to be replacing behavioral marital therapy) is a growing appreciation of *acceptance* of the partner while trying to encourage and support change. Based on earlier work by Rogers (Chapter 17) and Ellis (Chapter 18) and on Marsha Linehan's (1993a, 1993b) dialectical behavior therapy (p. 352), Neil Jacobson (1992), in collaboration with Andrew Christensen (Jacobson & Christensen, 1996), argues that behavior therapists have overlooked the importance of the ability of people in a committed relationship to accept their partner while at the same time hoping for and encouraging change.

The notion of acceptance has a time-honored history in clinical psychology and psychiatry, dating back at least to Sigmund Freud. As Jacobson indicates, the use of interpretation in psychoanalytic couples therapy (e.g., Scharff, 1995) can lead to greater acceptance of displeasing behavior by attributing it to childhood wounds, thereby fostering sympathy for the partner who is behaving in negative ways.* But the concept assumes greater meaning in the work of Carl Rogers, whose client-centered therapy rests on the belief that "conditions of worth" should not be set for others, rather, that we should try to accept them—and ourselves—as worthy people deserving of respect regardless of our behavior at any point in time. Ellis's rational-emotive behavioral approach also emphasizes acceptance by encouraging people to renounce many of the demands (shoulds) that they impose on themselves and on others.

In following up the results from an earlier outcome study (Jacobson, 1984), Jacobson noticed that after two years, of the

two-thirds of couples who had benefited from behavioral couples therapy, one-third had relapsed (Jacobson, Schmaling, & Holtzworth-Munroe, 1987). Thus, although the therapy was very effective for almost half the couples, it was *not* effective for the other half over an extended (two-year) period of time. This led to the question of what might be wrong or missing from behavioral couples therapy.

Predictors of poor outcome from this approach include being married for a long time, emotional disengagement, high severity of distress in the relationship, and rigidly held gender roles. It seemed to Jacobson and Christensen that a factor or theme common to these negative predictors might be low amenability to compromise with and to accommodate to the other person. And since behavioral couples therapy requires compromise—by, for example, trying to meet the partner's wishes in exchange for certain reinforcers—it may not be surprising that the approach works less well for people who cannot readily accommodate to the desires of their partners.

This should not be news to anyone who has tried to mediate in a marital problem or who has been in a distressed marriage. When a couple has been together for many years, there can be an accumulation of anger, hurt, resentment, and betrayal that makes it a challenge even to decide what restaurant to go to on a Friday evening. Good will is gone. Motives are constantly questioned. If a negative interpretation can be placed on a seemingly positive behavior, it will be. And if a behavior therapist asks the partners to do something nice for each other, the kind of couple Jacobson and Christensen are talking about will

cognitions and teaching them to monitor their thoughts associated with positive and negative interactions with their partner. For example, angry exchanges may follow one of the partner's blaming the other for a disappointing occurrence, even one that the partner could actually not have prevented, such as rain on the day of a planned barbecue party.

INTEGRATIVE BEHAVIORAL COUPLES THERAPY

Integrative behavioral couples therapy (IBCT) was developed by Andrew Christensen and Neil S. Jacobson and "represents both a continuation and a marked departure from previous attempts to apply behavioral theory to intervention with married couples" (Christensen, Jacobson, & Babcock, 1995, p. 31). IBCT uses reinforcement principles as well as behavioral exchange and communication training

strategies as described earlier by Jacobson and Margolin (1979), but it incorporates the Rogerian notion of acceptance and provides a series of procedures designed to foster acceptance in couples (Cordova & Jacobson, 1993) (Focus 19.2 contains more details on acceptance).

The assumption of IBCT is that traditional behavior therapy for couples focuses on superficial variables rather than trying to uncover the major controlling variables (see the discussion on p. 545 of underlying causes). For example, traditional behavior therapists might focus on discrete observable behavior, such as lack of sex or frequent arguments, rather than on a partner's feeling that he or she is not loved or valued by the other partner. This latter consideration would be the focus in IBCT. This shift in therapeutic attention is not new to psychoanalytically oriented couples therapists, and it is charac-

either not budge or, if they do make a specific change, will readily attribute it to the therapist's instruction, for example, "He doesn't *really* appreciate me for my good work at the office today; he's complimenting me only because Dr. Smith told him to." It is no accident that couples therapy sessions can be extraordinarily taxing for the therapist and unusually boisterous and noisy.

Another factor working against direct attempts to change is reactance, the resistance people can feel when another person is trying to change them (Brehm, 1966; Davison, 1973). Reactance is likely to be especially high when the would-be influencer is held in contempt by the would-be influencee. Since behavior therapy is characterized by open attempts to change people, this type of influence is unlikely to succeed when exchanges are encouraged between two partners who feel little affection and respect for each other.

With all this as context, what is acceptance in Jacobson and Christensen's terms? It refers to "a letting go of the struggle to change and in some cases even embracing those aspects of a partner which have…been precipitants of conflict…[it] implies that some conflicts cannot be resolved, and it attempts to turn areas of conflict into sources of intimacy and closeness" (Jacobson, 1992, p. 497).† As Jacobson points out, acceptance does imply change—but the change is in the partner who is giving up efforts to change the other! And, if reactance diminishes with acceptance, as indeed it might (see our earlier discussion of Shoham-Solomon's paradoxical therapy research on p. 542), more change in the partner may come about by giving up on trying to effect change!

Jacobson's behavioral roots show, however, in his suggestions about how therapists can bring about change within the context of acceptance. He gives the example of a wife who found her husband's unavailability objectionable. (Note: The assumption is that the man's unavailability was not due to such things as seeing other women. Jacobson is certainly attuned to the ethical and political dimensions of psychotherapy [cf. Jacobson, 1983, 1989]). In addition to the traditional goal of helping them improve their intimacy with each other, he encouraged the woman to develop some independent interests so that she would not rely so much on her husband on those occasions when he could not be present.

Is acceptance tantamount to resignation, to accepting a status quo that keeps one or both partners in a destructive relationship, one that perhaps demeans one partner in order to satisfy the selfish demands of the other? Jacobson argues that acceptance is actually affirmative, holding out the promise of even greater intimacy. And as suggested here, some behavioral changes that were formerly—and unsuccessfully—worked toward in behavioral couples therapy by direct change attempts might only be facilitated by embedding such efforts within a context of acceptance. Ultimately, if acceptance should maintain or increase the distress for which the couple has sought help, there is no moral imperative for the partners to stay together.

---

*At the same time, such historical attributions can be used by the patient as an excuse not to change. Therapists such as Fritz Perls are inclined to see such explanations as cop-outs. Behavioral and cognitive therapists take a similar tack.

†Some might say that this is the closest that psychologists come to defining love.

teristic of the humanistically oriented approach described next.

EMOTIONALLY FOCUSED THERAPY

The approach to conjoint treatment known as emotionally focused therapy (EFT) Alexander, Holtzworth-Munroe, & Jameson, 1994; Johnson & Greenberg, 1987, 1988, 1995) contains psychodynamic elements, but its humanistic emphasis on feelings strikes us as more salient. This therapy integrates components from attachment theory, which has been used to conceptualize adult romantic relationships (see also Bartholomew & Horowitz, 1991), and focuses on the "innate adaptive needs for protection, security, and connectedness with significant others" (Johnson & Greenberg, 1995, p. 124). From this vantage point, relationship distress occurs when the attachment needs have not been met and the relationship does not provide a secure base for one or both partners. The couple may engage in negative interaction cycles, such as blaming each other for sometimes minor problems. The overall goal of treatment is for couples to stop negative interaction cycles during the treatment session, maintain emotional engagement, and be accessible and responsive to each other.

GENERAL FEATURES

In all forms of couples therapy each partner is trained to listen empathically to the other and to state clearly to the partner what he or she understands is being said and what feelings underlie those remarks. One way to improve communication is to distinguish between the intent of a remark and its impact, in a manner similar to Aronson's analysis of a two-person exchange (see p. 562). Partner A, for example, may wish to be helpful by asking whether partner B would like him or her to get something from the store, but this question may have a negative impact if partner B would prefer partner A to stay home and help with a project. Partner A's intent, then, would be positive, but the question would affect partner B negatively. Research has shown that the communications of distressed and happy couples may not differ so much in intent as in impact. In one study Gottman and his colleagues (1976) found that both types of couples made the same number of positive statements to partners, but distressed spouses reported having *heard* fewer positive statements than satisfied spouses. Gottman proposed a technique for clarifying intent when two partners are in a heated argument. One partner calls, "Stop action," and asks the other to indicate what he or she believes the first is trying to say. The feedback indicates immediately whether remarks are having the intended impact.

An interaction pattern known as the demand-withdraw cycle is widely regarded as particularly destructive for couples. First described by MRI people (Watzlawick, Beavin, & Jackson, 1967) and a contemporary research focus of others (Christensen & Pasch, 1993; Christensen & Shenk, 1991), the demand-withdraw pattern is characterized by one partner attempting to discuss a problem and the other's avoiding or withdrawing from such efforts. This withdrawal generates more demand from the first spouse, who tries harder and harder to engage the other, only to be met with more avoidance. And so the cycle escalates. Christensen and Heavey (1990) suggest that there are sex differences in this pattern; women tend to assume the demanding role while men usually withdraw. This pattern is found in couples that have a conflict surrounding closeness; the person demanding change may be trying to generate closeness and the person avoiding the interaction may be struggling to seek or maintain autonomy (Christensen, 1987). The roles may also vary depending on who is seeking change and who prefers the relationship to remain as it is (Christensen & Pasch, 1993). Knowing who typically plays which role in a couple may benefit the couples therapist when planning intervention strategies to break this destructive cycle.

Couples and family therapy have for years made creative use of videotape equipment. A couple can be given a problem to solve during part of a therapy session, such as where to go on vacation, and can be videotaped while they attempt to solve it. The ways in which they push forward their own wishes—or fail

to—and the ways in which they accommodate the other's wishes—or fail to—are but one aspect of their communication patterns that a therapist can come to understand from later viewing the tape, often with the couple watching also. Patterns of communication and miscommunication can be readily discerned using this tool. The partners can agree to try out new ways of negotiating and new ways of dealing with conflictual issues (Margolin & Fernandez, 1985).

A common practice among family therapists is to give couples specific homework assignments to practice new patterns of interaction that they have learned during sessions and begin the important process of generalizing change from the consulting room to their everyday lives. Couples may be asked to practice paraphrasing each other's sentences for a specified time period, such as a half hour after dinner, as part of an active listening assignment. In essence couples are taught Rogerian empathy skills. They may also be instructed to practice a new parenting skill with their children. Some therapists ask couples to tape-record their assignment so that the therapist can review their progress during the next therapy session.

GENERAL ISSUES AND SPECIAL CONSIDERATIONS

The marital dysfunction treated by therapists is not all the same, as Margolin and Fernandez (1985) have pointed out. One couple may seek professional assistance when there is merely dissatisfaction in the relationship, but another may wait until the crisis is so great that one or both partners have already consulted a divorce lawyer. Thus there are different *stages* of marital distress (Duck, 1984; Weiss & Cerreto, 1980), and different therapeutic approaches may be used, depending on the point at which the therapist judges the couple to be. For example, a couple married for five years and on the verge of divorce, with some threat of physical violence, needs a more directive and more intensive approach than a couple who after ten years of reasonable content find themselves drifting apart (see Focus 19.3).

An important issue is deciding who the patient is. The term *identified patient* is often used when more than one family member is being seen by a therapist, especially when parents consult a therapist because of problems that their child is having. Also, treatment proceeds best when family members agree on what problem is to be addressed. Should, for example, the husband be less demanding and the wife more malleable—an issue that has been the subject of feminist writings for several decades? Difficulties also arise when one partner

FOCUS 19.3 MARITAL VIOLENCE

Marital violence can have devastating effects on the entire family, including physical injury, homicide, and suicide as well as the development of psychological problems such as alcohol abuse and depression, in one or both partners (e.g., Sonkin & Walker, 1985). The dramatic effects of such violence have been widely documented in magazines and news programs in recent years. In addition to its obvious effect on those directly involved, marital violence has been linked to a wide variety of childhood behavior and emotional problems (Cummings & Davies, 1994; Davies & Cummings, 1994; Grych & Fincham, 1990; Jenkins & Smith, 1991).

Despite the approximately equal frequencies of violent acts by husbands and wives, the physical damage done to wives by husbands is far greater than the reverse (Jacobson et al., 1994). Physical aggression by husbands results in more physical injury, health problems, depression, and psychosomatic symptoms than does aggression by wives (Cantos, Neidig, & O'Leary, 1994; Cascardi, Langhinrichsen, & Vivian, 1992; Stets & Straus, 1990). In 1991 the American Psychological Association's (APA) Committee on Women in Psychology established the APA's first Task Force on Male Violence Against Women, with a mandate to review research on the prevalence, causes, and impact of various forms of violence on women, to describe clinical and community interventions, and to recommend policy changes to address the problem (Goodman et al., 1993).

Without intervention many couples who are involved in physically abusive relationships will, over time, experience an increase in the severity, frequency, and intensity of physical aggression (Giles-Sims, 1983; Pagelow, 1981). There is a consensus that waiting to treat physical abuse after it has started may not be the best approach to the problem (Holtzworth-Munroe et al., 1995); however, most intervention programs treat couples only after the abuse has begun. The National Institute of Mental Health has recently recognized the importance of prevention programs directed at violence in couples (Coie et al., 1993). Conjoint therapy for violent couples is a controversial topic for several reasons (Margolin & Burman, 1993): (1) there is worry that including an abused wife in therapy will somehow suggest that she is partially responsible for her abuse; and (2) there is fear that husbands may use violence against their wives in response to issues they have brought up during therapy sessions.

Learning models view violence as a response to conflict that is acquired during childhood by observing adults, particularly one's parents, use violence to solve their problems. At the same time observers of this violence may fail to learn prosocial ways of handling conflict, making them more likely to resort to violence as a means of conflict management. Because they lack the skills to solve conflict, control anger, or express it in appropriately constructive and assertive ways, arguments are more likely to escalate into physical attacks. In addition, several risk factors have been identified that may increase the likelihood that certain men will engage in physical aggression against their partners. These factors include stress, inability to handle anger, alcohol and drug abuse, violence in family of origin, jealousy, and negative attitudes toward women (Holtzworth-Munroe et al., 1995).

Researchers from a variety of theoretical perspectives agree that an inability to handle anger and a lack of communication and problem-solving skills often result in the use of physical violence in relationships, especially for men (Eckhardt, Barbour, & Stuart, in press). In an articulated thoughts study, men who were violent in their marriages were less likely than nonviolent controls to verbalize anger-controlling thoughts while imagining themselves in an anger-provoking situation (wife talking and laughing with a mutual male acquaintance and acting somewhat flirtatiously toward him), suggesting poorly developed cognitive skills for reducing anger when provoked (Eckhardt, Barbour, & Davison, 1997). Researchers have also been working on preventive programs that will not only teach partners anger management and communication and problem-solving skills, but will also teach them how to safely walk away from or deescalate a conflict before it involves physical aggression. These programs include Markman's premarital Relationship Enhancement Program (PREP; Markman & Floyd, 1980; Markman et al., 1993) and Neidig's Stop Anger and Violence Escalation Program (SAVE; Neidig, 1989a, 1989b). The efficacy of these programs remains to be tested empirically.

Holtzworth-Munroe et al. (1995) have offered a new approach to violence prevention that differs from standard conjoint therapy because it place its emphasis on stopping physical violence rather than on saving the relationship. Husbands are encouraged to take responsibility for their aggression. Unlike traditional conjoint therapy, which focuses on preserving the relationship, termination of the relationship is not viewed as a negative outcome.

Goodman et al. (1993) have argued that programs directed at high risk couples and analysis of intrapsychic factors are not sufficient to address the problem of male violence against women. These authors remind us that changes in the social and cultural institutions that have given rise to the problem are necessary for any lasting solution.

wants to end the relationship and the other is desperate to save it. Finally, couples therapy varies depending on whether children are involved.

Family therapy is further complicated when sexual or nonsexual physical abuse is present. The therapist must consider what effect saving the relationship may have on the abused spouse and possibly on the abused children, for when there is spousal abuse there is a high likelihood of child abuse also. Regardless of who is the identified patient, the therapist must be sensitive to the needs of all those whose lives are affected by the relationship (Kadis & McClendon, 1995).

Other ethical considerations in family therapy include how to deal with the disclosure of secrets by one spouse when the other spouse is out of the room. Some therapists handle this at the outset of treatment by telling the couple that anything that is told to the therapist will be expected to come out during session, and therefore the therapist will not keep secrets from one spouse. Other therapists feel that this policy may keep them from obtaining valuable information (Kadis & McClendon, 1995).

An interesting line of research has focused on individual problems in one of the partners and how such problems respond to conjoint therapy versus an intervention targeted to the individual problem. Noting that depression in at least one of the partners is often a part of a distressed couple's relationship and that relapse into depression is more likely if the formerly depressed partner is in a troubled marriage (Hooley & Teasdale, 1989), researchers at Stony Brook (Beach & O'Leary, 1986; O'Leary & Beach, 1990) and at the University of Washington (Jacobson, Holtzworth-Munroe, & Schmaling, 1989; Jacobson et al., 1991) have studied behavioral marital therapy (BMT) as a treatment for depression. The findings indicate that Beck's individualized cognitive therapy for the depressed partner is no more effective than BMT in alleviating depression and that cognitive therapy is not as effective as BMT in enhancing marital satisfaction. Someone who is depressed and is also in a troubled relationship can be helped as much by a systems-oriented approach to the relationship as by an individualized intervention—with the advantage of also deriving benefit for relationship problems. This research highlights both the interpersonal nature of depression—a theme examined in Chapter 10 (p. 238)—and the role of depression in a distressed intimate relationship. Moreover, the finding that individualized cognitive therapy does not improve a marriage in the same way that improvement in a marriage lifts depression points up both the limits of a nonsystems individualized therapy, such as cognitive therapy, as well as the strengths of a systems approach, such as BMT.

EVALUATION OF COUPLES AND FAMILY THERAPY

A meta-analysis of twenty carefully selected outcome studies meeting stringent methodological standards concluded that overall, family therapy has beneficial effects for many family problems (Hazelrigg, Cooper, & Borduin, 1987). Comprehensive reviews of the area by Gurman and Kniskern (1978), Gurman, Kniskern, and Pinsoff (1986), Jacobson and Addis (1993), and Lebow and Gurman (1995) have reached the following specific conclusions about outcome and process in couples and family therapy:[4]

- Conjoint therapy for couples problems appears to be more successful than individual therapy with one partner. The state of about 10 percent of patients seen individually for couples problems worsens.

- The beneficial effects of behavioral couples therapy (BCT) have been demonstrated in more than two dozen studies in at least four countries (Hahlweg & Markman, 1988). Positive findings have also been reported for an experiential therapy (Greenberg & Johnson, 1988; Johnson & Greenberg, 1985) and an insight-oriented therapy (Snyder & Wills, 1989), although only a few such studies have been published. One study found an extremely low divorce rate in couples treated with an insight-oriented couples therapy (Snyder & Wills, 1989; Snyder, Wills, & Grady-Fletcher, 1991).

Jacobson and Addis (1993) have pointed out that almost all these positive findings are based on comparisons with no-treatment control groups, in which deterioration often occurs, thus making it all the easier for *any* intervention to do better than no formal treatment at all. Also, although statistically significant, the outcomes are not all *clinically significant* (Jacobson et al., 1984). For example, across all studies no more than half the treated couples were really happily married at the end of treatment (even if they had improved in a strictly statistical sense). Furthermore, few studies included much in the way of follow-ups, and those that did—and these were behaviorally oriented—found frequent relapse (Alexander, Holtzworth-Munroe, & Jameson, 1994; Jacobson, Schmaling, & Holtzworth-Munroe, 1987) and divorce (Snyder et al., 1991). As Jacobson and Addis have cautioned, these findings should temper premature

---

[4]A general caveat has been voiced by Jacobson and Addis (1993). When researchers evaluate their own treatments, the outcomes are better than when the evaluation is conducted by others. Are researchers hopelessly biased? Maybe. But it is possible also that when a putatively effective treatment is implemented by its proponents or creators, it is applied more efficaciously than when executed by nonspecialists.

enthusiasm for the efficacy of conjoint therapies, regardless of their theoretical bases.

- Direct comparisons of different couples therapies have not shown clear superiority of one approach over another (Baucom & Hoffman, 1986). Jacobson and Addis's (1993) judgment is that the longer a given approach has been around, the less startlingly superior its results seem to be as compared with other approaches.

- Although focused on the fearfulness of one partner, Barlow's exposure treatment, which involves encouragement and collaboration by the spouse, has proved effective in reducing agoraphobia (see Chapter 6, p. 138) and has avoided the deterioration in the marital relationship that has sometimes been reported when the agoraphobic partner gets better (Brown & Barlow, 1995; Himadi et al., 1986).

- The results of couples therapy are generally better for younger couples and when no steps have been taken toward divorce.

- Predictors of poor outcome include what Jacobson and Addis (1993) call "emotional disengagement," manifested by poor communication of feelings and by low frequency of sexual activity. Another sign of a poor prognosis in couples therapy is a relationship marked by rigidly held traditional gender roles, when the wife is oriented to affiliation and relationships and the husband is oriented primarily to work and autonomy (Jacobson, Follette, & Pagel, 1986). Finally, depression in one of the partners does not bode well for couples therapy (even though, as noted, behavioral couples therapy can have a positive impact both on a person's depression and on the relationship).

- Efforts to prevent distress in couples suggest that brief training in communication skills can enhance future satisfaction with the relationship and even lower divorce rates when compared with no-intervention controls (Markman et al., 1988). Since couples therapy generally works better when people are younger and highly involved with each other, prevention efforts seem particularly sensible and promising.

- Overall, most nonbehavioral approaches, such as the analytic and humanistic approaches, have not been subjected to as much controlled research as have behavioral and systems approaches, a probable reflection of the lesser research emphasis in these paradigms. Johnson and Greenberg (1985) did find superiority of a Gestalt therapy–based couples intervention that focused on uncovering unacknowledged feelings and needs (the emotion-focused therapy

mentioned earlier) as compared with the problem-solving component of behavioral couples therapy. As they speculated, it may be important for a couples intervention to work directly on increasing trust and sensitivity to one's own unmet needs and hidden fears as well as the fears and needs of one's partner. Behavioral couples therapists are paying increased attention to the affective dimensions of conflict, yet another sign of the move toward rapprochement among contrasting therapeutic orientations (p. 551). Another integrative direction was described earlier in Focus 19.2.

- Some studies have been conducted on **divorce mediation**, consultations occurring before a divorce has been obtained. An alternative to the usual adversarial process, mediation is conducted by a third party (a lawyer, counselor, or trained layperson) who strives for neutrality and whose goal is to help the distressed couple reach agreement on child custody and financial arrangements before involving their own lawyers. Mediation can help estranged couples continue functioning as parents even as they move toward divorce. Data indicate that mediation is associated with "(1) a higher rate of pretrial agreements; (2) a higher level of satisfaction with the agreements; (3) major reductions in the amount of litigation after final court orders; (4) an increase in joint custody agreements; and (5) … decrease in public expenses such as custody studies and court costs (Sprenkle and Storm, 1983)" (Gurman, Kniskern, & Pinsoff, 1986, p. 589).

COMMUNITY PSYCHOLOGY

We have previously described many examples of community psychology, for example, the prevention of cigarette smoking among young adolescents through school-based programs (p. 330), the prevention of HIV infection and AIDS through programs aimed at changing sexual practices among sexually active adults and adolescents (see p. 396), and efforts through Head Start programs to prevent educational deficits and their associated social and economic disadvantages among the poor (p. 432). We turn now to an examination of some general principles of community psychology and to a review of a number of noteworthy efforts.

THE FOCUS: PREVENTION

Community psychology's focus on prevention is often considered its defining trademark, and some leading community psychologists have declared prevention science a new research discipline in its own right (Coie et al., 1993). A recent typology presented by The Institute of Medicine, a branch of the National Academy of Sciences, distinguishes prevention from treatment and maintenance (Mrazek & Haggerty, 1994).

TREATMENT

Termed *tertiary prevention* by Caplan (1964), whose writings on prevention are seminal in community psychology, treatment refers to the various interventions presented thus far in this chapter and in Chapters 17 and 18. Treatment is therapy for mental disorders. It is preventive only in the sense that it aims to forestall the development of future mental illness problems. Treatment aims to reduce the duration or severity of a disorder or to increase the length of time between episodes, and it is not the focus of community psychology.

MAINTENANCE

Maintenance interventions are provided on a long-term basis for individuals who have met DSM-IV diagnostic levels and whose illness persists. Maintenance is continuing treatment for chronic or ongoing disorders in an effort to prevent relapse. These interventions seek to reduce disability associated with the more chronic and severe mental disorders. For example, efforts may be directed at increasing a patient's compliance with medication regimens. Aftercare, such as the halfway houses described later, is another example of maintenance.

PREVENTION

Rather than focusing on existing cases of disorder, **prevention** seeks to reduce the incidence or new cases of social and emotional problems in the population. Formerly called *primary* prevention, these efforts take place before the onset of a disorder. Whereas treatment is typically provided to individuals (or small groups) who have sought or been referred for help with an existing mental health problem, prevention occurs in much larger social settings that are usually nonclinical in nature, such as schools. Because prevention in community psychology often involves large groups and social systems, it usually requires a multidisciplinary approach and thus serves as a useful interface between abnormal psychology and the fields of criminology, developmental psychology, epidemiology, and education.

Under the general rubric of prevention finer distinctions can be made. A preventive intervention may be universal, selective, or indicated in its focus (Mrazek & Haggerty, 1994). A *universal* preventive intervention targets an entire population that has not been identified on the basis of particular individuals at risk. This approach makes no presumption of who is at a relatively higher risk for developing a problem, with messages often directed toward the general public. For example, the series of television commercials concerning the consequences of drug use ("This is your brain on drugs") would constitute an attempt at universal prevention. A *selective* preventive intervention targets a subgroup of the population whose risk of developing mental or behavioral problems is significantly higher than average. For example, a particular school may have a high drop-out rate, which is associated with juvenile delinquency; preventive efforts, such as remedial instruction to improve academic skills, might be directed toward the students in that school. *Indicated* preventive interventions are aimed at individuals who have exhibited some sign, symptom, or predisposition for a mental disorder but who do not yet meet diagnostic criteria for the disorder. An individual with a considerable family history of mental illness might be a suitable target for an indicated preventive intervention, for example, a youngster deemed to be at high risk for schizophrenia because both his parents are schizophrenic.

Altering stressful and depriving conditions in the environment and strengthening individuals so that they can resist stress and cope with adversity are two means of prevention. Examples include attention to such conditions as overcrowding, poor housing, job discrimination, poor neighborhood recreational facilities, and inadequate school curricula. Genetic counseling, prenatal care for inner-city mothers, school lunches, and Meals on Wheels are also prevention measures.

Although community psychologists concentrate their efforts on prevention, not all prevention efforts constitute community psychology, nor is prevention the exclusive province of community psychology. A clinical psychologist working individually in a private office with a healthy, fee-paying patient can be working at prevention of cardiovascular disease by encouraging the person to alter eating habits and lifestyle. This behavioral-medicine approach is not considered an instance of community psychology. Biologically oriented psychopathology research, such as Mednick's high-risk study of possible somatic diatheses for schizophrenia (p. 285), although it has prevention as a long-term goal, is seldom considered community psychology. (Perhaps it should be.) Thus, although prevention is an important feature of many community psychology efforts, other characteristics define the approach as well, in particular, the seeking orientation and a focus on organizations and institutions, discussed next.

THE ATTITUDE: SEEKING RATHER THAN WAITING

Nearly all the therapies reviewed thus far are administered by professional persons with advanced degrees who make themselves available by appointment in offices, clinics, and hospitals. They provide assistance to individuals who initiate the contact themselves or are referred by the courts. Such delivery of services operates in a *waiting mode* (Rappaport & Chinsky, 1974). Community psychology, in contrast, typically (though not always) operates in the *seeking mode*, that is, those who are believed likely one day to be in psychological trouble are sought out by community workers, some of whom are paraprofessionals (discussed later) supervised by psychologists, psychiatrists, or social workers.

Rappaport and Chinsky (1974) proposed that every type of mental health care has two components, the delivery and the conceptual. The delivery component relates to the difference between seeking and waiting, that is, the *attitude* about making services available. As noted, community psychology usually has a seeking orientation. The conceptual component consists of the *theoretical* and *data-based underpinnings* of the services. Two possible theoretical approaches are the psychoanalytic and learning approaches. For example, a mass media campaign to persuade people to practice safer sex would be in the community psychology seeking mode. But how *specifically* the messages are phrased depends on the conceptual mode. One effort might take a psychoanalytic approach, emphasizing the desirability of subliminating sexual urges into nonsexual pursuits; another might follow a cognitive-behavioral tack, assuming that people need to learn assertive skills in order better to decline unsafe sexual overtures. These two campaigns would distribute different kinds of messages—but both would be delivering community psychology. The question whether a particular conceptual orientation is more suited to one delivery mode than to the other is a separate and crucial issue and causes ongoing controversy among community psychologists and psychiatrists.

VALUES AND THE QUESTION OF WHEN TO INTERVENE

Rappaport (1977), a leading writer in the field, proposed another way to understand community psychology. He suggested viewing society as composed of four levels: the individual, the small group, the organization, and the institution. Therapists intervene at a given level, depending on their values and goals for people. For example, human problems may be seen as *individual in nature*, and treatment therefore focuses on changing the individual. This treatment is pursued in a number of ways—from behavior therapy to psychoanalysis to chemotherapy—but in all these modes of intervention, society is considered good and people in need of adjustment to it.

Alternatively, human problems may be assumed to derive from *interpersonal difficulties*, such as conflicts within families, at work, and in other *small groups*. The therapist applies family and encounter therapy to help members of the group communicate better. The therapist does not just try to change the individual, because the problem is assumed to lie in group processes.

Psychologists who consider that *organizations* lie at the root of human disorders blame the way in which such units as schools and prisons operate. To help a child who is failing in school, for example, community psychologists examine the school curriculum and how it is implemented by principals and teachers; they do not provide remedial tutoring for the pupil. Community psychology operates at this level as well as at the *institutional* level, which is closely related but is more abstract and all-inclusive. Institutions refer not to physical entities, such as school buildings and prisons, but to the basic values and ideologies that characterize a society, its religion, and its politics. For example, the community psychologist may assert that people are unhappy because of a lopsided distribution of wealth and power. Professional efforts would then be directed at political parties, the courts, legislatures, and the like, not to encourage them to function more efficiently, but to shift their goals and basic assumptions so that they might work toward a more equitable social distribution of wealth and power.

Rappaport's analysis makes it clear why some community psychologists tend to be impatient with individual and group therapy. They do not believe that problems lie with the individual or a small group, and they assert that by concentrating on these levels the therapist "blames the victim" (Ryan, 1971) and overlooks the real problems of organizations and institutions. Community psychologists work in the seeking mode on large-scale social problems and make no pretense, as some individual and group therapists do, of being politically and ethically neutral.

COMMUNITY PSYCHOLOGY IN ACTION

With the foregoing as conceptual context, let us turn to a few noteworthy examples of community psychology as implemented. We focus on projects whose effectiveness has been evaluated empirically and on a broad range of topics that will give a flavor for the scope of this field.

SUICIDE PREVENTION CENTERS AND TELEPHONE CRISIS SERVICES

Many suicide prevention centers are modeled after the Los Angeles Suicide Prevention Center, founded in 1958 by Farberow and Shneidman. There are at present more than 200 such centers in the United States, and there are many abroad as well (Lester, 1995). Staffed largely by nonprofessionals under the supervision of psychologists or psychiatrists, these centers attempt to provide twenty-four-hour consultation to people in suicidal crises. Usually the initial contact is made by telephone. The center's phone number is well publicized in the community. The worker tries to assess the likelihood that the caller will make a serious suicide attempt and, most important, tries to establish personal contact and dissuade the caller from suicide. (Recall the earlier discussion of the prevention of suicide, p. 257.)

Such community facilities are potentially valuable because people who attempt suicide give warnings—cries for help—before taking their lives (see p. 255). Ambivalence about living or dying is the hallmark of the suicidal state (Shneidman, 1976). Usually, pleas are directed first to relatives and friends, but many potential suicide victims are isolated from these sources of emotional support; a hot-line service may save the lives of such individuals.

Victims of suicide include survivors, especially if they are among the unfortunate 25 percent who

were speaking to or in the presence of the person when the act was committed (Andress & Corey, 1978). Sometimes these survivors are therapists or hospital emergency room personnel. All are subject to strong feelings of guilt and self-recrimination, second-guessing what they might have done to prevent the suicide. Even dispassionate analysis does not invariably allay the guilt and anger. Grieving tends to last much longer than when deaths are not self-inflicted. For these many reasons, peer support groups exist to help survivors cope with the aftermath of a suicide. They provide social support, opportunities to ventilate feelings, constructive information, and referrals to professionals if that seems advisable (Fremouw et al., 1990).

It is exceedingly difficult to do controlled research on suicide, and outcome studies have yielded inconsistent results. A meta-analysis of five studies on the effectiveness of suicide prevention centers failed to demonstrate that rates decline after the implementation of services (Dew et al., 1987). A similarly negative finding was recently reported from Canada (Leenaars & Lester, 1995). However, another study found that suicide rates declined in the years following the establishment of suicide prevention centers in several cities (Lester, 1991). Once again, we are left with conflicting and inconclusive evidence. Human lives are precious, however, and since many people who contact prevention centers weather a suicidal crisis successfully, these efforts will continue.

THE USE OF MEDIA AND MASS EDUCATION TO CHANGE HARMFUL LIFESTYLES

Cardiovascular diseases, such as high blood pressure and coronary heart disease, are responsible for more deaths in the United States than is any other single group of illnesses. In many respects the lifestyle of an affluent, industrialized society increases the risk of premature cardiovascular diseases—little need for physical exertion and plenty of high-calorie foods rich in fat. One way to try to change harmful lifestyles is to use the mass media to inform people of what they can do to reduce their risks for such illnesses.

A group of researchers in the Stanford Heart Disease Prevention Program, led by Nathan Maccoby (Maccoby & Altman, 1988), a psychologist noted for his work in communications, undertook such a task. For the Three Communities Project they chose a media campaign and a direct, intensive, instructional program (Maccoby & Alexander, 1980; Maccoby et al., 1977; Meyer et al., 1982).

Three towns in northern California were the subjects of their investigation. Watsonville and Gilroy were the two experimental towns, and Tracy was

Suicide hot-line services, staffed by paraprofessinals, are an example of community psychology.

the control town. For two years both experimental towns were bombarded by a mass media campaign to inform citizens about cardiovascular diseases (an example of a universal preventive intervention). The campaign consisted of television and radio spots, weekly newspaper columns, and newspaper advertisements and stories urging people to stop smoking, exercise more, and eat foods low in cholesterol. Posters in buses and in stores conveyed briefly and graphically such vital information as the desirability of eating fewer eggs, since yolks are rich in cholesterol. In addition, a selective preventive intervention had a sample of Watsonville residents at high risk for heart disease receive intensive instruction in group sessions and individual home counseling over a ten-week period. The researchers wanted to examine whether information (e.g., how to select and prepare foods low in fat and cholesterol) and exhortations to alter lifestyle delivered face-to-face might add to whatever positive benefits derived from the mass media campaign.

The control town, Tracy, had media services that were quite different from those of the two experimental towns. Tracy is separated from Watsonville and Gilroy by a range of low mountains and therefore, at the time, had entirely separate local television stations. The inhabitants of Tracy were of course not imprisoned in their hometown for the duration of the two-year study, but for the most part they did not receive through their media the messages conveyed to the citizens of the two experimental towns. Because all three towns had a sizable Spanish-speaking population, all media messages were in Spanish as well as in English.

The findings revealed that citizens of Watsonville and Gilroy significantly increased their knowledge of cardiovascular risk factors; people in the control town did not gain in such knowledge. Egg consumption was reduced more in Watsonville and Gilroy than in Tracy, and clinically significant decreases in blood pressure were observed in the two experimental towns, in contrast with small increases in the control town. The high-risk people of Watsonville who participated in the special, intensive instruction program reaped even greater benefits in lower egg consumption and blood pressure. Finally, the researchers considered the townspeople's overall measure of risk, a weighted average of the several known physical risk factors—high blood levels of cholesterol, smoking cigarettes, and not exercising enough. They found highly significant drops in risk in the people in the experimental towns, an important result, since we know from previous research, the Framingham, Massachusetts, longitudinal study of risk factors in cardiovascular diseases (Truett, Cornfield, & Kannel, 1967), that elevated risk scores predict reasonably well the incidence of heart disease over a twelve-year period.

These positive findings led to a more ambitious and larger-scale program called the Stanford Five City Project, which extended face-to-face instructional programs to a variety of community settings such as schools, community colleges, hospitals, and work sites and involved many more people across a broader age range. An important goal was to embed the education programs in existing community organizations so that any beneficial effects might persist well after the researchers had left the scene (Altman, Flora, & Farquhar, 1986). Dependent measures included actual illness and death from cardiovascular diseases. Begun in 1978 and continuing well into the 1990s, results support the efficacy of the interventions in significantly reducing several risk factors, such as cigarette usage, elevated cholesterol levels, low levels of physical activity, and high blood pressure (Farquhar, 1991; Farquhar et al., 1990; Jackson et al., 1991; Maccoby & Altman, 1988; Schooler, Flora, & Farquhar, 1993).

The work of the Stanford group and similar projects in Finland (Tuomilehto et al., 1986) and in South Africa (Farquhar et al., 1990) are important as community psychology efforts for they demonstrate that laypeople can learn from properly designed and delivered mass media and other large-scale educational programs how to reduce their overall risk for cardiovascular diseases. The multiyear span of these studies is considerable and highly unusual as far as experiments in psychology are concerned. But in terms of the serious health problems that can develop through certain long-standing detrimental behavior patterns, five or ten or more years is not a very long time at all.

There is great potential for such community-based programs to reduce the incidence and seriousness of many medical illnesses beyond what is achievable by strictly medical practices, for it is

Media campaigns have been used successfully by community psychologists to change behaviors that have negative consequences on health.

increasingly accepted that people's physical health is primarily in their own hands and that changing lifestyle practices is often the best means of reducing the risk of illness (Bandura, 1986).

BEHAVIORAL MEDICINE AT THE WORK SITE

Some of the behavioral medicine approaches reviewed earlier (e.g., pp. 538–541) are being followed in programs conducted by companies for their employees at the work site. Particular attention is paid to reducing the risk of cardiovascular diseases by helping employees lose weight, exercise more and regularly, eat more nutritionally, and stop smoking. Stress management, originally a buzzword in industry, is also a frequent focus, with workers being trained in muscle relaxation, time management, and other procedures for handling the challenges of their work.

Results thus far are mixed. For example, though weight-reduction and smoking-cessation programs can be successful in the short term (e.g., Jeffrey, Forster, & Schmid, 1989), relapse and drop-out rates as high as 75 percent are the rule rather than the exception. But if companies would offer encouragement to their workers, for instance, by lowering their health insurance premiums as a reward for weight loss and lower cholesterol, the effectiveness of these preventive work-site efforts might be enhanced. All things considered, the same criticism can be applied to such programs as is properly directed at individual psychotherapy: as long as the person is exposed to factors outside the treatment environment that do not support the objectives of the program and that often even work against them, the success of such efforts is bound to be limited.

SCHOOL-BASED PREVENTIVE INTERVENTIONS

Preventive interventions in community psychology are often implemented within school settings for both practical and theoretical reasons. Children and adolescents spend thirty or more hours a week in school, which allows for implementation of programs under fairly controlled conditions. We previously reviewed such programs aimed at discouraging junior high school students from taking up smoking (p. 330).

A program aimed at much younger children was designed to teach ways to resolve everyday problems and social conflicts (Shure & Spivack, 1988), common when youngsters undergo the transition from home to a school setting, where they must interact with others unrelated and often unknown to them at first. Shure and Spivack taught problem-

Corporate health programs are designed to lower work stress, improve health, and increase productivity.

solving skills to help the children manage these new interactions. (Their earlier work laid the foundation for the social problem-solving therapies for adults reviewed in Chapter 18, p. 533.) The children were encouraged to think of alternatives when faced with a problem and to stop and take stock of problematic situations before acting impulsively. Also, they were reminded of how aggressive and belligerent behavior can lead to unwanted consequences, such as counter-aggression, rather than to a solution to perceived conflict, such as getting to play for a while with a desired toy. At a two-year follow-up, children taught these skills by their own teachers exhibited significantly less disruptive behavior and were more at ease in school than were no-intervention controls.

HALFWAY HOUSES AND AFTERCARE

Some people function too well to remain in a mental hospital and yet do not function independently enough to live on their own or even within their own families. For such individuals there are halfway houses, a classic example being Fairweather's "community lodge" (Fairweather et al., 1969). These are protected living units, typically located in large, formerly private residences. Here patients discharged from a mental hospital live, take their meals, and gradually return to ordinary community life by holding a part-time job or going to school. Living arrangements may be relatively unstructured; some houses set up money-making enterprises that help to train and support the residents. Depending on how well funded the halfway house is, the staff may include psychiatrists or clinical psychologists. The most important staff members are paraprofessionals, often graduate students in clinical psychology or social work who live in the house and act both as administrators and as friends to the residents. Group meetings, at which residents talk out their frustrations and learn to relate to others in honest and constructive ways, are often part of the routine.

The nation's requirements for effective halfway houses for ex-mental patients cannot be underestimated, especially in light of deinstitutionalization efforts that have seen tens of thousands of patients discharged from mental hospitals when thirty years ago they would have remained in the protected hospital setting. Although civil rights issues are very important in shielding mental patients from ill-advised and even harmful detention—a topic dealt with in depth in Chapter 20—discharge has all too often led to shabbily dressed former patients left to fend for themselves in the streets (see p. 617) or being rehospitalized in what has been called the revolving-door syndrome. Discharge is a desirable goal, but ex-patients usually need follow-up community-based services, and these are scarce.

A model of what aftercare can be is provided by the Paul and Lentz (1977) comparative treatment study discussed in Chapter 18 (p. 522). When patients were discharged from any of the three wards of the program, social learning, milieu therapy, or routine hospital management, they usually went to live in nearby boarding homes. These homes, often converted motels, were staffed by workers who had been trained by the Paul–Lentz project to treat the ex-patients according to social-learning principles. The workers, some of whom had B.A. degrees, attended to the specific problems of the ex-patients, using rewards, including tokens, to encourage more independence and normal functioning. They positively reinforced appropriate behavior of the residents and did not attend much to bizarre behavior.

Because assessment was careful and ongoing, the staff knew at all times how a particular patient was doing. The mental health center project—and this is of paramount importance—acted as consultant to these community boarding homes in order to help their staff work with the ex-patients in as effective a manner as possible. Some boarding homes for ex-mental patients are supported financially by the state as part of the mental health system, but only rarely have the procedures followed in these homes been carefully planned and monitored by professional mental health staff.

In spite of many practical problems, such as staff layoffs, the results were as positive as those of the social-learning ward program. The ex-patients derived significant benefit from the aftercare; more

than 90 percent of the patients discharged from the social-learning ward were able to remain continuously in the community residences during the year-and-a-half follow-up period, and some for as long as four years more. The revolving-door syndrome in this instance was halted. Finally, in a finding rather critical in these days of diminishing public funds, the social-learning program—the mental health center treatment combined with the after-care—was much less expensive than the institutional care such patients usually receive.

Encouraging findings on milieu-therapy community programs in nonhospital residential settings have also been reported. Mosher and his colleagues (Mosher & Burti, 1989; Mosher et al., 1986) found results equivalent to those of a well-staffed inpatient unit. The patients were young adults experiencing their first psychotic episodes (and therefore very different from the chronic patients in the Paul–Lentz project). The hospital treatment relied heavily on psychotropic drugs, whereas the alternative setting employed Jones's therapeutic community principles, reviewed earlier (p. 523). The positive outcomes for the community-based program indicate that hospitalization may not even be necessary for some acutely disturbed patients.

COMPETENCE ENHANCEMENT AND FAMILY PROBLEMS

Competence enhancement refers to increasing an individual's adaptive coping resources and capabilities to manage a wide range of environmental stressors. These kinds of competencies are especially important for success in meeting life transitions (see Felner, Farber, & Primavera, 1983). For example, beginning middle school or high school, becoming a parent, or starting a new job are all transitions that introduce major changes into one's social environment. These changes often require a different set of competencies or skills that may not have been previously mastered. Examples of competencies include problem-solving and decision-making skills, assertiveness, and stress management (Botvin & Tortu, 1988; Caplan et al., 1992; Shure & Spivack, 1988; Weissberg, Caplan, & Harwood, 1991).

The negative effects that *nonsexual* child abuse has on perpetrators, the victim, and other family members render this problem one of considerable social and psychological importance. A number of preventive approaches have been studied (Rosenberg & Reppucci, 1985). One approach emphasizes competence enhancement in the form of instruction in parenting skills so that the various challenges of child rearing are more familiar and less daunting. If parents know what to expect in child development—that contrariness and selfishness are normal in two- and three-year-olds, for example—they may react less negatively when their children act in this fashion. Also, learning how to cope with their children's behavior and to control them in non-aversive ways may help parents be less emotionally coercive and physically punitive. Some programs utilize live or videotaped skits that model assertive problem-solving (Gray, 1983, reported in Rosenberg & Reppucci, 1985). Results from several large-scale programs suggest positive attitudinal changes, but an actual impact on lessening child abuse has yet to be demonstrated (Wolfe, Reppucci, & Hart, 1995).

Similarly indeterminate are the effects of community-wide media campaigns and hot lines available to parents under stress. Indications are that crisis services such as hot lines are utilized less often to prevent child abuse than to report abuse or to seek referrals for handling abuse that has already occurred. Better validation exists for efforts directed at high-risk groups, families that are more likely than others to have child abuse and neglect problems, for example, teenage-mother and single-parent families. One such study (Olds, 1984, reported in Rosenberg & Reppucci, 1985) added regular visits by a nurse to other postnatal services during the baby's first two years of life. Special intervention included parent education and enhancement of social-support networks. Results indicated that nurse-visited mothers had fewer conflicts with their babies and punished them less, and most important, the frequency of child abuse and neglect was less than with controls.

Some efforts to reduce child *sexual* abuse focus on children themselves, such as instructing them in their rights to control access to their bodies and in assertive behaviors when adults talk to or touch them in discomfiting ways (recall our discussion on p. 371). Data are lacking on the effectiveness of such efforts, however, and there are indications of occasional negative effects of such open discussions, for example, nightmares. The overall impact on prevalence is quite unclear (Reppucci, 1989; Reppucci, Jones, & Cook, 1994).

Community researchers have also focused on children of divorced couples. In their Children of Divorce Intervention Program, Pedro-Carroll and Cowen (1985) and Pedro-Carroll et al. (1986) had school-based groups of fourth-, fifth-, and sixth-graders discuss common concerns in a supportive group atmosphere and learn useful skills such as anger control. In a subsequent program some of the youngsters served on an expert panel, fielding questions from peers about coping with their parents' divorce. Children who participated in these groups generally demonstrated fewer adjustment problems in the classroom and lower anxiety levels as compared with control groups. Similar programs (e.g., Stolberg & Garrison, 1985) have reported encouraging findings as well. What remains unexamined in these and in most other prevention studies is the degree to which they truly reduce the incidence of psychopathology.

Instruction in parenting and child development illustrates a community psychology approach to preventing child abuse.

OUTREACH FOR CHILDREN'S STRESS FROM THE PERSIAN GULF WAR

The Persian Gulf campaign against Iraq's invasion of Kuwait, beginning in late July 1990 with the mobilization of allied forces (Desert Shield) and culminating in a short but intense war, principally from the air, in February 1991 (Desert Storm), appeared to be deceptively easy on service personnel. There were, after all, very few casualties on the allied side, very strong support from citizens around the world, and an engagement that overwhelmed Iraq with strategic, technological, and personnel superiority. Yet mental health professionals recognized that those who were dispatched to the Middle East for this war would not be shielded from the stressors of wartime. Nor indeed would their families, especially their children, for whom the war was brought home in telecasts unique in their immediacy and vividness. Unlike the troops in

Vietnam, the service personnel deployed in the Persian Gulf included many reservists, people well into their thirties and beyond and much more settled in civilian living; few of them—with good reason—ever expected to be called to active duty.

In response to the ominous situation in the Gulf, the American Psychological Association and the Kent State University Applied Psychology Center Task Force on War-Related Stress convened a group of trauma and intervention experts to discuss the nature of combat-related stress and to publish a general article for dissemination to psychologists (Hobfoll et al., 1991). The intent was to provide state-of-the-art information on the nature, prevention, and treatment of stress and posttraumatic stress disorder. Covering much of the material we reviewed in Chapter 6, this task force had some especially useful things to say about the predicament of children, whose stress reactions to the dangers of war—especially when a parent is called up for duty thousands of miles away—can sometimes be overlooked or underestimated by adults. Their recommendations, which have general relevance for helping children deal with other disaster situations, included the following:

- Parents and teachers need to learn to listen empathically and nonjudgmentally to children's concerns.

- Adults need to provide reassurance without minimizing the children's worries. It is usually not a good idea to try to comfort a child by promising that nothing bad could possibly happen. A better tack is to point out the measures taken to maximize the safety of service personnel and of the world in general—something that could not have been easy during the earliest stages of the Persian Gulf campaign.

- Adults must try their utmost not to burden children with their own concerns about the war. Sometimes children are stressed by seeing adult figures, especially parents, under strain. For this reason alone, adults would do well to seek professional assistance for their own emotional difficulties, so that they can better meet the needs of children in their charge.[5]

- Adults should try to instill in children a sense of self-efficacy (Bandura, 1982, 1997), a belief

that although the road ahead is rough, they will be able to cope.

- Like adults, children can benefit from being involved in helping behaviors, for example, writing letters to service personnel, sending little gifts, and so on.

The task force recommended that health professionals be proactive in disseminating information about war-related stress, through psychoeducational messages in the media and through schools, community groups, military organizations, and support groups. Via such community psychological outreach, the largest numbers of people can benefit from theory and research on the nature of posttraumatic stress and its prevention and amelioration. These outreach efforts have been used for more contemporary events also, including the Oklahoma City bombing in 1995 and the war in Bosnia throughout the 1990s.

EVALUATION OF COMMUNITY PSYCHOLOGY WORK

It has been suggested that the results of community psychology have not lived up to the rhetoric (Bernstein & Nietzel, 1980; Phares & Trull, 1997), but in recent years some projects have shown their worth.

One infrequently discussed reason for the limited effectiveness of prevention efforts may be that some of the problems community psychologists are trying to prevent are not readily amenable to environmental or social manipulation because they have major genetic or biological components that are left untouched by the kinds of community-based interventions described in this chapter. As we saw in Chapter 11, for example, there is very strong evidence that schizophrenia has some kind of biological diathesis. Although an environmental preventive effort may conceivably reduce the amount of stress that a predisposed individual is subject to in normal daily living, it seems unlikely that any realistic social change will be able to keep stress levels low enough to prevent schizophrenic episodes from occurring or recurring in high-risk people. Family therapy for reducing expressed emotion (p. 289) is a prototype of what might be necessary on a societal scale to have a positive impact on the recurrence of schizophrenic episodes. How practical is it, however, to apply such an approach on a broad scale?

Evaluation of community psychology efforts is particularly challenging because the interventions occur in the field, where it is difficult to set up experimental controls and thus harder to draw causal inferences (Linney, 1989). There are many alternative

---

[5]This raises a general issue for health providers, namely, does one always tell a patient the truth? In this case, does the parent who remains at home serve the child's best interests by minimizing or even concealing extreme worry about the loved one in the war theater? At what point do such efforts to shield children become an unjustifiable and impractical deception?

explanations for the effect of a preventive intervention. For example, if a reduction in gang activity follows a school-based intervention aimed at that goal, it may be that a community center, such as the YMCA, or even a single, inspirational teacher had something to do with the observed change. Another concern in the current practice of prevention science is the problem of attrition, or loss of participants (Mrazek & Haggerty, 1994). Those who drop out of an intervention must be monitored in some fashion, for these individuals could be at the highest risk and may constitute the group with which preventive efforts are most appropriate.

Some exemplary preventive interventions that have survived the test of empirical scrutiny have been reviewed, and others can be found as well, in *14 Ounces of Prevention*, a volume created by the American Psychological Association's Task Force on Prevention (Price et al., 1988). All the programs described in the APA report used randomized experimental designs and creative strategies to deal with the methodological challenges that are inherent to field research.

Many of the cases outlined in *14 Ounces* concern competence-enhancement programs, consonant with the recent emphasis in prevention science on increasing more generalized positive outcomes (rather than decreasing the occurrence of a specific negative outcome). But it is difficult to demonstrate that general competency skills of some kind have been enhanced because researchers may disagree about what constitutes the competency in question, for example, parenting skills. In contrast, some of the prevention programs of old focused on reducing a readily identifiable behavior, and thus there may have been less disagreement concerning measurement of the behavior in question. For example, measuring changes in school drop-out rates (negative outcome) may be easier than measuring an increase in goal-setting skills (a general competency skill). Despite these new challenges, many leading researchers believe that competence enhancement is a crucial focus for community psychology. The next phase for research programs in prevention science might be to assume a more longitudinal focus, where the acquisition of general competencies can be linked to a decrease in the longer-term development of specific behavior problems (Mrazek & Haggerty, 1994).

POLITICAL AND ETHICAL FACTORS IN COMMUNITY PSYCHOLOGY

The study of both community psychology, and to a lesser extent community mental health (see below), raises the question of why there was a shift in the 1960s and 1970s to community activism in the prevention of mental disorders. The answer is complex. For many years it was obvious that few people could avail themselves of psychotherapeutic services, which were usually very expensive, in short supply, and apparently geared to so-called YAVIS clients—individuals who are young, attractive, verbal, intelligent, and successful (Schofield, 1964). Eysenck (1952) had earlier questioned the effectiveness of most kinds of psychotherapy, finding treated patients' rates of improvement no better than the spontaneous remission rate. Although Eysenck's criticisms were compellingly rebutted by a number of scholars (e.g., Bergin, 1971), the idea took hold among mental health professionals that psychotherapy aimed at changing the individual might not be the best way to alleviate the psychological problems of the majority of people. Focus began to shift from repressions, conflicts, and neurotic fears to large-scale social problems, such as poverty, overcrowding, poor education, segregation, the alienation felt in large cities, and the impersonal nature of many aspects of present-day living. Community psychology's emphasis on prevention has become especially important in the United States, where there has developed a large gap between the need for mental health care and the availability of services (Weissberg, Caplan, & Sivo, 1989).

The shift from intrapsychic to social factors probably also reflected the Zeitgeist, or tenor of the times. The 1960s and early 1970s were a period of tremendous social upheaval and activism. Institutions of all kinds were being challenged. Cities and college campuses erupted in riots, and a range of minority groups, from African-Americans to gays, charged racism and political repression. This social upheaval, which at times seemed to border on revolution, further encouraged looking at social institutions for causes of individual suffering. At the same time the Kennedy and Johnson administrations (1961–1968) lent the monetary clout of the federal government to a progressive liberalism. John Kennedy's New Frontier and Lyndon Johnson's Great Society programs poured tens of millions of dollars into attempts at bettering the human condition.

Whatever the reasons for the growth of community-based efforts, enthusiasm must unfortunately be tempered with awareness of social reality—the conditions of deprivation that community psychologists assume are important in producing and maintaining disordered behavior. To train an African-American youngster for a specific vocational slot can have a beneficial long-term outcome for the individual only to the extent that society at large provides the appropriate opportunity to use these skills. Those who work in community psychology are aware that racial and social prejudices play a central role in limiting the access of many minority groups to the rewards of the culture at large. Although efforts to improve the sociocultural milieu must of course continue if our society has any commitment to fostering social and mental well-being, programs may raise expectations that will only be dashed by the realities of the larger culture. This is the quandary of any mental health professional who ventures forth from the consulting room into the community.

Community psychology has as its goal the change of large systems and groups of people rather than treating individual problems. And it is primarily in the seeking mode; psychologists take the initiative in serving people, rather than waiting for individuals in need to come to them. On the face of it, this is a tall order. What do we know about the principles that operate to produce change in societal values and institutions? When a community psychologist organizes a rent strike, for example, what is the best way of doing so, that is, of persuading the greatest number of tenants to work together in the joint effort? Will gentle persuasion be most effective, or does the situation call for harangues against the landlord? Further, if the community psychologist hopes to take actions that meet the wishes and needs of the community, how does he or she determine them? Recall from Chapters 3 and 4 the difficulties the psychologist has in assessing the needs of an individual client with whom there is extensive direct contact. How much more difficult, then, to assess the needs of thousands of people!

Community psychologists become social activists to some degree, which raises the danger that these well-meaning professionals may *impose* values and goals on their clients. John Kennedy's launching of the community mental health movement (see below) proclaimed that the federal government is rightfully concerned about improving the mental health of Americans. But what is mental health? Who is to decide? To what extent do the people being served by community psychologists have a say in how they are to be helped? These are but a few of the nettlesome questions that must continually be posed if community psychology is to act responsibly and effectively. The focus of this field is on large-scale factors. Many people are involved; many lives, then, will be affected by decisions and actions. Questions of values and of effectiveness are inherent in any effort to alter the human condition, but they are of special importance when the clients themselves do not seek the intervention.

COMMUNITY MENTAL HEALTH

In 1955 Congress authorized the Joint Commission on Mental Illness and Health to examine the state mental hospitals. On the basis of its six-year survey, the commission concluded that the care offered was largely custodial and that steps must be taken to provide effective treatment. Its 1961 report recommended that no additional large hospitals be built and that instead community mental health clinics be established. In 1963, President Kennedy sent a message to Congress calling for a "bold new approach," proposing the Community Mental Health Centers Act to provide comprehensive services in the community and to implement programs for the prevention and treatment of mental disturbances. The act was passed. For every 100,000 people a mental health center was to provide outpatient therapy, short-term inpatient care, day hospitalization for those able to go home at night, twenty-four-hour emergency services, and consultation and education to other agencies in the community.

Additional impetus came from the 1965 Swampscott Conference (Bennett et al., 1966), organized out of the growing dissatisfaction felt by many clinical psychologists with the inherent limitations of traditional delivery of mental health services and for what they perceived as the need for a new commitment to the promotion of human welfare on a broad scale. Though the political climate in the country in the 1980s was not particularly supportive of such efforts, five NIMH-sponsored Preventive Intervention Research Centers were operating in the late 1980s (Gesten & Jason, 1987).

GOALS OF COMMUNITY MENTAL HEALTH

The principal objective of a community mental health center is to provide outpatient mental health care in a person's own community and at a cost that is not beyond the means of most people. The hope is that the increased availability of such clinical services will result in fewer individuals requiring institutionalization, instead being able to remain with their families and friends and continuing to work while receiving therapy locally several times a week. The community health center also provides short-term inpatient care, usually on a psychiatric ward of a community general hospital, again, where relatives and friends of patients may conveniently visit them. When it is needed, partial hospitalization, during the day or sometimes for the night, is usually available on a psychiatric ward. A

FOCUS 19.4   COMMUNITY PSYCHOLOGY AND COMMUNITY MENTAL HEALTH—RELATED BUT DIFFERENT

Although related, community psychology and the community mental health movement should be distinguished from each other. Community psychology is concerned predominantly with prevention, intervening before dysfunctions are evident. Community psychology shows its concern for individuals by trying to alter social systems on the institutional level and by creating different and, it is hoped, better environments for people to live in, both to reduce the forces that are thought to bring maladaptions and to promote opportunities for individuals to realize their potential. Community psychology concerns intervention with the entire range of social institutions, including the courts, police, schools, and city services and planning agencies. Political more than clinical skills are required for such work; in fact, relatively little time is spent dealing directly with the individuals affected by the larger social forces.

Community mental health, in contrast, focuses much more on treatment, particularly with troubled low-income people who have traditionally been underserved by the mental health professions. Its orientation is often as individualistic as traditional consulting room therapy of the kind discussed in Chapters 17 and 18. On the staffs of mental health centers are psychiatrists, clinical and counseling psychologists, and social workers who conduct individual or group therapy in offices at

Providing better housing for low-income families is an excellent illustration of a community psychology activity.

the center. The two movements are sometimes equated, but their differences are as important to appreciate as their similarities.

---

twenty-four-hour walk-in crisis service offers emergency consultation around the clock and rap sessions for members of the community. In Chapter 14 we discussed rape crisis work, a service often run by community mental health centers.

Centers are staffed by psychiatrists, psychologists, social workers, and nurses, and sometimes by paraprofessionals who live in the neighborhood and can help bridge the gap between the middle- and upper-middle-class professionals and community members to whom mental health service is sometimes an alien concept. Paraprofessionals and volunteers can provide needed staffing within the limited budgets of the centers. The inclusion of paraprofessionals in the service delivery process has been hailed as an efficient and useful way to expand human resources by converting 'helpees' into helpers (Riessman, 1990), and some observers believe that they can be as effective as professionals under certain circumstances (Christensen & Jacobson, 1994). Paraprofessionals, as indigenous members of the community, may have a unique understanding of relevant cultural and social variables, thereby facilitating the relevance and accept-

ability of an intervention to the people being served. Enlisting paraprofessionals also exploits the helper-therapy principle, whereby the process of helping those in need enhances the mental health of those providing the help (Riessman, 1965, 1990). This opportunity for a mutually beneficial exchange has remained an enduring legacy of the community mental health movement. A wide range of services is included under the rubrics of consultation and education. A primary service is the education of other community workers—teachers, clergy, and police—in the principles of preventive mental health and in how to extend help themselves (see Focus 19.4 for contrasts between community psychology and community mental health).

EVALUATION OF COMMUNITY MENTAL HEALTH

Fewer than 800 of the 2000 community mental health centers envisioned by Congress in the 1960s were established, and during the Reagan and Bush administrations of the 1980s centers across the United States suffered a loss of political support and federal funding (see Mosher & Burti, 1989) to the degree that federal support of community mental health centers has been virtually phased out in the mid- and late-1980s (Rappaport, 1992). One can gain an idea of the politicization of the movement by considering the suggestion that the withdrawal of federal funding occurred not because there was no longer a need for such services, but rather because political conservatives decided that a social problem more deserving of attention and money was substance abuse. In this way, Lyndon Johnson's War on Poverty in the social activist 1960s became Ronald Reagan's War on Drugs in the 1980s (Humphrey & Rappaport, 1993). It was suggested further that substance abuse was a more acceptable target for conservative policy makers because it provided a focus on individual defects and moral character, a dimension not readily apparent within the socioenvironmental concerns of the community mental health (and community psychology) movement. Rather than increase support for human services through the existing community mental health centers, policy makers moved to the problem of substance abuse and essentially employed an internal-defect model, which assumes that substance abuse arises from moral or physical flaws rather than from social or political environments. Hence, substance abusers ought to be able to "Just Say No," as Nancy Reagan and others repeatedly urged. And what began primarily as a Republican initiative in the 1980s seems to be attracting continuing support from Democrats in the 1990s.

Problems of community mental health centers were examined twenty-five years ago in a controversial critique by Ralph Nader's Center for Study of Responsive Law (Holden, 1972). This report held that the centers were based on a good and commendable set of ideas but that the implementation had been rather poor. Often the problem was one of old wine in new bottles. Nader's group pointed out that centers were usually controlled by psychiatrists, whose training and outlook were tied to one-to-one therapy, typically along psychoanalytic lines. The fit between treatment and the problems of lower-income people, who were the centers' primary clients, was often poor. A study conducted by Hollica and Milic (1986) in a Connecticut community mental health center indicated that assignment to psychotherapy was made more often for patients of higher social class, who had more education and better employment status. On the plus side was the finding that lower-income patients had indeed been able to obtain some access to outpatient therapy, so-called categorical treatment that focused on specific problems such as alcohol and drug abuse. What this

study did not address was who was better off in the respective treatment assignment.

CULTURAL AND RACIAL FACTORS IN PSYCHOLOGICAL INTERVENTION

As we close our three-chapter discussion of intervention, we revisit the issue of cultural diversity that has been addressed many times already throughout this book. This is important to highly heterogeneous countries, such as the United States and Canada, but it is of importance to other countries as well because most of our discussion of psychopathology and intervention is presented within the context and constraints of western European society. Despite our increasing understanding of biological factors in the nature of mental illness and how to prevent and treat many disorders, social circumstances are ignored only at great risk.

For a variety of historical and socioeconomic reasons many minorities in the United States have had contact with the mental health system primarily through lower-cost agencies such as community mental health centers, where the therapists they see are often paraprofessionals. Frequently these helpers come from the same backgrounds as those receiving services; they have some training but do not have typical credentials for mental health work. The prevailing belief is that these individuals will better know the life circumstance of those in need, and, most important, will be more acceptable to them. Extensive research on modeling provides some justification for these assumptions. Participants in studies of learning through observation are found to acquire information more readily from models who are perceived as credible and relevant to them; similarity of age and background are important determinants of credibility and relevance (Rosenthal & Bandura, 1978). We can therefore expect that individuals unaccustomed to the standard middle-class fare of a professional office and formal appointments will find the activities and advice of helpers similar to themselves more acceptable.

It would be a mistake, however, to assume that services rendered by paraprofessionals are good enough for ethnic and racial minorities or that the kinds of professional interventions reviewed in this and the two preceding chapters are not suitable for minorities. Many middle- and upper-class minorities avail themselves of the services of mental health professionals, and all people are entitled to the best services available. It has not been shown that minorities do less well in psychotherapy (which in the United States is provided primarily by whites) than do whites (Sue, Zane, & Young, 1994), nor has it been demonstrated that better outcomes are achieved when patient and therapist are similar in race or ethnicity (Beutler et al., 1994). Moreover, many of those who cannot afford professional help belong to the minority culture. The following discussion is as relevant to the traditional settings discussed in Chapters 17 and 18 as to the community-oriented work just examined. That minorities are overrepresented among the clientele of paraprofessionals and community psychology workers is an accident of history and discrimination.

A final caveat: our discussion of racial factors in intervention runs the risk of stereotyping because we review generalizations that experts make about the way a *group* of people react to psychological assistance. People from minority groups are *individuals* who can differ as much from each other as their racial group differs from another racial group. However, a consideration of group characteristics is important and is part of a developing specialty called minority mental health.

AFRICAN-AMERICANS AND PSYCHOLOGICAL INTERVENTION

African-American clients report higher levels of rapport with African-American therapists than with white therapists, prefer African-American therapists to white, and report greater satisfaction with them (Atkinson, 1983, 1985). One study found that African-American clients engage in more self-exploration with counselors of their own race (Jackson, 1973). At the same time, studies suggest that racial differences are *not* insurmountable barriers to understanding between counselor and client (Beutler et al., 1994). Therapists with considerable empathy are perceived as more helpful by clients, regardless of the racial mix.

African-Americans who have not fully accepted the values of white America generally react differently to whites than to other African-Americans: with African-Americans they are more open and spontaneous, whereas with whites they tend to be more guarded and less talkative (Gibbs, 1980; Ridley, 1984). Therapists need to accept that virtually all African-Americans have encountered prejudice and racism and many must wrestle with their anger and rage at a majority culture that is sometimes insensitive to and unappreciative of the emotional consequences of growing up as a member of a feared, resented, and sometimes hated minority (Hardy & Laszloffy, 1995). On the other hand, as

Greene (1985) cautioned, therapists' sensitivity to social oppression should not translate into a paternalism that removes personal responsibility and individual empowerment from the African-American client.

LATINOS AND PSYCHOLOGICAL INTERVENTION

Findings about how Mexican-Americans react to non-Latino therapists are mixed. However, with improved experimental designs in three interrelated studies, Lopez et al. (1991) found that Mexican Americans reported a clear preference for ethnically similar therapists, especially when the clinical problem related to ethnic concerns (e.g., a woman's feeling pressure from Mexican parents to marry rather than have a career). Less acculturated Latinos have been shown to view ethnically similar counselors as more credible sources of help than Anglo counselors (Ponce & Atkinson, 1989). Therapy with most Latinos should appreciate their difficulty in expressing psychological concerns; men in particular may have great trouble expressing weakness and fear, which may be exacerbated by the growing independence of many Latina women as wage earners.

Cognitive behavior therapy may be more acceptable than insight-oriented psychotherapy to traditionally oriented Latinos because it aims more at symptom relief, giving advice and guidance, and problem-solving around issues of immediate importance. (These characteristics would seem to apply generally to lower-income people, regardless of race or ethnicity.) The didactic style of cognitive behavior therapy may also serve to demystify the process and render it more educational than psychotherapeutic in nature, thus reducing the possible stigmatizing effects of "having one's head shrunk" (Organista & Munoz, 1996).

ASIAN-AMERICANS AND PSYCHOLOGICAL INTERVENTION

Asian-Americans comprise more than two dozen distinct subgroups (e.g., Filipino, Chinese, Japanese, Vietnamese) and differ also on such dimensions as how well they speak English, whether they immigrated or came as refugees from war or terrorism in their homeland, and the degree to which they identify with their native land or that of their parents if they were born in the United States (Yoshioka et al., 1981, as cited in Sue & Sue, 1992). With this diversity in mind, therapists should nonetheless be aware of greater tendencies among these groups than among whites to be ashamed of emotional suffering and, coupled with a relative lack of assertiveness (according to U.S. standards), to seek out professional help with great reluctance. Above all, the stereotype of Asian-Americans as having made it, as invariably being highly educated, earning good salaries, and being emotionally well-adjusted, is belied by the facts. The discrimination suffered by Asians in the United States and in many other countries appears to be as severe as that endured by other racial and ethnic minority groups (Sue & Sue, 1992).

There are many implications for how to conduct psychotherapy with Asian-Americans. Sue and Sue (1992) advise therapists to be sensitive to the personal losses that many Asian refugees have suffered and, especially in light of the great importance that family connections have for them, to the likelihood that they are very stressed from these losses. Another way to put this is to appreciate the role of posttraumatic stress in Asian-Americans who have come to this country as refugees. Therapists should also be aware that Asian-Americans have a tendency to "somaticize," that is, to experience and to talk about stress in physical terms, such as headaches and fatigue. Their values are also different from the Western values of the majority culture in the United States. For example—and allowing for considerable individual variation—Asians respect structure and formality in interpersonal relationships, whereas a Western therapist is likely to favor informality and a less authoritarian attitude. Respect for authority may take the form of agreeing readily to what the therapist does and proposes—and perhaps, rather than discussing differences openly, just not showing up for the next session. The acceptability of psychotherapy as a way to handle stress is likely to be much lower among Asian-Americans, who tend to see emotional duress as something to be handled on one's own and through willpower (Kinzie, 1985). Asian-Americans may consider some areas off-limits for discussion with a therapist, for example, the nature of the marital relationship, and especially sex.

Asian-Americans born in the United States are often caught between two cultures. One form of a resolution is to identify vigorously with majority values and denigrate anything Asian, a kind of racial self-hate. Others, torn by conflicting loyalties, experience (poorly expressed) rage at a discriminatory Western culture but at the same time question aspects of their Asian background. Finally, the therapist may have to be more directive and active than he or she otherwise might be, given the preference of many Asian-Americans for a structured approach over a reflective one (Atkinson, Maruyama, & Matsui, 1978; Iwamasa, 1993).

NATIVE AMERICANS AND PSYCHOLOGICAL INTERVENTION

As with other minorities, Native Americans are a highly heterogeneous group, with about 500 tribes residing in the United States. With due regard for individual differences, such as the degree to which the person is assimilated into the majority culture, some generalizations can be made that pertain to therapeutic approaches (Sue & Sue, 1992; Sue, Zane, & Young, 1994).

Because Native American children are often looked after in the households of various relatives, the pattern of a child's or young adult's moving among different households is not necessarily a sign of trouble. A youngster's avoidance of eye contact is a traditional sign of respect but may be misconstrued by someone unfamiliar with the culture as quite the opposite and regarded as a problem to be remedied (Everett, Proctor, & Cartmell, 1989). As with other minorities, conflicts about identification can be severe—young people can be torn between traditional values and those of the (decidedly more privileged) majority culture, which may underlie the high rates of truancy, substance abuse, and suicide among Native American young people (Red Horse, 1982). Drug abuse, especially alcoholism, is a widespread problem in some tribes and frequently leads to child abuse, an issue that also needs to be considered when there is family conflict. A value placed on cooperativeness rather than competitiveness can be misinterpreted by a culturally unaware therapist as lack of motivation. The importance of family may make it advisable to conduct treatment in the home with family members present and an integral part of the intervention.

Very little controlled research has been conducted on Native Americans in therapy (Sue et al., 1994). A recent sign of the professional inattention to these groups of people can be found in an otherwise exemplary special issue of the journal *Cognitive and Behavioral Practice* (vol. 3, no. 2, 1996), devoted entirely to ethnic and cultural diversity in cognitive and behavioral practice. There are articles on African-Americans, Latinos, Japanese, orthodox Jews, gays, and older adults, but none on Native Americans.

TOWARD A MORE COMPLETE SCIENCE OF BEHAVIOR

Regardless of whether the therapist has the same skin color or ethnicity as the client, it is important that the mental health professional be aware of and sensitive to the different value structures and life experiences of the client. The same can be said of the treatment of any client who is different from the therapist in ways that affect attitudes and behavior. The study of ethnic or racial factors in psychological intervention, as well as their role in clinical assessment (p. 96), can be seen in the broader context of the social and scientific importance of including such variables in the study of human behavior. The inclusion of diversity can enhance our scientific understanding of people (Betancourt & Lopez, 1993; Rokeach, 1979). If membership in a particular subculture plays a role, for example, in how readily emotion is expressed, then neglecting culture as a variable may limit our understanding of the role of expressing emotion in psychopathology. And such a constraint may vitiate not only our data-based knowledge but our ability to meet our social responsibilities. Culture and values are increasingly recognized as key factors in how a society structures its science and makes its policy. Our sensitivity throughout this book to paradigms in science reflects this understanding. In our final chapter, we further examine the complex interplay between scientific knowledge and the use to which that knowledge is put in affecting people's lives.

Summary

Although therapy is sometimes conducted in groups only as a way to deliver individual treatment efficiently, group therapy usually takes advantage of some special properties of the group itself. A group can exert strong social pressure for change. Members also benefit from sharing common concerns and aspirations. Sensitivity training and encounter groups enable people to learn how they affect others and are affected by them. Efforts are made to get behind the social facades that people present to the world, so that they may deal honestly and more effectively with one another. Controlled research on outcome and process in group therapy of all kinds is just beginning to be done, but it is fair to say that many people can benefit from the experience of group therapy.

In family therapy the problems of the identified patient are considered the manifestation of disturbances within the family unit. Family members learn how their behavior and attitudes affect one another, that flexibility and changing communication patterns can bring greater harmony. Marital or couples therapy helps distressed couples resolve the conflicts inevitable in any ongoing relationship of two adults living together. One technique consists of caring days—one partner at a time concentrates on giving pleasure to the other, breaking the cycle of bitterness and hostility plaguing them. Couples therapists of all theoretical allegiances try to improve partners' communication of needs and wants to each other. An act may be well-intentioned but have a negative impact. Talking openly about this problem appears to ease the tensions of many couples. Continuing research in family and couples therapy promises to elucidate the problems for which these therapies are appropriate and the processes by which they bring relief.

Community psychology and the related community mental health movement try to prevent mental disorders from developing, to seek out troubled people, to find the social conditions that may be causing or exacerbating human problems, and to make available affordable mental health services. Examples include suicide prevention centers, mass media campaigns to change harmful lifestyles, teaching problem-solving skills to children in schools, and teaching parenting skills to groups at high risk for abusing their children. Community workers must make their values explicit, for they are often fostering social change rather than helping individuals adjust to what some consider untenable social conditions. Deinstitutionalization, the policy of having former mental patients live, if at all possible, at home or in small residences, is part of this movement. Much work needs to be done, however, in designing and supplying adequate, sheltered residences and care that will help these individuals live in the community in an acceptable fashion. Prevention is difficult to institute, a reflection of our inadequate knowledge of how disordered behavior develops. More needs to be learned about how to determine the needs of a community and how to mobilize large groups of people for change.

Finally, the cultural and racial backgrounds of patients present a variety of considerations. Particular issues surround the treatment of African-Americans, Latinos, Asian-Americans, and Native Americans, including the kinds of problems these groups may have and the kinds of sensitivities clinicians should possess in order to deal respectfully and effectively with patients from minority groups.

KEY TERMS

group therapy
couples (marital) therapy
family therapy
community psychology

community mental health
sensitivity training group
  (T-group)
encounter group

family systems approach
divorce mediation
prevention

Robert Vickrey, "Cops,"
1988

LEGAL AND ETHICAL ISSUES

20

Amendment 1   Congress shall make no law respecting an establishment of religion, or prohibiting the free exercise thereof; or abridging the freedom of speech, or of the press; or the right of the people peaceably to assemble, and to petition the Government for a redress of grievances.

Amendment 4   The right of the people to be secure in their persons, houses, papers, and effects, against unreasonable searches and seizures, shall not be violated. ...

Amendment 5   No person...shall be compelled in any criminal case to be a witness against himself, nor be deprived of life, liberty, or property, without due process of law. ...

Amendment 6   In all criminal prosecutions, the accused shall enjoy the right to a speedy and public trial ...; to be confronted with the witnesses against him; to have compulsory process for obtaining witnesses in his favor, and to have the Assistance of Counsel for his defense.

Amendment 8   Excessive bail shall not be required, nor excessive fines imposed, nor cruel and unusual punishment inflicted.

Amendment 13 ... Neither slavery nor involuntary servitude, except as a punishment for crime whereof the party shall have been duly convicted, shall exist within the United States, or any place subject to their jurisdiction. ...

Amendment 14 ... No State shall ... deprive any person of life, liberty, or property, without due process of law; nor deny to any person within its jurisdiction the equal protection of the laws.

Amendment 15 ... The right of citizens of the United States to vote shall not be denied or abridged by the United States or by any State on account of race, color, or previous condition of servitude.

These eloquent statements describe and protect some of the rights of U.S. citizens and others residing in the United States. Against what are these rights being protected? Be mindful of the circumstances under which most of these statements were issued. After the Constitutional Convention had delineated the powers of government in 1787, the first Congress saw fit in 1789 to amend what had been framed and to set specific limits on the federal government. Amendments beyond the original ten have been added since that time. The Fourteenth Amendment is directed to the states, which are playing increasingly important roles in the protection of the rights of mental patients. The philosoph-

ical ideal of the U.S. government is to allow citizens the maximum degree of liberty consistent with preserving order in the community at large.

We open our final chapter in this way because the legal and mental health systems collaborate continually, although often subtly, to deny a substantial proportion of the U.S. population their basic civil rights. With the best of intentions, judges, governing boards of hospitals, bar associations, and professional mental health groups have worked over the years to protect society at large from the actions of people regarded as mentally ill or mentally defective and considered dangerous to themselves or to others. But in so doing they have abrogated the rights of thousands of people in both criminal and civil commitment proceedings. Mentally ill individuals who have broken the law or who are alleged to have done so are subject to **criminal commitment**, a procedure that confines a person in a mental institution either for determination of competency to stand trial or after acquittal by reason of insanity. **Civil commitment** is a set of procedures by which a mentally ill and dangerous person who has not broken a law can be deprived of liberty and incarcerated in a mental hospital. Both commitments in effect remove individuals from the normal processes of the law. In this chapter we look at these legal procedures in depth. Then we turn to an examination of some important ethical issues as they relate to therapy and research.

CRIMINAL COMMITMENT

We examine first the role of psychiatry and psychology in the criminal justice system. Almost as early as the concept of *mens rea*, or "guilty mind," and the rule "No crime without an evil intent" had begun to be accepted in English common law, insanity had to be taken into consideration, for a disordered mind may be regarded as unable to formulate and carry out a criminal purpose (Morse, 1992). In other words, a disordered mind cannot be a guilty mind; only a guilty mind can engender culpable actions. At first insanity was not a trial defense, but the Crown sometimes granted pardons to people who had been convicted of homicide if they were judged completely and totally mad (A. A. Morris, 1968). By the reign of Edward I (1272–1307) the concept of insanity had begun to be argued in court and could lessen punishment. During the course of the fourteenth century it became the rule of law that a person proved to be wholly and continually mad could be defended against a criminal charge.

In today's courts judges and lawyers call on psychiatrists and clinical psychologists for assistance in dealing with criminal acts thought to result from the accused's disordered mental state and not from free will. Are such emotionally disturbed perpetrators less criminally responsible than those who are not distraught but commit the same crimes? Should such individuals even be brought to trial for transgressions against society's laws? Although efforts to excuse or protect the accused through the insanity defense or by judging them incompetent to stand trial are undoubtedly well-intentioned, invoking these doctrines can often subject those accused to a greater denial of liberties than they would otherwise experience.

THE INSANITY DEFENSE

The **insanity defense** is the legal argument that a defendant should not be held responsible for an illegal act if it is attributable to mental illness that interferes with rationality or that results in some other excusing circumstance, such as not knowing right from wrong. A staggering amount of material has been written on the insanity defense, even though it is pleaded in less than one percent of all cases that reach trial and is rarely successful (N. Morris, 1968; Morse, 1982b; Steadman, 1979; Steadman et al., 1993). Alan A. Stone (1975), a professor of law and psychiatry at Harvard University, proposed an intriguing reason for this great interest in finding certain people not guilty by reason of insanity (NGRI). Criminal law rests on the assumption that people have free will and that if they do wrong, they have *chosen* to do so, are blameworthy, and should therefore be punished. Stone suggests that the insanity defense strengthens the concept of free will by pointing to the few people who constitute an exception because they do not have it, namely, those judged to be insane. These individuals are assumed to have less responsibility for their actions because of a mental defect, an inability to distinguish between right and wrong, or both. They lack the degree of free will that would justify holding them legally accountable for criminal acts. By exclusion, everyone else *has* free will! "The insanity defense is in every sense the exception that proves the rule. It allows the courts to treat every other defendant as someone who chose 'between good and evil'" (Stone, 1975, p. 222).

LANDMARK CASES AND LAWS

In modern Anglo-American criminal law, several court rulings and established principles bear on the problems of legal responsibility and mental illness.

The so-called *irresistible impulse* concept was formulated in 1834 in a case in Ohio. According to this concept if a pathological impulse or drive that the person could not control had compelled that person to commit the criminal act, an insanity defense was legitimate. The irresistible-impulse test was confirmed in two subsequent court cases, *Parsons* v. *State* and *Davis* v. *United States*.[1]

The second well-known concept, the *M'Naghten* rule, was announced in the aftermath of a murder trial in England in 1843. The defendant, Daniel M'Naghten, had set out to kill the British prime minister, Sir Robert Peel, but had instead mistaken Peel's secretary for Peel. M'Naghten claimed that he had been instructed to kill Lord Peel by the "voice of God." The judges ruled that

to establish a defense of insanity, it must be clearly proved that, at the time of the committing of the act, the party accused was labouring under such a defect of reason, from disease of the mind, as not to know the nature and quality of the act he was doing; or if he did know it, that he did not know he was doing what was wrong.

By the beginning of the twentieth century this right–wrong test was being used in all the states except New Hampshire and in all federal courts. By the late 1980s it was the sole test in eighteen states and in several others was applied in conjunction with irresistible impulse. However, a committee of the American Psychiatric Association expressed the view that understanding the difference between right and wrong was out of step with modern conceptions of insanity. It was in this context that a third important court decision was made.

Judge David Bazelon ruled in 1954, in the case of *Durham* v. *United States*,[2] that the "accused is not criminally responsible if his unlawful act was the product of mental disease or mental defect." Bazelon believed that by referring simply to mental illness he would leave the profession of psychiatry free to apply its full knowledge. It would no longer be limited to considering impulses or knowledge of right and wrong. Bazelon purposely did not incorporate in what would be called the Durham test any particular symptoms of mental disorder that might later become obsolete. The psychiatrist was accorded great liberty to convey to the court his or her own evaluation of the accused's mental condition. Forcing the jury to rely to this extent on expert testimony did not prove workable courtroom practice, however. Since 1972 the Durham test has not been used in any jurisdiction, and Bazelon eventually

---

[1]*Parsons* v. *State*, 2 So. 854, 866–67 (Ala. 1887); *Davis* v. *United States*, 165 U.S. 373, 378 (1897).

[2]*Durham* v. *United States*, 214 F.2d 862, 876 (D.C. Cir. 1954).

withdrew his support for it, feeling that it allowed too much leeway to expert witnesses.

In 1962 the American Law Institute (ALI) proposed its own guidelines, which were intended to be more specific and informative to lay jurors than were other tests.

1. A person is not responsible for criminal conduct if at the time of such conduct as a result of mental disease or defect he lacks substantial capacity either to appreciate the criminality (wrongfulness) of his conduct or to conform his conduct to the requirements of law.

2. As used in the Article, the terms "mental disease or defect" do not include an abnormality manifested only by repeated criminal or otherwise antisocial conduct. (The American Law Institute, 1962, p. 66)

The first ALI guideline combines the M'Naghten rule and the irresistible impulse concept. The second guideline concerns those who are repeatedly in trouble with the law; they are not to be deemed mentally ill only because they keep committing crimes. Indeed, the phrase "substantial capacity" in the first guideline is designed to limit an insanity defense to those with the most serious mental disorders. Until 1984 the ALI test was in use in more than half the states and in all federal courts. Some scholars, however, have argued that such words like *substantial* and *appreciate* introduce ambiguities that foster disagreements among expert witnesses as well as jurors as to whether a defendant's state of mind is sufficiently disturbed to justify a verdict of not guilty by reason of insanity (Simon & Aaronson, 1988).

In the 1980s a fifth major effort began in the United States to clarify the legal defense of insanity, strength-ened by the controversy created by the NGRI verdict in the highly publicized trial of John Hinckley, Jr., for an assassination attempt against President Ronald Reagan in March 1981. Judge Parker, who presided over the trial, received a flood of mail from outraged citizens that a would-be assassin of a U.S. president had not been held criminally responsible and had only been committed to an indefinite stay in a mental hospital until deemed mentally healthy enough for release. (As we write this in mid-1997, Hinckley has been incarcerated in St. Elizabeth's Hospital, a public mental hospital in Washington, D.C., for over sixteen years, but can be released whenever his mental health is deemed adequate.)

Because of the publicity of the trial and the public outrage at the NGRI verdict, the insanity defense became a target of vigorous and sometimes vituperative criticism from many quarters. As Judge Parker put it: "For many, the [Hinckley] defense was a clear manifestation of the failure of our criminal justice system to punish individuals who have clearly violated the law" (Simon & Aaronson, 1988, p. vii).

As a consequence of political pressures to get tough on criminals, Congress enacted in October 1984 the Insanity Defense Reform Act, addressing the insanity defense for the first time. This new law, which has been adopted in all federal courts, contains several provisions.

- It eliminates the irresistible impulse component of the ALI rules, which referred to inability of the person to conform to the requirements of the law as a result of a mental disease or defect. This volitional and behavioral aspect of the ALI

John Hinckley, President Reagan's assailant, wrote this letter to actress Jodie Foster expressing his dream of marrying her and becoming president.

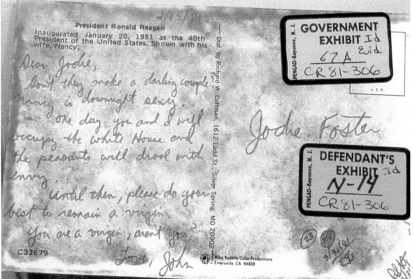

guidelines had been strongly criticized because one could regard *any* criminal act as arising from an inability to stay within the limits of the law, which would exclude all criminals from the usual processes of the criminal justice system.

- It changes the ALI's lack of "substantial capacity … to appreciate" to "unable to appreciate." This alteration in the cognitive component of the law is intended to tighten the grounds for an insanity defense by making more stringent the criterion for impaired judgment.

- The act also stipulates that the mental disease or defect must be "severe," the intent being to exclude insanity defenses on the bases of nonpsychotic disorders, such as antisocial personality disorder. (The ALI guidelines were developed to impose similar restrictions by the use of the word *substantial* to describe incapacity; this apparently was not considered strong enough in the immediate aftermath of the Hinckley acquittal.) Also abolished by the act were defenses relying on "diminished capacity" or "diminished responsibility," based on such mitigating circumstances as extreme passion or "temporary insanity."

- It shifts the burden of proof from the prosecution to the defense. Instead of the prosecution's having to prove that the person was sane beyond a reasonable doubt at the time of the crime (the most stringent criterion, consistent with the constitutional requirement that people are considered innocent until proved guilty), the defense must prove that the defendant was not sane and must do so with "clear and convincing evidence" (a less stringent but still demanding standard of proof). The importance of this shift can be appreciated by keeping in mind that if the prosecution bears the burden of proof beyond a reasonable doubt, then the defense need only introduce a reasonable doubt to defeat the prosecution's efforts to prove sanity. The heavier burden now placed on the defense is, like the other provisions, designed to make it more difficult to relieve a defendant of moral and legal responsibility.[3]

- Finally, the new act responds to what many felt to be the most troublesome feature of the existing laws, namely, that the person could be released from commitment after a shorter period of time than would be allowed under an ordinary sentence. With this act, if the person is judged to have recovered from mental illness, then instead of allowing release from the prison hospital, the period of incarceration can be extended to the maximum allowable for the actual crime.

Over a dozen states have since supplemented the NGRI defense with what seems to be a compromise verdict—guilty but mentally ill (GBMI). Initially adopted by Michigan in 1975, this principle allows an accused person to be found legally guilty of a crime—thus maximizing the chances of incarceration—but allows for psychiatric judgment of how to deal with the convicted person if he or she is considered to have been mentally ill when the act was committed. Thus, even a seriously ill person can be held morally and legally responsible, but can then be committed to a prison hospital or other suitable facility for psychiatric treatment rather than to a regular prison for punishment.

This trend reflects the uneasiness of the legal and mental health professions in excusing a person who, in Thomas Szasz's terms, is *descriptively* responsible for a crime—that is, there is no disputing that he or she actually committed the act—without being held *ascriptively* responsible—that is, without having to suffer some sort of societal negative consequence for breaking the law (see Focus 20.1). This legal modification avoids the irony of a situation in which (1) it is determined that a person committed a crime, (2) it is determined that he or she is not to be held legally responsible because of insanity at the time of the crime—the NGRI defense—and then (3) by the time the person is to be criminally committed, he or she is judged to be no longer mentally ill, and (4) the person is *not* incarcerated (or is released after a confinement shorter than it would have been had the person been found guilty of the crime he or she committed).[4] A GBMI verdict allows the usual sentence to be imposed for being found guilty of a given crime but also allows for the person to be treated for mental illness during incarceration, a proposal Szasz made in the 1960s. So far, however, evidence does not indicate that the GBMI alternative per se results in appropriate psychiatric treatment for those convicted (Fentiman, 1985; Steadman et al., 1993).

---

[3]According to Simon and Aaronson (1988), this provision arose in large measure from the inability of the prosecution to prove John Hinckley's sanity when he shot Reagan and three others. Several members of the jury testified after the trial to a subcommittee of the Senate Judiciary Committee that the judge's instructions on the burden of proof played a role in their verdict of NGRI. Even before the act, almost half the states required that the defendant must prove insanity, but only one, Arizona, had the "clear and convincing" standard. About two-thirds of the states now place the burden of proof on the defense, albeit with the least exacting of legal standards of proof, "by a preponderance of the evidence."

---

[4]Things can go the other way, however, as demonstrated in the case of *Jones* v. *United States* described shortly.

In general, the insanity defense requires applying an abstract principle to specific life situations. As in all aspects of the law, terms can be defined in a number of ways—by defendants, defense lawyers, prosecutors, judges, and jurors—and testimony can be presented in diverse fashion, depending on the skill of the interrogators and the intelligence of the witnesses. Furthermore, because the defendant's mental condition *only at the time the crime was committed* is in question, retrospective, often speculative, judgment on the part of attorneys, judges, jurors, and psychiatrists is required. And disagreement between defense and prosecution psychiatrists and psychologists is the rule.

A final point should be emphasized. There is an important difference between insanity and mental illness or defect. A person can be diagnosed as mentally ill and yet be held responsible for a crime. *Insanity* is a legal, not a psychiatric or psychological concept. This distinction was made vivid by the February 15, 1992, conviction of Jeffrey Dahmer in Milwaukee, Wisconsin. He had been accused of and had admitted to butchering, cannibalizing, and having sex with the corpses of fifteen boys and young men. Pleading guilty but mentally ill, Dahmer's sanity was the sole focus of an unusual trial that had jurors listening to conflicting testimony from mental health experts about the defendant's state of mind during the serial killings to which he had confessed. They had to decide whether he had been suffering from a mental disease that prevented him from knowing right from wrong or from being able to control his action (note the blend of the ALI guidelines, M'Naghten, and irresistible impulse). Even though there was no disagreement that he was mentally ill, diagnosable as having some sort of paraphilia, Dahmer was deemed sane and therefore legally responsible for the grisly murders. He was sentenced by the judge to fifteen consecutive life terms (Associated Press, 1992).

THE CASE OF *JONES* V. *UNITED STATES*

CASE DESCRIPTION To illustrate the predicament that a person can get into by raising insanity as an excusing condition for a criminal act, we consider a celebrated—some would call it infamous—Supreme Court case.[5] Michael Jones was arrested, unarmed, on September 19, 1975, for attempting to steal a jacket from a department store in Washington, D.C. He was charged the following day with attempted petty larceny, a misdemeanor punishable by a maximum prison sentence of one year. The court ordered that he be committed to St. Elizabeth's Hospital for a determination of his competency to stand trial. On March 2, 1976, almost six months after the alleged crime, a hospital psychologist reported to the court that Jones was competent to stand trial, although he suffered from "schizophrenia, paranoid type." The psychologist also reported that the alleged crime resulted from Jones's condition, his paranoid schizophrenia. This comment is noteworthy because the psychologist was not asked to offer an opinion on Jones's state of mind during the crime, only on whether Jones was competent to stand trial. Jones then decided to plead not guilty by reason of insanity. Ten days later, on March 12, the court found him not guilty by reason of insanity and formally committed him to St. Elizabeth's Hospital for treatment of his mental disorder.

On May 25, 1976, a customary fifty-day hearing was held to determine whether Jones should remain in the hospital any longer. A psychologist from the hospital testified that Jones still suffered from paranoid schizophrenia and was therefore a danger to himself and to others. A second hearing was held on February 22, 1977, seventeen months after the commission of the crime and Jones's original commitment to St. Elizabeth's for determination

Insanity is a legal concept and differs from the psychological concept of mental illness. Jeffrey Dahmer, a serial killer and paraphiliac, seemed clearly psychopathological but was not judged insane because he was regarded as knowing right from wrong and able to control his behavior.

---

[5]*Jones* v. *United States*, 463 U.S. 354 (1983).

FOCUS 20.1 THOMAS S. SZASZ AND THE CASE AGAINST FORENSIC PSYCHIATRY AND PSYCHOLOGY

HIS POLEMIC

By codifying acts of violence as expressions of mental illness, we neatly rid ourselves of the task of dealing with criminal offenses as more or less rational goal-directed acts, no different in principle from other forms of conduct. (Szasz, 1963, p. 141)

This quotation from one of Thomas Szasz's most widely read books enunciates the basic theme of his argument against the weighty role that his own profession of psychiatry plays in the legal system. (Note that the quote is from 1963. Mental health specialists play an even greater role in the courts today.) We have already mentioned Szasz's distinction between descriptive and ascriptive responsibility. To hold a person criminally responsible is to *ascribe* legal responsibility for an act for which the person is *descriptively* responsible. A given social group makes the judgment that the person who is descriptively responsible for a criminal act will receive criminal punishment. As Szasz points out, being criminally responsible is not an inherent trait that society uncovers. Rather, society at a given time and for a given criminal act decides that it will hold the perpetrator legally responsible and will punish him or her.

Szasz suggests that mental illness began to be used as an explanation for criminal behavior when people acted in a way that was considered particularly irrational and threatening to society. According to Szasz, these exceptional cases all involved violence against people of high social rank. In the shooting of an English nobleman in 1724, a man named Arnold was believed to have as little understanding of his murderous act as "a wild beast." Another man, James Hadfield, was deemed deranged for attempting to assassinate King George III as he sat in a box at the Theatre Royal in 1800. And a third person, named Oxford, was regarded as insane for trying to kill Queen Victoria in 1840. The best-known case has already been mentioned, that of David M'Naghten (1943), who killed Sir Robert Peel's private secretary after mistaking him for Peel. In all these cases from English law, which forms the basis for U.S. law, people of low social rank openly attacked their superiors. Szasz believes that "the issue of insanity may have been raised in these trials in order to obscure the social problems which the crimes intended to dramatize" (1963, p. 128).

Other cases here and abroad, such as the assassinations of John and Robert Kennedy, South African prime minister Hendrik

Noted psychiatrist, Thomas S. Szasz, argues strongly against the use of the insanity defense.

Verwoerd, Martin Luther King, Jr., and John Lennon, and the attempted assassinations of Ronald Reagan and Pope John Paul II, may to a degree reflect the social ills of the day. Moreover, events in the former Soviet Union provide examples of the role of politics in criminal and civil commitment. In *A Question of Madness*, the well-known Russian biochemist Zhores Medvedev (1972) told how Soviet psychiatrists collaborated with the state in attempting to muzzle his criticism of the government. They diagnosed him as suffering from paranoid delusions, multiple personality, and other mental ailments that would make it dangerous for him to be at large in society.

of competency. The defendant demanded release since he had already been hospitalized longer than the one-year maximum sentence he would have served had he been found guilty of the theft of the jacket. The court denied the request and returned him to St. Elizabeth's.

The District of Columbia Court of Appeals agreed with the original court. Ultimately, in November 1982, more than seven years after his hospitalization, Jones's appeal to the Supreme Court was heard. On June 29, 1983, by a five-to-four decision, the Court affirmed the earlier decision:

Of course Szasz does not claim that all insanity pleas involve some sort of silent conspiracy of the Establishment to cover up social problems, for the vast majority of pleas of insanity are made in far more ordinary cases. Szasz sets forth a polemic much broader in scope. His basic concern is with individual freedom and responsibility for one's actions, which include the right to deviate from prevailing mores and the duty to assume responsibility for one's behavior.* (Recall Szasz's argument that people should not be forcibly prevented from committing suicide; p. 258.) Far from advocating that people be held *less* accountable for antisocial acts, he argues that legal responsibility should be extended to *all*, even to those whose actions are so far beyond the limits of convention that some explain their behavior in terms of mental illness. Szasz's overall lament is that instead of recognizing the deviant as an individual different from those who would judge him or her, but nonetheless worthy of their respect, he or she is first discredited as a self-responsible human being and then subjected to humiliating punishment defined and disguised as treatment (1963).

EVALUATION OF SZASZ'S POSITION

The Insanity Defense Reform Act of 1984, as well as changes in civil commitment to be described shortly, is consistent with the arguments that Szasz has put forward since the 1960s. These shifts toward holding mentally ill persons accountable for their actions and thereby more deserving of protection of their civil rights are probably due in large measure to Szasz's unrelenting attacks on the liaison between the law and the mental health professions.

However, Szasz has been criticized by those who believe that psychiatry and psychology should have an important role in deciding how to deal with people whose criminal acts seem attributable to mental illness. The abuses documented by Szasz should not blind us to the fact that—for whatever combination of biological and psychological reasons—some people are at times a danger to others and to themselves. Although Szasz and others object to mental illness as an explanation, it is difficult to deny that there is madness in the world. People *do* occasionally imagine persecutors, whom they sometimes act against with force. Some people *do* hallucinate and on this basis may behave in a dangerous fashion. Our concern for the liberties of one individual has always been tempered with our concern for the rights of others.

But does it help a criminal acquitted by reason of insanity to be placed in a prison mental hospital with an indeterminate sentence, pending rehabilitation? The answer cannot be an unqualified yes. Should such a person, then, be treated like any other convicted felon and be sent to a penitentiary? Considering the psychic damage that we know may occur in ordinary prisons, a yes to this question cannot be enthusiastic either. But a prison sentence is more often a finite term of incarceration. If we cannot demonstrate that people are rehabilitated in mental hospitals, perhaps it is just as well to rely on our prisons and on the efforts of penologists to improve these institutions and to find ways of helping inmates alter their behavior so that they will not be antisocial after release.

Stephen J. Morse, a University of Pennsylvania law professor and a leading theorist in forensics, has also written on the need to treat mentally ill people as responsible individuals and on the associated need to improve the prison system.

If involuntary commitment is abolished, there may well be an increase in the processing of cases of relatively mild deviance through the criminal justice system and increased numbers of crazy persons may spend some time in unpleasant and often terrible jails. But, if crazy persons are almost always responsible for their behavior, and if incarceration in a jail is justified, there is no reason why they should not go to jail. This outcome is in fact more respectful of the dignity and autonomy of crazy persons than assuming that they are nonresponsible and must be "fixed." Jails and locked hospitals are both massive intrusions on liberty. The best response to the argument that jails are bad places, as they surely are for non-crazy and crazy inmates alike, is to clean them up. Using unjustified hospitalization—merely another form of incarceration that offers little if any of the benefits it promises—to avoid jails is not a sensible solution to the problems of criminal justice: it merely allows us to avoid those problems. (Morse, 1982a, p. 98)

---

*In a provocative book, *The Abuse Excuse*, Alan Dershowitz, a well-known and high-profile law professor at Harvard University, argues that more and more lawbreakers are trying to avoid responsibility for their criminal acts by invoking one or another hardship in their past histories as a reason for their unlawful actions (Dershowitz, 1994a). One such excuse is the so-called adopted child syndrome, which holds that children who are given up by their biological parents for adoption feel such a profound sense of rejection that they should not be blamed for some of their antisocial behavior as adults. One lawyer employed this novel defense in claiming that his client murdered seventeen women, most of them prostitutes, because he had been rejected by his birth-mother and he murdered repeatedly to alleviate the pain of that rejection (Dershowitz, 1994b).

Jones was to remain at St. Elizabeth's. His public defender lawyer reports that Jones has spent most of his years committed in St. Elizabeth's, living in the community for a period of time in the late 1980s but always returning to the hospital (Harry Fulton, personal communication, April 22, 1997).

THE DECISION OF THE SUPREME COURT. The basic question that Jones took to the Supreme Court was whether someone "who was committed to a mental hospital upon being acquitted of a criminal offense by reason of insanity must be released because he has been hospitalized for a period longer than he might have served in prison had he been convicted" (*Jones* v. *United States*, p. 700). Having already spent more time in the prison hospital than he would have served in prison had he been convicted, Jones believed that he should be released. The Supreme Court, however, viewed matters differently (S Rep No. 1170, 84th Cong, 1st Sess 13 [1955], as cited in *Jones* v. *United States*):

> An insanity acquittee is not entitled to his release merely because he has been hospitalized for a period longer than he could have been incarcerated if convicted. The length of a sentence for a particular criminal offense is based on a variety of considerations, including retribution, deterrence, and rehabilitation. However, *because an insanity acquittee was not convicted, he may not be punished*. The purpose of his commitment is to treat his mental illness and protect him and society from his potential dangerousness. There simply is no necessary correlation between the length of the acquittee's hypothetical criminal sentence and the length of time necessary for his recovery. (p. 700, emphasis added)[6]
>
> Where [the] accused has pleaded insanity as a defense to a crime, and the jury has found that the defendant was, in fact, insane at the time the crime was committed, it is just and reasonable … that the insanity, once established, should be presumed to continue and that the accused should automatically be confined for treatment until it can be shown that he has recovered. (p. 705)
>
> And because it is impossible to predict how long it will take for any given individual to recover—or indeed whether he ever will recover—Congress has chosen, as it has with respect to civil commitment, to leave the length of commitment indeterminate, subject to periodic review of the patient's suitability for release. (p. 708)

Essentially, the Supreme Court ruled that since Jones was acquitted he could not be punished for the crime; to be punished, the individual must be blameworthy. Jones's insanity left him legally blameless, for he could not possess *mens rea*, a guilty mind. His free will to have committed the theft was deemed to have been superseded by his disturbed mental state. This is the logic of the insanity defense. Furthermore, according to the Court, since punishment cannot have any of its intended individual or societal effects on a mentally disturbed person—rehabilitation, deterrence, or retribution—it was irrelevant that Jones was being held longer than a normal prison sentence. Jones would clearly have been better off not to have pleaded insanity.

CRITIQUE OF THE SUPREME COURT DECISION In this case, the burden of proof was on Jones, the acquittee, to prove that he was no longer mentally ill or dangerous to society, whereas in the normal practice of justice in the United States a person's *accusers* have the burden of proving him or her guilty. This situation differs as well from civil commitment, in which the government, not the person, bears the burden of proof. Jones was denied this civil right.

The Court was concerned about Jones's illness-produced dangerousness. Jones argued in his petition to the Supreme Court that his theft of the jacket was not dangerous because it was not a violent crime. The Court stated, however, that for there to be violence in a criminal act, the act itself need not be dangerous. It cited a previous decision that a nonviolent theft of an article such as a watch may frequently result in violence through the efforts of the criminal to escape, or of the victim to protect his or her property, or of the police to apprehend the fleeing thief.[7]

The dissenting justices of the Court commented that the longer someone such as Jones had to remain in the hospital, the harder it would be for him to demonstrate that he was no longer a dangerous person nor mentally ill. Extended institutionalization would likely make it more difficult for him to afford medical experts other than those associated with the hospital and to behave like someone who was not mentally ill.

> The current [use of] psychotropic drugs … may render mental patients docile … but it does not "cure" them or allow them to demonstrate that they would remain non-violent if they were not drugged. … At petitioner's May 1976 hearing, the Government relied on testimony [from hospital mental health experts] that petitioner was "not always responsive in a positive way to what goes on" and was "not a very active participant in the informal activities on the Ward" to support its contention that he had not recovered. (p. 716, n. 16)

Jones's case is unusual, even Kafkaesque. Most NGRI decisions are for crimes considerably more heinous than stealing a jacket. But the Jones case did reach the Supreme Court, and it illustrates some of the reasons that the insanity defense remains a controversial and emotionally charged issue for a society that values the rule of law and civil rights for its citizens.

COMPETENCY TO STAND TRIAL

The insanity defense concerns the accused's mental state *at the time of the crime*. A question that arises before the issue of what kind of defense an accused

---

[6]At the time, this absence of correlation between the criminal act and the length of incarceration could also work the other way, namely, "no matter how serious the act committed by the acquittee, he may be released within fifty days of his acquittal if he has recovered" (p. 708).

[7]*Overholser* v. *O'Beorne*, 302 F.2d 852, 861 (D.C. Cir. 1961).

person offers is whether the person is competent to stand trial *at all*. It is obviously possible for a person to be judged competent to stand trial yet be acquitted by reason of insanity.

Far greater numbers of people are committed to prison hospitals after being judged incompetent to stand trial than are tried and acquitted by reason of insanity. The U.S. criminal justice system is organized such that the fitness of individuals to stand trial must be decided before it can be determined whether they are responsible for the crime of which they are accused.

With the Supreme Court case *Pate* v. *Robinson*[8] as precedent, the defense attorney, prosecutor, or judge may raise the question of mental illness whenever there is reason to believe that the accused's mental condition might interfere with his or her upcoming trial. Another way to look at competency is that the courts do not want a person to be brought to trial *in absentia* ("not present")—which is a centuries-old principle of English common law—referring here to the person's mental state, not his or her physical presence. If after examination the person is deemed too mentally ill to participate meaningfully in a trial, the trial is routinely delayed and the accused is incarcerated in a prison hospital with the hope that means of restoring adequate mental functioning can be found. This is what happened to Jones immediately after his arrest.

If a court fails to order a hearing when there is evidence that raises a reasonable doubt about competency to stand trial, or if it convicts a legally incompetent defendant, there is a violation of due process.[9] Once competency is questioned there must be a preponderance of evidence showing that the defendant is competent to stand trial.[10] The test to be applied is whether the defendant shows sufficient ability to consult with his or her lawyer with a reasonable degree of understanding and whether he or she has a rational as well as a factual understanding of the proceedings.[11] The court has to consider evidence such as irrational behavior as well as any medical or psychological data that might bear on the defendant's competency.[12] However, analogous to the insanity defense, just being deemed mentally ill does not necessarily mean that the person is incompetent to stand trial; a person with schizophrenia, for example, may still understand legal proceedings and be able to assist in his or her defense (Winick, 1996).

Being judged incompetent to stand trial can have severe consequences for the individual. Bail is automatically denied, even if it would be routinely granted if the question of incompetency had not been raised. The accused is usually kept in a facility for the criminally insane for the pretrial examination. During this period the accused is supposed to receive treatment to render him or her competent to stand trial.[13] In the meantime, the accused may lose employment and undergo the trauma of being separated from family and friends and from familiar surroundings for months or even years, perhaps making his or her emotional condition even worse and thus making it all the more difficult to show competency to stand trial. Until the 1970s, some people languished in a prison hospital for many years waiting to be found competent to stand trial.

A 1972 Supreme Court case, *Jackson* v. *Indiana*,[14] forced the states to a speedier determination of incompetency. The case concerned a mentally retarded deaf and mute man who was deemed not only incompetent to stand trial but unlikely ever to become competent. The Court ruled that the length of pretrial confinement must be limited to the time it takes to determine whether treatment during this detainment is likely to render the defendant competent to stand trial. If the defendant is unlikely ever to become competent, the state must after this period either institute civil commitment proceedings or release the defendant. It has been suggested that lawyers participate with mental health professionals in making the competency determination, for a knowledgeable lawyer understands exactly what the defendant must be able to do to participate in the trial (Roesch & Golding, 1980). Legislation has been drafted in most states to define more precisely the minimal requirements for competency to stand trial, ending the latitude that has deprived thousands of people of their rights to due process (Fourteenth Amendment) and a speedy trial (Sixth Amendment). Defendants today cannot be committed for determination of competency for a period longer than the maximum possible sentence they face.[15]

Modern medicine has had an impact on the competency issue. The concept of "synthetic sanity"

---

[8]*Pate* v. *Robinson*, 383 U.S. 375 (1966).

[9]*United States* v. *White*, 887 F.2d 705 (6th Cir. 1989); *Wright* v. *Lockhart*, 914 F.2d 1093, *cert. denied*, 111 S.Ct. 1089 (1991).

[10]*United States* v. *Frank*, 956 F.2d 872, *cert. denied*, 113 S.Ct. 363 (1992); *United States* v. *Blohm*, 579 F.Supp. 495 (1983).

[11]*United States* v. *Frank*; *Wright* v. *Lockhart*.

[12]*United States* v. *Hemsi*, 902 F.2d 293 (2d Cir. 1990); *Balfour* v. *Haws*, 892 F.2d 556 (7th Cir. 1989).

[13]*United States* v. *Sherman*, 912 F.2d 907 (7th Cir. 1990).

[14]*Jackson* v. *Indiana*, 406 U.S. 715 (1972).

[15]*United States* v. *DeBellis*, 649 F.2d 1 (1st Cir. 1981); *State* v. *Moore*, 467 N.W. 2d 201 (Wis. Ct. App. 1991).

FOCUS 20.2 DISSOCIATIVE IDENTITY DISORDER AND THE INSANITY DEFENSE

Imagine that as you are having a cup of coffee one morning you hear pounding at the front door. You hurry to answer and find two police officers staring grimly at you. One of them asks, "Are you John Smith?" "Yes," you reply. "Well, sir, you are under arrest for grand theft and for the murder of Jane Doe." The officer then reads you your Miranda rights against self-incrimination, handcuffs you, and takes you to the police station, where you are allowed to call your lawyer.

This would be a scary situation for anybody, but what is particularly frightening and puzzling to you and your lawyer is that you have absolutely no recollection of having committed the crime that a detective later describes to you. You are aghast that you cannot account for the time period when the murder was committed—in fact, your memory is startlingly blank for that entire time. And, as if this were not bizarre enough, the detective then shows you a videotape in which you are clearly firing a shotgun at a bank teller during a holdup. "Is that you in the videotape?" asks the detective. You confer with your lawyer, saying that it certainly looks like you, including the clothes, but you are advised not to admit anything one way or the other.

Let's move forward in time now to your trial some months later. Witnesses have come forward and identified you beyond a reasonable doubt. There is no one you know who can testify that you were somewhere other than at the bank on the afternoon of the robbery and the murder. And it is clear that the jury is going to find you, in Szasz's terms, descriptively responsible for the crimes. But did *you* murder the teller in the bank? You are able to assert honestly to yourself and to the jury that you

did not. And yet even you have been persuaded that the person in the videotape is you, and that that person committed the robbery and the murder.

Because of the strange nature of the case your lawyer arranged prior to the trial to have you interviewed by a psychiatrist and a clinical psychologist, both of them well-known experts in forensics. Through extensive questioning they have decided that you suffer from dissociative identity disorder (DID, formerly multiple personality disorder), and that the crimes were committed not by you, John Smith, but by your rather violent alter, Dick. Indeed, during one of the interviews, Dick emerged and boasted about the crime, even chuckling over the fact that you, John, would be imprisoned for it.

This fictional account is not as far-fetched as you might think (recall the discussion of dissociative identity disorder in Chapter 7). Mental health lawyers have for some time been concerned with such scenarios as they have wrestled with various aspects of the insanity defense. But nearly all the people who successfully use this defense are diagnosable as schizophrenic (or more generally, as psychotic), and DID is regarded as a dissociative disorder (and used to be classified as one of the neuroses). Can DID be an excusing condition for a criminal act? Should John Smith be held ascriptively responsible for a crime committed by his alter, Dick? The quandary is clearly evident in the title of an article that addresses the DID issue: "Who's on Trial?" (Appelbaum & Greer, 1994).

Consider the widely accepted legal principle that people accused of crimes should be punished only if they are blameworthy. The several court decisions and laws we have reviewed

(Schwitzgebel & Schwitzgebel, 1980) has been used to argue that if a drug, such as Thorazine, temporarily produces a modicum of rationality in an otherwise deranged defendant, the trial may proceed. The likelihood that the defendant will again become incompetent to stand trial if the drug is withdrawn does not disqualify the person from going to court.[16] However, the individual rights of the defendant are to be protected against forcible medication, because there is no guarantee that such treatment would render the person competent to stand trial and there is a chance that it might cause harm. A recent Supreme Court ruling[17] held that a

criminal defendant could not be forced to take psychotropic medication in an effort to render him competent to stand trial. One of the Justices expressed strong reservations that a drugged defendant could ever really get a fair trial. In general, the courts have responded to the existence of powerful psychoactive medications by requiring safeguards against their involuntary use, to ensure that the defendant's civil rights are protected, even when a drug might restore legal competency to stand trial.[18] The implications of this ruling for legal and civil rights continue to be debated in the mental health law literature (e.g., Winick, 1993).

Finally, if the defendant wishes, the effects of the medication must be explained to the jury, lest—if the defendant is pleading NGRI—the jury conclude

---

[16]*State* v. *Hampton*, 218 So.2d 311 (La. 1969); *State* v. *Stacy*, no. 446 (Crim. App., Knoxville, Tenn., August 4, 1977); *United States* v. *Hayes*, 589 F.2d 811 (1979).

[17]*Riggins* v. *Nevada*, 504 U.S. 127 (1992).

[18]*United States* v. *Waddell*, 687 F.Supp. 208 (1988).

The film, *Primal Fear*, portrayed an insanity defense in a case of dissociative identity disorder.

in this chapter all rest on this principle. In recent reviews of the DID literature and of its forensic implications, Elyn Saks (1992, 1997) of the University of Southern California Law Center argues that DID should be regarded as a special case in mental health law, that a new legal principle should be established, "irresponsibility by virtue of multiple personality disorder."

What is intriguing about Saks's argument is that she devotes a major portion of it to defining personhood. *What is a person?* Is a person the body we inhabit? Well, most of the time our sense of who we are as a person does not conflict with the body we have come to know as our own, or rather, as *us*. But in DID there is a discrepancy. The body that committed the crimes

at the bank was John Smith. But it was his alter, Dick, who committed the crimes. Saks argues that, peculiar as it may sound, the law should be interested in the body only as a container for the person. It is the person who may or may not be blameworthy, not the body. Nearly all the time they are one and the same, but in the case of DID they are not. In a sense, Dick committed the murder by using John's body.

Then is John blameworthy? The person John did not commit the crime; he did not even know about it.* For the judge to sentence John, or more specifically, the body in the courtroom who usually goes by that name, would be unjust, argues Saks, for John is descriptively innocent. To be sure, sending John to prison would punish Dick, for whenever he would emerge, he would find himself imprisoned. But what of John? Saks concludes that we cannot imprison John because he is not blameworthy. Rather, we must find him not guilty by reason of dissociative identity disorder and remand him for treatment of the disorder.

Saks is optimistic about the effectiveness of therapy for DID and believes that people like John/Dick can be integrated into one personality and then released to rejoin society. Saks goes so far as to argue that people with DID who are judged dangerous but who have not committed a crime should be subject to civil commitment, even though this would be tantamount to preventive detention. In this way, she suggests, future crimes might be avoided.

---

*One might ask whether the situation would be different if John had coconsciousness of Dick, that is, if John were aware even during the criminal acts of what Dick was doing. Saks argues that this would not matter, unless it could be shown that John could have prevented Dick from his felonious behavior.

---

from his or her relatively calm and rational drug-produced demeanor that the defendant could not have been insane at the time of the crime.[19] This ruling relates to the difficulty of drawing a conclusion from retrospective evidence as to a defendant's mental state at the time of committing the crime, perhaps years earlier than the trial. This legal principle acknowledges that juries form their judgments of legal responsibility or insanity at least in part on how the defendant appears *during the trial*. If the defendant appears normal, the jury may be less likely to believe that the crime was an act of a disturbed mental state rather than of free will. Focus 20.2 discusses the unusual challenge posed by dissociative identity disorder in criminal commitments.

---

[19]*State v. Jojola*, 553 F.2d 1296 (N.M. Ct. App. 1976).

CIVIL COMMITMENT

Civil commitment affects far greater numbers of people than criminal commitment. It is beyond the scope of this book to examine in detail the variety of state civil commitment laws and regulations; each state has its own, and they are in almost constant flux. Our aim is to present an overview that will provide a basic understanding of the issues and of current directions of change.

In virtually all states a person can be committed to a psychiatric hospital against his or her will if a judgment is made that he or she is (1) mentally ill and (2) a danger to self—that is, unable to provide for the basic physical needs of food, clothing, and shelter—or a danger to others (Warren, 1982). At present, dangerousness to others is more often the second criterion, and recent court rulings point to *imminent* dangerousness as the principal criterion (e.g., the person is right on the verge of committing a violent act).[20] Such commitment is supposed to last for only as long as the person remains dangerous.[21]

Historically, governments have had the duty to protect their citizens from harm. We take for granted the right and duty of government to set limits on our freedom for the sake of protecting us. Few drivers, for example, question the legitimacy of the state's imposing limits on them by providing traffic signals that often make them stop when they would rather go. Most people go along with the Food and Drug Administration when it bans uncontrolled use of drugs that cause cancer in laboratory animals, although some people feel they have the right to decide for themselves what risks to take with their own bodies. Government has a long-established right as well as an obligation to protect us both from ourselves—the *parens patriae*, "power of the state"—and from others—the police power of the state. Civil commitment is one further exercise of these powers.

Specific commitment procedures generally fit into one of two categories, formal or informal. Formal or judicial commitment is by order of a court. It can be requested by any responsible citizen; usually the police, a relative, or a friend seeks the commitment. If the judge believes that there is a good reason to pursue the matter, he or she will order a mental health examination. The person has the right to object to these attempts to "certify" him or her, and a court hearing can be scheduled to allow the person to present evidence against commitment.

Informal, emergency commitment of mentally ill persons can be accomplished without initially involving the courts. For example, if a hospital administrative board decides that a voluntary patient requesting discharge is too disturbed and dangerous to be released, it is able to detain the patient with a temporary, informal commitment order.

Any person acting wildly may be taken immediately to a mental hospital by the police. Perhaps the most common informal commitment procedure is the 2PC, or two physicians' certificate. In most states two physicians, not necessarily psychiatrists, can sign a certificate that allows a person to be incarcerated for some period of time, ranging from twenty-four hours to as long as twenty days. Detainment beyond this period requires formal judicial commitment.

---

[20]*Suzuki* v. *Yuen*, 617 F.2d 173 (9th Cir. 1980).

[21]*United States* v. *DeBellis*.

PREVENTIVE DETENTION AND PROBLEMS IN THE PREDICTION OF DANGEROUSNESS

Despite the widespread perception that mentally ill people are dangerous and that they account for a significant proportion of the violence that besets contemporary society (Monahan, 1992), only about 3 percent of the violence in the United States is clearly linked to mental illness (Swanson et al., 1990). Moreover, about 90 percent of people diagnosed as psychotic (primarily schizophrenic) are not violent (Swanson et al., 1990). Mentally ill persons—even allowing for their small numbers relative to people not given DSM diagnoses of psychosis—account for a very small fraction of violent offenses, especially when compared to substance abusers and people who are in their teens and twenties, are male, and are poor (Mulvey, 1994). At best, mental illness makes a trivial contribution to the overall level of violence in society (Monahan, 1992).

Yet there is a strong connection in the public mind between violence and mental illness, and this belief is central to society's justification of civil commitment (Monahah & Shah, 1989) as well as to the stigma attached to having been a patient in a psychiatric institution (Link et al., 1987).

Civil commitment is necessarily a form of preventive detention; the prediction is made that a person judged mentally ill may in the future behave in a dangerous manner and should therefore be detained. Ordinary prisoners, however, are released from penitentiaries even though statistics show that most will commit additional crimes. Moreover, conviction by a court of law and subsequent imprisonment occur only after a person has done some harm to others (some may equate this situation with closing the barn door after the horses have thundered out). But our entire legal and constitutional system is organized to protect people from preventive detention. Even if witnesses have seen a person commit a serious crime, he or she is assumed innocent until proved guilty by the courts. The person who openly threatens to inflict harm on others, such as an individual who for an hour each day stands in the street and shouts threats to people in a nearby apartment house, is another matter. Does the state have to wait until the person acts on the threats? No. In such a case the civil commitment process can be brought into play, although the person must be deemed not only an imminent danger to others but mentally ill as well (Schwitzgebel & Schwitzgebel, 1980). Most mental health professionals, in agreement with laypeople, would conclude that a person has to be psychotic to behave in this way.

The likelihood of committing a dangerous act is central to civil commitment, but is dangerousness easily predicted? Early studies examining the reliability of predictions that a person would commit a dangerous act found that mental health professionals were poor at making this judgment (e.g., Kozol, Boucher, & Garofalo, 1972; Monahan, 1973, 1976; Stone, 1975). Some workers went on to argue that civil commitment for the purposes of preventive detention should be abolished. Monahan (1978), however, carefully scrutinized these studies and concluded that the professional's ability to predict violence had not been adequately assessed. Most of the studies conformed to the following methodological pattern.

- People were institutionalized for mental illness and for being a danger to the community.
- While these people were in the hospital, some of them were again predicted to be violent if they were released into the community.
- After a period of time, these people were released, thus putting together the conditions for a natural experiment.
- Checks on the behavior of the released patients over the next several years did not reveal much dangerous behavior.

What is wrong with such research? Monahan pointed out that little if any consideration was given to changes that institutionalization itself might have effected. In the studies reviewed, the period of incarceration ranged from several months to fifteen years. Prolonged periods of enforced hospitalization might very well make patients more docile, if for no other reason than that they become that much older. Furthermore, conditions in the open community where the predicted violence would occur can vary widely. Thus we should not expect this kind of prediction to have great validity (Mischel, 1968).

These studies, although flawed, have been used in arguments against civil commitment. Yet neither these studies nor any others have examined this specific issue. Monahan has theorized that prediction of dangerousness is probably far easier and surer in true emergency situations than after extended periods of hospitalization. When an emergency commitment is sought, the person may appear out of control and be threatening violence in his or her own living room or, like the person in the street, may be shouting threats. He or she may also have been violent in the past—a good predictor of future violence—and victims and weapons may be on hand. A dangerous outburst seems imminent.

Thus, unlike the danger to society predicted in the aforementioned studies, violence that requires an emergency commitment is expected almost immediately and in a known situation. Common sense tells us that such predictions of violence are likely to be very accurate. To test the validity of these expectations, we would have to leave alone half the people predicted to be immediately violent and later compare their behavior with that of persons hospitalized in such emergency circumstances. Such an experiment would be ethically irresponsible. Mental health professionals must apply logic and make the most prudent judgments possible.

Reconsideration of earlier research suggests that greater accuracy can be achieved in predicting dangerousness (Monahan, 1984; Monahan & Steadman, 1994). Violence prediction is most accurate under the following conditions (note the role played by situational factors, sometimes in interaction with personality variables) (e.g., Campbell, Stefan, & Loder, 1994).

- If a person has been repeatedly violent in the recent past, it is reasonable to predict that he or she will be violent in the near future unless there have been major changes in the person's attitudes or in their environment. Thus, if a violent person is placed in a restrictive environment, such as a prison or high-security psychiatric hospital facility, he or she may well not be violent given the markedly changed environment.
- If violence is in the person's distant past, if it was even just a single but a very serious act, and if that person has been incarcerated for a period of time, then violence can be expected on release if there is reason to believe that the person's predetention personality and physical abilities have not changed and if the person is going to return to the same environment in which he or she was previously violent.
- Even with no history of violence, violence can be predicted if the person is judged to be on the brink of a violent act, for example, if the person is pointing a loaded gun at an occupied building.

Convincing data on the ability of mental health professionals to predict violence are difficult to obtain, and some experts still voice extreme caution about locking people up on the basis of predictions of dangerousness, which continue to be viewed as fallible (Morse, 1996). Litwack (1975) argued that at the very least social scientists have the tools to gather the kinds of information that seem useful in predicting violence, for example, interview procedures that can uncover violent intentions as well as other assessment techniques that can determine whether a person still has personality characteristics that are believed to have contributed to violent behavior in the past. It is believed that support services, such as halfway houses in which people can live after their discharge from a mental hospital (p. 580), can markedly reduce the chances that a person who might otherwise be prone to committing a violent act will actually commit one (Dvoskin & Steadman, 1994).

One example of preventive detention is provided by laws recently passed in seven states that enable some repeat and dangerous sex offenders to be deemed mentally ill when they are about to be released from prison and then to be civilly committed to a prison hospital for an indefinite period—until treatment cures them of their presumed illness. Although this appears to be unconstitutional—detaining a person for a crime that he or she *may* commit in the future—many argue that it makes sense to keep sexual predators out of society.

Proponents of these laws, usually called sexually violent predator acts, point to rapists and child molesters with long histories of recidivism. If the probability is high—based on past experience and sometimes on comments made by the prisoners themselves (for example, one man said that the only way to keep him from victimizing children on his release would be to execute him)—that they will harm children after their release, should they not be prevented from doing so? In December 1996 a dispute between the state of Kansas and an imprisoned sex offender affected by the Kansas sexual predator law went to the U.S. Supreme Court (*Kansas* v. *Hendricks*). The constitutional issue here is that we don't detain other kinds of criminals when they have served their time only because of the probability that they will be recidivists. However, if a person is deemed mentally ill and dangerous, he or she *can* be civilly committed; this feature of civil commitment laws may allow these sexual predator laws to stand. The Supreme Court decision is bound to be controversial (Savage, 1996; Savage & Dolan, 1996).

How good must a prediction be to warrant interfering with someone's civil rights? Some have argued that being able to make only probabilistic predictions about future violence, such as, "Mr. Jones is likely, though not certain, to harm others if he is released," does not render this practice unethical (Grisso & Appelbaum, 1992). Once again, there is a balancing act between individual liberty and the obligation of government to protect its citizens. Different degrees of certainty are required for dif-

ferent legal and societal purposes. For example, the Supreme Court case of *Addington* v. *Texas*[22] requires clear and convincing evidence of proneness to violence and of mental illness to justify *extended* civil commitment; presumably evidence of a lesser quality would be enough for short-term, emergency commitment. If confinement is to be relatively brief (e.g., a few days), the downside risk for the individual detained would be only a few days' loss of freedom, whereas the possible benefit to society would be saving another from harm or murder. This is a legal[23] and moral decision, not a psychological or psychiatric one (see also Focus 20.3).

RECENT TRENDS FOR GREATER PROTECTION

The United States Constitution is a remarkable document. It lays down the basic duties of elected federal officials and guarantees a set of civil rights. But there is often some distance between the abstract delineation of a civil right and its day-to-day implementation. Moreover, judges must *interpret* the Constitution as it bears on specific contemporary problems. Since nowhere in this cornerstone of U.S. democracy is there specific mention of committed mental patients, lawyers and judges interpret various sections of the document to justify what they consider necessary in society's treatment of people whose mental health is in question.

In 1972 voluntary admissions to mental hospitals began to outnumber involuntary admissions. But a great number of people are still admitted and retained against their wishes, and it is impossible to know how many of those who admit themselves voluntarily do so under threat of civil commitment. One survey (Gilboy & Schmidt, 1971) revealed that 40 percent of patients who had voluntarily admitted themselves to a psychiatric hospital in Chicago had actually been threatened with commitment by the police officers who had taken them there. The issue of enforced hospitalization is still very much with us. Even though psychiatrists, psychologists, the courts, and hospital staff are growing more reluctant to commit, tens of thousands of mentally ill patients are in hospitals against their will.

---

[22]*Addington* v. *Texas*, 441 U.S. 418 (1979). The clear and convincing standard of proof, however, still protects the person less than would application of the criminal standard of beyond a reasonable doubt. The criminal standard—beyond a reasonable doubt—is referred to as the 90 percent standard; the clear and convincing standard is set at 75 percent certainty.

[23]*United States* v. *Sahhar*, 917 F.2d 1197, *cert. denied*, 111 S.Ct. 1591 (1991).

FOCUS 20.3   THE TARASOFF CASE—THE DUTY TO WARN AND TO PROTECT

The client's right to privileged communication—the legal right of a client to require that what goes on in therapy remain confidential—is an important protection, but it is not absolute. Society has long stipulated certain conditions in which confidentiality in a relationship should not be maintained because of the harm that can befall others. A famous California court ruling in 1974* described circumstances in which a therapist not only may but should breach the sanctity of a client's communication. First, what appear to be the facts in the case:

In the fall of 1968, Prosenjit Poddar, a graduate student from India studying at the University of California at Berkeley, met Tatiana (Tanya) Tarasoff at a folk dancing class. They saw each other weekly during the fall, and on New Year's Eve she kissed him. Poddar interpreted this act as a sign of formal engagement (as it might have been in India, where he was a member of the Harijam or "untouchable caste"). [But] Tanya told him that she was involved with other men, and indicated that she did not wish to have an intimate relationship with him.

Poddar was depressed as a result of the rebuff, but he saw Tanya a few times during the spring (occasionally tape recording their conversations in an effort to understand why she did not love him). Tanya left for Brazil in the summer, and Poddar at the urging of a friend went to the student health facility where a psychiatrist referred him to a psychologist for psychotherapy. When Tanya returned in October 1969, Poddar discontinued therapy. Based in part on Poddar's stated intention to purchase a gun, the psychologist notified the campus police, both orally and in writing, that Poddar was dangerous and should be taken to a community mental health center for psychiatric commitment.

The campus police interviewed Poddar, who seemed rational and promised to stay away from Tanya. They released him and notified the health service. No further efforts at commitment were made because the supervising psychiatrist apparently decided that such was not needed and, as a matter of confidentiality, requested that the letter to the police as well as certain therapy records be destroyed.

On October 27, Poddar went to Tanya's home armed with a pellet gun and a kitchen knife. She refused to speak to him. He shot her with the pellet gun. She ran from the house, was pursued, caught, and repeatedly and fatally stabbed. Poddar was found guilty of voluntary manslaughter rather than first- or second-degree murder. The defense established with the aid of the expert testimony of three psychiatrists that Poddar's diminished mental capacity, paranoid schizophrenia, precluded the malice necessary for first- or second-degree murder. After his prison term, he returned to India, where, according to his own report, he is happily married. (Schwitzgebel & Schwitzgebel, 1980, p. 205)

Under the privileged communication statute of California (see p. 621), the counseling center psychologist properly breached the confidentiality of the professional relationship and took steps to have Poddar civilly committed, for he judged Poddar to be an imminent danger. Poddar had stated that he intended to purchase a gun, and by his other words and actions he had convinced the therapist that he was desperate enough to harm Tanya. What the

Prosenjit Poddar was convicted of manslaughter in the death of Tatiana Tarasoff. The court ruled that his therapist, who had become convinced Prosenjit might harm Tatiana, should have warned her of the impending danger.

psychologist did not do, and what the court decided he should have done, was to warn the likely victim, Tanya Tarasoff, that her former friend had bought a gun and might use it against her. Such a warning would have been consistent with previous court decisions requiring physicians to warn the public when they are treating people with contagious diseases and requiring mental institutions to warn others when a dangerous patient has escaped (Knapp & Vandecreek, 1982). Or, as stated by the California Supreme Court in *Tarasoff*: "Once a therapist does in fact determine, or under applicable professional standards reasonably should have determined, that a patient poses a serious danger of violence to others, he bears a duty to exercise reasonable care to protect the foreseeable victims of that danger." The *Tarasoff* ruling, now being applied in other states as well,[†] requires clinicians, in deciding when to violate confidentiality, to use the very imperfect skill of predicting dangerousness.

A subsequent California court ruling[‡] held by a bare majority that foreseeable victims include those in close relationship to the identifiable victim. In this instance a mother was hurt by a shotgun fired by the dangerous patient, and her seven-year-old son was present when the shooting took place. The boy later sued the psychologists for damages brought on by emotional trauma. Since a young child is likely to be in the company of his or her mother, the court concluded in *Hedlund* that the *Tarasoff* ruling extended to the boy.

In the years since the *Tarasoff* ruling, health professionals have wondered whether it would have a negative effect, perhaps even a chilling effect, on psychotherapists. If clients are informed of this limitation to the confidentiality of what they say to their therapists, they may become reluctant to express feelings of extreme anger to therapists for fear that therapists will notify the people at whom they are angry. Clients might become less open with their therapists, perhaps derive less benefit from therapy, and even become *more* likely to inflict harm on others if they have not disclosed their fury as a first step toward controlling it. The welfare of the people whom the *Tarasoff* decision intended to protect might be endangered by the very ruling itself! It is unclear whether these concerns are well founded.

A survey of more than 1200 psychologists and psychiatrists in California soon after *Tarasoff* became law indicated that the *Tarasoff* decision was affecting their thinking and practices (Wise, 1978). On the plus side, one-third reported consulting more often with colleagues concerning cases in which violence was an issue. This practice should have a good outcome, since input from other professionals may improve the solitary clinician's decision making, presumably to the benefit of the client. Consultation can also demonstrate that the clinician took extra steps to adhere to *Tarasoff*, which can reduce legal liability if the patient later harms someone (Monahan, 1993). On the minus side, about 20 percent of the respondents indicated that they avoided asking their clients questions about violence, an ostrichlike stance that may keep the clinician from obtaining important information and yet reduces his or her legal liability should the client harm another person. A substantial number of

therapists were keeping less detailed records, again in an effort to reduce legal liability. Twenty years later, the emerging picture is that *Tarasoff* has not hobbled the practice of psychotherapy. Therapists seem to be managing to balance the rights of others with respect for the confidentiality of their patients (Mangalmurti, 1994). Psychotherapists in other countries are not as yet bound by such rulings. For example, in the United Kingdom, no such duty to warn or to protect has been placed on therapists, but that could change (Kennedy & Jones, 1995).

A 1983 decision of a federal circuit court in California[§] extended *Tarasoff*. The court ruled that Veterans Administration psychiatrists should earlier have warned the murdered lover of an outpatient, Phillip Jablonski, that she was a foreseeable victim, even though the patient had never made an explicit threat against her to the therapists. The reasoning was that Jablonski, having previously raped and otherwise harmed his wife, would likely direct his continuing "violence … against women very close to him" (p. 392).

The court also found the hospital psychiatrists negligent in not obtaining Jablonski's earlier medical records. These records showed a history of harmful violent behavior, which, together with the threats his lover was complaining about, should have moved the hospital to institute emergency civil commitment. The court ruled that the failure to warn was a proximate or immediate cause of the woman's murder. Proper consideration of the medical records, said the judge, would have convinced the psychiatrists that Jablonski was a real danger to others and should be committed.

This broadening of the duty to warn and protect now places mental health professionals in California in an even more difficult predicament, for the potentially violent patient need not even mention whom specifically he or she may harm. It is up to the therapist to deduce who are possible victims, based on what he or she can learn of the patient's past and present circumstances. Ironically, Jablonski's lover realized that she was in danger; she had moved out of the apartment she was sharing with him and had complained to her priest and to the Veterans Administration psychiatrists themselves that she feared for her safety. One of the psychiatrists had even advised her to leave Jablonski, at least while he was being evaluated at the medical center. But "when [she] responded, 'I love him,' [the psychiatrist] did not warn her further because he believed she would not listen to him" (p. 393). The court found this warning "totally unspecific and inadequate under the circumstances" (p. 398).

Tarasoff was further extended by a Vermont State Supreme Court ruling, *Peck* v. *Counseling Service of Addison County*,[‖] which held that a mental health practitioner has a duty to warn a third party if there is a danger of *damage of property*. The case involved a twenty-nine-year-old male patient who, after a heated argument with his father, told his therapist that he wanted to get back at his father and indicated that he might do so by burning down his father's barn. He proceeded to do just that. No people or animals were harmed in the fire; the barn housed no animals and was located 130 feet away from the parents' home. The court's conclusion that the therapist had a duty to warn was based on reasoning that arson is a violent act and therefore a lethal threat to people who may be in the vicinity of the fire. This ruling can be seen as an expansion of the *Hedlund* court decision as well; whereas *Hedlund* speaks of humans who may be at risk because of possible physical proximity to the endangered victim, *Peck* speaks of humans who could be harmed via threat to an inanimate object.

Many courts have augmented the duty to warn and protect to foreseeable victims of child abuse and even to possible victims as yet unknown. In one such case,[#] a medical student underwent a training analysis as one of the requirements to become a psychoanalyst. During the therapy he admitted that he was a pedophile. Later in his training he saw a male child as a patient as part of his psychiatric residency and sexually assaulted the boy. The court decided that the training analyst, who was not just the student's therapist but an instructor in the school, had reason to know that his patient-student "posed a specific threat to a specific group of persons, namely future minor patients, with whom [the student] would necessarily interact as part of his training" (p. 8). Even though, at the time the student revealed his pedophilia he did not have child patients (and thus there were no specific people whom the instructor could warn and take steps to protect), the supervisor—as his instructor, not just his therapist—was judged to have sufficient control over the student's professional training and activities (specifically, the power to keep the student from pursuing his interests in working with children) for the *Tarasoff* ruling to be relevant. The court decided that the supervisor could have and therefore *should have* "redirect[ed] the student's] professional development without even compromising the confidentiality of [the student's] disclosures to him" (p. 8). Instead, the supervisor and, by virtue of his faculty status, the college in which he worked allowed the patient-student to pursue his interests in child psychiatry, which resulted in the sexual molestation of a child patient.

In Chapter 14 (p. 399) we questioned whether *Tarasoff* is applicable when a therapist has reason to believe that his or her HIV-positive patient may endanger others by engaging in unprotected sex without notifying partners. So far no legal rulings bear on this difficult question, but that situation may change soon, especially if there is a clearly identifiable third party, such as the unknowing partner of an infected patient (Sizemore, 1995). A relevant factor may be the mental competence of the patient. Some people who are HIV positive or have AIDS have impairments in their judgment and reasoning processes, which may prevent them from fully understanding the dangers their seropositive status poses to others through unsafe sex or needle sharing. Under such conditions health professionals may have the legal and ethical duty to follow *Tarasoff* (Searight & Pound, 1994). Legal scholars as well as mental health professionals are beginning to debate the issue (e.g., Daniolos & Holmes, 1995; McGuire et al., 1995).

As problematic as *Tarasoff* and associated rulings may be for the mental health professions, the situation may not be as worrisome as it originally appeared. When the 1974 *Tarasoff* ruling was reaffirmed in 1976 by the California Supreme Court, the duty to warn was broadened to a duty to *protect* (see the earlier quotation from the 1976 decision), and it is this seemingly slight change that makes it possible for practitioners to adhere to *Tarasoff* without necessarily breaking confidentiality, that is, without having always to warn a potential victim. As Appelbaum (1985) pointed out, clinicians can undertake such preventive measures as increased frequency of sessions, initiation of or changes in psychotropic medication, and, in general, closer supervision of the patient. He suggested further that if such measures are judged reasonable, the therapist is unlikely to be held liable if the patient does ultimately harm somebody.

One strategy described by Appelbaum involved an eighteen-year-old patient who threatened during a session that he would beat up his landlady for not permitting her son to associate with him. On the basis of other information about the patient, the therapist determined that *Tarasoff* was relevant. He decided to involve the patient in the discussion, explaining his legal responsibility to protect a potential victim but also his reluctance to break therapeutic confidentiality. He presented to the patient the choice between hospitalization (the patient was indeed sometimes psychotic) and warning the landlady. The patient preferred to stay out of the hospital and did not object to the therapist's calling the landlady. When the landlady was called, she told the therapist that the young man had threatened her previously and that she knew how to take care of herself. In other words, she did not take the threats seriously. Appelbaum observed that the patient's threats seemed to be manipulative—he succeeded in once again issuing a verbal threat to his landlady, this time through his psychotherapist. But the psychotherapist succeeded in involving the patient in the decision making as well as preserving trust in the therapeutic relationship.

As anxiety–provoking as *Tarasoff* can be to clinicians, it does not call for therapists to reflexively pick up the phone to call a possible victim whenever a patient expresses a threat. Many other responsible options are available, such as directly asking the patient or relatives whether he or she has previously assaulted someone and taking care to check hospital records of a potentially dangerous patient (Monahan, 1993).

---

*Tarasoff v. *Regents of the University of California*, 529 P.2d 553 (Cal. 1974), *vacated, reheard in bank, and affirmed*, 131 Cal. Rptr. 14, 551 P.2d 334 (1976). The 1976 California Supreme Court ruling was by a four-to-three majority.

†*White* v. *United States*, 780 F.2d 97 (D.C. Cir. 1986); *Soutear* v. *United States*, 646 F.Supp. 524 (1986); *Dunkle* v. *Food Services East Inc.*, 582 A.2d. 1342 (1990); *People* v. *Clark*, 50 Cal. 3d 583, 789 P.2d 127 (1990).

‡*Hedlund* v. *Superior Court*, 34 Cal.3d 695 (1983).

§*Jablonski by Pahls* v. *United States*, 712 F.2d 391 (1983).

∥*Peck* v. *Counseling Service of Addison County*, 499 A.2d 422 (Vt. 1985).

#*Almonte* v. *New York Medical College*, 851 F. Supp. 34, 40 (D. Conn. 1994) (denying motion for summary judgment).

In a democratic society the most grievous wrong that can be suffered by a citizen is loss of liberty. The rights accorded to ordinary citizens, and even to criminals, are gradually being extended to those threatened with civil commitment and to those who have been involuntarily hospitalized. It is no longer assumed that deprivation of liberty for purposes of mental health care is a reason to deny to the individual his or her other rights.

For example, a 1976 federal court decision in Wisconsin, *Lessard* v. *Schmidt*,[24] gives a person threatened with civil commitment the right to timely, written notice of the proceeding, opportunity for a hearing with counsel, the right to have the hearing decided by jury, Fifth Amendment protection against self-incrimination, and other similar procedural safeguards already accorded defendants in criminal actions, including being present at any hearing to decide the need for commitment.[25] Such protections are to be provided even under emergency commitment conditions.[26] As mentioned earlier, and as implemented in recent lower court rulings,[27] a 1979 Supreme Court decision, *Addington* v. *Texas*, further provides that the state must produce clear and convincing evidence that a person is mentally ill and dangerous before he or she can be involuntarily committed to a psychiatric hospital. In 1980 the Ninth Circuit Court of Appeals ruled that this danger must be imminent.[28] Clearly the intent is to restrict the state's power to curtail individual freedoms because of mental illness. Although protection of the rights of mentally ill individuals adds tremendously to the burden of both civil courts and state and county mental hospital staffs, it is a price a free society must pay.

> Given the record … of legal commitment used to warehouse American citizens, it is … important that the individual feel sure that the [present] mental health system [in particular] cannot be so used and abused … for while the average citizen may have some confidence that if called by the Great Inquisitor in the middle of the night and charged with a given robbery, he may have an alibi or be able to prove his innocence, he may be far less certain of his capacity, under the press of fear, to instantly prove his sanity. (Stone, 1975, p. 57)

LEAST-RESTRICTIVE ALTERNATIVE

As noted earlier, civil commitment rests on presumed dangerousness, a condition that may vary depending on the surrounding circumstances. Thus a person may be deemed dangerous if allowed to live in an apartment, but not dangerous if living in a boarding home and taking prescribed psychoactive drugs every day under medical supervision. The least restrictive alternative to freedom is to be provided when treating disturbed people and protecting them from harming themselves and others. A number of court rulings require that only those mentally ill patients who cannot be adequately looked after in less restrictive homes be confined in hospitals.[29] Thus commitment is no longer necessarily in an institution; rather, a patient might well be required to reside in a supervised boarding home or in other sheltered quarters. In general terms, mental health professionals have to provide the treatment that restricts the patient's liberty to the least possible degree while remaining workable.[30] It is unconstitutional to confine a nondangerous mentally ill patient who is capable of surviving on his or her own or with the help of willing and responsible family or friends.[31] Of course, this principle will have meaning only if society provides suitable residences and treatments, something that has not yet happened.

In a thought-provoking analysis of how principles of civil commitment are actually implemented, Turkheimer and Parry (1992) concluded that the dangerousness criterion is less frequently followed in actual practice than is a judgment of "grave disability." This latter criterion is concerned with whether a patient might be unable to take care of himself or herself and would thus become a burden or a nuisance to society if not involuntarily institutionalized. This disability criterion is *not* supposed to be sufficient for civil commitment, yet it often is.

Least restrictive alternatives were supposed to be created when the deinstitutionalization movement took hold in the 1970s, but since the virtual cessation of federal funding for community mental health centers and other nonhospital placements in the 1980s, society has been faced with a growing number of people, usually ex-mental hospital patients, who are no longer dangerous and yet in need of more care than is available outside a hospital. A vivid example of what can happen is detailed in Focus 20.4. Turkheimer and Parry argue that an awareness of the dearth of less restrictive alternatives has led to rather desultory protection of civil rights (e.g., attorneys may not argue vigorously against commitment) and to commitment of people even when they are not judged dangerous.

[24]*Lessard* v. *Schmidt*, 349 F.Supp. 1078 (E.D. Wisc. 1972), *vacated and remanded on other grounds*, 94 S.Ct. 713 (1974), *reinstated in* 413 F.Supp. 1318 (E.D. Wisc. 1976).

[25]*In Re: Lawaetz*, 728 F.2d 225 (3d Cir. 1984).

[26]*Doremus* v. *Farrell*, 407 F.Supp. 509 (1975).

[27]*Dautremont* v. *Broadlawns Hospital*, 827 F.2d 291 (8th Cir. 1987).

[28]*Suzuki* v. *Yuen*.

[29]*Lake* v. *Cameron*; *Lessard* v. *Schmidt*.

[30]*In Re: Tarpley*, 556 N.E.2d 71, *superseded by* 581 N.E.2d 1251 (1991).

[31]*Project Release* v. *Prevost*, 722 F.2d 960 (2d Cir. 1983).

Civil commitment supposedly requires that the person be dangerous. But in actual practice the decision to commit can be based
on a judgment of severe disability as in the case of some homeless persons.

RIGHT TO TREATMENT

Another aspect of civil commitment that has come
to the attention of the courts is the so-called right to
treatment, a principle first articulated by Birnbaum
(1960). If a person is deprived of liberty because he
or she is mentally ill and is a danger to self or others, is not the state required to provide treatment to
alleviate these problems? Is it not unconstitutional
(and even indecent) to incarcerate someone without
afterward providing the help he or she is supposed
to need? This important question has been the subject of several court cases since Birnbaum first articulated the issue.

The right to treatment has gained in legal status
since the 1960s and was extended to all civilly committed patients in a landmark case, *Wyatt* v.
Stickney.[32] In that case an Alabama federal court
ruled in 1972 that the only justification for the civil
commitment of patients to a state mental hospital is
treatment. As stated by Judge Frank Johnson, "to
deprive any citizen of his or her liberty upon the
altruistic theory that the confinement is for humane
and therapeutic reasons and then fail to provide
adequate treatment violates the very fundamentals
of due process." Committed mental patients "have
a constitutional right to receive such individual
treatment as will give each of them a realistic
opportunity to be cured or to improve his or her

mental condition." This ruling, upheld on appeal, is
frequently cited as ensuring protection of people
confined by civil commitment, at least to the extent
that the state cannot simply put them away without
meeting minimal standards of care. In fact, when
mentally retarded patients (as opposed to those
judged to be mentally ill) are released from an institution, health officials are not relieved of their constitutional duty to provide reasonable care and safety as well as appropriate training.[33]

The *Wyatt* ruling was significant, for previously
the courts had asserted that it was beyond their
competence to pass judgment on the care given to
mentally ill patients, and they had assumed that
mental health professionals possessed special and
exclusive knowledge about psychopathology and
its treatment. Repeated reports of abuses, however,
gradually prodded the U.S. judicial system to rule
on what goes on within the walls of mental institutions. The *Wyatt* decision set forth very specific
requirements—dayrooms of at least forty square
feet; curtains or screens for privacy in multipatient
bedrooms; bedrooms limited to a maximum of five
persons; a comfortable bed; one toilet per eight persons; the right of the patient to wear any clothing he
or she wishes, provided it is not deemed dangerous;
opportunities to interact with members of the opposite sex; and no physical restraints except in emergency situations. Further, to provide care twenty-
four hours a day, seven days a week, there should
be, for every 250 patients, at least two psychiatrists,
three additional physicians, twelve registered nurses, ninety attendants, four psychologists, and seven
social workers. When the *Wyatt* action was taken,
Alabama state mental facilities averaged one physician per 2000 patients, an extreme situation
indeed.[34] The *Wyatt* requirements are still good law,
and similar protections have been extended to the
mentally retarded.[35]

The trend of the *Wyatt* ruling may have been
weakened by a later Supreme Court decision,
Youngberg v. *Romeo*,[36] regarding the treatment of a
mentally retarded boy, Nicholas Romeo, who had

[32]*Wyatt* v. *Stickney*, 325 F.Supp. 781 (M.D. Ala. 1971), *enforced in*
334 F.Supp. 1341 (M.D. Ala. 1971), 344 F.Supp. 373, 379 (M.D. Ala.
1972), *aff'd sub nom Wyatt* v. *Anderholt*, 503 F.2d 1305 (5th Cir.
1974).

[33]*Thomas S.* v. *Flaherty*, 902 F.2d 250, *cert. denied*, 111 S.Ct. 373
(1990).

[34]The underlying assumption is that patients civilly committed to
public mental hospitals will receive adequate care, but the evidence for this level of care is weak. Even though the extremely
negligent conditions that the *Wyatt* decision remedied in
Alabama are seldom found today, it is questionable, argued
Morse (1982c), whether forced hospitalization benefits patients.
At the very least, however, public mental hospitals can provide
shelter, food, protection, and custodial care, which many deinstitutionalized patients lack.

[35]*Feagley* v. *Waddill*, 868 F.2d 1437 (5th Cir. 1989).

[36]*Youngberg* v. *Romeo*, 102 S.Ct. 2452 (1982).

Focus 20.4   The Strange Case of Billie Boggs

The conflict between individual civil rights and the responsibility of the government to care for its citizens was played out in an almost surreal way in the mid-1980s in the case of Billie Boggs, a forty-year-old New York City homeless woman (Hornblower & Svoboda, 1987; Kasindorf, 1988). Her real name is Joyce Brown, and she achieved notoriety in 1987 when New York's sometimes flamboyant and always forthright mayor, Edward Koch, concerned about the living conditions of his city's homeless population, decided in October to round up those homeless people who seemed to be mentally ill and to hospitalize them even if they did not want it. Mayor Koch had come under intense political pressure to do something about homeless people's freezing to death in the shadows of luxurious Manhattan skyscrapers. He had started Project HELP in 1982, but it was stymied by difficulties in getting mentally ill people hospitalized. The incident involving Brown arose from a reinterpretation of case law that city attorneys told Koch would permit commitment if a person could be judged a danger to self or others "in the reasonably foreseeable future" rather than at the moment.

On a tour with other city officials Koch came upon Brown lying near a heating grate, her jaw swollen. When told that she could not be committed, Koch remarked to one of the officials, "You're loony yourself." Brown was taken involuntarily to Bellevue Hospital with the diagnosis of paranoid schizophrenia, based on such behavior as screaming and cursing at African-American men on the street ("Come suck my d—k, you black motherf——r"), lifting her skirt to expose her bare buttocks and shouting, "Kiss my black ass, you motherf——g nigger," defecating in her clothes or on the pavement, tearing up and burning money, and talking to herself—in addition to living in the streets.

Brown's family background was a conventional middle-class one. She graduated from high school and worked for ten years as a secretary. She lived at home with her mother, who died in 1979. Brown had been a heavy user of cocaine and heroin since high school, and she ultimately lost her job in 1983 because of spotty attendance and bizarre behavior, for example, swearing at people for no reason. After she lost her job, her life began to come apart; she would hear voices and talk to herself. One day she went into a store with one of her sisters and, seeing a security guard, began to curse at him loudly. "It was 'motherf——r this and motherf——r that,'" reported a sister (Kasindorf, 1988, p. 38). Brown also developed the idea that she would marry a handsome, professional white man, and started to make harassing phone calls based on this notion. From time to time she lived with one or more of her four sisters. In 1985 she was removed from a Newark, New Jersey, shelter because of disruptive behavior. Brown was seen by more than one psychiatrist, was prescribed Thorazine (which she refused to take), and had numerous mental health clinic contacts. During this time she became obsessed with Bill Boggs, the host of a local

television talk show, and tried to engage him in conversation when she visited the television station. Boggs reported that the conversations never made any sense to him. Brown thereafter adopted his name. Her sisters attempted more than once to commit her after trying to house her in their own homes or in apartments they found for her and partially paid for.

Five days after being picked up on Koch's orders, Brown appeared before a judge who ruled on whether she could be detained longer against her will. Brown was calm and articulate, explaining away much of her unusual behavior; for example, because the nearest public toilet was so far away, she would sometimes defecate in her pants. Four city psychiatrists testified that she was mentally ill, but she was declared sane by three psychiatrists hired by American Civil Liberties Union (ACLU) attorneys, who had taken a civil rights interest in Brown's case. When she testified on her own behalf, Brown was lucid, calm, and intelligent, which her attorneys claimed showed that she was not mentally ill but which the city psychiatrists claimed was irrelevant in that mentally ill people do not necessarily have mental retardation nor do they always appear disturbed.

Unable to obtain guidance from the diametrically opposed psychiatric testimonies of the city and the patient, the judge focused on Brown's in-court demeanor and determined that, even if she were mentally ill, she was neither malnourished, suicidal, nor dangerous to others. He declared further that, although living in the streets may be an "offense to aesthetic senses, freedom, constitutionally guaranteed, is the right of all, no less of those who are mentally ill ... beggars can be choosers" (*Time*, 1988, p. 29).

While the city contested the judge's ruling to release her, Brown was detained in Bellevue. On several appeals, the ACLU and other civil rights–minded people claimed that all the mayor was concerned about was cleaning up the streets so that rich constituents would not be confronted with destitute homeless people. Koch and others claimed that the city had a responsibility to help the helpless. The public debate was loud and bitter, Brown's lawyers calling Koch a demagogue and Koch calling them loonies. During her enforced stay at Bellevue, Brown cooperated not at all with any treatment program and refused all psychotropic medication.

In January 1988, Brown was released from Bellevue and became a cause célèbre in the ongoing efforts of advocates for homeless people to force city and state government to provide adequate housing and, for the mentally ill, appropriate outpatient mental health services. She appeared on several local New York talk programs and even on CBS's *60 Minutes*. Two weeks after a February 1988 appearance at the Harvard Law School Forum, where she was as big a hit as she had been on the television programs, she was back on the streets again, panhandling and swearing at African-Americans.

been placed in physical restraints on occasion to keep him from hurting himself and others. While maintaining that patients have a right to reasonable care and safety, this 1982 decision deferred to the professional judgment of the mental health professionals responsible for the boy: "courts must show deference to the judgment exercised by a qualified professional … the decision, if made by a professional, is presumptively valid" (pp. 322, 323). On the other hand, the 1990 *Thomas S.* v. *Flaherty* decision held that professional judgment is not the final word when it comes to constitutional protections of mentally retarded patients in public mental hospitals. The situation seems to be in flux.

In a celebrated case, *O'Connor* v. *Donaldson*,[37] which eventually found its way to the Supreme Court, a civilly committed mental patient sued two state hospital doctors for his release and for monetary damages, on the grounds that he had been incarcerated against his will for fourteen years without being treated and without being dangerous to himself or to others. In January 1957, at the age of forty-nine, Kenneth Donaldson was committed to the Florida state hospital at Chattahoochee on petition of his father, who felt that his son was delusional. At a brief court hearing a county judge found that Donaldson suffered from paranoid schizophrenia and committed him for "care, maintenance, and treatment." The Florida statute then in effect allowed for such commitment on the usual grounds of mental illness and dangerousness, the latter defined as inability to manage property and to protect oneself from being taken advantage of by others.

In 1971, Donaldson sued Dr. O'Connor, the hospital superintendent, and Dr. Gumanis, a hospital psychiatrist, for release. Evidence presented at the trial in a U.S. district court in Florida indicated that the hospital staff could have released Donaldson at any time following a determination that he was not a dangerous person. Testimony made it clear that at no time during his hospitalization had Donaldson's conduct posed any real danger to others or to himself. Furthermore, just before his commitment in 1957 he had been earning a living and taking adequate care of himself (and immediately on discharge he secured a job in hotel administration). Nonetheless, O'Connor had repeatedly refused the patient's requests for release, feeling it was his duty to determine whether a committed patient could adapt successfully outside the institution. His judgment was that Donaldson could not. In deciding the question of dangerousness on the basis of how well

Kenneth Donaldson, displaying a copy of the Supreme Court opinion stating that nondangerous mental patients cannot be confined against their will under civil commitment.

the patient could live outside the institution, O'Connor was applying a more restrictive standard than that required by most state laws.

Several responsible people had attempted to obtain Donaldson's release by guaranteeing that they would look after him. In 1963 a halfway house formally requested that Donaldson be released to its care, and between 1964 and 1968 a former college classmate made four separate attempts to have the patient released to his custody. O'Connor refused, saying that the patient could be released only to his parents, who by this time were quite old.

The evidence indicated that Donaldson received only custodial care during his hospitalization. No treatment that could conceivably alleviate or cure his assumed mental illness was undertaken. The milieu therapy that O'Connor claimed Donaldson was undergoing consisted of being kept in a large room with sixty other patients, many of whom were under criminal commitment. Donaldson had been denied privileges to stroll around the hospital grounds or even to discuss his case with Dr. O'Connor. O'Connor also regarded as delusional Donaldson's expressed desire to write a book about his hospital experiences (which Donaldson did after his release; the book sold well).

The original trial and a subsequent appeal concluded that Donaldson was not dangerous and had been denied his constitutional right to treatment, based on the Fifth Amendment. Throughout this litigation Donaldson declared that he was neither

---

[37]*O'Connor* v. *Donaldson*, 95 S.Ct. 2486 (1975).

dangerous nor mentally ill. *But*, went his claim, *even if* he were mentally ill, he should be released because he was not receiving treatment.

The Supreme Court ruled on June 26, 1975, that "a State cannot constitutionally confine … a non-dangerous individual who is capable of surviving safely in freedom by himself or with the help of willing and responsible family members or friends." In 1977 Donaldson settled for $20,000 from Dr. Gumanis and from the estate of Dr. O'Connor, who had died during the appeals process.

The Supreme Court decision on *O'Connor* v. *Donaldson* created a stir when it was issued and has since given mental health professionals pause in detaining patients. Although this decision is often cited as yet another affirmation of the right to treatment, the Supreme Court did not, in fact, rule on the constitutionality of this doctrine. Indeed, Chief Justice Warren E. Burger issued some warnings about the right to treatment.

Given the present state of medical knowledge regarding abnormal behavior and its treatment, few things would be more fraught with peril than [for] a State's power to protect the mentally ill [to depend on its ability to provide] such treatment as will give them a realistic opportunity to be cured. Nor can I accept the theory that a State may lawfully confine an individual thought to need treatment and justify that deprivation of liberty solely by providing such treatment. Our concepts of due process would not tolerate such a "trade off." (*O'Connor* v. *Donaldson*, pp. 588–589)

The *Donaldson* decision did say that a committed patient's status must be periodically reviewed, for the grounds on which a patient was committed cannot be assumed to continue in effect forever. In other words, people can change while in a mental hospital and may no longer require confinement. This position seems straightforward enough, yet it may still be overlooked. For example, a 1986 court decision involved a woman with mental retardation who had spent her entire adult life in a state institution for the retarded after having been committed at age fifteen; during her twenty years of confinement she was never given a hearing to reconsider the grounds for the original commitment.[38]

RIGHT TO REFUSE TREATMENT

If a committed patient has the right to expect appropriate treatment, since the need for help has resulted in loss of freedom, does he or she have the right to *refuse* treatment or a particular kind of treatment? The answer is yes, albeit with qualifications, for a right to obtain treatment does not oblige the patient

to *accept* treatment (Schwitzgebel & Schwitzgebel, 1980).

A state hospital may have adequate staff to provide up-to-date chemotherapy as well as group therapy but lack the professional resources to offer individual therapy. Suppose that a patient refuses the available modalities and insists on individual therapy. Would the patient later be able to sue the hospital for not offering the specific services requested? If the patient has the right to refuse certain forms of treatment, how far should the courts go in ensuring this right, remaining at the same time realistic about the state's ability to provide alternatives? When should the judgment of a professional override the wishes of a patient, especially one who is severely psychotic? Are the patient's best interests always served if he or she can veto the plans of those responsible for care (Stone, 1975; Winick, 1994), especially if refusing to take a therapeutic drug keeps a criminal defendant from being considered competent to stand trial (Winick, 1993) (recall the *Riggins* v. *Nevada* case discussed earlier, p. 602)? Does the right to refuse treatment mean that patients have the freedom to "rot with their rights on" (Appelbaum & Gutheil, 1980)?

The right of committed patients to refuse psychotropic drugs is hotly debated. Although somatic therapies such as electroconvulsive therapy and psychosurgery have for some time been subject to judicial review and control, only recently has close attention been paid to drugs used with patients in mental institutions. Significant legal and ethical issues surround the use of psychotropic medications; the side effects of most antipsychotic drugs are often aversive to the patient and sometimes harmful and irreversible in the long run, and the drugs do not truly address all of the patient's psychosocial problems (see the discussion of negative symptoms on p. 287). Moreover, antipsychotic drugs are often the only kind of treatment a patient in a state hospital receives with any regularity.

Some court decisions illustrate the thorny issues that arise when the right to refuse treatment is debated. In a 1979 decision on some cases in which "unjustified polypharmacy" and "force or intimidation" had allegedly been applied without due consideration for the serious negative side effects of drugs, the judge in a New Jersey federal district court concluded that drugs can actually inhibit recovery and that therefore, except in emergencies, even an involuntarily committed patient can refuse to take them, based on the rights of privacy (First Amendment) and due process (Fourteenth Amendment).[39] The judge

---

[38]*Clark* v. *Cohen*, 794 F.2d 79, *cert. denied*, 479 U.S. 962 (1986).

[39]*Rennie* v. *Klein*, Civil Action No. 77-2624, Federal District Court of New Jersey, 14 September 1979.

ordered that advocates be available in each state mental hospital to help patients exercise the right to refuse treatment and that a listing of all the side effects of the drugs that might be given to the patients be posted in each hospital ward. In a reconsideration of this case, however, the judge stated that the opinion of the health professional must take precedence over the right to refuse treatment when patients are a danger to themselves or to others, in other words, in emergency situations.[40]

The question of the right to refuse medication continues to be the subject of lawsuits on behalf of both involuntary and voluntary mental hospital patients. Decisions on behalf of patients judged incompetent are frequently made by the hospital's professional staff. Although there is inconsistency across jurisdictions and the forensic picture is still developing, there is a trend toward granting even involuntarily committed patients certain rights to refuse psychotropic medication, based on the constitutional protections of freedom from physical invasion, freedom of thought, and the right to privacy.[41] In an extension of the least restrictive treatment principle, *United States* v. *Charters* ruled that the government cannot force antipsychotic drugs on a person only on the supposition that at some future time he or she might become dangerous. Threat to the public safety has to be clear and imminent to justify the risks and restrictions that such medications pose, and it must be shown that less intrusive intervention will not likely reduce impending danger to others. In other words, forcible medication necessarily restricts liberty in addition to whatever physical risks it could bring; there has to be a very good reason to deprive even a committed mental patient of liberty and privacy via such intrusive measures.

The hands of mental health professionals are not tied, however. For example, it was ruled in a 1987 case that forcing a psychoactive drug on a former mental patient did not violate his constitutional rights because he had been threatening to assassinate the president of the United States, posed a threat to his own safety, and could be shown by clear and convincing evidence to be seriously mentally impaired.[42] Decisions of health professionals, though, are subject to judicial review.[43]

Opponents of the right to refuse treatment are concerned that mental hospitals will revert to being warehouses of poorly treated patients. Psychiatrists fear that lawyers and judges will not accept that some people are too mentally deranged to be believed, too mentally disturbed to be able to make sound judgments about their treatment. In a recent book on what he calls America's mental health crisis, psychiatrist E. Fuller Torrey asserts that upwards of 90 percent of psychotic patients have no insight into their condition. Believing that they do not need any treatment, they subject themselves and their loved ones to sometimes desperate and frightening situations by refusing medication or other modes of therapy, most of which involve hospitalization (Torrey, 1996). When someone already hospitalized is believed to be too psychotic to give informed consent about a treatment, mental health law sometimes invokes the doctrine of *substituted judgment*, the decision that the patient *would have made* if he or she had been able or competent to make a decision.[44] This principle creates as many problems as it solves. Deciding when a patient is competent to refuse treatment is one of the most controversial topics in the mental health law literature (e.g., Appelbaum & Grisso, 1995; Grisso & Appelbaum, 1995; Winick, 1997).

LAW, FREE WILL, AND ETHICS

Mental health law construes voluntariness somewhat differently from the way many social scientists do. Social scientists operate within paradigms that tend to assign less importance to the concept of free will than does the law, which rests utterly on that idea (Morse, 1992). As psychologists familiar with actual practices in mental hospitals, we are sensitive to the subtle coercion that can operate on hospitalized patients, even those who entered voluntarily. A hospital patient is subject to strong persuasion and pressure to accept the treatment recommendations of professional staff. Although one could argue that this is as it should be, the fact remains that even a "voluntary" and informed decision to take psychotropic medication or to participate in any other therapy regimen is often (maybe usually) less than free. The issue thus is more complicated and thorny than mental health law usually considers it to be— and the arguments of the legal profession do not lack for complexity and thorniness!

We are dealing ultimately with an ethical issue that is sometimes obscured by legal argumentation.

The most important force behind the notion of a patient's right to reject therapy is the recognition that the weighing of risks and benefits inherent in a decision to

---

[40]*Rennie* v. *Klein*, 720 F.2d 266 (3d Cir. 1983).

[41]*United States* v. *Charters*, 829 F.2d 479 (1987); *United States* v. *Watson*, 893 F.2d 970 (1990).

[42]*Dautremont* v. *Broadlawns Hospital*.

[43]*United States* v. *Charters*, 863 F.2d 302, *cert. denied*, 494 U.S. 1016 (1990).

[44]*Guardianship of Weedon*, 565 N.E. 2d 432, 409 Mass. 196 (1991).

undergo or to defer treatment is value-laden. Personal preferences play a role in determining which risks are unacceptable and which benefits are desirable. For instance, the doctor's decision to treat an objecting patient with psychotropic drugs is a value judgment; it reflects the physician's view that freedom from psychosis outweighs the costs of overriding the patient's wishes and of exposing him or her to side effects. This means, at a minimum, that a physician and patient may not always agree on what constitutes the "best" therapy. ... [Furthermore, the argument that the psychiatrist is acting only in the patient's best interests] assumes a general entitlement to intervene in another's best interest. Society, however, does not generally overrule an individual's decisions merely because they are not objectively self-regarding, to say nothing of not being in his or her best interest. People are permitted to engage in all sorts of dangerous activities, from hang-gliding to cigarette smoking. (Clayton, 1988, pp. 19–20)

Related questions of freedom of choice are discussed in Focus 20.5 (p.624).

RIGHTS TO TREATMENT, TO REFUSE TREATMENT, AND TO BE TREATED IN THE LEAST RESTRICTIVE SETTING—CAN THEY BE RECONCILED?

We have reviewed several legal principles developed over the years that guide the courts and mental health professionals in meeting their constitutional obligations to civilly committed mental patients. Actions taken to implement one principle may conflict with another, however. The basic question is whether the right to be treated in the least restrictive fashion can be reconciled with both the right to treatment and the right to refuse treatment. A creative proposal was put forth in the 1970s by Paul and Lentz (1977) in their report on social-learning and milieu therapies at a mental health center (see p. 522). They argued that under certain conditions a committed mental patient can and should be coerced into a particular therapy program, even if the patient states that he or she does not wish to participate, and that these conditions do not, as *Rennie* v. *Klein* requires, have to be emergencies.

Paul and Lentz proposed that some hospital treatments have minimal and others optimal goals, and that institutions should have the right and the duty to do whatever is reasonable to move patients toward minimal goals. Achievement of minimal goals—self-care, such as getting up in the morning, bathing, eating meals, and the like; communication with others on the most basic level; and the absence of violence—will allow patients to move into a less restrictive residence. The elimination of symptomatic behavior would also be regarded as a minimal goal if the local community required patients to conform, at least to some extent, to community standards.[45] Paul and Lentz argued further that if empirical evidence indicates that particular treatments do achieve minimal goals—as the social-learning program did in their study—patients might justifiably be forced to participate in them, even if they or their legal guardians do not give consent voluntarily. Protection of their interests would be the responsibility of an institutional review board, a group of professionals and laypeople who would review all therapy and research activities for a given hospital. The board would decide *for* patients which therapy is likely to achieve minimal goals that would allow them to leave the hospital.

If it is determined that the patient is operating above minimal levels, he or she should have the right to refuse treatments that have optimal goals, such as acquiring vocational skills, obtaining a high school diploma, and other luxury items that can enhance the quality of a patient's life. According to Paul and Lentz, these goals are not considered so vital that the patient should be forced into working toward them.

DEINSTITUTIONALIZATION, CIVIL LIBERTIES, AND MENTAL HEALTH

The cumulative impact of court rulings such as *Wyatt* v. *Stickney* and *O'Connor* v. *Donaldson* was to put mental health professionals on notice that they must be more careful about keeping people in mental hospitals against their will and that they must attend more to the specific treatment needs of committed patients. Pressure was placed on state governments to upgrade the quality of care in mental institutions. In view of the abuses that have been documented in hospital care, these are surely encouraging trends. But the picture is not all that rosy. For judges to declare that patient care must meet certain minimal standards does not automatically translate into that praiseworthy goal. Money is not in unlimited supply, and the care of mentally ill individuals has not been one of government's high priorities since the 1960s, nor has support of research in the social and behavioral sciences—an important consideration, given how much more needs to be learned about the nature of psychopathology, its prevention, and its treatment.

Since the 1960s, many states have embarked on a policy of deinstitutionalization, discharging as

---

[45]Many therapists are accused of forcing patients to conform to community standards that are themselves open to question. The basic issue here is not whether mentally ill patients wear clean pants with a belt to hold them up, but whether they wear pants at all.

many patients as possible from mental hospitals and discouraging admissions. Civil commitment is more difficult to achieve now than it was in the fifties and sixties, and committed patients are able, with the help of civil rights–minded lawyers, to refuse much of the treatment made available to them in the hospital. The population of state mental hospitals peaked in the 1950s at almost half a million patients; by the mid-1990s the population had dropped to around 100,000. The maxim is now "Treat them in the community," the assumption being that virtually anything is preferable to institutionalization.

But what is this community that former mental hospital patients are supposed to find more helpful to them on discharge? Facilities outside hospitals are not prepared to cope with the influx of these patients. Some promising programs were described in Chapter 19, but these are very much the exception, not the rule. The state of affairs in many large metropolitan areas is an unrelenting social crisis, for hundreds of thousands of chronically ill mental patients have been released without sufficient job training and without community services to help them. It is doubtful, too, that deinstitutionalization has reduced the rate of chronic mental illness. As Gralnick (1987) argued, acutely ill persons are largely neglected because it is difficult to commit them unless they are found to be a danger to themselves and others, a condition that can take years to develop; by that time the problems may have become chronic and more difficult to deal with. The irony is that deinstitutionalization may be contributing to the very problem it was designed to alleviate, chronic mental illness.

Indeed, *de*institutionalization may be a misnomer. *Trans*institutionalization may be more apt, for declines in the census of public mental hospitals have occasioned *increases* in the presence of mentally ill people in prisons, nursing homes, and the mental health departments of nonpsychiatric hospitals (Kiesler, 1991), and these settings are by and large not equipped to handle the particular needs of mental patients. The oft-mentioned revolving door is seen in the increase in readmission rates from 25 percent before the deinstitutionalization movement to around 80 percent by the 1980s (Paul & Menditto, 1992).

Many patients discharged from mental hospitals are eligible for benefits from the Veterans Administration and for Social Security Disability Insurance, but a large number are not receiving these benefits. Homeless persons do not have fixed addresses and need assistance in establishing eligibility and residency for the purpose of receiving benefits. A study by the Community Service Society (Baxter & Hopper, 1981), an old and respected social agency in New York City, found people who had been discharged from psychiatric hospitals living in the streets, in train and bus terminals, in abandoned buildings, on subways, in cavernous steam tunnels running north from Grand Central Station, and in shelters operated by public agencies, churches, and charitable organizations. The lives of these people are desperate, and although this report was made in 1981, the situation has not changed.

[In a train station at 11:00 P.M.] … the attendant goes off duty and women rise from separate niches and head for the bathroom. There they disrobe, and wash their clothes and bodies. Depending on the length of [the] line at the hand dryers, they wait to dry their clothes, put them in their bags or wear them wet. One woman cleans and wraps her ulcerated legs with paper towels every night. The most assertive claim toilet cubicles, line them with newspapers for privacy and warmth and sleep curled around the basin. Once they are taken, the rest sleep along the walls, one on a box directly beneath the hand dryer which she pushes for warm air. One of the women regularly cleans up the floors, sinks and toilets so that no traces of their uncustomary use remain. (Baxter & Hopper, 1981, p. 77)

No one knows how many homeless individuals are deinstitutionalized mental hospital patients. Those who are not homeless live marginal and unhealthful lives in nursing homes, jails, and rundown hotels. Although a visible part of the population, their visibility may be diminishing as many other people have been dispossessed from their homes and have lost their jobs. The state of homelessness undoubtedly exacerbates the emotional suffering of former mental patients. Whatever their numbers, mentally ill persons remain an especially defenseless segment of the homeless population.

The relationships between homelessness and mental health were enumerated and analyzed by a committee of the National Academy of Sciences (NAS; Committee on Health Care for Homeless People, 1988, as summarized in Leeper, 1988). It was estimated that 25 to 40 percent of the homeless population were alcoholics; similar proportions had some form of serious mental illness, usually schizophrenia. Such problems were probably aggravated by their nomadic and dangerous existence; homeless people, especially women, are likely victims of violence and rape, even when living in shelters for the homeless (D'Ercole & Struening, 1990). Children are also found among the homeless population, a fact the committee termed "a national disgrace"; these youngsters are forced to live their formative years in chaotic and dangerous situations, with parents under severe stress. One committee member noted in an interview that "many children have developmental delays. I've seen two-year-olds who can't walk, six-month-olds who don't cuddle in your arms, and four-year-olds acting like mothers to one-year-olds because their mother isn't giving them the care they need" (Leeper, 1988, p. 8). That these children often drop out of school and suffer from anxiety, depression, and substance abuse and are subject to physical and sexual abuse should come as no surprise.

Do such appalling facts, which hold in the late 1990s, justify reversing the policy of deinstitutionalization? The NAS committee thought not, because in its view the problem lies with the failure of communities to provide suitable living and rehabilitation conditions, a theme sounded earlier in this book.

[The] vulnerability [of former patients]…became clear in January 1982, when a sixty-one-year-old former psychiatric patient was found dead in a cardboard box on a New York City street. She had been living in the box for eight months after her entitlements were revoked for failure to appear for recertification. She had refused the efforts of various agencies to relocate her, and she died of hypothermia hours before a court order was obtained directing her removal to a hospital.

This case led to the creation of Project HELP, the Homeless Emergency Liaison Project, which is a mobile, psychiatric outreach team that identifies homeless people in need of psychiatric aid, and has authority under State and local laws to involuntarily remove homeless people in danger to themselves to a hospital for help and evaluation. *(Committee on Government Operations, 1985, p. 5)*[46]

Fears have been expressed that schizophrenic individuals are increasingly being seen as misfits, drug abusers, and panhandlers rather than as ill people in need of professional care (Gralnick, 1986). They end up more often in jails, shelters, and church basements than in mental wards. A large-scale field study (Teplin, 1984) found that police officers were 20 percent more likely to arrest people if they were showing signs of mental disorder than if they were (merely) committing offenses for which arrest was an option. Furthermore, any treatment

made available to these individuals is likely to be biological and drug based because such treatment is cheaper and more straightforward and does not require the close interpersonal relationship that is intrinsic to any psychotherapy (Gralnick, 1986). Biological factors are emphasized *to the exclusion of* psychological factors.[47] This focus threatens to interfere with achieving full understanding of serious mental illness, which most workers in the field view as a complex interaction between biological diatheses and environmental stressors. Gralnick recommends that the psychiatric hospital be restored to its previous position as the place of choice to treat and research schizophrenia and that research be more vigorously pursued in aftercare for patients who are discharged.

ETHICAL DILEMMAS IN THERAPY AND RESEARCH

In this textbook we have examined a variety of theories and a multitude of data focusing on *what is* and *what is thought to be*. Ethics and values, often embodied in our laws, are a different order of discussion. They concern *what ought to be*, having sometimes little to do with *what is*. It is extremely important to recognize the difference. Within a given scientific paradigm we are able to examine what we believe is reality. As the study of philosophy and ethics reveals, however, the statements that people have made for thousands of years about what *should* be are another matter. The Ten Commandments are such statements. They are prescriptions and proscriptions about human conduct. For example, the Eighth Commandment, Thou shalt not steal, in no way describes human conduct, for stealing is not uncommon. It is, instead, a pronouncement of an ideal to which people should aspire. The integrity of an ethical code that proscribes stealing does not depend on any evidence concerning the percentage of people who steal. Morals and data are two separate realms of discourse.

The legal trends reviewed thus far in this chapter place limits on the activities of mental health professionals. These legal constraints are important, for

---

[46]There are signs that the pendulum may begin to swing back in the direction of more involuntary hospitalization, even when the person does not pose a real danger to self or to others, but is "only" wandering homeless on the streets and living in squalor. Being "persistently and acutely disabled" is, in some jurisdictions, replacing being a danger to oneself or to others (Shogren, 1994). It remains to be seen how this trend will develop in the light of laws and court rulings that have been making it more and more difficult to keep people institutionalized against their will.

[47]Gralnick is not arguing that major advances are not being made in biological approaches to diagnosis, etiology, and treatment—one would have to be out of contact with reality to believe this. Rather, he is concerned that scientific advances will be *coupled to* a distancing from the personal plight of people with schizophrenia and lead to a scientifically unjustified and socially questionable neglect of their sad living situation in the era of what he and others regard as misguided deinstitutionalization.

laws are one of society's strongest means of encouraging all of us to behave in certain ways. Psychologists and psychiatrists also have professional and ethical constraints. All professional groups promulgate shoulds and should nots, and by guidelines and mandates they limit to some degree what therapists and researchers should do with their patients, clients, and subjects. Courts as well have ruled on some of these questions. Most of the time what we believe is unethical is also illegal, but sometimes existing laws are in conflict with our moral sense of right and wrong. We examine now the ethics of making psychological inquiries and interventions into the lives of other human beings.

ETHICAL RESTRAINTS ON RESEARCH

Basic to the nature of science is that what can be done will be attempted. The most reprehensible ethical insensitivity was evidenced in the brutal experiments conducted by German physicians on concentration camp prisoners during World War II. One experiment, for example, investigated how long people lived when their heads were bashed repeatedly with a heavy stick. Even if important information might be obtained from this kind of experiment (which seems extremely doubtful), such actions violate our sense of decency and morality. The Nuremberg trials, conducted by the Allies following the war, brought these and other barbarisms to light and meted out severe punishment to some of the soldiers, physicians, and Nazi officials who had engaged in or contributed to such actions, even when they claimed that they had merely been following orders.

It would be reassuring to be able to say that such gross violations of human decency take place only during incredible and cruel epochs such as the Third Reich, but unfortunately this is not the case. Spurred on by a blind enthusiasm for their work, researchers in the United States and other countries have sometimes dealt with human subjects in reproachable ways.[48]

Henry K. Beecher, a research professor at Harvard Medical School, surveyed medical research since 1945 and found that "many of the patients [used as subjects in experiments] never had the risk satisfactorily explained to them, and ... further hundreds

have not known that they were the subjects of an experiment although grave consequences have been suffered as the direct result" (1966, p. 1354). One experiment compared penicillin with a placebo as a treatment to prevent rheumatic fever. Even though penicillin had already been acknowledged as the drug of choice to give people with a streptococcal respiratory infection in order to protect them from later contracting rheumatic fever, placebos were administered to 109 service personnel without their knowledge or permission. More subjects received penicillin than received the placebo, but three members of the control group contracted serious illnesses—two had rheumatic fever and one acute nephritis, a kidney disease. None of those who had received penicillin contracted such illnesses.

Half a century later, in January 1994, spurred on by Eileen Welsome, a journalist who won a Pulitzer Prize for her investigative reporting on the issue, the United States Energy Department began to publicize numerous experiments conducted in the 1950s through the 1970s that had exposed hundreds of subjects—usually without their informed consent or prior knowledge—to harmful doses of radiation. Particular concern was expressed because the overwhelming majority of participants were people of low socioeconomic status, members of racial minorities, people with mental retardation, nursing home patients, or prisoners. That the scientists, for the most part supported in their research with federal funds, understood the risks were great even though relatively little was known about the harmful effects of radiation at the time, is reflected in the fact that "they were doing it to poor and black people. You didn't see them doing it at the Mayo Clinic" (lawyer arguing for compensation for some of the subjects, as quoted in Healy, 1994). Some of these experiments involved giving women in the third trimester of pregnancy a radioactive tonic to determine safe levels of exposure and irradiating the testicles of prisoners to find out the degree of radiation that service personnel could endure without negative effects on sperm production. That these experiments took place many years after the Nuremberg Trials is particularly troubling.

The training of scientists equips them splendidly to pose interesting questions, sometimes even important ones, and to design research that is as free as possible of confounds. They have no special qualifications, however, for deciding whether a particular line of inquiry that involves humankind *should* be followed. Society needs knowledge, and a scientist has a right in a democracy to seek that knowledge. However, the ordinary citizens employed as participants in experiments must be

---

[48]Scientists who conduct research on animals have also sometimes dealt with their subjects in gratuitously harsh fashion. The American Psychological Association has guidelines for handling laboratory animals that are intended to minimize their discomfort and danger. Strict standards have also been promulgated by the National Institutes of Health.

protected from unnecessary harm, risk, humiliation, and invasion of privacy.[49]

Several international codes of ethics pertain to the conduct of scientific research—the Nuremberg Code formulated in the aftermath of the Nazi war-crime trials, the Declaration of Helsinki, and statements from the British Medical Research Council. In the early 1970s the U.S. Department of Health, Education, and Welfare began to issue guidelines and regulations governing scientific research that employs human subjects. In addition, a blue-ribbon panel, the National Commission for the Protection of Human Subjects of Biomedical and Behavioral Research, conducted hearings and inquiries into restrictions that the federal government might impose on research performed with patients in psychiatric institutions, prisoners, and children. For several years the proposals of behavioral researchers, many of whom conduct experiments related to psychopathology and therapy, have been reviewed for safety and general ethical propriety by institutional review boards in hospitals, universities, and research institutes. Such committees—and this is very significant—comprise not only behavioral scientists, but also citizens from the community, lawyers, students, and specialists in a variety of disciplines, such as professors of English, history, and comparative religion. They are able to block any research proposal or require questionable aspects to be modified if in their collective judgment the research will put participants at too great a risk. It has recently been suggested that such committees also pass judgment on the scientific merits of proposals, the rationale being that it is not ethical to recruit participants for studies that will not yield valid data (Rosenthal, 1995).

INFORMED CONSENT

Participation in research brings up the all-important concept of **informed consent**. Just as committed mental patients are gaining some right to refuse treatment, so may anyone refuse to be a participant in an experiment. The investigator must provide enough information to enable people to judge whether they want to accept any risks inherent in being a participant. Prospective participants must be legally capable of giving consent, and there must be no deceit or coercion in obtaining it. For example, an experimental psychologist might wish to determine whether imagery helps college students associate one word with another. One group of students will be asked to associate pairs of words in

their minds by generating a fanciful image connecting the two, such as a cat riding on a bicycle. If a prospective participant decides that the experiment is likely to be boring, that person may decline to participate; in fact, anyone may withdraw from the experiment at any time without fear of penalty.

Paired-associates research such as that just described is relatively innocuous, but what if the experiment poses real risks, such as ingesting a drug? Or what if the prospective participant is a committed mental patient, or a child with mental retardation, unable to understand fully what is being asked? Such a person may not feel free or even be able to refuse participation. And what of the rights of the researcher, which often are not as carefully considered as those of participants, and of the cost to society of important research left undone? Will scientists become reluctant to undertake certain types of work because review committees make the process of obtaining informed consent unduly onerous?

A further complication is that it is not easy to demonstrate that a researcher has obtained informed consent. Epstein and Lasagna (1969) found that only one-third of those volunteering for an experiment really understood what the experiment entailed. In a more elaborate study, Stuart (1978) discovered that most college students could not accurately describe a simple experiment, even though it had just been explained to them and they had agreed to participate. A signature on a consent form is no assurance that informed consent has been obtained, which poses a challenge to investigators and members of review panels who are committed to upholding codes of ethics governing participation of human subjects in research. Similar problems have been found in clinical settings, where there is a question of whether patients understand the nature of antipsychotic medication. Irwin et al. (1985) found that although most patients *said* they understood the benefits and side effects of their drugs, only a quarter of them could actually demonstrate such understanding when queried specifically. The authors concluded that simply reading information to hospitalized patients—especially the more disturbed ones—is no guarantee that they fully comprehend; therefore, *informed* consent cannot be said to have been obtained.

In general, as with the right to refuse treatment, there is increasing recognition that being judged mentally ill—more specifically, being diagnosed with schizophrenia and being hospitalized—does not necessarily mean that the person is not capable of giving informed consent (Appelbaum & Gutheil, 1991; Grisso, 1986). An experiment by Grisso and

---

[49]This very statement is an ethical, not an empirical, one.

Applebaum (1991) found that, although schizophrenic patients on average understood issues relating to treatment involving medication less well than did nonpsychiatric patients, there was a wide *range* of understanding among the schizophrenic patients; some showed as good understanding as that of nonpsychiatric patients. These results pointed to the importance of examining each person individually for ability to give informed consent, rather than assuming that a person is unable to do so by virtue of being hospitalized for schizophrenia. Before a mental patient can give informed consent in New York state hospitals, for example, a licensed psychologist or psychiatrist must certify that the person is capable of doing so. Thus, although professional judgment is required, and may therefore be erroneous, there is the real possibility that being judged mentally ill will not *ipso facto* deny a patient the ability to give informed consent.

CONFIDENTIALITY AND PRIVILEGED COMMUNICATION

When an individual consults a physician, psychiatrist, or clinical psychologist, he or she is assured by professional ethics codes that what goes on in the session will remain confidential; **confidentiality** means that nothing will be revealed to a third party, except only to other professionals and those intimately involved in the treatment, such as a nurse or medical secretary.

A **privileged communication** goes even further. It is communication between parties in a confidential relationship that is protected by law. The recipient of such a communication cannot legally be compelled to disclose it as a witness. The right of privileged communication is a major exception to the access that courts have to evidence in judicial proceedings. Society believes that in the long term the interests of people are best served if communications to a spouse and to certain professionals remain off limits to the prying eyes and ears of the police, judges, and prosecutors. The privilege applies to such relationships as husband–wife, physician–patient, pastor–penitent, attorney–client, and psychologist–patient. The legal expression is that the patient or client "holds the privilege," which means that only he or she may release the other person to disclose confidential information in a legal proceeding.

There are important limits to a client's right of privileged communication, however. For example, according to the current California psychology licensing law (similar elements are present in other state laws), this right is eliminated for any of the following reasons.

- If the client has accused the therapist of malpractice; the therapist, in other words, can divulge information about the therapy in order to defend himself or herself in any legal action initiated by the client.

- If the client is under sixteen years old and the therapist has reason to believe that the child has been a victim of a crime such as child abuse. In fact, the psychologist is *required* to report to the police or to a child welfare agency within thirty-six hours any suspicion he or she has that the child client has been physically abused, including any suspicion of sexual molestation.

- If the client initiated therapy in hopes of evading the law for having committed a crime or for planning to do so.

- If the therapist judges that the client is a danger to self or to others and if disclosure of information is necessary to ward off such danger (recall Focus 20.3).

WHO IS THE CLIENT OR PATIENT?

Is it always clear to the clinician who the client is? In private therapy, when an adult pays a clinician a fee for help with a personal problem that has nothing to do with the legal system, the consulting individual is clearly the client. But an individual may be seen by a clinician for an evaluation of his or her competency to stand trial, or the clinician may be hired by an individual's family to assist in civil commitment proceedings. Perhaps the clinician is employed by a state mental hospital as a regular staff member and sees a particular patient about problems in controlling aggressive impulses. It should be clear, although it seldom *is* clear, that in these instances the clinician is serving more than one client. In addition to the patient, he or she serves the family or the state, and it is incumbent on the mental health professional to inform the patient that this is so. This dual allegiance does not necessarily indicate that the patient's own interests will be sacrificed, but it does mean that discussions will not inevitably remain secret and that the clinician may in the future act in a way that displeases the individual.

CHOICE OF GOALS

Ideally the client sets the goals for therapy, but in practice it is naive to assume that some are not imposed by the therapist and may even go against the wishes of the client. For example, a school sys-

Which environment best fosters learning: typical classroom (left) or "open" classroom (right)?

tem may want to institute a program that will teach children to "be still, be quiet, be docile" (Winett & Winkler, 1972, p. 499). Many behavior therapists have assumed that young children *should* be compliant, not only because the teacher can then run a more orderly class but because children are assumed to learn better when they are so. But do we really know that the most efficient and most enjoyable learning takes place when children are forced to remain quietly in their seats? Some advocates of open classrooms believe that curiosity and initiative, even in the youngest elementary schoolchild, are at least as important as the acquisition of academic skills. As is generally the case in psychology, evidence is less plentiful than are strongly held and vehemently defended opinions. But it is clear that any professionals consulted by a school system have to be mindful of their own personal biases with respect to goals and should be prepared to work toward different ones if the parents and school personnel so wish. Any therapist has the option of not working for a client whose goals and proposed means of attaining them are abhorrent in his or her view.

This question of goals is particularly complex in family and couples therapy (Margolin, 1982). If several people are clients simultaneously—inevitable in family treatment—an intervention that benefits one or more individuals may well work to the disadvantage of one or more others. This can happen if one partner in couples therapy really wants to end the relationship, but the other sees the therapy as a way to save it. Because people often do not openly express their real concerns and wishes at the very

beginning of therapy, the therapist can already be deeply enmeshed in their lives before learning that the two partners have conflicting goals (Gurman & Kniskern, 1981).

Although the plight of people who voluntarily consult therapists is in no way as confining as that of institutionalized patients, there are constraints on their freedom. This issue was addressed by Seymour Halleck (1971), a psychiatrist, who asserts that the neutrality of the therapist is a myth. In his opinion therapists influence their clients in ways that are subtle yet powerful.

At first glance, a model of psychiatric [or psychological] practice based on the contention that people should just be helped to learn to do the things they want to do seems uncomplicated and desirable. But it is an unobtainable model. Unlike a technician, a psychiatrist [or psychologist] cannot avoid communicating and at times imposing his own values upon his patients. The patient usually has considerable difficulty in finding the way in which he would wish to change his behavior, but as he talks to the psychiatrist his wants and needs become clearer. In the very process of defining his needs in the presence of a figure who is viewed as wise and authoritarian, the patient is profoundly influenced. He ends up wanting some of the things the psychiatrist thinks he should want. (p. 19)

Research supports the contention that clients are indeed influenced by the values of their therapists (e.g., Rosenthal, 1955). A person not only seeks out a therapist who suits his or her taste and meets what the person believes are his or her needs but also adopts some of the ideals, sometimes even the mannerisms, of the therapist. Most therapists are keenly aware of this modeling after themselves, which increases the already heavy responsibilities of their professional role. Perry London (1964, 1985), a leading writer on the ethics of therapeutic intervention, suggested that therapists are contemporary society's secular priests, purveyors of values and ethics to help clients live "the good life" (see Focus 20.5).

CHOICE OF TECHNIQUES

The end does not justify the means. This canon is said to be intrinsic to a free society. For years questions concerning behavioral techniques have been debated among professionals and have been the subject of court rulings. Perhaps because the various insight therapies deemphasize direct efforts to change behavior, they have seldom been scrutinized as has behavior therapy. The very concreteness, specificity, and directiveness of behavioral techniques have called attention to them, as has their alignment with experimental psychology. It is offensive to some to believe that our understanding of human beings could possibly be advanced by employing rats and pigeons as analogues to humans.

Particular concern has been expressed about the ethics of inflicting pain for purposes of therapy. For some people the term *behavior therapy* conjures up an image of the violent protagonist in Kubrick's classic film *Clockwork Orange*, eyes propped open with a torturous apparatus, being made nauseous by a drug while scenes of violence flash on a screen. Aversion therapy programs never reach this level of coercion and drama, but certainly any such procedure entails making the patient uncomfortable, sometimes extremely so. Making patients vomit or cringe with pain from electric shock applied to the extremities are two aversion techniques worthy of their name. Can there be any circumstances that justify therapists' inflicting pain on clients?

Before quickly exclaiming, "No!" consider the following report.

The patient was a nine-month-old baby who had already been hospitalized three times for treatment of vomiting and chronic rumination (regurgitating food and rechewing it in the mouth). A number of diagnostic tests, including an EEG, plus surgery to remove a cyst on the right kidney, had revealed no biological basis for the problems, and several treatments, including a special diet, had been attempted without success. When referred to Lang and Melamed (1969), two behavior therapists, the child was in critical condition and was being fed by tubes leading from the nose directly into the stomach. The attending physician had stated that the infant's life was in imminent danger if the vomiting could not be halted.

Treatment consisted of delivering a series of one-second-long electric shocks to the infant's calf each time he showed signs of beginning to vomit. Sessions followed feeding and lasted under an hour. After just two sessions, shock was rarely required, for the infant learned quickly to stop vomiting in order to avoid the shock. By the sixth session he was able to fall asleep after eating. Nurses reported that the in-session inhibition of vomiting generalized as the infant progressively reduced his vomiting during the rest of the day and night. About two weeks later the mother began to assume some care of the hospitalized child, and shortly thereafter the patient was discharged with virtually complete elimination of the life-threatening pattern of behavior. Throughout the three weeks of treatment and observation, the child gained weight steadily. One month after discharge the child weighed twenty-one pounds and was rated as fully recovered by the attending physician. Five months later he weighed twenty-six pounds and was regarded as completely normal, both physically and psychologically.

The use of aversion therapy has been subject to an understandably high degree of regulation. An additional reason for administrative and judicial concern is that aversion techniques smack more of research than of standard therapy. The more established a therapeutic procedure, whether medical or psychological, the less likely it is to attract the attention of the courts or other governmental agencies. Paul and Lentz (1977) had a few very assaultive patients. Their account of administrative problems demonstrates that patients might be subject to more extreme procedures because of restrictions placed on the use of new techniques.

Some consideration was given to the contingent use of mild electric shock. ... However, early in the explorations of the necessary safeguards and review procedures to be followed before evaluating such methods, the department director telephoned to explain that aversion conditioning was a politically sensitive issue. Therefore, more than the usual proposal, preparation, documentation, and committee reviews would be required—to the extent that approval would probably take about eighteen months. Instead, it was suggested that convulsive shock ... be employed since "ECT is an accepted medical treatment." With those alternatives, our choice was to abandon either use of shock. (p. 499)

Mindful that short-term application of electric shock can sometimes keep children with mental retardation or autism from their self-destructive acts, Martin (1975) proposed that

the test should be that aversive therapy might be used where other therapy has not worked, where it can be

Focus 20.5   Not Can but Ought: An Opinion on the Treatment of Homosexuality

Several psychologists have argued that the social pressures on homosexual individuals to become heterosexual make it difficult to believe that the small minority of people who consult therapists for help in changing from same-sex to opposite-sex partners act with free choice (Begelman, 1975; Davison, 1974, 1976, 1991; Silverstein, 1972). Although most states have dropped their sodomy laws, which used to be enforced selectively against homosexual acts, some legal pressure against homosexuality remains. A 1986 U.S. Supreme Court decision*, still valid, refused to find constitutional protection in the right to privacy for consensual adult homosexual activity and thereby upheld a Georgia law that prohibits oral–genital and anal–genital acts, even in private and between consenting adults. Studies indicate the existence of considerable pressure on gay men and women to change their sexual orientation: 90 percent of lesbian women and gay men report having been the objects of threats or other verbal abuse and more than 30 percent have suffered physical violence because of their homosexuality (Adams et al., 1996; Fassinger, 1991).

It has further been suggested that the mere availability of change-of-orientation programs serves to condone the prejudice against homosexuality. Clinicians develop procedures and study their effects only if they are concerned about the problem that their techniques address. The therapy literature contains much less material on helping homosexual persons develop as individuals without changing their sexual orientation than on how best to discourage homosexual behavior and substitute for it heterosexual patterns. Aversion therapy used to be the most widely used behavioral technique (Davison & Wilson, 1973; Henkel & Lewis-Thomé, 1976). "What are we really saying to our clients when, on the one hand, we assure them that they are not abnormal and on the other hand, present them with an array of techniques, some of them painful, which are aimed at eliminating that set of feelings and behavior that we have just told them is okay?" (Davison, 1976, p. 161).

For these reasons it has been proposed that therapists not help homosexual clients to become heterosexual even when such treatment is requested. This radical proposal, held by a small minority of clinicians, has evoked some strong reactions. Gay-activist groups consider this suggestion concrete support for the belief that homosexuality per se is not a mental disorder. But many psychologists and psychiatrists are concerned about limiting the choices available to people seeking therapy. Why should a therapist decide for potential clients what options should be available? Is it not the responsibility of therapists to satisfy the needs expressed by their clients (Sturgis & Adams, 1978)? A reply to this important criticism would be that therapists decide what therapy will be available when they refuse to take as clients people with whose goals they disagree. The request of a patient for a certain kind of treatment has never been sufficient justification for providing that treat-

ment (see Davison, 1978). Therapists do not operate from a position of ethical neutrality (London, 1964).

It has been asserted that continued research will help develop sexual-reorientation programs that are more effective than those already available (Sturgis & Adams, 1978), and that to discourage such work would deprive today's homosexual clients of promising therapies and tomorrow's homosexual clients of improved treatments. However, the fact that we *can* do something does not mean that we *should* do it. The proposal to deny sexual-reorientation therapy is philosophical and ethical in nature, not empirical. The decision whether to change sexual orientation will have to be made on moral grounds.

Will numbers of people be hurt by eliminating the option of sexual-reorientation? Some have raised the specter of an upsurge in suicides among homosexual clients if therapists refuse to help them switch. These are very serious concerns, but they overlook the possibility, some would say the fact, that far greater numbers of people have been hurt over the years by the availability of sexual-reorientation programs. As suggested earlier, the existence of these treatments is consistent with societal prejudices and discrimination against homosexuals.

It is noteworthy that since 1975 there has been a dramatic reduction in the use of aversion therapy for changing homosexual orientation to heterosexual (Rosen & Beck, 1988) and a sharp decrease also in reports of other procedures for altering homosexuality (Campos & Hathaway, 1993). Other signs of increased acceptance of homosexuality as a lifestyle are the elimination of ego-dystonic homosexuality from the DSM and the establishment within the American Psychological Association of the Division of Lesbian and Gay Psychologists and the Committee on Lesbian and Gay Concerns on the Board of Social and Ethical Responsibility.

The proponents who wish to terminate change-of-orientation programs believe that much good can come of their proposal. Homosexual individuals would be helped to think better of themselves, and greater attention could be directed to the problems they have rather than to the issue of homosexuality.

It would be nice if an alcoholic homosexual, for example, could be helped to reduce his or her drinking without having his or her sexual orientation questioned. It would be nice if a homosexual fearful of interpersonal relationships, or incompetent in them, could be helped without the therapist assuming that homosexuality lies at the root of the problem. It would be nice if a nonorgasmic or impotent homosexual could be helped as a heterosexual would be rather than [being guided] to change-of-orientation regimens ... the hope [is] that therapists will concentrate their efforts on such human problems rather than focusing on the most obvious "maladjustment"—loving members of one's own sex. (Davison, 1978, p. 171)

---

*Bowers v. Hardwick, 106 S.Ct. 2841 (1986).

administered to save the individual from immediate and continuing self-injury, when it allows freedom from physical restraints which would otherwise be continued, when it can be administered for only a few short instances and when its goal is to make other nonaversive therapy possible. Such an aversive program certainly requires consent from a guardian and immediate review of the results of each separate administration. (p. 77)[50]

Such extra precautions are necessary when treatment deliberately inflicts pain on a patient; they are especially important when the patient cannot realistically be expected to give informed consent. But should we be concerned only with physical pain? The anguish we suffer when a loved one dies is psychologically painful. It is perhaps more painful than an electric shock of 1500 microamperes. Who is to say? Since we allow that pain can be psychological, should we forbid a Gestalt therapist from making a patient cry by confronting the patient with feelings that have been avoided for years? Should we forbid a psychoanalyst from guiding a patient to an insight that will likely cause great anguish, all the more so for the conflict's having been repressed for years?

THE ETHICAL AND LEGAL DIMENSIONS OF RECOVERED MEMORIES

In Chapter 7 we examined the scientific controversies raised by so-called recovered memories (p. 174). The growing debate over the validity and reliability of reports of child abuse that surface when adults are in therapy has created considerable ethical and legal concern. One of the most important of the guidelines issued by the American Psychiatric Association (1993) stipulates that therapists should remain neutral when a patient reports abuse. Because a given symptom, for example, avoidance of sexual contact, may have many possible origins, it is not ethical according to the APA to attribute such symptoms to repressed memories of childhood sexual abuse without corroborating evidence.

A problem with this laudable stance is explored in Focus 20.5, which challenges the notion that therapists can maintain neutrality. Furthermore, as mentioned in Chapter 14, some experts on sexual dysfunctions recommend that therapists inquire into possible sexual abuse whenever patients, especially women, report aversions to or disinterest in sex (p. 378). The basic problem, then, is that many therapists are predisposed by their theorizing or by personal biases to believe that sexual abuse lies behind a wide range of psychological disorders. By the same token, therapists who do *not* believe that traumatic memories are often repressed may overlook childhood sexual abuse when it has taken place.

An incorrect diagnosis of repressed memories of sexual abuse can harm not only the patient, but also the persons whom the patient accuses of having molested her years earlier. Courts in some jurisdictions have held that in addition to their duty to their patients, therapists have a duty to those wrongly accused of abuse as a result of revelations during psychotherapy.[51]

This legal stance opens the door to lawsuits brought by the person against the alleged abuser. The statute of limitations has been extended in such cases, allowing those who believe they were abused as children to file suit twenty or more years after the abuse purportedly occurred. However, there has been a backlash to these kinds of lawsuits as accused parents have begun to deny such charges vigorously, and some patients have recanted their allegations. This turn of events has resulted in lawsuits being filed against therapists both by the accused parties and by the patients (MacNamara, 1993).

Probably the best known legal incident concerned Gary Romona, a man who claimed that irresponsible therapy had implanted false memories into his adult daughter's mind. The daughter sued her father for having molested her when she was a child, but the father sued her therapist for having planted this erroneous idea into his daughter's mind, and won a nearly half-million-dollar judgment (Kramer, 1995), at which point the daughter's suit against her father was dismissed. It is estimated that thousands of parents and other third parties have either already filed or plan to file lawsuits against therapists (Lazo, 1995). In addition to possible therapist bias, the concern is with particular treatments that may increase susceptibility to suggestion, such as hypnosis and sodium amytal (truth serum).

With the scientific status of the validity of recovered memories very much in dispute, legal scholars as well as professional associations advise extreme caution in dealing with the issue. The danger of false positives—concluding that there was abuse when there wasn't—is as serious a matter as the danger of false negatives—concluding that there was no abuse when there was.

An underlying theme of this book concerns the nature of knowledge. How do we decide that we

---

[50]In addition to being humane, Martin's suggestions are consistent with an established legal principle that holds that therapy should begin with the technique that intrudes least on the patient's freedom and exposes him or her to the least possible risk (Morris, 1966).

[51]See, for example, *Montoya v. Bensee*, 761 P.2d 285 (Colo. Ct. App. 1988); *Peterson v. Walentiny*, No. 93-C-399-K (N.D. Okla. Jan. 6, 1995) (denying motion for summary judgment); but see *Bird v. W.C.W.*, 868 S.W. 2d 767 (Tex.1994).

understand a phenomenon? The rules of science that govern our definition of and search for knowledge require theories that can be tested, experiments that can be replicated, and data that are public. But given the complexity of abnormal behavior and the vast areas of ignorance, far more extensive than the domains that have already been mapped by science as it is currently practiced, we have great respect for theoreticians and clinicians, those inventive souls who make suppositions, offer hypotheses, follow hunches—all based on rather flimsy data but holding some promise that scientific knowledge will be forthcoming (Davison & Lazarus, 1995).

This final chapter demonstrates again something emphasized at the very beginning of this book, namely, that the behavioral scientists and mental health professionals who conduct research and give treatment are only human beings. They suffer from the same foibles that sometimes plague nonspecial-ists. They occasionally act with a certainty their evidence does not justify, and they sometimes fail to anticipate the moral and legal consequences of the ways in which they conduct research and apply the tentative findings of their young discipline. When society acts with great certainty on the basis of expert scientific opinion, particularly when that opinion denies to an individual the rights and respect accorded others, it may be well to let Szasz (1963) remind us that Sir Thomas Browne, a distinguished English physician, testified in an English court of law in 1664 that witches did indeed exist, "as everyone knew."

We hope that we have communicated in some measure our love for our subject matter and, more importantly our commitment to the kind of questioning, doubting stance that wrests useful knowledge from nature and will yield more as new generations of scholars build on the achievements of their predecessors.

SUMMARY

There are many legal and ethical issues related to treatment and research in psychopathology and intervention. Some civil liberties are rather routinely set aside when mental health professionals and the courts judge that mental illness has played a decisive role in determining an individual's behavior.

Criminal commitment sends a person to a hospital either before a trial for an alleged crime, because the person is deemed incompetent to stand trial, or after an acquittal by reason of insanity. Several landmark cases in Anglo-American law inform current thinking about the conditions under which a person who has committed a crime might be excused from legal responsibility for it. These decisions involve the presence of an irresistible impulse, the notion that some people may not be able to distinguish between right and wrong (the M'Naghten rule), and the principle that a person should not be held criminally responsible if his or her unlawful act is the product of mental disease or mental defect (the Durham principle). The Insanity Defense Reform Act makes it harder for accused criminals to argue insanity as an excusing condition. Today the U.S. legal system relies on one or more of these notions, supplemented in some states by a new kind of verdict, guilty but mentally ill. This emergent legal doctrine reflects an uneasiness in legal and mental health circles about not holding people ascriptively responsible for crimes for which they are descriptively responsible. There is an important difference between mental illness and insanity. The latter is a legal concept. A person can be diagnosed as mentally ill and yet be deemed sane enough both to stand trial and to be found guilty of a crime.

A person who is considered mentally ill and dangerous to self and to others, though he or she has not broken a law, can be civilly committed to an institution. Recent court rulings have provided greater protection to all committed mental patients, particularly those under civil commitment. They have the right to written notification, to counsel, to a jury decision concerning their commitment, and to Fifth Amendment protection against self-incrimination; the right to the least restrictive treatment setting; the right to be treated; and in most circumstances, the right to refuse treatment, particularly any procedure that entails considerable risk. However, there is a trend toward preventive detention when, for example, convicted sexual predators are about to be released from prison with every indication that they will harm others again.

There are a number of moral issues concerning therapy and research: ethical restraints on research, the duty of scientists to obtain informed consent from prospective human subjects, the right of clients to confidentiality, the setting of therapy goals, the choice of techniques, and memories of sexual abuse in childhood recovered during psychotherapy when the person is an adult.

KEY TERMS

criminal commitment
civil commitment

insanity defense
informed consent

confidentiality
privileged communication

GLOSSARY

abnormal behavior. Patterns of emotion, thought, and action deemed pathological for one or more of the following reasons: infrequent occurrence, violation of norms, personal distress, disability or dysfunction, and unexpectedness.

accurate empathic understanding. In client-centered therapy, an essential quality of the therapist, referring to the ability to see the world through the client's phenomenology as well as from perspectives of which the client may be only dimly aware.

acetylcholine. A *neurotransmitter*[1] of the central, somatomotor, and *parasympathetic nervous systems* and of the ganglia and the neuron—sweat gland junctions of the *sympathetic nervous system*.

acquaintance (date) rape. Forcible sex when the people involved know each other, sometimes occurring on a date.

acute stress disorder. New in DSM-IV, a short-lived anxiety reaction to a traumatic event; if it lasts more than a month, it is diagnosed as *posttraumatic stress disorder*.

addiction. See *substance dependence*.

adrenal glands. Two small areas of tissue located just above the kidneys. The inner core of each gland, the medulla, secretes *epinephrine* and *norepinephrine*; the outer cortex secretes *cortisone* and other steroid hormones.

adrenaline. A hormone that is secreted by the *adrenal glands*; also called *epinephrine*.

adrenergic system. All the nerve cells for which *epinephrine* and *norepinephrine* are the transmitter substances, as contrasted with the *cholinergic system*, which consists of the nerve cells activated by *acetylcholine*.

advanced accurate empathy. A form of *empathy* in which the therapist infers concerns and feelings that lie behind what the client is saying; it represents an *interpretation*. Compare with *primary empathy*.

affect. A subjective feeling or emotional tone often accompanied by bodily expressions noticeable to others.

age effects. The consequences of being a given chronological age. Compare with *cohort effects*.

ageism. Discrimination against someone because of his or her age.

agoraphobia. A cluster of fears centering on being in open spaces and leaving the home. It is often linked to *panic disorder*.

AIDS (acquired immunodeficiency syndrome). A fatal disease transmitted by transfer of the human immunodeficiency virus, usually during sexual relations or by using needles previously infected by an HIV-positive person; it compromises the immune system to such a degree that the person ultimately dies from cancer or from one of any number of infections.

alcoholism. A behavioral disorder in which consumption of alcoholic beverages is excessive and impairs health and social and occupational functioning; a physiological dependence on alcohol. See *substance dependence*.

alkaloid. An organic base found in seed plants, usually in mixture with a number of similar alkaloids. Alkaloids are the active chemicals that give many drugs their medicinal properties and other powerful physiological effects.

alogia. A *negative symptom* in *schizophrenia*, marked by poverty of speech and of speech content.

alternate form reliability. See *reliability*.

altruistic suicide. As defined by Durkheim, self-annihilation that the person feels will serve a social purpose, such as the self-immolations practiced by Buddhist monks during the Vietnam War.

Alzheimer's disease. A *dementia* involving a progressive atrophy of cortical tissue and marked by memory impairment, involuntary movements of limbs, occasional convulsions, intellectual deterioration, and psychotic behavior.

ambivalence. The simultaneous holding of strong positive and negative emotional attitudes toward the same situation or person.

American Law Institute guidelines. Rules proposing that *insanity* is a legitimate defense plea if during criminal conduct, an individual could not judge right from wrong or control his or her behavior as required by law. Repetitive criminal acts are disavowed as a sole criterion. Compare *M'Naghten rule* and *irresistible impulse*.

amino acid. One of a large class of organic compounds important as the building blocks of proteins.

amnesia. Total or partial loss of memory that can be associated with a *dissociative disorder*, brain damage, or *hypnosis*.

amniocentesis. A prenatal diagnostic technique in which fluid drawn from the uterus is tested for birth defects, such as *Down syndrome*.

amphetamines. A group of stimulating drugs that produce heightened levels of energy and, in large doses, nervousness, sleeplessness, and paranoid *delusions*.

anal personality. An adult who, when anal retentive, is found by psychoanalytic theory to be stingy and sometimes obsessively clean; when anal expulsive, to be aggressive. Such traits are assumed to be caused by *fixation* through either excessive or inadequate gratification of id impulses during the *anal stage* of psychosexual development.

anal stage. In psychoanalytic theory, the second *psychosexual stage*, which occurs during the second year of life

---

[1]Italicized words or variants of these terms are themselves defined elsewhere in the glossary.

when the anus is considered the principal *erogenous* zone.

analgesia. An insensitivity to pain without loss of consciousness, sometimes found in *conversion disorder*.

analogue experiment. An experimental study of a phenomenon different from but related to the actual interests of the investigator.

analysand. A person being psychoanalyzed.

analysis of defenses. The study by a *psychoanalyst* of the ways in which a patient avoids troubling topics by the use of *defense mechanisms*.

analyst. See *psychoanalyst*.

analytical psychology. A variation of Freud's psychoanalysis introduced by Carl Jung and focusing less on biological drives and more on factors such as self-fulfillment, collective unconscious, and religious symbolism.

anesthesia. An impairment or loss of sensation, usually of touch but sometimes of the other senses, that is often part of *conversion disorder*.

anger-in theory. The view that *psychophysiological disorders*, such as *essential hypertension*, arise from a person's not expressing anger or resentment.

angina pectoris. See *coronary heart disease*.

anhedonia. A *negative symptom* in *schizophrenia* in which the individual is unable to feel pleasure.

animal phobia. The fear and avoidance of small animals.

anomic suicide. As defined by Durkheim, self-annihilation triggered by a person's inability to cope with sudden and unfavorable change in a social situation.

anorexia nervosa. A disorder in which a person refuses to eat or to retain any food or suffers a prolonged and severe diminution of appetite. The individual has an intense fear of becoming obese, feels fat even when emaciated, refuses to maintain a minimal body weight, and loses at least 25 percent of his or her original weight.

anoxia. A deficiency of oxygen reaching the tissues that is severe enough to damage the brain permanently.

Antabuse (trade name for disulfiram). A drug that makes the drinking of alcohol produce nausea and other unpleasant effects.

antidepressant. A drug that alleviates *depression*, usually by energizing the patient and thus elevating mood.

antipsychotic drug. Psychoactive drugs, such as *Thorazine*, that reduce *psychotic* symptoms but have long-term side effects resembling symptoms of neurological diseases.

antisocial personality. Also called a psychopath or a sociopath, a person with this disorder is superficially charming and a habitual liar, has no regard for others, shows no remorse after hurting others, has no shame for behaving in an outrageously objectionable manner, is unable to form relationships and take responsibility, and does not learn from punishment.

anxiety. An unpleasant feeling of fear and apprehension accompanied by increased physiological arousal. In learning theory it is considered a drive that mediates between a threatening situation and avoidance behavior. Anxiety can be assessed by self-report, by measuring physiological arousal, and by observing overt behavior.

anxiety disorders. Disorders in which fear or tension is overriding and the primary disturbance: *phobic disorders, panic disorder, generalized anxiety disorder, obsessive-compulsive disorder;* and *posttraumatic stress disorder*. These disorders form a major category in DSM-IV and cover most of what used to be referred to as the *neuroses*.

anxiety neurosis. DSM-II term for what are now diagnosed as *panic disorder* and *generalized anxiety disorder*.

anxiolytics. Tranquilizers; drugs that reduce anxiety.

aphasia. The loss or impairment of the ability to use language because of lesions in the brain: *executive*, difficulties in speaking or writing the words intended; *receptive*, difficulties in understanding written or spoken language.

apnea. Cessation of breathing for short periods of time, sometimes occurring during sleep.

applied behavior analysis. The study of the antecedent conditions and *reinforcement* contingencies that control behavior. See also *operant conditioning*.

aptitude test. A paper-and-pencil assessment of a person's intellectual functioning that is supposed to predict how the person will perform at a later time; well-known examples include the Scholastic Aptitude Test and the Graduate Record Examination.

aptitude-treatment interaction. The suitability of a particular therapeutic intervention to a particular patient characteristic.

arousal. A state of behavioral or physiological activation.

ascriptive responsibility. The social judgment assigned to someone who has committed an illegal act and who is expected by society to be punished for it. Contrast with *descriptive responsibility*.

asociality. A *negative symptom* of *schizophrenia* marked by an inability to form close relationships and to feel intimacy.

assertion training. *Behavior therapy* procedures that attempt to help a person more easily express thoughts, wishes, beliefs, and legitimate feelings of resentment or approval.

asthma. A *psychophysiological disorder* characterized by narrowing of the airways and increased secretion of mucus, often causing extremely labored and wheezy breathing.

asylums. Refuges established in western Europe in the fifteenth century to confine and provide for the mentally ill; the forerunners of the mental hospital.

attention-deficit/hyperactivity disorder (ADHD). A disorder in children marked by difficulties in focusing adaptively on the task at hand, by inappropriate fidgeting and antisocial behavior, and by excessive non-goal-directed behavior.

attribution. The explanation a person has for his or her behavior.

autistic disorder. An absorption in self or fantasy as a means of avoiding communication and escaping objective reality. In this *pervasive developmental disorder*, the child's world is one of profound aloneness.

automatic thoughts. In Beck's theory, the things people picture or tell themselves as they make their way in life.

autonomic lability. Tendency for the *autonomic nervous system* to be easily aroused.

autonomic nervous system (ANS). The division of the nervous system that regulates involuntary functions; innervates *endocrine glands, smooth muscle,* and heart muscle; and initiates the physiological changes that are part of the expression of emotion. See *sympathetic* and *parasympathetic nervous systems.*

aversion therapy. A *behavior therapy* procedure that pairs a noxious stimulus, such as a shock, with situations that are undesirably attractive to make the situations less appealing.

aversive conditioning. Process believed to underlie the effectiveness of *aversion therapy.*

aversive stimulus. A stimulus that elicits pain, fear, or avoidance.

avoidance conditioning. Learning to move away from a stimulus that has previously been paired with an *aversive stimulus* such as electric shock.

avoidance learning. An experimental procedure in which a neutral stimulus is paired with a noxious one so that the organism learns to avoid the previously neutral stimulus.

avoidant personality disorder. Individuals with this disorder have poor self-esteem and thus are extremely sensitive to potential rejection and remain aloof even though they very much desire affiliation and affection.

avolition. A *negative symptom* in *schizophrenia* in which the individual lacks interest and drive.

barbiturates. A class of synthetic *sedative* drugs that are addictive and in large doses can cause death by almost completely relaxing the diaphragm.

baseline. The state of a phenomenon before the *independent variable* is manipulated, providing a standard against which the effects of the variable can be measured.

behavior genetics. The study of individual differences in behavior that are attributable to differences in genetic makeup.

behavior modification. A term sometimes used interchangeably with *behavior therapy.*

behavior rehearsal. A *behavior therapy* technique in which a client practices new behavior in the consulting room, often aided by demonstrations and role-play by the therapist.

behavior therapy. A branch of psychotherapy narrowly conceived as the application of *classical* and *operant conditioning* to the alteration of clinical problems, but more broadly conceived as applied experimental psychology in a clinical context.

behavioral assessment. A sampling of ongoing cognitions, feelings, and overt behavior in their situational context. Contrast with *projective test* and *personality inventory.*

behavioral medicine. An interdisciplinary field concerned with integrating knowledge from medicine and behavioral science to understand health and illness and to prevent as well as to treat *psychophysiological disorders*

and other illnesses in which a person's psyche plays a role. See also *health psychology.*

behavioral observation. A form of *behavioral assessment* that entails careful observation of a person's overt behavior in a particular situation.

behavioral pediatrics. A branch of *behavioral medicine* concerned with psychological aspects of childhood medical problems.

behaviorism. The school of psychology associated with John B. Watson, who proposed that observable behavior, not consciousness, is the proper subject matter of psychology. Currently, many who consider themselves behaviorists do use *mediational* concepts, provided they are firmly anchored to observables.

bell and pad. A *behavior therapy* technique for eliminating nocturnal *enuresis*; if the child wets, an electric circuit is closed and a bell sounds, waking the child.

bilateral ECT. *Electroconvulsive therapy* in which electrodes are placed on each side of the forehead and an electrical current is passed between them through both hemispheres of the brain.

binge eating disorder. Categorized in DSM-IV as a diagnosis in need of further study; includes recurrent episodes of unrestrained eating.

biofeedback. Procedures that provide an individual immediate information on minute changes in muscle activity, skin temperature, heart rate, blood pressure, and other somatic functions. It is assumed that voluntary control over these bodily processes can be achieved through this knowledge, thereby ameliorating to some extent certain *psychophysiological disorders.*

biological paradigm. A broad theoretical view that holds that mental disorders are caused by some aberrant somatic process or defect.

bipolar I disorder. A term applied to the disorder of people who experience episodes of both *mania* and *depression* or of mania alone.

bisexuality. Sexual desire or activity directed toward both men and women.

blocking. A disturbance associated with thought disorders in which a train of speech is interrupted by silence before an idea is fully expressed.

body dysmorphic disorder. A *somatoform disorder* marked by preoccupation with an imagined or exaggerated defect in appearance, for example, facial wrinkles or excess facial or body hair.

borderline personality disorder. People with a borderline personality are impulsive and unpredictable, with an uncertain self-image, intense and unstable social relationships, and extreme swings of mood.

brain stem. The part of the brain connecting the spinal cord with the *cerebrum.* It contains the *pons* and *medulla oblongata* and functions as a neural relay station.

brief reactive psychosis. A disorder in which a person has a sudden onset of *psychotic* symptoms—*incoherence, loose associations, delusions, hallucinations*—immediately after a severely disturbing event; the symptoms last more than a few hours but no more than two weeks. See *schizophreniform disorder.*

brief therapy. Time-limited psychotherapy, usually

ego-analytic in orientation and lasting no more than twenty-five sessions.

Briquet's syndrome. See *somatization disorder*.

bulimia nervosa. A disorder characterized by episodic uncontrollable eating binges followed by purging either by vomiting or by taking laxatives.

Cannabis sativa. See *marijuana*.

cardiovascular disorder. A medical problem involving the heart and the blood circulation system, such as *hypertension* or *coronary heart disease*.

case study. The collection of historical or biographical information on a single individual, often including experiences in therapy.

castration. The surgical removal of the *testes*.

castration anxiety. The fear of having the genitals removed or injured.

catatonic immobility. A fixity of posture, sometimes grotesque, maintained for long periods, with accompanying muscular rigidity, trancelike state of consciousness, and *waxy flexibility*.

catatonic schizophrenia. A subtype of *schizophrenia* whose primary symptoms alternate between stuporous immobility and excited agitation.

catecholamines. *Monoamine* compounds, each having a catechol portion. Catecholamines known to be *neurotransmitters* of the central nervous system are *norepinephrine* and *dopamine*; another, *epinephrine*, is principally a hormone.

categorical classification. An approach to assessment in which the basic decision is whether a person is or is not a member of a discrete grouping. Contrast with *dimensional classification*.

cathartic method. A therapeutic procedure introduced by Breuer and developed further by Freud in the late nineteenth century whereby a patient recalls and relives an earlier emotional catastrophe and reexperiences the tension and unhappiness, the goal being to relieve emotional suffering.

central nervous system. The part of the nervous system that in vertebrates consists of the brain and spinal cord, to which all sensory impulses are transmitted and from which motor impulses pass out; it also supervises and coordinates the activites of the entire nervous system.

cerebellum. An area of the hindbrain concerned with balance, posture, and motor coordination.

cerebral atherosclerosis. A chronic disease impairing intellectual and emotional life, caused by a reduction in the brain's blood supply through a buildup of fatty deposits in the arteries.

cerebral contusion. A bruising of neural tissue marked by swelling and hemorrhage and resulting in coma; it may permanently impair intellectual functioning.

cerebral cortex. The thin outer covering of each of the *cerebral hemispheres*; it is highly convoluted and composed of nerve cell bodies which constitute the *gray matter* of the brain.

cerebral hemisphere. Either of the two halves that make up the *cerebrum*.

cerebral hemorrhage. Bleeding onto brain tissue from a ruptured blood vessel.

cerebral thrombosis. The formation of a blood clot in a cerebral artery that blocks circulation in that area of brain tissue and causes paralysis, loss of sensory functions, and possibly death.

cerebrovascular disease. An illness that disrupts blood supply to the brain, such as a *stroke*.

cerebrum. The two-lobed structure extending from the *brain stem* and constituting the anterior (frontal) part of the brain. The largest and most recently developed portion of the brain, it coordinates sensory and motor activities and is the seat of higher cognitive processes.

character disorder. The old term for *personality disorder*.

child sexual abuse. Sexual contact with a minor.

chlorpromazine. One of the *phenothiazines*, the generic term for one of the most widely prescribed *antipsychotic drugs*, sold under the name *Thorazine*.

cholinergic system. All the nerve cells for which *acetylcholine* is the transmitter substance, in contrast to the *adrenergic system*.

choreiform. Pertaining to the involuntary, spasmodic, jerking movements of the limbs and head found in *Huntington's chorea* and other brain disorders.

chromosomes. The threadlike bodies within the nucleus of the cell, composed primarily of DNA and bearing the genetic information of the organism.

chronic. Of lengthy duration or recurring frequently, often with progressing seriousness.

chronic brain syndrome. See *senile dementia*.

chronic schizophrenic. A *psychotic* patient who deteriorated over a long period of time and has been hospitalized for more than two years.

civil commitment. A procedure whereby a person can be legally certified as mentally ill and hospitalized, even against his or her will.

classical conditioning. A basic form of learning, sometimes referred to as Pavlovian conditioning, in which a neutral stimulus is repeatedly paired with another stimulus (called the **unconditioned stimulus**, UCS) that naturally elicits a certain desired response (called the **unconditioned response**, UCR). After repeated trials the neutral stimulus becomes a **conditioned stimulus** (CS) and evokes the same or a similar response, now called the **conditioned response** (CR).

classificatory variables. The characteristics that people bring with them to scientific investigations, such as sex, age, and mental status; studied by *correlational* research and *mixed designs*.

client-centered therapy. A *humanistic-existential insight therapy*, developed by Carl Rogers, which emphasizes the importance of the therapist's understanding the client's subjective experiences and assisting the client to gain more awareness of current motivations for behavior; the goal is not only to reduce anxieties but also to foster actualization of the client's potential.

clinical interview. General term for conversation between a clinician and a patient that is aimed at determining diagnosis, history, causes for problems, and possible treatment options.

clinical psychologist. An individual who has earned a Ph.D. degree in psychology or a Psy.D. and whose training has included an internship in a mental hospital or clinic.

clinical psychology. The special area of psychology concerned with the study of psychopathology, its diagnosis, causes, prevention, and treatment.

clinician. A health professional authorized to provide services to people suffering from one or more pathologies.

clitoris. The small, heavily innervated structure located above the vaginal opening; the primary site of female responsiveness to sexual stimulation.

clonidine. An antihypertensive drug that shows some promise in helping people wean themselves from *substance dependence*.

cocaine. A pain-reducing, stimulating, and addictive *alkaloid* obtained from coca leaves, which increases mental powers, produces euphoria, heightens sexual desire, and in large doses causes *paranoia* and *hallucinations*.

cognition. The process of knowing; the thinking, judging, reasoning, and planning activities of the human mind; behavior is now often explained as depending on these processes.

cognitive paradigm. General view that people can best be understood by studying how they perceive and structure their experiences.

cognitive restructuring. Any *behavior therapy* procedure that attempts to alter the manner in which a client thinks about life so that he or she changes overt behavior and emotions.

cognitive therapy (CT). A *cognitive restructuring* therapy associated with the psychiatrist Aaron T. Beck, concerned with changing negative *schemata* and certain cognitive biases or distortions that influence a person to construe life in a depressing or otherwise maladaptive way.

cohort effects. The consequences of having been born in a given year and having grown up during a particular time period with its own unique pressures, problems, challenges, and opportunities. To be distinguished from *age effects*.

coitus. Sexual intercourse.

collective unconscious. Jung's concept that every human being has within the wisdom, ideas, and strivings of those who have come before.

community mental health. The delivery of services to needy, underserved groups through centers that offer outpatient therapy, short-term inpatient care, day hospitalization, twenty-four-hour emergency services, and consultation and education to other community agencies, such as the police.

community psychology. An approach to therapy that emphasizes prevention and the seeking out of potential difficulties rather than waiting for troubled individuals to initiate consultation. The location for professional activities tends to be in the person's natural surroundings rather than in the therapist's office. See *prevention*.

comorbidity. The co-occurrence of two disorders, as when a person is both depressed and alcoholic.

competency to stand trial. A legal decision as to whether a person can participate meaningfully in his or her own defense.

compulsion. The irresistible impulse to repeat an irrational act over and over again.

concordance. As applied in *behavior genetics*, the similarity in psychiatric diagnosis or in other *traits* within a pair of twins.

concurrent (descriptive) validity. See *validity*.

concussion. A jarring injury to the brain produced by a blow to the head that usually involves a momentary loss of consciousness followed by transient disorientation and memory loss.

conditioned response (CR). See *classical conditioning*.

conditioned stimulus (CS). See *classical conditioning*.

conduct disorder. Patterns of extreme disobedience in youngsters, including theft, vandalism, lying, and early drug use; may be precursor of *antisocial personality* disorder.

confabulation. Filling in gaps in memory caused by brain dysfunction with made-up and often improbable stories that the person accepts as true.

confidentiality. A principle observed by lawyers, doctors, pastors, psychologists, and psychiatrists that dictates that the goings-on in a professional and private relationship are not divulged to anyone else. See *privileged communication*.

conflict. A state of being torn between competing forces.

confounds. Variables whose effects are so intermixed that they cannot be measured separately, making the design of an *experiment* internally invalid and its results impossible to interpret.

congenital. Existing at or before birth but not acquired through heredity.

conjoint therapy. *Couples* or *family therapy* where partners are seen together and children are seen with their parents and possibly with an extended family.

construct. An entity inferred by a scientist to explain observed phenomena. See also *mediator*.

construct validity. The extent to which scores or ratings on an assessment instrument relate to other variables or behaviors according to some theory or hypothesis.

contingency. A close relationship, especially of a causal nature, between two events, one of which regularly follows the other.

control group. Those in an *experiment* for whom the *independent variable* is not manipulated, thus forming a *baseline* against which the effects of the manipulation of the experimental group can be evaluated.

controlled drinking. A pattern of alcohol consumption that is moderate and avoids the extremes of total abstinence and of inebriation.

conversion disorder. A *somatoform disorder* in which sensory or muscular functions are impaired, usually suggesting neurological disease, even though the bodily organs themselves are sound; *anesthesias* and paralyses of limbs are examples.

convulsive therapy. See *electroconvulsive therapy*.

coronary heart disease (CHD). Angina pectoris, chest pains caused by insufficient supply of blood and thus oxygen to the heart; and myocardial infarction, or heart attack, in which the blood and oxygen supply is reduced so much that heart muscles are damaged.

corpus callosum. The large band of nerve fibers connecting the two *cerebral hemispheres*.

correlation. The tendency for two variables, such as height and weight, to co-vary.

correlation coefficient. A statistic that measures the degree to which two variables are related.

correlational method. The research strategy used to establish whether two or more variables are related. Relationships may be positive—as values for one variable increase, those for the other do also—or negative—as values for one variable increase, those for the other decrease.

cortisone. A hormone secreted by the *adrenal* cortices.

co-twin. In *behavior genetics* research using the *twin method*, the member of the pair who is tested later to determine whether he or she has the same diagnosis or trait discovered earlier in the birth partner.

counseling psychologist. A doctoral level mental health professional whose training is similar to that of a *clinical psychologist*, though usually with less emphasis on research and serious *psychopathology*.

counterconditioning. Relearning achieved by eliciting a new response in the presence of a particular stimulus.

countertransference. Feelings that the *psychoanalyst* unconsciously directs to the *analysand*, stemming from his or her own emotional vulnerabilities and unresolved *conflicts*.

couples (marital) therapy. Any professional intervention that treats relationship problems of a couple.

covert sensitization. A form of *aversion therapy* in which the person is told to imagine undesirably attractive situations and activities while unpleasant feelings are being induced by imagery.

criminal commitment. A procedure whereby a person is confined in a mental institution either for determination of *competency to stand trial* or after acquittal by reason of insanity.

critical period. A stage of early development in which an organism is susceptible to certain influences and during which important irreversible patterns of behavior are acquired.

cross-dependent. Acting on the same receptors, as *methadone* does with *heroin*. See *heroin substitutes*.

cross-sectional studies. Studies in which different age groups are compared at the same time. Compare with *longitudinal studies*.

CT scan. Refers to computerized axial tomography, a method of diagnosis in which X rays are taken from different angles and then analyzed by computer to produce a representation of the part of the body in cross section; often used on the brain.

cultural-familial retardation. A mild backwardness in mental development with no indication of brain pathology but evidence of similar limitation in at least one of the parents or siblings.

cunnilingus. The oral stimulation of female genitalia.

Cushing's syndrome. An endocrine disorder usually affecting young women, produced by oversecretion of *cortisone* and marked by mood swings, irritability, agitation, and physical disfigurement.

cyclical psychodynamics. The reciprocal relations between current behavior and *repressed* conflicts, such that they mutually reinforce each other.

cyclothymic disorder. Chronic swings between elation and depression not severe enough to warrant the diagnosis of *bipolar disorder*.

defense mechanisms. In psychoanalytic theory, reality-distorting strategies unconsciously adopted to protect the ego from anxiety.

delay of reward gradient. The learning theory term for the finding that rewards and punishments lose their effectiveness the further they are removed in time from the response in question.

delayed echolalia. See *echolalia*.

delirium. A state of great mental confusion in which consciousness is clouded, attention cannot be sustained, and the stream of thought and speech is incoherent. The person is probably disoriented, emotionally erratic, restless or lethargic, and often has *illusions, delusions*, and *hallucinations*.

delirium tremens (DTs). One of the *withdrawal* symptoms that sometimes occurs when a period of heavy alcohol consumption is terminated; marked by fever, sweating, trembling, cognitive impairment, and *hallucinations*.

delusional (paranoid) disorder. A disorder in which the individual has persistent persecutory *delusions* or *delusional jealousy* and is very often contentious but has no *thought disorder* or *hallucinations*.

delusional jealousy. The unfounded conviction that one's mate is unfaithful; the individual may collect small bits of "evidence" to justify the *delusion*.

delusions. Beliefs contrary to reality, firmly held in spite of evidence to the contrary; common in *paranoid disorders*; **of control,** belief that one is being manipulated by some external force such as radar, television, or a creature from outer space; **of grandeur,** belief that one is an especially important or powerful person; **of persecution,** belief that one is being plotted against or oppressed by others.

dementia. Deterioration of mental faculties—memory, judgment, abstract thought, control of impulses, intellectual ability—that impairs social and occupational functioning and eventually changes the personality.

dementia praecox. An older term for *schizophrenia*, chosen to describe what was believed to be an incurable and progressive deterioration of mental functioning beginning in adolescence.

demographic variable. A varying characteristic that is a vital or social statistic of an individual, sample group, or population, for example, age, sex, *socioeconomic status*, racial origin, education.

demonology. The doctrine that a person's abnormal behavior is caused by an autonomous evil spirit.

denial. *Defense mechanism* in which a thought, feeling, or action is disavowed by the person.

dependent personality disorder. Lacking in self-confidence, such people passively allow others to run their lives and make no demands on them so as not to endanger these protective relationships.

dependent variable. In a psychological *experiment*, the behavior that is measured and is expected to change with manipulation of the *independent variable*.

depersonalization. An alteration in perception of the self in which the individual loses a sense of reality and feels estranged from the self and perhaps separated from the body. It may be a temporary reaction to stress and fatigue or part of *panic disorder, depersonalization disorder*, or *schizophrenia*.

depersonalization disorder. A *dissociative disorder* in which the individual feels unreal and estranged from the self and surroundings enough to disrupt functioning. People with this disorder may feel that their extremities have changed in size or that they are watching themselves from a distance.

depression. A disorder marked by great sadness and apprehension, feelings of worthlessness and guilt, withdrawal from others, loss of sleep, appetite, sexual desire, loss of interest and pleasure in usual activities, and either lethargy or agitation. Called *major depression* in DSM-IV and *unipolar depression* by others. It can be an associated symptom of other disorders.

derealization. Loss of the sense that the surroundings are real; present in several psychological disorders, such as *panic disorder, depersonalization disorder*, and *schizophrenia*.

descriptive responsibility. In legal proceedings, the judgment that the accused performed an illegal act. Contrast with *ascriptive responsibility*.

deterioration effect. In abnormal psychology, a harmful outcome from being in psychotherapy.

detoxification. The initial stage in weaning an addicted person from a drug; involves medical supervision of the sometimes painful *withdrawal*.

detumescence. The flow of blood out of the genital area.

diagnosis. The determination that the set of symptoms or problems of a patient indicates a particular disorder.

dialectical behavior therapy. A therapeutic approach to *borderline personality* disorder that combines client-centered empathy and acceptance with behavioral problem solving, social-skills training, and limit setting.

diathesis. *Predisposition* toward a disease or abnormality.

diathesis–stress paradigm. As applied in *psychopathology*, a view that assumes that individuals predisposed toward a particular mental disorder will be particularly affected by stress and will then manifest abnormal behavior.

dichotic listening. An experimental procedure in which a person hears two different taped messages simultaneously through earphones, one in each ear, usually with the instruction to attend to only one of the messages.

diencephalon. The lower area of the forebrain, containing the *thalamus* and *hypothalamus*.

dimensional classification. An approach to assessment according to which a person is placed on a continuum. Contrast with *categorical classification*.

directionality problem. A difficulty that arises in the *correlational method* of research when it is known that two variables are related but it is unclear which is causing the other.

discriminative stimulus. An event that informs an organism that if a particular response is made, reinforcement will follow.

disease. The medical concept that distinguishes an impairment of the normal state of the organism by its particular group of symptoms and its specific cause.

disease model. See *medical model*.

disorder of written expression. Difficulties writing without errors in spelling, grammar, or punctuation.

disorganized schizophrenia. In this subtype of *schizophrenia* the person has diffuse and regressive symptoms; the individual is given to silliness, facial grimaces, and inconsequential rituals and has constantly changeable moods and poor hygiene. There are few significant remissions and eventually considerable deterioration. This form of *schizophrenia* was formerly called hebephrenia.

disorganized speech (thought disorder). Speech found in schizophrenics that is marked by problems in the organization of ideas and in speaking so that others can understand.

disorientation. A state of mental confusion with respect to time, place, identity of self, other persons, and objects.

displacement. A *defense mechanism* whereby an emotional response is unconsciously redirected from an object or concept perceived as dangerous to a substitute less threatening to the *ego*.

dissociation. A process whereby a group of mental processes is split off from the mainstream of consciousness, or behavior loses its relationship with the rest of the personality.

dissociative amnesia. A *dissociative disorder* in which the person suddenly becomes unable to recall important personal information to an extent that cannot be explained by ordinary forgetfulness.

dissociative disorders. Disorders in which the normal integration of consciousness, memory, or identity is suddenly and temporarily altered; *dissociative amnesia, dissociative fugue, dissociative identity disorder (multiple personality)*, and *depersonalization disorder* are examples.

dissociative fugue. Disorder in which the person experiences total amnesia, moves, and establishes a new identity.

dissociative identity disorder (DID). A rare *dissociative disorder* in which two or more fairly distinct and separate personalities are present within the same individual, each with his or her own memories, relationships, and behavior patterns, with only one of them dominant at any given time. Formerly called multiple personality disorder.

divorce mediation. A form of *couples (marital) therapy* in which a distressed couple is helped to collaborate on issues such as child custody outside the adversarial framework of a formal legal process.

dizygotic (DZ) twins. Birth partners who have developed from separate fertilized eggs and who are only 50 percent alike genetically, no more so than siblings born from different pregnancies; sometimes called fraternal twins.

dominant gene. One of a pair of *genes* that predominates over the other and determines that the *trait* it fosters will prevail in the *phenotype*.

dopamine. A *catecholamine* that is both a precursor of *norepinephrine* and itself a *neurotransmitter* of the central nervous system. Disturbances in certain of its tracts apparently figure in *schizophrenia* and *Parkinson's disease*.

dopamine activity theory. The view that *schizophrenia* arises from an increase in the number of *dopamine* receptors.

double-bind theory. An interpersonal situation in which an individual is confronted over long periods of time by mutually inconsistent messages to which she or he must respond, formerly believed by some theorists to cause *schizophrenia*.

double-blind procedure. A method for reducing the biasing effects of the expectations of research participant and experimenter; neither is allowed to know whether the *independent variable* of the *experiment* is being applied to the participant.

Down syndrome (trisomy 21). A form of *mental retardation* generally caused by an extra *chromosome*. The child's IQ is usually less than 50, and the child has distinctive physical characteristics, most notably slanted eyes.

dream analysis. A key psychoanalytic technique in which the unconscious meanings of dream material are uncovered.

drive. A *construct* explaining the motivation of behavior, or an internal physiological tension impelling an organism to activity.

drug abuse. See *substance abuse*.

drug addiction. See *substance dependence*.

DSM-IV. The current *Diagnostic and Statistical Manual* of the American Psychiatric Association.

dualism. Philosophical doctrine, advanced most definitively by Descartes, that a human being is both mental and physical and that these two aspects are separate but interacting. Contrast with *monism*.

Durham decision. A 1954 U.S. court ruling that an accused person is not *ascriptively responsible* if his or her crime is judged attributable to mental disease or defect.

dysfunction. An impairment or disturbance in the functioning of an organ, organ system, behavior, or cognition.

dyslexia. A disturbance in the ability to read; it is one of the *learning disorders*.

dyspareunia. Painful or difficult sexual intercourse; the pain or difficulty is usually caused by infection or a physical injury, such as torn ligaments in the pelvic region.

dysthymic disorder. State of depression that is long lasting but not severe enough for the diagnosis of *major depression*.

echolalia. The immediate repetition of the words of others, often found in autistic children. In **delayed echolalia** this inappropriate echoing takes place hours or weeks later.

eclecticism. In psychology, the view that more is to be gained by employing concepts and techniques from various theoretical systems than by restricting oneself to a single approach.

Ecstasy. A relatively new *hallucinogen* that is chemically similar to *mescaline* and the *amphetamines*.

ego. In psychoanalytic theory, the predominantly conscious part of the personality, responsible for decision making and for dealing with reality.

ego analysis. An important set of modifications of classical *psychoanalysis*, based on a conception of the human being as having a stronger, more autonomous *ego* with gratifications independent of *id* satisfactions. Sometimes called ego psychology.

ego analysts. Those who practice *ego analysis*.

ego-alien. Foreign to the self, such as a *compulsion*.

ego-dystonic homosexuality. According to DSM-III, a disorder of people who are persistently dissatisfied with their *homosexuality* and wish instead to be attracted to members of the opposite sex.

egoistic suicide. As defined by Durkheim, self-annihilation committed because the individual feels extreme alienation from others and from society.

elective mutism. A pattern of continuously refusing to speak in almost all social situations, including school, even though the child understands spoken language and is able to speak.

Electra complex. See *Oedipus complex*.

electrocardiogram. A recording of the electrical activity of the heart, made with an electrocardiograph.

electroconvulsive therapy (ECT). A treatment that produces a convulsion by passing electric current through the brain. Though an unpleasant and occasionally dangerous procedure, it can be useful in alleviating profound *depression*.

electrodermal responding. A recording of the minute electrical activity of the sweat glands on the skin, allowing the inference of an emotional state.

electroencephalogram (EEG). A graphic recording of electrical activity of the brain, usually of the *cerebral cortex*, but sometimes of lower areas.

empathy. Awareness and understanding of another's feelings and thoughts. See *primary empathy* and *advanced accurate empathy*.

empty-chair technique. A *Gestalt therapy* procedure for helping the client become more aware of denied feelings; the client talks to important people or to feelings as though they were present and seated in a nearby vacant chair.

encephalitis. Inflammation of brain tissue caused by a number of agents, the most significant being several viruses carried by insects.

encephalitis lethargica. Known as sleeping sickness, a form of encephalitis that occurred early in this century and was characterized by lethargy and prolonged periods of sleeping.

encopresis. A disorder in which, through faulty control of the sphincters, the person repeatedly defecates in his or her clothing after an age at which continence is expected.

encounter group. See *sensitivity training group*.

endocrine gland. Any of a number of ductless glands that release *hormones* directly into the blood or lymph. The secretions of some endocrine glands increase during emotional arousal.

endogenous. Attributable to internal causes.

endorphins. Opiates produced within the body; they may have an important role in the processes by which the body builds up *tolerance* to drugs and is distressed by their withdrawal.

enuresis. A disorder in which, through faulty control of the bladder, the person wets repeatedly during the night (nocturnal enuresis) or during the day after an age at which continence is expected.

enzyme. A complex protein produced by the cells to act as a catalyst in regulating metabolic activities.

epidemiology. The study of the frequency and distribution of illness in a population.

epilepsy. An altered state of consciousness accompanied by sudden changes in the usual rhythmical electrical activity of the brain.

epinephrine. A hormone (a *catecholamine*) secreted by the medulla of the *adrenal gland*; its effects are similar, but not identical, to those of stimulating the *sympathetic* nerves. It causes an increase in blood pressure, inhibits peristaltic movements, and liberates glucose from the liver. Also called *adrenaline*.

erogenous. Capable of giving sexual pleasure when stimulated.

Eros (libido). Freud's term for the life-integrating instinct or force of the *id*, sometimes equated with sexual drive. Compare *Thanatos*.

essential hypertension. A *psychophysiological disorder* characterized by high blood pressure that cannot be traced to an organic cause. Over the years it causes degeneration of small arteries, enlargement of the heart, and kidney damage.

estrogen. A female sex hormone produced especially in the ovaries that stimulates the development and maintenance of the secondary sex characteristics, such as breast enlargement.

etiological validity. See *validity*.

etiology. All the factors that contribute to the development of an illness or disorder.

eugenics. The field concerned with improving the hereditary qualities of the human race through social control of mating and reproduction.

ex post facto **analysis.** In the *correlational method* of research, an attempt to reduce the *third-variable problem* by picking people who are matched on characteristics that may be *confounds*.

excitement phase. As applied by Masters and Johnson, the first stage of sexual arousal, which is initiated by any appropriate stimulus.

executive aphasia. See *aphasia*.

executive functioning The *cognitive* capacity to plan how to do a task, how to devise strategies, and how to monitor one's performance.

exhibitionism. Marked preference for obtaining sexual gratification by exposing one's genitals to an unwilling observer.

existential analysis. See *existential therapy*.

existential therapy. An insight therapy that emphasizes choice and responsibility to define the meaning of one's life. In contrast with *humanistic therapy*, it tends to be less cheerful or sanguine in outlook, focusing more on the anxiety that is inherent to confronting one's ultimate aloneness in the world.

exogenous. Attributable to external causes.

exorcism. The casting out of evil spirits by ritualistic chanting or torture.

experiment. The most powerful research technique for determining causal relationships, requiring the manipulation of an *independent variable*, the measurement of a *dependent variable*, and the *random assignment* of participants to the several different conditions being investigated.

experimental effect. A statistically significant difference between two groups experiencing different manipulations of the *independent variable*.

experimental hypothesis. What the investigator assumes will happen in a scientific investigation if certain conditions are met or particular variables are manipulated.

expressed emotion (EE). In the literature on *schizophrenia*, the amount of hostility and criticism directed from other people to the patient, usually within a family.

expressive language disorder. Difficulties expressing oneself in speech.

external validity. See *validity*.

extinction. The elimination of a *classically conditioned* response by the omission of the *unconditioned stimulus*. In *operant conditioning*, the elimination of the *conditioned response* by the omission of *reinforcement*.

extradural hematoma. Hemorrhage and swelling between the skull and dura mater when a *meningeal* artery is ruptured by a fractured bone of the skull.

factitious disorders. Disorders in which the individual's physical or psychological symptoms appear under voluntary control and are adopted merely to assume the role of a sick person. The disorder can also involve a parent producing a disorder in a child and is then called factitious disorder by proxy.

falsifiability. The extent to which a scientific assertion is amenable to systematic probes, any one of which could negate the scientist's expectations.

familiar. In witchcraft, a supernatural spirit often embodied in an animal and at the service of a person.

family interaction method. A procedure for studying family behavior by observing family members' interactions in a structured laboratory situation.

family method. A research strategy in *behavior genetics* in which the frequency of a *trait* or of abnormal behavior is determined in relatives who have varying percentages of shared genetic background.

family systems approach. A general approach to *etiology* and treatment that focuses on the complex interrelationships within families.

family therapy. A form of *group therapy* in which members of a family are helped to relate better to one another.

fear drive. In the Mowrer–Miller theory, an unpleasant internal state that impels avoidance. The necessity to reduce a fear drive can form the basis for new learning.

fear of performance. Being overly concerned with one's behavior during sexual contact with another, postulated by Masters and Johnson as a major factor in sexual dysfunction.

fear response. In the Mowrer–Miller theory, a response to a threatening or noxious situation that is covert and unobservable but that is assumed to function as a stimulus to produce measurable physiological changes in the body and observable overt behavior.

female orgasmic disorder. A recurrent and persistent delay or absence of orgasm in a woman during sexual activity adequate in focus, intensity, and duration; in many instances the woman may experience considerable sexual excitement.

female sexual arousal disorder. Formally called frigidity, the inability of a female to reach or maintain the lubrication–swelling stage of sexual excitement or to enjoy a subjective sense of pleasure or excitement during sexual activity.

fetal alcohol syndrome. Retarded growth of the developing fetus and infant; cranial, facial, and limb anomalies; and *mental retardation* caused by heavy consumption of alcohol by the mother during pregnancy.

fetishism. Reliance on an inanimate object for sexual arousal.

first-rank symptoms. In *schizophrenia*, specific *delusions* and *hallucinations* proposed by Schneider as particularly important for its more exact diagnosis.

fixation. In psychoanalytic theory, the arrest of *psychosexual* development at a particular stage through too much or too little gratification at that stage.

flashback. An unpredictable recurrence of *psychedelic* experiences from an earlier drug trip.

flat affect. A deviation in emotional response wherein virtually no emotion is expressed whatever the stimulus, emotional expressiveness is blunted, or a lack of expression and muscle tone is noted in the face.

flight of ideas. A symptom of *mania* that involves a rapid shift in conversation from one subject to another with only superficial associative connections.

flooding. A *behavior therapy* procedure in which a fearful person is exposed to what is frightening, in reality or in the imagination, for extended periods of time and without opportunity for escape.

follow-up study. A research procedure whereby individuals observed in an earlier investigation are contacted at a later time for further study.

forced rape. The legal term for rape, forced sexual intercourse or other sexual activity with another person. **Statutory rape** is sexual intercourse between an adult male and someone who is under the age of consent, as fixed by local statute.

forced-choice item. A format of a *personality inventory* in which the response alternatives for each item are equated for *social desirability*.

forensic psychiatry or psychology. The branch of psychiatry or psychology that deals with the legal questions raised by disordered behavior.

fragile X syndrome. Malformation (or even breakage) of the X *chromosome* associated with *moderate mental retardation*. Symptoms include large, underdeveloped ears, a long, thin face, a broad nasal root, and enlarged

testicles in males; many individuals show attention deficits and hyperactivity.

free association. A key psychoanalytic procedure in which the *analysand* is encouraged to give free rein to his or her thoughts and feelings, verbalizing whatever comes into the mind without monitoring its content. The assumption is that over time, *repressed* material will come forth for examination by the *analysand* and *psychoanalyst*.

freebase. The most potent part of *cocaine*, obtained by heating the drug with ether.

free-floating anxiety. Continual anxiety not attributable to any specific situation or reasonable danger. See *generalized anxiety disorder*.

frontal lobe. The forward or upper half of each *cerebral hemisphere*, in front of the central *sulcus*, active in reasoning and other higher mental processes.

fugue. See *dissociative fugue*.

functional social support. The quality of a person's relationships, for example, a good versus a distressed marriage. Contrast with *structural social support*.

gay. A colloquial term for *homosexual*, now often adopted by homosexuals who have openly announced their sexual orientation.

gay liberation. The often militant movement seeking to achieve civil rights for homosexuals and recognition of the normality of *homosexuality*.

gender identity. The deeply ingrained sense a person has of being either a man or a woman.

gender identity disorders. Disorders in which there is a deeply felt incongruence between anatomic sex and the sensed gender; *transsexualism* and gender identity disorder of childhood are examples.

gene. An ultramicroscopic area of the *chromosome*; the gene is the smallest physical unit of the DNA molecule that carries a piece of hereditary information.

general adaptation syndrome (GAS). Hans Selye's model to describe the biological reaction of an organism to sustained and unrelenting stress; there are several stages, culminating in death in extreme circumstances.

general paresis. See *neurosyphilis*.

generalized anxiety disorder (GAD). In this *anxiety disorder*, anxiety is so chronic, persistent, and pervasive that it seems *free-floating*. The individual is jittery and strained, distractible, and apprehensive that something bad is about to happen. A pounding heart, fast pulse and breathing, sweating, flushing, muscle aches, a lump in the throat, and an upset gastrointestinal tract are some of the bodily indications of this extreme anxiety.

genital stage. In psychoanalytic theory, the final *psychosexual stage*, reached in adulthood, in which *heterosexual* interests predominate.

genotype. An individual's unobservable, genetic constitution; the totality of *genes* possessed by an individual. Compare *phenotype*.

genuineness. In *client-centered therapy*, an essential quality of the therapist, referring to openness and authenticity.

germ theory (of disease). The general view in medicine that disease is caused by infection of the body by minute organisms and viruses.

gerontology. The interdisciplinary study of aging and of the special problems of the elderly.

Gestalt therapy. A *humanistic therapy* developed by Fritz Perls, which encourages clients to satisfy emerging needs so that their innate goodness can be expressed, to increase their awareness of unacknowledged feelings, and to reclaim parts of their personality that have been denied or disowned.

gestation period. The length of time, normally nine months in human beings, during which a fertilized egg develops into an infant ready to be born.

glans. The heavily innervated tip of the *penis.*

glove anesthesia. A *hysterical* lack of sensation in the part of the arm that would be covered by a glove.

grandiose delusions. Found in *paranoid schizophrenia, delusional disorder,* and *mania,* an exaggerated sense of one's importance, power, knowledge, or identity.

Graves' disease. An endocrine disorder resulting from oversecretion of the hormone thyroxin, in which metabolic processes are speeded up, producing apprehension, restlessness, and irritability.

gray matter. The neural tissue made up largely of nerve cell bodies that constitutes the cortex covering the *cerebral hemisphere,* the *nuclei* in lower brain areas, columns of the spinal cord, and the ganglia of the *autonomic nervous system.*

grimace. A distorted facial expression, often a symptom of *schizophrenia.*

group therapy. Method of treating psychological disorders whereby several persons are seen simultaneously by a single therapist.

gyrus. A ridge or convolution of the *cerebral cortex.*

habituation. In physiology, a process whereby an organism's response to the same stimulus lessens with repeated presentations.

halfway house. A homelike residence for people who are considered too disturbed to remain in their accustomed surroundings but do not require the total care of a mental institution.

hallucinations. Perceptions in any sensory modality without relevant and adequate external stimuli.

hallucinogen. A drug or chemical whose effects include *hallucinations.* Hallucinogenic drugs such as *LSD, psilocybin,* and *mescaline* are often called *psychedelic.*

hashish. The dried resin of the *Cannabis* plant, stronger in its effects than the dried leaves and stems that constitute *marijuana.*

health psychology. A branch of psychology dealing with the role of psychological factors in health and illness. See also *behavioral medicine.*

hebephrenia. See *disorganized schizophrenia.*

helplessness. A *construct* referring to the sense of having no control over important events; considered by many theorists to play a central role in *anxiety* and *depression.* See *learned helplessness theory.*

hermaphrodite. A person with parts of both male and female genitalia.

heroin. An extremely addictive *narcotic* drug derived from *morphine.*

heroin antagonists. Drugs, such as naloxone, that prevent a heroin user from experiencing any high.

heroin substitutes. Narcotics, such as *methadone,* that are *cross-dependent* with *heroin* and thus replace it and the body's craving for it.

heterosexual. A person who desires or engages in sexual relations with members of the opposite sex.

high-risk method. A research technique involving the intensive examination of people who have a high probability of later becoming abnormal.

histrionic personality disorder. This person is overly dramatic and given to emotional excess, impatient with minor annoyances, immature, dependent on others, and often sexually seductive without taking responsibility for flirtations; formerly called hysterical personality.

homophobia. Fear of or aversion to *homosexuality.*

homosexuality. Sexual desire or activity directed toward a member of one's own sex.

homovanillic acid. A major metabolite of *dopamine.*

hormone. A chemical substance produced by an *endocrine gland* and released into the blood or lymph for the purpose of controlling the function of a distant organ or organ system. Metabolism, growth, and development of secondary sexual characteristics are among the functions so controlled.

humanistic and existential therapies. A generic term for insight psychotherapies that emphasize the individual's subjective experiences, free will, and ever-present ability to decide on a new life course.

humanistic therapy. An insight therapy that emphasizes freedom of choice, growth of human potential, the joys of being a human being, and the importance of the patient's phenomenology; sometimes called an experiential therapy. See also *existential therapy.*

Huntington's chorea. A fatal disease passed on by a single *dominant gene.* Symptoms include spasmodic jerking of the limbs, psychotic behavior, and mental deterioration.

5-hydroxyindoleacetic acid (5-HIAA). The major metabolite of *serotonin.*

hyperactivity. See *attention-deficit/hyperactivity disorder.*

hyperkinesis. See *attention-deficit/hyperactivity disorder.*

hypertension. Abnormally high arterial blood pressure, with or without known organic causes. See *essential hypertension.*

hyperventilation. Very rapid and deep breathing associated with high levels of anxiety; causes the level of carbon dioxide in blood to be lowered with possible loss of consciousness.

hypnosis. A trancelike state or behavior resembling sleep, induced by suggestion, characterized primarily by increased suggestibility.

hypoactive sexual desire disorder. The absence of or deficiency in sexual fantasies and urges.

hypochondriasis. A *somatoform disorder* in which the person, misinterpreting rather ordinary physical sensations, is preoccupied with fears of having a serious disease and is not dissuaded by medical opinion. Difficult to distinguish from *somatization disorder.*

hypomania. An above-normal elevation of mood, but not as extreme as *mania*.

hypothalamus. A collection of *nuclei* and fibers in the lower part of the *diencephalon* concerned with the regulation of many visceral processes, such as metabolism, temperature, and water balance.

hysteria. A disorder known to the ancient Greeks in which a physical incapacity—a paralysis, an *anesthesia*, or an *analgesia*—is not due to a physiological dysfunction, for example, *glove anesthesia*; an older term for *conversion disorder*. In the late nineteenth century *dissociative disorders* were identified as such and considered hysterical states.

hysterical neurosis. The DSM-II category for *dissociative* and *somatoform disorders*.

id. In psychoanalytic theory, that part of the personality present at birth, composed of all the energy of the *psyche*, and expressed as biological urges that strive continually for gratification.

ideas of reference. *Delusional* thinking that reads personal significance into seemingly trivial remarks and activities of others and completely unrelated events.

identity crisis. A developmental period in adolescence marked by concerns about who one is and what one is going to do with his or her life.

idiographic. In psychology, relating to investigative procedures that consider the unique characteristics of a single person, studying them in depth, as in the *case study*. Contrast with *nomothetic*.

idiot savant. An individual with a rare form of *mental retardation*, extraordinarily talented in one or a few limited areas of intellectual achievement; sometimes called autistic savant.

illusion. A misperception of a real external stimulus, such as hearing the slapping of waves as footsteps.

imipramine. An *antidepressant* drug, one of the *tricyclic* group, trade name Tofranil.

in absentia. Literally, "in one's absence." Courts are concerned that a person be able to participate personally and meaningfully in his or her own trial and not be tried *in absentia* because of a distracting mental disorder.

in vivo. As applied in psychology, taking place in a real-life situation.

inappropriate affect. Emotional responses that are out of context, such as laughter when hearing sad news.

incest. Sexual relations between close relatives, most often between daughter and father or between brother and sister.

incidence. In epidemiological studies of a particular disorder, the rate at which new cases occur in a given place at a given time. Compare with *prevalence*.

incoherence. In *schizophrenia*, an aspect of *thought disorder* wherein verbal expression is marked by disconnectedness, fragmented thoughts, and jumbled phrases.

independent variable. In a psychological *experiment*, the factor, experience, or treatment that is under the control of the experimenter and that is expected to have an effect on participants as assessed by changes in the *dependent variable*.

index case (proband). The person who in a genetic investigation bears the diagnosis or *trait* in which the investigator is interested.

individual psychology. A variation of Freud's psychoanalysis introduced by Alfred Adler and focusing less on biological drives and more on such factors as people's conscious beliefs and goals for self-betterment.

infectious disease. An illness caused when a microorganism, such as a bacterium or a virus, invades the body, multiplies, and attacks a specific organ or organ system; pneumonia is an example.

informed consent. The agreement of a person to serve as a research participant or to enter therapy after being told the possible outcomes, both benefits and risks.

inhibited male orgasm. A recurrent and persistent delay or absence of ejaculation after an adequate phase of sexual excitement.

insanity defense. The legal argument that a defendant should not be held *ascriptively responsible* for an illegal act if the conduct is attributable to mental illness.

insight therapy. A general term for any *psychotherapy* that assumes that people become disordered because they do not adequately understand what motivates them, especially when their needs and drives conflict.

instrumental learning. See *operant conditioning*.

intelligence quotient (IQ). A standardized measure indicating how far an individual's raw score on an *intelligence test* is from the average raw score of his or her chronological age group.

intelligence test. A standardized means of assessing a person's current mental ability, for example, the Stanford–Binet test and the Wechsler Adult Intelligence Scale.

internal validity. See *validity*.

interpersonal therapy. A psychodynamic psychotherapy that focuses on the patient's interactions with others and that directly teaches how better to relate to others.

interpretation. In *psychoanalysis*, a key procedure in which the *psychoanalyst* points out to the *analysand* where *resistance* exists and what certain dreams and verbalizations reveal about impulses repressed in the *unconscious*; more generally, any statement by a therapist that construes the client's problem in a new way.

interrater reliability. See *reliability*.

introjection. In psychoanalytic theory, the unconscious incorporation of the values, attitudes, and qualities of another person into the individual's own ego structure.

introspection. A procedure whereby trained subjects are asked to report on their conscious experiences. This was the principal method of study in early twentieth-century psychology.

irrational beliefs. Self-defeating assumptions that are assumed by *rational-emotive* therapists to underlie psychological distress.

irresistible impulse. The term used in an 1834 Ohio court ruling on criminal responsibility that determined that an *insanity defense* can be established by proving that the accused had an uncontrollable urge to perform the act.

Korsakoff's psychosis. A chronic brain disorder marked by loss of recent memories and associated *confabulation* and by additional lesions in the *thalamus*.

la belle indifférence. The blasé attitude people with *conversion disorder* have toward their symptoms.

labeling theory. The general view that serious *psychopathology,* such as *schizophrenia,* is caused by society's reactions to unusual behavior.

labile. Easily moved or changed, quickly shifting from one emotion to another, or easily aroused.

language disorder. Difficulties understanding spoken language (receptive) or expressing thoughts verbally (expressive).

latency period. In psychoanalytic theory, the years between ages six and twelve, during which *id* impulses play a minor role in motivation.

latent content. In dreams, the presumed true meaning hidden behind the *manifest content.*

law of effect. A principle of learning that holds that behavior is acquired by virtue of its consequences.

learned helplessness theory. The theory that individuals acquire passivity and a sense of being unable to act and to control their lives; this happens through unpleasant experiences and traumas against which their efforts were ineffective; according to Seligman, this brings on *depression.*

learning disabilities. General term for *learning disorders,* communication disorders, and *motor skills disorder.*

learning disorders. A set of developmental disorders encompassing *dyslexia, mathematics disorder,* and disorder of written expression and characterized by failure to develop in a specific academic area to the degree expected by the child's intellectual level. Not diagnosed if the disorder is due to a sensory deficit.

learning (behavioral) paradigm. In abnormal psychology, a set of assumptions that abnormal behavior is learned in the same way as other human behavior.

least restrictive alternative. The legal principle according to which a committed mental patient must be treated in a setting that imposes as few restrictions as possible on his or her freedom.

lesion. Any localized abnormal structural change in organ or tissue caused by disease or injury.

libido. See *Eros.*

Life Change Unit (LCU) score. A score produced by totaling ratings of the stressfulness of recently experienced life events; high scores are found to be related to the contraction of a number of physical illnesses.

life-span developmental psychology. The study of changes in people as they grow from infancy to old age.

lifetime prevalence rate. The proportion of a sample that has ever had a disorder.

limbic system. The lower parts of the *cerebrum,* made up of primitive cortex; controls visceral and bodily changes associated with emotion and regulates drive-motivated behavior.

linkage analysis. A technique in genetic research whereby occurrence of a disorder in a family is evaluated alongside a known genetic marker.

lithium carbonate. A drug useful in treating both *mania* and *depression* in *bipolar disorder.*

lobotomy. A brain operation in which the nerve pathways between the *frontal lobes* of the brain and lower brain structures are cut in hopes of effecting beneficial behavioral change.

logotherapy. An *existential psychotherapy,* developed by Viktor Frankl, aimed at helping the demoralized client restore meaning to life by placing his or her suffering in a larger spiritual and philosophical context. The individual assumes responsibility for his or her existence and for pursuing a meaningful life.

longitudinal studies. Investigation that collects information on the same individuals repeatedly over time, perhaps over many years, in an effort to determine how phenomena change. Compare with *cross-sectional studies.*

loose associations (derailment). In *schizophrenia,* an aspect of *thought disorder* wherein the patient has difficulty sticking to one topic and drifts off on a train of associations evoked by an idea from the past.

LSD. *d*-lysergic acid diethylamide, a drug synthesized in 1938 and discovered to be a *hallucinogen* in 1943.

Luria–Nebraska test. A battery of *neuropsychological tests* that can detect impairment in different parts of the brain.

magical thinking. The conviction of the individual that his or her thoughts, words, and actions may in some manner cause or prevent outcomes in a way that defies the normal laws of cause and effect.

magnetic resonance imaging (MRI). A technique for measuring the structure or activity of the living brain. The person is placed inside a large circular magnet that causes hydrogen atoms to move; the return of the atoms to their original positions when the current to the magnet is turned off is translated by a computer into pictures of brain tissue.

mainstreaming. A policy of placing children with disabilities in regular classrooms; although special classes are provided as needed, the children share as much as possible in the opportunities and ambience afforded youngsters without disabilities.

maintenance dose. An amount of a drug designed to enable a patient to continue to benefit from a therapeutically effective regimen of medication. It is often less than the dose required to initiate the positive change.

major (unipolar) depression. A disorder of individuals who have experienced episodes of *depression* but not of *mania.*

male erectile disorder. A recurrent and persistent inability to attain or maintain an erection until completion of sexual activity.

male orgasmic disorder. See *inhibited male orgasm.*

malingering. Faking a physical or psychological incapacity in order to avoid a responsibility or gain an end; the goal is readily recognized from the individual's circumstances. To be distinguished from *conversion disorder,* in which the incapacity is assumed to be beyond voluntary control.

malleus maleficarum ("the witches' hammer"). A manual written by two Dominican monks in the fifteenth century to provide rules for identifying and trying witches.

mammillary body. Either of two small rounded structures located in the *hypothalamus* and consisting of *nuclei.*

mania.   An emotional state of intense but unfounded elation evidenced in talkativeness, *flight of ideas,* distractibility, grandiose plans, and spurts of purposeless activity.

manic-depressive illness, manic-depressive psychosis. Originally described by Kraepelin, a *mood disorder* characterized by alternating euphoria and profound sadness or by one of these moods. Called *bipolar disorder* in DSM-IV.

manifest content.   The immediately apparent, conscious content of dreams. Compare with *latent content.*

marathon group.   A group therapy session run continuously for a day or even longer, typically for *sensitivity training,* the assumption being that defenses can be worn down by the physical and psychological fatigue generated through intensive and continuous group interaction.

marijuana.   A drug derived from the dried and ground leaves and stems of the female hemp plant, *Cannabis sativa.*

marital therapy.   See *couples therapy.*

masochism.   See *sexual masochism.*

mathematics disorder.   Difficulties dealing with arithmetic symbols and operations; one of the *learning disorders.*

mediational theory of learning.   In psychology, the general view that certain stimuli do not directly initiate an overt response but activate an intervening process, which in turn initiates the response. It explains thinking, drives, emotions, and beliefs in terms of stimulus and response.

mediator.   In psychology, an inferred state intervening between the observable stimulus and response, activated by the stimulus and in turn initiating the response; in more general terms, a thought, drive, emotion, or belief. Also called a *construct.*

medical (disease) model. As applied in abnormal psychology, a set of assumptions that conceptualizes abnormal behavior as similar to physical diseases.

medulla oblongata.   An area in the *brain stem* through which nerve fiber tracts ascend to or descend from higher brain centers.

megalomania.   A paranoid *delusion of grandeur* in which an individual believes that he or she is an important person or is carrying out great plans.

melancholia.   A vernacular diagnosis of several millennia's standing for profound sadness and depression. In *major depression* with melancholia the individual is unable to feel better even momentarily when something good happens, regularly feels worse in the morning and awakens early, and suffers a deepening of other symptoms of depression.

meninges.   The three layers of nonneural tissue that envelop the brain and spinal cord. They are the dura mater, the arachnoid, and the pia mater.

meningitis.   An inflammation of the *meninges* through infection, usually by a bacterium, or through irritation. *Meningococcal,* the epidemic form of the disease, takes the lives of 10 percent of those who contract it and causes cerebral palsy, hearing loss, speech defects, and other forms of permanent brain damage in one of four people who recover.

mental age.   The numerical index of an individual's cognitive development determined by standardized *intelligence tests.*

mental retardation.   Subnormal intellectual functioning associated with impairment in adaptive behavior and identified at an early age.

meprobamate.   Generic term for *Miltown,* an *anxiolytic,* the first introduced and for a time one of the most widely used.

mescaline.   A *hallucinogen* and *alkaloid* that is the active ingredient of *peyote.*

mesmerize.   The first term for *hypnotize,* after Franz Anton Mesmer, an Austrian physician who in the late eighteenth century treated and cured hysterical or *conversion disorders* with what he considered the animal magnetism emanating from his body and permeating the universe.

meta-analysis.   A quantitative method of analyzing and comparing various therapies by standardizing their results.

metabolism.   The sum of the intracellular processes by which large molecules are broken down into smaller ones, releasing energy and wastes, and by which small molecules are built up into new living matter by consuming energy.

metacognition.   The knowledge people have about the way they know their world, for example, recognizing the usefulness of a map in finding their way in a new city.

methadone.   A synthetic addictive *heroin substitute* for treating *heroin* addicts that acts as a substitute for heroin by eliminating its effects and the craving for it.

methedrine.   A very strong *amphetamine,* sometimes shot directly into the veins.

3-methoxy-4-hydroxyphenylethylene glycol (MHPG) A major metabolite of *norepinephrine.*

midbrain.   The middle part of the brain that consists of a mass of nerve fiber tracts connecting the spinal cord and *pons, medulla,* and *cerebellum* to the *cerebral cortex.*

migraine headaches.   Extremely debilitating headaches caused by sustained dilation of the extracranial arteries, the temporal artery in particular; the dilated arteries trigger pain-sensitive nerve fibers in the scalp.

mild mental retardation.   A limitation in mental development measured on IQ tests at between 50–55 and 70; children with such a limitation are considered the educable mentally retarded and are usually placed in special classes.

milieu therapy.   A treatment procedure that attempts to make the total environment and all personnel and patients of the hospital a *therapeutic community,* conducive to psychological improvement; the staff conveys to the patients the expectation that they can and will behave more normally and responsibly.

Miltown.   The trade name for *meprobamate,* one of the principal *anxiolytics.*

Minnesota Multiphasic Personality Inventory (MMPI). A lengthy *personality inventory* by which individuals are diagnosed through their true–false replies to groups of statements indicating states such as *anxiety, depression,* masculinity–femininity, and *paranoia.*

mixed design.   A research strategy in which both *classificatory* and experimental *variables* are used; assigning people from discrete populations to two experimental conditions is an example.

mixed receptive-expressive language disorder. Difficulties producing and understanding spoken language.

M'Naghten rule.   An 1843 British court decision stating that an *insanity defense* can be established by proving that the defendant did not know what he or she was doing or did not realize that it was wrong.

modeling.   Learning by observing and imitating the behavior of others.

moderate mental retardation.   A limitation in mental development measured on IQ tests between 35–40 and 50–55; children with this degree of retardation are often institutionalized, and their training is focused on self-care rather than on development of intellectual skills.

mongolism.   See *Down syndrome.*

monism.   Philosophical doctrine that ultimate reality is a unitary organic whole and that therefore mental and physical are one and the same. Contrast with *dualism.*

monoamine.   An organic compound containing nitrogen in one amino group (NH). Some of the known *neurotransmitters* of the central nervous system, called collectively brain amines, are *catecholamines* and indoleamines, which are monoamines.

monoamine oxidase (MAO).   An enzyme that deactivates *catecholamines* and indoleamines within the presynaptic neuron, indoleamines in the *synapse.*

monoamine oxidase inhibitors.   A group of *antidepressant* drugs that prevent the enzyme *monoamine oxidase* from deactivating *neurotransmitters* of the central nervous system.

monozygotic (MZ) twins.   Genetically identical siblings who have developed from a single fertilized egg; sometimes called identical twins.

mood disorders.   Disorders in which there are disabling disturbances in emotion.

moral anxiety.   In psychoanalytic theory, the *ego*'s fear of punishment for failure to adhere to the *superego*'s standards of proper conduct.

moral treatment.   A therapeutic regimen, introduced by Philippe Pinel during the French Revolution, whereby mental patients were released from their restraints and were treated with compassion and dignity rather than with contempt and denigration.

morbidity risk.   The probability that an individual will develop a particular disorder.

morphine.   An addictive narcotic *alkaloid* extracted from *opium,* used primarily as an analgesic and as a *sedative.*

motor skills disorder.   A *learning disability* characterized by marked impairment in the development of motor coordination that is not accounted for by a physical disorder such as cerebral palsy.

mourning work.   In Freud's theory of *depression,* the recall by a depressed person of memories associated with a lost one, serving to separate the individual from the deceased.

multiaxial classification.   Classification having several dimensions, each of which is employed in categorizing; DSM-IV is an example.

multifactorial.   Referring to the operation of several variables influencing in complex fashion the development or maintenance of a phenomenon.

multimodal therapy.   A cognitive-behavioral therapy introduced by Arnold Lazarus, which employs techniques from diverse approaches in an effort to help people make positive changes in their BASIC IB: behavior, affects, sensations, images, cognitions, interpersonal relationships, and biological functioning.

multiple personality disorder (MPD).   See *dissociative identity disorder (DID).*

multiple-baseline design.   An experimental design in which two behaviors of a single person are selected for study and a treatment is applied to one of them. The behavior that is not treated serves as a baseline against which the effects of the treatment can be determined. This is a common design in *operant conditioning* research.

mutism.   The inability or refusal to speak.

myocardial infarction.   Heart attack. See *coronary heart disease.*

narcissistic personality disorder.   Extremely selfish and self-centered, people with a narcissistic personality have a grandiose view of their uniqueness, achievements, and talents and an insatiable craving for admiration and approval from others. They are exploitative to achieve their own goals and expect much more from others than they themselves are willing to give.

narcosynthesis.   A psychiatric procedure originating during World War II in which a drug was employed to help stressed soldiers recall the battle traumas underlying their disorders.

narcotics.   Addictive *sedative* drugs, for example, *morphine* and *heroin,* that in moderate doses relieve pain and induce sleep.

negative reinforcement.   The strengthening of a tendency to exhibit desired behavior by rewarding responses in that situation with the removal of an aversive stimulus.

negative symptoms.   Behavioral deficits in *schizophrenia,* such as *flat affect* and *apathy.*

negative triad.   In Beck's theory of depression, a person's baleful views of the self, the world, and the future; the triad is in a reciprocal causal relationship with pessimistic assumptions (*schemata*) and cognitive biases such as *selective abstraction.*

neo-Freudian.   A person who has contributed to the modification and extension of Freudian theory.

neologism.   A word made up by the speaker that is usually meaningless to a listener.

nerve impulse.   A change in the electric potential of a neuron; a wave of depolarization spreads along the neuron and causes the release of *neurotransmitter.*

neurofibrillary tangles.   Abnormal protein filaments present in the cell bodies of brain cells in patients with *Alzheimer's disease.*

neurologist. A physician who studies the nervous system, especially its structure, functions, and abnormalities.

neuron. A single nerve cell.

neuropsychological tests. Psychological tests, such as the *Luria–Nebraska*, that can detect impairment in different parts of the brain.

neuropsychologist. A psychologist concerned with the relationships among cognition, affect, and behavior on the one hand, and brain function on the other.

neuroses. A large group of non-*psychotic* disorders characterized by unrealistic *anxiety* and other associated problems, for example, *phobic* avoidances, *obsessions*, and *compulsions*.

neurosyphilis (general paresis). Infection of the central nervous system by the spirochete *Treponema pallidum*, which destroys brain tissue; marked by eye disturbances, tremors, and disordered speech as well as severe intellectual deterioration and *psychotic* symptoms.

neurotic anxiety. In psychoanalytic theory, a fear of the consequences of expressing previously punished and *repressed id* impulses; more generally, unrealistic fear.

neurotransmitter. A chemical substance important in transferring a nerve impulse from one *neuron* to another; for example, *serotonin* and *norepinephrine.*

nicotine. The principal *alkaloid* of tobacco (an addicting agent).

Niemann-Pick disease. An inherited disorder of lipid (fat) metabolism that produces *mental retardation* and paralysis and brings early death.

nitrous oxide. A gas that, when inhaled, produces euphoria and sometimes giddiness.

nomenclature. A system or set of names or designations used in a particular discipline, such as the DSM-IV.

nomothetic. Relating to the universal and to the formulation of general laws that explain a range of phenomena. Contrast with *idiographic*.

norepinephrine. A *catecholamine* that is a *neurotransmitter* of the central nervous system. Disturbances in its tracts apparently figure in *depression* and *mania*. It is also a neurotransmitter secreted at the nerve endings of the *sympathetic nervous system*, a hormone liberated with *epinephrine* in the adrenal medulla and similar to it in action, and a strong vasoconstrictor.

normal curve. As applied in psychology, the bell-shaped distribution of a measurable trait depicting most people in the middle and few at the extremes.

nosology. A systematic classification of diseases.

nucleus. In anatomy, a mass of nerve cell bodies (*gray matter*) within the brain or spinal cord by which descending nerve fibers connect with ascending nerve fibers.

object choice. In the psychology of sex, the type of person or thing selected as a focus for sexual desire or activity.

objective (realistic) anxiety. In psychoanalytic theory, the *ego's* reaction to danger in the external world; realistic fear. Contrast with *neurotic anxiety.*

observer drift. The tendency of two raters of behavior to begin to agree with each other, achieving unusually high levels of *reliability*; their way of coding behavior differentiates their scores from those of another pair of raters. This is regarded as a threat to reliable and valid *behavioral assessment.*

obsession. An intrusive and recurring thought that seems irrational and uncontrollable to the person experiencing it.

obsessive-compulsive disorder (OCD). An *anxiety disorder* in which the mind is flooded with persistent and uncontrollable thoughts or the individual is compelled to repeat certain acts again and again, causing significant distress and interference with everyday functioning.

obsessive-compulsive personality disorder. People with an obsessive-compulsive personality have inordinate difficulty making decisions, are overly concerned with details and efficiency, and relate poorly to others because they demand that things be done their way. They are unduly conventional, serious, formal, and stingy with their emotions.

occipital lobe. The posterior area of each *cerebral hemisphere*, situated behind the *parietal lobe* and above the *temporal lobes*, responsible for reception and analysis of visual information and for some visual memory.

Oedipus complex. In Freudian theory, the desire and conflict of the four-year-old male child who wants to possess his mother sexually and to eliminate the father rival. The threat of punishment from the father causes *repression* of these *id* impulses. Girls have a similar sexual desire for the father, which is repressed in analogous fashion and is called the *Electra complex*.

operant behavior. A response that is supposedly voluntary and operates on the environment, modifying it so that a reward or goal is attained.

operant conditioning. The acquisition or elimination of a response as a function of the environmental contingencies of *reward* and *punishment*.

operationism. A school of thought in science that holds that a given concept must be defined in terms of a single set of identifiable and repeatable operations that can be measured.

opiates. A group of addictive *sedatives* that in moderate doses relieve pain and induce sleep.

opium. One of the opiates, the dried, milky juice obtained from the immature fruit of the opium poppy. This addictive *narcotic* produces euphoria and drowsiness and reduces pain.

oppositional defiant disorder. An undercontrolled disorder of children marked by high levels of disobedience to authority but lacking the extremes of *conduct disorder.*

oral stage. In psychoanalytic theory, the first *psychosexual stage*, which extends into the second year; during it the mouth is the principal *erogenous* zone.

organismic variable. The physiological or psychological factor assumed to be operating "under the skin"; these variables are a focus of *behavioral assessment.*

orgasm (climax). The involuntary, intensely pleasurable, climactic phase in sexual arousal that lasts a number of seconds and usually involves muscular contractions and ejaculation in the male and similar contractions in the genitalia of the female.

orgasmic reorientation. A *behavior therapy* technique for altering classes of stimuli to which people are sexually attracted; individuals are confronted by a conventionally arousing stimulus while experiencing *orgasm* for another, undesirable reason.

outcome research. Research on the efficacy of *psychotherapy*. Contrast with *process research*.

overcontrolled (behavior). In reference to childhood disorders, problems that create distress for the child, such as *anxiety* and *social withdrawal*.

pain disorder. A *somatoform disorder* in which the person complains of severe and prolonged pain that is not explainable by organic pathology; it tends to be stress-related or permits the patient to avoid an aversive activity or to gain attention and sympathy.

panic disorder. An *anxiety disorder* in which the individual has sudden and inexplicable attacks of jarring symptoms, such as difficulty breathing, heart palpitations, dizziness, trembling, terror, and feelings of impending doom. In DSM-IV, said to occur with or without *agoraphobia*.

paradigm. A set of basic assumptions that outlines the universe of scientific inquiry, specifying both the concepts regarded as legitimate and the methods to be used in collecting and interpreting data.

paradoxical intervention. A therapeutic strategy that asks patients to increase or observe the frequency or intensity of a symptom, for example, having anxious patients make themselves more anxious or note when and how severely they become anxious.

paranoia. The general term for *delusions of persecution*, of *grandiosity*, or both; found in several pathological conditions, *paranoid disorders*, *paranoid schizophrenia*, and *paranoid personality* disorder. It can also be produced by large doses of certain drugs, such as *cocaine* or alcohol.

paranoid disorder. See *delusional disorder*.

paranoid personality disorder. The person with this personality expects to be mistreated by others, becomes suspicious, secretive, jealous, and argumentative. He or she will not accept blame and appears cold and unemotional.

paranoid schizophrenia. A type of *schizophrenia* in which the patient has numerous systematized *delusions* as well as *hallucinations* and *ideas of reference*. He or she may also be agitated, angry, argumentative, and sometimes violent.

paraphilias. Sexual attraction to unusual objects and sexual activities unusual in nature.

paraphrenia. A term sometimes used to refer to *schizophrenia* in an older adult.

paraprofessional. In clinical psychology, an individual lacking a doctoral degree but trained to perform certain functions usually reserved for clinicians, for example, a college student trained and supervised by a behavioral therapist to shape the behavior of *autistic* children through contingent reinforcers.

parasympathetic nervous system. The division of the *autonomic nervous system* that is involved with maintenance; it controls many of the internal organs and is active primarily when the organism is not aroused.

paresthesia. *Conversion disorder* marked by a sensation of tingling or creeping on the skin.

parietal lobe. The middle division of each *cerebral hemisphere*, situated behind the central *sulcus* and above the lateral sulcus; the receiving center for sensations of the skin and of bodily positions.

Parkinson's disease. A disease characterized by uncontrollable and severe muscle tremors, a stiff gait, a masklike, expressionless face, and withdrawal.

pathology. The anatomical, physiological, and psychological deviations of a disease or disorder; the study of these abnormalities.

PCP. See *phencyclidine*.

Pearson product moment correlation coefficient (*r*). A statistic, ranging in value from -1.00 to +1.00; the most common means of denoting a *correlational* relationship. The sign indicates whether the relationship is positive or negative, and the magnitude indicates the strength of the relationship.

pedophiles. People with a marked preference for obtaining sexual gratification through contact with youngsters defined legally as underage; pedophilia is a *paraphilia*.

penile plethysmograph. A device for detecting blood flow and thus for recording changes in size of the penis.

perseveration. The persistent repetition of words and ideas, often found in *schizophrenia*.

personality disorders. A heterogeneous group of disorders, listed separately on Axis II, regarded as long-standing, inflexible, and maladaptive personality *traits* that impair social and occupational functioning.

personality inventory. A self-report questionnaire by which an examinee indicates whether statements assessing habitual tendencies apply to him or her.

personality structure. See *trait*.

pervasive developmental disorders. Severe childhood problems marked by profound disturbances in social relations and oddities in behavior. *Autistic disorder* is one.

PET scan. Computer-generated picture of the living brain, created by analysis of radioactive particles from isotopes injected into the bloodstream.

peyote. A *hallucinogen* obtained from the root of the peyote cactus; the active ingredient is *mescaline*, an *alkaloid*.

phallic stage. In psychoanalytic theory, the third *psychosexual stage*, extending from ages three to six, during which maximal gratification is obtained from genital stimulation.

phencyclidine (PCP). Also known as angel dust, PeaCE Pill, zombie, and by other street names, this very powerful and hazardous drug causes profound disorientation, agitated and often violent behavior, and even seizures, coma, and death.

phenomenology. As applied in psychology, the philosophical view that the phenomena of subjective experience should be studied because behavior is considered to be determined by how people perceive themselves and the world, rather than by objectively described reality.

phenothiazine. The name for a group of drugs that relieve psychotic symptoms; their molecular structure, like that of the *tricyclic drugs*, consists of three fused rings. An example is *chlorpromazine (Thorazine)*.

phenotype. The totality of observable characteristics of a person. Compare with *genotype*.

phenylketonuria (PKU). A genetic disorder that, through a deficiency in a liver enzyme, phenylalanine hydroxylase, causes severe *mental retardation* unless phenylalanine can be largely restricted from the diet.

phobia. An *anxiety disorder* in which there is intense fear and avoidance of specific objects and situations, recognized as irrational by the individual.

phonological disorder. A *learning disability* in which some words sound like baby talk because the person is not able to make certain speech sounds.

physiology. The study of the functions and activities of living cells, tissues, and organs and of the physical and chemical phenomena involved.

placebo. Any inactive therapy or chemical agent, or any attribute or component of such a therapy or chemical, that affects a person's behavior for reasons related to his or her expectation of change.

placebo effect. The action of a drug or psychological treatment that is not attributable to any specific operations of the agent. For example, a tranquilizer can reduce anxiety both because of its special biochemical action and because the recipient expects relief. See *placebo*.

plaques. Small, round areas composed of remants of lost neurons and beta-amyloid, a waxy protein deposit; present in the brains of patients with *Alzheimer's disease*.

plateau phase. According to Masters and Johnson, the second stage in sexual arousal, during which excitement and tension have reached a stable high level before *orgasm*.

play therapy. The use of play as a means of uncovering what is troubling a child and of establishing *rapport*.

pleasure principle. In psychoanalytic theory, the demanding manner by which the *id* operates, seeking immediate gratification of its needs.

plethysmograph. An instrument for determining and registering variations in the amount of blood present or passing through an organ.

polydrug abuse. The misuse of more than one drug at a time, such as drinking heavily and taking cocaine.

pons. An area in the *brain stem* containing nerve-fiber tracts that connect the *cerebellum* with the spinal cord and with motor areas of the *cerebrum*.

positive reinforcement. The strengthening of a tendency to behave in a certain situation by presenting a desired reward following previous responses in that situation.

positive spikes. An EEG pattern recorded from the *temporal lobe* of the brain, with frequencies of 6 to 8 cycles per second and 14 to 16 cycles per second, often found in impulsive and aggressive people.

positive symptoms. In *schizophrenia*, behavioral excesses, such as *hallucinations* and bizarre behavior. Compare with *negative symptoms*.

posttraumatic stress disorder (PTSD). An *anxiety disorder* in which a particularly stressful event, such as military combat, rape, or a natural disaster, brings in its aftermath intrusive reexperiencings of the trauma, a numbing of responsiveness to the outside world, estrangement from others, a tendency to be easily startled, and nightmares, recurrent dreams, and otherwise disturbed sleep.

poverty of content. Reduced informational content in speech, one of the *negative symptoms* of *schizophrenia*.

poverty of speech. Reduced amount of talking, one of the *negative symptoms* of *schizophrenia*.

predictive validity. See *validity*.

predisposition. An inclination or *diathesis* to respond in a certain way, either inborn or acquired; in abnormal psychology, a factor that lowers the ability to withstand stress and inclines the individual toward *pathology*.

prefrontal lobotomy. A surgical procedure that destroys the tracts connecting the *frontal lobes* to lower centers of the brain; once believed to be an effective treatment for *schizophrenia*.

premature ejaculation. Inability of the male to inhibit his *orgasm* long enough for mutually satisfying sexual relations.

premorbid adjustment. In research on *schizophrenia*, the social and sexual adjustment of the individual before the onset or diagnosis of the symptoms. Patients with good premorbid adjustment are those found to have been relatively normal earlier; those with poor premorbid adjustment had inadequate interpersonal and sexual relations.

preparedness. In *classical conditioning* theory, a biological *predisposition* to associate particular stimuli readily with the *unconditioned stimulus*.

prevalence. In *epidemiological* studies of a disorder, the percentage of a population that has the disorder at a given time. Compare with *incidence*.

prevention. *Primary* prevention comprises efforts in *community psychology* to reduce the incidence of new cases of psychological disorder by such means as altering stressful living conditions and genetic counseling; *secondary* prevention includes efforts to detect disorders early, so that they will not develop into full-blown, perhaps chronic, disabilities; *tertiary* prevention attempts to reduce the long-term consequences of having a disorder, equivalent in most respects to therapy.

primary empathy. A form of *empathy* in which the therapist understands the content and feeling of what the client is saying and expressing from the client's *phenomenological* point of view. Compare with *advanced accurate empathy*.

primary prevention. See *prevention*.

primary process. In psychoanalytic theory, one of the *id's* means of reducing tension, by imagining what it desires.

privileged communication. The communication between parties in a confidential relation that is protected by statute. A spouse, doctor, lawyer, pastor, psychologist, or psychiatrist cannot be forced, except under unusual circumstances, to disclose such information.

proband. See *index case*.

process research. Research on the mechanisms by which a therapy may bring improvement. Compare with *outcome research*.

process-reactive dimension (of schizophrenia). A dimension used to distinguish people with *schizophrenia*; patients with process schizophrenia suffer long-term and gradual deterioration before the onset of their illness, whereas those with reactive schizophrenia have a better premorbid history and a more rapid onset of symptoms. See *premorbid adjustment*.

profound mental retardation. A limitation in mental development measured on IQ tests at less than 20–25; children with this degree of retardation require total supervision of all their activities.

progestins. Steroid progestational hormones that are the biological precursors of androgens, the male sex hormones.

prognosis. A prediction of the likely course and outcome of an illness. Compare with *diagnosis*.

projection. A *defense mechanism* whereby characteristics or desires unacceptable to the *ego* are attributed to someone else.

projective hypothesis. The notion that highly unstructured stimuli, as in the *Rorschach*, are necessary to bypass defenses in order to reveal unconscious motives and conflicts.

projective test. A psychological assessment device employing a set of standard but vague stimuli on the assumption that unstructured material will allow unconscious motivations and fears to be uncovered. The *Rorschach* series of inkblots is an example.

pronoun reversal. A speech problem in which the child refers to himself or herself as "he," "she," or "you" and uses "I" or "me" in referring to others; often found in the speech of children with *autistic disorder*.

pseudocommunity. An illusory world built up by a *paranoid* person, dominated by false beliefs that are not properly verified and shared by others.

psilocybin. A *psychedelic* drug extracted from the mushroom *Psilocybe mexicana*.

psyche. The soul, spirit, or mind as distinguished from the body. In psychoanalytic theory, it is the totality of the *id*, *ego*, and *superego*, including both conscious and unconscious components.

psychedelic. A drug that expands consciousness. See also *hallucinogen*.

psychiatrist. A physician (M.D.) who has taken specialized postdoctoral training, called a residency, in the diagnosis, treatment, and prevention of mental and emotional disorders.

psychoactive drugs. Chemical compounds having a psychological effect that alters mood or thought process. Valium is an example.

psychoanalysis. A term applied primarily to the therapy procedures pioneered by Freud, entailing *free association*, *dream analysis*, and *working through* the *transference neurosis*. More recently the term has come to encompass the numerous variations on basic Freudian therapy.

psychoanalyst (analyst). A therapist who has taken specialized postdoctoral training in psychoanalysis after earning an M.D. or a Ph.D. degree.

psychoanalytic (psychodynamic) paradigm. General view based on *psychoanalysis*.

psychodynamics. In psychoanalytic theory, the mental and emotional forces and processes that develop in early childhood and their effects on behavior and mental states.

psychogenesis. Development from psychological origins, as distinguished from somatic origins. Contrast with *somatogenesis*.

psychological autopsy. The analysis of an individual's *suicide* through the examination of his or her letters and through interviews with friends and relatives in the hope of discovering why the person committed suicide.

psychological deficit. The term used to indicate that performance of a pertinent psychological process is below that expected of a normal person.

psychological dependency. The term sometimes applied as the reason for *substance abuse*; a reliance on a drug but not a physiological addiction.

psychological factor influencing a medical condition. A diagnosis in DSM-IV that a physical illness is caused in part or exacerbated by psychological *stress*.

psychological tests. Standardized procedures designed to measure a person's performance on a particular task or to assess his or her personality.

psychopath. See *antisocial personality*.

psychopathologists. Mental health professionals who conduct research into the nature and development of mental and emotional disorders. Their academic backgrounds can differ; some are trained as experimental psychologists, others as psychiatrists, and still others as biochemists.

psychopathology. The field concerned with the nature and development of mental disorders.

psychopathy. See *antisocial personality*.

psychophysiological disorders. Disorders with physical symptoms that may involve actual tissue damage, usually in one organ system, and that are produced in part by continued mobilization of the *autonomic nervous system* under stress. Hives and ulcers are examples. No longer listed in DSM-IV in a separate category, such disorders are now diagnosed on Axis I as *psychological factors influencing a medical condition*; on Axis III the specific physical condition is given.

psychophysiology. The discipline concerned with the bodily changes that accompany psychological events.

psychosexual stages. In psychoanalytic theory, critical developmental phases that the individual passes through, each stage characterized by the body area providing maximal erotic gratification. The adult personality is formed by the pattern and intensity of instinctual gratification at each stage.

psychosexual trauma. As applied by Masters and Johnson, an earlier frightening or degrading sexual experience that is related to a present *sexual dysfunction*.

psychosis. A severe mental disorder in which thinking and emotion are so impaired that the individual is seriously out of contact with reality.

psychosocial stages of development. In Erik Erikson's theory, phases through which people pass from infancy through old age, each characterized by a particular challenge or crisis.

psychosomatic (disorder). See *psychophysiological disorders.*

psychosurgery. Any surgical technique in which neural pathways in the brain are cut in order to change behavior. See *lobotomy.*

psychotherapy. A primarily verbal means of helping troubled individuals change their thoughts, feelings, and behavior to reduce distress and to achieve greater life satisfaction. See *insight therapy* and *behavior therapy.*

psychotic (delusional) depression. A profound sadness and unjustified feelings of unworthiness, which also include *delusions.*

punishment. In psychological experiments, any noxious stimulus imposed on an organism to reduce the probability that it will behave in an undesired way.

random assignment. A method of assigning people to groups in an *experiment* that gives each person an equal chance of being in each group. The procedure helps to ensure that groups are comparable before the experimental manipulation begins.

rape. See *forced rape.*

rapid-smoking treatment. A *behavior therapy* technique for reducing cigarette smoking in which the person is instructed to puff much more quickly than usual in an effort to make the whole experience aversive.

rapport. A close, trusting relationship, believed to be essential for effective psychotherapy.

rational-emotive behavior therapy (REBT). New term for *rational-emotive therapy.*

rational-emotive therapy (RET). A *cognitive-restructuring behavior therapy* introduced by Albert Ellis and based on the assumption that much disordered behavior is rooted in absolutistic demands that people make on themselves. The therapy aims to alter the unrealistic goals individuals set for themselves, such as, "I must be universally loved."

rationalization. A *defense mechanism* in which a plausible reason is unconsciously invented by the *ego* to protect itself from confronting the real reason for an action, thought, or emotion.

Raynaud's disease. A *psychophysiological disorder* in which capillaries, especially of the fingers and toes, are subject to spasm. It is characterized by cold, moist hands, is commonly accompanied by pain, and may progress to gangrene.

reaction formation. A *defense mechanism* whereby an unconscious and unacceptable impulse or feeling that would cause anxiety is converted into its opposite so that it can become conscious and can be expressed.

reaction-time test. A procedure for determining the interval between the application of a stimulus and the beginning of the subject's response.

reactivity (of behavior). The phenomenon whereby behavior is changed by the very fact that it is being observed.

reading disorder. See *dyslexia.*

reality principle. In psychoanalytic theory, the manner in which the *ego* delays gratification and otherwise deals with the environment in a planned, rational fashion.

receptive aphasia. See *aphasia.*

receptor. Proteins embedded in the membrane covering a neural cell that interact with one or more *neurotransmitters.*

recessive gene. A *gene* that must be paired with one identical to it in order to determine a *trait* in the *phenotype.*

recovery time. The period it takes for a physiological process to return to *baseline* after the body has responded to a stimulus.

refractory phase. The brief period after stimulation of a nerve, muscle, or other irritable element during which it is unresponsive to a second stimulus; or the period after intercourse during which the male cannot have another orgasm.

regression. A *defense mechanism* in which anxiety is avoided by retreating to the behavior patterns of an earlier *psychosexual stage.*

reinforcement. In *operant conditioning,* increasing the probability that a response will recur either by presenting a contingent positive event or by removing a negative one.

reliability. The extent to which a test, measurement, or classification system produces the same scientific observation each time it is applied. Some specific kinds of reliability include **test-retest,** the relationship between the scores that a person achieves when he or she takes the same test twice; **interrater,** the relationship between the judgments that at least two raters make independently about a phenomenon; **split half,** the relationship between two halves of an assessment instrument that have been determined to be equivalent; **alternate form,** the relationship between scores achieved by people when they complete two versions of a test that are judged to be equivalent.

repression. A *defense mechanism* whereby impulses and thoughts unacceptable to the *ego* are pushed into the *unconscious.*

residual schizophrenia. Diagnosis given to patients who have had one episode of schizophrenia but who presently show no psychotic symptoms, though signs of the disorder do exist.

resistance. During *psychoanalysis,* the defensive tendency of the unconscious part of the *ego* to ward from consciousness particularly threatening *repressed* material.

resistance to extinction. The tendency of a *conditioned response* to persist in the absence of any *reinforcement.*

resolution phase. The last stage in the sexual arousal cycle, during which sexual tensions abate.

response cost. An *operant conditioning punishment* procedure in which the misbehaving person is fined already earned reinforcers.

response deviation. A tendency to answer questionnaire items in an uncommon way, regardless of their content.

response hierarchy. The ordering of a series of responses according to the likelihood of their being elicited by a particular stimulus.

response prevention. A *behavior therapy* technique in which the person is discouraged from making an accustomed response; used primarily with *compulsive* rituals.

response set. The tendency of an individual to respond in a particular way to questions or statements on a test —for example, with a False—regardless of the content of each query or statement.

reticular formation. Network of *nuclei* and fibers in the central core of the *brain stem* that is important in arousing the cortex and maintaining alertness, in processing incoming sensory stimulation, and in adjusting spinal reflexes.

retrospective reports. Recollections by an individual of past events.

reversal (ABAB) design. An experimental design in which behavior is measured during a baseline period (A), during a period when a treatment is introduced (B), during the reinstatement of the conditions that prevailed in the baseline period (A), and finally during a reintroduction of the treatment (B). It is commonly used in *operant* research to isolate cause–effect relationships.

reward. Any satisfying event or stimulus that, by being contingent on a response, increases the probability that the person will make that response again.

Rh factor. A substance present in the red blood cells of most people. If the Rh factor is present in the blood of a fetus but not in that of the mother, her system produces antibodies that may enter the bloodstream of the fetus and indirectly damage the brain.

right to refuse treatment. A legal principle according to which a committed mental patient may decline to participate in treatment.

right to treatment. A legal principle according to which a committed mental patient must be provided some minimal amount and quality of professional intervention, enough to afford a realistic opportunity for meaningful improvement.

risk factor. A condition or variable that, if present, increases the likelihood of developing a disorder.

role-playing. A technique that teaches people to behave in a certain way by encouraging them to pretend that they are in a particular situation; it helps people acquire complex behaviors in an efficient way. See also *behavior rehearsal*.

Rorschach Inkblot Test. A *projective test* in which the examinee is instructed to interpret a series of ten inkblots reproduced on cards.

Rosenthal effect. The tendency for results to conform to experimenters' expectations unless stringent safeguards are instituted to minimize human bias; named after Robert Rosenthal, who performed many of the original experiments revealing the problem.

rubella (German measles). An infectious disease that, if contracted by the mother during the first three months of pregnancy, has a high risk of causing *mental retardation* and physical deformity in the child.

sadism. See *sexual sadism*.

schema. A mental structure for organizing information about the world. *Pl.* schemata.

schizoaffective disorder. Diagnosis applied when a patient has symptoms of both mood disorder and either *schizophreniform disorder* or *schizophrenia*.

schizoid personality disorder. The person with a schizoid personality is emotionally aloof, indifferent to the praise, criticism, and feelings of others, and usually a loner with few, if any, close friends and with solitary interests.

schizophrenia. A group of *psychotic* disorders characterized by major disturbances in thought, emotion, and behavior; disordered thinking in which ideas are not logically related; faulty perception and attention; bizarre disturbances in motor activity; flat or inappropriate emotions; and reduced tolerance for stress in interpersonal relations. The patient withdraws from people and reality, often into a fantasy life of *delusions* and *hallucinations*. See *schizoaffective disorder, schizophreniform disorder,* and *brief reactive psychosis*.

schizophreniform disorder. Diagnosis given to people who have all the symptoms of *schizophrenia*, except that the disorder lasts more than two weeks but less than six months. See *brief reactive psychosis*.

schizophrenogenic mother. A cold, dominant, conflict-inducing mother formerly believed to cause *schizophrenia* in her child.

schizotypal personality disorder. The person with a schizotypal personality is eccentric, has oddities of thought and perception (*magical thinking, illusions, depersonalization, derealization*), speaks digressively and with overelaborations, and is usually socially isolated. Under stress he or she may appear *psychotic*.

school phobia. An acute, irrational dread of attending school, usually accompanied by somatic complaints. It is the most common *phobia* of childhood.

science. The pursuit of systematized knowledge through reliable observation.

secondary gain. Benefits that a person unconsciously obtains from a disability.

secondary prevention. See *prevention*.

secondary process. The reality-based decision-making and problem-solving activities of the *ego*. Compare with *primary process*.

secondhand smoke. The smoke from the burning end of a cigarette, which contains higher concentrations of ammonia, carbon monoxide, nicotine, and tar than does the smoke inhaled by the smoker.

sedative. A drug that slows bodily activities, especially those of the central nervous system; it is used to reduce pain and tension and to induce relaxation and sleep.

selective abstraction. A cognitive bias in Beck's theory of depression whereby a person picks out from a complex situation only certain features and ignores aspects that could lead to a different conclusion.

selective mortality. A possible confound in *longitudinal studies*, whereby the less healthy people in a sample are more likely to drop out over time.

self-actualization. Fulfilling one's potential as an always growing human being; believed by *client-centered therapists* to be the master motive.

self-efficacy. In Bandura's theory, the person's belief that he or she can achieve certain goals.

self-instructional training. A cognitive-behavioral approach that tries to help people improve their overt behavior by changing how they silently talk to themselves.

self-monitoring. In *behavioral assessment,* a procedure whereby the individual observes and reports certain aspects of his or her own behavior, thoughts, or emotions.

self-psychology. Kohut's variant of psychoanalysis, in which the focus is on the development of the person's self-worth from acceptance and nurturance by key figures in childhood.

senile plaques. Small areas of tissue degeneration in the brain, made up of granular material and filaments.

sensate focus. A term applied to exercises prescribed at the beginning of the Masters and Johnson sex therapy program; partners are instructed to fondle each other to give pleasure but to refrain from intercourse, thus reducing anxiety about sexual performance.

sensitivity training group (T-group). A small group of people who spend a period of time together both for therapy and for educational purposes; participants are encouraged or forced to examine their interpersonal functioning and their often overlooked feelings about themselves and others.

sensory-awareness procedures. Techniques that help clients tune into their feelings and sensations, as in *sensate-focus* exercises, and to be open to new ways of experiencing and feeling.

separation anxiety disorder. A disorder in which the child feels intense fear and distress when away from someone on whom he or she is very dependent; said to be a significant cause of *school phobia.*

serotonin. An indoleamine that is a *neurotransmitter* of the central nervous system. Disturbances in its tracts apparently figure in *depression.*

severe mental retardation. A limitation in mental development measured in IQ tests at between 20–25 and 35–40. Individuals often cannot care for themselves, communicate only briefly, and are listless and inactive.

sex-reassignment surgery. An operation removing existing genitalia of a *transsexual* and constructing a substitute for the genitals of the opposite sex.

sexual and gender identity disorders. In DSM-IV, disorders comprising the *paraphilias, sexual dysfunctions,* and *gender identity disorders.*

sexual aversion disorder. Avoidance of nearly all genital contact with other people.

sexual dysfunctions. Dysfunctions in which the appetitive or psychophysiological changes of the normal sexual response cycle are inhibited.

sexual masochism. A marked preference for obtaining or increasing sexual gratification through subjection to pain or humiliation.

sexual orientation disturbance. An earlier term for DSM-III's *ego-dystonic homosexuality.*

sexual response cycle. The general pattern of sexual physical processes and feelings, building to an orgasm by stimulation and made up of five phases: *interest, excitement, plateau, orgasm,* and *resolution.*

sexual sadism. A marked preference for obtaining or increasing sexual gratification by inflicting pain or humiliation on another person.

sexual script. Rules people have for guiding their actions in sexual situations.

sexual value system. As applied by Masters and Johnson, the activities that an individual holds to be acceptable and necessary in a sexual relationship.

shaping. In *operant conditioning,* reinforcing responses that are successively closer approximations to the desired behavior.

shell shock. A term from World War I for what is now referred to as *posttraumatic stress disorder;* it was believed to be due to sudden atmospheric changes from nearby explosions.

significant difference. See *statistical significance.*

single-subject experimental design. A design for an experiment conducted with a single subject, for example, the *reversal* and *multiple-baseline designs* in *operant conditioning* research.

situational determinants. The environmental conditions that precede and follow a particular piece of behavior, a primary focus of *behavioral assessment.*

skeletal (voluntary) muscle. Muscle that clothes the skeleton of the vertebrate, is attached to bone, and is under voluntary control.

Skinner box. A laboratory apparatus in which an animal is placed for an *operant-conditioning* experiment. It contains a lever or other device that the animal must manipulate to obtain a reward or avoid punishment.

sleeping sickness. See *encephalitis lethargica.*

smooth (involuntary) muscle. Thin sheets of muscle cells associated with *viscera* and walls of blood vessels, performing functions not usually under direct voluntary control.

social desirability. In completion of *personality inventories,* the tendency of the responder to give what he or she considers the socially acceptable answer, whether or not it is accurate.

social phobia. A collection of fears linked to the presence of other people.

social problem solving. A form of cognitive behavior therapy that has people construe their psychological difficulties as stemming from soluble problems in living and then teaches them how to generate useful solutions.

social selection theory. An attempt to explain the correlation between social class and *schizophrenia* by proposing that people with schizophrenia move downward in social status.

social worker. A mental health professional who holds a master of social work (M.S.W.) degree.

social-skills training. *Behavior therapy* procedures for teaching socially unknowledgeable individuals how to meet others, talk to them and maintain eye contact, give and receive criticism, offer and accept compliments, make requests and express feelings, and otherwise improve their relations with other people. *Modeling* and *behavior rehearsal* are two such procedures.

socioeconomic status. A relative position in the community as determined by occupation, income, and level of education.

sociogenic hypothesis. Generally, an idea that seeks causes in social conditions, for example, that being in a low social class can cause one to become *schizophrenic*.

sociopath. See *antisocial personality*.

sodomy. Originally, penetration of the male organ into the anus of another male; later broadened in English law to include heterosexual anal intercourse and by some U.S. state statutes to cover unconventional sex in general.

soma. The totality of an organism's physical makeup.

somatic nervous system. That part of the nervous system that controls muscles under voluntary control.

somatic weakness. The vulnerability of a particular organ or organ system to psychological stress and thereby to a particular *psychophysiological disorder*.

somatization disorder (Briquet's syndrome). A *somatoform disorder* in which the person continually seeks medical help for recurrent and multiple physical symptoms that have no discoverable physical cause. The medical history is complicated and dramatically presented. Compare with *hypochondriasis*.

somatoform disorders. Disorders in which physical symptoms suggest a physical problem but have no known physiological cause; they are therefore believed to be linked to psychological conflicts and needs but not voluntarily assumed. Examples are *somatization disorder* (Briquet's syndrome), *conversion disorder, pain disorder, hypochondriasis*.

somatoform pain disorder. A *somatoform disorder* in which the person complains of severe and prolonged pain that is not explainable by organic pathology; it tends to be stress related or permits the patient to avoid an aversive activity or to gain attention and sympathy.

somatogenesis. Development from bodily origins, as distinguished from psychological origins. Compare with *psychogenesis*.

SORC. An acronym for the four sets of variables that are the focus of *behavioral assessment: situational determinants, organismic variables,* (overt) *responses,* and *reinforcement contingencies*.

specific phobia. An unwarranted fear and avoidance of a specific object or circumstance, for example, fear of nonpoisonous snakes or fear of heights.

specific-reaction theory. The hypothesis that an individual develops a given *psychophysiological disorder* because of the innate tendency of the *autonomic nervous system* to respond in a particular way to stress, for example, by increasing heart rate or developing tension in the forehead.

spectator role. As applied by Masters and Johnson, a pattern of behavior in which the individual's focus on and concern with sexual performance impedes his or her natural sexual responses.

split-half reliability. See *reliability*.

stability–lability. A dimension of classifying the responsiveness of the *autonomic nervous system*. Labile individuals are those in whom a wide range of stimuli can elicit autonomic *arousal*; stable individuals are less easily aroused.

standardization. The process of constructing an assessment procedure that has norms and meets the various psychometric criteria for *reliability* and *validity*.

state-dependent learning. The phenomenon whereby an organism shows the effects of learning that took place in a special condition, such as while intoxicated, better than in another condition.

state-dependent memory. The phenomenon whereby people are more able to remember an event if they are in the same state as when it occurred. If they are in a greatly different state when they try to remember— happy now, and sad then, for example—memory is poorer.

statistical significance. A result that has a low probability of having occurred by chance alone and is by convention regarded as important.

statutory rape. See *forced rape*.

stepping-stone theory. The belief that the use of one kind of drug, such as *marijuana*, leads to the use of a more dangerous one, such as *cocaine*.

stimulant. A drug that increases alertness and motor activity and at the same time reduces fatigue, allowing an individual to remain awake for an extended period of time. Examples are *cocaine* and *amphetamines*.

strategic processing. The use of *cognitive* strategies to solve problems; said to be defective in people with *mental retardation*.

stress. State of an organism subjected to a *stressor*; it can take the form of increased *autonomic* activity and in the long term can cause the breakdown of an organ or development of a mental disorder.

stress management. A range of psychological procedures that help people control and reduce their *stress* or *anxiety*.

stressor. An event that occasions *stress* in an organism, for example, loss of a loved one.

stroke. A sudden loss of consciousness and control followed by paralysis; caused when a blood clot obstructs an artery or by hemorrhage into the brain when an artery ruptures.

structural social support. A person's network of social relationships, for example, number of friends. Contrast with *functional social support*.

stuttering. One of the communication disorders of childhood, marked by frequent and pronounced verbal dysfluencies, such as repetitions of certain sounds.

subdural hematoma. Hemorrhage and swelling of the arachnoid torn by a fractured bone of the skull.

subintentioned death. A form of *suicide* that is believed to have been caused in some measure by the person's unconscious intentions.

substance abuse. The use of a drug to such an extent that the person is often intoxicated throughout the day and fails in important obligations and in attempts to abstain, but there is no physiological dependence. See *psychological dependency*.

substance dependence. The abuse of a drug sometimes accompanied by a physiological dependence on it, made evident by *tolerance* and *withdrawal* symptoms; also called addiction.

substance-related disorders. Disorders in which drugs such as *alcohol* and *cocaine* are abused to such an extent that behavior becomes maladaptive; social and occupational functioning are impaired, and control or abstinence becomes impossible. Reliance on the drug may be either psychological, as in *substance abuse*, or physiological, as in *substance dependence*, or addiction.

successive approximations. Responses that closer and closer resemble the desired response in *operant conditioning*. See *shaping*.

suicide. The taking of one's own life intentionally.

suicide prevention centers. Based on the assumption that people are often ambivalent about taking their own lives, these centers are staffed primarily by paraprofessionals who are trained to be *empathic* and to encourage suicidal callers to consider nondestructive ways of dealing with what is bothering them.

sulcus (fissure). A shallow furrow in the *cerebral cortex* separating adjacent convolutions or *gyri*.

superego. In psychoanalytic theory, the part of the personality that acts as the conscience and reflects society's moral standards as learned from parents and teachers.

symbolic loss. In *psychoanalytic* theory, the unconscious interpretation by the *ego* of an event such as the rebuff of a loved one as a permanent rejection.

sympathetic nervous system. The division of the *autonomic nervous system* that acts on bodily systems—for example, contracting the blood vessels, reducing activity of the intestines, and increasing the heartbeat—to prepare the organism for exertion, emotional stress, or extreme cold.

symptom. An observable physiological or psychological manifestation of a disease, often occurring in a patterned group to constitute a *syndrome*.

synapse. A small gap between two *neurons* where the nerve impulse passes from the axon of the first to the dendrites, cell body, or axon of the second.

syndrome. A group or pattern of *symptoms* that tend to occur together in a particular *disease*.

systematic desensitization. A major *behavior therapy* procedure that has a fearful person, while deeply relaxed, imagine a series of progressively more fearsome situations. The two responses of relaxation and fear are incompatible and fear is dispelled. This technique is useful for treating psychological problems in which *anxiety* is the principal difficulty.

systematic rational restructuring. A variant of *rational-emotive therapy* in which the client imagines a series of increasingly anxiety-provoking situations while attempting to reduce distress by talking about them to the self in a more realistic, defusing fashion.

systems perspective. A general viewpoint that holds that a phenomenon, for example, a child's conduct problem, is best understood in the broad context in which it occurs, for example, the child's family and school environments.

tachycardia. A racing of the heart, often associated with high levels of *anxiety*.

tardive dyskinesia. A muscular disturbance of older patients who have taken *phenothiazines* for a very long time, marked by involuntary lip smacking and chin wagging.

Taylor Manifest Anxiety Scale. Fifty items drawn from the MMPI, used as a self-report questionnaire to assess *anxiety*.

temporal lobe. A large area of each *cerebral hemisphere* situated below the lateral *sulcus* and in front of the *occipital lobe*; contains primary auditory projection and association areas and general association areas.

tertiary prevention. See *prevention*.

testes. Male reproductive glands or gonads; the site where sperm develop and are stored.

testosterone. Male sex hormone secreted by the *testes* that is responsible for the development of sex characteristics, such as enlargement of the testes and growth of facial hair.

test-retest reliability. See *reliability*.

tetrahydrocannabinol (THC). The major active chemical in *marijuana* and *hashish*.

T-group. See *sensitivity training group*.

thalamus. A major brain relay station consisting of two egg-shaped lobes located in the *diencephalon*; it receives impulses from all sensory areas except the olfactory and transmits them to the *cerebrum*.

Thanatos. In psychoanalytic theory, the death instinct; with *Eros*, the two basic instincts within the *id*.

Thematic Apperception Test (TAT). A *projective test* consisting of a set of black-and-white pictures reproduced on cards, each depicting a potentially emotion-laden situation. The examinee, presented with the cards one at a time, is instructed to make up a story about each situation.

theory. A formally stated and coherent set of propositions that purport to explain a range of phenomena, order them in a logical way, and suggest what additional information might be gleaned under certain conditions.

therapeutic community. A concept in mental health care that views the total environment as contributing to *prevention* or treatment.

thiamine. One of the complex of B vitamins.

third-variable problem. The difficulty in the *correlational method* of research whereby the relationship between two variables may be attributable to a third factor.

Thorazine. Trade name for *chlorpromazine*, one of the *antipsychotic drugs* and a member of the *phenothiazine* group.

thought disorder. A symptom of *schizophrenia*, evidenced by problems such as *incoherence*, *loose associations*, poverty of speech, and poverty of content of speech.

thyroid gland. An endocrine structure whose two lobes are located on either side of the windpipe; it secretes thyroxin.

time-of-measurement effects. A possible confound in *longitudinal studies* whereby conditions at a particular point in time can have a specific effect on a variable that is being studied over time.

time-out. An *operant conditioning* punishment procedure in which, after bad behavior, the person is temporarily removed from a setting where reinforcers can be obtained and placed in a less desirable setting, for example, in a boring room.

token economy. A *behavior therapy* procedure, based on *operant conditioning* principles, in which institutionalized patients are given scrip rewards, such as poker chips, for socially constructive behavior. The tokens can be exchanged for desirable items and activities such as cigarettes and extra time away from the ward.

tolerance. A physiological process in which greater and greater amounts of an addictive drug are required to produce the same effect. See *substance dependence*.

trait. A somatic characteristic or an enduring psychological *predisposition* to respond in a particular way, distinguishing one individual from another.

tranquilizer. A drug that reduces anxiety and agitation, such as *Valium*. See *anxiolytics*.

transference. The venting of the *analysand*'s emotions, either positive or negative, by treating the *psychoanalyst* as the symbolic representative of someone important in the past. An example is the analysand's becoming angry with the psychoanalyst to release emotions actually felt toward his or her father.

transference neurosis. A crucial phase of *psychoanalysis* during which the *analysand* reacts emotionally toward the *psychoanalyst,* treating the analyst as a parent and reliving childhood experiences in his or her presence. It enables both psychoanalyst and analysand to examine hitherto *repressed* conflicts in the light of present-day reality.

transsexual. A person who believes he or she is opposite in sex to his or her biological endowment; *sex-reassignment surgery* is usually desired.

transvestic fetishism. The practice of dressing in the clothing of the opposite sex, usually for the purpose of sexual arousal.

trauma. A severe physical injury or wound to the body caused by an external force, or a psychological shock having a lasting effect on mental life. *Pl.* traumata.

traumatic disease. An illness produced by external assault, such as poison, a blow, or stress; for example, a broken leg.

tremor. An involuntary quivering of voluntary muscle, usually limited to small musculature of particular areas.

triadic reciprocality. The influence of cognition and behavior on each other through the relationships among thinking, behavior, and the environment.

tricyclic drugs. A group of *antidepressants* with molecular structures characterized by three fused rings. Tricyclics are known to interfere with the reuptake of *norepinephrine* and *serotonin* by a *neuron* after it has fired.

trisomy. A condition wherein there are three rather than the usual pair of homologous *chromosomes* within the cell nucleus.

tumescence. The flow of blood into the genitals.

tumor (neoplasm). Abnormal growth that when located in the brain can either be malignant and directly destroy brain tissue or be benign and disrupt functioning by increasing intracranial pressure.

twin method. Research strategy in *behavior genetics* in which *concordance* rates of *monozygotic* and *dizygotic twins* are compared.

two-factor theory. Mowrer's theory of *avoidance learning* according to which (1) fear is attached to a neutral stimulus by pairing it with a noxious *unconditioned stimulus*, and (2) a person learns to escape the fear elicited by the *conditioned stimulus*, thereby avoiding the *unconditioned stimulus*. See *fear-drive*.

Type A behavior pattern. One of two contrasting psychological patterns revealed through studies seeking the cause of *coronary heart disease*. Type A people are competitive, rushed, hostile, and overcommitted to their work, and are believed to be at heightened risk for heart disease. Those who meet the other pattern, Type B people, are more relaxed and relatively free of pressure.

unconditional positive regard. According to Rogers, a crucial attitude for the *client-centered* therapist to adopt toward the client, who needs to feel complete acceptance as a person in order to evaluate the extent to which current behavior contributes to *self-actualization*.

unconditioned response (UCR). See *classical conditioning*.

unconditioned stimulus (UCS). See *classical conditioning*.

unconscious. A state of unawareness without sensation or thought. In psychoanalytic theory, it is the part of the personality, in particular the *id* impulses, or id energy, of which the *ego* is unaware.

undercontrolled (behavior). In reference to childhood disorders, problem behavior of the child that creates trouble for others, such as disobedience and aggressiveness.

undifferentiated schizophrenia. Diagnosis given for patients whose symptoms do not fit any listed category or meet the criteria for more than one subtype.

unilateral ECT. *Electroconvulsive therapy* in which electrodes are placed on one side of the forehead so that current passes through only one brain hemisphere.

unipolar depression. A term applied to the disorder of individuals who have experienced episodes of *depression* but not of *mania*; referred to as *major depression* in DSM-IV.

vagina. The sheathlike female genital organ that leads from the uterus to the external opening.

vaginal barrel. The passageway of the vaginal canal leading from the external opening to the uterus.

vaginal orgasm. Sexual climax experienced through stimulation of the *vagina*.

vaginal plethysmograph. A device for recording the amount of blood in the walls of the *vagina* and thus for measuring arousal.

vaginismus. Painful, spasmodic contractions of the outer third of the *vaginal barrel,* which make insertion of the *penis* impossible or extremely difficult.

validity. Different types of validity include **internal,** the extent to which experimental results can be confidently attributed to the manipulation of the *independent variable;* **external,** the extent to which research results may be generalized to other populations and settings. Validity as applied to psychiatric diagnoses includes **concurrent,** the extent to which previously undiscovered features are found among patients with the same diagnosis; **predictive,** the extent to which predictions can be made about the future behavior of patients with the same diagnosis; **etiological,** the extent to which a disorder in a number of patients is found to have the same cause or causes. See also *construct validity.*

Valium. An anxiety-reducing drug, or *anxiolytic,* believed to be the most widely prescribed of those available to physicians.

value self-confrontation. A procedure whereby a person's values and behavior are changed by demonstrating that the values of people he or she wishes to emulate are different from the ones currently held by the person.

variable. A characteristic or aspect in which people, objects, events, or conditions vary.

vasoconstriction. A narrowing of the space within the walls (lumen) of a blood vessel; implicated in diseases such as *hypertension.*

vicarious learning. Learning by observing the reactions of others to stimuli or by listening to what they say.

Vineland Adaptive Behavior Scale. An instrument for assessing how many age-appropriate, socially adaptive behaviors a child engages in.

viscera. The internal organs of the body located in the great cavity of the trunk proper.

vitamins. Various organic substances that are, as far as is known, essential to the nutrition of many animals, acting usually in minute quantities to regulate various metabolic processes.

voyeurism. Marked preference for obtaining sexual gratification by watching others in a state of undress or having sexual relations.

vulnerability schema. The schema of people who are socially anxious and who generally think about danger, harm, and unpleasant events that may come to them.

waxy flexibility. An aspect of *catatonic immobility* in which the patient's limbs can be moved into a variety of positions and maintained that way for unusually long periods of time.

white matter. The neural tissue, particularly of the brain and spinal cord, consisting of tracts or bundles of myelinated (sheathed) nerve fibers.

withdrawal. Negative physiological and psychological reactions evidenced when a person suddenly stops taking an addictive drug; cramps, restlessness, and even death are examples. See *substance abuse.*

woolly mammoth. A metaphor for the way in which the *repressed conflicts* of *psychoanalytic* theory are encapsulated in the *unconscious,* making them inaccessible to examination and alteration; thus maintained, the conflicts cause disorders in adulthood.

working through. In *psychoanalysis,* the arduous, time-consuming process through which the *analysand* confronts *repressed conflicts* again and again and faces up to the validity of the *psychoanalyst's interpretations* until problems are satisfactorily solved.

Zeitgeist. The German word for the trends of thought and feeling of culture and taste of a particular time period.

zygote. The fertilized egg cell formed when the male sperm and female ovum unite.

REFERENCES

Abel, G.G., Mittelman, M.S., & Becker, J.V. (1985). Sexual offenders: Results of assessment and recommendations for treatment. In M.H. Ben-Aron, S.J. Hucker, & C.D. Webster (Eds.), *Clinical criminology: The assessment and treatment of criminal behavior.* Toronto: M & M Graphics.

Abrams, R., Swartz, C.M., & Vedak, C. (1991). Antidepressant effects of high-dose right unilateral electroconvulsive therapy. *Archives of General Psychiatry, 48,* 746–748.

Abramson, L.Y., Metalsky, G.I., & Alloy, L.B. (1989). Hopelessness depression: A theory-based subtype of depression. *Psychological Review, 96,* 358–372.

Abramson, L.Y., Seligman, M.E.P., & Teasdale, J.D. (1978). Learned helplessness in humans: Critique and reformulation. *Journal of Abnormal Psychology, 87,* 49–74.

Achenbach, T.M., & Edelbrock, C.S. (1978). The classification of child psychopathology: A review of empirical efforts. *Psychological Bulletin, 85,* 1275–1301.

Ackerman, N.W. (1966). *Treating the troubled family.* New York: Basic Books.

Adams, H.E., Wright, L.W., Jr., & Lohr, B.A. (1996). Is homophobia associated with homosexual arousal? *Journal of Abnormal Psychology, 105,* 440–445.

Adams, K.M. (1980). In search of Luria's battery: A false start. *Journal of Consulting and Clinical Psychology, 48,* 511–516.

Addis, M.E. (1997). Evaluating the treatment manual as a means of disseminating empirically validated psychotherapies. *Clinical Psychology: Science and Practice, 4,* 1–11.

Adelmann, P.K. (1994). Multiple roles and psychological well-being in a national sample of older adults. *Journal of Gerontology, 49,* S277–S285.

Adler, A. (1929). *Problems of neurosis.* New York: Harper & Row.

Agras, W.S., Rossiter, E.M., Arnow, B., Schneider, J.A., Telch, C.F., Raeburn, S.D., Bruce, B., Perl, M., & Koran, L.M. (1992). Pharmacologic and cognitive-behavioral treatment for bulimia nervosa: A controlled comparison. *American Journal of Psychiatry, 149,* 82–87.

Akbarian, S., Kim, J.J., Potkin, S.G., Hagman, J.O., Tafazzoli, A., et al. (1995). Gene expression for glutamic acid decarboxylase is reduced without loss of neurons in prefrontal cortex of schizophrenics. *Archives of General Psychiatry, 52,* 258–266.

Akillas, E., & Efran, J.S. (1995). Symptom prescription and reframing: Should they be combined? *Cognitive Therapy and Research, 19,* 263–279.

Albano, A.M., Marten, P.A., Holt, C.S., Heimberg, R.G., et al. (1995). Cognitive-behavioral group treatment for social phobia in adolescents: A preliminary study. *Journal of Nervous and Mental Disease, 183,* 649–656.

Albee, G.W., Lane, E.A., & Reuter, J.M. (1964). Childhood intelligence of future schizophrenics and neighborhood peers. *Journal of Psychology, 58,* 141–144.

Alcohol, Drug Abuse, and Mental Health Administration. (1996). Reports of the Secretary's Task Force on Youth Suicide. *Vols. 1–4,* Washington, DC. U.S. Government Printing Office.

Alexander, F. (1950). *Psychosomatic medicine.* New York: Norton.

Alexander, F., & French, T.M. (1946). *Psychoanalytic therapy.* New York: Ronald Press.

Alexander, J.F., Holtzworth-Munroe, A., & Jameson, P. (1994). The process and outcome of marital and family therapy: Research review and evaluation. In A.E. Bergin & S.L. Garfield (Eds.), *Handbook of psychotherapy and behavior change.* Fourth edition (pp. 595–630). New York: Wiley.

Alexander, P.C., & Lupfer, S.L. (1987). Family characteristics and long-term consequences associated with sexual abuse. *Archives of Sexual Behavior, 16,* 235–245.

Allderidge, P. (1979). Hospitals, mad houses, and asylums: Cycles in the care of the insane. *British Journal of Psychiatry, 134,* 321–324.

Allen, G.J., Chinsky, J.M., Larsen, S.W., Lockman, J.E., & Selinger, H.V. (1976). *Community psychology and the schools: A behaviorally oriented multilevel preventive approach.* Hillsdale, NJ: Erlbaum.

Allen, M.G. (1976). Twin studies of affective illness. *Archives of General Psychiatry, 33,* 1476–1478.

Allison, R.B. (1984). Difficulties diagnosing the multiple personality syndrome in a death penalty case. *International Journal of Clinical and Experimental Hypnosis, 32,* 102–117.

Alloy, L.B., Kelly, K.A., Mineka, S., & Clements, C.M. (1990). Comorbidity in anxiety and depressive disorders: A helplessness/hopelessness perspective. In J.D. Maser & C.R. Cloninger (Eds.), *Comorbidity in anxiety and mood disorders.* Washington, DC: American Psychiatric Press.

Allport, G.W. (1937). *Personality: A psychological interpretation.* New York: Holt, Rinehart & Winston.

Allport, G.W. (1961). *Pattern and growth in personality.* New York: Holt, Rinehart & Winston.

Almada, S.J. (1991). Neuroticism and cynicism and risk of death in middle aged men: The Western Electric study. *Psychosomatic Medicine, 53,* 165–175.

Altman, D.G., Flora, J.A., & Farquhar, J.W. (1986, August). *Institutionalizing community-based health promotion programs.* Paper presented at the annual meeting of the American Psychological Association, Washington, DC. As cited in Maccoby & Altman (1988).

Altshuler, L.L., Post, R.M., Leverich, G.S., Mikalauskas, K., Rusoff, A., & Ackerman, L. (1995). Antidepressant-induced mania and cycle acceleration: A controversy revisited. *American Journal of Psychiatry, 152,* 1130–1138.

Amador, X.F., Flaum, M., Andreasen, N.C., Strauss, D.H., Yale, S.A., et al. (1994). Awareness of illness in schizophrenia and schizoaffective and mood disorder. *Archives of General Psychiatry, 51,* 826–836.

Aman, M.G., & Kern, R.A. (1989). Review of fenfluramine in the treatment of the developmental disabilities. *Journal of the American Academy of Child and Adolescent Psychiatry, 28,* 549–565.

American Association of Mental Retardation. (1992). *Mental retardation: Definition, classification, and systems of support.* Washington, DC: Author.

American Law Institute. (1962). *Model penal code: Proposed official draft.* Philadelphia: Author.

American Psychiatric Association (1994). *Diagnostic and statistical manual of mental disorders. Fourth edition (DSM-IV).* Washington, DC: Author.

American Psychiatric Association Board of Trustees. (1993). *Statement on memories of sexual abuse.* Washington, DC: American Psychiatric Association.

American Psychiatric Association. (1992). AIDS policy: Guidelines for outpatient psychiatric services. *American Journal of Psychiatry, 149,* 721.

American Psychiatric Association. (1993).

Practice guidelines for major depressive disorder in adults. *American Journal of Psychiatry, 150,* All.

American Psychiatric Association. *Diagnostic and statistical manual of mental disorders.* First edition, 1952; second edition, 1968; third edition, 1980; revised, 1987. Washington, DC: Author.

Ames-Frankel, J., Devlin, M.J., Walsh, B.T., Strasser, T.J., & Sadick, C. (1992). Personality disorder diagnoses in patients with bulimia nervosa. *Journal of Clinical Psychiatry, 53,* 90–96.

Amoss, P.T., & Harrell, S. (1981). Introduction: An anthropological perspective on aging. In P.T. Amoss & S. Harrell (Eds.), *Other ways of growing old* (pp. 1–24). Stanford, CA: Stanford University Press.

Anastasi, A. (1990). *Psychological testing* (6th ed.). New York: Macmillan.

Anderson, B.J., & Wolf, F.M. (1986). Chronic physical illness and sexual behavior: Psychological issues. *Journal of Consulting and Clinical Psychology, 54,* 168–175.

Anderson, B.L. (1983). Primary orgasmic dysfunction: Diagnostic considerations and review of treatment. *Psychological Bulletin, 93,* 105–136.

Anderson, B.L. (1992). Psychological interventions for cancer patients to enhance quality of life. *Journal of Consulting and Clinical Psychology, 60,* 552–568.

Anderson, C.A. (1991). How people think about causes: Examination of the typical phenomenal organization of attributions for success and failure. *Social Cognition, 9,* 295–329.

Anderson, G.M., & Hoshino, Y. (1987). Neurochemical studies of autism. In D.J. Cohen, A.M. Donnellan, & R. Paul (Eds.), *Handbook of autism and pervasive developmental disorders* (pp. 166–191). New York: Wiley.

Anderson, J.C., Williams, S., McGee, R., & Silva, A. (1987). DSM-III disorders in pre-adolescent children: Prevalence in a large sample from the general population. *Archives of General Psychiatry, 44,* 69–76.

Anderson, L.T., Campbell, M., Adams, P., Small, A.M., Perry, R., & Shell, J. (1989). The effects of haloperidol on discrimination learning and behavioral symptoms in autistic children. *Journal of Autism and Developmental Disorders, 19,* 227–239.

Andreasen, N.C. (1979). Thought, language, and communication disorders: 2. Diagnostic significance. *Archives of General Psychiatry, 36,* 1325–1330.

Andreasen, N.C., & Olsen, S.A. (1982). Negative versus positive schizophrenia. Definition and validation. *Archives of General Psychiatry, 39,* 789–794.

Andreasen, N.C., Flaum, M., Swayze, V.W., Tyrrell, G., & Arndt, S. (1990). Positive and negative symptoms in schizophrenia: A critical reappraisal. *Archives of General Psychiatry, 47,* 615–621.

Andreasen, N.C., Olsen, S.A., Dennert, J.W., & Smith, M.R. (1982). Ventricular enlargement in schizophrenia: Relationship to positive and negative symptoms. *American Journal of Psychiatry, 139,* 297–302.

Andreasen, N.C., Rice, J., Endicott, J., Coryell, W., Grove, W.W., & Reich, T. (1987). Familial rates of affective disorder. *Archives of General Psychiatry, 44,* 461–472.

Andreasen, N.C., Swayze, V.W., Flaum, M. et al. (1990). Ventricular enlargement in schizophrenia evaluated with computed tomographic scanning: Effects of gender, age, and stage of illness. *Archives of General Psychiatry, 47,* 1008–1015.

Andress, V.R., & Corey, D.M. (1978). Survivor-victims: Who discovers or witnesses suicide? *Psychological Reports, 42,* 759–764.

Angold, A., & Rutter, M. (1992). Effects of age and pubertal status on depression in a large clinical sample. *Development and Psychopathology, 4,* 5–28.

Angrist, B., Lee, H.K., & Gershon, S. (1974). The antagonism of amphetamine-induced symptomatology by a neuroleptic. *American Journal of Psychiatry, 131,* 817–819.

Anthony-Bergstone, C., Zarit, S.H., & Gatz, M. (1988). Symptoms of psychological distress among caregivers of dementia patients. *Psychology and Aging, 3,* 245–248.

Antoni, M.H., Baggett, L., Ironson, G., LaPerriere, A., August, S., Klimas, N., Schneiderman, N., & Fletcher, M.A. (1991). Cognitive-behavioral stress management intervention buffers distress responses and immunologic changes following notification of HIV-1 seropositivity. *Journal of Consulting and Clinical Psychology, 59,* 906–915.

Antoni, M.H., Schneiderman, N., Fletcher, M.A., Goldstein, D.A., Ironson, G., & Laperriere, A. (1990). Psychoneuroimmunology and HIV-1. *Journal of Consulting and Clinical Psychology, 58,* 38–49.

Antonovsky, H., Sadowsky, M., & Maoz, B. (1990). Sexual activity of aging men and women: An Israeli study. *Behavior, Health, and Aging, 1,* 151–161.

Apfelbaum, B. (1989). Retarded ejaculation: A much-misunderstood syndrome. In S.R. Leiblum & R.C. Rosen (Eds.), *Principles and practice of sex therapy: Update for the 1990s* (pp. 168–206). New York: Guilford.

Appel, L.J., Moore, T.J., Obarzanek,E.,

Vollmer, W.M., Svetkey, L.P., Sacks, F.M., Bray, G.A., Vogt, T.M., Cutler, J.A., Windhauser, M.M., Lin, P-H, Karanja, N., for the DASH Collaborative Research Group. (1997). A clinical trial of the effects of dietary patterns on blood pressure. *New England Journal of Medicine, 336,* 1117–1124.

Appelbaum, P.S. (1985). *Tarasoff* and the clinician: Problems in fulfilling the duty to protect. *American Journal of Psychiatry, 142,* 425–429.

Appelbaum, P.S., & Greer, A. (1994). Who's on trial? Multiple personalities and the insanity defense. *Hospital and Community Psychiatry, 45,* 965–966.

Appelbaum, P.S., & Grisso, T. (1995). The MacArthur Treatment Competence Study: 1. Mental illness and competence to consent to treatment. *Law and Human Behavior, 19,* 105–126.

Appelbaum, P.S., & Gutheil, T. (1980). The Boston State Hospital case: "Involuntary mind control," the Constitution, and the "right to rot." *American Journal of Psychiatry, 137,* 720–727.

Appelbaum, P.S., & Gutheil, T. (1991). *Clinical handbook of psychiatry and the law.* Baltimore: Williams & Wilkins.

Appleby, P.R. (1995). *Rationalizing risk: Sexual behavior of gay male couples.* Unpublished masters thesis, University of Southern California.

Apt, C., & Hurlbert, D.H. (1994). The sexual attitudes, behavior, and relationships of women with histrionic personality disorder. *Journal of Sex and Marital Therapy, 20,* 125–133.

Arbuthnot, J., & Gordon, D.A. (1986). Behavioral and cognitive effects of a moral reasoning development intervention for high-risk behavior disordered adolescents. *Journal of Consulting and Clinical Psychology, 54,* 208–216.

Ard, B.N., Jr. (1977). Sex in lasting marriages: A longitudinal study. *Journal of Sex Research, 13,* 274–285.

Arentewicz, G., & Schmidt, G. (1983). *The treatment of sexual disorders: Concepts and techniques of couple therapy.* New York: Basic Books.

Arieti, S. (1979). New views on the psychodynamics of phobias. *American Journal of Psychotherapy, 33,* 82–95.

Arkowitz, H. (1989). The role of theory in psychotherapy integration. *Journal of Integrative and Eclectic Psychotherapy, 8,* 8–16.

Arkowitz, H. (1992). Integrative theories of therapy. In D. Freedheim (Ed.), *The history of psychotherapy: A century of change.* Washington, DC: American Psychological Association.

Arndt, I.O., Dorozynsky, L., Woody, G.E., McLellan, A.T., & O'Brien, C.P. (1992). Desipramine treatment of cocaine dependence in methadone-maintained patients. *Archives of General Psychiatry, 49,* 888–893.

Arnow, B., Kenardy, J., & Agras, W.S. (1992). Binge eating among the obese. *Journal of Behavioral Medicine, 15,* 155–170.

Aronson, E. (1972). *The social animal.* San Francisco: Freeman.

Aronson, E., & Carlsmith, J.R. (1968). Experimentation in social psychology. In G. Lindzey & E. Aronson (Eds.), *The handbook of social psychology: Vol 2. Research methods.* Menlo Park, CA: Addison-Wesley.

Artiles, A.J., & Trent, S.C. (1994). Overrepresentation of minority students in special education: A continuing debate. *Journal of Special Education, 27,* 410–437.

Ascher, L.M., & Turner, R.M. (1979). Paradoxical intention and insomnia: An experimental investigation. *Behaviour Research and Therapy, 17,* 408–411.

Associated Press. (1996, October 5). Congress adds to penalty for using "date-rape" drugs. *Los Angeles Times,* p. A3.

Asthana, S., Craft, S., Baker, L.D., Raskind, M.A., Avery, E., Lofgreen, C., Wilkinson, C.W., Falzgraf, S., Veith, R.C., & Plymate, S.R. (1996). Transdermal estrogen improves memory in women with Alzheimer's Disease. Annual meeting of the Society for Neuroscience, November (abstract).

Atchley, R. (1980). Aging and suicide: Reflection of the quality of life. In S. Haynes & M. Feinleib (Eds.), *Proceedings of the Second Conference on the Epidemiology of Aging.* National Institute of Health, Washington, DC: U.S. Government Printing Office.

Atkeson, B.M., Calhoun, K.S., Resick, P.A., & Ellis, E.M. (1982). Victims of rape: Repeated assessment of depressive symptoms. *Journal of Consulting and Clinical Psychology, 50,* 96–102.

Atkinson, D. (1985). Karl Marx and group therapy. *Counseling and Values, 29,* 183–184.

Atkinson, D.R., Maruyama, M., & Matsui, S. (1978). The effects of counselor race and counseling approach on Asian Americans' perception of counselor credibility and utility. *Journal of Counseling Psychology, 25,* 76–83.

Austin, L.S., Lydiard, R.B., Forey, M.D., & Zealberg, J.J. (1990). Panic and phobic disorders in patients with obsessive personality disorder. *Journal of Clinical Psychiatry, 51,* 456–458.

Awad, G.A., & Saunders, E. (1989). Adolescent child molesters: Clinical observations. *Child Psychiatry and Human Development, 19,* 195–206.

Ayllon, T., & Azrin, N.H. (1968). *The token economy: A motivational system for therapy and rehabilitation.* New York: Appleton-Century-Crofts.

Azrin, N.H., Sisson, R.W., Meyers, R., & Godley, M. (1982). Alcoholism treatment by disulfiram and community reinforcement therapy. *Journal of Behaviour Therapy and Experimental Psychiatry, 13,* 105–112.

Azrin, N.H., Sneed, T.J., & Foxx, R.M. (1973). Dry bed: A rapid method of eliminating bedwetting (enuresis) of the retarded. *Behaviour Research and Therapy, 11,* 427–434.

Bach, G.R. (1966). The marathon group: Intensive practice of intimate interactions. *Psychological Reports, 181,* 995–1002.

Bachrach, H., Galatzer-Levy, R., Skolnikoff, A., & Waldron, S. (1991). On the efficacy of psychoanalysis. *Journal of the American Psychoanalytic Association, 39,* 871–916.

Badeau, D. (1995). Illness, disability and sex in aging. *Sexuality and Disability, 13,* 219–237.

Badian, N.A. (1983). Dyscalculia and nonverbal disorders of learning. In H.R. Myklebust (Ed.), *Progress in learning disabilities* (Vol. 5). New York: Grune & Stratton.

Baer, J.S., & Lichtenstein, E. (1988). Cognitive assessment. In D.M. Donovan & G.A. Marlatt (Eds.), *Assessment of addictive behaviors* (pp. 189–213). New York: Guilford.

Baer, L., Jenike, M.A., Ricciardi, J.N., Holland, A.D., Seymour, R.J., et al. (1990). Standardized assessment of personality disorders in obsessive compulsive disorder. *Archives of General Psychiatry, 47,* 826–831.

Baer, L., & Jenike, M.A. (1992). Personality disorders in obsessive-compulsive disorder. *Psychiatric Clinics of North America, 15,* 803–812.

Baer, L., Rauch, S.L., Ballantine, H.T., Martuza, R., Cosgrove, R., et al. (1995). Cingulatomy for intractable obsessive-compulsive disorder. *Archives of General Psychiatry, 52,* 384–392.

Bailey, A., LeCouteur, A., Gottesman, I., Bolton, P., Simonoff, E., Yuzda, E., & Rutter, M. (1995). Autism as a strongly genetic disorder: Evidence from a British twin study. *Psychological Medicine, 25,* 63–77.

Baker, T., & Brandon, T.H. (1988). Behavioral treatment strategies. In *A report of the Surgeon General: The health consequences of smoking: Nicotine addiction.* Rockville, MD: U.S. Department of Health and Human Services.

Bakwin, H. (1973). The genetics of enuresis. In J. Kolvin, R.C. MacKeith, & S.R. Meadow (Eds.), *Enuresis and encopresis.* Philadelphia: Lippincott.

Ball, J.C., & Chambers, C.D. (Eds.). (1970). *The epidemiology of opiate addiction in the United States.* Springfield, IL: Charles C. Thomas.

Ball, J.C., & Ross, A. (1991). *The effectiveness of methadone maintenance treatment.* New York: Springer-Verlag.

Ball, S.A., Carroll, K.M., & Rounsaville, B.T. (1994). Sensation seeking, substance abuse, and psychopathology in treatment-seeking and community cocaine abusers. *Journal of Consulting and Clinical Psychology,* 1053–1057.

Ball-Rokeach, S.J., Rokeach, M., & Grube, J.W. (1984). *The great American values test.* New York: Free Press.

Ballard, E.L. (1995). Attitudes, myths, and realities: Helping family and professional caregivers cope with sexuality in the Alzheimer's patient. *Sexuality and Disability, 13,* 255–270.

Ballenger, J.C., Burrows, G.O., DuPont, R.L., Lesser, M., Noyes, R.C., Pecknold, J.C., Rifkin, A., & Swinson, R.P. (1988). Alprazolam in panic disorder and agoraphobia, results from multicenter trial. *Archives of General Psychiatry, 45,* 413–421.

Baltes, M.M. (1988). The etiology and maintenance of dependency in the elderly: Three phases of operant research. *Behavior Therapy, 19,* 301–319.

Bancroft, J. (1988). Sexual desire and the brain. *Sexual and marital therapy, 3,* 11–29.

Bancroft, J.H. (1989). *Human sexuality and its problems* (2nd ed.). Edinburgh: Churchill Livingston.

Bandura, A. (1969). *Principles of behavior modification.* New York: Holt, Rinehart & Winston.

Bandura, A. (1977). Self-efficacy: Toward a unifying theory of behavioral change. *Psychological Review, 84,* 191–215.

Bandura, A. (1982). The psychology of chance encounters. *American Psychologist, 37,* 747–755.

Bandura, A. (1986). *Social foundations of thought and action: A social cognitive theory.* Englewood Cliffs, NJ: Prentice-Hall.

Bandura, A. (1997). *Self-efficacy: The exercise of control.* New York: Freeman.

Bandura, A., & Menlove, F.L. (1968). Factors determining vicarious extinction of avoidance behavior through symbolic modeling. *Journal of Personality and Social Psychology, 8,* 99–108.

Bandura, A., & Perloff, B. (1967). Relative efficacy of self-monitored and externally imposed reinforcement systems. *Journal of Personality and Social Psychology, 7,* 111–116.

Bandura, A., & Rosenthal, T.L. (1966). Vicarious classical conditioning as a function of arousal level. *Journal of Personality and Social Psychology, 3,* 54–62.

Bandura, A., & Walters, R.H. (1963). *Social learning and personality development.* New York: Holt, Rinehart & Winston.

Bandura, A., Blanchard, E.B., & Ritter, B. (1969). Relative efficacy of desensitization and modeling approaches for inducing behavioral, affective, and attitudinal changes. *Journal of Personality and Social Psychology, 13,* 173–199.

Bandura, A., Grusec, J.E., & Menlove, F.L. (1967). Vicarious extinction of avoidance behavior. *Journal of Personality and Social Psychology, 5,* 16–23.

Bandura, A., Jeffrey, R.W., & Bachicha, D.L. (1974). Analysis of memory codes and cumulative rehearsal in observational learning. *Journal of Research in Personality, 7,* 295–305.

Banis, H.T., Varni, J.W., Wallander, J.L., Korsch, B.M., Jay, S.M., Adler, R., Garcia-Temple, E., & Negrete, V. (1988). Psychological and social adjustment of obese children and their families. *Child: Care, Health, and Development, 14,* 157–173.

Bank, L., Marlowe, J.H., Reid, J.B., Patterson, G.R., & Weinrott, M.R. (1991). A comparative evaluation of parent-training interventions for families of chronic delinquents. *Journal of Abnormal Child Psychology, 19,* 15–33.

Barabee, H.E., Marshall, W.L., Yates, E., & Lightfoot, L. (1983). Alcohol intoxication and deviant sexual arousal in male social drinkers. *Behaviour Research and Therapy, 21,* 365–373.

Barbarin, O.A., & Soler, R.E. (1993). Behavioral, emotional, and academic adjustment in a national probability sample of African-American children: Effects of age, gender, and family structure. *Journal of Black Psychology, 19,* 423–446.

Barber, T.X., & Silver, M.J. (1968). Fact, fiction, and the experimenter bias effect. *Psychological Bulletin, Monograph Supplement, 70,* 1–29.

Barclay, D.R., & Houts, A.C. (1995). Childhood enuresis. In C. Schaefer (Ed.), *Clinical handbook of sleep disorders in children* (pp. 223–252). Northvale, NJ: Jason Aronson.

Barefoot, J.C., Dahlstrom, G., & Williams, R.B. (1983). Hostility, CHD incidence, and total mortality: A 25-year follow-up study of 255 physicians. *Psychosomatic Medicine, 45,* 59–63.

Barefoot, J.C., Peterson, B.L., Dahlstrom, W.G., Siegler, I.C., Anderson, N.B., et al. (1991). Hostility patterns and health implications: Correlates of Cook-Medley hostility scale scores in a national survey. *Health Psychology, 10,* 18–24.

Barkley, R.A. (1981). *Hyperactive children: A handbook for diagnosis and treatment.* New York: Guilford.

Barkley, R.A. (1990). *Attention-deficit hyperactivity disorder: A handbook for diagnosis and treatment.* New York: Guilford.

Barkley, R.A. (1997). Behavioral inhibition, sustained attention, and executive function: Constructing a unifying theory of ADHD. *Psychological Bulletin, 121,* 65–94.

Barkley, R.A., Copeland, A.P., & Sivage, C. (1980). A self-control classroom for hyperactive children. *Journal of Autism and Developmental Disorders, 10,* 75–89.

Barkley, R.A., DuPaul, G.J., & McMurray, M.B. (1990). A comprehensive evaluation of attention deficit disorder with and without hyperactivity defined by research criteria. *Journal of Consulting and Clinical Psychology, 58,* 775–789.

Barkley, R.A., Fischer, M., Edelbrock, C.S., & Smallish, L. (1990). The adolescent outcome of hyperactive children diagnosed by research criteria: 1. An 8 year prospective follow-up study. *Journal of the American Academy of Child and Adolescent Psychiatry, 29,* 546–557.

Barkley, R.A., Grodzinsky, G., & DuPaul, G.J. (1992). Frontal lobe functions in attention deficit disorder with and without hyperactivity: A review and research report. *Journal of Abnormal Child Psychology, 20,* 163–188.

Barkley, R.A., Karlsson, J., & Pollard, S. (1985). Effects of age on the mother–child interactions of hyperactive children. *Journal of Abnormal Child Psychology, 13,* 631–638.

Barlow, D.H. (1988). *Anxiety and its disorders: The nature and treatment of anxiety and panic.* New York: Guilford.

Barlow, D.H., Abel, G.G., & Blanchard, E.B. (1979). Gender identity change in transsexuals. *Archives of General Psychiatry, 36,* 1001–1007.

Barlow, D.H., Becker, R., Leitenberg, H., & Agras, W.S. (1970). A mechanical strain gauge for recording penile circumference. *Journal of Applied Behavior Analysis, 3,* 73–76.

Barlow, D.H., Blanchard, E.B., Vermilyea, J.A., Vermilyea, B.B., & DiNardo, P.A. (1986). Generalized anxiety and generalized anxiety disorder: Description and reconceptualization. *American Journal of Psychiatry, 143,* 40–44.

Barlow, D.H., Cohen, A.B., Waddell, M.T., Vermilyea, B.B., Klosko, J.S., Blanchard, E.B., & DiNardo, P.A. (1984). Panic and generalized anxiety disorders: Nature and treatment. *Behavior Therapy, 15,* 431–449.

Barlow, D.H., Craske, M.G., Cerny, J.A., & Klosko, J.S. (1989). Behavioral treatment of panic disorder. *Behavior Therapy, 26,* 261–282.

Barlow, D.H., Reynolds, E.J., & Agras, W.S. (1973). Gender identity change in a transsexual. *Archives of General Psychiatry, 29,* 569–576.

Barlow, D.H., et al. (1985). The phenomenon of panic. *Journal of Abnormal Psychology, 94,* 320–328.

Baron, M., Risch, N., Levitt, M., & Gruen, R. (1985). Familial transmission of schizotypal and borderline personality disorders. *American Journal of Psychiatry, 142,* 927–934.

Barr, L.C., Goodman, W.K., McDougle, C.J., Delgado, P.L., Heninger, G.R., et al. (1994). Tryptophan depletion in patients with obsessive-compulsive disorder who respond to serotonin reuptake blockers. *Archives of General Psychiatry, 51,* 309–317.

Barsky, A.J., Brener, J., Coeytaux, R.R., & Cleary, P.D. (1995). Accurate awareness of heartbeat in hypochondriacal and non-hypochondriacal patients. *Journal of Psychosomatic Research, 39,* 489–487.

Bartholomew, K., & Horowitz, L.M. (1991). Attachment styles among young adults: A test of a four-category model. *Journal of Personality and Social Psychology, 61,* 226–244.

Bartlett, F. (1932). *Remembering.* Cambridge: Cambridge University Press.

Bartlett, J. (1992). *Familiar quotations: A collection of passages, phrases and proverbs traced to their sources in ancient and modern literature.* Boston: Little, Brown and Company.

Bartlett, J.G. (1993). *The Johns Hopkins Hospital guide to medical care of patients with HIV infection.* Baltimore: Williams & Wilkins.

Bartzokis, G., Liberman, R.P., & Hierholzer, R. (1990). Behavior therapy in groups. In I.L. Kutash & A. Wolf (Eds.), *The group psychotherapist's handbook: Contemporary theory and technique.* New York: Columbia University Press.

Basco, M.R., & Rush, A.J. (1996). *Cognitive-behavioral therapy for bipolar disorder.* New York: Guilford.

Bass, E., & Davis, L. (1994). *The courage to heal: A guide for women survivors of child sexual abuse.* New York: Harper Collins.

Bastani, B., Nash, J.F., & Meltzer, H.Y. (1990). Prolactin and cortisol responses to MK-212, a serotonin agonist, in obsessive compulsive disorder. *Archives of General Psychiatry, 47,* 833–839.

Bates, G.W. (1990). *Social anxiety and self-presentation: Conversational behaviours and articulated thoughts of heterosexually anxious males.* Unpublished doctoral dissertation, University of Melbourne, Australia.

Bates, G.W., Campbell, T.M., & Burgess, P.M. (1990). Assessment of articulated thoughts in social anxiety: Modification of the ATSS procedure. *British Journal of Clinical Psychology, 29,* 91–98.

Baucom, D., Epstein, N., & Rankin, L. (1995). Integrative couple therapy. In N.S. Jacobson & A.S. Gurman (Eds.), *Clinical handbook of couple therapy* (pp. 65–90). New York: Guilford.

Baucom, D.H., Epstein, N., Sayers, S.L., & Sher, T.G. (1989). The role of cognitions in marital relationships: Definitional, methodological, and conceptual issues. *Journal of Consulting and Clinical Psychology, 57,* 31–38.

Baucom, D.H., & Hoffman, J.A. (1986). The effectiveness of marital therapy: Current status and application to the clinical setting. In N.S. Jacobson & A.S. Gurman (Eds.), *Clinical handbook of marital therapy* (pp. 597–620). New York: Guilford.

Baumeister, A.A., Kupstas, F.D., & Klindworth, L.M. (1991). The new morbidity: A national plan of action. *American Behavioral Scientist, 34,* 468–500.

Baumeister, R.F. (1990). Suicide as escape from self. *Psychological Review, 97,* 90–113.

Baumgartner, G.R., & Rowen, R.C. (1987). Clonidine vs. chlordiazepoxide in the management of acute alcohol withdrawal. *Archives of Internal Medicine, 147,* 1223–1226.

Baxter, E., & Hopper, K. (1981). *Private lives/public places: Homeless adults on the streets of New York City.* New York: Community Service Society.

Baxter, L.R., Schwartz, J.M., Bergman, K.S., Szuba, M.P., Guze, B.H., Mazziotta, J.C., Alazraki, A., Selin, C.E., Ferng, H., Munford, P., & Phelps, M.E. (1992). Caudate glucose metabolic rate changes with both drug and behavior therapy for obsessive-compulsive disorder. *Archives of General Psychiatry, 49,* 681–689.

Beach, S.R.H., & O'Leary, K.D. (1986). The treatment of depression occurring in the context of marital discord. *Behavior Therapy, 17,* 43–49.

Beach, S.R.H., Sandeen, E.E., & O'Leary, K.D. (1990). *Depression in marriage.* New York: Guilford.

Beck, A.T. (1967). *Depression: Clinical, experimental and theoretical aspects.* New York: Harper & Row.

Beck, A.T. (1976). *Cognitive therapy and the emotional disorders.* New York: International Universities Press.

Beck, A.T. (1986a). Cognitive therapy: A sign of retrogression or progress. *The Behavior Therapist, 9,* 2–3.

Beck, A.T. (1986b). Hopelessness as a predictor of eventual suicide. In J.J. Mann & M. Stanley (Eds.), *Psychobiology of suicidal behavior.* New York: New York Academy of Sciences.

Beck, A.T. (1987). Cognitive models of depression. *Journal of Cognitive Psychotherapy: An International Quarterly, 1,* 5–37.

Beck, A.T., & Ward, C.H. (1961). Dreams of depressed patients: Characteristic themes in manifest content. *Archives of General Psychiatry, 5,* 462–467.

Beck, A.T., Brown, G., Berchick, R.J., Stewart, B.L., & Steer, R.A. (1990). Relationship between hopelessness and ultimate suicide: A replication with psychiatric outpatients. *American Journal of Psychiatry, 147,* 190–195.

Beck, A.T., Brown, G., Steer, R.A., Eidelson, J.I., & Riskind, J.H. (1987). Differentiating anxiety and depression: A test of the cognitive-content-specificity hypothesis. *Journal of Abnormal Psychology, 96,* 179–183.

Beck, A.T., Kovacs, M., & Weissman, A. (1975). Hopelessness and suicidal behavior: An overview. *Journal of the American Medical Association, 234,* 1146–1149.

Beck, A.T., Kovacs, M., & Weissman, A. (1979). Assessment of suicidal ideation: The Scale for Suicide Ideation. *Journal of Consulting and Clinical Psychology, 47,* 343–352.

Beck, A.T., Schuyler, D., & Herman, I. (1974). Development of suicidal intent scales. In A.T. Beck, H.L.P. Resnik, & D.J. Lettieri (Eds.), *The prediction of suicide.* Bowie, MD: Charles Press.

Beck, A.T., Steer, R.A., Kovacs, M., & Garrison, B. (1985). Hopelessness and eventual suicide: A 10-year prospective study of patients hospitalized with suicidal ideation. *American Journal of Psychiatry, 142,* 559–563.

Beck, J.G. (1995). Hypoactive sexual desire disorder: An overview. *Journal of Consulting and Clinical Psychology, 63,* 919–927.

Beck, J.G., & Bozman, A. (1995). Gender differences in sexual desire: The effects of anger and anxiety. *Archives of Sexual Behavior, 24,* 595–612.

Beck, M. (1979, November 12). Viet vets fight back. *Newsweek,* pp. 44–49.

Becker, J.V. (1990). Treating adolescent sexual offenders. *Professional Psychology: Research and Practice, 21,* 362–365.

Becker, J.V., Kaplan, M.S., Cunningham-Rathner, J., & Kavoussi, R.J. (1986). Characteristics of adolescent incest sexual perpetrators: Preliminary findings. *Journal of Family Violence, 1,* 85–97.

Becker, J.V., Kaplan, M.S., Tenke, C.E., & Tartaglini, A. (1991). The incidence of depressive symptomatology in juvenile sex offenders with a history of abuse. *Child Abuse and Neglect, 15,* 531–536.

Becker, J.V., Skinner, L.J., Abel, G.G., & Cichon, J. (1986). Level of postassault sexual functioning in rape and incest victims. *Archives of Sexual Behavior, 15,* 37–49.

Bedell, J.R., Archer, R.P., & Marlow, H.A. (1980). A description and evaluation of a problem-solving skills training program. In D. Upper & S.M. Ross (Eds.), *Behavioral group therapy: An annual review* (pp. 3–35). Champaign, IL: Research Press.

Bednar, R.L., & Kaul, T.J. (1994). Experiential group research: Can the canon fire? In A.E. Bergin & S.L. Garfield (Eds.), *Handbook of psychotherapy and behavior change* (4th edition.) New York: Wiley.

Beecher, H.K. (1966). Ethics and clinical research. *New England Journal of Medicine, 274,* 1354–1360.

Begelman, D.A. (1975). Ethical and legal issues of behavior modification. In M. Hersen, R. Eisler, & P.M. Miller (Eds.), *Progress in behavior modification.* New York: Academic Press.

Beidel, D.C. (1991). Social phobia and overanxious disorder in school-age children. *Journal of the American Academy of Child and Adolescent Psychiatry, 30,* 545–552.

Bell, J.E. (1961). *Family group therapy.* Washington, DC: U.S. Department of Health, Education, and Welfare.

Bellack, A.S., & Mueser, K.T. (1993). Psychosocial treatments for schizophrenia. *Schizophrenia Bulletin, 19,* 317–336.

Bellack, A.S., Hersen, M., & Turner, S.M. (1976). Generalization effects of social skills training in chronic schizophrenics: An experimental analysis. *Behavior Research and Therapy, 14,* 391–398.

Bellack, A.S., Morrison, R.L., & Mueser, K.T. (1989). Social problem solving in schizophrenia. *Schizophrenia Bulletin, 15,* 101–116.

Ben-Porath, Y.S., & Butcher, J.N. (1989). The comparability of MMPI and MMPI-2 scales and profiles. *Psychological Assessment, 1,* 345–347.

Ben-Tovim, M.V., & Crisp, A.H. (1979). Personality and mental state within anorexia nervosa. *Journal of Psychosomatic Research, 23,* 321–325.

Benes, F.M., McSparren, J., Bird, T.D., San-Giovanni, J.P., Vincent, S.L., et al. (1991). Deficits in small interneurons in prefrontal and cingulate cortices of schizophrenic and schizoaffective patients. *Archives of General Psychiatry, 48,* 986–1001.

Benkelfat, C., Ellenbogen, M.A., Dean, P., Palmour, R.M., & Young, S.N. (1994b). Mood-lowering effect of tryptophan depletion: Enhanced susceptibility in young men at genetic risk for major affective disorders. *Archives of General Psychiatry, 51,* 687–700.

Bennett, C.C., Anderson, L.S., Cooper, S., Hassol, L., Klein, D.C., & Rosenblum, G. (Eds.). (1966). *Community psychology: A report of the Boston Conference on the ed-*

ucation of psychologists for community mental health. Boston: Boston University Press.

Bennett, I. (1960). *Delinquent and neurotic children.* London: Tavistock.

Bennett, V. (1997, February 22). Russia's forgotten children. *Los Angeles Times,* pp. A1, A10.

Benson, H., Beary, J.F., & Carl, M.P. (1974). The relaxation response. *Psychiatry, 37,* 37.

Berger, K.S., & Zarit, S.H. (1978). Late life paranoid states: Assessment and treatment. *American Journal of Orthopsychiatry, 48,* 528–537.

Bergin, A.E. (1971). The evaluation of therapeutic outcomes. In A.E. Bergin & S.L. Garfield (Eds.), *Handbook of psychotherapy and behavior change: An empirical analysis.* New York: Wiley.

Bergin, A.E., & Garfield, S.L. (Eds.). (1994). *Handbook of psychotherapy and behavior change.* Fourth edition. New York: Wiley.

Bergin, A.E., & Lambert, M.J. (1978). The evaluation of therapeutic outcomes. In S.L. Garfield & A.E. Bergin (Eds.), *Handbook of psychotherapy and behavior change: An empirical analysis* (2nd ed.). New York: Wiley.

Berlin, F.S., & Meinecke, C.F. (1981). Treatment of sex offenders with antiandrogenic medication: Conceptualization, review of treatment modalities, and preliminary findings. *American Journal of Psychiatry, 138,* 601–607.

Berman, A.L., & Jobes, D.A. (1996). *Adolescent suicide: Assessment and intervention.* Washington, DC: American Psychological Association.

Berman, E.M., & Lief, H.I. (1976). Sex and the aging process. In W.W. Oaks, G.A. Melchiode, & I. Ficher (Eds.), *Sex and the life cycle.* New York: Grune & Stratton.

Berman, J.S., & Norton, N.C. (1985). Does professional training make a therapist more effective? *Psychological Bulletin, 98,* 401–407.

Bernstein, D.A., & Nietzel, M.T. (1980). *Introduction to clinical psychology.* New York: McGraw-Hill.

Bernstein, D.P., Useda, D., & Siever, L.J. (1993). Paranoid personality disorder: Review of the literature and recommendations. *Journal of Personality Disorders, 7,* 53–62.

Berrettini, W.H., Goldin, L.R., Gelernter, J., Geiman, P.Z., Gershon, E., et al. (1990). X-chromosome markers and manic-depressive illness: Rejection of linkage to Xq28 in nine bipolar pedigrees. *Archives of General Psychiatry, 47,* 366–373.

Berry, J.C. (1967). *Antecedents of schizophrenia, impulsive character and alcoholism in males.* Paper presented at the 75th An-

nual Convention of the American Psychological Association, Washington, DC.

Besdine, R.W. (1980). Geriatric medicine: An overview. In C. Eisodorfer (Ed.), *Annual review of gerontology and geriatrics.* New York: Springer.

Betancourt, H., & Lopez, S. (1993). The study of culture, ethnicity, and race in American psychology. *American Psychologist, 48,* 629–637.

Bettelheim, B. (1967). *The empty fortress.* New York: Free Press.

Bettelheim, B. (1973). Bringing up children. *Ladies Home Journal, 90,* 28.

Bettelheim, B. (1974). *A home for the heart.* New York: Knopf.

Beutler, L.E. (1979). Toward specific psychological therapies for specific conditions. *Journal of Consulting and Clinical Psychology, 47,* 882–897.

Beutler, L.E. (1983). *Eclectic psychotherapy: A systematic approach.* New York: Pergamon.

Beutler, L.E. (1991). Have all won and must all have prizes? Revisiting Luborsky et al.'s verdict. *Journal of Consulting and Clinical Psychology, 59,* 226–232.

Beutler, L.E. (1997). The psychotherapist as a neglected variable in psychotherapy: An illustration by reference to the role of therapist experience and training. *Clinical Psychology: Science and Practice, 4,* 44–52.

Beutler, L.E., & Davison, E.H. (1995). What standards should we use? In S.C. Hayes, V.M. Follette, R.M. Dawes, & K.E. Grady (Eds.), *Scientific standards of psychological practice: Issues and recommendations* (pp. 11–24). Reno, NV: Context Press.

Beutler, L.E., & Harwood, T.M. (1995). Prescriptive psychotherapies. *Applied and Preventive Psychology, 4,* 89–100.

Beutler, L.E., Crago, M., & Arizmendi, T.G. (1986). Therapist variables in psychotherapy process and outcome. In S.L. Garfield & A.E. Bergin (Eds.), *Handbook of psychotherapy and behavior change* (3rd ed.). New York: Wiley.

Beutler, L.E., Machado, P.P.P., & Neufeldt, S.A. (1994). Therapist variables. In A.E. Bergin & S.L. Garfield (Eds.), *Handbook of psychotherapy and behavior change.* Fourth edition (pp. 229–269). New York: Wiley.

Beutler, L.E., Scogin, F., Kirkish, P., Schretlen, D., Corbishley, A., Hamblin, D., Meredith, K., Potter, R., Bamford, C.R., & Levenson, A.I. (1987). Group cognitive therapy and alprazolam in the treatment of depression in older adults. *Journal of Consulting and Clinical Psychology, 55,* 550–556.

Biederman, J., Newcorn, J., & Sprich, S.

(1991). Comorbidity of attention deficit hyperactivity disorder with conduct, depressive, and other disorders. *American Journal of Psychiatry, 148,* 564–577.

Biederman, J., Rosenbaum, J., Hirschfeld, D., Faraone, S., Bolduc, E., & et al. (1990). Psychiatric correlates of behavioral inhibition in young children of parents with and without psychiatric disorders. *Archives of General Psychiatry, 47,* 21–26.

Billings, A. (1979). Conflict resolution in distressed and nondistressed married couples. *Journal of Consulting and Clinical Psychology, 47,* 368–376.

Billings, A.G., Cronkite, R.C., & Moos, R.H. (1983). Social-environmental factors in unipolar depression: Comparisons of depressed patients and nondepressed controls. *Journal of Abnormal Psychology, 92,* 119–133.

Bion, W. (1959). *Experiences in groups.* New York: Basic Books.

Birbaumer, H. (1977). Biofeedback training: A critical review of its clinical applications and some possible future directions. *European Journal of Behavioral Analysis and Modification, 4,* 235–251.

Birnbaum, M. (1960). The right to treatment. *American Bar Association Journal, 46,* 499–505.

Birren, J.E., & Schaie, K.W. (Eds). (1996). *Handbook of the psychology of aging.* Fourth edition. San Diego, CA: Academic Press.

Bisette, G., Smith, W.H., Dole, K.C., Crain, B., Ghanbari, B., Miller, B., & Nemeroff, C.B. (1991). Alterations in Alzheimer's disease-associated protein in Alzheimer's disease frontal and temporal cortex. *Archives of General Psychiatry, 48,* 1009–1011.

Blackburn, I.M., Eunson, K.M., & Bishop, S. (1986). A two-year naturalistic follow-up of depressed patients treated with cognitive therapy, pharmacotherapy, and a combination of both. *Journal of Affective Disorders, 10,* 67–75.

Blake, W. (1973). The influence of race on diagnosis. *Smith College Studies in Social Work, 43,* 184–192.

Blanchard, E.B. (1994). Behavioral medicine and health psychology. In A.E. Bergin & S.L. Garfield (Eds.), *Handbook of psychotherapy and behavior change.* Fourth edition (pp. 701–733). New York: Wiley.

Blanchard, E.B., Andrasik, F., Neff, D.F., Arena, J.G., Ashles, T.A., Jurish, S.E., Pallmeyer, T.P., Saunders, N.L., & Teders, S.J. (1982). Biofeedback and relaxation training with three kinds of headache: Treatment effects and their prediction. *Journal of Consulting and Clinical Psychology, 50,* 562–575.

Blanchard, E.B., Miller, S.T., Abel, G.G.,

Haynes, M.R., & Wicker, R. (1979). Evaluation of biofeedback in the treatment of borderline essential hypertension. *Journal of Applied Behavior Analysis, 12,* 99–109.

Blaske, D.M., Borduin, C.M., Hengeler, S.W., & Mann, B.J. (1989). Individual, family, and peer characteristics of adolescent sex offenders and assaultive offenders. *Developmental Psychology, 25,* 846–855.

Blatt, B. (1966). The preparation of special educational personnel. *Review of Educational Research, 36,* 151–161.

Blau, Z.S., Oser, G.T., & Stephens, R.C. (1979). Aging, social class, and ethnicity: A comparison of Anglo, Black, and Mexican-American Texans. *Pacific Sociological Review, 22,* 501–525.

Blazer, D., George, L.K., & Hughes, D. (1991). The epidemiology of anxiety: An age comparison. In C. Salzman & B.D. Lebovitz (Eds.), *Anxiety in the elderly.* New York: Springer.

Blazer, D., Hughes, D., & George, L.K. (1987). Stressful life events and the onset of a generalized anxiety syndrome. *American Journal of Psychiatry, 144,* 1178–1183.

Blazer, D.G. (1982). *Depression in late life.* St. Louis: Mosby.

Blazer, D.G., & Williams, C.D. (1980). Epidemiology of dysphoria and depression in the elderly population. *American Journal of Psychiatry, 137,* 439–444.

Blazer, D.G., Bachar, J.R., & Manton, K.G. (1986). Suicide in late life: Review and commentary. *Journal of the American Geriatrics Society, 34,* 519–525.

Blazer, D.G., Kessler, R.C., & McGonagle, K.A. (1994). The prevalence and distribution of major depression in a national community sample: The National Comorbidity Survey. *American Journal of Psychiatry, 151,* 979–986.

Blechman, E.A., McEnroe, M.J., Carella, E.T., & Audette, D.P. (1986). Childhood competence and depression. *Journal of Abnormal Psychology, 95,* 223–227.

Blehar, M.C., & Rosenthal, N.E. (1989). Seasonal affective disorders and phototherapy: Report of a National Institute of Mental Health–sponsored workshop. *Archives of General Psychiatry, 46,* 469–474.

Blenker, M. (1967). Environmental change and the aging individual. *Gerontologist, 7,* 101–105.

Bliss, E.L. (1980). Multiple personalities: A report of 14 cases with implications for schizophrenia and hysteria. *Archives of General Psychiatry, 37,* 1388–1397.

Bliss, E.L. (1983). Multiple personalities, related disorders, and hypnosis. *American Journal of Clinical Hypnosis, 26,* 114–123.

Bliwise, D., Carskadon, M., Carey, E., & Dement, W. (1984). Longitudinal development of sleep-related respiratory disturbance in adult humans. *Journal of Gerontology, 39,* 290–293.

Block, A.P. (1990). Rape trauma syndrome as scientific expert testimony. *Archives of Sexual Behavior, 19,* 309–323.

Block, J. (1971). *Lives through time.* Berkeley, CA: Bancroft Books.

Bloomfield, H.H. (1973). Assertive training in an outpatient group of chronic schizophrenics: A preliminary report. *Behavior Therapy, 4,* 277–281.

Blumstein, A., & Cohen, J. (1987). Characterizing criminal careers. *Science, 237,* 985–991.

Bockhoven, J. (1963). *Moral treatment in American psychiatry.* New York: Springer.

Bohart, A.C., & Greenberg, L.S. (1997) (Eds.), *Empathy reconsidered: New directions in psychotherapy.* Washington, DC: American Psychological Association.

Bolger, N., Foster, M., Vinokur, A.D., & Ng, R. (1996). Close relationships and adjustment to a life crisis: The case of breast cancer. *Journal of Personality and Social Psychology, 70,* 283–294.

Boll, T.J. (1985). Developing issues in clinical neuropsychology. *Journal of Clinical and Experimental Neuropsychology, 7,* 473–485.

Bolton, P., MacDonald, H., Pickles, A., Rios, P., Goode, S., Crowson, M., Bailey, A., & Rutter, M. (1994). A case-control family history study of autism. *Journal of Child Psychology and Psychiatry, 35,* 877–900.

Bond, I.K., & Hutchinson, H.C. (1960). Application of reciprocal inhibition therapy to exhibitionism. *Canadian Medical Association Journal, 83,* 23–25.

Bootzin, R.R., & Engle-Friedman, M. (1987). Sleep disturbances. In L.L. Carstensen & B.A. Edelstein (Eds.), *Handbook of clinical gerontology.* New York: Pergamon.

Bootzin, R.R., Engle-Friedman, M., & Hazelwood, L. (1983). Sleep disorders and the elderly. In P.M. Lewinsohn & L. Teri (Eds.), *Clinical geropsychology: New directions in assessment and treatment.* New York: Pergamon.

Borduin, C.M., Mann, B.J., Cone, L.T., Henggeler, S.W., Fucci, B.R., Blaske, D.M., & Williams, R.A. (1995). Multisystemic treatment of serious juvenile offenders: Long-term prevention of criminality and violence. *Journal of Consulting and Clinical Psychology, 63,* 569–578.

Borkovec, T.D., & Costello, E. (1993). Efficacy of applied relaxation and cognitive behavioral therapy in the treatment of generalized anxiety disorder. *Journal of Consulting and Clinical Psychology, 61,* 611–619.

Borkovec, T.D., & Inz, J. (1990). The nature of worry in generalized anxiety disorder: A predominance of thought activity. *Behaviour Research and Therapy, 28,* 153–158.

Borkovec, T.D., & Mathews, A. (1988). Treatment of nonphobic anxiety disorders: A comparison of nondirective, cognitive and coping desensitization therapy. *Journal of Consulting and Clinical Psychology, 56,* 877–884.

Borkovec, T.D., & Roemer, L. (1994). Generalized anxiety disorder. In M. Hersen & R.T. Ammerman (Eds.), *Handbook of prescriptive treatments for adults* (pp. 261–281). New York: Plenum.

Borkovec, T.D., & Whisman, M.A. (1996). Psychosocial treatment for generalized anxiety disorder. In M. Mavissakalian & R.E. Prien (Eds.), *Long-term treatment of anxiety disorders* (pp. 171–199). Washington, DC: American Psychiatric Association.

Borkovec, T.D., Roemer, L., & Kinyon, J. (1995). Disclosure and worry: Opposite sides of the emotional processing coin. In J.W. Pennebaker (Ed.), *Emotion, disclosure, and health.* Washington, DC: American Psychological Association.

Bornstein, P.E., Clayton, P.J., Halikas, J.A., & Robins, E. (1973). The depression of widowhood after thirteen months. *British Journal of Psychiatry, 122,* 561–566.

Bornstein, R.F., Leone, D.R., & Galley, D.J. (1987). The generalizability of subliminal mere exposure effects: Influence of stimuli perceived without awareness on social behavior. *Journal of Personality and Social Psychology, 53,* 1070–1079.

Botvin, G.J., & Tortu, S. (1988). Peer relationships, social competence, and substance abuse prevention: Implications for the family. *Journal of Chemical Dependency Treatment, 1,* 245–273.

Bouchard, T.J., Lykken, D.T., McGue, M., Segal, N.L., & Tellegen, A. (1990). Sources of human psychological differences: The Minnesota Study of Twins Reared Apart. *Science, 250,* 223–228.

Boudreaux, R. (1996, September 29). HIV now haunts streets of former Soviet model city. *Los Angeles Times,* pp. A1, A14.

Bowers, J., Jorm, A.F., Henderson, S., & Harris, P. (1990). General practitioners' detection of depression and dementia in elderly patients. *The Medical Journal of Australia, 153,* 192–196.

Bowers, K.S., & Meichenbaum, D. (Eds.). (1984). *The unconscious reconsidered.* New York: Praeger.

Bowers, M.B., Jr. (1974). Central dopamine turnover in schizophrenic syndromes. *Archives of General Psychiatry, 31,* 50–54.

Bowers, M.K., Brecher-Marer, S., Newton, B.W., Piotrowski, Z., Spyer, T.C., Taylor, W.S., & Watkins, J.G. (1971). Therapy of multiple personality. *International Journal of Clinical and Experimental Hypnosis, 19*, 57–65.

Bowlby, J. (1980). *Attachment and loss: Sadness and depression.* New York: Basic Books.

Boxall, B. (1995, September 3). Young gays stray from safer sex, new data shows. *Los Angeles Times*, pp. A1, A24.

Boyle, M. (1991). *Schizophrenia: A scientific delusion?* New York: Routledge.

Bozman, A., & Beck, J.G. (1991). Covariation of sexual desire and sexual arousal: The effects of anger and anxiety. *Archives of Sexual Behavior, 20*, 47–60.

Bradley, B.P., Mogg, K., Millar, N., & White, J. (1995). Selective processing of negative information: Effects of clinical anxiety, concurrent depression, and awareness. *Journal of Abnormal Psychology, 104*, 532–536.

Bradley, L., & Bryant, P.E. (1985). *Rhyme and reason in reading and spelling.* Ann Arbor: University of Michigan Press.

Brady, E., & Kendall, P. (1992). Comorbidity of anxiety and depression in children and adolescents. *Psychological Bulletin, 111*, 244–255.

Brady, J.P., Davison, G.C., DeWald, P.A., Egan, G., Fadiman, J., Frank, J.D., Gill, M.M., Hoffman, I., Kempler, W., Lazarus, A.A., Raimy, V., Rotter, J.B., & Strupp, H.H. (1980). Some views on effective principles of psychotherapy. *Cognitive Therapy and Research, 4*, 269–306.

Brandon, Y.H., Zelman, D.C., & Baker, T.B. (1987). Effects of maintenance sessions on smoking relapse: Delaying the inevitable? *Journal of Consulting and Clinical Psychology, 55*, 780–782.

Brandt, J., Buffers, N., Ryan, C., & Bayog, R. (1983). Cognitive loss and recovery in chronic alcohol abusers. *Archives of General Psychiatry, 40*, 435–442.

Bransford, J.D., & Johnson, M.K. (1973). Considerations of some problems of comprehension. In W.G. Chase (Ed.), *Visual information processing.* New York: Academic Press.

Braswell, L., & Kendall, P.C. (1988). Cognitive-behavioral methods with children. In K.S. Dobson (Ed.), *Handbook of cognitive-behavioral therapies.* New York: Guilford.

Brecher, E.M., & the Editors of Consumer Reports. (1972). *Licit and illicit drugs.* Mount Vernon, NY: Consumers Union.

Breen, M.J. (1989). Cognitive and behavioral differences in ADHD boys and girls. *Journal of Child Psychology and Psychiatry, 30*, 711–716.

Brehm, J.W. (1966). *A theory of psychological reactance.* New York: Academic Press.

Brehm, S.S., & Brehm, J.W. (1981). *Psychological reactance: A theory of freedom and control.* New York: Academic Press.

Breier, A., Charney, D.S., & Heninger, G.R. (1986). Agoraphobia with panic attacks. *Archives of General Psychiatry, 43*, 1029–1036.

Breier, A., Schreiber, J.L., Dyer, J., & Pickar, D. (1991). National Institute of Mental Health longitudinal study of chronic schizophrenia: Prognosis and predictors of outcome. *Archives of General Psychiatry, 48*, 239–246.

Bremner, J.D., Southwick, S.M., Darnell, A., & Charney, D.S. (1996). Chronic post-traumatic stress disorder in Vietnam combat veterans: Course of illness and substance abuse. *American Journal of Psychiatry, 153*, 369–375.

Breslau, N., Davis, G. C., Andreski, D., & Peterson, E. (1991). Traumatic events and post-traumatic stress disorder in an urban population. *Archives of General Psychiatry, 48*, 216–222.

Bretschneider, J.G., & McCoy, N.L. (1988). Sexual interest and behavior in healthy 80 to 102-year-olds. *Archives of Sexual Behavior, 17*, 109–129.

Brettle, R.P., & Leen, L.S. (1991). The natural history of HIV and AIDS in women. *AIDS, 5*, 1283–1292.

Breuer, J., & Freud, S. (1982). *Studies in hysteria.* (J. Strachey, Trans. and Ed., with the collaboration of A. Freud). New York: Basic Books. (Original work published 1895)

Brewerton, T.D., Lydiard, B.R., Laraia, M.T., Shook, J.E., & Ballenger, J.C. (1992). CSF Beta-endorphin and dynorphin in bulimia nervosa. *American Journal of Psychiatry, 149*, 1086–1090.

Brickel, C.M. (1984). The clinical use of pets with the aged. *Clinical Gerontologist, 2*, 72–75.

Brickman, A.S., McManus, M., Grapentine, W.L., & Alessi, N. (1984). Neuropsychological assessment of seriously delinquent adolescents. *Journal of the American Academy of Child Psychiatry, 23*, 453–457.

Bridge, T.B., & Wyatt, R.J. (1980). Paraphrenia: Paranoid states of late life. 2. American research. *Journal of the American Geriatrics Society, 28*, 205–210.

Bridger, W.H., & Mandel, I.J. (1965). Abolition of the PRE by instructions in GSR conditioning. *Journal of Experimental Psychology, 69*, 476–482.

Brody, N. (1985). The validity of tests of intelligence. In B.B. Wolman (Ed.), *Handbook of intelligence* (pp. 353–389). New York: Wiley.

Brookoff, D., Cook, C.S., Williams, C., & Mann, C.S. (1994). Testing reckless drivers for cocaine and marijuana. *The New England Journal of Medicine, 331*, 518–522.

Brown, G.L., & Goodwin, F.K. (1986). Cerebrospinal fluid correlates of suicide attempts and aggression. *Annals of the New York Academy of Science, 487*, 175–188.

Brown, G.P., Hammen, C.L., Craske, M.G., & Wickens, T.D. (1995). Dimensions of dysfunctional attitudes as vulnerabilities to depressive symptoms. *Journal of Abnormal Psychology, 104*, 431–435.

Brown, G.W., & Birley, J.L.T. (1968). Crises and life changes and the onset of schizophrenia. *Journal of Health and Social Behavior, 9*, 203–214.

Brown, G.W., & Harris, T.O. (1978). *Social origins of depression.* London: Tavistock.

Brown, G.W., Bone, M., Dalison, B., & Wing, J.K. (1966). *Schizophrenia and social care.* London: Oxford University Press.

Brown, H.D., Kosslyn, S.M., Breiter, H.C., Baer, L., & Jenike, M.A. (1994). Can patients with obsessive-compulsive disorder discriminate between percepts and mental images? A signal detection analysis. *Journal of Abnormal Psychology, 103*, 445–454.

Brown, S.A., Vik, P.W., McQuaid, J.R., Patterson, T.L., Irwin, M.R., et al. (1990). Severity of psychosocial stress and outcome of alcoholism treatment. *Journal of Abnormal Psychology, 99*, 344–348.

Brown, T.A., & Barlow, D.H. (1995). Long-term outcome in cognitive-behavioral treatment of panic disorder: Clinical predictors and alternative strategies for assessment. *Journal of Consulting and Clinical Psychology, 63*, 754–765.

Brown, T.A., Barlow, D.H., & Liebowitz, M.R. (1994). The empirical basis of generalized anxiety disorder. *American Journal of Psychiatry, 151*, 1272–1280.

Brownell, K.D., & Rodin, J. (1994). The dieting maelstrom: Is it possible or advisable to lose weight? *American Psychologist, 49*, 781–791.

Brownell, K.D., & Wadden, T.A. (1992). Etiology and treatment of obesity: Toward understanding a serious, prevalent, and refractory disorder. *Journal of Consulting and Clinical Psychology, 60*, 505–517.

Brownell, K.D., Hayes, S.C., & Barlow, D.H. (1977). Patterns of appropriate and deviant sexual arousal: The behavioral treatment of multiple sexual deviations. *Journal of Consulting and Clinical Psychology, 45*, 1144–1155.

Brownell, K.D., Stunkard, A.J., & Albaum, J.M. (1980). Evaluation and modification of exercise patterns in the natural environment. *American Journal of Psychiatry, 137*, 1540–1545.

Brownmiller, S. (1975). *Against our will:*

Men, women and rape. New York: Simon & Schuster.

Bruch, H. (1980). Preconditions for the development of anorexia nervosa. *American Journal of Psychoanalysis, 40,* 169–172.

Bruck, M. (1987). The adult outcomes of children with learning disabilities. *Annals of Dyslexia, 37,* 252–263.

Bryant, R.A. (1995). Autobiographical memory across personalities in dissociative identity disorder. *Journal of Abnormal Psychology, 4,* 625–632.

Bryant, R.A., & McConkey, K.M. (1989). Visual conversion disorder: A case analysis of the influence of visual information. *Journal of Abnormal Psychology, 98,* 326–329.

Buchsbaum, M.S., Kessler, R., King, A., Johnson, J., & Cappelletti, J. (1984). Simultaneous cerebral glucography with positron emission tomography and topographic electroencephalography. In G. Pfurtscheller, E.J. Jonkman, & F.H. Lopes da Silva (Eds.), *Brain ischemia: Quantitative EEG and imaging techniques.* Amsterdam: Elsevier.

Buckley, P.F., Buchanan, R.W., Schulz, S.C., & Tamminga, C.A. (1996). Catching up on schizophrenia: The Fifth International Congress on Schizophrenia Research, Warm Springs, VA, April 8–12, 1995. *Archives of General Psychiatry, 53,* 456–462.

Bulfinch's mythology. (1979). New York: Avenel Books.

Bunney, W.E., Goodwin, F.K., & Murphy, D.L. (1972). The "Switch Process" in manic-depressive illness. *Archives of General Psychiatry, 27,* 312–317.

Bunney, W.E., Murphy, D.L., Goodwin, F.K., & Borge, G.F. (1970). The switch process from depression to mania: Relationship to drugs which alter brain amines. *Lancet, 1,* 1022.

Burgess, A.W., & Holmstrom, L.L. (1974). *Rape: Victim of crisis.* Bowie, MD: Robert J. Brady Company.

Burgio, L.D., Burgio, K.L., Engel, B.T., & Tice, L.M. (1986). Increasing distance and independence of ambulation in elderly nursing home residents. *Journal of Applied Behavior Analysis, 19,* 357–366.

Burnam, M.A., Stein, J.A., Golding, J.M., Siegel, J.M., Sorenson, S.B., Forsythe, A.B., & Telles, C.A. (1988). Sexual assault and mental disorders in a community population. *Journal of Consulting and Clinical Psychology, 56,* 843–850.

Burns, A. (1991). Affective symptoms in Alzheimer's disease. *International Journal of Geriatric Psychiatry, 6,* 371–376.

Buss, A.H. (1966). *Psychopathology.* New York: Wiley.

Butcher, J.N., Dahlstrom, W.G., Graham, J.R., Tellegen, A., & Kraemer, B. (1989).

Minnesota Multiphasic Personality Inventory-2: Manual for administration and scoring. Minneapolis: University of Minnesota Press.

Butler, G., & Mathews, A. (1983). Cognitive processes in anxiety. *Advances in Behaviour Research and Therapy, 5,* 51–62.

Butler, L., Miezitis, S., Friedman, R., & Cole, I.D. (1980). The effect of two school-based intervention programs on depressive symptoms. *American Educational Research Journal, 17,* 111–119.

Butler, L.D., Duran, E.F., Jasinkaitis, P., Koopman, C., & Spiegel, D. (1996). Hypnotizability and traumatic experience: A diathesis-stress model of dissociative symptomatology. *American Journal of Psychiatry, 153,* 42–63.

Butler, R.N. (1963). The life review: An interpretation of reminiscence in the aged. *Psychiatry, 119,* 721–728.

Butler, R.N., & Lewis, M.I. (1982). *Aging and mental health: Positive psychosocial approaches* (3rd ed.). St. Louis: Mosby.

Butterfield, E.C., & Belmont, J.M. (1977). Assessing and improving the cognitive functions of mentally retarded people. In I. Bialer & M. Sternlicht (Eds.), *The psychology of mental retardation: Issues and approaches.* New York: Psychological Dimensions.

Caccioppo, J.T., Glass, C.R., & Merluzzi, T.V. (1979). Self-statements and self-evaluations: A cognitive-response analysis of heterosexual social anxiety. *Cognitive Therapy and Research, 3,* 249–262.

Caddy, G.R. (1983). Alcohol use and abuse. In B. Tabakoff, P.B. Sutker, & C.L. Randell (Eds.), *Medical and social aspects of alcohol use.* New York: Plenum.

Caddy, G.R. (1985). Cognitive behavior therapy in the treatment of multiple personality. *Behavior Modification, 9,* 267–292.

Cadoret, R.J. (1978). Evidence for genetic inheritance of primary affective disorder in adoptees. *American Journal of Psychiatry, 135,* 463–466.

Cadoret, R.J., & Stewart, M.A. (1991). An adoption study of attention deficit/aggression and their relationship to adult antisocial personality. *Archives of General Psychiatry, 47,* 73–82.

Cadoret, R.J., Yates, W.R., Troughton, E., Woodworth, G., & Stewart, M.A. (1995a). Adoption study demonstrating two genetic pathways to drug abuse. *Archives of General Psychiatry, 52,* 42–52.

Cadoret, R.J., Yates, W.R., Troughton, E., Woodworth, G., & Stewart, M.A. (1995b). Genetic-environment interaction in the genesis of aggressivity and conduct disorders. *Archives of General Psychiatry, 52,* 916–924.

Calhoun, J.B. (1970). Space and the strategy of life. *Ekistics, 29,* 425–437.

Calhoun, K.S., & Atkeson, B.M. (1991). *Treatment of rape victims.* Elmsford, NY: Pergamon.

Calhoun, K.S., Atkeson, B.M., & Resick, P.A. (1982). A longitudinal examination of fear reactions in victims of rape. *Journal of Counseling Psychology, 29,* 655–661.

Cameron, D.J., Thomas, R.I., Mulvhill, M., & Bronheim, H. (1987). Delirium: A test of the Diagnostic and Statistical Manual III criteria on medical inpatients. *Journal of the American Geriatrics Society, 35,* 1007–1010.

Cameron, N. (1959). The paranoid pseudocommunity revisited. *American Journal of Sociology, 65,* 52–58.

Cameron, N., & Magaret, A. (1951). *Behavior pathology.* Boston: Houghton Mifflin.

Campbell, J., Stefan, S., & Loder, A. (1994). Putting violence in context. *Hospital and Community Psychiatry, 45,* 633.

Campbell, M., Anderson, L.T., & Small, A.M. (1990). Pharmacotherapy in autism: A summary of research at Bellevue/New York University. *Brain Dysfunction, 3,* 299–307.

Campbell, M., Anderson, L.T., Small, A.M., Adams, P., Gonzales, N.M., & Ernst, M. (1993). Naltrexone in autistic children: Behavioral symptoms and attentional learning. *Journal of the American Academy of Child and Adolescent Psychiatry, 32,* 1283–1291.

Campbell, M., Rosenbloom, S., Perry, R., George, A.E., Kercheff, I.I., Anderson, L., Small, A.M., & Jennings, S.J. (1982). Computerized axial tomography in young autistic children. *American Journal of Psychiatry, 139,* 510–512.

Campbell, S.B. (1990). *Behavioral problems in preschoolers: Clinical and developmental issues.* New York: Guilford.

Camper, P.M., Jacobson, N.S., Holtzworth-Munroe, A., & Schmaling, K.B. (1988). Causal attributions for interactional behaviors in married couples. *Cognitive Therapy and Research, 12,* 195–209.

Campos, P.E., & Hathaway, B.E. (1993). Behavioral research on gay issues 20 years after Davison's ethical challenge. *The Behavior Therapist, 16,* 193–197.

Canetto, S.S. (1992). Gender and suicide in the elderly. *Suicide and Life-Threatening Behavior, 22,* 80–97.

Cangelosi, A., Gressard, C.F., & Mines, R. A. (1980). The effects of a rational thinking group on self-concepts in adolescents. *The School Counselor, 27,* 357–361.

Cannon, D.S., Baker, T.B., Gino, A., & Nathan, P.E. (1986). Alcohol-aversion therapy: Relation between strength of aversion and abstinence. *Journal of Consulting and Clinical Psychology, 54,* 825–830.

Cannon, T.D., Mednick, S.A., & Parnas, J. (1990). Antecedents of predominantly negative and predominantly positive-symptom schizophrenia in a high-risk population. *Archives of General Psychiatry, 47,* 622–632.

Cannon, T.D., Mednick, S.A., Parnas, J., Schulsinger, F., Praestholm, J., & Vestergaard, A. (1994). Developmental brain abnormalities in the offspring of schizophrenic mothers: 2. Structural brain characteristics of schizophrenia and schizotypal personality disorder. *Archives of General Psychiatry, 51,* 955–962.

Cannon, T.D., Zorilla, L.E., Shtasel, D., Gur, R.E., Gur, R.C., et al. (1994). Neuropsychological functioning in siblings discordant for schizophrenia and healthy volunteers. *Archives of General Psychiatry, 51,* 651–661.

Cantor, N., Markus, H., Niedenthal, P., & Nurius, P. (1986). On motivation and the self-concept. In R.M. Sorrentino & E.T. Higgins (Eds.), *Handbook of motivation and cognition: Foundations of social behavior* (pp. 96–121). New York: Guilford.

Cantos, A.L., Neidig, P.H., & O'Leary, K.D. (1994). Injuries of women and men in a treatment program for domestic violence. *Journal of Family Violence, 9,* 113–124.

Cantwell, D.P., Baker, L., & Rutter, M. (1978). Family factors. In M. Rutter & E. Schopler (Eds.), *Autism: A reappraisal of concepts and treatment.* New York: Plenum.

Caplan, G. (1964). *Principles of preventive psychiatry.* New York: Basic Books.

Caplan, M., Weissberg, R.P., Grober, J.S., Sivo, P.J., et al. (1992). Social competence promotion with inner-city and suburban young adolescents: Effects on social adjustment and alcohol use. *Journal of Consulting and Clinical Psychology, 66,* 56–63.

Cardon, L.R., Smith, S.D., Fulker, D.W., Kimberling, W.J., Pennington, B.F., & DeFries, J.C. (1994). Quantitative trait locus for reading disability on chromosome 6. *Science, 266,* 276–279.

Carey, G., & Gottesman, I.I. (1981). Twin and family studies of anxiety, phobic, and compulsive disorders. In D.F. Klein & J.G. Rabkin (Eds.), *Anxiety: New research and changing concepts.* New York: Raven.

Carnelly, K.B., Pietomonaco, P.R., & Jaffe, K. (1994). Depression, working models of others and relationship functioning. *Journal of Personality and Social Psychology, 66,* 127–141.

Carney, R.M., Freedland, K.E., Rich, M.W., & Jaffe, A.S. (1995). Depression as a risk factor for cardiac events in established coronary heart disease: A review of possible mechanisms. *Annals of Behavioral Medicine, 17,* 142–149.

Carone, B.J., Harrow, M., & Westermeyer, J.F. (1991). Posthospital course and outcome in schizophrenia. *Archives of General Psychiatry, 48,* 247–253.

Carr, A.T. (1971). Compulsive neurosis: Two psychophysiological studies. *Bulletin of the British Psychological Society, 24,* 256–257.

Carr, E.G., Schreibman, L., & Lovaas, O.I. (1975). Control of echolalic speech in psychotic children. *Journal of Abnormal Child Psychology, 3,* 331–351.

Carroll, B.J. (1982). The dexamethasone suppression test for melancholia. *British Journal of Psychiatry, 140,* 292–304.

Carroll, J.M., Touyz, S.M., & Beumont, P.J. (1996). Specific comorbidity between bulimia nervosa and personality disorders. *International Journal of Eating Disorders, 19,* 159–170.

Carroll, K.M. (1996). Relapse prevention as a psychosocial treatment: A review of controlled clinical trials. *Experimental and Clinical Psychopharmacology, 4,* 46–54.

Carroll, K.M., Rounsaville, B.J., Gordon, L.T., Nich, C., Jatlow, P., Bisighini, R.M., & Gawin, F.H. (1994). Psychotherapy and pharmacotherapy for ambulatory cocaine abusers. *Archives of General Psychiatry, 51,* 177–187.

Carroll, K.M., Rounsaville, B.J., Nich, C., Gordon, L.T., & Gawin, F. (1995). Integrating psychotherapy and pharmacotherapy for cocaine dependence: Results from a randomized clinical trial. In L.S. Onken, J.D. Blaine & J.J. Boren (Eds.), *Integrating behavioral therapies with medications in the treatment of drug dependence* (pp. 19–36). Rockville, MD: National Institute on Drug Abuse.

Carroll, K.M., Rounsaville, B.J., Nich, C., Gordon, L.T., Wirtz, P.W., & Gawin, F. (1994). One-year follow-up of psychotherapy and pharmacotherapy for cocaine dependence. *Archives of General Psychiatry, 51,* 989–997.

Carstensen, L.L. (1996). Evidence for a life-span theory of socioemotional selectivity. *Current Directions in Psychological Science, 4,* 151–156.

Carter, M.M., Hollon, S.D., Carson, R., & Shelton, R.C. (1995). Effects of a safe person on induced distress following a biological challenge in panic disorder with agoraphobia. *Journal of Abnormal Psychology, 104,* 156–163.

Carver, C.S., Pozo, C., Harris, S.D., Noriega, V., Scheier, M., Robinson, D., Ketcham, A., Moffat, F.L., & Clark, K. (1993). How coping mediates the effect of optimism on distress: A study of women with early stage breast cancer. *Journal of Personality and Social Psychology, 65,* 375–390.

Cashman, J.A. (1966). *The LSD story.* Greenwich, CT: Fawcett.

Casriel, D. (1971). The dynamics of Synanon. In R.W. Siroka, E.K. Siroka, & G.A. Schloss (Eds.), *Sensitivity training and group encounter.* New York: Grosset & Dunlap.

Castellanos, F.X., Giedd, J.N., Marsh, W.L., Hamburger, S.D., Vaituzis, A.C., Dickstein, D.P., Sarfatti, S.E., Vauss, Y.C., Snell, J.W., Lange, N., Kaysen, D., Krain, A.L., Ritchie, G.F., Rajapaske, J.C., & Rapoport, J.L. (1996). Quantitative brain magnetic resonance imaging in attention-deficit/hyperactivity disorder. *Archives of General Psychiatry, 53,* 607–616.

Castle, D.J., & Murray, R.M. (1993). The epidemiology of late-onset schizophrenia. *Schizophrenia Bulletin, 19,* 691–700.

Catania, J.A., Turner, H., Kegeles, S.M., Stall, R., et al. (1989). Older Americans and AIDS: Transmission risks and primary prevention research needs. *Gerontologist, 29,* 373–381.

Cautela, J.R. (1966). Treatment of compulsive behavior by covert sensitization. *Psychological Record, 16,* 33–41.

Caven, R.S. (1973). Speculations on innovations to conventional marriage in old age. *The Gerontologist, 13,* 409–411.

Centers for Disease Control. (1994). *HIV/AIDS surveillance report.* Atlanta: Centers for Disease Control.

Cerny, J.A., Barlow, D.H., Craske, M.G., & Himadi, W.G. (1987). Couples treatment of agoraphobia: A two year follow-up. *Behavior Therapy, 18,* 401–415.

Chambers, K.C., & Bernstein, I.L. (1995). Conditioned flavor aversions. In R.L. Doty (Ed.), *Handbook of olfaction and gustation* (pp. 745–773). New York: Marcel Dekker.

Chambless, D.L., Sanderson, W.C., Shoham, V., Johnson, S.B., Pope, K.S., Crits-Christoph, P., Baker, M., Johnson, B., Woody, S.R., Sue, S., Beutler, L.E., Williams, D.A., & McCurry, S. (1996). An update on empirically validated therapies. *The Clinical Psychologist, 49,* 5–18.

Chambliss, C.A., & Murray, E.J. (1979). Efficacy attribution, locus of control, and weight loss. *Cognitive Therapy and Research, 3,* 349–353.

Chaney, E.F., O'Leary, M.R., & Marlatt, G.A. (1978). Skills training with alcoholics. *Journal of Consulting and Clinical Psychology, 46,* 1092–1104.

Chapman, L.J., & Chapman, J.P. (1969). Illusory correlation as an obstacle to the use of valid psychodiagnostic signs. *Journal of Abnormal Psychology, 74,* 271–287.

Charney, D.S., Woods, S.W., Goodman, W.K., & Heninger, G.R. (1987). Neurobiological mechanisms of panic anxiety: Biochemical and behavioral correlates of yohimbine-induced panic attacks. *American Journal of Psychiatry, 144,* 1030–1036.

Chassin, L., Curran, P.J., Hussong, A.M., & Colder, C. R. (1996). The relation of parent alcoholism to adolescent substance abuse: A longitudinal follow-up. *Journal of Abnormal Psychology, 105,* 70–80.

Chelune, G.J., Ferguson, W., Koon, R., & Dickey, T.O. (1986). Frontal lobe disinhibition in attention deficit disorder. *Child Psychiatry and Human Development, 16,* 264–281.

Chemtob, C., Roitblat, H.C., Hamada, R.S., Carlson, J.G., & Twentyman, C.T. (1988). A cognitive action theory of posttraumatic stress disorder. *Journal of Anxiety Disorders, 2,* 253–275.

Cherner, J. (1990). *A smoke-free America.* New York: Smokefree Educational Services.

Chernoff, R., & Davison, G. C. (1997, August). Values and their relationship to HIV/AIDS risk behavior. Paper presented at the annual convention of the American Psychological Association, Chicago.

Chesney, M.A., & Folkman, S. (1994). Psychological impact of HIV disease and implications for intervention. *Psychiatric Clinics of North America, 17,* 163–182.

Chiariello, M.A., & Orvaschel, H. (1995). Patterns of parent-child communication: Relationship to depression. *Clinical Psychology Review, 15,* 395–407.

Christensen, A., & Heavey, C.L. (1990). Gender and social structure in the demand/withdraw pattern of marital interaction. *Journal of Personality and Social Psychology, 59,* 73–81.

Christensen, A., & Jacobson, N.S. (1993). Who or what can do psychotherapy? *Psychological Science, 5,* 8–14.

Christensen, A., Jacobson, N.S., & Babcock, J.C. (1995). Integrative behavioral couples therapy. In N.S. Jacobson & A.S. Gurman (Eds.), *Clinical handbook of couples therapy* (pp. 31–64). New York: Guilford.

Christensen, A., & Shenk, J.L. (1991). Communication, distress, and psychological distance in nondistressed, clinic, and divorcing couples. *Journal of Consulting and Clinical Psychology, 59,* 458–463.

Christie, A.B. (1982). Changing patterns in mental illness in the elderly. *British Journal of Psychiatry, 140,* 154–159.

Chua, S.T., & McKenna, P.T. (1995). Schizophrenia—A brain disease? *British Journal of Psychiatry, 166,* 563–582.

Churchill, D.W. (1969). Psychotic children and behavior modification. *American Journal of Psychiatry, 125,* 1585–1590.

Cimons, M. (1992, May 22). Record number of Americans stop smoking. *Los Angeles Times,* p. A4.

Cimons, M. (1995, December 16). Smoking, illegal drug use still rising among teens, national survey shows. *Los Angeles Times,* p. A25.

Cimons, M. (1996, March 19). Firm adjusted nicotine in cigarettes, affidavits say. *Los Angeles Times,* pp. A1, A13.

Cinciripini, P.M., Lapitsky, L., Seay, S., Wallfisch, A., Kitchens, K., & Van Vunakis, H. (1995). The effect of smoking schedules on cessation outcome: Can we improve on common methods of gradual and abrupt nicotine withdrawal? *Journal of Consulting and Clinical Psychology, 63,* 388–399.

Cinciripini, P.M., Lapitsky, L.G., Wallfisch, A., Mace, R., Nezami, E., & Van Vunakis, H. (1994). An evaluation of a multicomponent treatment program involving scheduled smoking and relapse prevention procedures: Initial findings. *Addictive Behaviors, 19,* 13–22.

Clark, D.F. (1988). The validity of measures of cognition: A review of the literature. *Cognitive Therapy and Research, 12,* 1–20.

Clark, D.M. (1986). A cognitive approach to panic. *Behavior Research and Therapy, 24,* 461–470.

Clark, L.A., Watson, D., & Mineka, S. (1994). Temperament, personality, and the mood and anxiety disorders. *Journal of Abnormal Psychology, 103,* 92–102.

Clark, R.F., & Goate, A.M. (1993). Molecular genetics of Alzheimer's disease. *Archives of Neurology, 50,* 1164–1172.

Clarke, G., Hops, H., Lewinsohn, P.M., Andrews, J., Seeley, J.R., & Williams, J. (1992). Cognitive-behavioral group treatment of adolescent depression: Prediction of outcome. *Behavior Therapy, 23,* 341–354.

Clarke, K., & Greenberg, L. (1986). Differential effects of the gestalt two chair intervention and problem solving in resolving decisional conflict. *Journal of Counseling Psychology, 33,* 48–53.

Clarkin, J.F., Marziali, E., & Munroe-Blum, H. (Eds.). (1992). *Borderline personality disorder: Clinical and empirical perspectives.* New York: Guilford.

Clausen, J.A., & Kohn, M.L. (1959). Relation of schizophrenia to the social structure of a small city. In B. Pasamanick (Ed.), *Epidemiology of mental disorder.* Washington, DC: American Association for the Advancement of Science.

Clayton, E.W. (1988). From Rogers to Rivers: The rights of the mentally ill to refuse medications. *American Journal of*

Law and Medicine, 13, 7–52.

Clayton, P.J. (1973). The clinical morbidity of the first year of bereavement: A review. *Comparative Psychiatry, 14,* 151–157.

Clayton, R.R., Catterello, A., & Walden, K.P. (1991). Sensation seeking as a potential mediating variable for school-based prevention intervention: A two-year follow-up of DARE. *Health Communication, 3,* 229–239.

Cleckley, H. (1976). *The mask of sanity* (5th ed.). St. Louis: Mosby.

Climko, R.P., Roehrich, H., Sweeney, D.R., & Al-Razi, J. (1987). Ecstasy: A review of MDMA and MDA. *International Journal of Psychiatry in Medicine, 16,* 359–372.

Clomipramine Collaborative Study Group. (1991). Clomipramine in the treatment of patients with obsessive-compulsive disorder. *Archives of General Psychiatry, 48,* 730–738.

Cloninger, R.C., Bohman, M., & Sigvardsson, S. (1981). Inheritance of alcohol abuse: Cross-fostering analysis of adopted men. *Archives of General Psychiatry, 38,* 861–868.

Cloninger, R.C., Martin, R.L., Guze, S.B., & Clayton, P.L. (1986). A prospective follow-up and family study of somatization in men and women. *American Journal of Psychiatry, 143,* 713–714.

Clunies-Ross, G.G. (1979). Accelerating the development of Down's syndrome infants and young children. *The Journal of Special Education, 13,* 169–177.

Coates, S., & Person, E.S. (1985). Extreme boyhood femininity: Isolated behavior or pervasive disorder? *Journal of the American Academy of Child Psychiatry, 24,* 702–709.

Cody, M., Wendt, P., Dunn, D., Ott, J., Pierson, J., & Pratt, L. (1997) Friendship formation and community development on the Internet. International Communication Association Meeting, Montreal, May.

Cohen, D., Eisdorfer, C., Prinz, P., Breen, A., Davis, M., & Gadsby, A. (1983). Sleep disturbances in the institutionalized aged. *Journal of the American Geriatrics Society, 31,* 79–82.

Cohen, D.J., Solnit, A.J., & Wohlford, P. (1979). Mental health services in Head Start. In E. Zigler & J. Valentine (Eds.), *Project Head Start.* New York: Free Press.

Cohen, L.J., & Roth, S. (1987). The psychological aftermath of rape: Long-term effects and individual differences in recovery. *Journal of Social and Clinical Psychology, 5,* 525–534.

Cohen, P., Cohen, J., Kasen, S., Velez, C.N., Hartmark, C., Johnson, J., Rojas, M., Brook, J., & Streuning, E.L. (1993). An epidemiological study of disorders in late childhood and adolescence: 1. Age and gender-specific prevalence. *Journal of Child Psychology and Psychiatry, 34,* 851–867.

Cohen, S., & Herbert, T.B. (1996). Health psychology: Psychological factors and physical disease from the perspective of human psychoneuroimmunology. In J.T. Spence, J.M. Darley, & D.J. Foss (Eds.), *Annual review of psychology* (pp. 123–142). Stanford, CA: Stanford University Press.

Cohen, S., & Wills, T.A. (1985). Stress, social support, and the buffering process. *Psychological Bulletin, 98,* 310–357.

Cohen, S., Tyrell, D.A.J., & Smith, A.P. (1991). Psychological stress and susceptibility to the common cold. *New England Journal of Medicine, 325,* 606–612.

Cole, D., & Turner, J., Jr. (1993). Models of cognitive mediation and moderation in child depression. *Journal of Abnormal Psychology, 102,* 271–281.

Cole, D.A., Martin, J.M., Powers, B., & Truglio, R. (1990). Modeling causal relations between academic and social competence and depression: A multitrait-multimethod longitudinal study of children. *Journal of Abnormal Psychology, 105,* 258–270.

Cole, J., Watt, N., West, S., Hawkins, J., Asarnow, J., Markman, H., Ramey, S., Shure, M., & Long, B. (1993). The science of prevention: A conceptual framework and some directions for a national research program. *American Psychologist, 48,* 1013–1022.

Cole, J.D. (1988). Where are those new anti-depressants they promised us? *Archives of General Psychiatry, 45,* 193–194.

Cole, K.C. (1996, November 22). Trying to solve the riddle of the rock. *Los Angeles Times,* pp. A1, A29.

Collaborative study of children treated for phenylketonuria, preliminary report 8. (1975, February). R. Koch, principal investigator. Presented at the Eleventh General Medicine Conference, Stateline, NV.

Colletti, G., & Kopel, S.A. (1979). Maintaining behavior change: An investigation of three maintenance strategies and the relationship of self-attribution to the long-term reduction of cigarette smoking. *Journal of Consulting and Clinical Psychology, 47,* 614–617.

Collins, L.F., Maxwell, A.E., & Cameron, C. (1962). A factor analysis of some child psychiatric clinic data. *Journal of Mental Science, 108,* 274–285.

Collins, S., & King, M. (1996). Ten year follow-up of 50 patients with bulimia nervosa. *British Journal of Psychiatry, 110,* 86–108.

Combs, G., Jr., & Ludwig, A.M. (1982). Dissociative disorders. In J.H. Greist, J.W. Jefferson, & R.L. Spitzer (Eds.), *Treatment of mental disorders.* New York: Oxford University Press.

Comfort, A. (1980). Sexuality in later life. In J.E. Birren & R.B. Sloane (Eds.), *Handbook of mental health and aging.* Englewood Cliffs, NJ: Prentice-Hall.

Comfort, A. (1984). Sexuality and the elderly. In J.P. Abrahams & V. Crooks (Eds.), *Geriatric mental health.* Orlando, FL: Grune & Stratton.

Committee on Government Operations. (1985). *The federal response to the homeless crisis.* Washington, DC: U.S. Government Printing Office.

Committee on Health Care for Homeless People. (1988). *Homelessness, health, and human needs.* Washington, DC: National Academic Press.

Compas, B.E., Ey, S., & Grant, K.E. (1993). Taxonomy, assessment and diagnosis of depression during adolescence. *Psychological Bulletin, 144,* 323–344.

Compton, D.R., Dewey, W.L., & Martin, B.R. (1990). Cannabis dependence and tolerance production. *Advances in Alcohol and Substance Abuse, 9,* 129–147.

Condelli, W.S., Fairbank, J.A., Dennis, M.L., & Rachal, J.V. (1991). Cocaine use by clients in methadone programs: Significance, scope, and behavioral interventions. *Journal of Substance Abuse Treatment, 8,* 203–212.

Conger, J.J. (1951). The effects of alcohol on conflict behavior in the albino rat. *Quarterly Journal of Studies on Alcohol, 12,* 129.

Connelly, M. (1992, March 7). 3 found dead after inhaling laughing gas. *Los Angeles Times,* pp. A1, A23.

Conners, C.K. (1969). A teacher rating scale for use in drug studies with children. *American Journal of Psychiatry, 126,* 884–888.

Conners, F.A., Caruso, D.R., & Detterman, D.K. (1986). Computer-assisted instruction for the mentally retarded. In N.R. Ellis & N.W. Bray (Eds.), *International review of research in mental retardation* (Vol. 14). New York: Academic Press.

Conoley, C.W., Conoley, J.C., McConnell, J.A., & Kimzey, C.E. (1983). The effect of the ABCs of rational emotive therapy and the empty-chair technique of Gestalt therapy on anger reduction. *Psychotherapy: Theory, Research, and Practice, 20,* 112–117.

Consumer Reports. (1995, November). Mental health: Does therapy help? *Consumer Reports,* pp. 734–739.

Conwell, Y. (1994). Suicide in elderly patients. In L.S. Schneider, C.F. Reynolds, III, B.D. Lebowitz, & A.J. Friedhoff (Eds.), *Diagnosis and treatment of depression in late life* (pp. 397–418). Washington, DC: American Psychiatric Press.

Cook, B., Blatt, S.J., & Ford, R.Q. (1995). The prediction of therapeutic response to long-term intensive treatment of seriously disturbed young adult inpatients. *Psychotherapy Research, 5,* 218–230.

Cook, M., & Mineka, S. (1989). Observational conditioning of fear to fear-relevant versus fear-irrelevant stimuli in rhesus monkeys. *Journal of Abnormal Psychology, 98,* 448–459.

Coons, P.M., & Milstein, V. (1992). Psychogenic amnesia: A clinical investigation of 25 cases. *Dissociation: Progress in the Dissociative Disorders, 5,* 73–79.

Cooper, A.F., Garside, R.F., & Kay, D.W.K. (1976). A comparison of deaf and non-deaf patients with paranoid and affective psychoses. *British Journal of Psychiatry, 129,* 532–538.

Cooper, A.F., Kay, D.W.K., Curry, A.R., Garside, R.F., & Roth, M. (1974). Hearing loss in paranoid and affective psychoses of the elderly. *Lancet, 2,* 851–854.

Cooper, J.E., Kendell, R.E., Gurland, B.J., Sharpe, L., Copeland, J.R.M., & Simon, R. (1972). *Psychiatric diagnosis in New York and London.* London: Oxford University Press.

Cooper, M.L., Frone, M.R., Russell, M., & Mudar, P. (1995). Drinking to regulate positive and negative emotion: A motivational model of alcoholism. *Journal of Personality and Social Psychology, 69,* 961–974.

Cooper, P.J., Coker, S., & Fleming, C. (1994). Self-help for bulimia nervosa: A preliminary report. *International Journal of Eating Disorders, 16,* 401–404.

Coppen, A., Prange, A.J., Whybrow, P.C., & Noguera, R. (1972). Abnormalities in indoleamines in affective disorders. *Archives of General Psychiatry, 26,* 474–478.

Corbitt, E.M., & Widiger, T.A. (1995). Sex differences in the personality disorders: An exploration of the data. *Clinical Psychology: Science and Practice, 2,* 225–238.

Cordova, J.V., & Jacobson, N.S. (1993). Couple distress. In D.H. Barlow (Ed.), *Clinical handbook of psychological disorders* (2nd ed., pp. 461–512). New York: Guilford.

Cornblatt, B., & Erlenmeyer-Kimling, L.E. (1985). Global attentional deviance in children at risk for schizophrenia: Specificity and predictive validity. *Journal of Abnormal Psychology, 94,* 470–486.

Cornelius, J.R., Salloum, I.M., Mezzich, J., Cornelius, M.D., Fabrega, H., & et al. (1995). Disproportionate suicidability in patients with comorbid major depression and alcoholism. *American Journal of Psychiatry, 152,* 358–364.

Corwin, M. (1996). Heroin's new popularity claims unlikely victims. *Los Angeles Times.*

Coryell, W., Leon, A., Winokur, G., Endicott, J., Keller, M., et al. (1996). Importance of psychotic features to long-term course in major depressive disorder. *American Journal of Psychiatry, 153,* 483–489.

Coryell, W., Winokur, G., Shea, T., Maser, J.W., Endicott, J., & Akiskal, H.S. (1994). The long-term stability of depressive subtypes. *American Journal of Psychiatry, 151,* 199–204.

Costa, P.T., Jr., & McCrae, R.R. (1992). *NEO-PI-R.* Odessa, FL: Psychological Assessment Resources.

Costa, P.T., Jr., & McCrae, R.R. (1988). Personality in adulthood: A six-year longitudinal study of self-reports and spouse ratings on the NEO Personality Inventory. *Journal of Personality and Social Psychology, 54,* 853–863.

Costa, P.T., Jr., Zonderman, A.B., McCrae, R.R., Cornoni-Huntley, J., Locke, B.Z., & Barbano, H.E. (1987). Longitudinal analyses of psychological well-being in a national sample: Stability of mean levels. *Journal of Gerontology, 42,* 50–55.

Costello, E.J., Costello, A.J., Edelbrock, C., Burns, B.J., Dulcan, M.K., Brent, D., & Janiszewski, S. (1988). Psychiatric disorders in pediatric primary care. *Archives of General Psychiatry, 45,* 1107–1116.

Courchesne, E., Yeung-Courchesne, R., Press, G.A., Hesselink, J.R., & Jernigan, T.L. (1988). Hypoplasia of cerebellar vermal lobules VI and VII in autism. *New England Journal of Medicine, 318,* 1349–1354.

Covi, L., Lipman, R.S., Derogatis, L.R., Smith, J.E., & Pattison, J.H. (1974). Drugs and group psychotherapy in neurotic depression. *American Journal of Psychiatry, 131,* 191–197.

Cox, A., Rutter, M., Newman, S., & Bartak, L. (1975). A comparative study of infantile autism and specific developmental language disorders: 2. Parental characteristics. *British Journal of Psychiatry, 126,* 146–159.

Cox, D.J., Freundlich, A., & Meyer, R.G. (1975). Differential effectiveness of electromyographic feedback, verbal relaxation instructions, and medication placebo with tension headaches. *Journal of Consulting and Clinical Psychology, 43,* 892–898.

Coyne, J.C. (1976). Depression and the response of others. *Journal of Abnormal Psychology, 85,* 186–193.

Craft, M.J. (1969). The natural history of psychopathic disorder. *British Journal of Psychiatry, 115,* 39–44.

Craig, M.M., & Glick, S.J. (1963). Ten years' experience with the Glueck social prediction table. *Crime and Delinquency, 9,* 249–261.

Craighead, L.W., & Agras, W.S. (1991).

Mechanisms of action in cognitive-behavioral and pharmacological interventions for obesity and bulimia nervosa. *Journal of Consulting and Clinical Psychology, 59,* 115–125.

Craighead, W.E., Evans, D.D., & Robins, C.J. (1992). Unipolar depression. In S.M. Turner, K.S. Calhoun, & H.E. Adams (Eds.), *Handbook of clinical behavior therapy* (2nd ed., pp. 99–116). New York: Wiley.

Craske, M.G., Brown, A.T., & Barlow, D.H. (1991). Behavioral treatment of panic disorder: A two-year follow-up. *Behavior Therapy, 22,* 289–304.

Craske, M.G., Maidenberg, E., & Bystritsky, A. (1995). Brief cognitive-behavioral versus nondirective therapy for panic disorder. *Journal of Behavior Therapy & Experimental Psychiatry, 26,* 113–120.

Craske, M.G., Rapee, R.M., & Barlow, D.H. (1992). Cognitive-behavioral treatment of panic disorder, agoraphobia, and generalized anxiety disorder. In S.M. Turner, K.S. Calhoun, & H.E. Adams (Eds.), *Handbook of clinical behavior therapy* (2nd ed. pp. 39–65). New York: Wiley.

Creer, T.L. (1982). Asthma. *Journal of Consulting and Clinical Psychology, 50,* 912–921.

Creer, T.L., Renna, C.M., & Chai, H. (1982). The application of behavioral techniques to childhood asthma. In D.C. Russo & J.W. Varni (Eds.), *Behavioral pediatrics: Research and practice.* New York: Plenum.

Crick, N.R., & Dodge, K.A. (1994). A review and reformulation of social information-processing mechanisms in children's social adjustment. *Psychological Bulletin, 115,* 74–101.

Crisp, A.H., Callender, J.S., Haleck, C., & Hsu, L.K.G. (1992). Long-term mortality in anorexia nervosa. *British Journal of Psychiatry, 161,* 104–107.

Crits-Christoph, P. (1992). The efficacy of brief dynamic psychotherapy. *American Journal of Psychiatry, 149,* 151–158.

Cronan, T.A., Cruz, S.G., Arriaga, R.I., & Sarkin, A.J. (1996). The effects of a community-based literacy program on young children's language and conceptual development. *American Journal of Community Psychology, 24,* 251–272.

Crow, T.J. (1980). Molecular pathology of schizophrenia: More than one disease process? *British Medical Journal, 280,* 784–788.

Crowe, R.R., Noyes, R., Pauls, D.I., & Slyman, D.J. (1983). A family study of panic disorder. *Archives of General Psychiatry, 40,* 1065–1069.

Crowe, R.R., Noyes, R., Wilson, A.F., Elston, R.C., et al. (1987). A linkage study

of panic disorder. *Archives of General Psychiatry, 44,* 933–937.

Culter, S.E., & Nolen-Hoeksema, S. (1991). Accounting for sex differences in depression through female victimization: Childhood sexual abuse. *Sex Roles, 24,* 425–438.

Cummings, E.M., Davies, P.T., & Simpson, K.S. (1994). Marital conflict, gender, and children's appraisals and coping efficacy as mediators of child adjustment. *Journal of Family Psychology, 8,* 141–149.

Cunningham, P.J., & Mueller, C.D. (1991). Individuals with mental retardation in residential facilities: Findings from the 1987 National Medical Expenditure Survey. *American Journal on Mental Retardation, 96,* 109–117.

D'Amicis, L., Goldberg, D., LoPiccolo, J., Friedman, J., & Davies, L. (1985). Clinical follow-up of couples treated for sexual dysfunction. *Archives of Sexual Behavior, 14,* 461–483.

D'Ercole, A., & Struening, E. (1990). Victimization among homeless women: Implications for service delivery. *Journal of Community Psychology, 18,* 141–152.

D'Zurilla, T.J. (1986). *Problem-solving therapy: A social competence approach to clinical intervention.* New York: Springer.

D'Zurilla, T.J. (1990). Problem-solving training for effective stress management and prevention. *Journal of Cognitive Psychotherapy: An International Quarterly, 4,* 327–355.

D'Zurilla, T.J., & Goldfried, M.R. (1971). Problem-solving and behavior modification. *Journal of Abnormal Psychology, 78,* 107–126.

D'Zurilla, T.J., & Sheedy, C.F. (1991). Relation between social problem-solving ability and subsequent level of psychological stress in college students. *Journal of Personality and Social Psychology, 61,* 841–846.

D'Zurilla, T.J., & Sheedy, C.F. (1992). The relation between social problem-solving ability and subsequent level of academic competence in college students. *Cognitive Therapy and Research, 16,* 589–599.

Dackis, C.A., & Gold, M.S. (1985). Pharmacological approaches to cocaine addiction. *Journal of Substance Abuse Treatment, 2,* 139–145.

DaCosta, M., & Halmi, K.A. (1992). Classifications of anorexia nervosa: Question of subtypes. *International Journal of Eating Disorders, 11,* 305–313.

Daneman, E.A. (1961). Imipramine in office management of depressive reactions (a double-blind study). *Diseases of the Nervous System, 22,* 213–217.

Daniolos, P.T., & Holmes, V.F. (1995). HIV public policy and psychiatry: An examination of ethical issues and professional guidelines. *Psychosomatics, 36,* 12–21.

Dare, C., LeGrange, D., Eisler, I., & Rutherford, J. (1994). Redefining the psychosomatic family: Family process of 26 eating disordered families. *International Journal of Eating Disorders, 16,* 211–226.

Davies, P.T., & Cummings, E.M. (1994). Marital conflict and child adjustment: An emotional security hypothesis. *Psychological Bulletin, 116,* 387–411.

Davila, J., Hammen, C.L., Burge, D., Paley, B., & Daley, S.E. (1995). Poor interpersonal problem solving as a mechanism of stress generation in depression among adolescent women. *Journal of Abnormal Psychology, 104,* 592–600.

Davis, J.M. (1978). Dopamine theory of schizophrenia: A two-factor theory. In L.C. Wynne, R.L. Cromwell, & S. Matthysse (Eds.), *The nature of schizophrenia.* New York: Wiley.

Davis, K.L., Kahn, R.S., Ko, G., & Davidson, M. (1991). Dopamine and schizophrenia: A review and reconceptualization. *American Journal of Psychiatry, 148,* 1474–1486.

Davison, E.H. (1996). Women and aging. Unpublished manuscript, University of California at Santa Barbara.

Davison, G.C. (1964). A social learning therapy programme with an autistic child. *Behaviour Research and Therapy, 2,* 146–159.

Davison, G.C. (1966). Differential relaxation and cognitive restructuring in therapy with a "paranoid schizophrenic" or "paranoid state." *Proceedings of the 74th Annual Convention of the American Psychological Association.* Washington, DC: American Psychological Association.

Davison, G.C. (1968a). Elimination of a sadistic fantasy by a client-controlled counterconditioning technique. *Journal of Abnormal Psychology, 73,* 84–90.

Davison, G.C. (1968b). Systematic desensitization as a counterconditioning process. *Journal of Abnormal Psychology, 73,* 91–99.

Davison, G.C. (1973). Counter countrol in behavior modification. In L.A. Hamerlynck, L.C. Handy, & E.J. Mash (Eds.), *Behavior change: Methodology, concepts and practice.* Champaign, IL: Research Press.

Davison, G.C. (1974). *Homosexuality: The ethical challenge.* Presidential address to the Eighth Annual Convention of the Association for Advancement of Behavior Therapy, Chicago.

Davison, G.C. (1976). Homosexuality: The ethical challenge. *Journal of Consulting and Clinical Psychology, 44,* 157–162.

Davison, G.C. (1978). Not can but ought: The treatment of homosexuality. *Journal of Consulting and Clinical Psychology, 46,* 170–172.

Davison, G.C. (1991). Constructionism and therapy for homosexuality. In J. Gonsiorek & J. Weinrich (Eds.), *Homosexuality: Research findings for public policy.* Newbury Park, CA: Sage.

Davison, G.C., & Darke, L. (1991). Managing pain. In R. Bjork & D. Druckman (Eds.), *In the mind's eye: Understanding the basis of human performance.* Washington, DC: National Academy Press.

Davison, G.C., & Lazarus, A.A. (1995). The dialectics of science and practice. In S.C. Hayes, V.M. Follette, T. Risley, R.D. Dawes, & K. Grady (Eds.), *Scientific standards of psychological practice: Issues and recommendations* (pp. 95–120). Reno, NV: Context Press.

Davison, G.C., & Neale, J.M. (1996). *Abnormal psychology.* Revised sixth edition. New York: Wiley.

Davison, G.C., & Rosen, R.C. (1972). Lobeline and the reduction of cigarette smoking. *Psychological Reports, 31,* 443–456.

Davison, G.C., & Thompson, R.F. (1988). Stress management. In D. Druckman & J.A. Swets (Eds.), *Enhancing human performance: Issues, theories, and techniques.* Washington, DC: National Academic Press.

Davison, G.C., & Valins, S. (1969). Maintenance of self-attributed and drug-attributed behavior change. *Journal of Personality and Social Psychology, 11,* 25–33.

Davison, G.C., & Wilson, G.T. (1973). Attitudes of behavior therapists toward homosexuality. *Behavior Therapy, 4,* 686–696.

Davison, G.C., & Zighelboim, V. (1987). Irrational beliefs in the articulated thoughts of college students with social anxiety. *Journal of Rational-Emotive Therapy, 5,* 238–254.

Davison, G.C., Feldman, P.M., & Osborn, C.E. (1984). Articulated thoughts, irrational beliefs, and fear of negative evaluation. *Cognitive Therapy and Research, 8,* 349–362.

Davison, G.C., Haaga, D.A., Rosenbaum, J., Dolezal, S.L., & Weinstein, K.A. (1991). Assessment of self-efficacy in articulated thoughts: "States of Mind" analysis and association with speech anxious behavior. *Journal of Cognitive Psychotherapy: An International Quarterly, 5,* 83–92.

Davison, G.C., Navarre, S.G., & Vogel, R.S. (1995). The articulated thoughts in simulated situations paradigm: A think-aloud approach to cognitive assessment. *Current Directions in Psychological Science, 4,* 29–33.

Davison, G.C., Robins, C., & Johnson, M.K. (1983). Articulated thoughts during simulated situations: A paradigm for studying cognition in emotion and behavior. *Cognitive Therapy and Research, 7,* 17–40.

Davison, G.C., Tsujimoto, R.N., & Glaros, A.G. (1973). Attribution and the maintenance of behavior change in falling asleep. *Journal of Abnormal Psychology, 82,* 124–133.

Davison, G.C., Williams, M.E., Nezami, E., Bice, T.L., & DeQuattro, V. (1991). Relaxation, reduction in angry articulated thoughts, and improvements in borderline essential hypertension and heart rate. *Journal of Behavioral Medicine, 14,* 453–468.

Dawes, R.M. (1994). *House of cards: Psychology and psychotherapy built on myth.* New York: Free Press.

Dawson, G., & Lewy, A. (1989). Reciprocal subcortical-cortical influences in autism. In G. Dawson (Ed.), *Autism: Nature, diagnosis, and treatment* (pp. 144–173). New York: Guilford.

Dawson, M.E., Schell, A.M., & Banis, H.T. (1986). Greater resistance to extinction of electrodermal responses conditioned to potentially phobic CSs: A noncognitive process? *Psychophysiology, 23,* 552–561.

Deacon, S., Minichiello, V., & Plummer, D. (1995). Sexuality and older people: Revisiting the assumptions. *Educational Gerontology, 21,* 497–513.

DeJong, W., & Kleck, R.E. (1986). The social psychological effects of overweight. In C.P. Herman, M.P. Zanna, & E.T. Higgins (Eds.), *Physical appearance, stigma, and social behavior.* Hillside, NJ: Erlbaum.

Delgado, P.L., Charney, D.S., Price, L.H., Aghajanian, G.K., Landis, H., et al. (1990). Serotonin function and the mechanism of antidepressant action: Reversal of antidepressant induced remission by rapid depletion of plasma tryptophan. *Archives of General Psychiatry, 47,* 411–418.

deLint, J. (1978). Alcohol consumption and alcohol problems from an epidemiological perspective. *British Journal of Alcohol and Alcoholism, 17,* 109–116.

Dement, W.C., Laughton, E., & Carskadon, M.A. (1981). "White paper" on sleep and aging. *Journal of the American Geriatrics Society, 30,* 25–50.

DeMyer, M. (1975). The nature of the neuropsychological disability of autistic children. *Journal of Autism and Childhood Schizophrenia, 5,* 109–127.

Depression Guideline Panel. (1997). *Depression in primary care: Detection and diagnosis.* Rockville, MD: U.S. Department of Health and Human Services.

Depue, R.A., & Monroe, S.M. (1978). Learned helplessness in the perspective of the depressive disorders: Conceptual and definitional issues. *Journal of Abnormal Psychology, 87,* 3–20.

Dershowitz, A. (1994a, May 15). "Abuse Excuse" du jour victimizes many. *Los Angeles Times.*

Dershowitz, A. (1994b). *The abuse excuse: And other cop-outs, sob stories, and evasions of responsibility.* Boston: Little Brown.

DeRubeis, R.J., Hollon, S.D., Evans, M.D., & Bemis, K.M. (1982). Can psychotherapies for depression be discriminated? A systematic investigation of cognitive therapy and interpersonal therapy. *Journal of Consulting and Clinical Psychology, 50,* 744–760.

Detterman, D.K. (1979). Memory in the mentally retarded. In N.R. Ellis (Ed.), *Handbook of mental deficiency, psychological theory and research* (2nd ed.). Hillsdale, NJ: Erlbaum.

Deutsch, A. (1949). *The mentally ill in America.* New York: Columbia University Press.

Devanand, D.P., Dwork, A.J., Hutchinson, E.R., Bolwig, T.G., & Sackeim, H.A. (1994). Does ECT alter brain structure? *American Journal of Psychiatry, 151,* 957–970.

Devanand, D.P., Sano, M., Tang, M., Taylor, S., Gurland, B., et al. (1996). Depressed mood and the incidence of Alzheimer's disease in the elderly living in the community. *Archives of General Psychiatry, 53,* 148–158.

Devine, V., Adelson, R., Goldstein, J., Valins, S., & Davison, G.C. (1974). Controlled test of the analgesic and relaxant properties of nitrous oxide. *Journal of Dental Research, 53,* 486–490.

DeVries, H.A. (1975). Physiology of exercise and aging. In D.S. Woodruff & J.E. Birren (Eds.), *Aging: Scientific perspectives and social issues.* New York: Van Nostrand-Reinhold.

Dew, M.A., Bromet, E.J., Brent, D., & Greenhouse, J.B. (1987). A quantitative literature review of the effectiveness of suicide prevention centers. *Journal of Consulting and Clinical Psychology, 55,* 239–244.

Dewys, W.D., Begg, C., & Lavin, P.T. (1980). Prognostic effect of weight loss prior to chemotherapy in cancer patients. *American Journal of Medicine, 69,* 491–497.

Diamond, S., Baldwin, R., & Diamond, R. (1963). *Inhibition and choice.* New York: Harper & Row.

DiClemente, C.C. (1993). Changing addictive behaviors: A process perspective. *Current Directions in Psychological Science, 2,* 101–106.

Didion, J. (1979). *The white album.* New York: Simon & Schuster.

Dietz, P.E., Hazelwood, R.R., & Warren, J. (1990). The sexually sadistic criminal and his offenses. *Bulletin of the American Academy of Psychiatry and the Law, 18,* 163–178.

DiFranza, J.R., Richards, J.W., Paulman, P.M., Wolf-Gillespie, N., Fletcher, C., et al. (1991). RJR Nabisco's cartoon camel promotes Camel Cigarettes to children. *Journal of the American Medical Association, 266,* 3149–3153.

DiMascio, A., Weissman, M.M., Prusoff, B.A., Neu, C., Zwilling, M., & Klerman, G.L. (1979). Differential symptom reduction by drugs and psychotherapy in acute depression. *Archives of General Psychiatry, 36,* 1450–1456.

DiNardo, P.A., Guzy, L.T., Jenkins, J.A., Bak, R.M., Tomasi, S.F., & Copland, M. (1988). Etiology and maintenance of dog fears. *Behaviour Research and Therapy, 26,* 241–244.

DiNardo, P.A., O'Brien, G.T., Barlow, D.H., Waddell, M.T., & Blanchard, E.B. (1993). Reliability of the DSM-III-R anxiety disorders categories using the Anxiety Disorders Interview Schedule-Revised (ADIS-R). *Archives of General Psychiatry, 50,* 251–256.

Dobson, K.S. (1989). A meta-analysis of the efficacy of cognitive therapy for depression. *Journal of Consulting and Clinical Psychology, 57,* 414–419.

Dobson, K.S., & Jackman-Cram, S. (1996). Common change processes in cognitive-behavioral therapies. In K.S. Dobson & K.D. Craig (Eds.), *Advances in cognitive-behavioral therapy.* (pp. 63–82). Thousand Oaks, CA: Sage Publications.

Dobson, K.S., & Shaw, B.F. (1986). Cognitive assessment with major depressive disorders. *Cognitive Therapy and Research, 10,* 13–29.

Dodge, K.A., & Coie, J.D. (1987). Social information-processing factors in reactive and proactive aggression in children's peer groups. *Journal of Personality and Social Psychology, 53,* 1146–1158.

Dodge, K.A., & Frame, C.L. (1982). Social cognitive biases and deficits in aggressive boys. *Child Development, 53,* 620–635.

Doerfler, L.A., Moran, P.W., Barriera, P., Chaplin, M., & Brown, L. (in press). Marital satisfaction and marital communication in depressed, manic, and normal couples. *Behavior Therapy.*

Doerr, P., Fichter, M., Pirke, K.M., & Lund, R. (1980). Relationship between weight gain and hypothalamic-pituitary-adrenal function in patients with anorexia nervosa. *Journal of Steroid Biochemistry, 13,* 529–537.

Dohrenwend, B.P., Levav, P.E., Schwartz, S., Naveh, G., Link, B.G., Skodol, A.E., & Stueve, A. (1992). Socioeconomic status and psychiatric disorders: The causation-selection issue. *Science, 255,* 946–952.

Dolan, B. (1991). Cross-cultural aspects of anorexia and bulimia: A review. *International Journal of Eating Disorders, 10,* 67–78.

Dollard, J., & Miller, N.E. (1950). *Personality and psychotherapy.* New York: McGraw-Hill.

Doran, A.R., Pickar, D., Boronow, J., et al. (1985). *CT scans in schizophrenics, medical and normal controls.* Annual meeting of the American College of Neuropsychopharmacology, Maui, HI.

Dougher, M.J. (1988). Clinical assessment of sex offenders. In B.K. Schwartz (Ed.), *A practitioner's guide to treating the incarcerated male sex offender* (pp. 77–84). Washington, DC: U.S. Department of Justice.

Dowd, J.J., & Bengston, V.L. (1978). Aging in minority populations: An examination of the double jeopardy hypothesis. *Journal of Gerontology, 33,* 427–436.

Dowson, J.H. (1992). Associations between self-induced vomiting and personality disorder in patients with a history of anorexia nervosa. *Acta Psychiatrica Scandinavica, 86,* 399–404.

Draguns, J.G. (1989). Normal and abnormal behavior in cross-cultural perspective: Specifying the nature of their relationships. In J.J. Berman (Ed.), *Nebraska symposium on motivation.* Lincoln: University of Nebraska Press.

Dubbert, P. (1995). Behavioral (life style) modification in the prevention and treatment of hypertension. *Clinical Psychology Review, 15,* 187–216.

Duck, S. (1984). A perspective on the repair of personal relationships. In S. Duck (Ed.), *Personal relationships: 5. Repairing personal relationships.* New York: Academic Press.

Duggan, C.E., Marks, I., & Richards, D. (1993). Clinical audit of behavior therapy training of nurses. *Health Trends, 25,* 25–30.

Duggan, C.F., Lee, A.S., & Murray, R.M. (1991). Do different subtypes of hospitalized depressives have different long term outcomes? *Archives of General Psychiatry, 48,* 308–312.

Duke, M.P. (1994). Chaos theory and psychology: Seven propositions. *Genetic, Social, & General Psychology Monographs, 120,* 267–286.

Dunham, H.W. (1965). *Community and schizophrenia: An epidemiological analysis.* Detroit: Wayne State University Press.

DuPaul, G.J. (1991). Parent and teacher ratings of ADHD symptoms: Psychometric properties in a community-based sample. *Journal of Clinical Child Psychology, 20,* 245–253.

Dura, J.R., Stukenberg, K.W., & Kiecolt-Glaser, J.K. (1991). Anxiety and depressive disorders in adult children caring for demented parents. *Psychology and Aging, 6,* 467–473.

Durkheim, E. (1951). *Suicide.* (J.A. Spaulding & G. Simpson, Trans.). New York: Free Press. (Original work published 1897; 2nd ed., 1930)

duVerglas, G., Banks, S.R., & Guyer, K.E. (1988). Clinical effects of fenfluramine on children with autism: A review of the research. *Journal of Autism and Developmental Disorders, 18,* 297–308.

Dvoskin, J.A., & Steadman, H.J. (1994). Using intensive case management to reduce violence by mentally ill persons in the community. *Hospital and Community Psychiatry, 45,* 679–684.

Dworkin, R.H., & Lenzenwenger, M.F. (1984). Symptoms and the genetics of schizophrenia: Implications for diagnosis. *American Journal of Psychiatry, 141,* 1541–1546.

Dworkin, R.H., Lenzenwenger, M.F., & Moldin, S.O. (1987). Genetics and the phenomenology of schizophrenia. In P.D. Harvey and E.F. Walker (Eds.), *Positive and negative symptoms of psychosis.* Hillsdale, NJ: Erlbaum.

Dykens, E., Leckman, J., Paul, R., & Watson, M. (1988). Cognitive, behavioral, and adaptive functioning in fragile X and non-fragile A retarded men. *Journal of Autism and Developmental Disorders, 18,* 41–52.

Dysken, M.W. (1979). Clinical usefulness of sodium amobarbital interviewing. *Archives of General Psychiatry, 36,* 789–794.

Eagles, J.M., Johnston, M.I., Hunter, D., Lobban, M., & Millar, H.R. (1995). Increasing incidence of anorexia nervosa in the female population of northeast Scotland. *American Journal of Psychiatry, 152,* 1266–1271.

Eaker, E.D., Pinsky, J., & Castelli, W.P. (1992). Myocardial infarction and coronary death among women: Psychosocial predictors from a 20 year follow-up of women in the Framingham study. *American Journal of Epidemiology, 135,* 854–864.

Earleywine, M., & Gann, M.K. (1995). Challenging recovered memories in the courtroom. In J. Ziskin (Ed.), *Coping with psychiatric and psychological testimony* (pp. 1100–1134). Los Angeles: Law and Psychology Press.

Eastwood, M.R., Corbin, S., Reed, M., Nobbs, H., & Kedward, M.B. (1985). Acquired hearing loss and psychiatric illness: An estimate of prevalence and comorbidity in a geriatric setting. *British Journal of Psychiatry, 147,* 552.

Eaton, W.W., Kramer, M., Anthony, J.C., Dryman, A., Shapiro, S., et al. (1989). The incidence of specific DIS/DSM-III mental disorders: Data from the NIMH Epidemiologic Catchment Area Programs. *Acta Psychiatrica Scandinavaica, 79,* 163–178.

Eckhardt, C.I., Barbour, K.A., & Davison, G.C. (1997). Articulated thoughts of maritally violent and nonviolent men during anger arousal. Unpublished manuscript, University of North Carolina, Wilmington.

Eckhardt, C.I., Barbour, K.A., & Stuart, G.L. (in press). Anger and hostility in maritally violent men: Conceptual distinctions, measurement issues, and literature review. *Clinical Psychology Review.*

Egan, G. (1975). *The skilled helper.* Monterey, CA: Brooks/Cole.

Egan, T. (1990). As memory and music faded, Alzheimer patient met death. *The New York Times, 89,* pp. A1, A16.

Egeland, J.A., Gerhard, D.S., Pauls, D.L., Sussex, J.N., Kidd, K.K., Allen, C.R., Hosterer, A.M., & Housman, D.E. (1987). Bipolar affective disorders linked to DNA markers on chromosome 11. *Nature, 325,* 783–787.

Ehrhardt, A., & Money, J. (1967). Progestin-induced hermaphroditism: IQ and psychosexual identity in a study of ten girls. *Journal of Sex Research, 3,* 83–100.

Eiberg, H., Berendt, I., & Mohr, J. (1995). Assignment of dominant inherited nocturnal enuresis to chromosome 13Q. *Nature Genetics, 10,* 354–356.

Eiser, C., Eiser, R.J., Town, C., & Tripp, J. (1991). Discipline strategies and parental perceptions of preschool children with asthma. *British Journal of Medical Psychology, 64,* 45–53.

Eisler, R.M., & Blalock, J.A. (1991). Masculine gender role stress: Implications for the assessment of men. *Clinical Psychology Review, 11,* 45–60.

Elias, M., & Clabby, J.F. (1989). *Social decision making skills: A curriculum for the elementary grades.* Rockville, MD: Aspen Publishers.

Elkin, I. (1994). Treatment of Depression Collaborative Research Program: Where we began and where we are. In A.E. Bergin & S.L. Garfield (Eds.), *Handbook of psychotherapy and behavior change.* Fourth edition (pp. 114–139). New York: Wiley & Sons.

Elkin, I., Gibbons, R.D., Shea, M.T., & Shaw, B.F. (1996). Science is not a trial (but it can sometimes be a tribulation). *Journal of Consulting and Clinical Psychology, 64,* 92–103.

Elkin, I., Gibbons, R.D., Shea, M.T., Sotsky, S.M., Watkins, J.T., Pilkonis, P.A., & Hedeker, D. (1995). Initial severity and differential treatment outcome in the NIMH Treatment of Depression Collaborative Research Program. *Journal of Consulting and Clinical Psychology, 63,* 841–847.

Elkin, I., Parloff, M.B., Hadley, S.W., & Autry, J.H. (1985). NIMH Treatment of Depression Collaborative Research Program. *Archives of General Psychiatry, 42,* 305–316.

Elkin, I., Shea, M.T., Watkins, J.T., Imber, S.D., Sotsky, S.M., Collins, J.F., Glass, D.R., Pilkonis, P.A., Leber, W.R., Docherty, J.P., Fiester, S.J., & Parloff, M.B. (1989). NIMH Treatment of Depression Collaborative Research Program: 1. General effectiveness of treatments. *Archives of General Psychiatry, 46,* 971–983.

Elkin, I., Shea, T., Imber, S., Pilkonis, P., Sotsky, S., Glass, D., Watkins, J., Leber, W., & Collins, J. (1986). *NIMH Treatment of Depression Collaborative Research Program: Initial outcome findings.* Paper presented to the American Association for the Advancement of Science.

Elkis, H., Friedman, L., Wise, A., & Meltzer, H.T. (1995). Meta-analysis of studies of ventricular enlargement and cortical sulcal prominence in mood disorders. *Archives of General Psychiatry, 52,* 735–746.

Ellenberger, H.F. (1972). The story of "Anna O": A critical review with new data. *Journal of the History of the Behavior Sciences, 8,* 267–279.

Ellis, A. (1962). *Reason and emotion in psychotherapy.* New York: Lyle Stuart.

Ellis, A. (1984). Rational-emotive therapy. In R.J. Corsini (Ed.), *Current psychotherapies* (3rd ed.). Itasca, IL: Peacock Press.

Ellis, A. (1991). The revised ABC's of rational-emotive therapy (RET). *Journal of Rational-Emotive and Cognitive Behavior Therapy, 9,* 139–172.

Ellis, A. (1993a). Changing rational-emotive therapy (RET) to rational emotive behavior therapy (REBT). *The Behavior Therapist, 16,* 257–258.

Ellis, A. (1993b). Fundamentals of rational-emotive therapy for the 1990s. In W. Dryden & L. Hill (Eds.), *Innovations in rational-emotive therapy.* Newbury Park, CA: Sage.

Ellis, A. (1995). Changing rational-emotive therapy (RET) to rational emotive behavior therapy (REBT). *Journal of Rational-Emotive and Cognitive Behavior Therapy, 13,* 85–89.

Ellis, H. (1906). *Studies in the psychology of sex.* New York: Random House.

Ellis, H. (1910). *Studies in the psychology of sex.* Philadelphia: FA Davis.

Ellis, N.R., Deacon, J.R., & Wooldridge, P.W. (1985). Structural memory deficits of mentally retarded persons. *American*

Journal of Mental Deficiency, 89, 393–402.

Elmore, A.M., & Tursky, B. (1978). The biofeedback hypothesis: An idea in search of a theory and method. In A.A. Sugerman & R.E. Tarter (Eds.), *Expanding dimensions of consciousness.* New York: Springer.

Elmore, J.L., & Sugerman, A.A. (1975). Precipitation of psychosis during electroshock therapy. *Diseases of the Nervous System, 3,* 115–117.

Emery, R.E., & O'Leary, K.D. (1979). *Children's perceptions of marital discord and behavior problems of boys and girls.* Paper presented at the annual meeting of the Association for Advancement of Behavior Therapy, San Francisco.

Emmelkamp, P.M.G. (1986). Behavior therapy with adults. In S.L. Garfield & A.E. Bergin (Eds.), *Handbook of psychotherapy and behavior change* (3rd ed.). New York: Wiley.

Emmelkamp, P.M.G., Visser, S., & Hoekstra, R.J. (1988). Cognitive therapy versus exposure *in vivo* in the treatment of obsessive-compulsives. *Cognitive Therapy and Research, 12,* 103–114.

Emmons, R.A., & Diener, E. (1986). Situation selection as a moderator of response consistency and stability. *Journal of Personality and Social Psychology, 51,* 1013–1019.

Emory, L.E., Williams, D.H., Cole, C.M., Amparo, E.G., & Meyer, W.J. (1991). Anatomic variation of the corpus callosum in persons with gender dysphoria. *Archives of Sexual Behavior, 20,* 409–417.

Emrick, C.D., Tonigan, J.S., Montgomery, H., & Little, L. (1993). Alcoholics Anonymous: What is currently known? In B.S. McCrady & W.R. Miller (Eds.), *Research on Alcoholics Anonymous: Opportunities and alternatives* (pp. 41–76). New Brunswick, NJ: Rutgers Center of Alcohol Studies.

English, H.B. (1929). Three cases of the "conditioned fear response." *Journal of Abnormal and Social Psychology, 34,* 221–225.

Enright, J.B. (1970). An introduction to Gestalt techniques. In J. Fagan & I.L. Shepherd (Eds.), *Gestalt therapy now: Theory, techniques, applications.* Palo Alto, CA: Science & Behavior Books.

Epping-Jordan, J.E., Compas, B.E., & Howell, D.C. (1994). Predictors of cancer progression in young adult men and women: Avoidance, intrusive thoughts, and psychological symptoms. *Health Psychology, 13,* 539–547.

Epstein, L.C., & Lasagna, L. (1969). Obtaining informed consent. *Archives of Internal Medicine, 123,* 682–688.

Epstein, L.H., Beck, S., Figneroa, J., Farkas, G., Kazdin, A.E., Danema, D., & Becker, D. (1981). The effects of point economy and parent management on urine glucose and metabolic control in children with insulin dependent diabetes. *Journal of Applied Behavior Analysis, 14,* 365–375.

Epstein, L.H., Masek, B.J., & Marshall, W.R. (1978). A nutritionally based school program for control of eating in obese children. *Behavior Therapy, 9,* 766–788.

Epstein, L.H., Wing, R.R., Thompson, J.K., & Griffen, W. (1980). Attendance and fitness in aerobics exercise: The effects of contract and lottery procedures. *Behavior Modification, 4,* 465–479.

Epstein, S. (1979). The stability of behavior: On predicting most of the people much of the time. *Journal of Personality and Social Psychology, 37,* 1097–1126.

Erdberg, P., & Exner, J.E., Jr. (1984). Rorschach assessment. In G. Goldstein & M. Hersen (Eds.), *Handbook of psychological assessment.* New York: Pergamon.

Erikson, E.H. (1950). *Childhood and society.* New York: Norton.

Erikson, E.H. (1959). *Identity and the life cycle. Selected papers.* New York: International Universities Press.

Erikson, E.H. (1968). *Identity: Youth and crisis.* New York: Norton.

Erlenmeyer-Kimling, L.E., & Cornblatt, B. (1987). The New York high-risk project: A follow-up report. *Schizophrenia Bulletin, 13,* 451–461.

Ernst, M., Liebenauer, L.L., King, A.C., Fitzgerald, G.A., Cohen, R.M., & Zametkin, A.J. (1994). Reduced brain metabolism in hyperactive girls. *Journal of the American Academy of Child and Adolescent Psychiatry, 33,* 858–868.

Escobar, J.I., Burnam, M.A., Karno, M., Forsythe, A., Golding, J.M., et al. (1987). Somatization in the community. *Archives of General Psychiatry, 44,* 713–720.

Esler, J., Julius, S., Sweifler, A., Randall, O., Harburg, E., Gardiner, H., & DeQuattro, V. (1977). Mild high-renin essential hypertension: A neurogenic human hypertension. *New England Journal of Medicine, 296,* 405–411.

Estes, C.L. (1995). Mental health services for the elderly: Key policy elements. In M. Gatz (Ed.), *Emerging issues in mental health and aging* (pp. 303–327). Washington, DC: American Psychological Association.

Etringer, B.D., Gregory, V.R., & Lando, H.A. (1984). Influence of group cohesion on the behavioral treatment of smoking. *Journal of Consulting and Clinical Psychology, 52,* 1080–1086.

Evans, M.D., Hollon, S.D., DeRubeis, R.J., Piasecki, J.M., Grove, W.M., et al. (1992). Differential relapse following cognitive therapy, pharmacotherapy, and combined cognitive-pharmacotherapy for depression. *Archives of General Psychiatry, 49,* 802–808.

Evans, P.D., & Edgerton, N. (1990). Life events as predictors of the common cold. *British Journal of Medical Psychology, 64,* 35–44.

Evans, R.I., Rozelle, R.M., Maxwell, S.E., Raines, B.E., Dill, C.A., Guthrie, T.J., Henderson, A.H., & Hin, P.C. (1981). Social modelling films to deter smoking in adolescents: Results of a three-year field investigation. *Journal of Applied Psychology, 66,* 399–414.

Everett, F., Proctor, N., & Cartmell, B. (1989). Providing psychological services to American Indian children and families. In D.R. Atkinson, G. Morten, & D.W. Sue (Eds.), *Counseling American minorities* (3rd ed.). Dubuque, IA: W.C. Brown.

Everill, J.T., & Waller, G. (1995). Reported sexual abuse and eating psychopathology: A review of the evidence for a causal link. *International Journal of Eating Disorders, 18,* 1–11.

Exner, J.E. (1978). *The Rorschach: A comprehensive system: Vol. 2. Current research and advanced interpretation.* New York: Wiley.

Exner, J.E., Jr. (1986). *The Rorschach: A comprehensive system: Vol. 1. Basic foundations* (2nd ed.). New York: Wiley.

Eysenck, H.J. (1952). The effects of psychotherapy: An evaluation. *Journal of Consulting Psychology, 16,* 319–324.

Eysenck, H.J. (1975). Crime as destiny. *New Behaviour, 9,* 46–49.

Fairbank, J.A., & Brown, T.A. (1987). Current behavioral approaches to the treatment of posttraumatic stress disorder. *The Behavior Therapist, 3,* 57–64.

Fairbank, J.A., DeGood, D.E., & Jenkins, C.W. (1981). Behavioral treatment of a persistent post-traumatic startle response. *Journal of Behaviour Therapy and Experimental Psychiatry, 12,* 321–324.

Fairburn, C., Jones, R., Peveler, R., Hope, R., & O'Connor, M. (1993). The longer-term effects of interpersonal psychotherapy, behavior therapy, and cognitive therapy. *Archives of General Psychiatry, 50,* 419–428.

Fairburn, C.G. (1985). Cognitive-behavioral treatment for bulimia. In D.M. Garner, & P.E. Garfinkel (Eds.), *Handbook of psychotherapy for anorexia nervosa and bulimia* (pp. 160–192). New York: Guilford.

Fairburn, C.G., Agras, W.S., & Wilson, G.T. (1992). The research on the treatment of bulimia nervosa: Practical and theoretical implications. In G.H. Anderson & S.H. Kennedy (Eds.), *The biology of feast and famine: Relevance to eating disorders.* New York: Academic Press.

Fairburn, C.G., Jones, R., Peveler, R.C., Carr, S.J., Solomon, R.A., O'Connor, M.E., Burton, J., & Hope, R.A. (1991). Three psychological treatments for bulimia nervosa. *Archives of General Psychiatry, 48,* 463–469.

Fairburn, C.G., Jones, R., Peveler, R.C., Hope, R.A., & O'Connor, M.E. (1993). Psychotherapy and bulimia nervosa: The longer-term effects of interpersonal psychotherapy, behavior therapy, and cognitive therapy. *Archives of General Psychiatry, 50,* 419–428.

Fairburn, C.G., Marcus, M.D., & Wilson, G.T. (1993). Cognitive behaviour therapy for binge eating and bulimia nervosa: A comprehensive treatment manual. In C.G. Fairburn & G.T. Wilson (Eds.), *Binge eating: Nature, assessment, and treatment.* New York: Guilford.

Fairburn, C.G., Norman, P.A., Welch, S.L., O'Connor, M.E., Doll, H.A., & Peveler, R.C. (1995). A prospective study of outcome in bulimia nervosa and the long-term effects of three psychological treatments. *Archives of General Psychiatry, 52,* 304–312.

Fairburn, C.G., Peveler, R.C., Jones, R., Hope, R.A., & Doll, H.A. (1993). Predictors of twelve-month outcome in bulimia nervosa and the influence of attitudes to shape and weight. *Journal of Consulting and Clinical Psychology, 61,* 696–698.

Fairburn, C.G., Welch, S.L., & Hay, P.J. (1993). The classification of recurrent overeating: The "binge eating disorder" proposal. *International Journal of Eating Disorders, 13,* 155–159.

Fairburn, C.G., Welch, S.L., Norman, P.A., O'Conner, M.E., & Doll, H.E. (1996). Bias and bulimia nervosa: How typical are clinic cases? *American Journal of Psychiatry, 153,* 386–391.

Fairweather, G.W. (Ed.). (1964). *Social psychology in treating mental illness: An experimental approach.* New York: Wiley.

Fairweather, G.W., Sanders, D.H., Maynard, H., & Cressler, D.L. (1969). *Community life for the mentally ill: An alternative to institutional care.* Chicago: Aldine-Atherton.

Falkner, B., Kusher, H., Oresti, G., & Angelakus, E.T. (1981). Cardiovascular characteristics in adolescents who develop essential hypertension. *Hypertension, 3,* 496–505.

Falloon, I.R.H., Boyd, J.L., McGill, C.W., Razani, J., Moss, H.B., & Gilderman, A.N. (1982). Family management in the prevention of exacerbation of schizophrenia: A controlled study. *New England Journal of Medicine, 306,* 1437–1440.

Falloon, I.R.H., Boyd, J.L., McGill, C.W., Williamson, M., Razani, J., Moss, H.B., & Gilderman, A.M., & Simpson, G.M.

(1985). Family management in the prevention of morbidity of schizophrenia. *Archives of General Psychiatry, 42,* 887–896.

Faraone, S.V., Biederman, J., Chen, W.J., Milberger, S., Warburton, R., & Tsuang, M.T. (1995). Neuropsychological functioning among the nonpsychotic relatives of schizophrenic patients: A diagnostic efficiency anaylsis. *Journal of Abnormal Psychology, 104,* 286–304.

Faraone, S.V., Kremen, W.S., & Tsuang, M.T. (1990). Genetic transmission of affective disorders: Quantitative models and linkage analysis. *Psychological Bulletin, 108,* 109–127.

Farina, A. (1976). *Abnormal psychology.* Englewood Cliffs, NJ: Prentice- Hall.

Farkas, G., & Rosen, R.C. (1976). The effects of alcohol on elicited male sexual response. *Studies in Alcohol, 37,* 265–272.

Farquhar, J.W. (1991). The Stanford cardiovascular disease prevention programs. *Annals of the New York Academy of Sciences, 623,* 327–331.

Farquhar, J.W., Fortmann, S.P., Flora, J.A., & Maccoby, N. (1990). Methods of communication to influence behaviour. In W. Holland, R. Detels, & G. Knox (Eds.), *Oxford textbook of public health* (2nd ed.). New York: Oxford University Press.

Farquhar, J.W., Fortmann, S.P., Flora, J.A., Taylor, B., Haskell, W.L., Williams, P.T., Maccoby, N., & Wood, P.D. (1990). Effects of communitywide education on cardiovascular disease risk factors: The Stanford Five-City Project. *Journal of the American Medical Association, 264,* 359–365.

Farris, E.J., Yeakel, E.H., & Medoff, H. (1945). Development of hypertension in emotional gray Norway rats after air blasting. *American Journal of Physiology, 144,* 331–333.

Fassinger, R. (1991). The hidden minority: Issues and challenges in working with lesbian women and gay men. *Counseling Psychologist, 19,* 157–176.

Fawcett, J., Epstein, P., Fiester, S.J., Elkin, I., & Autry, J.H. (1987). Clinical Management—Imipramine/placebo administration manual: NIMH Treatment of Depression Collaborative Research Program. *Psychopharmacology Bulletin, 23,* 309–324.

Fedora, O., Reddon, J.R., & Yeudall, L.T. (1986). Stimuli eliciting sexual arousal in genital exhibitionists: A possible clinical application. *Archives of Sexual Behavior, 15,* 417–427.

Fein, D., Pennington, B., Markowitz, P., Braverman, M., & Waterhouse, L. (1986). Toward a neuropsychological model of infantile autism: Are the social deficits primary? *Journal of the American*

Academy of Child Psychiatry, 25, 198–212.

Feingold, B.F. (1973). *Introduction to clinical allergy.* Springfield, IL: Charles C. Thomas.

Feinsilver, D.B., & Gunderson, J.G. (1972). Psychotherapy for schizophrenics—Is it indicated? *Schizophrenia Bulletin, 1,* 11–23.

Feldman, H.A., Goldstein, I., Hatzichristou, G., Krane, R.J., & McKinlay, J.B. (1994). Impotence and its medical and psychosocial correlates: Results of the Massachusetts male aging study. *Journal of Urology, 151,* 54–61.

Felner, R.D., Farber, S.S., & Primavera, J. (1983). Transition and stressful events: A model for primary prevention. In R.A. Felner, L.A. Jason, J.N. Mortisugu, & S.S. Farber (Eds.), *Preventive psychology: Theory, research, and practice* (pp. 199–229). New York: Pergamon.

Fenigstein, A. (1979). Self-consciousness, self-attention, and social interaction. *Journal of Personality and Social Psychology, 37,* 75–86.

Fenigstein, A., Scheier, M.F., & Buss, A.H. (1975). Public and private self-consciousness: Assessment and theory. *Journal of Consulting and Clinical Psychology, 43,* 522–527.

Fentiman, L.C. (1985). Guilty but mentally ill: The real verdict is guilty. *Boston College Law Review, 26,* 601–653.

Ferguson, K.J., & Spitzer, R.L. (1995). Binge eating disorder in a community-based sample of successful and unsuccessful dieters. *International Journal of Eating Disorders, 18,* 167–172.

Ferster, C.B. (1961). Positive reinforcement and behavioral deficits of autistic children. *Child Development, 32,* 437–456.

Fillmore, K.M. (1987). Prevalence, incidence and chronicity of drinking patterns and problems among men as a function of age: A longitudinal and cohort analysis. *British Journal of Addiction, 82,* 77–83.

Fillmore, K.M., & Caetano, R. (1980, May 22). *Epidemiology of occupational alcoholism.* Paper presented at the National Institute on Alcohol Abuse and Alcoholism's Workshop on Alcoholism in the Workplace, Reston, VA.

Fils-Aime, M.L., Eckardt, M.J., George, D.T., Brown, G.L., Mefford, I., & Linnoila, M. (1996). Early-onset alcoholics have lower cerebrospinal fluid 5-hydroxyindoleacetic acid levels than late-onset alcoholics. *Archives of General Psychiatry, 53,* 211–216.

Finkelhor, D. (1979). *Sexually victimized children.* New York: Free Press.

Finkelhor, D. (1983). Removing the child—Prosecuting the offender in cases of sexual abuse: Evidence from the national reporting system for child abuse and neglect. *Child Abuse and Neglect, 7,* 195–205.

Finkelhor, D. (1993). Epidemiological factors in the clinical identification of child sexual abuse. *Child Abuse and Neglect, 17,* 67–70.

Finkelhor, D., & Araji, S. (1986). Explanations of pedophilia: A four-factor model. *Journal of Sex Research, 22,* 145–161.

Finkelhor, D., Hotaling, G., Lewis, I.A., & Smith, C. (1990). Sexual abuse in a national survey of adult men and women: Prevalence, characteristics, and risk factors. *Child Abuse and Neglect, 14,* 19–28.

Finn, S.E. (1982). Base rates, utilities, and DSM-III: Shortcomings of fixed-rule systems of psychodiagnosis. *Journal of Abnormal Psychology, 91,* 294–302.

Fiore, J., Becker, J., & Coppel, D.B. (1983). Social network interactions: A buffer or a stress? *American Journal of Community Psychology, 11,* 423–439.

Fiore, M.C., Novotny, T.F., Pierce, J.P., Giovino, G.A., Hatziandreu, E.J., Newcomb, P.A., Surawicz, T.S., & Davis, R.M. (1990). Methods used to quit smoking in the United States: Do cessation programs help? *Journal of the American Medical Association, 263,* 2760–2765.

Fiore, M.C., Smith, S.S., Jorenby, D.E., & Baker, T.B. (1994). The effectiveness of the nicotine patch for smoking cessation: A meta-analysis. *Journal of the American Medical Association, 271,* 1940–1947.

Fischer, M. (1971). Psychoses in the offspring of schizophrenic monozygotic twins and their normal co-twins. *British Journal of Psychiatry, 118,* 43–52.

Fischetti, M., Curran, J.P., & Wessberg, H.W. (1977). Sense of timing. *Behavior Modification, 1,* 179–194.

Fishbain, D.A., & Goldberg, M. (1991). The misdiagnosis of conversion disorder in a psychiatric emergency service. *General Hospital Psychiatry, 13,* 177–181.

Fisher, J.E., & Noll, J.P. (1996). Anxiety disorders. In L.L. Carstensen, B.A. Edelstein, & L. Dornbrand (Eds.), *The practical handbook of clinical gerontology* (pp. 304–323). Thousand Oaks: Sage.

Fisher, J.E., Goy, E.R., Swingen, D.N., & Szymanski, J. (1994, November). The functional context of behavioral disturbances in Alzheimer's disease patients. Paper presented at the annual convention of the Association for Advancement of Behavior Therapy.

Fishler, K., Azen, C.G., Henderson, R., Friedman, E.G., & Koch, R. (1987). Psychoeducational findings among children treated for phenylketonuria. *American Journal of Mental Deficiency, 92,* 65–73.

Fishman, D.B., Rodgers, F., & Franks,

C.M. (Eds.). (1988). *Paradigms in behavior therapy: Present and promise* (pp. 254–293). New York: Springer.

Fitts, S.N., Gibson, P., Redding, C.A., & Deiter, P.J. (1989). Body dysmorphic disorder: Implications for its validity as a DSM-III-R clinical syndrome. *Psychological Reports, 64,* 655–658.

Fitzgerald, R.V. (1973). *Conjoint marital therapy.* New York: Jason Aronson.

Fleming, J.E., & Offord, D.R. (1990). Epidemiology of childhood depressive disorders: A critical review. *Journal of the American Academy of Child and Adolescent Psychiatry, 29,* 571–580.

Fluoxetine Bulimia Nervosa Collaborative Study Group. (1992). Fluoxetine in the treatment of bulimia nervosa: A multicenter, placebo-controlled, double blind trial. *Archives of General Psychiatry, 49,* 139–147.

Foa, E.B., & Kozak, M.J. (1986). Emotional processing of fear: Exposure to corrective information. *Psychological Bulletin, 99,* 20–35.

Foa, E.B., Feske, U., Murdock, T. B., Kozak, M.J., & McCarthy, P.R. (1991). Processing of threat-related information in rape victims. *Journal of Abnormal Psychology, 100,* 156–165.

Foa, E.B., Kozak, M.J., Steketee, G.S., & McCarthy, P.R. (1992). Treatment of depressive and obsessive-compulsive symptoms in OCD by imipramine and behavior therapy. *British Journal of Clinical Psychology, 31,* 279–292.

Foa, E.B., Steketee, G.S., & Ozarow, B.J. (1985). Behavior therapy with obsessive-compulsives: From theory to treatment. In M. Mavissakalian, S.M. Turner, & L. Michelson (Eds.), *Obsessive-compulsive disorder: Psychological and pharmacological treatment.* New York: Plenum.

Foa, E.B., Zinbarg, R., & Rothbaum, B.O. (1992). Uncontrollability and unpredictability in post-traumatic stress disorder: An animal model. *Psychological Bulletin, 112,* 218–238.

Fodor, I. (1978). Phobias in women: Therapeutic approaches. In *Helping women change: A guide for professional counseling.* New York: BMA Audio Cassette Program.

Folkman, S., & Lazarus, R.S. (1985). If it changes it must be a process: Study of emotions and coping during 3 stages of college examination. *Journal of Personality and Social Psychology, 48,* 150–170.

Folkman, S., Bernstein, L., & Lazarus, R.S. (1987). Stress processes and the misuse of drugs in older adults. *Psychology and Aging, 2,* 366–374.

Folks, D.G., Ford, C.V., & Regan, W.M. (1984). Conversion symptoms in a general hospital. *Psychosomatics, 25,* 285–295.

Follette, V.M. (1994). Acceptance and commitment in the treatment of incest survivors: A contextual approach. In S.C. Hayes, N.S. Jacobson, V.M. Follette, & M. Dougher (Eds.), *Acceptance and change: Content and context in psychotherapy.* Reno, NV: Context Press.

Folstein, S., & Rutter, M. (1977a). Genetic influences and infantile autism. *Nature, 265,* 726–728.

Folstein, S., & Rutter, M. (1977b). Infantile autism: A genetic study of 21 twin pairs. *Journal of Child Psychology and Psychiatry, 18,* 291–321.

Ford, C.S., & Beach, F.A. (1951). *Patterns of sexual behavior.* New York: Harper.

Ford, C.V. (1995). Dimensions of somatization and hypochondriasis. Special Issue: Malingering and conversion reactions. *Neurological Clinics, 13,* 241–253.

Ford, C.V., & Folks, D.G. (1985). Conversion disorders: An overview. *Psychosomatics, 26,* 371–383.

Ford, D.H., & Urban, H.B. (1963). *Systems of psychotherapy: A comparative study.* New York: Wiley.

Fordyce, W.E. (1994). Pain and suffering: What is the unit? *Quality of Life Research: An International Journal of Quality of Life Aspects of Treatment, Care, and Rehabilitation, 3,* S51–S56.

Fordyce, W.E., Brockway, J.A., Bergman, J.A., & Spengler, D. (1986). Acute back pain: A control-group comparison of behavioral vs. traditional methods. *Journal of Behavioral Medicine, 9,* 127–140.

Foreyt, J.P. (1990). Behavioral medicine. In C.M. Franks, G.T. Wilson, P.C. Kendall, & J.P. Foreyt (Eds.), *Annual review of behavior: Theory and practice* (Vol. 12). New York: Guilford.

Forsythe, W.I., & Redmond, A. (1974). Enuresis and spontaneous cure rate: Study of 1129 enuretics. *Archives of Disease in Childhood, 49,* 259–263.

Forth, A.E., & Hare, R.D. (1989). The contingent negative variation in psychopaths. *Psychophysiology, 26,* 676–682.

Foucault, M. (1965). *Madness and civilization.* New York: Random House.

Foulkes, S.H. (1964). *Therapeutic group analysis.* New York: International Universities Press.

Foy, D.W., Resnick, H.S., Carroll, E.M., & Osato, S.S. (1990). Behavior therapy. In A.S. Bellack & M. Hersen (Eds.), *Handbook of comparative treatments for adult disorders* (pp. 302–315). New York: Wiley.

Foy, D.W., Resnick, H.S., Sipprelle, R.C., & Carroll, E.M. (1987). Premilitary, military, and postmilitary factors in the development of combat-related posttraumatic stress disorder. *The Behavior Therapist, 10,* 3–9.

Frame, C., Matson, J.L., Sonis, W.A., Fialkov, M.J., & Kazdin, A.E. (1982). Behavioral treatment of depression in a prepubertal child. *Journal of Behaviour Therapy and Experimental Psychiatry, 3,* 239–243.

Frances, A., Pincus, H.A., Widiger, T.A., Davis, W.W., & First, M.B. (1990). DSM-IV: Work in progress. *American Journal of Psychiatry, 147,* 1439–1448.

Frances, R., Franklin, J., & Flavin, D. (1986). Suicide and alcoholism. *Annals of the New York Academy of Science, 287,* 316–326.

Frank, E., & Kupfer, D.J. (1994). Maintenance therapy in depression: In reply. *Archives of General Psychiatry, 51,* 504–505.

Frank, E., & Spanier, C. (1995). Interpersonal psychotherapy for depression: Overview, clinical efficacy, and future directions. *Clinical Psychology: Science and Practice, 2,* 349–369.

Frank, E., Anderson, C., & Kupfer, D.J. (1976). Profiles of couples seeking sex therapy and marital therapy. *American Journal of Psychiatry, 133,* 559–562.

Frank, E., Anderson, C., & Rubenstein, D. (1978). Frequency of sexual dysfunctions in "normal" couples. *New England Journal of Medicine, 299,* 111–115.

Frank, E., Kupfer, D.J., Perel, J.M., Cornes, C., Jarrett, D.B., et al. (1990). Three-year outcomes for maintenance therapies in recurrent depression. *Archives of General Psychiatry, 47,* 1093–1099.

Frank, E., Kupfer, D.J., Wagner, E.F., McEachran, A.B., & Cornes, C. (1991). Efficacy of interpersonal psychotherapy as a maintenance treatment of recurrent depression: Contributing factors. *Archives of General Psychiatry, 48,* 1053–1059.

Frank, J.D. (1961). *Persuasion and healing.* Baltimore: Johns Hopkins University Press. Second edition, 1973; third edition, 1978.

Frank, J.D. (1971). Therapeutic factors in psychotherapy. *American Journal of Psychotherapy, 25,* 350–361.

Frank, J.D. (1976). Psychotherapy and the sense of mastery. In R.L. Spitzer & D.F. Klein (Eds.), *Evaluation of psychotherapies: Behavioral therapies, drug therapies and their interactions.* Baltimore: Johns Hopkins University Press.

Frank, J.D. (1982). Therapeutic components shared by all psychotherapies. In J.H. Harvey & M.M. Parks (Eds.), *The Master Lecture Series: Vol. 1. Psychotherapy research and behavior change* (pp. 73–122). Washington, DC: American Psychological Association.

Frankenhaeuser, M.U., Lundberg, M., Fredriksson, B., Melin, M., Thomisto, A., et al. (1989). Stress on and off the job as related to sex and occupational status in whitecollar workers. *Journal of Organizational Behavior, 10,* 321–346.

Frankl, V. (1959). *From death camp to existentialism.* Boston: Beacon.

Frankl, V. (1963). *Man's search for meaning.* New York: Washington Square.

Frankl, V. (1967). *Psychotherapy and existentialism.* New York: Simon & Schuster.

Franklin, J.C., Schiele, B.C., Brozerk, J., & Keys, A. (1948). Observations on human behavior in experimental semistarvation and rehabilitation. *Journal of Clinical Psychology, 4,* 28–45.

Franks, C.M., Wilson, G.T., Kendall, P.C., & Foreyt, J.P. (1990). *Review of behavior therapy: Theory and practice.* New York: Guilford.

Frazier, P.A. (1990). Victim attributions and post-rape trauma. *Journal of Personality and Social Psychology, 59,* 298–304.

Frederickson, B.L., & Carstensen, L.L. (1990). Choosing social partners: How old age and anticipated endings make people more selective. *Psychology and Aging, 5,* 335–347.

Freeman, A., & Reinecke, M.A. (1995). Cognitive therapy. In A.S. Gurman & S.B. Messer (Eds.), *Essential psychotherapies: Theory and practice.* New York: Guilford.

Fremouw, W.J., Perczel, W.J., & Ellis, T.E. (1990). *Suicide risk: Assessment and response guidelines.* Elmsford, NY: Pergamon.

Freud, A. (1946). *The ego and mechanisms of defense.* New York: International Universities Press.

Freud, A. (1966). *The ego and the mechanisms of defense.* New York: International Universities Press.

Freud, S. (1917). Mourning and melancholia. In *Collected papers* (Vol. 4). London: Hogarth and the Institute of Psychoanalysis, 1950.

Freud, S. (1937). Analysis terminable and interminable. *International Journal of Psychoanalysis, 18,* 373–391.

Freud, S. (1955). Lines of advance in psychoanalytic therapy. In *The complete psychological works of Sigmund Freud.* J. Strachey (Ed. and Trans.) London: Hogarth and the Institute of Psychoanalysis. (Original work published 1918)

Freud, S. (1956). Analysis of a phobia in a five-year-old boy. In *Collected works of Sigmund Freud* (Vol. 10). London: Hogarth. (Original work published 1909)

Freund, K., & Kuban, M. (1994). The basis of the abused abuser theory of pedophilia: A further elaboration on an earlier study. *Archives of Sexual Behavior, 23,* 553–563.

Friedman, J.M. (1978). Sexual adjustment of the postcoronary male. In J. LoPiccolo & L. LoPiccolo (Eds.), *Handbook of sex therapy.* New York: Plenum.

Friedman, J.M., & Hogan, D.R. (1985). Sexual dysfunction: Low sexual desire. In D.H. Barlow (Ed.), *Clinical handbook of psychological disorders.* New York: Guilford.

Friedman, M., & Ulmer, D. (1984). *Treating type A behavior and your heart.* New York: Fawcett Crest.

Friedman, M., Thoresen, C.E., Gill, J.J., Powell, L.H., Ulmer, D., Thompson, L., Price, V.A., Rabin, D.D., Breall, W.S., Dixon, T., Levy, R., & Bourg, E. (1984). Alteration of type A behavior and reduction in cardiac recurrences in postmyocardial infarction patients. *American Heart Journal, 108,* 237–248.

Friedman, M., Thoresen, C.E., Gill, J.J., Ulmer, D., Thompson, L., Powell, L., Price, A., Elek, S.R., Rabin, D.D., Breall, W.S., Piaget, G., Dixon, T., Bourg, E., Levy, R., & Tasto, D.I. (1982). Feasibility of altering type A behavior pattern after myocardial infarction. *Circulation, 66,* 83–92.

Friedman, M. (1969). *Pathogenesis of coronary artery disease.* New York: McGraw-Hill.

Friedman, R., & Dahl, L.K. (1975). The effects of chronic conflict on the blood pressure of rats with a genetic susceptibility to experimental hypertension. *Psychosomatic Medicine, 37,* 402–416.

Frisch, M.B., & Higgins, R.L. (1986). Instructional demand effects and the correspondence among role-play, self-report, and naturalistic measures of social skill. *Behavioral Assessment, 8,* 221–236.

Frith, U. (1989). *Autism: Explaining the enigma.* Cambridge, MA: Basil Blackwell.

Fromm-Reichmann, F. (1948). Notes on the development of treatment of schizophrenics by psychoanalytic psychotherapy. *Psychiatry, 11,* 263–273.

Fromm-Reichmann, F. (1952). Some aspects of psychoanalytic therapy with schizophrenics. In E. Brady & F.C. Redlich (Eds.), *Psychotherapy with schizophrenics.* New York: International Universities Press.

Frude, N. (1982). The sexual nature of sexual abuse: A review of the literature. *Child Abuse and Neglect, 6,* 211–223.

Fuller, R.K. (1988). Disulfiram treatment of alcoholism. In R.M. Rose & J.E. Barrett (Eds.), *Alcoholism: Treatment and outcome.* New York: Raven.

Fuller, R.K., Branchey, L., Brightwell, D.R., Derman, R.M., Emrick, C.D., Iber, F.L., James, K.E., & Lacoursiere, R.B. (1986). Disulfiram treatment of alcoholism: A Veterans Administration cooperative study. *Journal of the American Medical Association, 256,* 1449–1455.

Furnham, A., & Baguma, P. (1994). Cross-cultural differences in the evaluation of male and female body shapes. *International Journal of Eating Disorders, 15,* 81–89.

Fyer, A.J., Mannuzza, S., Chapman, T.F., Martin, L.Y., & Klein, D.F. (1995). Specificity in familial aggregation of phobic disorders. *Archives of General Psychiatry, 52,* 564–573.

Fyer, A.J., Sandberg, D., & Klein, D.F. (1991). The pharmacological treatment of panic disorder and agoraphobia. In J.R. Walker, G.R. Norton, & C.A. Ross (Eds.), *Panic disorder and agoraphobia: A comprehensive guide for the practitioner* (pp. 211–251). Belmont, CA: Brooks/Cole.

Gabbay, F.H. (1992). Behavior genetic strategies in the study of emotion. *Psychological Science, 3,* 50–55.

Gagnon, J.H. (1977). *Human sexualities.* Chicago: Scott, Foresman.

Gaines, J. (1974). The founder of Gestalt therapy: A sketch of Fritz Perls. *Psychology Today, 8,* 117–118.

Galaburda, A.M. (1989). Ordinary and extraordinary brain development: Anatomical variation in developmental dyslexia. *Annals of Dyslexia, 39,* 67–80.

Galaburda, A.M. (1993). Neuroanatomical basis of developmental dyslexia. *Neurologic Clinics, 11,* 161–173.

Galanter, M., & Castaneda, R. (1985). Self-destructive behavior in the substance abuser. *Psychiatric Clinics of North America, 8,* 251–261.

Galin, D., Diamond, R., & Braff, D. (1977). Lateralization of conversion symptoms: More frequent on the left. *American Journal of Psychiatry, 134,* 578–580.

Gallagher, D., & Thompson, L.W. (1982). *Elders' maintenance of treatment benefits following individual psychotherapy for depression: Results of a pilot study and preliminary data from an ongoing replication study.* Paper presented at the annual meeting of the American Psychological Association, Washington, DC.

Gallagher, D., & Thompson, L.W. (1983). Cognitive therapy for depression in the elderly. A promising model for treatment and research. In L.D. Breslau & M.R. Haug (Eds.), *Depression and aging: Causes, care and consequences.* New York: Springer.

Gallagher, D., Breckenridge, J.N., Thompson, L.W., Dessonville, C., & Amaral, P. (1982). Similarities and differences between normal grief and depression in older adults. *Essence, 5,* 127–140.

Gallagher-Thompson, D., & Thompson, L.W. (1995a). Efficacy of psychotherapeutic interventions with older adults. *The Clinical Psychologist, 48,* 24–30.

Gallagher-Thompson, D., & Thompson, L.W. (1995b). Psychotherapy with older adults in theory and practice. In B. Bon-

gar & L.E. Beutler (Eds.), *Comprehensive textbook of psychotherapy: Theory and practice* (pp. 359–379). New York: Oxford University Press.

Gann, M.K. (1995). Challenging personality testing: 2. The Rorschach and other projective methods. In J. Ziskin (Ed.), *Coping with psychiatric and psychological testimony.* Los Angeles: Law & Psychology Press.

Garber, J., Kriss, M.R., Koch, M., & Lindholm, L. (1988). Recurrent depression in adolescents: A follow-up study. *Journal of the American Academy of Child and Adolescent Psychiatry, 27,* 49–54.

Garber, J., Weiss, B., & Shanley, N. (1993). Cognitions, depressive symptoms, and development in adolescents. *Journal of Abnormal Psychology, 102,* 47–57.

Garbutt, J.C., Mayo, J.P., Little, K.Y., Gillette, G.M., Mason, G.A., et al. (1994). Dose-response studies with protirelin. *Archives of General Psychiatry, 51,* 875–883.

Garcia, J., McGowan, B.K., & Green, K.F. (1972). Biological constraints on conditioning. In A.H. Black & W.F. Prokasy (Eds.), *Classical conditioning: 2. Current research and theory.* New York: Appleton-Century-Crofts.

Gardner, H. (1997, January 19). [Review of "The Creation of Dr. B."] *Los Angeles Times,* Book Review, p. 3.

Garfield, S.L. (1978). Research on client variables in psychotherapy. In S.L. Garfield & A.E. Bergin (Eds.), *Handbook of psychotherapy and behavior change* (2nd ed.). New York: Wiley.

Garfield, S.L., & Bergin, A.E. (1986b). Introduction and historical overview. In S.L. Garfield & A.E. Bergin (Eds.), *Handbook of psychotherapy and behavior change* (3rd ed.). New York: Wiley.

Garfield, S.L., & Bergin, A.E. (Eds.). (1986a). *Handbook of psychotherapy and behavior change* (3rd ed.). New York: Wiley.

Garland, R.J., & Dougher, M.J. (1991). Motivational interviewing in the treatment of sex offenders. In W.R. Miller & S. Rollnick (Eds.), *Motivating interviewing: Preparing people to change addictive behavior* (pp. 303–313). New York: Guilford.

Garner, D.M., & Wooley, S.C. (1991). Confronting the failure of behavioral and dietary treatments of obesity. *Clinical Psychology Review, 11,* 729–780.

Garner, D.M., Garfinkel, P.E., Schwartz, D., & Thompson, M. (1980). Cultural expectation of thinness in women. *Psychological Reports, 47,* 483–491.

Garner, D.M., Olmsted, M.P., & Polivy, J. (1981). The Eating Disorder Inventory: A measure of cognitive-behavioral dimensions of anorexia nervosa and bulimia. In P.L. Darby, P.E. Garfinkel, D.M.

Garner, & D.V. Coscina (Eds.), *Anorexia nervosa: Recent developments in research.* New York: Liss.

Garner, D.M., Olmsted, M.P., & Polivy, J. (1983). Development and validation of a multi-dimensional eating disorder inventory for anorexia nervosa and bulimia. *International Journal of Eating Disorders, 2,* 15–34.

Garner, D.M., Rockert, W., Davis, R., Garner, M.V., Olmsted, M.P., & Eagle, M. (1993). Comparison between cognitive-behavioral and supportive-expressive therapy for bulimia nervosa. *American Journal of Psychiatry, 150,* 37–46.

Garrison, C.Z., McKeown, R.E., Valois, R.F., & Vincent, M.L. (1993). Aggression, substance use, and suicidal behaviors in high school students. *American Journal of Public Health, 83,* 179–184.

Garssen, B., Buikhuisen, M., & Van Dyck, R. (1996). Hyperventilation and panic attacks. *American Journal of Psychiatry, 153,* 513–518.

Gatchel, R.J., Baum, A., & Krantz, D.S. (1989). *An introduction to health psychology* (2nd ed.). New York: Random House.

Gatz, M., & Pearson, C.G. (1988). Ageism revised and the provision of psychological services. *American Psychologist, 43,* 184–188.

Gatz, M., & Smyer, M.A. (1992). The mental health system and older adults in the 1990s. *American Psychologist, 47,* 741–751.

Gatz, M., Bengtson, V.L., & Blum, M.J. (1990). Caregiving families. In J.E. Birren & K.W. Schaie (Eds.), *Handbook of the psychology of aging.* (3rd ed., pp. 404–426). New York: Academic Press.

Gatz, M., Kasl-Godley, J.E., & Karel, M.J. (1996). Aging and mental disorders. In J.E. Birren & K.W. Schaie (Eds.), *Handbook of the psychology of aging* San Diego: Academic Press.

Gatz, M., Pearson, C., & Fuentes, M. (1984). Older women and mental health. In A.U. Rickel, M. Gerrard, & I. Iscoe (Eds.), *Social and psychological problems of women: Prevention and crisis intervention.* Washington, DC: Hemisphere.

Gauthier, Y., Fortin, C., Drapeau, P., Breton, J., Gosselin, J., Quintal, L., Weisnagel, J., & Lamarre, A. (1978). Follow-up study of 35 asthmatic preschool children. *Journal of the American Academy of Child Psychiatry, 17,* 679–694.

Gauthier, Y., Fortin, C., Drapeau, P., Breton, J., Gosselin, J., Quintal, L., Weisnagel, J., Tetreault, L., & Pinard, G. (1977). The mother-child relationship and the development of autonomy and self-assertion in young (14–30 months) asthmatic children. *Journal of the American Academy of Child Psychiatry, 16,*

109–131.

Gebhard, P.H., Gagnon, J.H., Pomeroy, W.B., & Christenson, C.V. (1965). *Sex offenders.* New York: Harper & Row.

Geer, J.H., Davison, G.C., & Gatchel, R.I. (1970). Reduction of stress in humans through nonveridical perceived control of aversive stimulation. *Journal of Personality and Social Psychology, 16,* 731–738.

Geer, J.H., Heiman, J., & Leitenberg, H. (1984). *Human sexuality.* Englewood Cliffs, NJ: Prentice-Hall.

Gelernter, C.S., Uhde, T.W., Cimbolic, P., Arnkoff, D.B., Vittone, B.J., et al. (1991). Cognitive behavioral and pharmacological treatments of social phobia: A controlled study. *Archives of General Psychiatry, 48,* 938–945.

Gendlin, E.T. (1962). *Experiencing and the creation of meaning: A philosophical and psychological approach to the subject.* New York: Free Press.

General Register Office. (1968). *A glossary of mental disorders.* London: Author.

George, L.K. (1980). *Role transitions in later life.* Monterey, CA: Brooks/Cole.

George, L.K. (1994). Social factors and depression in late life. In L.S. Schneider, C.F. Reynolds, III, B.D. Lebowitz, & A.J. Friedhoff (Eds.), *Diagnosis and treatment of depression in late life* (pp. 131–153). Washington, DC: American Psychiatric Press.

George, L.K., & Weiler, S.J. (1981). Sexuality in middle and late life: The effects of age, cohort, and gender. *Archives of General Psychiatry, 38,* 919–923.

George, L.K., Landoman, R., Blazer, D.G., & Anthony, J.C. (1991). Cognitive impairment. In L.N. Robins & D.A. Regier (Eds.), *Psychiatric disorders in America.* New York: Free Press.

Gerber, L.M. (1983). Ethnicity still matters: Socio-demographic profiles of the ethnic elderly in Ontario. *Canadian Ethnic Studies, 15,* 60–80.

Gergen, K.J. (1982). *Toward transformation in social knowledge.* New York: Plenum.

Gerin, W., Rosofsky, M., Pieper, C., & Pickering, T.G. (1994). A test of generalizability of cardiovascular reactivity using a controlled ambulatory procedure. *Psychosomatic Medicine, 56,* 360–368.

Gershon, E.S. (1990). Genetics. In F.K. Goodwin & K.R. Jamison (Eds.), *Manic depressive illness.* New York: Oxford University Press.

Gesten, E.L., & Jason, L.A. (1987). Social and community interventions. *Annual Review of Psychology, 38,* 427–460.

Ghoneim, M.M., & Mewaldt, S.P. (1990). Benzodiazepines and human memory: A review. *Anesthesiology, 72,* 926–938.

Gibbons, D.C. (1975). *Delinquent behavior.* Englewood Cliffs, NJ: Prentice-Hall.

Gibbs, J.T. (1980). The interpersonal orientation in mental health consultation: Toward a model of ethnic variations in consultation. *American Journal of Orthopsychiatry, 45,* 430–445.

Gibson, D., & Harris, A. (1988). Aggregated early intervention effects for Down's syndrome persons: Patterning and longevity of benefits. *Journal of Mental Deficiency Research, 32,* 1–17.

Gielen, A.C., Faden, R.R., O'Campo, P., Kass, N., & Anderson, J. (1994). Women's protective sexual behaviors: A test of the health belief model. *AIDS Education and Prevention, 6,* 1–11.

Gilbert, F.S. (1991). Development of a "steps questionnaire." *Journal of Studies on Alcohol, 52,* 353–360.

Gilboy, J.A., & Schmidt, J.R. (1971). "Voluntary" hospitalization of the mentally ill. *Northwestern University Law Review, 66,* 429–439.

Gillberg, C. (1991). Outcome in autism and autistic-like conditions. *Journal of the American Academy of Child and Adolescent Psychiatry, 30,* 375–382.

Gillberg, C., & Steffenburg, S. (1987). Outcome and prognostic factors in infantile autism and similar conditions: A population-based study of 46 cases followed through puberty. *Journal of Autism and Developmental Disorders, 17,* 273–287.

Gillberg, C., & Svendsen, P. (1983). Childhood psychosis and computed tomographic brain scan findings. *Journal of Autism and Developmental Disorders, 13,* 19–32.

Ginsburg, A.B., & Goldstein, S.G. (1974). Age bias in referral to psychological consultation. *Journal of Gerontology, 29,* 410–415.

Ginzburg, H.M. (1986). Naltrexone: Its clinical utility. In B. Stimmel (Ed.), *Advances in alcohol and substance abuse* (pp. 83–101). New York: Haworth.

Gitlin, M.J. (1993). Pharmacotherapy of personality disorders: Conceptual framework and clinical strategies. *Journal of Clinical Psychopharmacology, 13,* 343–353.

Gittelman, R., Abikoff, H., Pollack, E., Klein, D., Katz, F., & Mattes, J. (1980). A controlled trial of behavior modification and methylphenidate in hyperactive children. In C. Whalen & B. Henker (Eds.), *Hyperactive children: The social ecology of identification and treatment* (pp. 221–246). New York: Academic Press.

Gittelman, R., Mannuzza, S., Shenker, R., & Bonagura, N. (1985). Hyperactive boys almost grown up. *Archives of General Psychiatry, 42,* 937–947.

Gladue, B.A. (1985). Neuroendocrine response to estrogen and sexual orientation. *Science, 230,* 961.

Gleaves, D.H., & Eberenz, K.P. (1994). Sexual abuse histories among treatment-resistant bulimia nervosa patients. *International Journal of Eating Disorders, 15,* 227–231.

Gleick, J. (1987). *Chaos: Making a new science.* New York: Penguin Books.

Goff, D.C., & Simms, C.A. (1993). Has multiple personality disorder remained consistent over time? A comparison of past and present cases. *Journal of Nervous and Mental Disease, 181,* 595–600.

Goldberg, E.M., & Morrison, S.L. (1963). Schizophrenia and social class. *British Journal of Psychiatry, 109,* 785–802.

Goldbloom, D.S., Garfinkel, P.E., & Shaw, B.F. (1991). Biochemical aspects of bulimia nervosa. *Journal of Psychosomatic Research, 35,* 11–22.

Golden, C.J. (1981a). The Luria-Nebraska Children's Battery: Theory and formulation. In G.W. Hynd & J.E. Obrzut (Eds.), *Neuropsychological assessment and the school-age child: Issues and procedures.* New York: Grune & Stratton.

Golden, C.J. (1981). A standardized version of Luria's neuropsychological tests: A quantitative and qualitative approach to neuropsychological evaluation. In S.B. Filskov & T.J. Boil (Eds.), *Handbook of clinical neuropsychology.* New York: Wiley.

Golden, C.J., Hammeke, T., & Purisch, A. (1978). Diagnostic validity of a standardized neuropsychological battery derived from Luria's neuropsychological test. *Journal of Consulting and Clinical Psychology, 46,* 1258–1265.

Goldfried, M.R. (1971). Systematic desensitization as training in self-control. *Journal of Consulting and Clinical Psychology, 37,* 228–234.

Goldfried, M.R. (1980). Toward the delineation of therapeutic change principles. *American Psychologist, 35,* 991–999.

Goldfried, M.R. (1991). Research issues in psychotherapy integration. *Journal of Psychotherapy Integration, 1,* 5–25.

Goldfried, M.R., & D'Zurillia, T.J. (1969). A behavioral-analytic model for assessing competence. In C.D. Speilberger (Ed.), *Current topics in clinical and community psychology* (Vol. 1). New York: Academic Press.

Goldfried, M.R., & Davison, G.C. (1994). *Clinical behavior therapy.* Expanded edition. New York: Wiley.

Goldfried, M.R., Greenberg, L.S., & Marmar, C. (1990). Individual psychotherapy: Process and outcome. *Annual Review of Psychology, 41,* 659–688.

Goldfried, M.R., Padawer, W., & Robins, C. (1984). Social anxiety and the semantic structure of heterosocial interactions. *Journal of Abnormal Psychology, 93,* 87–97.

Golding, J.M., Smith, G.R., & Kashner,

T.M. (1991). Does somatization disorder occur in men? Clinical characteristics of women and men with unexplained somatic symptoms. *Archives of General Psychiatry, 48,* 231–235.

Goldmeier, J. (1988). Pets or people: Another research note. *The Gerontologist, 26,* 203–206.

Goldstein, A. (1994). *Addiction: From biology to drug policy.* New York: W.H. Freeman.

Goldstein, A.J., & Chambless, D.L. (1978). A reanalysis of agoraphobic behavior. *Behavior Therapy, 9,* 47–59.

Goldstein, M.J., & Rodnick, E. (1975). The family's contribution to the etiology of schizophrenia: Current status. *Schizophrenia Bulletin, 14,* 48–63.

Goldstein, R.B., Weissman, M.M., Adams, P.B., Horwath, E., Lish, J.D., et al. (1994). Psychiatric disorders in relatives of probands with panic disorder or major depression. *Archives of General Psychiatry, 51,* 383–394.

Goldstein, S.E., & Birnbom, F. (1976). Hypochondriasis and the elderly. *Journal of the American Geriatrics Society, 24,* 150–154.

Goleman, D. (1995). *Emotional intelligence.* New York: Bantam.

Gomez, F.C., Piedmont, R.L., & Fleming, M.Z. (1992). Factor analysis of the Spanish version of the WAIS: The Escala de Inteligencia Wechsler para Adultos (EIWA). *Psychological Assessment, 4,* 317–321.

Goodenow, C., Reisine, S.T., & Grady, K.E. (1989). Quality of social support and associated social and psychological functions in women with rheumatoid arthritis. *Health Psychology, 9,* 266–284.

Goodman, L.A., Koss, M.P., Fitzgerald, L.F., Russo, N.F., et al. (1993). Male violence against women: Current research and future directions. *American Psychologist, 48,* 1054–1058.

Goodman, R., & Stevenson, J. (1989). A twin study of hyperactivity: 2. The aetiological role of genes, family relationships, and perinatal adversity. *Journal of Child Psychology and Psychiatry, 30,* 691–709.

Goodwin, D.W. (1979). Alcoholism and heredity: A review and hypothesis. *Archives of General Psychiatry, 36,* 57–61.

Goodwin, D.W. (1982). Substance induced and substance use disorders: Alcohol. In J.H. Griest, I.W. Jefferson, & R.L. Spitzer (Eds.), *Treatment of mental disorders.* New York: Oxford University Press.

Goodwin, D.W., & Guze, S.B. (1984). *Psychiatric diagnosis* (3rd ed.). New York: Oxford University Press.

Goodwin, D.W., Schulsinger, F., Hermansen, L., Guze, S.B., & Winokur, G.A.

(1973). Alcohol problems in adoptees raised apart from alcoholic biological parents. *Archives of General Psychiatry, 128,* 239–243.

Goodwin, F., & Jamison, K. (1990). *Manic-depressive illness.* New York: Oxford University Press.

Gorenstein, E.E. (1991). A cognitive perspective on antisocial personality. In P.A. Magaro (Ed.), *Cognitive bases of mental disorders.* Newbury Park, CA: Sage.

Gorenstein, E.E., & Newman, J.P. (1980). Disinhibitory psychopathology: A new perspective and a model for research. *Psychological Review, 87,* 301–315.

Gorman, J.M. (1994). New and experimental pharmacological treatments for panic disorder. In B.E. Wolfe & J.D. Maser (Eds.), *Treatment of panic disorder: A consensus development conference* (pp. 83–90). Washington, DC: American Psychiatric Press.

Gorman, J.M., Fyer, M.R., Goetz, R., Askanazi, J., Leibowitz, M.R., Fyer, A.J., Kinney, J., & Klein, D.F. (1988). Ventilatory physiology of patients with panic disorder. *Archives of General Psychiatry, 45,* 53–60.

Gotesdam, K.G., & Agras, W.S. (1995). General population-based epidemiological survey of eating disorders in Norway. *International Journal of Eating Disorders, 18,* 119–126.

Gotlib, I.H. (1982). Self-reinforcement and depression in interpersonal interaction: The role of performance level. *Journal of Abnormal Psychology, 93,* 19–30.

Gotlib, I.H., & Asarnow, R.F. (1979). Interpersonal and impersonal problem-solving skills in mildly and clinically depressed students. *Journal of Consulting and Clinical Psychology, 47,* 86–95.

Gotlib, I.H., Lewinsohn, P.M., Seeley, J.R., Rohde, P., & Rednew, J.E. (1993). Negative cognitions and attributional style in depressed adolescents: An examination of stability and specificity. *Journal of Abnormal Psychology, 102,* 607–615.

Gotlib, I.H., & Robinson, L.A. (1982). Responses to depressed individuals: Discrepancies between self-report and observer-rated behavior. *Journal of Abnormal Psychology, 91,* 231–240.

Gottesman, I., & Shields, J. (1972). *Schizophrenia and genetics: A twin study vantage point.* New York: Academic Press.

Gottesman, I.I., & Goldsmith, H.H. (1994). Developmental psychopathology of antisocial behavior: Inserting genes into its ontogenesis and epigenesis. In C.A. Nelson (Ed.), *Threats to optimal development.* Hillside, NJ: Erlbaum.

Gottesman, I.I., McGuffin, P., & Farmer, A.E. (1987). Clinical genetics as clues to the "real" genetics of schizophrenia.

Schizophrenia Bulletin, 13, 23–47.

Gottlieb, J. (1990). Mainstreaming and quality education. *American Journal on Mental Retardation, 95,* 16.

Gottman, J.M. (1979). *Marital interaction: Experimental investigations.* New York: Academic Press.

Gottman, J.M., Notarius, C., Gonso, J., & Markman, H. (1976). *A couple's guide to communication.* Champaign, IL.: Research Press.

Gottman, J.M., & Krokoff, L.J. (1989). Marital interaction and satisfaction: A longitudinal view. *Journal of Consulting and Clinical Psychology, 57,* 47–52.

Gould, M.S., Wallenstein, S., & Kleinman, M.H. (1990). Time-space clustering of teenage suicide. *American Journal of Epidemiology, 131,* 71–78.

Gove, W.R. (1970). Societal reaction as an explanation of mental illness: An evaluation. *American Sociological Review, 35,* 873–884.

Gove, W.R., & Fain, T. (1973). The stigma of mental hospitalization. *Archives of General Psychiatry, 28,* 494–500.

Goyer, P., Andreason, P.J., Semple, W.E., Clayton, A.H., et al. (1994). Positron-emission tomography and personality disorders. *Neuropsychopharmacology, 10,* 21–28.

Goyette, C.H., & Conners, C.K. (1977). *Food additives and hyperkinesis.* Paper presented at the 85th Annual Convention of the American Psychological Association.

Graham, J.R. (1988). *Establishing validity of the revised form of the MMPI.* Symposium presentation at the 96th Annual Convention of the American Psychological Association, Atlanta.

Graham, J.R. (1990). *MMPI-2: Assessing personality and psychopathology.* New York: Oxford University Press.

Graham, J.W., Johnson, C.A., Hansen, W.B., Flay, B.R., & Gee, M. (1990). Drug use prevention programs, gender, and ethnicity: Evaluation of three seventh-grade Project SMART cohorts. *Preventive Medicine, 19,* 305–313.

Graham, P.J., Rutter, M.L., Yule, W., & Pless, I.B. (1967). Childhood asthma: A psychosomatic disorder? Some epidemiological considerations. *British Journal of Preventive Medicine, 21,* 78–85.

Gralnick, A. (1986). Future of the chronic schizophrenic patient: Prediction and recommendation. *American Journal of Psychotherapy, 40,* 419–429.

Grandin, T. (1986). *Emergence: Labeled autistic.* Novato, CA: Arena Press.

Grandin, T. (1995). *Thinking in pictures.* New York: Doubleday.

Gratzer, T., & Bradford, J.M.W. (1995). Offender and offense characteristics of sexual sadists: A comparative study.

Journal of Forensic Sciences, 40, 450–455.

Gray, E.B. (1983). *Final report: Collaborative research of community and minority group action to prevent child abuse and neglect: Vol. 3. Public awareness and education using the creative arts.* Chicago: National Committee for Prevention of Child Abuse.

Green, R. (1969). Mythological, historical and cross-cultural aspects of transsexualism. In R. Green & J. Money (Eds.), *Transsexualism and sex reassignment.* Baltimore: Johns Hopkins University Press.

Green, R. (1974). *Sexual identity conflict in children and adults.* New York: Basic Books.

Green, R. (1976). One hundred ten feminine and masculine boys: Behavioral contrasts and demographic similarities. *Archives of Sexual Behavior, 5,* 425–446.

Green, R. (1985). Gender identity in childhood and later sexual orientation: Follow-up of 78 males. *American Journal of Psychiatry, 142,* 339–341.

Green, R. (1987). *The "sissy boy syndrome" and the development of homosexuality.* New Haven: Yale University Press.

Green, R. (1992). *Sexual science and the law.* Cambridge, MA: Harvard University Press.

Green, R., & Blanchard, R. (1995). Gender identity disorders. In H.I. Kaplan & B.J. Sadock (Eds.), *Comprehensive textbook of psychiatry.* (pp. 1347–1360). Baltimore, MD: Williams & Wilkins.

Green, R., & Fleming, D.T. (1990). Transsexual surgery follow-up: Status in the 1990s. In J. Bancroft, C. Davis, & D. Weinstein (Eds.), *Annual review of sex research* (pp. 163–174).

Green, R., & Money, J. (1969). *Transsexualism and sex reassignment.* Baltimore: Johns Hopkins University Press.

Greenberg, J. (1996, August 21). Teen drug use has doubled in 4 years, U.S. says. *Los Angeles Times,* pp. A1, A17.

Greenberg, L., Elliott, R., & Lietaer, G. (1994). Research on experiential therapies. In A.E. Bergin & S.L. Garfield (Eds.), *Handbook of psychotherapy and behavior change* (pp. 509–539). New York: Wiley.

Greenberg, L., Fine, S.B., Cohen, C., Larson, K., Michaelson-Baily, A., Rubinton, P., & Glick, I.D. (1988). An interdisciplinary psychoeducation program for schizophrenic patients and their families in an acute care setting. *Hospital and Community Psychiatry, 39,* 277–281.

Greenberg, L.S., & Johnson, S.M. (1988). Curative principles in marital therapy: A response to Wile. *Journal of Family Psychology, 2,* 28–31.

Greenberg, L.S., & Johnson, S.M. (1988). *Emotionally focussed couples therapy.* New York: Guilford.

Greenberg, L.S., & Rice, L.N. (1981). The specific effects of a gestalt intervention. *Psychotherapy: Theory, Research, and Practice, 18,* 31–37.

Greenberg, L.S., & Safran, J. (1984). Integrating affect and cognition: A perspective on the process of therapeutic change. *Cognitive Therapy and Research, 8,* 559–578.

Greenblatt, M., Solomon, M.H., Evans, A.S., & Brooks, G.W. (Eds.). (1965). *Drugs and social therapy in chronic schizophrenia.* Springfield, IL: Charles C. Thomas.

Greene, B.A. (1985). Considerations in the treatment of black patients by white therapists. *Psychotherapy, 22,* 115–122.

Greene, B.L. (1960). Marital disharmony: Concurrent analysis of husband and wife. *Diseases of the Nervous System, 21,* 1–6.

Greer, S., Morris, T., & Pettigale, K.W. (1979). Psychological response to breast cancer: Effect on outcome. *Lancet, 2,* 785–787.

Gregerson, H.B., & Sailer, L. (1993). Chaos theory and its implications for social science. *Human Relations, 46,* 777–802.

Grigorenko, E.L., Wood, F.B., Meyer, M.S., Hart, L.A., Speed, W.C., Shuster, A., & Pauls, D.L. (in press). Susceptibility loci for distinct components of developmental dyslexia on chromosome 6 and 15. *American Journal of Human Genetics.*

Grilo, C.M., Shiffman, S., & Carter-Campbell, J.T. (1994). Binge eating antecedents in normal weight nonpurging females: Is there consistency? *International Journal of Eating Disorders, 16,* 239–249.

Grings, W.W., & Dawson, M.E. (1978). *Emotions and bodily responses: A psychophysiological approach.* New York: Academic Press.

Grinker, R.R., & Spiegel, J.P. (1944). *Management of neuropsychiatric casualties in the zone of combat: Manual of military neuropsychiatry.* Philadelphia: W.B. Saunders.

Grinker, R.R., & Spiegel, J.P. (1979). *War neuroses.* New York: Arno Press.

Grinspoon, L., & Bakalar, J.B. (1995). Marijuana as medicine: A plea for reconsideration. *Journal of the American Medical Association, 273,* 1875–1876.

Grisso, T. (1986). *Evaluating competencies: Forensic assessments and instruments.* New York: Plenum.

Grisso, T., & Appelbaum, P.S. (1991). Mentally ill and non-mentally ill patients' abilities to understand informed consent disclosures for medication: Preliminary data. *Law and Human Behavior, 15,* 377–388.

Grisso, T., & Appelbaum, P.S. (1992). Is it unethical to offer predictions of future violence? *Law and Human Behavior, 16,* 621–633.

Grisso, T., & Appelbaum, P.S. (1995). The MacArthur Treatment Competence Study: 3. Abilities of patients to consent to psychiatric and medical treatments. *Law and Human Behavior, 19,* 149–174.

Gross, M.D. (1984). Effects of sucrose on hyperkinetic children. *Pediatrics, 74,* 876–878.

Grosz, H.J., & Zimmerman, J. (1970). A second detailed case study of functional blindness: Further demonstration of the contribution of objective psychological laboratory data. *Behavior Therapy, 1,* 115–123.

Groth, N.A., & Burgess, A.W. (1977). Sexual dysfunction during rape. *New England Journal of Medicine, 297,* 764–766.

Groth, N.A., Hobson, W.F., & Guy, T.S. (1982). The child molester: Clinical observations. In J. Conte & D.A. Shore (Eds.), *Social work and child sexual abuse.* New York: Haworth.

Grove, W.R., Eckert, E.D., Heston, L., Bouchard, T., et al. (1990). Heritability of substance abuse and antisocial behavior in monozygotic twins reared apart. *Biological Psychiatry, 27,* 1293–1304.

Grych, J.H., & Fincham, F.D. (1990). Marital conflict and children's adjustment: A cognitive-contextual framework. *Psychological Bulletin, 108,* 267–290.

Guerra, N., & Slaby, R. (1990). Cognitive mediators of aggression in adolescent offenders: 2. Intervention. *Developmental Psychology, 26,* 269–277.

Guidano, V.F., & Liotti, G. (1983). *Cognitive processes and emotional disorders.* New York: Guilford.

Gunderson, J.G., Kolb, J.E., & Austin, V. (1981). The diagnostic interview for borderline patients. *American Journal of Psychiatry, 138,* 896–903.

Gunn, J. (1993). Castration is not the answer. *British Medical Journal, 307,* 790–791.

Gur, R.E., & Pearlson, G.D. (1993). Neuroimaging in schizophrenia research. *Schizophrenia Bulletin, 19,* 337–353.

Gurian, B., & Miner, J.H. (1991). Clinical presentation of anxiety in the elderly. In C. Salzman & B.D. Lebowitz (Eds.), *Anxiety in the elderly.* New York: Springer.

Gurland, B. (1991). Epidemiology of psychiatric disorders. In J. Sadavoy, L.W. Lazarus, & L.F. Jarvik (Eds.), *Comprehensive review of geriatric psychiatry* (pp. 25–40). Washington, DC: American Psychiatric Press.

Gurland, B.J., & Cross, P.S. (1982). Epidemiology of psychopathology in old age. In L.F. Jarvik & G.W. Small (Eds.), *Psychiatric Clinics of North America.*

Philadelphia: Saunders.

Gurman, A.S., & Kniskern, D.P. (1978). Research on marital and family therapy: Progress, perspective, and prospect. In S.L. Garfield & A.E. Bergin (Eds.), *Handbook of psychotherapy and behavior change: An empirical analysis* (2nd ed.). New York: Wiley.

Gurman, A.S., & Kniskern, D.P. (1981). Family therapy outcome research: Knowns and unknowns. In A.S. Gurman & D.P. Kniskern (Eds.), *Handbook of family therapy.* New York: Brunner/Mazel.

Gurman, A.S., Kniskern, D.P., & Pinsoff, W.M. (1986). Research on the process and outcome of marital and family therapy. In S.L. Garfield & A.E. Bergin (Eds.), *Handbook of psychotherapy and behavior change* (3rd ed.). New York: Wiley.

Gustafson, Y., Berggren, D., Bucht, B., Norberf, A., Hansson, L.I., & Winblad, B. (1988). Acute confusional states in elderly patients treated for femoral neck fracture. *Journal of the American Geriatrics Society, 36,* 525–530.

Guze, S.B. (1967). The diagnosis of hysteria: What are we trying to do? *American Journal of Psychiatry, 124,* 491–498.

Guze, S.B. (1993). Genetics of Briquet's syndrome and somatization disorder: A review of family, adoption, and twin studies. *Annals of Clinical Psychiatry, 5,* 225–230.

Gwynther, L.P., & George, L.K. (1986). Caregivers for dementia patients: Complex determinants of well-being and burden. *The Gerontologist, 26,* 245–247.

Haaga, D.A. (1987a). *Smoking schemata revealed in articulated thoughts predict early relapse from smoking cessation.* Paper presented at the 21st Annual Convention of the Association for Advancement of Behavior Therapy, Boston.

Haaga, D.A. (1987b). Treatment of the type A behavior pattern. *Clinical Psychology Review, 7,* 557–574.

Haaga, D.A. (1988). *Cognitive aspects of the relapse prevention model in the prediction of smoking relapse.* Paper presented at the 22nd Annual Convention of the Association for Advancement of Behavior Therapy, New York.

Haaga, D.A., & Davison, G.C. (1989). Outcome studies of rational-emotive therapy. In M.E. Bernard & R. DiGiuseppe (Eds.), *Inside rational-emotive therapy.* New York: Academic Press.

Haaga, D.A.F. (1989). Articulated thoughts and endorsement procedures for cognitive assessment in the prediction of smoking relapse. *Psychological Assessment: A Journal of Consulting and Clinical Psychology, 1,* 112–117.

Haaga, D.A.F. (1990). Issues in relating self-efficacy to smoking relapse: Importance of an "Achilles' Heel" situation and of prior quitting experience. *Journal of Substance Abuse, 2,* 191–200.

Haaga, D.A.F., & Davison, G.C. (1991). Cognitive change methods. In F.H. Kanfer & A.P. Goldstein (Eds.), *Helping people change: A textbook of methods* (4th ed.). Elmsford, NY: Pergamon.

Haaga, D.A.F., & Davison, G.C. (1992). Disappearing differences do not always reflect healthy integration: An analysis of cognitive therapy and rational-emotive therapy. *Journal of Psychotherapy Integration, 1,* 287–303.

Haaga, D.A.F., Dyck, M.J., & Ernst, D. (1991). Empirical status of cognitive theory of depression. *Psychological Bulletin, 110,* 215–236.

Haas, G.L., Glick, I.D., Clarkin, J.F., Spencer, J.H., & Lewis, A.B. (1990). Gender and schizophrenia outcome: A clinical trial of an outpatient intervention. *Schizophrenia Bulletin, 16,* 277–292.

Hafner, R.J. (1982). Marital interaction in persisting obsessive-compulsive disorders. *Australian and New Zealand Journal of Psychiatry, 16,* 171–178.

Hafner, R.J., Gilchrist, P., Bowling, J., & Kalucy, R. (1981). The treatment of obsessional neurosis in a family setting. *Australian and New Zealand Journal of Psychiatry, 15,* 145–151.

Hagerman, R.J. (1995). Molecular and clinical correlations in Fragile X syndrome. *Mental Retardation and Developmental Disabilities Research Reviews, 1,* 276–280.

Hahlweg, K., & Markman, H.J. (1988). The effectiveness of behavioral marital therapy: Empirical status of behavioral techniques in preventing and alleviating marital distress. *Journal of Consulting and Clinical Psychology, 56,* 440–447.

Hale, A.S. (1993). New antidepressants: Use in high-risk patients. *Journal of Clinical Psychiatry, 54,* 61–70.

Haley, S.A. (1978). Treatment implications of post-combat stress response syndromes for mental health professionals. In C.R. Figley (Ed.), *Stress disorders among Vietnam veterans.* New York: Brunner/Mazel.

Haley, W.E., Levine, E.G., Brown, S.L., Berry, J.W., & Hughes, G.H. (1987). Psychological, social, and health consequences of caring for a relative with senile dementia. *Journal of the American Geriatrics Society, 35,* 405–411.

Hall, C.S., Lindzey, G., Loehlin, J.C., & Manosevitz, M. (1985). *Introduction to theories of personality.* New York: Wiley.

Hall, G.C., Hirschman, R., & Oliver, L.L. (1995). Sexual arousal and arousability to pedophilic stimuli in a community sample of normal men. *Behavior Therapy, 26,* 681–694.

Hall, S.M., Munoz, R.F., & Reus, V.I. (1994). Cognitive-behavioral intervention increases abstinence rates for depressive-history smokers. *Journal of Consulting and Clinical Psychology, 62,* 141–146.

Hall, S.M., Munoz, R.F., Reus, V.I., Sees, K.L., Duncan, C., Humfleet, G.L., & Hartz, D.T. (1996). Mood management and nicotine gum in smoking treatment: A therapeutic contract and placebo-controlled study. *Journal of Consulting and Clinical Psychology, 64,* 1003–1009.

Halleck, S.L. (1971). *The politics of therapy.* New York: Science House.

Hamilton, E.W., & Abramson, L.Y. (1983). Cognitive patterns and major depressive disorder: A longitudinal study in a hospital setting. *Journal of Abnormal Psychology, 92,* 173–184.

Hammen, C., & Compas, B.E. (1994). Unmasking unmasked depression in children and adolescents: The problem of comorbidity. *Clinical Psychology Review, 14,* 585–603.

Hammen, C.L. (1980). Depression in college students: Beyond the Beck Depression Inventory. *Journal of Consulting and Clinical Psychology, 48,* 126–128.

Hammen, C.L. (1991). Generation of stress in the course of unipolar depression. *Journal of Abnormal Psychology, 100,* 555–561.

Hammen, C.L., & Cochran, S.D. (1981). Cognitive correlates of life stress and depression in college students. *Journal of Abnormal Psychology, 90,* 23–27.

Hampe, E., Noble, H., Miller, L.C., & Barrett, C.L. (1973). Phobic children one and two years posttreatment. *Journal of Abnormal Psychology, 82,* 446–453.

Hannappel, M., Calsyn, R.J., & Allen, G. (1993). Does social support alleviate the depression of caregivers of dementia patients? *Journal of Gerontological Social Work, 20,* 35–51.

Hansen, W.B. (1992). School-based substance abuse prevention: A review of the state of the art in curriculum, 1980–1990. *Health Education Research: Theory and Practice, 7,* 403–430.

Hansen, W.B. (1993). School-based alcohol prevention programs. *Alcohol Health and Research World, 18,* 62–66.

Hansen, W.B., & Graham, J.W. (1991). Preventing alcohol, marijuana, and cigarette use among adolescents: Peer pressure resistance training versus establishing conservative norms. *Preventive Medicine, 20,* 414–430.

Hansen, W.B., Johnson, C.A., Flay, B.R., Graham, J.W., & Sobel, J. (1988). Affective and social influence approaches to the prevention of multiple substance abuse among seventh grade students. *Preventive Medicine, 17,* 135–154.

Hanusa, B.H., & Schulz, R. (1977). Attributional mediators of learned helplessness. *Journal of Personality and Social Psychology, 35,* 602–611.

Haracz, J.L. (1982). The dopamine hypothesis: An overview of studies with schizophrenic patients. *Schizophrenia Bulletin, 8,* 438–469.

Hardy, B.W., & Waller, D.A. (1988). Bulimia as substance abuse. In W.G. Johnson (Ed.), *Advances in eating disorders.* New York: JAI.

Hardy, J. (1993). Genetic mistakes point the way to Alzheimer's disease. *Journal of NIH Research, 5,* 46–49.

Hardy, K.V., & Laszloffy, T.A. (1995). Therapy with African Americans and the phenomenon of rage. *In Session: Psychotherapy in Practice, 1,* 57–70.

Hare, E. (1969). *Triennial statistical report of the Royal Maudsley and Bethlem Hospitals.* London: Bethlem and Maudsley Hospitals.

Hare, R.D. (1978). Electrodermal and cardiovascular correlates of sociopathy. In R.D. Hare & D. Schalling (Eds.), *Psychopathic behaviour: Approaches to research.* New York: Wiley.

Hare, R.D., Harpur, T.J., Hakstian, R.A., Forth, A.E., Hart, S.D., et al. (1990). The revised Psychopathy Checklist: Reliability and factor structure. *Psychological Assessment, 2,* 338–341.

Hare, R.D., Hart, S.D., & Harpur, T.J. (1991). Psychopathy and the DSM-IV criteria for antisocial personality disorder. *Journal of Abnormal Psychology, 100,* 391–398.

Harpur, T.J., & Hare, R.D. (1990). Psychopathy and attention. In J. Enns (Ed.), *The development of attention: Research and theory.* Amsterdam: New Holland.

Harris, M.J., & Jeste, D.V. (1988). Late-onset schizophrenia: A review. *Schizophrenia Bulletin, 14,* 39–55.

Harrison, J., Chin, J., & Ficarrotto, T. (1989). Warning: Masculinity may be dangerous to your health. In M.S. Kimmel & M.A. Messner (Eds.), *Men's lives* (pp. 296–309). New York: Macmillan.

Hart, S.D., & Hare, R.D. (1989). Discriminant validity of the Psychopathy Checklist in a forensic psychiatric population. *Psychological Assessment, 1,* 211–218.

Hartley, D.E., & Strupp, H.H. (1983). The therapeutic alliance: Its relationship to outcome in brief psychotherapy. In J. Masling (Ed.), *Empirical studies of psychoanalytical theories* (Vol. 1). Hillsdale, NJ: Analytical Press.

Hartmann, H. (1958). *Ego psychology and the problem of adaptation.* New York: International Universities Press.

Harvard Mental Health Letter. (1995). Schizophrenia update, Pt. 2. *Harvard Mental Health Letter, 12,* 1–5.

Harvard Mental Health Letter. (1996a). Pt. 1. *Harvard Mental Health Letter, 13,* 1–4.

Harvard Mental Health Letter. (1994a, July). Borderline personality—Part III, *11,* 1–3.

Harvard Mental Health Letter. (1994b, July). Borderline personality—Part I and II, *Special Supplement, 11,* 1–3.

Harvard Mental Health Letter. (1995, July). Schizophrenia update—Part II, *12,* 1–5.

Harvard Mental Health Letter. (1996a, August). Treatment of alcoholism—Part I, *13,* 1–4.

Harvard Mental Health Letter. (1996b, February). Personality disorders: The anxious cluster—Part I, *12,* 1–3.

Harvard Mental Health Letter. (1996c, March). Personality disorders: The anxious cluster—Part II, *12,* 1–3.

Hastrup, J.L., Light, K.C., & Obrist, P.A. (1982). Parental hypertension and cardiovascular response to stress in healthy young adults. *Psychophysiology, 19,* 615–622.

Hathaway, S.R., & McKinley, J.C. (1943). *MMPI manual.* New York: Psychological Corporation.

Hawton, K., Catalan, J., & Fagg, J. (1992). Sex therapy for erectile dysfunction: Characteristics of couples, treatment outcome, and prognostic factors. *Archives of Sexual Behavior, 21,* 161–176.

Hawton, K., Catalan, J., Martin, P., & Fagg, J. (1986). Long-term outcome of sex therapy. *Behaviour Research and Therapy, 24,* 665–675.

Hay, D.P. (1991). Electroconvulsive therapy. In J. Sadavoy, L.W. Lazarus, & L.F. Jarvik (Eds.), *Comprehensive review of geriatric psychiatry* (pp. 469–485). Washington, DC: American Psychiatric Press.

Hayashi, K., Toyama, B., & Quay, H.C. (1976). A cross-cultural study concerned with differential behavioral classification: 1. The Behavior Checklist. *Japanese Journal of Criminal Psychology, 2,* 21–28.

Hayes, R.L., Halford, W.K., & Varghese, F.T. (1995). Social skills training with chronic schizophrenic patients: Effects on negative symptoms and community functioning. *Behavior Therapy, 26,* 433–449.

Hayes, S.C. (1987). A contextual approach to therapeutic change. In N.S. Jacobson (Ed.), *Psychotherapists in clinical practice: Cognitive and behavioral perspectives.* New York: Guilford.

Haynes, S.N., & Horn, W.F. (1982). Reactivity in behavioral observation: A review. *Behavioral Assessment, 4,* 369–385.

Hazelrigg, M.D., Cooper, H.M., & Borduin, C.M. (1987). Evaluating the effectiveness of family therapies: An integrative review and analysis. *Psychological Bulletin, 101,* 428–442.

Healy, M. (1994, January 8). Science of power and weakness. *Los Angeles Times,* pp. A1, A12.

Heatherton, T.F., & Baumeister, R.F. (1991). Binge eating as escape from self-awareness. *Psychological Bulletin, 110,* 86–108.

Heatherton, T.F., Herman, C.P., & Polivy, J. (1991). Effects of physical threat and ego threat on eating behavior. *Journal of Personality and Social Psychology, 60,* 138–143.

Heatherton, T.F., Nichols, P., Mahamedi, F., & Keel, P. (1995). Body weight, dieting, and eating disorder symptoms among college students, 1982 to 1992. *American Journal of Psychiatry, 152,* 1623–1630.

Hechtman, L., Weiss, G., & Perlman, T. (1984). Hyperactives as young adults: Past and current substance abuse and antisocial behavior. *American Journal of Orthopsychiatry, 54,* 415–425.

Hecker, M.H.L., Chesney, M., Black, G.W., & Frautsch, N. (1988). Coronary-prone behavior in the Western Collaborative Group Study. *Psychosomatic Medicine, 50,* 153–164.

Heidrich, S.M. (1993). The relationship between physical health and psychological well-being in elderly women: A developmental perspective. *Research in Nursing and Health, 16,* 123–130.

Heilman, K.M., Voeller, K.K., & Nadeau, S.E. (1991). A possible pathophysiologic substrate of attention deficit hyperactivity disorder. *Journal of Child Neurology, 6,* S76–S81.

Heiman, J.R., & Verhulst, J. (1990). Sexual dysfunction and marriage. In F.D. Fincham, & T.N. Bradbury (Eds.), *The psychology of marriage: Basic issues and applications* (pp. 299–322). New York: Guilford.

Heiman, J.R., Rowland, D.L., Hatch, J.P., & Gladue, B.A. (1991). Psychophysiological and endocrine responses to sexual arousal in women. *Archives of Sexual Behavior, 20,* 171–186.

Heimberg, R.G., & Juster, H.R. (1994). Treatment of social phobia in cognitive-behavioral groups. *Journal of Clinical Psychiatry, 55,* 38–46.

Heimberg, R.G., Salzman, D.G., Holt, C.S., & Blendell, K. (1993). Cognitive behavioral group treatment for social phobia: Effectiveness at five-year follow-up. *Cognitive Therapy and Research, 17,* 325–339.

Heller, J. (1966). *Something happened.* New York: Knopf.

Heller, K.A., Holtzman, W.H., & Messick,

S. (Eds.). (1982). *Placing children in special education: A strategy for equity.* Washington, DC: National Academy Press.

Helzer, J.E., Burnam, A., & McEvoy, L.T. (1991). Alcohol abuse and dependence. In L. Robins & D. Reiger (Eds.), *Psychiatric disorders in America: The Epidemiologic Catchment Area Study* (pp. 9–38). New York: Free Press.

Helzer, J.E., Robins, L.N., & McEvoy, L. (1987). Post-traumatic stress disorder in the general population. *New England Journal of Medicine, 317,* 1630–1634.

Hembree, W.C., Nahas, G.G., & Huang, H.F.S. (1979). Changes in human spermatozoa associated with high dose marihuana smoking. In G.G. Nahas & W.D.M. Paton (Eds.), *Marihuana: Biological effects.* Elmsford, NY: Pergamon.

Hendin, H. (1982). *Suicide in America.* New York: Norton.

Henkel, H., & Lewis-Thomé, J. (1976). *Verhaltenstherapie bei männlichen Homosexuellen.* Diplomarbeit der Studierenden der Psychologie. University of Marburg, Germany.

Henry, J.P., Ely, D.L., & Stephens, P.M. (1972). Changes in catecholamine-controlling enzymes in response to psychosocial activation of defense and alarm reactions. In *Physiology, emotion, and psychosomatic illness.* Ciba Symposium 8. Amsterdam, Netherlands: Associated Scientific Publishers.

Henry, R.M. (1996). Psychodynamic group therapy with adolescents: Exploration of HIV-related risk taking. *International Journal of Group Psychotherapy, 46,* 229–253.

Henry, W.P., & Strupp, H.H. (1994). The therapeutic alliance as interpersonal process. In A. Horvath & L. Greenberg (Eds.), *The working alliance: Theory, research and practice* (pp. 51–84). New York: Guilford.

Henry, W.P., Strupp, H.H., Schacht, T.E., & Gaston, L. (1994). Psychodynamic approaches. In A.E. Bergin & S.L. Garfield (Eds.), *Handbook of psychotherapy and behavior change.* Fourth edition (pp. 467–508). New York: Wiley.

Herbert, J.D. (1995). An overview of the current status of social phobia. *Applied and Preventive Psychology, 4,* 39–51.

Herbert, M. (1982). Conduct disorders. In B.B. Lahey & A.E. Kazdin (Eds.), *Advances in clinical child psychology* (Vol. 5). New York: Plenum.

Herman, C.P., & Polivy, J. (1980). Restrained Eating. In A. Stunkard (Ed.), *Obesity.* Philadelphia: Sanders.

Herman, C.P., Polivy, J., Lank, C., & Heatherton, T.F. (1987). Anxiety, hunger, and eating. *Journal of Abnormal Psychology, 96,* 264–269.

Hersen, M., & Barlow, D.H. (1976). *Single case experimental designs: Strategies for studying behavior change.* New York: Pergamon.

Hersen, M., & Van Hasselt, V.B. (1992). Behavioral assessment and treatment of anxiety in older adults. *Clinical Psychology Review, 12,* 619–640.

Hersen, M., Bellack, A.S., Himmelhoch, J.M., & Thase, M.E. (1984). Effects of social skill training, amitriptyline, and psychotherapy in unipolar depressed women. *Behavior Therapy, 15,* 21–40.

Hester, R.K., & Miller, W.R. (1989). Self-control training. In R.K. Hester & W.R. Miller (Eds.), *Handbook of alcoholism treatment approaches: Effective alternatives* (pp. 141–149). New York: Pergamon.

Heston, L.L. (1966). Psychiatric disorders in foster home reared children of schizophrenic mothers. *British Journal of Psychiatry, 112,* 819–825.

Heston, L.L. (1987). The paranoid syndrome after mid-life. In N.E. Miller & G.D. Cohen (Eds.), *Schizophrenia and aging* (pp. 249–257). New York: Guilford.

Heston, L.L., & White, J.A. (1991). *The vanishing mind.* New York: Freeman.

Hewett, F.M. (1965). Teaching speech to an autistic child through operant conditioning. *American Journal of Orthopsychiatry, 33,* 927–936.

Hewitt, P.L., Flett, G.L., & Ediger, E. (1996). Perfectionism and depression: Longitudinal assessment of a specific vulnerability hypothesis. *Journal of Abnormal Psychology, 105,* 276–280.

Heyd, D., & Bloch, S. (1981). The ethics of suicide. In S. Bloch & P. Chodoff (Eds.), *Psychiatric ethics.* New York: Oxford University Press.

Hietala, J., Syvalahti, E., Vuorio, K., Nagren, K., Lehikoinen, P., et al. (1994). Striatal D2 dopamine receptor characteristics in drug-naive schizophrenic patients studied with positive emission tomography. *Archives of General Psychiatry, 51,* 116–123.

Hill, C.E., O'Grady, K.E., & Elkin, I. (1992). Applying the Collaborative Study Psychotherapy Rating Scale to rate therapist adherence to cognitive-behavior therapy, interpersonal therapy, and clinical management. *Journal of Consulting and Clinical Psychology, 60,* 73–79.

Hill, J.H., Liebert, R.M., & Mott, D.E.W. (1968). Vicarious extinction of avoidance behavior through films: An initial test. *Psychological Reports, 12,* 192.

Hill, S.Y. (1980). Introduction: The biological consequences. In *Alcoholism and alcohol abuse among women: Research issues.* Rockville, MD: National Institute on Alcohol Abuse and Alcoholism.

Himadi, W.G., Cerny, J.A., Barlow, D.H., Cohen, S., & O'Brien, G.T. (1986). The relationship of marital adjustment to agoraphobia treatment outcome. *Behaviour Research and Therapy, 24,* 107–115.

Hinshaw, S.P. (1987). On the distinction between attentional deficits/hyperactivity and conduct problems/aggression in child psychopathology. *Psychological Bulletin, 101,* 443–463.

Hinshaw, S.P. (1991). Stimulant medication and the treatment of aggression in children with attentional deficits. *Journal of Clinical Child Psychology, 20,* 301–312.

Hinshaw, S.P., Henker, B., & Whalen, C.K. (1984). Cognitive-behavioral and pharmacologic interventions for hyperactive boys: Comparative and combined effects. *Journal of Consulting and Clinical Psychology, 52,* 739–749.

Hinshaw, S.P., Henker, B., & Whalen, C.K. (1984). Self-control in hyperactive boys in anger-inducing situations: Effects of cognitive-behavioral training and of methylphenidate. *Journal of Abnormal Child Psychology, 12,* 55–77.

Hirschi, T. (1969). *Causes of delinquency.* Berkeley, CA: University of California Press.

Hite, S. (1976). *The Hite Report: A nationwide study of female sexuality.* New York: Dell.

Hobbs, S.A., Beck, S.J., & Wansley, R.A. (1984). Pediatric behavioral medicine: Directions in treatment and prevention. In M. Hersen, R.M. Eisler, & P.M. Miller (Eds.), *Progress in behavior modification* (Vol. 16). New York: Academic Press.

Hobfoll, S.E., Spielberger, C.D., Breznitz, S., Figley, C., Folkman, S., Lepper-Green, B., Meichenbaum, D., Milgram, N.A., Sandler, I., Sarason, I., & van der Kolk, B. (1991). War-related stress: Addressing the stress of war and other traumatic events. *American Psychologist, 46,* 848–855.

Hodges, L.F., Rothbaum, B.O., Kooper, R., Opdyke, D., Meyer, T., de Graff, J.J., & Williford, J.S. (1994). Presence as the defining factor in a VR application: Virtual reality graded exposure in the treatment of acrophobia. *Tech Rep GIT-GVU-94–96,* Georgia Institute of Technology.

Hodgson, R.J., & Rachman, S.J. (1972). The effects of contamination and washing on obsessional patients. *Behaviour Research and Therapy, 10,* 111–117.

Hodson, D.S., & Skeen, P. (1994). Sexuality and aging: The hammerlock of myths. *Journal of Applied Gerontology, 13,* 219–235.

Hoebel, B.G., & Teitelbaum, P. (1966). Weight regulation in normal and hypothalamic hyperphagic rats. *Journal of Comparative and Physiological Psychology, 61,* 189–193.

Hoffman, M.L. (1970). Moral development. In P.H. Mussen (Ed.), *Carmichael's manual of child psychology.* London: Wiley.

Hofmann, S.G., Newman, M.G., Ehlerr, A., & Roth, W. (1995). Psychophysiological differences between subgroups of social phobia. *Journal of Abnormal Psychology, 104,* 224–231.

Hogan, D. (1978). The effectiveness of sex therapy: A review of the literature. In J. LoPiccolo & L. LoPiccolo (Eds.), *Handbook of sex therapy.* New York: Plenum.

Hogarty, G.E. (1993). Prevention of relapse in chronic schizophrenic patients. *Journal of Clinical Psychiatry, 54,* 18–23.

Hogarty, G.E., Anderson, C.M., Reiss, D.J., Kornblith, S.J., Greenwald, D.P., et al. (1986). Family psychoeducation, social skills training, and maintenance chemotherapy in the aftercare treatment of schizophrenia: 1. One-year effects of a controlled study on relapse and expressed emotion. *Archives of General Psychiatry, 43,* 633–642.

Hogarty, G.E., Anderson, C.M., Reiss, D.J., Kornblith, S.J., Greenwald, D.P., Ulrich, R.F., Carter, M., & The Environmental–Personal Indicators in the Course of Schizophrenia (EPICS) Research Group. (1991). Family psychoeducation, social skills training, and maintenance chemotherapy in the aftercare treatment of schizophrenia. *Archives of General Psychiatry, 48,* 340–347.

Hogarty, G.E., McEvoy, J.P., Ulrich, R.F., DiBarry, A.L., Bartone, P., et al. (1994). Pharmacotherapy of impaired affect in recovering schizophrenic patients. *Archives of General Psychiatry, 52,* 29–41.

Hokanson, J.E., & Burgess, M. (1962). The effects of three types of aggression on vascular processes. *Journal of Abnormal and Social Psychology, 65,* 446–449.

Hokanson, J.E., Burgess, M., & Cohen, M.F. (1963). Effects of displaced aggression on systolic blood pressure. *Journal of Abnormal and Social Psychology, 67,* 214–218.

Hokanson, J.E., Willers, K.R., & Koropsak, E. (1968). Modification of autonomic responses during aggressive interchange. *Journal of Personality, 36,* 386–404.

Holden, C. (1972). Nader on mental health centers: A movement that got bogged down. *Science, 177,* 413–415.

Holder, H., Longabaugh, R., Miller, W.R., & Rubonis, A.V. (1991). The cost effectiveness of treatment for alcoholism: A first approximation. *Journal of Studies on Alcohol, 52,* 517–540.

Holinger, P.C. (1987). *Violent deaths in the United States.* New York: Guilford.

Hollander, E., Cohen, L.J., & Simeon, D. (1993). Body dysmorphic disorder. *Psychiatric Annals, 23,* 359–364.

Hollander, E., DeCaria, C.M., Nitescu, A.,

Gully, R., Suckow, R.F., et al. (1992). Serotonergic function in obsessive-compulsive disorder: Behavioral and neuroendocrine responses to oral m-chlorophenylpiperazine and fenfluramine in patients and healthy volunteers. *Archives of General Psychiatry, 49,* 21–27.

Hollander, E., Stein, D.J., Decaria, D.M., Cohen, L.J., Saond, J.B., et al. (1994). Serotonergic sensitivity in borderline personality disorder. *American Journal of Psychiatry, 151,* 277–280.

Hollifield, M., Katon, W., Spain, D., & Pule, L. (1990). Anxiety and depression in a village in Lesotho, Africa: A comparison with the United States. *British Journal of Psychiatry, 156,* 343–350.

Hollingshead, A.B., & Redlich, F.C. (1958). *Social class and mental illness: A community study.* New York: Wiley.

Hollon, S.D., & Beck, A.T. (1986). Cognitive and cognitive-behavioral therapies. In S.L. Garfield & A.E. Bergin (Eds.), *Handbook of psychotherapy and behavior change* (3rd ed.). New York: Wiley.

Hollon, S.D., & Beck, A.T. (1994). Cognitive and cognitive behavioral therapies. In A.E. Bergin & S.L. Garfield (Eds.), *Handbook of psychotherapy and behavior change.* Fourth edition (pp. 428–466). New York: Wiley.

Hollon, S.D., & Kendall, P.C. (1980). Cognitive self-statements in depression: Development of an automatic thoughts questionnaire. *Cognitive Therapy and Research, 4,* 383–395.

Hollon, S.D., De Rubeis, R.J., & Evans, M.D. (1996). Cognitive therapy in the treatment and prevention of depression. In P.M. Salkovskis (Ed.), *Frontiers of cognitive therapy* (pp. 293–317). New York: Guilford.

Hollon, S.D., DeRubeis, R.J., & Seligman, M.E.P. (1992). Cognitive therapy and the prevention of depression. *Applied and Preventive Psychology, 1,* 89–95.

Hollon, S.D., DeRubeis, R.J., Evans, M.D., Wiemer, J.J., Garvey, J.G., Grove, W.M., & Tuason, V.B. (1992). Cognitive therapy and pharmacotherapy for depression: Singly and in combination. *Archives of General Psychiatry, 49,* 774–781.

Hollon, S.D., DeRubeis, R.J., Tuason, V.B., Weimer, M.J., Evans, M.D., & Garvey, M.J. (1989). *Cognitive therapy, pharmacotherapy, and combined cognitive-pharmacotherapy in the treatment of depression: 1. Differential outcome.* Unpublished manuscript, Vanderbilt University, Nashville, TN.

Holm, V.A., & Varley, C.K. (1989). Pharmacological treatment of autistic children. In G. Dawson (Ed.), *Autism: Nature, diagnosis, and treatment* (pp.

386–404). New York: Guilford.

Holme, I. (1990). An analysis of randomized trials on cholesterol reduction on total mortality and coronary heart disease risk. *Circulation, 82,* 1916–1924.

Holmes, T.H., & Rahe, R.H. (1967). The social readjustment rating scale. *Journal of Psychosomatic Research, 11,* 213–218.

Holmes, T.S., & Holmes, T.H. (1970). Short-term intrusions into the life style routine. *Journal of Psychosomatic Research, 14,* 121–132.

Holroyd, K., Penzien, D., Hursey, K., Tobin, D., Rogen, L., Holm, J., Marcille, P., Hall, J., & Chila, A. (1984). Change mechanisms in EMG biofeedback training: Cognitive changes underlying improvements in tension headache. *Journal of Consulting and Clinical Psychology, 52,* 1039–1053.

Holtzworth-Munroe, A., Markman, H., O'Leary, K.D., Neidig, P., Leber, D., Heyman, R., Hulbert, D., & Smutzler, N. (1995). The need for marital violence prevention efforts: A behavioral cognitive secondary prevention program for engaged and newly married couples. *Applied and Preventive Psychology, 4,* 77–88.

Holzman, P.S. (1985). Eye movement dysfunctions and psychosis. *Review of Neurobiology, 27,* 179–205.

Honigfeld, G., & Howard, A. (1978). *Psychiatric drugs: A desk reference* (2nd ed.). New York: Academic Press.

Hooley, J.M., & Teasdale, J.D. (1989). Predictors of relapse in unipolar depressives: Expressed emotion, marital distress, and perceived criticism. *Journal of Abnormal Psychology, 98,* 229–235.

Hoon, E.F., & Hoon, P.W. (1978). Styles of sexual expression in women: Clinical implications of multivariate analyses. *Archives of Sexual Behavior, 7,* 105–116.

Hope, D.A., Heimberg, R.G., & Bruch, M.A. (1995). Dismantling cognitive-behavioral group therapy for social phobia. *Behaviour Research and Therapy, 33,* 637–650.

Horn, A.S., & Snyder, S.H. (1971). Chlorpromazine and dopamine: Confirmational similarities that correlate with the anti-psychotic activity of phenothiazine drugs. *Proceedings of the National Academy of Sciences, 68,* 2325–2328.

Horn, W.F., Wagner, A.E., & Ialongo, N. (1989). Sex differences in school-aged children with pervasive attention deficit hyperactivity disorder. *Journal of Abnormal Child Psychology, 17,* 109–125.

Hornblower, M., & Svoboda, W. (1987, November 23). Down and out—But determined: Does a mentally disturbed woman have the right to be homeless? *Time,* p. 29.

Horney, K. (1939). *New ways in psycho-*

analysis. New York: International Universities Press.

Horney, K. (1942). *Self-analysis*. New York: Norton.

Horovitz, B. (1992, March 10). Cigarette ads under fire. *Los Angeles Times*, pp. D1, D6.

Horowitz, M.J. (1975). Intrusive and repetitive thoughts after experimental stress. *Archives of General Psychiatry, 32*, 223–228.

Horowitz, M.J. (1986). *Stress response syndromes*. Northvale, NJ: Aronson.

Horowitz, M.J. (1988). *Introduction to psychodynamics: A new synthesis*. New York: Basic Books.

Horowitz, M.J. (1990). Psychotherapy. In A.S. Bellack & M. Hersen (Eds.), *Handbook of comparative treatments for adult disorders* (pp. 289–301). New York: Wiley.

Horwath, E., Wolk, S.I., Goldstein, R.B., Wickramaratne, P., Sobin, C., et al. (1995). Is the comorbidity between social phobia and panic disorder due to familial cotransmission or other factors? *Archives of General Psychiatry, 52*, 574–581.

Horwitz, L. (1974). *Clinical prediction in psychotherapy*. New York: Jason Aronson.

House, J.S., Landis, K.R., & Umberson, D. (1988). Social relationships and health. *Science, 241*, 540–544.

Houston, B.K., & Vavak, C.R. (1991). Cynical hostility: Developmental factors, psychosocial correlates, and health behaviors. *Health Psychology, 10*, 9–17.

Houts, A.C. (1991). Nocturnal enuresis as a biobehavioral problem. *Behavior Therapy, 22*, 133–151.

Houts, A.C., Berman, J., & Abramson, H. (1994). Effectiveness of psychological and pharmacological treatments for nocturnal enuresis. *Journal of Consulting and Clinical Psychology, 62*, 737–745.

Houts, P.S., & Serber, M. (Eds.). (1972). *After the turn-on, what? Learning perspectives on humanistic groups*. Champaign, IL: Research Press.

Howard, K.I., Orlinsky, D.E., Saunders, S.M., Bankoff, E., Davidson, C., & O'Mahoney, M. (1991). Northwestern University–University of Chicago Psychotherapy Research Program. In L. Beutler & M. Crago (Eds.), *Psychotherapy research*. Washington, DC: American Psychological Association.

Howard, R., Almeida, O.P., & Levy, R. (1993). Schizophrenic symptoms in late paraphrenia. *Psychopathology, 26*, 95–101.

Howard, R., Castle, D., O'Brien, J., Almeida, O., & Levy, R. (1991). Permeable walls, floors, ceilings, and doors: Partition delusions in late paraphrenia.

International Journal of Geriatric Psychiatry, 7, 719–724.

Howard, R., Castle, D., Wessely, S., & Murray, R. (1993). A comparative study of 470 cases of early-onset and late-onset schizophrenia. *British Journal of Psychiatry, 163*, 352–357.

Howes, J.L., & Vallis, T.M. (1996). Cognitive therapy with nontraditional populations: Application to post-traumatic stress disorder and personality disorders. In K.S. Dobson & K.D. Craig (Eds.), *Advances in cognitive-behavioral therapy* (pp. 237–272). Thousand Oaks, CA: Sage.

Howitt, D. (1995). Pornography and the paedophile: Is it criminogenic? *British Journal of Medical Psychology, 68*, 15–27.

Hser, Y., Anglin, M.D., & Powers, K. (1993). A 24-year follow-up of California narcotics addicts. *Archives of General Psychiatry, 50*, 577–584.

Hsu, L.K.G. (1990). *Eating disorders*. New York: Guilford.

Hudson, J.I., Pope, H.G., Yurgelun-Todd, D., Jonas, J.M., & Frankenburg, F.R. (1987). A controlled study of lifetime prevalence of affective and other psychiatric disorders in bulimic patients. *American Journal of Psychiatry, 144*, 1283–1287.

Huesmann, L.R., & Miller, L.S. (1994). Long-term effects of repeated exposure to media violence in childhood. In L.R. Huesmann (Ed.), *Aggressive behavior: Current perspectives* (pp. 153–186). New York: Plenum.

Hughes, J.R., & Hatsukami, D.K. (1992). The nicotine withdrawal syndrome: A brief review and update. *International Journal of Smoking Cessation, 1*, 21–26.

Hughes, J.R., Higgins, S.T., Bickel, W.K., Hunt, W.K., & Fenwick, J.W. (1991). Caffeine self-adminstration, withdrawal, and adverse effects among coffee drinkers. *Archives of General Psychiatry, 48*, 611–617.

Hughes, J.R., Higgins, S.T., & Hatsukami, D.K. (1990). Effects of abstinence from tobacco: A critical review. In L.T. Kozlowski, H. Annis, H.D. Cappell, F. Glaser, M. Goodstadt, Y. Israel, H. Kalant, E.M. Sellers, & J. Vingilis (Eds.), *Research advances in alcohol and drug problems*. New York: Plenum.

Humphrey, L.L. (1986). Family relations in bulimic-anorexic and nondistressed families. *International Journal of Eating Disorders, 5*, 223–232.

Humphreys, K., & Rappaport, J. (1993). From the community mental health movement to the war on drugs: A study in the definition of social problems. *American Psychologist*, 892–901.

Hunt, W.A., & Bespalec, D.A. (1974). An evaluation of current methods of modi-

fying smoking behavior. *Journal of Clinical Psychology, 30*, 431–438.

Hunter, J.E. (1986). Cognitive ability, cognitive aptitudes, job knowledge, and job performance. *Journal of Vocational Behavior, 29*, 340–362.

Hurst, J. (1992, March). Blowing smoke. *Los Angeles Times*, pp. A3, A29.

Hussian, R.A., & Lawrence, P.S. (1980). Social reinforcement of activity and problem-solving training in the treatment of depressed institutionalized elderly patients. *Cognitive Therapy and Research, 5*, 57–69.

Hutt, C., Hutt, S.J., Lee, D., & Ounsted, C. (1964). Arousal and childhood autism. *Nature, 204*, 908–909.

Hyland, M.E. (1990). The mood-peak flow relationship in adult asthmatics: A pilot study of individual differences and direction of causality. *British Journal of Medical Psychology, 63*, 379–384.

Iacono, W.G., Morean, M., Beiser, M., Fleming, J.A., et al. (1992). Smooth pursuit eye-tracking in first episode psychotic patients and their relatives. *Journal of Abnormal Psychology, 101*, 104–116.

Imber, S.D., Elkin, I., Watkins, J.T., Collins, J.F., Shea, M.T., Leber, W.R., & Glass, D.R. (1990). Mode-specific effects among three treatments for depression. *Journal of Consulting and Clinical Psychology, 58*, 352–359.

Ingram, C. (1996, September 26). Bill signed to let police tell of sex offenders' whereabouts. *Los Angeles Times*, pp. A3, A19.

Ingram, R.E., & Kendall, P.C. (1987). The cognitive side of anxiety. *Cognitive Therapy and Research, 11*, 523–536.

Insell, T.R. (1986). The neurobiology of anxiety. In B.F. Shaw, Z.V. Segal, T.M. Wallis, & F.E. Cashman (Eds.), *Anxiety disorders*. New York: Plenum.

Institute of Medicine. (1990a). Matching. In *Broadening the base of treatment for alcohol problems* (pp. 279–302). Washington, DC: National Academy Press.

Institute of Medicine. (1990b). *Treating drug problems*. Washington, DC: National Academy Press.

Insull, W. (Ed.). (1973). *Coronary risk handbook*. New York: American Heart Association.

Irwin, M., Lovitz, A., Marder, S.R., Mintz, J., Winslade, W.J., Van Putten, T., & Mills, M.J. (1985). Psychotic patients' understanding of informed consent. *American Journal of Psychiatry, 142*, 1351–1354.

Isen, A.M., Shaiken, T.F., Clark, M., & Karp, L. (1978). Affect, accessibility of material in memory, and behavior: A cognitive loop? *Journal of Personality and Social Psychology, 36*, 1–12.

Issidorides, M.R. (1979). Observations in chronic hashish users: Nuclear aberrations in blood and sperm and abnormal acrosomes in spermatozoa. In G.G. Nahas & W.D.M. Paton (Eds.), *Marihuana: Biological effects.* Elmsford, NY: Pergamon.

Istvan, J., & Matarazzo, J.D. (1984). Tobacco, alcohol and caffeine use: A review of their interrelationships. *Psychological Bulletin, 95,* 301–326.

Ivanoff, A., Jang, S.J., Smyth, N.J., & Linehan, M.M. (1994). Fewer reasons for staying alive when you are thinking of killing yourself: The Brief Reasons for Living Inventory. *Journal of Psychopathology and Behavioral Assessment, 16,* 1–13.

Iwamasa, G.Y. (1993). Asian Americans and cognitive behavioral therapy. *The Behavior Therapist, 16,* 233–235.

Jablensky, A., Sartorius, N., Cooper, J.E., Anker, A., Korten, A., & Bertelson, A. (1994). Culture and schizophrenia. *British Journal of Psychiatry, 165,* 434–436.

Jackson, A.M. (1973). Psychotherapy: Factors associated with the race of the therapist. *Psychotherapy: Theory, Research, and Practice, 10,* 273–277.

Jackson, C., Winkleby, M.A., Flora, J.A., & Fortmann, S.P. (1991). Use of educational resources for cardiovascular risk reduction in the Stanford Five- City Project. *American Journal of Preventive Medicine, 7,* 82–88.

Jackson, R.L., & Weinstein, H. (1996, March 16). Liggett agrees to pay 5 states for tobacco illnesses. *Los Angeles Times,* pp. A1, A15.

Jacobs, M., Jacobs, A., Gatz, M., & Schaible, T. (1973). Credibility and desirability of positive and negative structured feedback in groups. *Journal of Consulting and Clinical Psychology, 40,* 244–252.

Jacobson, A., & Herald, C. (1990). The relevance of childhood sexual abuse to adult psychiatric inpatient care. *Hospital and Community Psychiatry, 41,* 154–158.

Jacobson, A., & McKinney, W.T. (1982). Affective disorders. In J.H. Griest, J.W. Jefferson, & R.L. Spitzer (Eds.), *Treatment of mental disorders.* New York: Oxford University Press.

Jacobson, E. (1929). *Progressive relaxation.* Chicago: University of Chicago Press.

Jacobson, N.A., Dobson, K.S., Truax, P.A., Addis, M.E., Koerner, K., Gollan, J.K., Gortner, E., & Prince, S.E. (1996). A component analysis of cognitive behavioral treatment for depression. *Journal of Consulting and Clinical Psychology, 64,* 285–304.

Jacobson, N.S. (1984). A component analysis of behavioral marital therapy: The relative effectiveness of behavior exchange and problem solving training. *Journal of Consulting and Clinical Psychology, 52,* 295–305.

Jacobson, N.S. (1992). Behavioral couple therapy: A new beginning. *Behavior Therapy, 23,* 493–506.

Jacobson, N.S., & Addis, M.E. (1993). Research on couples and couple therapy: What do we know? Where are we going? *Journal of Consulting and Clinical Psychology, 61,* 85–93.

Jacobson, N.S., & Christensen, A. (1996). *Integrative couple therapy: Promoting acceptance and change.* New York: Norton.

Jacobson, N.S., Gottman, J.M., Waltz, J., Rushe, R., Babcock, J., & Holtzworth-Munroe, A. (1994). Affect, verbal content, and psychophysiology in the arguments of couples with a violent husband. *Journal of Consulting and Clinical Psychology, 62,* 982–988.

Jacobson, N.S., & Hollon, S.D. (1996). Cognitive-behavior therapy versus pharmacotherapy: Now that the jury's returned its verdict, it's time to present the rest of the evidence. *Journal of Consulting and Clinical Psychology, 64,* 74–80.

Jacobson, N.S., & Margolin, G. (1979). *Marital therapy: Strategies based on social learning.* New York: Brunner/Mazel.

Jacobson, N.S., Dobson, K., Fruzzetti, A.E., Schmaling, K.B., & Salusky, S. (1991). Marital therapy as a treatment for depression. *Journal of Consulting and Clinical Psychology, 59,* 547–557.

Jacobson, N.S., Follette, W.C., & Pagel, N. (1986). Predicting who will benefit from behavioral marital therapy. *Journal of Consulting and Clinical Psychology, 54,* 518–522.

Jacobson, N.S., Follette, W.C., Revenstorf, D., Baucom, D.H., Hahlweg, K., & Margolin, G. (1984). Variability of outcome and clinical significance of behavioral marital therapy: A reanalysis of outcome data. *Journal of Consulting and Clinical Psychology, 52,* 497–504.

Jacobson, N.S., Fruzzetti, A.E., Dobson, K., Whisman, M., & Hops, H. (1993). Couple therapy as a treatment for depression. 2: The effects of relationship quality and therapy on depressive relapse. *Journal of Consulting and Clinical Psychology, 61,* 516–519.

Jacobson, N.S., Holzworth-Munroe, A., & Schmaling, K.B. (1989). Marital therapy and spouse involvement in the treatment of depression, agoraphobia, and alcoholism. *Journal of Consulting and Clinical Psychology, 57,* 5–10.

Jacobson, N.S., Schmaling, K.B., & Holtzworth-Munroe, A. (1987). Component analysis of behavioral marital therapy: Two-year follow-up and prediction of relapse. *Journal of Marital and Family Therapy, 13,* 187–195.

Jacobson, N.S., Waldron, H., & Moore, D. (1980). Toward a behavioral profile of marital distress. *Journal of Consulting and Clinical Psychology, 48,* 696–703.

Jaffe, J.H. (1985). Drug addiction and drug abuse. In *Goodman and Gilman's the pharmacological basis of therapeutic behavior.* New York: Macmillan.

James, N., & Chapman, J. (1975). A genetic study of bipolar affective disorder. *British Journal of Psychiatry, 126,* 449–456.

Jamison, K.R. (1979). Manic-depressive illness in the elderly. In O.J. Kaplan (Ed.), *Psychopathology of aging.* New York: Academic Press.

Jamison, K.R. (1992). *Touched with fire: Manic depressive illness and the artistic temperament.* New York: Free Press.

Jampole, L., & Weber, M.K. (1987). An assessment of the behavior of sexually abused and nonsexually abused children with anatomically correct dolls. *Child Abuse and Neglect, 11,* 187–192.

Jandorf, L., Deblinger, E., Neale, J.M., & Stone, A.A. (1986). Daily vs. major life events as predictors of symptom frequency. *Journal of General Psychology, 113,* 205–218.

Janicak, P.G., Davis, J.M., Preskorn, S.H., & Ayd, F.J. (1993). *Principles and practice of psychopharmacological therapy.* Baltimore: Williams & Wilkins.

Janoff-Bulman, R. (1992). *Shattered assumptions: Toward a new psychology of trauma.* New York: Free Press.

Jansen, M.A., Arntz, A., Merckelbach, H., & Mersch, P.P.A. (1994). Personality disorders and features in social phobia and panic disorder. *Journal of Abnormal Psychology, 103,* 391–395.

Jansen, M.A., Glynn, T., & Howard, J. (1996). Prevention of alcohol, tobacco and other drug abuse. *American Behavioral Scientist, 39,* 790–807.

Jarrell, M.P., Johnson, W.G., & Williamson, D.A. (1986). *Insulin and glucose response in the binge purge episode of bulimic women.* Paper presented at the annual convention of the Association for Advancement of Behavior Therapy, Chicago.

Jarvelin, M.R., Moilanen, I., Vikevainen-Tervonen, L., & Huttunen, N.P. (1990). Life changes and protective capacities in enuretic and non-enuretic children. *Journal of Child Psychology and Psychiatry, 31,* 763–774.

Jary, M.L., & Stewart, M.A. (1985). Psychiatric disorder in the parents of adopted children with aggressive conduct disorder. *Neuropsychobiology, 13,* 7–11.

Jasnoski, M.L., & Kugler, J. (1987). Relaxation, imagery, and neuroimmunomodulation. *Annals of the New York Academy of Sciences, 496,* 722–730.

Jay, S.M., Elliott, C.H., Ozolins, M., & Olson, R.A. (1982). *Behavioral management of children's distress during painful medical procedures.* Paper presented at the annual meeting of the American Psychological Association, Washington, DC.

Jay, S.M., Elliott, C.J., Woody, P.D., & Siegel, S. (1991). An investigation of cognitive-behavioral therapy combined with oral Valium for children undergoing painful medical procedures. *Health Psychology, 10,* 317–322.

Jeans, R.F.I. (1976). An independently validated case of multiple personality. *Journal of Abnormal Psychology, 85,* 249–255.

Jeffrey, D.B. (1974). A comparison of the effects of external control and self-control on the modification and maintenance of weight. *Journal of Abnormal Psychology, 83,* 404–410.

Jeffrey, R.W. (1991). Weight management and hypertension. *Annals of Behavioral Medicine, 13,* 18–22.

Jeffrey, R.W., Forster, J.L., & Schmid, T.L. (1989). Worksite health promotion: Feasibility testing of repeated weight control and smoking cessation classes. *American Journal of Health Promotion, 3,* 11–16.

Jellinek, E.M. (1952). Phases of alcohol addiction. *Quarterly Journal of Studies on Alcohol, 13,* 673–684.

Jenike, M.A. (1986). Theories of etiology. In M.A. Jenike, L. Baer, & W.E. Minichiello (Eds.), *Obsessive-compulsive disorders.* Littleton, MA: PSG Publishing.

Jenike, M.A. (1990). Psychotherapy. In A.S. Bellack & M. Hersen (Eds.), *Handbook of comparative treatments for adult disorders* (pp. 245–255). New York: Wiley.

Jenike, M.A., & Rauch, S.L. (1994). Managing the patient with treatment-resistant obsessive-compulsive disorder: Current strategies. *Journal of Clinical Psychiatry, 55,* 11–17.

Jenike, M.A., Baer, L., & Minichiello, W.E. (1986). *Obsessive-compulsive disorders: Theory and management.* Littleton, MA: PSG Publishing.

Jenkins, C.D. (1976). Recent evidence supporting psychologic and social risk factors for coronary disease. *New England Journal of Medicine, 294,* 987–994, 1033–1038.

Jenkins, J.M., & Smith, M.A. (1991). Marital disharmony and children's behaviour problems: Aspects of a poor marriage that affect children adversely. *Journal of Child Psychology & Psychiatry & Allied Disciplines, 32,* 793–810.

Jensen, J.P., Bergin, A.E., & Greaves, D.W. (1990). The meaning of eclecticism: New survey and analysis of components. *Professional Psychology: Research and Practice, 21,* 124–130.

Jeste, D.V., Harris, M.J., Pearlson, G.D., Rabins, P.V., Lesser, I., Miller, B., Coles, C., & Yassa, R. (1988). Late-onset schizophrenia: Studying clinical validity. *Psychiatric Annals of North America, 11,* 1–13.

Jeste, D.V., Lacro, J.P., Gilbert, P.L., Kline, J., & Kline, N. (1993). Treatment of late-life schizophrenia with neuroleptics. *Schizophrenia Bulletin, 19,* 817–830.

Jeste, D.V., Manley, M., & Harris, M.J. (1991). Psychoses. In J. Sadavoy, L.W. Lazarus, & L.F. Jarvik (Eds.), *Comprehensive review of geriatric psychiatry* (pp. 353–368). Washington, DC: American Psychiatric Press.

Jimerson, D.C., Lesem, M.D., Kate, W.H., & Brewerton, T.D. (1992). Low serotonin and dopamine metabolite concentrations in cerebrospinal fluid from bulimic patients with frequent binge episodes. *Archives of General Psychiatry, 49,* 132–138.

Johnson, B.A. (1991). Cannabis. In I.B. Glass (Ed.), *International handbook of addiction behavior.* London: Tavistock/Routledge.

Johnson, C.L., Rifkind, B.M., & Sempos, C.T., et al. (1993). Declining serum total cholesterol levels among U.S. adults. *Journal of the American Medical Association, 269,* 3002–3008.

Johnson, D.R. (1987). The role of the creative arts therapist in the diagnosis and treatment of psychological trauma. *The Arts in Psychotherapy, 14,* 7–13.

Johnson, J., Horvath, E., & Weissman, M.M. (1991). The validity of depression with psychotic features based on a community study. *Archives of General Psychiatry, 48,* 1075–1081.

Johnson, J., Weissman, M.M., & Klerman, G.L. (1990). Panic disorder, comorbidity, and suicide attempts. *Archives of General Psychiatry, 47,* 805–808.

Johnson, L. (1995). *Psychotherapy in the age of accountability.* New York: Norton.

Johnson, M.K., & Raye, C.L. (1981). Reality monitoring. *Psychological Review, 88,* 67–85.

Johnson, S.M., & Greenberg, L.S. (1985). Differential effects of experiential and problem-solving interventions in resolving marital conflict. *Journal of Consulting and Clinical Psychology, 53,* 175–184.

Johnson, S.M., & Greenberg, L.S. (1987). Emotionally focused marital therapy: An overview. *Psychotherapy, 24,* 552–560.

Johnston, M.B., Whitman, T.L., & Johnson, M. (1980). Teaching addition and subtraction to mentally retarded children: A self-instructional program. *Applied Research in Mental Retardation, 1,* 141–160.

Joiner, T.E. (1995). The price of soliciting and receiving negative feedback: Self-verification theory as a vulnerability to depression theory. *Journal of Abnormal Psychology, 104,* 364–372.

Joiner, T.E., & Metalsky, G.I. (1995). A prospective test of an integrative interpersonal theory of depression: A naturalistic study of college roommates. *Journal of Personality and Social Psychiatry, 69,* 778–789.

Joiner, T.E., Alfano, M.S., & Metalsky, G.I. (1992). When depression breeds contempt: Reassurance seeking, self-esteem, and rejection of depressed college students by their roommates. *Journal of Abnormal Psychology, 101,* 165–173.

Jones, M. (1953). *The therapeutic community.* New York: Basic Books.

Jones, M.C. (1924). A laboratory study of fear: The case of Peter. *Pedagogical Seminary, 31,* 308–315.

Jones, R.T. (1980). Human effects: An overview. In *Marijuana research findings.* Washington, DC: U.S. Government Printing Office.

Julkunen, J.T., Salonen, R., Kaplan, G.A., Chesney, M.A., & Salonen, J.T. (1994). Hostility and the progression of carotid atherosclerosis. *Psychosomatic Medicine, 56,* 519–525.

Junginger, J., Barker, S., & Coe, D. (1992). Mood theme and bizarreness of delusions in schizophrenia and mood psychosis. *Journal of Abnormal Psychology, 101,* 287–292.

Jutai, J.W., & Hare, R.D. (1983). Psychopathy and selective attention during performance of a complex perceptual-motor task. *Psychophysiology, 20,* 140–151.

Kagan, J., & Snidman, N. (1991a). Infant predictors of inhibited and uninhibited profiles. *Psychological Science, 2,* 40–44.

Kahana, R.J. (1987). Geriatric psychotherapy: Beyond crisis management. In J. Sadavoy & M. Leszcz (Eds.), *Treating the elderly with psychotherapy.* Madison, CT: International Universities Press.

Kahn, R.L., Zarit, S.H., Hilbert, N.M., & Niederehe, G. (1975). Memory complaint and impairment in the aged: The effect of depression and altered brain function. *Archives of General Psychiatry, 32,* 1569–1573.

Kahneman, D. (1973). *Attention and effort.* Englewood Cliffs, NJ: Prentice-Hall.

Kaiser, F.E., Viosca, S.P., Morley, J.E., Mooradian, A.D., Davis, S.S., & Korenman, S.G. (1988). Impotence and aging: Clinical and hormonal factors. *Journal of the American Geriatrics Society, 36,* 511–519.

Kalichman, S.C. (1991). Psychopathology

and personality characteristics of criminal sexual offenders as a function of victim age. *Archives of Sexual Behavior, 20,* 187–198.

Kalichman, S.C. (1995). *Understanding AIDS: A guide for mental health professionals.* Washington, DC: American Psychological Association.

Kalichman, S.C. (1996). *Answering your questions about AIDS.* Washington, DC: American Psychological Association.

Kalichman, S.C., Sikkema, K., & Somlai, A. (1995). Assessing persons with human immunodeficiency virus (HIV) infection using the Beck Depression Inventory: Disease processes and other potential confounds. *Journal of Personality Assessment, 64,* 86–100.

Kamarck, T.W., Annunziato, B., & Amateau, L.M. (1995). Affiliations moderate the effects of social threat on stress-related cardiovascular responses: Boundary conditions for a laboratory model of social support. *Psychosomatic Medicine, 57,* 183–194.

Kammen, D.P. van, Bunney, W.E., Docherty, J.P., Jimerson, J.C., Post, R.M., et al. (1977). Amphetamine induced catecholamine activation in schizophrenia and depression. *Advances in Biochemical Psychopharmacology, 16,* 655–659.

Kandel, D.B. (1984). Marijuana users in young adulthood. *Archives of General Psychiatry, 41,* 200–209.

Kandel, D.B., & Andrews, K. (1987). Processes of socialization by parents and peers. *International Journal of the Addictions, 22,* 319–342.

Kandel, D.B., Davies, M., Karus, D., & Yamaguchi, K. (1986). The consequences in young adulthood of adolescent drug involvement. *Archives of General Psychiatry, 43,* 746–754.

Kandel, D.B., Murphy, D., & Karus, D. (1985). *National Institute on Drug Abuse Research Monograph Series 61.* Washington, DC: NIDA.

Kane, J., Honigfeld, G., Singer, J., Meltzer, H., and the Clozapine Collaborative Study Group. (1988). Clozapine for treatment resistant schizophrenics. *Archives of General Psychiatry, 45,* 789–796.

Kane, J.M., Woerner, M., Weinhold, P., Wegner, J., Kinon, B., & Bernstein, M. (1986). Incidence of tardive dyskinesia: Five-year data from a prospective study. *Psychopharmacology Bulletin, 20,* 387–389.

Kane, R.L., Parsons, D.A., & Goldstein, G. (1983). Statistical relationships and discriminative accuracy of the Halstead–Reitan, Luria–Nebraska, and Wechsler IQ scores in the identification of brain damage. *Journal of Clinical and Experimental Neuropsychology, 7,* 211–223.

Kanfer, F.H., & Busenmeyer, J.R. (1982). The use of problem-solving and decision making in behavior therapy. *Clinical Psychology Review, 2,* 239–266.

Kanfer, F.H., & Phillips, J.S. (1970). *Learning foundations of behavior therapy.* New York: Wiley.

Kanner, L. (1943). Autistic disturbances of affective contact. *Nervous Child, 2,* 217–250.

Kanner, L., & Eisenberg, L. (1955). Notes on the follow-up studies of autistic children. In P. Hoch & J. Zubin (Eds.), *Psychopathology of childhood.* New York: Grune & Stratton.

Kanter, J., Lamb, R., & Loeper, G. (1987). Expressed emotions in families: A critical review. *Hospital and Community Psychiatry, 38,* 374–380.

Kantorovich, N.V. (1930). An attempt at associative-reflex therapy in alcoholism. *Psychological Abstracts, 4,* 493.

Kaplin, H.I., & Sadock, B.J. (1991). *Synopsis of psychiatry: Behavioral sciences, clinical psychiatry.* Baltimore: Williams & Williams.

Kaplan, H.S. (1974). *The new sex therapy.* New York: Brunner/Mazel.

Kaplan, H.S. (1991). Sex therapy with older patients. In W.A. Myers (Ed.), *New techniques in the psychotherapy of older patients* (pp. 21–37). Washington, DC: American Psychiatric Press.

Karasek, R.A. (1979). Job demands, job decision latitude, and mental strain: Implications for job redesign. *Administrative Science, 24,* 285–308.

Karasu, T.B., Stein, S.P., & Charles, E.S. (1979). Age factors in the patient-therapist relationship. *Journal of Nervous and Mental Disease, 167,* 100–104.

Karno, M., & Golding, J.M. (1991). Obsessive-compulsive disorder. In L.N. Robinson & D.A. Regier (Eds.), *Psychiatric disorders in America.* New York: Free Press.

Kasanin, J. (1933). The acute schizoaffective psychoses. *American Journal of Psychiatry, 13,* 97–123.

Kashani, J.H., Beck, N.C., Hoeper, E.W., Fallahi, C., Corcoran, C.M., McAllister, J.A., Rosenberg, T.K., & Reid, J.C. (1987). Psychiatric disorders in a community sample of adolescents. *American Journal of Psychiatry, 144,* 584–589.

Kashani, J.H., & Carlson, G.A. (1987). Seriously depressed preschoolers. *American Journal of Psychiatry, 144,* 348–350.

Kashani, J.H., Holcomb, W.R., & Orvaschel, H. (1986). Depression and depressive symptoms in preschool children from the general population. *American Journal of Psychiatry, 143,* 1138–1143.

Kashani, J.H., Orvaschel, H., Rosenberg, T.K., & Reid, J.C. (1989). Psychopathology in a community sample of children and adolescents: A developmental perspective. *Journal of the American Academy of Child and Adolescent Psychiatry, 28,* 701–706.

Kasindorf, J. (1988, May 2). The real story of Billie Boggs: Was Koch right—Or the civil libertarians? *New York,* pp. 36–44.

Kasl, S.V., & Cobb, S. (1970). Blood pressure changes in men undergoing job loss: A preliminary report. *Psychosomatic Medicine, 32,* 19–38.

Kaslow, N.J., & Racusin, G.R. (1990). Childhood depression: Current status and future directions. In A.S. Bellack, M. Hersen, & A.E. Kazdin (Eds.), *International handbook of behavior modification and therapy* (2nd ed.). New York: Plenum.

Kaslow, N.J., Stark, K.D., Printz, B., Livingston, R., & Tsai, Y. (1992). Cognitive Triad Inventory for Children: Development and relationship to depression and anxiety. *Journal of Clinical Child Psychology, 21,* 339–347.

Kasprowicz, A.L., Manuck, S.B., Malkoff, S., & Kranz, D.S. (1990). Individual differences in behaviorally evoked cardiovascular response: Temporal stability and hemodynamic patterning. *Psychophysiology, 27,* 605–619.

Kaszniak, A.W., Nussbaum, P.D., Berren, M.R., & Santiago, J. (1988). Amnesia as a consequence of male rape: A case report. *Journal of Abnormal Psychology, 97,* 100–104.

Katz, E.R. (1980). Illness impact and social reintegration. In J. Kellerman (Ed.), *Psychological aspects of childhood cancer.* Springfield, IL: Charles C. Thomas.

Katz, E.R., Kellerman, J., & Siegel, S.E. (1980). Behavioral distress in children with leukemia undergoing bone marrow aspirations. *Journal of Consulting and Clinical Psychology, 48,* 356–365.

Katz, R.C., Gipson, M.T., Kearl, A., & Kriskovich, M. (1989). Assessing sexual aversion in college students: The Sexual Aversion Scale. *Journal of Sex and Marital Therapy, 15,* 135–140.

Kaufmann, P.G., Jacob, R.G., Ewart, C.K., Chesney, M.A., Muenz, L.R., Doub, N., Mercer, W., & HIPP Investigators. (1988). Hypertension intervention pooling project. *Health Psychology, 7,* 209–224.

Kay, D.W.K., Cooper, A.F., Garside, R.F., & Roth, M. (1976). The differentiation of paranoid from affective psychoses by patient's premorbid characteristics. *British Journal of Psychiatry, 129,* 207–215.

Kaye, W.H., Weltzin, T.E., Hsu, L.K.G., & Bulik, C.M. (1991). An open trial of fluoxetine in patients with anorexia nervosa. *Journal of Clinical Psychiatry, 52,*

464–471.

Kazdin, A.E. (1985). *Treatment of antisocial behavior in children and adolescents*. Homewood, IL: Dorsey Press.

Kazdin, A.E. (1986). Research designs and methodology. In S.L. Garfield & A.E. Bergin (Eds.), *Handbook of psychotherapy and behavior change* (3rd ed.). New York: Wiley.

Kazdin, A.E. (1994). Psychotherapy for children and adolescents. In A.E. Bergin & S.L. Garfield (Eds.), *Handbook of psychotherapy and behavior change*. Fourth edition (pp. 543–594). New York: Wiley.

Kazdin, A.E., & Kagan, J. (1994). Models of dysfunction in developmental psychopathology. *Clinical Psychology: Science and Practice, 1*, 35–52.

Keane, T.M. (in press). The role of exposure therapy in the psychological treatment of PTSD. *PTSD Clinical Quarterly.*

Keane, T.M., & Wolfe, J. (1990). Co-morbidity in post-traumatic stress disorder: An analysis of community and clinical studies. *Journal of Applied Social Psychology, 20*, 1776–1788.

Keane, T.M., Fairbank, J.A., Caddell, J.M., & Zimering, R.T. (1989). Implosive (flooding) therapy reduces symptoms of PTSD in Vietnam combat veterans. *Behavior Therapy, 20*, 245–260.

Keane, T.M., Fisher, L.M., Krinsley, K.E., & Niles, B.L. (1994). Posttraumatic stress disorder. In M. Hersen & R.T. Ammerman (Eds.), *Handbook of prescriptive treatments for adults* (pp. 237–260). New York: Plenum.

Keane, T.M., Foy, D.W., Nunn, B., & Rychtarik, R.G. (1984). Spouse contracting to increase Antabuse compliance in alcoholic veterans. *Journal of Clinical Psychology, 40*, 340–344.

Keane, T.M., Gerardi, R.J., Quinn, S.J., & Litz, B.T. (1992). Behavioral treatment of post-traumatic stress disorder. In S.M. Turner, K.S. Calhoun, & H.E. Adams (Eds.), *Handbook of clinical behavior therapy* (2nd ed., pp. 87–97). New York: Wiley.

Keane, T.M., Zimering, R.T., & Caddell, J. (1985). A behavioral formulation of posttraumatic stress disorder in Vietnam veterans. *The Behavior Therapist, 8*, 9–12.

Keefe, F.J., & Gil, K.M. (1986). Behavioral concepts in the analysis of chronic pain syndromes. *Journal of Consulting and Clinical Psychology, 54*, 776–783.

Keith, J. (1982). *Old people as people*. Boston: Little, Brown.

Keller, M.B., Beardslee, W., Lavori, P.W., Wunder, J., Dils, D.L., & Samuelson, H. (1988). Course of major depression in non-referred adolescents: A retrospective study. *Journal of Affective Disorders, 15*, 235–243.

Keller, M.B., Shapiro, R.W., Lavori, P.W., & Wolpe, N. (1982). Relapse in major depressive disorder: Analysis with the life table. *Archives of General Psychiatry, 39*, 911–915.

Kellerman, J. (1989). *Silent partner*. New York: Bantam Books.

Kellerman, J., & Varni, J.W. (1982). Pediatric hematology/oncology. In D.C. Russo & J.W. Varni (Eds.), *Behavioral pediatrics: Research and practice*. New York: Plenum.

Kellner, R. (1982). Disorders of impulse control (not elsewhere classified). In J.H. Griest, J.W. Jefferson, & R.L. Spitzer (Eds.), *Treatment of mental disorders*. New York: Oxford University Press.

Kelly, G.A. (1955). *The psychology of personal constructs*. New York: Norton.

Kelly, J.A. (1985). Group social skills training. *The Behavior Therapist, 8*, 93–95.

Kelly, J.A. (1995). *Changing HIV risk behavior: Practical strategies*. New York: Guilford.

Kelly, J.A., & St. Lawrence, J.S. (1988a). *The AIDS health crisis: Psychological and social interventions*. New York: Plenum.

Kelly, J.A., & St. Lawrence, J.S. (1988b). AIDS prevention and treatment: Psychology's role in the health crisis. *Clinical Psychology Review, 8*, 255–284.

Kelly, J.A., Murphy, D., Sikkema, K., & Kalichman, S.C. (1993). Psychological interventions are urgently needed to prevent HIV infection: New priorities for behavioral research in the second decade of AIDS. *American Psychologist, 48*, 1023–1034.

Kelly, J.A., St. Lawrence, J.S., Betts, R., Brasfield, T., & Hood, H. (1990). A skills training group intervention model to assist persons in reducing risk behaviors for HIV infection. *AIDS Education and Prevention, 2*, 24–35.

Kelly, J.A., St. Lawrence, J.S., Hood, H., & Brasfield, T. (1989). Behavioral intervention to reduce AIDS risk activities. *Journal of Consulting and Clinical Psychology, 57*, 60–67.

Kempster, N. (1996, August 25). Clinton orders tracking of sex offenders. *Los Angeles Times*, p. A20.

Kendall, P., Haaga, D.A.F., Ellis, A., Bernard, M., DiGiuseppe, R., & Kassinove, H. (1995). Rational-emotive therapy in the 1990s and beyond: Current status, recent revisions, and research questions. *Clinical Psychology Review, 15*, 169–185.

Kendall, P.C. (1990). Cognitive processes and procedures in behavior therapy. In C.M. Franks, G.T. Wilson, P.C. Kendall, & J.P. Foreyt (Eds.), *Review of behavior therapy: Theory and practice* (Vol. 12, pp. 103–137). New York: Guilford.

Kendall, P.C., & Braswell, L. (1985). *Cogni-*

tive-behavioral therapy for impulsive children. New York: Guilford.

Kendall, P.C., & Ingram, R.E. (1989). Cognitive-behavioral perspectives: Theory and research on depression and anxiety. In P.C. Kendall & D. Watson (Eds.), *Anxiety and depression: Distinctive and overlapping features* (pp. 27–54). New York: Academic Press.

Kendell, R.E. (1975). *The role of diagnosis in psychiatry*. London: Blackwell.

Kendler, K., Pedersen, N., Johnson, L., Neale, M.C., & Mathe, A. (1993). A Swedish pilot twin study of affective illness, including hospital and population-ascertained subsamples. *Archives of General Psychiatry, 50*, 699–706.

Kendler, K.S. (1993). Twin studies of psychiatric illness: Current status and future directions. *Archives of General Psychiatry, 50*, 905–914.

Kendler, K.S., & Diehl, S.R. (1993). The genetics of schizophrenia: A current, genetic-epidemiologic perspective. *Schizophrenia Bulletin, 19*, 87–113.

Kendler, K.S., & Gruenberg, A.M. (1984). Independent analysis of Danish adoption study of schizophrenia. *Archives of General Psychiatry, 41*, 555–562.

Kendler, K.S., Neale, M.C., Kessler, R.C., Heath, A.C., & Eaves, L.J. (1992). Generalized anxiety disorder: Same genes, (partly) different environments. *Archives of General Psychiatry, 49*, 716–722.

Kennedy, E., Spence, S.H., & Hensley, R. (1989). An examination of the relationship between childhood depression and social competence amongst primary school children. *Journal of Child Psychology and Psychiatry, 30*, 561–573.

Kennedy, M., & Jones, E. (1995). Violence from patients in the community: Will UK courts impose a duty of care on mental health professionals? *Criminal Behaviour and Mental Health, 5*, 209–217.

Kennedy, S.H., & Garfinkel, P.E. (1992). Advances in the diagnosis and treatment of anorexia nervosa and bulimia nervosa. *Canadian Journal of Psychiatry, 37*, 309–315.

Kent, J.S., & Clopton, J.R. (1992). Bulimic women's perceptions of their family relationships. *Journal of Clinical Psychology, 48*, 281–292.

Kent, R.N., O'Leary, K.D., Diament, C., & Dietz, A. (1974). Expectation biases in observational evaluation of therapeutic change. *Journal of Consulting and Clinical Psychology, 42*, 774–780.

Kernberg, O.F. (1985). *Borderline conditions and pathological narcissism*. Northvale, NJ: Jason Aronson.

Kerr, S.L., & Neale, J.M. (1993). Emotion perception in schizophrenia: Specific deficit or further evidence of generalized poor performance? *Journal of Abnormal Psychology, 102,* 312–326.

Kessel, N., & Grossman, G. (1961). Suicide in alcoholics. *British Medical Journal, 2,* 1671–1672.

Kessler, R.C., McGonagle, K.A., Shanyang, Z., Nelson, C.B., Hughes, M., Eshleman, S., Wittchen, H.U., & Kendler, K. (1994). Lifetime and 12-month prevalence of DSM-III-R psychiatric disorders in the United States. *Archives of General Psychiatry, 51,* 8–19.

Kessler, R.C., McGonagle, K.A., Zhao, S., Nelson, C.B., Hughes, M., et al. (1994). Lifetime and 12-month prevalence rates of DSM-III-R psychiatric disorders in the United States: Results from the National Comorbidity Survey. *Archives of General Psychiatry, 51,* 8–19.

Kety, S.S., Rosenthal, D., Wender, P.H., & Schulsinger, F. (1968). The types and prevalence of mental illness in the biological and adoptive families of adopted schizophrenics. In D. Rosenthal & S.S. Kety (Eds.), *The transmission of schizophrenia.* Elmsford, NY: Pergamon.

Kety, S.S., Rosenthal, D., Wender, P.H., & Schulsinger, F. (1975). Mental illness in the adoptive and biological families of adopted individuals who have become schizophrenic. In R.R. Fieve, D. Rosenthal, & H. Brill (Eds.), *Genetic research in psychiatry.* Baltimore: Johns Hopkins University Press.

Kety, S.S., Wender, P.H., Jacobsen, B., Ingraham, L.T., Jansson, L., et al. (1994). Mental illness in the biological and adoptive relatives of schizophrenic adoptees: Replication of the Copenhagen study in the rest of Denmark. *Archives of General Psychiatry, 51,* 442–468.

Keys, A., Taylor, H.L., et al. (1971). Mortality and coronary heart disease in men studied for 23 years. *Archives of Internal Medicine, 128,* 201–214.

Kidder, T. (1978). Soldiers of misfortune. *The Atlantic Monthly, 241,* 41–52.

Kiecolt-Glaser, J., Dura, J.R., Speicher, C.E., & Trask, O. (1991). Spousal caregivers of dementia victims: Longitudinal changes in immunity and health. *Psychosomatic Medicine, 54,* 345–362.

Kiecolt-Glaser, J., Glaser, R., Strain, E., Stout, J.C., Tarr, K.L., Holliday, J.E., & Speicher, C.E. (1986). Modulation of cellular immunity in medical students. *Journal of Behavioral Medicine, 9,* 5–21.

Kiecolt-Glaser, J.K., Garner, W., Speicher, C.E., Penn, G.M., Holliday, J., & Glaser, R. (1984). Psychosocial modifiers of immunocompetence in medical students. *Psychosomatic Medicine, 46,* 7–14.

Kiecolt-Glaser, J.K., Glaser, R., Williger, D., Stout, J., Messick, G., Sheppard, S.,

Ricker, D., Romischer, S.C., Briner, W., Bonnell, G., & Donnerberg, R. (1985). Psychosocial enhancement of immunocompetence in a geriatric population. *Health Psychology, 4,* 25–41.

Kiesler, C.A. (1991). Changes in general hospital psychiatric care. *American Psychologist, 46,* 416–421.

Kihlstrom, J.F., & Tataryn, D. J. (1991). Dissociative disorders. In P.B. Sutker & H.E. Adams (Eds.), *Comprehensive handbook of psychopathology* (2nd ed.). New York: Plenum.

Kihlstrom, J.F. (1994). Dissociative and conversion disorders. In D.J. Stein & J.E. Young (Eds.), *Cognitive science and clinical disorders.* San Diego, CA. Academic Press.

Kihlstrom, J.F. (1997). Exhumed memory. In S.J. Lynn, K.M. McConkey, & N.P. Spanos (Eds.), *Truth in memory.* New York: Guilford.

Killen, J.D., Fortmann, S.P., Newman, B., & Varady, A. (1990). Evaluation of a treatment approach combining nicotine gum with self-guided behavioral treatments for smoking relapse prevention. *Journal of Consulting and Clinical Psychology, 58,* 85–92.

Killen, J.D., Taylor, C.B., Hayward, C., Wilson, D.M., Haydel, K.F., et al. (1994). Pursuit of thinness and onset of eating disorders in a community sample of adolescent girls. *International Journal of Eating Disorders, 16,* 227–238.

Killen, J.D., Taylor, C.B., Telch, M.J., Saylor, K.E., Maron, D.J., & Robinson, T.N. (1986). Self-induced vomiting and laxative and diuretic use among teenagers: Precursors of the binge-purge syndrome. *Journal of the American Medical Association, 255,* 1447–1449.

Kilpatrick, D.G., & Best, C.L. (1990, April). *Sexual assault victims: Data from a random national probability sample.* Paper presented at the annual convention of the Southeastern Psychological Association, Atlanta.

Kilpatrick, D.G., Best, C.L., Veronen, L.J., Amick, A.E., Villeponteaux, L.A., & Ruff, G.A. (1985). Mental health correlates of criminal victimization: A random community survey. *Journal of Consulting and Clinical Psychology, 53,* 866–873.

Kilpatrick, D.G., Edmunds, C.N., & Seymour, A.K. (1992). *Rape in America: A report to the nation.* Arlington, VA: National Victim Center.

Kimble, G.A., Garmezy, N., & Zigler, E. (1980). *Principles of general psychology.* New York: Wiley.

King, D.W., King, L.A., Gudanowski, D.M., & Vreven, D.L. (1995). Alternative representations of war zone stressors: Relationship to posttraumatic stress dis-

order in male and female Vietnam veterans. *Journal of Abnormal Psychology, 104,* 184–196.

King, M.B. (1990). Sneezing as a fetishistic stimulus. *Sexual and Marital Therapy, 5,* 69–72.

Kingsley, L.A., Kaslow, R., Rinaldo, C.R., Detre, K., Odaka, N., Van-Raden, M., Detels, R., Polk, B.F., Chmiel, J., Kelsey, S.F., Ostrow, D., & Visscher, B. (1987). Risk factors for seroconversion to human immunodeficiency virus among male homosexuals. *Lancet, 1,* 345–348.

Kinsey, A.C., Pomeroy, W.B., & Martin, C.E. (1948). *Sexual behavior in the human male.* Philadelphia: Saunders.

Kinsey, A.C., Pomeroy, W.B., Main, C.E., & Gebhard, P.H. (1953). *Sexual behavior in the human female.* Philadelphia: Saunders.

Kinsman, R.A., Spector, S.L., Shucard, D.W., & Luparello, T.J. (1974). Observations on patterns of subjective symptomatology of acute asthma. *Psychosomatic Medicine, 36,* 129–143.

Kinzie, J.D. (1985). Overview of clinical issues in the treatment of Southeast Asian refugees. In T.C. Owan (Ed.), *Southeast Asian mental health treatment, prevention services, training, and research.* Washington, DC: National Institute of Mental Health.

Kipke, M.D., Montgomery, S., & MacKenzie, R.G. (1993). Substance use among youth who attend community-based health clinics. *Journal of Adolescent Health, 14,* 289–294.

Kirmayer, L.J., Robbins, J.M., & Paris, J. (1994). Somatoform disorders: Personality and social matrix of somatic distress. *Journal of Abnormal Psychology, 103,* 125–136.

Kivlighan, D.M., & Mullison, D. (1988). Participants' perception of therapeutic factors in group counseling: The role of interpersonal style and stage of group development. *Small Group Development, 19,* 452–468.

Kleeman, S.T. (1967). Psychiatric contributions in the treatment of asthma. *Annals of Allergy, 25,* 611–619.

Klein, D. (1992, April 1). The empty pot. *Los Angeles Times,* pp. A3, A14.

Klein, D.F. (1993). False suffocation alarms, spontaneous panics, and related conditions: An integrative hypothesis. *Archives of General Psychiatry, 50,* 306–317.

Klein, D.F. (1996). Preventing hung juries about therapy studies. *Journal of Consulting and Clinical Psychology, 64,* 81–87.

Klein, D.F., & Ross, D.C. (1993). Reanalysis of the National Institute of Mental Health Treatment of Depression Collaborative Research Program general effectiveness report. *Neuropsychopharmacology*, *8*, 241–251.

Klein, D.N., Taylor, E.B., Dickstein, S., & Harding, K. (1988). Primary early-onset dysthymia: Comparison with primary nonbipolar nonchronic major depression on demographic, clinical, familial, personality, and socioenvironmental characteristics and short-term outcome. *Journal of Abnormal Psychology*, *97*, 387–398.

Klerman, G.L. (1983). Problems in the definition and diagnosis of depression in the elderly. In M. Hauge & L. Breslau (Eds.), *Depression in the elderly: Causes, care, consequences*. New York: Springer.

Klerman, G.L. (1988). Depression and related disorders of mood (affective disorders). In A.M. Nicholi, Jr. (Ed.), *The new Harvard guide to psychiatry*. Cambridge, MA: Harvard University Press.

Klerman, G.L. (1988). The current age of youthful melancholia. *British Journal of Psychiatry*, *152*, 4–14.

Klerman, G.L. (1990). Treatment of recurrent unipolar major depressive disorder. *Archives of General Psychiatry*, *47*, 1158–1162.

Klerman, G.L., & Weissman, M.M. (Eds.), (1993). *New applications of interpersonal psychotherapy*. Washington, DC: American Psychiatric Press.

Klerman, G.L., Weissman, M.M., Markowitz, J.C., Glick, I., Wilner, P.J., Mason, B., & Shear, M.K. (1994). Medication and psychotherapy. In A.E. Bergin & S.L. Garfield (Eds.), *Handbook of psychotherapy and behavior change*. Fourth edition (pp. 734–782). New York: Wiley.

Klerman, G.L., Weissman, M.M., Rounsaville, B.J., & Chevron, E.S. (1984). *Interpersonal psychotherapy of depression*. New York: Basic Books.

Klinnert, M.D., Mrazek, P.J., & Mrazek, D.A. (1994). Early asthma onset: The interaction between family stressors and adaptive parenting. *Psychiatry*, *57*, 51–61.

Klosko, J.S., Barlow, D.H., Tassinari, R., & Cerny, J.A. (1990). A comparison of alprazolam and behavior therapy in treatment of panic disorder. *Journal of Consulting and Clinical Psychology, 58*, 77–84.

Kluft, R.P. (1984a). An introduction to multiple personality disorder. *Psychiatric Annals*, *7*, 19–24.

Kluft, R.P. (1984b). Multiple personality in childhood. *Psychiatric Clinics of North America*, *7*, 121–134.

Kluft, R.P. (1984c). Treatment of multiple personality disorder: A study of 33 cases. *Psychiatric Clinics of North America*, *7*, 929.

Kluft, R.P. (1985). The treatment of multiple personality disorder (MPD): Cur-

rent concepts. In F.F. Flach (Ed.), *Directions in psychiatry*. New York: Hatherleigh.

Knapp, S., & Vandecreek, L. (1982). Tarasoff: Five years later. *Professional Psychology*, *13*, 511–516.

Knaus, W., & Bokor, S. (1975). The effect of rational-emotive education lessons on anxiety and self-concept in sixth grade students. *Rational Living*, *10*, 7–10.

Knight, B. (1983). An evaluation of a mobile geriatric team. In M.A. Smyer & M. Gatz (Eds.), *Mental health and aging: Programs and evaluations*. Beverly Hills, CA: Sage.

Knight, B.G. (1996). *Psychotherapy with older adults*. 2nd ed. Thousand Oaks, CA: Sage.

Knight, B. G., Kelly, M., & Gatz, M. (1992). Psychotherapy and the older adult. In D.K. Freedheim (Ed.), *History of psychotherapy: A century of change* (pp. 528–551). Washington, DC: American Psychological Association.

Knight, B.G., Lutzky, S.M., & Olshevski, J.L. (1992). A randomized comparison of stress reduction training to problem solving training for dementia caregivers: Processes and outcomes. Unpublished manuscript, University of Southern California, Los Angeles.

Knopp, E.H. (1984). *Retraining adult sex offenders*. New York: Safer Society Press.

Kobak, K.A., Rock, A.L., & Greist, J.H. (1995). Group behavior therapy for obsessive-compulsive disorder. *Journal for Specialists in Group Work*, *20*, 26–32.

Koegel, R.L., Schreibman, L., Britten, K.R., Burkey, J.C., & O'Neill, R.E. (1982). A comparison of parent training to direct child treatment. In R.L. Koegel, A. Rincover, & A.L. Egel (Eds.), *Educating and understanding autistic children*. San Diego, CA: College-Hill.

Koenig, H.G., & Blazer, D.G. (1992). Mood disorders and suicide. In J.E. Birren, R.B. Sloane, & G.D. Cohen (Eds.), *Handbook of mental health and aging* (pp. 379–407). San Diego: Academic Press.

Koenig, K., & Masters, J. (1965). Experimental treatment of habitual smoking. *Behaviour Research and Therapy*, *3*, 235–243.

Koenigsberg, H.W., & Handley, R. (1986). Expressed emotion: From predictive index to clinical construct. *American Journal of Psychiatry*, *143*, 1361–1373.

Kohn, M.L. (1968). Social class and schizophrenia: A critical review. In D. Rosenthal & S.S. Kety (Eds.), *The transmission of schizophrenia*. Elmsford, NY: Pergamon.

Kohut, H. (1971). *The analysis of the self*. New York: International Universities Press.

Kohut, H. (1977). *The restoration of the self*.

New York: International Universities Press.

Kohut, H., & Wolf, E.S. (1978). The disorders of the self and their treatment: An outline. *International Journal of Psychoanalysis*, *59*, 413–425.

Kolden, G.G. (1991). The generic model of psychotherapy: An empirical investigation of patterns of process and outcome relationships. *Psychotherapy Research*, *1*, 62–73.

Kolmen, B.K., Feldman, H.E., Handen, B.L., & Janosky, J.E. (1995). Naltrexone in young autistic children: A double-blind, placebo-controlled crossover study. *Journal of the American Academy of Child and Adolescent Psychiatry*, *34*, 223–231.

Kolvin I., McKeith, R.C., & Meadows, S.R. (1973). *Bladder control and enuresis*. Philadelphia: Lippincott.

Konig, P., & Godfrey, S. (1973). Prevalence of exercise-induced bronchial liability in families of children with asthma. *Archives of Diseases of Childhood*, *48*, 518.

Korchin, S.J. (1976). *Modern clinical psychology*. New York: Basic Books.

Kornetsky, C. (1976). Hyporesponsivity of chronic schizophrenic patients to dextroamphetamine. *Archives of General Psychiatry*, *33*, 1425–1428.

Koss, M.P. (1985). The hidden rape victim: Personality, attitudinal, and situational characteristics. *Psychology of Women Quarterly*, *9*, 193–212.

Koss, M.P., & Butcher, J.N. (1986). Research on brief psychotherapy. In S.L. Garfield & A.E. Bergin (Eds.), *Handbook of psychotherapy and behavior change* (3rd ed.). New York: Wiley.

Koss, M.P., & Shiang, J. (1994). Research of brief psychotherapy. In A.E. Bergin & S.L. Garfield (Eds.), *Handbook of psychotherapy and behavior change*. Fourth edition (pp. 664–700). New York: Wiley.

Kosten, T.R., Mason, J.W., Giller, E.L., Ostroff, R., & Harkness, I. (1987). Sustained urinary norepinephrine and epinephrine elevation in posttraumatic stress disorder. *Psychoneuroendocrinology*, *12*, 13–20.

Kosten, T.R., Morgan, C.M., Falcione, J., & Schottenfeld, R.S. (1992). Pharmacotherapy for cocaine-abusing methadone-maintained patients using amantadine or desipramine. *Archives of General Psychiatry*, *49*, 894–898.

Kovacs, M. (1990). Comorbid anxiety disorders in childhood-onset depressions. In J.D. Maser & C.R. Cloninger (Eds.), *Comorbidity of mood and anxiety disorders* (pp. 272–281). Washington, DC: American Psychiatric Press.

Kovacs, M., Feinberg, T.L., Crouse-Novack, M.A., Paulauskas, S.L., & Finkelstein, R. (1984). Depressive disorders in childhood: 1. A longitudinal prospective study of characteristics and recovery. *Archives of General Psychiatry, 41,* 229–237.

Kovacs, M., Feinberg, T.L., Crouse-Novak, M.A., Paulauskas, S.L., Pollack, M., & Finkelstein, R. (1984). Depressive disorders in childhood: 4. A longitudinal study of comorbidity with and risk for anxiety disorders. *Archives of General Psychiatry, 41,* 776–782.

Kovacs, M., Rush, A.J., Beck, A.T., & Hollon, S.D. (1981). Depressed outpatients treated with cognitive therapy or pharmacotherapy: A one-year follow-up. *Archives of General Psychiatry, 38,* 33–39.

Kowalik, D.L., & Gotlib, I.H. (1987). Depression and marital interation: Concordance between intent and perception of communication. *Journal of Abnormal Psychology, 96,* 127–134.

Kowall, N.K., & Beal, M.F. (1988). Cortical somatostatin, neuropeptide Y, and NADPH diphorase neurons: Normal anatomy and alterations in Alzheimer's disease. *Annals of Neurology, 23,* 105–113.

Kozel, N.J., & Adams, E.H. (1986). Epidemiology of drug abuse: An overview. *Science, 234,* 970–974.

Kozel, N.J., Crider, R.A., & Adams, E.H. (1982). National surveillance of cocaine use and related health consequences. *Morbidity and Mortality Weekly Report 31,* 20, 265–273.

Kozlowski, L.T., Skinner, W., Kent, C., & Pope, M. (1989). Prospects for smoking treatment in individuals seeking treatment for alcohol and other drug problems. *Addictive Behaviors, 14,* 273–279.

Kozol, H., Boucher, R., & Garofalo, R. (1972). The diagnosis and treatment of dangerousness. *Crime and Delinquency, 18,* 37–92.

Kraepelin, E. (1981). *Clinical psychiatry.* (A.R. Diefendorf, Trans.). Delmar, NY: Scholars' Facsimiles and Reprints. (Original work published 1883)

Kramer, E.F. (1995). Controversial litigation issue may be shifting our focus away from a more serious problem. *Res Gestae,* 12.

Krantz, S., & Hammen, C.L. (1979). Assessment of cognitive bias in depression. *Journal of Abnormal Psychology, 88,* 611–619.

Kranzler, H.R., Burleson, J.A., Del Boca, F.K., Babor, T.F., Korner, P., et al. (1994). Busipirone treatment of anxious alcoholics: A controlled trial. *Archives of General Psychiatry, 51,* 720–731.

Kring, A.M., & Neale, J.M. (1996). Do schizophrenics show a disjunctive relationship among expressive, experiential and physiological components of emotion? *Journal of Abnormal Psychology,*

105, 249–257.

Kringlen, E. (1970). Natural history of obsessional neurosis. *Seminars in Psychiatry, 2,* 403–419.

Krystal, J.H., Karper, L.P., Seibyl, J.P., Freeman, G.K., Delaney, R., et al. (1995). Subanesthetic effects of the non-competitive NMDA antagonist, ketamine, in humans: Psychotomimetic, perceptual, cognitive, and neuroendocrine effects. *Archives of General Psychiatry, 51,* 199–214.

Krystal, J.H., Kosten, T.R., Southwick, S., Mason, J.W., Perry, B.D., & Giller, E.L. (1989). Neurobiological aspects of PTSD: Review of clinical and preclinical studies. *Behavior Therapy, 20,* 177–198.

Kucharski, L.T., White, R.M., & Schratz, M. (1979). Age bias, referral for psychological assistance and the private physician. *Journal of Gerontology, 34,* 423–428.

Kuhn, T.S. (1962). *The structure of scientific revolutions.* Chicago: University of Chicago Press.

Kundera, M. (1991). *Immortality.* New York: Grove Press.

Kunst-Wilson, W.R., & Zajonc, R.B. (1980). Affective discrimination of stimuli that cannot be recognized. *Science, 207,* 557–558.

Kuriansky, J.B., Deming, W.E., & Gurland, B.J. (1974). On trends in the diagnosis of schizophrenia. *American Journal of Psychiatry, 131,* 402–407.

Kutchinsky, B. (1970). *Studies on pornography and sex crimes in Denmark.* Copenhagen: New Social Science Monographs.

Lacey, J.I. (1967). Somatic response patterning and stress: Some revisions of activation theory. In M.H. Appley & R. Trumball (Eds.), *Psychological stress.* New York: McGraw-Hill.

Ladd, G.W. (1981). Effectiveness of a social learning method for enhancing children's social interaction and peer acceptance. *Child Development, 52,* 171–178.

Lahey, B.B., Piacentini, J.C., McBurnett, K., Stone, P., Hartdagen, S., & Hynd, G. (1988). Psychopathology in the parents of children with conduct disorder and hyperactivity. *Journal of the American Academy of Child and Adolescent Psychiatry, 27,* 163–170.

Lam, R.W., Zis, A.P., Grewal, A., Delgado, P.L., Charney, D.S., & Krystal, J.H. (1996). Effects of rapid tryptophan depletion in patients with seasonal affective disorder in remission after light therapy. *Archives of General Psychiatry, 53,* 41–46.

Lambert, M.J., & Bergin, A.E. (1994). The effectiveness of psychotherapy. In A.E. Bergin & S.L. Garfield (Eds.), *Handbook of psychotherapy and behavior change.* Fourth edition (pp. 143–189). New

York: Wiley.

Lambert, M.J., Bergin, A.E., & Collins, J.L. (1977). Therapist-induced deterioration in psychotherapy. In A.S. Gurman & A.M. Razin (Eds.), *Effective psychotherapy: A handbook of research.* Elmsford, New York: Pergamon.

Lambert, M.J., Shapiro, D.A., & Bergin, A.E. (1986). The effectiveness of psychotherapy. In S.L. Garfield & A.E. Bergin (Eds.), *Handbook of psychotherapy and behavior change* (3rd ed.). New York: Wiley.

Landman, J.T., & Dawes, R. (1982). Psychotherapy outcome: Smith and Glass's conclusions stand up under scrutiny. *American Psychologist, 37,* 504–516.

Lando, H.A. (1977). Successful treatment of smokers with a broad-spectrum behavioral approach. *Journal of Consulting and Clinical Psychology, 45,* 361–366.

Lane, E.A., & Albee, G.W. (1965). Childhood intellectual differences between schizophrenic adults and their siblings. *American Journal of Orthopsychiatry, 35,* 747–753.

Lang, A.R., Goeckner, D.J., Adessor, V.J., & Marlatt, G.A. (1975). Effects of alcohol on aggression in male social drinkers. *Journal of Abnormal Psychology, 84,* 508–518.

Lang, P.J., & Lazovik, A.D. (1963). Experimental desensitization of a phobia. *Journal of Abnormal and Social Psychology, 66,* 519–525.

Lang, P.J., & Melamed, B.G. (1969). Case report: Avoidance conditioning therapy of an infant with chronic ruminative vomiting. *Journal of Abnormal Psychology, 74,* 1–8.

Lange, A.J., & Jakubowski, P. (1976). *Responsible assertive behavior.* Champaign, IL: Research Press.

Langeluddeke, A. (1963). *Castration of sexual criminals.* Berlin: de Gruyter.

Langenbucher, J.W., & Chung, T. (1995). Onset and staging of DSM-IV alcohol dependence using mean age and survival hazard methods. *Journal of Abnormal Psychology, 104,* 346–354.

Langer, E.J. (1981). Old age: An artifact? In J. McGaugh & S. Kiesler (Eds.), *Aging: Biology and behavior.* New York: Academic Press.

Langer, E.J. (1989). *Mindfulness.* Reading, MA: Addison-Wesley.

Langer, E.J., & Abelson, R.P. (1974). A patient by any other name . . . : Clinician group difference in labelling bias. *Journal of Consulting and Clinical Psychology, 42,* 4–9.

Langer, E.J., & Rodin, J. (1976). The effects of choice and enhanced personal responsibility for the aged. *Journal of Personality and Social Psychology, 34,* 191–198.

Lanyon, R.I. (1986). Theory and treatment of child molestation. *Journal of Consulting and Clinical Psychology, 54*, 176–182.

Lara, M.E., & Klein, D.N. (in press). Processes underlying chronicity in depression.

LaRue, A. (1992). *Aging and neuropsychological assessment.* New York: Plenum.

LaRue, A., Dessonville, C., & Jarvik, L.F. (1985). Aging and mental disorders. In J.E. Birren & K.W. Schaie (Eds.), *Handbook of psychology of aging* (2nd ed.). New York: Van Nostrand-Reinhold.

Lassano, D., del Buono, G., & Latapano, P. (1993). The relationship between obsessive-compulsive personality and obsessive-compulsive disorder: Data obtained by the personality disorder examination. *European Psychiatry, 8*, 219–221.

Last, C.G., & Strauss, C.C. (1990). School refusal in anxiety-disordered children and adolescents. *Journal of the American Academy of Child and Adolescent Psychiatry, 29*, 31–35.

Laub, J.H., & Sampson, R.J. (1995). The long term effects of punitive discipline. In J. McCord (Ed.), *Coercion and punishment in long-term perspective* (pp. 247–258). Cambridge, MA: Cambridge University Press.

Laumann, E.O., Gagnon, J.H., Michael, R.T., & Michaels, S. (1994). *The social organization of sexuality.* Chicago: University of Chicago Press.

Lavelle, T.L., Metalsky, G.I., & Coyne, J.C. (1979). Learned helplessness, test anxiety, and acknowledgment of contingencies. *Journal of Abnormal Psychology, 88*, 381–387.

Law, M., & Tang, J.L. (1995). An analysis of the effectiveness of interventions intended to help people stop smoking. *Archives of Internal Medicine, 155*, 1933–1941.

Lawler, B.A., Sunderland, T., Mellow, A.M., Hill, J.L., Molchan, S.E., et al. (1989). Hyperresponsivity to the serotonin agonist m-chlorophenylpiperazine in Alzheimer's disease. *Archives of General Psychiatry, 46*, 542–548.

Layne, C. (1986). Painful truths about depressives' cognitions. *Journal of Clinical Psychology, 39*, 848–853.

Lazar, I. (1979). Social services in Head Start. In E. Zigler & J. Valentine (Eds.), *Project Head Start.* New York: Free Press.

Lazarus, A.A. (1961). Group therapy of phobic disorders by systematic desensitization. *Journal of Abnormal and Social Psychology, 63*, 504–510.

Lazarus, A.A. (1965). Behavior therapy, incomplete treatment, and symptom substitution. *Journal of Nervous and Mental Disease, 140*, 80–86.

Lazarus, A.A. (1968a). Behavior therapy in groups. In G.M. Gazda (Ed.), *Basic approaches to group psychotherapy and counseling.* Springfield, IL: Charles C. Thomas.

Lazarus, A.A. (1968b). Learning theory and the treatment of depression. *Behavior Research and Therapy, 6*, 83–89.

Lazarus, A.A. (1971). *Behavior therapy and beyond.* New York: McGraw-Hill.

Lazarus, A.A. (1973). Multimodal behavior therapy: Treating the basic ID. *Journal of Nervous and Mental Disease, 156*, 404–411.

Lazarus, A.A. (1989). *The practice of multimodal therapy.* Baltimore: Johns Hopkins University Press.

Lazarus, A.A. (1997). *Brief but comprehensive psychotherapy: The multimodal way.* New York: Springer.

Lazarus, A.A., & Davison, G.C. (1971). Clinical innovation in research and practice. In A.E. Bergin & S.L. Garfield (Eds.), *Handbook of psychotherapy and behavior change: An empirical analysis.* New York: Wiley.

Lazarus, A.A., & Messer, S.B. (1991). Does chaos prevail? An exchange on technical eclecticism and assimilative integration. *Journal of Psychotherapy Integration, 1*, 143–158.

Lazarus, A.A., Davison, G.C., & Polefka, D. (1965). Classical and operant factors in the treatment of school phobia. *Journal of Abnormal Psychology, 70*, 225–229.

Lazarus, R.S. (1966). *Psychological stress and the coping process.* New York: McGraw-Hill.

Lazarus, R.S., & Folkman, S. (1984). *Stress, appraisal, and coping.* New York: Springer.

Lazo, J. (1995). True or false: Expert testimony on repressed memory. *Loyola of Los Angeles Law Review, 28*, 1345–1413.

Leach, S., & Roy, S.S. (1986). Adverse drug reactions: An investigation on an acute geriatric ward. *Age and Ageing, 15* 241–246.

Lebow, J.L., & Gurman, A.S. (1995). Research assessing couple and family therapy. *Annual Review of Psychology, 46*, 27–57.

Lee, D., DeQuattro, V., Cox, T., Pyter, L., Foti, A., Allen, J., Barndt, R., Azen, S., & Davison, G.C. (1987). Neurohormonal mechanisms and left ventricular hypertrophy: Effects of hygienic therapy. *Journal of Human Hypertension, 1*, 147–151.

Lee, S. (1994). The Diagnostic Interview Schedule and anorexia nervosa in Hong Kong. *Archives of General Psychiatry, 51*, 251–252.

Lee, V.E., Brooks-Gunn, J., & Schnur, E. (1988). Does Head Start work? A 1-year follow-up comparison of disadvantaged children attending Head Start, no preschool, and other preschool programs. *Developmental Psychology, 24*, 210–222.

Leenaars, A.A., & Lester, D. (1995). Impact of suicide prevention centers on suicide in Canada. *Crisis, 16*, 39.

Leeper, P. (1988). Having a place to live is vital to good health. *News Report, 38*, 5–8.

Leff, J.P. (1976). Schizophrenia and sensitivity to the family environment. *Schizophrenia Bulletin, 2*, 566–574.

Legido, A., Tonyes, L., Carter, D., Schoemaker, A., DiGeorge, A., & Grover, W.D. (1993). Treatment variables and intellectual outcome in children with classic phenylketonuria: A single-center-based study. *Clinical Pediatrics, 32*, 417–425.

Lehrer, P.M., & Woolfolk, R.L. (1993) *Principles and practice of stress management* (2nd ed.). New York: Guilford.

Lehrer, P.M., Hochron, S.M., Mayne, T., Isenberg, S., & et al. (1994). Relaxation and music therapies for asthma among patients prestabilized on asthma medication. *Journal of Behavioral Medicine, 17*, 1–24.

Lehrer, P.M., Isenberg, S., & Hochron, S.M. (1993). Asthma and emotion: A review. *Journal of Asthma, 30*, 5–21.

Leiblum, S.R., & Rosen, R.C. (Eds.). (1988). *Sexual desire disorders.* New York: Guilford.

Leitenberg, H., Gross, H., Peterson, H., & Rosen, J.C. (1984). Analysis of an anxiety model in the process of change during exposure plus response prevention treatment of bulimia nervosa. *Behavior Therapy, 15*, 3–20.

Leland, J. (1995). A risky Rx for fun. *Newsweek*, p. 74.

Lenane, M.C., Swedo, S.F., Leonard, H., Pauls, D.L., Sceery, W., et al. (1990). Psychiatric disorders in first degree relatives of children and adolescents with obsessive compulsive disorder. *Journal of the American Academy of Child and Adolescent Psychiatry, 29*, 407–412.

Lenzenwenger, M.F., Dworkin, R.H., & Wethington, E. (1991). Examining the underlying structure of schizophrenic phenomenology: Evidence for a 3-process model. *Schizophrenia Bulletin, 17*, 515–524.

Leon, G.R., Fulkerson, J.A., Perry, C.L., & Early-Zald, M.B. (1995). Prospective analysis of personality and behavioral vulnerabilities and gender influences in the later development of disordered eating. *Journal of Abnormal Psychology, 104*, 140–149.

Lerer, B., Bleich, A., Kotler, M., Garb, R., Hertzberg, M., & Levin, B. (1987). Posttraumatic stress disorder in Israeli combat veterans. *Archives of General Psychiatry, 44*, 976–981.

Lerman, C., & Glanz, K. (1997). Stress, coping, and health behavior. In K. Glanz, F. Lewis, & B. Rimer (Eds.), *Health behavior and health education: Theory, research and practice* San Francisco: Jossey-Bass.

Lerman, C., Schwartz, M.D., Miller, S.M., Daly, M., Sands, C., & Rimer, B.K. (1996). A randomized trial of breast cancer risk counseling: Interacting effects of counseling, educational level, and coping style. *Health Psychology, 15,* 75–83.

Lerner, H.P. (1983). Contemporary psychoanalytic perpectives on gorge-vomiting: A case illustration. *International Journal of Eating Disorders, 3,* 47–63.

Lesage, A., & Lamontagne, Y. (1985). Paradoxical intention and exposure *in vivo* in the treatment of psychogenic nausea: Report of two cases. *Behavioral Psychotherapy, 13,* 69–75.

Lesperance, F., Frasure-Smith, N., & Talajic, M. (1996). Major depression before and after myocardial infarction: Its nature and consequences. *Psychosomatic Medicine, 58,* 99–110.

Lester, D. (1991). Do suicide prevention centers prevent suicide? *Homeostasis in Health and Disease, 33,* 190–194.

Leuchter, A.F. (1985). Assessment and treatment of the late-onset psychoses. *Hospital and Community Psychiatry, 36,* 815–818.

Levenson, M. (1972). *Cognitive and perceptual factors in suicidal individuals.* Unpublished doctoral dissertation, University of Kansas, Lawrence.

Levin, R.L. (1992). The mechanisms of human female sexual arousal. *Annual Review of Sex Research, 3,* 1–48.

Levine, S.B., & Yost, M.A. (1976). Frequency of sexual dysfunction in a general gynecological clinic: An epidemiological approach. *Archives of Sexual Behavior, 5,* 229–238.

Levitsky, A., & Perls, F.S. (1970). The rules and games of Gestalt therapy. In J. Fagan & I.L. Shepherd (Eds.), *Gestalt therapy now: Theory, techniques, applications.* Palo Alto, CA: Science & Behavior Books.

Levy, S.M., Herberman, R.B., Whiteside, T., Sanzo, K., Lee, J., & Kirkwood, J. (1990). Perceived social support and tumor estrogen/progesterone receptor status as predictors of natural killer cell activity in breast cancer patients. *Psychosomatic Medicine, 52,* 73–85.

Lewinsohn, P.M. (1974). A behavioral approach to depression. In R.J. Friedman and M.M. Katz (Eds.), *The psychology of depression: Contemporary theory and research.* Washington, DC: Winston-Wiley.

Lewinsohn, P.M., Clarke, G.N., Hops, H., & Andrews, J. (1990). Cognitive-behavioral treatment for depressed adolescents. *Behavior Therapy, 21,* 385–401.

Lewinsohn, P.M., Hops, H., Roberts, R.E., Seeley, J.R., & Andrews, J.A. (1993). Adolescent psychopathology: 1. prevalence and incidence of depression and other DSM-III disorders in high school students. *Journal of Abnormal Psychology, 102,* 133–144.

Lewinsohn, P.M., Mischef, W., Chapion, W., & Barton, R. (1980). Social competence and depression: The role of illusory self-perceptions. *Journal of Abnormal Psychology, 89,* 203–212.

Lewinsohn, P.M., Roberts, R.E., Seeley, J.R., Rohde, P., Gotlib, I.H., & Hops, H. (1994). Adolescent psychopathology: 2. Psychosocial risk factors for depression. *Journal of Abnormal Psychology, 103,* 302–315.

Lewinsohn, P.M., Rohde, P., Fischer, S.A., & Seeley, J.R. (1991). Age and depression: Unique and shared effects. *Psychology and Aging, 6,* 247–260.

Lewinsohn, P.M., Steimetz, J.L., Larsen, D.W., & Franklin, J. (1981). Depression related cognitions: Antecedent or consequences? *Journal of Abnormal Psychology, 90,* 213–219.

Lewinsohn, P.M., Weinstein, M., & Alper, T. (1970). A behavioral approach to the group treatment of depressed persons: A methodological contribution. *Journal of Clinical Psychology, 26,* 525–532.

Ley, R. (1987). Panic disorder: A hyperventilation interpretation. In L. Michelson & L.M. Asher (Eds.), *Anxiety and stress disorders.* New York: Guilford.

Li, T-K., Lumeng, L., McBride, W.J., & Waller, M.B. (1981). Indiana selection studies on alcohol related behaviors. In R.A. McClearn, R.A. Deitrich, & V.G. Erwin (Eds.), *Development of animal models as pharmacogenetic tools.* Washington, DC: U.S. Government Printing Office.

Liberman, R.P. (1972). Reinforcement of social interaction in a group of chronic mental patients. In R. Rubin et al., *Advances in behavior therapy.* New York: Academic Press.

Liberman, R.P. (1994). Psychosocial treatments for schizophrenia. *Psychiatry: Interpersonal and Biological Processes, 57,* 104–114.

Liberman, R.P. (Ed.) (1992). *Handbook of psychiatric rehabilitation.* New York: Macmillan.

Liberman, R.P., DeRisi, W.J., & Mueser, K.T. (1989). *Social skills training for psychiatric patients.* Elmsford, NY: Pergamon.

Liberto, J.G., Oslin, D.W., & Ruskin, P.E. (1996). Alcoholism in the older population. In L.L. Carstensen, B.A. Edelstein, & L. Dornbrand (Eds.), *The practical handbook of clinical gerontology* (pp. 324–348). Thousand Oaks, CA: Sage.

Liebenluft, E. (1996). Women with bipolar illness: Clinical and research issues. *American Journal of Psychiatry, 153,* 163–173.

Lieberman, M.A., Yalom, J.D., & Miles, M.B. (1973). *Encounter groups: First facts.* New York: Basic Books.

Liebert, R.M., Neale, J.M., & Davidson, E.S. (1973). *The early window.* Elmsford, NY: Pergamon.

Liebson, I. (1967). Conversion reaction: A teaming theory approach. *Behaviour Research and Therapy, 7,* 217–218.

Lief, H.I. (1988). Foreword. In S.R. Leiblum & R.C. Rosen (Eds.), *Sexual desire disorders.* New York: Guilford.

Lief, H.I., & Hubschman, L. (1993). Orgasm in the postoperative transsexual. *Archives of Sexual Behavior, 22,* 145–155.

Lifton, R.J. (1976). Advocacy and corruption in the healing profession. In N.L. Goldman & D.R. Segal (Eds.), *The social psychology of military service.* Beverly Hills, CA: Sage.

Light, E., & Lebowitz, B.D. (Eds.). (1991). *The elderly with chronic mental illness.* New York: Springer.

Light, K.C., Dolan, C.A., Davis, M.R., & Sherwood, A. (1992). Cardiovascular responses to an active coping challenge as predictors of blood pressure patterns 10 to 15 years later. *Psychosomatic Medicine, 54,* 217–230.

Light, L.L. (1990). Interactions between memory and language in old age. In J.E. Birren & K.W. Schaie (Eds.), *Handbook of the psychology of aging* (pp. 275–290). San Diego: Academic Press.

Lindemann, E. (1944). Symptomatology and management of acute grief. *American Journal of Psychiatry, 101,* 141–148.

Linehan, M.M. (1985). The reasons for living inventory. In P. Keller & L. Ritt (Eds.), *Innovations in clinical practice: A sourcebook* (pp. 321–330). Sarasota, FL: Professional Resource Exchange.

Linehan, M.M. (1987). Dialectical behavior therapy for borderline personality disorder. *Bulletin of the Menninger Clinic, 51,* 261–276.

Linehan, M.M. (1993a). *Behavioral skills training manual for treating borderline personality disorder.* New York: Guilford Press.

Linehan, M.M. (1993b). *Cognitive behavioral treatment of borderline personality disorder: The dialectics of effective treatment.* New York: Guilford.

Linehan, M.M., & Shearin, E.N. (1988). Lethal stress: A social-behavioral model of suicidal behavior. In S. Fisher & J. Reason (Eds.), *Handbook of life stress, cognition, and health.* New York: Wiley.

Linehan, M.M., Armstrong, H.E., Suarez, A., Allmon, D., & Heard, H.L. (1991).

Cognitive-behavioral treatment of chronically parasuicidal borderline patients. *Archives of General Psychiatry, 48,* 1060–1064.

Linehan, M.M., Camper, P., Chiles, J.A., Strosahl, K., & Shearin, E.N. (1987). Interpersonal problem-solving and parasuicide. *Cognitive Therapy and Research, 11,* 1–12.

Linehan, M.M., Goodstein, J.L., Nielsen, S.L., & Chiles, J.A. (1983). Reasons for staying alive when you are thinking of killing yourself. *Journal of Consulting and Clinical Psychology, 51,* 276–286.

Linehan, M.M., Heard, H.L., & Armstrong, H.E. (1992). *Naturalistic follow-up of a behavioral treatment for chronically parasuicidal borderline patients.* Unpublished manuscript, University of Washington, Seattle.

Link, B., Cullen, F., Frank, J., & Wozniak, J. (1987). The social rejection of former mental patients: Understanding why labels matter. *American Journal of Sociology, 92,* 1401–1500.

Linney, J.A. (1989). Optimizing research strategies in the schools. In L.A. Bond & B.E. Compas (Eds.), *Primary prevention and promotion in the schools* (pp. 50–76). Newbury Park, CA: Sage.

Lion, J.R. (1978). Outpatient treatment of psychopaths. In W.H. Reid (Ed.), *The psychopath: A comprehensive study of antisocial disorders and behaviors.* New York: Brunner/Mazel.

Lipowski, C.J. (1990). *Acute confusional states.* New York: Oxford University Press.

Lipowski, P., Kerkhofs, M., VanOnderbergen, A., Hubain, P., Copinschi, G., & et al. (1994). The 24 hour profiles of cortisol, prolactin, and growth hormone secretion in mania. *Archives of General Psychiatry, 51,* 616–624.

Lipowski, Z.J. (1980). *Delirium: Acute brain failure in man.* Springfield, IL: Charles C. Thomas.

Lipowski, Z.J. (1983). Transient cognitive disorders (delirium and acute confusional states) in the elderly. *American Journal of Psychiatry, 140,* 1426–1436.

Liskow, B. (1982). Substance induced and substance use disorders: Barbiturates and similarly acting sedative hypnotics. In J.H. Greist, J.W. Jefferson, & R.L. Spitzer (Eds.), *Treatment of mental disorders.* New York: Oxford University Press.

Liston, E.H. (1982). Delirium in the aged. In L.E. Jarvik & G.W. Small (Eds.), *Psychiatric clinics of North America.* Philadelphia: Saunders.

Litwack, T.R. (1985). The prediction of violence. *The Clinical Psychologist, 38,* 87–90.

Livesley, W.J., Schroeder, M.L., & Jackson, D.N. (1990). Dependent personality and attachment problems. *Journal of Personality Disorders, 4,* 131–140.

Livesley, W.J., Schroeder, M.L., Jackson, D.N., & Jung, K.L. (1994). Categorical distinctions in the study of personality disorder: Implications for classification. *Journal of Abnormal Psychology, 103,* 6–17.

Lobitz, W.C., & Post, R.D. (1979). Parameters of self-reinforcement and depression. *Journal of Abnormal Psychology, 88,* 33–41.

Loeber, R., & Keenan, K. (1994). Interaction between conduct disorder and its comorbid conditions: Effects of age and gender. *Clinical Psychology Review, 14,* 497–523.

Loeber, R., Lahey, B., & Thomas, C. (1991). Diagnostic conundrum of oppositional defiant disorder and conduct disorder. *Journal of Abnormal Psychology, 100,* 379–390.

Loeber, R., Stouthamer-Loeber, M., Van Kammen, W., & Farrington, D.P. (1989). Development of a new measure of self-reported antisocial behavior for young children: Prevalence and reliability. In M. Klein (Ed.), *Cross-national research in self-reported crime and delinquency* (pp. 203–226). Boston: Kluwer-Nijhoff.

Loftus, E.F. (1993). The reality of repressed memories. *American Psychologist, 48,* 518–537.

Loftus, E.F., & Ketchum, K. (1994). *The myth of repressed memory: False memories and allegations of sexual abuse.* New York: St. Martin's Press.

London, P. (1964). *The modes and morals of psychotherapy.* New York: Holt, Rinehart & Winston.

London, P. (1986). *The modes and morals of psychotherapy* (2nd ed.). New York: Hemisphere.

Loney, J., Langhorne, J.E., Jr., & Paternite, C.E. (1978). An empirical basis for subgrouping the hyperkinetic-minimal brain dysfunction syndrome. *Journal of Abnormal Psychology, 87,* 431–441.

Long, W.R. (1995, November 24). A changing world proves deadly to Brazil Indians. *Los Angeles Times,* pp. A1, A47, A48.

Looman, J. (1995). Sexual fantasies of child molesters. *Canadian Journal of Behavioural Science, 27,* 321–332.

Lopez, S.R. (1989). Patient variable biases in clinical judgment: Conceptual overview and methodological considerations. *Psychological Bulletin, 106,* 184–203.

Lopez, S.R. (1994). Latinos and the expression of psychopathology: A call for direct assessment of cultural influences. In C. Telles & M. Karno (Eds.), *Latino mental health: Current research and policy perspectives.* Los Angeles: UCLA.

Lopez, S.R. (1996). Testing ethnic minority children. In B.B. Wolman (Ed.), *The encyclopedia of psychology, psychiatry, and psychoanalysis.* New York: Henry Holt.

Lopez, S.R., & Hernandez, P. (1986). How culture is considered in evaluations of psychopathology. *Journal of Nervous and Mental Disease, 176,* 598–606.

Lopez, S.R., & Romero, A. (1988). Assessing the intellectual functioning of Spanish-speaking adults: Comparison of the EIWA and the WAIS. *Professional Psychology: Research and Practice, 19,* 263–270.

Lopez, S.R., & Taussig, I.M. (1991). Cognitive-intellectual functioning of Spanish-speaking impaired and nonimpaired elderly: Implications for culturally sensitive assessment. *Psychological Assessment: A Journal of Consulting and Clinical Psychology, 3,* 448–454.

Lopez, S.R., Lopez, A.A., & Fong, K.T. (1991). Mexican Americans' initial preferences for counselors: The role of ethnic factors. *Journal of Counseling Psychology, 38,* 487–496.

LoPiccolo, J. (1977). Direct treatment of sexual dysfunction in the couple. In J. Money & H. Musaph (Eds.), *Handbook of sexology.* New York: Elsevier/North-Holland.

LoPiccolo, J. (1991). Counseling and therapy for sexual problems in the elderly. *Clinics in Geriatric Medicine, 7,* 161–179.

LoPiccolo, J. (1992a). Post-modern sex therapy for erectile failure. In R.C. Rosen & S.R. Leiblum (Eds.), *Erectile failure: Assessment and treatment.* New York: Guilford.

LoPiccolo, J. (1992b). Psychological evaluation of erectile failure. In R. Kirby, C. Carson, & G. Webster (Eds.), *Diagnosis and management of male erectile failure dysfunction.* Oxford: Butterworth-Heinemann.

LoPiccolo, J. (in press). Sex therapy: A post-modern model. In S.J. Lynn & J.P. Garske (Eds.), *Contemporary psychotherapies: Models and methods.* New York: Merrill.

LoPiccolo, J., & Friedman, J. (1988). Broad-spectrum treatment of low sexual desire: Integration of cognitive, behavioral, and systemic therapy. In S. Leiblum & R.C. Rosen (Eds.), *Sexual desire disorders.* New York: Guilford.

LoPiccolo, J., & Friedman, J.M. (1985). Sex therapy: An integrated model. In S.J. Lynn & J.P. Garskee (Eds.), *Contemporary psychotherapies: Models and methods.* New York: Merrill.

LoPiccolo, J., & Hogan, D.R. (1979). Multidimensional treatment of sexual dysfunction. In O.F. Pomerleau & J.P. Brady (Eds.), *Behavioral medicine: Theory and practice.* Baltimore: Williams & Wilkins.

LoPiccolo, J., & Stock, W.E. (1987). Sexual function, dysfunction, and counseling in gynecological practice. In Z. Rosenwaks, F. Benjamin, & M.L. Stone (Eds.), *Gynecology*. New York: Macmillan.

LoPiccolo, J., Heiman, J., Hogan, D., & Roberts, C. (1985). Effectiveness of single therapists vs. co-therapy teams in sex therapy. *Journal of Consulting and Clinical Psychology, 53*, 287–294.

Loranger, A., Oldham, J., Russakoff, L.M. & Susman, V. (1987). Structured interviews and borderline personality disorder. *Archives of General Psychiatry, 41*, 565–568

Loranger, A.W., Sartorius, N., Andreoli, A., Berger, P., Buchleim, P., et al. (1994). The International Personality Disorders Examination: The World Health Organization/Alcohol, Drug Abuse and Mental Health Administration international pilot study of personality disorders. *Archives of General Psychiatry, 51*, 215–223.

Lotter, V. (1974). Factors related to outcome in autistic children. *Journal of Autism and Childhood Schizophrenia, 4*, 263–277.

Lotter, V. (1978). Follow-up studies. In M. Rutter & E. Schopler (Eds.), *Autism: A reappraisal of concepts and treatment*. New York: Plenum.

Lovaas, O.I. (1987). Behavioral treatment and normal educational and intellectual functioning in young autistic children. *Journal of Consulting and Clinical Psychology, 55*, 3–9.

Lovaas, O.I., Berberich, J.P., Perloff, B.F., & Schaeffer, B. (1966). Acquisition of imitative speech by schizophrenic children. *Science, 151*, 705–707.

Lovaas, O.I., Freitag, G., Gold, V.J., & Kassoria, I.C. (1965). Experimental studies in childhood schizophrenia: Analysis of self-destructive behavior. *Journal of Applied Behavior Analysis, 6*, 131–166.

Lovaas, O.I., Newsom, C., & Hickman, C. (1987). Self-stimulatory behavior and perceptual reinforcement. *Journal of Applied Behavior Analysis, 20*, 45–68.

Lovass, O.I., Schreibman, L., Koegel, R., & Rehm, R. (1971). Selective responding by autistic children to multiple sensory input. *Journal of Abnormal Psychology, 77*, 221–222.

Lubin, B. (1983). Group therapy. In I.B. Weiner (Ed.), *Clinical methods in psychology* (2nd ed.). New York: Wiley.

Luborsky, L., & Spence, D.P. (1978). Quantitative research on psychoanalytic therapy. In S.L. Garfield & A.E. Bergin (Eds.), *Handbook of psychotherapy and behavior change: An empirical analysis* (2nd ed.). New York: Wiley.

Luborsky, L., Barber, J.P., & Crits-Christoph, P. (1990). Theory-based research for understanding the process of dynamic psychotherapy. *Journal of Consulting and Clinical Psychology, 58*, 281–287.

Luborsky, L., Crits-Christoph, P., Melon, J., & Auerbach, A. (1988). *Who will benefit from psychotherapy: Predicting therapeutic outcomes*. New York: Basic Books.

Luepnitz, R.R., Randolph, D.L., & Gutsch, K.U. (1982). Race and socioeconomic status as confounding variables in the accurate diagnosis of alcoholism. *Journal of Clinical Psychology, 38*, 665–669.

Lykken, D.T. (1957). A study of anxiety in the sociopathic personality. *Journal of Abnormal and Social Psychology, 55*, 6–10.

Lynam, D.R. (1996). Early identification of chronic offenders: Who is the fledgling psychopath? *Psychological Bulletin, 120*, 209–234.

Lyon, G.R., & Moats, L.C. (1988). Critical issues in the instruction of the learning disabled. *Journal of Consulting and Clinical Psychology, 56*, 830–835.

Lyons, M.J., True, W.S., Eisen, A., Goldberg, J., Meyer, J.M., et al. (1995). Differential heritability of adult and juvenile antisocial traits. *Archives of General Psychiatry, 52*, 906–915.

Lystad, M.M. (1957). Social mobility among selected groups of schizophrenics. *American Sociological Review, 22*, 288–292.

Maccoby, N., & Alexander, J. (1980). Use of media in lifestyle programs. In P.O. Davidson & S.M. Davidson (Eds.), *Behavioral medicine: Changing health lifestyles*. New York: Brunner/Mazel.

Maccoby, N., & Altman, D.G. (1988). Disease prevention in communities: The Stanford Heart Disease Prevention Program. In R.H. Price, E.L. Cowen, R.P. Lorion, & J. Ramos-McKay (Eds.), *14 ounces of prevention: A casebook for practitioners* (pp. 165–174). Washington, DC: American Psychological Association.

Maccoby, N., Farquhar, J.W., Wood, P.D., & Alexander, J. (1977). Reducing the risk of cardiovascular disease: Effects of a community-based campaign on knowledge and behavior. *Journal of Community Health, 3*, 100–114.

MacLeod, C., & Hemsley, D.R. (1985). Visual feedback of vocal intensity in the treatment of hysterical aphonia. *Journal of Behaviour Therapy and Experimental Psychiatry, 4*, 347–353.

MacLeod, C., Mathews, A., & Tata, P. (1986). Attentional bias in emotional disorders. *Journal of Abnormal Psychology, 95*, 15–20.

MacNamara, M. (1993). Fade away: The rise and fall of the repressed memory theory in the courtroom. *California Lawyer, 15*, 36–41.

Madonna, P.G., Van Scoyk, S., & Jones, D.B. (1991). Family interactions within incest and nonincest families. *American Journal of Psychiatry, 148*, 46–49.

Magee, W.J., Eaton, W.W., Wittchern, H.U., McGonagle, K.A., & Kessler, R.C. (1996). Agoraphobia, simple phobia and social phobia in the National Comorbidity Survey. *Archives of General Psychiatry, 53*, 159–168.

Maher, B.A. (1966). *Principles of psychopathology: An experimental approach*. New York: McGraw-Hill.

Maher, B.A. (1974). *Journal of Consulting and Clinical Psychology, 42*, 1–3 [Editorial].

Mahoney, L.J. (1977). Early diagnosis of breast cancer: The breast self-examination problem. *Progress in Clinical and Biological Research, 12*, 203–206.

Mahoney, M.J. (1974). *Cognition and behavior modification*. Cambridge, MA: Ballinger.

Mahoney, M.J. (1982). Psychotherapy and human change processes. In *Psychotherapy research and behavior change* (Vol. 1). Washington, DC: American Psychological Association.

Mahoney, M.J. (1991). *Human change processes: Notes on the facilitation of human development*. New York: Basic Books.

Mahoney, M.J. (1991). *Human change processes: The scientific foundations of psychotherapy*. New York: Basic Books.

Mahoney, M.J. (1993). Theoretical developments in the cognitive psychotherapies. *Journal of Consulting and Clinical Psychology, 7*, 138–157.

Mahoney, M.J., & Moes, A.J. (1997). Complexity and psychotherapy: Promising dialogues and practical issues. In F. Masterpasque & A. Perna (Eds.), *The psychological meaning of chaos: Self-organization in human development and psychotherapy*. Washington, DC: American Psychological Association.

Malamuth, N.M., & Check, J.V.P. (1983). Sexual arousal to rape depictions: Individual differences. *Journal of Abnormal Psychology, 92*, 55–67.

Malatesta, C.Z., & Izard, C.E. (1984). The facial expression of emotion: Young, middle-aged, and older adult expressions. In C.Z. Malatesta & C.E. Izard (Eds.), *Emotion in adult development* (pp. 253–273). Beverly Hills, CA: Sage.

Maletzky, B.M. (1991). *Treating the sexual offender*. Newbury Park, CA: Sage.

Mandler, G. (1966). Anxiety. In D.L. Sills (Ed.), *International encyclopedia of the social sciences*. New York: Macmillan.

Mandler, G. (1972). Helplessness: Theory and research in anxiety. In C.D. Spielberger (Ed.), *Anxiety: Current trends in theory and research*. New York: Academic

Press.

Mangalmurti, V.S. (1994). Psychotherapists' fear of *Tarasoff*: All in the mind? *Journal of Psychiatry and Law, 22,* 379–409.

Manji, H.K., Chen, G., Shimon, H., Hsiao, J.K., Potter, W.Z., & Belmaker, R.H. (1995). Guanine nucleotide-binding proteins in bipolar affective disorder: Effects of long-term lithium treatment. *Archives of General Psychiatry, 52,* 135–144.

Mann, V.A., & Brady, S. (1988). Reading disability: The role of language deficiencies. *Journal of Consulting and Clinical Psychology, 56,* 811–816.

Mannuzza, S., Klein, R.G., Bonagura, N., Malloy, P., Giampino, T.L., & Addalli, K.A. (1991). Hyperactive boys almost grown up: 5. Replication of psychiatric status. *Archives of General Psychiatry, 48,* 77–83.

Mannuzza, S., Schneier, F.R., Chapman, T.F., Leibowitz, M.R., Klein, D.F., & Fyer, A.J. (1995). Generalized social phobia: Reliability and validity. *Archives of General Psychiatry, 52,* 230–237.

Manos, N., Vasilopoulou, E., & Sotiriou, M. (1987). DSM-III diagnoses of borderline disorder and depression. *Journal of Personality Disorders, 1,* 263–268.

Manton, K.G., Blazer, D.G., & Woodbury, M.A. (1987). Suicide in middle age and later life: Sex and race specific life table and cohort analyses. *Journal of Gerontology, 42,* 219–227.

Manuck, S.B., Kaplan, J.R., Adams, M.R., & Clarkson, T.B. (1989). Behaviorally elicited heart rate reactivity and atherosclerosis in female cynomolgus monkeys (*Macaca fascicularis*). *Psychosomatic Medicine, 51,* 306–318.

Manuck, S.B., Kaplan, J.R., & Clarkson, T.B. (1983). Behaviorally induced heart rate reactivity and atherosclerosis in cynomolgus monkeys. *Psychosomatic Medicine, 49,* 95–108.

March, J.S. (1995). Cognitive-behavioral psychotherapy for children and adolescents with OCD: A review and recommendations for treatment. *Journal of the American Academy of Child and Adolescent Psychiatry, 34,* 7–18.

Marcus, J., Hans, S.L., Nagier, S., Auerbach, J.G., Mirsky, A.F., & Aubrey, A. (1987). Review of the NIMH Israeli Kibbutz-City and the Jerusalem infant development study. *Schizophrenia Bulletin, 13,* 425–438.

Marder, S.R., & Meibach, R.C. (1994). Risperidone in the treatment of schizophrenia. *American Journal of Psychiatry, 151,* 825–836.

Marder, S.R., Wirshing, W.C., Mintz, J., McKenzie, J., Johnston, K., et al. (1996). Two-year outcome of social-skills train-ing and group psychotherapy for outpatients with schizophrenia. *American Journal of Psychiatry, 153,* 1585–1592.

Marder, S.R., Wirshing, W.C., VanPutten, T., Mintz, J., McKenzie, R.N., et al. (1994). Fluphenazine vs. placebo supplementation for prodromal sign of relapse in schizophrenia. *Archives of General Psychiatry, 51,* 280–287.

Marengo, J., & Westermeyer, J.F. (1996). Schizophrenia and delusional disorder. In L.L. Carstensen, B.A. Edelstein, & L. Dornbrand (Eds.), *The practical handbook of clinical gerontology* (pp. 255–273). Thousand Oaks, CA: Sage.

Margolin, G. (1981). Behavior exchange in happy and unhappy marriages: A family cycle perspective. *Behavior Therapy, 12,* 329–343.

Margolin, G. (1982). Ethical and legal considerations in marital and family therapy. *American Psychologist, 37,* 788–801.

Margolin, G., & Burman, B. (1993). Wife abuse vs. marital violence: Different terminologies, explanations, and solutions. *Clinical Psychology Review, 13,* 59–73.

Margolin, G., & Fernandez, V. (1985). Marital dysfunction. In M. Hersen & A.S. Bellack (Eds.), *Handbook of clinical behavior therapy with adults.* New York: Plenum.

Margolin, G., & Wampold, B.F. (1981). Sequential analysis of conflict and accord in distressed and non-distressed marital partners. *Journal of Consulting and Clinical Psychology, 49,* 554–567.

Marijuana research findings. (1980). Washington, DC: U.S. Government Printing Office.

Margraf, J., Ehlers, A., & Roth, W.T. (1986). Sodium lactate infusions and panic attacks: A review and critique. *Psychosomatic Medicine, 48,* 23–51.

Markman, H.J., Floyd, F.J., Stanley, S.M., & Storaasli, R.D. (1989). Prevention of marital distress: A longitudinal investigation. *Journal of Consulting and Clinical Psychology, 56,* 210–217.

Markman, H.J., Silvern, L., Clements, M., & Kraft-Hanak, S. (1993). Men and women dealing with conflict in heterosexual relationships. *Journal of Social Issues, 49,* 107–125.

Markovitz, J.H., Matthews, K.A., Kiss, J., & Smitherman, T.C. (1996). Effects of hostility on platelet reactivity to stress in coronary heart disease patients and in healthy controls. *Psychosomatic Medicine, 58,* 143–149.

Markowitz, J.C., Rabkin, J., & Perry, S. (1994). Treating depression in HIV-positive patients. *AIDS, 8,* 403–412.

Marks, I.M. (1969). *Fears and phobias.* New York: Academic Press.

Marks, I.M. (1995). Advances in behavioral-cognitive therapy of social phobia. *Journal of Clinical Psychiatry, 56,* 25–31.

Marks, I.M., & Gelder, M.G. (1967). Transvestism and fetishism: Clinical and psychological changes during faradic aversion. *British Journal of Psychiatry, 113,* 711–729.

Marks, I.M., Gelder, M.G., & Bancroft, J. (1970). Sexual deviants two years after electrical aversion. *British Journal of Psychiatry, 117,* 73–85.

Marlatt, G.A. (1983). The controlled drinking controversy: A commentary. *American Psychologist, 38,* 1097–1110.

Marlatt, G.A. (1985). Relapse prevention: Theoretical rationale and overview of the model. In G.A. Marlatt & J. Gordon (Eds.), *Relapse prevention: Maintenance strategies in addictive behavior change.* New York: Guilford.

Marlatt, G.A., & Gordon, J.R. (1985). (Eds.), *Relapse prevention: Maintenance strategies in the treatment of addictive behaviors.* New York: Guilford.

Marmar, C., & Horowitz, M.J. (1988). Diagnosis and phase-oriented treatment of post-traumatic stress disorders. In J. Wilson (Ed.), *Human adaptation to extreme stress: From the Holocaust to Vietnam.* New York: Brunner/Mazel.

Marmor, J. (1962). Psychoanalytic therapy as an educational process: Common denominators in the therapeutic approaches of different psychoanalytic schools. In J.H. Masserman (Ed.), *Science and psychoanalysis: Vol. 5. Psychoanalytic education.* New York: Grune & Stratton.

Marmor, J. (1971). Dynamic psychotherapy and behavior therapy: Are they irreconcilable? *Archives of General Psychiatry, 24,* 22–28.

Marrazzi, M.A., & Luby, E.D. (1986). An auto-addiction model of chronic anorexia nervosa. *International Journal of Eating Disorders, 5,* 191–208.

Marsh, B. (1996, July 7). Meth at work: In virtually every industry, use among employees is on the rise [editorial]. *Los Angeles Times,* pp. D1-D4.

Marshall, W.L., Barabee, H.E., & Christophe, D. (1986). Sexual offenders against female children: Sexual preferences for age of victims and type of behavior. *Canadian Journal of Behavioural Science, 18,* 424–439.

Marshall, W.L., Jones, R., Ward, T., Johnston, P., & Barabee, H.E. (1991). Treatment outcomes with sex offenders. *Clinical Psychology Review, 11,* 465–485.

Martin, J.E., Dubbert, P.M., & Cushman, W.C. (1991). Controlled trial of aerobic exercise in hypertension. *Circulation, 81,* 1560–1567.

Martin, P.A., & Bird, H.W. (1953). An approach to the psychotherapy of marriage partners—The stereoscopic technique. *Psychiatry, 16,* 123–127.

Martin, R. (1975). *Legal challenges to behavior modification: Trends in schools, corrections, and mental health.* Champaign, IL.: Research Press.

Maruish, M.E., Sawicki, R.F., Franzen, M.D., & Golden, C.J. (1984). Alpha coefficient reliabilities for the Luria–Nebraska Neuropsychological Battery summary and localization scales by diagnostic category. *The International Journal of Clinical Neuropsychology, 7,* 10–12.

Marziali, E. (1984). Prediction of outcome of brief psychotherapy from therapist interpretive interventions. *Archives of General Psychiatry, 41,* 301–304.

Masling, J. (1960). The influences of situational and interpersonal variables in projective testing. *Psychological Bulletin, 57,* 65–85.

Maslow, A.H. (1968). *Toward a psychology of being.* New York: Van Nostrand-Reinhold.

Masson, J.M. (1984). *The assault on truth: Freud's suppression of the seduction theory.* New York: Farrar, Strauss, Giroux.

Masters, W.H., & Johnson, V.E. (1966). *Human sexual response.* Boston: Little, Brown.

Masters, W.H., & Johnson, V.E. (1970). *Human sexual inadequacy.* Boston: Little, Brown.

Masters, W.H., Johnson, V.E., & Kolodny, R.C. (1988). *Human sexuality* (3rd ed.). Boston: Little Brown.

Mathe, A., & Knapp, P. (1971). Emotional and adrenal reactions of stress in bronchial asthma. *Psychosomatic Medicine, 33,* 323–329.

Mathews, A., & MacLeod, C. (1994). Cognitive approaches to emotion and emotional disorders. In L.W. Porter & M.R. Rosenzweig (Eds.), *Annual Review of Psychology* (pp. 25–50). Stanford, CA: Stanford University Press.

Matsumoto, A., Murakami, S., & Arai, Y. (1988). Neurotropic effects of estrogen on the neonatal preoptic area grafted into the adult rat brain. *Cell and Tissue Research, 252,* 33–37.

Matthews, K.A. (1982). Psychological perspectives on the type A behavior pattern. *Psychological Bulletin, 91,* 293–323.

Matthews, K.A., & Rakaczky, C.J. (1987). Familial aspects of type A behavior and physiologic reactivity to stress. In T. Dembroski & T. Schmidt (Eds.), *Behavioral factors in coronary heart disease.* Heidelberg: Springer-Verlag.

Matthews, K.A., Meilan, E., Kuller, L.M., Kelsey, S.F., Caggiula, A., et al. (1989). Menopause and risk factors in coronary heart disease. *New England Journal of Medicine, 321,* 641–646.

Matthews, K.A., Glass, D.C., Rosenman, R.H., & Bonner, R.W. (1977). Competi-

tive drive, pattern A, and coronary heart disease: A further analysis of some data from the Western Collaborative Group Study. *Journal of Chronic Diseases, 30,* 489–498.

Matthews, K.A., Woodall, K.L., Jacob, T., & Kenyon, K. (1995). Negative family environment as a predictor of boy's future status on measures of hostile attitudes, interview behavior, and anger expression. *Health Psychology, 15,* 30–37.

Mattick, R.P., & Andrews, G. (1994). Social phobia. In M. Hersen & R.T. Ammerman (Eds.), *Handbook of prescriptive treatments for adults* (pp. 157–177). New York: Plenum.

Mattson, M.E., Allen, J.P., Longabaugh, R., Nickless, C.J., Connors, G.J., & Kadden, R.M. (1994). A chronological review of empirical studies matching alcoholic clients to treatment. *Journal of Studies on Alcohol, 55,* 16–29.

Maugh, T.H.I. (1996a, July 10). AIDS forum addresses ways to help women. *Los Angeles Times,* p. A6.

Maugh, T.H. (1996b, July 7). Experts alarmed by HIV spread, hopeful on prevention. *Los Angeles Times,* p. A6.

Maugh, T.H. (1996c, July 4) New AIDS drug therapies could check epidemic. *Los Angeles Times,* pp. A1, A24.

Maugh, T.H. (1996d, July 11). New AIDS test may predict disease's course. *Los Angeles Times,* pp. A1, A8.

Mavissikalian, M., Hammen, M.S., & Jones, B. (1990). DSM-III personality disorders in obsessive-compulsive disorder. *Comprehensive Psychiatry, 31,* 432–437.

Mays, D.T., & Franks, C.M. (1980). Getting worse: Psychotherapy or no treatment-The jury should still be out. *Professional Psychology, 11,* 78–92.

McArthur, D.S., & Roberts, G.E. (1982). *Roberts Apperception Test for Children Manual.* Los Angeles: Western Psychological Services.

McBride, P.A., Anderson, G.M., & Shapiro, T. (1996). Autism research: Bringing together approaches to pull apart the disorder. *Archives of General Psychiatry, 53,* 980–983.

McCarthy, B.W. (1986). A cognitive-behavioral approach to understanding and treating sexual trauma. *Journal of Sex and Marital Therapy, 12,* 322–329.

McConaghy, N. (1990). Sexual deviation. In A.S. Bellack, M. Hersen, & A.E. Kazdin (Eds.), *International handbook of behavior modification and therapy* (2nd ed., pp. 565–580). New York: Plenum.

McConaghy, N. (1994). Paraphilias and gender identity disorders. In M. Hersen & R.T. Ammerman (Eds.), *Handbook of prescriptive treatments for adults* (pp.

317–346). New York: Plenum.

McConaghy, N., Blaszczynski, A., & Kidson, W. (1988). Treatment of sex offenders with imaginal desensitization and/or medroxyprogesterone. *Acta Psychiatrica Scandinavica, 77,* 199–206.

McCord, W., & McCord, J. (1964). *The psychopath: An essay on the criminal mind.* New York: Van Nostrand-Reinhold.

McCrady, B.S. (1985). Alcoholism. In D.H. Barlow (Ed.), *Clinical handbook of psychological disorders.* New York: Guilford.

McCrady, B.S., Noel, N.E., Abrams, D.B., Stout, R.L., Nelson, H.F., & Hay, W.M. (1986). Comparative effectiveness of three types of spouse involvement in outpatient behavioral alcoholism treatment. *Journal of Studies on Alcohol, 47,* 459–467.

McCrady, B.S., Stout, R., Noel, N., Abrams, D., & Nelson, H.F. (1991). Effectiveness of three types of spouse-involved behavioral alcoholism treatment. *British Journal of the Addictions, 86,* 1415–1424.

McCrady, B.S., Stout, R.L., Noel, N.E., Abrams, D.B., & Nelson, H.F. (in press). Comparative effectiveness of three types of spouse involved behavioral alcoholism treatment: Outcomes 18 months after treatment. *British Journal of Addictions.*

McCrae, R.R., & Costa, P.T., Jr. (1990). *Personality in adulthood.* New York: Guilford.

McCutchan, J.A. (1990). Virology, immunology, and clinical course of HIV infection. *Journal of Consulting and Clinical Psychology, 58,* 5–12.

McDougle, C.J., Black, J.E., Malison, R.T., Zimmerman, R.C., Kosten, T.R., et al. (1994). Noradrenergic dysregulation during discontinuation of cocaine rise in addicts. *Archives of General Psychiatry, 51,* 713–719.

McDougle, C.J., Goodman, W.K., Leckman, J.F., Lee, N.C., Heninger, G.R., & Price, L.H. (1994). Haloperidal addition in fluvoxamine-refractory obsessive-compulsive disorder: A double-blind, placebo controlled study in patients with and without tics. *Archives of General Psychiatry, 51,* 302–308.

McDougle, C.J., Naylor, S.T., Volkmar, F.R., Heninger, G.R., & Price, L.H. (1996). A double-blind placebo-controlled study of fluvoxamine in adults with autistic disorder. *Archives of General Psychiatry, 53,* 1001–1008.

McEachin, J.J., Smith, T., & Lovaas, O.I. (1993). Long-term outcome for children with autism who received early intensive behavioral treatment. *American Journal on Mental Retardation, 97,* 359–372.

McElroy, S.L., Phillips, K.A., Keck, P.E.,

Hudson, J.I., & Pope, H.G. (1993). Body dysmorphic disorder: Does it have a psychiatric subtype? *Journal of Clinical Psychiatry, 54,* 389–395.

McFall, R.M., & Hammen, C.L. (1971). Motivation, structure, and self-monitoring: Role of nonspecific factors in smoking reduction. *Journal of Consulting and Clinical Psychology, 37,* 80–86.

McFall, R.M., & Lillesand, D.B. (1971). Behavior rehearsal with modeling and coaching in assertion training. *Journal of Abnormal Psychology, 77,* 313–323.

McGee, R., & Feehan, M. (1991). Are girls with problems of attention underrecognized? *Journal of Psychopathology and Behavioral Assessment, 13,* 187–198.

McGee, R., & Williams, S. (1988). A longitudinal study of depression in nine-year-old children. *Journal of the American Academy of Child and Adolescent Psychiatry, 27,* 49–54.

McGee, R., Williams, S., & Silva, P. (1987). A comparison of girls and boys with teacher-identified problems of attention. *Journal of the American Academy of Child and Adolescent Psychiatry, 26,* 711–717.

McGhie, A., & Chapman, I.S. (1961). Disorders of attention and perception in early schizophrenia. *British Journal of Medical Psychology, 34,* 103–116.

McGlynn, F.D. (1994). Simple phobia. In M. Hersen & R.T. Ammerman (Eds.), *Handbook of prescriptive treatments for adults* (pp. 179–196). New York: Plenum.

McGrady, A.V., & Bernal, G.A.A. (1986). Relaxation-based treatment of stress induced syncope. *Journal of Behavior Therapy and Experimental Psychiatry, 17,* 23–27.

McGue, M., Pickens, R.W., & Svikis, D.S. (1992). Sex and age effects on the inheritance of alcohol problems: A twin study. *Journal of Abnormal Psychology, 101,* 3–17.

McGuffin, P., Katz, R., Watkins, S., & Rutherford, J. (1996). A hospital-based twin registry study of the heritability of DSM-IV unipolar depression. *Archives of General Psychiatry, 53,* 129–136.

McGuiness, D. (1981). Auditory and motor aspects of language development in males and females. In A. Ansara (Ed.), *Sex differences in dyslexia.* Towson, MD: The Orton Dyslexia Society.

McGuire, J., Nieri, D., Abbott, D., Sheridan, K., et al. (1995). Do *Tarasoff* principles apply in AIDS-related psychotherapy? Ethical decision making and the role of therapist homophobia and perceived client dangerousness. *Professional Psychology: Research and Practice, 26,* 608–611.

McGuire, R.J., Carlisle, J.M., & Young, B.G. (1965). Sexual deviations as conditioned behaviour: A hypothesis. *Behaviour Research and Therapy, 2,* 185–190.

McIntosh, J.L. (1995). Suicide prevention in the elderly (65–99). In M.M. Silverman & R.W. Maris (Eds.), *Suicide prevention toward the year 2000* (pp. 180–192). New York: Guilford.

McIntosh, J.L., Santos, J.F., Hubbard, R.W., & Overholser, J.C. (1994). *Elder suicide: Research, theory, and treatment.* Washington, DC: American Psychological Association.

McIntyre-Kingsolver, K., Lichtenstein, E., & Mermelstein, R.J. (1986). Spouse training in a multicomponent smoking-cessation program. *Behavior Therapy, 17,* 67–74.

McKeon, P., & Murray, R. (1987). Familial aspects of obsessive-compulsive neurosis. *British Journal of Psychiatry, 151,* 528–534.

McKibben, A., Proulx, J., & Lusignan, R. (1994). Relationships between conflict, affect, and deviant sexual behaviors in rapists and pedophiles. *Behaviour Research and Therapy, 32,* 571–575.

McKim, W.A. (1991). *Drugs and behavior: An introduction to behavioral pharmacology.* Englewood Cliffs, NJ: Prentice-Hall.

McLarnon, L.D., & Kaloupek, D.G. (1988). Psychological investigation of genital herpes recurrence: Prospective assessment and cognitive-behavioral intervention for a chronic physical disorder. *Health Psychology, 7,* 231–249.

McMullen, S., & Rosen, R.C. (1979). Self-administered masturbation training in the treatment of primary orgasmic dysfunction. *Journal of Consulting and Clinical Psychology, 47,* 912–918.

McNally, R.J. (1987). Preparedness and phobias: A review. *Psychological Bulletin, 101,* 283–303.

McNally, R.J. (1994). *Panic disorder: A critical analysis.* New York: Guilford.

McNally, R.J., Caspi, S.P., Riemann, B.C., & Zeitlin, S.B. (1990). Selective processing of threat cues in posttraumatic stress disorder. *Journal of Abnormal Psychology, 99,* 398–406.

McNeal, E.T., & Cimbolic, P. (1986). Antidepressants and biochemical theories of depression. *Psychological Bulletin, 99,* 361–374.

McNeil, E. (1967). *The quiet furies.* Englewood Cliffs, NJ: Prentice-Hall.

Mednick, S.A., & Schulsinger, F. (1968). Some premorbid characteristics related to breakdown in children with schizophrenic mothers. In D. Rosenthal & S.S. Kety (Eds.), *The transmission of schizophrenia.* Elmsford, NY: Pergamon.

Mednick, S.A., Gabrielli, W.F., & Hutchings, B. (1984). Genetic influences in criminal convictions: Evidence from an adoption cohort. *Science, 224,* 891–894.

Mednick, S.A., Huttonen, M.O., & Machon, R.A. (1994). Prenatal influenza infections and adult schizophrenia. *Schizophrenia Bulletin, 20,* 263–268.

Mednick, S.A., Machon, R., Hottunen, M.O., & Bonett, D. (1988). Fetal viral infection and adult schizophrenia. *Archives of General Psychiatry, 45,* 189–192.

Medvedev, Z. (1972). *A question of madness.* New York: Knopf.

Meehl, P.E. (1962). Schizotaxia, schizotypy, schizophrenia. *American Psychologist, 17,* 827–838.

Meehl, P.E. (1986). Diagnostic taxa as open concepts: Methodological and statistical questions about reliability and construct validity in the grand strategy of nosological revision. In T. Millon & G.L. Klerman (Eds.), *Contemporary directions in psychopathology.* New York: Wiley.

Meichenbaum, D.H. (1971). Examination of model characteristics in reducing avoidance behavior. *Journal of Personality and Social Psychology, 17,* 298–307.

Meichenbaum, D.H., & Asarnow, J. (1979). Cognitive-behavioral modification and metacognitive development: Implications for the classroom. In P.C. Kendall & S.D. Hollon (Eds.), *Cognitive-behavioral interventions: Theory, research, and procedures.* New York: Academic Press.

Melamed, B.G., & Siegel, L.J. (1975). Reduction of anxiety in children facing hospitalization and surgery by use of filmed modeling. *Journal of Consulting and Clinical Psychology, 43,* 511–521.

Melamed, B.G., Hawes, R.R., Heiby, E., & Glick, J. (1975). Use of filmed modeling to reduce uncooperative behavior of children during dental treatment. *Journal of Dental Research, 54,* 797–801.

Mellinger, G.D., Balter, M.B., & Uhlenhuth, E.H. (1985). Insomnia and its treatment. *Archives of General Psychiatry, 42,* 225–232.

Mello, N.K., & Mendelson, J.H. (1970). Experimentally induced intoxication in alcoholics: A comparison between programmed and spontaneous drinking. *Journal of Pharmacology and Experimental Therapy, 173,* 101.

Mellor, C.S. (1970). First rank symptoms of schizophrenia. *British Journal of Psychiatry, 117,* 15–23.

Meltzer, H.Y., Cola, P., & Way, L.E. (1993). Cost effectiveness of clozapine in neuroleptic-resistant schizophrenia. *American Journal of Psychiatry, 150,* 1630–1638.

Mendels, J. (1970). *Concepts of depression.* New York: Wiley.

Mendels, J., Stinnett, J.L., Burns, D., & Frazer, A. (1975). Amine precursors and depression. *Archives of General Psychia-*

try, 32, 22–30.

Mendlewicz, J., & Rainer, J.D. (1977). Adoption study supporting genetic transmission in manic-depressive illness. *Nature, 268*, 327–329.

Merzenich, M.M., Jenkins, W.M., Johnson, P., Schreiner, C., Miller, S.L., & Tallal, P. (1996). Temporal processing deficits of language-learning impaired children ameliorated by training. *Science, 271*, 77–81.

Meschino, W., & Lennox, A. (1994). Workshop report: Genetic testing programs for familial Alzheimer's disease. *Alzheimer's Disease and Associated Disorders, 8*, 68–70.

Messer, S.B., Sass, L.A., & Woolfolk, R.L. (Eds.). *Hermeneutics and psychological theory: Integrative perspectives on personality, psychotherapy and psychopathology.* New Brunswick, NJ: Rutgers University Press.

Metalsky, G.I., Halberstadt, L.J., & Abramson, L.Y. (1987). Vulnerability and invulnerability to depressive mood reactions: Toward a more powerful test of the diathesis–stress and causal mediation components of the reformulated theory of depression. *Journal of Personality and Social Psychology, 52*, 386–393.

Meyer, J.J. (1988). Impotence: Assessment in the private-practice office. *Postgraduate Medicine, 84*, 87–91.

Meyer, J.J., & Reter, D.J. (1979). Sex reassignment follow-up. *Archives of General Psychiatry, 36*, 1010–1015.

Meyer, J.K. (1995). Paraphlias. In H.I. Kaplan & B.J. Sadock (Eds.), *Comprehensive textbook of psychiatry* (pp. 1334–1347). Baltimore: Williams & Wilkins.

Meyer, V. (1966). Modification of expectations in cases with obsessional rituals. *Behaviour Research and Therapy, 4*, 273–280.

Meyer, V., & Chesser, E.S. (1970). *Behavior therapy in clinical psychiatry.* Baltimore: Penguin.

Meyer-Bahlburg, H. (1979). Sex hormones and female homosexuality: A critical examination. *Archives of Sexual Behavior, 8*, 101–119.

Meyerowitz, B.E., & Chaiken, S. (1987). The effect of message framing on breast self-examination attitudes, intentions, and behavior. *Journal of Personality and Social Psychology, 52*, 500–510.

Mezzich, A.C., Moss, H., Tarter, R.E., Wolfenstein, M., et al. (1994). Gender differences in the pattern and progression of substance use in conduct disordered adolescents. *American Journal on Addiction, 3*, 289–295.

Michelson, L., Mavissakalian, M., & Marchione, K. (1985). Cognitive and behavioral treatments of agoraphobia: Clinical, behavioral, and psychophysiolog-

ical treatments of agoraphobia. *Journal of Consulting and Clinical Psychology, 53*, 913–925.

Michelson, L., Sugai, D.P., Wood, R.P., & Kazdin, A.E. (1983). *Social skills assessment and training with children: An empirically based handbook.* New York: Plenum.

Mikhliner, M., & Solomon, Z. (1988). Attributional style and post-traumatic stress disorder. *Journal of Abnormal Psychology, 97*, 308–313.

Miklich, D.R., Rewey, H.H., Weiss, J.H., & Kolton, S. (1973). A preliminary investigation of psychophysiological responses to stress among different subgroups of asthmatic children. *Journal of Psychosomatic Research, 17*, 1–8.

Miklowitz, D.J. (1985). *Family interaction and illness outcome in bipolar and schizophrenic patients.* Unpublished Ph.D. thesis, University of California at Los Angeles.

Miklulineen, M., & Solomon, Z. (1988). Attributional style and posttraumatic stress disorder. *Journal of Abnormal Psychology, 97*, 308–313.

Miles, L.E., & Dement, W.C. (1980). Sleep and aging. *Sleep, 3*, 119–220.

Miller, H.R. (1981). Psychiatric morbidity in elderly surgical patients. *British Journal of Psychiatry, 128*, 17–20.

Miller, N.E. (1948). Studies of fear as an acquirable drive: I. Fear as motivation and fear-reduction as reinforcement in the learning of new responses. *Journal of Experimental Psychology, 38*, 89–101.

Miller, N.E. (1959). Liberalization of basic S-R concepts: Extensions to conflict behavior, motivation, and social learning. In S. Koch (Ed.), *Psychology: A study of a science* (Vol. 2). New York: McGraw-Hill.

Miller, N.S. (1995). History and review of contemporary addiction treatment. *Alcoholism Treatment Quarterly, 12*, 1–22.

Miller, S.B. (1994). Parasympathetic nervous system control of heart rate responses to stress in offspring of hypertensives. *Psychophysiology, 31*, 11–16.

Miller, S.M., Shoda, Y., & Hurley, K. (1996). Applying cognitive-social theory to health-protective behavior: Breast self-examination in cancer screening. *Psychological Bulletin, 119*, 70–94.

Miller, S.O. (1989). Optical differences in cases of multiple personality disorder. *Journal of Nervous and Mental Disease, 177*, 480–487.

Miller, T.Q., Markides, K.S., Chiriboga, D.A., & Ray, L.A. (1995). A test of the psychosocial and health behavior models of hostility: Results from an 11-year follow-up of Mexican Americans. *Psychosomatic Medicine, 57*, 572–581.

Miller, W.R., & Rollnick, S.(Eds). (1991).

Motivational interviewing: Preparing people to change addictive behavior. New York: Guilford.

Miller, W.R., Zweben, A., DiClemente, C.C., & Rychtarik, R.G. (1992). Motivational Enhancement Therapy manual: A clinical research guide for therapists treating individuals with alcohol abuse and dependence. *NIAA Project MATCH Monograph, Vol. 2*, DHHS Publication No. (ADM) 92–1894.

Millon, T. (1996). *Disorders of personality: DSM-IV and beyond.* (2nd ed.). New York: Wiley.

Millsaps, C.L., Azrin, R.L., & Mittenberg, W. (1994). Neuropsychological effects of chronic cannabis use on the memory and intelligence of adolescents. *Journal of Child and Adolescent Substance Abuse, 3*, 47–55.

Milton, F., & Hafner, J. (1979). The outcome of behavior therapy for agoraphobia in relation to marital adjustment. *Archives of General Psychiatry, 36*, 807–811.

Mineka, S. (1985). Animal models of anxiety-based disorders: Their usefulness and limitations. In A.H. Tuma & J.D. Maser (Eds.), *Anxiety and the anxiety disorders.* Hillsdale, NJ: Erlbaum.

Mineka, S. (1992). Evolutionary memories, emotional processing, and the emotional disorders. In D. Medin (Ed.), *The psychology of learning and motivation* (Vol. 28). New York: Academic Press.

Mineka, S., Davidson, M., Cook, M., & Keir, R. (1984). Observational conditioning of snake fear in rhesus monkeys. *Journal of Abnormal Psychology, 93*, 355–372.

Mintz, E. (1967). Time-extended marathon groups. *Psychotherapy, 4*, 65–70.

Mintz, J. (1983). Integrating research evidence. *Journal of Consulting and Clinical Psychology, 51*, 71–75.

Mintz, M. (1991). Tobacco roads: Delivering death to the third world. *Progressive, 55*, 24–29.

Mintz, R.S. (1968). Psychotherapy of the suicidal patient. In H.L.P. Resnik (Ed.), *Suicidal behaviors.* Boston: Little, Brown.

Minuchin, S., Baker, L., Rosman, B.L., Lieberman, R., Milman, L., & Todd, T.C. (1975). A conceptual model of psychosomatic illness in children. *Archives of General Psychiatry, 32*, 1031–1038.

Mirenda, P.L., Donnellan, A.M., & Yoder, D.E. (1983). Gaze behavior: A new look at an old problem. *Journal of Autism and Developmental Disorders, 13*, 397–409.

Mischel, W. (1968). *Personality and assessment.* New York: Wiley.

Mischel, W. (1977). On the future of personality assessment. *American Psychologist, 32*, 246–254.

Mishkind, M.E., Rodin, J., Silberstein,

L.R., & Striegel-Moore, R.H. (1986). The embodiment of masculinity: Cultural, psychological, and behavioral dimensions. *American Behavioral Scientist, 29,* 545–562.

Mitchell, J., McCauley, E., Burke, P.M., & Moss, S.J. (1988). Phenomenology of depression in children and adolescents. *Journal of the American Academy of Child and Adolescent Psychiatry, 27,* 12–20.

Mitchell, J.E. (1992). Subtyping of bulimia nervosa. *International Journal of Eating Disorders, 11,* 327–332.

Mitchell, J.E., & Pyle, R.L. (1985). Characteristics of bulimia. In J.E. Mitchell (Ed.), *Anorexia nervosa and bulimia: Diagnosis and treatment.* Minneapolis: University of Minnesota Press.

Mittleman, M.A., Maclure, M., Sherwood, J.B., Murly, R.P., Tofler, G.A., et al., (1997). Triggering of acute myocardial infarction onset by episodes of anger. *Circulation, 92,* 1720–1725.

Modestin, J. (1987). Quality of interpersonal relationships: The most characteristic DSM-III BPD characteristic. *Comprehensive Psychiatry, 28,* 397–402.

Modestin, J. (1992). Multiple personality disorder in Switzerland. *American Journal of Psychiatry, 149,* 88–92.

Moffatt, M.E.K., Kato, C., & Pless, I.B. (1987). Improvements in self-concept after treatment of nocturnal enuresis: Randomized controlled trial. *The Journal of Pediatrics, 110,* 647–652.

Moffitt, T.E. (1990). Juvenile delinquency and attention deficit disorder: Boys' developmental trajectories from age 13 to 15. *Child Development, 61,* 893–910.

Moffitt, T.E. (1993). Adolescence-limited and life-course-persistent antisocial behavior: A developmental taxonomy. *Psychological Review, 100,* 674–701.

Moffitt, T.E., Lynam, D., & Silva, P.A. (1994). Neuropsychological tests predict persistent male delinquency. *Criminology, 32,* 101–124.

Mohr, D.C., & Beutler, L.E. (1990). Erectile dysfunction: A review of diagnostic and treatment procedures. *Clinical Psychology Review, 10,* 123–150.

Mohr, D.C., & Beutler, L.E. (1990). Erectile dysfunction: A review of diagnostic and treatment procedures. *Clinical Psychology Review, 10,* 123–150.

Mohr, J.W., Turner, R.E., & Jerry, M.B. (1964). *Pedophilia and exhibitionism.* Toronto: University of Toronto Press.

Molgaard, C.A., Nakamura, C.M., Stanford, E.P., Peddecord, K.M., & Morton, D.J. (1990). Prevalence of alcohol consumption among older persons. *Journal of Community Health, 15,* 239–251.

Monahan, J. (1973). The psychiatrization of criminal behavior. *Hospital and Community Psychiatry, 24,* 105–107.

Monahan, J. (1976). The prevention of violence. In J. Monahan (Ed.), *Community mental health and the criminal justice system.* Elmsford, NY: Pergamon.

Monahan, J. (1978). Prediction research and the emergency commitment of dangerous mentally ill persons: A reconsideration. *American Journal of Psychiatry, 135,* 198–201.

Monahan, J. (1984). The prediction of violent behavior: Toward a second generation of theory and policy. *American Journal of Psychiatry, 141,* 10–15.

Monahan, J. (1992). Mental disorder and violent behavior: Perceptions and evidence. *American Psychologist, 47,* 511–521.

Monahan, J. (1993). Limiting therapist exposure to *Tarasoff* liability: Guidelines for risk containment. *American Psychologist, 48,* 242–250.

Monahan, J., & Shah, S. (1989). Dangerousness and commitment of the mentally disordered in the United States. *Schizophrenia Bulletin, 15,* 541–553.

Monahan, J., & Steadman, H. (1994). Toward a rejuvenation of risk assessment research. In J. Monahan & H. Steadman (Eds.), *Violence and mental disorder: Developments in risk assessment.* Chicago: University of Chicago Press.

Moniz, E. (1936). *Tentatives operatoires dans le traitement de ceretaines psychoses.* Paris: Mason.

Monroe, S.M., & Simons, A.D. (1991). Diathesis-stress theories in the context of life stress research: Implications for the depressive disorders. *Psychological Bulletin, 110,* 406–425.

Moran, M. (1991). Psychological factors affecting pulmonary and rheumatological diseases: A review. *Psychosomatics, 32,* 14–23.

Moreau, D., Mufson, L., Weissman, M.M., & Klerman, G.L. (1992). Interpersonal psychotherapy for adolescent depression: Description of modification and preliminary application. *Journal of the Academy of Child and Adolescent Psychiatry, 30,* 642–651.

Morenz, B., & Becker, J.V. (1995). The treatment of youthful sexual offenders. *Applied and Preventive Psychology, 4,* 247–256.

Morey, L.C. (1988). Personality disorders in DSM-III and DSM-IIIR: Convergence, coverage, and internal consistency. *American Journal of Psychiatry, 145,* 573–577.

Morgan, C.A., Grillon, C., Southwick, S.M., Davis, M., & Charney, D.S. (1996). Exaggerated acoustic startle reflex in Gulf War veterans with post-traumatic stress disorder. *American Journal of Psychiatry, 153,* 64–68.

Morgan, K. (1992). Sleep, insomnia, and mental health. *Reviews in Clinical Gerontology, 2,* 246–253.

Morin, C.M., & Azrin, N.H. (1988). Behavioral and cognitive treatments of geriatric insomnia. *Journal of Consulting and Clinical Psychology, 56,* 748–753.

Morokoff, P., & Gilliland, R. (1993). Stress, sexual functioning, and marital satisfaction. *Journal of Sex Research, 30,* 43–53.

Morokoff, P.J. (1988). Sexuality in perimenopausal and postmenopausal women. *Psychology of Women Quarterly, 12,* 489–511.

Morris, A.A. (1968). Criminal insanity. *Washington Review, 43,* 583–622.

Morris, N. (1966). Impediments to legal reform. *University of Chicago Law Review, 33,* 627–656.

Morris, N. (1968). Psychiatry and the dangerous criminal. *Southern California Law Review, 41,* 514–547.

Morse, R.M. (1988). Substance abuse among the elderly. *Bulletin of the Menninger Clinic, 52,* 259–268.

Morse, S.J. (1982a, June 23). In defense of the insanity defense. *Los Angeles Times.*

Morse, S.J. (1982b). Failed explanation and criminal responsibility: Experts and the unconscious. *Virginia Law Review, 678,* 971–1084.

Morse, S.J. (1982c). A preference for liberty: The case against involuntary commitment of the mentally disordered. *California Law Review, 70,* 54–106.

Morse, S.J. (1992). The "guilty mind": Mens rea. In D.K. Kagehiro & W.S. Laufer (Eds.), *Handbook of psychology and law* (pp. 207–229). New York: Springer-Verlag.

Morse, S.J. (1996). Blame and danger: An essay on preventive detention. *Boston University Law Review, 76,* 113–155.

Moscicki, E.K. (1995). Epidemiology of suicidal behavior. In M.M. Silverman & R.W. Maris (Eds.), *Suicide prevention: Toward the year 2000* (pp. 22–35). New York: Guilford.

Moser, C., & Levitt, E.E. (1987). An exploratory-descriptive study of a sadomasochistically oriented sample. *The Journal of Sex Research, 23,* 322–337.

Moser, P.W. (1989, January). Double vision: Why do we never match up to our mind's ideal? *Self Magazine,* pp. 51–52.

Moses, J.A. (1983). Luria–Nebraska Neuropsychological Battery performance of brain dysfunctional patients with positive or negative findings on current neurological examination. *International Journal of Neuroscience, 22,* 135–146.

Moses, J.A., & Schefft, B.K. (1984). Interrater reliability analyses of the Luria–Nebraska Neuropsychological Battery. *The International Journal of Clinical Neuropsychology, 7,* 31–38.

Mosher, L.R., & Burti, L. (1989). *Commu-*

nity mental health: Principles and practice. New York: Norton.

Mosher, L.R., Kresky-Wolff, M., Mathews, S., & Menn, A. (1986). Milieu therapy in the 1980s: A comparison of two residential alternatives to hospitalization. *Bulletin of the Menninger Clinic, 50,* 257–268.

Moss, H.B. (1990). Pharmacotherapy. In A.S. Bellack & M. Hersen (Eds.), *Handbook of comparative treatments for adult disorders* (pp. 506–520). New York: Wiley.

Mowrer, O.H. (1939). A stimulus-response analysis of anxiety and its role as a reinforcing agent. *Psychological Review, 46,* 553–565.

Mowrer, O.H. (1947). On the dual nature of learning—A reinterpretation of "conditioning" and "problem-solving." *Harvard Educational Review, 17,* 102–148.

Mowrer, O.H. (1950). *Learning theory and personality dynamics.* New York: Ronald Press.

Mowrer, O.H., & Mowrer, W.M. (1938). Enuresis: A method for its study and treatment. *American Journal of Orthopsychiatry, 8,* 436–459.

Mrazek, P.J., & Haggerty, R.J. (1994). *Reducing risks for mental disorders: Frontiers for preventive intervention research.* Washington, DC: National Academy Press.

Mueser, K., Bellack, A.S., & Blanchard, J.J. (1992). Co-morbidity of schizophrenia and substance abuse: Implications for treatment. *Journal of Consulting and Clinical Psychology, 60,* 845–856.

Mueser, K.T., & Liberman, R.P. (1995). Behavior therapy in practice. In B. Bongar & L.E. Beutler (Eds.), *Comprehensive textbook of psychotherapy: Theory and practice* (pp. 84–110). New York: Oxford University Press.

Mulligan, T., & Palguta, R.F. (1991). Sexual interest, activity, and satisfaction among male nursing home residents. *Archives of Sexual Behavior, 20,* 199–204.

Mulligan, T., Retchin, S.M., Chinchilli, V.M., & Bettinger, C.B. (1988). *Journal of the American Geriatrics Society, 36,* 520–524.

Mulvey, E.P. (1994). Assessing the evidence of a link between mental illness and violence. *Hospital and Community Psychiatry, 45,* 663–668.

Mumford, D.B., Whitehouse, A.M., & Choudry, I.Y. (1992). Survey of eating disorders in English-medium schools in Lahore, Pakistan. *International Journal of Eating Disorders, 11,* 173–184.

Munjack, D.J. (1984). The onset of driving phobias. *Journal of Behavior Therapy and Experimental Psychiatry, 15,* 305–308.

Murdoch, D., Pihl, R.O., & Ross, D. (1990). Alcohol and crimes of violence: Present issues. *International Journal of Addiction,*

25, 1059–1075.

Murphy, J. (1976). Psychiatric labeling in cross-cultural perspective. *Science, 191,* 1019–1028.

Murphy, J.K., Stoney, C.M., Alpert, B.S., & Walker, S.S. (1995). Gender and ethnicity in children's cardiovascular reactivity: 7 years of study. *Health Psychology, 14,* 48–55.

Muscettola, G., Potter, W.Z., Pickar, D., & Goodwin, F.K. (1984). Urinary 3-methoxy-4-hydroxyphenyl glycol and major affective disorders. *Archives of General Psychiatry, 41,* 337–342.

Muse, M. (1986). Stress-related, posttraumatic chronic pain syndrome: Behavioral treatment approach. *Pain, 25,* 389–394.

Musetti, L., Perugi, G., Soriani, A., Rossi, V.M., Cassano, G.B., & Akiskal, H.S. (1989). Depression before and after age 65: A re-examination. *British Journal of Psychiatry, 155,* 330–336.

Myers, J.K., Weissman, M.M., Tischler, G.L., Holzer, C.E., Leaf, P.J., Orvaschel, H.A., Anthony, J.C., Boyd, J.H., Burke, J.E., Kramer, M., & Stoltzman, R. (1984). Six-month prevalence of psychiatric disorders in three communities: 1980–1982. *Archives of General Psychiatry, 41,* 959–967.

Nagy, Z., Esiri, M.M., Jobst, K.A., Morris, J.H., et al. (1995). Relative roles of senile plaques and tangles in the dementia of Alzheimer's disease: Correlations using three sets of neuropathological indicators. *Dementia, 6,* 21–31.

Nahas, G.G., & Manger, W.M. (1995). Marijuana as medicine: In reply. *Journal of the American Medical Association, 274,* 1837–1838.

National Cancer Institute. (1977). *The smoking digest: Progress report on a nation kicking the habit.* Washington, DC: U.S. Department of Health, Education and Welfare.

National Center for Child Abuse and Neglect. (1988). *Study of national incidence and prevalence of child abuse and neglect, 1988.* Washington, DC: U.S. Department of Health and Human Services.

National Center for Health Statistics (1989). *National nursing home survey* (DHHS Publication No. PHS 89–1758, Series 13, No. 97). Washington, DC: U.S. Government Printing Office.

National Center for Health Statistics. (1988). Advance report of final mortality statistics, 1986. *NCHS Monthly Vital Statistics Report, 37* (Suppl. 6).

National Center for Health Statistics. (1994). Advance report of final mortality statistics, 1991. *Monthly Vital Statistics Report, 42.*

National Institute on Drug Abuse. (1979). *National Survey on Drug Abuse.* Wash-

ington, DC: Author.

National Institute on Drug Abuse. (1982). *National Survey on Drug Abuse.* Washington, DC: Author.

National Institute on Drug Abuse. (1983a). *National Survey on Drug Abuse: Main Findings 1982* (DHHS Publication No. ADM 83–1263). Washington, DC: U.S. Government Printing Office.

National Institute on Drug Abuse. (1983b). *Population projections, based on the National Survey on Drug Abuse, 1982.* Rockville, MD: Author.

National Institute on Drug Abuse. (1988). *National household survey on drug abuse: Main findings 1985.* Washington, DC: Department of Health and Human Services.

National Institute on Drug Abuse. (1991). *National Household Survey on Drug Abuse: Population Estimates, 1991.* Washington, DC.

Nauss, D.W. (1996, March 9). Kevorkian found not guilty of aiding two suicides. *Los Angeles Times,* pp. A1, A15.

Nawas, M.M., Fishman, S.T., & Pucel, J.C. (1970). The standardized densensitization program applicable to group and individual treatment. *Behaviour Research and Therapy, 6,* 63–68.

Neale, J.M., & Liebert, R.M. (1986). *Science and behavior: An introduction to methods of research* (3rd ed.). Englewood Cliffs, NJ: Prentice-Hall.

Neale, J.M., & Oltmanns, T. (1980). *Schizophrenia.* NY: Wiley.

Neisser, U. (1976). *Cognition and reality.* San Francisco: Freeman.

Neisser, U., & Harsch, N. (1991). Phantom flashbulbs: False recognitions of hearing the news about *Challenger.* In E. Winograd & U. Neisser (Eds.), *Affect and accuracy of recall: Studies of "flashbulb" memories.* New York: Cambridge University Press.

Nelson, R.E., & Craighead, W.E. (1977). Selective recall of positive and negative feedback, self-control behaviors, and depression. *Journal of Abnormal Psychology, 86,* 379–388.

Nelson, R.O., Lipinski, D.P., & Black, J.L. (1976). The reactivity of adult retardates' self-monitoring: A comparison among behaviors of different valences, and a comparison with token reinforcement. *Psychological Record, 26,* 189–201.

Nemeroff, C.F., Stein, R.I., Diehl, N.S., & Smilack, K.M. (1994). From the Cleavers to the Clintons: Role choices and body orientation as reflected in magazine article content. *International Journal of Eating Disorders, 16,* 167–176.

Nemeroff, C.J., & Karoly, P. (1991). Operant methods. In F.H. Kanfer & A.P. Goldstein (Eds.), *Helping people change: A textbook of methods* (4th ed.) Elmsford,

NY: Pergamon.

Nemetz, G.H., Craig, K.D., & Reith, G. (1978). Treatment of female sexual dysfunction through symbolic modeling. *Journal of Consulting and Clinical Psychology, 46,* 62–73.

Neron, S., Lacroix, D., & Chaput, Y. (1995). Group vs. individual cognitive behaviour therapy in panic disorder: An open clinical trial with a six month follow-up. *Canadian Journal of Behavioural Science, 27,* 379–392.

Nestadt, G., Romanoski, A., Chahal, R., Merchant, A., et al. (1990). An epidemiological study of histrionic personality disorder. *Psychological Medicine, 20,* 413–422.

Nettelbeck, T. (1985). Inspection time and mild mental retardation. In N.R. Ellis & N.W. Bray (Eds.), *International review of research in mental retardation* (Vol. 13). New York: Academic Press.

Neugarten, B.L. (1977). Personality and aging. In J.E. Birren & K.W. Schaie (Eds.), *Handbook of the psychology of aging* (pp. 626–649). New York: Van Nostrand.

Neugebauer, R. (1979). Mediaeval and early modern theories of mental illness. *Archives of General Psychiatry, 36,* 477–484.

Neuringer, C. (1964). Rigid thinking in suicidal individuals. *Journal of Consulting Psychology, 28,* 54–58.

Newlin, D.B., & Thomson, J.B. (1990). Alcohol challenge with sons of alcoholics: A critical review and analysis. *Psychology Bulletin, 108,* 383–402.

Newman, J.P., Patterson, C.M., & Kosson, D.S. (1987). Response perseveration in psychopaths. *Journal of Abnormal Psychology, 96,* 145–149.

Nezu, A.M. (1986). Efficacy of a social problem-solving therapy approach for unipolar depression. *Journal of Consulting and Clinical Psychology, 54,* 196–202.

Nezu, A.M., Nezu, C.M., D'Zurilla, T.J., & Rothenberg, J.L. (1996). Problem-solving therapy. In J.S. Kantor (Ed.), *Clinical depression during addiction recovery* (pp. 187–219). New York: Marcel Dekker.

Nezworski, M.T., & Wood, J.M. (1995). Narcissism in the Comprehensive System for the Rorschach. *Clinical Psychology: Science and Practice, 2,* 179–199.

Nicholson, R.A., & Berman, J.S. (1983). Is follow-up necessary in evaluating psychotherapy? *Psychological Bulletin, 93,* 261–278.

Nietzel, M.T., & Harris, M.J. (1990). Relationship of dependency and achievement/autonomy to depression. *Clinical Psychology Review, 10,* 279–297.

Nigg, J.T., & Goldsmith, H.H. (1994). Genetics of personality disorders: Perspectives from personality and psychopathology research. *Psychological Bulletin, 115,* 346–380.

Nihira, K., Foster, R., Shenhaas, M., & Leland, H. (1975). *AAMD-Adaptive Behavior Scale.* Washington, DC: American Association on Mental Deficiency.

Nisbett, R.E., & Wilson, T.D. (1977). Telling more than we can know: Verbal reports on mental processes. *Psychological Review, 84,* 231–259.

Nobler, M.S., Sackeim, H.A., Prohovnik, I., Moeller, J.R., Mukherjee, S., et al. (1994). Regional cerebral blood flow in mood disorders, 3. Treatment and clinical response. *Archives of General Psychiatry, 51,* 884–896.

Nocks, B.C., Learner, R.M., Blackman, D., & Brown, T.E. (1986). The effects of a community-based long term care project on nursing home utilization. *The Gerontologist, 26,* 150–157.

Nolen-Hoeksema, S., & Girgus, J.S. (1994). The emergence of gender differences in depression during adolescence. *Psychological Bulletin, 115,* 424–443.

Norgaard, J.P. (1989a). Urodynamics in enuretics: 1. Reservoir function. *Neurourology and Urodynamics, 8,* 199–211.

Norgaard, J.P. (1989b). Urodynamics in enuretics: 2. A pressure/flow study. *Neurourology and Urodynamics, 8,* 213–217.

North, A.F. (1979). Health services in Head Start. In E. Zigler & J. Valentine (Eds.), *Project Head Start.* New York: Free Press.

Norton, J.P. (1982). *Expressed emotion, affective style, voice tone and communication deviance as predictors of offspring schizophrenia spectrum disorders.* Unpublished doctoral dissertation, University of California at Los Angeles.

Noshirvani, H.F., et al. (1991). Gender-divergent factors in obsessive-compulsive disorder. *British Journal of Psychiatry, 158,* 260–263.

Nottelmann, E.D., & Jensen, P.S. (1995). Comorbidity of disorders in children and adolescents: Developmental perspectives. *Advances in Clinical Child Psychology, 17,* 109–155.

Nowlan, R., & Cohen, S. (1977). Tolerance to marijuana: Heart rate and subjective "high." *Clinical Pharmacology Therapeutics, 22,* 550–556.

Noyes, R., Reich, J., Christiansen, J., Suelzer, M., Pfohl, B., et al. (1990). Outcome of panic disorder: Relationship to diagnostic subtypes and comorbidity. *Archives of General Psychiatry, 47,* 809–818.

Noyes, R., Kathol, R.G., Fisher, M.M., Phillips, S.B., & Suezer, M.T. (1994). Psychiatric comorbidity among patients with hypochondriasis. *General Hospital Psychiatry, 16,* 78–87.

Noyes, R., Woodman, C., Garvey, M.J., Cook, B.C., Suezer, M., & et al. (1992). Generalized anxiety disorder versus panic disorder: Distinguishing characteristics and patterns of comorbidity. *Journal of Nervous and Mental Disease, 180,* 369–379.

Nunn, R.G., Newton, K.S., & Faucher, P. (1992). 2.5 year follow-up of weight and body mass index values in the weight control for life program. *Addictive Behaviors, 17,* 579–585.

Nyth, A.L., Gottfries, C.G., Blennow, F., Brane, G., & Wallin, A. (1991). Heterogeneity in the course of Alzheimer's disease: A differentiation of subgroups. *Dementia, 2,* 18–24.

O'Conner, M.C. (1989). Aspects of differential performance by minorities on standardized tests: Linguistic and sociocultural factors. In B.R. Gifford (Ed.), *Test policy and test performance: Education, language, and culture* (pp. 129–181). Boston: Kluwer Academic Publishers.

O'Connor, D.W., Pollitt, P.A., Roth, M., Brook, P.B., & Reiss, B.B. (1990). Memory complaints and impairment in normal, depressed, and demented elderly persons identified in a community survey. *Archives of General Psychiatry, 47,* 224–227.

O'Connor, R.D. (1969). Modification of social withdrawal through symbolic modeling. *Journal of Applied Behavior Analysis, 2,* 15–22.

O'Donohue, W., & Plaud, J.J. (1994). The conditioning of human sexual arousal. *Archives of Sexual Behavior, 23,* 321–344.

O'Donohue, W.T. (1987). The sexual behavior and problems of the elderly. In L.L. Carstensen & B.A. Edelstein (Eds.), *Handbook of clinical gerontology.* New York: Pergamon.

O'Leary, K.D., & Beach, S.R.H. (1990). Marital therapy: A viable treatment for depression and marital discord. *American Journal of Psychiatry, 147,* 183–186.

O'Leary, K.D., Pelham, W.E., Rosenbaum, A., & Price, G.H. (1976). Behavioral treatment of hyperkinetic children: An experimental evaluation of its usefulness. *Clinical Pediatrics, 15,* 510–515.

O'Leary, K.D., & Wilson, G.T. (1987). *Behavior therapy: Application and outcome.* Englewood Cliffs, NJ: Prentice-Hall.

O'Malley, S.S., Jaffe, A.J., Chang, G., Rode, S., Schottenfeld, R., et al. (1996). Six month follow-up of naltrexone and psychotherapy for alcohol dependence. *Archives of General Psychiatry, 53,* 217–224.

O'Neal, J.M. (1984). First person account: Finding myself and loving it. *Schizophrenia Bulletin, 10,* 109–110.

O'Neil, P.M., & Jarrell, M.P. (1992). Psychological aspects of obesity and dieting. In T.A. Wadden & T.B. Vanltallie (Eds.), *Treatment of the seriously obese patient* (pp. 231–251). New York: Guilford.

Obrist, P.A., Gaebelein, C.J., Teller, E.S., Langer, A.W., Grignolo, A., Light, K.C., & McCubbin, J.A. (1978). The relationship among heart rate, carotid *dP/dt*, and blood pressure in humans as a function of the type of stress. *Psychophysiology, 15*, 102–115.

Ochitil, H. (1982). Conversion disorder. In J.H. Greist, J.W. Jefferson, & R.L. Spitzer (Eds.), *Treatment of mental disorders.* New York: Oxford University Press.

Offord, D.R., Boyle, M.H., Szatmari, P., Rae-Grant, N.I., Links, P.S., Cadman, D.T., Byles, J.A., Crawford, J.W., Blum, H.M., Byrne, C., Thomas, H., & Woodward, C.A. (1987). Ontario Child Health Study: 2. Six-month prevalence of disorder and rates of service utilization. *Archives of General Psychiatry, 44*, 832–836.

Ogilvie, D.M., Stone, P.J., & Shneidman, E.S. (1983). A computer analysis of suicide notes. In E.S. Shneidman, N. Farberow, & R. Litman (Eds.), *The psychology of suicide* (pp. 249–256). New York: Jason Aronson.

Ogloff, J.R., & Wong, S. (1990). Electrodermal and cardiovascular evidence of a coping response in psychopaths. *Criminal Justice and Behavior, 17*, 231–245.

Öhman, A., Erixon, G., & Loftberg, I. (1975). Phobias and preparedness: Phobic versus neutral pictures as conditional stimuli for human autonomic responses. *Journal of Abnormal Psychology, 84*, 41–45.

Öhman, A., & Soares, J.J.F. (1994). "Unconscious anxiety": Phobic responses to masked stimuli. *Journal of Abnormal Psychology, 103*, 231–240.

Olds, D.L. (1984). *Final report: Prenatal/early infancy project.* Washington, DC: Maternal and Child Health Research, National Institute of Health.

Olivardia, R., Pope, H.G., Mangweth, B., & Hudson, J.I. (1995). Eating disorders in college men. *American Journal of Psychiatry, 152*, 1279–1284.

Oltmanns, T.F., Broderick, J.E., & O'Leary, K.D. (1976). *Marital adjustment and the efficacy of behavior therapy with children.* Paper presented at the Association for the Advancement of Behavior Therapy, New York.

Oltmanns, T.F., Neale, J.M., & Davison, G.C. (1995). *Case studies in abnormal psychology.* Fourth edition. New York: Wiley.

Organista, K.C., & Munoz, R.F. (1996). Cognitive behavioral therapy with Latinos. *Cognitive and Behavioral Practice, 3*, 255–270.

Orleans, C.T., Schoenbach, V.J., Wagner, E.H., Quade, D., Salmon, M.A., Pearson, D.C., Fiedler, J., Porter, C.Q., & Kaplan, B.H. (1991). Self-help quit smoking interventions: Effects of self-help materials, social support instructions, and telephone counseling. *Journal of Consulting and Clinical Psychology, 59*, 439–448.

Orne, M.T., Dinges, D.F., & Orne, E.C. (1984). The differential diagnosis of multiple personality in the forensic court. *International Journal of Clinical and Experimental Hypnosis, 32*, 118–169.

Ornitz, E. (1973). Childhood autism: A review of the clinical and experimental literature. *California Medicine, 118*, 21–47.

Ornitz, E.M. (1989). Autism at the interface between sensory and information processing. In G. Dawson (Ed.), *Autism: Nature, diagnosis, and treatment* (pp. 174–207). New York: Guilford.

Orr, S.P., Lasko, N.B., Shalev, A.Y., & Pitman, R.K. (1995). Physiological responses to loud tones in Vietnam veterans with post-traumatic stress disorder. *Journal of Abnormal Psychology, 104*, 75–82.

Orth-Gomer, K., & Unden, A.L. (1990). Type A behavior, social support, and coronary risk: Interaction and significance for mortality in cardiac patients. *Psychosomatic Medicine, 52*, 59–72.

Ost, L-G. (1987a). Age of onset in different phobias. *Journal of Abnormal Psychology, 96*, 223–229.

Ost, L-G. (1987b). Applied relaxation: Description of a coping technique and review of controlled studies. *Behaviour Research and Therapy, 25*, 397–409.

Ost, L-G. (1992). Blood and injection phobia: Background and cognitive, physiological, and behavioral correlates. *Journal of Abnormal Psychology, 101*, 68–74.

Ost, L-G., Fellenius, J., & Sterner, U. (1991). Applied tension, exposure in vivo, and tension-only in the treatment of blood phobia. *Behaviour Research and Therapy, 29*, 561–574.

Ouimette, P.C., Finney, J.W., & Moos, R.H. (1997). Twelve-step and cognitive-behavioral treatment for substance abuse: A comparison of treatment effectiveness. *Journal of Consulting and Clinical Psychology, 65*, 230–240.

Overholser, J.C., & Beck, S. (1986). Multimethod assessment of rapists, child molesters, and three control groups on behavioral and psychological measures. *Journal of Consulting and Clinical Psychology, 54*, 682–687.

Page, A.C. (1994). Blood-injection phobia. *Clinical Psychology Review, 14*, 443–461.

Pahkala, K. (1990). Social and environmental factors and atypical depression

in old age. *International Journal of Geriatric Psychiatry, 5*, 99–113.

Palmer, T. (1984). Treatment and the role of classification: Review of basics. *Crime and Delinquency, 30*, 245–267.

Paris, J., Zweig, F.M., & Guzder, J. (1994). Psychological risk factors for borderline personality disorder in female patients. *Comprehensive Psychiatry, 35*, 301–305.

Parker, K.C.H., Hanson, R.K., & Hunsley, J. (1988). MMPI, Rorschach, and WAIS: A meta-analytic comparison of reliability, stability, and validity. *Psychological Bulletin, 103*, 367–373.

Parker, S.R., Mellins, R.B., & Sogn, D.D. (1989). Asthma education: A national strategy. *American Journal of Respiratory Disease, 140*, 848–853.

Parkes, C.M., & Brown, R.J. (1972). Health after bereavement: A controlled study of young Boston widowers. *Psychosomatic Medicine, 34*, 49–461.

Parkinson, L., & Rachman, S. (1981). Intrusive thoughts: The effects of an uncontrived stress. *Advances in Behavior Research and Therapy, 3*, 111–118.

Parks, C.V., Jr., & Hollon, S.D. (1988). Cognitive assessment. In A.S. Bellack & M. Hersen (Eds.), *Behavioral assessment* (3rd ed.). Elmsford, NY: Pergamon.

Parsons, O.A. (1975). Brain damage in alcoholics: Altered states of consciousness. In M.M. Gross (Ed.), *Alcohol intoxication and withdrawal.* New York: Plenum.

Patel, C., Marmot, M.G., Terry, D.J., Carruthers, M., Hunt, B., & Patel, M. (1985). Trial of relaxation in reducing coronary risk: Four year follow-up. *British Medical Journal, 290*, 1103–1106.

Pato, M.T., Zohar-Kadouch, R., Zohar, J., & Murphy, D.L. (1988). Return of symptoms after discontinuation of clomipramine and patients with obsessive-compulsive disorder. *American Journal of Psychiatry, 145*, 1521–1525.

Patrick, C.J. (1994). Emotion and psychopathy: Some startling new insights. *Psychophysiology, 31*, 319–330.

Patrick, M., Hobson, R.P., Dastie, D., Howard, R., et al. (1994). Personality disorder and the mental representation of early social experience. *Development and Psychopathology, 6*, 375–388.

Patterson, C.M., & Newman, J.P. (1993). Reflectivity and learning from aversive events: Toward a psychological mechanism for the syndromes of disinhibition. *Psychological Review, 100*, 716–736.

Patterson, G., & Chamberlain, P. (1992). A functional analysis of resistance (a neobehavioral perspective). In H. Arkowitz (Ed.), *Why people don't change: New perspectives in resistance and noncompliance.* New York: Guilford.

Patterson, G.R. (1974). A basis for identifying stimuli which control behaviors in natural settings. *Child Development, 45,* 900–911.

Patterson, G.R., Crosby, L., & Vuchinich, S. (1992). Predicting risk for early police arrest. *Journal of Quantitative Criminology, 8,* 335–355.

Patterson, G.R., Ray, R.S., Shaw, D.A., & Cobb, J.A. (1969). *Manual for coding of family interactions.* New York: ASIS/NAPS, Microfiche Publications.

Paul, G.L. (1966). *Insight vs. desensitization in psychotherapy.* Stanford, CA: Stanford University Press.

Paul, G.L. (1969). Chronic mental patient: Current status–future directions. *Psychological Bulletin, 71,* 81–94.

Paul, G.L., & Lentz, R.J. (1977). *Psychosocial treatment of chronic mental patients: Milieu versus social learning programs.* Cambridge, MA: Harvard University Press.

Paul, G.L., & Menditto, A.A. (1992). Effectiveness of inpatient treatment programs for mentally ill adults in public psychiatric facilities. *Applied and Preventive Psychology: Current Scientific Perspectives, 1,* 41–63.

Paul, G.L., & Shannon, D.T. (1966). Treatment of anxiety through systematic desensitization in therapy groups. *Journal of Abnormal Psychology, 71,* 124–135.

Paul, G.L., Stuve, P., & Cross, J.V. (in press). Real-world inpatient programs: Shedding some light. *Applied and Preventive Psychology.*

Paul, G.L., Stuve, P., & Menditto, A.A. (in press). Social-learning program (with token economy) for adult psychiatric inpatients. *The Clinical Psychologist.*

Paul, R. (1987). *Communication.* In D.J. Cohen, A.M. Donnellan, & R. Paul (Eds.), *Handbook of autism and pervasive developmental disorders* (pp. 61–84). New York: Wiley.

Paykel, E.S., Brayne, L., Huppert, F.A., Gill, C., Barkley, L., et al. (1994). Incidence of dementia in a population older than 75 years in the United Kingdom. *Archives of General Psychiatry, 51,* 325–332.

Pearlin, L.I., Mullan, J.T., Semple, S.J., & Skaff, M.M. (1990). Caregiving and the stress process: An overview of concepts and their measures. *Gerontologist, 30,* 583–594.

Pearlson, G.D., & Rabins, P.V. (1988). The late-onset psychoses: Possible risk factors. *Psychiatric Clinics of North America, 11,* 15–32.

Pearlson, G.D., Wong, D.F., Tune, L.E., Ross, C.A., Chase, G.A., et al. (1995). In vivo D2 dopamine receptor density in psychotic and non-psychotic patients with bipolar disorder. *Archives of General Psychiatry, 52,* 471–477.

Pearson, C., & Gatz, M. (1982). Health and mental health in older adults: First steps in the study of a pedestrian complaint. *Rehabilitation Psychology, 27,* 37–50.

Pedro-Carroll, J.L., & Cowen, E.L. (1985). The children of divorce intervention program: An investigation of the efficacy of a school-based prevention program. *Journal of Consulting and Clinical Psychology, 53,* 603–611.

Pedro-Carroll, J.L., Cowen, E.L., Hightower, A.D., & Guare, J.C. (1986). Preventive intervention with latency-aged children of divorce: A replication study. *American Journal of Community Psychology, 14,* 277–290.

Pelham, W.E., Carlson, C., Sams, S.E., Vallano, G., Dixon, M.J., & Hoza, B. (1993). Separate and combined effects of methylphenidate and behavior modification on boys with attention deficit/hyperactivity disorder in the classroom. *Journal of Consulting and Clinical Psychology, 61,* 506–515.

Pelham, W.E., McBurnett, K., Harper, G.W., Milich, R., Murphy, D.A., Clinton, J., & Thiele, C. (1990). Methylphenidate and baseball playing in ADHD children: Who's on first? *Journal of Consulting and Clinical Psychology, 58,* 130–133.

Penn, D.L., & Mueser, K.T. (1996). Research update on the psychosocial treatment of schizophrenia. *American Journal of Psychiatry, 153,* 607–617.

Pennebaker, J., Kiecolt-Glaser, J.K., & Glaser, R. (1988). Disclosure of traumas and immune function: Health implications for psychotherapy. *Journal of Consulting and Clinical Psychology, 56,* 239–245.

Pennebaker, J.W. (1990). *Opening up: The healing power of confiding in others.* New York: William Morrow & Co.

Pennington, B.F. (1995). Genetics of learning disabilities. *Journal of Child Neurology, 10,* S69–S77.

Pentoney, P. (1966). Value change in psychotherapy. *Human Relations, 19,* 39–46.

Peplau, L.A., & Cochran, S.D. (1988). Value orientations in the intimate relationships of gay men. In J. De Cecco (Ed.), *Gay relationships* (pp. 195–216). New York: Harrington Park Press.

Perkins, D.D. (1995). Speaking truth to power: Empowerment ideology as social intervention and policy. *American Journal of Community Psychology, 23,* 765–794.

Perley, M.J., & Guze, S.B. (1962). Hysteria—The stability and usefulness of clinical criteria. *New England Journal of Medicine, 266,* 421–426.

Perls, F.S. (1947). *Ego, hunger, and aggression.* New York: Vintage.

Perls, F.S. (1969). *Gestalt therapy verbatim.*

Moab, UT: Real People Press.

Perls, F.S. (1970). Four lectures. In J. Fagan & I.L. Shepherd (Eds.), *Gestalt therapy now: Therapy, techniques, applications.* Palo Alto, CA: Science & Behavior Books.

Perls, F.S., Hefferline, R.F., & Goodman, P. (1951). *Gestalt therapy: Excitement and growth in the human personality.* New York: Julian Press.

Perry, R., Campbell, M., Adams, P., Lynch, N., Spencer, E.K., Curren, E.L., & Overall, J.E. (1989). Long-term efficacy of haloperidol in autistic children: Continuous versus discontinuous administration. *Journal of the American Academy of Child and Adolescent Psychiatry, 28,* 87–92.

Persons, J. (1989). *Cognitive therapy in practice: A case formulation approach.* New York: Norton.

Persons, J.B., Thase, M.E., & Crits-Christoph, P. (1996). The role of psychotherapy in the treatment of depression: Review of two practice guidelines. *Archives of General Psychiatry, 53,* 283–290.

Peters, M. (1977). Hypertension and the nature of stress. *Science, 198,* 80.

Peterson, C., & Seligman, M.E.P. (1984). Causal explanations as a risk factor for depression: Theory and evidence. *Psychological Review, 91,* 347–374.

Peterson, D. (1995). The reflective educator. *American Psychologist, 50,* 975–984.

Pfeiffer, E. (1977). Psychopathology and social pathology. In J.E. Birren & K.W. Schaie (Eds.), *Handbook of psychology and aging.* New York: Van Nostrand- Reinhold.

Pfeiffer, E., Verwoerdt, A., & Wang, H.H. (1969). The natural history of sexual behavior in a biologically advantaged group of aged individuals. *Journal of Gerontology, 24,* 193–198.

Pfeiffer, E., Verwoerdt, A., & Wang, H.S. (1968). Sexual behavior in aged men and women: 1. Observations on 254 community volunteers. *Archives of General Psychiatry, 19,* 753–758.

Phares, E.J., & Trull, T.J. (1997). *Clinical psychology.* Pacific Grove, CA: Brooks/Cole.

Phelps, L., Wallace, D., & Waigant, A. (1989, August). *Impact of sexual assault: Post assault behavior and health status.* Paper presented at the annual convention of the American Psychological Association, New Orleans. As cited in Calhoun & Atkeson (1991).

Phillips, D.P. (1974). The influence of suggestion on suicide: Substantive and theoretical implications of the Werther effect. *American Sociological Review, 39,* 340–354.

Phillips, D.P. (1977). Motor vehicle fatalities increase just after publicized suicide stories. *Science, 196,* 1464–1465.

Phillips, D.P. (1985). The found experiment: A new technique for assessing impact of mass media violence on real-world aggressive behavior. In G. Comstock (Ed.), *Public communication and behavior* (Vol. 1). New York: Academic Press.

Phillips, K.A., McElroy, S.L., Keck, P.E., Pope, H.G., & Hudson, J.L. (1993). Body dysmorphic disorder: 30 cases of imagined ugliness. *American Journal of Psychiatry, 150,* 302–308.

Phillips, L. (1953). Case history data and prognosis in schizophrenia. *Journal of Nervous and Mental Disease, 117,* 515–525.

Pigott, T.A., Pato, M.T., Bernstein, S.E., Grover, G.N., Hill, J.L., et al. (1990). Controlled comparison of clomipramine and fluoxetine in the treatment of obsessive-compulsive disorder. *Archives of General Psychiatry, 47,* 926–932.

Pilowsky, I. (1970). Primary and secondary hypochondriasis. *Acta Psychiatrica Scandinavica, 46,* 273–285.

Pinel, P. (1962). *A treatise on insanity, 1801.* English (D.D. Davis, Trans.). New York: Hafner.

Pinkston, E., & Linsk, N. (1984). Behavioral family intervention with the impaired elderly. *The Gerontologist, 24,* 576–583.

Piper, W.E., Azim, F.A., Joyce, S.A., McCallum, M., Nixon, G., & Segal, P.S. (1991). Quality of object relations vs. interpersonal functioning as predictors of alliance and outcome. *Archives of General Psychiatry, 48,* 946–953.

Piran, N., Kennedy, S., Garfinkel, P.E., & Owens, M. (1985). Affective disturbance in eating disorders. *Journal of Nervous and Mental Disease, 173,* 395–400.

Pirsig, R.M. (1974). *Zen and the art of motorcycle maintenance: An inquiry into values.* New York: Morrow.

Pitman, R.K., Orr, S.P., Forgue, D.F., Altman, B., deJong, J.B., et al. (1990). Psychophysiologic responses to combat imagery of Vietnam veterans with post-traumatic stress disorder vs. other anxiety disorders. *Journal of Abnormal Psychology, 99,* 49–54.

Piven, J., Arndt, S., Bailey, J., Havercamp, S., Andreasen, N.C., & Palmer, P. (1995). An MRI study of brain size in autism. *American Journal of Psychiatry, 152,* 1145–1149.

Pliner, P., & Haddock, G. (1996). Perfectionism in weight-concerned and unconcerned women: An experimental approach. *International Journal of Eating Disorders, 19,* 381–389.

Plotkin, D.A., Mintz, J., & Jarvik, L.F. (1985). Subjective memory complaints in geriatric depression. *American Journal of Psychiatry, 142,* 1103–1105.

Pokorny, A.D. (1968). Myths about suicide. In H.L.P. Resnik (Ed.), *Suicidal behaviors.* Boston: Little, Brown.

Polich, J.M., Armor, D.J., & Braiker, H.B. (1980). Patterns of alcoholism over four years. *Journal of Studies on Alcohol, 41,* 397–415.

Polivy, J. (1976). Perception of calories and regulation of intake in restrained and unrestrained eaters. *Addictive Behaviors, 1,* 237–244.

Polivy, J., & Herman, C.P. (1985). Dieting and binging: A causal analysis. *American Psychologist, 40,* 193–201.

Polivy, J., Heatherton, T.F., & Herman, C.P. (1988). Self-esteem, restraint and eating behavior. *Journal of Abnormal Psychology, 97,* 354–356.

Polivy, J., Herman, C.P., & Howard, K. (1980). The Restraint Scale. In A. Stunkard (Ed.), *Obesity.* Philadelphia: Saunders.

Polivy, J., Herman, C.P., & McFarlane, T. (1994). Effects of anxiety on eating: Does palatability moderate distress-induced overeating in dieters? *Journal of Abnormal Psychology, 103,* 505–510.

Pollak, M.H. (1994). Heart rate reactivity to laboratory tests and in two daily life settings. *Psychosomatic Medicine, 56,* 271–276.

Pollak, R. (1997). *The creation of Dr. B.* New York: Simon & Schuster.

Pollard, C.A., Pollard, H.J., & Corn, K.J. (1989). Panic onset and major events in the lives of agoraphobics: A test of contiguity. *Journal of Abnormal Psychology, 98,* 318–321.

Polusny, M.A., & Follette, V.M. (1995). Long-term correlates of child sexual abuse: Theory and review of the empirical literature. *Applied and Preventive Psychology, 4,* 143–166.

Ponce, F., & Atkinson, D. (1989). Mexican-Americans and acculturation, counselor ethnicity, counseling style, and perceived counselor credibility. *Journal of Counseling Psychology, 36,* 203–208.

Pope, K.S. (1995). What psychologists better know about recovered memories, research, lawsuits, and the pivotal experiment: A review of "The Myth of Repressed Memory: False Memories and Allegations of Sexual Abuse," by Elizabeth Loftus and Katherine Ketcham. *Clinical Psychology: Science and Practice, 2,* 304–315.

Posner, M.I. (1992). Attention as a cognitive and neural system. *Current Directions in Psychological Science, 1,* 11–14.

Post, F. (1978). The functional psychosis. In A.D. Isaacs & F. Post (Eds.), *Studies in geriatric psychiatry.* Chichester, England: Wiley.

Post, F. (1980). Paranoid, schizophrenia-like and schizophrenic states in the aged. In J.E. Birren & R.B. Sloane (Eds.), *Handbook of mental health and aging.* Englewood Cliffs, NJ: Prentice-Hall.

Post, F. (1987). Paranoid and schizophrenic disorders among the aging. In L.L. Carstensen & B.A. Edelstein (Eds.), *Handbook of clinical gerontology.* New York: Pergamon.

Post, S.G. (1994). Genetics, ethics, and Alzheimer's disease. *Journal of the American Geriatrics Society, 42,* 782–786.

Poster, D.S., Penta, J.S., Bruno, S., & Macdonald, J.S. (1981). Delta 9-tetrahydrocannabinol in clinical oncology. *Journal of the American Medical Association, 245,* 2047–2051.

Potashnik, S., & Pruchno, R. (1988, November). *Spouse caregivers: Physical and mental health in perspective.* Paper presented at the meeting of the Gerontological Society of America, San Francisco.

Powell, L.H., Friedman, M., Thoresen, C.E., Gill, J.J., & Ulmer, D.K. (1984). Can the type A behavior pattern be altered after myocardial infarction? A second year report from the Recurrent Coronary Prevention Project. *Psychosomatic Medicine, 46,* 293–313.

Praderas, K., & MacDonald, M.L. (1986). Telephone conversational skills training with socially isolated impaired nursing home residents. *Journal of Applied Behavior Analysis, 19,* 337–348.

Premack, D. (1959). Toward empirical behavior laws: 1. Positive reinforcement. *Psychological Review, 66,* 219–233.

Pressman, B., & Sheps, A. (1994). Treating wife abuse: An integrated model. *International Journal of Group Psychotherapy, 44,* 477–498.

Price, L.H., Charney, D.S., Rubin, A.L., & Heninger, G.R. (1986). Alpha-2 adrenergic receptor function in depression. *Archives of General Psychiatry, 43,* 849–860.

Price, R.A., Cadoret, R.J., Stunkard, A.J., & Troughton, E. (1987). Genetic contributions to human fatness: An adoption study. *American Journal of Psychiatry, 144,* 1003–1008.

Price, V.A. (1982). *Type A behavior pattern: A model for research and practice.* New York: Academic Press.

Prien, R.F., & Potter, W.Z. (1993). Maintenance treatment for mood disorders. In D.L. Dunner (Ed.), *Current psychiatric therapy.* Philadelphia: Saunders.

Prieto, S.L., Cole D.A., & Tageson, C.W. (1992). Depressive self-schemas in clinic and nonclinic children. *Cognitive Therapy and Research, 16,* 521–534.

Prinz, P., & Raskind, M. (1978). Aging and sleep disorders. In R. Williams & R.

Karacan (Eds.), *Sleep disorders: Diagnosis and treatment*. New York: Wiley.

Prioleau, L., Murdock, M., & Brody, N. (1983). An analysis of psychotherapy versus placebo studies. *The Behavioral and Brain Sciences, 6*, 275–310.

Prochaska, J.O. (1984). *Systems of psychotherapy* (2nd ed.). Homewood, IL: Dorsey Press.

Project Match Research Group. (1997). Matching alcoholism treatments to client heterogeneity: Project MATCH posttreatment drinking outcomes. *Journal of Studies on Alcohol, 58*, 7–29.

Pryor, T., Wiederman, M.W., & McGilley, B. (1996). Clinical correlates of anorexia subtypes. *International Journal of Eating Disorders, 19*, 371–379.

Pu, T., Mohamed, E., Imam, K., & El-Roey, A.M. (1986). One hundred cases of hysteria in eastern Libya. *British Journal of Psychiatry, 148*, 606–609.

Puig-Antich, J., Goetz, D., Davies, M., Kaplan, T., Davies, S., Ostrow, L., Asnis, L., Twomey, J., Iyengar, S., & Ryan, N.D. (1989). A controlled family history study of prepubertal major depressive disorder. *Archives of General Psychiatry, 46*, 406–418.

Puig-Antich, J., Kaufman, J., Ryan, N.D., Williamson, D.E., Dahl, R.E., Lukens, E., Todak, G., Ambrosini, P., Rabinovich, H., & Nelson, B. (1993). The psychosocial functioning and family environment of depressed adolescents. *American Academy of Child and Adolescent Psychiatry, 32*, 244–253.

Puig-Antich, J., Lukens, E., Davies, M., Goetz, D., Brennan-Quattrock, J., & Todak, G. (1985). Psychosocial functioning in prepubertal major depressive disorders: 1. Interpersonal relationships during the depressive period. *Archives of General Psychiatry, 42*, 500–507.

Puig-Antich, J., Perel, J.M., Lupatkin, W., Chambers, W.J., Tabrizi, M.A., King, J., Goetz, R., Davies, M., & Stiller, R.L. (1987). Imipramine in prepubertal major depressive disorders. *Archives of General Psychiatry, 44*, 81–89.

Purcell, K., & Weiss, J.H. (1970). Asthma. In C.G. Costello (Ed.), *Symptoms of psychopathology: A handbook*. New York: Wiley.

Purdie, F.R., Honigman, T.B., & Rosen, P. (1981). Acute organic brain syndrome: A view of 100 cases. *Annals of Emergency Medicine, 10*, 455–461.

Putnam, F.W., Guroff, J.J., Silberman, E.K., Barban, L., & Post, R.M. (1986). The clinical phenomenology of multiple personality disorder: Review of 100 recent cases. *Journal of Clinical Psychiatry, 47*, 285–293.

Putnam, F.W., Post, R.M., & Guroff, J.J. (1983). *100 cases of multiple personality disorder*. Paper presented at the annual meeting of the American Psychiatric Association, New York.

Putnam, F.W., Zahn, T.P., & Post, R.M. (1990). Differential autonomic nervous system activity in multiple personality disorder. *Psychiatry Research, 31*, 251–260.

Quay, H.C. (1979). Classification. In H.C. Quay & J.S. Werry (Eds.), *Psychopathological disorders of childhood* (2nd ed.). New York: Wiley.

Quay, H.C., & Parskeuopoulos, I.N. (1972, August). *Dimensions of problem behavior in elementary school children in Greece, Iran, and Finland*. Paper presented at the 20th International Congress of Psychology, Tokyo.

Rabavilas, A., & Boulougouris, J. (1974). Physiological accompaniments of ruminations, flooding and thought-stopping in obsessional patients. *Behaviour Research and Therapy, 12*, 239–244.

Rabins, P.V., & Folstein, M.F. (1982). Delirium and dementia: Diagnostic criteria and fatality rates. *British Journal of Psychiatry, 140*, 149–153.

Rabkin, J.G. (1974). Public attitudes toward mental illness: A review of the literature. *Schizophrenia Bulletin, 9*, 9–33.

Raboch, J., & Faltus, F. (1991). Sexuality of women with anorexia nervosa. *Acta Psychiatrica Scandinavica, 84*, 9–11.

Rachman, S.J. (1966). Sexual fetishism: An experimental analogue. *Psychological Record, 16*, 293–296.

Rachman, S. & deSilva, P. (1978). Abnormal and normal obsessions. *Behaviour Research and Therapy, 16*, 233–248.

Rachman, S.J., & Hodgson, R.J. (1980). *Obsessions and compulsions*. Englewood Cliffs, NJ: Prentice-Hall.

Rachman, S.J., & Wilson, G.T. (1980). *The effects of psychological therapy* (2nd ed.). Elmsford, NY: Pergamon.

Rahe, R.H., & Lind, E. (1971). Psychosocial factors and sudden cardiac death: A pilot study. *Journal of Psychosomatic Research, 15*, 19–24.

Raj, B.A., Corvea, M.H., & Dagon, E.M. (1993). The clinical characteristics of panic disorder in the elderly: A retrospective study. *Journal of Clinical Psychiatry, 54*, 150–155.

Ramsey, J.M., Andreason, P., Zametkin, A.J., Aquino, T., King, A.C., Hamburger, S.D., Pikus, A., Rapoport, J.L., & Cohen, R.M. (1992). Failure to activate the left tempoparietal cortex in dyslexia: An oxygen 15 positron emission tomographic study. *Archives of Neurology, 49*, 527–534.

Ramsey, J.M., Zametkin, A.J., Andreason, P., Hanahan, A.P., Hamburger, S.D., Aquino, T., King, A.C., Pikus, A., & Cohen, R.M. (1994). Normal activation of frontotemporal language cortex in dyslexia, as measured with oxygen 15 positron emission tomography. *Archives of Neurology, 51*, 27–38.

Rapaport, D. (1951). *The organization and pathology of thought*. New York: Columbia University Press.

Rapp, S.R., Parisi, S.A., & Walsh, D.A. (1988). Psychological dysfunction and physical health among elderly medical inpatients. *Journal of Consulting and Clinical Psychology, 56*, 851–855.

Rapp, S.R., Parisi, S.A., Walsh, D.A., & Wallace, C.E. (1988). Detecting depression in elderly medical impatients. *Journal of Consulting and Clinical Psychology, 56*, 509–513.

Rappaport, J. (1977). *Community psychology: Values, research, and action*. New York: Holt, Rinehart & Winston.

Rappaport, J., & Chinsky, J.M. (1974). Models for delivery of service from a historical and conceptual perspective. *Professional Psychology, 5*, 42–50.

Raskin, F., & Rae, D.S. (1981). Psychiatric symptoms in the elderly. *Psychopharmacology Bulletin, 17*, 96–99.

Raskind, M.A., Carta, A., & Bravi, D. (1995). Is early-onset Alzheimer disease a distinct subgroup within the Alzheimer disease population? *Alzheimer Disease and Associated Disorders, 9*, S2–S6.

Rasmussen, D.X., Brandt, J., Martin, D.B., & Folstein, M.F. (1995). Head injury as a risk factor in Alzheimer's disease. *Brain Injury, 9*, 213–219.

Rather, B.C., Goldman, M.S., Roehrich,L., & Brannick, M. (1992). Empirical modeling of an alcohol expectancy memory network using multidimensional scaling. *Journal of Abnormal Psychology, 101*, 174–183.

Rauch, S.L., & Jenike, M.A. (1993). Neurobiological models of obsessive-compulsive disorder. *Psychosomatics, 34*, 20–30.

Rauch, S.L., Jenike, M.A., Alpert, N.M., Baer, L., Breiter, H.C.R., et al. (1994). Regional cerebral blood flow measured during symptom provocation in obsessive-compulsive disorder using oxygen-15 labeled carbon dioxide and positron emission tomography. *Archives of General Psychiatry, 51*, 62–70.

Red Horse, Y. (1982). A cultural network model: Perspectives for adolescent services and paraprofessional training. In S. Manson (Ed.), *New directions in prevention among American Indians and Alaskan Native communities*. Portland: Oregon Health Sciences University.

Redmond, D.E. (1977). Alterations in the function of the nucleus locus coeruleus. In I. Hanin & E. Usdin (Eds.), *Animal models in psychiatry and neurology*. New York: Pergamon.

Reed, S.D., Katkin, E.S., & Goldband, S. (1986). Biofeedback and behavioral medicine. In F.H. Kanfer & A.P. Goldstein (Eds.), *Helping people change: A textbook of methods* (3rd ed.). Elmsford, NY: Pergamon.

Rees, L. (1964). The importance of psychological, allergic and infective factors in childhood asthma. *Journal of Psychosomatic Research, 7,* 253–262.

Regier, D.A., Boyd, J.H., Burke, J.D., Jr., Rae, D.S., Myers, J.K., Kramer, M., Robins, L.N., George, L.K., Karno, M., & Locke, B.Z. (1988). One-month prevalence of mental disorders in the United States. *Archives of General Psychiatry, 45,* 977–1986.

Reich, J. (1990). Comparison of males and females with DSM-III dependent personality disorder. *Psychiatry Research, 33,* 207–214.

Reifler, B.V. (1994). Depression: Diagnosis and comorbidity. In L.S. Schneider, C.F. Reynolds, III, B.D. Lebowitz, & A.J. Friedhoff (Eds.), *Diagnosis and treatment of depression in late life* (pp. 55–59). Washington, DC: American Psychiatric Press.

Reifler, B.V., Larson, E., & Hanley, R. (1982). Coexistence of cognitive impairment and depression in geriatric outpatients. *American Journal of Psychiatry, 139,* 623–626.

Reiss, D., Heatherington, E.M., Plomin, R., Howe, G.W., Simmens, S.J., et al. (1995). Genetic questions for environmental studies: Differential parenting and psychopathology in adolescence. *Archives of General Psychiatry, 52,* 925–936.

Reiss, I.L., & Leik, R.K. (1989). Evaluating strategies to avoid AIDS: Number of partners vs. use of condoms. *The Journal of Sex Research, 26,* 411–433.

Rekers, G.A., & Lovaas, O.I. (1974). Behavioral treatment of deviant sex role behaviors in a male child. *Journal of Applied Behavioral Analysis, 7,* 173–190.

Renshaw, D.C. (1988). Profile of 2376 patients treated at Loyola Sex Clinic between 1972 and 1987. *Sexual and Marital Therapy, 3,* 111–117.

Renvoize, E.B., & Beveridge, A.W. (1989). Mental illness and the late Victorians: A study of patients admitted to three asylums in York, 1880–1884. *Psychological Medicine, 19,* 19–28.

Reppucci, N.D., & Haugaard, J.J. (1989). Prevention of child sexual abuse: Myth or reality. *American Psychologist, 44,* 1266–1275.

Reppucci, N.D., Jones, L.M., & Cook, S.L. (1994). Involving parents in child sexual abuse prevention programs. *Journal of Child and Family Studies, 3,* 137–142.

Rescorla, R.A. (1988). Pavlovian conditioning: It's not what you think it is.

American Psychologist, 43, 151–160.

Resick, P.A. (1992). Cognitive treatment of crime-related post-traumatic stress disorder. In R. Peters, R. McMahon, & V. Quinsey (Eds.), *Aggression and violence throughout the life span.* (pp. 171–191). Newbury Park, CA: Sage.

Resick, P.A. (1993). The psychological impact of rape. *Journal of Interpersonal Violence, 8,* 223–255.

Resick, P.A., & Schnicke, M.K. (1992). Cognitive processing therapy for sexual assault victims. *Journal of Consulting and Clinical Psychology, 60,* 748–756.

Resick, P.A., Veronen, L.J., Calhoun, K.S., Kilpatrick, D.G., & Atkeson, B.M. (1986). Assessment of fear reactions in sexual assault victims: A factor-analytic study of the Veronen–Kilpatrick Modified Fear Survey. *Behavioral Assessment, 8,* 271–283.

Reynolds, C.R., Chastain, R.L., Kaufman, A.S., & McLean, J.E. (1997). Demographic characteristics and IQ among adults: Analysis of the WAIS-R standardization sample as a function of the stratification variables. *Journal of School Psychology, 25,* 323–342.

Riccardi, N., & Leeds, J. (1997, February 24). Megan's law calling up old, minor offenses. *Los Angeles Times,* pp. A1, A16.

Richardson, J.L., Dwyer, K.M., McGuigan, K., Hansen, W.B., Dent, C.W., Johnson, C.A., Sussman, S.Y., Brannon, B., & Flay, B. (1989). Substance use among eighth grade students who take care of themselves after school. *Pediatrics, 84,* 556–566.

Richman, D.D. (1996). HIV therapeutics. *Science, 272,* 1886–1888.

Ricks, D.M. (1972). *The beginning of vocal communication in infants and autistic children.* Unpublished doctoral dissertation, University of London.

Ridley, C.R. (1984). Clinical treatment of the nondisclosing black client. *American Psychologist, 39,* 1234–1244.

Rieder, R.O., Mann, L.S., Weinberger, D.R., van Kammen, D.P., & Post, R.M. (1983). Computer tomographic scans in patients with schizophrenia, schizoaffective, and bipolar affective disorder. *Archives of General Psychiatry, 40,* 735–739.

Riesmann, F. (1990). Restructuring help: A human services paradigm for the 1990s. *American Journal of Community Psychology, 18,* 221–231.

Riggs, D. et al. (1991). Post-traumatic stress disorder following rape and nonsexual assault: A predictive model. Unpublished manuscript.

Rimland, B. (1964). *Infantile autism.* New York: Appleton-Century-Crofts.

Ringwalt, C., Ennett, S.T., & Holt, K.D. (1991). An outcome evaluation of Project DARE (Drug Abuse Resistance Education). *Health Education Research, 6,* 327–337.

Ritter, B. (1968). The group treatment of children's snake phobias, using vicarious and contact desensitization procedures. *Behaviour Research and Therapy, 6,* 1–6.

Rittig, S., Knudsen, U.B., Norgaard, J.P., Pedersen, E.B., & Djurhuus, J.C. (1989). Abnormal diurnal rhythm of plasma vasopressin and urinary output in patients with enuresis. *American Journal of Physiology, 256,* 664–671.

Ritvo, E.R., Freeman, B.J., Geller, E., & Yuwiler, A. (1983). Effects of fenfluramine on 14 outpatients with the syndrome of autism. *Journal of the American Academy of Child Psychiatry, 22,* 549–558.

Roan, S. (1992, October 15). Giving up coffee tied to withdrawal symptoms. *Los Angeles Times,* p. A26.

Roberts, M.C., Wurtele, S.K., Boone, R.R., Ginther, L.J., & Elkins, P.D. (1981). Reduction of medical fears by use of modeling: A preventive application in a general population of children. *Journal of Pediatric Psychology, 6,* 293–300.

Robins, L.N. (1966). *Deviant children grown up.* Baltimore: Williams & Wilkins.

Robins, L.N. (1978). Sturdy childhood predictors of adult antisocial behavior: Replications from longitudinal studies. *Psychological Medicine, 8,* 611–622.

Robins, L.N., Helzer, J.E., Przybec, T.R., & Regier, D.A. (1988). Alcohol disorders in the community: A report from the Epidemiological Catchment Area. In R.M. Rose & J.E. Barrett (Eds.), *Alcoholism: Origins and outcome.* NY: Raven.

Robins, L.N., Helzer, J.E., Weissman, M.M., Orvaschel, H., Gruenberg, E., Burke, J.D., & Reiger, D.A. (1984). Lifetime prevalence of specific psychiatric disorders in three sites. *Archives of General Psychiatry, 41,* 942–949.

Robinson, N.M., & Robinson, H.B. (1976). *The mentally retarded child* (2nd ed.). New York: McGraw-Hill.

Robinson, N.S., Garber, J., & Hillsman, R. (1995). Cognitions and stress: Direct and moderating effects on depression versus externalizing symptoms during the junior high school transition. *Journal of Abnormal Psychology, 104,* 453–463.

Rodin, J. (1980). Managing the stress of aging: The control of control and coping. In H. Ursin & S. Levine (Eds.), *Coping and health.* New York: Academic Press.

Rodin, J. (1983). Behavioral medicine: Beneficial effects of self-control training in aging. *International Review of Applied Psychology, 32,* 153–181.

Rodin, J. (1986). Aging and health: Effects of the sense of control. *Science, 233,*

1271–1276.

Rodin, J., & Ickovics, J.R. (1990). Women's health: Review and research agenda as we approach the 21st century. *American Psychologist, 45*, 1018–1034.

Rodin, J., & Langer, E.J. (1977). Long-term effects of a control-relevant intervention with the institutionalized aged. *Journal of Personality and Social Psychology, 35*, 897–902.

Rodin, J., McAvay, G., & Timko, C. (1988). A longitudinal study of depressed mood and sleep disturbances in elderly adults. *Journal of Gerontology: Psychological Sciences, 43*, 45–53.

Roesch, R., & Golding, S.L. (1980). *Competency to stand trial*. Urbana: University of Illinois Press.

Rogers, C.R. (1942). *Counseling and psychotherapy: New concepts in practice*. Boston: Houghton Mifflin.

Rogers, C.R. (1951). *Client-centered therapy*. Boston: Houghton Mifflin.

Rogers, C.R. (1961). *On becoming a person: A therapist's view of psychotherapy*. Boston: Houghton Mifflin.

Rogers, C.R. (1970). *Carl Rogers on encounter groups*. New York: Harper & Row.

Rogers, J.H., Widiger, T.A., & Krupp, A. (1995). Aspects of depression associated with borderline personality disorder. *American Journal of Psychiatry, 152*, 288–290.

Rogler, L.H., & Hollingshead, A.B. (1985). *Trapped: Families and schizophrenia* (3rd ed.). Maplewood, NJ: Waterfront Press.

Rohde, P., Lewinsohn, P.M., & Seeley, J.R. (1991). Comorbidity of unipolar depression: 2. Comorbidity with other mental disorders in adolescents and adults. *Journal of Abnormal Psychology, 54*, 653–660.

Rokeach, M. (1973). *The nature of human values*. New York: Free Press.

Rokeach, M. (1979). Some unresolved issues in theories of beliefs, attitudes, and values. *Proceedings of the Nebraska Symposium on Motivation*. Lincoln: University of Nebraska Press.

Romanczyk, R.G., Diament, C., Goren, E.R., Trundeff, G., & Harris, S.L. (1975). Increasing isolate and social play in severely disturbed children: Intervention and postintervention effectiveness. *Journal of Autism and Childhood Schizophrenia, 43*, 730–739.

Romero, D. (1992, March 7). Two drugs crash the party scene. *Los Angeles Times*, pp. A1, A22–23.

Ronningstam, E., & Gunderson, J.G. (1990). Identifying criteria for narcissistic personality disorder. *American Journal of Psychiatry, 147*, 918–922.

Root, M.P. (1990). Disordered eating in women of color. *Sex Roles, 22*, 525–536.

Rooth, F.G. (1973). Exhibitionism, sexual violence, and pedophilia. *British Journal of Psychiatry, 122*, 705–710.

Rorsman, B., Hagnell, O., & Lanke, J. (1986). Prevalence and incidence of senile and multi-infarct dementia in the Lundby Study: A comparison between time periods 1947–1957 and 1957–1972. *Neuropsychobiology, 15*, 122–129.

Rorty, M., Yager, J., & Rossotto, E. (1994). Childhood sexual, physical, and psychological abuse in bulimia nervosa. *American Journal of Psychiatry, 151*, 1122–1126.

Rose, D.T., Abramson, L.Y., Hodulik, C.J., Halberstadt, L., & Gaye, L. (1994). Heterogeneity of cognitive style among depressed inpatients. *Journal of Abnormal Psychology, 103*, 419–429.

Rose, J. (1996). Anger management: A group treatment program for people with mental retardation. *Journal of Developmental and Physical Disabilities, 8*, 133–149.

Rose, S.D. (1986). Group methods. In F.H. Kanfer & A.P. Goldstein (Eds.), *Helping people change: A textbook of methods* (3rd ed.). Elmsford, NY: Pergamon.

Rosen, E., Fox, R., & Gregory, I. (1972). *Abnormal psychology* (2nd ed.). Philadelphia: Saunders.

Rosen, R.C. (1991). Alcohol and drug effects on sexual response: Human experimental and clinical studies. *Annual Review of Sex Research, 2*, 119–180.

Rosen, R.C., & Beck, J.G. (1988). *Patterns of sexual arousal: Psychophysiological processes and clinical applications*. New York: Guilford.

Rosen, R.C., & Hall, E. (1984). *Sexuality*. New York: Random House.

Rosen, R.C., & Leiblum, S.R. (1995). Treatment of sexual disorders in the 1990s: An integrated approach. *Journal of Consulting and Clinical Psychology, 63*, 877–890.

Rosen, R.C., & Rosen, L. (1981). *Human sexuality*. New York: Knopf.

Rosen, R.C., Leiblum, S.R., & Spector, I. (1994). Psychologically based treatment for male erectile disorder: A cognitive-interpersonal model. *Journal of Sex and Marital Therapy, 20*, 67–85.

Rosenbaum, M. (1980). The role of the term schizophrenia in the decline of diagnoses of multiple personality. *Archives of General Psychiatry, 37*, 1383–1385.

Rosenberg, M.S., & Reppucci, N.D. (1985). Primary prevention of child abuse. *Journal of Consulting and Clinical Psychology, 53*, 576–585.

Rosenfarb, I.S.,. Goldstein, M.J., Mintz, J., & Neuchterlein, K.H. (1994). Expressed emotion and subclinical psychopathology observable within transactions between schizophrenics and their family members. *Journal of Abnormal Psychology, 104*, 259–267.

Rosenman, R.H., Brand, R.J., Jenkins, C.D., Friedman, M., Straus, R., & Wurm, M. (1975). Coronary heart disease in the Western Collaborative Group Study: Final follow-up experience of 8 years. *Journal of the American Medical Association, 233*, 872–877.

Rosenman, R.H., Friedman, M., Straus, R., Wurm, M., Kositichek, R., Hahn, W., & Werthessen, N.T. (1964). A predictive study of coronary heart disease. *Journal of the American Medical Association, 189*, 103–110.

Rosenthal, D. (1955). Changes in some moral values following psychotherapy. *Journal of Consulting Psychology, 19*, 431–436.

Rosenthal, D. (1970). *Genetic theory and abnormal behavior*. New York: McGraw-Hill.

Rosenthal, N.E., Carpenter, C.J., James, S.P., Parry, B.L., Rogers, S.L.B., & Wehr, T.A. (1986). Seasonal affective disorder in children and adolescents. *American Journal of Psychiatry, 143*, 356–358.

Rosenthal, R. (1966). *Experimenter bias in behavioral research*. New York: Appleton-Century-Crofts.

Rosenthal, R. (1995). Critiquing Pygmalion: A 25 year perspective. *Current Directions in Psychological Science, 4*, 171–172.

Rosenthal, T.L., & Bandura, A. (1978). Psychological modeling: Theory and practice. In S.L. Garfield & A.E. Bergin (Eds.), *Handbook of psychotherapy and behavior change: An empirical analysis* (2nd ed.). New York: Wiley.

Rosenzweig, R., & Fillit, H. (1992). Probable heterosexual transmission of AIDS in an aged woman. *Journal of the American Geriatric Society, 40*, 1261–1264.

Rosman, B.L., Minuchin, S., & Liebman, R. (1975). Family lunch session: An introduction to family therapy in anorexia nervosa. *American Journal of Orthopsychiatry, 45*, 846–852.

Rosman, B.L., Minuchin, S., & Liebman, R. (1976). Input and outcome of family therapy of anorexia nervosa. In J.L. Claghorn (Ed.), *Successful psychotherapy*. New York: Brunner/Mazel.

Ross, C.A. (1989). *Multiple personality disorder: Diagnosis, clinical features, and treatment*. New York: Wiley.

Ross, C.A. (1991). Epidemiology of multiple personality disorder and dissociation. *Psychiatric Clinics of North America, 14*, 503–517.

Ross, C.A., Miller, S.D., Reagor, P., Bjornson, L., & Fraser, G.A. (1990). Structured interview data on 102 cases of multiple personality from four centers.

American Journal of Psychiatry, 147, 596–600.

Ross, D.M., & Ross, S.A. (1982). *Hyperactivity: Research, theory, and action.* New York: Wiley.

Roth, D., & Rehm, L.P. (1980). Relationships among self-monitoring processes, memory, and depression. *Cognitive Therapy and Research, 4,* 149–157.

Roth, M. (1955). The natural history of mental disorder in old age. *Journal of Mental Science, 99,* 439–450.

Roth, M., & Kay, D.W.K. (1956). Affective disorder arising in the senium: 2. Physical disability as an etiological factor. *Journal of Mental Science, 102,* 141–150.

Rothbaum, B.O., & Foa, E.B. (1992). Exposure therapy for rape victims with posttraumatic stress disorder. *the Behavior Therapist, 15,* 219–222.

Rothbaum, B.O., Foa, E.B., Murdock, T., Riggs, D.S., & Walsh, W. (1992). A prospective examination of post-traumatic stress disorder in rape victims. *Journal of Traumatic Stress, 5,* 455–475.

Rothbaum, B.O., Hodges, L., Watson, B.A., Kessler, G.D., et al. (1996). Virtual reality exposure therapy in the treatment of fear of flying: A case report. *Behaviour Research and Therapy, 34,* 477–481.

Rothbaum, B.O., Hodges, L.F., Kooper, R., Opdyke, D., Williford, J.S., & North, M. (1995a). The efficacy of virtual reality graded exposure in the treatment of acrophobia. *American Journal of Psychiatry, 152,* 626–628.

Rothbaum, B.O., Hodges, L.F., Kooper, R., Opdyke, D., Williford, J.S., & North, M. (1995b). Virtual reality graded exposure in the treatment of acrophobia. A case report. *Behavior Therapy, 26,* 547–554.

Rounsaville, B.J., Chevron, E.S., & Weissman, M.M. (1984). Specification of techniques in interpersonal psychotherapy. In J.B.W. Williams & R.L. Spitzer (Eds.), *Psychotherapy research: Where are we and where should we go?* New York: Guilford.

Rovner, B.W., Kafonek, S., Filipp, L., Lucas, M.J., & Folstein, M.F. (1986). Prevalence of mental illness in a community nursing home. *American Journal of Psychiatry, 143,* 1446–1449.

Rowston, W.M., & Lacey, H.J. (1992). Stealing in bulimia nervosa. *International Journal of Social Psychiatry, 38,* 309–313.

Roy, A. (1982). Suicide in chronic schizophrenia. *British Journal of Psychiatry, 141,* 171–180.

Roy, A. (1994). Recent biologic studies on suicide. *Suicide and Life Threatening Behaviors, 24,* 10–24.

Roy, A. (1995). Suicide. In H.I. Kaplan & B.J. Sadock (Eds.), *Comprehensive textbook of psychiatry* (pp. 1739–1752). Balti-

more: Williams & Wilkins.

Roy, A., & Linnoila, M. (1986). Alcoholism and suicide. *Suicide and Life Threatening Behaviors, 16,* 244–259.

Roy, A., Everett, D., Pickar, D., & Paul, S.M. (1987). Platelet tritiated imipramine binding and serotonin uptake in depressed patients. *Archives of General Psychiatry, 44,* 320–327.

Roy, A., Segal, N., Centerwall, B., & Robinette, D. (1991). Suicide in twins. *Archives of General Psychiatry, 48,* 29–36.

Ruberman, W., Weinblatt, E., Goldberg, J.D., & Chaudhary, B.S. (1984). Psychosocial influences on mortality after myocardial infarction. *New England Journal of Medicine, 311,* 552–559.

Rubin, P., Holm, S., Madsen, R.L., Friberg, L., et al. (1993). Regional cerebral blood flow in newly diagnosed schizophrenic and schizophreniform disorders. *Psychiatry Research, 53,* 57–75.

Rubin, R.T., Phillips, J.J., Sadow, T.F., & McCracken, J.T. (1995). Adrenal gland volume in major depression: Increase during the depressive episode and decrease with successful treatment. *Archives of General Psychiatry, 52,* 213–218.

Ruch, L.O., & Leon, J.J. (1983). Sexual assault trauma and trauma change. *Women and Health, 8,* 5–21.

Rush, A.J., Beck, A.T., Kovacs, M., & Hollon, S.D. (1977). Comparative efficacy of cognitive therapy and pharmacotherapy in the treatment of depressed outpatients. *Cognitive Therapy and Research, 1,* 17–39.

Rush, A.J., Beck, A.T., Kovacs, M., Weissenberger, J., & Hollon, S.D. (1982). Comparison of the effects of cognitive therapy on hopelessness and self-concept. *American Journal of Psychiatry, 139,* 862–866.

Russell, M.A.H., Feyerabend, C., & Cole, P.V. (1976). Plasma nicotine levels after cigarette smoking and chewing nicotine gum. *British Medical Journal, 290,* 1043–1046.

Russo, D.C., & Varni, J.W. (1982). Behavioral pediatrics. In D.C. Russo & J.W. Varni (Eds.), *Behavioral pediatrics: Research and practice.* New York: Plenum.

Rutter, M. (1967). Psychotic disorders in early childhood. In A.J. Cooper (Ed.), *Recent developments in schizophrenia* [Special publication]. *British Journal of Psychiatry.*

Rutter, M. (1971). Parent–child separation: Psychological effects on the children. *Journal of Child Psychology and Psychiatry, 12,* 233–260.

Rutter, M., & Schopler, E. (1987). Autism and pervasive developmental disorders: Concepts and diagnostic issues.

Journal of Autism and Developmental Disorders, 17, 159–186.

Ryall, R. (1974). Delinquency: The problem for treatment. *Social Work Today, 15,* 98–104.

Ryan, W. (1971). *Blaming the victim.* New York: Random House.

Rybstein-Blinchik, E. (1979). Effects of different cognitive strategies on chronic pain experience. *Journal of Behavioral Medicine, 2,* 93–101.

Sabin, J.E. (1975). Translating despair. *American Journal of Psychiatry, 132,* 197–199.

Sachs, J.S. (1983). Negative factors in brief psychotherapy: An empirical assessment. *Journal of Consulting and Clinical Psychology, 51,* 557–564.

Sackeim, H.A., Nordlie, J.W., & Gur, R.C. (1979). A model of hysterical and hypnotic blindness: Cognition, motivation and awareness. *Journal of Abnormal Psychology, 88,* 474–489.

Sacks, O. (1985). The twins. In *The man who mistook his wife for a hat and other clinical tales.* New York: Harper & Row.

Sacks, O. (1995). *An anthropologist on Mars.* New York: Knopf.

Safer, D.J., & Krager, J.M. (1988). A survey of medication treatment for hyperactive/inattentive students. *Journal of the American Medical Association, 260,* 2256–2258.

Saffer, H. (1991). Alcohol advertising bans and alcohol abuse: An international perspective. *Journal of Health Economics, 10,* 65–79.

Safran, J.D., Vallis, T.M., Segal, Z.V., & Shaw, B.F. (1986). Assessment of core cognitive processes in cognitive therapy. *Cognitive Therapy and Research, 10,* 509–526.

Sager, C.J. (1990). Foreword. In I.L. Kutash & A. Wolf (Eds.), *The group psychotherapist's handbook: Contemporary theory and technique.* New York: Columbia University Press.

Sakel, M. (1938). The pharmacological shock treatment of schizophrenia. *Nervous and Mental Disease Monograph, 62.*

Saks, E. (1997). *Jekyll on trial: MPD and criminal law.* New York: New York University Press.

Salan, S.E., Zinberg, N.E., & Frei, E. (1975). Antiemetic effect of delta-9-THC in patients receiving cancer chemotherapy. *New England Journal of Medicine, 293,* 795–797.

Salovey, P., & Singer, J.A. (1991). Cognitive behavior modification. In F.H. Kanfer & A.P. Goldstein (Eds.), *Helping people change: A textbook of methods* (4th ed.). Elmsford, NY: Pergamon.

Salter, A. (1949). *Conditioned reflex therapy.* New York: Farrar, Straus.

Saltzman, D. (1995). *The jester has lost his*

jingle. Palos Verdes Estates, CA: The Jester Company.

Salzman, L. (1980). *Psychotherapy of the obsessive personality.* New York: Jason Aronson.

Salzman, L. (1985). Psychotherapeutic management of obsessive-compulsive patients. *American Journal of Psychotherapy, 39,* 323–330.

Sanday, P.R. (1981). The socio-cultural context of rape: A cross-cultural study. *The Journal of Social Issues, 37,* 5–27.

Sanderson, W.C., DiNardo, P.A., Rapee, R.M., & Barlow, D.H. (1990). Syndrome comorbidity in patients diagnosed with a DSM-IIIR anxiety disorder. *Journal of Abnormal Psychology, 99,* 308–312.

Sanderson, W.C., Rapee, R.M., & Barlow, D.H. (1989). The influence of an illusion of control on panic attacks induced via inhalation of 5.5% carbon dioxide-enriched air. *Archives of General Psychiatry, 46,* 157–162.

Sandler, J. (1986). Aversion methods. In F.H. Kanfer & A.P. Goldstein (Eds.), *Helping people change: A textbook of methods* (3rd ed.). Elmsford, NY: Pergamon.

Sandler, J. (1991). Aversion methods. In F.H. Kanfer & A.P. Goldstein (Eds.), *Helping people change: A textbook of methods.* Elmsford, NY: Pergamon.

Sano, M., Ernesto, C., Thomas, R. G., Klauber, M. R., Schafer, K., Grundman, M., Woodbury, P., Growdon, J., Cotman, C. W., Pfeiffer, E., Schneider, L. S., Thai, L. J., for the Members of the Alzheimer's Disease Cooperative Study. (1997). A controlled trial of selegiline, alpha-tocopherol, or both as treatment for Alzheimer's disease. *New England Journal of Medicine, 336,* 1216–1222.

Sartorius, N., Shapiro, R., & Jablonsky, A. (1974). The international pilot study of schizophrenia. *Schizophrenia Bulletin, 2,* 21–35.

Saunders, E.A. (1991). Rorschach indicators of chronic childhood sexual abuse in female borderline patients. *Bulletin of the Menninger Clinic, 55,* 48–71.

Savage, D.G. (1996, December 11). High court debates sexual predator law. *Los Angeles Times,* p. A26.

Savage, D.G., & Dolan, M. (1996, December 12). Sex predator law faces high court challenge. *Los Angeles Times,* pp. A1, A22.

Sayette, M.A., & Wilson, G.T. (1991). Intoxication and exposure to stress: Effects of temporal patterning. *Journal of Abnormal Psychology, 100,* 56–62.

Sbrocco, T., Weisberg, R.B., & Barlow, D.H. (1995). Sexual dysfunction in the older adult: Assessment of psychosocial factors. *Sexuality and Disability, 13,* 201–218.

Scarborough, H.S. (1990). Very early language deficits in dyslexic children. *Child Development, 61,* 128–174.

Scarlett, W. (1980). Social isolation from age-mates among nursery school children. *Journal of Child Psychology and Psychiatry, 21,* 231–240.

Schaie, K.W., & Hertzog, C. (1982). Longitudinal methods. In B.B. Wolman (Ed.), *Handbook of developmental psychology.* Englewood Cliffs, NJ: Prentice-Hall.

Schall, P.L., Landsbergis, P.A., & Baker, D. (1994). Job strain and cardiovascular disease. *Annual Review of Public Health, 15,* 381–411.

Scharff, J.S. (1995). Psychoanalytic marital therapy. In N.S. Jacobson & A.S. Gurman (Eds.), *Clinical handbook of couple therapy.* New York: Guilford.

Schatzberg, A.F. (1991). Overview of anxiety disorders: Prevalence, biology, course, and treatment. *Journal of Clinical Psychiatry, 52,* 5–9.

Scheerer, M., Rothman, E., & Goldstein, K. (1945). A case of "idiot savant": An experimental study of personality organization. *Psychological Monographs, 58* (Whole No. 269).

Scheff, T.J. (1966). *Being mentally ill: A sociological theory.* Chicago: Aldine.

Schellenberg, G.D., Bird, T.D., Wijsman, E.M., Moore, D.K., Boehkne, E.M., Bryant, E.M., Lampe, T.H., Nochlin, D., Sumi, S.M., Deeb, S.S., Bayreuther, K., & Martin, G.M. (1988). Absence of linkage of chromosome 21q21 markers to familial Alzheimer's disease. *Science, 241,* 1507–1510.

Schinke, S.P., & Gilchrist, L.D. (1985). Preventing substance abuse with children and adolescents. *Journal of Consulting and Clinical Psychology, 53,* 596–602.

Schleifer, M. (1995). Should we change our views about early childhood education? *Alberta Journal of Educational Research, 41,* 355–359.

Schlundt, D.G., & Johnson, W.G. (1990). *Eating disorders: Assessment and treatment.* Needham Heights, MA: Allyn & Bacon.

Schmitt, B.D. (1982). Nocturnal enuresis: An update on treatment. *Pediatric Clinics of North America, 29,* 21–37.

Schnall, P.L., Landsbergis, P.A., & Baker, D. (1994). Job Strain and cardiovascular disease. *Annual Review of Public Health, 15,* 381–411.

Schneider, J. (1996). Geriatric psychopharmacology. In L.L. Carstensen, B.A. Edelstein, & L. Dornbrand (Eds.), *The practical handbook of clinical gerontology* (pp. 481–542). Thousand Oaks, CA: Sage.

Schneider, K. (1959). *Clinical psychopathology.* New York: Grune & Stratton.

Schneider, N.G. (1987). Nicotine gum in smoking cessation: Rationale, efficacy, and proper use. *Comprehensive Therapy,*

13, 32–37.

Schoenbach, V., Kaplan, B.H., Fredman, L., & Kleinaum, D.G. (1986). Social ties and mortality in Evans County, Georgia. *American Journal of Epidemiology, 123,* 577–591.

Schoeneman, T.J. (1977). The role of mental illness in the European witch-hunts of the sixteenth and seventeenth centuries: An assessment. *Journal of the History of the Behavioral Sciences, 13,* 337–351.

Schofield, W. (1964). *Psychotherapy: The purchase of friendship.* Englewood Cliffs, NJ: Prentice-Hall.

Schooler, C., Flora, J.A., & Farquhar, J.W. (1993). Moving toward synergy: Media supplementation in the Stanford Five-City Project. *Communication Research, 26,* 587–610.

Schopler, E., Short, B., & Mesibov, G.B. (1989). Comments. *Journal of Consulting and Clinical Psychology, 157,* 162–167.

Schuckit, M.A. (1983). The genetics of alcoholism. In B. Tabakoff, P.B. Sulker, & C.L. Randall (Eds.), *Medical and social aspects of alcohol use.* New York: Plenum.

Schuckit, M.A. (1994). Low level of response to alcohol as a predictor of future alcoholism. *American Journal of Psychiatry, 151,* 184–189.

Schuckit, M.A., & Smith, T.L. (1996). An 8-year follow-up of 450 sons of alcoholic and control subjects. *Archives of General Psychiatry, 53,* 202–210.

Schultz, J. (1991). Smoking-attributable mortality and years of potential life lost: U.S., 1988. *Morbidity and Mortality Weekly Report, 40,* 63–71.

Schultz, R., & Brenner, G. (1977). Relocation of the aged: A review and theoretical analysis. *Journal of Gerontology, 32,* 323–333.

Schulz, R. (1982). Emotionality and aging: A theoretical and empirical analysis. *Journal of Gerontology, 37,* 42–51.

Schulz, R., & Williamson, G.M. (1991). A 2-year longitudinal study of depression among Alzheimer's caregivers. *Psychology and Aging, 6,* 569–578.

Schwalberg, M.D., Barlow, D.H., Alger, S.A., & Howard, L.J. (1992). Comparison of bulimics, obese binge eaters, social phobics, and individuals with panic disorders on comorbidity across DSM-III anxiety disorders. *Journal of Abnormal Psychology, 101,* 675–681.

Schwartz, G.E. (1973). Biofeedback as therapy: Some theoretical and practical issues. *American Psychologist, 28,* 666–673.

Schwartz, G.E., & Weiss, S. (1977). What is behavioral medicine? *Psychosomatic Medicine, 36,* 377–381.

Schwartz, J.E., Warren, K., & Pickering, T.G. (1994). Mood, location, and physical posture as predictors of ambulatory blood pressure: Application of a multilevel random effects model. *Annals of Behavioral Medicine, 16,* 210–220.

Schwartz, M.S. (1946). The economic and spatial mobility of paranoid schizophrenics. Unpublished master's thesis, University of Chicago.

Schwartz, R., & Schwartz, L.J. (1980). *Becoming a couple.* Englewood Cliffs, NJ: Prentice-Hall.

Schwartz, R.M., & Gottman, J.M. (1976). Toward a task analysis of assertive behavior. *Journal of Consulting and Clinical Psychology, 44,* 910–920.

Schwartz, S.H., & Inbar-Saban, N. (1988). Value self-confrontation as a method to aid in weight loss. *Journal of Personality and Social Psychology, 54,* 396–404.

Schwarz, J.R. (1981). *The Hillside Strangler: A murderer's mind.* New York: New American Library.

Schweizer, E., et al. (1990). Long-term therapeutic use of benzodiazapines: Effects of gradual taper. *Archives of General Psychiatry, 47,* 908–915.

Schwitzgebel, R.L., & Schwitzgebel, R.K. (1980). *Law and psychological practice.* New York: Wiley.

Scientific perspectives on cocaine abuse. (1987). *Pharmacologist, 29,* 20–27.

Scoggin, F., & McElreath, L. (1994). Efficacy of psychosocial treatments for geriatric depression: A quantitative review. *Journal of Consulting and Clinical Psychology, 62,* 69–74.

Searight, H.R., & Pound, P. (1994). The HIV-positive psychiatric patient and the duty to protect: Ethical and legal issues. *International Journal of Psychiatry in Medicine, 24,* 259–270.

Seeman, P., & Nizik, H.B. (1990). Dopamine receptors and transporters in Parkinson's disease and schizophrenia. *Federation of Associated Society of Experimental Biology, 4,* 2737–2744.

Seeman, T.E., & Syme, S.L. (1987). Social networks and coronary artery disease: A comparison of the structure and function of social relations as predictors of disease. *Psychosomatic Medicine, 49,* 381–406.

Segal, Z.V., & Shaw, B.F. (1988). Cognitive assessment: Issues and methods. In K.S. Dobson (Ed.), *Handbook of cognitive behavioral therapies* (pp. 39–81). New York: Guilford.

Segal, Z.V., Gemar, M., Truchon, C., Guirguis, M., & Horowitz, L.M. (1995). A priming methodology for studying self-representation in major depressive disorder. *Journal of Abnormal Psychology, 104,* 205–213.

Segraves, K.B., & Segraves, R.T. (1991). Hypoactive sexual desire disorder: Prevalence and comorbidity in 906 subjects. *Journal of Sex and Marital Therapy, 17,* 55–58.

Segraves, R.T. (1990). Theoretical orientations in the treatment of marital discord. In F.D. Fincham & T.N. Bradbury (Eds.), *The psychology of marriage: Basic issues and applications* (pp. 281–298). New York: Guilford.

Segraves, R.T., & Segraves, K.B. (1995). Human sexuality and aging. *Journal of Sex Education and Therapy, 21,* 88–102.

Selemon, L.D., Rajkowska, G., & Goldman-Rakic, P.S. (1995). Abnormally high neuronal density in the schizophrenic cortex: A morphometric analysis of prefrontal area 9 and occipital area 17. *Archives of General Psychiatry, 52,* 805–818.

Seligman, L. (1990). *Selecting effective treatments: A comprehensive, systematic guide to treating adult mental disorders.* San Francisco: Jossey- Bass.

Seligman, M.E.P. (1971). Phobias and preparedness. *Behavior Therapy, 2,* 307–320.

Seligman, M.E.P. (1974). Depression and learned helplessness. In R.J. Friedman & M.M. Katz (Eds.), *The psychology of depression: Contemporary theory and research.* Washington, DC: Winston-Wiley.

Seligman, M.E.P. (1995). The effectiveness of psychotherapy: The Consumer Reports study. *American Psychologist, 50,* 965–974.

Seligman, M.E.P. (1996). Science as an ally of practice. *American Psychologist, 51,* 1072–1079.

Seligman, M.E.P., Abramson, L.V., Semmel, A., & Von Beyer, C. (1979). Depressive attributional style. *Journal of Abnormal Psychology, 88,* 242–247.

Seligman, M.E.P., & Binik, U. (1977). The safety signal hypothesis. In H. Davis & H. Horowitz (Eds.), *Operant-Pavlovian interaction.* Hillsdale, NJ: Erlbaum.

Seligman, M.E.P., Castellon, C., Cacciola, J., Schulman, P., Luborsky, L., Ollove, M., & Downing, R. (1988). Explanatory style change during cognitive therapy for unipolar depression. *Journal of Abnormal Psychology, 97,* 13–18.

Selling, L.S. (1940). *Men against madness.* New York: Greenberg.

Seltzer, L.F. (1986). *Paradoxical strategies in psychotherapy: A comprehensive overview and guidebook.* New York: Wiley.

Selye, H. (1950). *The physiology and pathology of exposure to stress.* Montreal: Acta.

Settin, J.M. (1982). Clinical judgment in geropsychology practice. *Psychotherapy: Theory, Research and Practice, 19,* 397–404.

Shader, R.I., & DiMascio, A. (1970). *Psychotropic drug side-effects: Clinical and theoretical perspectives.* Baltimore: Williams & Wilkins.

Shalev, A.Y., Peri, T., Canetti, L., &

Schreiber, S. (1996). Predictors of post-traumatic stress disorder in injured trauma survivors: A prospective study. *American Journal of Psychiatry, 153,* 219–225.

Sham, P.C., Jones, P., Russell, A., Gilvarry, K., Bebbington, P., et al. (1994). Age of onset, sex and familial psychiatric morbidity in schizophrenia. *British Journal of Psychiatry, 165,* 466–473.

Shaper, A.G. (1990). Alcohol and mortality: A review of prospective studies. *British Journal of Addiction, 85,* 837–847.

Shapiro, D., Goldstein, I.B., & Jamner, L.D. (1995). Effects of anger and hostility, defensiveness, gender and family history of hypertension on cardiovascular reactivity. *Psychophysiology, 32,* 425–435.

Shapiro, D., Jamner, L.D., & Goldstein, I.B. (1993). Ambulatory stress psychophysiology: The study of "compensatory and defensive counterforces" and conflict in a natural setting. *Psychosomatic Medicine, 55,* 309–323.

Shapiro, D., Tursky, B., & Schwartz, G.E. (1970). Control of blood pressure in man by operant conditioning. *Circulation Research, 26,* 127–132.

Shapiro, D.A., & Shapiro, D. (1983). Comparative therapy outcome research: Methodological implications of meta-analysis. *Journal of Consulting and Clinical Psychology, 51,* 42–53.

Shaw, B.F. (1977). Comparison of cognitive therapy and behavior therapy in the treatment of depression. *Journal of Consulting and Clinical Psychology, 45,* 543–551.

Shaw, B.F. (1984). Specification of the training and evaluation of cognitive therapists for outcome studies. In J.B.W. Williams & R.L. Spitzer (Eds.), *Psychotherapy research: Where are we and where should we go?* New York: Guilford.

Shaywitz, S.E., Shaywitz, B.A., Fletcher, J.M., & Escobar, M.D. (1990). Prevalence of reading disability in boys and girls. *Journal of the American Medical Association, 264,* 998–1002.

Shea, M.T., Elkin, I., Imber, S.D., Sotsky, S.M., Watkins, J.T., Collins, J.F., Beckham, E., Glass, D.R., Dolan, R.T., & Parloff, M.B. (1992). Course of depressive symptoms over follow-up: Findings from the National Institute of Mental Health Treatment of Depression Collaborative Research Program. *Archives of General Psychiatry, 49,* 782–787.

Shea, M.T., Pilkonis, P.A., Beckham, E., Collins, J.F., Elkin, I., Sotsky, S.M., & Docherty, J.P. (1990). Personality disorders and treatment outcome in the NIMH Treatment of Depression Collaborative Research Program. *American Journal of Psychiatry, 147,* 711–718.

Shekelle, R.B., Honey, S.B., Neaton, J., Billings, J., Borlani, N., Gerace, T., Jacobs, D., Lasser, N., & Stander, J. (1983). Type A behavior pattern and coronary death in MRFIT. *American Heart Association Cardiovascular Disease Newsletter, 33,* 34.

Sher, K.J., & Levenson, R.W. (1982). Risk for alcoholism and individual differences in the stress-response-dampening effects of alcohol. *Journal of Abnormal Psychology, 91,* 350–367.

Sher, K.J., Frost, R.O., Kushner, M., Crew, T.M., & Alexander, J.E. (1989). Memory deficits in compulsive checkers in a clinical sample. *Behaviour Research and Therapy, 27,* 65–69.

Sher, K.J., & Otto, R. (1983). Cognitive deficits in compulsive checkers: An exploratory study. *Behaviour Research and Therapy, 21,* 357–363.

Sher, K.J., Walitzer, K.S., Wood, P.K., & Brent, E.F. (1991). Characteristics of children of alcoholics: Putative risk factors, substance use and abuse, and psychopathology. *Journal of Abnormal Psychology, 100,* 427–448.

Sherwin, B.B. (1991). The psychoendocrinology of aging and female sexuality. *Annual Review of Sex Research, 2,* 181–198.

Shneidman, E.S. (1973). Suicide. In *Encyclopedia Britannica.* Chicago: Encyclopedia Britannica.

Shneidman, E.S. (1976). A psychological theory of suicide. *Psychiatric Annals, 6,* 51–66.

Shneidman, E.S. (1985). *Definition of suicide.* New York: Wiley.

Shneidman, E.S. (1987). A psychological approach to suicide. In G.R. VandenBos & B.K. Bryant (Eds.), *Cataclysms, crises, and catastrophes: Psychology in action.* Washington, DC: American Psychological Association.

Shneidman, E.S., & Farberow, N.L. (1970). A psychological approach to the study of suicide notes. In E.S. Shneidman, N.L. Farberow, & R.E. Litman (Eds.), *The psychology of suicide.* New York: Jason Aronson.

Shneidman, E.S., Farberow, N.L., & Litman, R.E. (Eds.). (1970). *The psychology of suicide.* New York: Jason Aronson.

Shoda, Y., Mischel, W., & Wright, J.C. (1994). Intraindividual stability in the organization and patterning of behavior: Incorporating psychological situations into the idiographic analysis of personality. *Journal of Personality and Social Psychology, 67,* 674–687.

Shogren, E. (1994, August 18). Treatment against their will. *Los Angeles Times,* pp. A1, A16.

Shoham, V., Bootzin, R.R., Rohrbaugh, M., & Urry, H. (1995). Paradoxical versus relaxation treatment for insomnia: The moderating role of practice. *Sleep Research, 25a,* 365.

Shoham, V., Rohrbaugh, M., & Patterson, J. (1995). Problem- and solution-focused couple therapies: The MRI and Milwaukee models. In N.S. Jacobson & A.S. Gurman (Eds.), *Clinical handbook of couple therapy* (pp. 142–163). New York: Guilford.

Shoham-Salomon, V., & Rosenthal, R. (1987). Paradoxical interventions: A meta-analysis. *Journal of Consulting and Clinical Psychology, 55,* 22–27.

Shoham-Salomon, V., Avner, R., & Neeman, R. (1989). You're changed if you do and changed if you don't: Mechanisms underlying paradoxical interventions. *Journal of Consulting and Clinical Psychology, 57,* 590–598.

Shontz, F.C., & Green, P. (1992). Trends in research on the Rorschach: Review and recommendations. *Applied and Preventive Psychology, 1,* 149–156.

Shopsin, B., Friedman, E., & Gershon, S. (1976). Parachlorophenylalanine reversal of tranylcypromine effects in depressed patients. *Archives of General Psychiatry, 33,* 811–819.

Shulman, K.I. (1993). Mania in the elderly. *International Review of Psychiatry, 5,* 445–453.

Shure, M., & Spivack, G. (1988). Interpersonal cognitive problem-solving. In R. Price, E. Cowen, R. Lorion, & X. Ramos-McKay (Eds.), *14 ounces of prevention* (pp. 111–122). Washington, DC: American Psychological Association.

Siegel, J.M., Sorenson, S.B., Golding, J.M., Burnam, M.A., & Stein, J.A. (1987). The prevalence of childhood sexual assault: The Los Angeles Epidemiological Catchment Area Project. *American Journal of Epidemiology, 126,* 1141–1153.

Siegel, R.K. (1982). Cocaine smoking. *Journal of Psychoactive Drugs, 14,* 277–359.

Siegler, I.C., & Costa, P.T., Jr. (1985). Health behavior relationships. In J.E. Birren & K.W. Schaie (Eds.), *Handbook of the psychology of aging* (2nd ed.). New York: Van Nostrand-Reinhold.

Siever, L.J., Amin, P., Coccaro, E.P., Trestman, R., Silverman, J., et al. (1993). CSF homovanillic acid in schizotypal personality disorder. *American Journal of Psychiatry, 150,* 149–151.

Sifton, D.W. (1988). *PDR drug interactions and side effects index.* Oradell, NJ: Medical Economics.

Sigman, M., Ungerer, J.A., Mundy, P., & Sherman, T. (1987). Cognition in autistic children. In D.J. Cohen, A.M. Donnellan, & R. Paul (Eds.), *Handbook of autism and pervasive developmental disorders* (pp. 103–120). New York: Wiley.

Silk, K.R., Lee, S., Hill, E.M., & Lohr, N. (1995). Borderline personality disorder symptoms and severity of sexual abuse. *American Journal of Psychiatry, 152,* 1053–1057.

Silverman, J.M., Li, G., Zaccario, M.L., Smith, C., Schmeidler, J., et al. (1994). Patterns of risk in first-degree relatives with Alzheimer's disease. *Archives of General Psychiatry, 51,* 568–576.

Silverman, K., Evans, S.M., Strain, E.C., & Griffiths, R.R. (1992). Withdrawal syndrome after the double-blind cessation of caffeine consumption. *New England Journal of Medicine, 327,* 1109–1114.

Silverstein, B., Feld, S., & Kozlowski, L.T. (1980). The availability of low-nicotine cigarettes as a cause of cigarette smoking among teenage females. *Journal of Health and Social Behavior, 21,* 383–388.

Silverstein, C. (1972). *Behavior modification and the gay community.* Paper presented at the annual convention of the Association for Advancement of Behavior Therapy, New York.

Simeons, A.T.W. (1961). *Man's presumptuous brain: An evolutionary interpretation of psychosomatic disease.* New York: Dutton.

Simon, R.J., & Aaronson, D.E. (1988). *The insanity defense: A critical assessment of law and policy in the post-Hinckley era.* New York: Praeger.

Simons, A.D., Garfield, S.L., & Murphy, G.E. (1984). The process of change in cognitive therapy and pharmacotherapy for depression: Changes in mood and cognition. *Archives of General Psychiatry, 41,* 45–51.

Simons, A.D., Lustman, P.J., Wetzel, R.D., & Murphy, G.E. (1985). Predicting response to cognitive therapy of depression: The role of learned resourcefulness. *Cognitive Therapy and Research, 9,* 79–89.

Simons, A.D., Murphy, G.E., Levine, J.L., & Wetzel, R.D. (1985). Sustained improvement one year after cognitive and/or pharmacotherapy of depression. *Archives of General Psychiatry, 43,* 43–48.

Simons, M. (1996, June 28). For first time, court defines rape as war crime. *New York Times.* p. 1.

Sinclair, J.J., Larzelere, R.E., Paine, M., Jones, P., et al. (1995). Outcome of group treatment for sexually abused adolescent females living in a group home setting: Preliminary findings. *Journal of Interpersonal Violence, 10,* 533–542.

Singer, J.L. (1984). The private personality. *Personality and Social Psychology Bulletin, 10,* 7–30.

Singer, M., & Wynne, L.C. (1963). Differentiating characteristics of the parents of childhood schizophrenics. *American Journal of Psychiatry, 120,* 234–243.

Sinnott, J.D. (1986). *Sex roles and aging:*

Theory and research from a systems perspective. Basel, Switzerland: Karger.

Sintchak, G.H., & Geer, J.H. (1975). A vaginal plethysmograph system. *Psychophysiology, 12,* 113–115.

Siris, S.G., Bermanzohn, P.C., Mason, S.E., & Shuwall, M.A. (1994). Maintenance imipramine therapy for secondary depression in schizophrenia: A controlled trial. *Archives of General Psychiatry, 51,* 109–115.

Sisson, R.W., & Azrin, N.H. (1989). The community reinforcement approach. In R.K. Hester & W.R. Miller (Eds.), *Handbook of alcohol treatment approaches: Effective alternatives.* Elmsford, NY: Pergamon.

Sisson, R.W., & Azrin, N.H. (1989). The community-reinforcement approach. In R.K. Hester & W.R. Miller (Eds.), *Handbook of alcoholism treatment approaches: Effective alternatives* (pp. 242–258). New York: Pergamon.

Sizemore, C.C., & Pittillo, E.S. (1977). *I'm Eve.* Garden City, NY: Doubleday.

Sizemore, J.P. (1995). Alabama's confidentiality quagmire: Psychotherapists, AIDS, mandatory reporting, and *Tarasoff. Law and Psychology Review, 19,* 241–257.

Skinner, B.F. (1953). *Science and human behavior.* New York: Macmillan.

Sklar, L.A., & Anisman, H. (1979). Stress and coping factors influence tumor growth. *Science, 205,* 513–515.

Slater, E. (1961). The thirty-fifth Maudsley lecture: Hysteria 311. *Journal of Mental Science, 107,* 358–381.

Slater, E., & Glithero, E. (1965). A followup of patients diagnosed as suffering from hysteria. *Journal of Psychosomatic Research, 9,* 9–13.

Slavson, S.R. (1950). *Analytic group psychotherapy with children, adolescents and adults.* New York: Columbia University Press.

Sloane, R.B. (1980). Organic brain syndrome. In J.E. Birren & R.B. Sloane (Eds.), *Handbook of mental health and aging.* Englewood Cliffs, NJ: Prentice-Hall.

Small, G.W., & Jarvik, L.F. (1982). The dementia syndrome. *Lancet,* 1443–1446.

Small, G.W., Komanduri, R., Gitlin, M., & Jarvik, L.F. (1986). The influence of age on guilt expression in major depression. *International Journal of Geriatric Psychiatry, 1,* 121–126.

Small, G.W., Kuhl, D.E., Riege, W.H., Fujikawa, D.G., Ashford, J.W., et al. (1989). Cerebral glucose metabolic patterns in Alzheimer's disease: Effects of gender and age at dementia onset. *Archives of General Psychiatry, 46,* 527–533.

Small, J.C., Klapper, M.H., Milstein, V., Kellans, J.J., Miller, M.J., et al. (1991). Carbamazapine compared with lithium

in the treatment of mania. *Archives of General Psychiatry, 48,* 915–921.

Smith, D. (1982). Trends in counseling and psychotherapy. *American Psychologist, 37,* 802–809.

Smith, D.W., Bierman, E.L., & Robinson, N.M. (1978). *The biologic ages of man: From conception through old age.* Philadelphia: Saunders.

Smith, G.T., Goldman, M.S., Greenbaum, P.E., & Christiansen, B.A. (1995). Expectancy for social facilitation from drinking: The divergent paths of high expectancy and low expectancy adolescents. *Journal of Abnormal Psychology, 104,* 32–40.

Smith, J., Frawley, P.J., & Polissar, L. (1991). Six- and twelve-month abstinence rates in inpatient alcoholics treated with aversion therapy compared with matched inpatients from a treatment registry. *Alcoholism: Clinical and Experimental Research, 15,* 862–870.

Smith, K.F., & Bengston, V.L. (1979). Positive consequences of institutionalization: Solidarity between elderly parents and their middle aged children. *The Gerontologist, 5,* 438–447.

Smith, M.L., Glass, G., & Miller, T. (1980). *The benefits of psychotherapy.* Baltimore: Johns Hopkins University Press.

Smith, P.B. (1975). Controlled studies of the outcome of sensitivity training. *Psychological Bulletin, 82,* 597–622.

Smith, S.S., & Newman, J.P. (1990). Alcohol and drug dependence in psychopathic and nonpsychopathic criminal offenders. *Journal of Abnormal Psychology, 99,* 430–439.

Smith, T., Snyder, C.R., & Perkins, S.C. (1983). Self-serving function of hypochondriacal complaints: Physical symptoms as self-handicapping strategies. *Journal of Personality and Social Psychology, 44,* 787–797.

Smith, T.W. (1983). Change in irrational beliefs and the outcome of rational-emotive psychotherapy. *Journal of Consulting and Clinical Psychology, 51,* 156–157.

Smolowe, J. (1996, Fall). Older, longer. *Time, 148 (Special Issue),* 76–80.

Smyer, M.A., & Gatz, M. (1995). The public policy context of mental health care for older adults. *The Clinical Psychologist, 48,* 31–36.

Smyer, M.A., Zarit, S.H., & Qualls, S.H. (1990). Psychological interventions with the aging individual. In J.E. Birren & K.W. Schaie (Eds.), *Handbook of the psychology of aging* (3rd ed., pp. 375–403). New York: Academic Press.

Smyth, C., Kalsi, G., Brynjofsson, J., O'Neill, J., Curtis, D., et al. (1996). Further tests for linkage of bipolar affective disorder to the tyrosine hydroxylase

gene of chromosome 11p15 in a new series of multiplex British affective disorder pedigrees. *American Journal of Psychiatry, 153,* 271–274.

Snyder, D.K., & Wills, R.M. (1989). Behavioral versus insight-oriented marital therapy: Effects of individual and interspousal functioning. *Journal of Consulting and Clinical Psychology, 57,* 39–46.

Snyder, D.K., Wills, R.M., & Grady-Fletcher, A. (1991). Long-term effectiveness of behavioral vs. insight-oriented marital therapy. *Journal of Consulting and Clinical Psychology, 59,* 138–141.

Snyder, M. (1983). The influence of individuals on situations: Implications for understanding the links between personality and social behavior. *Journal of Personality, 51,* 497–516.

Snyder, M., & White, E. (1982). Moods and memories: Elation, depression, and remembering the events of one's life. *Journal of Personality, 50,* 149–167.

Snyder, S.H. (1974). *Madness and the brain.* New York: McGraw-Hill.

Sobell, L.C., Toneatto, A., & Sobell, M.B. (1990). Behavior therapy. In A.S. Bellack & M. Hersen (Eds.), *Handbook of comparative treatments for adult disorders* (pp. 479–505). New York: Wiley.

Sobell, M.B., & Sobell, L.C. (1976). Second-year treatment outcome of alcoholics treated by individualized behavior therapy: Results. *Behaviour Research and Therapy, 14,* 195–215.

Sobell, M.B., & Sobell, L.C. (1993). *Problem drinkers: Guided self-change treatment.* New York: Guilford.

Society of Behavioral Medicine. (1989). *Bylaws of the Society of Behavioral Medicine.* Washington, DC: Author.

Solomon, Z., Mikulincev, M., & Flum, H. (1988). Negative life events, coping response, and combat-related psychopathology: A prospective study. *Journal of Abnormal Psychology, 97,* 302–307.

Sonda, P., Mazo, R., & Chancellor, M.B. (1990). The role of yohimbine for the treatment of erectile impotence. *Journal of Sex and Marital Therapy, 16,* 15–21.

Sorenson, S.B., & Brown, V.B. (1990). Interpersonal violence and crisis intervention on the college campus. *New Directions for Student Services, 49,* 57–66.

Soueif, M.I. (1976). Some determinants of psychological deficits associated with chronic cannabis consumption. *Bulletin of Narcotics, 28,* 25–42.

Southwick, S.M., Krystal, J.H., Morgan, C.A., Johnson, D., Nagy, L.M., & et al. (1993). Abnormal noradrenergic function in posttraumatic stress disorder. *Archives of General Psychiatry, 50,* 266–274.

Spacapan, S., & Oskamp, S. (1989). Introduction to the social psychology of aging. In S. Spacapan & S. Oskamp (Eds.), *The social psychology of aging* (pp. 9–24). Newbury Park, CA: Sage.

Spanos, N.P., Weekes, J.R., & Bertrand, L.D. (1985). Multiple personality: A social psychological perspective. *Journal of Abnormal Psychology, 94,* 362–376.

Spar, J.E., & LaRue, A. (1990). *Geriatric psychiatry.* Washington, DC: American Psychiatric Press.

Sparrow, S.S., Ballo, D.A., & Cicchetti, D.V. (1984). *Vineland Adaptive Behavior Scales.* Circle Pines, MI: American Guidance Service.

Spector, I.P., & Carey, M.P. (1990). Incidence and prevalence of the sexual dysfunctions: A critical review of the empirical literature. *Archives of Sexual Behavior, 19,* 389–408.

Spencer, G. (1989). *Projections of the population of the United States, by age, sex, and race: 1988 to 2080.* Washington, DC: U.S. Department of Commerce.

Spengler, A. (1977). Manifest sado-masochism of males: Results of an empirical study. *Archives of Sexual Behavior, 6,* 441–456.

Spiegel, D. (1990). Can psychotherapy prolong cancer survival? *Psychosomatics, 31,* 361–366.

Spiegel, D., Bloom, J.R., & Yalom, I. (1981). Group support for patients with metastatic cancer: A randomized prospective outcome study. *Archives of General Psychiatry, 38,* 527–534.

Spiegel, D., Bloom, J.R., Kraemer, H.C., & Gottheil, E. (1989). Effect of psychosocial treatment on survival of patients with metastatic breast cancer. *Lancet, 2,* 888–891.

Spiers, P.A. (1982). The Luria-Nebraska Neuropsychological Battery revisited: A theory in practice or just practicing? *Journal of Consulting and Clinical Psychology, 50,* 301–306.

Spiess, W.F.J., Geer, J.H., & O'Donohue, W.T. (1984). Premature ejaculation: Investigation of factors in ejaculatory latency. *Journal of Abnormal Psychology, 93,* 242–245.

Spinetta, J.J. (1980). Disease-related communication: How to tell. In J. Kellerman (Ed.), *Psychological aspects of childhood cancer.* Springfield, IL: Charles C. Thomas.

Spitzer, R.L., Endicott, J., & Gibbon, M. (1979). Crossing the border into borderline personality and borderline schizophrenia. *Archives of General Psychiatry, 36,* 17–24.

Spitzer, R.L., Gibbon, M., & Williams, J.B.W. (1986). *Structured clinical interview of DSM-IV Axis I disorders.* New York: N.Y. State Psychiatric Institute, Biometrics Research Department.

Spitzer, R.L., Skodol, A.E., Gibbon, M., & Williams, J.B.W. (1981). *DSM-III casebook.* Washington, DC: American Psychiatric Press.

Spitzer, R.M., Stunkard, A., Yanovski, S., Marcus, M.D., Wadden, T., et al. (1993). Binge eating disorders should be included in DSM-IV. *International Journal of Eating Disorders, 13,* 161–169.

Sprague, R.L., & Gadow, K.D. (1976). The role of the teacher in drug treatment. *School Review, 85,* 109–140.

Sprenkle, D.H., & Storm, C.L. (1983). Divorce therapy outcome research: A substantive and methodological review. *Journal of Marital and Family Therapy, 9,* 239–258.

Spunt, B., Goldstein, P., Brownstein, H., & Fendrich, M. (1994). The role of marijuana in homicide. *International Journal of the Addictions, 29,* 195–213.

Squires-Wheeler, E., Skodal, A., Agamo, O.M., Bassett, A.S., et al. (1993). Personality features and disorder in the subjects in the New York High-Risk Project. *Journal of Psychiatric Research, 27,* 379–393.

Srole, L., Langner, T.S., Michael, S.T., Opler, M.K., & Rennie, T.A.C. (1962). *Mental health in the metropolis: The midtown Manhattan study.* New York: McGraw-Hill.

St. Lawrence, J., Jefferson, K.W., Banks, P.G., Cline, T.R., et al. (1994). Cognitive-behavioral group intervention to assist substance-dependent adolescents in lowering HIV infection. *AIDS Education and Prevention, 6,* 425–435.

St. Lawrence, J.S., & Madakasira, S. (1992). Evaluation and treatment of premature ejaculation: A critical review. *International Journal of Psychiatry in Medicine, 22,* 77–97.

Staats, A.W., & Staats, C.K. (1963). *Complex human behavior.* New York: Holt, Rinehart & Winston.

Stacy, A.W., Newcomb, M.D., & Bentler, P.M. (1991). Cognitive motivation and drug use: A 9-year longitudinal study. *Journal of Abnormal Psychology, 100,* 502–515.

Stacy, A.W., Sussman, S., Dent, C.W., Burton, D., & Flay, B.R. (1992). Moderators of peer social influence in adolescent smoking. *Personality and Social Psychology Bulletin, 18,* 163–172.

Stall, R.D., McKusick, L., Wiley, J., Coates, T., & Ostrow, D. (1986). Alcohol and drug use during sexual activity and compliance with safe sex guidelines for AIDS: The AIDS Behavioral Research Project. *Health Education Quarterly, 13,* 359–371.

Stampfer, M.J., Colditz, G.A., Willett, W.C., Speizer, F.E., & Hennekens, C.H. (1988). A prospective study of moderate alcohol consumption and risk of coronary disease and stroke in women. *New England Journal of Medicine, 319,* 267–273.

Stanley, M.A., & Turner, S.M. (1995). Current status of pharmacological and behavioral treatment of obsessive-compulsive disorder. *Behavior Therapy, 26,* 163–186.

Stanley, M.A., Beck, J.G., & Glassco, J.D. (1997). Treatment of generalized anxiety disorder in older adults: A preliminary comparison of cognitive-behavioral and supportive approaches. *Behavior Therapy, 27,* 565–581.

Stansfield, J.M. (1973). Enuresis and urinary tract infection. In I. Kolvin, R.C. MacKeith, & S.R. Meadow (Eds.), *Bladder control and enuresis* (pp. 102–103). London: William Heinemann.

Stanton, A.H., Gunderson, J.G., Knapp, P.H., Frank, A.E., Vanicelli, M.L., Schnitzer, R., & Rosenthal, R. (1984). Effects of psychotherapy in schizophrenia. *Schizophrenia Bulletin, 10,* 520–563.

Stanton, A.L., & Snider, P. (1993). Coping with breast cancer diagnosis: A prospective study. *Health Psychology, 12,* 16–23.

Stanton, M.D., & Bardoni, A. (1972). Drug flashbacks: Reported frequency in a military population. *American Journal of Psychiatry, 129,* 751–755.

Starfield, B. (1972). Enuresis: Its pathogenesis and management. *Clinical Pediatrics, 11,* 343–350.

Stark, K.D., Kaslow, N.J., & Reynolds, W.M. (1987). A comparison of the relative efficacy of self-control therapy and a behavioral problem-solving therapy for depression in children. *Journal of Abnormal Child Psychology, 15,* 91–113.

Stark, K.D., Linn, J.D., MacGuire, M., & Kaslow, N.J. (in press). The social functioning of depressed and anxious children: Social skills, social knowledge, automatic thoughts, and physical arousal. *Journal of Clinical Child Psychology.*

Stark, K.D., Napolitano, S., Swearer, S., Schmidt, K., Jaramillo, D., & Hoyle, J. (1996). Issues in the treatment of depressed children. *Applied and Preventive Psychology, 5,* 59–83.

Stark, K.D., Schmidt, K., Joiner, T.E., & Lux, M.G. (in press). Depressive cognitive triad: Relationship to severity of depressive symptoms in children, parents' cognitive triad, and perceived parental messages about the child him or herself, the world, and the future. *Journal of Abnormal Child Psychology.*

Starr, B.D., & Weiner, M.B. (1981). *The Starr-Weiner report on sex and sexuality in the mature years.* New York: Stein & Day.

Steadman, H.J. (1979). *Beating a rap: Defendants found incompetent to stand trial.*

Chicago: University of Chicago Press.

Steadman, H.J., McGreevy, M.A., Morrissey, J.P., Callahan, L.A., Robbins, P.C., & Cirincione, C. (1993). *Before and after Hinckley: Evaluating insanity defense reform.* New York: Guilford.

Steele, C.M., & Josephs, R.A. (1988). Drinking your troubles away: 2. An attention-allocation model of alcohol's effects on psychological stress. *Journal of Abnormal Psychology, 97,* 196–205.

Stephens, B.J. (1985). Suicidal women and their relationships with husbands, boyfriends, and lovers. *Suicide and Life-Threatening Behavior, 15,* 77–89.

Stephens, J.H., & Kamp, M. (1962). On some aspects of hysteria: A clinical study. *Journal of Nervous and Mental Disease, 134,* 305–315.

Stephens, R.S., Roffman, R.A., & Simpson, E.E. (1993). Adult marijuana users seeking treatment. *Journal of Consulting and Clinical Psycology, 61,* 1100–1104.

Stern, D.B. (1977). Handedness and the lateral distribution of conversion reactions. *Journal of Nervous and Mental Disease, 164,* 122–128.

Stern, R.S., & Cobb, J.P. (1978). Phenomenology of obsessive-compulsive neurosis. *British Journal of Psychiatry, 132,* 233–234.

Sternberger, R.T., Turner, S.M., Beidel, D.C., & Calhoun, K.S. (1995). Social phobia: An analysis of possible developmental pathways. *Journal of Abnormal Psychology, 104,* 526–531.

Stets, J.E., & Straus, M.A. (1989). The marriage license as a hitting license: A comparison of assaults in dating, cohabiting, and married couples. *Journal of Family Violence, 4,* 161–180.

Steuer, J.L. (1982). Psychotherapy with older women: Ageism and sexism in traditional practice. *Psychotherapy: Theory, research and practice, 19,* 429–436.

Stevenson, J., & Jones, I.H. (1972). Behavior therapy technique for exhibitionism: A preliminary report. *Archives of General Psychiatry, 27,* 839–841.

Stevenson, J.S., & Topp, R. (1990). Effects of moderate and low intensity long-term exercise by older adults. *Research in Nursing and Health, 13,* 209–213.

Stewart, B.D., Hughes, C., Frank, E., Anderson, B., Kendall, K., & West, D. (1987). Profiles of immediate and delayed treatment seekers. *Journal of Nervous and Mental Disease, 175,* 90–94.

Stinson, F.S., & DeBakey, S.F. (1992). Alcohol-related mortality in the United States 1979–1988. *British Journal of Addiction, 87,* 777–783.

Stolbach, L.L., Brandt, U.C., Borysenko, J.Z., Benson, H., Maurer, S.N., Lesserman, J., Albright, T.E., & Albright, N.L. (1988, April). *Benefits of a mind/body group program for cancer patients.* Paper presented at the annual meeting of the Society for Behavioral Medicine, Boston.

Stolberg, A.L., & Garrison, K.M. (1985). Evaluating a primary prevention program for children of divorce. *American Journal of Community Psychology, 13,* 111–124.

Stolberg, S. (1996a, August 24). Clinton imposes wide crackdown on tobacco firms. *Los Angeles Times,* pp. A1, A10.

Stolberg, S. (1996b, October 1). Ending life on their own terms. *Los Angeles Times,* pp. A1, A14.

Stoller, E.P., & Gibson, R.C. (1994). *Worlds of difference: Inequality in the aging experience.* Thousand Oaks, CA: Pine Forge Press.

Stoller, F.H. (1968). Accelerated interaction: A time-limited approach based on the brief intensive group. *International Journal of Group Psychotherapy, 18,* 220–235.

Stom, M., French, S.A., Resnick, M.D., & Blum, R.W. (1995). Ethnic/racial and socioeconomic differences in dieting behaviors and body image perceptions in adolescents. *International Journal of Eating Disorders, 18,* 173–179.

Stone, A.A. (1975). *Mental health and law: A system in transition.* Rockville, MD: National Institute of Mental Health.

Stone, A.A., & Neale, J.M. (1982). Development of a methodology for assessing daily experiences. In A. Baum and J. Singer (Eds.), *Environment and health.* Hillsdale, NJ: Erlbaum.

Stone, A.A., & Neale, J.M. (1984). The effects of "severe" daily events on mood. *Journal of Personality and Social Psychology, 46,* 137–144.

Stone, A.A., Bovbjerg, D.H., Neale, J.M., Napoli, A., Valdimarsdottir, H., et al. (1992). Development of common cold symptoms following experimental rhinovirus infection is related to prior stressful life events. *Behavioral Medicine, 18,* 115–120.

Stone, A.A., Cox, D.S., Valdimarsdottir, H., Jandorf, L., & Neale, J.M. (1987). Evidence that secretory IgA antibody is associated with daily mood. *Journal of Personality and Social Psychology, 52,* 988–993.

Stone, A.A., Reed, B.R., & Neale, J.M. (1987). Changes in daily event frequency precede episodes of physical symptoms. *Journal of Human Stress, 13,* 70–74.

Stone, G. (1982). Health psychology, a new journal for a new field. *Health Psychology, 1,* 1–6.

Stone, L.J., & Hokanson, J.E. (1967). Arousal reduction via self-punitive behavior. *Journal of Personality and Social Psychology, 12,* 72–79.

Stone, M.H. (1986). Exploratory psychotherapy in schizophrenia-spectrum patients: A reevaluation in the light of long-term follow-up of schizophrenic and borderline patients. *Bulletin of the Menninger Clinic, 50,* 287–306.

Stone, M.H. (1987). Psychotherapy of borderline patients in light of long-term follow-up. *Bulletin of the Menninger Clinic, 51,* 231–247.

Stone, M.H. (1993). *Abnormalities of personality. Within and beyond the realm of treatment.* New York: Norton.

Stone, S.V., & Costa, P.T. (1990). Disease-prone personality or distress-prone personality? The role of neuroticism in coronary heart disease. In H.S. Friedman (Ed.), *Personality and Disease.* New York: Wiley.

Stormer, S.M., & Thompson, J.K. (1996). Explanations of body image disturbance: A test of maturational status, negative verbal commentary, and sociological hypotheses. *International Journal of Eating Disorders, 19,* 193–202.

Story, M., French, S.A., Resnick, M.D., & Blum, R.W. (1995). Ethnic/racial and socioeconomic differences in dieting behaviors and body image perceptions in adolescents. *International Journal of Eating Disorders, 18,* 173–179.

Strauss, J.S., Carpenter, W.T., & Bartko, J.J. (1974). The diagnosis and understanding of schizophrenia: Part 3. Speculations on the processes that underlie schizophrenic signs and symptoms. *Schizophrenia Bulletin, 1,* 61–69.

Strauss, M.E., & Ogrocki, P.K. (1996). Confirmation of an association between family history of affective disorder and the depressive syndrome in Alzheimer's disease. *American Journal of Psychiatry, 153,* 1340–1342.

Stringer, A.Y., & Josef, N.C. (1983). Methylphenidate in the treatment of aggression in two patients with antisocial personality disorder. *American Journal of Psychiatry, 140,* 1365–1366.

Strober, M., Morrell, B., Burroughs, J., Salkin, B., & Jacobs, C. (1985). A controlled family study of anorexia nervosa. *Journal of Psychiatric Research, 19,* 239–246.

Strober, M., Salkin, B., Burroughs, J., & Morrell, W. (1982). Validity of the bulimia-restrictor distinction in anorexia nervosa. *Journal of Nervous and Mental Disease, 170,* 345–351.

Strong, R., Huang, J.S., Huang, S.S., Chung, H.D., Hale, C., et al. (1991). Degeneration of the cholinergic innervation of the locus ceruleus in Alzheimer's disease. *Brain Research, 542,* 23–28.

Strub, R.L., & Black, F.W. (1981). *Organic*

brain syndromes: An introduction to neurobehavioral disorders. Philadelphia: F.A. Davis.

Strunin, L., & Hingson, R. (1987). Acquired immunodeficiency syndrome: Knowledge, beliefs, attitudes, and behaviors. Pediatrics, 79, 825–828.

Strupp, H.H. (1989). Psychotherapy: Can the practitioner learn from the researcher? American Psychologist, 44, 717–724.

Strupp, H.H., Hadley, S.W., & Gomes-Schwartz, B. (1977). Psychotherapy for better or worse: An analysis of the problem of negative effects. New York: Jason Aronson.

Stuart, I.R., & Greer, J.G. (Eds.). (1984). Victims of sexual aggression: Treatment of children, women and men. New York: Van Nostrand-Reinhold.

Stuart, R.B. (1976). An operant interpersonal program for couples. In D.H.L. Olson (Ed.), Treating relationships. Lake Mills, IA: Graphic Publishing.

Stuart, R.B. (1978). Protection of the right to informed consent to participate in research. Behavior Therapy, 9, 73–82.

Stunkard, A.J., & Rush, J. (1974). Dieting and depression reexamined: A critical review of reports of untoward responses during weight reduction for obesity. Annals of Internal Medicine, 81, 526–533.

Sturgis, E.T., & Adams, H.E. (1978). The right to treatment: Issues in the treatment of homosexuality. Journal of Consulting and Clinical Psychology, 46, 165–169.

Suddath, R.L., Christison, G.W., Torrey, E.F., Cassonova, M.F., Weinberger, D.R. et al. (1990). Anatomical abnormalities in the brains of monozygotic twins discordant for schizophrenia. New England Journal of Medicine, 322, 789–793.

Sue, D.W., & Sue, D. (1992). Counseling the culturally different (2nd ed.). New York: Wiley.

Sue, S., Zane, N., & Young, K. (1994). Research on psychotherapy with culturally diverse populations. In A.E. Bergin & S.L. Garfield (Eds.), Handbook of psychotherapy and behavior change. Fourth edition (pp. 783–820). New York: Wiley.

Suinn, R.M., & Richardson, R. (1971). Anxiety management training: A nonspecific behavior therapy program for anxiety control. Behavior Therapy, 2, 498–510.

Sukhai, R.N., Mol, J., & Harris, A.S. (1989). Combined therapy of enuresis alarm and desmopressin in the treatment of nocturnal enuresis. European Journal of Pediatrics, 148, 465–467.

Sullivan, H.S. (1953). The interpersonal theory of psychiatry. New York: Norton.

Sullivan, P.F. (1995). Mortality in anorexia nervosa. American Journal of Psychiatry, 152, 1073–1075.

Suls, J., & Fletcher, B. (1985). The relative efficacy of avoidant and nonavoidant coping strategies: A meta-analysis. Health Psychology, 4, 249–288.

Sultenfuss, J., & Geczy, B., Jr. (1996). Group therapy on state hospital chronic wards: Some guidelines. International Journal of Group Psychotherapy, 46, 163–176.

Sundin, O., Ohman, A., Palm, T., & Strom, G. (1995). Cardiovascular reactivity, Type A behavior, and coronary heart disease: Comparisions between myocardial infarction patients and controls during laboratory-induced stress. Psychophysiology, 32, 28–35.

Suppes, T., Baldessarini, R.J., Faedda, G.L., & Tohen, M. (1991). Risk of recurrence following discontinuation of lithium treatment in bipolar disorder. Archives of General Psychiatry, 48, 1082–1087.

Susser, E., & Wanderling, J. (1994). Epidemiology of nonaffective acute remitting psychosis versus schizophrenia: Sex and sociocultural setting. Archives of General Psychiatry, 51, 294–301.

Susser, E., Neugebauer, R., Hoek, H.W., Brown, A.S., Lin, S., et al. (1996). Schizophrenia after prenatal famine: Further evidence. Archives of General Psychiatry, 53, 25–31.

Sussman, S. (1996). Development of a school-based drug abuse prevention curriculum for high-risk youth. Journal of Psychoactive Drugs, 28, 169–182.

Sussman, S., Dent, C.W., Burton, D., Stacy, A.W., & Flay, B.R. (1995). Developing school-based tobacco use prevention and cessation programs. Thousand Oaks, CA: Sage.

Sussman, S., Dent, C.W., McAdams, L., Stacy, A.W., Burton, D., & Flay, B.R. (1994). Group self-identification and adolescent cigarette smoking: A 1-year prospective study. Journal of Abnormal Psychology, 103, 576–580.

Sussman, S., Dent, C.W., Simon, T.R., Stacy, A.W., Galaif, E.R., Moss, M.A., Craig, S., & Johnson, C.A. (1995). Immediate impact of social influence-oriented substance abuse prevention curricula in traditional and continuation high schools. Drugs and Society, 8, 65–81.

Sussman, S., Stacy, A.W., Dent, C.W., Simon, T.R., & Johnson, C.A. (in press). Marijuana use: Current issues and new research directions. The Journal of Drug Issues.

Sussman, S., Dent, C.W., Stacy, A.W., Burciage, C., Raynor, A., et al. (1990). Peer-group association and adolescent tobacco use. Journal of Abnormal

Psychology, 99, 349–352.

Sutcliffe, J.P., & Jones, J. (1962). Personal identity, multiple personality, and hypnosis. International Journal of Clinical and Experimental Hypnosis, 10, 231–269.

Sutker, P.B., Davis, J.M., Uddo, M., & Ditta, A. (1995). Warzone stress, personal resources, and post-traumatic stress disorder in Persian Gulf War returnees. Journal of Abnormal Psychology, 104, 444–453.

Svartberg, M., & Stiles, T.C. (1991). Comparative effects of short-term psychodynamic psychotherapy: A meta-analysis. Journal of Consulting and Clinical Psychology, 59, 704–714.

Swain, A., & Suls, J. (1996). Reproducibility of blood pressure and heart rate reactivity: A meta-analysis. Psychophysiology, 33, 162–174.

Swan, N. (1994). Marijuana, other drug use among teens continues to rise. NIDA Notes: National Institute on Drug Abuse, 10, 8–9.

Swann, W.B., Jr. (1996). Self-traps: The elusive quest for higher self-esteem. New York: W.H. Freeman.

Swanson, J.W., Holzer, C.E., Ganju, V.K., & Jono, R.T. (1990). Violence and psychiatric disorder in the community: Evidence from the Epidemiological Catchment Area surveys. Hospital and Community Psychiatry, 41, 761–770.

Swartz, M., Blazer, D., George, L., & Landerman, R. (1986). Somatization disorder in a community population. American Journal of Psychiatry, 143, 1403–1408.

Swartz, M., Blazer, D., George, L., & Winfield, I. (1990). Estimating the prevalence of borderline personality in the community. Journal of Personality Disorders, 1990, 257–272.

Sweet, J.J., Carr , M.A., Rossini, E., & Kasper, C. (1986). Relationship between the Luria–Nebraska Neuropsychological Battery and the WISC-R: Further examination using Kaufman's factors. International Journal of Clinical Neuropsychology, 8, 177–180.

Sweet, R.A., Mulsant, B.H., Gupta, B., Rifai, A.H., Pasternak, R.E., et al. (1995). Duration of neuroleptic treatment and prevalence of tardive dyskinesia in late life. Archives of General Psychiatry, 52, 478–486.

Sweeting, H.W. (1995). Family life and health in adolescence. Social Science and Medicine, 40, 163–175.

Syndulko, K. (1978). Electrocortical investigations of sociopathy. In R.D. Hare & D. Schalling (Eds.), Psychopathic behaviour: Approaches to research. New York: Wiley.

Szasz, T. (1986). The case against suicide prevention. American Psychologist, 41, 806–812.

Szasz, T.S. (1963). *Law, liberty, and psychiatry.* New York: Macmillan.

Szasz, T.S. (Ed.). (1974). *The age of madness: The history of involuntary hospitalization.* New York: Jason Aronson.

Szatmari, P., Offord, D.R., & Boyle, M.H. (1989). Ontario child health study: Prevalence of attention deficit disorder with hyperactivity. *Journal of Child Psychology and Psychiatry, 30,* 219–230.

Tallal, P., Miller, S.L., Bedi, G., Byma, G., Wang, X., Nagarajan, S.S., Schreiner, C., Jenkins, W.M., & Merzenich, M.M. (1996). Language comprehension in language-learning impaired children improved with acoustically modified speech. *Science, 271,* 81–84.

Tallmadge, J., & Barkley, R.A. (1983). The interactions of hyperactive and normal boys with their mothers and fathers. *Journal of Abnormal Child Psychology, 11,* 565–579.

Tanzi, R.E., Gusella, F., Watkins, P.C., Bruns, G.A.P., St. George-Hyslop, P., Van Keunen, M.L., et al. (1987). Amyloid B protein gene: cDNA, mRNA distribution, and genetic linkage near the Alzheimer locus. *Science, 235,* 880–884.

Task Force on Promotion and Dissemination of Psychological Procedures. (1995). Training in and dissemination of empirically-validated psychological treatments: Report and recommendations. *The Clinical Psychologist, 48,* 3–23.

Tate, B.G., & Baroff, G.S. (1966). Aversive control of self-injurious behavior in a psychotic boy. *Behaviour Research and Therapy, 4,* 281–287.

Taylor, C.B. (1983). DSM-III and behavioral assessment. *Behavioral Assessment, 5,* 5–14.

Taylor, S.E., & Brown, J.D. (1988). Illusion and well-being: A social psychological perspective on mental health. *Psychological Bulletin, 103,* 193–210.

Taylor, S.E., Kemeny, M.E., Aspinwall, L.G., Schneider, S.G., Rodriguez, R., & Herbert, M. (1992). Optimism, coping, psychological distress, and high-risk sexual behavior among men at risk for acquired immunodeficiency syndrome (AIDS). *Journal of Personality and Social Psychology, 63,* 460–473.

Teasdale, J.D., Fennell, M.J.V., Hibbert, G.A., & Amies, P.L. (1984). Cognitive therapy for major depressive disorder in primary care. *British Journal of Psychiatry, 44,* 400–406.

Telch, C.F., & Telch, M.J. (1986). Group coping skills instruction and supportive group therapy for cancer patients: A comparison of strategies. *Journal of Consulting and Clinical Psychology, 54,* 802–808.

Telch, M.J., & Harrington, P.J. (in press). Anxiety sensitivity and expectedness of

arousal in mediating affective response to 35% carbon dioxide inhalation.

Teplin, L.A. (1984). Criminalizing mental disorder: The comparative arrest rate of the mentally ill. *American Psychologist, 29,* 794–803.

Teri, L., & Lewinsohn, P.M. (1986). Individual and group treatment of unipolar depression: Comparison of treatment outcome and identification of predictors of successful treatment outcome. *Behavior Therapy, 17,* 215–228.

Teri, L., & Logsdon, R.G. (1992). The future of psychotherapy with older adults. *Psychotherapy, 29,* 81–87.

Teri, L., & Reifler, B.V. (1987). Depression and dementia. In L.L. Carstensen & B.A. Edelstein (Eds.), *Handbook of clinical gerontology.* New York: Pergamon.

Terman, L.M. (1995). *Genetic studies of genius.* Stanford, CA: Stanford University Press.

Theodor, L.H., & Mandelcorn, M.S. (1973). Hysterical blindness: A case report using a psychophysical technique. *Journal of Abnormal Psychology, 82,* 552–553.

Thibaut, J.W., & Kelley, H.H. (1959). *The social psychology of groups.* New York: Wiley.

Thigpen, C.H., & Cleckley, H. (1954). *The three faces of Eve.* Kingsport, TN: Kingsport Press.

Thomas, S., Gilliam, A., & Iwrey, C. (1989). Knowledge about AIDS and reported risk behaviors among black college students. *Journal of American College Health, 31,* 61–66.

Thompson, G.O.B., Raab, G.M., Hepburn, W.S., Hunter, R., Fulton, M., & Laxen, D.P.H. (1989). Blood-lead levels and children's behaviour—Results from the Edinburgh lead study. *Journal of Child Psychology and Psychiatry, 30,* 515–528.

Thompson, L.W., Gallagher, D., & Breckenridge, J.S. (1987). Comparative effectiveness of psychotherapies for depressed elders. *Journal of Consulting and Clinical Psychology, 55,* 385–390.

Thoresen, C.E., Friedman, M., Powell, L.H., Gill, J.J., & Ulmer, D.K. (1985). Altering the type A behavior pattern in postinfarction patients. *Journal of Cardiopulmonary Rehabilitation, 5,* 258–266.

Thyer, B.A., & Curtis, G.C. (1984). The effects of ethanol on phobic anxiety. *Behaviour Research and Therapy, 22,* 599–610.

Tiefer, L., Pedersen, B., & Melman, A. (1988). Psychosocial follow-up of penile prosthesis implant patients and partners. *Journal of Sex and Marital Therapy, 14,* 184–201.

Tienari, P. (1991). Interaction between genetic vulnerability and family environment: The Finnish adoptive family study of schizophrenia. *Acta Psychiatrica*

Scandinavica, 84, 460–465.

Tillich, P. (1952). *The courage to be.* New Haven, CT: Yale University Press.

Tollefson, D.J. (1972). *The relationship between the occurrence of fractures and life crisis events.* Unpublished Master of Nursing thesis, University of Washington, Seattle.

Tollefson, G.D., Rampey, A.H., Jr., Potvin, J.H., Jenike, M.A., Rush, A.J., et al. (1994). A multicenter investigation of fixed-dose fluoxetine in the treatment of obsessive-compulsive disorder. *Archives of General Psychiatry, 51,* 552–558.

Tomasson, K., Kent, D., & Coryell, W. (1991). Somatization and conversion disorders: Comorbidity and demographics at presentation. *Acta Psychiatrica Scandinavica, 84,* 288–293.

Toran-Allerand, C.D. (1976). Sex steroids and the development of the newborn mouse hypothalamus and preoptic area in vitro: Implications for sexual differentiation. *Brain Research, 106,* 407–412.

Torgersen, S. (1983). Genetic factors in anxiety disorders. *Archives of General Psychiatry, 40,* 1085–1089.

Torgersen, S. (1986). Genetics of somatoform disorder. *Archives of General Psychiatry, 43,* 502–505.

Torrey, E.F. (1996). *Out of the shadows: Confronting America's mental health crisis.* New York: Wiley.

Torrey, E.F., Taylor, E., Bowler, A., & Gottesman, I. (1994). *Schizophrenia and manic depressive disorder. The biological roots of mental illness as revealed by the landmark study of identical twins.* New York: Basic Books.

Tramontana, J., & Stimbert, V. (1970). Some techniques of behavior modification with an autistic child. *Psychological Reports, 27,* 498.

Traskman, L., Asberg, M., Bertilsson, L., & Sjostrand, L. (1981). Monoamine metabolites in CSF and suicidal behavior. *Archives of General Psychiatry, 38,* 631–639.

Treffert, D.A., McAndrew, J.B., & Dreifuerst, P. (1973). An inpatient treatment program and outcome for 57 autistic and schizophrenic children. *Journal of Autism and Childhood Schizophrenia, 3,* 138–153.

Trickett, P.K., & Putnam, F.W. (1993). Impact of child sexual abuse on females: Toward a developmental, psychobiological integration. *Psychological Science, 4,* 81–87.

True, W.R., Rice, J., Eisen, S.A., Heath, A.C., Goldberg, J., et al. (1993). A twin study of genetic and environmental contributions to liability for posttraumatic stress disorder. *Archives of General Psychiatry, 50,* 257–264.

Truett, J., Cornfield, J., & Kannel, W.

(1967). Multivariate analysis of the risk of coronary heart disease in Framingham. *Journal of Chronic Disease, 20,* 511–524.

Trull, T.J., Widiger, T.A., & Frances, A. (1987). Covariation of criteria for avoidant, schizoid, and dependent personality disorders. *American Journal of Psychiatry, 144,* 767–771.

Tsai, G., Parssani, L.A., Slusher, B.S., Carter, R., Baer, L., et al. (1995). Abnormal excitatory neurotransmitter metabolism in schizophrenic brains. *Archives of General Psychiatry, 52,* 829–836.

Tsoi, W.F. (1990). Developmental profile of 200 male and 100 female transsexuals in Singapore. *Archives of Sexual Behavior, 19,* 595–605.

Tsuang, M.T., & Faraone, S.V. (1990). *The genetics of mood disorders.* Baltimore: Johns Hopkins University Press.

Tucker, J.A., Vuchinich, R.E., & Downey, K.K. (1992). Substance abuse. In S.M. Turner, K.S. Calhoun, & H.E. Adams (Eds.), *Handbook of clinical behavior therapy* (pp. 203–223). New York: Wiley.

Tune, L.E., Wong, D.F., Pearlson, G.D., Strauss, M.E., Young, T., et al. (1993). Dopamine D2 receptor density estimates in schizophrenia: A positron-emission tomography study with "C-methylspiperone." *Psychiatry Research, 49,* 219–237.

Tuomilehto, J., Geboers, J., Salonen, J.T., Nissinen, A., Kuulasman, K., & Puska, P. (1986). Decline in cardiovascular mortality in North Karelia and other parts of Finland. *British Medical Journal, 293,* 1068–1071.

Turk, D.C. (1996). Cognitive factors in chronic pain and disability. In K.S. Dobson & K.D. Craig (Eds.), *Advances in cognitive-behavioral therapy* (pp. 83–115). Thousand Oaks, CA: Sage.

Turk, D.C., Meichenbaum, D.H., & Genest, M. (1983). *Pain and behavioral medicine: A cognitive behavioral perspective.* New York: Guilford.

Turk, D.C., Wack, J.T., & Kerns, R.D. (1985). An empirical examination of the "pain behavior" construct. *Journal of Behavioral Medicine, 8,* 119–130.

Turk-Charles, S., Rose, T., & Gatz, M. (1996). The significance of gender in the treatment of older adults. In L.L. Carstensen, B.A. Edelstein, & L. Dornbrand (Eds.), *The practical handbook of clinical gerontology* (pp. 107–128). Thousand Oaks, CA: Sage.

Turkat, I.D., & Maisto, S.A. (1985). Personality disorders: Application of the experimental method to the formulation and modification of personality disorders. In D.H. Barlow (Ed.), *Clinical handbook of psychological disorders.* New York: Guilford.

Turkewitz, H., & O'Leary, K.D. (1977). *A comparison of communication and behavioral marital therapy.* Paper presented at the Eleventh Annual Convention of the Association for Advancement of Behavior Therapy, Atlanta.

Turkheimer, E. (in press). Heritability and biological explanation.

Turkheimer, E., & Parry, C.D. (1992). Why the gap? Practice and policy in civil commitment hearings. *American Psychologist, 47,* 646–655.

Turner, B.F., & Adams, C.G. (1988). Reported change in preferred sexual activity. *The Journal of Sex Research, 25,* 289–303.

Turner, L.A., Althof, S.E., Levine, S.B., Risen, C.B., Bodner, D.R., Kursh, E.D., & Resnick, M.I. (1989). Self-injection of papaverine and phentolamine in the treatment of psychogenic impotence. *Journal of Sex and Marital Therapy, 15,* 163–176.

Turner, R.J., & Sternberg, M.P. (1978). Psychosocial factors in elderly patients admitted to a psychiatric hospital. *Age and Aging, 7,* 171–177.

Turner, R.J., & Wagonfeld, M.O. (1967). Occupational mobility and schizophrenia. *American Sociological Review, 32,* 104–113.

Turner, R.M. (1993). Dynamic-cognitive-behavior therapy. In T. Giles (Ed.), *Handbook of effective psychotherapy* (pp. 437–454). New York: Plenum.

Turner, R.M. (1994). Borderline, narcissistic, and histrionic personality disorders. In M. Hersen & R.T. Ammerman (Eds.), *Handbook of prescriptive treatments for adults* (pp. 393–420). New York: Plenum.

Turner, S.M., Beidel, D.C., & Cooley-Quille, M.R. (1995). Two-year follow-up of social phobics treated with Social Effectiveness Therapy. *Behaviour Research and Therapy, 33,* 553–555.

Turner, S.M., Beidel, D.C., & Townsley, R.M. (1992). Behavioral treatment of social phobia. In S.M. Turner, K.S. Calhoun, & H.E. Adams (Eds.), *Handbook of clinical behavior therapy* (2nd ed., pp. 13–37). New York: Wiley.

Tuschen, B., & Bent, H. (1995). Intensive brief inpatient treatment of bulimia nervosa. In K.D. Brownell & C.G. Fairburn (Eds.), *Eating disorders and obesity: A comprehsive handbook.* New York: Guilford.

Twentyman, C.T., & McFall, R.M. (1975). Behavioral training of social skills in shy males. *Journal of Consulting and Clinical Psychology, 43,* 384–395.

Tye, J. (1991). *Stop teenage addiction to tobacco.* Springfield, MA: Stop Teenage Addiction to Tobacco.

Tykra, A.R., Cannon, T.D., Haslam, N., Mednick, S.A, Schulsinger, F., et al.

(1995). The latent structure of schizotypy. I. Premorbid indicators of a taxon of individuals at risk for schizophrenia spectrum disorders. *Journal of Abnormal Psychology, 104,* 173–184.

U. S. Department of Health and Human Services (1991). *Health United States: 1990.* Washington, DC. U.S. Government Printing Office.

U.S. Bureau of the Census (1990). *Statistical abstract of the United States.* Washington, DC.

U.S. Bureau of the Census. (1986). *Statistical brief.* Washington, DC: U.S. Government Printing Office.

U.S. Department of Health and Human Services, National Center for Health Statistics. (1990a, August 30). *Monthly vital statistics.*

U.S. Department of Health and Human Services. (1982). Prevention in adulthood: Self-motivated quitting. In *Cancer: The health consequences of smoking, a report of the Surgeon General.* Washington, DC: U.S. Government Printing Office.

U.S. Department of Health and Human Services. (1989). *Reducing the health consequences of smoking: 25 years of progress. A report of the Surgeon General, Executive summary* (DHHS Publication No. CDC 89–8411). Washington, DC: U.S. Government Printing Office.

U.S. Department of Health and Human Services. (1990b). *The health benefits of smoking cessation: A report of the surgeon general.* Alexandria, VA: Author.

U.S. Department of Health and Human Services. (1993). *Eighth special report to the U.S. Congress on alcohol and health.* Alexandria, VA: Author.

U.S. Department of Health and Human Services. (1994). *National survey results on drug use from the Monitoring the Future Study, 1975–1993.* Rockville, MD: National Institute on Drug Abuse.

U.S. Department of Health and Human Services. (1997). *Alcohol and health.* Washington, DC: NIH.

Ullmann, L., & Krasner, L. (1975). *A psychological approach to abnormal behavior* (2nd ed.). Englewood Cliffs, NJ: Prentice-Hall.

Upper, D., & Ross, S.M. (Eds.). (1980). *Behavioral group therapy 1980: An annual review.* Champaign, IL: Research Press.

Vaillant, G.E. (1979). Natural history of male psychologic health: Effects of mental health on physical health. *New England Journal of Medicine, 301,* 1249–1254.

Vaillant, G.E. (1983). *The natural history of alcoholism: Causes, patterns, and paths to recovery.* Cambridge, MA: Harvard University Press.

Vaillant, G.E. (1996). A long-term follow-up of male alcohol abuse. *Archives of General Psychiatry, 53,* 243–250.

Valdes, M., Garcia, L., Treserra, J., & et al. (1989). Psychogenic pain and depressive disorders: An empirical study. *Journal of Affective Disorders, 16,* 21–25.

van Broeckhoven, C.L. (1995). Molecular genetics of Alzheimer disease: Identification of genes and gene mutations. *European Neurology, 35,* 8–19.

van den Broucke, S., Vandereycken, W., & Vertommen, H. (1995). Marital Communication in Eating Disorders: A Controlled Observational Study. *International Journal of Eating Disorders, 17,* 1–23.

Van der Kolk, B., Greenberg, M., Boyd, H., & Krystal, J.H. (1985). Inescapable shock, neurotransmitters, and addiction to trauma: Toward a psychobiology of posttraumatic stress. *Biological Psychiatry, 20,* 314–325.

van der Kolk, B.A., Dreyfuss, D., Michaels, M., Shera, D., Berkowitz, R., et al. (1994). Fluoxetine in posttraumatic stress disorder. *Journal of Clinical Psychiatry, 15,* 517–523.

van Egeren, L.F., & Madarasmi, S. (1987). A computerized diary for ambulatory blood pressure monitoring. In N. Schneiderman (Ed.), *Handbook on methods and measurements in cardiovascular behavioral medicine.* New York: Plenum.

van Praag, H., Plutchik, R., & Apter, A. (Eds.), (1990). *Violence and suicidality.* New York: Brunner/Mazel.

van Reekum, R., Conway, C.A., Gansler, D., & White, R. (1993). Neurobehavioral study of borderline personality disorder. *Journal of Psychiatry and Neuroscience, 18,* 121–129.

vanKammen, D.P., Bunney, W.E., Docherty, J.P., Jimerson, D.C., Post, R.M., Sivis, S., Ebart, M., & Gillin, J.C. (1977). Amphetamine-induced catecholamine activation in schizophrenia and depression. *Advances in Biochemical Psychopharmacology, 16,* 655–659.

vanKammen, D.P., Hommer, D.W., & Malas, K.L. (1987). Effects of pimozide on positive and negative symptoms in schizophrenic patients: Are negative symptoms state dependent? *Neuropsychobiology, 18,* 113–117.

vanKammen, W.B., Loeber, R., & Stouthamer-Loeber, M. (1991). Substance use and its relationship to conduct problems and delinquency in young boys. *Journal of Youth and Adolescence, 20,* 399–413.

Vanzi, M. (1996, August 31). Drug castration bill passes, goes to Gov. Wilson. *Los Angeles Times,* pp. A1, A26.

Vardaris, R.M., Weisz, D.J., Fazel, A., & Rawitch, A.B. (1976). Chronic administration of delta-9–tetrahydrocannabinol to pregnant rats: Studies of pup behavior and placental transfer. *Pharmacology and Biochemistry of Behavior, 4,* 249–254.

Varner, R.V., & Gaitz, C.M. (1982). Schizophrenic and paranoid disorders in the aged. In L.F. Jarvik & G.W. Small (Eds.), *Psychiatric Clinics of North America.* Philadelphia: Saunders.

Varni, J.W. (1981). Self-regulation techniques in the management of chronic arthritic pain in hemophilia. *Behavior Therapy, 12,* 185–194.

Varni, J.W., & Bernstein, B.H. (1991). Evaluation and management of pain in children with rheumatoid diseases. *Pediatric Rheumatology, 17,* 985–1000.

Varni, J.W., & Dietrich, S.L. (1981). Behavioral pediatrics: Towards a reconceptualization. *Behavioral Medicine Update, 3,* 5–7.

Varni, J.W., & Wallander, J.L. (1984). Adherence to health-related regimens in pediatric chronic disorders. *Clinical Psychology Review, 4,* 585–596.

Varni, J.W., Blount, R.L., Waldron, S.A., & Smith, A.J. (1997). Management of pain and distress. In M.C. Roberts (Ed.), *Handbook of pediatric psychology.* New York: Guilford.

Vaughn, C.E., & Leff, J.P. (1976). The influence of family and social factors on the course of psychiatric illness. A comparison of schizophrenic and depressed neurotic patients. *British Journal of Psychiatry, 129,* 125–137.

Ventura, J., Neuchterlein, K.H., Lukoff, D., & Hardesty, J.D. (1989). A prospective study of stressful life events and schizophrenic relapse. *Journal of Abnormal Psychology, 98,* 407–411.

Vernberg, E.M., LaGreca, A.M., Silverman, W.K., & Prinstein, M.J. (1996). Prediction of post-traumatic stress symptoms in children after hurricane Andrew. *Journal of Abnormal Psychology, 105,* 237–249.

Viederman, M. (1986). Somatoform and factitious disorders. In A.M. Cooper, A.J. Frances, & M.H. Sacks (Eds.), *The personality disorders and neuroses.* Philadelphia: Lippincott.

Vinogradov, S., & Yalom, I. (1989). *Group therapy.* Washington, DC: American Psychiatric Press.

Vitousek, K., & Manke, F. (1994). Personality variables and disorders in anorexia nervosa and bulimia nervosa. *Journal of Abnormal Psychology, 103,* 137–147.

Vogel, V.G., Graves, D.S., Vernon, S.W., Lord, J.A., Winn, R.J., & Peters, G.N. (1990). Mammographic screening of women with increased risk of breast cancer. *Cancer, 66,* 1613–1620.

Volpicelli, J.R., Watson, N.T., King, A.C., Shermen, C.E., & O'Brien, C.P. (1995). Effects of naltrexone on alcohol "high" in alcoholics. *American Journal of Psychiatry, 152,* 613–617.

von Krafft-Ebing, R. (1902). *Psychopathia sexualis.* Brooklyn, NY: Physicians and Surgeons Books.

Vygotsky, L.S. (1978). *Mind in society: The development of higher psyhological processes* (M. Cole, V. John-Steiner, S. Scribner, & E. Souberman, Eds. and Trans.). Cambridge, MA: Harvard University Press.

Wachtel, E.F., & Wachtel, P.L. (1986). *Family dynamics in individual psychotherapy: A guide to clinical strategies.* New York: Guilford.

Wachtel, P.L. (1977). *Psychoanalysis and behavior therapy: Toward an integration.* New York: Basic Books.

Wachtel, P.L. (1982). Vicious circles: The self and the rhetoric of emerging and unfolding. *Contemporary Psychoanalysis, 18,* 259–273.

Wachtel, P.L. (1993). *Therapeutic communication: Principles and effective practice.* New York: Guilford.

Wachtel, P.L. (1997). *Psychoanalysis, behavior therapy and the relational world.* Washington, DC: American Psychological Association.

Wahl, O.F. & Harrman, C.R. (1989). Family views of stigma. *Schizophrenia Bulletin, 15,* 131–139.

Wakefield, H., & Underwager, R. (1994). *Return of the furies: An investigation into recovered memory therapy.* Chicago: Open Court Publishing.

Wakefield, J. (1992). Disorder as dysfunction: A conceptual critique of DSM-III-R's definition of mental disorder. *Psychological Review, 99,* 232–247.

Walco, G.A., Varni, J.W., & Ilowite, N.T. (1992). Cognitive-behavioral pain management in children with juvenile rheumatoid arthritis. *Pediatrics, 89,* 1075–1079.

Waldenger, R.J., & Frank, A.E. (1989). Clinicians' experiences in combining medication and psychotherapy in the treatment of borderline patients. *Hospital and Community Psychiatry, 40,* 712–718.

Waldron, I. (1976). Why do women live longer than men? *Journal of Human Stress, 2,* 1–13.

Walen, S., Hauserman, N.M., & Lavin, P.J. (1977). *Clinical guide to behavior therapy.* Baltimore: Williams & Wilkins.

Walitzer, K.S., & Connors, G.J. (1994). Psychoactive substance use disorders. In M. Hersen & R.T. Ammerman (Eds.), *Handbook of prescriptive treatments for adults* (pp. 53–71). New York: Plenum.

Walker, E.F., Davis, D.M., & Savoie, T.D. (1994). Neuromotor precursors of schizophrenia. *Schizophrenia Bulletin, 20,* 441–451.

Walker, E.F., Grimes, K.E., Davis, D.M., & Adina, J. (1993). Childhood precursors of schizophrenia: Facial expressions of emotion. *American Journal of Psychiatry, 150,* 1654–1660.

Walker, J.L., Lahey, B.B., Russo, M.F., Frick, P.J., Christ, M.A.G., McBurnett, K., Loeber, R., Stouthamer-Loeber, M., & Green, S.M. (1991). Anxiety, inhibition, and conduct disorder in children: 1. Relations to social impairment. *Journal of the American Academy of Child and Adolescent Psychiatry, 30,* 187–191.

Wallace, C.J., Boone, S.E., Donahoe, C.P., & Foy, D.W. (1985). The chronically mentally disabled: Independent living skills training. In D.H. Barlow (Ed.), *Clinical handbook of psychological disorders.* New York: Guilford.

Waller, D.A., Kiser, S., Hardy, B.W., Fuchs, I., & Feigenbaum, L.P. (1986). Eating behavior and plasma beta-endorphin in bulimia. *American Journal of Clinical Nutrition, 4,* 20–23.

Wallerstein, R.S. (1986). *Forty-two lives in treatment: A study of psychoanalysis and psychotherapy.* New York: Guilford.

Wallerstein, R.S. (1989). The Psychotherapy Research Project of the Menninger Foundation: An overview. *Journal of Consulting and Clinical Psychology, 57,* 195–205.

Walling, M., Anderson, B.L., & Johnson, S.R. (1990). Hormonal replacement therapy for postmenopausal women: A review of sexual outcomes and related gynecologic effects. *Archives of Sexual Behavior, 19,* 119–137.

Walsh, D.C., & Hingson, R.W. (1991). A randomized trial of treatment for alcohol abusing workers. *New England Journal of Medicine, 325,* 775–782.

Walters, E., & Kendler, K.S. (1994). Anorexia nervosa and anorexia-like symptoms in a population based twin sample. *American Journal of Psychiatry, 152,* 62–71.

Walters, E.E., Neale, M.C., Eaves, L.J., Lindon, J., & Heath, A.C. (1992). Bulimia nervosa and major depression: A study of common genetic and environmental factors. *Psychological Medicine, 22,* 617–622.

Ward, C.H., Beck, A.T., Mendelson, M., Mock, E., & Erbaugh, J.K. (1962). The psychiatric nomenclature: Reasons for diagnostic disagreement. *Archives of General Psychiatry, 7,* 198–205.

Warren, C.A.B. (1982). *The court as last resort: Mental illness and the law.* Chicago: University of Chicago Press.

Wartenberg, A.A., Nirenberg, T.D., Liepman, M.R., Silvia, L.Y., Begin, A.M., & Monti, P.M. (1990). Detoxification of alcoholics: Improving care by symptom-triggered sedation. *Alcoholism: Clinical and Experimental Research, 14,* 71–75.

Waskow, I.E. (1984). Specification of the technique variable in the NIMH Treatment of Depression Collaborative Research Program. In J.B.W. Williams & R.L. Spitzer (Eds.), *Psychotherapy research: Where are we and where should we go?* New York: Guilford.

Watkins, J.G. (1984). The Bianchi (L.A. Hillside Strangler) case: Sociopath or multiple personality? *International Journal of Clinical and Experimental Hypnosis, 32,* 67–101.

Watson, D., & Pennebaker, J.W. (1989). Health complaints, stress, and distress: Exploring the central role of negative affectivity. *Psychological Review, 96,* 234–254.

Watson, G.C., & Buranen, C. (1979). The frequency and identification of false positive conversion reactions. *Journal of Nervous and Mental Disease, 167,* 243–247.

Watson, J.B. (1913). Psychology as the behaviorist views it. *Psychological Review, 20,* 158–177.

Watson, J.B., & Rayner, R. (1920). Conditioned emotional reactions. *Journal of Experimental Psychology, 3,* 1–14.

Watt, N.F. (1974). Childhood and adolescent roots of schizophrenia. In D. Ricks, A. Thomas, & M. Roll (Eds.), *Life history research in psychopathology* (Vol. 3). Minneapolis: University of Minnesota Press.

Watt, N.F., Stolorow, R.D., Lubensky, A.W., & McClelland, D.C. (1970). School adjustment and behavior of children hospitalized for schizophrenia as adults. *American Journal of Orthopsychiatry, 40,* 637–657.

Wattis, J.P. (1990). Diagnostic issues in depression in old age. *International Clinical Psychopharmacology, 5,* 1–6.

Watzlawick, P., Beavin, J., & Jackson, D.D. (1967). *Pragmatics of human communication: A study of interactional patterns, pathologies, and paradoxes.* New York: Norton.

Weaver, T.L., & Clum, G.A. (1993). Early family environments and traumatic experiences associated with borderline personality disorder. *Journal of Consulting and Clinical Psychology, 61,* 1068–1075.

Webb, W.B., & Campbell, S.S. (1980). Awakenings and the return to sleep in an older population. *Sleep, 3,* 41–66.

Weber, T. (1996, December 2). Tarnishing the golden years with addiction. *Los Angeles Times,* pp. A1, A37.

Wechsler, D. (1968). *Escala de Inteligencia Wechsler para Adultos.* New York: Psychological Corporation.

Wechsler, H., Davenport, A., Dowdell, G., Moeykens, B., & Castillo, S. (1994). Health and behavioral consequences of binge drinking in college: A national survey of students at 140 campuses. *Journal of the American Medical Association, 272,* 1672–1677.

Wechsler Intelligence Scale for Children. Third Edition. (1991). San Antonio: The Psychological Corporation.

Weg, R.B. (Ed.). (1983). *Sexuality in the later years: Roles and behavior.* New York: Academic Press.

Wegner, D.M., Schneider, D.J., Carter, S.R., & White, T.L. (1987). Paradoxical effects of thought suppression. *Journal of Personality and Social Psychology, 53,* 5–13.

Wegner, D.M., Schneider, D.J., Knutson, B., & McMahon, S.R. (1991). Polluting the stream of consciousness: The effect of thought suppression on the mind's environment. *Cognitive Therapy and Research, 15,* 141–152.

Weicz, J.R., Suwanlert, S., Chaiyasit, W., & Walter, B.R. (1987). Over-and undercontrolled referral problems among children and adolescents from Thailand and the United States: The *wat* and *wai* of cultural differences. *Journal of Consulting and Clinical Psychology, 55,* 719–726.

Weidner, G., & Collins, R.L. (1993). Gender, coping, and health. In H.W. Krohne (Ed.), *Attention and avoidance.* New York: Springer-Verlag.

Weidner, G., & Griffin, K.W. (1995). Psychological aspects of cholesterol-lowering. *Cardiovascular Risk Factors, 5,* 1–7.

Weidner, G., Connor, S.L., Hollis, J.F., & Connor, W.E. (1992). Improvements in hostility and depression in relation to dietary change and cholesterol lowering. *Annals of Internal Medicine, 117,* 820–823.

Weidner, G., Sexton, G., McLellarn, R., Connor, S.L., & Matarazzo, J.D. (1987). The role of Type A behavior and hostility in the elevation of plasma lipids in adult women and men. *Psychosomatic Medicine, 49,* 136–146.

Weidner, G., Friend, R., Ficarroto, T.J., & Mendell, N.R. (1989). Hostility and cardiovascular reactivity to stress in women and men. *Psychosomatic Medicine, 51,* 36–45.

Weikel, D. (1996, April 7). Meth labs: How young lives are put in peril. *Los Angeles Times,* pp. A1, A18.

Weiler, P.G., Mungas, D., & Pomerantz, S. (1988). AIDS as a cause of dementia in the elderly. *Journal of the American Geriatrics Society, 36,* 139–141.

Weinberger, D.R. (1987). Implications of normal brain development for the pathogenesis of schizophrenia. *Archives of General Psychiatry, 44,* 660–669.

Weinberger, D.R., Berman, K.F., & Illowsky, B.P. (1988). Physiological dysfunction of dorsolateral prefrontal cortex in schizophrenia: 3. A new cohort and evidence for a monoaminergic mechanism. *Archives of General Psychiatry, 45,* 609–615.

Weinberger, D.R., Cannon-Spoor, H.E., Potkin, S.G., & Wyatt, R.J. (1980). Poor premorbid adjustment and CT scan abnormalities in chronic schizophrenia. *American Journal of Psychiatry, 137,* 1410–1413.

Weinberger, D.R., Wagner, R.L., & Wyatt, R.J. (1983). Neuropathological studies of schizophrenia: A selective review. *Schizophrenia Bulletin, 9,* 193–212.

Weiner, B. (1986). *An attributional theory of motivation and emotion.* Unpublished manuscript, University of California at Los Angeles.

Weiner, B., Frieze, L., Kukla, A., Reed, L., Rest, S., & Rosenbaum, R.M. (1971). *Perceiving the causes of success and failure.* New York: General Learning Press.

Weiner, H. (1977). *Psychobiology and human disease.* New York: Elsevier.

Weingartner, H., & Silverman, E. (1982). Models of cognitive impairment: Cognitive changes in depression. *Psychopharmacology Bulletin, 18,* 27–42.

Weinstein, H. (1996, March 7). Assisted deaths ruled legal: 9th Circuit lifts ban of doctor-aided suicide. *Los Angeles Times,* pp. A1, A16.

Weinstein, H., & Groves, M. (1996, March 14). Tobacco firm agrees to settle a health suit. *Los Angeles Times,* pp. A1, A12.

Weinstein, K.A., Davison, G.C., DeQuattro, V., & Allen, J.W. (1986). *Type A behavior and cognitions: Is hostility the bad actor?* Paper presented at the 94th Annual Convention of the American Psychological Association, Washington, DC.

Weintraub, S., Liebert, D.E., & Neale, J.M. (1975). Teacher ratings of children vulnerable to psychopathology. *American Journal of Orthopsychiatry, 45,* 838–845.

Weintraub, S., Prinz, R., & Neale, J.M. (1978). Peer evaluations of the competence of children vulnerable to psychopathology. *Journal of Abnormal Child Psychology, 6,* 461–473.

Weiss, B., Weisz, J.R., & Bromfield, R. (1986). Performance of retarded and nonretarded persons on information-processing tasks: Further tests of the similar structure hypothesis. *Psychological Bulletin, 100,* 157–175.

Weiss, G. (1983). Long-term outcome: Findings, concepts, and practical implications. In M. Rutter (Ed.), *Developmental neuropsychiatry.* New York: Guilford.

Weiss, G., & Hechtman, L. (1986). *Hyperactive children grown up.* New York: Guilford.

Weiss, R.L., & Cerreto, M.C. (1980). The Marital Status Inventory: Development of a measure of dissolution potential. *American Journal of Family Therapy, 8,* 80–85.

Weiss, S. (1986). Introduction and overview. In K.A. Matthews, S.J. Weiss, T. Detre, T.M. Dembroski, B. Falkner, S.B. Manuck, & R.B. Williams (Eds.), *Handbook of stress, reactivity, and cardiovascular disease.* New York: Wiley.

Weissberg, R.P., Caplan, M., & Harwood, R.L. (1991). Promoting competent young people in competence-enhancing environments: A systems-based perspective on primary prevention. *Journal of Consulting and Clinical Psychology, 59,* 830–841.

Weissberg, R.P., Gesten, E.L., Rapkin, B.D., Cowen, E.L., Davidson, E., deApodaca, R.F., & McKim, B.J. (1981). Evaluation of a social-problem-solving training program for suburban and inner-city third-grade children. *Journal of Consulting and Clinical Psychology, 49,* 251–261.

Weissman, A.N., & Beck, A.T. (1978). *Development and validation of the Dysfunctional Attitude Scale: A preliminary investigation.* Paper presented at the annual meeting of the American Educational Research Association, Toronto.

Weissman, M.M. (1993). The epidemiology of personality disorders: A 1990 update. *Journal of Personality Disorders, 7,* 44–61.

Weissman, M.M. (1995). *Mastering depression: A patient's guide to interpersonal psychotherapy.* New York: Graywind.

Weissman, M.M., & Markowitz, J.C. (1994). Interpersonal psychotherapy: Current status. *Archives of General Psychiatry, 51,* 599–605.

Weissman, M.M., Klerman, G.L., & Paykel, E.S. (1971). Clinical evaluation of hostility in depression. *American Journal of Psychiatry, 128,* 261–266.

Weissman, M.M., Klerman, G.L., Paykel, E.S., Prusoff, A., & Hanson, B. (1974). Treatment effects on the social adjustment of depressed patients. *Archives of General Psychiatry, 30,* 771–778.

Weissman, M.M., Prusoff, B.A., DiMascio, A., New, C., Goklaney, M., & Klerman, G.L. (1979). The efficacy of drugs and psychotherapy in the treatment of acute depressive episodes. *American Journal of Psychiatry, 36,* 555–558.

Weisz, J.R., & Weiss, B. (1991). Studying the "referability" of child clinical problems. *Journal of Consulting and Clinical Psychology, 59,* 266–273.

Weisz, J.R., & Yeates, K.D. (1981). Cognitive development in retarded and nonretarded persons: Piagetian tests of the similar structure hypothesis. *Psychological Bulletin, 90,* 153–178.

Weisz, J.R., Suwanlert, S., Chaiyasit, W., Weiss, B., Walter, B.R., & Anderson, W.W. (1988). Thai and American perspectives on over- and undercontrolled child behavior problems: Exploring the threshold model among parents, teachers, and psychologists. *Journal of Consulting and Clinical Psychology, 56,* 601–609.

Weitzenhoffer, A.M., & Hilgard, E.R. (1959). *Stanford hypnotic susceptibility scale, Forms A and B.* Palo Alto, CA: Consulting Psychologists Press.

Welch, S.L., & Fairburn, C.G. (1994). Sexual abuse and bulimia nervosa: Three integrated case-control comparisons. *American Journal of Psychiatry, 151,* 402–407.

Wells, C.E., & Duncan, G.W. (1980). *Neurology for psychiatrists.* Philadelphia: F.A. Davis.

Wender, P.H., Kety, S.S., Rosenthal, D., Schulsinger, F., Ortmann, J., & Lunde, I. (1986). Psychiatric disorders in the biological and adoptive families of adopted individuals with affective disorders. *Archives of General Psychiatry, 43,* 923–929.

Wenzlaff, R.M., Wegner, D.M., & Klein, S.B. (1991). The role of thought suppression in the bonding of thought and affect. *Journal of Personality and Social Psychology, 60,* 500–508.

West, D.J. (1977). *Homosexuality re-examined.* Minneapolis: University of Minnesota Press.

Wester, P., Eriksson, S., Forsell, A., Puu, G., & Adolfsson, R. (1988). Monoamine metabolite concentrations and cholinesterase activities in cerebrospinal fluid of progressive dementia patents: Relation to clinical parameters. *Acta Neurologica Scandinavica, 77,* 12–21.

Whalen, C.K. (1983). Hyperactivity, learning problems, and the attention deficit disorders. In T.H. Ollendick & M. Hersen (Eds.), *Handbook of child psychopathology.* New York: Plenum.

Whalen, C.K., & Henker, B. (1985). The social worlds of hyperactive (ADDH) children. *Clinical Psychology Review, 5,* 447–478.

Whalen, C.K., & Henker, B. (1991). Therapies for hyperactive children: Comparisons, combinations, and compromises. *Journal of Consulting and Clinical Psychology, 59,* 126–137.

Whalen, C.K., Henker, B., Hinshaw, S.P., Heller, T., & Huber-Dressler, A. (1991). Messages of medication: Effects of actual versus informed medication status on hyperactive boys' expectancies and self-evaluations. *Journal of Consulting and Clinical Psychology, 59,* 602–606.

White, J., Davison, G.C., Haaga, D.A.F., & White, K. (1992). Articulated thoughts and cognitive distortion in depressed and nondepressed psychiatric patients. *Journal of Nervous and Mental Disease, 180*, 77–81.

White, K., & Cole, J.O. (1990). Pharmacotherapy. In A.S. Bellack & M. Hersen (Eds.), *Handbook of comparative treatments for adult disorders* (pp. 266–284). New York: Wiley.

White, P.F. (1986). Patient-controlled analgesia: A new approach to the management of postoperative pain. *Seminars in Anesthesia, 4*, 255–266.

Whitehead, W.E., Burgio, K.L., & Engel, B.T. (1985). Biofeedback treatment of fecal incontinence in geriatric patients. *Journal of the American Geriatrics Society, 33*, 320–324.

Whitford, R., & Parr, V. (1995). Use of rational emotive behavior therapy with juvenile sex offenders. *Journal of Rational-Emotive and Cognitive Behavior Therapy, 13*, 273–282.

Whitlock, F.A. (1967). The aetiology of hysteria. *Acta Psychiatrica Scandinavica, 43*, 144–162.

Whitman, T.L. (1990). Self-regulation and mental retardation. *American Journal on Mental Retardation, 94*, 347–362.

Whyte, S., Bayreuther, K., & Masters, C.L. (1994). Rational therapeutic strategies for Alzheimer's disease. In D.B. Calne (Ed.), *Neurodegenerative diseases.* Philadelphia: Saunders.

Wickens, D.D., Allen, C.K., & Hill, F.A. (1963). Effects of instruction on extinction of the conditioned GSR. *Journal of Experimental Psychology, 66*, 235–240.

Widiger, T.A., & Costa, P.T., Jr. (1994). Personality and personality disorders. *Journal of Abnormal Psychology, 95*, 43–51.

Widiger, T.A., Frances, A., & Trull, T.J. (1987). A psychometric analysis of the social-interpersonal and cognitive-perceptual items for the schizotypal personality disorder. *Archives of General Psychiatry, 44*, 741–745.

Widiger, T.A., Frances, A., Spitzer, R.L., & Williams, J.B.W. (1988). The DSM-III personality disorders: An overview. *American Journal of Psychiatry, 145*, 786–795.

Wig, N.N., & Varma, V.K. (1977). Patterns of long-term heavy cannabis use in North India and its effects on cognitive functions. A preliminary report. *Drug and Alcohol Dependence, 2*, 211–219.

Wigdor, B., & Morris, G. (1977). A comparison of twenty-year medical histories of individuals with depressive and paranoid states. *Journal of Gerontology, 32*, 160–163.

Wikler, A. (1980). *Opioid dependence: Mechanisms and treatment.* NY: Plenum.

Willi, J., & Grossman, S. (1983). Epidemiology of anorexia nervosa in a defined region of Switzerland. *American Journal of Psychiatry, 140*, 564–567.

Williams, D.A., Compas, B., Leitenberg, H., & Haaga, D.A.F. (in press). Empirically supported psychological treatments: A sampling from health psychology. *Journal of Consulting and Clinical Psychology.*

Williams, H., & McNicol, K.N. (1969). Prevalence, natural history and relationship of wheezy bronchitis and asthma in children: An epidemiological study. *British Medical Journal, 4*, 321–325.

Williams, J.B.W., Gibbon, M., First, M.B., Spitzer, R.L., Davies, M., et al. (1992). The Structured Clinical Interview for DSM-III-R (SCID): 2. Multisite test-retest reliability. *Archives of General Psychiatry, 49*, 630–636.

Williams, J.M., Little, M.M., Scates, S., & Blackman, N. (1987). Memory complaints and abilities among depressed older adults. *Journal of Consulting and Clinical Psychology, 55*, 595–598.

Williams, K., Goodman, M., & Green, R. (1985). Parent-child factors in gender role socialization in girls. *Journal of the American Academy of Child Psychiatry, 26*, 720–731.

Williams, L.M. (1995). Recall of childhood trauma: A prospective study of women's memories of child sexual abuse. *Journal of Consulting and Clinical Psychology, 62*, 1167–1176.

Williams, M.E., Davison, G.C., Nezami, E., & DeQuattro, V. (1992). Cognitions of type A and type B individuals in response to social criticism. *Cognitive Therapy and Research, 16*, 19–30.

Williams, R.B. (1987). Psychological factors in coronary artery disease: Epidemiological evidence. *Circulation, 76*, 117–123.

Williams, R.B., Barefoot, J.C., Haney, T.H., Harrell, F.E., Blumenthal, J., Pryor, D.B., & Peterson, B. (1986). *Type A behavior and angiographically documented coronary atherosclerosis in a sample of 2,289 patients.* Paper presented at the annual meeting of the Psychosomatic Society.

Williams, S.L., & Rappoport, A. (1983). Cognitive treatment in the natural environment for agoraphobics. *Behavior Therapy, 14*, 299–313.

Williamson, D.A., Goreczny, A.J., Davis, C.J., Ruggiero, L., & MacKenzie, S.L. (1988). Psychophysiological analysis of the anxiety model of bulimia nervosa. *Behavior Therapy, 19*, 1–9.

Wills, T.A., DuHamel, K., & Vaccaro, D. (1995). Activity and mood temperament as predictors of adolescent substance use: Test of a self-regulation model. *Journal of Personality and Social Psychology, 68*, 901–916.

Wilsnak, S.C. (1984). Drinking, sexuality, and sexual dysfunction in women. In S.C. Wilsnak & L.J. Beckman (Eds.), *Alcohol problems in women: Antecedents, consequences, and intervention* (pp. 189–227). New York: Guilford.

Wilson, G. T. (in press). Manual-based treatment and clinical practice. *Clinical Psychology: Science and Practice.*

Wilson, G.T. (1991). Chemical aversion conditioning in the treatment of alcoholism: Further comments. *Behaviour Research and Therapy, 29*, 405–420.

Wilson, G.T. (1995). Empirically validated treatments as a basis for clinical practice: Problems and prospects. In S.C. Hayes, V.M. Follette, R.M. Dawes, & K.E. Grady (Eds.), *Scientific standards of psychological practice: Issues and recommendations.* Reno, NV: Context Press.

Wilson, G.T. (1996). Manual-based treatments: The clinical application of research findings. *Behaviour Research and Therapy, 34*, 295–314.

Wilson, G.T., & Davison, G.C. (1971). Processes of fear reduction in systematic desensitization. Animal studies. *Psychological Bulletin, 76*, 1–14.

Wilson, G.T., & Lawson, D.M. (1976). The effects of alcohol on sexual arousal in women. *Journal of Abnormal Psychology, 85*, 489–497.

Wilson, G.T., & Pike, K.M. (1993). Eating disorders. In D.H. Barlow (Ed.), *Clinical handbook of psychological disorders* (pp. 278–317). New York: Guilford.

Wilson, G.T., & Rachman, S. (1983). Meta-analysis and the evaluations of psychotherapy outcome: Limitations and liabilities. *Journal of Consulting and Clinical Psychology, 51*, 54–64.

Wilson, G.T., Eldredge, K.L., Smith, D., & Niles, B. (1991). Cognitive-behavioural treatment with and without response prevention for bulimia. *Behaviour Research and Therapy, 29*, 575–583.

Wilson, T.D., Goldin, J.C., & Charbonneau-Powis, M. (1983). Comparative efficacy of behavioral and cognitive treatments of depression. *Cognitive Therapy and Research, 7*, 111–124.

Wilson, W.R. (1975). *Unobtrusive induction of positive attitudes.* Unpublished doctoral dissertation, University of Michigan.

Winchel, R.M., Stanley, B., & Stanley, M. (1990). Biochemical aspects of suicide. In S.J. Blumenthal & D.J. Kupfer (Eds.), *Suicide over the life cycle: Risk factors, assessment and treatment of suicidal patterns* (pp. 97–126). Washington, DC: American Psychiatric Press.

Wincze, J.P., & Carey, M.P. (1991). *Sexual dysfunction: A guide for assessment and treatment.* New York: Guilford.

Winett, R.A., & Winkler, R.C. (1972). Current behavior modification in the classroom: Be still, be quiet, be docile. *Journal of Applied Behavior Analysis, 5,* 499–504.

Wing, L. (1976). Diagnosis, clinical description, and prognosis. In L. Wing (Ed.), *Early childhood autism: Clinical, educational, and social aspects.* New York: Pergamon.

Wing, L., & Attwood, A. (1987). Syndromes of autism and atypical development. In D.J. Cohen, A.M. Donnellan, & R. Paul (Eds.), *Handbook of autism and pervasive developmental disorders* (pp. 3–19). New York: Wiley.

Winick, B.J. (1993). Psychotropic medication in the criminal trial process: The constitutional and therapeutic implications of *Riggins v. Nevada. New York Law School Journal of Human Rights, 10,* 637–709.

Winick, B.J. (1994). The right to refuse mental health treatment: A therapeutic jurisprudence analysis. *International Journal of Law and Psychiatry, 17,* 99–117.

Winick, B.J. (1996). The MacArthur Treatment Competence Study: Legal and therapeutic implications. *Psychology, Public Policy, and Law, 2,* 137–166.

Winick, B.J. (1997) *The right to refuse mental health treatment.* Washington, DC: American Psychological Association.

Winick, C. (1962). Maturing out of narcotic addiction. *Bulletin on Narcotics, 14,* 1–7.

Winkler, R. (1977). What types of sex-role behavior should behavior modifiers promote? *Journal of Applied Behavior Analysis, 10,* 549–552.

Winters, K.C., & Neale, J.M. (1985). Mania and low self-esteem. *Journal of Abnormal Psychology, 94,* 282–290.

Winters, K.C., Weintraub, S., & Neale, J.M. (1981). Validity of MMPI code types in identifying DSM-III schizophrenics, unipolars and bipolars. *Journal of Consulting and Clinical Psychology, 49,* 486–487.

Wirz-Justice, A., Graw, P., Krauchi, K., Gisin, B., Jochum, A., et al. (1993). Light therapy in seasonal affective disorder is independent of time of day or circadian Phase. *Archive of General Psychiatry, 50,* 927–940.

Wischik, C. (1994). Molecular neuropathology of Alzheimer's disease. In C.L.A. Katona (Ed.), *Dementia disorders: Advances and prospects.* London: Chapman and Hall.

Wise, T. (1978). Where the public peril begins: A survey of psychotherapists to determine the effects of Tarasoff. *Stanford Law Review, 31,* 165–190.

Wiseman, C.V., Gray, J.J., Mosimann, J.E., & Arhens, A.H. (1992). Cultural expectations of thinness in women: An up-

date. *International Journal of Eating Disorders, 11,* 85–89.

Wittchen, H.U., Zhao, S., Kessler, R.C., & Eaton, W.W. (1994). DSM-III-R generalized anxiety disorder in the national comorbidity survey. *Archives of General Psychiatry, 51,* 355–364.

Wold, D.A. (1968). *The adjustment of siblings to childhood leukemia.* Unpublished medical thesis, University of Washington, Seattle.

Wolf, A. (1949). The psychoanalysis of group. *American Journal of Psychotherapy, 3,* 16–50.

Wolf, A., & Kutash, I.L. (1990). Psychoanalysis in groups. In I.L. Kutash & A. Wolf (Eds.), *The group psychotherapist's handbook: Contemporary theory and technique.* New York: Columbia University Press.

Wolf, M., Bally, H., & Morris, R. (1986). Automaticity, retrieval processes, and reading: A longitudinal study in average and impaired readers. *Child Development, 57,* 988–1000.

Wolfe, D.A., Reppucci, N.D., & Hart, S. (1995). Child abuse prevention: Knowledge and priorities. *Journal of Clinical Child Psychology, 24,* 5–22.

Wolfe, J.L. (1995). Rational emotive behavior therapy women's groups: A twenty year retrospective. *Journal of Rational-Emotive and Cognitive Behavior Therapy, 13,* 153–170.

Wolfe, R., Morrow, J., & Frederickson, B.L. (1996). Mood disorders in older adults. In L.L. Carstensen, B.A. Edelstein, & L. Dornbrand (Eds.), *The practical handbook of clinical gerontology* (pp. 274–303). Thousand Oaks, CA: Sage.

Wolfe, V.V. (1990). Sexual abuse of children. In A.S. Bellack, M. Hersen, & A.E. Kazdin (Eds.), *International handbook of behavior modification and therapy* (2nd ed., pp. 707–729). New York: Plenum.

Wolin, S.J. (1980). Introduction: Psychosocial consequences. In *Alcoholism and alcohol abuse among women: Research issues.* Rockville, MD: National Institute on Alcohol Abuse and Alcoholism.

Wolitzky, D. (1995). Traditional psychoanalytic psychotherapy. In A.S. Gurman & S.B. Messer (Eds.), *Essential psychotherapies: Theory and practice.* New York: Guilford.

Wolitzky, D.L., & Eagle, M.N. (1990). Psychotherapy. In A.S. Bellack & M. Hersen (Eds.), *Handbook of comparative treatments for adult disorders* (pp. 123–143). New York: Wiley.

Wolpe, J. (1958). *Psychotherapy by reciprocal inhibition.* Stanford, CA: Stanford University Press.

Wolraich, M., Milich, R., Stumbo, P., & Schultz, F. (1985). The effects of sucrose ingestion on the behavior of hyperac-

tive boys. *Pediatrics, 106,* 675–682.

Wong, D.F., Wagner, H.N., Tune, L.E., Dannals, R.F., Pearlson, G.D., Links, J.M., et al. (1986). Positron emission tomography reveals elevated D2 dopamine receptors in drug-naive schizophrenics. *Science, 234,* 1558–1562.

Wong, N. (1995). Group psychotherapy, combined individual and group psychotherapy, and psychodrama. In H.I. Kaplan & B.J. Sadock (Eds.), *Comprehensive textbook of psychiatry* (pp. 1821–1838). Baltimore: Williams & Wilkins.

Wood, J.M., Nezworski, M.T., & Stejskal, W.J. (1996). The Comprehensive System for the Rorschach: A critical examination. *Psychological Science, 7,* 3–10.

Wood, L.F., & Jacobson, N.S. (1985). Marital distress. In D.H. Barlow (Ed.), *Clinical handbook of psychological disorders.* New York: Guilford.

Woodside, D.B., Shekter-Wolfson, L.F., Garfinkel, P.E., & Olmsted, M.P. (1995). Family interactions in bulimia nervosa: Study design, comparisons to established population norms and changes over the course of an intensive day hospital treatment program. *International Journal of Eating Disorders, 17,* 105–115.

Woody, G.M., McLellan, T., Luborsky, L., & O'Brien, C.P. (1995). Psychotherapy in community methadone programs: A validation study. *American Journal of Psychiatry, 152,* 1302–1308.

World Health Organization. (1948). *Manual of the international statistical classification of diseases, injuries, and causes of death.* Geneva: Author.

World Health Organization. (1993). *1992 world health statistics annual.* Geneva: Author.

Worling, J.R. (1995). Sexual abuse histories of adolescent male sex offenders: Differences on the basis of the age and gender of their victims. *Journal of Abnormal Psychology, 104,* 610–613.

Wortman, C.B., & Brehm, J.W. (1975). Responses to uncontrollable outcomes: An integration of the reactance theory and the learned helplessness model. In L. Berkowitz (Ed.), *Advances in social psychology.* New York: Academic Press.

Wright, D.S. (1971). *The psychology of moral behavior.* Harmondsworth, England: Penguin.

Wright, J.C. (1976). A comparison of systematic desensitization and social skill acquisition in the modification of social fear. *Behavior Therapy, 7,* 205–210.

Wright, M.J. (1991). Identifying child sexual abuse using the Personality Inventory for Children. *Dissertation Abstracts International, 52,* 1744.

Wulsin, L., Bachop, M., & Hoffman, D. (1988). Group therapy in manic-depressive illness. *American Journal of Psychotherapy, 2,* 263–271.

Wurtele, S.K., & Miller-Perrin, C.L. (1987). An evaluation of side-effects associated with participation in a child sexual abuse prevention program. *Journal of School Health, 57,* 228–231.

Wynne, L.C., & Singer, M.T. (1963). Thought disorder and family relations in schizophrenia. 2: A classification of forms of thinking. *Archives of General Psychiatry, 9,* 199–206.

Yalom, I.D. (1980). *Existential psychotherapy.* New York: Basic Books.

Yalom, I.D. (1985). *The theory and practice of group psychotherapy* (3rd ed.). New York: Basic Books.

Yalom, I.D., Green, R., & Fisk, N. (1973). Prenatal exposure to female hormones: Effect on psychosexual development in boys. *Archives of General Psychiatry, 28,* 554–561.

Yates, A. (1989). Current perspectives on the eating disorders. *Journal of the American Academy of Child and Adolescent Psychiatry, 28,* 813–828.

Yetman, N.R. (1994). Race and ethnic inequality. In C. Calhoun & G. Ritzer (Eds.), *Social problems.* New York: McGraw-Hill.

Yirmiya, N., & Sigman, M. (1991). High functioning individuals with autism: Diagnosis, empirical findings, and theoretical issues. *Clinical Psychology Review, 11,* 669–683.

Yoshioka, R.B., Tashima, N., Chew, M., & Murase, K. (1981). *Mental health services for Pacific/Asian Americans.* San Francisco: Pacific American Mental Health Project.

Young, G.C. (1965). The aetiology of enuresis in terms of learning theory. *Medical Officer, 113,* 19–22.

Yurgelon-Todd, D., Waternaux, C.M., Cohen, B.N., Gruber, S.A., English, C.D., & Renshaw, P.F. (1996). Functional magnetic resonance imagery of schizophrenia patients and comparison subjects during word production. *American Journal of Psychiatry, 153,* 200–206.

Zakowski, S., Hall, M.H., & Baum, A. (1992). Stress, stress management, and the immune system. *Applied and Preventive Psychology, 1,* 1–13.

Zanarini, M.C., Gunderson, J.G., Marino, M.F., Gunderson, J., Marino, M., Schwartz, E., & Frankenburg, F. (1988). DSM-III disorders in the families of borderline outpatients. *Journal of Personality Disorders, 2,* 292–302.

Zane, M.D. (1984). Psychoanalysis and contextual analysis of phobias. *Journal of the American Academy of Psychoanalysis, 12,* 553–568.

Zarit, S.H. (1980). *Aging and mental disorders: Psychological approaches to assessment and treatment.* New York: Free Press.

Zarit, S.H. (1989). Issues and directions in family intervention research. In E. Light & B. Lebowitz (Eds.), *Alzheimer's Disease treatment and family stress: Directions for research* (Publication No. ADM 89–1569, pp. 458–486). Washington, DC: U.S. Department of Health and Human Services.

Zarit, S.H., Eiler, J., & Hassinger, M. (1985). Clinical assessment. In J.E. Birren & K.W. Schaie (Eds.), *Handbook of psychology of aging* (2nd ed.). New York: Van Nostrand-Reinhold.

Zarit, S.H., Todd, P.A., & Zarit, I.M. (1986). Subjective burden of husbands and wives as caregivers: A longitudinal study. *The Gerontologist, 26,* 260–266.

Zeaman, D., & Hanley, P. (1983). Stimulus preferences as structural features. In T.J. Tighe & B.E. Shepp (Eds.), *Perception, cognition, and development.* Hillsdale, NJ: Erlbaum.

Zeiss, A.M., & Steffen, A.M. (1996). Interdisciplinary health care teams: The basic unit of geriatric care. In L.L. Carstensen, B.A. Edelstein, & L. Dornbrand (Eds.), *The practical handbook of clinical gerontology* (pp. 423–450). Thousand Oaks, CA: Sage.

Zeiss, A.M., Zeiss, R.A., & Dornbrand, L. (1988, November). *Assessing and treating sexual problems in older couples.* Paper presented at the meeting of the Gerontological Society of America, San Francisco.

Zeitlin, S.B., & McNally, R.J. (1991). Implicit and explicit memory bias for threat in post-traumatic stress disorder. *Behaviour Research and Therapy, 29,* 451–457.

Zellner, D.A., Harner, D.E., & Adler, R.L. (1989). Effects of eating abnormalities and gender of perceptions of desirable body shape. *Journal of Abnormal Psychology, 98,* 93–96.

Ziegler, F.J., Imboden, J.B., & Meyer, E. (1960). Contemporary conversion reactions: A clinical study. *American Journal of Psychiatry, 116,* 901–910.

Zigler, E. (1967). Familial mental retardation: A continuing dilemma. *Science, 155,* 292–298.

Zigler, E., Hodapp, R.M., & Edison, M.R. (1990). From theory to practice in the care and education of mentally retarded individuals. *American Journal on Mental Retardation, 95,* 1–12.

Zilbergeld, B., & Evans, M. (1980). The inadequacy of Masters and Johnson. *Psychology Today, 14,* 28–43.

Zilboorg, G., & Henry, G.W. (1941). *A history of medical psychology.* New York: Norton.

Zimbardo, P.G., Andersen, S.M., & Kabat, L.G. (1981). Paranoia and deafness: An experimental investigation. *Science, 212,* 1529–1531.

Zimbardo, P.G., LaBerge, S., & Butler, L.D. (1993). Psychophysiological consequences of unexplained arousal: A posthypnotic suggestion paradigm. *Journal of Abnormal Psychology, 102,* 466–473.

Zimmer, L., & Morgan, J.P. (1995). *Exposing marijuana myths: A review of the scientific evidence.* New York: The Lindemith Center.

Zimmerman, M. (1988). Why are we rushing to publish DSM-IV? *Archives of General Psychiatry, 45,* 1135–1138.

Zimmerman, M. (1994). Diagnosing personality disorders: A review of issues and research methods. *Archives of General Psychiatry, 51,* 225–245.

Zimmerman, M., & Coryell, W. (1989). DSM-III personality disorder diagnoses in a nonpatient sample. *Archives of General Psychiatry, 46,* 682–689.

Zimmerman, M., Coryell, W., Pfohl, B., & Staid, D. (1986). The validity of four types of endogenous depression. *Archives of General Psychiatry, 43,* 234–245.

Zoccolillo, M., & Rogers, K. (1991). Characteristics and outcome of hospitalized adolescent girls with conduct disorder. *Journal of the American Academy of Child and Adolescent Psychiatry, 30,* 973–981.

Zucker, K.J., Finegan, J.K., Deering, R.W., & Bradley, S.J. (1984). Two subgroups of gender-problem children. *Archives of Sexual Behavior, 13,* 27–39.

Zucker, K.J., Green, R., Garofano, C., Bradley, S.J., et al. (1994). Prenatal gender preference of mothers of feminine and masculine boys: Relation to sibling sex composition and birth order. *Journal of Abnormal Child Psychology, 22,* 1–13.

Quotation and Illustration Credits

Permission was obtained for use of the following copyrighted material.

Page 22, figure 1.2: From Langer E. J., & Abelson, R. P. (1974). A look at how different theoretical orientations might affect the ways in which trained clinicians view the "adjustment" of a person. *Journal of Consulting and Clinical Psychology, 42,* 4–9. Copyright © 1974 by the American Psychological Association. Reprinted with permission.

Page 58–59, table 3.1: DSM-IV multiaxial classification system. *Diagnostic and Statistical Manual of Mental Disorders, Fourth Edition.* Copyright © 1994 by the American Psychiatric Association. Reprinted by permission.

Page 64, table 3.2: Manic-like episodes that are clearly caused by somatic antidepressant treatment (e.g., medication, electroconvulsive therapy, light therapy) should not count toward a diagnosis of Bipolar I Disorder. Copyright © 1994 by the American Psychiatric Association: *Diagnostic and Statistical Manual of Mental Disorders, Fourth Edition.* Reprinted with permission.

Page 74, figure 4.1: First, M. B., Spitzer, R. L., Williams, J. B. W., and Gibbon, M. (1997). From research version of Structured Clinical Interview for DSM-IV Axis I Disorders (SCID). Copyright © 1997 by New York State Psychiatric Institute, Biometrics Research Department. Used by permission.

Page 76, table 4.1: Hathaway, S. R. & McKinley, J. C. (1943). Topical clinical interpretations of items similar to those on the MMPI-2. *MMPI Manual.* Revised 1989 Butcher et al.

Page 105: figure 5.1: Miller, N. E. (1959). An illustration of the advantages of using anxiety as a theoretical concept. In S. Koch (Ed.), *Psychology: A study of a science* (Vol. 2), 278. Reprinted by permission of McGraw-Hill Book Company.

Page 109, table 5.1: Kessler, R. C., McGonagle, K. A., Zhao, S., Nelson, C. B., Hughes, M., et al. (1994). Lifetime and 12-month prevalence rates of DSM-III-R psychiatric disorders in the United States: Results from the National Comorbidity Survey. *Archives of General Psychiatry, 51,* 8–19. Reprinted by permission of American Medical Association.

Page 113, figure 5.3: Pennebaker, J., Kiecolt-Glaser, J. K., & Glaser, R. (1988). *Journal of Consulting and Clinical Psychology, 56,* 243. Copyright © 1988 by the American Psychological Association. Reprinted with permission.

Page 117, figure 5.4: Tate, B. G., & Baroff, G. S. (1966). Effects of a treatment for self-injurious behavior in an experiment with an ABAB single-subject design. *Behavior Research and Therapy, 4,* 281–287. Copyright © 1966, with kind permission from Elsevier Science Ltd., The Boulevard, Langford Lane, Kidlington OX5 1GB, UK.

Page 146, quotation: Spitzer, R. L., Skodol, A. E., Gibbon, M., & Williams, J. B. W. (1981). *DSM-III casebook.* Washington, DC: American Psychiatric Press.

Page 157, figure 7.1: Netter, F. H. Adapted. Anesthesias in conversion disorder can be distinguished from true neurological dysfunctions. The CIBA Collection of Medical Illustrations, plates 5 and 6. Copyright © CIBA Pharmaceutical Company, Division of CIBA-GEIGY Corporation. Reprinted by permission.

Page 182, table 8.2: Holmes, T. H. & Rahe, R. H. (1967). Social Readjustment Scale. *Journal of Psychosomatic Research, 11*(2), 213–218. Copyright © 1967 Elsevier Science Inc. Reprinted by permission of Pergamon Press Ltd., Oxford, England.

Page 184, figure 8.2: Stone, A. A. & Neale, J. M. (1982). Sample page from Stone & Neale's Assessment of Daily Experience scale. In A. Baum, & J. Singer (Eds.), *Environment and health.* Reprinted by permission of authors and Laurence Erlbaum Associates Inc.

Pages 184–185, figures 8.3 and 8.4: Stone, A. A., Reed, B. R. & Neale, J. M. (1987). Number of undesirable events for the ten days preceding an episode of respiratory infection. *Journal of Human Stress, 13,* 70–74. Copyright © 1987. Reprinted with permission of the Helen Dwight Reid Educational Foundation. Published by Heldref Publications, 1319 Eighteenth Street, NW, Washington, DC 20036-1802.

Page 185, table 8.3: Carver, C. S. (1993). Scales and sample items from the SCOPE. *Journal of Personality and Social Psychology, 65,* 375–390, Appendix 390. Copyright © 1993 by the American Psychological Association. Reprinted with permission.

Page 599, quotation: Morse, S. J. (1982). A preference for liberty: The case against involuntary commitment of mentally disordered. *California Law Review, 70,* 98. Copyright © 1982 by California Law Review Inc. Reprinted by permission.

Pages 615–616, quotation: Clayton, E. W. (1988). From Rogers to Rivers: The rights of the mentally ill to refuse medications. *American Journal of Law and Medicine, 13,* 19–20. Copyright © 1987 by American Journal of Law & Medicine, XIII. Reprinted with the permission of the American Society of Law, Medicine & Ethics and Boston University School of Law.

Page 617, quotation: Baxter, E. & Hopper, K. (1981). Private lives/public places: Homeless adults on the streets of New York City. Reprinted by permission of Community Service Society.

Pages 624–625, quotation: Schwitzgebel, R. L. & Schwitzgebel, R. K. (1980). Law and psychological practice. Copyright © 1980 by John Wiley & Sons, Inc. Reprinted by permission of John Wiley & Sons, Inc.

PHOTO CREDITS

Chapter 1

Opener: "What the Earth Is Really Like" by Jedd Garet, 1984. Courtesy of the Robert Miller Gallery. Page 6: Steven E. Sutton/Duomo Photography, Inc. Page 7 (top): John Maher/Stock, Boston/PNI. Page 7 (bottom): John Ficara/Woodfin Camp & Associates. Page 8: Bill Aron/ Photo Researchers. Page 9: Frank Siteman/Rainbow. Page 10 (top): From Sander L. Gilman, "Seeing the Insane," New York: Wiley, (1982). Courtesy Sander Gilman. Page 10 (bottom): Topham/The Image Works. Pages 11, 13, 14 (top) and 15 (bottom): Corbis-Bettmann. Pages 12 and 15 (top): Culver Pictures, Inc. Page 14 (bottom): Historical Picture Services. Page 17: Eric Roth/The Picture Cube. Page 19 (top): Jean-Loup Charmet/Photo Researchers. Pages 19 (bottom) and 20 (left): Corbis-Bettmann. Page 20 (right): Courtesy Lucy Freeman Walker & Co., New York.

Chapter 2

Opener: "La Ruta" by Juan Genovese, 1980. Courtesy Marlborough Gallery. Page 26: Will & Deni McIntyre/ Photo Researchers. Page 27: Porterfield/Chickering/ Photo Researchers. Page 30: National Library of Medi-cine/Science Photo Library/Photo Researchers. Page 31 (top): Myrleen Ferguson/PhotoEdit. Page 31 (bottom): Richard Nowitz/Photo Researchers. Page 32 (top): Jeff Isaac Greenberg/Photo Researchers. Page 32 (bottom): Ken Cavanagh/Photo Researchers. Page 34 : Courtesy The National Library of Medicine. Page 35 (top): Courtesy Alfred Adler Consultation Center. Page 35 (bot-tom): Courtesy Jon Erikson. Page 36: John Eastcott/YVA Momatiuk/Photo Researchers. Page 38: Richard Nowitz/Photo Researchers. Page 40: Culver Pictures, Inc. Page 41: Rick Friedman/Black Star. Page 42 (top): Ken Cavanagh/Photo Researchers. Page 42 (bottom): Omikron/Photo Researchers. Page 44: Jerry Howard/ Stock, Boston. Page 47 (left): Institute for Rational-Emo-tive Therapy. Page 47 (right): Dan Miller/New York Times Pictures. Page 49 (left): Peter Southwick/Stock, Boston/PNI. Page 49 (right): Wesley Bocxe/Photo Researchers.

Chapter 3

Opener: "David, Celia, Stephen, and Ian" by David Hockney, London, 1982. Oil on Canvas, 72x80; © David Hockney. Page 57: Bob Daemmrich/Stock, Boston. Page 59: Arlene Collins/Monkmeyer Press Photo. Page 60: Richard Nowitz/Photo Researchers. Page 61 (top): Andrew Lichtenstein/Impact Visuals/PNI. Page 61 (bot-tom): J.L. Bohin/Explorer/Photo Researchers. Page 63: Will & Deni McIntyre/Science Source/Photo Research-ers. Page 67: Richard Nowitz/Photo Researchers. Page 68: Michael Newman/PhotoEdit/PNI.

Chapter 4

Opener: "Liberty" by Max Papart, 1981. Courtesy Nahan Galleries. Page 78 (top): Lew Merrim/Monkmeyer Press Photo. Page 78 (bottom): Richard Nowitz/Photo Researchers. Page 79 (left): Courtesy Dr. Henri F. Ellenberger. Page 79 (right): Archives of the History of American Psychology. Page 81: Jeff Isaac Greenberg/ Photo Researchers. Page 83: George Chin/DOTS/Elec-tronic Diary courtesy Saul Shiffman, Ph.D., University of Pittsburgh Smoking Research Group. Page 85: Renata Hiller/Monkmeyer Press Photo. Pages 88 (top) and 89: Dan McCoy/Rainbow. Page 88 (bottom): Courtesy Deborah A. Yurgelun-Todd, Ph.D. Page 90: Richard Nowitz/Photo Researchers. Page 91: Ulrike Welsch Photography. Page 93 (top): Richard Nowitz/Photo Researchers. Page 93 (bottom): Doug Plummer/Photo Researchers. Page 95: Steven E. Sutton/Duomo Photogra-phy, Inc. Page 96: Jacques Jangoux/Photo Researchers. Page 97: Lawrence Migdale/Photo Researchers. Page 99: Courtesy Columbia University Department of Psychology.

Chapter 5

Opener: "Magnifying Glass" by Roy Lichtenstein, 1963. Photograph by Rudolph Burckhardt/Courtesy Leo Castelli Gallery. Page 104: Courtesy NASA Goddard Laboratory for Atmospheres. Page 105: Peter Vander-mark/Stock, Boston. Page 107: Geral Martineau/The Washington Post. Page 109: Ken Cavanagh/Photo Re-searchers. Page 115: Martin Rogers/Woodfin Camp & Associates.

Chapter 6

Opener: "Germs Are Everywhere" by Sandy Skoglund, 1984. © Sandy Skoglund. Page 125 (top): Harvey Stein. Page 125 (bottom): Rich Iwasaki/PNI. Page 126: Bill Gallery/Stock, Boston/PNI. Page 127: Richard Nowitz/ Photo Researchers. Page 128: Courtesy Prof. Benjamin Harris, University of Wisconsin, Parkside. Page 129: Courtesy Dr. Susan Mineka. Page 132: Sheila Terry/ Science Photo Library/Photo Researchers. Page 133: Mimi Forsyth/Monkmeyer Press Photo. Page 134: Laura Dwight/Peter Arnold, Inc. Page 136: B & C Alexander/ Photo Researchers. Page 143: Courtesy New York Public Library, Astor, Lenox and Tilden Foundations. Page 147: J. Pat Carter/Gamma Liaison. Page 148: Christopher Morris/Black Star. Page 150: Christopher Brown/Stock, Boston/PNI. Page 151: J.P. Laffont/Sygma.

Chapter 7

Opener: "Man with Entanglements" by Goodenough, 1982. Page 156: Schell/Mullaney Health Care Marketing. Page 157: Joseph Nettis/Photo Researchers. Page 159: Courtesy Sun-Sentinel. Page 162: Courtesy Daniel Weinberger, M.D., National Institute of Mental Health. Page 163: Hank

Morgan/Photo Researchers. Page 165: Bob Pizarro/Comstock, Inc. Page 166: Bob Daemmerich/Stock, Boston. Page 167: Springer/Corbis-Bettmann. Page 169: Courtesy Jerry Ohlinger's. Page 171: AP/Wide World Photos. Page 173: Comstock, Inc. Page 175 (top): Dion Ogust/The Image Works. Page 175 (bottom): Oscar Burriel/Latin Stock/Science Photo Library/Photo Researchers.

Chapter 8
Opener: "Nervosa" by Ed Paschke, 1939/SUPERSTOCK. Page 181 (top): Borrfdon/Explorer/Photo Researchers. Page 181 (bottom): Bruce Ayres/Tony Stone Images/New York, Inc. Page 183 (top left): Cindy Karp/Black Star. Page 183 (top right): Will McIntyre/Photo Researchers. Page 183 (bottom): Herve Donnezan/Photo Researchers. Page 185: Michael P. Gadomski/Science Source/Photo Researchers. Page 187: Benelux/Photo Researchers. Page 190: Emily Strong/The Picture Cube. Page 191 (top): Thomas S. England/Photo Researchers. Page 191 (bottom): Donna Binder/Impact Visuals/PNI. Page 196: Simon Fraser/Photo Researchers. Page 198: Hattie Young/Photo Researchers. Page 200: Dan McCoy/Rainbow. Page 203: Courtesy American Cancer Society. Page 204: Dick Luria/Photo Researchers.

Chapter 9
Opener: "Girl Before a Mirror" by Pablo Picasso, 1932; © 1997 Estate of Pablo Picasso/Artist Rights Society (ARS), New York/SUPERSTOCK. Page 207: AP/Wide World Photos. Page 208: Richard T. Nowitz/Photo Researchers. Page 212 (left): Giraudon/Art Resource. Page 212 (right): Maria C. Valentino/Sygma. Page 212 (bottom): Jill Greenberg; © 1996 The Walt Disney Co. Reprinted with permission of *Discover* Magazine. Page 212 (center): Eve Arnold/Magnum Photos, Inc. Page 213 (top): Aaron Haupt/Photo Researchers. Page 213 (bottom): Eric Draper/AP/Wide World Photos. Page 214: Phyllis Picardi/Stock, Boston/PNI. Page 215: Phyllis Picardi/Stock, Boston/PNI. Page 216: Robert Brenner/PhotoEdit/PNI. Page 219: Blair Seitz/Photo Researchers.

Chapter 10
Opener: "Blue Woman in Red" by Sherri Silverman, 1993/SUPERSTOCK. Page 227: Steve Granitz/Retna. Page 228: Paul Gauguin, National Gallery of Art, Washington D.C./SUPERSTOCK. Page 230: Griffin/The Image Works. Page 232: Richard Hutchings/Photo Researchers. Page 245: Will & Deni McIntyre/Photo Researchers. Page 249: Jeff Greenberg/Photo Researchers. Page 253: Murray & Associates/Tony Stone Images/ New York, Inc. Page 254: Kevin Estrada/Retna. Page 255: Rogerio Reis/Black Star. Page 257: Mark Antman/The Image Works. Page 259: Corbis-Bettmann. Page 260: Blake Discher/Sygma.

Chapter 11
Opener: "Eyes" by Gyorgy Kepes, 1941. Courtesy Gyorgy and Juliette Kepes/Alpha Gallery. Page 266: Courtesy Mrs. Heidi Schneider . Page 268: From Sander L. Gilman, "Seeing the Insane". Page 269 (top): Radio Times Hulton Picture Library. Page 269 (bottom): Corbis-Bettmann.

Page 275: Joseph Sohm/Chromosohm/Photo Researchers. Page 277: Courtesy Dr. William Iacono, University of Minnesota. Page 281: From Lieberman, et. al., 1992; © *American Journal of Psychiatry*. Reproduced with permission. Page 283: Alain Evrard/Photo Researchers. Page 285: Courtesy Sarnoff Mednick. Page 286: Courtesy Museum of Modern Art Film Stills Archive. Page 288: Chestnut Lodge Hospital, Rockville, Maryland.

Chapter 12
Opener: "A La Buvette" by Henri De Toulouse-Lautrec. Christie's Images, London/SUPERSTOCK. Page 296: Culver Pictures, Inc. Page 297: Timothy Shonnard/Tony Stone Images/New York, Inc. Page 298: Corbis-Bettmann. Page 300: Dr. James A. Hanson. Page 302: Custom Medical Stock Photo. Page 303: Culver Pictures, Inc. Page 304: Richard Hutchings/Photo Researchers. Page 306: Dr. Jeremy Burgess/Science Photo Library/Photo Researchers. Page 307: National Library of Medicine/Photo Researchers. Page 310 (top): Dr. Morley Read/Science Photo Library/Photo Researchers. Page 310 (bottom): Russell Einhon/Gamma Liaison. Page 312: Corbis-Bettmann. Page 315: Eric Brissaud/Gamma Liaison. Page 316: Photo by Lisa Rosier. © 1997 by The New York Times Company. Reprinted with permission. Page 320: Hank Morgan/Photo Researchers. Page 325: John Giordano/Picture Group. Page 328: Jim Selby/Photo Researchers.

Chapter 13
Opener: "Heads" by Bette Alexande, 1991. Page 338: Photofest. Page 340: Culver Pictures, Inc. Page 341: Courtesy Susan Kohut. Page 342: Gamma Liaison. Page 347: Ken Cavanagh/Photo Researchers. Page 349: Blair Seitz/Photo Researchers. Page 352 (top): Courtesy Dr. Otto Kernberg, The New York Hospital-Cornell Medical Center, Westchester Division. Page 352 (bottom): Courtesy Dr. Marsha M. Linehan, Dept. of Psychology, University of Washington. Page 355: Bob Daemmrich/Tony Stone Images/ New York, Inc.

Chapter 14
Opener: "The Conversation" by Henri Matisse, 1909; © 1997 Succession H. Matisse, Paris/Artists Rights Society (ARS), New York/Scala/Art Resource. Page 360: Antonello Nusca/Gamma Liaison. Page 361: Francene Keery/Stock, Boston. Page 363 (left): Robin Laurence/New York Times Pictures. Page 363 (right): Corbis-Bettmann. Page 366: Frank Fournier/Contact Press Images, Inc. Page 371: Jacques Chenet/Woodfin Camp & Associates. Page 372: Jeff Greenberg/Photo Researchers. Page 379 (top): Andrew Kaiser-G.A.F.F./Sipa Press. Page 379 (bottom): Everett Collection, Inc. Page 383: Vanessa Vick/Photo Researchers. Page 384 (top): Ira Wyman/Sygma. Page 384 (bottom): Bernard Gotfryd/Woodfin Camp & Associates. Page 398: Vanessa Vick/Photo Researchers. Page 399: Jane Rosett/Sygma.

Chapter 15
Opener: "The Way Home" by Elizabeth Barakah Hodges, 1994/SUPERSTOCK. Page 442: © Rosalie Winard. Page

409: Paula Lerner/Woodfin Camp & Associates. Page 412: Richard Phelps/Photo Researchers. Page 413 (top): Lew Merrim/Monkmeyer Press Photo. Page 413 (bottom): Ken Lax/Photo Researchers. Page 417: Rick Kopstein/ Monkmeyer Press Photo. Page 421: Hattie Young/Photo Researchers. Page 425 (left): Gene Peach/Gamma Liaison. Page 425 (right): Joseph Rodriguez/Black Star. Page 428: James Schnepf/Gamma Liaison. Page 430: Kunkel/ Phototake. Page 432: James Keyser/© Time, Inc. Page 433 (top): Jacques Chenet/Woodfin Camp & Associates. Page 433 (bottom): Nancy Pierce/Photo Researchers. Page 434: Richard Hutchings/Photo Researchers. Page 436: Will & Deni McIntyre/Photo Researchers. Page 441: Nancy Pierce/Photo Researchers.

Chapter 16
Opener: "Mirror II" by George Tooker (1920-1938), 1963; Egg tempera on gesso panel, 20 x 20 in., 1968.4. Gift of R.H. Donnelley Erdman (PA 1956); © Addison Gallery of American Art, Phillips Academy, Andover, Massachusetts. All Rights Reserved. Page 453: Mike Nelson, Pool/AP/Wide World Photos. Page 454 (top): Hulton Getty. Page 454 (bottom): Bob Daemmrich/The Image Works. Page 456 (left): Martin Rotker/Phototake. Page 456 (right): Alfred Pasieka/Science Photo Library/Photo Researchers. Page 460: R.T. Nowitz/Photo Researchers. Page 464: Suzanne Goldstein/Photo Researchers. Page 466: Susan Oliver Young/Courtesy of Ivar Lovaas. Page 470: James Prince/Photo Researchers. Page 474: Will & Deni McIntyre/Photo Researchers. Page 478 (left): David Portnoy/Black Star. Page 478 (right): McMichael/Photo Researchers. Page 480: Charles Gupton/Stock, Boston. Page 481: Cindy Charles/Gamma Liaison.

Chapter 17
Opener: "The Human Condition" by Rene Magritte, 1934. 1.00 x .81 m.; © 1997 C. Herscovici, Brussels/Artists Rights Society (ARS) New York. National Gallery of Art, Washington, D.C./Giraudon/Art Resource, NY. Page 491 (left): Richard Nowitz/Photo Researchers. Page 491 (right): Jeff Isaac Greenberg/Photo Researchers. Page 501 (top): UPI/Corbis-Bettmann. Page 501 (bottom): Courtesy William Alanson White Psychiatric Foundation. Page 505: Michael Rougier/Life Magazine/©Time, Inc. Page 509 (top): UPI/Corbis-Bettmann. Page 509 (bot-

tom): Bernard Gotfryd. Page 512 (top): Courtesy Gestalt Institute of Cleveland. Page 512 (bottom): Peter Byron/Monkmeyer Press Photo.

Chapter 18
Opener: "When the Mirror Dreams With Another Image" by Alfredo Castañeda, 1988. Oil on canvas, 11 3/8 x 15 in. Courtesy Mary-Anne Martin/Fine Art. Page 519: Courtesy Public Relations Department, Temple University Health Sciences Center. Page 521: Bob Daemmrich/The Image Works. Page 522 (top): Courtesy Anthony Menditto, Ph.D. Page 522 (bottom): Courtesy Gordon Paul. Page 526: Courtesy Mrs. Andrew Salter. Page 531: Andy Levin/Photo Researchers. Page 539 (top): R.B./J.O./Gamma Liaison. Page 539 (bottom): Larry Mulvehill/Photo Researchers. Page 540: Lori Ginker. Page 547: Richard T. Nowitz. Page 552: Courtesy Dr. Arnold Lazarus.

Chapter 19
Opener: "The Family" by Marisol Escobar, 1962; © 1997 Marisol Escobar. Painted wood and other materials in three sections, overall, 6' 10 5/8" x 65 1/2" x 15 1/2" (209.8 x 166.3 x 39.3 cm). The Museum of Modern Art, New York. Advisory Committee Fund. Photograph © 1997 The Museum of Modern Art, New York. Licensed by VAGA, New York, NY. Page 561: Joe Sohm/Stock, Boston. Page 562: Charles Harbutt/Actuality. Page 568: Richard Nowitz/Photo Researchers. Page 578: Mary Kate Denny/PhotoEdit/PNI. Page 579: Tony Freeman/ PhotoEdit/PNI. Page 580: Charles Thatcher/Thatcher Productions. Page 582: Kermani/Gamma Liaison. Page 586: Margaret Miller/Photo Researchers.

Chapter 20
Opener: "Cops" by Robert Vickrey, 1988; © 1997 Robert Vickrey. Licensed by VAGA, New York, NY. Page 595: R. Mims/Sygma. Page 597: Courtesy Thomas Szasz/G. Szilasi Photography. Page 597: Sygma. Page 603: Courtesy Jerry Ohlinger's. Page 607: AP/Wide World Photos. Page 611: Joseph Sohm/Chromosohm/Photo Researchers. Page 613: AP/Wide World Photos. Page 622 (left): Bill Bachmann/The Image Works. Page 622 (right): Larry Kolvoord/The Image Works.

NAME INDEX

Subject Index